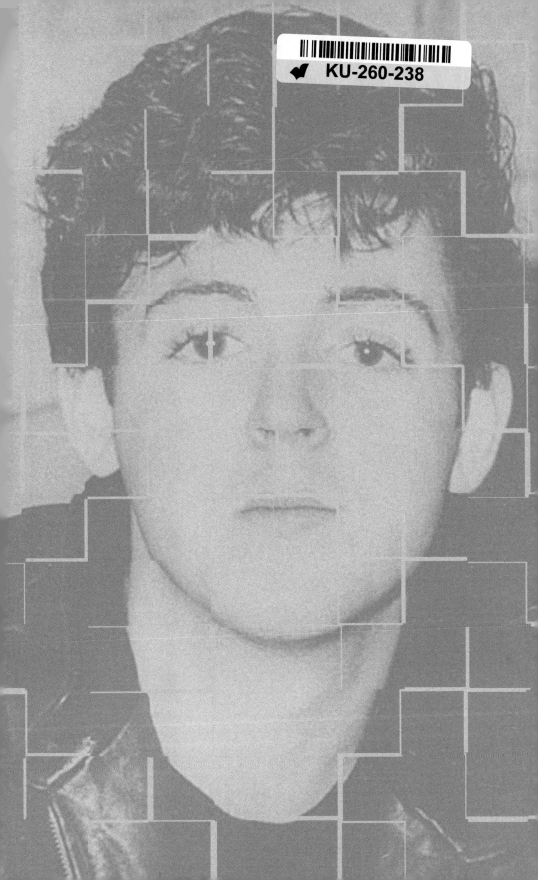

ALL THESE YEARS

Tune In

Also by Mark Lewisohn

The Beatles Live! (1986)
The Beatles: 25 Years In The Life (1987) [USA: Day By Day, 1990]
The [Complete] Beatles Recording Sessions (1988)
*In My Life: John Lennon Remembered (1990)
The Complete Beatles Chronicle (1992)
*The Beatles' London (1994)
Radio Times Guide To TV Comedy (1998)
Funny, Peculiar: The True Story Of Benny Hill (2002)
Radio Times Guide To TV Comedy (2nd edition, 2003)
*The Beatles' London (2nd edition, 2008)

*co-author

ALL THESE YEARS

Volume 1: Tune In

MARK LEWISOHN

Little, Brown

LITTLE, BROWN

First published in Great Britain in 2013 by Little, Brown
Reprinted 2013

A CIP catalogue record for this book
is available from the British Library.

ISBN 978-0-316-72960-4

Typeset in Transitional 521 by M Rules
Printed and bound in Great Britain by
Clays Ltd, St Ives plc

Papers used by Little, Brown are from well-managed forests
and other responsible sources.

MIX
Paper from
responsible sources
FSC
www.fsc.org   FSC® C104740

Little, Brown
An imprint of
Little, Brown Book Group
100 Victoria Embankment
London EC4Y 0DY

An Hachette UK Company
www.hachette.co.uk

www.littlebrown.co.uk

For Richard, who gets it,
and Neil, who got it but went too soon,
and Liverpudlians everywhere, whose heritage this is

Contents

Introduction   ix
The pre-1971 British monetary system explained   xiii

THE PROLOGUE: Another Lennon-McCartney Original (January 1958)   1

OLD BEFORE OUR BIRTH   13

1   In My Liverpool Home (1845–1945)   15
2   Boys (1945–54)   33
3   'Who you lookin' at?' (1954–5)   62
4   Scufflers to Skifflers (1956)   82
5   Guaranteed Not to Split (January–June 1957)   105
6   Come Go With Me (6 July 1957)   126
7   'He'll get you into trouble, son' (July–December 1957)   133

YEAR 1, 1958: THINKING OF LINKING   155

8   'Where we going, Johnny?' (January–May 1958)   157
9   'This is my life' (June–December 1958)   181

YEAR 2, 1959: THREE COOL CATS   205

10   'A sort of violent Teddy Boy' (January–July 1959)   207
11   'Come viz me to ze Casbah' (July–December 1959)   222

Contents

YEAR 3, 1960: COMPETENCE, CONFIDENCE & CONTINUITY — 249

12 The Swish of the Curtain — 251
13 'Hi-yo, hi-yo Silver – away!' (January–May 1960) — 281
14 'Where's the bloody money?' (18–30 May 1960) — 313
15 Drive and Bash (31 May–15 August 1960) — 326
16 'Mach Schau!' (15 August–30 September 1960) — 358
17 A Cellarful of Oiks (1 October–31 December 1960) — 377

YEAR 4, 1961: THE ROCK AGE — 407

18 The Big Beat Boppin' Beatles (January–March 1961) — 409
19 Piedels on Prellies (April–June 1961) — 440
20 Soup and Sweat and Rock 'n' Roll (July–September 1961) — 469
21 Les Nerk Twins à Paris (1–14 October 1961) — 501
22 'Right then, Brian – manage us' (15 October–3 December 1961) — 507
23 The Boys (December 1961) — 535

YEAR 5, 1962: ALWAYS BE TRUE — 555

24 Choices (1 January–5 February 1962) — 557
25 'A tendency to play music' (6 February–8 March 1962) — 578
26 'Us against them' (9 March–10 April 1962) — 605
27 'He could easily have been *the* Beatle' (10–13 April 1962) — 625
28 You Better Move On (13 April–2 June 1962) — 631
29 Under Marching Orders (2–6 June 1962) — 662
30 The Undesirable Member (7 June–18 August 1962) — 674
31 Some Other Guy (19 August–4 October 1962) — 707
32 Friday 5 October 1962 – The Sixties Start Here — 745
33 'We've got it, and here we are with it' (6–31 October 1962) — 756
34 'Show me I'm wrong' (1–15 November 1962) — 786
35 New Look, New Sound (16 November–17 December 1962) — 796
36 And Who Knows! (18–31 December 1962) — 827

Notes — 841
Appeal — 903
Credits — 904
Picture Credits — 913
Index — 915

Introduction

Every once in a while, life conjures up a genuine ultimate.

It can be said without fear of hyperbole: this is what the Beatles were and are, and fifty-plus years after they leapt into view – *fifty* – there's little hint it's going to change. So many would-be successors have come and gone, there's now an acceptance that no one can be bigger or better. John Winston Lennon, James Paul McCartney, George Harrison and Richard Starkey hold on strong, universally acknowledged as a cultural force, still somehow current and woven into the fabric of modern lives. *John, Paul, George and Ringo,* the four Liverpool lads who pumped the heart of the decade that also won't shut up, the 1960s.

If it was necessary to 'sell' the Beatles you could point to many achievements, but their music underpins everything: one game-changing album after another and one game-changing single after another, 214 tracks recorded in seven crowded years in a kaleidoscope of styles. This music is known, loved, respected, discussed, imitated, cherished and studied; it continues to inspire new artists and be reshaped impressively in every genre; its song titles and words are adapted for headlines in twenty-first-century media, quoted and folded into everyday vocabulary, chanted in football stadiums. Infused with the Beatles' energy and personalities, this music still lifts the spirit and is passed joyfully from generation to generation.

Clearly, something special happened here – but *what? How?*
Consider too . . .

- how the Beatles repeatedly married cutting-edge originality with immense mainstream popularity, when for almost anyone else these are mutually exclusive, and how (and why) they ditched their winning ideas every time the world raced to copy them;

- how they did everything with down-to-earth humour, honesty, optimism, style, charisma, irreverence, intelligence and a particularly spiky disdain for falseness; how they were articulate, bold, curious, direct, instinctive, challenging, blunt, sharp, polite, rude, prickers of pomposity, rule-breakers never cowed by convention;
- how they created a profound and sustained connection to their public, and how they resisted branding, commercial sponsorship and corporate affiliation and hype: the Beatles were free of artifice and weren't the product of market research or focus groups or TV talent shows, they were original and developed organically when everyone was looking the other way.

I've been waiting for the book this sweeping story demands, one that stares unflinchingly at how it happened and what it was all about – a book to shoot adrenalin back into extraordinary events crushed under the weight of fifty years' telling (and not always very good telling at that). I've wanted a history of deep-level enquiry where the information is tested accurate, and free of airbrushing, embellishment and guesswork, written with an open mind and even hands, one that unfolds lives and events in context and without hindsight, the way they occurred, and sets the Beatles fully among their contemporaries – they *never* existed in isolation and were always part of musical scenes with friends and rivals, young turks together in clubs and night-clubs.

I've also wanted a book that explains how the society that shaped the Beatles first received them and was then shaped *by* them, that looks at how John, Paul, George and Ringo dealt with each other as friends and bandmates, and how they so deftly handled the media and such phenomenal celebrity. I've wanted it shown how they transformed the worldwide music industry, and shook global youth culture awake, and induced a revolution in how people listened to and played music. The Beatles didn't invent the electric guitar and weren't the first 'guitar group', but every rock band since 1963 is fulfilling their legacy, especially if they write their own songs.

In 2003, I decided to have a go. As a professional historian-researcher who had worked around (and sometimes for) the Beatles for thirty years, I could draw on long periods of access to the right people and resources. Beyond that, I was aware that mountains of unfound knowledge – vibrant colour, vital details – were out there if you knew where to look.

But, one book? *Way* too much of relevance and interest happened in and around the Beatles to fit into one book. This is a richly epic tale; cramming it into a single volume would mean cutting reams of material essential to the understanding. This book, *Tune In,* is the first in a trilogy titled *All These Years* that I hope will do the subject justice. (It is, at any rate, my best shot.) It's an objective and independent three-volume series that begins at the beginning and will go on until it reaches the end. Primary sources are central: an array of research discoveries, and every conceivable form of archive document found in private and public hands – letters, contracts, photos, recordings and so much more, and this story has a fantastically rich paper trail – augmented entirely by direct quotes. I'm tracking whatever was said by the Beatles (and those close to them) to anyone at any time – and there are hundreds of frank and revealing interviews unused since they were carried out. I've also traced and talked to hundreds of authentic witnesses, many of them overlooked until now. George Harrison's cautionary words are a constant companion – 'In their bid to tell what they know, sometimes people tell *more* than what they know'* – but fictions fall quicker through the sieve.

It's been a continually surprising experience. I've likened the challenge (which is ongoing) to assembling a multi-million-piece jigsaw puzzle of lives and moments: the more pieces you have and can place right where they belong, where they *really* fit, the clearer the picture becomes both in vivid close-up and broadly detailed context.

Tune In takes the Beatles from before their childhoods right up to the final night of 1962 when, after packing several years into the previous three, they know success is theirs to grasp but have no clue they're on the cusp of a whole new kind of fame, a white-hot and ever-royal celebrity. These, then, are the formative years, the less visible years, the pre-madness years – and in many respects the most absorbing and entertaining period of them all. (This can also be claimed for the others, of course.)

What the research yells loudly is that the Beatles didn't begin to be remarkable when they upped and took over Britain or (all the more amazingly) America and the rest of the world, and that they didn't suddenly become funny when they filmed *A Hard Day's Night*, or beguiling when recording *Rubber Soul*. It shouts that their compelling urge to move on fast, to innovate and progress, didn't start with *Revolver* or *Sgt Pepper* – or even when, in the last chapters of this book, their first record came out. Everything was already revved up and running in the halls, houses and streets of an exceptional city, the only place these people could have come from, the only place these events could have happened: Liverpool, that great matrix of Anglo-Celtic alchemy. From her Second World War bombsites rose a thriving live music scene the like of which

---

* Said during evidence given at the Royal Courts of Justice, London, 6 May 1998.

existed nowhere else, a scene in which the Beatles were sharper-smarter-faster-funnier than their many rivals – and where they also polished, well before they had hits, that tightly engaged relationship with their public. In other words, those later world-changing Beatles are *these* Beatles, just lesser-known, local not global. They're the same blokes with the same instinctive, intuitive originality and humour, the same bluntness and abhorrence of sham, living the present to the full . . . and sowing seeds that would flower later.

Again, though, *how*? I've tried to thread together the lives and relationships of John, Paul, George, Richy, Stuart, Pete, Brian Epstein, George Martin and other crucial players. Everyone is in their context and worlds run on parallel and occasionally interweaving tracks before properly connecting – characters creating the circumstances to dictate an outcome. The Lennon and McCartney partnership is one among many deep explorations, told thoroughly in their words and deeds. George and Ringo were essential to the Beatles but John and Paul drove the bus and wrote the catalogue, and theirs is an especially fascinating tale – two needle-sharp grammar-school boys and then young men steeped in post-war British culture but with a passion for America and its great music, close friends with a deep admiration for each other's talent and understanding of each other's moods and personalities. Their determination, their egos and their creative rivalry made them the greatest songwriters of the age, and I've tried to show how it began.

The Beatles manifestly rejected labels and categories in all they did, so it doesn't matter if you call them the ultimate rock band or the ultimate pop group or whatever else. They just *were*, and theirs is the best story. Every performer, band, producer, impresario has one, and many of them are great and worthy of fine biographies, but there's nothing like the Beatles story to legitimately go everywhere and strongly connect everything to everyone. It's a blockbuster history with surprises at every turn, many heroes and a few villains, unparalleled triumphs, great joys and genuine tragedies, the ebbs and flows of human lives – plus an avalanche of fortuitous chances and coincidences that defy the laws of probability.

From the project's conception I've seen it as the Beatles in their times – them in their world and the world right about them. And now it's all this . . .

Mark Lewisohn
England, 2013

The pre-1971 British monetary system explained

Until switching to the decimal system in 1971, the currency was pounds, shillings and pence – often abbreviated in print as L.S.D. or l.s.d., from the Latin librae, solidi, denarii. One pound (£1) was broken down into twenty shillings, and each shilling had twelve pence, so there were 240 pence in the pound.

In speech, eight shillings and sixpence (for example) was said as 'eight and six'; in writing, this could be shown as 8s 6d, or 8/6, or even 8/6d. Unless quoting original documents that had it differently, this book adopts the style 8s 6d.

The pound had nicknames, most commonly 'a quid'; £5 and £10 notes were known then as now as 'a fiver' and 'a tenner'. A shilling was 'a bob': a tenshilling note was 'ten bob'; a record might cost six bob; £1 10s could be written as 30s and said as 'thirty bob'. Similarly, coins took on nicknames: two pence (2d) was known as 'tuppence', the 3d coin 'threppence' or 'thruppence', the 6d (sixpence) 'a tanner', and the large silver coin worth 'two and six' (2s 6d) was 'half a crown' or 'a half-crown'. Fractions of a penny were known as the 'ha'penny' (half-penny) and 'farthing' (quarter of a penny, phased out in 1960). Something costing just pennies, e.g. 4d, would be referred to as 'four penn'orth', short for 'four pennies' worth'.

The value of £1 in these years, comparable to 2013

1850	£72.10	1930	£43.46	1947	£33.49	1955	£22.66
1860	£64.71	1940	£37.35	1948	£31.37	1956	£21.58
1870	£63.08	1941	£34.52	1949	£30.51	1957	£20.82
1880	£66.40	1942	£34.31	1950	£29.63	1958	£20.21
1890	£78.86	1943	£34.50	1951	£27.15	1959	£20.09
1900	£81.40	1944	£34.19	1952	£24.85	1960	£19.89
1910	£74.21	1945	£33.75	1953	£24.11	1961	£19.23
1920	£27.58	1946	£33.70	1954	£23.67	1962	£18.45

Source: Bank of England/International Monetary Fund

The Prologue
Another Lennon-McCartney Original
(January 1958)

Jim McCartney would no more let Paul skip school than allow *that boy* in the house, so subterfuge was vital. Afternoon sessions, two till five, ended with a hurried wafting around of smoke and washing of dirty dishes … though by then they'd often written another song.

'He'll get you into trouble, son,' Jim warned Paul. Parents had been saying that about John Lennon since he was five – and rightly so, because he did. But this hadn't stopped a solid gang of pals – intelligent grammar-school boys, as Paul McCartney was – idolising him as their leader. And what high and hysterical times he gave them in return.

In 1956–7, when John was 16, he turned his gang into his group, the Quarry Men, and for a while they rode the skiffle craze, up on stage belting out rhythmic prison songs of the American South. John sang and played guitar, forever the front man. But he was – first, last, always – a rocker, and his group was now charging headlong in that direction; newspaper ads for the dances they played were already calling them Rock 'n' Skiffle, though actually it was rock all the way. And later, when John – now 17 and clearly the coolest kid on the block – generously invited Paul to join them, the 15-year-old was so keen to make himself indispensable that deceiving Dad was but the flimsiest of obstacles.

Paul was conscious of the age gap. To him, John was 'the fairground hero, the big lad riding the dodgems',[1] a grown-up Teddy Boy who swore, smoked, scrapped, had sex, got drunk and went to college, who strutted around with Elvis Presley sideburns, upturned collar, hunched shoulders and an intimidating stare (which Paul would soon learn was born of insecurity and acute short-sightedness). Lennon radiated a life-force that turned heads everywhere:

he was wickedly funny and fast with it, he was abrasive, incisive and devastatingly rude, and he was musical, literate and beguilingly creative. Whether painting, conceiving strangely comic poems, or committing cruel drawings and odd stories to the written page, he was a boy beyond convention and control, a lone ranger. He was everything his friends wanted to be, and said everything they wanted to say but wouldn't dare. John Lennon always dared.

He had long dispensed with one of the taboos of childhood, befriending whoever he liked even if they were younger. One of his closest pals, Ivan Vaughan, was born the same day as Paul McCartney in June 1942 (and Ivan had introduced them). Age didn't matter to John if the friend brought something interesting to the table. If anyone had a problem with a 17-year-old college student hanging around with a 15-year-old schoolboy it was theirs alone to deal with, though if they chose to voice it near him they were risking a thump. As for Paul, at their first meeting six months earlier he'd felt too young to be John's friend, the wrong side of 'the cusp'; he'd impressed the hell out of him though, and now, invited in, he wasn't going to let it slip. He would be – and was – sharp, sure and impressive enough to hold John's attention.

Paul had only recently sung in a church choir, arrived home wet from scout camp, and been allowed to wear long trousers to school – but, instantly, such things were history. From late 1957, he grew up fast. 'Once I got to know John it all changed,' he'd recall a decade later. 'I went off in a completely new direction.'[2] Paul had much to offer, and John had seen it. He had a great musical talent, an instinctive and untutored gift; he played piano and was a confident and characteristic guitarist who always knew more chords than John and was much better at remembering words. At 13, before rock and roll changed his life, Paul composed two catchy piano tunes, dance-band numbers like those his dad had played around Liverpool ballrooms in the 1920s with his own Jim Mac's Band. Then, when the guitar came along in 1957, Paul was hooked.

He was also a funny storyteller and mimic, a cartoonist and able caricaturist. The eldest son of particular parents, Paul knew how to behave socially. John, who'd also been brought up well, bothered less with social niceties. Paul liked to create the best impression and say the right things, exuding a breezy confidence and wanting people to think highly of him. He was charming, sharp, mentally strong and rarely outmanoeuvred. John saw it all and welcomed it: though he had to be dominant, he respected no one who didn't stand up to him. Paul did, despite being twenty months his junior; but John also knew that if Paul ever challenged his natural supremacy, at least before he was ready to abdicate it, he'd see him off.

The more hours John and Paul spent together the more they found these things out, uncovering humour and harmony right down the line. They'd both read *Alice In Wonderland* and *Just William*, though Paul had read *Alice* once or twice whereas John still feasted on it every few months and had folded Lewis Carroll's vocabulary into his own. They also shared a strong interest in television, and knew BBC radio personalities and northern comedians, quoting current and vintage catchphrases. Both were consumed by *The Goon Show* and talked the talk familiar only to those who imbibed the lingo; they made each other laugh all the time and began to develop an attuned shorthand humour beyond others' comprehension.

Then there were girls. Paul, despite the age gap, matched John in his ceaseless lust; John was already a sexual adventurer, Paul wasn't far behind. Both had shed their virginity and were eager for whatever action they could get. Birdspotting was a way of life and often now a combined quest. They also shared the same goddesses, the fantasy figures who kept men awake at night in the late 1950s, women such as Anita Ekberg, Juliette Gréco and Brigitte Bardot. The Parisienne Bardot, an actress as well as a model, was the ultimate in pin-ups. When *And God Created Woman* and *Mam'selle Striptease* were in the local cinemas, Liverpool could have been powered on the heat generated in the stalls. John and Paul were there. On the ceiling above his bed, John had the original French poster of *Et Dieu ... Créa la femme*, a drawing of the topless Bardot, long blonde hair cascading over ample breasts.

But top of their hit parade, always, was American rock and roll music – hearing it and playing it. Two years earlier it wasn't known to them, now it was what they lived and breathed for. There weren't yet a hundred recordings to cherish but John and Paul knew them all, and when they weren't listening to or playing them they were talking about them, thrilling to the minutiae. 'Worshipping' is the word Paul has used.[3] They both revered Little Richard, the dynamic singer from Macon, Georgia, who, according to the weekly British music papers, had just given it all up and disappeared into the Church. But they would always have Long Tall Sally, Tutti Frutti, Slippin' And Slidin' and Lucille, and John was floored by Paul's uncanny ability to mimic that screaming and hollering voice. *Everyone* was amazed by it. Ian James, Paul's best friend before John came along, says Paul would often break into it without warning, as if Little Richard was trapped inside him and occasionally had to surface for air.

There were other heroes – Carl Perkins, Gene Vincent, Eddie Cochran, Jerry Lee Lewis and more – but no one was ever greater, for either, than Elvis, who'd already cut the soundtrack of their youth. Elvis Presley was God, it was as simple as that. John and Paul listened to his records in the way only besotted fans do, catching and trying to analyse all the little inexplicable sounds, like the laugh he couldn't stifle at the end of Baby Let's Play House, and the muttered asides at the end of Hound Dog.[4]

Just recently, the Crickets had burst into their lives too, a breakthrough almost as essential. Under their leader Buddy Holly, the Crickets introduced the *group sound*: vocal, electric guitar, bass and drums. Three singles – That'll Be The Day, Peggy Sue and Oh Boy! – had arrived in Britain at the perfect moment, their easy-to-play music encouraging thousands of bored skiffle groups to begin making the switch to pop and rock. It was the start of everything. John and Paul loved the Crickets (even the name had their regard) and were inspired to write songs in Buddy's vocal and musical style. Towards the end of 1957, John wrote Hello Little Girl and Paul came up with I Lost My Little Girl; the similarity in their titles was apparently coincidental but both were steeped in the Crickets' sound.

John and Paul's passion for rock and roll wedded them heart and soul, and Liverpool Corporation's education committee also played a part. Unless the Quarry Men had a booking somewhere, Jim McCartney's disapproval of John meant Paul couldn't see his friend at night. They had to be more shrewd. Situated up the hill from the city centre, Liverpool College of Art – where John, newly enrolled, was already proving himself a handful – happened to adjoin Liverpool Institute, Paul's grammar school. The two buildings had been one, so with a quick dash through their respective exits John and Paul would arrive together on the same stretch of street at the same moment and were truants for the afternoon – 'sagging off'. John would have his guitar ready.

From a stop on Catharine Street, they'd board the 86 bus, a green double-decker like those driven by Harry Harrison, father of Paul's young schoolfriend George. They found their way upstairs and had a smoke, strumming strings while the bus bounced them out to the southern suburbs, along Upper Parliament Street – Toxteth, with its immigrant West Indian ghetto – past Sefton General Hospital to the roundabout at Penny Lane and then beyond to Allerton. Within thirty minutes of sneaking out, they'd be inside Paul's terraced council house at 20 Forthlin Road, empty in the daytime. The McCartneys had only been here six months when Paul's mother Mary died, and now Jim, 55, was trying to cope alone with their two teenage boys and maintain his wife's high standards and principles. His brothers and sisters rallied round – they were a strong, close-knit family, the women big on motherly advice, the men strong on Liverpool wit and repartee, characters all. Paul's Auntie Gin and Auntie Mill came over to clean, iron and cook for them on alternate Monday afternoons: Paul's sessions with John were only possible Tuesdays to Fridays. There was the irony. It was only because Jim wanted Paul to stay away from the troublemaker Lennon that he was sagging off school, courting trouble like he'd never done before. (So it was 'Dad's fault'.)

They'd go into what the McCartneys called the front parlour, a standard, basic 1950s front room: a sofa with antimacassars crocheted by Paul's aunties, cotton covers hiding the broken springs of Jim's armchair, a tiny black-and-white TV in the corner, a record player, a piano, and threadbare runners on the wooden floorboards that did for a carpet. John and Paul would sit opposite each other by the fireplace. As Paul was left-handed their guitars went the same way and each could enjoy the mirror effect of watching the other's fingers shape the chords as if they were his own. Paul would later call these 'eyeball to eyeball sessions', and he'd be treated to something few witnessed: John put his glasses on. Only rarely did they leave his pocket, even though without them he could barely see a thing. Almost in each other's faces, John and Paul quickly gained an unusual closeness, little or nothing hidden. Paul noticed that 'John had beautiful hands'.[5]

Paul weaned John off the banjo chords taught him by his mother Julia. John had musical flair in his family line too, but it was more rough and ready than Paul's: John could play banjo, guitar and harmonica, often more with aggression than precision. Afternoons were whiled away playing guitars to records, singing, revelling in the joy of chords, finding out how almost every rock song they knew could be played with C, F and G or G7. They laughed over a sticker visible through the soundhole of John's guitar: GUARANTEED NOT TO SPLIT it said, and *by 'eck it 'adn't*. They toiled hours, weeks, trying to work out how Buddy Holly played the intro to That'll Be The Day, before John eventually figured it out, celebrating with a puff on Jim's spare pipe. They'd no tobacco, but a quick raid on the tea caddy produced a few pinches of Twinings or Typhoo; the pipe passed between them, each pulling hard while agreeing on its terrible taste.

Buddy Holly was the springboard to John and Paul's songwriting. As John later said, 'Practically every Buddy Holly song was three chords, so why not write your own?'[6]

Stated so matter-of-factly, it could seem that writing songs was an obvious next move, but it wasn't. Teenagers all over Britain liked Buddy Holly and rock and roll, but of that large number only a fraction picked up a guitar and tried playing it, and fewer still – in fact hardly anyone – used it as the inspiration to write songs themselves. John and Paul didn't know anyone else who did it, no one from school or college, no relative or friend . . . and yet somehow, by nothing more than fate or fluke, they'd found each other, discovered they both wrote songs, and decided to try it together. Paul recalls the method: 'We'd sit down and say, "OK, what are we going to do?" and we'd just start off strumming and one or the other of us would kick off some kind of idea and then we'd just develop it and bounce off each other.'[7]

It had only taken seconds to discover that both had strong and distinctive voices for rock – in all its styles and tempos – and that they sounded great together. They could blend in perfect harmony, with Paul tending to take the higher key and John holding the lower. The Crickets' influence was again strong, and so too were the crafted melodic harmonies of the Everly Brothers, whose first record, Bye Bye Love, was issued in Britain the day before John met Paul, 5 July 1957. (Throughout this history, the timing of everything is always perfect.) Now, in the last week of January 1958, the bestselling chart produced by Liverpool's newest record shop Nems – published in *The Record Mirror* the same day John and Paul led the Quarry Men through some rock 'n' skiffle down the Cavern – had Peggy Sue by Buddy Holly at number 1, Oh Boy! by the Crickets at 2 and Great Balls Of Fire by Jerry Lee Lewis at 3. Here was inspiration on a stick.

Their first song was Too Bad About Sorrows. It was never properly recorded, possibly never completed, and John and Paul only ever let out the first couple of lines:

> Too bad about sorrows, too bad about love,
> There'll be no tomorrow, for all of your life.[8]

They sang the vocal in unison, as they did most of these songs.
They called their second song Just Fun.

> They said our love was just fun / The day that our friendship begun.
> There's no blue moon that I can see / There's never been in history.

They knew the final line was a stinker and left the song unfinished after failing to come up with anything better. Paul had a tendency to perfection but John was always restless to move on, keen to try something new.

Another number seems to have been called Because I Know You Love Me So. The words were about someone who wakes up feeling blue because his lover doesn't treat him right, but then reads her letters and finds she does care. It had appealing Holly-like changes and John and Paul sang it together in harmony like the Everlys, each encouraging good music from the other.[9]

These were not songs they played with the Quarry Men. The group's three other members (Eric, Len and Colin) never knew much about them: a rift had taken place, the front two getting together without their bandmates. Only certain people heard these new songs – select friends, Paul's dad, brother and a few relatives. John may not have played them to anyone but Paul liked to demonstrate them, enjoying the resulting praise. Their harshest critics were always themselves. Paul has said that the two of them never reckoned any of these early songs, not even at the time; they knew they were unsophisticated, just a step.[10] John in particular was never slow to say if something was 'crap', even if it was his own.

John's first two attempts at songwriting, a year earlier, had already vanished from his memory, never to return, so he and Paul knew they had to keep proper track of their ideas. They'd no means of recording them and neither could read or write music, so Paul appropriated a Liverpool Institute exercise book, maybe forty-eight feint-ruled pages, in which every new song had a fresh page. In his neat left-handed script, generally using a fountain pen, he wrote the words (they were always *words*, never lyrics) with chords shown by their alphabetical letter. Unable to describe the melody, they decided early on that if they couldn't remember something the next day, they could hardly expect it to stick in the mind of anyone else, in which case it was 'crap' and deserved to go. But sometimes Paul wrote atmospheric directions. For one song it was 'Ooh ah, angel voices'.

And on the top of every new page, above the song title, Paul wrote:

ANOTHER LENNON-MCCARTNEY ORIGINAL

The influence for this wasn't rock and roll so much as the great American songwriting teams of older generations, the likes of Rodgers and Hammerstein, Rodgers and Hart, Lerner and Loewe and other famous combinations who wrote for Hollywood and Broadway.[11] From the outset, John and Paul settled on Lennon-McCartney as a partnership, with that name order. Lennon came before McCartney alphabetically, and he was almost two years older, and it was his invitation, and, surpassing any other consideration, it was simply the way of things: John *always* came first. While equal in terms of contribution, Paul had to accept that one of them was just a little more equal than the other. Second billing wasn't in his nature, though. Paul accepted it from his fairground hero and positively no one else. 'We were really looking at being Rodgers and Hammerstein, and famous writing duos always had their name the same way. You didn't hear "Hammerstein and Rodgers", it just didn't sound as good. So we always wanted to have people say, "Oh, that's a Lennon-McCartney song."'[12]

Neither planned to do anything with these songs (to send them off to singers, publishers or record companies) but they agreed – by actually discussing it, albeit briefly – that each could continue to operate independently, writing songs on his own and then bringing them to the other for approval and the joint Lennon-McCartney credit. 'We decided on that very early on,' says Paul. 'It was just for simplicity really, and – so as to not get into the ego thing – we were very pure with it.'[13]

Competition was nonetheless an ever-essential component. John had complete admiration for Paul's facility with harmony and melody, his musicianship and invention; Paul respected John's musical talent and envied his original repartee. Yet while combining their skills as a team, they remained competitive as individuals, each trying to outdo the other. It became a vital artistic spur: John would call it 'a sibling rivalry ... a *creative* rivalry', Paul spoke of 'competitiveness in that we were ricocheting our ideas'.[14] Each tried to impress the other out of sheer fear of what he might say in return. Both were rarely less than candid, and the thought that a new song might be branded 'crap' was usually more than enough to continually raise standards.

John and Paul had an abundance of ambition, and top of their lists was *to be rich*. John's Aunt Mimi, his surrogate parent since the age of five, told him 'possessions don't bring happiness but they make misery a lot easier', which was one comfort, but mostly John wanted money to avoid having to work.[15] Art college was only a means of delaying the inevitable another four or five years, though he was unlikely even then to have a clear idea how to earn a living. He could only ever see himself as a painter or poet or writer or musician and they didn't give out those jobs down the Labour Exchange. John Lennon and conformity were ugly bedfellows – he'd no discipline or desire for office or factory work, and had his own dismissive phrase for such jobs: 'brummer striving'.

Before she died, Mary McCartney had wanted Paul to become a doctor; Jim hoped he'd go to university and become a teacher or writer ... but Paul wanted to be a star and had the confidence and talent to shoot for it. And with stardom he'd be rich. About £75,000 would cover what he wanted. As he later said, 'If you'd asked me for my fantasies when I was 16 years old, standing at a bus stop waiting to go to Garston on the 86, I'd have said "guitar, car and a house", in that order. That was it – the entire thing.'[16]

These would have been among the thoughts crowding Paul's mind as he walked from Allerton to Woolton to visit John. By road it was one and a half miles, but on foot or by bike there was a short-cut across Allerton Municipal Golf Course, emerging from the greens on to a bank above Menlove Avenue, diagonally opposite John's house. Both boys rode bikes to get around, but usually walked if carrying their guitars, not having cases. A long way from streetlamps, the golf course was pitch-black after dark. When Paul was heading home on late winter afternoons he'd try to steady his nerve by playing guitar and singing at the top of his voice. If anybody came along he'd immediately stop and pretend it hadn't been him, but on one occasion he was halted by a policeman. Paul felt sure he'd be arrested for a breach of the peace but the cop asked him for guitar lessons.[17]

John's house, on a busy dual-carriageway, was a semi-detached suburban villa given the name Mendips by its previous occupants. Paul came here less frequently than John's covert visits to Forthlin Road, turning up mostly on weekends. Conditions at Mendips were different: there was no need for stealth but Mimi made clear what could and couldn't be done in her house. After the first visit, Paul knew not to use the front door but to walk down the side and knock at the back, which led into the kitchen. (The front was rarely used.) Mimi would call upstairs, 'John, your little friend's here.' She had always been patronising about his friends, telling him in plain language if she considered them lower class or in some other way not good enough for him. When Mimi said this the first time, John assured Paul, 'That's just the way she is, you mustn't be offended.'[18] Paul watched the two of them with a curious fascination.

> I thought John and Mimi had a very special relationship. She would always be making fun of him and he never took it badly; he was always very fond of her, and she of him. She struck me as being an honest woman who looked after John's interests and would take the mickey, but she would also say these [belittling] things, purposeful put-downs. I never minded it, in fact I think she quite liked me – out of a put-down I could glean the knowledge that she liked me.[19]

Mimi's husband (John's Uncle George) had died, and as the combination of a modest rental income and her widow's state pension was barely going to fund John's feeding and raising, she took in lodgers, students from Liverpool University. There was always at least one in residence, sometimes three or four, and their need for quiet study meant that Mimi frequently had to remind John to keep the noise down. Also, like her nephew, she was a gluttonous reader and relished peace and quiet.

Mimi didn't deny John and Paul space to play their guitars, but insisted they used the porch. It was standing room only in here, another breath exchange, one boy with his back to the front of the house, the other with his back to the internal front door.[20] (Despite Mimi's 'little friend' jibe, Paul and John were the same height, almost fully grown.) The porch was no hardship because with its high roof, art nouveau leaded windows and black and white check tiled floor it provided highly prized echo. Budding rock and rollers would do anything for that reverb, to be at least close to the heavenly slap echo sound of the great Elvis records. But for the traffic noise from Menlove Avenue – buses and cars speeding past – they could have been in Sun Studio, Memphis, Tennessee.

It was in the porch ('vestibule' in Paul's vocabulary) that John and Paul cracked the chords to Elvis's Blue Moon, one of his first and best Sun records. In a sudden moment of joy, they found it was the same as Paul Anka's recent hit Diana, C–A minor–F–G, known to them from this point as 'the Diana chords'. Presley's cover of Rodgers-Hart's Blue Moon was an eerily minimalist blues and lent itself perfectly to the tiny echoing space. The porch was also good for whistling; Paul, who whistled well, appreciated anyone else who could do it tunefully and John was one of the best around. He often blew as accompaniment to Paul's singing or playing.

When Mimi went out shopping they would steal up to John's little bedroom – the 'box room' over the front of the house – and play records. By early 1958, John had amassed a fair collection (some bought, others stolen) of Elvis and Lonnie Donegan. Paul remembers how they spent time trying to anticipate the next music trend, so they could write a song in that style. Convinced that rock and roll would die at any moment, corporate America was trying to kill it, to save time, by kicking off the next kooky craze. John and Paul gave it some thought too, conjuring odd fusions like Latin-rock and rock-rumba and ... then gave up. They learned that forcing an idea never worked, that songs had to come naturally. Plenty did: they hoped to write at least one in every session, and in this early period amassed perhaps twenty.

Few are known beyond their title. I've Been Thinking That You Love Me, If Tomorrow Ever Comes, That's My Woman, and Won't You Please Say Goodbye. A song called Years Roll Along ('It might have been winter when you told me ...') was never completed. One that was, which they both recognised as the best of this first batch of Lennon-McCartney Originals, was Love Me Do. Paul would recall it as a 50:50 effort with John, written in the front parlour at Forthlin Road, but John said it was almost entirely Paul's. No recording of Love Me Do exists before the song changed shape and musical direction after four years had rolled along, but John and Paul both said how everything they wrote in this period was heavily influenced by Buddy Holly, including the vocal style.[21]

Another early number, written mostly by John, was I Call Your Name, which he would describe as 'my effort at a kind of blues'.[22] It went down in the book as ANOTHER LENNON-MCCARTNEY ORIGINAL but Paul's contribution may have been confined only to constructive criticism; he remembers working on it in John's bedroom.

Mendips was a window to another world for Paul. John used a portable typewriter to hammer out song words and also his poetry, and because he was a punchy and impatient typist, keystroke errors inevitably added to the jokes.[23] John had been writing for years, creating his own cartoons, comics and newspapers with wild wordplay and ideas; songwriting was merely a recent addition to his locker. He ran the two on parallel tracks with no crossover – it was *these* ideas and words for the printed page and *those* ideas and words for the songs. Paul, who knew no one else with a typewriter and counted no other poet among his friends, was heavily impressed. John was *deep*, and there were few higher compliments. Paul would never forget (and always laugh at) the final lines of 'The Tale Of Hermit Fred', a poem John let him see, published in the Quarry Bank school magazine just before he left.

> I peel the bagpipes for my wife
> And cut all negroes' hair
> As breathing is my very life
> And stop I do not dare.

The McCartneys had always lived in council houses, cheek-by-jowl with the working classes. It gave them a usefully solid grounding in that particular reality, although Paul's strongly aspirational mother made sure they considered themselves a cut above. By Paul's personal definition, John was middle-class, and though there was much about his friend's domestic situation he didn't yet know or understand, this was how Paul saw and admired it. 'John's family was rather middle-class and it was a lot of his appeal to me. I'm attracted to that type of person, particularly in the British. John had relatives up in Edinburgh and one of them was a *dentist* – none of us knew people like that. So I was attracted to that. It wasn't a social climbing thing, it's just that I find it attractive.'[24]

Paul spotted several other signposts to indicate John's higher standing. In Mendips' front room was a full bookshelf that included Sir Winston Churchill's four-volume A *History Of The English-Speaking Peoples* and six-volume *The Second World War* – ten leather-bound folio editions John said he'd read, and had. They didn't just have cats, they had *pedigree* cats. Paul had aunties, but Mimi was John's *aunt*. Then there was Mendips itself – 'a house with a name, that was very posh; no one had houses with names where I came from, you were numbers'.[25]

It was all irresistibly magnetic, but Paul's predicament never changed: his dad didn't approve. This wasn't going to stop him, but he loved his dad and valued his own good reputation too much to openly rebel like John. It made John mad, and all the more determined to be the troublemaker Jim said he was.

> Paul always wanted the home life. He liked it with daddy and the brother ... and obviously missed his mother. And his dad was the whole thing. Just simple things, [like] he wouldn't go against his dad and wear drainpipe trousers. He treated Paul like a child all the time, cut his hair and telling him

what to wear, at 17, 18. I was always saying, 'Don't take that shit off him!' I was brought up by a woman so maybe it was different – but I wouldn't let the old man treat *me* like that.[26]

Through sheer force of personality, John Lennon changed others' lives, and many went willingly on the journey. For Paul McCartney, who had a fundamental need to be noticed, stepping forward with John was a natural move – he was aligning himself with someone people couldn't avoid, and who thrust two fingers up to things in a way he envied but would rarely do in full view. At the same time, Paul could apply gloss, where needed, to minimise John's trail of damage. Their musical group was formed in John's image and driven ever onward by his restlessness, but without Paul he would have upset too many people too many times to make the progress they both craved. Paul's other strengths were his great talent, his burning ambition and his high self-regard . . . and when John felt them becoming overbearing he'd pull him down a peg or two, as only he could.

And so Lennon-McCartney stood shoulder to shoulder as equals, connected at every level, their considerable talents harmonised, their personalities meshed, their drive unchecked, their goal in focus. They were a union, stronger than the sum of their parts, and everything was possible.

OLD BEFORE OUR BIRTH

1

In My Liverpool Home (1845–1945)

The significance of the location was unknown to those present that murky day in 1962 when four lads stood in front of a huge tea warehouse by Liverpool's dock road, having photos taken to publicise their first record. John Lennon certainly had no idea that the clearing of land on Saltney Street on which he was standing was where his family began their life in the city, just a few among the hordes of starving and mostly illiterate Irish fleeing the potato famine in their homeland.

At least one and a half million stricken Irish men, women and children sailed into Liverpool between 1845 and 1854. Plenty travelled on again, to America, Canada, Mexico and Australia, but a vast number stayed and few of those went very far: Saltney Street was hard by the docks of this great global seaport, ocean liners steaming up and down the River Mersey right at the end of the street. It's still there today, though the horrors of its cholera-infested housing have been swept away. In Liverpool, history is everywhere you look.

John Lennon – family background

James Lennon was the first to put down roots. Born about 1829 in County Down, one of the nine counties to form the province of Ulster, he was married in 1849 on Scotland Road, the slum-ridden heart of Liverpool's immigrant Catholic community. He fathered at least eight children before his wife died in the act of delivering another, and probably the third of these, in January 1855, was John Lennon, grandfather.

John (sometimes Jack) Lennon grew into an intelligent, happy-go-lucky soul who sang loud and often in ale-houses, worked mostly as a freight clerk, and led an intriguing life of mysteries, dead-ends and deceptions. After marrying twice, his longest relationship was with a Protestant woman, Mary 'Polly' Maguire. Their first seven babies all died, and of the seven that followed, the fifth was Alfred Lennon, born in December 1912 at the family home in Copperfield Street, Toxteth. After this, they got married.*

When cirrhosis of the liver killed his father in 1921, Alf was eight. Malnutrition had visited rickets upon the lad, a common condition among the poor, and he wore leg-irons for a considerable part of his childhood. Three years later he was offered a place at the excellent Blue Coat School, in the district of Wavertree, the city's oldest charitable foundation for the free education of orphans and fatherless children. There was one proviso: Protestants only, and several certificates were sought to prove a half-truth. Alf received a fine education here, and like every Blue Coat boy was regularly marched down to Bioletti's, the barber's shop at the nearby Penny Lane roundabout, for a severe scissoring.

On leaving in 1929, he was found an office placement with a shipping company, and three weeks later, while ambling with his slightly unsteady gait through Sefton Park – one of Liverpool's many fine green spaces – he met 15-year-old Julia Stanley.

John Lennon's maternal family was essentially Protestant. His great-grandfather, William Stanley, born 1846 in Birmingham, had moved to Liverpool by 1868. He and wife Eliza (born in Omagh, County Tyrone, another of the Ulster counties) set up home in Everton, in the north end of the city, and in 1874 gave birth to their third son, George – the 'Pop' John Lennon would know until losing him at the age of eight.

By 1898, George Stanley, a merchant seaman, had united with Annie Milward (born Chester, 1873) and begun to produce a family. For reasons as inexplicable as John Lennon and Polly Maguire's situation at the same time, they did this outside of marriage, and their experiences were similarly tragic – their first two children died. The third lived, however: Mary Elizabeth Stanley, known as Mimi, was born in Windsor Street, Toxteth, in 1906, just a shout from the Lennons on Copperfield Street.

John Lennon isn't known to have been aware that both his father and his Aunt Mimi, key figures in his life, were, in the literally used word of the day,

---

* The first of their fourteen children was another John Lennon, born 1894, died of diarrhoea 1895. John and Polly claimed marital status right down the line, yet there appears to have been no impediment to their tying the knot before they did, beyond the usual (considerable) problem of mixing Catholic and Protestant.

bastards. What he did know is that the Stanleys always believed they were several notches above the Lennons, claiming better breeding, education, nationality, religion, refinement, resources and aspiration, at least some of which is debatable.

Post-marriage, four more girls were born to George and Annie, all to live long and to create, with Mimi, a posse of five sisters whose allegiances would prove strong in the decades that followed, and whose influence on John Lennon would be of great significance. The third of that final four, Julia – born in March 1914 on the proverbial eve of the Great War – was John's mother. She was given licence within the family as the wild one, free-spirited, her notable wit and pranks enjoyed by all. Her father – the girls called him Dada – taught her banjo and she was talented, able to pick up tunes by ear. She was soon plucking and singing along to popular songs of the day, like Girl Of My Dreams and Ramona, which came across from America in 1927 as sheet music and then via three inventions that progressed rapidly during these years: the wireless, the gramophone and the talking pictures.

Julia left school in 1929 and met Alf Lennon soon after taking her first job. He wasn't the kind of young man to object if someone found him funny. Creating an impression was the thing, even if he was being laughed at, which he was. 'You look silly' were the first words said to him by Julia, naturally drawn to the daft. 'You look lovely,' he replied, and a relationship was born.

At the start of the 1930s, Alf left his office job and became a merchant seaman, beginning a long and highly colourful nautical career. Generally known to his shipmates as Lennie (sometimes he was Freddie; he mostly called himself Alf), the sea was for him. The comradeship of his sailor pals was wonderful, there was a thriving black market to make extra loot on the side, he really did get to see the world, and the work was something he did well enough to earn several promotions: shipping records show that he went from bellboy to silver room boy, saloon steward, assistant steward and other, similar positions.

Alf's best decade at sea was the first. His close friend Billy Hall laughs as he recalls:

> He was a rascal. An *absolute* character. You wouldn't think of going out anywhere without dragging Lennie along. He was always part of the fun – and if there wasn't any, he'd make some.
>
> He was an ale drinker, but once he started drinking he'd drink anything. If there was a bottle, he'd stay with it. He was a happy drunk, he just did stupid things on the spur of the moment. Most times he'd get away with it and laugh like hell.[1]

Alf had now reached his full adult height, 5ft 3in, and compensated for cat-calls by being the comedian. He whistled, played harmonica and loved to sing: he particularly enjoyed Red Sails In The Sunset, except he did it as 'Red suns in the sailset, all blue I feel day', having found that twisting words would winkle another laugh.

Though only sporadically back in Liverpool, Alf always claimed he was faithful to Julia. She, however, was nonplussed about his absences, scarcely reacted when he left, and never went to the docks to see him off. He'd recall how, even though he wrote to her, she never wrote back; and how, when he was home in Liverpool, she treated him coolly. He appears to have been her plaything, an amusing friend repeatedly ambling back into her life and then going away again, at which point she – a rebel spirit with a strong allure to men and a playful, vivacious character – did whatever she pleased. With their higher opinion of themselves, most (or all) of the Stanleys saw Alf as 'low', and there was also the religious schism, Protestant against Catholic, a gulf that violently divided Liverpool in these years.

Julia worked through the 1930s as an usherette at the Trocadero, one of several sumptuous film palaces newly built in the centre of town. With her lively personality, iridescent appeal to men, and a job that brought her into constant contact with many of them, it's not credible (though it's been claimed) that Julia resisted all male overtures because Alf was her one true love. When they married, it was for a dare, a lark. He'd later recall how Julia goaded him, claiming that, through sheer cowardice, he'd never propose.[2] That did it. Alf popped the question and Julia said yes. He fixed the wedding for Liverpool register office on 3 December 1938, just before he had to sail off to the West Indies. Their first married hours comprised an afternoon at the pictures (watching an awful Tommy Trinder comedy called *Almost A Honeymoon*), then Alf took his wife back to 22 Huskisson Street and went home to 57 Copperfield Street.*

The news was poorly received at the Stanleys, as Mimi later remembered: 'We were all shocked. She just thought it was clever to defy the family. She soon regretted it when she realised it was not so clever. Julia was a beautiful girl, headstrong. I loved Julia. She was so witty and amusing, always laughing. We all make mistakes. Julia's was not realising the seriousness of a defiant "prank". The only good thing that came out of it was John.'[3]

---

* The Stanleys had moved to Huskisson Street in recent months from 71a Berkley Street.

Paul McCartney – family background

McCartney isn't an English name, but efforts to establish when this specific line of the family arrived in England have proved fruitless, so many are the possibilities. Genealogists ascribe the name's journey to a start in Scotland as the Mackintosh clan, followed by a migration to Ireland, during the course of which they switched from Catholic to Protestant.

A clear and traceable line in Liverpool begins in 1864 when James McCartney (Paul's great-grandfather) married Elizabeth Williams, he the son of an upholsterer who may have fled the Great Famine, she the daughter of a boilermaker. They lived on Scotland Road, that heaving thoroughfare with Catholic and Protestant immigrants packed into dingy properties, from airless cellars to gusty rafters, unturned cheek by bloodied jowl. Their first child was Joseph (Joe), and by the time he came along, in 1866, they'd the misfortune to be in the despicable court housing on parallel Great Homer Street.

From the leaving of school until the leaving of his life, Joe McCartney worked for Cope Brothers & Co, importers of tobacco and manufacturers of all its related products. He was a journeyman cutter and stover for almost fifty years – hefty labour in hot conditions. A quiet and likeable man, teetotal, he blew the huge E-flat bass tuba in his works' brass band – warm and nurturing north-country music played at church fetes and on park bandstands. Joe was the first in the still-continuing line of male McCartney musicians to perform in public.[4]

In 1896, Joe married Florence (Florrie, Flo) Clegg, whose family were from Onchan in the Isle of Man, and they settled in Everton. There was the usual heartbreak: two of their nine children died in infancy. Paul McCartney's father, James – known to all as Jim – was the fifth, born in July 1902. The McCartneys were a no-nonsense, close-knit family and would always remain so. The seven surviving children – known as Jack, Jim, Joe, Edie, Mill (or Milly), Annie and Gin (or Ginny) – lived and looked out for one another and spoke with down-to-earth Liverpool wit and wisdom. Several could sing well, and Jim's favoured instrument was the piano. Around 1916, the McCartneys bought a secondhand upright from a nearby music shop called Nems, and Jim – self-taught, and despite being almost deaf in one ear – had natural flair, good rhythm and the ability to pick up all the popular tunes.*

---

* Nems will play a huge part in this history. At this point, however, it was not yet owned by the Epstein family. Paul bought back his father's piano in 1981 (it had previously been sold) and still plays it. Jim got his hearing problem when, as a child, he fell off a wall in the narrow back alley ('jigger') behind their house at 3 Solva Street.

Jim McCartney exuded courtesy and civility all through his life, being someone to whom charm came naturally. (Paul remembers him habitually raising his
hat to women at the bus stop and bidding them 'Good morning', and insisting
Paul raise his school cap similarly. 'Oh Dad, do I *have* to?' 'Yes son, you do.'[5])
A keen reader, and a self-schooled whizz at crosswords, he entered employment
at 14, doing well to get work as a sample boy for A. Hannay & Co, cotton bro-
kers annexed to Liverpool's great Cotton Exchange.

It was at a Hannay's staff soirée that Jim first played music for the public. The
year was 1919 and the latest musical explosion in America, ragtime, had crossed
the Atlantic, landing first in Liverpool because this was where the great ocean
liners came and went. The immense popularity of ragtime, swiftly followed by
jazz, fuelled and fed a boom in dancing and the evolution of the gramophone
record into a standard format – typically ten-inch, made of shellac and spinning
at 78 revolutions per minute (rpm), so harnessing the length of a song to about
three minutes. Together with family and friends of family, Jim Mac's Band
played Merseyside's many dance/music venues until 1924, though not very
often. Were they any good? Jim had a pat and typically self-deprecating answer.
'Band?' he'd say. 'Band? I've seen better bands around a man's hat.'

They played all the great tunes coming out of New York's gold-laden Tin Pan
Alley, and also a more modest piece of music Jim made up, the first ever
McCartney composition, an instrumental piano shuffle he called Eloise. A wife
for Gentleman Jim, however, was not so easy. He went through his teens, twenties and almost all his thirties before finding her.[6]

Paul McCartney's mother was Mary Patricia Mohin, born in Fazakerley (north
Liverpool) in 1909. She was of strong Irish stock, Roman Catholic on both
sides; though she married outside her kind, Catholicism was significant in her
life.

On her father's side, the genealogy is almost comical, undergoing three arbitrary changes of a similar-sounding surname in rapid succession. Her father,
Owen Mohin, was born Owen Mohan, and his father before him was Owen
Moan. Born about 1880 and known as 'Ownie', Owen Mohin was one of nine
born into a poor rural farming family in County Monaghan. At 12, the boy
escaped and got to Scotland, where he lived in a Glasgow inner-city tenement
and worked as a coal delivery boy, which must have been exceedingly rough. In
1905, he married Mary Theresa Danher in an RC church local to her home in
Liverpool; how they met isn't known. Born in 1877, Mary was the daughter of
John Danher, who'd arrived in England from Limerick (on the west coast of
Ireland) in the 1860s.

Ownie and Mary brought four, almost five, children into the world. When giving birth to the fifth, Mary succumbed to pneumonia and died with the baby. Mary Patricia was the second. The distress of losing her mother at the age of nine was then compounded by her father suddenly taking her and her two brothers to Ireland, where he made a failed attempt to get back into farming – and when they all returned to Liverpool, broke, he had a new wife and stepchildren, all of which was strongly opposed by Mary and her siblings.

The first time the Danher and McCartney families got together was in 1925, when Mary's cousin Bert (one of Jim Mac's Band) married Jim's sister Annie. Mary and Jim must have met at the wedding, but it would be another sixteen years before they began their relationship. Mary knew all the McCartneys and liked them as they liked her, and by the end of the 1930s she'd moved in with Gin, the youngest of the breed but soon to become matriarch. Now in her twenties, the daughter of an uneducated and poor man, Mary was determined to work hard and elevate her station in life. Set truly on the path of self-improvement, she went into nursing, with midwifery her speciality. She reached 30 as a ward sister and what people always called 'a spinster'.

George Harrison – family background

Down the male line at least, the Harrisons were Liverpool English through and through: Protestant, bright, labouring class and, from the end of the nineteenth century, citizens of Wavertree. Once a self-governing authority, with its own history and fine Gothic municipal buildings, it bridges factory and greenery and has a foot in both. Though much of the housing was drab and basic, there were plenty worse places to live in Liverpool.

Despite being illiterate – like many others, his mark was an X – Edward Harrison (George's great-grandfather) was an artist with his hands, practising the trade of stonemasonry on public buildings. In 1868 he married Manchester girl Elizabeth Hargreaves and they had a substantial family; one of the boys was Henry, known as Harry, who also went into the building business. As his grandson George would appreciatively explain, 'My father's father, who I never knew, built all these great Victorian, or maybe Edwardian, houses in Prince's Road in Liverpool, which used to be where all the doctors lived. And in those days they knew how to build: good masonry, good bricks, good timber.'[7]

When Harry was killed, fighting for his country in the Great War, it didn't only forestall the continued Harrison imprint on Liverpool architecture, it widowed a wife, robbed seven children of a father and caused them all great financial hardship. He'd married Jane Thompson in 1902, whose father was Scottish and mother from the Isle of Man; the fourth of their seven offspring, born at home in Wavertree in 1909, was Harold Hargreaves Harrison, father of George. With no assistance for bereaved families, everything was threadbare.

Harold, known to all as Harry, was by nature quiet and resolute, with a dogged strength and wry sense of humour. After leaving school at 14, he lied about his age and joined the merchant navy. From 1926 he was a steward with the White Star Line, plying the same routes and doing the same job as Alf Lennon. He first visited the United States in 1927; America was seen enviously as 'the land of plenty', because it was, and the Harrison household soon began to accumulate American gear, including a radio, wind-up gramophone, records and a guitar. Then, at home between voyages, Harry met a vivacious 18-year-old called Louise French, and by 1930 their lives were entwined.

On George's mother's side the influence is Irish – the known history stretches back to the Norman knights who sailed from France to Ireland around 1169 and settled as powerful Catholic landowners in County Wexford. The peasant locals called them French, which came to be misspelled Ffrench. These landowners received a brutal shock in 1649 in the form of the Parliamentarian invasion from London. When Oliver Cromwell's bloody conquest was complete, and Ireland part of the British Empire, huge tracts of land had been confiscated, and for the next 250 years the Ffrench toiled in the soil they'd once owned.

George's grandfather, John French, was born in 1870 into a family that doesn't appear to have been as destitute as those around them, or even too badly stricken by the potato famine. Still, he left and settled in Liverpool in the late 1890s, where he met the woman who'd share his last four decades.

Louise Woollam, the grandmother George knew until he was almost six, was Protestant, not Catholic, and hers wasn't a Liverpool family but a Shropshire one, gardeners and farmers. Her parents lived rurally – in Little Crosby, north of Liverpool – and Louise, born in 1879, was their third child. From 1905 to 1924, she and John French had seven children, all raised as staunch Catholics, but they weren't married. 'Mr and Mrs French', poor but respectable folk of Wavertree, were the proverbial dark horses, free to marry but not bothering. Born in March 1911, the fourth of the seven was named after the mother, Louise.

It's not clear if all this was known to their offspring, but John and Louise's efforts to keep their status secret had ramifications beyond the point where its origin was necessarily remembered. So concerned were they that their situation should not be exposed, they maintained a marked suspicion about 'nosy neighbours', guarding information about themselves. Their daughter Louise – George Harrison's mother – always felt strongly about anyone knowing more about her family than she wished, and passed it down to her children.

*

Louise and Harry Harrison always said they married in 1930, putting distance between this and the 1931 birth of their first baby, another Louise. The actual interval between the two events was three months, and no doubt the domestic circumstances were heavy. The oil and water mix of Catholic and Protestant was always a major problem, to say nothing of the fact there had clearly been 'relations' before marriage. They put their name down for a Liverpool Corporation house but knew they'd have to wait, and in the meantime rented a tiny terraced house at 12 Arnold Grove, a standard British 'two-up-two-down' typical of all these lives: downstairs was a small front room (used maybe three times a year) and a kitchen, upstairs were two small bedrooms. No heating, no bathroom, and no toilet except the privy in the minuscule and draughty back yard.

Louise gave birth a second time in 1934, to Harold (known as Harry, maintaining a generations-long confusion of names), and then Harry quit the White Star Line in 1936 so his wife wouldn't have to raise the children alone. He struggled for almost two years to find work: it was the Depression, and times grew very tough for the Harrisons. The guitar was pawned, never retrieved. At the end of 1937, though, Harry passed some exams to become a Corporation ('Corpy') bus conductor, and by 1939 he'd qualified to drive and was behind the wheel – a quiet, rock steady, punctual character flashing his genuine lop-sided smile at those he met.

Richard 'Richy' Starkey – family background

Above the last docks in Liverpool, on the streets that take the hill from the Mersey, the nineteenth century brought petroleum stores, gas works, factories, chimneys and a hundred different manufacturing eyesores, swiftly accompanied by block after block of narrow streets and alleys packed tight with cramped terraced houses built to poor specifications. The area was known as the Dingle. Not everything here was bad – there was an authentically strong community, people pulled together and took care of their own, and housewives were as houseproud as could be. But there was no hiding the infestations, the damp, the decay and subsidence, or the malnourished and barefoot children. A high proportion of the Dingle's adult population – generally Protestant, few Irish, and entirely working-class – was jobless and penniless, drinking and singing their lives away in its many pubs. In Liverpool, where you're never far away from a run-down area, the Dingle – the 'South End' – had a reputation for roughness and alcoholism all its own.

Richy Starkey's family were Dingle through and through. Dot an old map with the addresses of his ancestors and they're all within a square mile. On official documents this isn't the Dingle at all but Toxteth, or Toxteth Park, Liverpool 8, and these places are within the same precinct of poverty as the Lennons on Copperfield Street and the Stanleys on Berkley Street ... but the Dingle is just a bit further south and more depressed. That word 'Toxteth' wasn't used in everyday conversation. Lads were 'Dingle boys' – a phrase that could spark fear in others, such was the violence and vandalism of its gangs of deadbeat youths. Other Liverpudlians generally kept away.

A key distinction between Dingle men was those who were unemployed and those who were unemployable, the work-keen versus the work-shy. Richy Starkey's family, on both sides, were workers, and generally had some. His father's father, a journeyman boilermaker, was born John (Johnny) Parkin in 1890. At some point between 1903 and 1910, his mother took up 'living in sin' with a married man named Starkey, a situation considered so sordid that, to avoid difficulties and gossip, Ma Parkin switched her surname to that of her new man, and her son, to maintain the illusion, changed his too. Johnny Parkin became Johnny Starkey overnight, just like that.

Johnny Parkin's father was a seaman working a lightship at Formby, up the coast from Liverpool. He was also John Parkin, born in 1865, and he in turn was the son of a seaman born about 1823 in Hull, across the other side of England. This man, yet another John Parkin (there were at least three generations of them), was married to a Hull woman and they moved coasts to settle in the Dingle about 1862.

The young man who flipped from Johnny Parkin to Johnny Starkey was married in 1910 to Annie Bower, born 1889, whose father was a tinsmith. They had four children together, the second of them – Richard Henry Parkin Starkey – arriving in October 1913. Known as Richy, he was the father of the boy born twenty-seven years later who, against inconceivable odds, would force his way out of a dreary dead-end Dingle destiny in the most spectacular fashion.

Johnny Starkey would play a crucial role in the raising of his grandson, and by all accounts he was a full-on 'wacker' (a much-used word for working-class Liverpool men and boys), being a drinker, labourer, gambler and brawler. No pushover herself, Annie was something of a twentieth-century witch, invoking the name of the devil and concocting her own remedies and potions when tending the sick. The Starkeys' was quite a household – noisy and poor. Their boy Richy became a confectioner, making sweets and cakes, and it was while working in a bakery in 1935 that he met the woman he'd marry, a doughty Dingle girl by the name of Elsie Gleave.

The Gleaves had been in the Dingle over fifty years before Elsie's birth in October 1914. They lived in all the same streets and her family line was also steeped in boilermaking, that dirty but vital ancillary industry in a city of ships. Her father John was one, his father too, and his as well, by which time the documents have stretched back to the middle of the nineteenth century.

Elsie's mother provided a little more variation. Catherine 'Kitty' Johnson was of Dingle parents but her father was the son of a mariner born in the Shetland Islands, off the north coast of Scotland, and her mother was the daughter of a gardener from Mayo – the only trace of Irish in this genealogy. They could have been Catholics, but it's unlikely: the Gleaves were street-marching Protestants in Liverpool, Elsie included.

John and Kitty married in 1914, and of Elsie's seven younger siblings, three didn't survive infancy. Life was grim for the Gleaves, especially after John went through front-line trench action in the Great War; Elsie was in the care of a grandmother for at least part of her childhood, and was out of school and into work at 14. She had a variety of jobs, one of them in the bakery where worked Richard Starkey.

In the throes of a chaotic time in her life, Elsie was receptive to Richy's offer of stability through marriage, and in October 1936 the bells rang out at St Silas Church. He was 23 and she 22. With nothing set aside, they moved into the cramped and boisterous Starkey household at 59 Madryn Street, and, like all the generations before them, tried to make the best of things.

Everyone knew a war with Hitler was coming, and everyone knew Liverpool would be devastated, but the city's preparations were poor and inadequate. Not that the first bombs to explode here in 1939 were German. The Irish Republican Army (IRA) began a fresh wave of mainland terrorism that summer, and – in spite of its vast Irish population – Liverpool was a repeated target. On 3 May, a tear-gas bomb exploded under a seat in the Trocadero cinema. It wasn't designed to kill and there was no loss of life, but this was only realised later; there was a loud explosion, a great panic, and fifteen people were rushed to hospital. The *Evening Express* ran a photo of three usherettes in their match-ing uniforms and pill-box hats receiving first-aid on the street outside. Julia Lennon isn't in it, but it's likely she was on duty and among the shaken staff who, with admirable calmness, ushered patrons to safety. The *Daily Mirror* headline the next day was 3000 FLEE FROM IRA GAS.*

---

* The trade magazine *Kinematograph Weekly* reported (11 May 1939) that when the gas had cleared and the Trocadero resumed its programme, the organist struck up Dancing With Tears In My Eyes.

Four months later, on 3 September, Britain stood up to Germany's aggression and declared war. The Merseyside time signal – the 'one o'clock gun' fired every day at Birkenhead – was silenced. From the outlying quarry village of Woolton to the slums of Scotland Road, from Toxteth and the Dingle to Everton and Wavertree, all of Liverpool – as shockingly ill-equipped and under-prepared as she was – held their collective breath and waited, more or less unprotected, for the Nazis to come and bomb the hell out of them.

The British government's National Service (Armed Forces) Act compelled the call-up of men between the ages of 18 and 41, but as a merchant seaman, bus driver and cake-maker respectively, Alf Lennon (26), Harry Harrison (30) and Richy Starkey (25) were in 'reserved occupations' and excused duty, and Jim McCartney (37) was spared because of his impaired hearing. He became a part-time fire-watcher, and Harry Harrison may have gone into his works' Home Guard. Richy Starkey's access to the means of production meant his family had sugar, tightly rationed for everyone else.

Elsie fell pregnant about four weeks after war was declared, after which she and her husband moved out of Ma and Pa Starkey's at 59 Madryn Street and into a place of their own. Despite the certainty of heavy bombing right here – the adjacent docks were a clear target – they didn't go far: they carted their possessions just twenty-five houses along the terrace to a rented house at number 9.

George and Annie Stanley also moved when war was announced, renting a terraced three-bedroom house at 9 Newcastle Road, Wavertree, an area generally referred to as Penny Lane because of the nearby bus and tram terminus that took the name.[8] Their three at-home children made the move with them – unmarried Mimi and Anne, and Julia, now 25, whose husband – 'that Alf Lennon' – was at sea. It was Mimi's home for so few days it's doubtful she unpacked: she numbered among the many who rushed to marry when war was announced. On 15 September, age 33, she pledged herself to George Smith, a Woolton cowkeeper, 36, whom she'd known ten years. In one move, Mimi broke away from an imposing father, gained a devoted husband, moved into an inherited small cottage in Woolton, and had a little cash in hand – new and understandably welcome experiences in uncertain times.

Mimi would later remark that Julia swiftly regretted marrying Alf, and accepted that she'd allowed defiance of her family to cloud her judgement, but it was unlikely to have been for the sake of defiance that Julia conceived Alf's baby. The *Duchess Of York* was in port between 5 and 13 January 1940 and Alf had removed his waiter's white gloves for a week of unabashed revelry in and around 9 Newcastle Road. Always one for candour, he'd later boast how they made the baby on the kitchen floor.[9] Then he set sail again, helping to maintain the increasingly dangerous North Atlantic trade route. What just years earlier had been an enjoyable job had turned into a hellish nightmare, U-boats lurking in the deep.

Ten minutes into Sunday 7 July 1940, in an upstairs bedroom at 9 Madryn Street, Elsie Starkey gave birth to a boy. He was a week overdue and the delivery was tricky, but he appeared to be a healthy, podgy ten-pounder screaming his lungs out. Fourteen days later, Richy and Elsie were back at the scene of their wedding, St Silas Church, to have their son baptised Protestant, Church of England. In working-class tradition, they named him after his father, so now there were two Richards, a Big Richy and a Little Richy.

Having babies now was tricky, as Louise Harrison was also finding out. In July, she gave birth to her third, Peter ... and then, shortly after midnight on 17 August, the Germans finally began their attack on Liverpool. The first bombs fell on the southern docks, and when the sirens sounded Elsie and Big Richy jumped out of bed, grabbed the baby and panicked through the blackout to the pathetic shelter of the tiny under-stairs cupboard. It was only when the baby wouldn't stop screaming that Elsie realised she was holding him to her shoulder feet first. Years later, when he was old enough to understand, Elsie would tell her son the Second World War had started because of his birth – it was the only way it could be celebrated.[10]

Julia Lennon didn't give birth in an air-raid. Wednesday 9 October 1940 offered a rare window of respite from the falling bombs. Her baby was born in Liverpool Maternity Hospital on Oxford Street, Mimi as companion and the first to appreciate it was a boy – very welcome in a female-dominated family. John Winston Lennon's arrival was registered by Alf on 11 November. The name John might have been Mimi's suggestion, one that Alf, the informant, could have changed had he wished – but maybe it was his idea. It was, after all, his dad's name, and so the infant connected him to the memory of Liverpool's original John Lennon, 1855–1921. The middle name was in honour of Churchill at this time of fervent patriotism – the Stanleys, certainly Julia and Mimi, are said to have loved Britain's wartime leader – but the timing of the registration may also have been an influence: 11 November is Armistice Day, always a sombre date in Britain, when everyone wears a poppy and remembers the Great War dead. Now, in the midst of another do-or-die struggle against the Germans, the occasion had a focused poignancy.

Home for baby John was Newcastle Road with his parents (although Alf was about to sail away again), his Aunt Anne and his grandparents (Pop and Mama), with a dash for the shelter when the air-raid sirens sounded, and already frequent visits to his Aunt Mimi and Uncle George two miles away in Woolton, where the not-so-young newlyweds, stable adults with no children of their own on the horizon, were already forming a singular attachment to this one.

In the north end of town, in Norris Green, Jim McCartney too was seeing plenty of enemy action. He spent every night as a fire-watcher and, when called to duty, fireman. Day to day, though, his life was in turmoil. The British government's sudden wartime decision to nationalise the buying of cotton forced the closure of the Cotton Exchange; all work there ended and a new job had to be found. Matters were suddenly moving in his personal life too. Mary Mohin was visiting Florrie McCartney one night when the sirens sounded and she was forced to stay over. Jim and Mary had talked together many times, but if there was ever a spark of interest between them, it hadn't much ignited. This time, chatting for several more hours, it finally did. How long they courted isn't known, but relationships accelerate in times of war, and, as their loved ones were doubtless pointing out, neither of them was getting any younger.

On 15 April 1941, two weeks after losing his job, Jim Mac married Mary Mohin. He was 38 and she 31. He was Protestant by birth and agnostic by choice, but because religion was important to Mary, they married in a Catholic chapel. Jim found work at a factory making piston engines for British fighter planes, then he became a lathe-turner on a production line. They lived in a rented house at 10 Sunbury Road, Anfield (next door to a couple called Lennon), and Mary worked on the maternity ward at nearby Walton Hospital.

All Merseyside continued to suffer heavily from the bombs, especially in the Blitz week of May 1941, when Germany attempted to obliterate Liverpool, to wipe it off the map as a prelude to a land invasion. In that one week, 3966 people were killed and 3812 seriously injured; 10,000 homes were destroyed and 184,000 damaged – as if many of them weren't decrepit enough to start with. Liverpudlians, for whom tough times were a way of life, buried their dead, swept the rubble into piles and carried on. They couldn't be extinguished any more than their humour. One street-corner chip shop ('chippie') simply put up a sign – 'Owing to Hitler, our portions are littler' – and kept the home fryers burning.

The ensuing months were quieter, however, and in the middle of the pause, in September, Mary McCartney fell pregnant. As maternity ward sister at Walton Hospital she was accorded the luxury of a private room there when giving birth to a boy on Thursday 18 June 1942. It was just as well, because there was a complication. Interpreting signs that the delivery would be difficult, the midwife (who'd trained Mary) summoned the urgent assistance of a doctor. In the terminology of the time, the baby was born in a state of White Asphyxia, a condition that typically required direct cardiac massage and mouth-to-mouth resuscitation. It was an emergency, but a brief one: the infant suddenly began screaming and all was well. Jim and Mary named him James Paul – the first from Jim, the second, maybe, from Jim's grandad, Paul Clegg (c.1815–79). To avoid the kind of confusion common in many households, they called him by his middle name. He was baptised Catholic, but on King Billy's Day (12 July), the most important date in the Protestant calendar, when Liverpool was full of marchers.

A month or so before these events, Louise Harrison fell pregnant once more. She and Harry were still in the tiny house at Arnold Grove, the one they'd rented pro-tem eleven years earlier. Though they'd no intention of adding to the army of local families squeezing ten or more kids into a room, they wanted Peter to have a sibling around his age, just as Louise and Harry had each other. With Liverpool now free of bombs, and those elder children back from a temporary evacuation to Wales, bus driver Harry Harrison's house had room for just one more on top.

The baby was close to three weeks overdue when he emerged into the cold front-upstairs bedroom ten minutes into Thursday 25 February 1943.[11] No one could sleep through Louise's labour pains, and each in turn was invited to see the latest and last addition to the family, another boy. The strong similarity between father and son wasn't lost on Harry, who later said, 'There he was, a miniature version of me. "Oh no," I thought, "we just couldn't be so alike."'[12] He trooped off next day to register the birth. He and Louise hadn't discussed a name, so Harry gave it some thought as he walked the short way to Wavertree Town Hall. When he got back, Louise asked what he'd chosen. 'George.' 'Why George?' 'If it's good enough for the King it should be good enough for him.' The baby was baptised Catholic, and after a spell in his parents' bedroom a place was found for him in the children's – he had a small wooden cot, Harry and Peter now shared a single bed, and Louise had another. Along with a small chest of drawers, nothing more could possibly be squeezed into the tiny space.

Paul and George were fortunate to have a settled home life. The same could not be said for young Richy Starkey, whose parents split up some time after his third birthday. They'd been married seven years and it was over. There was no divorce (yet), just a parting of the ways, the child sticking with his mother. While Johnny and Annie Starkey would always maintain a close relationship with their daughter-in-law and grandson, their son provided his estranged wife and child with little support and Elsie was forced to raise Richy on whatever shillings she could scrimp. From 1943 she was taking any job going, but they remained firmly on the breadline. Elsie later said that Little Richy didn't seem too upset about it all, though he did complain about lack of company. 'When it was raining he used to look out of the window and say, "I wish I had brothers and sisters. There's nobody to talk to when it's raining."'[13]

John Lennon was also feeling the effects of marital discord. The longest period he spent within a standard family unit was probably about two months, when Alf was home for a spell and Mimi and George let him, Julia and John stay at their place, 120a Allerton Road, the cottage George had inherited from his father. It was spring 1943, after Alf had completed a succession of voyages to and from New York on the *Moreton Bay*. John was two and a half.

Alf would later say how shocked he was to find that, during his time at sea, Julia had been going out most nights to local pubs and to dances, mixing and singing with men of the forces, a married woman enjoying the life of one unmarried. And his next absence was much longer, because Alf got himself into trouble: first he deserted one of his ships, and then, on his next voyage, he was arrested for possession of broached cargo, landing up in a naval court in Bône, north-east Algeria, where he was sentenced to a month in prison. Back in Liverpool, Julia may have had no idea of her husband's fate. Down at the Mercantile Marine Offices there was no pay ('family allotment') to collect, Alf's letters home stopped, and all went quiet. Here ended whatever vestiges of marital fidelity she still maintained.

It's not difficult to imagine what a hit Julia was when she took a job as barmaid at the Brook House pub on Smithdown Road. She soon began a relationship with a soldier from Wales – history records his name only as Taffy Williams – and he evidently spent a fair bit of time at Newcastle Road, in John's company, because John would remember him. He'd also keep a particular memory of Julia at this time, when she sang to him I'm Wishing from Walt Disney's animated film *Snow White And The Seven Dwarfs*. 'Want to know a secret? / Promise not to tell? / We are standing by a wishing well.' It could be something she sang in the pub, because, like Alf, Julia enjoyed providing saloon entertainment.

The following November, when Alf knocked on the door of 9 Newcastle Road, it was eighteen months since he'd gone away. 'Give us a kiss,' appealed the guileless wacker, suggesting his long absence could be put behind them with a kiss and a cuddle and a roaring great yarn about Algeria. But Julia stopped him short and announced, 'I'm in the family way.' Out tumbled a tale to explain her pregnancy (she was two months gone) by Taffy Williams and a domestic scene blew up involving all parties, which the four-year-old John witnessed and would remember but never fully understand. Mimi watched ever more anxiously from the sidelines, concerned about the impact of events searing into her nephew's fertile mind.

That December, Alf took John away to Maghull, ten miles north of Liverpool, to stay with his brother Syd, his wife Madge and John's cousin Joyce. They left after about three weeks and then suddenly made a surprise and, in John's case, indefinite return: Joyce says he lived with them for several months – maybe three – staying in their small semi-detached house at 27 Cedar Grove.

He was here long enough for Madge to seek his admission to the local school in the coming September, and for she and Syd to form such an attachment that they hoped to become his legal guardians. Julia never came to see him, which left them a long way short of impressed. Then, probably in April 1945, Alf came and took John away. Joyce, who'd been getting along great with her younger cousin, never met him again. She remembers, 'My parents were devastated when he left – and not only for themselves. They knew John was going back to being dragged from one parent to the other.'[14]

The McCartneys, meanwhile, had begun a succession of short-term lets; Jim had found new work in an armament plant, and Mary had fallen pregnant again. Paul gained a brother in January 1944 – Peter Michael, known as Michael or Mike, and to his parents as Mick. The age gap was one and a half years, the distinction of older and younger brother always clear. Mary then became a municipal midwife for the Corporation, delivering babies around the north end of the city, which enabled the family to rent a reserved tenement flat in Everton.

VE Day, Victory in Europe. Little Richy Starkey, who'd lost a parent but not as a result of the war, sat down to a few severely rationed treats at an open-air party in Madryn Street, and George Harrison, youngest in a family of six, did the same in Arnold Grove.[15] Alf Lennon, back in Liverpool between voyages, was with his mum on Copperfield Street, his bizarre marriage in tatters. Julia had charge of their four-year-old John and was about to pop with another man's baby.* Mimi and husband George had taken out a mortgage on a semi-detached house on Menlove Avenue, a leafy but busy boulevard in Woolton. For the McCartney family, VE Day would be ever tinged with sadness. Just a few hours before, Jim's mother Florrie died from a heart attack. Paul and Mike would never remember her, and with her passing they lost their last grandparent. In their stead, they had aunties, uncles and cousins galore to provide them with the most energising and memorable of family lives.

Much of the Liverpool in which all these people lived was in ruins, the city fathers having made distressingly few efforts to bandage its open wounds during

---

* A girl, Victoria Elizabeth Lennon, was born in June 1945 in a Salvation Army maternity home in the Mossley Hill district, a short walk from Penny Lane. Julia then allowed that organisation to arrange an adoption and the baby was assigned to a local woman and her Norwegian-born seaman husband. She spent her childhood just north of Liverpool and never met her mother, father or half-brother John. Her identity was made public in 1998 – her name had been changed from Victoria Lennon to Ingrid Pedersen, adopted daughter of Peder and Margaret. They show up in 1950s phone directories at 88 The Northern Road, Crosby, Liverpool 23.

the four post-Blitz years – certainly nothing like as much as Britain's other bombed cities were doing. But on this great day, the 8th of May 1945, everyone put the trauma of the six-year war behind them and looked forward to a brighter future. Schoolchildren were given the day off, streets were bedecked with bunting, flags were waved, and crowds gathered outside Liverpool Town Hall to hear the BBC broadcast by Winston Churchill and an address by the Lord Mayor – a great mass of people the like of which wouldn't be seen again at this place for about another twenty years.

2
Boys (1945–54)

Not long after war's end, Julia Lennon found herself a new man. She'd taken a job at another big local pub, the Coffee House at Wavertree, where she met customer John Dykins. He'd been spared active war service because of a lingering childhood chest complaint, since when he'd developed a twitch and was often nervously clearing his throat. He worked as a door-to-door salesman and was also involved in the local black market. He and Julia began an affair – confusingly, she called him Bobby – and again her family frowned on it. As before, John Lennon was often looked after by Mimi, who was expressing grave concern for his welfare.

Three miles away, in the Toxteth end of the Dingle, Johnny and Annie Starkey were helping care for their grandson Richy (or Dicky, or 'that bloody Noddler', as his grandad called him) – especially when he was ailing. Annie would make him either a bread poultice (slices of white bread soaked in boiling water, wrapped in muslin and applied to the skin) or a hot toddy (a spirit, usually whisky, with hot water). Richy especially loved the hot toddies, not to mention all the fuss that went with being ill. Annie was shocked her little grandson was left-handed; she announced he'd been possessed by witches, or the devil, and took it upon herself to exorcise it. Over a long time, but persistently, she defeated the evil, forcing the child to ditch his natural tendency and use his right hand instead. Not for nothing, and never without love, would Richy come to describe Granny Starkey as 'the voodoo queen of Liverpool'.[1]

Having been conceived about four weeks after war began, Richy started school ten days after it officially ended, on 25 August 1945. He was enrolled at St Silas, a large red-brick Victorian building annexed to the now bombed-out church where his parents had married. Elsie walked him there and said, 'On your way, son.' He instantly hated it. Elsie would tell the story of how he walked home at dinner-time and announced they'd all been given the afternoon off, and how she gullibly believed him until she saw other kids walking past their window, returning to school. He had nearly conned her, and there'd be hundreds of times when he did.

Elsie was scraping together around £3 a week through no end of toil – scrubbing steps and serving in a greengrocery, doing anything decent to bring in the pennies – and it was around this time that her estranged husband quit his parents' house and left the area, probably moving to Crewe, about forty miles south of Liverpool. He saw very little of his Richy again, would retain few sympathetic memories, and stopped supporting his wife and child altogether. Unable to meet the rent on 9 Madryn Street, Elsie loaded their possessions on to a cart and wheeled them across High Park Street, then down the narrow 'play street' that was Admiral Grove to their new home – a tiny 'two-up-two-down' in a terrace which, Richy would always say, had already been condemned for ten years. He'd recall sitting on the back of the cart, his legs dangling over the side, as his earliest memory.[2]

Rented at ten shillings a week, 10 Admiral Grove had a wooden V (for Victory) sign only recently affixed over the front door ... but there wasn't much in the way of celebration going on inside. Elsie was angry with her husband's behaviour and didn't hide her opinions from their son, who'd later use the word 'brainwashed' to describe his intake; he expressed pain incoherently when he expressed it at all.[3] There were pubs at either end of the street and Elsie worked as a barmaid in at least one of them, needing the company and the laughs.

Home life was much steadier for Paul McCartney, now aged three, and also a natural left-hander (left unchallenged). Jim and Mary seem to have quickly established the kind of balanced domesticity experienced by only some families: Jim was mild-mannered, softly spoken, even-tempered and attentive; if he was cross, he kept it inside. Mary – quiet, firm, presentable, respectable – was more serious but also more demonstrably affectionate, though not overly so. She'd smack Paul or Mike if the need arose, but her biggest threat would be verbal: 'You'll get a smacked bottom from your father.'[4]

George Harrison was also being nurtured within a strong family, led by the indomitable Louise and steadfast Harry, Liverpool-sharp with decency. Harry had become an official with the local Transport & General Workers Union (TGWU), active at his bus depot. Though people considered him a quiet man, every so often he'd be up on a soapbox telling his worker brothers his thoughts and beliefs, and how he felt their lives could be improved.[5]

Still waiting for the Corporation to give them somewhere bigger to live, the Harrisons spent much of their time in Arnold Grove's cramped kitchen. There was usually a fire in the grate, with its adjacent oven where Louise baked bread; mantle-lights were lit by gas fed through a shilling meter; and the cooker was a two-ring burner on top of an upside-down tea-chest – from which lucky equipment, and using the government's scanty rations, Louise somehow made three meals a day for six. Once a week here (as in Madryn Street, Newcastle Road and some of the places the McCartneys lived), a zinc tub would be brought into the kitchen and everyone – adults and children in turn – would bathe or be bathed with hot water poured from a jug into their 'bungalow bath'. Photos of George at this age show a blond-haired boy, podgy-cheeked and with his father's lop-sided smile, and every story of his childhood paints a picture of a lad singlemindedly self-reliant. 'George was always a very independent child,' Louise would explain. 'He liked to do things by himself, no one to help him. He was also very intelligent and fun-loving, and helped a lot around the house.'[6]

John Lennon started school on 12 November 1945, at Mosspits Lane Primary, a suburban establishment typical of its kind. It was a short distance from Newcastle Road and Julia walked him there in the morning and collected him in the afternoon, working the Coffee House lunchtime session in between, and sometimes singing from its stage. Like Richy Starkey at St Silas, John began in the nursery class; unlike Richy, John saw clearly how he stood out from the crowd. He was exceptional, being advanced at reading, writing, drawing and painting, as well as at thinking creatively and communicating. But this gifted and lively mind was set in perpetual whirl by the adults around him. Problems beyond John's ken and control had been hurtling at him since the womb – and now came the decisive episode.

At the end of March 1946, Julia moved in with Bobby Dykins, and took John with her. It wasn't only a one-bedroom flat in Gateacre Village (close to Woolton), it was a one-*bed* flat – one double-bed in which Julia and her man were sleeping with her five-year-old son.[7] Considering with what fervour and frequency newly cohabiting couples usually enjoy sex, John's intimate exposure to such a situation was truly shocking, no matter how discreetly the adults may have been behaving. Mimi went straight over to express her view, Dykins ordered her out, and she returned with a senior official from the Public Assistance Committee. This department of Liverpool City Council – the Social Services of its day – played everything straight. It wasn't in the business of separating a mother from her child unless there was good reason, but an unmarried couple sharing a bed with a young infant was one such. As a consequence, for the time being at least, Mimi found herself John's primary carer. He moved in with her and his Uncle George at their house on Menlove Avenue.

While all this was going on, Alf finally accepted he'd been taken for a mug.

His next engagement was on the RMS *Queen Mary*, the great Cunard White Star flagship sailing from Southampton to New York – another 1600 GI brides exchanging ration books for endless bounty. But this was in stark contrast to his own predicament. Before leaving, he placed an advertisement in the *Liverpool Echo* – 'I, Alfred Lennon, recently of 9 Newcastle Road, Wavertree, Liverpool, will NOT be RESPONSIBLE for any DEBTS unless personally contracted'[8] – which as good as announced that the extraordinary seven-year marriage of Alfred Lennon and Julia Stanley was over. Not a single photograph of them together is known to have been taken.

One of Mimi's first actions was to remove John from Mosspits Lane and enrol him instead at Dovedale Road infants school – records show that he began here on 6 May 1946. The *Queen Mary* was back in England three weeks later; learning that his son was living with Mimi, Alf paid a visit to Menlove Avenue, one that seems to have been reasonably cordial. The next day, he said he was taking John out to the shops, but he didn't: they took the train to Blackpool and stayed there. The school 'withdrawal book' at Dovedale Road records the fact: 'Left district 31/5/46'.

Alf went to Blackpool because this was where his merchant navy friend Billy Hall lived, with his parents (the house is still there, 37 Ivy Avenue). Born in 1923, ten years younger than the man he knew as 'Lennie', Hall has for a long time been the only living witness to what transpired here, and the only person to relate the events impartially. (He calls John 'Johnny' because this was how Alf introduced him.)

Every account of Alf and John's time in Blackpool has turned on the vital fact that Alf brought his boy here prior to emigrating with him to New Zealand – the plan being that Billy's parents would emigrate and take John with them, to be joined later by Alf who'd work a passage there. This, insists Billy Hall, is fantasy.

> There's no truth at all in that. I said *I* would go to New Zealand, and Lennie said he might too, and also another mate of ours, and at some point it was mentioned that it would be a great place to raise Johnny – but no plans were ever made. Not only were my parents not planning to go, they didn't even know *I* was.
>
> The only actual plan that involved Johnny was that maybe he'd stay with my parents for two or three months until Lennie got something sorted out. But my mother was born in 1894 – she was already fifty-two. Though she looked after Johnny for the short time we were there, she didn't want to be responsible for a young kid at her age, and Lennie had to go back to sea. He *had* to go back. We were only on leave.

The final scene – probably 22 June 1946 – is painted vividly in John Lennon docudramas as the ultimate heartbreak moment for the youngster, the blameless participant in a devastating tug-of-love, forced to choose between his mother, who'd come up from Liverpool to fetch him back, and his father, who was about to sweep him off to New Zealand. Legend has the tear-stained infant first choosing Alf and then changing his mind, running in cinematic slow-motion down a Blackpool street as Julia walks dejectedly into a sepia sunset. Billy Hall recalls what actually happened.

> Lennie's wife came up with her boyfriend. I'll always remember him: he looked like a spiv, a wide-boy, with a trilby hat at a forty-five-degree angle, and a very thin moustache, like a smaller version of Terry-Thomas. He was probably there in case of trouble.
>
> They needed privacy, so we let them go in the front room – which normally no one went into, and which my mother kept spotless. They talked maybe half an hour and then Lennie came out and said, 'I'm letting Johnny go back with his mother – she's going to look after him properly.' I remember him saying 'properly' because Lennie felt pleased that he'd fixed it. There were no raised voices – had there been, I would have rushed in because I didn't know this Terry-Thomas character and my pal Lennie was only small. I really can't remember if Johnny was in there too, maybe he only went in later, but there was definitely no tug-of-love scene. Lennie's wife didn't leave the house until Lennie came and told us what they'd decided.[9]

John's 'choice' was not between his mother and father, it was between his mostly absent dad's friend's parents – in whose lives he had no place – and home and school back in Liverpool. There was no choice at all. But there was a goodbye, John parting decisively from his dad. From opening time that afternoon until closing time that night, Alf got hammered. Then, on 29 June, he sailed out of England on the *Almanzora* and continued life's riotous adventure ... while Julia and Bobby went back to Liverpool, and Julia (who was pregnant again) handed John over to Mimi and there was no further question, ever, about who would raise him.

John Lennon was now a child of Woolton, this self-sufficient village that was the least Irish, and so most English, suburb of Liverpool. Along with many other local children, he was enrolled in Sunday School at the handsome church on the hill, St Peter's; the sandstone that made it came from Woolton Quarry, from where excavating explosions regularly shook the area.

Like Mary McCartney and many others, Mimi Smith was trying to climb away from unvarnished working-class roots. George was now employed menially and on low pay, as a cleaner of trams and buses on the night-shift at Woolton depot, but they'd got a house that bordered on the affluent lower middle class – a semi-detached with a bathroom and indoor toilet, a telephone, picture rails, a couple of leaded-glass windows, and front and back gardens with lawns, trees and a shed. The previous occupants had pretensions of grandeur: not only did they give the house its name, Mendips, they called the middle downstairs room 'the morning room' and installed servants' bells – electrical fixtures that remained on the wall, but out of use, in the years John lived here. The Smiths had taken out a mortgage, and finding the monthly repayments was a stretch, achieved partly with rental income (from letting out a cottage George had inherited – it was now home to Mimi's sister Harriet and family) but mostly through prudent budgeting. Adding a child to the household was something Mimi had to manage with resourceful pragmatism. Though she gained John's ration book, she was never given the means to support him: there's no known indication that Alf or Julia helped foot the ongoing costs of their son's upbringing.

From June 1946, then, Mimi was the principal parental influence on John Lennon. Her character, which helped shape his, was later assessed by Mike Hennessey, a journalist who knew her:

> Aunt Mimi is a remarkable woman. Slender, dressed with severe simplicity and regarding the world with warm, brown, inquisitive eyes, she somehow communicates great inner strength and resolution and an independence of spirit, all mellowed by an irresistible sense of fun. She comes, she says, from a family of incessant talkers and certainly [she holds] free-flowing and intelligent conversation … She is extremely well-read, utterly self-sufficient, defiantly unsentimental and is sometimes mischievously irreverent. Her bookshelves are thick with biographies. She has a special regard for Osbert Sitwell but no time at all for slushy love stories. 'I couldn't possibly read that rubbish,' she says. 'If I read a book I want to be wiser afterwards.' Books are her only indulgence. She eats one simple meal a day, has never been to the hairdresser in her life and never wears make-up or jewellery. 'But if I go into Smith's, that's the end. I just can't resist books.'[10]

Already a keen reader, John became a bookworm at Mendips, digesting all the best juvenile literature and, while still a child, progressing to classic fiction, biographies, memoirs and histories – plus two daily papers, generally the *Daily Express* and *Liverpool Echo*, delivered and devoured. (John's reading skills were initially sharpened by Uncle George sitting him on his knee and poring over the

Echo.) John and Mimi often read the same books and discussed-argued their content. Mimi was fierce, stubborn, openly snobbish, pointed, bluntly uncompromising, nobody's fool – and John was never not aware of it and always 'gave back'. Though she might suddenly break into a Charleston dance to make him laugh (which he often copied), she was never demonstrative in her love, concealing it behind a coded series of verbal scoldings. She never hit him: her worst punishment was to ignore him, because he always had so much to say that needed to be heard. When she did, he'd plead, 'Don't 'nore me, Mimi!'[11]

She was never 'mum' to John, just Mimi or (when needling her deeper) Mary – and he stayed Lennon, never becoming John Smith. But he knew where he stood. He benefited enormously from her determination to provide what he'd never had in his tempestuous life to date: stability, assurance, certainty. She said she'd always be at home, that he'd never return to an empty house; she said she'd never go out in the evenings and subject him to the care of a child-sitter; and she got him put back into Dovedale Road school, where he shone, taking and fetching him every day. Her aim was to raise him as an individual. Both were as sharp as tacks, he exasperated her and she infuriated him, but theirs was always an earthy two-way relationship in which both could grow.

For a while, Julia came to the house and saw John, but then the visits stopped and Mimi encouraged distance to develop between the child and the woman he'd always call Mummy. Whether her judgement was right or wrong is subjective, but her motives were beyond question. If she was going to be the rock in John's life, she could not, at the same time, subject him to more of the emotional earthquakes he'd already suffered. This must have been traumatic for Julia at times (and Mimi too), but she never made any legal move to take him back, and none of their three voluble sisters made any noise about it either.

Mimi was one of two adult anchors in John's new life, because Uncle George was also important. Only three years older than his wife – 43 to her 40 – he seems somehow ancient in the photos, elderly before his time. He was tall, with a good head of silver hair, a kindly chap who, having served in the army, had seen a bit of the world; he could talk about things, sitting back to light his pipe and consider his view; he enjoyed salty jokes with his beer, and made Mimi's budgeting all the harder because he liked a 'flutter' on the horses. He and John formed a close bond and shared unimportant little secrets. He taught the boy to ride a bike and tried to demonstrate the finer techniques of cricket and football, though John had little aptitude for ball games. He also allowed affection: John insisted on giving him 'squeakers' – his word for kisses – before George put him to bed.

That Christmas of 1946, Mimi, George and John took the bus to Lewis's department store in the city and each sat for a series of Polyfotos. There's a physical ease about John Lennon here that is extraordinary considering his stormy life. Comfortable in front of the camera, in a school blazer and cap, he smiles naturally and appears happy.*

John's network of Woolton comforts also included family and friends. Running behind Mendips was Vale Road, where he found Pete, Nige and Ivan, his closest childhood pals – Masters Shotton, Walley and Vaughan. He formed them into a gang, four junior reprobates who persistently and sometimes dangerously terrorised the community for years to come. John was leader, because *he just was*. It was a position divined through natural unspoken process, by force of personality and, where necessary, by scrapping. Pete Shotton, a blond curly-haired lad, had the brazen guts to constantly challenge this and so became John's best mate. John Lennon liked to be confronted; by his code, if he found you were a pushover he'd push you over.

All three boys were younger than John, which was another reason he was the leader, but this demonstrated a further aspect of his unusual character: if you were different – an original thinker, in some way unconventional – age wasn't a particular problem. John's chosen friends were also intelligent – Ivan exceptionally so – and eager to follow their leader wherever he took them.

In early summer 1947, Richy Starkey fell dangerously ill. He'd never been the most robust infant, now he was sick beyond even the efficacy of Annie's medicinal compounds. An ambulance blue-lit him to Royal Liverpool Children's Hospital and appendicitis was diagnosed, but when they opened him up the picture was far worse: the appendix had burst and caused infected peritonitis. Barely conscious as he was wheeled into the operating theatre, Richy asked the nurse for a cup of tea. 'We'll give you one when you come round,' she answered – by which time ten weeks had passed.

Three times, doctors told Elsie he'd not survive the night. Still working all hours in all jobs, she was on the bus to the hospital every day, sometimes only allowed to see him through a pane of glass. One of the three desperate nights was 6 July, the eve of Richy's seventh birthday. But the boy was a born fighter, and would not surrender. When finally he stirred from his coma, he spent possibly another sixteen weeks slipping in and out of consciousness, and once this passed, at the start of 1948, he finally began a protracted and painful period of convalescence.

He was restricted to a cot with high sides, to allow his surgical scars to heal,

---

* The Polyfotos are on display at 251 Menlove Avenue, the house authentically re-created by the National Trust and open to the public.

so it was a time of utter, numbing boredom; there was simply *nothing* to do. Despite having been at school almost two years his progress had been unstartling, and at seven he'd not yet learned to read or write, so he couldn't even lose himself in a book. The nurses' instruction – *don't move* – held good until the day Richy wanted to show a boy in the next bed a toy bus he'd been given. As he leaned to pick it up, he overbalanced, fell out of the cot and ripped his stitches open, setting back his recovery another few months. 'Always remember, the sooner you're better, the sooner you're out' were the words he heard over and over, more times than he could count.[12]

In August 1947, a year after John Lennon had been relocated deeper into south Liverpool, Paul McCartney arrived there. The switch – seemingly the first time any of the McCartneys lived outside the north end – came through Mary's work. Her employers, Liverpool Corporation's Municipal Midwifery Service, needed a midwife resident on a new housing estate, and a rent-free house came with the job.

Speke was Liverpool's southernmost point and already the location of a small airport and industrial area; now it was to accommodate a vast new public housing project, effectively a whole new town. When the McCartneys moved into 72 Western Avenue they were among the earliest families to arrive: the road was still being constructed, grass verges were being sown and trees being planted ... but none of its much-vaunted British Utopian brightness would ever transfer from the architect's drawing-board. It was, instantly, *an estate* – nothing to do, nowhere to go, troubled.

Mrs M. P. McCartney SRN [State Registered Nurse], SCM [State Certified Midwife], her name etched on a brass plate on the gate, was a valued member of Speke's growing community. Paul had just turned five, and his earliest memory is of someone bringing her a plaster dog: she was brought gifts by many of the mothers she helped. Mary worked all hours (babies being no respecters of the clock), and, though the job was not well paid, she was dedicated and professional. Her attitude, Jim said, was never less than overly conscientious.[13]

The move more or less coincided with a welcome lift in Jim Mac's life: a return to cotton. He got a job at the reopened (though much-neutered) Cotton Exchange, and was even more fortunate to find himself back at Hannay's. It really wasn't like the old days though, and he had to accept what was called 'half-money', earning only about £10 a week before deductions. He felt acutely the 'shame' of not being a better provider for his family (a feeling imposed by no one but himself), but he was, nonetheless, back in his chosen career, a suited and courteous gent among friends in the business district.

Mary timed the move to coincide with the beginning of Paul's schooling. Jim didn't want him to go to a Catholic school, feeling they dispensed too much religion and not enough education.[14] Speke had a new Church of England school, Stockton Wood Road infants, and it was just behind the McCartneys' house; Paul began here as soon as they were in.

Things came more or less easily to him. He was naturally one of the brightest children – alert, upbeat, smart, gifted, funny. At the same time, since Speke was already a haven for young toughs, he could take care of himself, fighting to maintain position. Paul's only real difficulty was when anyone told him what to do. He was always one of the friendliest and keenest contributors, but the moment anyone – teacher, parent, friend – used the word 'should' or 'ought' to direct his actions, there'd usually be only one result: he would do the opposite, never doubting his right or ability to do so. As Paul says, 'I've never liked "ought". The minute I hear someone say *you ought to do this* I want to go the other way.'[15]

Sundays were the best days, at home, when Mary would whistle her way through making the best roast lunch rations could provide, and Jim would sit at his Nems upright piano, pipe in mouth, and allow his hands to find the melodies of old – some from those Roaring Twenties days of Jim Mac's Band, others more recent. The effect on his young sons, on Paul especially, was electrifying and permanent. 'I'd lie on the carpet and listen to him playing things like Stairway To Paradise or one I loved called Lullaby Of The Leaves, and a couple he made up himself. He'd just noodle around and it was lovely to listen to. He had a mate at the Cotton Exchange, another salesman called Freddie Rimmer, who'd come around and play as well, so there was always a musical atmosphere in the house.'[16]

Jim was reluctant to teach Paul the piano, so as not to pass on untutored bad habits, but it didn't matter because Paul listened and watched and *imbibed*, and his fingers did the rest. 'I started off with three fingers in the chord of C – C and E and G – and then I realised that if you moved the whole thing up a tone you got D minor, and if you moved it all up again you got E minor, and if you moved it all up again you got F, with the same shape.'[17]

John Lennon played his first instrument about the same time. The unsupported cost of raising him caused Mimi to take in lodgers at Mendips. Beginning autumn 1947, she had an ongoing arrangement with Liverpool University to accommodate students. They came usually in pairs, slept in the spare bedroom and used the ground-floor dining room for meals and quiet study. Because of this, John's youthful years were witnessed first-hand by a succession of bright young adults. They paid £3 a week for breakfast and evening meals, and Mimi asked for veterinary students because she had a dog and two cats (pets John adored) and they treated them free, needing the practice.

It was one of the first pair of house-guests, Harold Phillips – ex-Royal Navy, back in college as an English Lit student – who ignited in John the musical spark. He had a harmonica which John would not leave alone; one day Phillips held out the instrument and said John could keep it if he could play a tune by the following morning. The odds were narrow, but this boy had musical talent in his blood. Did he even know his dad and all his Lennon uncles played harmonica – or 'gob iron' to use Liverpool slang? John learned *two* tunes by the next day, and Phillips was as good as his word.[18] The instrument was now the boy's, although Mimi made him wait for it until Christmas. John could always tap into the excitement of waking up that Christmas morning in 1947: 'I felt the stocking and there was a mouth organ in it. A harmonica. That was one of the great moments of life, when I got my first harmonica.'[19]

A year after almost dying three times, by the summer of 1948 Richy Starkey was ready to convalesce at home. Elsie was thrilled to have him back and naturally more possessive. To Grandad Starkey, he was no longer just 'that bloody Noddler', he was Lazarus, the boy who'd cheated death. When finally Richy went back to school, however, he was hopelessly behind all the other children, and there wasn't much accommodation of the fact. Left to sink or swim, he sank.* It was much easier to 'sag off' than turn up: Richy and some pals would drift into nearby Prince's Park, or scamper down 'the Cazzy' (the Cast Iron Shore) and be *deserters*.[20]

Richy's decisive education in English came not from teachers but from a friend, Marie Maguire, four years his elder. Her mum Annie, newly a widow, had been Elsie's best buddy for years; the Maguires lived at 10 Madryn Street, opposite Elsie and Richy's former house at 9, and Marie always helped take care of the boy. Painstakingly, over a period of time at the kitchen tables of 10 Madryn Street and 10 Admiral Grove, even when Richy would *not* pay attention and threw things at her, Marie went over and over the *Dobbin* horse storybooks with him, pointing out each word and explaining how the letters formed sounds. Though he'd missed out on his education, Richy certainly wasn't stupid, and he also spoke better than many in the locality, not dropping letters from words and not adopting the Liverpool 'Scouse' accent; he just needed this extra tuition to get off the ground. His reading ambition would remain limited – he didn't progress much beyond comics for years to come, and his spelling was never good: he tended to write words phonetically, confusing 'wood' and

---

* After he'd spent several months in hospital, the school may have believed he wasn't coming back: the St Silas admission register records '21.11.47' as the date he left through 'Sickness'.

'would', and 'stake' and 'steak' – but, through dedication and perspiration, and thanks to Marie, he'd made a vital breakthrough.

Like the generations before him, Richy's life was bound up in the Dingle: home, family, friends, school, church, recreation. When he grew too big for a 'bungalow bath' in front of the fire, he'd scoot around to Steble Street baths and pay a few pennies for a hot tub. Music didn't yet feature much. A photo shows him holding a small accordion, but he didn't play it. His Starkey grand-parents played mandolin and banjo (or ukulele) at family sing-songs and gave him the instruments, but he'd no interest. At seven, he got a harmonica – same result. There was even, says Richy, 'a piano at home which I *walked* on'. The trigger came at the pictures, when he watched Gene Autry, on his horse Champion, singing South Of The Border, his three Mexican compadres adding the *ay-ay-ay-ays* as he rode along in a white cowboy hat, big wide-open prairie spaces all around. This eureka moment in Richy Starkey's life came together as sound and vision. He'd never forget it, and would call Autry 'the most sig-nificant musical force in my life'.[21]

From Autry onwards, Richy was and stayed a big fan of cowboys, of America and Americana, of country music, and of maudlin or melodic songs that tell the story of love lost and found. He harboured the dream of so many Liverpool sons: to become a merchant seaman and sail away to the USA, *the promised land*.

For a British boy intrigued by American country music, Liverpool certainly was the place to be. Merchant seamen (some known as 'Cunard Yanks') were bring-ing back goods unobtainable in British shops – cowboy boots, hats, jeans and records not issued by the companies in London – and that led to a small but vocal following of country and western (C&W) on Merseyside. The first guitar John Lennon ever saw was in the hands of 'a fully dressed cowboy in the middle of Liverpool, with his Hawaiian guitar . . . He had the full gear on.'[22]

Country music was also a great influence on George Harrison – the first guitar recordings he heard were Waiting For A Train and Blue Yodel No 4 (California Blues) by Jimmie Rodgers, America's original country star, a yodeller popularly known as the Singing Brakeman. The wind-up gramophone and records Harry brought back from New York in his 'merch' days bridged an ocean of magical discovery for his children. George's impressionable mind was spin-ning at 78 with Hank Williams, Stéphane Grappelli, the Ink Spots, Cab Calloway, Hoagy Carmichael and Josh White, and all the Harrisons loved the records they bought in Liverpool shops by George Formby, the toothy, north of England, banjulele-plucking star of music-hall and film comedies. These were real English songs of rhythm and sauce, and George was hooked. 'Those George Formby songs were always in the back of me life,' he'd explain fifty years later.

'They were either being played in the background or my mother was singing them when I was three or four.'[23]

John Lennon also loved Formby, and saw him on stage at Liverpool Empire in the 1948–9 pantomime season. An annual trip to the Empire panto was one of the two big treats he was allowed each year by Mimi and George, the other being a summer visit to the pictures to see Walt Disney's latest. Mostly, though, John read. In 1965, he was invited to list the books that had made a forceful impression on him, and for the period 'up to the age of eleven' he specified Lewis Carroll's *Alice In Wonderland* and *Alice Through The Looking-Glass* and Kenneth Grahame's *The Wind In The Willows*.[24] John was given the *Alice* books as birthday presents and re-read them once a year – though he never bothered to find out if Carroll wrote anything else. He was also in love with Richmal Crompton's *Just William* books, identifying himself with William Brown, the scruffy, rascally gangleader.

On the art front, John's favourite was Ronald Searle, creator of the St Trinian's School books. Searle's character-full cartoons catapulted John deeper into drawing, which took up great chunks of his time from about the age of eight. Though difficult to categorise, his work fell into two broad areas. The first was to draw, in careful detail, and then colour in, good copies of established art, like all the *Alice* characters and other fictional and historical personae; he used these to illustrate poems he was writing in the style of Carroll's *Jabberwocky*.[25] Another category was the Searle-like cartoons that gave a rough but dead-eye impression. In these, John hardly ever went into detail but would deliver the decisive feature – and most especially the humour – in a few speedy fountain-pen flourishes that cut to the core, saying everything in a few lines. He drew them fast and then moved on to the next.

Mendips' student lodgers would get used to the sight of John and Mimi quietly together in either the front room or 'the morning room', she reading, he reading or creating. John had to wear glasses, having become short-sighted by about the age of seven (just like Julia). Mimi took him into town and had him tested for a pair of 'goggles' issued free by the new National Health Service, round and wire-framed, with a curly circle of flex to run behind the ears (and abrade the skin). Julia's short-sightedness had been unaided for twenty or so years now and John started out in much the same direction: his glasses were for *inside* use only, as his friend Nigel Walley remembers. 'He didn't want to be seen out in them, and kept them in an inside pocket along with his mouth organ. He might slip them on to see something, but he'd whip them off again very quickly.'[26]

In August 1948, John went up into the junior section at Dovedale Road school. The infants had been mixed gender but now it was boys only and John wasn't slow or shy in ensuring a necessary dominance, fighting whoever wouldn't listen to reason. He also told Mimi she couldn't take him there any more, that he'd go alone ... and virtually these same words were also being said, at the same place and time, by George Harrison to his mum. Louise had sent her first two children to Catholic schools but let her third and fourth go Church of England. Peter was switched to Dovedale Road in April 1948 and George went there too, to start his schooling – though because of the age gap (and juniors used a different playground to the infants) he and John didn't know each other. Later, though, they'd have the same teachers and similar experiences to remember.

In Peter, George already had someone to take him to school and fetch him home again in the afternoons, and he didn't want his mum doing it. She took him the first day but then he put his five-year-old foot down: the scene at the gate was not for her. As Louise would recall, 'George was always against nosy mothers, and he used to hate all the neighbours who stood around gossiping.'[27]

Julia Lennon, Bobby Dykins and the child they'd had together – Julia Lennon, aka Julia Dykins, born March 1947 – had long since left the one-bed flat in Gateacre and been living back at Newcastle Road. Then George Stanley (John's grandad) died and they had to move. They applied to Liverpool Corporation for a council house, and as Julia was pregnant again at the time were given priority and assigned a pleasant three-bedroom semi-detached house on the Springwood estate, near Garston, at 1 Blomfield Road. It was under two miles from Mendips, though it's said Mimi kept this from John. To get the house, Julia and Bobby had to pretend they were married, and there was little chance of this becoming anything other than a deception because Alf Lennon wasn't minded to grant her a divorce, and wasn't around to discuss it. They show on the electoral roll as John Dykins and Julia Dykins, and no neighbour thought them otherwise. Also, while Julia's real husband was a waiter, on board ships, her 'husband' had chucked in door-to-door selling and become a waiter in a Liverpool hotel.

Julia was now settled for the first time in years. Giving birth to John hadn't stopped her leading a merry life, and her second baby had long gone for adoption, but at the third stroke she gave up work precisely to become a housewife and full-time mother. Her character remained unquenchable, of course: she still made people scream with her repartee and singing, and she went out shopping in six-inch stiletto heels, walking down the street like a petite doll. When, inevitably, a man gave her a wolf-whistle, she'd wolf-whistle back or shout 'Not bad yourself!' – although, with her poor eyesight, she'd no real idea what her admirer looked like.[28]

Julia had a bedroom to spare at Blomfield Road but John stayed at Mendips. He did see her though – there are photos of a summer 1949 family gathering at his Aunt Anne's house in Rock Ferry, 'over the water' (across the Mersey) from Liverpool: two shots of John with his cousins and half-sister, and one of him with Julia. It's the only known photo of John and Mummy. He's in short trousers, laughing as she tickles him under both arms, and she's wearing a baggy dress under which she's four or five months pregnant. That October, she gave birth to her and Bobby's second baby – Jacqueline Gertrude Lennon, aka Jacqueline Gertrude Dykins – so John now had two infant half-sisters, actually three.

It could have been because of Julia's past predicament that Mimi supported the Salvation Army's residence for the children of broken homes. Strawberry Field – Strawberry Fields most called it – was a Gothic mansion with turrets and towers, a rambling great edifice of Woolton sandstone, set in substantial private grounds.[29] Fun was had, and funds were raised, at its annual garden fete, an archetype of British summer life. Girls from the home – known as 'Strawbs' – went around the district in their summer striped-blue dresses, selling tickets door-to-door. Come the day, a brass band played, the children staged dancing and gymnastic displays, and there were stalls with little games, secondhand 'jumble', and homemade refreshments subject to rationing: tea, lemonade and cakes. Mimi always took John, until he went independently.

He knew the place well. To John, Pete, Nige and Ivan, Strawberry Fields meant the private grounds, not the big house. It was one of their prime hangouts: they'd scamper over the wall in Vale Road and disappear into the trees, with infinite opportunities for trouble, adventure, danger. One known peril was the groundsman – John called him 'the Cocky Watchman', or 'Cocky Watchtower' – a sour and sometimes vicious individual who hated all young trespassers, that Lennon gang in particular. He wouldn't think twice about giving them a good hiding, but had to catch them first. 'I suppose you realise this is private property!' he'd shout as they hightailed it into the wind . . .

The Liverpool of all these childhoods was in a sorry state as the 1940s turned into the 1950s. Little had gone right here in decades, just depression layered on downturn. Viewing it as would a stranger, a *Liverpolitan* magazine writer noted, 'What I saw made me almost ashamed of my home town. Once progressive and proud, the city is now dilapidated and dirty; shabby and down-and-out.'[30] True, the sounds of the place hadn't altered – the reinstated 'one o'clock gun' that reported every lunchtime, the seagulls, the foghorns, the laughter pouring from pub doorways – but its look had: the landscape was full of still-unrepaired bombsites, open lesions that had become children's playgrounds ('bommies') or eternal temporary car parks. The old place had plenty of fine public buildings, but everything was black with encrusted soot; ruined shops were riddled with police-dodging barrow boys; and people queued for almost everything, standing in long lines. The air was damp even when it wasn't raining – and instead of it being healthy air, fresh from the Irish Sea, it was (as the Liverpool novelist John Brophy noted in 1946) 'laden with smoke and soot and grease, and with smells from tanneries, breweries, oil-cake factories, margarine factories, smells from the engine-rooms of ships, from dockyards, from thousands of warehouses where every sort of cargo is stored'.[31]

Outsiders who had dealings with Liverpool were losing patience. A travellers' journal published by the great Thomas Cook & Son tried hard to apply gloss but it really wasn't easy. 'Let it be allowed that Liverpool took a tremendous pounding in her blitz week. Other cities took a hammering also, but somehow Liverpool never seems to have risen from the count.' In the London newspapers, Liverpool had become a word as dirty as its blackened buildings, and even *Liverpolitan* had to admit that the many charges against it were accurate – 'slovenly city, filthy tram cars, dilapidated buildings and dingy streets', the people 'ill-mannered savages', its women 'dowdy, shabbily dressed and carelessly groomed'.[32] But then, let them say what they like: Liverpudlians didn't like or trust Londoners anyway – they were 'soft' and 'bloody southerners'. Two fingers to the lot of 'em.

Liverpool's brain-drain, running since the 1930s or before, was accelerating now. Plenty with talent and ambition got out and made their lives elsewhere, while those who couldn't or wouldn't retreated further into the Liverpudlians' protective shell to keep them in and the rest out, Liverpool an enclave unto itself, nowhere else like it, its backside to the rest of the country, its people tightly together and, though sharply self-deprecating, acutely sensitive to an outsider's criticism. Deep down, pretty much everyone knew why people left, but those who stayed would disparage and hold a grudge against those who did.

Even its dream new housing estates, like the one at Speke, were soon plummeting in ambition; and it was here on New Year's Day 1950 that the Harrisons became the first residents at 25 Upton Green. It was eighteen years since Harry and Louise, then with one child, applied for a council house – so long ago that the child had grown up and gone. All the participants in the move – Harry (40), Louise (38), Harry (15), Peter (9) and George (6) – had lived their entire lives in Wavertree, compact but cosy. Quickly, having so long hankered for someplace else, they wanted to move back.

The novelty of being in a new house held good for a while – 25 Upton Green had no heating but it did have electricity, plumbing (an indoor loo at last, and even a bath), front and back gardens and, though the place was small, what seemed to George like *space*. He'd recall, 'After [living in] a two-up-two-down terrace house, you could go from the hall to the sitting-room then into the kitchen then into the hall again and back into the sitting-room. I just ran round and round it all that first day.'[33]

The main problem in Speke – as the McCartneys were also finding out less than a mile away in Western Avenue – was the undesirability of some of the neighbours. Upton Green was a close, a large oval bordered by identical estate houses; young kids played on the grass in the middle, older kids hung round the garden gates. When Louise tried to grow things, delinquents wrecked them – plants murdered in their beds. That got to George. As he'd later explain, 'As soon as we got to Speke we realised we had to get out of there, fast. The place was full of fear and people smashing things up. We got on another list.'[34] As for school, Louise decided against having George transferred to Speke, so he stayed at Dovedale Road, necessitating a long bus journey every morning and after-noon.

Alf Lennon didn't begin the new decade very well either. The *Dominion Monarch* docked at Tilbury before Christmas, after which he tomfooled around London with a few shipmates, waiting for it to sail again in mid-January. Alcohol was surely a fixture, opening time to closing with bottles between ses-sions, and late on Sunday 8 January they were laughing and shouting their way along Oxford Street when they stopped in front of a ladies' gown shop. A moment or two later the window was smashed and Alf and another Liverpool sailor, John Murphy, were dancing down Oxford Street with beautiful expen-sive dresses ... and waltzed right into the arms of the scuffers. The next morning, after sleeping off their drunkenness in the cells – Alf had probably cut himself too, because records show he needed a doctor – the Marlborough Street magistrate looked sternly upon Lennon and Murphy, both of 'no fixed abode'. Pleading guilty to a charge of breaking and entering, and stealing two gowns to the value of £42 8s 6d, they were each sentenced to six months. The ledger at the west London prison Wormwood Scrubs details Alf's incarceration: he arrived there from court on 9 January and was transferred to Brixton, south London, on 13 February, where he lived until gaining early release in the second week of May.[35]

This wasn't unknown behaviour for Alf – it was at least his third time in the clink. Always one for a laugh, the ale led him a merry life over which he exer-cised no apparent control. Friend Billy Hall remembers being with him in New Zealand in 1944 or '45 when they'd been drinking and Alf was shouting about smashing a jeweller's shop window. They didn't, but they did nick a bicycle and were making whoopee around the streets of Wellington until police stepped in and let them off with a warning.[36]

When the *Dominion Monarch* put to sea, Alf was marked down as AWOL. He was unable to explain himself until after release from Brixton, when the Merchant Service – taking a bleak view of events – dismissed him from duty. After twenty eventful years at sea, Alf Lennon was a sailor no more, beached at the age of 37, high but rarely dry.

His brothers despaired for him, but Alf received understanding and support from an unlikely source: Mimi. Using his best Blue Coat-educated grammar and script, and calling himself 'Alfred', he wrote to her (quite properly calling her 'Mary') and confessed to his situation. He corresponded first from prison and then from Copperfield Street, and Mimi – despite her consistent and now reinforced opinion of 'that Alf Lennon' – not only replied in kind but enclosed the first of at least two letters from John, friendly and chatty words from a nine-year-old lad to a dad he'd not seen in four years. She also enclosed some recent photos, so Alf could see his boy again. What Alf called 'white lies' were necessary between the adults, to prevent John discovering a certain embarrassing predicament, but it's clear from the letters that Mimi was trying to bring father and son closer. They were, at this moment, four miles apart, Toxteth to Woolton, but it was a wish that prompted Alf's retreat. Soon afterwards, he heard there might be a job going at Middleton Tower – a summer holiday camp in Morecambe, just up the coast from Liverpool – and went after it. He was on 'KP duty' (kitchen porter), up to his elbows in sudding dishes. And when the season ended, in September 1950, Alf hit the road and became an itinerant, going where the brew blew him.

The boy Lennon who had this sudden, unexpected contact with his dad had two still-evolving characters now, one for inside the house – reading, writing, drawing – the other for outside, a boy Mimi scarcely saw or would have recognised. This was the John Lennon of larks and dares, scraps and scrapes, games and guffaws, everything for laughs. There was plenty of boyish cruelty, verbal more than physical (though John was never shy to use his fists), and it was great to be in his gang even when he forced you to steal. John was now petty-thieving whenever and wherever he could. He called it 'slap leather', and all the gang had to do it. Shops were fair game, toy cars or sweets slipped into pockets with shopkeepers none the wiser. If there was trouble, though, if a Lennon plan went awry, he had the knack of disappearing. The gang members would turn around and their leader would be gone.

John's 'outside' vocabulary was now awash with swear words, instantly learned and put to inventive use, and he also adopted the lexicon of many a Liverpool kid, the local argot that Mimi Smith (and Mary McCartney and others) frowned upon but which Lennon, Starkey, McCartney and Harrison all used – where something good or great was 'gear', and stupid was 'soft', and out of fashion was 'down the nick'; and when taunting or teasing someone you'd shout 'Chickaferdy!'; and if someone was spineless they were 'nesh'; and you said 'Come 'ead!' ('come ahead', for 'come on'); and 'Eh oop!' had many uses, from 'hello' to 'let's go', and 'lad' was 'la'; and an interesting person was a 'skin' – so 'Eh la!' and 'Eh oop, la!' and ''E's a good skin'; and where (though swearing was muted on the street because people got upset if they overheard it) 'stupid get' ('stupid git') or 'yer daft get' were OK ... and then you said goodbye to your mates with a wacker's 'Tarrah well!'

John was the first of his pals to pick up some 'facts of life', information he readily passed on, and such was the way he conducted his life, adults swiftly singled him out as an undesirable. Each of his gang, and plenty of other boys in the district, heard the same words: 'Keep away from that John Lennon, he'll get you into trouble', or 'he's a bad influence', or 'he's a wrong 'un'. Many did, but some simply couldn't. As Nigel Walley says, 'He was a good buddy to have beside you: he wasn't a loner, he liked company, he was funny, he was generous, and he always supported his mates.'[37]

Three miles south, in Speke, Paul McCartney was now well established at Stockton Wood school, if not top of the class then certainly capable of it. Home life was settled, and he had a devoted playmate in his younger brother Mike. Paul led, egging 'our kid' into situations in which there could only ever be one casualty. In September 1950, Mary brought her midwifery career to an end, wanting a job where she was home nights and weekends. Paul and Mike were growing up fast and needed the benefit of closer attention. This meant relinquishing 72 Western Avenue, the house that had come with the job.

She was instantly appointed Speke's health visitor, administering advice and care around the district. Another Corporation house was found for them, deeper into the estate at 12 Ardwick Road – at least the seventh place Paul had lived in his eight years; it was rented, not free, but the McCartneys had two working adults. The worst thing about moving was that Paul and Mike had a longer walk to school. As they made their way back to Stockton Wood each day they'd pass close to Upton Green, which George Harrison was leaving to catch the bus up to Dovedale Road, he in his school cap, blazer and short trousers, they in theirs, passing as strangers. The *best* thing about Ardwick Road was that they were just half a mile from the eastern edge of the estate, beyond which it wasn't Liverpool any more but real Lancashire: different accents, woods, fields, farms and cliffs down to a more rural River Mersey. Years of happy adventuring lay ahead.

George rose from the infants to the juniors at Dovedale Road in August 1950 and would always remember being happy here. He reckoned himself a swift runner and liked playing football and cricket. He was comfortably bright, and he could take care of himself. Like a certain Dovedale boy two years his senior, George wasn't shy to use his fists. In the lingo of the day, he was 'handy'. The school's Punishment Book records the date he was caned for 'Disorderly behaviour in lines, despite repeated warnings'. It was 8 May 1951, when he was eight. A new teacher, Mr H. Lyon, administered a single stroke on George's hand. To what would be Lyon's regret, his aim was slightly askew; the cane thwacked across George's wrist and brought up a weal. As George would recall, 'When I got home my dad saw it, and the next day he came down to the school, got Mr Lyon out of the class and stuck one on him.'[38] Harry Harrison, the quiet man bestirred when he saw a wrong, was a hero to every child, but it wasn't the punishment he objected to, only Lyon's aim.

Richy Starkey was also fighting – he had to, where he lived. He won only rarely, and even then might have to face the retribution of his victim's big brother. Richy longed for a big brother who'd take care of the ruffians who picked on *him*, though Elsie certainly never fought shy of taking it to the opposition: 'My mother had many a fight for me. If anybody bigger picked on me, she'd be down knocking on the door and would deal with them.'[39]

Richy could have taken the Eleven-Plus exam in spring 1951 but St Silas didn't enter him. There was a Review, a filtering process, and it proved that the boy, so far behind in his education, had no chance of succeeding in such a test. Like most local kids, at 11 he ended up at Dingle Vale, a secondary modern school for the academically unexceptional, where boys and girls were segregated and streamed into A, B, C and D levels depending on ability. Richy was put in C, pretty much a no-hoper. His curriculum included gardening. The cane and slipper were liberally applied, and no GCE O-Level exams were taken: any child considered capable of sitting them was transferred to a technical or grammar school; all the others would leave empty-handed (some empty-headed) at 15, fit only for manual labour. Even the headmaster had to admit that the process had 'a deadening effect'.[40]

Richy's most-told memory of his years here is of going out on to Dingle Lane with mates Davy Patterson and Brian Briscoe and spending Elsie's 'dinner money' not on the school-provided meal but on a small loaf of Hovis bread, four penn'orth of chips and five Woodbines ('Woodies') – the cheapest brand of cigarette, the working man's fag. Like generations before and after, he'd scoop out the dough from the loaf, stuff it with chips (so making 'a chip butty', only without the butter), then return to school to eat, smoke and talk shit while lolling on the swings. Richy was a smoker from about 11.

Though he could make the best of not very much, Richy had experienced little real joy for a long time, so it was a great relief when, perhaps towards the end of 1951, Elsie suddenly had a man in her life again and the boy gained a father-figure, a dad like he'd never had. He was Harry Arthur Graves, born in Romford in 1913 – a year older than Elsie. Harry was a cockney, a West Ham supporter from the East End of London who, fantastically, forsook the slightly warmer climes and better living conditions of Romford to go and live in Liverpool 8. His explanation for the move – that he was ill and his doctor had suggested a change of air – warrants more questions than answers.[41] More likely he was getting away from a failed marriage: Harry was hitched in 1937 to a Romford girl and it hadn't worked, then in 1946 he arrived in the Dingle and rented a house on Jacob Street. (Harry and Elsie themselves couldn't marry yet because she was only separated from Richard Starkey, not divorced.)

Harry made friends fast. Liverpudlians never ceased to remind him he was 'a bloody soft southerner' and 'a cockney bastard', but most accepted him because he was a nice man, a sweet and gentle soul, softly spoken. Everybody liked Harry. 'All animals and children loved him,' Richy would say, adding, with touching respect, 'I learned gentleness from Harry.'[42] He was certainly a great and welcome ally for the lad. Employed as a painter and decorator for Liverpool Corporation, he was part of a team of men maintaining public buildings – respectable manual work; one job they had was out at the US Air Force base at Burtonwood, and Harry delighted Richy by bringing him back some highly desirable DC comics. They also went to the pictures together two or three times a week. Harry indulged the boy: when Elsie said he'd been giving her cheek and needed disciplining, he'd just shrug his shoulders and smile con-spiratorially. Richy needed and welcomed such a man in his life.

Dingle people actually had much in common with cockneys. Both were poor and working-class, both were predominantly English/Protestant, both suffered terrible bombing at the hands of the Germans, and both liked a good drink and boozy sing-song. One big reason Harry fitted right at home in Liverpool 8 was because he liked nothing better than to go to the pubs and clubs, get a few ales inside him and sing. He had a good voice and music in his ancestry. Harry's favourite songs, for which he earned a decent local reputation, were Night And Day, Star Dust, Bye Bye Blackbird, Dream, That Old Black Magic, and Moonglow. His musical tastes, and the gentle way he exposed Richy to singers such as Sarah Vaughan, Billy Daniels and Billy Eckstine, were a tremendous influence on the boy.[43]

The scene would be a pub – perhaps the Empress, yards from the house at the end of Admiral Grove. Elsie, Harry, relations, friends and workmates would drink and sing through the evening until closing time, and then, well bevvied, tumble into Elsie and Richy's tiny terraced house where the party carried on – more singing, more drinking, more swearing, Johnny and Annie Starkey on banjo and mandolin, the steam rising ever higher into the night. Most people in Liverpool had a 'turn', a party piece, and Richy had two. One was a song he sang in duet with his mum, the swing-jazzy Someone Like You. The other, sung solo, was Nobody's Child, a maudlin country tearjerker about a lonesome blind orphaned boy. Elsie's young Lazarus would look her square in the eye as he sang it, adding to the chorus line so it went 'I'm nobody's child, *Mum*', and she'd laugh or cry or both and affectionately instruct him to 'bugger off' or 'piss off'. The boy would always remember singing at home 'not in front of a coal fire but in front of a bottle of gin and a large bottle of brown', emphasising the point that, as many children have experienced down the years, the bond of good-time music and booze was significant. Years later, he would admit, 'My parents were alcoholics and I didn't realise it.'[44]

Many a Liverpool party included a punch-up – without one, people said, it just wasn't memorable – but an exception was the McCartney family's annual New Year's Eve knees-up, held usually at the Aintree house of Paul's Uncle Joe and Auntie Joan. These were great musical landmarks in his life – chaotic and raucous gatherings of uncles, aunties and cousins of every remove, with the adults getting bevvied and everyone singing happily. Jim played the piano, which showed Paul that a pianist would always get invited to parties, be the centre of the action and never have to buy a drink; glasses were lined up for him on the lid. Paul's much-loved aunties – Edie, Mill, Gin, Joan and others – sat around the room singing the old songs, 1920s favourites like Baby Face, When The Red, Red, Robin Comes Bob-Bob-Bobbin' Along, and the one that gained the biggest cheer of the night at every McCartney party, played at *just* the right moment, Carolina Moon, at which point everyone would be standing and swaying and drinking and singing, a family united in harmony.

The McCartney boys switched schools in September 1951. Speke's authorities had misjudged the numbers, and Stockton Wood was now bursting with fifteen hundred infants; as it happened, a school in another district – Joseph Williams primary, in Belle Vale, just beyond Gateacre – was short of older children. Paul made the move and Mike went too; a special shuttle bus was laid on to take them all to and fro, and instead of working the standard nine-to-four day they began and finished half an hour later. Great larks were had on the bus, especially on the top deck, and the fifty or so transplanted Speke kids formed a bond others at 'Joey Williams' didn't share. A photograph shows them outside their new school, and Paul, aged nine or ten, is the one who catches the eye – intentionally so. The rest are the usual motley jumble of post-war British children in varying degrees of 'it seemed smart at the time' raggedness; Paul is trim in a dark school cap and pulls a face while staring at an issue of the *Dandy*, the comic's colour pages clutched in his hands. Everyone is looking at the camera, Paul isn't, and he's the most knowing of it. His performance naturally steals the attention.

Paul and Mike had to share a room at 12 Ardwick Road, and such was their bedtime squabbling, Jim had the bright idea of rigging a set of Bakelite earphones by each bed, connected to the wireless downstairs under his control. The boys could put the earphones under their pillows and drift off to the sounds of the BBC Light Programme or Home Service. A similar set-up was also in place at Mendips, where Mimi let the wireless run up to John's bedroom (over the front door) by an extension speaker. The impact of radio on these fertile young minds was momentous. They all listened to the thriller and sci-fi serials and to the half-hour comedies like *Life With The Lyons*. This and others like it were conventional humour shows, funny if formulaic; but there was another comedy that operated in a world entirely its own and whose impact shaped the characters and personalities of many listeners: launched by the BBC in 1951, this was *The Goon Show*. These sensational half-hours broke every possible rule of comedy, of radio, of the *imagination*, and life was never the same again for its devoted fans. In Liverpool – on Menlove Avenue, Ardwick Road and Upton Green – schoolboys Lennon, McCartney and Harrison sat close to the speaker.

The Goon Show's residing genius was Spike Milligan, a writer, humorist, musician and humanitarian whose flights of comic fantasy and invention knew no bound; his cohorts were Peter Sellers (a uniquely talented voice artist), Harry Secombe (an explosive Welsh geyser of mouth-raspberries and song) and also, initially, Michael Bentine (a brilliantly resourceful nutcase). Its preposterous comedy situations, like floating Dartmoor Prison across the English Channel to France, and attempting to stop a flood by drinking the River Thames, made it the quintessential product of radio, with Milligan conjuring ideas and mind-pictures far beyond physical possibility. Schoolboys loved it, imitating the voices and phrases – 'you dirty rotten swine!' – for the rest of their days; Lennon, McCartney and Harrison separately and hungrily adopted Goon humour and its punning wordplay as their own, where it nestled among many other influences, not least Liverpool's own incessant comedy.

Milligan had no template – he was a true original – but he was everyone's template thereafter, and his surreal visual cartoonery gave John Lennon vital creative impetus ('My main influences for writing were always Lewis Carroll and *The Goon Show*, a combination of that'). Of equal merit, Milligan let John see that he wasn't alone in living with a creative whirlwind inside his mind. Whatever else was going on in his world, tuning the dial to the BBC Home

Service week after week reassured John that *it wasn't just him* – 'Their humour was the only proof that the WORLD was insane,' he would say.[45]

And there was always *something* going on in his world. In 1949, the aunt John regarded as his favourite (not counting Mimi), the widowed Elizabeth, called 'Mater', had married a Scotsman and gone to live in Edinburgh along with her son, John's older cousin Stanley. John's new uncle was a dentist, Robert 'Bert' Sutherland, and he had money in the bank; they bought a comfortable, late-Victorian stone-faced house in Ormidale Terrace, very close to Scotland's national rugby stadium at Murrayfield, and John spent the next six summers here. He travelled by bus, initially fetched by Stanley, and unescorted from the age of 13. (His trip in 1954 earned him a newer and better harmonica, gifted to him by the bus driver – another spike in his musical development.)

Edinburgh would always hold a unique place in John's heart; he had only to hear pipers to fall into a romantic reverie. As well as the house here, Bert had a croft at Durness, on the north-west tip of the British Isles, and no Scottish holiday was complete for John without a stay at this remote spot through the mountains. These visits were a formative influence on his life, instilling an abiding warmth for Scotland, its people and their accents, which he imitated lovingly, and always amusingly, on several recordings in later years.

Given all this extra-curricular input, and his natural intelligence, John couldn't help but shine at Dovedale Road. He was academically ready when the time came for the crucial Eleven-Plus, and aware of its importance. 'They hang it over you from age five,' he'd remember. 'If you don't pass, you're finished in life.'[46] Mimi knew he would fly through it and had already decided which school would educate him for at least the next five years – hoping it would become seven or even eight, with John taking A-Levels, then going on to university and emerging with a profession. She considered Liverpool Institute, but George's brother Alf was an English master there and Mimi didn't want John creating problems at school that would reverberate at home.* She opted instead for Quarry Bank High School for Boys; it was closer to home anyway, just a walk across Calderstones Park, and she'd be able to keep an eye on him. Before long, a letter arrived at Mendips indicating that John had indeed passed and that his place at Quarry Bank was confirmed, starting 4 September 1952.

John was delighted Pete Shotton would be with him – they'd not been at school together before. Theirs would be a Crazy Gang act through the Quarry Bank years: partners in crime, laughs all the time, standing and sinking together,

---

* A. J. Smith, although respected, was the kind of teacher kids liked to mimic: he spoke with pronounced sibilance and was somewhat effeminate; his 'Inny' nickname was Cissy.

scrapping with each other when they weren't fighting others, cycling together to and from Menlove, so inseparable that some called them LennonShotton or Shennon and Lotton. As Pete reflects, John needed to be in a partnership: 'He always had to have a support. He would never have gone and performed on his own. He always had to have a sidekick.' Michael Hill, who like John came to Quarry Bank from Dovedale Road, says that though John and Pete were close, John was definitely the leader. 'It was always "Lennon and Shotton", never "Shotton and Lennon". Pete wasn't without talent of his own but he was an acolyte of John's. We all were.'[47]

It could have come as a nasty shock that Quarry Bank planned to educate them, that they were meant to work, and work hard, continuously for years to come. Opened in 1922, the school had a reputation for high achievement, sending boys to Oxford and Cambridge. The teachers were 'masters' and wore gowns, and some wore mortar boards; boys called them 'Sir' but themselves were known only by their surname. The place was run along pseudo public school lines – prefects had the right to hit boys with a tennis shoe, and, like the masters, could hand out detentions. The headmaster, E. R. Taylor, was a lay preacher who did everything with 'strong Christian values', including the caning. The school motto was Ex Hoc Metallo Virtutem – more or less 'From this quarry, virtue is forged'. The school's founder, R. F. Bailey, its only head before Taylor, wrote the words to The Song Of The Quarry, the school hymn every boy learned and sang once every term and also at the annual prizegiving at Philharmonic Hall in the city. The sheet music says it must be sung *vigoroso*, and the opening verse runs:

> Quarry men old before our birth
> Straining each muscle and sinew.
> Toiling together, Mother Earth
> Conquered the Rock that was in you.

First-year boys weren't streamed, but how they performed in those initial ten months governed where they stood afterwards. John did some excellent work, but by the end of the first year, while first in Art, he'd picked up plenty of detentions – twenty in the summer term alone – and finished twenty-third out of thirty-three. He failed to make the 'A' stream for the following year – he would be in IIB. Shotton slipped down with him.

What had happened? On top of his usual behaviour, two things in particular. First, John experienced an early onset of puberty and found other things crowding his mind. Sex would consume his waking and somnambulant thoughts from now to the end of his days; he would be a sexual being to the extent of cursing it.[48]

Second, John had formed another gang, an inside-school outfit to run in parallel with his Vale Road posse, and he was determined to set an example. 'I wanted everybody to do what I told them to do,' he'd explain, 'to laugh at my jokes and let me be the boss.' Michael Hill recalls John as 'the chief clown. He could have the whole class in tears of laughter and the teacher in tears of pain. Looking back on it, it was awful. The teachers had to maintain discipline, but if we were given an inch we'd take a mile.'[49]

The biggest cloud on a boy's horizon in the 1950s was the call-up, conscription, National Service. You could say it different ways but you couldn't avoid it: everyone between 18 and 21 was expected to serve a two-year spell in the armed forces – eighteen months in active service and six more in reserve. Call-up papers would arrive soon after an 18th birthday. An army officer came to Quarry Bank to lecture on it; John Lennon, and also Richy Starkey, both born in 1940, were already wondering how to dodge it.

John's plan was to skip the country: 'I was always thinking I could go to Southern Ireland if it came to it [but] I didn't know what I was going to do there, I hadn't thought that far.' (He would have faced prison on his return.) Richy was also desperate to avoid the dreaded letter – 'The last place I wanted to go was in the army' – and surely would have done so on medical grounds. George Harrison was soon swearing to evade it any which way: 'I made up my mind when I was about 12 that I was not going in the army.' Paul McCartney was hoping to avoid it but consciously preparing for it. In the woods down by the Mersey, he climbed trees to spy on people, he used a stick for a bayonet and imagined himself running another man through, and he killed frogs and hung them on barbed wire, calling them 'Johnny Rebs' in the language of American Civil War films. Paul took Mike there to see them and he was horrified.[50]

This was a key period in Paul's life. He took the Eleven-Plus in February 1953 at Liverpool Institute. It was a daunting experience to step up to its great sweeping entrance then walk through wrought-iron gates into a marble-pillared hall, but he passed the test and would be an 'Inny' pupil come September.

Around this time, Jim and Mary were keen for Paul to have piano lessons, to build on his innate musical talent. To begin with, the teacher came to Ardwick Road, but neighbouring children were always knocking on the door to ask Paul out to play, so Jim said he should go to the teacher's house instead. Being made to go somewhere he didn't want to go, to do something he didn't really want to do, applied the brakes. Paul was happy playing piano his way, not somebody else's; he wanted to pick out tunes, not be forced to read music; and he certainly didn't want to bother with 'learning dots'. The end came when he was set homework. School homework was bad enough but it was compulsory, music wasn't; Paul abandoned the lessons after four or five weeks, saying the teacher's house 'smelled of old people'. Jim would reflect, 'He always seemed to know exactly what he wanted and usually knew how to get it.'[51]

Paul also failed an audition to become a choirboy at the Anglican Cathedral. It was Jim's idea he should join the Liverpool Cathedral Choristers' Guild – he felt sure his son's voice was good enough – so there Paul was in April 1953, dutifully lined up with other boys, waiting to audition one by one for choirmaster Ronald Woan. Jim later found out what happened: Paul failed not because he couldn't sing but because 'he deliberately cracked his voice'. It was subtle defiance – but, as it turned out, for the best. Had Paul passed, all subsequent events could have turned out very differently, for being in the choir involved a busy calendar of commitments for at least three years and possibly longer.[52]

Then came 2 June and the coronation of Queen Elizabeth II, which prompted the McCartneys to rent their first television, also the first in the street. All the neighbours and their children were invited to watch the seven-hour BBC coverage. Paul won a Liverpool Public Libraries prize for an essay anticipating the London spectacle ('after all this bother, many people will agree with me that it was well worth it') and collected it in a ceremony at Picton Hall, the splendid circular reading-room opposite the Empire Theatre. It was a prestigious event, and when the Lord Mayor announced 'And in the under-eleven age group, from Joseph Williams primary school in Gateacre, J. P. McCartney', and he had to walk up on the stage, his knees were 'rubbery'. 'It was my first ever experience of nerves,' he'd remember. 'I was shaking like a jelly.'[53]

Paul began his new life and new daily journey on 9 September – he was heading into town. The Latin motto at Liverpool Institute High School for Boys was Non Nobis Solum Sed Toti Mundo Nati – translated as 'Not for ourselves but for the whole world were we born'. Clearly, this was a school that took itself a mite seriously. Mary had high hopes Paul would become a doctor, Jim thought he'd become a scientist, but first Paul had to find his way around what *Liverpool and Merseyside Illustrated* called 'an overcrowded and ancient building'.[54] The school opened in the year of Queen Victoria's accession, 1837, and it was a confusion of dark dank passageways and staircases. Charles Dickens addressed a gathering here in 1844. Next door was Liverpool College of Art; it had been the same school until 1890, when doors were sealed up and they were separated. The headmaster was quite literally a Victorian: John 'Jack' Edwards, known to boys as The Baz, a feared individual, strict and humourless in his determination that every Institute scholar go on to Oxford or Cambridge. A number did, but those who didn't could be scorned as a waste of everyone's time.[55]

Pupils were in the 'Lower School' for the first three years – and began in what was confusingly called 'the third year'. Paul started in form 3C, an arbitrary decision, after which the forms were streamed according to ability. In his first year he was middling, ranked around twelfth – an impressive achievement considering his classmates were among the city's brightest boys and he was always one of the youngest in his year. He was popular too. Naturally funny, he showed a good talent for vocal mimicry by impersonating the masters, and drew witty cartoons that were passed around the class for laughs. Some pals called him Macca – the nickname stuck on many a Liverpool child whose surname starts with Mc or Mac. One boy he made friends with was John Lennon's close pal Ivan Vaughan, sometimes nicknamed Ive or Ivy. He was at the Institute solely *because* of John: his mother decided he couldn't go to Quarry Bank as 'that Lennon' was bound to derail his studies. Another boy starting at the Institute in September 1953 was Neil Aspinall, nicknamed Nell, from West Derby, north Liverpool. He too was in 3C, but on only nodding acquaintance with Paul at this time.

Paul's overall impression of the Institute was succinct and truthful: 'I didn't like it very much, but I didn't dislike it; and I quite enjoyed bits of it. What I didn't like was being told what to do.'[56] One particularly appealing aspect was its location. Until this time, Paul's life had played out in the suburbs; now he'd landed at the heart of the action. The school was in one of the best parts of Liverpool, just off Hope Street, a handsome thoroughfare with the Anglican Cathedral at one end, the Philharmonic Hall concert venue halfway along, and an art-house cinema, Hope Hall, at the far end. Very close by was Canning Street, the 'artistic quarter', peopled by the bohemians who studied or taught at the art school or did nothing very much at all except drink in the local pubs. Strides down the steep hill took Paul to the city's main streets: it was a thrill for him to spend solo time here, enjoying the spiel of the St John's Market traders, watching the escapologist wriggle his way out of chains on a 'bommy' opposite the Adelphi Hotel, and catching Codman's Punch and Judy show, a constant fixture by Lime Street station for decades.

George Harrison first went to the Liverpool Institute in February 1954, to take his Eleven-Plus. Though he'd done well at Dovedale Road, no one was sure he'd make grammar-school grade. His sister Louise had, his brothers Harry and Peter hadn't. The next day, when his Dovedale teacher asked who in the class felt they'd passed, George didn't put up his hand. But he had, and he'd be Institute-bound from September for at least five years, perhaps seven or eight.

The blond hair George had had since birth was now turning brown, and there was a major battle every time Harry tried to trim it: George always put up a fuss when forced into a haircut. He was growing into a self-sufficient and opinionated lad. Children were often being told to 'respect your elders and betters' but George didn't always feel they'd *earned* it. He was a born sceptic with

a reasoned disregard for some of his schoolteachers, and was experiencing a
rapid loss of faith in the Catholic Church owing to the way it was trying to control him. Louise had been sending George to mass on and off all his life at Our
Lady of Good Help, in Wavertree, where he'd also been going into the con-
fessional box from an early age, coming clean to the priest about his latest 'sins'.
At 11, he'd taken part in the Communion ceremony; but by this age, as he'd
explain, he already 'felt that there was some hypocrisy going on'.[57]

George observed the way supposedly God-fearing people carried on – how,
for instance, the men forced to go to church would far rather have been away
drinking somewhere: 'When I was about 11 I was sitting in this church with all
these people who could well have been in the Red Lion.' He'd overhear grown-
ups commenting on alleged infidelities: 'I always remember [adults] saying,
"You'll never believe that Mrs Jones – she's running around with Mr Badger.
She's a dark horse!"' And he also saw how, when priests came to Upton Green,
knocking on doors to collect money for the building of a new church, many
(and sometimes the Harrisons) would pretend they were out, lying low, turning off the lights and maintaining radio silence until God's messenger had
gone.

George was becoming dismissive of organised religion as he knew it, but he
kept the door ajar for God. 'The only thing that came across to me in the
church was these oil paintings of Christ struggling up the hill with the cross on
his back. I thought, "There's something going on there." But as to the rest of
the building and the priest and the people, I just thought it was stupid. [I
thought] "I can't get anything out of this!"' Though he was meant to be confirmed after his Communion, George dropped out. 'From then on,' he'd say, 'I
avoided the church.'[58]

3

'Who you lookin' at?' (1954–5)

As simplistic as it is to consider that fashion for young people didn't exist before the 1950s – that children reached 18 and then dressed like their parents – this was the essential truth of it. The suit-and-tie look was maintained daily in almost all walks of life by almost all men of all ages. Jim McCartney, George Smith, Harry Harrison and Harry Graves sat in a shirt and tie, or something similarly smart, at home in the evenings and at weekends, and certainly when going out, and almost every man had very short hair that was brushed or combed neatly into a parting and greased.

In London around 1948 there was a trend among upper-class Guards officers to wear handmade frock-coats with velvet collars and double-breasted waistcoats, echoing the style of royalty, politicians and businessmen in Edwardian (and previous) times. In the early 1950s, this style was taken up by gangs of working-class London youths, except they didn't ape the trend, they subverted it, extending the 'drape' jacket to the fingertips and knees in the manner of the American 'zoot suit'.* In May 1952 an advert ran in the *Daily Mirror* for 'crepe soled shoes, in 18 different styles', with a drawing of a young couple jiving to a jazz band and a blurb that exclaimed 'Not for him are the fashions of Grandfather's day'. These shoes, also known as 'brothel creepers', went brilliantly with the Edwardian jackets, and the outfit was completed with tight-legged 'drainpipe' trousers (to be known in Liverpool as 'drainies'); 'Slim Jim' bootlace ties; tight waistcoats; luminescent

---

* Worn by some black, Hispanic and Italian-American male youths in the late 1930s and '40s, the 'zoot suit' included high-waisted, wide-legged pegged trousers, and a long coat with wide lapels and wide padded shoulders.

socks; and, ever the crowning glory, a mop of hair swept back off the forehead into a piled quiff held in place with as much gunk as necessary. The hair at the back was separated and greased into two lanes, a style that took its name from what it looked like – in Britain a 'duck's arse', in America a 'duck's ass' or 'ducktail', the 'DA' for short. (The American film actor Tony Curtis, very popular among British kids, was the chief influence: people called it 'the Tony Curtis style'.) Finally, the 1950s Edwardian always carried a comb to keep his hair in order, and so much the better if it was steel and could double as a weapon.

Young Edwardians started to roam the streets in gangs rigorously demarcated into tight little districts or areas, and there were running battles with anyone who stepped in from outside. Juvenile delinquency was constantly in the news after the war but Edwardian activity was fairly low-key until January 1953, when an illiterate 19-year-old Londoner called Derek Bentley was found guilty of murdering an unarmed policeman, and was hanged for his crime. The subject was hot for a long time, and the popular press, noticing Bentley's appearance, began calling Edwardians 'Teddy Boys'. From now on, juvenile delinquents were Teddy Boys, and Teddy Boys were juvenile delinquents: the two were bootlace-tight.[1]

This sartorially savvy street-army instantly became the scapegoat for society's ills, a sickness of the age, the cause of all the problems. It was an unfair and illogical argument, but defending the line too strongly would obscure the fact that many a Ted enjoyed trouble, and plenty carried flick-knives, knuckle-dusters, studded belts or bicycle chains. Few were angels, no matter how much they loved their mum; if you saw even one Ted coming towards you on the street, it was always a good idea to run.

Inevitably, the more the Teddy Boy became public enemy number one, the more many found it attractive. Adopting the fashion of the reviled was a critical adolescent statement. Teddy Boys suddenly rose up all over Britain, especially in places of social deprivation – of which there were many. In Liverpool, gangs of Teds roamed more or less every little district, so just when Speke couldn't get much worse, Teds ensured it did.

> George: I was puny [but] I was a good runner – I'd just see a bunch of them coming and I'd avoid all that sort of scene. There was only once or twice I almost got done in.
>
> Paul: [It was] 'Who you lookin' at?' And if you answered wrong, either way, smack.[2]

Another major issue of the day was the creeping Americanisation of British society. Adults were scathing about it, but kids lapped it up. 'We were like the

Fifty-Ninth State in Britain,' John Lennon would say. 'We had all the Doris Day movies, and Heinz beans. (We all thought they were *English*.) I was brought up on Americana.'[3] Everyone was, especially when it came to films and music.

The early days of summer 1954 found John, Pete, Nige and Ivan in their latest favourite spot: a tree-shaded grassy knoll in Calderstones Park which they called The Bank. They sat around here and did what boys do: played games, talked crap, smoked 'Woodies' ('John was always saying "Give us a ciggie,"' recalls Nigel Walley) and teased and punched one another, always keeping a watchful eye out for the spoilsport park-keeper ('parkie'). Girls weren't invited, but, says Pete Shotton, 'There'd be a steady stream of them all want-ing to flirt with John.'[4] As crude and cutting as he was, John was a magnet for the 'birds'.

But The Bank was lads-only territory. John had the 'gob iron' and led them through rousing singalongs of recent American-made British hits such as Cool Water by Frankie Laine and at least three of Johnnie Ray's: Walkin' My Baby Back Home, The Little White Cloud That Cried, and Somebody Stole My Gal. John Lennon and pop music are linked here, decisively, for the first time.[5] He liked Laine and Ray, he also liked Sh-Boom by the Crew-Cuts, and when Tennessee Ernie Ford had a British number 1 with Give Me Your Word, he liked him too; he also enjoyed Caribbean by Mitchell Torok, a US country number 1 in 1953 that came to his attention by means unknown.

Around this time, John started seeing his mother again. It will never be known for certain how much contact they'd had in the preceding years – not none, but not a lot either.[6] It was John's cousin Stanley, down from Edinburgh, who took events into his own hands and let John accompany him on a visit to Julia at Blomfield Road. It was an encounter they kept secret from Mimi.

No doubt it was wonderful for John finally to be resuming a real relationship with Mummy after all these years, but it was probably also a time of great con-fusion. He once remarked how she was more like 'a young aunt or big sister' to him, as if the roles of Mimi and Julia were reversed in his mind.[7] He certainly made clear his feelings about Julia's de facto husband: he didn't much like him, just as he hadn't liked Taffy Williams. John called him Bobby to his face, but behind his back and to others he called him 'Twitchy', picking on Dykins' nerv-ous tic and throat-clearances.

John's schooling was now falling apart. His July 1954 report placed him thir-tieth out of thirty-four in his class, and he only just escaped being demoted, staying in the B stream for the third year. In Mimi's eyes he became 'bone-idle', but in certain respects he was more than active. John had started to draw captioned cartoons on scraps of paper, to be sneaked around the classroom during lessons, much as Paul was doing at the Institute. Many of these were inspired: a typical example featured a woman with a pram and ten tiny children, her husband burbling, 'But I do love you dear.' The artistic influence was US cartoonist James Thurber, the ideas were sprung from Milligan and also 'Professor' Stanley Unwin, the humorist who spoke in a mangled English known to aficionados (and John was one) as 'gobbledegook'. It wasn't long before these scraps of paper had evolved into John's own newspaper, *Daily Howl*, a school exercise book with an illustrated front cover and page after page of one-line gags, eccentric wordplay, spoof ads, cartoons and the first evidence of a lasting obsession with Negroes, Jews and human grotesques. John would write it at Mendips in the evenings and take the book into school next morning, to be read aloud and passed around – and then, after being confiscated by the teachers, enjoyed by the Quarry Bank staff before John got them back at the end of term.

Out of school, when he wasn't scrapping, John's main aim was to have a laugh and a shout. Michael Hill remembers how John would stand at the bus stop with a wellington boot on one foot and a football boot on the other, or he'd stick his leg out of the bus window. Nigel Walley says, 'He'd go upstairs on a bus and shout "All change!" and people would start scrambling downstairs, or "All tickets please!" and everyone would start fumbling for their tickets. Then he'd just sit down while someone mumbled, "Bloody teenagers."'

This word was a new American invention, arrived at after less likely attempts such as 'teenster' and 'teener'. Richy Starkey became one in July 1953 and had a new ambition: to become a tramp. If he couldn't ride the Prairie's wide-open spaces with his compadres, he'd wander the byways of Britain like Dick Whittington. Or, another plan: run away to sea. He'd heard that you could get out of National Service by serving eight uninterrupted years in the merchant navy – it was one of the few exemptions. Richy began his preparation by joining Dingle Sea Scouts, but was soon scuppered. 'I was thrown out because I ran away with a rifle. I never saw a boat. I was never in anything too long; I always did something that annoyed people.'[8]

He avoided school as much as possible. The only documented report from his years at Dingle Vale, Christmas 1952, shows that in the three months from September he was absent thirty-four times, which means he was away as much as he was there.[9] His form teacher wrote: 'A quiet, thoughtful type, although working rather slowly. Academic work will no doubt improve in time as he is trying to do his best. Helpful & willing.' He was twenty-third out of thirty-nine in his class. But he did achieve an A in Drama ('Takes a real interest and has done very well') because he loved playing roles – a trait he'd picked up from years of going to the Saturday-morning pictures.

Richy had a long walk when he went to school, from the north-east tip of the Dingle to its south-west corner. His usual route took him down Park Road, where there were shops, and one day – around early 1954 – he stopped outside a music store and stood staring at a drum in the window. 'They had guitars and banjos and mandolins, accordions and things like that, but this one drum, just a tom-tom, used to freak me out. I loved it and used to go and look at this tom-tom every day, walking to school and walking back.'[10] The drum was expensive, beyond his means, but the idea of owning it, of beating a sound on it, was unshakeable from his mind. 'I couldn't get over that price. But I couldn't get over the idea of a drum either. I don't know why.' Richy had been gifted a range of musical instruments in his childhood, none of which he'd asked for or bothered to do anything with; the drum was the first one *he* wanted. As he'd later put it, 'There was never any other instrument … I wanted to be a drummer.'[11]

At this time, ten years after separating, Elsie and Richard Starkey were divorced; both were remarried before the year was out. On 17 April, Elsie tied the knot with Harry Graves in a ceremony at the new register office on Mount Pleasant, a short walk up the hill from the city centre. The Graves family came up from London and there was a rare old party that night, cockneys in the Dingle, the ale flowing, the old songs sung, perhaps a fist or two thrown in boozed-up joy. Richy was a big part of the day. Elsie had asked his permission for all this, saying she wouldn't marry if he said no. It was a hefty weight for slight shoulders – he'd be having to share her, and maybe soon be competing with a new brother or sister. Elsie was only 39. On the other hand, Richy had loved Harry from the start, warming to his softly spoken and generous nature. So he said yes, and now Harry really was his stepfather. He didn't call him Dad, just Harry, and he took to calling his mum Elsie. They were his parents by deed if no longer by name. Harry moved into 10 Admiral Grove, so now there were three in the tiny house.

But not for long.

Most likely in May or June 1954, Richy fell seriously ill again. The problem this time was pleurisy, and once more Lazarus found himself out of school and in the Royal Liverpool Children's Hospital, where he'd lived through 1947–8. He was there for ten weeks this time, during which his condition developed into tuberculosis. Liverpool was very bad for TB: the industrial fug gave it one of the highest rates in Europe. The only cure was a long period of rest in cleaner air, so Richy was sent to the hospital's convalescence outpost in Heswall, on the leafy Wirral, the other side of the Mersey.

His recuperation promised to be a slow old process. No one had any real idea when he'd get out – a year, maybe two? – and this hammered the final nail into his school education. Recognising his plight, and that of his fellow young inmates, the hospital arranged for vocational teachers to come into the wards. Richy learned to knit, he painted, he made baskets, and he crafted a farm island from papier-mâché. Most stirringly of all, a music teacher came to the ward every fortnight with a collection of percussion instruments. She handed out tambourines, cymbals, triangles, maracas and six-inch drums, and put up an easel on which she pinned a large rolled-out music sheet with colour-coded notes; if she tapped red, the children with drums would have to strike them, green was for shaking the tambourine, and so on, in the hope that the cacoph-onous combination would approximate Three Blind Mice or London Bridge Is Falling Down.[12] Richy was obstinate in his refusal to join in unless the teacher gave him a drum. It was the first time he'd picked up a drumstick and the first time he'd hit something like a proper drum. The dream conceived at a Dingle shop window came to life in a Heswall hospital, and it was love at first strike.

In Liverpool on 5 July 1954, Richy Starkey was in hospital, John Lennon was rampaging at Quarry Bank, Paul McCartney was finishing his first year at the Institute, and George Harrison was ten days away from leaving primary school ... while, in Memphis, a 19-year-old singer-guitarist was recording a ses-sion in Sam Phillips' music studio at 706 Union Avenue. Over a few hours, gelling with local players Scotty Moore (guitar) and Bill Black (standup bass), the youth recorded four sides. Nobody looked anything like him, dressed any-thing like him, sounded anything like him, or had a name anything like his. He was Elvis Presley.

Phillips had opened his studio four years earlier and prayed for this: a white boy who sang country, the blues, anything, with a voice as rhythmic, as soulful, as tuneful, as dynamic and electrifying as the best he'd ever heard. When Elvis first walked into the studio and the receptionist asked what type of singer he was, who he sounded like, the boy had mumbled, 'I don't sound like nobody.' It was a statement of modesty, not brashness, and obviously true. On 19 July 1954, as he drew up a two-year contract for Elvis to sign, Phillips released the boy's first record, That's All Right c/w Blue Moon Of Kentucky.* Sun 209, bright yellow label. The A-side – aka That's All Right Mama – was originally an electric blues by Arthur 'Big Boy' Crudup, a black guitarist from the Mississippi Delta; Blue Moon Of Kentucky was a waltz number by country star Bill Monroe and his Bluegrass Boys. Elvis, Scotty and Bill did them uptempo and Sam

---

* There were two standard record business terms to denote the A- and B-sides of a single: c/w (short for 'coupled with') and b/w ('backed with'). This book will use c/w.

Phillips recorded them single track, live, no overdubs but lots of 'slap echo' (also 'slapback', simply achieved with tape by feeding the output signal from the playback head back to the recording head, the split-second delay between the two effecting an echo).

Reviewing the new record, *Billboard* magazine – one of the two main US music trade weeklies, along with *Cash Box* – called Presley a 'potent new chanter'. In his first advertised stage appearance, on 30 July, he demonstrated *wild* behaviour, his legs shaking and his hips swivelling and his pelvis thrusting and his top lip curling. News spread fast: the boy had a dangerous sexual image to go with his unique sound. The more the Memphis radio stations played the record, the more orders rolled into Sun.

Three months before this, on 12 April, Bill Haley and His Comets had gone into the Pythian Temple studio on West 70th Street, Manhattan, and recorded Rock Around The Clock, the song that would light the blue touchpaper under what, in America, was starting to be called 'rock and roll'. The phrase had been around for decades and meant different things to different people. In black gospel it meant the loving embrace and power of Jesus and God; in other black circles it meant *sex* – it was a synonym for 'fucking'. The sound itself was overwhelmingly rhythm and blues – written, played and sung by black artists for a black audience – music that was confident, assertive, exciting and irresistible, grooves that oozed swing, rhythm and beat, with punchy vocals that spoke of life, love and sex. It was called 'rock and roll' by Alan Freed, a rabidly enthusiastic white radio DJ from Cleveland, Ohio, whose incessant championing of the music he loved rode roughshod over all the conventions of the day to effect, ultimately, nothing less than unparalleled racial integration.* A huge success in Cleveland from 1951, Freed switched to the mighty New York AM station WINS in 1954, where he pumped rock and roll up and down the East Coast through a 50,000-watt transmitter.

Bill Haley was a guitarist, singer and former Indiana State yodelling champion who, sensing the coming direction, switched from cowboy music and 'western swing' to music with a slapped bass and swooping guitar solos. Slicking down a distinctive 'kiss curl' hair loop, Haley picked up the groove and changed the name of his group from the Saddlemen to the Comets.† They attacked Rock Around The Clock from the first snare double-beat, keeping a solid tempo through and beyond an exotic electric guitar solo in the bridge. The entire band

---

* It didn't matter if you wrote it as rock and roll or rock 'n' roll, just so long as you got the beat. Freed himself (mostly) wrote it as rock and roll.
† A childhood operation had left Haley blind in his left eye, which then took on a different appearance; the kiss curl was to distract people from noticing it.

honked and swung in a combination so infectious that the meaning of 'rock' wasn't considered – was Haley suggesting *partying* for a whole twelve hours or *bedroom activity*?

For the moment, few heard it. It was only a B-side, captured in two takes inside the last thirty minutes of a three-hour session. The record was issued in America in May and barely registered. It wasn't released in Britain at this time and nor was Elvis Presley, and no one yet sensed any sign of a musical uprising.

Finally, but also of major importance, another slow-burning revolutionary record was cut in London on 13 July, eight days after Elvis swung That's All Right Mama in Memphis. It was just another day at the Decca studio in West Hampstead and Chris Barber's Jazz Band had come in to make a ten-inch LP, *New Orleans Joys*. A popular element of Barber's live shows since 1952 was a supplementary spot where some of his musicians indulged in a little 'skiffle', a loose guitar-led jazz-band sound originating in 1920s black Chicago – rent party music played on basic instruments. Barber's singer-guitarist Lonnie Donegan and two others (Barber himself on standup bass, Beryl Bryden on washboard) quickly cut five songs, including Richy Starkey's party piece in Liverpool, Nobody's Child, and one called Rock Island Line, a chugging and then accelerating train song about a stretch of the Chicago Rock Island & Pacific railway line. *New Orleans Joys* came out, sold to the few British jazz aficionados who had the wherewithal to afford an LP, and that was that . . . for the time being.

George Harrison, one of the many British boys whose lives would be changed by Donegan, left Dovedale Road school two days later; like others in his situation, he was dismayed when the headmaster told them that, though they were the biggest children in the school now, at their next they'd be the little 'uns again. 'It seemed such a waste, after all that hustling to be one of the big lads,' George would reflect.[13]

George hated Liverpool Institute from the start. He resented the lessons and despised almost all the teachers. 'I was a real lout in my youth. When I was a kid I liked to run about, jump, do all those things kids do, but then they took me away and put me in high school where we didn't do anything except Latin and logarithms.'[14] On his first day, 8 September 1954, another new boy, Tony Workman, jumped on his back from behind a door and said, 'Do you wanna fight, la?' They did, and then became friends. George's closest Institute pal was Arthur Kelly, who lived in Edge Hill; along with Tony Workman, they all began in form 3E, and owing to alphabetical arrangement Harrison and Kelly were seated next to each other. They quickly found much in common, not least a comprehensive dislike of pretty much everything going on hereabouts. They and Tony became a terrible trio in the eyes of the school's begowned masters, intent upon doing as little work and extracting as much fun as possible, and if that meant being disruptive then it meant being disruptive. 'Harrison, Kelly and Workman – *get out!*' would be barked as frequently at the Institute as 'Lennon and Shotton – *get out!*' at Quarry Bank.

George's frustrations were expressed through unruly behaviour and use of fists. 'I was never a bully except in the first few years of grammar school, trying to deal with frustrations, punching a few people. You can't smile, and [it was] "Be here!" and "Shut up!", and exams every year, and the teachers were either old war veterans with no legs or eyes or [they were] fresh out of college. That's when the darkness came in, that was where my frustrations started. You would punch people just to get it out of your system.'[15]

If George wasn't already smoking by the age of 11, he was soon after. Though the demarcation in school years was emphatic, with little or no fraternisation between boys at different levels, the secluded area of the playground known as 'smokers' corner', behind the air-raid shelter, gathered a mixture of ages. This was where George first met Neil Aspinall, starting a lifelong friendship. 'I used to be with him behind the shelter at break-time saying, "Gis a drag,"' Neil would recall.[16] Someone would keep watch for masters on the prowl, and when none were around the lads imagined they'd put one over on them. The men weren't so easily fooled. As Arthur Kelly says, 'I remember a teacher saying to George, "Smoking well, Harrison?" "What do you mean, sir?" "Look at your fingers, boy, they're like Belisha beacons!" And they were – they were bright orange.'[17]

Paul McCartney, now in his second year at the Institute (form 4B), wasn't yet a smoker, but the day was coming fast. He and George had something else in common anyway: both were Speke boys who caught the bus to and from school every day, either the 82D or the express 500. George boarded one stop after Paul, and they tended to sit upstairs, where smoking was allowed. Establishing even so much as a rough date for when they first talked is impossible, but, recognising each other's school uniform, they did. 'Being close to each other in age, we talked,' Paul confirms, 'although I tended to talk down to him, because he was a year younger.' George, in 1963, when filling out a questionnaire that asked for his first impression of Paul, wrote 'fat and friendly'.[18]

In his thirteenth year, Paul was going through a pre-pubescent chubby stage. He was touchy about it, and 'had someone' at school (punched him hard) for making fun of him. The friendly phrase within the family was 'puppy fat', though brother Mike would call him 'Fatty!' before running away fast. He later remarked of this period in Paul's life that it was 'the only time that anything outwardly affected him'.[19]

A good photo of Paul, standing in front of a window announcing HOT DOG

CORNER, was taken at this time by Mike when the McCartney family were on holiday. In summer 1954 they took the train to the Butlin's camp at Pwllheli, on the north-west coast of Wales, and Jim was trusting enough to allow Mike use of the family's Kodak box camera. Mike was ten, and the moment he pressed the shutter a deep and lasting interest in photography clicked within him – much as Richy Starkey felt when he first hit a drum.[20]

The McCartneys were at Pwllheli through a family connection. Bett Danher (Jim's niece as well as Mary's cousin) had become engaged to Mike Robbins, who was working the summer season as a Butlin's Redcoat – an entertainer and all-round good sort. Paul was pleased to have an 'in' on this side of things, and one day saw five young men exit the ballroom, all identically dressed in tartan flat caps, grey crew-neck sweaters, tartan shorts and pumps. They came from Gateshead, and Paul watched as every head turned to look at them. In that second, he had an epiphany, seeing the potent impact of a group of performers all dressed alike. It was a vision he'd not forget.[21]

The first chart in Britain to rank sales of 'popular' records as opposed to classical records or sheet music sales had been launched by the weekly paper *New Musical Express* (to become known as the *NME*) in November 1952. In its first two years, almost every chart song was caked in goo, from syrupy beginning to saccharine end. There was nothing to fuel so much as a grain of youthful rebellion, nothing to make anyone snap off a disc in disgust. When records of rhythm and beat came along, when rock and roll exploded, it filled a vacuum none had realised existed, and so it seemed – no, *was* – radical, raucous, revolutionary, rousing, shocking and, like most new forms of music, a threat to the controlling powers.

Into this ultra-safe environment the week before Christmas 1954 exploded Shake, Rattle And Roll by Bill Haley and His Comets, the disc breaking through just as it had in America, where it spent ten weeks in the *Cash Box* top ten. The song penetrated Britain solely on the strength of promotion on Radio Luxembourg and some spins on AFN.* Nowhere could the BBC Light Programme accommodate this music: the network had no disc jockey shows,

---

* AFN – American Forces Network – served the needs of the United States' substantial body of European-based servicemen. Broadcast from a castle outside Frankfurt, the reception wasn't brilliant in Britain, but listeners were rewarded with a terrific quantity and variety of sounds. More popular and influential still, Radio Luxembourg beamed night-time programmes to Britain from the Grand Duchy of Luxembourg, its signal ebbing and flowing at 208 metres on the medium wave (AM). Unimpeded by any of the restrictions imposed on the BBC, Luxembourg was freer in tone and content, and strove for an American approach, commercials and all.

and was anyway prevented from unlimited playing of records by the so-called 'Needletime' agreement.*

In America, pretty much every adult who heard the new sound despised it, many fearing it as 'jungle music' or 'the devil's music' ... but young people loved it. In April 1955, *Alan Freed's Rock 'n' Roll Easter Jubilee* ran five times daily at the Brooklyn Paramount Theater, a galaxy of acts doing one song each, running on and off stage while Freed cranked the excitement in between. This delicious mayhem shattered the house record, grossing $107,000. The US entertainment industry was both disgusted and wowed.

A clinching factor in America's linkage of rock and roll with juvenile delinquency was the use of Bill Haley's Rock Around The Clock over the opening and closing credits of a new MGM movie, *Blackboard Jungle*. In this, teachers at an urban New York high school are confronted by hoodlum students: Spics, Jews, Niggers, Micks (their words), Italians and other insolent and violent elements. For teenagers, the film taught rebellion more than any movie before; for everyone, it coupled the sound of rock and roll with the image of foul-mouthed, flick-knife-wielding louts in leather jackets and strange hairstyles. Wherever *Blackboard Jungle* went, so did Rock Around The Clock. Decca reissued the former B-side and it tore up the US charts, settling at number 1 for eight straight weeks in the summer of 1955. Soon it would have the same effect in Britain.

Going to the pictures was beyond the reach of the boy still stuck in the Royal Liverpool Children's Hospital at Heswall. As 1954 clicked into 1955 and spring bloomed there remained no sign of when he might get out. Every clock had stopped but for the one that can't. Approaching 15, Richy Starkey was going through puberty. He'd had some sexual experiences at a much younger age but

---

* *Why there was never enough pop music on the BBC – aka 'Needletime in a nutshell'.*
In order to control broadcasting rights, in 1934 British record companies formed themselves into a central body called Phonographic Performance Ltd (PPL). The BBC couldn't play records without buying a PPL licence – an annual six-figure cost by the 1950s. The licence restricted the amount of time records could be played, and the influencing factor in negotiations was the Musicians' Union. Though not party to the agreements, the MU pulled PPL's strings, threatening industrial action against record companies if it granted the BBC too much 'Needletime', arguing that this could put musicians out of work. In 1952 it was set at twenty-two hours a week across all domestic BBC radio networks (twenty-eight hours from 1959), with BBC-tv allowed three hours; the BBC had to bolster its musical content with live and pre-recorded sessions. There were other restrictions too – e.g., in the 1950s, the BBC was only permitted to play a new record once a day in the first week of its release, to prevent over-exposure. Not without feeling was a BBC internal report about 'Needletime' titled *Radio's Bridle*. However, seen strictly in the light of this history, in the years 1962–5 it had some highly beneficial consequences.

that was just inquisitive stuff; now he was intent. He was feeling frisky, and asked for (and says he sometimes got) a fair old goodnight kiss from one or two of the younger nurses. There was also a bit of sneaking around between the boys' and girls' wards, but patients required patience: 'I'd stand there for hours trying to get a touch of tit,' he'd recall.[22]

The only other joy to break the monotony of month after month in hospital came through the drums. Richy had his first regular exposure here to the magic of television, boys and girls being allowed to watch the daily hour of BBC children's shows from five until six o'clock, and in the magazine programme *Jigsaw* he saw George Fierstone, a drummer who, as the boy would enthuse, could 'twiddle his sticks'. 'I went, "Wow! *Look* at this man, twiddling the sticks!"'[23] The combination of Fierstone's drumming skills and the fortnightly ward visit from the music teacher with her percussion instruments consumed the lad. There would be Richy Starkey – far from home, family and mates – a tough survivor, banging his drum as if beating out time.

John Lennon was out during the afternoon of Saturday 4 June 1955. Mimi and biochemistry student Michael Fishwick (the longest-staying lodger at Mendips, 1951–8) were finishing a meal when they heard her husband George start to make his way downstairs. He arrived near the bottom with a speed and a bump that sent Fishwick scurrying from the table. 'He was bleeding from the mouth. It was pretty obvious it came from the stomach, a haemorrhage.'[24] George was rushed to Sefton General Hospital but never recovered: he died the following day, a post-mortem establishing the cause as 'cirrhosis of liver (non alcoholic)' and burst abdomen. He was 52.

John had experienced much seismic upheaval in his life, but this was the first time he suffered the death of one so close: George wasn't only his uncle, he'd been his surrogate father for nine years. Mimi would later say, 'I think John was very shocked by George's death, but he never showed it'; but John would eventually be much more expressive on the matter. He'd recall that, as he didn't know how to be sad in public, he went up to his room with his cousin Liela Birch and they 'laughed and laughed', feeling guilty about it afterwards. Liela herself said only, 'It was a terrible shock to us all, but especially to John who looked on him as a father.' Paul McCartney remembers John saying (some years later) that, with his dad leaving him and Uncle George dying, he started to feel like he was a jinx on the male side of the family.[25]

A poem handwritten by John for Mimi on the day of George's funeral shows him far from heartless about her loss, and fearlessly open in his condemnation of her sisters, his mother included, for insufficiently stirring themselves in her hour of need. Mimi was, he wrote, 'the best of the five'.

MIMI

The worry and strife, that's been wont to her life,
Has driven her family to shame.
If they should survive, to one hundred and five,
They could never repay her again.
Each one in their turn, will finally learn
That she is the best of the five.
Each one of them slept, not one of them wept
At the struggle of her mate to survive.
7/6/55. *J. W. Lennon*

This sincere poem – lucid, forthright and notably mature for a 14-year-old – gave comfort to Mimi and she kept it always. It also has one other revealing dimension, because the third line – 'If they should survive, to one hundred and five' – is adapted from Frank Sinatra's Young At Heart, a 1954 American and British hit. In places, the cadence of John's piece just about fits the metre of Sinatra's recording too. This poem for Mimi is the first example of John Lennon expressing his feelings through popular song.[26]

It isn't known if he attended the funeral and burial, at St Peter's church. He never said he did (but no interviewer asked him). Mimi fell ill soon afterwards, suffering from stress. Yet as much as John gave comfort with his poem, the school report he brought home from Quarry Bank a month later caused her great anxiety. What had happened to the Dovedale Road high-flyer bright enough to be gliding through grammar school and beyond, to university and into a profession? His class positions were terrible: even in Art, where he was usually first, he was now fifteenth. He'd given up. Headmaster E. R. Taylor summarised it as 'A shocking report on work & conduct & attitude to school. He cannot escape relegation this year.' The boy who'd been in IIB and IIIB would next be in IVC . . . and again Pete Shotton went down with him. John's last report had been signed by George; this time the document received his widow's signature, and her raw feelings are shown in an extra comment scrawled at the bottom of the sheet: '6 of the best needed' – six lashes of the headmaster's cane, please. She wrote it to frighten John, she said later, but conceded that he never let the school see it anyway. Shortly afterwards, Mimi went into hospital for five weeks, suffering from shock, worry and ulcers, while John went to Edinburgh and Durness for what turned out to be his last-but-one Scottish summer holiday.

Paul McCartney became a teenager on 18 June 1955, lost his puppy fat and went straight into the raging-hormone stage. One day he had to face the consequence of his mother finding 'a dirty drawing' in his shirt pocket. It was a typically creative piece of work, a scrap of paper that had a clothed woman on the front but which, when unfolded, showed her gradually disrobing until naked. Mary was shocked and offended by such imagery, so palpably upset that when she confronted Paul he named and blamed another boy in his class. A fretful domestic impasse resulted. Paul says, 'It went three days, and my father was called in on the case. He grilled me, I still denied it and in the end he broke me down, and I admitted it and cried.'[27]

Several girls Paul's age lived in Ardwick Road and he gained a new nickname – 'the boy Casanova of Speke'. A fledgling boyfriend-girlfriend situation developed with Sheila Prytherch, from number 8. 'Paul McCartney was my first kiss,' she says, 'and we held hands. It was innocent and lovely – he was the first boy who made me feel like that.'[28] Paul would recall taking Sheila to the pictures one afternoon and announcing to her, 'I can sing better than Frank Sinatra!' Such was his self-belief, he felt he could. Paul's cousin Ian played trumpet in a local amateur jazz group, and during a family visit to his house in Huyton, Paul picked up the instrument for the first time; with only a little advice from Jim – 'purse the lips, son, purse the lips' – he managed to blow a few notes. *Impressive.*

Paul's birthday was coming up, so Jim took the opportunity to present him with a trumpet, bought secondhand at the oldest music store in Liverpool, Rushworth & Dreaper.[29] Paul set about mastering the instrument his way, untutored. Trumpet records were plumb in vogue at this time: the number 1 tune in Britain and America in the week of his 13th birthday was Cherry Pink And Apple Blossom White, so the instrument was at the pinnacle of its popularity. Paul felt he could crack it: 'Of course, I immediately fancied myself as Louis Armstrong, but I only got as far as learning When The Saints Go Marching In before I got fed up with it. It used to hurt my lip and I didn't fancy the thought of walking around like a beat-up boxer.'[30]

Into the last months of 1955 (and maybe as far as the spring of 1956) the sounds of Paul McCartney's trumpet playing spilled out into Ardwick Road like an avant-garde music-track to the street games of other children. He mastered the C scale and learned one or two other tunes beyond 'The Saints'. Ultimately, however, as the craze for trumpet records began to fade, as more exciting musical sounds reached Britain from America, and as Paul's lips suffered from the constant pursing, his attachment to the instrument ebbed away.

Eight months younger than Paul, George Harrison was still a boy, prepubescent. He and Arthur Kelly went everywhere together, and in July 1955 George saw his first Formula One Grand Prix, held at the new road-racing circuit added to the Grand National racecourse at Aintree. Engines were

George's sole sporting interest: as well as motor-racing, he also followed the bikes, sending away for photographs and autographs of the stars. At an Aintree practice day in September 1955 he clambered aboard one of the bikes for an evocative photograph, grinning away under his crash-helmet.[31]

This interest ran through the Harrison family: brothers Harry and Peter were also keen followers, and dad Harry had just bought his first car, which – as motor-fan George would always specifically recall – was a 1933 Austin 10 Saloon with running-boards, wire wheels and a luggage rack on the back. Virtually no family, friends or neighbours had a car, so they seemed like royalty. In July 1955, Harry and Louise took Peter and George on their first motoring holiday, a marathon trip down to South Devon. Their destination was the coastal town of Exmouth and what would become a camping and caravan park called Sandy Bay but was at this time just a field with a loo block. Here we see the British on holiday in the 1950s: spirit stoves, straw mattresses and rain. Soon after arriving, the Harrisons met another family, the Brewers, starting a friendship that would last the rest of their lives. Their daughter Jenny was the same age as George and they became good pals and pen-friends.

> I found Harry reticent and quiet; Lou was loud, vivacious, not shy at all – there wouldn't be silence in the room when she was there – and George was bubbly like his mum. They all bounced off each other and would do anything for anyone, and they all had a wonderful sense of humour, George especially. I threw a strop one day and threatened to walk to Budleigh Salterton. I stayed away a bit but all I really did was go to the loo and kill some time before coming back. After that, whenever George went to the loo he'd say, 'I'm just off to Budleigh Salterton . . .'[32]

Richy Starkey got out of hospital towards the end of 1955, under instructions to take life easy for a while. Before then, as a respite treat for his 15th birthday, Harry took him (and Elsie) on his annual trip home to Romford, staying with his parents in the house where he was born forty-two years earlier. It was Richy's first time in the south of England and his first glimpse of the capital – they went to see the annual Searchlight Tattoo at White City Stadium, where he enjoyed the swing of the American band, just as John Lennon had done in Edinburgh, and they went on a grand day out 'to see the sights'. A photo shows Richy patting a regimental horse. Somewhat dwarfed by the animal, he is a small lad, smart in a jacket but with his shirt and tie slightly askew, his hair brushed clear of the forehead into an impressive little quiff.[33]

Being 15, he was now beyond the minimum school-leaving age and this time there was no question of going back to find himself even further behind his

classmates – because they'd all left too. He returned only to pick up the sign-off
document qualifying him to collect his unemployment benefit – 'the dole'.
Initially, the school secretary couldn't find any record of his attendance, but
then she did and Dingle Vale provided him with a typed reference: 'Richard
Starkey is honest, cheerful and willing, and quite capable of making a satisfactory employee.'[34]

Where he might use such a lustrous testimonial was unclear. Elsie knew he
lacked the basic education to work in an office, and also, for at least a while
longer, the strength to do anything manual. On top of his dole money, Richy
earned a few bob singing in a church choir, and marking up papers in a
newsagency on High Park Street: he wasn't strong enough to be involved in
their delivery, and the future held nothing whatever in store for him.

With a broad taste in popular music, Richy spent these self-earned shillings
on a secondhand wind-up gramophone from a junk shop and a few discs to go
with it, some old and a few new. He bought the music-hall comedy record The
Laughing Policeman, by Charles Penrose; Love Is A Many Splendored Thing,
by the Four Aces; Eddie Calvert's 1954 trumpet hit Oh, Mein Papa; and
Mama, by David Whitfield. Besotted with drums, Richy strung wire across the
top of a biscuit tin and thwacked it with firewood, then he got his first proper
instrument: a single massive one-sided bass drum, fifty inches in diameter,
bought from a secondhand shop in Smithdown Road for thirty bob (£1 10s).
With this, he said, he 'used to drive 'em all mad . . . bashin' it to the BBC'.[35]
At family parties Richy wouldn't only sing Nobody's Child, he'd bring out the
big drum and pummel it with wood while everyone was doing their turn. 'Ah,
it's the kid,' people would say, sympathetically, 'let him have a go.' He could
hardly be seen behind it, but the *noise*! After a few minutes of tuneless thumping they'd all be shouting at him, 'Sling yer 'ook!'

Richy didn't buy Rock Around The Clock, which – on 25 November 1955,
soon after the X-certificate Blackboard Jungle opened in London – became the
first rock and roll number 1 in Britain. But he did love it, as did Paul
McCartney. All his life, Paul had heard people say that certain things 'give you
a tingle up your spine'; he first felt it when he heard Haley's record – a magical, emotional, unforgettable moment. On a visit to Blomfield Road, John
Lennon found Julia dancing around the kitchen to it – not Haley's version,
which he liked, but a Mills Brothers-like cover by the Deep River Boys which
he didn't. George Harrison eagerly saved his pocket money to buy it, and someone in the family went to the shop for him; he was crushed when they returned
saying, 'They sold out of Bill Haley so I got you this one instead,' presenting
him with the Deep River Boys. George would call Rock Around The Clock 'the
first record I didn't get'.[36]

An equally important figure for George at this time was Slim Whitman, the yodelling country and western singer from Florida who'd had two British hits in 1955, Indian Love Call and Rose Marie. Louise liked them so much she bought them, which meant George had unlimited exposure to the records, both of which had appealing steel guitar parts. George had been listening to guitar music since hearing his dad's Jimmie Rodgers records as a very young child, but he hadn't *seen* a guitar until catching sight of Whitman ... and he knew instantly he had to have one.*

Around this time, towards the end of 1955, George contracted nephritis (inflammation of the kidneys) and spent six weeks in hospital, obliged to force down an almost inedible spinach diet. One of his visitors reported grapevine news that an ex-Dovedale Road schoolmate, Raymond Hughes, had an acoustic guitar for sale. It was £3 10s – a lot of money, well beyond George's pocket, but he mentioned it to Mum and, ever a great encourager of her children, Louise found the cash. When George got out of hospital, he wasted no time in rushing round to Raymond's house, just off Penny Lane, emerging a short time later with his first guitar.

A snapshot: George in the front room of a Speke council house, a boy in his carpet slippers, fingers picking out notes at the eighth fret, one leg straight and the other crooked as he rises on his toes.[37]

He didn't play this guitar for long. Though costing £3 10s, it was really a cheap old thing, made in the Netherlands by a company called Egmond, and it had a bolt in the back of the neck. George kept wondering what would happen if he unscrewed it, so he did, and found out: the neck came off, and then he couldn't get it back on. Out of frustration and embarrassment at having broken something that had cost Louise all that money, he shoved the two pieces in a cupboard and closed the door, his guitar sentenced to a stretch of solitary.

This country music influence already affecting George and Richy was also significant for John Lennon. He was going to a friend's house and playing his Hank Williams records. This boy also had a guitar but neither of them could play it, so John would just hold the instrument while he sang, performing Honky Tonk Blues into the fireplace.[38]

It was probably Pat Boone's safe white cover version of Ain't That A Shame (the one played on radio rather than the original recording by Fats Domino) which John Lennon's mother Julia heard and liked, and which she taught him to play on banjo – the same instrument on which she was taught by her father.

---

* In later years, George couldn't recall if he saw Whitman on television or whether it was a photo in a magazine. The Harrison family rented their first TV in this period.

John had been a harmonica player for years and this interest in stringed instruments was new, kindled in those guitar-holding sessions miming to Hank Williams. He would later call Ain't That A Shame 'the first song I was able to accompany myself on, taught me by my mother. I learnt it on banjo.'[39] The words 'accompany myself' relate an equally vital dimension to Julia's teaching: without the harmonica, John was free to sing along with the chords his fingers were forming. And he could really *sing*; his was a voice that came naturally and honestly. His hands-on musical education also had balance. Julia showed him how to play at least four sweet songs from her youth: Don't Blame Me (1933), Little White Lies (1930), Ramona and Girl Of My Dreams (both 1927). All would remain lifelong favourites.

Julia was very much the girl of John's dreams. She was still the kicker of convention and bucker of trends she'd been all her life, and at 41 was simply an older version of himself, like him in drag: irreverent, iconoclastic, uninhibited, witty, with a huge personality and a wicked sense of fun. She stuck two fingers up to society and postponed housework duties whenever something daft could be done instead. A reliable witness to what he saw, Pete Shotton's first impression of Julia was of 'a slim, attractive woman dancing through the doorway with a pair of old woollen knickers wrapped around her head'; instead of shaking his hand, she stroked his hips and giggled girlishly. Pete was the first of many pals to come away thinking John's mum was *just bloody great*. This mother and son shared the same sense of the ridiculous: though Julia still shunned the glasses she needed for her acute short-sightedness, she sometimes put on empty frames; Pete once watched her talking to a neighbour and casually rubbing her eye through the lens-less centre. As it was with John so it was with Julia: the joke mattered, but even better was watching people react.[40]

'The part Julia played in John's life was more that of an indulgent young aunt than a responsible parent,' Pete comments. In a strange but logical role-reversal, John was giving Aunt Mimi the full adolescent spite typically meted out to a parent, while finding respite two miles away with Mum. Mimi probably always sensed that when John formed a real relationship with Julia it could undo her enduringly strenuous efforts to keep him on the straight and narrow. Though his Quarry Bank education was in freefall, she still clung to the hope – sharp and intelligent boy that he was – that he would somehow 'rally in the end' and quite literally make the grade. He would if *she* had anything to do with it. But here he was, on the brink of his critical year at grammar school – the year of his GCE O-Level exams – being encouraged to play truant by his mother. Any day that John, alone or with Pete, turned up on Julia's doorstep, she was always delighted to indulge him, remarking, 'It's lovely to see you. Don't worry about school, don't worry about a thing!' At a time when other parents were making heavy pronouncements about 'the future', urging sons to steel themselves for the challenges ahead, John's mother was preaching the polar opposite, and it was music to his ears.

For close to ten years, Mimi had maintained a line with John, tough, rock-solid, firm. They'd put each other to every test and survived, infuriated but intact. The pubescent John, however, encouraged to skip school by his mother, caused Mimi real grief. Their rows blazed, and with each one he spent less time at Mendips and more at Blomfield Road. A few hours became overnight, then weekends, then a week or more. John was now an adjunct of the Dykins family, and as no one – not their mother, father, John or any of their many relations – told Julia and Jacqui, eight and six, he was not their full brother, they thought he was.

Pete Shotton would also write that John's relationship with Julia was 'a source of unending confusion, much as he tried to give the impression of taking it all in his stride'. There were moments of emotional turmoil for a strongly sexual 15-year-old boy in the company of a woman who had a history of liberality uncommon in her time, a woman aware of her effect on men, a woman he knew to be his mother but didn't always act like it. As he'd recall in a personal audio diary:

> I was just remembering the time when I had my hand on my mother's tit. It's when I was about 14. Took a day off school. I was always doing that, and hanging out in her house. And we were lying on the bed and I was thinking, 'I wonder if I should do anything else?' And it was a strange moment, 'cause I actually had the hots for some rather lower-class female who lived on the opposite side of the road. But I always think I should have done it, presuming she would have allowed it.*

John's time with Julia was also complicated by the presence of 'Twitchy'. His relationship with Bobby Dykins was not all bad but neither was it particularly rosy. Pete Shotton isn't the only person to recall him as an alcoholic, and Dykins worked in a job that provided access to the means. Latterly, he'd become a waiter at one of Liverpool's foremost restaurants, the New Bear's Paw. Again the job entailed late shifts; he drove an Armstrong Siddeley car, returning home to south Liverpool at speed along deserted streets in the early hours. Pete says

---

* John Lennon said this on 5 September 1979 in the context of focusing on early memories, and because he only rarely filtered his thoughts before voicing them, and because this was a personal/private tape. Since it became public (c.1990) some writers have chosen to make more of the content than they can be certain was intended, one concluding that it reveals an incestuous relationship. This tape is the sole evidence, so such a conclusion is imaginary as well as unprovable.

Dykins wasn't best pleased at having John around the house ... which may or may not be tied to the problem of accommodating a teenager prone to entering rooms at inappropriate moments.

John's school report at Christmas 1955 was an improvement over the previous one – but only, he said later, because he more conscientiously cheated in exams and bullied other boys into letting him copy their work. Many elements of his life at this time show a duality: on the one hand he'd started drinking as well as smoking, swearing, stealing and being a sex-obsessed loudmouth; on the other he was a member of St Peter's church youth club, indulging in honest-to-goodness clean teenage fun.[41] Then there was the John Lennon who voluntarily put himself through Confirmation. Though later he said he did it 'for very materialistic reasons' (financial gifts from relatives), and rarely set foot in a church again, he also remarked, 'I've always suspected there was a God even when I thought I was an atheist.'[42]

All the while, National Service – the call-up – cast an ever longer shadow. These teenage boys knew their moment must come, but there *was* now a glimmer of hope. On John's 15th birthday, 9 October 1955, newspapers reported a speech by Prime Minister Anthony Eden announcing a gradual raising of the call-up age, which meant their turn wouldn't now come before they were 19. Richy Starkey and John Lennon would serve from 1959 to 1961, Paul McCartney 1961–3, and George Harrison 1962–4. People were also saying the intake might be relaxed further, or even that National Service might eventually be scrapped altogether; there were political and economic pressures for it. For these and other boys, it was time to pray: 'If the call-up is going to be scrapped, please, please could it happen before my turn?'

More was invested in this prayer than a simple wish to avoid army life. Those born during or soon after the war were having to contend with *endless* verbal and screen replays of the action. The conflict was too recent for any other topic to have taken over conversation, and in the teeth of everyday evidence shouting otherwise, the British were clinging to victory over the 'Krauts' as proof that they could overcome all adversity, and that the Empire was still mighty. It was inevitable, but mind-numbingly tedious for the first generation that followed. As John Lennon said, 'Our parents never stopped talking about the war. Yes it was very important, but not to us. We were alive because of what our parents did, but that was irrelevant to us, we were just *alive*. All the times they said "because of the war we didn't have matches, we didn't have milk", OK, too bad, but *I* got it! That's all we ever heard as kids in England – how lucky we were because of the fucking war.'[43]

4

Scufflers to Skifflers (1956)

Nineteen hundred and fifty-six began with Bill Haley at number 1 with Rock Around The Clock – which was also the title of rock's first real film. It was one that set the standard for most of those that followed – a swift cash-in before the bubble burst. For the moviegoing public, its only redeeming feature was the chance to see performers in action, miming to their latest record; the American showbiz term for the genre was 'juke-box musical'.

Haley didn't know that rock's regal robe, cloaked on him unbidden, was shortly to be yanked away by the hottest of hot young pretenders. Elvis Presley cut his first sides for RCA Victor in Nashville on 10 January, including I Got A Woman and Heartbreak Hotel. He'd just turned 21, and his arrival in the eyes and ears of mainstream America came eighteen nights later when he made his national TV debut on *Stage Show*. In a dark tweed jacket, black shirt and white tie, and sporting Marlon Brando-like looks, moody eyes and quivering lips, this strangely named young white man from Memphis put on a stunning spectacle of sexual power – whip-strumming an acoustic guitar with his right hand, jerking his legs, wheeling his hips, and bowing his torso dynamically and deeply after each of two songs. Parents and other adults recoiled, repulsed, but hundreds of thousands – or millions – of young Americans were floored. The battle lines were drawn.

These events were not yet known across the Atlantic. But breaking into that same first *NME* chart of 1956 was Rock Island Line, the eighteen-month-old recording credited to the Lonnie Donegan Skiffle Group, finally issued as a single by Decca when the Chris Barber LP on which it appeared had been excavated of other possibilities. The track had what seemed like a new sound – rudimentary, homemade rhythmic guitar music – but actually it was at least thirty years old, sourced in the 'rent parties' of poverty-stricken 1920s black America. First speaking it and then singing, Donegan delivered Rock Island Line as a rollicking yarn ('Now this here's the story . . .'), relating the rolling tale of a train driver who fools a tollgate-keeper on the railroad running down into New Orleans. One hearing was enough to engross British teenagers – boys especially – and sales began to pick up speed the same way Donegan's voice gradually accelerated through the two-and-a-half-minute recording.

Rock Island Line was never a huge hit – it spent five weeks in the top ten and peaked at 9 – but it hung around the chart for six months, during which time John Lennon, who never had much money, managed to buy or steal it. George Harrison also bought it – the first record he *did* get. Converts, instantly. His best friend Arthur Kelly remembers George in the Institute playground one morning raving, 'I've got this record you *really* must hear. It's called Rock Island Line, by Lonnie Donegan.' One listen for Arthur and, boom, fellow convert. His parents got him his first guitar soon afterwards, a Hoyer archtop acoustic that George always wanted to play.

The timely coincidence that the word 'rock' was in its title was enough to open certain ears, but it was the acoustic guitar sound on Rock Island Line that had the greatest impact. The instrument's appeal had kicked off with the Bill Haley records but Lonnie Donegan singlehandedly propelled the guitar high into the consciousness of young British males. For many, getting a guitar – and singing with it – would become a fixation, albeit, for most boys, one frustrated by lack of funds and the paucity of guitars in the shops. Lots of boys made them, a nation of young can-dos getting down to work with wood, glue and strings. Rock Island Line made a particular splash in Liverpool, where it spent two weeks in the 'Top 3'.[1] Rock Island Line's impact was that of a slow-ticking cultural time-bomb, the name Lonnie Donegan bandied about British school playgrounds as frequently as Bill Haley's.

Richy Starkey was beyond school, but had still to get a proper job. It was close on two years since he'd begun his second long stretch in hospital and several months since he'd come out. His health was not yet robust. It was all well and good having a piece of paper indicating his capability of 'making a satisfactory employee', but who would have him? He was relying on state support, and it wasn't only the future that promised no prospect. Because the Labour Exchange couldn't find anything for the lad, Harry Graves was putting the word around the pubs and clubs, telling people he was sure his stepson would do whatever he was offered. Eventually, someone said he knew of a job on the railways, as messenger boy. The starting pay was only £2 10s a week but Richy was considerably attracted to the uniform. New clothes weren't easily afforded at

10 Admiral Grove, much like heating: as he would say, 'Our house was very cold and damp. Everyone would huddle around the coal fire. When I started work you would jump out of bed, run down and put your feet in the oven to keep warm.'[2]

He was disappointed from the first day: expecting the full British Railways messenger boy's uniform, he was given only the cap. He grumped about it, but it made no difference – the rest of the outfit would follow, he was told. Only it didn't, because after he'd been in the job five weeks he had a medical exam and that was the end of that. Richy was sacked before the end of his probationary period, perhaps considered too much of a risk, a likely burden on the public payroll. He went back on the dole ... and had no choice but to be in 'the gang'.

Teddy Boys had risen unchecked in 1955 and 1956 and were now everywhere. Seldom a place for the faint-hearted, Merseyside had become a series of battlegrounds. Despite an established inter-city rivalry, it wasn't Teds from Liverpool fighting Teds from Manchester, it was Teds being territorial to the tiniest degree – Liverpudlians from one side of a main road fighting those from the other. The sworn enemies of Teds from the Dingle were the Teds from Garston, and they continually engaged in acts of warfare from minor skirmishes to pitched street-battles, fifty lads at a time all bundling in, with weapons. Richy Starkey was one of them. 'It was deadly serious – that's what life was about. In our area you had to be in one. If you weren't, you weren't protected and you'd be beaten up by *everybody*.'[3]

The word was 'walk'. You'd walk with a gang, a mass of youths strutting up and down High Park Street and Park Road and standing around on street corners, hungry for trouble. They'd beat people up and get beaten themselves, and go to the Gaumont or Beresford cinemas and create aggravation. Teds always fought with style, in their long colourful drape jackets, drainpipe trousers, crepe-sole shoes, and a belt studded with metal washers to double as a weapon. Some had the buckle ground down to form a sharp point, others carried bicycle chains; a few attached razor blades behind their coat lapels so, when grabbed, their assailants' fingers would be sliced. No one had a gun, but Richy witnessed lads being beaten with hammers and stabbed; on one occasion he saw someone's eye knifed out.

Every gang had a leader and Richy Starkey was never it – he was 'hospital boy', tagging along on the end, smaller, leaner, weaker than the strapping toughs he did his best to buddy up with. Their uniforms were clad around muscles; his gear came from a cousin several sizes bigger and he had to hitch up his drainies with a belt already heavy with washers. In such a rabid atmosphere, gangs could turn on themselves. As he'd remember, 'I didn't knife anyone or kill anybody but I got beaten up a few times – mainly by the people [I was] with, because it's that terrible craziness, that gang situation, where, if you're not fighting an outsider, you get crazy and start fighting amongst yourselves, like mad dogs.' Sometimes, even if you could sprint very fast – and Richy prided himself on his speed – there was no way of avoiding bother. When a Ted called out 'Oi, you lookin' at me?' you'd had it either way. Saying yes meant a certain beating; saying no got a 'Why not?' followed by a certain beating.

There were far fewer such dangers in Woolton, but no area was trouble-free. As John Lennon would say, 'It was a big part of one's life to look tough. I spent the whole of my childhood with shoulders up around the top of me head and me glasses off because glasses were cissy, and walking in complete fear, but with the toughest-looking little face you've ever seen. I'd get into trouble just because of the way I looked; I wanted to be this tough James Dean all the time.'[4]

The link between juvenile delinquency and rock music was now engrained in America, and Britain's perception ran close behind. By the time Heartbreak Hotel had given Elvis his first US number 1, the record was issued across the Atlantic, by EMI on 30 March 1956 under a half-century-old cross-licensing arrangement between His Master's Voice and RCA Victor. Elvis was a taste too foreign for most adult diets, including those who chose the content of the BBC Light Programme, but he was broadcast on Radio Luxembourg. Teenagers up and down the country eagerly tuned into its British evening service, trying to ride the signal that came and went over the medium wave, peaking and crashing across the European night skies. Listening to 'Luxy' was never less than an ordeal – ear pressed to the speaker, finger constantly micro-manipulating the tuning dial – but these broadcasts, and those on the American Forces Network (better at night but seldom a good signal either), contained treasure for anyone who loved rock and roll.

At some point in (probably) early April 1956, Heartbreak Hotel dropped into John Lennon's universe like an atom bomb with no four-minute warning.

When I first heard Heartbreak Hotel I could hardly make out what was being said. We'd never heard American voices singing like that – they'd always sung like Sinatra or enunciated very well, and suddenly there was this hillbilly, hiccuping on tape echo, and the bluesy background going on, and we didn't know what the hell Presley was singing about. To us it just sounded like a noise that was *great* … It just broke me up. I mean, that was the end. Me whole life changed from then on, I was just completely shaken by it … I remember rushing home with the record and saying, 'He sounds like Frankie Laine *and* Johnnie Ray *and* Tennessee Ernie Ford!' … I thought 'This is it!' and started trying to grow sideboards and all that gear.[5]

The Elvis Presley of 1956 would attract many fans around the world and John Lennon was ever among them. Richy Starkey was another: 'I couldn't believe it when Elvis came out. Just this lad with sideboards and shaking his pelvis and being absolutely naughty. Before Elvis we'd always had to listen to *men*, as opposed to guys who were just a bit older or around our own age ... Bill Haley was like my dad. When he came out, I was 14 or 15 and he was probably about 28.'[6]

Paul McCartney first read the name and saw the photo (for weeks there was just one wild photo of Elvis available in Britain) during a free period at Liverpool Institute. A friend had the *NME* and there was an advert for Heartbreak Hotel. 'I thought "He's *so* good-looking,"' Paul says, 'he just looked *perfect*.'[7] There was a buzz about him: boys seemed to know that Elvis was *it*, the Messiah, and it was confirmed for Paul when he first heard Heartbreak Hotel – he too became, in that instant, a lifelong and vocal Elvis fan.

The first time George Harrison heard Elvis would also remain etched in his memory. 'I was riding along on my bicycle and heard Heartbreak Hotel coming out of somebody's house. It was one of them things I'll never forget: what a sound, what a record! It changed the course of my life.'[8]

In the space of perhaps three weeks, John Lennon then experienced a second epiphany. The date was on or soon after 17 April, and Quarry Bank friend Michael Hill had just returned from an Easter school exchange visit to the Netherlands, during which he'd gone into an Amsterdam record store and bought a Belgian 78 by Little Richard, Long Tall Sally c/w Slippin' And Slidin'. Little Richard wasn't known in Britain, so when Hill said to his mate 'I've got a record by a singer who's better than Elvis', John – who'd clearly fallen head-over-heels for Presley – insisted (probably in two short words) that this simply *wasn't possible*. Hill lived on Dovedale Road and his mum worked in the daytime, which meant his house was available. One lunchtime, he, John, Pete Shotton and another friend, Don Beattie, raced there by bike and went into what Hill remembers as something of a routine: 'They'd cycle off to the fish and chip shop on Rose Lane to buy chips, and I'd go home to warm up the plates and prepare bread and butter, and I had a tin of cocoa hidden in my bedroom. We'd be at my house about forty-five minutes, eating chips, listening to records and sharing a Woodbine.'[9]

Hill lifted the wooden lid of his mother's Rushworth & Dreaper radiogram, in went the record, down went the needle, and Little Richard – the irrepressibly wild Richard Penniman from Macon, Georgia – burst screaming and yowling into suburban Liverpool.

Gonna tell Aunt Mary, 'bout Uncle John! He claim he has the misery but he's havin' a lot of fun!

'This record stopped John in his tracks,' Hill recalls. 'His reaction that day was something that stuck in everybody's memory, because he really was struck dumb by this record. He didn't know what to say, which for John was *most* unusual because he was always so quick with an answer, with a bit of repartee. So the record was played again, and again, and again. It made a huge impact on him. I felt good because John was so hard to impress.'

John spoke several times of the occasion, of how the record presented first a challenge and then a wedge that opened his mind to unconsidered possibilities.

> When I heard it [Long Tall Sally], it was so great I couldn't speak. You know how you're torn? I didn't want to leave Elvis. Elvis was bigger than religion in my life. We all looked at each other, but I didn't want to say anything against Elvis, not even in my mind. How could they be happening in my life, *both* of them? And then someone said, 'It's a nigger singing.' I didn't know Negroes sang [rock and roll]. So Elvis was white and Little Richard was black? 'Thank you, God,' I said. I thought about it for days at school, of the labels on the records. One [Richard] was yellow and one [Presley] was blue, and I thought of the yellow against the blue.[10]

So rock and roll wasn't only sung by whites ... John's education was on a steep curve: 'The first thing I learned about Negroes was that they were swinging like mad and that they had a great beat. Only later did I start meeting some of them. I didn't know a single black person in England, and I *worshipped* black people in America.'[11]

Those two recordings by Elvis Presley and Little Richard, totalling a little over four minutes, altered the course of John Lennon's life as sure as they did Richy Starkey's, Paul McCartney's, George Harrison's and a good many other young lads who happened to be the right age at this rightest of right times, 1956. Lennon later reflected:

> Somebody said that the blacks gave the middle-class whites back their bodies. It's something like that. It was the only thing to get through to me out of all the things that were happening when I was 15. Rock and roll was *real*. Everything else was unreal.
>
> Once I heard the music and got into it, that was life. Rock and roll was it – I thought of nothing else, night and day, apart from sex, food and money.
>
> I had no idea about doing music as a way of life until rock and roll hit me. That's the music that inspired me to play music.[12]

The influences began to flow thick and fast now. Beyond Elvis, and beyond Little Richard, there was also the sound of a young white singer-songwriter-guitarist from Tennessee who played country music with an uptempo or rock rhythm, called rockabilly – the word was coined in 1956 by *Cash Box* reviewer Ira Howard, combining 'rock' and 'hillbilly'. 'I suppose I started to get off-beat, musically, when I found I liked the Carl Perkins version of Blue Suede Shoes better than Presley's,' John said in 1963.[13] The two were in the charts simultaneously by the end of May 1956, and – Elvis disciple though Lennon was – Perkins' original was well worth the excitement. John got both versions (on 78) and was delighted to find another inspirational original number on Perkins' B-side, Honey Don't. This was rhythmic country and western – or, as John called it, 'crumbly and western'.[14] He loved it, and, with the intuitive thinking of a music aficionado, knew it was smarter to prefer Perkins' Blue Suede Shoes – more 'hip', to use the be-bop jargon also flowing across the Atlantic – because it was the less commercial of the two.

The music that had first inspired Paul McCartney to play was fading fast. The year had produced one more trumpet hit, Billy May's theme from Otto Preminger's controversial film *The Man With The Golden Arm*, in which Frank Sinatra played a jazz drummer with a heroin addiction, but the trumpet had tarnished in Paul's hands. When he wanted to play, he usually went to the piano.

At the end of April 1956, to Mary's great relief, the McCartneys moved out of Speke. Though Paul and Mike were sorry to be leaving friends behind, Paul would recall, 'It was getting a bit rough. I was wondering what was gonna happen – in a few more years would I have a gun?'[15] Mary always wanted better for them, and this time (it was at least the eighth home for Paul) 'better' meant another terraced council house in south Liverpool. It was at 20 Forthlin Road in the district of Allerton – a straight run south from the Penny Lane bus hub and not far from Woolton. It wasn't an estate and the area was much more agreeable: Forthlin Road was a short side-street off Mather Avenue, a busy tree-lined dual-carriageway into town. The McCartneys weren't its first residents but the house was only about four years old and similar in some respects to their place in Speke with its three small upstairs bedrooms, and an indoor toilet in addition to the back-garden privy. All this for £1 19s 10d a week.

The big hit record in Britain at this time was I'll Be Home by Pat Boone, which spent five weeks at number 1; perhaps because of its appropriate title – and that it was a sweet tune – it became the song of the McCartneys' first summer at Forthlin Road, heard and enjoyed many a Sunday lunchtime on *Two-Way Family Favourites* while Mary was cooking the roast. Sometimes the

BBC would play her favourite tune, the evocative light classical theme from the film *The Glass Mountain*. When the wireless was off, Mary would whistle around the house . . . and this wasn't the only music being created here.

Paul knew songwriting could be done. His father still played Eloise on the piano, the tune he'd composed in his teenage years, and now – as if a switch was flicked – Paul began to write music too.

It came naturally. He just sat at the piano and when his fingers found some interesting chords he started to explore around them, working in the key of C. His thinking was to write a tune for cabaret, night-club music, a song for Frank Sinatra to sing in a lounge, picked out by a spotlight through a smoky blue haze. Paul wrote two tunes in this vein: I Call It Suicide and a probably untitled piece that would become known some years later as When I'm Sixty-Four.[16] Suicide was perhaps the first, although it extended to only a first verse and chorus. Some of the words came while Paul was lying in bed; like all would-be writers, he kept a pencil and paper at hand and fancied his ability to write coherently in the dark.

Paul had about forty seconds of music, and it didn't get any further. He realised the key word 'suicide' presented a rhyming dilemma – the best he had was 'ruin, I'. But though the words wanted work (and didn't get it), it was a charming little tune, a dance-band piece with a dash of modernity, light, engaging and original . . . quite exceptional for a first attempt by a boy on the cusp of 14.

Paul thought about offering I Call It Suicide to Sinatra but didn't bother to write the letter (not at this time anyway). The Voice remained in the dark about it, as he did about Paul's second piano tune, the prototype When I'm Sixty-Four, which had no words yet. Jim Mac's Eloise never had any words, and there was a running joke in the McCartney family: could anyone think of any that fitted? No one did. Like I Call It Suicide, this second piece by his son possibly didn't extend any further than verse and chorus, but its tune was another quality dance-band piece, much like Jim Mac's would have played. Again, this was an exceptional achievement for a young teenager, a beginner. He felt so too. Mindful that no one else in his orbit was writing songs, Paul keenly played them to people, requesting their opinion. Yet, as much as he enjoyed their compliments and admiration, any perceived criticism stuck in his craw. '"It sounds a bit like a hymn" was one of the damning things people said about some of my early numbers,' he'd remember.[17]

Life was lived easier in Allerton. Paul and Mike (who also now went to Liverpool Institute) had a shorter school journey; their route was the 86, which meant Paul no longer rode the bus used by George Harrison, not unless George made the effort of changing buses in Garston, which sometimes he did and other times he didn't. Liverpool Institute periodically arranged for all staff and pupils to be photographed – extended panoramic shots taken in the playground – and a Lower School photo from April 1956 shows Paul and George at age 13 (far apart because they're with their respective year groups). Paul's hair is short and side-parted, George wears the lop-sided smile inherited from his dad, and long hair piled into a quiff. So impressive was this, and so daring was it for the 'Inny', Paul would always recall Arthur Kelly's awed exclamation, 'It's like a fuckin' turban!'[18]

Soon after the move, though, Mary McCartney started to suffer breast pains. She didn't tell Paul or Mike but she did tell Jim, saying she thought it was the menopause – she was 46. A doctor told her not to worry unduly, so Mary self-medicated BiSoDol, an antacid tablet taken for indigestion, and carried on as normal.

Richy Starkey landed his second job at this time, on the tramp steamer *St Tudno*. His new employer was the Liverpool & North Wales Steamship Company, which – oddly, considering he was 15 – hired Richy as a bar waiter. The TS *St Tudno* was the largest and swiftest of a fleet of three pleasure cruisers: it sailed daily from Liverpool to North Wales in the summer season, carrying up to 2500 day trippers a time, leaving Liverpool mid-morning, sailing to Llandudno, then on again through the Menai Straits to Menai Bridge, and returning to Liverpool before eight in the evening. The crew stayed on board one night a week.

Richy took the job because he still harboured hopes of joining the merchant navy, mindful that it remained one of the few legal methods of avoiding National Service. The way he understood it, you stood a better chance of being accepted in the merch if you had a few months' sea experience, even on a pleasure steamer. But the job also had another attraction: booze. Richy was now a confirmed drinker. Regular exposure to alcohol in and around the home was an influence, and it was what many boys did anyway, swear and smoke and drink at the first opportunity. Just as the appeal for *St Tudno* passengers (particularly the men) was its ever-open lounge bar, enabling them to drink when the pubs in Liverpool were closed, so Richy too enjoyed the same privilege, swigging bottles of ale in free moments, trying not to spill it down his waiter's tunic and tie. He and his workmates also headed to the pub after docking back in Liverpool in the evening, sinking as many beers as the coins in their pockets would buy. Being a sailor was something to boast about when chatting up 'judies', but, as Richy would recall, the gloating could be short-lived: '[I'd] say, "I'm in the navy. I just got back." And [she'd] say, "When did you leave?" and I'd say, "Ten o'clock this morning."'[19]

He lasted on the *St Tudno* no more than five weeks. One morning Richy arrived in a surly mood, hung-over from an all-night party. When his boss asked him to do something, he responded with insolence and was sacked on the spot. Any lingering desire to spend a life on the ocean waves was dashed. Richy had now had two jobs and been fired from both.

Harry Graves put the word around yet again – boy available, job wanted – and the call was answered immediately: there was a position at H. Hunt & Son, a long-established factory on Windsor Street which manufactured, supplied and fitted children's recreational equipment, everything from swings and slides for playgrounds to gymnasium gear for schools, even Olympic-quality diving boards.* The firm had contracts from local councils all over the country. Richy started work there five days shy of his 16th birthday and was set for a five-year woodworking apprenticeship, as a joiner. In 1961, if he played his cards right, he'd have the status that represented the pinnacle of aspiration for blue-collar workers: a trade for life. People were always saying to him, 'Get a trade, son, and you'll be OK,' so Richy was shooting for it – mindful too that being in an apprenticeship would qualify him for deferment of National Service.

Like all new boys, Richy started as the gofer, filling glue pots, getting sent out to buy chips, making tea, sweeping up and running errands with a handcart or the delivery bike; he earned the same £2 10s a week he'd been getting as a messenger boy on the railways. His 16th birthday came along on 7 July 1956, an age his loved ones had frequently believed he would never reach. But he had, and didn't everyone know it: as he'd remember, 'When I was 16 or 17 I thought that everyone at 60 should be shot, to make more space on the planet.'[20] This let off Elsie, who was only 41; spared the bullet, she gave Richy a birthday present he would cherish: a signet ring, his first piece of jewellery, something to show off to his latest group of workmates and the other Dingle Teds.

'Liverpool's Own Top 3' chart in the *Echo* on Richy Starkey's birthday showed Heartbreak Hotel at number 1. The record had been out more than three months and was now finally holding what many knew to be its rightful place. Two weeks earlier, the chart of Liverpool shop Nems, printed in *The Record Mirror*, had Carl Perkins' Blue Suede Shoes in second spot when it was 12 in the *NME*. A pattern was emerging where certain rock and skiffle records registered higher in Liverpool than nationally; and into this

---

* 85–93 Windsor Street, the top end, a short walk from Richy's house. The building was only the width of a triple garage, two storeys plus a basement, but it extended far back. It was demolished in the 1980s after the Toxteth riots.

frame hobbled crippled Gene Vincent with Be-Bop-A-Lula, a record that proved the theory: the discs *really* despised by adults were the ones most loved by teenagers.

To adults, Be-Bop-A-Lula was appalling; to kids, it was a sensation – a rocking, shuffling, echoing track with attitude, screams, two fabulous electric guitar solos and a girl who wears *red blue jeans* and has *flying feet*. Who knew what it meant? Being puzzled became part of the appeal. What would these incredible Americans come up with next? Just the first bar of Be-Bop-A-Lula was enough to send John Lennon into rapture. 'That beginning – "we-e-e-e-e-l-l-l-l!" – always made my hair stand on end.'[21] In this instant, John loved Gene Vincent like he loved Elvis, Carl and Little Richard. Three months earlier he'd existed without them, now he was really *living*, and these sounds were shaping his very future. As he would say of this period: 'When I was 15 I was thinking, "If only I can get out of Liverpool and be famous and be rich, wouldn't it be great?" I was always thinking I was going to be a famous artist. And possibly I'd have to marry a very rich old lady, or man, to look after me while I did my art; but then rock and roll came along and I thought, "Ah, *this* is the one." So I didn't have to marry anybody or live with them.'[22]

Be-Bop-A-Lula was the first record bought by Paul McCartney.

A friend at the Liverpool Institute said, 'There's this great record by Gene Vincent, called Be-Bop-A-Lula.' (If I'd have spent as much time on studies as talking about these rock and roll acts I think I'd be a nuclear physicist by now.) So I wrote it down and went to Curry's record shop in the city centre after school, went into the listening booth, and the echo and the whole atmosphere of it was so fantastic that I had to have it there and then. I got my hard-earned cash out, slipped it over the counter and I was a proud owner of Be-Bop-A-Lula. The whole song is purple in my mind because of the purple Capitol label. I loved the Capitol logo.[23]

John Lennon's report at the end of his fourth year at Quarry Bank shows where he was at academically at the age of 15: twentieth out of twenty-four in the lowest of the grammar school's three streams, almost the bottom of the bottom. He contrived to be absent for all the exams, and it isn't difficult to imagine where he spent those days. Julia had come up with a new term of affection for her son, Stinker (it wasn't in his nature to fart discreetly), and she was still showing him how to play banjo. John was also thrilled that his mother was an Elvis fan. Not as much as he was, of course – few people were *that* besotted – but she did like Elvis and was happy to hear his name mentioned any number of times, unlike Mimi, who remarked, 'Elvis Presley's all very well, John, but I don't want him for breakfast, dinner *and* tea.'

John and his gang still went every year to the garden fete at Strawberry Fields, and Nigel Walley has a cherished memory of laugh-a-minute Lennon somehow gaining possession of a monk's habit and spending the afternoon inclining a hooded head and dispensing twisted words of wisdom and phoney prophecies in a low murmur while people bowed to him. As it happens, though, John's own future direction – and the lives of untold numbers of others – was being determined this very same afternoon, Saturday 14 July, at another fete two hundred miles south.

The second annual Soho Fair was a week-long carnival organised to illustrate that there was another side to this London enclave than the goings-on depicted in the press and films. If you believed what you read and saw, Soho was Britain's post-war underworld, its rat-run streets a cloister of sweatshops, workshops and lurid bookshops, of pimps and prostitutes, drug-addled jazz musicians, small-time crooks and queer-smelling foreigners, of filmmakers, writers, agents, publishers, actors, deadbeat poets and no-good anarchists, all idling and con-spiring in its seedy coffee bars and darkly exotic restaurants. In truth, as well as being more than this, Soho *was* all of this. And because it was all of this, it was also the most diverse, cosmopolitan and cutting-edge 'village' in Britain.

On the Saturday of the 1956 Soho Fair, three bright chaps in their twenties, keen amateur guitarists devoted to the American folk- and workers'-song move-ment, acolytes of Pete Seeger, found themselves on the platform of a flatback lorry, singing and playing as it trundled around Soho Square, Wardour Street and Carnaby Street. The vehicle finally halted outside a small coffee bar on Old Compton Street, where they went in, bought coffees, sang and strummed as they sipped, and passed the hat around. When they rose to leave, the propri-etor asked if they would come back and play there again, perhaps for an evening: the place had a cellar and he could put up a little stage. And so it was that these three young men, who called themselves the Vipers, became the first attraction at the 2i's Coffee Bar. This chance encounter would light the fuse under the sound popularised all year by Lonnie Donegan, eventually trans-forming his skiffle hits into a fully fledged skiffle boom. While Donegan would always be its revered figurehead, the number of participants would soon be counted in tens of thousands. Why, if they'd made a film of it, it would have seemed trite.

This same summer, when the Harrisons caught up with their friends the Brewers again, back at the Sandy Bay holiday camp in Exmouth, George had a new obsession to share with his friend Jenny. 'He was now mad on music. He asked if I'd heard *the real one*. It was Heartbreak Hotel by Elvis Presley. I said, "Who?" "Elvis! Elvis Presley!" He didn't have his guitar with him, but he loved the music with a passion.'[24]

Peter Harrison was instrumental in getting George back on the guitar. George's cheap old Egmond had been sitting in pieces in the cupboard ever since George had taken a screwdriver to its neck. All the Harrison boys were useful with their hands: Harry repaired diesel engines for a living, and Peter – who left school at 15, in 1955 – had taken up automotive panel-beating, maintaining the Harrisons' interest in the motor trade; he also bought himself a motor-bike, which George loved. Peter set to work on George's guitar and managed to get it back in one piece. More than that, he showed him a couple of chords he'd been taught by someone. And so George got back in the habit of spending evenings practising the guitar, and he stuck at it. His intense single-minded dedication, hour after hour, day after day, was evident to all who saw it. And when his determination wavered there was his mum to give him every encouragement. 'You'll do it, son, you will, just keep at it, you'll do it.' Sometimes, Louise sat up with him until two or three in the morning, long after Harry had gone to bed, supplying endless pots of tea and watching and supporting while his fingers made the shapes.[25]

With rock and roll so restricted on radio and TV, the surest way of hearing the latest sounds was to go to the funfair. In the south end of Liverpool, the fair periodically visited a park in Garston and also Sefton Park. One night at the Sefton Park fair, dressed in his Teddy Boy drape, Richy Starkey bumped into a young lad he knew a little from Hunt's, Roy Trafford. He too was a Dingle boy, and almost instantly the pair became best mates, starting a strong and lifelong friendship. 'We had a good night there in the fair,' Roy recalls. 'They played all the top records. You couldn't afford to buy them but they played the best in the fairground, and the girls were there as well. It was the excitement of the fair, the waltzer and all that business. We hit it off as mates because we both liked the same kind of things. We became more like brothers – I was the nearest thing he ever had to one, and there was an instant affection there as men, as brothers. It was great. A nice feeling.'[26]

Richy and Roy not only worked in the same place, they loved rock and roll and American country music and wanted to play it: Roy was interested in the guitar and Richy was still thudding his great one-sided bass drum. They went to each other's houses (Roy lived in the Dingle, at 7 Paulton Street), listened to Radio Luxembourg together, dressed like Teds – Richy wore a black drape jacket, Roy blue – liked a drink and wanted girls. It was a perfect arrangement, and they quickly formed the kind of earthy bond George Harrison had with

Arthur Kelly and John Lennon had with Pete Shotton – solid friends who lived life similarly and shared attitudes, bluntness and candour.

Roy was quick to spot that though Richy remained physically weakened from his illnesses, 'he was *always* strong, mentally'. Never one to hold back from speaking his mind, Richy went to the management at H. Hunt & Son and complained, 'Come on, I'm here to be a joiner, not on the bike.'[27] Since there were no vacancies on the woodwork side, he was offered a fitter apprenticeship instead, metalwork, a junior member of the team making the diving stage for the 1958 Empire Games swimming pool. He joined a trade union – probably the Amalgamated Engineering Union (AEU) – was given a toolkit, and began learning how to make small parts, working at a bench and using the lathe and drilling machines. Though still paid £2 10s, his wage would rise incrementally to £6, and he faced the prospect of qualifying in 1961 on £12–15 a week, though he'd have to do part-time study for that. He worked weekdays from 8AM to 5.30PM, clocking on and clocking off with a punch-card, and took tea-breaks and lunch (everyone called it 'dinner') at a few tables in the basement, among the wood shavings. After work, he and Roy usually went for a few at the pub, perhaps the Sefton Arms or the Empress or Yates's Wine Lodge, where Elsie worked behind the bar. The minimum legal age for drinking was 18 but they were rarely refused. Richy was following a pattern established by most of his family for close on a century, leading *the Dingle life*, finding work, rest and play – and also the gang – within its bleak streets.

The new school year at Liverpool Institute was George Harrison's third, and his continued placement in the E stream (form L5E) set him only one rung above the bottom of the ladder. Of his own volition, he was well on the road to nowhere – or, at any rate, not where others hoped he would go. He still hated school, doing his damnedest to learn the minimum and disrupt the maximum. One way of rebelling was to subvert the school uniform: he wore big brother Harry's bright yellow waistcoat under his blazer, and his school cap (compulsory) sat high on top of his Elvis quiff, looking patently ridiculous. Masters were always hammering George over the length of his hair, but he stubbornly and heroically refused to yield.

Paul was now in form U5B, crossing the divide into the Upper School (though his parents still insisted he wear short trousers). Institute boys in the A, B and C streams were fast-tracked to sit some GCE O-Levels at 15, a year earlier than most schools, and Paul was set to take two (Spanish and Latin) in summer 1957, at the same time as John Lennon would be taking his at Quarry Bank. They were following a similar path in one other respect too: Paul slipped dramatically down his class during the school year 1955–6, from ninth to tenth to twentieth over three terms. There was strong resentment at always being told what to do, and his growing obsession with Elvis and rock and roll wasn't helping.

By the start of September, the film *Rock Around The Clock* had been out for six weeks. It played the Gaumont in Liverpool from 19 to 25 August: John didn't see it at this time; George went; Paul took a girl he knew from primary school; Richy had seen it a couple of weeks earlier, on the Isle of Man, and was one of the first to witness how it provoked great enthusiasm in the audiences.* It wasn't much, just *something*, and the Liverpool screening passed by uneventfully. Elsewhere, however, trouble was brewing.

It seems almost wish-fulfilled. DO WE WANT THIS SHOCKIN' ROCKIN'? queried Patrick Doncaster in the *Daily Mirror* on 16 August. 'Can it happen here – the trouble that goes with rock 'n' roll music in the United States?' The answer, perhaps too eagerly found, had come by the end of the month. At a showing of *Rock Around The Clock* in Paddington, west London, a 15-year-old boy punched the cinema manager. This routine incident was reported with the brand of relish spiced exclusively in Fleet Street: the punch landed while 'in-the-groove teenagers danced in the aisles'. Suddenly there were fresh incidents every day, sought out and covered by the papers as though they'd no part in their magnification. 1,000 ROCK 'N' ROLL RIOTERS TAKE CITY BY STORM headlined the *Daily Mirror* on 10 September, above one of those revved reports hypocritically blending disapproval with delight. 'A thousand screaming, jiving, rhythm-crazy teenagers surged through a city last night, sweeping aside a police cordon and stopping traffic. They had just left the day's third and last showing of the rock 'n' roll film *Rock Around The Clock* at the Gaiety Cinema, Manchester.'

Such headlines instantly attracted the kind of people irresistibly drawn to violence. This meant, among others, Teddy Boys. Rock and roll hadn't been their music, they pre-dated it, but here they were, desperate to dance, desirous to jive, ready to rip it up, to slash seats, smash lights and threaten cinema staff.

John Lennon remained an avid reader of the daily papers – every page of at least one every day, as well as at least one book a week – and seeing these *Rock Around The Clock* reports he rushed out to be part of it all. Though finished in Liverpool, the film was showing locally in Bootle and Wallasey. He was out of luck: although there was disorder at both venues, the night he went was

---

* It was common for British factories to have a summer closedown period so staff had their holidays and returned to work on the same date. Richy had been at H. Hunt & Son under a month when he had to have this break, and Granny and Grandad Starkey took him with them to the Isle of Man – which was akin to going abroad. He saw *Rock Around The Clock* at the Gaiety Theatre in Douglas.

trouble-free. (At least, there was none he could see: he wouldn't have had his glasses on. And he would have only *heard* the film.) 'I was most surprised,' he'd recall. 'Nobody was screaming and nobody was dancing. I'd read that everybody danced in the aisles. It must have all been done before I went. I was all set to tear up the seats too but nobody joined in.'[28]

Large-scale public disorder quickly becomes everybody's business, and within days the nation was in rockin' uproar. As with all press-created tempests, the *Rock Around The Clock* storm soon blew over, but the fallout would linger for years. Terror of Teddy Boys was now married to the repugnancy felt towards rock and roll. Just like in America. Rock wasn't just jungle music, rock wasn't simply sinister, or the music of the devil, it was the music of *violence*. The view painted rock fans into a corner – it shaped the way people thought about them, about the way they dressed, the music they liked and the instruments they played. Rock fans were pushed down Lonely Street to the edge of society.

In this light, skiffle was consciously sought out and promoted as rock's anti-dote. It was acoustic, not amplified, and it was cleaner: the lyrics weren't suggestive or smutty, and sometimes its practitioners were known to wash. On 8 September, plumb in the middle of the *Rock Around The Clock* drama, the *Daily Mirror* ran a feature by columnist Noel Whitcomb headlined THEY'RE JUST WILD ABOUT SKIFFLE! THE MUSIC THAT SENDS ROCK 'N' ROLL REELING. Rock, announced Whitcomb, was 'as old fashioned as aspidistras' while 'skif-fle-music is the coming craze'. His article confirmed Soho as the happening place, and explained how easily anyone could play it: it required only guitars, a washboard and, as a makeshift standup bass, 'an old tea-chest with a broom-handle stuck in the middle'.* Whitcomb enthused about the Vipers and singled out their songs It Takes A Worried Man To Sing A Worried Song, Pick A Bale Of Cotton, and Rock Me, Daddy-O (*sic*), 'all of which I am dead certain are bound right for the hit parade'.

Whitcomb knew what he was talking about because he'd not gone to the 2i's Coffee Bar alone to compile his report, he'd had the company of a young recording manager from EMI by the name of George Martin, who was desperate to save his under-threat Parlophone label by finding new talent. Tipped off about a young cockney singer from Bermondsey, Tommy Hicks, and the

---

* The handle, or any other kind of pole, was either inserted through a hole in the tea-chest or clamped to its outside. One end of a piece of string or cord was knotted tightly through (or at) the top, the other was tied through a hole in the chest, forming a triangle. Notes were produced by thumping or plucking the string while adjusting its tension by tilting the pole. The player would have one foot planted on the ground and the other (or his knee) on top of the chest, to keep it steady.

resident group who backed him, George went to check them out. Though not thinking much of the singer, he liked the backing group. EMI's standard penny-per-record contract was theirs for the taking, and they took it, thrilled at the prospect of appearing on Parlophone's blue Super Rhythm-Style label. So it was that George Martin became the first record producer to sign a skiffle group, and in so doing the first to sign a group whose name was drugs-related, 'viper' being 1930s slang for a cannabis smoker – a detail of which the Parlophone manager was blissfully unaware.[29]

Mary McCartney had her 47th birthday on 29 September, receiving all the usual felicitations for 'many happy returns'. She now knew otherwise. Around this time, amid discretion so great her two children knew nothing of it for a long time to come, she went into hospital for a mastectomy. Breast cancer had been diagnosed. Jim knew the score but adhered to Mary's wish that Paul and Mike not be told: mum was the word. The closest either came to finding anything amiss was when Mike investigated a curious sound coming from his mother's bedroom. 'I could just hear this strange noise, it sounded like crying, so I went into her room and there she was doing her rosary beads. I said, "What's wrong, Mum?" and she said [swiftly], "Nothing, son." She knew what was happening.'[30]

Mike assumed she was crying because he and Paul had been naughty. 'We could be right bastards,' he says. But then it all just happened so fast. The cancer had already spread and Mary went into the David Lewis Northern Hospital on 29 October very poorly, with a brain tumour. Paul and Mike visited, though still not knowing what was wrong. Mary put on a brave face, and they never saw her again. They were packed off to Park Lane, Aintree, to stay with Uncle Joe and Auntie Joan, and couldn't understand why this customary venue for the McCartney clan's uproarious New Year's Eve parties was so subdued. The boys loved Joe for his great Liverpool humour but even he was quiet. Paul and Mike slept in the same bed and wondered what on earth was going on.

The end came two days later. Jim put his hand on Mary's cheek and she said, 'Jim, I love you.' She told her sister-in-law Dill Mohin, 'I would have liked to have seen the boys growing up.' Rosary beads were tied around her wrist, a priest administered last rites, and she died.

Jim broke the news to the boys. Mike, who was especially close to his mother, burst into tears, a core part of him shattered irrevocably. Paul's response was less expected and not at all what Jim or anyone else wanted to hear. 'Mum was a working nurse. There wasn't a lot of money around – and she was half the family pay packet. My reaction was: "How are we going to get by without her money?" When I think back on it, I think, "Oh God, *what*? Did I *really* say that?" It was a terrible, logical thought which was preceded by the normal feelings of grief. It was very tough to take.'[31]

Paul and Mike stayed with Joe and Joan McCartney several more days; they didn't attend their mum's requiem mass or committal even though they took place on a Saturday when there was no school.[32] Eight years later, Mike looked back with candour on these first few days, reflecting on how he and Paul both felt the important thing was to show their cousins they weren't 'softies'. He referred to his brother's comment about the money – 'Paul made some flippant remark which sounded pretty callous at the time' – but he also added: 'Paul was far more affected by Mum's death than any of us imagined. His very character seemed to change and for a while he seemed like a hermit. He wasn't very nice to live with at this period, I remember. He became completely wrapped up in himself and didn't want people breaking in on his life.'[33]

Paul's way of dealing with the crisis was to seem unaffected by it. He just carried on. 'I learned to put a shell around me.'[34] Tough as it was to see or hear his dad crying, Paul got his head down and pushed forward.

His concern over how the family would manage without Mary's money was real. In Jim's ten post-war years back at Hannay's, the Liverpool cotton market had never really managed to pick up. He was bringing home only £400 a year – £8 a week – which wasn't much to pay the bills, feed and clothe two lads and leave something on the side for a flutter on the horses. On top of that, he was ever fearful of being made redundant.

Everyone felt for him, a widower at 54 and the single parent of boys aged 14 and 12. The McCartneys' domestic roles had always divided along lines that were traditional everywhere (though, if possible, even more rigorously applied in the north of England): men were breadwinners, not breadmakers. Men *worked*, whereas women merely ran everything in the house and managed everyone's lives. Jim was faced with having to learn to cook and clean in a house so new to them Mary hadn't left much of an imprint. The wider McCartney family – resolutely close-knit, comforting and down-to-earth – did all they could to help, which was a lot. Paul and Mike had always loved their relatives, and from this point these aunties, uncles and cousins assumed an even greater role in their lives, the relationships rooting deeper than ever, strong and safe.

John Lennon experienced the euphoria of hearing Little Richard in the spring of 1956 – that thrilling, life-changing moment – but it wasn't until November that the rest of Britain shared the joy, when Decca's London label issued Rip It Up c/w Ready Teddy as his first British single. Both tracks were in the same vein as Long Tall Sally and Slippin' And Slidin': big-band rave-ups with vocal, piano and saxophone, the sax accenting the sex. Richard screamed all over the place and provoked shivers. 'We'd never heard anybody sing like that in our lives, and all those saxes playing like crazy . . .' John would recall, adding, 'The most exciting thing about early Little Richard was when he screamed just before the solo; that howling. It used to make your hair stand on end.'[35]

Rip It Up c/w Ready Teddy was a bolt from the blue for Paul McCartney. He too experienced the epiphany: first Elvis *and now this*! 'Little Richard was this voice from heaven or hell, or both. This screaming voice seemed to come from the top of his head. I tried to do it one day and found I could. You had to lose every inhibition and *do it*.'[36] Jim McCartney didn't like it at all, but Paul was singing like a boy possessed, and in a very real sense he was. Absorbing Elvis, Little Richard and Gene Vincent was glorious, and it could block out other feelings. Paul revelled in the sounds of his great American heroes. He loved the way Little Richard hollered in his songs, a high-pitched 'Wooooooo!' evident in almost every recording, and found he had the range and talent to imitate this. Paul would know it as his 'Little Richard voice', though Richard himself admitted to having purloined it from Sister Rosetta Tharpe, Wynonie Harris, and Esquerita, the artist whose look, voice and sound he'd all but cloned.

The lure of the guitar was now irresistible to John Lennon. As much as he enjoyed playing the banjo at Julia's, the instrument was, well, a bit of a joke. Sure, it was good fun, but the banjo had for a long time been looked down on by musicians, the butt of all the gags in the musicians' joke book. It was *yesterday*. Gene Vincent played guitar, Elvis Presley played guitar, Lonnie Donegan played guitar. Rock meant guitar, and guitar meant rock. John yearned for one. As he'd recall in later years, 'Like everyone else, I used God for this one thing I wanted. "Please, God, *give me a guitar* . . ."'[37]

And, lo and behold, there came one. The winged messenger was a boy at school, his name unknown. Little is remembered of John Lennon's first guitar. The guitar he called his first guitar would come later, in March 1957, but before that he had this loan of someone else's, a cheap little acoustic, possibly an Egmond (the same as George Harrison's), the kind of instrument one would dispose of at the first opportunity and then usually forget to mention. But it *was* a guitar, and from approximately the last weeks of 1956 (it's impossible to be more precise than this) John became a strummer, using the banjo chords Julia taught him. And rubbish though this guitar was, the instrument and its temporary owner were seldom parted. Somehow or other now, John knew, he was going to be discovered. He 'waited for the big man with the cigar'.[38]

While John was using only the banjo's first four strings on his guitar, George was being taught all six. Harry Harrison had owned a guitar in his merchant seaman days, pawned in subsequent tough times, and he'd stayed in touch with one of his old shipmates who'd both played and kept his instrument. The man was Len Houghton, or Horton, and he was living above an off-licence (liquor store) which he also managed; the shop closed on Wednesday evenings and Harry arranged for George to go there a couple of hours at a time for probably a few weeks. The old seadog was pleased to teach his tricks to this keen and intense youngster, vamping 1920s tunes to demonstrate what George would fondly remember as 'old chords' on 'the top-of-the-line Hofner, called the Hofner Committee: it was in bird's-eye maple, a blond guitar modelled after the Gibson 400s'.[39]

Those old songs were also the ones Jim McCartney loved – and it was around now that George first got to know him, forming a relationship that was always respectful and cheekily playful. Chatting at school and on buses, George and Paul burst with shared passion for the new music, and this elevated their friendship. George rode his bike from Speke to Allerton in out-of-school hours to talk rock, country, blues and especially *guitars* – Paul, who hungered for one, and George, who (though eight months younger)* actually had one. The precise chronology is sketchy, but it was in this period that the pair first played music together. Paul could toot When The Saints Go Marching In on his trumpet, and George played the guitar and sang – sounds that bounced around the front parlour at 20 Forthlin Road and the back room of 25 Upton Green, when Paul cycled back to where he used to live.

Perhaps in or around November 1956, after having played his guitar only a short while, John Lennon hit upon the idea of forming a group.† No cigar man was going to find him playing on his own. And, as Pete Shotton noticed, not only did John evidently fear stepping out alone, so too would he never have considered fronting a collection of strangers. The first person he asked to join his group was

---

* Paul always said it was nine months and this became how both (with a revealing regularity) referred to it.

† Again, the date can be put no firmer than this. Recalling events from a distance of ten years, John said the group was not actually his conception but someone else's – 'I think the bloke whose idea it was didn't get into the group' (Davies, p20). This might have been a Quarry Bank lad called Geoff Lee, but no one is certain. John further remembered, 'We met at his house the first time,' though Pete Shotton says the first meeting was at *his* place. What's more, interviewed in 1971 (by Mike Hennessey for *Record Mirror*, though this section wasn't published), John said, 'I didn't have a guitar when I first joined the group, but a guy in the group had a guitar and we used to go to his house and listen to Lonnie Donegan [records].' The notion that John joined the group *before* he had a guitar (as well as this apparent confirmation that they were someone else's group to start with) also contradicts every known account.

his best mate, Pete himself, a subject John broached one day as they were walking across the Quarry Bank school yard. It didn't matter that Pete couldn't play anything – this was skiffle, definitely rough and ready. Could he strum a washboard? Pete knew there was an old metal one rusting away in his dad's garden shed. So he was in. Over the next days, or weeks, John and Pete found more members, including Eric Griffiths, who had a cheap acoustic guitar, and Bill Smith, who offered himself as player of the tea-chest bass. He remembers, 'We had a little meeting one afternoon standing in the yard outside the wood-work room. We discussed it [the group idea] and said, "Yes, let's go ahead." I stole a tea-chest from that woodwork room – I rode away with it on my bike.'*

The group lacked a name, and Bill Smith says he came up with Quarry Men. 'John didn't like it but the others agreed with me and it was three-to-one. John probably felt it was too "Establishment" but he didn't suggest anything else. As far as I remember, no other names were suggested.'[40] Pete Shotton also has a memory of being the one to think up the name. But whoever had the idea, its origin was evident to all, being the first line of R. F. Bailey's school song, sung every term: 'Quarry men old before our birth'.

This uncertainty over who decided what, when things happened, and all the many other whys and hows of the Quarry Men, will never be convincingly untangled. By definition, this was a group of teenage school lads getting together and doing things on a level rarely better than disorganised, quite often when 'bevvied'. No one kept diaries or documents, most of the activities were out of the public eye, and the numerous participants – there were soon several other Quarry Men – have always had conflicting memories, progressively more so with time. Just as it isn't crystal clear when John first got a guitar, or when the Quarry Men were formed, so there'll never be a roll of all the members (some lasted just one rehearsal or performance) or a full list of their engagements. Even the name itself is open to question – it's been written that they were originally the Blackjacks, maybe for a week, but no one can definitively confirm it. And was it Quarry Men or Quarrymen? Sometimes it was written as two words, other times

---

* The inclusion of the washboard in John Lennon's skiffle group shows the primary effect of Rock Island Line, on which it was used (played by Beryl Bryden). Since forming his actual Skiffle Group, Lonnie Donegan had distanced himself from the instrument, shunning it in his current recordings and stage shows. The only other outfit to make early use of it was Ken Colyer's Skiffle Group, whose records never got near the charts and were quite obscure. The Vipers used it too, but their first record, the George Martin-produced Ain't You Glad, wasn't issued until 23 November. And if (as some of its members insist) the formation of John Lennon's group dates to about November 1956 before the release of that Vipers disc, John wouldn't have heard or seen the tea-chest bass yet, merely read about it.

as one. Although Bill Smith thought up the name, he says he has no idea which spelling it was: 'I never visualised it written down'.*

Pete Shotton remembers the group's first rehearsal taking place in the not-yet-dismantled corrugated-iron Anderson air-raid shelter in his back garden. There was probably more swearing than singing, and definitely more smoking. They also rehearsed at Nigel Walley's house, when his fiery policeman father was at work. Walley let them in, with no idea of the startling talent he was about to witness. 'I'd known John since I was about five but I never knew he had a singing voice like that. We'd been in the choir together but we all had those "choir voices" then. When he started singing rock and roll I'd no idea he could do that.'[41]

The Quarry Men played skiffle, but no group with John Lennon in it was going to be stuck pickin' bales of cotton, lamenting long-lost John, pining for the glimpse of a train's flickering headlight and smuggling pig-iron past tollgate keepers.† Now he had a guitar, nothing and nobody was going to keep John from singing Elvis, Gene and Carl. And John *was* the leader, just as he'd been in his every activity since infancy. The only non-grammar-school boy among them was Colin Hanton, the drummer; he was 18, and joined through Eric Griffiths, but knew to whom he must answer. 'John didn't say "I am the leader", he just led, and we just followed him,' he recalls. 'There was never any discussion and it was never a problem. We just assumed John was the leader. He was the singer and whatever he wanted to sing we played.'[42]

Bill Smith was soon gone from the Quarry Men, unable to see the point in it, and perhaps because his father told him to stop messing about and start concentrating on his school studies. Colin Hanton aside, this was GCE O-Level year for all of them. In his place, plucking that single piece of string in some new definition of 'music', came John's Vale Road cronies – first Nigel Walley and then Paul McCartney's schoolfriend, the brilliant Institute academic Ivan Vaughan, who pinned a sign to the tea-chest: 'Jive with Ive, the ace on the bass'. Lennon's gang of scufflers at six had become Lennon's group of skifflers at 16.

*

---

* This book will use the two-word spelling. It's also not conclusive if they were the Quarry Men (or Quarrymen), a skiffle group, or the Quarry Men (Quarrymen) Skiffle Group, the last two words part of the name (as in the Lonnie Donegan Skiffle Group and the Vipers Skiffle Group). No one remembers, or much cares. Only one thing is certain: they were a *group*. Jazz musicians played in bands but skifflers played in groups.
† The flickering headlight was in Midnight Special, another Lead Belly penitentiary song recorded by Lonnie Donegan.

Harry Graves had done much for his stepson since marrying Elsie Starkey, but he wouldn't have welcomed anyone's congratulation for it. He and Richy simply rubbed along. They even went with ease to the pub together. The lad was benefiting from this love and friendship in all manner of ways, not the least of which was being found job after job after job. (Almost six months in, Richy at last seemed settled at Hunt's, and his health was finally stabilising too.)

Harry went south at Christmas, visiting his parents in Romford, and while there, his father, 68-year-old James Graves, said he'd heard that a local dance band was packing up and a set of drums was for sale.[43] Several of the Graves clubbed together and Harry's offer of £10 was accepted. It was something like a full kit, made in the early 1930s and far from first-rate but, still, a snare, a bass drum with a pedal, a hi-hat and one little tom-tom with a top cymbal. Harry carried it home, struggling manfully with it on the train from Romford to Liverpool Street, down to the Circle Line, around to Euston Square and along the road to Euston mainline station. He then popped it into the guard's van for the steam train up to Liverpool. He had a moment of panic at Lime Street when waiting for a taxi to the Dingle: while standing there, he noticed the famous bandleader Joe Loss walking towards him. Harry wondered what he'd say when Loss asked him whether he was a drummer ... but he walked straight past.

The last leg of this epic journey of Richy Starkey's first drum kit was up the tight staircase at 10 Admiral Grove and left, into the lad's freezing-cold backbedroom overlooking the privies of the houses on Grinshill Street. It was Boxing Day 1956, or thereabouts. Richy set it up, and for the first time in his life sat behind a drum kit. And then off he went, thrashing away. As he'd recall twenty years on, 'I was a load of crap. And then I heard from the bottom of the stairs, "Keep the noise down! The neighbours are complaining!" I only ever did it twice and got shouted at both times. I was just this mad thing, hitting drums. So I never practised. The only way I could practise was to join a group.'[44]

5

Guaranteed Not to Split
(January–June 1957)

In his attic room atop the former servants' staircase at Quarry Bank, 'Eggy' Bacon, the French master who doubled as careers adviser, surveyed the perpetual challenge that was John Lennon. The lad's schooling since 1945 had always been leading to this, the climactic 1957 when he must either do well enough in exams to stay in education, or leave to find work . . . or join the dole queue. Presently placed fifteenth in the lowest stream, class VC (5C), there was little hope he'd pass many O-Levels, so what would become of him? As John would point out years later, 'They ask, "What do you want to be?" Nobody ever said that I already *was*, and we already *are*.'[1] On the spur of the moment (probably) he said he could become a newspaper journalist, but Bacon pronounced this no respectable career for a Quarry Bank boy.

> I said, 'Well, present me with some alternative,' and they came up with veterinarian, doctor, dentist, lawyer – and I knew there was no hope in hell of me ever becoming that. So there was never anywhere for me to go. I [didn't] dare say 'artist' because of the social background I came from. Artsy-fartsy people were despised – they still are – in society. I used to say to my auntie, 'You like to read about artists and you worship them in museums, but you don't want 'em living around the house.'[2]

This ultra-sharp and edgy youth, this wolf in a grammar-school blazer, now carrying a guitar, was 16 going on 17. Many were repulsed by his attitude and behaviour – uncompromising, unpredictable, rude, cynical, sarcastic, anti-authoritarian, quickly bored – but to others he was sensational: a perpetual high-wire act who lived and communicated without a safety net, a faithful friend, generous, honest, gifted, literate, articulate and hugely funny. He dressed and looked tough and was no stranger to fighting, but his hostility was mostly verbal: he could shout louder than anyone else and lacerate with a brevity and wit that took the breath away. 'You didn't banter words with John or you were on a loser before you started,' concedes Pete Shotton.[3]

Ahead of John's GCE O-Levels, to be taken in June, came the 'mock' exams. Results in these gave school and pupil the clearest indication of the likely final outcome; John took six and passed only two, English and Art, experiencing plenty of distraction at the time – including, playing in Liverpool's cinemas, Alan Freed's latest juke-box musical *Don't Knock The Rock*. Here was Little Richard singing Long Tall Sally and Tutti Frutti, and nothing in John's world had ever seemed so dynamic. Decca's London label coupled the tracks as a new single and Long Tall Sally finally scorched to number 3 on the *NME* chart; Paul McCartney suddenly had another striking piece to add to his repertoire of Little Richard impersonations.

Though he paled alongside the vibrant Richard, the headlining star of *Don't Knock The Rock* was Bill Haley and this was still a heady period for rock's first monarch. With his kiss curl, Comets, wife, eccentric manager and his eccentric manager's 77-year-old mother, Haley was about to become the first American rock star to play Britain. His nationwide tour of one-night stands, a Lew & Leslie Grade promotion, was heading to Liverpool on 20 February, playing two houses on stage at the Odeon Cinema. Having thrilled to Rock Around The Clock, Paul McCartney was desperate to see him. As George Harrison would reflect, 'When Bill Haley came to Liverpool I couldn't afford a ticket. It was fifteen shillings, a lot of money for a schoolboy. I often wondered where Paul got his fifteen shillings from, because he got to see him.'[4]

Opting not to dash home and then back into town after school, Paul eagerly occupied his first-house Odeon seat in short trousers, Liverpool Institute cap stuffed deep into blazer pocket. The show began with disappointment, when Paul came face to face with an eternal truth of the music business: you don't always get what you want. It was a feeling he didn't like and would always remember. He believed he'd spent his hard-saved pocket money on an entire concert by Bill Haley, but first everyone had to sit through a long first half filled by the jazz-swing Vic Lewis Orchestra, the tin-whistle warbler Desmond Lane, and the double-act Kenneth Earle & Malcolm Vaughan (comedian and tenor singer).[5] After the interval, though, it happened exactly as Paul wanted it. The lights went down, the house quivered expectantly, there was a dramatic pause in the darkness, Haley and his Comets began the call-and-response 'On your marks, get set …' intro to Razzle Dazzle and then on the word 'Go!' the curtains flew open, the music started jumping and the lights picked them out. 'And there they all were,' Paul would remember with enthusiasm ever undimmed. 'They had tartan jackets on, which sounds terrible now, but it was great then. It was something special, and that's what I was after: *chills*.'⁶ Commissionaires kept fans in their seats, instructed to allow no dancing, but Paul was no passive spectator. The final number was Rock Around The Clock and it seemed the Odeon would explode with joy, but then two minutes later it was all over and, as usual, everyone was dashing to get out before the National Anthem.

And yet, despite the barely checked fervour of young McCartney and plenty of others, many left the Odeon that night dissatisfied, and it was a feeling experienced in cities all over the country. So strongly built up in advance, the tour ended on a curiously flat note. *Beat* magazine called it 'salesmanship, not musicianship ... one of the most embarrassing damp squibs for some years', and plans for a return visit later in 1957 collapsed when sales of Haley records fell through the floor: before the tour he'd had twelve different hits on the British chart, after it he had none. As hard as it was to get to the top, staying there was so much more difficult.

Rock and roll only figured in the minds of Liverpool's jazz fans and musicians when voicing their detestation of it, and this they could now do within their own exclusive venue. The Cavern Club opened on 16 January 1957 in a former fruit cellar at 10 Mathew Street – a dark cobblestoned alley of tall warehouses, replete with the wooden crates that brought produce from the ships for trading on the international Fruit Exchange. Construction of the club's music stage was done by Paul McCartney's uncle Harry Harris and his son, Paul's cousin Ian, who'd given Paul his first taste of the trumpet.

The three-tunnel vaulted storage cellar had been used as an air-raid shelter during the Second World War, now it was vacant, and a young jazz fanatic, 21-year-old Alan Sytner, had seen the possibilities. The Sytner family took holidays abroad at a time when few others had the funds or imagination to see beyond the seaside; Alan was an habitué of Le Caveau jazz club in Paris, and when he shone a torch around the gloomy basement at 10 Mathew Street his imagination gleamed. 'I was seeing a replica of Le Caveau. As Mathew Street looked like a little narrow street in the Latin Quarter in Paris, I felt I was bringing the Left Bank to Liverpool.'⁷ It was a heroic decision, as was his strict no-alcohol stance. Selling booze would have introduced problems Sytner didn't need, and he declined on moral grounds the temptation to intoxicate young people for profit. Anyone wanting to drink could obtain a pass-out and try the two pubs within yards of the club: the Grapes and the White Star. Most of the musicians spent much of the evenings in one or the other, threading their way back through the Cavern throng when it was time to climb on stage.

The Quarry Men first played the Cavern on a date unrecorded. Many of the local skiffle groups performed as interval attractions, not mentioned in the venue's *Liverpool Echo* adverts, and no club diary from that period has surfaced. John Lennon's combo was getting itself together through the first two or three months of 1957. Rod Davis, an academic Quarry Bank schoolboy and former Sunday School classmate, had bought a banjo and joined them, playing along-side John and Eric Griffiths (guitars), Pete Shotton (washboard), Colin Hanton (drums) and Ivan Vaughan (bass). Wrapped up in his studies, however, Ivan didn't stop long, and Len Garry – one of Ivan's schoolfriends from Liverpool Institute, whom he'd carefully introduced into John's gang a year or so earlier – stepped up to the tea-chest in his place. Nigel Walley was given the job of man-ager on an even share of whatever pittance they rarely received, and at a cost of 7s 6d had fifty business cards made by a Woolton printer:

Country · Western · Rock 'n' Roll · Skiffle
The Quarry Men
OPEN FOR ENGAGEMENTS
LEOSDENE, VALE ROAD, WOOLTON, LIVERPOOL.

Little would be remembered of their Cavern debut, of how long they played (thirty minutes maximum, probably less), of which songs they performed, of what they wore or how they went down, but there is one credible and endur-ing anecdote. 'We were doing skiffle numbers,' says Walley, 'but then John started singing a rock and roll song. Alan Sytner sent a note up: "Cut out the bloody rock."' Clearly, John Lennon on stage was the same as John Lennon off: he did what he wanted to do, and if it upset people that was their problem.

Bill Haley's tour coincided with other musical landmark events in Britain. The week he played in Liverpool saw the first great breakthrough in the presenta-tion of rock music on TV, courtesy of the BBC, which launched *Six-Five Special* on Saturday evenings. The show's producer and presiding genius was Jack Good, an Oxford graduate and Shakespearean actor-director whose elemental enthusiasm for excitement had shifted towards rock after witnessing a cinema audience going wild over *Rock Around The Clock*. Good looked and sounded posh but he was the archetypal rebel, and he battled with the BBC to make *Six-Five Special* as exciting as possible, setting the template for rock on the box: singers and musicians performing while teenagers danced around them.

The week Haley arrived in Britain, two recordings of Don't You Rock Me

Daddy-O were in the top ten of the *NME* chart at the same time – Lonnie Donegan's cover version (bought by John Lennon) and the Vipers' 'original'. Thirteen months after Rock Island Line had kicked it all off, the first week of February 1957 was definitively the start of 'the skiffle boom'. Groups were forming everywhere. Teenage boys nicked, begged or borrowed old washboards from mums, aunts and grannies, and they rummaged in attics, sheds and shops for tea-chests and broom handles.* They got guitars wherever and however possible, though demand far outstripped supply, emptying shops in an instant. *Melody Maker* reported on 16 February, 'The guitar is enjoying a boom period that surprises even the instrument manufacturers.' All this youthful activity was watched by adults who were bemused but didn't mind really because 'well, what harm can it do?'

The Quarry Men were one of scores of Liverpool skiffle groups – perhaps as many as two hundred – strumming and plucking away in every suburb. Merseyside was suddenly a disorderly young male voice choir finding joy in the rhythmic work- and prison-songs of the American South. And also, since it was rarely just about skiffle, a shed-load of thumping US rock and roll.

With a more or less settled line-up, Quarry Men rehearsals were now taking place fairly regularly, and ever chaotically, at drummer Colin's house . . . in guitarist Eric's house . . . at banjo picker Rod's house . . . in washboard strummer Pete's air-raid shelter . . . in manager Nigel's house . . . and most regularly of all in singer, guitarist and leader John's mother's house. They didn't rehearse at Mendips because Mimi emphatically didn't want the place full of kids, and also had to consider her lodgers who needed to study, but they were warmly welcomed by Julia, who was typically accommodating. Sessions often took place in the Dykins' none too spacious bathroom, John needing to hear his voice bounce off the shiny tiles, approximating the slap echo sound Sam Phillips had given Carl Perkins and Elvis at Sun Studio, Memphis.

It's hard to imagine the Quarry Men's sound being particularly impressive – Rod was a beginner on banjo, Colin was a novice on drums, the tea-chest bass was a crude instrument even in the most skilful of hands, and Pete was unmusical even with a washboard. Luckily, being skiffle, none of this mattered very much. John and Eric both had cheap guitars and could only play the banjo chords Julia was showing them, using four of the available six strings (they tuned to the fifth and John left the bottom E string loose, flapping about). Inevitably, this produced a thinner, more trebly sound than guitar chords. Aware

---

* A tea-chest bass was played on the Vipers' hit recording, bringing this homemade instrument mass attention for the first time.

of the problem, John and Eric found a guitar teacher in Hunt's Cross (south of Woolton, midway between there and Speke), though the tuition was definitively short-lived. As John would recall, 'I had one lesson, and it was so much like school that I gave up.'[8]

Richy Starkey had come to much the same conclusion. Practising at home on his old secondhand kit from Romford not only annoyed the neighbours, it was deathly boring. You couldn't drum *songs* on your own. Because he lacked any technique, and as it would be a chance to play, he was encouraged to have lessons. 'I went to this little man in a house [who] played drums, got a manuscript and wrote it all down. I had about three lessons and never went back – I just couldn't be bothered. It was too routine for me, all those paradiddles and that, I couldn't stand it.'[9]

It's likely these lessons highlighted a difficulty too, because when the man saw Richy playing he would have noticed a problem. It went back to his infancy, when superstitious Granny Starkey, convinced the boy's left-handedness meant he was possessed by the devil, forced him into being right-handed. The mysterious work of 'the voodoo queen of Liverpool' was effective when it came to changing his writing hand, but behind a drum kit his genetic programming was not so easily erased: it was custom to lead with the right but he always had to lead with his left. The combined forces of nature and Granny Annie's meddling would, in time, give Richy Starkey an unusual, actually unique drumming style. Once asked to define it, he called it 'some sort of rock lope'.[10]

Skiffle therefore arrived in Richy's life with miracle timing: it was music that embraced the boy beginner. He already liked Rock Island Line, and Take This Hammer (by Ken Colyer's Skiffle Group); now, with the boom, he became another of those hundreds of Liverpool lads rushing to join a group. While the Quarry Men were a grammar-school group, the Eddie Clayton Skiffle Group were a works group – the house skifflers at H. Hunt & Son. Clayton (quickly adopted as a stage name) was really Edward 'Eddie' Myles, two years Richy's senior, an apprentice fitter at Hunt's and already an accomplished musician, probably one of the best natural guitarists on Merseyside. He also happened to be Richy's next-door neighbour, living at 11 Admiral Grove. When Eddie put the word around that he was forming a group, enough of the other young lads at the factory stepped forward to fill the places: Peter Healey (second guitarist), John Docherty or sometimes Micky McGrellis (washboard) and Roy Trafford (tea-chest bass). And there was no more obvious contender for drums than Roy's best mate, as he remembers. 'Richy was always banging on the backs of chairs or tapping old coconut shells. He'd play on upturned biscuit tins with keys, he shook milk bottle-tops – he was always making a noise and he always had drumsticks very close. It was in him, and he had great rhythm.'[11]

Getting the group together for rehearsal presented no difficulty at all. Come lunchtime, the Windsor Street windows would rattle to the sound of skiffle. Roy Trafford again: 'It was only half an hour dinner, a quick sandwich and down the cellar. We couldn't wait to play the skiffle stuff, we just loved it. The other workmen were there and we'd play whatever songs came into our heads, sitting on bags of wood shavings. We were rough, but it got better.'

Perhaps it was because Myles lived next door that the Eddie Clayton Skiffle Group were able to grab additional rehearsal time at Richy's house. (At least this neighbour wasn't going to be offended by the noise.) Everyone somehow squeezed into the truly minuscule front room at number 10, even spectators. As Richy would remember, Elsie's best mate Annie Maguire liked to predict that one day he'd reach the very top of the entertainment tree, saying, 'See you on the Palladium, son. See your name in lights!' It was, of course, ridiculously unlikely. The venue was the established pinnacle of all British show business, even more so now that Lew Grade's ATV channel was beaming Britain's most popular television show, *Sunday Night At The London Palladium*, live from there every week. Yet with Annie Maguire's encouragement, even though it was a joke really, Richy nurtured the dream of making it to London and waving from the theatre's famous rotating stage at the end of the TV show. 'There was nothing bigger in the world than making it to the Palladium [so] I'd say, "Yeah, sure Annie, that's where we're going to go!"'[12]

If the internationally renowned London theatre was the top of the tree, the stump was the Labour Club on the corner of Peel Street, Dingle. The first public performance of the Eddie Clayton Skiffle Group happened here one evening in spring 1957 and it was a debut to remember. Playing for your work-mates at dinner time was one thing, it was quite another to feel the adrenalin rush of performing in front of people – people who expected not only to be entertained but to *dance*. As Richy would recall, 'We had no idea you had to keep the same tempo all the way through. We used to start off performing Maggie May at the right tempo and end up like an express train, we were all so excited. People had to dance to this!'[13]

He was playing without his full kit, unable to get around what would be his predicament for a long time to come. It was impossible for Richy to drag his drums around Liverpool: he couldn't afford taxis, and the journey to many venues necessitated changes of bus. Also, he well knew that no matter which end of Admiral Grove he exited, the moment he stepped out on to High Park Street or North Hill Street carrying his precious kit, he'd be set on by Teds – even by his own gang – and that would be the end of it. So Richy started playing in public with the bare minimum of gear, whatever he could run with: a snare drum on a hi-hat stand, hit with sticks or more often brushes; and because carrying a drum stool was impractical, he stood. Nothing for this boy ever came easy. If he did get to play a full kit it would be someone else's, begged off the drummer of another group on the bill. It was rough going, but, as he was the first to realise, good learning experience, and he was hungry for that.

The Eddie Clayton Skiffle Group did many of their early bookings for nothing, so great was their love of playing. This first one, in the Dingle, was for £1 a man – but, as Richy remembered, 'People were drinking, and when the time came to be paid the manager of the club was so drunk he refused to pay us. It was such a let down. My mother was there – everyone's mother was there – and all the aunties, and they got on the manager's case. He paid us two days later.'

Paul McCartney and George Harrison weren't in a group but both were certainly big skiffle fans. First it was Lonnie and now the Vipers. Paul headed back to his old stamping ground one evening, to the Speke estate, and followed George up to his bedroom where they tried to make sense of his guitar manual. Its technicalities had sapped even George's considerable reserves of patience: unable to work it out, he'd become angry and flung it into a cupboard. When he and Paul got their heads together they managed to glean some chords from it, C, F and G7, enough to be able to play Don't You Rock Me Daddy-O. George only had his ropey old Egmond guitar and Paul didn't have a guitar at all; Paul remembers they tried to make one, but never finished it.[14]

It was in this timeframe that Paul formed a closer friendship with Ian James, an Institute boy (in his year) he'd known since 1954. Ian was also into rock and skiffle and he'd recently been bought an acoustic guitar by his grandparents, at whose house he lived in the Dingle. (Every guitar had a maker's name: his was a Rex.) The two boys became good pals on the strength of it. While they tended not to see each other in the evenings, because they lived some distance apart, Paul often went to Ian's house for an hour or two after school – they walked there together down the hill from the Institute – and Ian sometimes went to Forthlin Road at weekends, taking his guitar with him.

Ian James held a triple attraction for Paul: he was an intelligent, decent and affable lad, he had some rock records, and he had a guitar – an unbeatable combination.

In the front room at home I had a table-top portable record player, three speed. I remember playing Blueberry Hill by Fats Domino over and over, just the first line and then I'd pick up the needle and put it back at the start. I also had Elvis Presley's first album, which we played time after time after time, with That's All Right Mama, Trying To Get To You, Lawdy Miss Clawdy, I'm Gonna Sit Right Down And Cry (Over You), Mystery Train . . . Elvis was the one to copy, he was the hero. He had everything: the charisma, the looks, the voice. Frank Sinatra had only one style but Elvis could do anything – gospel, blues, rock and roll, romantic ballads. There was nobody else like him. Paul and I talked about Elvis *all the time*.[15]

The Rex guitar was ever at hand. Ian showed and reinforced to Paul those three chord fundamentals that would get him started, C, F and G or G7, the basis for pretty much every song they loved. 'With those chords you could play most of the rock and skiffle stuff,' Ian says, having found what every budding guitarist in Britain was simultaneously thrilled to be discovering. Though naturally left-handed, Paul learned the chords as a right-hander – but still he was a very fast learner, a musical natural. Ian watched as Paul whooshed past him in no time at all.* But better though he was, Paul always had the frustration of going home to a trumpet and a piano. Somehow, he now knew, he *had* to get a guitar of his own.

John Lennon's first own guitar, to replace the one he'd borrowed, was bought for him by Julia. It's been said (though it's far from certain) he asked Mimi to buy it, but with his exams looming she was never likely to say yes. More likely he just asked Julia. (Nigel Walley remembers, 'If John needed new socks or a new shirt or some vests he'd say, "I'll go down Mum's and get them."' Julia had also just bought her beloved 'Stinker' his first coloured shirt, checked red and white.) Because the skiffle boom had temporarily stripped guitars from the shops, retailers were having to source them with greater cunning. John's was bought from a south London mail-order firm advertising in the popular low-brow weekly magazine *Reveille*. The ad appeared in the issue of 7 March 1957:

ROCK 'N ROLL GUITARS, REAL PROFESSIONAL, SENT FOR 20/-

That was enough to grab the eye, but the small print uncovered the real cost: it was £1 down and then twenty-one fortnightly payments of 20s 3d, for a total

---

* Ian also went to George Harrison's house once or twice, to show him some chords: 'He invited me round because he knew I'd done this with Paul.'

of £22 5s; or one instant payment of 19 guineas plus 5s carriage, total £20 4s. This was expensive. John (who always remembered it costing £10) later said it was bought 'on the never-never', which must mean Julia was committing to a shade over a pound from Bobby Dykins' wage-packet every two weeks all the way to the start of 1958.

For the mail-order company, the key was to find stocks of guitars in countries where rock had yet to catch fire. John's was shipped from Durban, South Africa. Though the ad made it sound like a dream machine, the Gallotone Champion was actually three-quarter size, made from laminates instead of solid wood, and its general tone and playability was poor. A sticker inside, visible through the soundhole, said GUARANTEED NOT TO SPLIT and (in Afrikaans) GEWAARBORG OM NIE TE BARS NIE. John conceded 'it was a bit crummy' but played it constantly, regardless of its quality or Mimi's curt words. A virtuoso he was not: 'All I ever wanted to do was vamp,' he'd recall. 'I only learned to play to back myself [singing].'[16]

John wrote his first song at this time – a calypso. Between the US and Britain, the flow of musical fads was strictly one-way: America never followed British trends and so stayed largely unaware of skiffle, but Britain always picked up on America's, and as the current obsession of the US music business was Caribbean calypso so it was confidently expected to arrive on British soil any day. CALYPSOMANIA! 'It's on the way, but will it stay?' pondered the *Daily Mirror* on 21 March 1957. An insatiable reader of the press, John was well aware of its coming. 'The first six months I got interested in rock, when Presley's Heartbreak Hotel came out in England they were saying "rock is going to die – is calypso going to take over?"'[17] John's first song was called Calypso Rock – though this is probably all that'll ever be known about it. The composition he usually talked about as his first was a subsequent piece; Calypso Rock he mentioned in only two interviews, and, apart from the title, all he said was that he could recall nothing more of it. He'd no means of recording and hadn't thought to come up with a way of memorising his ideas. 'The trouble was, I could never remember the song the next morning. What I had to learn to do was play the same phrase over and over again until it stuck and then go on to the next bit.'[18]

The calypso craze, corporate America's first attempt to fob off rock and roll, was a miserable failure ... though with a bright smile, great rhythm and happy tunes. Kids just didn't want it. The entertainment business couldn't grasp that rock was the purest movement of them all because it had grown organically out of rhythm and blues, and that, at its best, it was natural and thrilling. It couldn't be deposed by artifice.

The Quarry Men were now picking up the occasional booking, appearing again at the Cavern, at a sixth-formers' dance in Quarry Bank, and at St Peter's church youth club in Woolton, where some of them (John included) were still members.* They and the Eddie Clayton Skiffle Group appeared together on several occasions, enough for John to notice and admire Clayton's guitar playing even if he paid no special attention to their standup drummer. Promoters and dance-hall managers had clued into the fact that holding skiffle competitions or auditions ensured they'd be inundated with kids eager to perform for nothing. At best, the promoter's only expense was £10 or a trophy to be handed out at the end of the evening; most of the time they needed to do nothing at all except keep peace on the dance floor. Asked to name the favourite moment of his time in the Quarry Men, Eric Griffiths replied, 'The best gig we did was at the Locarno Ballroom, a competition. We played well but the audience wanted skiffle and we got booed off because we were playing Elvis Presley.'[19] John Lennon was getting up people's noses again. The date was probably 18 April 1957; though no records exist to show who won the contest, it may well be that Richy Starkey and his mates walked away with the prize. The Eddie Clayton Skiffle Group won several such competitions and Roy Trafford remembers one victory coming at the Locarno.

The evening of Friday 8 March – the day after the *Reveille* ad for the Gallotone guitar was published – John had a second experience that shaped his behaviour for many years to come. Quarry Bank's annual Speech Day had just taken place, as usual, at the Philharmonic Hall – all that boring singing and new headmaster Mr Pobjoy reminding them of the grammar school's very highest ideals. John and his gang couldn't wait to get out and sink a few bevvies in the pubs around Hope Street. As they walked along the roads, full of the ale, John was struck by how many deformed people there were – 'three-foot-high men selling newspapers', as he later put it. They'd always been there: Britain seemed full of paraplegics, dwarves and 'cripples' in those days, the casualties of two world wars and victims of poor sanitation, insufficient medical knowledge and inadequate diet and care. He hadn't really noticed them before, but now, as he waited for and caught the bus back to Woolton, they seemed to be everywhere. 'It got funnier and funnier and we couldn't stop laughing,' he'd remember.[20]

So began John's strange and prolonged obsession with deformities, one that dovetailed with his need to rattle on about anything that marked anyone out as different – blacks, Jews, queers and more – and wrap them up inside his humour. At any time now, John would contort his face into that of a 'crip' or

---

* No dates are known for any of these bookings. (And this was the word generally used when a group had an engagement to play somewhere; 'gig' or 'gigs' was not yet in common parlance. The pronunciation is worth mentioning too: in Liverpool, as book is like 'bewk' so booking is like 'boo-king', with an equal stress on the final letter.)

'spaz', the commonly used words of the period (for 'cripple' and 'spastic'), voiced without thought of offence by adults as well as children. He'd thrust his tongue inside his bottom lip, make 'spaz' noises and limp along the street – and the stage – hunching his back and dragging a leg like Quasimodo or those war casualties. He did it when he was feeling embarrassed or self-conscious, he did it when he ridiculed something, he did it when he thought someone was behaving like a prick, he did it off and on all the time at any moment – and, being John Lennon, he was cocky with it, always pushing to see how much he could get away with. Often, when he noticed a disabled person, he'd make a loud comment like 'Some people'll do anything to get out of the army' – rich stuff from a youth still scheming a disappearing act the moment his call-up papers hit the Mendips mat. Intolerable today, it was simply unremarkable in the 1950s for black people to be called 'wogs' or 'coons', Jews 'Yids', homosexuals 'queers' and 'poofs', and Down's syndrome sufferers 'mongols' or 'mongies', and for such language to appear in print and in comedians' jokes. It wasn't nice but it was said and done all the same, and while John's 'cripping' made some people nervous or uncomfortable (he naturally felt this was their problem, not his), it often made others laugh and join in with him.

In later times, some assumed John's antics to be a parody of Gene Vincent, one of his outright musical heroes, the untamed Virginia wildcat who dragged his shattered left leg behind him as he limped around the stage. Not so, but Vincent was first seen in Liverpool at precisely this time, in March 1957, when *The Girl Can't Help It* opened at the Scala Cinema on Lime Street. Previous rock and roll films were rightly recognised as trashy, but this movie earned a place at a higher table. *The Girl Can't Help It* was the first quality Hollywood film about rock, the first comedy, the first in colour, the first with proper production values and a storyline divorced from juvenile delinquency. Here, in particularly vivid De Luxe Color, was Little Richard performing three songs – like 'an animated golliwog', noted the *NME*[21] – and Gene Vincent singing Be-Bop-A-Lula. And what did he look like, this young god who gave John Lennon the shivers and made the first record bought by Paul McCartney? He was scruffy, dirty, ugly, scary and utterly wonderful. The Blue Caps, his backing group, all wore blue caps (known in Liverpool as 'twat 'ats' or 'cunt caps') which seemed to have been lowered on their heads by crane. The movie didn't mention delinquents but these guys sure looked the part.

Also featured were Fats Domino, the Treniers, the Platters and Eddie Cochran, a newcomer fictionally introduced as 'one of America's top rock and rollers'. He soon was. Cochran was 19, only just older than the boys and girls who instantly idolised him, and he looked vaguely weird in too much make-up and eye shadow; but his movements were good, his shoulders bouncing rhythmically, and he was playing a song called Twenty Flight Rock on his … *Good God, what is that gorgeous big guitar?* It was a Gretsch 6120 electric plugged into an amplifier – *want!* – and here too, instantly, was another great rock record to add to the pile.

Paul McCartney loved the whole film, start to finish, and not only for the music. He'd describe the way actor Tom Ewell ordered the standard screen into wide-screen at the beginning as 'the most fantastic trick ever, and of course added to that was Jayne Mansfield and her cantilevered cleavage – what more do young teenagers want?'[22] For kids hungry to know just how records were made, the film's recording studio scene made a deep impression. Everything was done live – orchestra, singers, backing singers and conductor waving his baton – and at the end the important man in the control box announced, 'I can assure you of another gold record!' So *that's* how they did it. This studio even had an automated vending machine dispensing apples. British eyes watched green with envy. The incredible luxuries they had in America!

It's impossible to overestimate the impact made by *The Girl Can't Help It* on Liverpool teenagers. *Rock Around The Clock* and *Don't Knock The Rock* played there just one week but *The Girl Can't Help It* ran and ran. It finally came off after seven weeks – forty-nine days and 195 performances. The Scala only seated 620 – it was an old fleapit, opened in 1916 – but by the time the projectionist packed the film away and sent it off to the suburbs to be watched by more, tens of thousands had seen it, and many of these were now joyously drunk on Little Richard, Gene Vincent and Eddie Cochran. Bang in the middle of the period supposedly dominated by skiffle, *The Girl Can't Help It* was seminal to everything that followed.

Paul wasted no time after seeing *The Girl Can't Help It*: he headed straight to Curry's and ordered Eddie Cochran's Twenty Flight Rock, having to wait because it wasn't out yet. John Lennon was contributing to a boom in record sales by buying Elvis's Blue Moon and Mystery Train, and other discs known to the enthusiasts included Come Go With Me by the Dell-Vikings – which only gained public exposure through Decca's purchased airtime on Radio Luxembourg[23] – and, at last, a second British single by Carl Perkins, Matchbox c/w Your True Love. Having already been bowled over by Blue Suede Shoes and Honey Don't, George Harrison was a definite fan of Perkins' seemingly effortless rockabilly guitar playing, just as he also loved Scotty Moore's work on the early Elvis records. Though George was interested in catching every guitar player around, craning for any glimpse of any instrument, that Sun style was his favourite and the one he spent most time studiously trying to copy.

Still only 14, George saw several live shows at this time: Frankie Lymon and the Teenagers at the Empire, Freddie Bell and the Bell Boys at the Empire, and the Vipers Skiffle Group at Grafton Ballroom (though how he gained entry to licensed premises at 14 he never let on). He was also awed by Big Bill Broonzy, the great American blues guitarist he caught when Jack Good booked him for *Six-Five Special*. Guitars were the only thing that mattered to George now, figuring in his mind pretty much the entire time. Still too young for girls, it was his sole obsession, while his only interest at Liverpool Institute was in seeing just how outrageously he could dress before being rapped over the knuckles. Arthur Kelly remembers George being stopped in the corridor by (John Lennon's uncle's brother) 'Cissy' Smith for wearing suede slip-on shoes. 'He shouted, "Harrison! They're *not* school shoes." George later said to me, "What the fuck are *school shoes?*"'

Rock and roll was encroaching hard on Paul McCartney's mind too at a time when Jim Mac wanted him to focus on his looming first GCE O-Level exams. Jim was always amazed how his son could do school homework and watch television at the same time; while he repeatedly told Paul his work would suffer, Paul kept assuring him it wouldn't, and generally his marks backed him up. Also, Jim noted, 'afterwards he usually knew more about the [TV] programme than I did. He seemed to have the sort of mind that could easily grasp things that used to take a lot of concentration from other boys.'[24] This period was the height of Paul's friendship with Ian James; as spring headed into summer, he spent many post-school afternoons at Ian's house in the Dingle, 43 Elswick Street. 'My grandmother was always on at me,' says Ian. 'I should have been studying for my exams, and all Paul and I were interested in was playing records. We played them so often I'm surprised some of them didn't wear out.'

Keeping tabs on all the new releases was an important after-school activity. The city centre had quite a few shops: Cranes, Curry's, Beaver Radio, the Top Hat, James Smith, Hessy's, Rushworth's, the record counters in Lewis's and Blackler's department stores and one or two other smaller places, and they shuttled between them as if on patrol. Ian remembers, 'We knew all the girls behind the counters. We'd ask "Is there anything new in?" and they'd play it for us in one of the booths; we'd either buy it or write down the words. Around this time I first heard the phrase "rhythm and blues", and when I asked the girl in the shop about it she said it was "some new kind of music from America". When I asked if she had any she put on a single by Chuck Berry . . .'[25]

Mostly, the pair played music together. If they were at Paul's house, Ian had the guitar while Paul played piano, both singing. Ian vividly remembers Jim Mac being on the phone in the back room, trying through the din to place horse-racing bets with his turf accountant: 'He'd often charge through to us and shout, "Can you keep that bloody noise down!"' They played more often at

Elswick Street.[26] Both boys now had Eddie Cochran's Twenty Flight Rock and wanted to learn it note-perfect. Ian's Rex acoustic deputised for Eddie's divine Gretsch 6120 and through repetition they learned all the flicks and tricks, and its intricate words about a man so tired after climbing twenty flights to see his girlfriend that when he gets there he's too tired to *rock*.

It was shaping up to be one of those rare good summers in Britain, hot from the end of May. Given study periods to revise for their O-Levels, Paul and Ian would buy a bag of chips from Vaughan's, on Falkner Street, and sunbathe on the tombstones in St James's Cemetery. And after school they'd carry the guitar into the tiny brick back yard at Elswick Street, by the privy, playing and basking in the sunshine: the sounds of Memphis, New Orleans and Los Angeles – mingled and mangled through a Liverpool filter – floating up and over Herculaneum Dock. Memorable times. There's no photo of Paul here, but he took a good one of Ian – his shirt off, his hair tousled into a quiff, cradling the precious guitar as they ran one more time through the songs of their heroes.[27]

Scenes like this were being played out all over the city. Six miles deeper into the south of Liverpool, on the Speke estate, a different back-yard photo shows George Harrison and Arthur Kelly playing their guitars, George squinting through the sunlight to check his fingers are on C.

It was around this time that George got a booking for *his* group, to play at the British Legion social club in Speke. Quite how he managed it isn't clear, but his mother Louise would recall him coming home to break the good news. 'I told him he must be daft: he hadn't even got a group. He said don't worry, he'd get one ... [On the night] they all left the house one by one, ducking down behind the hedge. George didn't want the nosy neighbours to know what they were doing.'[28]

George's group was a quartet: himself, his brother Pete and Arthur Kelly on guitars, and an older Speke boy called Alan Williams on tea-chest bass; there was no drummer. A James Dean fan, Arthur came up with their name, the Rebels, after *Rebel Without A Cause*. They made only this one unadvertised appearance, the date of which can't be pinpointed. However, since Arthur recalls their repertoire being Pick A Bale Of Cotton, Cumberland Gap, Hey Liley, Liley Lo and a couple of other early skiffle songs ('but we didn't do Freight Train because it required quite a bit of finesse'), the performance can be placed squarely in the second quarter of 1957. The booking was probably designed as a free audition, but they ended up with ten bob each for their labours.

George was never able to recall much of this event when asked about it in later years, but Arthur remembers it well:

We painted the tea-chest black and then painted the word REBELS in red, with a couple of musical symbols. George and I took turns to do the vocals.

We thought we were the support act, but when we got there we found we were the *only* act. The club was very quiet that night – there weren't more than half a dozen people in there – but we were just delighted to have a stage to stand on and microphones to sing into. Who had microphones? We only had six or seven numbers, so when somebody said 'Do more' we did them all again, and made them longer by repeating verses. When we finally came off, the bass player's fingers were bleeding profusely from all the plucking.[29]

There are fascinating photographs from this period. A picture of the Eddie Clayton Skiffle Group was taken on 23 May 1957, when they played for local promoter Charlie McBain ('Charlie Mac') at Wilson Hall, Garston. It's the earliest known photo of any Liverpool group playing any venue – truly the start of something.[30] Clayton is the main guitarist but Roy Trafford is centre-stage, singing; Richy is standing at the back, gazing forward, hitting his single snare with sticks or brushes. Though closing in on his 17th birthday, he's a young 16, small and skinny; while his illnesses are behind him, they've left their mark. Except for Eddie, who wears an open-neck shirt, the four other lads are wearing darkish shirts and black bootlace ties, group uniform being important.

On the same day, John Lennon lined up with the boys and masters of Quarry Bank for what would be his last school picture. He began at Quarry Bank a boy, he was to leave in July a young man, three months shy of 17, looking very much like the John Lennon people would come to know over the next few years, with strong features, a bony nose and a hard direct stare (though without glasses, he probably couldn't even see the photographer). Pete Shotton is by his right shoulder, as he'd been since the start. Two months more and they'd be gone from this place . . .

Either side of Easter had come the news for which so many boys were praying. The *Liverpool Echo* on 4 April was surely grabbed eagerly by lads all over Merseyside, much as other evening newspapers were being seized all around the country, for nestling within a five-year outline of government defence policy was an announcement that National Service, the dreaded call-up, would end in 1960. From this day, George Harrison knew he was spared the duty he was meaning to dodge, and Paul McCartney was almost certainly in the clear. He became definitively so on 27 May – the same day as John Lennon, Richy Starkey and others their age heard that boys born in 1940 would also be spared. They'd all escaped the call-up ordeal by the skin of their teeth. As John would recall: 'I remember the news coming through that it was "all those born before 1940", and I was thanking God for that. I'd always had this plan about [escaping to] Southern Ireland. I had no intention of going and fighting – I couldn't kill somebody, I couldn't charge at them.'[31]

Theirs became the first generation in Britain since pre-1939 not to be forced into army duty, and the first and only teenagers to have their own rebellious music – rock and roll. They had disillusionment to vanquish, money to squander, dreams to follow, and the drawing-board was blank. As Paul McCartney says, 'The turning point was the ending of National Service. It meant we were the first generation for so many years that didn't have that "we'll-make-a-man-of-you" threat hanging over [us]. We weren't going to be threaded through the system like so many before us – we were like errant schoolkids off the leash.'[32]

Into the celebratory atmosphere, on the opening day of June, jumped *Saturday Skiffle Club*, BBC radio's first teenage music show, given a half-hour slot in the Light Programme at 10AM. It wasn't much, but it offered skifflers a chance to pick up new songs, and was important in one other respect. Historically, any song with 'God' or 'Jesus' in its lyrics was avoided by the BBC because of complaints from devout listeners (diminishing in number but still a sizeable and powerful lobby). BBC producer Jimmy Grant argued that spirituals were an integral element of the skiffle repertoire and their exclusion would weaken the programme; through his persistence, and the popularity of skiffle, a more relaxed approach to the broadcasting of pop music lyrics was gradually introduced, and by one more notch the handbrake of control was eased.

That same Saturday, a boatload of British teenagers sailed to France on a *Rock Across The Channel* trip, intent on showing the Froggies (as everyone called them) just how to rip it up. The event was co-promoted by the 2i's Coffee Bar and one of the ten acts providing its soundtrack was Terry Dene, a boy hotly hyped as 'Britain's newest rock 'n' roll star'. He'd been 'discovered' at the 2i's and was (mis)managed by its proprietors Hunter and Lincoln, they and an agent creaming 50 per cent of his earnings. Dene's career stumbled from the start, the result of a fragile personality and terrible handling, but his 'arrival' again fingered Soho coffee bars as the hotbed of British rock and skiffle talent. As Parlophone A&R manager George Martin disclosed to the *Daily Mirror*, 'I make a regular visit. It has become a breeding ground for talent. Six months ago I wouldn't have dreamed of going there.'[33]

Dene's first record wasn't even rock and roll: it was a cover of Marty Robbins' American country hit A White Sports Coat (And A Pink Carnation), and both versions were easily beaten in the charts by another British act, the King

Brothers. It became Paul McCartney and Ian James' theme song as they swanned around Liverpool in the early summer. Paul had a white sports 'drape jacket' with a metallic thread that sparkled slightly; Ian had a pale blue coat which passed for white if you didn't look too hard. Though they skipped the carnations, they thought themselves the song's living embodiment, *flash*, and with their narrow black trousers and hair set high felt sure girls would fall at their feet. Collins Fun Fair visited Sefton Park for Whitsun week (7–15 June) and Paul and Ian, after grooming themselves in the mirror, went along with twin goals: to score and to catch all the latest sounds.

Paul would always recall his first hearing of a perennial favourite: 'I remember being in Sefton Park when the fair came to town and standing beside the waltzers as they were spinning around, and playing there at full volume was a track by Charlie Gracie called Fabulous.'[34] Ian James adds, 'The waltzer span round and round and up and down at the same time. It was always a favourite attraction because you'd take a girl on it and probably her skirt would blow up, and she'd be screaming and throw her arms around you for protection. And they always played great music.'

While their day at the fair delivered on the musical front, Paul and Ian had no luck chatting up the birds. Nothing. It was such a comedown, and they trooped back to Ian's house deflated, even in their white sports coats. The route took them past a record shop where Ian splashed the cash for Elvis Presley's Hound Dog. Paul would always invoke this moment when enthusing about rock's recuperative powers. Though rejected and dejected, they got back to Elswick Street, put on Hound Dog and instantly felt great once again, revived in a shade over two minutes by the miracle doctor from Memphis. 'After Ian put it on I swear the blues had gone,' Paul would say. 'We were like new people.'[35]

While Paul and Ian were unsuccessful, the same fair, at perhaps the exact same moment, was proving triumphant ground for Richy Starkey. He and Roy Trafford, both in their best Ted togs, found a pair of assenting judies and, after treating them to a few rides and trinkets, managed to lose their virginity simultaneously on a nearby grass verge, within range of the fairground's evocative sounds and smells. Richy was immediately addicted to the new fruit. 'Once in and you want to live there,' he would say. 'It [sex] was always on my mind, for a long time.'[36]

As the GCE O-Level exams approached, the Quarry Men suddenly had a flurry of bookings. On the morning of Sunday 9 June, they were in the queue that snaked around the Liverpool Empire, a ragged line of guitars, washboards and tea-chests, their owners clinging to the hope of impressing an established star-making impresario. Here, literally, was the man with the cigar John Lennon had

been awaiting. Strangely, this great fan of Lewis Carroll was now pinning his
hopes on Carroll Levis.

Levis was a particular player in British show business for a quarter-century,
an overweight, silver-haired Canadian in a tailored Savile Row suit who'd abandoned his own career as a Variety entertainer (his act was hypnotism and
necromancy) and arrived in Britain in the mid-1930s to start a touring talent-
spot show. Winners of his stage show were offered a spot in his fortnightly ATV
series, and everyone was desperate to appear in front of the cameras – this gold-
plated gateway to riches and happiness. In these early days of television, if you
appeared 'on the box' in any capacity you were instantly *a star*, treated differently by people from the moment they next saw you. They'd stop and gawp in
the street, amazed that *a TV personality* was before their very eyes. Film was
something else – you had to be an actor to be in the movies – but TV could
pick up ordinary folk and make them famous.

Levis in the theatre was the usual twice-nightly affair, the first half of each
performance filled with professional Variety acts (some were past discoveries
who'd 'made it' . . . this far) and the second showcasing between twenty and
twenty-four acts of local amateur talent, each given a couple of minutes on
stage to grab what Levis called 'the chance of a lifetime'. He was looking for two
winners twice a night, assessed on the strength of the audience's applause when
all the acts returned for another bow at the end. There was no technical apparatus for measuring this, but with all Levis's experience he could tell a winner
instinctively.* The qualifiers from the first five nights would then battle it out
in the week's climactic show, second-house Saturday, Levis promising the
champion a step up to 'the stairway to stardom' – that is, a couple of minutes
on TV before vanishing up their own ether, never to be heard of again. It was
a right old show-business racket.

This being summer 1957, skiffle was overwhelmingly popular among the
aspiring stars. When the Quarry Men got into the Empire, John Lennon filled
out the necessary form and, after a long wait in the auditorium, they finally
stepped on to the mighty stage, scene of all those magical pantomimes of his
childhood. Levis sat at a table stage left, John said, 'We're the Quarry Men,'
and a couple of minutes later the great man said, 'That's fine,' and booked
them for the show proper, the week after next. So far, so good.

That big *TV Star Search* week was 17–23 June, coinciding precisely with

---

* Levis didn't use a 'clapometer' to measure the strength of audience reaction – this device was
deployed solely (in later years) by Hughie Green, yet another self-important and insincere Canadian
'starmaker' based in Britain.

O-Levels. No lists survive to relate who appeared when, but Richy Starkey would remember playing Empire talent contests with the Eddie Clayton Skiffle Group and this was probably one of them, while another combo to qualify for the show proper were the Ravin' Texans, a skiffle group led by Al Caldwell and his mate Johnny Byrne, a couple of lads who'd not (as their name implied) flown over from Fort Worth but hopped the bus down from Broad Green. Colin Hanton and Rod Davis remember the Quarry Men's appearance being the Wednesday night (19 June). This was it, then. Success here, and again on the Saturday, and they'd be *on television*.

Banjo player Rod says they played one number, It Takes A Worried Man To Sing A Worried Song. Drummer Colin recalls they had quite a few supporters in the audience, though not as many as another group who not only got more applause but were also, he says, mysteriously given the chance to play a second number. The Quarry Men drew less applause than one or two other acts and weren't chosen to proceed to Saturday's final. It was over. TV stardom had been an illusion. Levis told them to stick at it, and any lingering sorrow was drowned in a few pints of ale.

The Quarry Men had other bookings lined up. They'd been asked to play at the annual garden fete of their local Woolton church, St Peter's, on Saturday 6 July, and at the end of the Levis week, on 22 June, they performed from the back of a flatbed coal lorry parked in Rosebery Street, Toxteth. At least three photographs were taken of them here – the first ever images of John Lennon as a musician. He's playing the Gallotone Champion guitar that Julia was still paying off, and wearing the checked shirt she'd bought him, and he's singing/laughing into a microphone powered by a cable fed through the window of a house. A crowd has gathered to watch them and one of the faces is black: this is Liverpool 8, the West Indian neighbourhood.[37]

Nigel Walley has a memory of John changing the words to the songs he was singing, though he doesn't recall which ones. It's entirely believable. John on stage was doing to song lyrics what he did with poetry and prose: perverting the vocabulary, creating something funnier than the original, thinking on his feet, performing not only the music but humour to go with it. 'Part of me would sooner have been a comedian,' he acknowledged when aged 40, 'I just don't have the guts to stand up and do it.'[38] Curiously, changing the words while singing was also a trick of Alf Lennon's; though John is unlikely to have known it, his talent was a hairyloom.

None of this activity during the Quarry Bank exam period seemed to faze Rod or Eric, who did well in the O-Levels. In fact, it didn't derail John either, who effortlessly succeeded in doing just what he'd planned: nothing whatever. Though the results wouldn't be known until August, everyone at Quarry Bank knew that John Lennon was, as his despised Maths teacher K. I. Lishman had prophesied, 'on the road to failure'. So how *would* he be filling his days after July? John himself still had no idea and no plans. But, without his knowledge, his future was being shaped at this very time by an interested party, an empathetic soul who'd been moved to tears of laughter by John's still-circulating comic paper *Daily Howl*.

Philip Burnett, John's English master, was one of that ever-welcome breed of teachers able to spot talent where others see only trouble. John's stock among the Quarry Bank masters was set low but Burnett wasn't like his colleagues. After graduating from Magdalen College, Oxford, where his tutor was C. S. Lewis, he'd worked at a school in Paris before joining Quarry Bank at 26. Burnett's girlfriend June Harry, a 20-year-old student at Liverpool College of Art, first saw him when he was reading Yeats's poetry in the Studio Club, just off Slater Street. 'His dress sense was shabby traditional, and he had a penchant for carousing with ladies of dubious virtue in dock road pubs,' she says. 'He was as rebellious as it was possible to be for a young middle-class man whose dad was still in holy orders. He was 27 and a frustrated artist, and he was kind to a fault.'[39]

One bright warm evening in the summer of 1957 the lovers met at Ye Cracke, a little pub near the art college, and Burnett produced from his pocket a crumpled collection of confiscated cartoons and writings by 'a Quarry Bank boy'. He spread them out on the table. Did June, he wondered, think their creator merited a place at the art college?

> I was intrigued by what I saw. They weren't academic drawings but hilarious and quite disturbing cartoons. The one which has stayed with me ever since was of an elderly granny pushing a pram. But the pram wasn't normal – the hood was oversize, presumably to accommodate the enormous misshapen head of the unseen horror heaving under a quilt. The caption was 'Be a good boy cuddles, we'll soon be home'. John explored this idea a few times – I later saw a similar cartoon with the caption 'Oochie-coochie Raymond' only this time a grizzly old granny was leaning over the pram. I thought they showed an original sense of humour not unlike our own.
>
> Phil enjoyed John's slant on life. He told me, 'He's a bit of a one-off. He's bright enough, but not much apart from music and doing his cartoons interests him.' 'So then he's just right for art college,' I said, and Phil looked pleased, [saying] 'It could be the making of him.'

6

Come Go With Me (6 July 1957)

The *Evening Express* headlined it the way British newspapers must: PHEW!
AGAIN TODAY MERSEYSIDE SIZZLES. It had been the hottest June in south
Liverpool since records began in 1939, and on Saturday 6 July – as John Lennon
had forecast in his *Daily Howl* – the weather was muggy (if not followed by tuggy
and weggy). Inevitably, complainers about winter cold were griping about
the heat.

Lonnie Donegan was top of the *NME* chart again, with a live recording of
Putting On The Style from the London Palladium. He was now a fixture of
British light entertainment, elevated from the grass-roots scene his Rock
Island Line had inspired. Quite how many skiffle groups were active in the
summer of 1957 was, it seems, everyone's guess. Between four and five hundred in the London area alone, the press reckoned. No one really knew the
true number, or ever will, but five thousand groups for the whole of Britain
might be about right, something like twenty to thirty thousand players, many
of them using instruments that could have come from the rubbish tip.
'There's a lively indiscipline and lack of inhibition about skiffle that exactly
suits the moods of this generation,' reflected *The World's Fair*, while the
Observer pondered skiffle's popularity more broadly and concluded with a
telling question: 'The remarkable thing is that in an age of high-fidelity
sound, long-players and tape recorders, the young should suddenly decide to
make their own music. It is fantastic. What are they going to do with all those
guitars when the craze ends?'[1]

What indeed. For the majority of skifflers, rock and roll was of at least equal
appeal. The many church committees that benevolently acceded to teenagers'
desires that summer and booked skiffle groups for fetes and garden parties

were unwittingly inviting that most feared of beasts through the door. St Peter's church in Woolton was happy to accommodate the Quarry Men in its grounds and hall, not realising their leader would be shouting the music of the devil.

There was, suddenly, plenty of it about. The *NME* Top Thirty at the end of June 1957 included for the first time together Elvis Presley, Chuck Berry and Little Richard, added to which there was already a buzz about the British release (on Friday 5 July) of Bye Bye Love, the present number 2 in America, by a new duo called the Everly Brothers. The young were beginning to get a grip on the music scene.

John Lennon bought (or 'slap leathered') Elvis's All Shook Up c/w That's When Your Heartaches Begin as well as that new one by Little Richard, Lucille c/w Send Me Some Lovin'. Of all the great records made by Richard in the first flush of a long career, Lucille could be the best, swept along by an irresistibly insistent piano, guitar and sax riff and crowned by a vocal of fabulous emotional intensity. Paul McCartney loved Lucille right away, and it too went straight into the 'Little Richard act' he would burst into, unbidden, at any moment.

Paul had an arrangement this Saturday, invited by his Institute friend Ivan Vaughan to accompany him to Woolton's church fete. 'Ivy' said a couple of his friends were playing in a skiffle group, and of course there was the perpetual hope of picking up a girl. Despite the sweltering weather, that white sports coat got another airing.

The fete began with a procession, leaving the church and finding its way back there by a circuitous route around the village. The line was headed by a brass band, followed by marching Girl Guides, Boy Scouts, Brownies and Cubs, with decorated flatbed lorries for the other attractions led by the new Rose Queen (flanked by attendants and boy soldiers in uniform); her crowning was to begin the main festivities at 3PM. Aboard the final lorry, as far from the brass band as possible, were the Quarry Men, bookending the experience of the Vipers fifty-one Saturdays before, in July 1956, when they'd trundled around the streets of Soho singing what became Don't You Rock Me Daddy-O. Just as the Vipers had grown tired of trying to compete acoustically with all the engine noise, so too did the Quarry Men: Rod Davis's father took photos of the procession as it passed his house on Kings Drive and the Quarry Men are sitting around on chairs.

In Soho in 1956, the Vipers had jumped from their lorry outside the 2i's Coffee Bar and, playing a couple of numbers inside, unwittingly started the skiffle craze. The direct consequence was the Quarry Men at Woolton in 1957. And when they got down from their lorry at the church, in the field where they were playing beyond the cemetery, John Lennon was watched by Paul McCartney and it was the start of everything else.

After Paul cycled over from Allerton, he and Ivy walked up the hill to the church, Paul feeling hip (and hot) in his coat and specially narrowed trousers, Ivy explaining the make-up of the group and who Paul would be meeting. As they paid their threepence admission they could hear the Quarry Men playing and went straight up to see them. Here, then, were Ivan's friends – and, right off, the singer *had it*. He looked strong and assertive, clearly the leader, cool in his checked red and white shirt. Paul, the keen guitarist, watched the fingers and couldn't work out what chords he was playing, not yet realising they were banjo chords. And also he noticed the song . . . 'He was singing Come Go With Me, which I thought was fabulous until I realised they weren't the right words. He was changing them. "Come go with me . . . down to the penitentiary" – he was nicking folk-song words and chain-gang words and putting them into the Dell-Vikings' song, a clever little bit of ingenuity.'[2]

With regular retelling, it became easy to underestimate the hurricane force of this primary experience. Come Go With Me wasn't merely a song they both knew, it was a song *few* knew; it was hidden gold, a shared secret, a connector of connoisseurs. John didn't have the Dell-Vikings' record and nor did Paul; they both knew it only from listening in record-shop booths or from its occasional airplay on Decca's Luxembourg shows. John didn't know it enough to have learned the words, Paul only knew it enough to know the words John was singing weren't the real ones.

Frequently asked what he thought of John Lennon this first time he saw him, Paul McCartney inevitably came to develop a pat response, what he would call 'a cute story', rounding it off, giving it a nice ring. The truth was deeper. 'My [real] first impression was that it was *amazing* how he was making up the words. He was singing Come Go With Me by the Dell-Vikings and he didn't know *one* of the words. He was making up every one as he went along. I thought it was great.'[3]

On stage at about 4.15, the Quarry Men's set probably lasted half an hour. A *Liverpool Weekly News* reporter, who took their names and some background details for the following week's front-page report, wrote that they performed Cumberland Gap, Maggie May and Railroad Bill (yet another traditional American train song popularised in Britain by Lonnie Donegan); others present have added to that list Rock Island Line, Lost John, Putting On The Style and Bring A Little Water, Sylvie. When John sang Putting On The Style, in place of the line 'it's only our poor preacher, boys, putting on the style' he substituted 'it's only Mr Pryce-Jones, putting on the style' – a cheeky name-check of the vicar of St Peter's. Another song John messed

about with was the Vipers' latest single Streamline Train, which he decided
should be called Long Black Train. That was the skiffle element. It isn't
remembered which rock songs they played but there would have been at least
a couple of Elvis numbers and, as well as Come Go With Me, John would
recall singing Be-Bop-A-Lula here because it was the first time he performed
Gene Vincent's song.

With good fortune, Woolton boy Geoff Rhind was at the fete and had
brought his camera, and as a schoolfriend of four of the Quarry Men (John,
Pete, Eric and Rod) he took their photo. It was just one shot but it was perfect,
destined to be reproduced in thousands of publications, the definitive photo
of the group's first phase, taken the very day John Lennon met Paul McCartney.
Paul isn't in it, and the crowd gathered around the small stage, some of them
on the stage, are young children. John is looking straight into Rhind's lens, right
hand strumming the Gallotone so vigorously it's a blur; there's the checked
shirt bought by Julia, sleeves rolled up to the elbows, his hair is a messy tousled
quiff, and he's singing into the one microphone supplied as PA while five other
Quarry Men beat out the rhythm.

Ten years later, John would recall 'I seemed to disgust everybody that day',
but didn't explain why, beyond saying that Mimi was appalled he'd finally gone
all out and dressed as a Teddy Boy – which the photo clearly disproves.[4] She was
at the fete along with other family members, passing close by husband George's
grave as she walked through the church grounds.

Ivan Vaughan had known John since infancy. In some ways they were
markedly different characters, especially in the way they applied themselves at
school, but Ivan admired his gangleader's many talents and paid full respect.
Introducing other people to John was a role he carried out with care: only 'great
fellows' would do. One was Len Garry, who'd been accepted into both the gang
and the Quarry Men; and now there was another 'great fellow' for John to meet.
After the group's first set, John wandered across to the scout hut to leave his
guitar safe for a while, and it was here that Ivan introduced him to his school-
mate Paul McCartney. There wouldn't have been a handshake and there wasn't
much talk; Pete Shotton, never far from John's side, says Paul was quiet and
remembers a certain wariness – 'they were almost standoffish' – but then this
wasn't meant to be a summit encounter or a meeting of like minds, it was just
lads standing around gassing, probably about music or birds.[5] Paul felt self-conscious about his age: like Ivan, he'd turned 15 only three weeks earlier, whereas
John was clearly much older, well on his way to 17 – a veritable chasm, boy to
man. 'I was just the wrong side of the cusp and they were just the right side of
it. That's the way I remember feeling.'[6] Paul also realised he'd seen John
Lennon before. 'I saw him a few times before I met him – "Oh he's *that* feller,

the Ted who gets on the bus." You notice who's hip . . . I wouldn't look at him too hard [on the bus] in case he hit me.'*

The fete carried on while the lads tootled around, perspiring in the humid eighty-degree heat. Over here a crowd was enjoying a demonstration of obedience and obstacle training by Liverpool City Police dogs; over there children queued for rides on a toy car worked by the Boy Scouts. Hydrogen-filled balloons were released from the church field with a prize offered to the person whose balloon travelled furthest, there were three fancy-dress competitions for the kiddies, the brass band played, and there was the assortment of sideshows and stalls typical of any rural British fete, of which this – despite the events happening off to the side – was just another, no more, no less.

According to the programme, the Quarry Men had to play a further stage spot, probably for half an hour from 5.45 as the festivities were winding to a close, but no one can definitively remember if they played or not.

There was a fourth appearance of the day to come, but not until well after eight: they were booked as the small-print name at the church-hall dance over the road, the interval filler for the George Edwards Band, a small-unit dance band playing waltzes and foxtrots. So, there was now much hanging around. A couple of the Quarry Men went home for tea, but a cluster of boys – including John Lennon, Pete Shotton, Len Garry, Colin Hanton, Ivan Vaughan and Paul McCartney – kicked their heels inside the hall while it was being prepared for the dance. They hung around by the stage and also in a small ante-room to the left which had a piano.

As they lounged around, so the talk hit on music. Not one to hold himself back, Paul asked John for a go on his guitar, and noticing its strange banjo tuning suggested he could retune it. The way he held the instrument upside down prompted a few sniggers, but after a minute or two of fiddling Paul suddenly stopped and burst into Twenty Flight Rock. Here, right away, was talent, already way out of John's league. And it wasn't just that Paul could get through

---

* *Was Woolton fete the first time John met Paul? A riddle in two paragraphs.*
In certain private company, Paul sometimes reveals that he hadn't only seen John on buses before the Woolton fete, but they'd also exchanged a few words. Paul says he was working as a paper-boy (on his bike, delivering the *Echo* to local houses in the evenings) when he once talked to John outside the newsagent's shop. John never mentioned it, and Paul has chosen, consistently for decades, never to say it publicly. He was a paper-boy after the McCartneys relocated to Forthlin Road in summer 1956, when he turned 14.
Paul is shy about giving away the shop's identity to anyone who'd print it, but one local family who knew him think it was 'Abbas'. At 166 Aigburth Road, close to the Cast Iron Shore, W. W. Abba would have been an oddly distant place of employment for a lad living and delivering three miles away in Allerton, and – as it was a mile further still from John's house – it's far from being a cast iron certainty. For now, there's merely the possibility to digest that McCartney first met Lennon outside a shop called Abba.

the song from start to finish, singing with a strong rocking voice and playing
those chords with confidence, it was knowing all the words. Twenty Flight Rock
was *tricky* . . . and it was another connoisseur's piece. It hadn't made the charts,
so anyone who'd learned it had gone out of his way – an expedition made only
by the passionate, not something you can fake.

After this, Paul went into full exhibition mode, showing off, confident of his
ability and aware of his audience. He demonstrated one or two chords he thought
the gathering might not have heard, and he played them some other numbers
(Be-Bop-A-Lula was one, something by Elvis surely another). Then, showing real
neck, he switched to piano and started belting out his Little Richard routine,
yelling alone into the quiet of a cavernous church hall. Paul couldn't have known
it, but by slipping into Long Tall Sally he was sliding into John's main artery. That
constantly thrilling, screaming black voice of Little Richard Penniman was now
coming out of Ivan's little mate from Allerton. No matter how much John
affected an air of coolness, his insides had to be leaping. Bullseye. Paul
McCartney had impressed the guy on whom making an impression was suddenly
so vital. He'd set out to do it and he'd achieved it; a tad eager but trying to hide
it, his eyebrows raised, probably biting his lip, talking slightly too fast, switched
on, and good. Really good. None of the Quarry Men could do anything like this.

Villagers ambled into the hall shortly before eight, men in suits and ties but
short-sleeve shirts, ladies in summer dresses; and even more extraordinary than
Geoff Rhind happening to take their photo during the afternoon, the Quarry
Men's evening performance was recorded on a Grundig reel-to-reel tape
machine heaved down the hill from his home on Kings Drive by a member of
the Bible class and youth club, Bob Molyneux. He captured most of the music
performed by both dance band and skiffle group, using several spools of tape,
standing by the side of the stage with the recorder plugged into the mains and
the microphone in his hand. If anyone noticed him then no one remembered
it, and it wasn't until 1994, thirty-seven years after the event, that Molyneux
disclosed the astonishing fact, selling the sole surviving spool of Emitape (tape
manufactured by EMI) that hadn't been lost during intervening house moves.
It includes two Quarry Men songs: the current chart number 1, Putting On The
Style, and Baby Let's Play House – John Lennon doing Elvis in front of the
vicar. It's by some distance his earliest known recording, and though the fidelity
is poor, and the hall's high-gabled ceiling swamps the sound in a booming echo,
one can plainly hear John Lennon through the thud.

And this, even more than its highly improbable existence, is the most
extraordinary thing about the tape: that it is unmistakably *John Lennon*.
Although inspired by Elvis and Lonnie, he's not attempting to imitate their
voices or their style, and more strikingly still he's not adopting any phoney

American or mid-Atlantic accent. Singers always start off as impersonators, mimicking whoever made the record they're performing, some perhaps going on to develop their own voice. That John Lennon already had it at Woolton, that he was so audibly *himself*, is the mark of a true original. Not only does he have a great rock voice, it's an honest one. His voice is who he is.

It was all over by ten o'clock. Paul says he then went with Ivan, John, Pete and some others to a pub, the 15-year-olds trying their best to appear of drinking age, but then tripping into a panic when word somehow reached them that a local hard-knock was on his way and spoiling for a fight. They didn't hang around, returning in haste to Vale Road where Paul collected his bike and cycled off home to Forthlin Road.

The quandary for John Lennon was whether or not to invite Paul McCartney to join his group. 'Was it better to have a guy who was better than the people I had in – obviously – or not? To make the group stronger or to let me be stronger? And [my] decision was to let Paul in, to make the group stronger . . . It went through my head that I'd have to keep him in line if I let him join, but he was good, so he was worth having. He also looked like Elvis. I dug him.'[7]

When this happened is unclear. Until the final interview John gave, it was established that the process was a gradual one, spanning days or even weeks, but here he explained, 'I turned around to him [Paul] right then, on first meeting, and said, "Do you want to join the group?" and I think he said yes the next day, as I recall it.'[8]

Pete Shotton has a different memory. He says that when he and John walked home at the end of that long day, John said, 'What would you think if I invited Paul to join the group?' Pete said he didn't mind. 'About ten days to two weeks later I was walking down Linkstor Road and Paul came around the corner on his bike, and it was exactly there, on the corner of Linkstor Road and Vale Road, that he stopped and we spoke. He said, "I've come up to see Ivan but he's not in," and I said, "Oh by the way, do you want to join the group?" And he looked at me and he kind of thought for a moment, or *pretended* to think for a moment, and then he said "OK", got on his bike and rode off. And that was it.'[9] Deceived by the age gap, Pete had no idea Paul was about to become his rival for John's closest friendship.

John Lennon didn't pick partners easily, but at 15 years of age Paul McCartney already had enough about him to impress the big league. A boy who believed he was it, and had the ability to back it up, had met another boy who clearly was it – and the fusion of their talents and personalities would change the world.

7

'He'll get you into trouble, son'
(July–December 1957)

Location filming for a new movie, *Violent Playground*, got underway across Liverpool on the Monday after Saturday's Woolton fete. It was clearly the place to shoot films about juvenile delinquency: another, *These Dangerous Years*, had only been released the week before. In this, Liverpool-born singing star Frankie Vaughan, 29, badly miscast as a Teddy Boy, played a troubled Dingle adolescent in hot water with the police and (after his call-up) the army. As if it wasn't hard enough for boys like Richy Starkey, Roy Trafford and Ian James to survive growing up in Liverpool 8, they had to hear a policeman yelling from the big screen, 'You Dingle boys are a menace and a nuisance to the district! Why don't you get some honest work?'

Playing skiffle with Eddie Clayton introduced a welcome way out from the street-corner existence Richy Starkey had known more than a year. It would take a long time to remove himself completely, but being with a group was an alternative to 'walking' with the gang, and when he and Roy weren't doing one or the other they were often dancing. Both were athletic and acrobatic jivers, accomplished rock and roll dancers able to flip, flop and fly their female partners, hold them up in the air and send them scooting through their legs.

> Richy was a good jiver and so was I. We used to go to all the hops, to the Rialto and the Cavern, and girls liked to dance with us because we could do it. We had denim suits and denim jackets so the lads and girls in the Cavern called us 'the Binmen'. We had regular jiving partners and loved it. But we were seriously threatened in the Rialto one night. Some feller got stabbed in the face with a pair of scissors and I was told, 'You and your mate are next.'

We were out of there like a shot. We didn't like that at all. That was me and Richy – out the door.

Liverpool living required acute environmental awareness: things could alter in a moment, around any corner. But it was far from all bad. Paul McCartney always knew the pluses, saying (in 1984), 'I swear to God I've never met any people more soulful, more intelligent, more kind [and] more filled with common sense than the people in Liverpool, people who can cut through problems like a hot knife through butter. [They're] the kind of people you need in life: salt of the earth.'[1]

At some point in July 1957, Paul finally got his first guitar. It had been a long time coming and he was desperate. As he couldn't afford to buy one he had the bright idea of swapping his trumpet for it, the one his dad had bought him two years earlier. Jim didn't mind – it was clear where Paul's interest was. 'I traded in the trumpet for a £15 Zenith guitar from Frank Hessy's. There was a feller there called Jim Gretty and he showed us (me and George) a great chord. I never knew its name – we called it "a jazz chord", like an F-shape with a couple of extra things on the first and second string.'[2] The Zenith Seventeen was a reasonably good new guitar, cheaper but better than John Lennon's Gallotone Champion though it too was manufactured from laminates. An archtop acoustic with f-holes, it was made in Germany, and inside the body was a label individually signed by the respected jazz and classical guitarist Ivor Mairants, stating that the instrument had been tested by him to his standards. So longingly and lovingly did these boys cherish their first guitars that Paul would later say of Mairants 'he was a God to us', much as John would always think of his first guitar as GUARANTEED NOT TO SPLIT.[3]

Having only played other people's guitars before, the time had come for Paul to address the problem caused by his left-handedness. Like most guitars, the Zenith was made for a right-handed player, so as before he turned it upside down, everything opposite where it should be, the top string now on the bottom. This didn't stymie his natural talent – when Paul impressed John in St Peter's church hall he was playing guitar upside down – but it wasn't ideal. The solution came when Paul chanced on a photo of Slim Whitman, possibly in a music press advert but more likely in a record shop, and saw that, though he was playing left-handed, his guitar was strung correctly.* Paul went home, unwound

---

* The American country musician is posing with his instrument on the cover of the 1956 British LP *Slim Whitman And His Singing Guitar*. A photograph of Whitman had inspired George Harrison to buy his first guitar; another was now instrumental in determining how Paul McCartney played his.

all six strings from the Zenith and threaded them back in what would usually be the reverse order but which, when the guitar was turned upside down for a southpaw, was 'correct'.

It needed some fixing: the top E string rattled in the tailpiece hole designed for the bottom E string, so Paul shaved a matchstick and wedged it in. There was only one problem he couldn't remedy: the scratchplate (pickguard) was in the wrong place, above rather than below the strings, but this didn't affect the playing . . . which he now did, *constantly*. Mike McCartney has said of Paul and his first guitar, 'He would get lost in another world. It was useless talking to him – I had better conversations with brick walls.' Paul played the guitar every-where, even on the bus. At home he played it in the bath and sitting on the loo. 'The fine acoustic of the toilet area was always very appealing to me. And it was also very private, about the only private place in the house. I used to sit there for hours – there and the bathroom. Dad would shout, "Paul, get off that toilet!" [And I'd reply] "I'm practising!"'[4]

If the Quarry Men had bookings in this period, Paul wasn't part of them. Rod Davis has a recollection of Paul dropping in to see a group rehearsal at (of all places) Mimi's house, and Eric Griffiths says the group all went to Paul's house one afternoon for a rehearsal together – something Paul has never men-tioned. (Like almost everything to do with the Quarry Men, solid information is lacking.) The invitation to join them had come out of the blue for Paul, who'd never expressed an interest in being in a group. He had one ambition – 'to be like Elvis', to sing with a guitar and be a great star.[5] His need to impress John Lennon had been merely to show off what he could do, to stir someone whose own talent he admired. It wasn't an audition.

Paul had two sort-of partners at this time. Ian James says he and Paul struck up an informal musical duo: 'We used to take our guitars around to parties and play a few numbers. Have guitar will travel – wherever we went our guitars went too. We played songs from that first Elvis LP: Trying To Get To You, Lawdy Miss Clawdy, Mystery Train – the tendency was to go for the faster or more rau-cous ones. Nobody took any notice of us but I don't recall being thrown out of anywhere.' His other collaborator was brother Mike, who didn't have an instru-ment but was game to add harmony. Getting their voices together was something they'd started a year or so earlier, when Disney's *Lady And The Tramp* was first on release. According to Mike, they enjoyed harmonising on The Siamese Cat Song, which was their 'turn' at family parties.[6] Paul's acqui-sition of the Zenith coincided with the arrival in the British charts of the Everly Brothers' Bye Bye Love; Paul became Don and Mike was Phil as they learned the parts together, Disney cartoon fun relegated in favour of this more mature piece.

On the last day of the school year, Paul took his Zenith into Liverpool Institute for the first time and treated his mates to the Little Richard act. 'All the class gathered round as I stood on the desk and did Tutti Frutti, I think it was.'[7] Although Paul was friends with George Harrison, enough sometimes to visit one another's houses and play music, year-by-year divisions at school held strong: boys stayed strictly within their own forms. Paul and George weren't great mates – when Ivan Vaughan asked Paul to go to Woolton fete, Paul didn't think to extend the invitation to George, no more than George had asked Paul to be a Rebel in their one and only performance.

This same last day of term, while Paul was doing his Little Richard act, George may well have been entertaining his own crowd. (He did in 1958. It's not clear whether it happened in 1957 too.) It was around this time that George ditched his ropey old Egmond and splashed out on his first really good guitar. Though younger than Paul, he was always at least one step ahead guitar-wise. The new model was another acoustic, a Hofner President, endorsed in music press ads by Tommy Steele and on sale for a handsome 32 guineas.[8] It represented a considerable upgrade, one careful owner having no plans to drive it beyond 25 Upton Green, but George's passion for guitars had so eclipsed everything in his life that the price didn't seem to matter, provided he could pay it off. He now spent most of his school lessons drawing impressive little sketches of guitars in his exercise book – cello guitars with f-holes (like his new President) and little solid-bodied guitars with cutaways – and when he wasn't doing this he was imagining himself playing one: '[I was] looking out the window, thinking about how I could be practising a guitar, while they were trying to teach me Pythagoras.'[9]

The curtain came down on John Lennon's five eventful years at Quarry Bank on 24 July. The O-Level results wouldn't be through for another few weeks but Mimi wasn't waiting: she went up to Quarry Bank for a meeting with the headmaster. Mr Pobjoy made the error of asking her what she was going to do with John after he left, and she shot back, 'No, what are *you* going to do with him? You've had him five years, you should have his future ready.' The head had just one thought, the one pressed on him by his enthused English master Philip Burnett: that John should go to Liverpool College of Art. Pobjoy relayed this to Mimi and offered to write a letter of reference. 'I had to say that he was "suitable" without doing too much violence to my conscience,' he would recall.[10]

John wasn't especially keen on the idea of going to college, but he had no other plans and it would put off having to work for a few more years. In their final meeting, Quarry Bank's headmaster told him frankly that if he didn't go then he may as well 'give up life'. John bristled at that, but agreed to assemble a small portfolio of material and go along for an interview, which he did in his late Uncle George's suit, shirt and tie. 'I thought it would be a crowd of old men but that I should make the effort to try and make something of myself ... [I had] an idea I might finish up drawing gorgeous girls for toothpaste posters.'[11] A letter arrived at Mendips soon afterwards, offering him a position on a four- to five-year course. His tuition fees would be free until the academic year 1959–60 and Mimi agreed to finance all his materials and daily expenses, and also to continue to provide at home. She'd come to John's rescue again, and tied herself to maintaining him to some extent until he was 20. This wasn't the future she'd foreseen when he started at Quarry Bank in 1952, but in the words of the popular phrase she herself uttered with some frequency, *any old port in a storm.*

Sales of skiffle records had petered out by autumn 1957 as the genre exhausted itself, but grass-roots interest remained, especially on Merseyside: whatever the musical fashion, it's always first in/last out in Liverpool. Richy Starkey was getting good experience as the drummer with the Eddie Clayton group, whose prowess as one of the best in town was emphasised when they qualified for the final of the Cavern's summer skiffle competition on the evening of 31 July, along with another local group, the Bluegenes. It was a big night for the new club, including too the Miss Cavern bathing beauty contest, which spectacle may be the cause of no one being able to recall the winning group. Another could be the drink: the Cavern was always a night on the town for Richy and Roy. As Richy would say, 'At the Cavern we'd get a pass-out, go to the pub – and then go back in and pass out.'[12] Though underage, they knew where they'd be all right. 'The Lisbon on Victoria Street and the Beaconsfield on North John Street were our regulars,' says Roy. 'We drank black velvet – pints of cider and Guinness mixed, and rum and blacks [blackcurrant] if we had any money. You think you can drink it all at that age – molten lead, anything – but we were only young lads and we'd be falling asleep when we went back in the Cavern. I didn't smoke but Richy did. He tried to get me on it but I just didn't like it. He hardly ever had one out of his hand.'

One week later, on 7 August, the Quarry Men played the Cavern again, and this time – for the first time – they were named in the *Liverpool Echo* ads.* Rod Davis wasn't there because he'd gone on holiday with his parents, and come September there'd be an unspoken parting of the ways. Where once there'd been four Quarry Men at Quarry Bank High School now he was the only one; out of sight, out of mind, Rod's days in the group were over. Also, Pete Shotton

---

* Regardless of genre – skiffle, jazz, folk, blues, rock – the *Echo* advertised all musical attractions under the generic heading 'Jazz'.

was making one of his last appearances. John had a way of making it plain if he felt someone wasn't up to scratch musically: in Pete's case, he engineered a blazing argument while they were out riding their bikes. Then, when the group played at a private party, they both got completely drunk and John smashed the washboard over Pete's head. Its centre section was pushed right out, leaving it framed around Shotton's neck. 'That solves that then, Pete,' the leader declared. Their great friendship – the bulwark in John's life since the year he'd turned six – would remain intact, but it was weakened by events. Now they'd left Quarry Bank, their lives headed in separate directions: John went to art college and Pete into the police force, a career choice that came as a complete shock to John, who greatly scorned it. And now that he was leaving the group, Pete's place at John's side on stage was taken by Paul McCartney. John and Pete would never forget the hundreds of great times they'd shared as the very best of buddies, but they were approaching the end of a chapter. And the Quarry Men, a six-piece group when Paul was invited to join them, was now a five-piece group with him: John, Eric, Paul, Len and Colin.

This Cavern booking would have been Paul's Quarry Men debut but for him being away with the Boy Scouts at summer camp – another ten days of wet feet, wind and Woodbines. The 19th City troop's destination this year was the Peak District – Callow Farm, Hathersage, Derbyshire – and both McCartney brothers went. Paul (inevitably) carted his Zenith along with his sleeping bag and tin mug. Almost as soon as they'd pitched tents, Mike had an altercation with an oak tree, badly breaking his arm; he was taken to hospital in Sheffield while Paul remained at the camp and entertained around the fire with Elvis's Trying To Get To You.[13]

Mike was in hospital four weeks, his plastered arm in a sling, and on the day of his release – the last full week of the school holidays – Jim arrived in Sheffield with Paul and revealed they were all heading straight off to Butlin's. Bett and Mike Robbins had fixed them seven days at Filey, on Yorkshire's east coast. Both were working there for the summer, Mike as a Redcoat and Bett as general factotum: it was her jolly voice that began each day with 'Wakey-wakey! Rise and shine, campers!' crackling over the Tannoy.

Ever the keen photographer, Mike operated the camera singlehandedly to take a fascinating photo of Paul on Filey beach with Bett Robbins and her infant son Ted. Paul is perched on Ted's pushchair and playing the much-travelled Zenith. The photo could be the closest taken to the date he met John Lennon, showing a 15-year-old who's come through his chubby period and is looking good: slim and like a real teenager – no longer a boy, not yet a man. He's wearing his white sports coat and his hair is piled high off the forehead, a keen youngster singing Elvis into the North Sea breeze at Filey Bay.[14]

A hero to the McCartney boys, Mike Robbins supervised the thrice-weekly morning auditions for campers wishing to try their luck in Butlin's National Talent Contest (sponsored by the *People* newspaper). Paul, probably in his white sports coat, urged Mike to go up with him, but Mike, technically too young anyway at 13, didn't feel like it, pointing out that he'd look a bit of a berk with his arm in a sling. Paul walked alone to the stage with his guitar, but just as Robbins was about to introduce him he whispered something . . . whereupon Robbins announced, 'This youngster is going to be joined on stage by his brother, a lad with a broken arm, so give him an extra round of applause!' Against his better judgement, realising Paul had yet again engineered just what he wanted, Mike went up and joined him. Robbins urged the audience to 'give a big hand for the McCartney Brothers' and they went into their Bye Bye Love duet. Then, says Mike, 'As soon as we'd finished and Paul's confidence had returned he shoved me off and went straight into his Little Richard routine.'[15] On whatever grounds the contestants were judged, the McCartneys – single-act or duo – got no further in the competition. However, it was here, around the last day of August 1957, at the Gaiety Theatre on site at Butlin's, Filey – rather than in the Cavern, Liverpool – that Paul McCartney first appeared on stage as a rock and roller.[16]

The Butlin's week came at a crunch time for Paul. He'd received his GCE results, and having taken Spanish and Latin a year earlier than most boys, he passed only the former. In the coming school year he'd go into the Removes, not progressing into the Lower Sixth like so many of his friends and contemporaries. Effectively, he was being kept back, stuck with boys a year younger, and he deeply resented both this and his lack of choice in the matter. In fact, Paul so hated it he considered quitting school completely – and being 15, he could have done. Jim felt sure Paul had failed Latin deliberately because he'd made such a strong point about it being necessary for university entrance – a proud attainment for a working-class family. 'He was always good at Latin but when I said he'd need the Latin for university he started slacking up. When he knew what was in my head Paul tried to stop himself doing well.'[17] Jim was certain Paul should stay on at school, and the Institute felt the same; while this made Paul think even harder about leaving, he didn't because he couldn't imagine what job he would do, and he wanted as much time as possible to play guitar.

Paul later described being in the Removes with younger boys as 'horrible', but it's no coincidence that from September 1957 he suddenly became much closer to George Harrison.[18] (George was now in class U5E. Paul was in RB, as were mates Neil Aspinall and Len Garry.) The curtain that had kept them apart was lifted, and there was a general shift in all Paul's school relationships.

Separated in their daily activities, Paul and Ian James lost the closeness in their friendship and it became Paul and George instead. Ian was surprised by this. 'They seemed totally different personalities. George always seemed a bit moody, morose, whereas Paul was light-hearted – he probably could have been a comedian if he'd wanted, he can tell a tale so well. George was nothing like that. I found it really strange that they were friends. He and Arthur Kelly were hard-knocks: George always walked round with long hair and wore drainpipe trousers to school, and probably beetle-crusher shoes.'[19]

Paul didn't replace Arthur Kelly as George's closest mate but was happily admitted to the circle, as Arthur remembers:

> Paul was great. He was full of fun and *desperate* to be Elvis. He did all the hair and everything, and he had a similar facial look, only he was prettier than Elvis. He didn't sag off like George and I did but we'd always see him in smokers' corner, and he drew great cartoons of members of staff – as soon as you looked at them you knew who they were. I stood next to Paul in assembly. There'd be the lesson for the day and the headmaster's speech, when he named whoever he wanted to thrash with his cane, and in every hymn we sang I never heard Paul sing the melody – he always did the harmony line. I used to stand there and think, 'How the fuck does he do that?'[20]

Paul and George's friendship was not a perfect fit. Paul had a need to remind George, one way or another and often without much subtlety, that he was 'nine months older', ensuring George didn't forget who held the aces. George, meanwhile, was still hitting out when he felt the need. Living on the Speke estate was keeping him 'handy', as the saying went. One day Paul was in the playground with Keith Ritson ('Ritter') – a boy his own age but now in the Lower Sixth – when George wandered along and Paul introduced them. For no reason, or a reason Paul never knew, George suddenly head-butted Ritter. 'Young George was a bit of a terror – him and his quiff,' says Paul. 'We were all talking and this guy must have said something to annoy him, so *bouff*, he nutted him.'[21]

Musically, Paul and George and the other more hip 'Inny' students had loads to talk about again this new term. Great new artists were pouring from that ever-open valve America. The Everly Brothers – siblings from Shenandoah, Iowa – sang in unusual harmony, parallel thirds, taking lines that could stand alone but sounded better blended. From the first strum of Bye Bye Love, their charmingly melodic country/rock ode to teenage romance, they had the top respect of every aficionado. Its impact on Merseyside was notable: while the record had entered the *NME* Top Thirty at 19, impressive in itself, it went straight in at the top of Disker's local *Liverpool Echo* list. (There was also much respect for its B-side, I Wonder If I Care As Much.)

Like so many of the new stars – Gene Vincent with Be-Bop-A-Lula, Elvis Presley with That's All Right Mama, Eddie Cochran with Twenty Flight Rock and Carl Perkins with Blue Suede Shoes – the Everlys hit the ground running with their first release, as did the Coasters, a distinctive black vocal group from Los Angeles whose debut on the New York label Atco gave parent company Atlantic Records its first US million-seller. Issued in Britain on 12 July, Searchin' c/w Young Blood was another of those imperative buried treasures: in terms of British sales it made almost no splash, but it gave deep joy to a dedicated few, establishing a prolonged interest not only in other Coasters records but also in the wittily inventive and quirkily rhythmic songs of composing team Leiber-Stoller, who could write rock and roll as radio melodrama.*

There was also a singer called Larry Williams, whose record Short Fat Fannie was clearly in the Little Richard vein and, judging by the wording on the London record label, came from the same source, Specialty Records of Hollywood. And then there was a stunning piece from a singer whose name was as new as his sound: Jerry Lee Lewis. Whole Lotta Shakin' Goin' On was released in Britain at the end of August in perfect time to be number 1 in schoolyard conversation. Here the London label said 'Recorded by Sun, Memphis' so its pedigree was definitely A1, coming from the same studio as Carl Perkins and Elvis. It wasn't a guitar tune either, it was piano, a thumping boogie with Lewis rolling his hands up and down the keys. Paul was soon unleashing it from the piano at 20 Forthlin Road ... much to Jim's restrained disdain. As Paul recalls, 'Dad didn't like rock and roll, but [because] his dad didn't like *his* music he was very tolerant – he knew I had to do something he wasn't going to like. He'd say, "That's very nice, son," but he never really liked it.'[22]

Paul and George had a quota of anecdotes from these early days of a strengthening friendship, like the time they heard how someone had a copy of the Coasters' Searchin' and made a long bus journey to Bootle or Kirkby or Knotty Ash (it varies in the telling but apparently it involved two changes) simply to ask this person if he'd play it to them. Why they didn't just buy it is never explained. However, as Paul once confessed, having accepted the generosity of this stranger, who let them sit in the living room and listen to his record, they relieved him of its ownership, doing a runner with the precious disc

---

* The record spent one week on the NME Top Thirty, at number 30, two months after release. The B-side title, Brooklynese for 'young chick', was sometimes written as Youngblood.

stuffed under a jacket.[23] Another of Paul's warm anecdotes is the one where he and George heard about somebody in a distant Liverpool suburb who knew the chord B7; again, they got out the bus map, planned a route, knocked on the unknown door and asked the man to show them.

How much any of this would have happened had Paul not been kept back in the Removes can only ever be speculation, but the consequence of another fact coinciding in September 1957 is resoundingly clear: it was John Lennon's enrolment at Liverpool College of Art that would bind the three close together. John had invited Paul to join his group and Paul was now close friends with George, and five days a week all three rode the bus from their respective suburbs into Hope Street to spend their days in adjoining buildings.

John Lennon's O-Level results were worse than even he expected. Here he was, going to art school, and he hadn't even passed in Art, in which he had such a gift. Pobjoy, Quarry Bank's headmaster, says he failed them narrowly, and John remarked ten years later that he managed to keep the results from Mimi: she believed he'd passed at least one and he let her think it.[24] But none of this mattered: he was accepted into Liverpool College of Art and on 16 September 1957 stood on the threshold of a whole new adventure.

The first challenge was what to wear. Apart from the optional art school scarf (blue, yellow and black), there was no uniform – students could dress how they liked. John wanted to wear jeans on the first day, and to avoid a scream-up with Mimi had them under another pair of trousers which he slipped off at the bus stop opposite Mendips. For a jacket, he wore his Quarry Bank blazer with the badge ripped off and the collar turned up.[25] From day two he kept people guessing: he was a Teddy Boy one day and a typical collegian the next, or just plain scruffy in his greasy hair and Uncle George's old tweed overcoat. Fellow student Bill Harry spotted John straight away and was impressed by his individuality. 'Everyone was dressed the same: navy blue, fawn or black duffel-coats, green polo-neck sweaters, and there was John Lennon striding around with a DA haircut, brothel-creepers, drape jacket. It was as if a Teddy Boy had walked in off the street into this strange place where everyone else was dressed the same.'[26]

Beyond its walls, out there in the public mind, art school students were young layabouts or just plain rebellious, but these were really quite polite radicals; they came generally from grammar schools and a variety of backgrounds across the social spectrum, some working-class, others middle-class from upmarket homes. There were boys who planned to become art teachers or were just putting off work for a few years; there were girls talented enough for a career in art or design, or who were merely filling in time between school and the duties of a housewife and mother, sent to college by parents who didn't want them working in shops before they married. Several had been students at the Junior College of Art across the street, on Gambier Terrace, and were less inclined to challenge the thinking. For John there was abundant scope and temptation to shock here, and it wouldn't take him long to kick off. Says another contemporary, Ann Mason, 'Art college was the perfect breeding ground for someone like John, a burster of bubbles. It was the only place that was both liberal and creative.'

Excepting the fact that membership of Sulca (Students' Union Liverpool College of Art) was compulsory, art school offered freedoms unknown to any maverick schoolboy. Students not only dressed how they pleased, they could also smoke in class, come and go from the premises, and drink in the pub at lunchtimes, often with the tutors. There was an expectation that the work must meet a certain standard, but the skilled skiver (and we know his name) could usually find a way out. The first year was a probationary period, not overly taxing: students were expected to learn perspective, an introduction to architecture, simple lettering, elements of design, modelling and craft ... and Life Drawing, which entailed lengthy study of the female nude – a great thrill, until it wore off.

John was one of only two boys from Quarry Bank's class of '57 to progress to art school, so during his years here he formed an entirely new social circle – not all coming right at the start, some developing slowly over time. John would befriend Bill Harry, and Bill would introduce him to his friend Stuart Sutcliffe, whose best friend was Rod Murray. As well as his former Quarry Bank alumnus Geoff Cain, one of John's earliest and most important friendships at art school was with Tony Carricker, whose passion for American music, especially rock and roll and rhythm and blues, had led to an outstanding record collection; and it was through Tony that John became close with a fascinating and complex individual named Jeff Mahomed. Then there was Derek Hodkin and Jon Hague, and for the first time since puberty John was in school with girls, among them Ann Mason, Mona Harris, Pat Jourdan, June Harry, Helen Anderson and Cynthia Powell. They would all be spending their final teenage years together in the college's large, light, airy rooms, sharing a wealth of experiences, seeing one another at their best and their worst – and all of them would have ample cause to remember John Lennon.

The ranks of Liverpool's college-going students were also swollen at this same time by Richy Starkey. Strange but true. From the second year of his five-year apprenticeship at H. Hunt & Son he was expected to attend a part-time course in engineering, studying towards a National Certificate. Though he'd hated school, Richy was happy to go because it was day-release – one day a week away from the factory, a day out, almost a day off. Instead of heading as usual to Windsor Street he took the bus down to Aigburth, to the area where he hoped to live one day, just beyond Liverpool Cricket Club, and joined the students heading into Riversdale Technical College. The college liked to encourage day-release students to take on evening study too, but Richy wasn't going to do that. He'd show them his face in work hours but he wasn't going to give up leisure time: he wanted to be out and about, drumming with Eddie, drinking and jiving with Roy.

Paul McCartney first played on stage with John Lennon and the Quarry Men the night of Friday 18 October 1957, in New Clubmoor Hall, situated in a little alley called Back Broadway, near Norris Green in the north end of Liverpool.[27] Also known as Maxwell Fyfe Hall (after the Conservative MP for Liverpool West Derby, Sir Maxwell Fyfe), it was the social venue of the Clubmoor Conservative Men's Club and a long way from home for the five of them, Paul being only 15 and all. Nigel Walley fixed the booking with Charlie McBain, the promoter who gave the Quarry Men more engagements than any other, though his opinion of their merit was definitely mixed: on the back of one of the group's business cards given to him by Walley he pencilled 'Good & Bad'.

Probably both aspects were reflected in this performance at New Clubmoor Hall, about which little is remembered save for one anecdote. During rehearsals, John and Paul decided one of their numbers should be Guitar Boogie by Arthur Smith and his Cracker-Jacks, and that Paul would handle the solo.* He was clearly the best guitarist in the group, better than John or Eric, and what did the best guitarist do if not play the solo in the middle of the song? Not for the first time in his life, however, the boy who routinely transmitted cheery confidence was suddenly beset by grand-scale nerves.

> My very first Quarry Men gig, at the Conservative Club in Broadway, was a disaster because I got sticky fingers and blew the solo in Guitar Boogie, which is one of the easiest things in the world to play ... I was just too frightened; it was too big a moment with everyone looking at the guitar player ... It's a twelve-bar and I just couldn't do it. The fingers stuck to the fretboard and wouldn't lift off, and I sweated and blushed. After that I said 'Forget me on lead' and I never played lead again on stage. It wiped me out as a lead guitar player, that night.[28]

---

* No one recalls where or when these rehearsals took place, or how many times; presumably it was once the school year began, say from mid-September.

There's no photograph to show what the Quarry Men looked like at this time, but one was taken when they came back to the hall five weeks later, on 23 November.[29] In images of the Quarry Men before Paul joined they're all wearing different clothes. In the first photo of the group with Paul they have a uniform look, and a sharp one at that: white shirts with black bootlace ties and black trousers, and John and Paul (only) are also wearing jackets on top, white or cream – it's Paul's 'white sports coat' and something similar John has managed to acquire. This was undoubtedly Paul's doing, reaching back to his experience at Butlin's in 1954 when he saw how a singing group in matching gear claimed everyone's attention. He'd brought the thinking early to John, and John had bought it. And something else is compelling about this Quarry Men photo: although it's John's group, new boy Paul is not at the back with Colin or Len, or to the side like Eric, he's up front with John. Lennon and McCartney are clearly the front line of the Quarry Men, strumming crummy Gallotone and upside-down Zenith, and they're the only ones with vocal microphones. The group is the two of them and three others. When one sings lead the other provides harmony; often they sing the lead in unison – and their voices go together.

One can only surmise what they sang into those microphones. Nigel Walley remembers plenty of rock in the repertoire in this period and not so much skiffle, including several Elvis numbers – All Shook Up, Blue Moon Of Kentucky, Heartbreak Hotel, Hound Dog, Lawdy Miss Clawdy, That's All Right Mama and Trying To Get To You – as well as Be-Bop-A-Lula, Blue Suede Shoes (Carl or Elvis), Come Go With Me and Twenty Flight Rock. All American songs, of course. Paul did some Little Richard – Long Tall Sally, Tutti Frutti, and probably Lucille – and John, who wanted to do Little Richard but couldn't sing high enough, found it easier to sing Larry Williams instead, taking on Short Fat Fannie. Not all of these were played this evening, although as the main act in Charlie Mac's *Liverpool Echo* advert they may have performed for an hour.

The hairiest part of the evening, as it would always be, was getting there and getting home again. Colin remembers John and Paul carrying their guitars without cases or bags, just the guitars, playing and singing upstairs on the bus as it wended its way to the city's northern suburbs. Colin put his drums in a large brown suitcase which he shoved under the stairs before going up for a ciggie with John, Paul, Len and Eric. Norris Green was a rough area: Teddy Boys and other hard-knocks claimed the streets. On 16 August Richy Starkey was here with the Clayton group, and they were set upon by a gang of fifteen thugs; in the melee, apart from all the bones that crunched, Eddie's handsome guitar was nabbed. In keeping with his prowess as one of the best players around, he'd just had it fitted with a pickup, going electric, so it was a devastating loss. Roy Trafford's sister wrote a letter to George Harrison, the *Evening Express* columnist, and he publicly appealed for the thug to surrender it. Six days later Harrison was able to publish good news: he was now in possession of the guitar, returned by the boy's mum, a divorced mother of six who didn't want her lad getting mixed up in any trouble.[30]

Another song highly likely to have been in the Quarry Men programme that first night was the Crickets' That'll Be The Day. Number 1 in America when issued in Britain, it came with built-in excitement. On the day that'll be, 20 September 1957, *The World's Fair* printed a unique notice, boxed and emboldened to attract the attention of the entire juke-box business: 'This will be really big in boxes for months to come. Be among the first to order. It will be a sell-out.'[31] It was no empty rhetoric: That'll Be The Day was as much a sensation among British boys as anything by Elvis Presley or Little Richard. If one can nail down a specific moment that the whole pop group business – the whole rock band industry – kicked off in Britain, it was when the needle dropped into the first groove of That'll Be The Day and boys were grabbed by its distinctive ringing guitar intro. The record came at the perfect time. Just when skiffle was fading, limited by sameness of repertoire and sound, all these grass-roots musicians – all these thousands of singers, guitarists and drummers around the country – suddenly discovered a whole wonderful new field to play in.

Big in America, the Crickets were so much bigger in Britain. Rock and roll was full of solo singers with backing musicians – Elvis, Little Richard, Jerry Lee Lewis, Carl Perkins, Gene Vincent, Chuck Berry, Eddie Cochran and the rest. The only group of note was the Coasters, and not many knew them yet; besides which, they were just vocalists with session musicians. The Crickets were another kind of group: vocals, electric guitar, bass, drums. When thousands of skifflers heard That'll Be The Day, those eternally uplifting two minutes, they were *converted*. It was like a well-drilled, willing and equipped army being given a new battle plan.

The Crickets certainly arrived at the right time for the Quarry Men. Without Rod Davis and Pete Shotton, they'd lost their banjo and washboard and were almost a skiffle group no longer, just three guitars, bass (tea-chest) and drums. Here was the big transition. In a letter of unqualified praise that John Lennon once typed about Buddy Holly, he went into capital letters to emphasise the point: 'EVERY GROUP TRIED TO BE THE CRICKETS'.[32]

Six weeks after release, That'll Be The Day was the bestselling record in Britain, and in Liverpool it got there in half that time, holding down the top spot in Nems' published chart well into November. It sold purely on sound: no one knew who the Crickets were, which area of America they came from or what they looked like. This knowledge only came when the record was already a hit, when the *NME* ran a feature article. So . . . there were four of them, they came from Texas, and the lead singer was an odd-looking bod in glasses (wire at this point, but by early 1958 black horn-rimmed) with the equally strange but desirously American name of Buddy Holly. His group's name was great too, admired in Britain for a punning dimension unrealised back home: it wasn't just the insect, it was also the sport; how very clever. It led to every kind of painfully contrived headline, like when the *NME* announced that Lew & Leslie Grade had signed them to a British tour in early 1958: CRICKETS TO BAT IN BRITAIN.[33]

Until now, John Lennon and Paul McCartney had soaked up rock and roll's small canon independently. That'll Be The Day was the first song they absorbed and learned together – the right song with the right sound arriving at exactly the right time. They loved the performance, the electric guitar, the harmonies, the lead singer's distinctive vocal style (with a kind of hiccup on certain phrases), and they were impressed with the name 'Crickets'. Paul says that when he first heard That'll Be The Day he didn't know if the singer was black or white and it didn't matter, he was simply electrified by its sound. This more than any other was the song that turned Paul on to the combination of guitar and vocal harmony.[34] John and Paul already knew their voices blended in an exciting way, and with That'll Be The Day they learned how to take parts. Paul's voice was naturally higher than John's, and his ear for melody and harmony, acquired through all those years of listening to Jim Mac's piano songs, meant he generally found the right notes without any difficulty.

Since getting his guitar, John had been only vamping, using the wrong chords; That'll Be The Day was the first pop/rock song he learned to play on his Gallotone, shown to him by Paul – and also, according to one (possibly suspect) quote, his mother. Apparently, Julia went through the song with him, demonstrating the tune on banjo while he tried to copy it on guitar. 'She made me go through it over and over again until I had it right. I remember her slowing down the record so that I could scribble out the words.'[35]

Through the last weeks of 1957, John and Paul began to see each other more frequently, socially and always with their guitars. They'd formed a strong connection; while they would see the other Quarry Men when they had bookings, or were rehearsing, they got together more often as a twosome, each finding out who the other was. It didn't take long for Paul to point out that the chords John was playing weren't proper guitar chords. Paul's dad then told John they weren't even proper banjo chords, though John felt sure they were – a conversation which was probably fairly abrupt and which got John and Jim's relationship off to a bad start, Paul's dad unwittingly maligning the banjo knowledge of John's mum. Paul showed John the guitar chords he knew, including that magical B7 recently learned (with his little friend George) from a distant stranger. He encouraged John to study his fingers, to jettison the banjo notes and learn the proper positions on the fretboard. It was a complicated and slow business, John copying Paul's fingers and then reversing them for the right-hander.[36]

The first time John turned up at 20 Forthlin Road, his new friend's younger brother happened to be gazing out of the window. 'By a million to one chance I'm in the front parlour and I just looked up and saw this Teddy Boy,' Mike McCartney would recall. '"Wow, he looks good!" He had sidies and drainies, and "Hold on ... he's coming down our path" – past me dad's lavender bush. "He looks good!"'[37]

Jim McCartney was nowhere near so enamoured. John wasn't your typical polite and respectful visitor, he was who he was, edgy and sarcastic. He knew manners but didn't necessarily use them, any more than he automatically showed respect to his elders. (He may also have let Jim see his 'crip' antics once or twice, because he was as liable to burst into them as Paul was to suddenly break into his screaming Little Richard voice.) Since primary-school days, parents had warned their children to 'keep away from that John Lennon', and Jim saw that here was *a character*. He knew his sort – Liverpool was full of them, and Jim was a man of the world – but this lad breezing into his house was a Teddy Boy, and everyone knew Teddy Boys were delinquents. Associating with John could well turn Paul into one, and this was all happening at a bad time, when Paul had just suffered that setback at school.

Jim was trying so hard to prevent Paul from becoming a Ted, even by (he thought) controlling the trousers he wore, and now Paul had gone and become friendly with one. Jim strongly disapproved of the way John dressed: his DA, his sideburns, his drape jacket, his drainies, his shoes. The boy was clearly going to be a bad influence. Mary probably wouldn't have had him in the house. Jim, determined to stand by his axiom of 'toleration and moderation', stopped short of banning him, but he made it plain to Paul that John wasn't welcome and urged him not to get involved, cautioning, 'He'll get you into trouble, son.'[38]

Right from the off, being John Lennon's friend presented challenges to Paul. But while he didn't court disapproval, he wasn't going to jettison a vital new friendship just because his dad didn't like him. The Latin exam failure had confirmed to Jim that his eldest son always rebelled when told what to do or think – 'It annoyed me when even my *dad* told me what to do,' Paul has said – and the outcome was invariably the same: he'd dig in his heels and do whatever he was being advised against, even to his own detriment. Nevertheless, maintaining the peace at home and a friendship with John would require diplomacy and skilful timing on Paul's part; it would mean keeping John out of Jim's way and evading John's repeated urgings: 'Face up to your dad! Tell him to fuck off!'[39]

Lennon and McCartney could not have come together at a more fertile time. Each enjoyed the other's great passion for Elvis. *Loving You*, his first starring movie, played at the Gaumont in Liverpool at the end of October. Unlike *The Girl Can't Help It*, it ran only a week, but it was compulsory viewing for every Presley fan. For the first time, British audiences could watch him sing, gyrate and sneer – all in glorious Vista-Vision Technicolor. Boys studied all his moves and aped his every mannerism, especially those slackly curled lips; aspiring guitarists watched the fingers; girls panted or just screamed.

On the downside, Little Richard carried through a threat to renounce the devil's music and stride into the Church; he tossed four diamond rings (valued at US$8000) into Hunter River, Sydney, during a tour of Australia, saying, 'If you want to live for the Lord you can't rock 'n' roll too. God doesn't like it.' On the upside, Chuck Berry disagreed – he said it'd *got to be* Rock And Roll Music in a single issued in Britain on 25 October, which was followed a week later by the Everly Brothers' Wake Up Little Susie, their second consecutive million-seller in America. November also brought the mellifluously soulful You Send Me by Sam Cooke, and a single by Buddy Holly intriguingly titled Peggy Sue.[40] John and Paul agreed it was fantastic, the perfect successor to That'll Be The Day: dynamic, inventive, with the same group-sound qualities ... and yet different. They were inspired by the ease with which Buddy sang and played guitar at the same time – *really* played guitar, not just strumming like Elvis – and they wondered how the fast drumming was done. John bought or nicked the record (Everyday was on the B-side – almost as wonderful) and he and Paul listened to it again and again, trying to figure it out. There was just so much to learn, and it was such great fun doing it.

Buddy Holly wasn't pure rock and roll, nor was he rhythm and blues, he was country and western with a beat. Holly, Carl Perkins, Jerry Lee Lewis and sometimes Elvis were all showing that rock could be country too, or gospel, or some interesting American popular song of the pre-Haley era, that it wasn't merely the one-dimensional 'jungle beat' so derided by critics. This message was received loud and clear – especially in Liverpool, historically a musical melting-pot anyway – and it directly informed the taste and direction of not only John Lennon and Paul McCartney but also George Harrison, Richy Starkey and the thousands of other teenage boys hooked on all these great American sounds.

Good music was good music no matter what, and to them it was all *rock*: origin, skin colour, rhythm and tempo were irrelevant. They were just as likely to appreciate Elvis's Hound Dog as Carl Perkins' rockabilly Glad All Over, one of the singles released in December from a new juke-box musical movie called *Jamboree*, extracts from which were shown on *Six-Five Special*. And here, seen in Britain for the first time, was the wildman Jerry Lee Lewis – from Ferriday, Louisiana, somewhere near Saturn – following Whole Lotta Shakin' Goin' On with the stupendously potent Great Balls Of Fire. It would shoot to number 1 and awe budding musicians, as would its B-side, Mean Woman Blues. And then, in the run-up to Christmas, Decca's Coral label put out another fabulous single by the Crickets, Oh Boy! c/w Not Fade Away.

Buddy Holly was a huge influence on George Harrison too. 'One of the greatest people for me was Buddy Holly, because first of all he sang, wrote his own tunes and was a guitar player, and he was very good. Buddy Holly was the first time I heard A to F sharp minor. Fantastic – he was opening up new worlds there. And then A to F. A, D, E, F and F sharp minor. He was sensational. I no longer had the fear of changing from A to F.'[41]

As well as Buddy, other guitarists figured high in George's mind. The Sun sound of Scotty Moore and Carl Perkins remained his favourite, and from the same Sam Phillips studio in Memphis at the end of 1957 came a twangy guitar instrumental, Raunchy, that would change George's life (the artist name on the record label was Bill Justis, who played sax; the guitarist was Sid Manker, the tune's co-writer). It was issued in Britain in mid-December, and George was quickly tuned in. His method was to play a section of a record over and over, lifting and lowering the stylus repeatedly and trying it on his guitar until he'd found the notes and learned them, then moving on to the next, and the next, until eventually he had the whole piece. It was slow and methodical but George always had great singlemindedness and patience. Paul was very impressed he'd mastered such a tricky piece and would boast 'I've got a mate who can play Raunchy'. He told John about it.

George also had a deep interest in the Nashville guitarist Chet Atkins, whose LPs he got as a regular supply (by 1963, he had eleven in his collection). Fellow Liverpool Institute pupil Les Chadwick, who often discussed guitars with George as they rode the bus into school, remembers George always enthusing about Atkins, saying he had an uncle who brought the LPs for him from North America.[42] Showing impressive reserves of application once again, George studied Atkins note by note, and he discovered inversions, realising how the same chords could be used in other positions. During his get-togethers with Paul they learned a piece called Bourrée from the 1957 Chet Atkins LP *Hi-Fi In Focus*. Actually a Bach composition for the lute, Atkins did it as a guitar two-hander, melody and bass simultaneous. Paul would remember Bourrée as 'a cod-Spanish piece – if anyone ever started talking seriously about the guitar, or any classics, George and I used to play this'.[43] They felt it important to have an extra dimension to their playing; rock and roll wasn't everyone's cup of tea and it was useful to have something else to show off. John's party-piece was his own arrangement of what people knew as 'The Harry Lime Theme' – Anton Karas's zither tune for the 1949 film *The Third Man*.* Paul also spent many solo hours practising a tune called Pink Champagne: 'I learned it, as an instrumental, so if anyone ever asked me if I could play a solo I'd say [in a deepened voice for added gravitas], "Well … do you know Pink Champagne?"'[44]

Few Quarry Men bookings in this period were advertised but they included three more for Charlie Mac (two at Wilson Hall in Garston and that return to the Conservative Club in Norris Green) and also a social club dance at the huge Stanley Abattoir, in a tough district of Liverpool called Old Swan. For the first of the Wilson Hall dances, on 7 November, they were advertised in the *Echo* as 'Quarrymen Rock 'N Skiffle Group'. Young lads were criss-crossing one another on the buses several nights a week, tea-chests and drums stowed under stairs by conductors, guitars strummed on the upper deck by smoking, swearing, sartorially savvy musicians out to entertain for the night … but paying child fares. Paul had to be at his persuasive best before Jim would let him out, especially if there was school the next day. It was the same old problem: because Paul wanted to dress like a Ted and grease his hair back with Vaseline, Jim assumed he'd be a Teddy Boy by attitude too, and get into fights. So – like John on his first day at college – Paul wore his drainies underneath trousers that Jim deemed acceptable, then stripped off on the top deck of the bus – a bit of an ordeal if people were watching.[45]

As ever, all the Quarry Men dates were arranged by John's mate Nigel Walley, who'd be at the shows too unless dogged by one of his asthma attacks. His father, the senior Liverpool police detective, said the whole thing was crazy, and bluntly told John and Paul too. 'He said to them, "You're wasting your time. Go out and find yourself a job. This business of a skiffle group is a load of nonsense!"' Nigel was still managing the Quarry Men for an even share of any income, which since many of the bookings didn't pay at all was more like an honorary position with occasional tips. Charlie Mac did pay – not a lot, perhaps £3 to £5 a night – and, says Walley, Paul quickly had a problem with his cut. 'Paul said that, as I wasn't

---

* This too was recorded by Chet Atkins, on an LP in George's collection, but Paul says the arrangement John did was his own.

playing, I shouldn't get as much as the group members. John stuck up for me, saying that if I hadn't got the engagement in the first place there'd be no money. Who else was going to do all the chasing about? They weren't interested in doing that – they just wanted to play. So I got the money and Paul didn't like it, and we never had the same relationship after that.'[46]

John came to Walley's aid this time, but wasn't always supportive: he'd often stand back and watch a situation naturally evolve. Walley remembers how Paul was critical of Colin Hanton's drumming (perhaps on Peggy Sue?) and made dismissive remarks about him. 'Paul would smile to your face and be catty about you behind your back,' Walley says. John did nothing, perhaps feeling Paul was doing him a favour. Paul was keen for the group to be always at their best musically and was trying to sharpen them up, and John took the leader's position of letting him get on with it. Another situation was Pete Shotton's reduced involvement. He was no longer in the group and no longer seeing John at school every day, but the pair remained great friends; Paul was now closer to John day-to-day, however, and Pete was jealous. The relationship between John's two mates would often carry an edge, but, again, John let it happen, and over the course of these months LennonShotton became LennonMcCartney.

John was continuing to divide his time between home with Aunt Mimi (plus some lodgers and cats) and his other home with Mum (plus two children and her make-believe husband Bobby 'Twitchy' Dykins). As much as it could in such circumstances, his life had settled down to a consistent pattern. Mimi provided the stability he professed not to need, but did; Julia provided the fun, and trumped his loathing of convention with her own. Her genuine interest in teenage music remained, and when she took in a stray cat she called it Elvis, even after it gave birth to a litter of kittens in the kitchen cupboard. Always a cat lover, John veritably melted.

It was with Julia in mind that John wrote another song in the final weeks of 1957. It was his third attempt, following Calypso Rock and a second piece about which he'd remember just as little. (He said only once, some years later, 'I did one which had the line "My love is like a bird with a broken wing" which I was very proud of.') Among the songs Julia liked to sing around 1 Blomfield Road was the 1939 dance-band and film number Scatterbrain, and John was fascinated by the rhythmic flow of such lines as 'When you smile it's so delightful / When you talk it's so insane / Still it's charming chatter, scatterbrain.'

John sat with his guitar and started playing around with chords and phrases in the Buddy Holly style and a new song began to emerge, words and music. (It isn't known which came first; they probably arrived simultaneously.) He called it Hello Little Girl, and though it's nothing like Scatterbrain, this was its spring.

The earliest known and surviving recording of Hello Little Girl is from 1960, and the Buddy Holly influence is overwhelming. For an early attempt at song-writing, it's a remarkably catchy tune, appealing and direct. The words are written in the first person: he's besotted with a girl but she never seems to see him standing there, he sends her flowers but she doesn't care, but still he hopes there'll come a day when she'll think of him and 'love, love, love'. And this time, having been unable to hang on to his earlier attempts, John found a way of remembering it, going over Hello Little Girl phrase by phrase until it was embedded in his head.[47]

While John Lennon was greeting his little girl and hoping for joy, Paul McCartney had lost his. He too wrote a song in this same period – his first on guitar – which he called I Lost My Little Girl. Again, the influence of Buddy Holly was crystal clear, and Paul described it in one interview as 'A funny little song, a nice little song, a corny little song, based on three chords – G, G7 and C.'[48] Again, it's not known whether words or music came first, but 'little' is the operative word: there probably wasn't much more to it than a couple of verses. The words were fairly simple and included a rhyme that would always make Paul cringe (though he never altered it): 'girl' with 'her hair didn't always curl'. The song was stronger musically, especially in its melodic counterpoint. These were native skills.[49]

As with his earlier piano tunes, Paul was never shy to play it to people. 'I liked the idea of being able to say "I wrote this",' he'd recall.[50] Ian James was among those treated to an early demonstration.

> I was in Forthlin Road once when Paul said, 'I've written this song.' I couldn't imagine what it would be like but we went up to his bedroom and while I stood there he sat on the edge of his bed and played me I Lost My Little Girl. Whether it was a good tune or not, I was impressed by the fact that he'd *written* something. I'd never thought about writing a song – I was only interested in playing what had been recorded. He didn't only want to strum to Elvis Presley or Jerry Lee Lewis, he was more interested in creating something himself. That spark was there from the start.[51]

Though they'd conceived their songs alone, it didn't take long for John and Paul to play them to each other. In 1957, Liverpool was packed with teenage boys strumming guitars, but very few were writing their own songs. Here in the city's southern suburbs they could have been the only two, and they'd found each other.

The next step was to write together.

YEAR 1, 1958:
THINKING OF LINKING

8

'Where we going, Johnny?'
(January–May 1958)

Paul McCartney's sticky-fingered solo the first time he performed with the group left a vacancy on lead guitar unfilled in the last months of 1957. John Lennon and Eric Griffiths weren't up to it. Paul told John he might know some-one – younger than him but talented – keen to play and properly equipped.

George Harrison's arrival in the Quarry Men took place over the course of up to four weeks soon after the start of 1958. Precisely where and when Paul first got him to audition for John's nod of approval has been subject to sev-eral contradictory recollections by those who were there (and maybe one or two who weren't), which makes it impossible to determine the true sequence of events.

Nine years later, in 1967, George recounted that Paul introduced him to John at a Quarry Men booking at Wilson Hall. Paul had said he should come along, though it seems George went there anyway from time to time to see if he could sit in with groups. He remembered the Quarry Men sharing a bill with the Eddie Clayton Skiffle Group, which means Lennon, McCartney, Harrison and Starkey were in the same hall for the night, playing to a floor full of hard Teds they knew would try to 'kill them' the moment they stepped off stage.[1] John, who rated the Dingle group, apparently said that if George could play guitar as well as Clayton he could consider himself *in*. Corralled by Paul, George played Raunchy, the twangy guitar instrumental released in December 1957 and climb-ing the charts at the start of February 1958. Though he isn't likely to have been as good as the handy Clayton, he was accomplished enough to impress.

Another encounter – John, Paul and George all talked about it – happened one night on an otherwise deserted top deck of a Corporation bus. They were all coming back from somewhere, probably heading towards the point where they'd split off home in different directions, when Paul urged George (who, naturally, had his guitar) to seize the moment and demonstrate Raunchy for John. As Paul recalls it: 'I said, "Go on, George, show him!" And Little George – he was always little – he got his guitar out of its case and by golly he played it. And we all fell about. "He's in, you're in, that's it!" Audition over.'[2]

For all Paul's encouragement, the decision whether or not to admit George into the group wasn't his and wasn't obvious. John was several months beyond 17, George a few days shy of 15 – a chasm. It was already big of John to befriend Paul, twenty months his junior, but to add *his* friend, eight months younger still, was really something to consider. Paul was about the same height as John but George was so much smaller, really still a boy. Nevertheless, though the judgement may not have been as instant as Paul suggests, John never lingered over things. When it came, the word was positive, and George Harrison became the Quarry Men's fourth guitarist, the only one designated 'lead'.

It very much helped George's situation that he could join Paul in finally eradicating John's banjo leanings, and share with him that most hotly sought-after commodity: new chords. It made quite a difference to John's playing – 'All I ever wanted to do was to vamp, then George and Paul came along and taught me other things,' he'd recall. And as George said, he didn't have to beg to join the Quarry Men: 'I was asked by John to join the group – I didn't twist his arm. He was very friendly with me; John and I had a good relationship from very early on.'[3]

In interviews, John generally focused on another aspect of the relationship, making it plain that the age gap bothered him, and that he struggled for some time to overcome it.

> He was a kid who played guitar and he was a friend of Paul's ... I didn't dig him on first sight. George looked even younger than Paul, and Paul looked about ten with his baby face. He came round once and asked me to go to the pictures with him but I pretended I was busy ... I couldn't be bothered with him, he used to follow me around like a bloody kid, hanging around all the time. It took me years to come round to him, to start considering him as an equal.[4]

Despite this frank if uncharitable purge of his feelings, John did want George in the group, seeing not only guitar skills but other attributes. George was *cool*. He dressed as an individual and often to shock, to goad reactions – usually admiration from his peers and dismay from adults. He could be quiet, and sometimes grumpy, but he was always honest and never intimidated or afraid, standing up for himself verbally and physically. 'He was cocky,' Paul would say, admiringly. 'He had a great sense of himself. He wasn't cowed by anything.'[5] When (not if) John aimed volleys of verbal missiles in his direction, George could fire back his own, and John saw and welcomed that this kid, though so much younger and smaller, was no pushover.

George's first impression of John, as recalled in a handwritten questionnaire five years later, was 'He doesn't get his hair cut either.' John was correct to see idolatry in George's attitude because, as George said, he was happy for it to be noticed. 'I was very impressed by John. Probably more than Paul, or I showed it more. I loved John's blue jeans and lilac shirt and sidies. He was very sarcastic, always trying to bring you down, but I either took no notice or gave him the same back, and it worked.'[6]

With Lennon as leader, humour within the ranks was crucial; being able to sing and play was one asset, capacity to have a laff and a shout another, and those who didn't join in – like the dour Eric Griffiths – could be ridiculed without much mercy.* The personalities had to dovetail, and in George's case it was an instant fit. Though often pointed, his wit was dressed in an endearing tone – wry, dry and droll – and he was an original thinker. It was a *Liverpool* humour, like theirs and plenty others' around. George was often funny and sometimes quite devastating; he delivered a line with a most unusual quality – a razor-sharp slowness – and his timing was almost as good as John's, whose comic timing was just sensational, the match of any great comedian. Much more so than John and Paul, George had a distinctive accent, not the full Scouse but *semi*, a wash of Wavertree with a smattering of Speke, and in combination with his delivery the result was victorious.

John and Paul's shared sense of fun was already strong, and laughing at cruelty was a big part of it. As Paul says, 'That was the kind of thing that separated us from other people. It meant we had our own world. A world of black humour and of nervousness at other people's afflictions.'[7] Though the timeframe will never be known, it didn't take George long to tune in, vamping in the shorthand wit, sourcing laughs from everything amusing and unkind and often

---

* Derek Taylor, a Merseysider in Los Angeles, said on his KRLA radio show in 1967: 'Laff is a great Liverpool word. "Had a laff and over dinner ..." It's a highly prized commodity, a laff, especially in Liverpool where there's hardly anything to laff at unless you laff at all the sadness and poverty. On Saturday nights in the old days the best night out was what you called "a laff and a shout" – that meant sitting in the pub all laffing and shouting, then going to the dance, laffing some more, falling over, bruising your knee, and if you woke up the next morning and could only remember a fraction of what had happened, you knew it had been a good night out.'

unseen by others. The door of their private in-joke circle opened to admit one new member and then slammed shut again.

George's joining also gave the relationships a whole new complexity. The chain – John brought in Paul, Paul brought in George – would never be unimportant or forgotten in all the years to come. Paul, to his credit, had recognised that young George was hip enough to risk introducing to John. On the other hand, while John was automatically revered by both of them – 'It was teenage hero worship', Paul has said[8] – Paul continued to remind George of their own age gap, that 'nine months younger' status. George had no one to lord it over, nor did he bother to jostle shoulder to shoulder with John and Paul on the front line, but he did expect – and, when necessary, demand – to be considered an equal . . . and was. In this group, John got his way by being boss and shouting louder (as the others said of him several times), Paul got it by charm or calculation, George got it almost unnoticed, but got it all the same.

Now George was in the Quarry Men, Arthur Kelly fell into their circle too. He'd come to know Paul quite well in the preceding months but hadn't met John until the day he and George were in Vaughan's, buying a bag of scallops.

> George and I were in the chippy one dinner-time when this Ted came in, his hair greased up the sides, a pale coloured sports jacket, black shirt, jeans, a big army belt and what we called chukka boots, like desert boots. He looked so fucking hard that I must admit I physically stepped back. And George just said, 'Oh, this is John.' But he was nice. He just *looked* hard: that nose and that look. All the other art school students had beards and sandals, typical bohemian, and John was *so* different.[9]

Though Kelly also played guitar, there was no suggestion he'd be invited to join the group. This was fine with him, he didn't have their need to do it, but he did start going around with them, getting in free at halls because he was 'with the group', maybe carrying a guitar. Right from the start, Arthur noticed how George's humour integrated with John's and Paul's.

> One time, they were playing a hall in Garston, one of those nights when you had to run like fuck at the end, with the instruments, because a gang of Teds had taken umbrage over something – probably the way their girls were eyeing up John and Paul. Paul was with a girlfriend this night who had huge tits. In those days we used to tap the end of a cigarette before we smoked it, and George tapped his on her tits. She didn't seem to be offended and we all completely fell apart. Tap-tap-tap on these enormous great sticky-out tits.[10]

The Quarry Men line-up remained as fluid as ever. Colin Hanton was in and out, playing some bookings and not others, which means they went without a drummer occasionally; and around the time George joined them they also got a pianist. This was John Lowe, two months older than Paul and in the same Removes class at the Institute. After first running the idea by John, Paul made the approach in the school playground: 'Do you want to join our group?' His full name was John Charles Duff Lowe and, inevitably, everyone called him Duff. As a piano player he was anything but, as Paul recalls: 'Duff was in because of that arpeggio at the front of Mean Woman Blues. He could play it great. No other pianist we knew could play an arpeggio, you had to be trained to do that. We could all play a chord but we couldn't keep it going all the way up.'[11]

It was now spring 1958, and their sound was changing: skiffle was out and Buddy was in, along with Little Richard, Jerry Lee, Carl and Elvis. Though Len Garry floated around the scene a while longer, as a friend of John and school-mate of Paul, and maybe sometimes he played something, there was little need now for his tea-chest. Duff only played if they knew the venue had a piano on stage. He also had a strict dad who prescribed an unmissable return time, so even when he did play he often had to leave before they'd finished. The others would turn around, wondering why they weren't hearing piano in a particular song, and the stool would be vacant. Having left his departure as late as possi-ble, Lowe was running up the street for the crosstown bus back to West Derby.

Paul saw to it that the addition of a lead guitarist and pianist meant a period of proper rehearsal, the like of which they hadn't had for some time. The obvi-ous venue was his house because Duff could use Jim Mac's piano. Boys would be drawn to Allerton on a Sunday afternoon from Speke, Woolton and West Derby as if by magnet, and the same thing was also happening in many other houses all over the city. Jim had to accept these visits to his house by John, which Paul had managed to talk him into, but it's likely he was still unaware the bad lad was popping over during the week and that Paul was sagging off school for their productive songwriting sessions, turning out those Lennon-McCartney Originals. Colin Hanton didn't usually come to these Sunday rehearsals because Jim was concerned the drum noise would penetrate the terraced house. Even without them, Duff has a recollection of Jim 'sitting at the end of the piano and waving his arms if we got too loud'.[12]

With his deep musical interest and knowledge, Jim found involvement irre-sistible. He felt there wasn't enough melody in rock and roll and suggested – possibly several times – the group add I'll Build A Stairway To Paradise to their repertoire, something George would always recall with amusement. Jim liked George. Though there appeared to be no reason why he should favour him over John, both being dressed as Teddy Boys, history played its part: Paul and George had been friends for some time, and a rapport had been established between child and adult – George called him 'Uncle Jim' and the older man found the youngster's impudence attractive. George wasn't going to influence Paul the same way John did, which was the prime reason Jim maintained his stand against the older lad. In fact, it went much further, as John discovered some time afterwards. '[Paul's] dad was always trying to get me out of the group behind me back, I found out later. He'd say to George, "Why don't you get rid of John, he's just a lot of trouble" [and also] "Cut your hair nice and wear baggy trousers", like I was the bad influence because I was the eldest and usually had all the gear first.'[13]

It can only have been to Jim's vexation that when Ian Harris asked his cousin Paul to round up some friends and perform at his wedding reception, this meant that Lennon would be at a McCartney family party. Ian was married in a Catholic church in Huyton on Saturday 8 March 1958, and the party took place at his parents' house, a detached property at 147 Dinas Lane – the biggest house in the McCartney family. Ian was 19 and his bride Jackie 16, so it was appropriate that 'teenage music' was among the entertainment, and all to the good that a cousin and his mates should provide it. They played in the dining room at the back of the house ('the back parlour') and it may have been George's first 'public' appearance with them. Mike McCartney, only 14, took an invaluable colour photograph as they played – the earliest (and, for four more years, only) colour shot of John, Paul and George.

Courtesy of Mike's application, so much is visible. Most striking is George's youth. He is indeed a *boy*, not even a young man. And yet, just eleven days beyond his 15th birthday, he has a quality that has brought him the company of elders – a triumphant act in itself. His thick hair has been brushed up all around and is set strong, Vaseline or sugar water enabling it to defy gravity; he also has splayed ears (of which he was self-conscious), dirty fingernails and a teenager's pustule in the middle of his chin.

George's Hofner President is evidently a quality instrument, and Paul's Zenith looks good, but John's guitar is clearly nasty (if not cheap). Performing in front of his beloved family, Paul's eyebrows are raised in the act of vocal expression. Again, there is uniformity of dress – a further indication of Paul's smart thinking about presentation, and also how very quickly George had joined their fold. All three are wearing light bluish sports jackets and black ties; John and Paul have identical blue shirts, George (who can't have had blue) is in white or pink. John is standing in the corner, furthest from Mike's lens; his hair is slicked up, and, without glasses, he has the look familiar to those who knew him: the young man who can hardly see a thing. His cheeks are flushed red – which, Paul maintains, is because John was 'bevvied'.[14]

In which case, this was probably a testing occasion for Paul. His family would have heard by now about the new friend, the troublemaker, and been watching him with particular attention. At the same time, as people in John's world were beginning to discover with some unease, John Lennon could be a horrible drunk, shedding the humour that vitally checked his roughest edges to become verbally abusive and physically aggressive, an unadulterated obnoxious pain in the backside. What a risk this was for Paul; he may have needed to keep John pacified in front of his aunties, uncles and cousins and the bride's family. Not that John would have been the only one 'aled up' here – it was a Liverpool party after all, famously steamy and frequently troublesome occasions.

While the photo seems to show only three musicians – John, Paul and George – when viewed at its widest extent, full frame, Mike also caught the headstock of an acoustic guitar by George's right elbow – a fourth player. It may have been the other Quarry Men guitarist Eric Griffiths. It's unlikely Duff or Colin were present, and no one can say how long they played. Buddy and Elvis are sure to have featured strongly.

The photo also reveals one further detail: Paul has bought a pickup for his Zenith. Though there's no trailing wire (so he wasn't using it on this occasion), he bought it when he got his first amplifier, a small green Elpico AC-55, which he recalls buying from the electrical store Curry's. Made of Bakelite, and capable of throwing out ten watts, it had a carrying handle and was, as he'd describe it, 'rather like a small green suitcase'.[15] For the first time, one of the Quarry Men is electric.

If that is Eric on the extreme of Mike McCartney's colour photo, it was a portent, for he was about to be edged out completely. George had walked into the Quarry Men and coolly wondered, what are all these people doing here? 'It was daft: they had no proper drummer but about eighteen guitarists, and people coming along for one night and not again ... who didn't seem to be doing anything, so I said, "Let's get rid of them" ... I conspired to get rid of Griff.'[16]

It says a great deal for John's leadership style – a kind of benign manoeuvring – that he'd allowed Paul to suggest the addition of George and Duff, and now he let the new and youngest boy ('a bloody kid') wield the axe over a founder member, John's old Quarry Bank schoolfriend.

Without telling Eric it was his only chance of staying, John and Paul first asked him to buy the hot new instrument on the scene, an electric bass guitar. Few groups had one, so the Quarry Men's stock would rise considerably if he said yes. It would mean buying not only the guitar but also an amplifier. Pretty much everyone in Liverpool and elsewhere bought goods by hire-purchase: a certain sum of money paid 'down' (right away) and the balance over a period of time – people called it 'buying on the never-never', 'on the knocker' or 'on the drip'. Even allowing for this, the bass and an amp represented real outlay, and Eric, who didn't have the cash, was unwilling to saddle his mum with the debt. He didn't know it, but he was signing his marching orders.

When it came down to it, neither John (whose group it was) nor Paul (implicit in the decision) nor George (who'd set the ball rolling) had the desire to sack Eric to his face. This, they decided, was the job of the manager. Says Nigel Walley:

> I was called to a meeting at John's house. It was John, Paul and me, and they said I had to go and get rid of Eric. It was 'You're the manager, so *you've* got to go and tell him. That's what you get paid for, that's why you get an equal share.'
>
> OK, Eric didn't fit into the situation. He had no personality whatsoever. You couldn't crack a smile out of him. He couldn't help it, that's the way he was. He'd play but never smile, whereas the others had the vim and vigour.
>
> I went either to Eric's house or a Woolton coffee bar, I can't now remember which, and broke the news to him. He was very upset – he said he was part of the group so why would they get rid of him? It was a sad day for him and for me: he thought I'd instigated it and never forgave me. They'd just sent the messenger boy out, and that was it. John and Paul never got in touch with him themselves.[17]

The Quarry Men was now John, Paul, George, Duff (when a venue had a piano) and Colin (if they told him what they were doing). The three guitarists were unimpressed with Colin's drumming and he would have been out too if a replacement was available, but one wasn't. He was on a limb, though: Paul and George (and Duff) were in school together at the Institute and John was next door at the art college, so there was much to which Colin just wasn't party. And Eric's sacking had annoyed him: the two were friends; he'd joined the group through Eric.

For Nigel, having to dismiss someone was not at all what he was in this for. It had been a tough task, made all the more so by John and Paul's attitude – particularly Paul's, he says. He was bruised. While his 'management' of the Quarry Men continued, he felt less and less enthused by it and his involvement began to ebb away.

For Paul and George, dinner-times became a regular highlight of school life. The Institute and art school were separated by nothing more than two side doors; only a courtyard cluttered with broken easels and desks stood between them. Through the second door and they were into the building, then down the stairs and straight into the canteen, the hub of art school life. It was like entering another world. John was here wolfing down his food one day when through they came, to be exposed immediately for what they were: schoolboys in blazers, self-evidently (and self-consciously) so much younger than anyone else in the room. John's friend Jon Hague remembers the first time it happened.

> When you're at art school and you're not a child any more it was unusual to invite in a couple of schoolboys in blazers. That's why John asked our permission, which he did, formally, because he must have felt we wouldn't want little schoolboys coming in. It would have been hard for him to ask, but he did it because he wanted them there. John was an extremely generous person – he would give you anything and do anything for you. He invited anybody into his world.[18]

Familiar only with the strictures of grammar school, Paul and George revelled in the relaxed atmosphere of the art college canteen, where instead of what George would satirise as 'school cabbage and boiled grasshoppers' they could eat spaghetti on toast for 7d, beans on toast for 8d or egg on toast for 9d, or sit on the small stage and tuck into scallops bought from Vaughan's. As George said, 'There'd be chicks and arty types [and] we could go in there and smoke without anyone giving us a bollocking. John would be friendly to us – but at the same time you could tell that he was always a bit on edge because I looked a bit too young, and so did Paul.'[19]

Nigel Walley managed to get the Quarry Men back into the Cavern in this period (not advertised, date unknown), a booking secured through the ever-thinning umbilical cord of skiffle, as well as a pretence that they could play the blues. Paul remembers, 'We announced songs like Long Tall Sally as being written by Blind Lemon Jefferson, and Blue Suede Shoes as "the famous creation of the legendary blues guitarist Lead Belly"'; George would recall, 'The owners sent up little notes to the stage complaining. We'd say, "Here's another one by Big Bill Broonzy called Rip It Up", and they threw us off.' John said they were 'banned from the Cavern for a year after that', nothing more doing until spring 1959, but actually it was more than this: it was the Quarry Men's final appearance here.[20]

George had started going out with his first girlfriend just before being invited into the group. Arthur Kelly went out one night with a girl named Ann Harvey, and afterwards when he asked to see her again she said, 'Only if you bring a friend for my friend.' This was how George (closing on 15) came to meet Iris Caldwell (almost 14) at the Palace Ice Rink on Prescot Road, Kensington. A foursome developed and the girls took to calling Arthur and George 'Azzer and Nazzer', though Iris can no longer remember why, except they too had a great sense of humour. After a date or three, just hanging around places, George went to her house and met her parents; and here began an important relationship that would long outlive his sweet but brief courtship with Iris.

Her brother Alan, often known as Al, was leader of the Texan Skiffle Group, aka the Texans, aka Al Caldwell's Texans and formerly the Ravin' Texans; whatever the name, they were reckoned one of Liverpool's better groups, regulars at the Cavern. Born in January 1938, Al developed a chronic stutter at the age of six when Iris was born, and could barely complete a sentence; 1950s medical science was tested to its limit in the hunt for a cure – he even underwent injections and hypnotism – but the stutter did lift, completely, miraculously, when he sang, especially when he aped an American accent. So he sang, with a twang. He loved skiffle and rock, and as a very good-looking lad with a stack of blond hair (like Iris), he had no shortage of female admirers – though less so after he spoke. He was also a fine athlete, competing in high-level track meetings. George liked Al immediately, and he became especially fond of Al and Iris's parents, Ernie and Vi, whose home at 54 Broad Green Road was an ever open house for their children's friends, any time of the day or night.*

Just before Paul got him into the Quarry Men, George had made a pitch to join the Texans. 'George was always playing the guitar,' says Iris, 'especially the old song Wedding Bells Are Breaking Up That Old Gang Of Mine. The main reason he went out with me was that he wanted to get in a group. He used to come around and play this to my brother, and my brother used to say, "Come back in a few years, son."'[21]

Vi Caldwell is remembered by Arthur Kelly as 'an Ethel Merman figure, and a great encourager'. With an unquenchable spirit, great sense of humour, love of people and generous, supportive nature, Vi was a true Liverpool character, endlessly chatting, laughing, joking, smoking, making fry-ups and brewing pots of tea. George loved her like a second mum, as did almost everyone who met her. As Iris says, 'I'm sure half the boyfriends I ever had and half the girlfriends my brother had was because they liked my mum so much. She was such a brilliant personality. People just used to love coming to our house and being part of it.'

During the course of these visits to the Caldwells, George heard plenty of enthusiastic (if stuttered) talk about a music club Al and Johnny Byrne (his Texan pardner from around the corner) were planning to open in the cellar of a

---

* Alan and Iris were born here. Like the general area of which it is part, Broadgreen can also be written like that, as one word.

big house a couple of hundred yards away. It was a nurses' residence, a detached Victorian property, and the woman in charge said they could use the basement as a teenagers' venue. They decided to call it the Morgue Skiffle Cellar, open for business two evenings a week, Tuesdays and Thursdays.* The club was unlawful – the boys never bothered to obtain licences – so when the opening session, on 13 March 1958, was advertised in the *Evening Express* they didn't give the address, which was close to useless. Attractions were detailed only on handouts typed on coloured sheets and individually signed 'Al Caldwell (manager)'. The Morgue was not at all in the Quarry Men's part of town, but John and Paul heard about it through George and they played here on the opening night in rotation with Al Caldwell's Texans, performing from the tiny makeshift stage.[22]

Except for three of the sessions, details of who played the Morgue and when have not been preserved, but the Quarry Men performed possibly several times, at least once as a trio of guitarists and at least once with Colin on drums (Duff never figured because there wasn't a piano). John, Paul and George also came along other times as clubgoers, because the place was full of nurses; however it was shut down by the end of April. Next-door neighbour Mr Brown complained about teenagers 'frolicking' in his garden, and there were also grumbles about litter and late-night noise in this residential district. John, Paul and George saw less of the Caldwells after that, but a bond had been created between them, to be rejuvenated in years to come.

It was to the Morgue Skiffle Cellar that they travelled the evening of Thursday 20 March, where they watched the Texans, the Bluegenes and the Sioux City Skiffle Group in action. But why they were here and not back in the city, at the Philharmonic Hall, remains unexplained, because this was the night Buddy Holly and the Crickets came to play in Liverpool – and these most devoted of fans chose not to go. It wasn't just because of the attractions at the Morgue: tickets for Holly had been on sale a month, before the cellar club was even known about. Nor was it the expense: tickets were reasonably priced, only four to twelve shillings. Even more oddly, they weren't the only absentees: the *Evening Express* reported afterwards how the combined audience for both houses at the Philharmonic would not have half-filled the Empire.

John, Paul and George were well aware Buddy and the Crickets were in the country because they'd been glued to TV the night of 2 March to watch them on *Sunday Night At The London Palladium*. As Paul says, 'That was the big

---

* The house was named Balgownie, at 25 Oakhill Park, six doors along from where Johnny lived and just around the corner from Alan. The Morgue was the second such venue in Liverpool. Another, similar club – also in the cellar of a large Victorian house – opened a week earlier in Hayman's Green, West Derby; it will appear shortly in this history (see chapter 10).

occasion – to watch his fingers, see what guitar he had, to see if he played the chords right, to see how he did that solo in Peggy Sue, see whether he used a capo or not, all the various technical things – that was where you got the info.'[23]

'I only saw them on the London Palladium [on TV],' John stated. 'He was great! It was the first time I saw a Fender guitar! Being played! While the singer sang!! Also the "secret" of the drumming on Peggy Sue was revealed ... live ... We did practically everything he put out. What he did with "3" chords made a songwriter out of me!! He was the first guy I ever saw with a capo. He made it OK to wear glasses! I WAS Buddy Holly.'[24]

Given such enthusiasm, it is astounding they didn't go to see him in person when it was so easy to do so. At four o'clock that afternoon, John came out of art college and Paul and George came out of school, and though Buddy Holly – *Buddy Holly!* – was just a couple of hundred yards along the same street, all the way over from Texas and rehearsing in 'the Phil' with the Crickets and his drool-over Fender Stratocaster guitar, they turned and went home. Then, after tea, they took a series of buses up to the Morgue.

Records by Buddy Holly and the Crickets were not to be missed, however. Like many other fine American discs, they were available in the Liverpool shops through licensing arrangements with British companies (almost entirely Decca's London label) ... and what rich pickings could be had in the first half of 1958, sourced from the thriving independent labels across the great continent:

- From Sam Phillips' Sun in Memphis came Breathless by Jerry Lee Lewis, and the rockabilly Lend Me Your Comb by Carl Perkins. From Josie in New York came the infectiously upbeat Do You Want To Dance by Bobby Freeman, and from Chicago, on the Chess subsidiary Checker, was The Walk by Jimmy McCracklin – a silly attempt to create a dance craze but a fine record with a swaggering beat.
- From Specialty in Hollywood came two dynamic Larry Williams singles, Bony Moronie and Dizzy Miss Lizzy (the B-side of which was the twelve-bar rocker Slow Down), and also the last rock recordings cut by Little Richard before he disappeared into the Church, Good Golly Miss Molly and Ooh! My Soul. John sang the Williams songs, Paul soon had Richard's down to sweet perfection.
- From studios in New York and New Mexico came not only three more inspirational singles by Buddy Holly and the Crickets – Maybe Baby, Listen To Me and Rave On – but also an entire LP, *The Chirping Crickets*, salivated over by their fans for the cover photo as well as the musical content: it was every British rocker's initial sight of a Fender Stratocaster. 'The first

time I ever saw a photograph of Buddy Holly with that Strat, you *cream yourself looking*,' remembered George Harrison.[25] This one guitar instantly occupied George's mind above all others, as proved by the drawings in his schoolbooks. 'You couldn't get one in the shops but he just loved the shape of it,' says Arthur Kelly. 'George used to sit and draw Strats all day long.'

- From Cadence in New York came Link Wray's Rumble, an extraordinary, distorted electric guitar track; and also All I Have To Do Is Dream by the Everly Brothers. ('When we first heard it, it blew us away,' says Paul.)[26]

- From Imperial in Hollywood came Stood Up, a good catchy rocker by the young American actor/singer Ricky Nelson, bought in Liverpool by Paul.

- And also from Chess in Chicago came two more singles by Chuck Berry, Sweet Little Sixteen c/w Reelin' And Rockin', and Johnny B. Goode c/w Around And Around. Johnny B. Goode didn't make the British charts (though it was a hit in the juke-boxes), yet both records cemented Berry's reputation in a nation where he'd always be a hero. John, Paul and George were diehard Berry fans from this moment. Paul's first real interest in the drums was stirred by the break around the kit in Sweet Little Sixteen; George would say, 'Everyone learned that guitar playing, everybody wanted to play like that';[27] John became especially possessive of Berry's music, not only singing the songs but instructing George that, though he was lead guitarist, *he*, John, was going to play these ones, OK? Methodical study was never John's style, but he rarely came closer to it than when he set his mind on being Chuck.

And just in case the bell-ringing guitar sound wasn't thrilling enough, Berry's words were extraordinary. No one else wrote so poetically about Americana – which, to British ears, now sounded ever more like nirvana. To this generation in cold, grey, austere post-war Britain, the promised land burst into ever more dazzling Technicolor through Chuck; if you closed your eyes you were halfway there, on *American Bandstand*, in Philadelphia PA, deep in the heart of Texas, 'round the 'Frisco Bay and by a log cabin deep down in Louisiana. John Lennon was *inspired*: 'He was well advanced of his time, lyric-wise, in a different class from the other performers. The lyrics were fantastic, even though we didn't know what he was saying half the time ... He's the greatest rock 'n' roll poet. When I hear rock, good rock, of the calibre of Chuck Berry, I just fall apart and have no other interest in life. The world could be ending if rock 'n' roll's playing. It's a disease of mine.'[28]

And then, of course, there was Elvis, whose success just seemed to grow and grow. All of them – Starkey, Lennon, McCartney and Harrison – went to see

Jailhouse Rock when it played the huge Forum cinema in Liverpool city centre at the end of March. Elvis's film character was bad boy Vince Everett and this most impressionable audience – playing at rock stars when they stepped on stage, dreaming of rock stardom as the day slipped away – was given another glimpse of the working practices inside a recording studio, one that pretty much confirmed the information in *The Girl Can't Help It*. When Everett cuts the first song for his own label, Laurel Records, the producer in the booth says, 'Laurel 101, Take 1!' and points the 'go' finger, everyone plays great together in one room, and after two minutes the picture dissolves to Everett and a glamour gal packing 45s into mailing cartons.

Elvis had now been in the lives of his fans for two years and it seemed nothing could ever halt his momentum. As Paul says, 'Buddy was a special thing for all of us when we were about 15 or 16, but we also had Elvis. We all loved Elvis – he was *so* hot. We were just *so* in love with him. He was just the greatest idol, always hamming it up, always doing a little funny thing. He was *so* great.'[29]

As it happened, however, in the very week they were watching *Jailhouse Rock* in Liverpool, Elvis was inducted into the US Army and everything changed. A neutering process was underway, starting when the star's great mane of black hair was shorn off in favour of a shortie.

While Elvis's posting suggested any visit to Britain would be delayed even longer, other American stars still made the trip, and Richy Starkey had a formative experience through seeing one. The still-popular Johnnie Ray was in Liverpool for a one-night stand at the Empire on Sunday 13 April and, like most big names, stayed at the Adelphi, a hotel then considered so exclusive that lesser mortals could only dream of the luxuries within, never expecting to walk among them. On this particular Sunday, Richy was in Liverpool with Roy Trafford when they noticed a crowd outside the Adelphi, and there was the great man at an upper-storey window, throwing down photo-publicity cards of himself.* Always a Johnnie Ray fan, Richy was struck significantly by the sight of the star at the window, up there in that wonderful hotel, literally looked up to by his fans. What a life that must be. 'I thought, "Wow, this is *fabulous*." It was one of the first times I thought, "This is the job for me."'[30]

Richy constantly contemplated stardom, and those words of family friend Annie Maguire glowed ever brighter in his mind. While the odds were a million

---

* Glossy black-and-white photographic postcards, literally called 'throwaways' in the business. Every artist had them, often with the logo of their record company printed under the photo and sometimes with a biographical blurb on the reverse. Freely available to fans, they and autograph books were the main items signed by the stars.

to one, Richy dared to dream: 'I was always gonna be "on the Palladium" – that was the aim when I was playing a club for ten bob a night. I knew some day I'd get that name in lights, that glossy thing. I just felt it.'[31]

For now, though, the Eddie Clayton Skiffle Group were stuck in Liverpool. As one of the best on the scene, admired by George Harrison as well as John Lennon,[32] they played the better venues, with regular dates at the Cavern and also, at least twice in April 1958, at midweek 'Rock' and 'Big Beat' dance nights at the huge Grafton Ballroom. Though they kept the skiffle label, their sound was contemporary: Roy Trafford had ditched the tea-chest and bought himself a Hofner guitar, for which Eddie made him a pickup from copper wires. The group were now fully electric. 'Eddie was an absolutely brilliant musician,' says Roy, 'he could play anything. He was the singer and I used to harmonise with him. Richy never sang.'[33]

Richy used his full kit whenever he could, but it remained too dangerous to lug around and he would dictate the tempo on that single snare. Though standing at the back, he attracted attention with his clothes: with a few quid in his pocket from the bookings and the job at H. Hunt & Son, he had become flash. As Eddie would remember, 'Richy was a trifle on the flamboyant side, particularly in his dress – he liked gold lamé waistcoats and snappy suits.'[34]

Eddie's group had much more stage time than the Quarry Men, their dates advertised regularly in the *Liverpool Echo*, on top of which they played plenty of private bookings. When Harry Graves' colleague, fellow Liverpool Corporation painter and decorator Harry Birch, mentioned he needed music for his wedding reception, Richy's stepdad said he knew just the group. The date was 25 January 1958 and the venue Fazakerley Public Hall in north Liverpool. As Birch recalls:

> We paid them £3 and whatever they wanted to drink, although if I remember rightly they had their own drinks with them. They did a great job, and what was amazing was that they could play dance music as well as skiffle. People were dancing to them, proper dancing. They put it across well and everyone had a really good time, it was a smashing night. And at the end, as was the ritual, they played God Save The Queen and everyone stood up – everyone except for my Welsh relatives, that is, who were spitting on the floor.[35]

Louise Harrison's invitation to John and Paul, to come and play their guitars at her house, provided useful new opportunities for the three to congregate somewhere welcoming. She was usually there with them, but sometimes was out at her part-time job and they would all sag off school, so to Speke – two boys unofficially absenting themselves from the Institute, John strolling out through the door as art college students could.

It was around this time that George joined Paul in going electric. George and Arthur Kelly both bought themselves pickups from Hessy's, and when Paul was around – and when they were on stage together – George plugged into a second input on Paul's Elpico; on other occasions, lacking an amp of their own, the boys had to improvise, plugging into Arthur's family radiogram.

As George knew several more guitar chords than John or Paul, every time he showed them a new one they tried to write a song around it[36] – and it was in this period, possibly at Upton Green, that Paul wrote one he called In Spite Of All The Danger, a chugging and melodic country-flavoured number with a couple of extended lead guitar solos created by George. For this reason, the song was a unique deviation from the Lennon-McCartney credit: it went down as McCartney-Harrison.

The tune of In Spite Of All The Danger was entirely Paul's, but it leaned heavily on the melody of Elvis's Trying To Get To You, a song that includes the lyric '[in] spite of all that I've been through'. Using an existing song as inspiration for the writing of another is standard practice, but the rock and roll era was already littered with outrageous examples of plagiarism seemingly free of legal action – possibly because the song being copied was not entirely original to that composer either.

Paul was now in full flow as a songwriter, keeping an ear cocked for any interesting phrases or sayings he could work into a new piece, not just thinking like a songwriter but *thinking* he was thinking like a songwriter, conscious of the process, seeing himself in a bigger picture. It was probably in this period that he seized on a catchphrase while out with George one evening at the pictures. One of the commercials was for Link furniture ('combine *contemporary* good looks with *ageless* glamour') and it ended with the tag-line 'Are *you* thinking of linking?' 'I came out of there [thinking] "That should be a song ... thinking of linking, people are going to get married, got to do that." But I could never really get past "thinking of linking can only be done by two" – pretty corny.'[37]

Going to the pictures was something they all did, as regularly as pocket money would permit, always provided that Paul was able to talk his dad into letting him out when he should have been revising for his O-Levels. They went in combinations and sometimes as a trio; one film they saw together was *Violent Playground*, the juvenile delinquency drama shot in Liverpool in summer 1957 and which opened there the following March. The main character was Johnny and one of the screen lines was 'What's it tonight, Johnny?' This was grabbed by John, Paul and George and, over time, became bastardised into 'Where we going, Johnny?', spoken with an exaggerated American whine.

It was their catchphrase, voiced not only when they were wondering where to go, but at any time, in any circumstance.

As well as George's house, or Paul's house (if Jim was out), and occasionally Mendips, John and Paul also had some 'eyeball to eyeball' sessions at Julia's. Like all John's other friends before him, Paul fell in love with her, finding her more like a big sister than a friend's mum. 'I always thought she was a very beautiful lady, with long red hair. I know John absolutely adored her: one, on the level that she was his mum, but also because she was a very beautiful woman and a very spirited woman. She was very lively.' Paul thought it was fabulous that she played banjo, finding her 'great, gorgeous and funny'. While observing John's awkward relationship with Twitchy, Paul could see how much he loved his mother – John 'idol-worshipped her', and when they left the house 'there was always a tinge of sadness' about him. Louise Harrison overheard John saying to Paul at her house one day, 'I don't know how you can sit there and act normal with your mother dead. If anything like that happened to me I'd go off me head.'[38]

The more Paul and John played guitar, sometimes with Julia and her banjo close to hand, the more they realised how they shared a liking for *old* songs too, like the 1920s standards she'd taught John a couple of years previously, Ramona, Little White Lies and Girl Of My Dreams, and Don't Blame Me (written 1933). Paul knew more of these tunes than John and shared some of the treasures. Both were inspired by the way some had unique introductions, a preliminary that didn't recur in the piece. Though rock and roll was first, second and third in Lennon-McCartney's list of obsessions, they snuck up their sleeve this other dimension to their musical knowledge and interest.

By this time, John was in the third and final term of his first year at Liverpool College of Art. From a work point of view, he rarely did more than the least he could get away with, and with minimal application. As fellow student Bill Harry says, 'John's strength was his spontaneity. If he did something, that was it – he'd scribble something down in maybe thirty seconds and that was all it needed. If he spent four hours doing the thing he wouldn't make it better, he'd make it worse.'[39]

Distractions were positively sought, and John's first real art school relationship happened in the summer term. Mona Harris, a year older, went out with John for a few weeks while her real boyfriend was away at university in London – and his return in July brought it to an end. They enjoyed good times in the interim. 'John took me to meet his mother,' she says. 'I remember her as small and lively, a real character, as full of wit and repartee as John was, and they sparked verbally. But we weren't there long because there was lots of washing hanging up to dry, all her young daughters' clothes around the place, and John said, "We're not stopping, it smells like old knickers here."'[40]

By some distance, friendships were the most attractive aspect of art school life for John. He and Tony Carricker gravitated towards each other on the basis of a shared love of music. As Tony puts it, 'Early rock freaks found each other like drug takers will find each other.' He still recalls their first conversation, as they walked down the hill into town: 'It was like an interrogation: "Have you got *this*?" "Have you heard *that*?" "Oh, you've got *that*, have you?" – it was like being vetted. I was in.'[41] Tony had Bloodshot Eyes by Wynonie Harris, he had red label Vogue 78s, he introduced John to Bobby Freeman's Do You Want To Dance, he had country blues and he loved Chuck Berry; when John found out Tony had memorised all the words of Roll Over Beethoven he got him to write them down for him. He recalls overhearing John saying to somebody, '*He's got all the records!*'

Tony was one of those enthusiasts not merely prepared to accept whatever was available in the local shops but to seek out scarce sounds. He was a gatherer, hungry to expand his knowledge. He'd discovered that the cultural department of the American Embassy in London loaned Smithsonian Institution and other rare records free to applicants, on trust. Packages containing discs by Bessie Smith, Ida Cox, Lead Belly, Big Bill Broonzy, Blind Willie Johnson, Sleepy John Estes and other such fabulously exotic creatures, remarkable field recordings from the American South and rare studio sessions of the 1920s to 1940s, would be despatched via Royal Mail from Grosvenor Square to Tony's tiny house in Widnes, the return postage prepaid.

Though John was indebted to Tony for broadening his musical horizons, Tony gained most from the friendship. 'I was an acolyte of John's, it was an acolytish relationship, because he had the personality. He was very much a force of nature – he was frightened of far fewer things than most people, he had no social fears, wasn't constrained by all the silly little things in life and had tremendous self-confidence and good fun. He was a very, very good mate.'

All the friendships in John's life were like this: he was the leader, respected and gratefully followed by others. But perhaps for the first time here at college there was an exception: John found a friend *he* revered. Being John, his choice was unconventional. Jeff Mahomed* was seven years his senior, a tall, bulky, swarthy man with tightly curled hair and sideburns. Born and raised just south of Manchester, he had a moneyed and exotic background: an Indian father and

---

* His birth certificate gives his name as Russell Geoffrey Mahomed but he used the middle name as his first and always spelled it Jeffrey, being known to everyone as Jeff.

Italian-French mother from the Vatican City. He'd been to boarding school and then completed a stint of National Service done the hard way, as a military policeman for the Commonwealth forces fighting insurrection in Malaya. Though his artistic talent was obvious, why Jeff Mahomed had enrolled at Liverpool College of Art remained a mystery to everyone. On the smallest of grants, he lived in a squalid basement flat in Liverpool 8, seemingly without other friends, racked by ruinous self-doubt, eating in the cheapest cafés, walking around in an old tweed coat not quite big enough for the job, collar turned against the cold and damp, hands thrust in pockets, feet wet from leaky shoes, a man who picked up cigarette butts from the gutter.[42]

George and Paul met Jeff. George would recall a man who 'looked like an Arab and talked like a German and was tanned all over'. It's not clear if they fully understood the complexity of John and Jeff's friendship. Ann Mason is sure John looked up to him as a father figure, which isn't inconceivable. In mid-1958, when John was coming up to 18, Jeff was rising 25 and going on 40; the younger man was desperate to experience everything and it seemed the elder man had. Another contemporary, Pat Jourdan, likens the relationship to uncle and nephew and is sure John was surprised Jeff had accepted him. 'He found his feet courtesy of Jeff,' she says.*

Visits to Jackson's art shop brought these students opposite a newly opened coffee bar at 23 Slater Street, one of the first in Liverpool and a venue that evidently catered for the city's more bohemian types. In the daytime, the Jacaranda was a standard ground-floor snack bar – tea, frothy espresso, beans on toast, bacon butties – but at night its downstairs area (a former coal cellar) became a separate enterprise, the Jacaranda Club, a members-only establishment. Its owner, Allan Williams, the son of one of Liverpool's oldest established dance promoters, had struck up a friendship with Tom Littlewood, day-to-day manager of the 2i's Coffee Bar in London, who'd explained how a coffee bar could register as a private club with a membership list and so stay open well beyond midnight.

Though unlicensed for alcohol, the Jacaranda – or 'the Jac' as it quickly became known – was always buzzing, Williams providing some unusual entertainment. He'd formed a good friendship with Trinidad-born Harold Phillips, one of the thousands of West Indians who sailed into Britain after the war.

---

* Jeff Mahomed died in 1974, aged 40. He was never interviewed about his friendship with John and there's no photograph of them together. In 1980 (when John himself was 40) he mentioned his old friend during a BBC interview and then cut across his anecdote to interject 'rest his soul'.

Phillips was leader of the Royal Caribbean Steel Band and Williams gave them a residency in the Jac, the sound of their eight forty-gallon steel oil-drums throbbing up the stairs and through the streets. Like all good calypsonians, Phillips adopted a noble moniker, this one chosen after his brand of cigarette: he was Lord Woodbine. Being Liverpool, the appellation was soon shortened, to Woody. 'The Jacaranda was a social revolution,' says Allan Williams, 'and great for anyone who worked anti-social hours, like nurses and people in the entertainment business. Villains generally steered clear because there was no booze and most of the people were intellectual conversationalists; they realised it wasn't their scene.'[43]

It was *the* scene of the city's art students. It was bound to be, because Allan and his wife Beryl, still in their twenties, were bohemians themselves. Society had shifted them to the edge because of their mixed-race marriage: he was white Liverpool-Welsh (born in Bootle, with a Welsh family background), she was born in Liverpool to Chinese parents, the daughter of a laundryman. Though Liverpool is often described as a melting-pot, Allan and Beryl ran up against open hostility; both sets of parents were against their marriage, and, says Allan, when out together in the street they were spat on and had to endure taunts like 'Oh look at him with that Chink'.

Allan was a City & Guilds-qualified plumber and Beryl a schoolteacher; they married in 1955 and soon afterwards went youth hostelling around Europe. At the same time as Alan Sytner was drawing inspiration from a Paris jazz club to open the Cavern, Allan and Beryl were in the same area of the Left Bank, the students' quarter, looking at cafés and clubs and pondering their own move. Back in Liverpool, Allan jacked in the plumbing, cashed in his insurance and opened the Jacaranda, launching himself into a colourful and highly eventful life as an entrepreneur. He had the basement decorated with vivid murals by two art school students, Rod Murray and Stuart Sutcliffe, who were paid in bottles of gin, baked beans on toast and coffee; Allan and Beryl rapidly established a close friendship with Sutcliffe, an intense and quite brilliant young art student.

John Lennon went to the Jacaranda to spend whatever remained of Mimi's weekly allowance. Paul and George and some of their friends went there too, though less often. At lunchtimes and in the late afternoons, the place was abuzz with college students, and much of their talk was of politics. In Pete Seeger's words, this was now the Frightened Fifties, the early years of the Cold War, a highly political time. The word 'beatnik' was coined on 2 April 1958 by the *San Francisco Chronicle* columnist Herb Caen and it soon jumped the Atlantic where the press liberally and pejoratively applied it to any young anti-war activist, layabout, bohemian, beardie, poet, writer, reader of beat novels or idler, and to most members of CND, the Campaign for Nuclear Disarmament, inaugurated in February 1958. (Some beatniks were actually all these things.) The Bomb was the single hottest and most divisive issue of the time, and a fifty-mile protest march by CND members, from London to the Atomic Weapons Research Establishment at Aldermaston, took place over the Easter holiday weekend in April. It received a very mixed press, and because anti-war songs were strummed by a few of the protesters the guitar was mentioned in despatches. Whether used for rock or peace, the instrument was seldom out of the headlines. In the hands of a rock and roller the guitar meant delinquency; in the hands of a beatnik it meant, to some, a threat like a gun.

Though John Lennon had become a college student at this revolutionary time, he showed no interest in engaging in any radical activities, in no peace or anti-Bomb protests. He'd arrived at his conclusions and that was that – no time for fussing or fighting, no need for further discussion.

In Britain, the nuclear issue went hand in hand with feelings of anti-Americanism, now rising steadily again to build on years of slow-burning post-war resentment, but America's front-line defence was always Britain's young. As John put it eight years later, 'America [was] the big youth place in everybody's imagination – America had teenagers and everywhere else just had people.'[44] In the eyes of British kids, the States was a milk and honey land of skyscrapers, cowboys, Cadillacs, Elvis, hamburgers, fabulous clothes, Hollywood, Little Richard, funny place names, Coca-Cola, Buddy Holly, wide prairies, Chuck Berry, DC comics and the very best sounds. In Liverpool especially, where American jeans, belts, boots, cowboy shirts and records were brought in by returning seamen, it was hard to find a young person with a bad word to say about the place.

The Quarry Men played on through the spring, picking up the odd date (and some of them were very odd) but no longer working the circuits of old. Again, as no bookings were advertised in the *Echo*, no dates are known. There is another photo, however, showing John, Paul and George standing with their guitars, Arthur Kelly in the background. Colin Hanton remembers it being taken after a booking in a Speke school, and that he was off to the side, dismantling his kit in a post-argument sulk. It was taken soon after Mike McCartney's colour photo, so George is still much smaller than John or Paul. Their matching stage outfit this time is white cowboy (western) shirts with black shoulders and white tasselled fringes. Everyone liked them, and Arthur remembers George saying he felt really good in his. They were obtained by Nigel Walley from a personal contact at a credit drapery shop – take now, pay later; but in spring 1958 Nigel was diagnosed with traces of TB and went into a sanatorium, and without his prompting, and to his acute personal embarrassment, the shirts were neither paid for nor returned.

This illness marked the end of Walley's tenure as manager of the Quarry Men. John and Paul visited him once or twice at the sanatorium, he says, taking their guitars for a sing-song around the bed, but while he stayed John's friend, as he'd been since the age of five, he walked away from the group . . . and without his endeavour on their behalf the bookings evaporated.

In their last shows, John and Paul were still side by side on the front line, eager to grab all the attention for themselves, singing together or backing each other. They didn't give George much of a look in. As John said, 'Paul and I really carved up the empire between us – we were [the] singers. George didn't sing when we brought him into the group. He was a guitarist. We maybe let him do one number – like "and here he is . . ." – but Paul and I did all the singing.'[45] Duff Lowe remembers these final bookings taking place on Saturday nights in 'various social clubs in the area. If we got paid it was very small, £1 each or less. I never took it that seriously. But Paul and John always gave it 120 per cent, it had to be perfect.'

It was at this time that John decided the Quarry Men should make a record, and the others needed no persuading – just 3s 6d each. This time the answer to 'Where we going, Johnny?' was 38 Kensington, where one Percy F. Phillips ran probably Liverpool's only recording studio and record press. It may be that George told him about it, because Johnny Byrne and Paul Murphy of the Texans cut a two-sided 78rpm disc here in 1957 and George probably heard it during the Morgue period. However they knew of it, the setting was appropriate. Elvis, Carl and Jerry Lee recorded for Sam Phillips in Memphis, John, Paul and George recorded for Percy Phillips in Liverpool.[46]

It was the five of them: John, Paul and George with their guitars (John and Paul acoustic, George using a pickup through Paul's Elpico amp), Colin with his drums, Duff on the studio piano. Though all the recording and disc-cutting gear was professional, it wasn't at all like the studios in *The Girl Can't Help It* and *Jailhouse Rock*: it was the small downstairs middle living room of a house in a Victorian terrace near a parade of shops on a main road. Traffic noise was dampened by curtains and carpets. The session cannot be dated with any certainty because the group's name doesn't show in the studio logbook, save for a note on the inside cover that reads merely 'Arthur Kelly of Quarrymen'. A plaque above the door of the house, unveiled in 2005, gives a precise session date of (Monday) 14 July 1958, but how this was arrived at has never been convincingly demonstrated; it could have been a month or two earlier.

Recollections of almost every aspect of the session are strewn with contradictions, but it seems probable they paid 17s 6d for a double-sided ten-inch disc, 78rpm, and recorded both sides straight to acetate to save what would have been an extra 2s 6d to go via tape.* Both recordings are live, the sounds captured by a single microphone suspended from the ceiling, balance non-existent. But it was *a record*! On what they considered the A-side they did That'll Be The Day, an appropriate salute to the Crickets for the song and sound that had changed everything, and on the other they did In Spite Of All The Danger, the composer credit – handwritten in ink under the title – saying 'McCartney, Harrison'.

Seventeen years later, without the advantage of hearing it in between times, John recalled what he could of the session: 'The first thing we ever recorded was That'll Be The Day, the Buddy Holly song, and one of Paul's called In Spite Of All The Danger. It cost us fifteen shillings and we made it in the front room of some guy's house that he called a recording studio. It had all the equipment, and it was a 78. And I sang both sides. I was such a bully in those days I didn't even let Paul sing his own song. That's the actual first recording we ever made.'[47]

The sound is rough, but here they are then, the Quarry Men. It is, again, unmistakably John Lennon's voice on That'll Be The Day, with Paul providing the 'ah' backing and George taking the guitar solo. The harmonies work really well. They shave seven seconds off the Crickets' version by going faster, probably through nerves. It isn't brilliant and was never likely to be, but it is live and they get through it, and the only hiccups are the right ones, when John pays homage to Buddy's distinctive vocal signature.

John again sings lead on In Spite Of All The Danger, Paul provides more fine harmonies throughout, and George adds an 'ah' backing. It's said Colin and Duff hadn't heard the song before, and so were feeling their way through it, but it's not solely for this reason that it plods somewhat. Though the debt to Trying To Get To You is clear, it's still an original number and an interesting, attractive one at that, written by a boy of 15 – a fantastic achievement. The B7 chord gleaned by Paul and George from that stranger way over town makes an appearance. The song is long: the lead guitar solo that Paul mistakenly believed merited George a co-composer credit comes around not once but twice, so by the time they were done three and a half minutes had elapsed; anecdotes have Percy Phillips waving his arms at them, hurrying them to a finish, because he could see the disc-cutting lathe reaching its ultimate point, almost at the centre label.[48]

---

* An acetate, or lacquer, was an aluminium disc with a nitrocellulose lacquer coating; because the grooves were softer than a conventionally pressed record, the sound quality deteriorated by degrees each time it was played. Acetates were much used in the music business as the quickest and easiest means of distributing recorded sound.

Paul says the entire session lasted a quarter of an hour, though what happened next is again unclear. In his only published interview about it, Percy Phillips said the group had just fifteen shillings, not the full 17s 6d, and someone ('I think it was John') had to return a couple of days later with the other 2s 6d in order to collect the record.[49] But Colin and Duff both have a clear memory of the five of them standing together on Kensington that day, holding the prized disc in their hands and just gazing at it. None of them could quite believe their eyes. Black gold. Duff also has an extra memory: that Percy Phillips popped the disc into a sleeve for protection, from a Parlophone record.

Equal owners, they agreed to divvy the disc around. John had it first (of course), then Paul and George, and Colin and Duff got it later. Others also had it for a while – a friend of Duff's kept it for a bit, and Tony Carricker swears he had it for a long time in 1959: he used it as collateral to get back from John an Elvis LP he'd loaned him. Somehow or other, though, it ended up with Duff.[50]

The record That'll Be The Day c/w In Spite Of All The Danger is the culmination of an era for the Quarry Men, the end of the road for now. It's not representative of their sound at any time other than this moment, which was a long way from the rough skiffle scuffle of tea-chest bass, washboard and banjo that was its start. Where once the group had been John's schoolboy gang, now it was John, Paul and George and a couple of others. Duff left Liverpool Institute in July and scarcely saw them again; Colin had a huge row with them after a performance and walked away: he didn't contact them, they didn't contact him, it was over.* Three boys were left, all guitarists – a nucleus.

After all the upset of the previous year, Jim McCartney did what he could to make Paul keep to his revision timetable, his main tranche of GCE O-Level exams due in June. Paul was already looking beyond them. In the spring, he wrote an undated letter to Mike Robbins asking for summer jobs at a Butlin's camp – not music but 'any kind of work' – on behalf of himself, Len (Garry, presumably) and John (Lennon). Though he mentioned in passing that his group had a 'smashing' new guitarist, George was simply too young for work. 'Both of my friends look 17,' Paul blarneyed, cognisant of Butlin's employment rules. In fact, while John was approaching 18, Len was 16 and Paul only closing in on that age; he was hoping Robbins could pull some strings for them. 'We would do any kind of work,' Paul assured him, adding that they'd be free from the middle of July …

---

* As usual, where and when this was remains unknown, but other events in their lives suggest it could have been before the summer.

9

'This is my life' (June–December 1958)

As an alcoholic with a restaurant job in the city, Julia Lennon's 'husband' John Albert Dykins – aka Bobby and (to John Lennon) Twitchy – had been courting trouble for years, driving home to the southern suburbs in the early hours. Just after midnight on Friday 20 June, however, half an hour into Saturday morning, his luck ran out. He was driving drunk along Menlove Avenue, just beyond Mendips, when he was observed by a constable walking his beat. Though the car was going at normal speed, its engine was racing. Dykins should have turned right at the lights but, seeing the policeman, shot left, and the car mounted the reservation between Menlove Avenue and Vale Road. The constable got to the road and flashed a torch, signalling him to stop, but Dykins drove on and came to a halt further along Vale Road. Noticing that the driver's breath smelled strongly of drink, and that his speech was slurred, the policeman asked him to get out; Dykins opened the door and fell out, and had to be helped to his feet. Told he was being arrested, Dykins became aggressive and abusive, shouting, 'You —— fool, you can't do this to me, I'm the press!'[1]

Dykins was taken to Woolton police station where a doctor certified him unfit to drive. Held overnight in a cell, he was charged in the morning and taken straight to the court, to be remanded on bail of £5. When he reappeared there on 1 July, his solicitor entered a guilty plea and Dykins was fined £25 plus costs, had his licence endorsed, and was disqualified from driving for a year. The incident was reported in both of the city evening papers and also twice in the local *Liverpool Weekly News*, which will have caused no little embarrassment in the family.[2] The Stanley sisters did not think highly of Julia's man-friend.

He immediately left or lost his job: either he was dismissed or gave it up, incapable of getting home late from the city, taxis unaffordable. The drink-driving incident had set in motion a sequence of events that reached a terrible calamity two weeks later.

Julia was often at Mimi's. Their original relationship had been rekindled since John began shuttling between them. Her visit on Tuesday 15 July had a purpose, though. The summer term at Liverpool College of Art had ended on Friday the 4th, three days after Bobby Dykins lost his licence and his job and had been fined the equivalent of about three weeks' wages, cash they may not have had. Financially, things were suddenly tight at 1 Blomfield Road, and Dykins had told Julia a stark truth as he saw it: they could no longer afford to have John staying at the house. It was going to be hard enough to feed the two girls without a gluttonous young man eating them out of house and home. If Julia didn't agree, then perhaps discussions became heated, because – heavy-hearted or otherwise – she ended up going to Mendips to convey this very message. John was at Blomfield Road when she left to pay the visit.[3]

Having said what she'd gone there to say, Julia left for home at 9.45. She had three choices: to walk all the way, perhaps cutting across the golf course; to walk down to Woolton Road and catch the bus to Garston (and then walk); or to cross Menlove Avenue and catch the bus going north, towards Penny Lane, and then change for a bus cutting back south again, to Springwood. She chose the last. On another day, Bobby might have come to collect her ... if right here on Menlove Avenue he hadn't lost his licence ... but for which she mightn't have been here at all.

Mimi sometimes walked Julia to the bus stop, but this summer's evening they parted at the gate. A number 4 was due within a couple of minutes. Just as Julia was about to head off, Nigel Walley came along, hoping to find John at home.

> Mimi said John was out, then Julia said, 'Oh Nigel, you've just arrived in time to escort me to the bus stop.' Julia said her goodbyes to Mimi and I started walking with her. When we got to Vale Road I turned up while she crossed Menlove Avenue, and at that moment I heard a car skidding and a thump and I turned to see her body flying through the air. I rushed over. It wasn't a gory mess but she must have had severe internal injuries. To my mind, she'd been killed instantly. I can still see her gingery hair fluttering in the breeze, blowing across her face.[4]

Walley ran to Mendips but the commotion had already brought Mimi back outside. By chance, long-term lodger Michael Fishwick was there too. 'Mimi and I heard the screech of brakes. We looked at each other and took off in full-flight out of the house. We ran up the road and across and there was Julia, looking quite peaceful, bloodied only at the back of her head. A crowd gathered. Someone ran off to ring for an ambulance. She gave one final breath and died.'[5]

Mimi, still in her carpet slippers, went in the back of the ambulance that sped Julia's body to Sefton General Hospital. What hell that must have been. Fishwick followed with her shoes and handbag, and then the police took them to Blomfield Road where no one yet had any idea of the terrible events.

Mimi would recall John being out at the time, but when he came in and was told the news he broke down, saying, 'Oh God, oh God.' John's own recollection, when talking about it nine years later, was different. He remembered a policeman coming to the door and, as if in a film scene, asking for confirmation he was Julia Dykins' son. When John mumbled a yes, the constable replied, 'I'm sorry to tell you your mother's dead.'[6]

Bobby phoned for a taxi to get him and John to the hospital. As John would recall, 'He [Twitchy] said, "Who's going to look after the kids?" and I hated him. Bloody selfishness.'[7] John gabbled hysterically all the way, but when they got to the hospital, unlike Bobby, he couldn't bring himself to see the body. 'It was the worst thing that ever happened to me. We'd caught up so much, me and Julia, in just a few years. We could *communicate*. We got on. She was great. I thought, "Fuck it, fuck it, fuck it. That's really fucked everything. I've no responsibilities to anyone now."'[8]

The funeral was the following Monday, 21 July, at Allerton Cemetery. John never spoke of it publicly and there's only one reliable witness to confirm he was in some way part of it. His cousin Liela (while not saying explicitly that John was or wasn't at the cemetery) would relate how she and John were at The Cottage, 120a Allerton Road, afterwards, for post-funeral sandwiches. 'John and I just sat there on the couch, him with his head on my lap. I never said a word. I can't even recall telling him I was sorry. There *was* nothing you could say. We were both numb with anguish.'[9]

The grief was not John's alone. In one instant, four children had lost a mother, an estranged husband lost a wife, a man lost his partner, four women lost a loved sister, three nephews and a niece lost an aunt, and Liverpool lost one of its colourful characters. The fallout was widespread.

Julia's two youngest daughters, Julia and Jacqui, weren't at the funeral and for many months weren't told their mum was dead or why they weren't seeing her, nor did they carry on living with their father. For reasons that aren't clear (but may be related to Bobby's comment in the taxi, or the family's knowledge of the accident's wider cause), they were allowed to be made 'wards of court' and raised by their Aunt Harrie and Uncle Norman at The Cottage. As a consequence of losing a mother they lost their father too, and were never really told why.

Because the law ruled there had to be an inquest, newspaper reports were inevitable, and in these the secret of Julia's surname spilled out. The first mention in the *Liverpool Weekly News* called her Mrs Juliette Dykins, aged 40, the second – correctly – Mrs Julia Lennon, 44.[10] The authorities finally realised that the long-time occupants of the council house at 1 Blomfield Road weren't who they'd said they were, that the property had been obtained on the lie of a pretence marriage. Julia and Bobby Dykins were instantly exposed to one and all as having 'lived in sin', their two girls illegitimate in the eyes of the law and the morals of the day. This could explain why Bobby was so quickly gone from the house. In the space of weeks, perhaps even days, he lost his car, his job, his wife, his children and his home. Strangely, though, his new home was better situated than Blomfield Road: 97 School Lane wasn't on an estate but among trees, backing on to Woolton Golf Course and facing Woolton Woods, an ordinary council house but on a quiet and pleasant rural lane.

The fatal accident hardened, irrevocably, John Lennon's view of the Establishment, and especially the police. Coming to believe the driver who killed his mother was 'a drunk off-duty cop', his respect for authority, and especially the law, crumbled and would only ever worsen. Where most people saw law and order, John would only see rank hypocrisy. The driver, Eric Clague, was an off-duty cop; he was also a learner-driver and shouldn't have been on the road unaccompanied, and was suspended from the force because of it; but he was never charged with being drunk, and alcohol wasn't mentioned at the inquest. Though it's possible it was suppressed, it's also possible this cornerstone of John's lasting grudge against the police was set in misinformation.

Julia's husband took the news badly. Alf Lennon probably hadn't seen his wife in twelve years, not since the eventful Blackpool episode of 1946, when John was five. They'd never divorced, and this meant he was entitled to her estate. When Julia's sisters tried to claim on her life insurance it was made clear that the man they still thought of as 'that Alf Lennon' – another of Julia's winners; where was he? in prison? drunk somewhere no doubt – would have to be found and persuaded to let them keep the money.

Alf later said he learned of Julia's death two months after the fact – 'I was out of work in London at the time, living in a doss house in King's Cross.'[11] He received word after getting in touch with his youngest brother Charles, who then sent him a cutting from the *Liverpool Echo*. Alf took it badly. He wasn't one for bitterness or grudges – he lived for the present, each day a fresh start – but this was painful news. He hit the road again and somehow managed to break a leg ... and it was while in this condition, resting in a Salvation Army hostel in London, that another letter from Charles reached him, explaining his entitlement to Julia's legacy.

Little in Alf's life was clear-cut. What happened next depends on which of two conflicting accounts is correct, assuming either is. Both are his own. In one, he dragged his broken leg to Liverpool only to be told by the Dale Street solicitor that Julia's sisters had somehow swindled him out of the money. In the other, the solicitor told him £530 (a *fortune*) was his for the taking ... and he, a gambler and down-and-out, heroically refused it, all of it, and said it should be held in trust for John at 21.[12] Whatever happened, Julia's death was another bitter blow. Alf had spent seven summers washing dishes at Middleton Tower holiday camp in Morecambe, but even this had come to an end; instead, he continued a well-established pattern: menial jobs in hotels (usually washing-up) and vagrancy, the down-at-heel but never down-at-heart Alf, the happy drinker falling in the muck but coming up with a smile and a song.

He seems to have made no attempt to contact his son, John Winston Lennon, the abandoned boy who was now broken. He had 'lost' his mother at five and now lost her again with appalling finality at 17, and so soon after establishing a profound connection. It was the most tremendous and irreconcilable heartbreak. As he would put it, with customary deafening economy, she had him but he never had her. He was scarred for life, and more embittered, more cynical, more harsh, more uncompromising, more edgy, more volatile than ever. It was also the second death of a close loved-one in three years, because that's all it was since his dear Uncle George, his father figure, had gone at the age of 52. Life was still dealing John Lennon bad cards. As he would recall in 1980: '[It] was really a hard time for me and it just absolutely made me very, very bitter. The underlying chip on my shoulder I'd had as a youth was really big then. Being a teenager, and rock and roll and sideboards and art school and mother being killed just when I was re-establishing a relationship with her – it was very traumatic for me.'[13]

Accounts vary about John's reaction in the first weeks after the accident. Some have him burying his feelings, going quiet; others have him raging and rampaging, drunk and vitriolic. The witnesses are reliable. Everyone agrees that he never talked about it. *Internalise* would have been the word, had it existed.

It was Mimi's role in life to have backbone, and to show it: the eldest of the five surviving Stanley sisters, the family matriarch after their mother's death, John's surrogate mother from the age of five, the reliable provider for husband, nephew and lodgers. Now the sole caring adult in John's life, she would continue to do her best and to protect him – but it was going to be a fiery old time, especially as he no longer had the Blomfield Road bolt-hole for days, evenings, weekends. Thunderous verbal exchanges were inevitable. Mimi was going to have this damaged youth undiluted, for good and for ill.

Despite John's very mixed feelings about Twitchy, they maintained some semblance of a relationship at least a little longer. Dykins got a job in the Viscount restaurant at Liverpool Airport, and when John was looking for summer work, the chance to earn a few quid until college went back, Dykins obliged. For perhaps three or four weeks, probably in August 1958, John did some basic restaurant work here: washing up, waiting at tables, packing sandwiches. It was his first ever job. As his later friend and assistant Derek Taylor would recall, however,[14] when they were passing through the airport on a particularly momentous occasion in 1964, 'John advised anyone who would listen not to eat cheese sandwiches at Speke Airport; he said he'd once been employed there as a packer and used to spit in them for spite.'*

Richy Starkey turned 18 on 7 July. Free of illness for almost three years, he was in more vigorous health now than at any time. He'd stopped growing at 5ft 8in, neither giant nor shrimp, and he had a bigger-than-normal nose that people weren't slow to tell him about; yet while his visage was naturally downcast, which meant people thought he was glum, or even miserable, he was generally contented – 'I always feel I was born happy,' he would say. He was also a bolshie teenager, full of robust views loudly broadcast. At 16, he'd declared everyone should be shot at 60 to create more space on the planet; he'd since revised that figure – 'When I was 18 I thought that thirty was the time to die.'[15] It was all about *now*. Eighteen was only *a* birthday – not the big coming-of-age marker, which was 21 – but it meant legal drinking. Richy celebrated with Roy, knocking 'em back in the city-centre pubs where they'd been underage customers; when they shared their deceit with the manageress at the Lisbon, she feigned anger and then they all had a bloody good laugh about it.

It was to Richy's credit, and his parents', that he was always prepared to put in a good shift of work to earn his ale money, unlike so many of Dingle's work-shy men who just lived off the dole. The fruit of his labour at H. Hunt & Son must have been a source of real pride in the family when the Sixth British Empire and Commonwealth Games opened in Cardiff on 18 July: there, on television, was the diving board Richy had helped make, the springboard to an English victory, no less. Generally, however, Richy found work at Hunt's a mixed but mostly dull bag: the bosses got on his nerves and he hated one of the foremen who lorded it over him but knew less about the work than he did. Years later, asked to describe his time here, Richy said only, 'I was lugging metal about

---

* Oblivious to this past association, the airport was renamed Liverpool John Lennon Airport in 2002, and the art deco terminal building where he worked, and spat in the sandwiches, is now Crowne Plaza Liverpool John Lennon Airport Hotel. (He's sure to have come up with a pithier name.)

and chopping it up and things, which got me down.'[16] Another thing that got him down was Hunt's relocation from Windsor Street to Woodend Avenue, Speke. Instead of a short walk to and from the factory, he now had to get up half an hour earlier and catch the 80 bus, passing George Harrison who was heading to school by bus in the other direction. Richy did this four days a week; on the other he'd either go to his day-release class at Riversdale Tech or sag off and head into town, perhaps to take in a Cavern midday session. OK, it was jazz, but it was live music.

Richy began his first long-term relationship about this time. Geraldine McGovern was a dark-haired girl, one year older, who lived in Kent Gardens, midway between the Dingle and town, and worked at an upholsterer's. They met, she would recall, at a dance in the north end of Liverpool, and went out together when Richy wasn't playing with the Eddie Clayton group or messing about with Roy. Richy called her Gerry, although his friend Marie Maguire says he introduced her as 'Gelatine'. The Roy and Richy double-act frequently became a foursome with Gerry and one other. As Roy remembers, 'He'd try to bung me off with one of Gerry's mates. I'd get the "she's yours" tactic and would go along with it just to please him.'[17]

Richy and Gerry's relationship became serious but has stayed private: not much is known of it. It seems clear there was a religious schism between his family and hers, Protestant versus Roman Catholic, and that this caused some friction; it's clearer still that the couple's harmony was undercut by percussion. Gerry had little time for her boyfriend's interest in the drums, which was bad timing because ever since seeing Johnnie Ray throwing photos from the Adelphi Hotel, Richy had defined his destiny: 'I decided, when I was 18, this is my life.'[18]

Pursuing this, Richy had just bought his first new drum kit, in May, replacing the secondhand set Harry Graves and his Romford relatives generously gave him at Christmas 1956. It was time to upgrade, and Richy had his eye on a £57 Ajax Edgware single-headed kit being sold at Hessy's. Canny lad that he was, he went to his beloved Grandad Starkey for the loan of a good deposit, £46. Elsie would remember, 'If his grandad even refused him a shilling he'd do a war dance. This time his grandad came to see me. "Hey, do you know what that bloody Noddler of yours wants?"'[19]

The bloody Noddler knew exactly how to pull his grandad's strings, *and* he knew where the old man kept his gambling winnings (when he had any) – in a sock in the wardrobe upstairs at 59 Madryn Street. Richy pledged to pay him back at the rate of £1 a week from his wages. It seemed worth the outlay: Eddie 'Clayton' Myles ran a really good group and continued to get the best bookings around. They even played the main dance at the annual Liverpool Show, at

Wavertree on 18 July, an especially prestigious booking. For Richy Starkey, this was one date where only the full kit would do.

For Paul McCartney and George Harrison, the school year ended seven days later. Boys could bring musical instruments into Liverpool Institute classrooms on the last day of term, and even more so than in 1957 it was guitars, guitars, guitars and a few more guitars besides. Paul and George performed together, plugged into the Elpico.

Asked some years later to describe how he'd been able to help John cope with the loss of Julia, Paul could remember nothing of the period at all. It could be they didn't see much of each other in the summer of 1958. John was working at the airport, and Paul and George went on holiday together – adventurous for boys of 16 and 15. But Louise Harrison would recall how she encouraged George to visit John at Mendips, 'so he wouldn't be alone with his thoughts'. The awful fact that both his mates had lost their mothers terrified George: the penny dropped that his might die any moment too. 'He'd watch me carefully all the time. I told him not to be so silly, I wasn't going to die.'[20]

Paul and John shared tragedies of sudden severity – Paul lost his mother at 14 in 1956 with literally no warning, John lost his at 17 in 1958, the same way. Not that they spoke of it, as Paul says:

> We had a bond there that we never talked about – but each of us knew that had happened to the other . . . I know he was shattered, but at that age you're not *allowed* to be devastated, and particularly as young boys, teenage boys, you just shrug it off. That's a lot of what we did – we had private tears. It's not that either of us was remotely hard-hearted about it, it *shattered* us, but we knew you had to get on with your life. I'm sure I formed shells and barriers in that period that I've got to this day. John certainly did.[21]

Paul's hope that Mike Robbins might swing them summer jobs at Butlin's came to nothing; the plan would anyway have been wrecked by Julia's death. But Paul and George did have that holiday, their first together, away from their parents. Some of the details are sketchy, but they ended up in a farmhouse bungalow in Harlech, just around the west Wales coast from Pwllheli.* John

---

* One of the sketchy details is how they got here from Liverpool and back again. Paul says they hitch-hiked – quite a risk considering their youth. They certainly hitch-hiked on a second such holiday in 1959.

Brierley, the then 16-year-old son of the farm owners, remembers Paul and George 'wandering around':

> They didn't know us. It was just 'Can we stop in your field?' We had quite a bit of land at the back. Mum said that was fine, so they put up this crappy little tent and started camping. It poured with rain during the night, and because their tent was useless they were wet through. So Mum said, 'You can't stop out there, come in.' They stayed in the bungalow, both of them sharing a double-bed, and Mum fed and watered them for the duration of their stay.
>
> My abiding memory is Paul playing my crummy acoustic guitar upside down for the left-hander. George also played it, and we had a piano in what we called 'the bottom room'. Buddy Holly's Think It Over had just come out and I remember Paul working on it and working on it until he'd completely figured out the piano solo in the middle. My younger brother Bernard loved the way Paul pounded away at the Little Richard songs and kept bothering him to play them again, over and over, and Paul was always happy to oblige.[22]

Paul remembers a week of playing snooker (there was a half-size table in the same room as the piano) and repeated spins of Elvis's first LP, Rock 'n' Roll, which John Brierley owned – those fabulous early Sun recordings burning deeper and deeper into their psyche. George noticed how one of the farm's Alsatian dogs had an arthritic hind leg, and told it as a joke for years: 'Heard the one about the woman who had a dog with no legs? Every morning she'd take it out for a slide.'[23]

The week's high point, perhaps, was when Paul and George sat in for a few minutes with Harlech skifflers the Vikings in a performance at the Queens Hotel pub. John Brierley was one of their singer/guitarists, and a couple of the lads stepped down to allow Paul and George use of their guitars. Beyond this, nothing at all is remembered of the occasion, except Paul says he was drunk.[24]

The GCE O-Level results were good enough for Paul. He failed History, Geography, Scripture and German but passed four: English Language, English Literature, Art and Maths. With the Spanish obtained a year earlier he now had five passes, enough to leave the Removes and progress into the sixth-form (class 6BM2), where he decided to study for two A-Levels, English Literature and Art, to be taken in summer 1960. With George automatically moving from the E stream into the Removes (form RC), the clear school year gap between them was restored.

Paul's two-year English Lit A-Level course delivered him into the hands of one of the most inspirational figures of his life, the English master Alan Durband. Known to one and all as 'Dusty', he had that innate ability to inspire a classroom collectively and connect with students individually. His age was a strong advantage: he was just 31, only fifteen years older than Paul. He was also a 'Lioban' (Liverpool Institute old boy) of humble origins who'd dragged himself up, worked hard and done well, studying under F. R. Leavis at Cambridge. Paul was particularly impressed that Durband had written a story broadcast by the BBC.

Another key was his understanding of what would drive the boys' interest. To get them stoked up about Chaucer's *The Miller's Tale*, for instance, he disclosed its many rude bits ('he kissed her naked arse full savorly' and more). In an instant, Paul was 'totally turned on to Chaucer'. Shakespeare's *Hamlet* followed, and suddenly a little-evident literary interest was awakened in Paul McCartney. He started reading plays – *Salome* by Oscar Wilde, *Camino Real* by Tennessee Williams, and works by Shaw, Sheridan and Hardy. Just as he liked to see himself as a songwriter, so now Paul saw himself, in his imagination, as a stage director.[25]

George, meanwhile, hated the Removes as Paul had done twelve months before. It was demeaning to be lumped in with boys a year younger. As he put it, with characteristic brevity, 'I did one day in Mike McCartney's class and then I thought fuck this and went over the railings.'[26] More than ever now, it was fun or nothing. Arthur Kelly recalls a moment in Art class when Stan Reed, for them the only good master, momentarily sat in George's seat to demonstrate a particular technique. Reed had black sideburns, and George, standing behind him, stage-whispered, 'Sing us a song, Sideburns!' – a line from the Elvis film *Loving You*.

Just as Pete Shotton's Quarry Bank descent had matched John Lennon's, so Arthur Kelly was set on the same path as George. This was O-Level year for them both and neither gave a fig about it. Many days they didn't go in at all, just sagged off. When they did deign to attend, at least one teacher struck an arrangement with them: if they promised not to disrupt the lesson, he'd let them sleep at the back of the class. George's school uniform became even more outlandish, so extreme even by his own standards that he knew it was 'very risky – it felt like all day, every day, I was going to get busted'. One of its many pieces was Twitchy Dykins' black double-breasted waiter's waistcoat that John had given him. (How John got it, he didn't necessarily make clear.) John also gave him powder-blue drainies with turn-ups, which George then dyed black for school. (John and George were already this close.)

And what of John? To everyone, his behaviour now seemed worse by degrees. He was the definitively gifted yet troubled young man, the mix that defined him: artistic and sarcastic, literate and cruel, brutal and tender, swift and funny, contemptuous of all pretence. His obsession with deformities, race and religion seemed to have gone up a few notches and absolutely everything was done for laughs, to amuse the audience he always needed. Jeff Mahomed exposed this one day when he jumped on a passing bus while John was pointing at something in a shop window. Jon Hague witnessed it and says, 'He was furious at being left alone like that.'

John told none of his college friends straightforwardly about Julia's death and the news spread sporadically, some learning it right away, others not for ages. Tony Carricker discovered it only when John was skint (his regular state) and looking to cadge money (his regular solution). Tony said to him one day, 'Can't you borrow some money off your mother?' The reply and the succinctness of its delivery shook him rigid. 'He just said, "Me mother's dead." And I said, "Jesus! When did that happen?" It turned out she'd already been dead a few months. John said, "What could I have said to people – 'Oh, by the way, me mother's died'?" It did explain to me why he was being a lot more cruel than he had been before.'[27]

The full colour spectrum of John's personality could usually be witnessed in the pub. The students' main hang-out was Ye Cracke – 'the Cracke' – a small and basic bar on Rice Street with a quaint little nook called the War Office where older men sat and drank. Art school student Rod Murray had many a session in the Cracke with John and mostly enjoyed them. 'Provided he wasn't picking on you for something, John was very amusing company. He was an endless source of amusement in the pub – largely at somebody else's expense, that is, which was only fine so long as it *was* somebody else.'[28]

It was in the Cracke that John developed the beginnings of a strong friendship with Stuart Sutcliffe. Four months older than John, Stuart had entered art school a year earlier and was in every respect a different kind of student. He had an outstanding talent, and his strong sole focus was on learning and developing as an artist. Where John was brash, Stuart was meek; where John seemed tough, Stuart was delicate to the point of being weedy. Where John only rarely wore his glasses, Stuart kept them on. They appeared to have nothing in common at all, but then found out, steadily through the 1958–9 academic year, that there was a good friendship. Bill Harry, who introduced them, says, 'Stuart was very much the introvert and John was the extrovert, but the two of them became so very, very close – they each had something the other found quite valuable.'[29] Pat Jourdan insists John was closer to Jeff Mahomed than to Stuart, but an abiding kinship evolved along similar lines. John was impressed with Stuart's talent and dedication; also, Stuart had *grown up*: he'd left home at 16, in 1956, and taken a flat near the college with Rod Murray, his best friend – the first in a series of scarcely furnished or unfurnished rooms they rented in the grand but deteriorating houses by the college, where Liverpool 1 meets Liverpool 8, the haunt of bohemians, great empty rooms with bare floors, high ceilings and no heating. They presently had first-floor rooms at 9 Percy Street, one block behind Hope Street. Rod watched Stuart and John's friendship develop: 'Even though Stuart was physically more slight, I think John looked up to him as a mentor in art, and also in general knowledge about things. And he admired Stuart's talent as an artist. You couldn't dislike Stuart – I can't remember Stuart saying anything nasty about anybody or being malicious, he was a really nice guy. John could be very abrasive and mean, but not Stuart.'

John's girlfriend in the autumn of 1958 was Thelma Pickles, a new and interesting student at the art school, just turning 17. Initially, she thought him 'a smartarse', then changed her mind when she witnessed his reaction to a girl who asked if what she'd heard about his mother was true. 'She said, "Hey John, I hear your mother's dead." He didn't flinch. He simply said, "Yeah." She carried on, "It was a policeman that knocked her down, wasn't it?" Again he didn't react, he just said, "That's right, yeah." I was stunned by his detachment, and impressed that he was brave enough not to break down or show any emotion. Of course, it was all a front.'[30]

Soon afterwards, John and Thelma sat talking at the Queen Victoria Monument and each revealed being deserted by their dads. 'He pissed off and left me when I was a baby,' John said of Alf, which was far from correct but no doubt how he felt. Thelma's father had left home when she was ten; she was sensitive to the stigma of having only one parent and emotional when anyone mentioned it. 'I couldn't sustain the detachment John managed,' she says. 'I thought it was quite an achievement to be able to behave like that.'

Suddenly, John and Thel, as he called her, were 'going out'. The shared soul-baring cemented it, and also they fancied each other. Thelma was the first female John allowed to get close after Julia's terrible death. She was given glimpses of his other side.

> When we discussed it between ourselves I realised he was clearly more sensitive than he appeared. He spoke of the pure shock of losing his mother, and he said what a *loss* it was (though I don't think he used the word 'loss'). At such times, he spoke in a much softer, more explanatory way than usual, and though he never demonstrated extremes of emotion, his pain was clear. The other side of the coin was that he'd detect any minor frailty in somebody with a laser-like homing device. I thought he was hilarious, but it wasn't funny to the recipients.[31]

Thelma was witness to a rare occasion at Mendips, when John, Paul and George all stood in the kitchen and played their guitars. Mimi was out, and before she was expected back Thelma and the two lads scarpered. John knew Mimi didn't want them in the house and would raise merry hell about it, and he just didn't need the headache. For a while, though, John and Thel took regular advantage of Mimi's going out (it seems she went to play bridge one night a week). The plan, carefully formulated by John, was for Thel (who lived in Knotty Ash) to take the bus to Woolton; she and John would meet and sit across Menlove Avenue in a shelter on the edge of the golf course, and when Mimi left and walked down the street, over they'd go. 'I only ever saw Mimi from a distance, in the dark,' Thelma says.

Mostly, Thel found John 'enormous fun to be with, always witty, and when we were alone together he was really soft, thoughtful and generous-spirited'. He made them tea and toast, he made her laugh, and he made love to her in his little bedroom above the porch. 'We didn't call it sex – that word wasn't really used by people then. John called it "going for a five-mile run", because he'd read or heard this was the amount of energy a man spent.' They used no protection, trusting only to luck, and John told Thel he was glad she was no 'edge of the bed virgin' – his euphemism for the kind of girl who would take him half the way there but no further.

John and Thel often took afternoons off from art school to go to the pictures. He liked the old horror films at the equally old Palais de Luxe on Lime Street, and they also went to see Elvis's final pre-army film, *King Creole*, which reached Liverpool Odeon in mid-October 1958. Though John very occasionally wore his glasses at college, he definitely didn't do so in public, and without them, even sitting near the front of the stalls, he could hardly make out how his idol was faring up there on the big screen. He kept nudging Thelma, nagging her to describe all the action: 'What's he doing now, Thel?'

King Creole arrived in Liverpool just when his loyal subjects were maturing into wage earners. Skiffle was as good as gone,* and though plenty of groups disbanded and many lads gave up performing altogether – going into jobs, further education or relationships – a strong and solid core soldiered on. While the record business (in both Britain and America) focused entirely on solo singers, in Liverpool it was still all about *groups*, mates together, adopting the Crickets' template: vocals, electric guitar, rhythm guitar, bass guitar, drums. Their music

* *Liverpool Echo*'s weekly Mersey Beat music column on 15 November 1958 called skiffle 'as much out of fashion as a five-year-old Paris design'.

drew on the widest range of American rock: some groups incorporated a piano and leaned towards Jerry Lee Lewis and Fats Domino; some went for the instrumental sound of Bill Justis and new guitar star Duane Eddy; some went for a more country influence; and many were wedded to the beat of Chuck Berry, the thrill of Elvis and Little Richard, and the harmonies of the Crickets and the Everly Brothers. For all of them, the invention of the electric bass guitar meant the tea-chest was put back wherever it belonged and the standup bass stayed in jazz. Hessy's and Liverpool's other instrument shops enjoyed another spike in business as boys persuaded parents to serve again as guarantors while they upgraded instruments on the drip.

Because all the available music clubs in town were devoted to jazz, Liverpool's live rock and roll scene took off in the working-class suburbs, generally to the north and east of the city, in scruffy ballrooms and bleak public halls. It was a process that took a leap in the final months of 1958 and owed entirely to the efforts of a handful of interesting individuals, ordinary men doing extraordinary things, blokes who fancied themselves as dance promoters and risked situations just this side of hell to put on entertainment and make a few quid for their trouble. As the old guard melted away, the first of the new wave was Sam Leach, a 22-year-old from Norris Green who decided to put on groups in a local hall for no other reason than he was a mad rock and roll fan.

Never a deskbound businessman, Leach's promotions were ambitious and chaotic. In his first real venture he set himself up as manager of Mossway Jiving Club, which opened for business on 28 November at Mossway Hall in Croxteth. From such tiny acorns, planted in the blood and crunch of appalling Teddy Boy violence, a huge scene would unfold. Members signed up to a six-page booklet of club rules Leach nicked first to last from the Cavern's. The club secretary was a quiet tax-office clerk, Richard (Dick) Matthews, 28, Leach's good mate and a gifted amateur photographer – his pictures would capture in stunning monochrome the first era of Merseyside rock. Together they drew up a leaflet for the Mossway that specified a four-point plan, their manifesto, in which they promised patrons:

1) Three-and-a-half hours of solid rock 'n' roll.
2) The very best bands on Merseyside plus the top records.
3) Good companionship, where guy meets doll.
4) One of the best halls in Liverpool.

John, Paul and George played no part in this emerging scene. Just when it was all going forwards they seemed to be going backwards. Their group was gone. They had nicknames for each other – Lennie, Macca and Hazza[32] – and got together only to go to the pictures, chat up girls, play guitars, have lots of laughs, and keep up with current records. Among their playgrounds was 97 School Lane in Woolton, Bobby Dykins' new place. Knowing when Twitchy was at work, or heading out to the local pub, John led his accomplices around the back of the house, where the larder window was kept open. Someone (George, if he was with them) would squeeze through, open the front door and they'd pile in. The others took the lead from John's attitude, having little regard for Dykins' property: one time Paul broke his record player; another time he scratched one of Dykins' own records (which Paul says Dykins subsequently gave him hell for); George plugged the pickup of his guitar through the radiogram and blew the speaker. They also raided the larder, made themselves tea and sandwiches and then snuck away before he returned, after a not always wholly successful attempt at restoring everything the way they'd found it.[33]

It was around this time that Jim McCartney tried again to make Paul learn the piano properly. Paul was keen, but kind of hoped that Dad would show him; Jim still declined, knowing he'd be passing on untutored bad habits to a boy with a great natural gift. He found the money for lessons for both Paul and Mike, and thoughtfully picked a young man to teach them, Leonard Milne, a 21-year-old piano graduate and tutor who lived just across the other side of Mather Avenue.

> I gave Paul one lesson a week, at a grand piano I had in the lounge at my parents' house, 237 Mather Avenue. He started on *The Adult Beginner's Guide To Musical Notation* but this didn't last long because he said he wanted to learn by 'chord symbols', letters printed under the notes – like 'C7', say. It's a musical shorthand he would have known as a guitar player. He didn't want to learn the real technique, he wanted to rush ahead – he was clearly a boy with talent who didn't want to be held back. I also didn't set homework because Paul made it clear he wanted to press on, not fiddle around with paper.[34]

To Milne's disappointment, but not surprise, the lessons quickly came to an end. Paul put up with them about as long as he'd endured his previous tuition, when the McCartneys had lived in Speke. Not only did he not want to be told rules, feeling he'd already gone a long way beyond them, he wasn't going to be bounced into anything either. 'I always had great [attitude] difficulties with it, I couldn't get interested ... there was no way I wanted to go back to simple exercises, I just couldn't do it, it seemed boring, like homework ... I didn't like to have to come back to the hard, rigid discipline.'[35]

Jim was despairing. He did what he could to keep the leash on Paul's passive rebellion but Paul was just so skilled at winning his way ... on top of which 'that John Lennon' was constantly barking seditious thoughts in his ear ('Tell him to fuck off!'). Though Jim no longer took Paul to Bioletti's, the barber at the Penny Lane roundabout, he still told him when he must take himself there. As Paul pedalled along the road, so his grumbles projected into the future, when *he* would be a father – 'No way am I going to be like my dad! I'm not going to be as strict as he is! If any one of my kids wants to wear long hair, they can do it!' He'd return home later with, so far as Jim was concerned, either the merest of trims or no trim at all. 'It would just look the same, and I'd say, "Was it closed, then?" He just wore me down.'[36]

Paul was also still getting together with John to write songs. Though their productivity seems to have slowed by autumn 1958, their ideas were merely branching out. Around October, perhaps during the half-term week at the end of the month, Paul made another visit to Mendips ('John! Your little friend's here again!') and was happy to find John typing a new poem. Actually, it wasn't a poem, it was more of a lunatic short story. Paul took one look and loved the wordplay, the typical Lennon phrases like 'a cup of teeth' and 'in the early owls of the morecombe'. John called it 'On Safairy With Whide Hunter' and its origin was clear: it was from *White Hunter*, an adventure serial being shown by Granada (the local ITV station) – weekly yarns about 'the surest and fastest shot in Africa', overblown scripts brimming with 'bwana'.

John let Paul join in and the satire became a way-out Lennon-McCartney Original.* Though some lines are characteristically John's, especially the trade-mark renaming of the lead character every time he was mentioned (Whide Hunter is also Wipe Hudnose, Whide Hungry, Wheat Hoover and Whit Monday), others are probably Paul's ('Could be the Flying Docker on a case' and also 'No! but mable next week it will be my turn to beat the bus now standing at platforbe nine'). One imagines the two of them in stitches when they came up with lines like 'All too soon they reached a cleaner in the jumble and set up cramp.' Another sentence – 'Jumble Jim, whom shall remain nameless, was slowly but slowly asking his way through the underpants' – could well have been a reference to Jim McCartney.[37]

Perhaps emboldened by their Safairy – or, more likely and much less pro-saically, because they were having a laff – John and Paul also started to write a play. Two pages of an exercise book were filled with dialogue about a Jesus-like figure they called Pilchard, who lived in a working-class slum in the north of England. Coinciding with Paul's Durband-inspired literary phase, the hero

---

* Or as John put it, when it was part of a bestselling book six years later, 'Written in conjugal with Paul'.

was not going to be seen but merely referred to, as in 'He's upstairs praying'. Things ground to a halt when it hit the writers that plays need structure; theirs didn't have one, and they couldn't be bothered to put in the effort. Paul says it had 'a suburban parlour setting' which squares with its first description in print, four years later, when he told writer-poet Adrian Mitchell (then of the *Daily Mail*) it was 'about a feller called Pilchard who was Jesus come back into the slums'.[38] At this same time, Lennon-McCartney wrote a comedy song called I Fancy Me Chances, set in a Liverpool dance hall and designed to be sung in a thick adenoidal Scouse voice. If connected to the play, it would have made it a musical.

> I fancy me chances with you / I fancy me chances with you.
> When we're at the dances, I fancy me chances / I fancy me chances
>   with you.[39]

John, Paul and George performed only a handful of times at most in these last months of 1958, a private party or two, a low-key dance here and maybe there, nothing advertised, details non-existent. They went out as a trio of singing guitarists and, if challenged over the absence of a drummer, had a ready-made reply they felt was close to unanswerable: 'The rhythm's in the guitars' – said with as much bluff as they could muster (which was quite a lot). The group name changed on a whim. Once they were the Rainbows because they all wore different colour shirts. Everything was done for laughs: at one party they turned up with cabbages and a workman's red lamp pinched along the way. In spite of the absence of opportunity, the three lads still hungered for fame, riches and freedom from tyranny: Tony Carricker was deeply impressed when John said to him at this time, 'I'll play me guitar in pubs but I'm not *working* for a living, I'm not going to actually *work*.' As Tony notes, 'This was revolutionary talk in 1958.' But how on earth could it be achieved?

And then, right on cue, back into their lives came the Savile Row-suited star-maker himself, Carroll Levis, dangling the promise of a spot on his weekly ATV show.

It was close on eighteen months since phase one of the Quarry Men auditioned for and played in a Levis show at Liverpool Empire, before Paul and George had joined. Quite how they found themselves back in the Canadian's orbit this time is a mystery, but George seems to have been the propelling force, somehow hearing of an audition being held in the Manchester area. They got there by train and weren't the only Liverpudlians to make the journey: George recognised and chatted to a quiet lad from the Dingle, an Elvis fan called Ronnie Wycherley, who had a solo act, singing his own song (Margo) while playing acoustic guitar. There are few degrees of separation in Liverpool: Wycherley was Arthur Kelly's cousin.

This time Lennie, Macca and Hazza called themselves Johnny and the Moondogs and only Paul and George played guitar.[40] John's Gallotone Champion was GUARANTEED NOT TO SPLIT but not GUARANTEED NOT TO BE PULVERISED. Having been on the receiving end of some heavy Lennon aggression in recent times, the once precious possession, bought for him on the drip by Julia, was now in pieces – 'smashed in half' was how he described it. His next move was predictable: on their way out of the Manchester theatre after auditioning for Levis, John spotted a guitar propped up against a wall and 'slap leathered' it. Three boys and two guitars arrived in Manchester, three boys and three guitars left. According to Arthur Kelly, John's new instrument was a piece of garbage, even worse than the old Gallotone. 'It wasn't even a nice guitar shape and I never once saw John play it. I said to George, "Couldn't he have nicked something better?"'[41]

Johnny and the Moondogs were told they'd hear by post if they were needed back for the actual *TV Star Search* stage show, and Louise would always remember George's excitement when he arrived home from the Institute one day to find a letter saying they'd passed the audition.[42] It specified a particular night (in the week commencing Monday 24 November) when, second half of the second house, they were expected to perform at Manchester Hippodrome. John, Paul and George, with their supporter Arthur, took the train to Manchester a second time; Paul remembers them rehearsing the Buddy Holly numbers Think It Over and Rave On along the way.

The *Manchester Evening News* review of the opening show declared, 'Never have so many electric guitars been plugged into amplifiers in such a short time, or so many incomprehensible words yelled in would-be Western accents.' Despite Levis's desire for complete Variety, most of the would-be stars were teenage boys performing rock and roll. It was big in Manchester too – not as big as in Liverpool, but still big. One of the acts was a pair of local lads, Ricky & Dane, actually Allan Clarke and Graham Nash. The latter would recall how Johnny and the Moondogs 'had a raw edge – they looked as if they didn't give a shit about being there'.[43]

John didn't bring the stolen guitar back to Manchester in case it was recognised, so the three agreed to stand together, Moondogs flanking Johnny who stood slightly behind them, his arms around their shoulders. The effect must have pleased the eye: as Paul was left-handed and George right-handed, both guitars were pointing out towards the audience. Their appearance wouldn't have looked nearly as good had George still been small, as he was in Mike McCartney's March photo, but he'd had a good growth spurt and was now close to John and Paul's height. Restricted to performing one song, they did Think

It Over; Paul remembers John effecting a casual look while he sang, and Paul and George added the *ba-ba-baah* backing. It isn't known if they plugged into Paul's Elpico amp or just used the house PA; either way, they'll have struggled to project their sound into the gods of the two-thousand-capacity Hippodrome.

The Levis set-up was the same as usual: acts did their one piece then ran off and were expected to return to the stage at the end of the night, when Levis would determine the winning act on the strength of audience applause. Arthur Kelly had done his best to set the right tone during their spot – 'my job was to clap and yell and make as much noise as possible' – and of course he'd repeat this in the finale. There was plenty of hanging about in between, and all the lads were busy ogling Jackie Collins, the younger sister of starlet actress Joan, who was Levis's compere throughout his 1958 stage tour. Arthur clearly remembers her: 'She was wearing quite a low-cut dress and seemed well-endowed. John said, "Look at the fuckin' tits on 'er!" – as if we wouldn't have noticed them ourselves.'

The peril of appearing second house and having to wait for the end of the show was the possibility of missing the last train home to Liverpool. The local station, Ardwick, closed after the rush-hour, so Johnny and the Moondogs had to get back to Manchester Central by walking, running or hoping for a bus. They had no real idea where they were and no money to stay overnight; they were also expected home at a certain time and due in school the next morning. The last Liverpool train from Manchester Central left at 10.35 and even this would only deposit them back in south Liverpool close to midnight, so there came a point in the evening when they knew they had to 'leg it'. It might have been only minutes before Jackie Collins was announcing, 'And let's welcome again Johnny and the Moondogs!', but when she did, there none came. Would they have won? Had they missed out again on the chance (of a chance) of Levis's weekly ATV show, or his BBC radio series? Quite possibly, because George remembers, 'We thought we were really good.'[44] Arthur Kelly confirms the three were far from pleased with the way it had all worked out: 'They were cross about it. We didn't actually wreck the train carriage on the way back but we jumped about and spat on the mirror – 1950s petty vandalism. It wasn't quite "tearing up the seats" but someone would have had to go in and clean up after us.'

John, Paul and George's belief that stars were made like this, 'discovered overnight', was more than mere cliché – it seemed to be all around them, especially when Britain's best-known rock 'n' roll manager Larry Parnes came to Merseyside and signed up Arthur Kelly's cousin. Young Ronnie Wycherley was a boy who, like the Quarry Men, had paid to have a record made by Percy Phillips; a boy who, like Johnny and the Moondogs, had just been to Manchester to impress Carroll Levis; a boy from rough tough Dingle who'd been in the same form at St Silas primary school as Richy Starkey, and who, just like Richy, had been in and out of children's hospitals and missed much of his education. Now, suddenly, with one wave of Parnes' wand, Ronnie Wycherley was gone in a puff of Woodbines and it was long live Billy Fury, kitted out in sleek suits, signed to Decca, appearing on TV, every inch 'a star' (though he hadn't yet sold a record). Ronnie had talent, certainly, but if it could happen to him then it could happen to anyone.

Something similar was occurring with another habitué of the Soho coffee bars, 17-year-old Harry Webb, a Ricky Nelson and Elvis fan from just north of London. Webb was signed by Norrie Paramor to the Columbia label on EMI's usual penny-per-record contract, but only after Decca turned him down.* His next few months were a blur, embodying every good, bad and ugly side of the British music business. First he was given a change of name, to Cliff Richard; then Franklyn Boyd, a music publisher, forced him to record as his debut disc *Schoolboy Crush*, an American cover version he was pushing, which Webb wouldn't have chosen; and then Paramor imposed session musicians on his backing group the Drifters.

Cliff Richard's breakthrough happened because Jack Good, a music man, flipped the record, heard Move It!, and flipped out. It was a terrific track; and when Good saw the boy's photo he knew he'd look great on camera. This was just what Good needed for his first ITV rock show – *Oh Boy!* – to be launched on 13 September in direct opposition to his tired old *Six-Five Special* on the BBC. Under Good's characteristic instruction, Cliff went for maximum excitement, ramping up the pouting and writhing like a pre-army Elvis. 'I got him to be mean, moody and magnificent,' Good says.[45] Cliff Richard exploded into stardom inside two and a half minutes that Saturday evening. EMI made Move It! the A-side and it almost cracked the top of the charts, and deservedly so. Up in Liverpool it was immediately noted by John Lennon and Tony Carricker. 'We thought Move It! was absolutely fucking brilliant,' says Tony. 'It was *British* but head and shoulders above anything else.' John confirmed it was a good record – at long last, something made in Britain that sounded American: 'Move It! by Cliff Richard was the first one that had anything like the right echo on it. Before that there had been *nothing*, just nothing at all. Nothing had ever got anywhere near [the American sound].'[46]

---

* Decca didn't meet Webb but heard a demo disc, recorded in the tiny studio within the HMV record shop on Oxford Street. Decca's Dick Rowe also turned down another Parnes signing, Reg Smith, renamed Marty Wilde.

The American sound itself remained the real deal, of course. Paul splashed some pocket money on *Elvis's Golden Records*, the first compilation of Presley's greatest hits – fourteen tracks, ten of them million-sellers in America. It set him back just a halfpenny under £2 – the most expensive LP he'd bought – but it served up endless joy and introduced him, John and George to songs they'd not heard before, old tracks but new to them, which they soon added to their guitar sessions, such as the Sun-recorded country songs I'll Never Let You Go (Little Darlin') and I Forgot To Remember To Forget. Paul liked to sing the first of these, while the second became one of the very few numbers they let George sing, and he also revelled in the Scotty Moore guitar solo; at the same time, there was a new Chuck Berry single, Carol, which John sang and on which he insisted he played lead (provided he had use of a guitar).

Other new records in the last months of 1958 that appealed strongly to them and which they either bought, stole from shops or pocketed at parties were Whole Lotta Loving c/w Coquette by Fats Domino, Eddie Fontaine's Nothin' Shakin' (But The Leaves On The Trees) – George bought this – the Coasters' Yakety Yak c/w Zing Went The Strings Of My Heart – Paul bought this – and one they all loved, To Know Him Is To Love Him by the Teddy Bears, a quirkily original harmony ballad in 6/8 time, the label of which showed just a single surname for the composer: Spector. The development of John, Paul and George's harmony singing took shape with this arresting song; they switched the 'him' to 'her' and set about correctly pitching their voices. As Paul would recall, '"To know-know-know is to love-love-love" was the first three-part we ever did. We learned that in my house in Liverpool. We just *loved* singing three-part.' Paul also says his dad helped them with the technique.[47]

The last day of term for John, Paul and George was Friday 19 December, and the next day they had a booking, a family do, invited to play at the wedding reception for George's big brother Harry and his bride Irene. Here it was, in the front bar of the Childwall Abbey Hotel – a historic pub on Childwall Abbey Road – that Japage 3 made their public debut.*

It had all started one day when John was in town with art school friend Derek Hodkin:

We were in Lewis's having a cup of tea when John said, 'Somebody said you've got a tape recorder, Derek.' I'd done my National Service with the RAF and been given £200 in compensation after a motor-cycle accident. I bought

---

* Childwall pronounced 'Chilled-wall'.

a Magnafon FRS tape recorder from Beaver Radio, suitcase-size but portable, with a carrying handle, so I had something John wanted. He was only my friend because I had a tape recorder, but I was quite happy about that: I was pleased to show off.[48]

The consequence of this conversation came one foggy night, probably at the end of November 1958, when Hodkin lugged the machine from his home in Widnes up to Allerton, to tape a musical get-together at 20 Forthlin Road. 'I was almost 22 and smoking a pipe, a serious young man in a duffel-coat. The first thing Paul's dad said to me was "Good to meet you, Derek – I'm glad they've got someone sensible with them."'

John, Paul and George were joined on this occasion by a drummer – Paul's brother Mike. The four of them and their instruments plus Derek and his recorder all squeezed into the front parlour. The precise origin of Mike's drum kit remains unclear. The way he puts it, Paul cobbled it together while its true owners were looking the other way, adding, 'We didn't ask any questions about how he got it [but] I think he acquired it for me so that I could be the drummer in the group.'[49] Regrettably, Mike's technique was hampered by a bad arm. Despite intensive physiotherapy, including electric shock treatment, it hadn't properly recovered from being fractured at the 1957 scout camp. Paul also practised with the drums and, inevitably, was a much better player, working out how to sweep around the kit like the drummer in Chuck Berry's Sweet Little Sixteen. However, Paul emphatically ruled out any prospect of being the drummer that he, John and George so sorely needed. Why would he want to play drums when he could be out front, playing guitar and singing?

As Derek Hodkin remembers it, the recording session was 'an hour of repartee, jokes, laughs, practice, songs, and quite a few ribald remarks about my French girlfriend'.

> I liked classical music and didn't really know rock and roll. I'd only heard of Elvis Presley. So when John said to Paul, 'Do your Little Richard,' and he sang Long Tall Sally, it sounded incredible there in the front room, a terrific sound, so loud and exciting. It was like they all had party pieces. John said, 'George, play that bit for Derek ...' I thought George was a bit of a show-off – he played guitar the best and let us know it, but everyone liked it. Then John and Paul started singing a little ditty that went 'I fancy me chances with you, I fancy me chances with you ...'[50]

Hodkin filled a seven-inch spool of Emitape then played it back for them – an experience he says they all enjoyed immensely. It was exciting, and ideas formed

in the bubble. Derek remembers, 'They said to me, "You can be our manager!"'
He didn't mind the suggestion at all.

Along with his recording gear Derek carried an RAF notebook, and when
John, Paul and George started to pitch and toss ideas for a new group name he
wrote them down in pencil. He still has the book, where the ideas remain, a
moment frozen in time:

THE POLECATS
THE RAVENS
THE BLACKBIRDS
THE JACKDAWS
THE JAYBIRDS

The Ravens is the only name underlined, so it was probably favourite for a
while, but the last of the five evidently sparked a new mode of thinking
because, above all of them – in larger letters, dominant – Hodkin wrote
JAPAGE 3.

As Hodkin explains it, Japage – pronounced as 'Jaypage' – came from the 'J'
for John, 'pa' for Paul and 'ge' for George, and it was '3' because they were staying a trio, having no intention of keeping Mike as drummer. Playing for a
recorded rehearsal was one thing, going on stage another. He wasn't even 15 and
was like a one-armed bandit.

Before leaving Forthlin Road that evening Hodkin offered John, Paul and
George the tape, but they couldn't afford to repay him its cost (about thirty
shillings), besides which they had no means of playing it, so he took it home.
He set to work right away: 'When I got home to Widnes I insisted on my parents listening to this tape. They both pronounced it "noisy rubbish" but I said
I was going to manage them.' He then took a tabbed A–Z phone directory and
wrote across the front '"The Japage 3" Engagements Book'. This records that
on 2 December 1958 he carried out his first duties, contacting (probably by
letter) the Territorial Army's Entertainments Officer at the Drill Hall in
Widnes; he also contacted the man who handled bookings at La Scala
Ballroom, Runcorn. Underneath each entry Hodkin wrote '£4', indicating the
fee he was seeking – perhaps a pound for each of them.

But Japage 3's first booking wasn't arranged by their manager and he knew
nothing of it: it was at George's brother's wedding party. There's a fine photo
of the trio playing here, framed in the window of Childwall Abbey Hotel: John
is again without a guitar (not even bothering with the rubbish one he'd swiped
in Manchester), they're dressed in neat uniform dark suits and ties, and they
all have quiffs. History doesn't record what they sang, but George would recall

them being drunk, and the groom remembers John's most singular contribution to the event: pouring his pint of ale over the head of an elderly lady pianist and wedding guest and announcing, 'I anoint thee David.' Outlandish behaviour was so typical at Liverpool parties, no one took against John for his action, not even the beer-soaked woman; she just walked off, silently but stickily, to try to dry herself.[51]

Two-thirds of Japage 3 saw their manager again a couple of days later, at his house, as Derek Hodkin recalls:

> I threw a party for Monique, my 'French girlfriend', who was visiting me. For Englishmen at that time, the very thought of a French girl was erotic. I chose not to invite George but this didn't stop John and Paul coming – they knew I'd have some pretty girls there. Though I didn't ask them to bring guitars, Paul did and he was busy playing and chatting up all the girls; John was in his usual tight trousers, black T-shirt and jacket, very beatnikish. Neither of them got off with anyone. My eighty-something grandfather said they were 'ne'er-do-wells'.

John and Paul were closer than ever at the end of 1958, a double-act forged through so many dimensions. No one ever made Paul laugh more than John, and right here at Christmastime came an incident he would always tell with great fondness. After leaving Forthlin Road late one night without his glasses, John told Paul he saw on Mather Avenue 'some mad people sitting in their front porch playing cards at one o'clock in the bloody morning'. *What?!* The next time Paul went past he looked for himself, and it was an illuminated nativity scene. Cue hysterics.

Reflecting on this period less than a decade later, Paul remarked how 'Each year seemed five years'[52] – but they were growing up fast. At the McCartney clan's annual New Year's Eve knees-up in Aintree, Paul was now deemed old enough to work behind the bar (a plank of wood on a few crates), pouring ale from the barrel, learning about 'gin and it' and 'rum and black'. There was his dad leading the singing from the piano, playing all the wonderful tunes of the 1920s and '30s; there was his dear Uncle Jack cracking great jokes to all the kids; there was the entire bevvied Liverpool lot of them swaying to Carolina Moon; there was the lone piper entering the house at midnight; and there was Paul, filled to the gills with black velvet, seeing in 1959 in the time-honoured fashion ... by throwing up.[53]

YEAR 2, 1959:
THREE COOL CATS

10

'A sort of violent Teddy Boy'
(January–July 1959)

The mainspring of so much joy and inspiration was cruelly shut off on Tuesday 3 February 1959 when Buddy Holly was killed in a plane crash at the age of 22. News reached his Liverpool disciples the following morning. Thelma Pickles remembers John discussing it in the art school canteen at lunchtime, though not seeming particularly affected. Another death of someone special to him. He had barriers for such upset. Paul McCartney would recall how word went around Liverpool Institute: 'I remember being in my old school playground. We used to get there in the morning and go to what we called smokers' corner, where we'd smoke a quick Woodbine before we went into classes. Someone had a *Daily Mirror* and there was the headline that Buddy Holly had died. The rug was pulled from underneath us. It was quite shocking.'[1]

At the same time, Derek Hodkin's management of Japage 3 was petering out, the first flush of interest having dissipated. Only four pages in '"The Japage 3" Engagements Book' have handwriting. Most intriguingly, he made contact with a Sergeant Head, who ran the NCO club on the United States Air Force base at Burtonwood, sixteen miles from Liverpool. Had Japage 3 played here they would have been seen by an American audience for the first time; but despite several discussions between Hodkin and Head over a £5 Sunday booking, it never materialised.

The only date Japage 3's manager successfully fixed was at La Scala Ballroom, Runcorn, where they had an on-stage audition during the Teenage Night on 2 March, while the resident Stan Clarke Orchestra took an interval break. The fee was a refund of their return train fares from Liverpool. Hodkin couldn't be present, so Tony Carricker – who lived in Widnes, just across the river from Runcorn – took it upon himself to be their guide, which included leading them on the half-mile walk from station to ballroom.

> It was just John and his mates Paul and George, and they only had acoustic guitars. There *might* have been another guy, a piano player, because in my mind they were the Japage 4, but I could be wrong. I do remember a group of girls bursting into our train carriage, girls I saw on my daily journey, so my stock with the guys went up considerably. The only other thing I remember is sitting on the edge of the stage with John when two local girls came up and asked us if we wanted to dance. We both looked at each other and said no. We didn't fancy the idea of dancing with strangers.[2]

Soon afterwards, Hodkin was able to tell John that La Scala liked Japage 3 and was offering a £4 booking on 8 May. Accepted. But one date is all it was going to be – Hodkin was finding rock management a complete bore. He cheerfully admits the group were never his priority: 'I was going out with a different girl every night of the week and that was *so* much more interesting than Japage 3.' Also, he found the lads demanding. 'George would say to me, "Have you got us any more dates, Derek?" and I thought he was cocky and aggressive, rather too full of himself for a 15-year-old. I was 22 and he treated me as though I should be doing things for him.'[3]

George's desire to play guitar in every moment prompted him to begin what he later called 'freelancing' – and in spring 1959 he joined another group, the Les Stewart Quartet.[4] He didn't leave John and Paul, he just joined Stewart's outfit at the same time, replacing another lad to become their fourth member. Stewart was the lead guitarist* and George played rhythm; there was also another guitarist – a guy with glasses called Ken Brown – and a drummer, Ray Skinner. George was just turning 16 and the youngest of the four, but Stewart (coming up to 18) says it hardly mattered. 'I never thought about George being younger, he was just a neat guy. I liked him a lot, and he was a pretty decent guitarist: he used to practise and practise and practise until he got things note-perfect. This was something I never did – I just used to wing it all the time and didn't have much patience.'[5]

The position had come George's way through a Saturday job he'd taken to pay for his Hofner President. He was a butcher's delivery boy, cycling around Hunt's Cross and Speke with bleeding white paper parcels. Because he was always talking music, George learned that another lad there had a Dobro

---

* Charles Leslie Stewart (b.1941); he played banjo, mandolin and piano in addition to the guitar.

resonator guitar, the first one George ever saw. As Les remembers it, this other chap, Tommy Askew, went to Old Swan Technical College with him, and this is how the link was established. Les lived at 32 Ballantyne Road, between Tuebrook and West Derby in the north end of Liverpool, so George had a multiple bus journey every time he rehearsed or played with the Quartet. This didn't stop him. Just like his dad, when George's mind was set on something nothing could ever shift it.

Looking back on this period thirty-five years later, George recalled only the odd booking with the Les Stewart Quartet. In fact, they played regularly at a British Legion club, and every Sunday night in a West Derby club called Lowlands. Like the Morgue in Broad Green, Lowlands opened in March 1958 and occupied the cellar of a substantial detached Victorian house, this one situated in quiet residential Hayman's Green. But while the Morgue had operated outside the law and was quickly shut down, Lowlands was the HQ of West Derby Community Association, bastion of a good neighbourhood. Its weekly teenage music sessions were in a low-ceilinged cellar named the Pillar Club, complete with its own integral coffee bar; committee-organised with efficiency and imagination, it was an established success for several years.

George's second group played different music. Of course they did Jerry Lee Lewis, Chuck Berry, Elvis Presley and Gene Vincent, but they were also one of the very few Merseyside groups to play real blues – the music of Big Bill Broonzy, Josh White, Lead Belly, Muddy Waters, Woody Guthrie, and Sonny Terry & Brownie McGhee. With only a little knowledge of the blues, George had to work hard to keep pace, learning all the time. The group's dedicated and only follower, Shelagh Maguire – Les Stewart's girlfriend, and from 1961 his wife – says their star number was a bluesy working of You Are My Sunshine, and remembers that George added one or two Carl Perkins songs to the set, which he sang.

George often took John with him to Lowlands or to the group's regular rehearsals at Les's house, and sometimes he took Paul. Les has a crystal-clear memory of John joining the group on the little Lowlands stage – at least once, he says. No further details are remembered, and there's also, unfortunately, no known photograph of George playing with the group. The period, though, was most likely February/March 1959.

George hammered the final nail into his schooling at this time. He'd just taken his 'mock' O-Levels and fared dismally, failing everything but Art; in English Language his mark was 2 per cent. The headmaster, The Baz, let it be known that, unofficially, he and the school were washing their hands of him, and if George, who hardly came in anyway, didn't bother to turn up during the summer term, that was fine. A stiffer fate befell Arthur Kelly. He'd been expecting for a long time to go straight into art school, like John, but then discovered late in the day that the college was implementing new admission rules, requiring three GCE passes. His only chance was to cheat in the exams – he did so, and was caught. Summoned to The Baz's chamber, it was made quite clear to Kelly that he should leave grammar school and not return. 'I wasn't expelled as such but I left at Easter 1959. Not long afterwards a relative pulled some strings and got me a four-pound-a-week office job at Cunard.'[6]

Knowing he'd be leaving in July, and now without the company of his best mate, George simply sagged off the entire time, not going into school for three months from April. He had no idea what he'd do with the rest of his life, and didn't care. Something would turn up. Knowing his dad would be furious at this latest turn of events, George felt it better not to tell his parents. He just pocketed the dinner money Louise gave him and went off on the bus every morning as usual, but instead of going into school he hung around Liverpool as a deserter. He spent a lot of time with his sister-in-law Irene at the flat she and Harry were renting as newlyweds. George would urge her, 'Don't tell me mum,' and Irene – who loved Louise and Harry – kept his secret uncomfortably but kept it all the same. Sometimes George would ask her, 'Where are you going today?' and when Irene reached wherever it was, there he'd be, to hang around with her some more.[7]

John and Thelma had been going out about six months when their relationship fell apart. The art school held a regular dance in the canteen, usually on the third Saturday of each month, and although they didn't always go, they went to one held around Easter. During the course of this, John leaned over to Thel and asked if she fancied 'going for a five-mile run'. She agreed, and they slipped upstairs to the Art History room, assuming it would be free. 'It was dark but we could tell there were other couples in there, probably having a five-mile run of their own, or trying to,' Thelma recalls. 'I told John I was uneasy about doing it in a place like that, especially with other people there, and he wasn't happy with my attitude. When I insisted on going, and got up to leave, he became rough and whacked me one – his fist connected somewhere between my shoulder and my head, around my neck.'[8]

Thelma stormed off, and decided that was the end of their relationship. She did her best to avoid John through the following week, and when this wasn't possible she simply ignored him. He started to mock her but she resisted his jibes, and this went on for several days until reaching its culmination in the Cracke. 'He was still mocking me, in front of others, and then he called me "an edge of the bed virgin". That really pissed me off because we both knew it wasn't true. He was just being sarcastic and wounding because he was pissed off with me, and I got so enraged I shouted back, "Don't blame me just because your mother's dead!" It was a cruel remark, but he knew all about those. It just seemed the easiest way to get back at him.'

John and Thelma had reached the end of the line, though they'd remain friends and keep in touch for several years. In an interview in 1980, John reflected on his teenage behaviour: 'Hitting females is something I'm always ashamed of and still can't talk about – I'll have to be a lot older before I can face that in public, about how I treated women as a youngster.'[9] Except that he *was* talking about it, and with the sort of candour customary even when it was to his own detriment. In 1967, John mentioned it within a song lyric and spoke about it to his biographer Hunter Davies. 'I was in a blind rage for two years,' he said. 'I was either drunk or fighting. There was something the matter with me.'[10]

This was also, of course, the way it was in many other relationships, and had been for a long time and would be in the future, especially in the north of England. It wasn't excusable but nor was it unusual, and such attitudes were reinforced constantly in receptive minds by the silver screen. 'Not only did we dress like James Dean and walk around like that,' John later remarked, 'but we acted out those cinematic charades. The he-man was supposed to smack a girl across the face, make her succumb in tears and then make love. Most of the guys I knew in Liverpool thought that's how you do it.'[11]

In terms of dress, John continued to interchange between college scarf and Teddy Boy drape, though being a Ted was always more a state of mind for him.[12] The persona remained very much part of his attraction to Paul and George, however – as Paul says, 'We looked up to him as a sort of violent Teddy Boy, which was attractive at the time. He got drunk a lot and once he kicked the telephone-box in . . . [and] what might have been construed as good old-fashioned rudeness I always had to put down to ballsiness.'[13]

In turn, Tony Carricker remembers how he and John used to watch Stuart Sutcliffe with admiration. 'He looked aloof, cool, very self-contained. He didn't have a good complexion or good skin but he created a very good impression and had a great James Dean haircut.' John's friendship with Stuart was strong now. Paul and George also got to know him, and George took a particular shine, admiring not only Stuart's obvious artistic talent but also his personality. 'I liked Stuart a lot; he was always very gentle. John had a slight superiority complex at times but Stuart didn't discriminate against Paul and me because we weren't from the art school.'[14] Stuart enjoyed hearing John, Paul and George play music together and enthused about them at a time when few others were doing so. He fixed it for them to play a party or two, and went along to encourage.

The Liverpool rock and roll scene remained far beyond their reach. Sam Leach was still active in Croxteth, and interest was picking up in other suburbs too.

A Crosby man called Brian Kelly, who ran an audio hire company called Alpha Sound, used the name Beekay to promote 'jive dances' in ballrooms in the north end, including Lathom Hall in Seaforth and Litherland Town Hall. Troubled places. And in the south end a young man named Wally Hill was taking his first steps as an independent promoter at the bloodshed that was the Winter Gardens in Garston, and also at Holyoake Hall, a Co-op ballroom close to Penny Lane bus depot.

Hill's enterprise swiftly attracted a like-minded soul, when Garston man Bob Wooler offered his services as disc jockey and MC (master of ceremonies). He would soon become known as the 'Daddy-O' of Merseyside rock and roll DJs, the city's very own Alan Freed ... or not: Wooler was quietly spoken, soberly suited, pedantic and punctual, but nonetheless a man blessed with clarity of thought and expression, a great wit, a fine grasp of English and clear diction. He was a born communicator, a wizard with words, and a pun-merchant beyond restraint. By day he was a railways clerk at Garston Docks, by night he became the soul of Liverpool rock and roll, the dean of the scene, organising all aspects of promotions and doing everything he could to advise and encourage the musicians. Born in 1926, Wooler was a secretive bachelor in his thirties who loved playing records and watching live music, so he lopped off six years and said he was born in 1932. That was already old enough. As he said, he didn't want Daddy-O to become Grandaddy-O.[15]

As the various halls opened up, so came the groups to play in them. In spring 1959 the *Liverpool Echo*'s 'Jazz' classifieds started to sprout new names, the first members of the first generation of Liverpool rock groups: Duke Duval's Rockers, the Rocking Rhythm Coasters, the Remo Quartet, the Swinging Bluegenes and the Raving Texans.* Al Caldwell and Johnny Byrne were going strong with their four-piece group, now all-electric; Caldwell's skill for self-promotion was second to none in Liverpool, undercut only by his peculiar habit of changing the group's name every five minutes. Still, he managed to get a good profile of 'the Texans' published in the new national paper *Disc* – a first – and at just about this time the drummer named in that article left and enquiries were made with a certain young man from the Dingle.[16]

It has proved impossible to determine dates or even the exact sequence of events for Richy Starkey in 1959. What's clear is that the Eddie Clayton Skiffle

---

* The Remo Quartet, technically gifted guitar players, included Colin Manley and Don Andrew, who were friendly with Paul and George at Liverpool Institute. The Swinging Bluegenes (sometimes just Bluegenes) weren't rock but a hybrid of jazz, folk, pop and comedy. The Les Stewart Quartet were never in the newspaper because Lowlands didn't advertise and their other bookings were parochial. Nor were Japage 3 ever listed.

Group had broken up by the spring. Skiffle had gone, and with it some momentum; on top of that, Clayton – Eddie Myles – was engaged and planning to marry by the end of the year. Relationships put paid to many a musical career in Liverpool, as elsewhere: it was time for young men to 'stop messing about', 'get serious' and 'settle down', to do away with raving and start saving. Rare was the girlfriend whose idea of a good night out was to stand at the side of a stage, watch other women eyeing up her man and maybe feel a few raked fingernails for her trouble. So, Eddie's boys went their separate ways.

This could have been the end for Richy and music, except he was fully committed to pressing on. So resolute and strong-minded was he that when there seemed no prospect of joining another group, he formed his own. 'I had my own band when I was 18, for three weeks. We had a clarinet player who could only play in B-flat, a pianist who could only play in C, a guitarist who was quite good, a tea-chest bass, and a trumpeter who could only play When The Saints Go Marching In. The band folded after two rehearsals, but it was a good try.'[17]

Some identities can be applied – Roy Trafford was the 'quite good' guitarist, Jimmy Roughley was on clarinet and Johnny Mooney on trumpet, with Richy on drums, of course – and the rehearsals took place in a small hall down High Park Street.[18] The group didn't have a name and their musical direction was never really explored because they could only ever play The Saints. They seem so motley a collection as to be almost avant-garde, and it was strange for a tea-chest to be used again – the death of skiffle had otherwise banished them back to garden sheds. Roy retired from the scene when Richy's short-lived band ground to a halt. Having been with the Eddie Clayton group for two years and this new one for two rehearsals, he put down his guitar and only picked it up again at parties. But he would remain Richy's lifelong close mate.

It could be that Richy's combo ended because he suddenly got a call to join the Darktown. They were, as John Lennon once noted, 'the biggest group in Liverpool'.[19] Not only had they had the most copious local newspaper coverage throughout 1957 and '58, they'd twice been to London to appear on BBC-tv's Six-Five Special. It's a barometer of Richy's already solid reputation that the Darktown turned to him when they had a vacancy … though this does also seem to have been downtime for the group, a period of restructuring, with fewer bookings than before. And though Richy was with them for possibly as long as four months, the period overlapped with his appointment in the Raving Texans. Like George Harrison, Richy Starkey was a member of two groups at the same time.

Richy was invited to *audition* for the Texans, something he'd never had to do before. Al Caldwell and Johnny Byrne gave Richy the thumbs-up with one reservation: Al was flash and his group had to be too, but Richy had turned up looking like an old Ted. 'I was still in me black drape and me hair back, look-ing a bit rough, so they were a bit insecure about me. But I got the job because I was a good player.'[20] Being in two groups meant, on occasion, playing with both on the same night. One time he even played with three groups – the Darktown, the Texans and a third outfit who turned up without a drummer. It was invaluable experience, having to adapt to the different musical styles and keep time with all the players, but Richy could do it. He just sat on the drum stool all evening, changing into a different jacket for each group and then walk-ing away with thirty bob at the end, ten bob from each.

One of his earliest bookings with the Raving Texans was on 23 and 24 May 1959 at the Cavern, still a jazz venue. Richy would always remember this because Johnny Byrne somehow managed to plug his guitar through a radio. The electric guitar had only been seen at the Cavern in the hands of Sister Rosetta Tharpe and other blues players; in the hands of a young rock and roll yob it was scandalous. Richy remembers them being thrown off.[21]

Another reason Richy may not have created the best of first impressions with Al and Johnny was because, by 18, his hair had developed a peculiar and promi-nent grey streak just above his right ear. As he later described it, 'this whole side went grey'. Richy believed it was due to trauma from all his illnesses. He also realised it looked bloody odd and created another unwanted problem: 'Liverpool's a tough place. People would grab me and say, "Who do you think you are, Jeff Chandler?" Any excuse to beat you up.'[22]

Also this year, Richy followed the lead of Eddie Myles and got engaged. He and Gerry McGovern had been going steady for twelve months or more when he proposed and she accepted. It isn't known if they fixed a wedding date, but per-haps they had 1961 in mind, when Richy's five-year apprenticeship at H. Hunt & Son would be completed; as a man with 'a trade' he'd be able to *provide*, and they'd get a house or flat somewhere in the Toxteth/Dingle area or, if his pipe-dreams came true, that little place in Aigburth. In the meantime, Gerry started preparing her 'bottom drawer' – collecting clothes and household goods in antic-ipation of setting up a marital home – and they bought each other engagement rings, which for Richy was his second piece of hand jewellery, complementing the signet Elsie gave him when he turned 16. Religion was still a divisive issue between their respective families and it remained to be seen how this would be settled, but of one thing Richy was quietly (or not-so-quietly) certain: if Gerry thought he was going to give up his drums for her, she was mistaken.

Plenty more great American records were issued by the British companies in the first half of 1959. Gene Vincent, becoming a forgotten man in the States but revered across the Atlantic, recorded the uptempo Say Mama and contemporary versions of the *Porgy And Bess* song Summertime and the *Wizard Of Oz* hit Over The Rainbow, the latter some distance from rock and roll but still enjoyed by his fans. Eddie Cochran followed Summertime Blues with an even bigger hit, the song that joyously stirred teenage rebellion, C'mon Everybody – his first British top ten success. And Chuck Berry was still turning out records of cutting-edge originality. Little Queenie c/w Almost Grown was not only a dynamic 45 but influential to budding songwriters. As Paul McCartney recalls, 'Little Queenie was the first time we heard somebody *talk* in a record – "meanwhile I's thinking".'[23] There was also yet another driving 45 by Larry Williams, especially liked by John Lennon – She Said 'Yeah' c/w Bad Boy – while the singer so many of Williams' fans associated him with, Little Richard, was back in the British charts yet again with a characteristically fran-tic Kansas City. As the *NME* noted, 'Little Richard's widespread popularity among British fans is quite startling, despite the fact that he still hasn't been seen here in person' – and there was also the fact that he hadn't recorded in almost two years. Kansas City was dug up from 1955.[24]

The writers of Kansas City were Jerry Leiber and Mike Stoller, the brilliantly inventive composers and producers who also continued to come up with records for the Coasters. Searchin' was the first to make a splash in Liverpool and there'd been several others; then, in March 1959, they cooked up another fine pairing: Charlie Brown c/w Three Cool Cats, again blending stagey satire with memorable vocal harmonies and sax breaks. These weren't just songs, they were playlets, rhythm and blues with plotlines, wit, atmosphere, incidents and accidents. John, Paul and George liked Charlie Brown and they *consumed* Three Cool Cats: they learned it with joyful care and sang it standing close together, taking all the different parts, perfecting the intricate timing essential to a suc-cessful performance. Once Three Cool Cats went into their stage set it remained a favourite for years.*

History doesn't tell if Japage 3 sang Three Cool Cats when they performed at La Scala Ballroom in Runcorn on Friday 8 May. This was the £4 date earned from their March audition but they weren't named in the local news-paper ad, which merely stated it was the Old Quay Workshops Social Club Dance, 8PM to 1AM, licensed bar, admission five shillings. It was the end of the line for the Japage boys and their manager. Derek Hodkin had fixed the book-ing but didn't turn up to see how it went. 'I had the flu,' he says. 'A couple of days later, at college, John said, "Where were you then?" That was the end of

* All the records mentioned were released in Britain by Decca's London label except for Gene Vincent (on EMI's Capitol).

it, really – they didn't want to know any more, and nor did I. That was the end of my participation.'

Hodkin's disaffection with 'management', the expiry of what had only ever been a whim, was confirmed over the following five weeks, to his lasting regret. The appeal of magnetic recording tape was that, while expensive to buy, it was reusable. Though Hodkin had briefly managed a rock and roll trio, the classics remained his favourite music, and during the course of two mornings, 31 May and 14 June 1959, he recorded extracts from the BBC Home Service programme *Your Concert Choice* over the one and only Japage 3 session, that Forthlin Road evening the previous November. Hodkin retains the spool of tape to this day, but where the larks, laffs and songs of Lennon, McCartney and Harrison were is Elgar's *The Wand Of Youth* and Bizet's *Jeux d'enfants*.

The end of Japage 3 mattered least to George. He was playing every Sunday at Lowlands with the Les Stewart Quartet, and it was at this time that he moved even further beyond John and Paul in terms of guitars, buying a secondhand Hofner Club 40 from Ray Ennis of the Swinging Bluegenes. It was George's first fully electric guitar and he was thrilled: 'I thought it was the most fantastic guitar ever.'[25] The name provided value too – John called it a 'Club Footy' and they all did the same. This was now very much their shared humour, and where George led, John wasn't far behind: every time he played the Club Footy he liked it, so now he wanted to go electric too. For much of 1959 he badgered Mimi into putting down the deposit and signing as guarantor on a new guitar to be bought on the drip from Frank Hessy's. It was something Julia probably would have done for him without much hesitation, but Mimi was always reluctant to support something she knew would distract John from study. 'His training would last, but these things come and go. One week everybody's clamouring for a guitar, then they disappear and nobody ever hears of them again. And what was I going to do if I had a boy of 21 thrown back on me hands qualified for nothing?'[26] Beyond this, how anyway would John be able to repay her and meet Hessy's weekly terms? He was useless with money; he spent it – drank it – like water and was always flat broke and on the scrounge. Mimi's final word on the matter – and she probably made quite certain John heard it – was that he would have to show willing, to prove he could fund a good chunk of the cost himself, before she'd even consider getting involved in buying a guitar. This, she surely imagined, would put paid to the matter once and for all.*

---

* There are no references to John playing his harmonica in these years. After finding the guitar in 1956 he seems to have left it alone for a long stretch of time.

Although John and Paul weren't playing in a group for much of this period, they were far from inactive. It will always be impossible to attach precise dates of creation to the early Lennon-McCartney Originals but quite a number can be ascribed with some certainty to 1959. At the same time, while they were still sagging off for fun afternoons in the front parlour at 20 Forthlin Road, and pressing close together in the echoey porch of Mendips, Tennessee, neither happened as frequently as before, and they were mostly creating alone. Most (possibly all) of the new songs from this timeframe were written by one and then appraised and perhaps improved by the other, and Paul was by far the more prolific. This was partly because much of the time John either didn't have a guitar or didn't have one he wanted to play, and also because most of his creativity was going into the written word, his funny poetry and prose. He himself would reflect, 'We used to write things separately because Paul was always more advanced than I was. He was always a couple of chords ahead and his songs usually had more chords in them. His dad played the piano – he was always playing pop and jazz standards and Paul picked things up from him.'[27]

In no particular order, the Lennon-McCartney Originals from this period include:

- Love Of The Loved. Paul remembers coming up with this on the Zenith and also late one night as he walked home to Allerton: either he'd taken a girl out or been at John's and was braving the dark short-cut home over the golf course, in which case it may be from one of those times he played guitar and sang at the top of his voice into the scary pitch blackness. Structurally and harmonically, the middle-eight leaned on the same section of the Teddy Bears' (Phil Spector's) To Know Him Is To Love Him, but the song smartly transcended its influences.* The title might have been a phrase Paul heard and seized on – a technique he'd already used with Thinking Of Linking.
- I'll Follow The Sun. Paul came up with this rhythmic ballad alone, words and music, on his Zenith guitar.
- What Goes On. Written by John, probably at Mendips. Strong Buddy Holly influence.†
- A World Without Love. A song fragment conceived by Paul during a dark, late-night walk home. He rarely made any bold claims for this one because

---

* John, Paul and George always called the bridge section in the middle of a song 'the middle-eight', not realising that, as a count of the bars, it could vary.
† At this point substantially different to the version recorded for disc six years later; only the chorus was the same.

of John and George's reaction to the opening line when he first demonstrated it. As Paul remembers, 'I came in and said, "Listen to this song,
fellers. 'Please lock me away . . .'" and everyone laughed. And that was it.'
Paul never did change the opening line, and on the occasions he played
it, when he sang 'Please lock me away' John would interject 'Yes, OK', and
end it there.[28]

- I'll Be On My Way. A Paul song with which John always happily declared
  no association. Written on the Zenith, with an attractively simple melody
  but the kind of lyric these writers usually spurned ('When the June light
  turns to moonlight').

- Like Dreamers Do. Another interesting McCartney song. George felt it
  exuded the influence of Jim McCartney, in the vein of his Gershwin
  favourite I'll Build A Stairway To Paradise.[29]

- You'll Be Mine. A 1960 recording of this Paul song was performed with
  overblown drama, but it's not clear if it was intended that way.

- Several guitar instrumentals, mostly and perhaps entirely composed by
  Paul. It seems they were created this way, that they weren't merely songs
  lacking a lyric: Hot As Sun, Cayenne, Catswalk, Looking Glass, Winston's
  Walk. (Though Winston was John's middle name it isn't known for certain if this was his tune.)

Some of these would remain unheard but – along with the already written
Love Me Do, I Call Your Name and the tune of what would become When I'm
Sixty-Four – several went on to become very well known, and one an American
number 1. This is extraordinary, considering that most people's early attempts
at songwriting are stuck crudely and often laughably at first base. A few early
Lennon-McCartney Originals were undoubtedly unsophisticated and unpolished – as the work of beginners, aged 16 to 18, they were bound to be – but
quite patently there was also something very special happening here.

In terms of group activity, the spring and summer of 1959 represents the quietest period for John, Paul and George. The answer to 'Where we going,
Johnny?' appeared to be 'nowhere', yet these months strengthened the partnership; it was a time when the friendships grew ever tighter, when they enjoyed
one another's company not by performing but simply by going round to each
other's houses, larking and smoking and drinking and burping and farting, playing guitars and records, hanging out. It's a period about which relatively little
is known, but it was fundamental to the future. It's interesting that though
George enjoyed playing with the Les Stewart Quartet, and though the other
members liked him, he never made the connection with them that he had with
John and Paul; he stayed closer to the group that wasn't playing than the one

that was. As he would put it, 'I loved my association with John and Paul because I had something in me which I recognised in them – which they must have or could have recognised in me, which is why we ended up together. And it was just great knowing there's somebody else in life who feels similar to yourself.'[30]

At the end of his second year in art school, John took the Intermediate Examination (tested in Life Drawing and Lettering) and failed. It isn't known if he broke the news to Mimi. A re-sit was possible, but his prospects were beginning to look bleak. If he cared, it didn't stop him pursuing his usual good time at an end-of-term party, held in tutor Arthur Ballard's room on Friday 3 July. Someone carted in a record player, a few people brought in 45s, and there was booze.

John had been secretly admired for much of the term by one of the quietest girls on the course, Cynthia Powell, who came to college every day by train from Hoylake, on the north-west Wirral coast. Liverpudlians regard Hoylake as posh, and John certainly thought Cynthia was. 'She was a right Hoylake runt, dead snobby,' he would remember. 'We used to poke fun at her and mock her, me and my mate Jeff Mahomed. "Quiet please," we'd shout, "no dirty jokes. It's Cynthia."'[31] The only class they took together was Lettering, all day Thursday in the Lecture Theatre, when John usually arrived late, sat behind Cynthia and constantly asked to borrow her equipment. He had nothing and she had every-thing, all neatly laid out; then she'd arrive home and find she was missing a ruler or a brush, whatever John had borrowed. John hated these classes: 'They were all neat fuckers in Lettering – they might as well have put me in skydiving for all the use I was.'[32]

One day, though, during a lecture by Dr Warburg, Cynthia saw Helen Anderson casually stroke John's hair and she was flushed with jealousy. It brought her up with a start, to realise she had feelings for such a brutish, intim-idating young man; yet as the weeks passed she could think of nothing and no one else. It was infatuation – 'He was the most outrageous character I'd ever met and I loved him for it.'[33]

Jeff Mahomed kept telling John that Cynthia secretly fancied him, and at this July party – where John rapidly became drunk – Jeff was egging him on: 'Ask her to dance.' So he did. John and Cynthia had a slow, smoochy shuffle around the classroom; she was in silent bliss and something clicked for him too. John asked if she'd like to go out with him some time and Cynthia replied, 'I'm awfully sorry, I'm engaged to this fellow in Hoylake.' John shot back, 'I didn't ask you to marry me, did I?'[34]

Before long, everyone piled into the Cracke for a good drinking session, the young men downing pints of black velvet. John appeared to be ignoring

Cynthia, and she and her close friend Phyllis McKenzie – they went everywhere together – were about to leave when the Lennon voice rose above the hubbub. 'Didn't you know Miss Powell was a nun, then?' That did it: she stayed, then the two of them left the pub, bought fish and chips at Vaughan's and snuck up to Stuart's room at 9 Percy Street where Cynthia proved she wasn't a nun. They risked pregnancy right from the start. Cynthia next had a couple of weeks with her mother and family in Buckinghamshire, but they agreed to meet as soon as she returned.*

The year at Liverpool Institute ended on 23 July – guitars in the classrooms again – and it was the end of an era for many. Paul's friend Ian James left, awaiting successful A-Level results that would arrive during August. Paul himself was one year behind, at the halfway point in his two-year A-Level courses. Neil Aspinall had taken his O-Levels and was quitting come what may; in August, he found he'd passed in eight subjects. And George Harrison left. He *went back* to leave, not having shown his face in the place since April. The three-month period of sagging off finally over, he turned up to collect his final report and also his testimonial – the piece of paper he could produce for prospective employers. It was written by The Baz, who wasn't a man much given to sentimentality: 'I can't tell you what his work has been like because he hasn't done any. [He] has taken part in no school activity whatsoever.'[35] With this document George was meant to make his way in the world. As it was of no use to him at all, and given that his report betrayed in black and white the post-Easter absences he'd successfully obscured from his parents, George felt his only course of action was to burn both before he got home to Speke. He walked in through the door of 25 Upton Green a free boy, no longer in education . . . and not fit for any particular employment.

He and Paul planned to take another holiday together towards the end of August, this time hitch-hiking around the West Country. In the meantime, Paul got himself a summer job, working for a few weeks as second man on a delivery van at Lewis's department store.[36]

John was unable to go with Paul and George because he too had a job. Tony

---

* Cynthia Powell was born 10 September 1939 in a Blackpool boarding house (601 Promenade South) to which her mother had evacuated one week before, at the start of the Second World War. Her parents were Liverpudlians: Charles (born 1899, a travelling salesman of electrical goods for GEC; he smoked untipped cigarettes and died of lung cancer in 1956) and Lillian (née Roby, born 1900). They married in 1926 and settled in Hoylake during the war. Cynthia was an unplanned third child following brothers born in 1927 and 1931. Post-1956, with both sons gone from home, mother and daughter occupied 18 Trinity Road alone but for the occasional lodger brought in to pay the bills.

Carricker's dad was general foreman on a building site in Scarisbrick, the Lancashire town just inland from Southport, twenty miles from home. A new waterworks was being constructed and Tony had fixed it for himself and John to be general labourers for the summer, on good money – about £5 a week. It was going to be tough work, the first physical labour John had ever attempted, but he had the purest of motives: that new electric guitar. Mimi had thrown down the gauntlet – if you want it, prove it – and John was fixed on doing just that.

11

'Come viz me to ze Casbah'
(July–December 1959)

John Lennon was not cut out for labouring. 'He absolutely *hated* it,' says Tony Carricker. 'He told me he used to pray every morning the train would crash.'

John's desire to buy an electric guitar, and at the same time show Mimi he could get it if he really wanted, came at the cost of blood, sweat and possibly a new world record in swearing. Tony and his father drove to Scarisbrick each day without him. 'We didn't take John because we lived in Widnes and it was a different route – and also because me dad couldn't stand him.' As the working day began at eight, John had to get up around five, which for a teenager who loved sleep and hated going to bed early was a constant problem. His journey entailed train changes and a crosstown walk before he got to distant Ormskirk, where the Carrickers collected him. If John was late and missed them he had to make further train changes to finally land up at Bescar Lane, a tiny station in the middle of Lancashire fields. From there he would trudge along country lanes to the building site. And that was before his working day even began, when those artistic hands grabbed the pick-axe in ineffective anger. As Tony says, 'We weren't skilled, we were the lowest of the pecking order, doing the lighter end of the work: wielding pick-axes, shovelling. I found that labouring didn't hurt me. Once the hands stopped bleeding, after a couple of weeks, I could enjoy it. John hated every minute of it – he had no physical reserves at all.'[1]

It must have been Murphy's law that dictated John Lennon's labour pains should occur during one of those rare golden summers in Britain, the sun beating down every day without respite, a month or more of heatwave and everyone complaining. The purpose of their work was to ready the ground for the construction of a new water pumping station, excavating and preparing foundations, but whatever the stresses and strains, they couldn't complain about £5 a week. John's new guitar homed closer into view with every f-f-f-f-flourish of that pick-axe.

George was also involved in construction work at this time – of a sort. He'd been 'freelancing' with the Les Stewart Quartet about six months when, as Stewart clearly recalls, a woman approached them all one Sunday night outside Lowlands youth club after a show. She lived just across the road, she explained, in a similar house at number 8, and was planning to open a rival club in her cellar. It was going to be made by teenagers for teenagers, and have a resident live group. Did they want to have a look around?

The woman was Mrs Mona Best, a dusky-skinned Anglo-Indian who'd sailed into Liverpool at Christmas 1945 as the wartime bride of Johnny Best, the city's well-known boxing promoter. Mona's eldest son – she called him Peter – was born in Madras and four years old when their ship docked in Liverpool. Known to his friends as Pete, he was now a very quiet though sporty 17-year-old, halfway through his A-Level course at Liverpool Collegiate grammar school. The combination of two factors – Peter bringing home friends and Mona's urge to foster that, as well as the good nights he'd had at Lowlands – inspired her to announce they could have a place just like it in their very own house. What better way for Peter and his younger brother Rory to be surrounded by friends than having their own exclusive club? And she could do it: Mona Best was a perpetual can-do woman, a human hurricane to whom everything was possible, especially for her adored sons.

George went to have a look around the place with Les and the others. It was going to be interesting – strangely, a second members-only teenagers' coffee-bar club on this quiet, leafy lane, a clone of Lowlands but more trendy. They accepted Mona's invitation to get involved. As Shelagh Maguire remembers, 'Mrs Best said if we would help convert her cellar into a club then she would give the group the weekly residency. So Les, Ray, Ken, George, me and one or two others all started to paint the place and get it ready, working evenings and weekends.'[2]

Paul's temporary job with Lewis's gave him real money for the first time, a fabulous feeling, and he was both flush and well placed to inject some impetus into his record collection. A succession of important buys and experiences came together in this short space of time – memories he would always recall with affection.

One was the new Chuck Berry single, Back In The USA c/w Memphis,

Tennessee, issued in Britain on the consistently superb London label. Paul (or John) bought it, and shared the joys together. 'I remember learning Memphis up in John's bedroom – it had the greatest guitar riff *ever*,' Paul says.[3] It also had an impact on songwriters Lennon-McCartney: Paul would always cite the line 'hurry-home drops on her cheek' as a lesson in lyrical economy, much as they admired the Buddy Holly line in I'm Looking For Someone To Love 'drunk man – streetcar – foot slip – there you are'. This was their poetry.

Another new release that resonated – though with Paul alone, not at all with John or George – was The Honeymoon Song, a tender and sweetly melodic Mediterranean ballad by the Marino Marini Quartet, issued by Decca UK's Italian label Durium. Several other important new singles were then issued as August headed into September. The Everly Brothers had ('Til) I Kissed You, another great harmony piece, and death hadn't stopped Buddy Holly releasing records: Peggy Sue Got Married c/w Crying, Waiting, Hoping made a big impression and few realised the elaborate production work that turned Holly's rough home demos into finished masters. (John, Paul and George particularly liked the catchy B-side, another good harmony piece for them to practise.) Other hot new 45s included, on Parlophone, the driving R&B rocker Leave My Kitten Alone by Little Willie John; and Linda Lu by Ray Sharpe, the B-side of which was a swinging rock update of the old number Red Sails In The Sunset – as sung by Alf Lennon in many a floating Pig & Whistle saloon in the 1930s. All these went into their collective bag.*

Unless Paul was out late on Saturdays with John and George, the day that began with a lie-in to the sounds of *Saturday Club* ended with the radio tuned to the same Light Programme for *Pick Of The Pops*, running up to midnight with an hour of chart hits and new releases.† On 25 July, host David Jacobs played the new single by Ray Charles – in fact, he played both sides of it: What'd I Say was one long track, at 6.25, split into two parts for the disc, its electric piano and call-and-response vocals spinning joyously on and on. Passion for a new song can sometimes be instant, and this was one such time: Paul leaned out of bed, scribbled it down and bought it on release date. Few others

---

* Parlophone released many US masters, primarily through its arrangement with the Cincinnati-based King Records. George Martin was rarely involved in deciding these issues – it was usually handled by another EMI department.

† Two hours of music 'designed for teenage appeal', *Saturday Club* was presented by Brian Matthew and broadcast by the BBC Light Programme every week from 4 October 1958, a successor to the half-hour *Saturday Skiffle Club* launched on 1 June 1957. David Jacobs also hosted BBC-tv's newest pop show, *Juke Box Jury*, copied under licence from its American originator, the LA DJ Peter Potter. It went out every week from 1 June 1959, a panel of four guests voting a selection of new 45s a 'Hit' or a 'Miss'.

in Britain did the same, which meant that What'd I Say didn't break into the
NME Top Thirty, but its impact was colossal. This one recording constructed
the bridge back from rock and roll to rhythm and blues; it was gospel too, and
a major step towards the breakthrough of soul music. It was a great favourite
of John, Paul and George, as Paul recalls: 'Ray Charles's What'd I Say was one
of our favourites: this record *blew our socks off*.'[4]

As the summer holidays progressed, Paul and George set out on their second
consecutive adventure together, their plan being to hitch-hike from the north-
west to the south-west of England, down the spine, and then take it from there.
The first destination was the only known factor: Sandy Bay holiday camp in
Exmouth, where George had been with his mum and dad in 1955 and '56,
befriending Jenny Brewer, with whom he was maintaining a warm pen-pal relationship. Paul and George each had a haversack into which they stuffed a towel
and swimming trunks, one or two changes of clothes, toothbrush and toothpaste, comb and hair grease. Paul took his guitar, and it seems George took one
too.[5] They had a small cooking stove heated by methylated spirit, and one or
two cans of spaghetti and rice pudding, to be eaten straight from warmed-up
tins. They had cigarettes, a camera and little money, just £2 10s each, planning
to hitch-hike everywhere and sleep any place they could find for nothing. It
turned out to be a week of hungry days, cold nights and general discomfort,
but, these things being what they are, they'd love remembering the good bits.

They set out on Saturday 15 August, 'thumbing a ride' – crooking a digit at
passing motorists in the direction of travel. Though Britain's first motorway
wasn't yet open, they managed to cover two hundred miles this first day and by
Sunday lunchtime had hitched the extra seventy miles down to Sandy Bay. This
was their destination, but they stayed just one night. Paul says they had twin
aims – to pull birds, and show the local groups how to play guitar – and maybe
Exmouth didn't provide the opportunities. The following morning they were
back on the road and heading deeper into the West Country; there was talk of
Torquay, but really they'd be going *wherever*, like one of those 'mystery tour'
coach trips advertised in the resort shop-windows. A third aim of the week was
to drink as much beer as possible, provided barmen turned a blind eye to their
youth. In one pub they met a drunk whose name, he said, was Oxo Whitney.
Paul and George thought it hysterically funny and repeated it the rest of the
holiday. This Monday night was spent on the beach at Paignton where, though
temporarily warmed by a couple of 'Salvation Army girls' (as George would
remember them), they shivered for hours, waking with aching limbs.[6]

A ride thumbed on Tuesday took them back inland, at which point – by
design or otherwise – they left the West Country behind. In need of a proper
bed, Paul had the idea they could gatecrash Butlin's in Pwllheli, where Bett and

Mike Robbins would surely see them right. They headed back north, reached Wales by the Aust Ferry, and when eventually they arrived at Butlin's were met with the barbed-wire fences erected to keep non-payers out (and payers in). In tandem with the grim chalets – still the old naval training base huts – it put George in mind of a German prisoner-of-war camp from any one of a dozen 1950s British films. And though they saw Bett and Mike Robbins, they couldn't stay at the camp without paying, or else it was full, because they moved on again, around the coast to Harlech and back to the Brierleys' farmhouse where they'd stayed a week in 1958. This time they spent the last couple of nights here.

They planned to be back in Liverpool by the Saturday afternoon, 22 August, because George had an evening booking with the Les Stewart Quartet at a British Legion social club. Either they set off late or they had difficulty hitching a lift because by the time George arrived in West Derby it was all over . . . bar the shouting, as Les Stewart recalls:

> It was only me and Ray Skinner [drums] who showed up. No Ken Brown and no George Harrison. I had to do it all myself and it was really horrible. I was pretty steamed about the whole thing, and just as we were leaving the guys showed up. I chewed them out about it and basically told them to get lost. Mona Best's club was due to open the following week and they asked me what would happen about it, and I said, 'Well you take it. I don't want to do it.' I broke up the group and gave up the residency at the new club, after all the time I'd put in cleaning up and painting that cellar.[7]

It wasn't only the end of the line for the Les Stewart Quartet, it was a headache for Mona Best, who'd lost her new club's resident group just days before its opening. She did have a name for the place though. As she surveyed the redecoration, the cellar's nooks and crannies put her in mind of the film *Algiers*, starring Hedy Lamarr and Charles Boyer; it was set in the native quarter of Algeria's capital, the walled citadel – the Casbah – with its narrow alleys and souks. She took this as her inspiration: it would be called the Casbah Coffee Club, known to one and all simply as the Casbah.

But who would play the opening night? George Harrison and Ken Brown could hardly play as a duo. Each did sing a song or two but they couldn't hold together a whole performance, besides which they'd no desire to strike out as a pair: they weren't particular friends, they were simply the backing bit of the Quartet.[8] It was a problem, but George knew the solution. He told Mrs Best there were a couple of other lads likely to be keen and available, then phoned John and Paul to break the news: there was a booking, and an open-ended Saturday-night residency if they went down well. It was nearly four months since the last Japage 3 performance and dates had been few and far between all through 1959. They grabbed at it.

During the week, Paul and John and John's new girlfriend Cynthia – he usually called her Cyn – joined George and Ken at the house to take a look around. Mrs Best was never backward in coming forward: she made sure they were all given a paintbrush and set to work. She asked John to paint a ceiling in black matt. Her son Pete remembers how, much to everyone's amusement, John first painted some of his characteristic cartoon figures, sexless humans with grotesque limbs and three toes, and then obliterated them as he completed the job ... though perhaps because of his short-sightedness he used gloss instead of matt and Mrs Best worried it wouldn't dry in time.[9] Paul was also busy with a brush, painting a ceiling in stripes of varying colours – 'It was great to be involved in the birth of a coffee bar, they were such important places then. The concrete and wood in the basement had been stripped and we painted each part a different colour. And after we'd painted it up, it was "our club".'[10]

Pete Best watched the three lads who, with Ken, were looking around the cellar of his house. He noticed how the *arty* one, John, 'looked and acted the leader from the start', and how he alone decided where they would play 'while Paul and George hovered in the background silently agreeing'.[11] John chose a spot in a cosy nook right under Paul's multicoloured ceiling. All that remained was to talk with Ken Brown about what songs they'd be likely to do, and have a quick, loose rehearsal. George knew Ken's style of playing and the sound he got from his Hofner Senator, and John and Paul had seen him with Les's Quartet. Though disappointed that instead of a drummer or bass player they were getting yet another guitarist – even more *rhythm in the guitars* – Ken did have a Watkins 'Westminster' ten-watt amplifier with three inputs. George could plug in, and when he got his new guitar so could John; Paul could plug into his Elpico. They'd be an all-electric band.[12]

Saturday's Casbah date gave John's decision a deadline, and he bought himself his first good guitar on the Friday, 28 August 1959. He chose the same instrument as George, a Hofner Club 40, and Hessy's hire-purchase document shows that a £17 deposit was put down, requiring him to pay a further five shillings a week for fifty-three weeks for a total outlay of £30 9s.[13] Confusion remains over who paid the £17: Mimi always said she did, and perhaps that's so, but this was why John had been sweating and swearing at Scarisbrick all these weeks, and he had the cash. His occupation is written on the document as 'Student' while Mary Elizabeth Smith – Mimi – is his guarantor, legalising the contract by signing her name across a postage stamp (effectively paying a small government tax), so she was certainly present in the shop. There'd been some battle to reach this moment. Mimi was still lecturing John that he must try to resist distractions and focus on his studies, so he could qualify and get a proper job. Tired of repeating herself over and over, Mimi distilled her cautionary advice into a saying that would be aired many times during the next few years and become something of a joke between them: 'The guitar's all right for a hobby but it won't earn you any money.'[14]

All the same, having challenged John to show just how much he wanted this guitar, having seen how he was even prepared to suffer blistered hands for it, working on a building site, Mimi had to concede that in his summer-of-glove John had done just that. Resignedly, she accepted that this guitar business was something he needed to get out of his system; and John's timing was as good as ever because he was sacked at Scarisbrick this same day. His employment card records the fact that he began work there on 20 July and left on 28 August – a total of six weeks – and the reason for his departure is given as 'Unsuitable'. As Tony Carricker recalls, John's time as a labourer came to an end when 'he burned the arse out of the kettle', putting a fire under it without first filling it with water.

The Casbah opened twenty-four hours later. It was a very pleasant summer's evening, the cherry on a lovely day, and in tucked-away Hayman's Green queues stretched along the Woolton-sandstone walls. Lowlands had competition. Kids paid a shilling admission and had to sign up as members at half a crown a year – blue membership cards for boys, pink for girls. The smell of fresh paint mingled attractively with cigarette smoke, hot dogs, espresso coffee, Brylcreem, hairspray and teenage perspiration. Records were played on a portable Dansette deck. Everyone admired the decor, especially a great white-and-red dragon painted the entire length of a black wall. And then there was the group: John, Paul, George and Ken ... the group whose name was ...

Not much thought, or even less, had been given to this. The novelty of Japage had worn off and wasn't relevant anyway unless they changed it to something like Japageken, which they definitely weren't going to do. Johnny and the Moondogs? The Rainbows might have worked, given Paul's painted ceiling just above their heads. None appealed, and it's evident no new name came to mind, not even to that inspired wordsmith John Lennon, because they went back to the Quarrymen.* Given that John had hardly liked the name in the first place,

---

* Just as the spelling was never definitively settled 1956–8, Quarry Men or Quarrymen, the same holds true for this revival. It survives written in only three places: twice in local newspaper articles (though one informed the other) and once in Mona Best's hand in a Casbah club diary. These have it as Quarrymen, so that is the spelling used here; however it could still have been Quarry Men. As before, no one cared.

and that any relevance to Quarry Bank High School was long past, why they went back to it is a conundrum, one that was never explained and never will be.

Ken Brown became a group member for the time being, but never – in the eyes of John, Paul and George – one of them. They lived in the south of the city and he in the north, in Norris Green; they didn't socialise with him and he wasn't admitted into their tight circle; he was just a feller they saw when they played the Casbah, who had an amp and let them use it, and who took his fifteen shillings quarter-share of the £3 paid out in silver by Mrs Best. Mostly he sat quietly at the back and strummed away; he sang one, perhaps two numbers, his main contribution being the light, sweetly-twee ballad I'll Be With You In Apple Blossom Time. Arthur Kelly, present at most Quarrymen sessions at the Casbah, remembers how John, Paul and George 'slipped little guitar riffs behind Brown's strict tempo to make it sound rockier'. As ever, Arthur's duty was to report back about their sound and songs. 'I'd sit and watch, and when they finished they'd be asking, "What was that song like? What did so-and-so sound like?" I'd tell them where they were too loud or not loud enough, whatever adjustments were necessary.'

Also up with the Quarrymen, witnessing their unexpected resuscitation, was Tony Carricker:

Ken Brown didn't fit in with anything – he wore suits with wide lapels, in pastel colours, didn't have a very good haircut and wore glasses. The others turned down the volume on his guitar a bit, and turned George's up. George took them all by surprise that first night because he did the That'll Be The Day solo and hadn't said anything about it. John was *John*, but for me the most impressive of the two of them was Paul, because he could sing like Little Richard and Sun-take Presley. He was the obvious vocalist. Paul could do early Presley better than anyone apart from Elvis himself.

Just before the Casbah's opening, Pete Best had been on holiday at an international students camp in Colomendy, North Wales, along with Collegiate friends Bill Barlow and Chas Newby. Both played in Lowlands group the Barmen and were among the many Pillar Club regulars who also went to the Casbah; Newby had seen George play with Les Stewart and now he was impressed by the Quarrymen. 'They were good. When they sang Three Cool Cats they *harmonised* on it, which was brilliant. Though they played the same stuff as everybody else – Chuck Berry, Buddy Holly and all that – it was all guitars, no drums, and they could all sing.'[15]

Members entered the Casbah through a door in the garden that led directly into the cellar. Up above was the extensive Best household, fifteen good-size rooms which, apart from a living room converted into a cloakroom for coats, were out of bounds to everyone but the inner circle. Through their weekly appearances here, John, Paul and George entered the Bests' world, one quite unlike any they knew. The famous man of the house was scarcely seen. Johnny Best made it plain to Mona he wanted nothing to do with the Casbah and kept away; his disapproval was never going to stop her, of course – it was for the boys. Their marriage was in difficulties; some Casbah members swear Johnny had already moved out when the club opened, others say he was still there but only rarely. Soon he would be gone completely.

Mona Best was 35, small and round, exuding a beauty that bewitched men of all ages. She was full of life and in love with fun, but didn't suffer fools and stood no nonsense from anyone. She was amusing and generous, sharp and uncompromising, ever the boss. If you weren't in, you were out. The Casbah began to open up on other nights, mostly as a venue for playing records and drinking Coke; and then in November 1959 a second group night was added, Sundays, in unbidden house-to-house combat with neighbouring Lowlands. One club was an established youth community centre not for profit, the other a private enterprise. Mona decreed that any Casbah group who then played Lowlands would not be booked again, and very few dared cross her.

This was, too, a family with secrets. No one knew it, but Mona had had her two boys with different men. Johnny Best, doing war service in India as a physical training instructor, did not father her firstborn. The boy known as Pete Best was really Randolph Peter Scanland, born in the Egmore district of Madras on 24 November 1941 to 17-year-old Alice Mona Shaw and marine engineer Donald Peter Scanland. There is no record of their marriage. She married John Best at St Thomas Cathedral, Bombay, when Randolph Peter was two years and three months, then John Rory Best was born in January 1945.[16] It was as a foursome that they sailed into Liverpool at the end of that year. Johnny Best accepted Randolph Peter – known as Peter – as his son, and became the only real father the boy would know, but Peter had climbed far inside a shell, and until the end of her life it was Mona's mission to entice him out of it. Peter and his mother – he called her 'Mo' – had a relationship of quite extraordinary intensity. She was right behind him all the way, pushing, encouraging, dominating, cajoling, controlling, influencing, speaking for him, doing all she could – more than most mothers would ever consider – to bring a closed flower into bloom. Everyone who saw it talks about it: they simply idolised each other.

Pete grew into a strong, muscly lad, exceptional at sports and carrying no excess weight, eminently capable of taking care of himself in a physical confrontation, which in Liverpool could always happen at any moment. He was also handsome, and knew it, trading on an introverted personality to project a studied bashfulness – the shyly sullen face, dark eyes looking up appealingly from bowed head, just a few words spoken in quiet monotone. Many girls flocked to him (and Pete showed them he wasn't always shy). 'Pete Best used to *hover* a lot at the Casbah,' Tony Carricker says. 'He was definitely a presence – he was a very good-looking boy and had obviously decided to develop a moody pose at an early age.' Cyn remembers a private moment, also from the Casbah's opening night: 'I was upstairs in the house with John and Paul and then Pete came in and I thought how much he reminded me of the film star Jeff Chandler. What a handsome man ... but so quiet, there with his mother.'[17]

The 1959–60 academic year at Liverpool College of Art began on 14 September, when a full-on relationship rocketed under the noses of John and Cyn's amazed fellow students. With her in 'the ladies', Pat Jourdan witnessed Cynthia dressing-to-please. 'She was putting on yet another layer of mascara, and she had on a black sweater and a very, very short tartan skirt with a fringe which she was moving upwards. Then she said, "Pat, will you walk through the canteen with me? All the printing students are there and they'll wolf-whistle." She wanted to be chaperoned past them just after she'd spent fifteen minutes titivating herself. What I didn't know then was that it was all for *John*.'[18]

It was lust-and-love and love-and-lust, and with John as the driver everything went at 200mph. No third party can ever know what binds a relationship, and though many joked that the only thing they had in common was short-sightedness – without glasses both were as blind as bats – difference was probably key to this attraction.

For all her quiet personality and posh Hoylake credentials, Cyn met John's needs. Her love for him was total and loyal, and yet she stood up to him; he was desperate for such assurance and stability, still only twelve months after the shattering ordeal of his mother's death. Also, he'd been imagining himself falling for a beautiful artist and must have thought she was the one. Several years later he remarked, 'I always had this dream of meeting an artist woman that I would fall in love with, even from art school.'[19] He said this when speaking of another, but clearly he was thinking about it, looking for it, wishing it, now.

As for Cyn herself, she was a quiet girl who'd never expressed herself with much boldness, so with John she was evidently rebelling in a huge way. She'd recently been engaged to a Hoylake window-cleaner and now found herself attached to a human whirlwind, hooked on his danger and outrageousness and believing her love could penetrate his extraordinary aggression. As she says, 'His attitude was extremely "don't look at me 'cause I'll kill yer if you do" – but he wanted to be loved.'[20] They also fancied each other like mad. Sex was big for them, grabbed where and when opportunities arose, though with both still living 'at home' this wasn't easy.

Over time, as their relationship became 'steady', so their families entered the picture. Lillian Powell, for understandable reasons, formed the same instant opinion of John as almost every parent since his infancy: she didn't like him at all. This made life tough for Cyn, who was close to her widowed mother and somewhat under the thumb of her dominating personality. John didn't much care for Lillian either, so Cyn was left on the high-wire.

John clearly sought the approval of his family. At some point, probably before the end of 1959, he took Cyn up to Edinburgh to meet his Aunt Elizabeth (Mater) and Uncle Bert, and cousin Stanley, hitch-hiking there and back; and they also found favour in Woolton with John's Aunt Harrie and Uncle Norman, in whose home John not only had a cousin but also his two young half-sisters, Julia's daughters. It's said they all liked Cyn and she liked them. Mimi, of course, was adept at finding fault with everyone John brought home, even though Cyn was the model of good behaviour and politeness.

Then came the moment when Mimi and Lillian had to meet. John and Mimi took the train over to Hoylake for Sunday tea, to the tiny terraced house at 18 Trinity Road, leading down to the beach. The two indomitable and fiercely protective fifty-something widows maintained decorum for a while and then did away with pleasantries, each accusing the other's child of distracting theirs from study. According to Cyn, it became so aerated that John ran out of the house in tears.[21]

He was, she says, unable to stand the conflict. If so, it's a sharp insight into the insecure and churned-up mind of John Lennon in 1959, because he was himself a constant source of conflict and turmoil to everyone around him. Cyn has spoken often of the 'unreasonable rages' John inflicted on her, of his obsessive and addictive possessiveness and the loudly shouted unbridled jealousy he exhibited without any cause. Her dedication to the relationship was incredible – she knew he'd dismiss her in a second if she didn't stand up to him, and he tested this endurance endlessly. 'I was really quite terrified of him for 75 per cent of the time,' she says.[22] Being with John was a white-knuckle ride in a Force Ten storm and Cyn held on only in the hope of finding calmer waters ahead, believing she could be the one to steer him there. It was love.

John's third year at art school was in the lap of the gods and the hands of the principal, W. L. Stevenson, and the advice he took from some of his senior colleagues was that John should be allowed to stay on, despite having failed the Intermediate exam. He would have to re-sit it in May 1960, and if he failed that he'd be out; in the meantime, he began working towards the National Diploma in Design (NDD) qualification, beginning a second two-year course that would end in summer 1961.

Encouraged and inspired by Stuart Sutcliffe, who was taking the same course but one year ahead, John pursued his NDD in the Department of Painting. As Cyn chose Illustration, their tutorials were separate, and with Stuart's help – and freed from the intricate precision of Lettering – John suddenly threw himself into his work, using what Cyn would describe as 'an orgy of oil paint, sand, sawdust, in fact anything he could lay his hands on to create paintings that were truly individual'.[23] If John belonged anywhere at art school, it was here in the Department of Painting, but this doesn't mean he agreed with his fellow students' thinking – quite the reverse; he rebelled against them all, and it brought him to a crucial creative junction. 'The thing to do then was to paint and destroy [the paintings] or just keep them in your own room. It's hypocrisy. So I made the decision that what I did I wanted everybody to see, that I wasn't going after the asceticism of the monastery or the lone artist who supposedly doesn't care what people think about his work. I care a lot whether people hate it or love it because it's part of me.'[24]

Pat Jourdan, with John since they'd started at college two years previously, and ever a canny observer of his character, was awestruck not only by his creativity but also by the mind behind it.

As an artist, John was quick, swift, dexterous, sharp. I don't remember him being fired up by any particular artist – he was just *John*, sufficient being himself. He would see what somebody was doing, assimilate it, do it once and then drop it. We had a man called Tony Byrne come across from Birkenhead – he'd been to the American exhibition in London and started painting on the floor, on big pieces of hardboard. John walked in and said, 'When are you going to add an egg?', which was the advert at the time: 'Add an egg'. Tony grumped. John then did a perfect painting on the floor, better than Tony's, and never did another one again. That's the sort of thing he'd do. He could look at people from the other end of a telescope, take in what they were about and move on. John lived a hundred lives while we had only one.[25]

John's friendship with Stuart was also growing stronger, and – mirroring his relationship with Cyn – few others could see the attraction, and in particular what it was about John that made Stuart want to be with him. Being John's friend wasn't easy, because he took the piss out of everyone, no exceptions, but they inspired each other, and they laughed, drank, painted and read together. Along with Rod Murray, they played snooker in the Philharmonic pub, and also in a hall near the Royal Court theatre; Rod wasn't very good, John was worse and Stuart completely hopeless – every time he went down on a shot they almost spilled their beer laughing, waiting for the baize to rip. But Stuart was recognised by almost everyone as the most talented artist in college, the star student, a sensitive and intuitive soul who saw that underneath his harsh exterior John Lennon had special qualities.

With George no longer at school, Paul snuck alone into the college canteen to see John, but probably less frequently than before. Cyn observed how he 'tried hard to impress John, posing and strutting with his hair slicked back to prove that he was cool, because John was very much the leader'.[26] Paul was now in his final year at 'the Inny', class 6AM2, one of the oldest boys in the school. Apart from Ivan Vaughan, his main mates had left.*

Paul was now deep into his Dusty Durband-inspired literary phase. Lacking company but content to be alone, he went to see plays at the Royal Court and the Playhouse, not enjoying it very much but still accumulating the knowledge he'd need if, as his father now hoped, he became an English teacher. Just as he didn't only write songs but was aware of seeing himself in that songwriter image, so Paul was now consciously projecting the look of a deep thinker. He became the intellectual young man on the 86, thoughtfully puffing a pipe on the top deck while reading *Under Milk Wood* or *Waiting For Godot*, their titles visible. 'I did most of my reading in [that] little period of my life . . . I thought it was a bit swotty, a good image . . . I felt like I was at university.' Paul went on ferries from the Pier Head with not only a book of poetry but also a pen and paper – '[I'd] think of myself as a bit of a poet, observing people; sit on a bench and write a little about what I saw. I was very conscious of gathering material. I really fancied myself as an artist . . . my mind was full of it.'[27] He also dropped into the nobs' bookshop, the university-appointed Philip, Son & Nephew, which specialised in plays, poems and novels: when he could afford them, Paul bought intellectually weighty books; when he couldn't, and if there was no one watching, he'd nick 'em.

George Harrison was idling. No need now for the pretence of going into town every day simply to kill time – he could stay at home and do it. When he needed money he tapped his parents; as Louise would recall, 'All I heard was "'eh Mum, lend us the bus fare, eh, and I'll pay you back when I'm famous."'[28] If she was applying any force to his backside, to make him get out and get a job, it wasn't

---

* His brother Mike was still there, now in the Removes.

shifting him; Harry kicked harder, and set up an interview and entrance exam with Liverpool Corporation for George to become an apprentice bus mechanic. It was the usual deal – he'd qualify with 'a trade' after five years, in summer 1964. George loathed the very thought of it, but was in no position to refuse; yet it was a bittersweet moment when he found he'd failed the exam. He didn't want the job but it was a jolt to his ego, an Institute boy failing where lads from secondary modern schools hadn't. As he later reflected, 'The people who went to work for the Corporation weren't exactly the sharpest people around.'[29]

Staring at a dead end, George flirted with emigration. First he tried to persuade his parents to consider a family move to Australia, which they rejected. Then he thought of emigrating alone, a 16-year-old planning to live in Malta (he'd seen it in some travel brochures) or Canada. He went as far as requesting the application forms but lost heart when he saw parental authority was needed. He didn't even bother asking.[30]

When he could charm a bob or two from his mum and dad, George continued to take himself into Liverpool. On several afternoons, John and Cyn emerged from art school in the hope of a quiet time to themselves only to be hailed or whistled at by George as they walked down the street. He would catch them up and say, 'Where you two off to?' and 'Can I come?' Neither had the heart to tell him to push off, and so, much to Cyn's disappointment and annoyance, he'd trail around with them. As John would remember, 'George'd be following us down the street, two hundred yards away, and she'd be saying, "What does he want?" I said, "He just wants to hang out. Should we take him with us?" She'd say, "Oh, OK, we'll take him to the bloody movies." And we used to allow him to come to the movies with us and things like that.'[31]

This was an active period for Richy Starkey, still drumming with both the Darktown and Texans, and trying the patience of his fiancée, who didn't appreciate having his divided attention. As Elsie and Harry had no home phone, Richy's bandmates could only reach him by calling Mr Jones, the newsagent on High Park Street for whom he'd briefly worked; Len Jones would send someone to knock on Richy's door and he'd scurry round from Admiral Grove to the back of the shop to take the call and get the latest news on where he was wanted . . . and what new name Al Caldwell had cooked up for his group.

Possibly inspired by US group Johnny and the Hurricanes – not yet big in Britain but having hits in America – the Texans had just become Al Storm and his Hurricanes, and the switch coincided with a sudden upswing in activity, when Richy Starkey found himself in Liverpool's busiest rock and roll group. Any lingering note of skiffle or an acoustic sound was done, gone, *finito*: Johnny Byrne had bought himself a new Antoria electric guitar, which would become his trademark, so now it was rock all the way; and while Al certainly wasn't the greatest singer around, such was his flash and flair they could impress in spite of it.* On Saturday 5 September, when yet another new club opened on Merseyside – 'The Jive Hive' at St Luke's Hall in Crosby – Al Storm and his Hurricanes got the residency.

The other Hurricanes lived in the Broad Green/Old Swan area, so the group mostly played north of the city, a bus ride away and always at least two for Richy. Afterwards, if the last bus had gone, pretty Iris Caldwell would thumb a lift while the lads hid in bushes, waiting with their gear for a car to stop. Despite the risk of attack by Teddy Boy gangs, Richy carried his full kit now and it was always a sod to transport. The worst part was getting a bus home: even if people helped him aboard they weren't with him when he reached his destination. He would recall: 'One miserable night when I got off at my stop – it was half a mile to the house and I had four cases. I had to run twenty yards with two cases, keeping my eye on the other two left behind, then go back, pick them up and run forty yards with those, drop those, go back, and so on. It was the most miserable thing and all I thought was, "Shit, I need a car."'[32]

The last thing Richy needed now was his studies. The third year of his part-time college course at Riversdale Tech was evenings only, no longer day-release, and he drew the line. That's enough of *that*. Abandoning it meant, in the fourth of his five years, jeopardising his apprenticeship. And just at the time all this was going on, he suffered a tragedy: his beloved Grandad Starkey passed away on 3 October, dying from a chronic peptic ulcer while in care at Sefton General Hospital, and it all happened fast. Johnny Parkin Starkey had filled the place of his absent son, who'd left his child at three; he'd always been there for his Lazarus, his bloody Noddler, the boy who'd just finished paying back the money borrowed for his drum kit.

Richy would describe it as one of the saddest moments of his life. He held himself together until the burial, four days later at Allerton Cemetery, but as he watched his grandad being lowered into the ground he broke down, sobbing beyond consolation. Soon afterwards, widowed Granny Annie gave him a precious keepsake, Johnny's wedding ring. Richy was going to need it when he married Gerry. Such was his love for Grandad, and his passion for rings, he slipped the broad gold band on his finger right away and said he'd never remove it.

He now wore three rings. Wearing two hadn't been all that unusual, but three

---

* The rest of the Hurricanes' line-up was fluid at this time but the two main guys were bass guitarist and occasional singer Walter Eymond, known as Wally, and rhythm guitarist Charles O'Brien, known as Chas. There's a tendency in Liverpool to stress the final syllable of words, so 'Hurricanes' is usually pronounced to fully include 'canes' at the end.

caught the eye. Every ring told a story, and he was happy to tell it when people asked – 'this one's from me mum I got when I was 16, this one's an engagement ring from me girlfriend, and this one's me grandad's wedding ring I got when he died'. Three was a collection, and people started to call him 'Rings'.

Rings Starkey played his last booking with the Darktown on 16 October, at the Cavern. It was the usual story: the other guys drifted off to be fitters or mechanics or to get married, leaving their youth behind. He now gave all his playing energy to Al Storm and his Hurricanes. Unable to get in at the Casbah because a group called the Quarrymen had the residency, they played a few Sunday sessions at Lowlands. They also took part in the return to Liverpool of Carroll Levis's TV *Star Search*, passing the Empire audition and then going through the usual rigmarole, a winning spot during the week earning them a place in Saturday's finale. The Hurricanes came very close to securing the great prize, a TV appearance, finishing overall runners-up.

There's no explanation for why the Quarrymen didn't enter Levis's contest this time. Twelve months earlier, when the group was in limbo, John, Paul and George went to great lengths to take part, twice going to Manchester as Johnny and the Moondogs. Now it was back on their home turf, they were playing together every week with an improved repertoire and better equipment, and they let it pass. Others didn't. As well as Al Storm and his Hurricanes, another local rock group, Derry and the Seniors, entered and impressed. They had a beefy Little Richard sound, fronted by a dynamic young black singer from Toxteth, Derry Wilkie, and with a large individual named Howard 'Howie' Casey on sax. Their name was a spin on Danny and the Juniors, the white vocal group from Philadelphia, PA, who scored a great hit in 1958 with At The Hop.

The rise of the Liverpool rock group was now evident, and it was happening in complete contrast to the national scene. Almost every hit on the British charts in 1959 was by a solo singer, and rock's apparent decline was noted when *Disc* ran a feature looking at the diminishing success of beat and rock package shows in British theatres. Among those quoted was Neil Brooks, manager of the Liverpool Empire, who observed how 'rock is growing less and less popular'.[33] At his high end of the market it may have been, but at grass-roots level the Empire was becoming encircled by clubs and halls just bursting with urban working-class rock and roll. The promoter Wally Hill, with his sage MC Bob Wooler, opened for business at a second Co-op venue, Blair Hall in Walton Road, where (the *Echo* ad announced) Gerry Marsden's Pacemakers would be playing. Another hot new group was Cass and the Cassanovas – singer Brian Cassar and some big lads from Liverpool 8 who could take care of themselves as well as their music. They rented the Temple jazz club on Sunday afternoons and turned it into a rock venue – the city centre's first.

Change was also in the air at that bastion of jazz the Cavern Club. It had been open two and a half years when the man who'd made it all possible, Alan Sytner, went down to London to work for the National Jazz Federation and didn't come back. The Cavern was no longer doing so well: he'd taken his eye off the ball and his crowds were evaporating. He left it in the hands of his father, Dr Joseph Sytner, who in turn came to rely on a man at the accountancy firm balancing the club's books, Andrew Raymond McFall, known to all as Ray McFall. At the age of 32, McFall had some money and fancied a career break; he offered to buy the Cavern outright, and a deal was done for £2750. From Saturday 3 October 1959 the club operated under new ownership. Though there was no obvious change of musical policy, bookings for rock groups became more frequent, especially for Al Storm and his Hurricanes who played here eight times in the last three months of the year, not quite able to rock and roll but venturing close.

After a further lengthy period, and under his dad's pointed prompting – 'Don't you think you'd better get a job?' – George Harrison finally bowed to the inevitable and did. An officer from the Juvenile Employment Bureau flicked through some cards and informed him of a vacancy for a window-dresser at Blackler's, the department store extending along Great Charlotte Street. George wasn't enthused but knew it would put a few pounds in his pocket and get Dad off his back.

When George arrived at Blackler's he found the window-dressing job gone but there was another vacancy, for an apprentice electrician in the maintenance department – the very kind of job Harry was hoping his son would get. Forms had to be signed, and George seems to have committed to a five-year programme, to be completed at Christmas 1964, starting on £3 10s a week and with (at most) two weeks' holiday a year.* All apprentices and trainees were paid on Fridays, called forward individually and handed cash and a payslip inside a sealed envelope. From about the first week of November 1959, then, George Harrison was a working man.

In the light of all that followed, George rarely spoke much about his only real job outside music. 'I enjoyed it,' he said in 1967. 'It was better than school, and

---

* Twenty years later, George remembered his weekly pay as thirty bob (£1 10s), but one of his friends there, on the same money, is certain it was £3 10s. This was before he had to surrender a slice to the taxman.

with the winter coming on it was nice to be in a big warm shop. We used to play darts most of the time.' Ten years later, he added, 'Occasionally we broke the lifts so we could have a skive in the lift-shaft . . . I also learned how to drink fourteen pints of beer and three rum and blackcurrants and eat two Wimpys [burgers] all in one session.'[34]

The boy who snagged the window-dressing job before George could get there, Peter Cottenden, became his best pal at Blackler's. He was just a year older than George and their friendship was rooted in a quickly discovered mutual love of Chuck Berry and Buddy Holly. 'George was a nice lad, really a very nice lad, and we got on well. He had to wear a grey boiler-suit all day and every day. I remember one job he did: he had a bucket of water, a rag, a paint-brush and a stepladder, and he had to clean out the fluorescent lights. It wasn't exactly electrical, but it was where an apprentice began.'

Almost the first thing George did after joining Blackler's was nip around to Hessy's on Whitechapel to buy another guitar. It was payday, 20 November, and he picked out a solid-body electric made in Czechoslovakia by the Delicia company, a guitar given the space-age name Futurama by the company that imported them into Britain, Selmer. The instrument sold on the strength of its visual similarity to the Fender Stratocaster; the heavenly Strat – used by Buddy Holly and featured in so many of George's dreams and drawings – couldn't be had, but the Futurama was anyone's for 55 guineas (£57 15s). George also bought a case, and by the time hire-purchase interest was added he was staring at a bill totalling £74 6s – more than half his annual take-home pay. He put £10 'down' – probably a combination of his own money and some from his ever-supportive mum – and committed to a weekly sixteen-shillings repayment plan that stretched ahead to summer 1961.*

Thirty-five years later, George described how Paul was with him at Hessy's when he chose the instrument. Paul plugged it into an amp and turned it up high, and when George pressed one of the instrument's three piano-like rocker switches, a great booming sound sent other guitars crashing down from the wall.[35] Paul says he first laid eyes on the Futurama in Mrs Best's house the next evening: 'I remember George, upstairs in the front parlour, opening up the guitar case and there it was, like the Holy Grail . . . It was like heaven; it was nirvana time when a new guitar arrived in its case.'[36] Rory Best didn't play guitar but raved about George's beautiful Futurama so much that Mona went out and bought him one, just in case he felt like playing. He never did, but he was able

---

* George liked to repeat the popular line about buying a guitar on the drip from Frank Hessy – to pay a certain sum down and the rest 'when Frank catches me'.

to loan it to George when George's broke. Arthur Kelly, too, was most impressed
with his best friend's greatest acquisition yet.

> Everyone else at the Casbah had to queue up to get into the cellar but we'd
> always go in through the house. The front room was like the bandroom. I
> remember going there with George when he first had his Futurama. John was
> sitting there picking his nose – he was always picking his nose – and then
> George produced his new guitar out of the case. It was the closest he could
> get to a Strat, simply amazing. He put on the whammy bar [the tremolo arm,
> to change the pitch and add a vibrato effect] and when someone asked what
> it was for, George – for some strange reason – said, 'It's a wigwam to wind up
> the sun.'[37]

This was George's fourth guitar, which contrasted sharply with Paul, still
playing his first – the inexpensive Zenith acoustic he'd got in summer 1957, to
which he'd added a pickup. John bought his Club Footy because George had
one, so now they had different guitars again.*

The Futurama gave the Quarrymen another change of sound, which probably caused some shift in their repertoire. Playing together every week for the
first time, they were surely improving, but while much is known about their
Casbah appearances there's nothing to gauge how good they were. The
strong likelihood is that their instrumental technique wasn't as accomplished as their singing. Paul sang Elvis and Little Richard so well he almost
touched the untouchables, John did great Chuck Berry and Buddy Holly,
George did a nice Carl Perkins, and there were always some highly effective
harmonies. At its best, the Quarrymen's Casbah sound was probably four
electric guitars lightly strumming while John, Paul and George weaved their
way through Crying, Waiting, Hoping, or the tricky three-part To Know Her
Is To Love Her.

It's unlikely they sang any Lennon-McCartney Originals here. John and Paul
had little belief in them and felt sure audiences only wanted to hear what they
knew. But they did do arrangements. One Quarrymen speciality was to mod-
ernise old songs – all their rock heroes did it, so it was far from unusual. In early
1960, when Paul wrote a letter hoping to get them a booking, he mentioned as
staples of their act Ain't She Sweet, Moonglow, You Were Meant For Me,

---

* George kept his Club 40 but didn't use it. Paul didn't buy it from him and doesn't seem to have
had access to it. The guitar was given away as a prize in 1966.

Home, and You Are My Sunshine. This being so, they must have played them at the Casbah because there were no other performances in between.

The Quarrymen played through autumn 1959 as a four-guitar group, always lacking bass and drums. No contender stepped forward for either position – no one at the Casbah had a drum kit or bass and volunteered himself. Jon Hague says that John invited him to be their drummer. 'In art school one day he said, "Get some drums and join us," but I think he said it to everybody at the time. I couldn't do it – I was totally non-musical.'[38]

John, Paul and George's desire to add a bassman to the line-up now stretched back eighteen months, since they'd tried to coerce Eric Griffiths into buying one. *They* weren't going to play it: bass is an unsexy position in a group, almost as 'Leppo' as drums. They never suggested Ken Brown swap his guitar for one, but Tony Carricker says John asked him to buy a bass and join them. 'I thought it was absurd. It was beyond me. There were those who wanted to make the sounds and those who just wanted to listen to them, and I was one of those who wanted to listen.'[39] Arthur Kelly was also approached. 'George said to me, "Why don't you get a bass?" I was earning £4 a week at Cunard and the bass cost about £60, even more with an amp, and I just couldn't afford it. Besides which, my uncle had pulled some strings to get me the job and I didn't want to let him down. I'd already let down my family with my schooling and wasn't going to do it again.'[40]

How many others were asked will never be known, but probably the strangest invitations were issued to Stuart Sutcliffe and Rod Murray, when John, Paul and George were hanging out with them one day at 9 Percy Street. Rod wasn't into rock and couldn't play guitar but fancied having a go; without money, and keen on woodwork, he told them he'd *make* a bass in the college workshop. It wasn't likely to take long. Stuart had an acoustic guitar but couldn't really play it, nor did he have the money for a bass, but he always supported them, going occasionally to the Casbah. And through his relationship with John he was getting ever more interested in rock. As Cyn has noted, 'The influence John had over Stuart was very strong and the urge to communicate with John on every level was important to him at that time.'[41]

Stuart was also occupied with his art. This was the 'sending-in' period for *The John Moores Liverpool Exhibition 2*, to be held at the Walker Art Gallery for two months from 17 November; Rod and Stuart both submitted pieces, Stuart's being a vast abstract work, a mosaic of angular shapes and colours painted on two boards totalling eight feet square. He called it *Summer Painting* and its influence was the Parisian abstract artist Serge Poliakoff. The work was accepted, though just one of his two painted boards was used. As Rod Murray remembers, 'We carried half of Stuart's painting down the hill to Jackson's, opposite the Jacaranda – the shop was a holding agent for the exhibition: people took their work there and they forwarded it to the gallery. On our way back to collect the second half we stopped in the Cracke and, well, we never made it back to Jackson's.'[42]

Offering unrivalled prize money, and reviewed by the national press and BBC radio, Moores' exhibition was the biggest of its type in Britain. Five rooms at the Walker housed 157 pieces of art from canvases to sculptures, whittled down from two thousand submissions. Only 10 per cent of the artists were from Merseyside and Stuart Sutcliffe was the sole student, his work appearing alongside pieces by Henry Moore, Barbara Hepworth and Victor Pasmore. More than fifteen thousand were expected to see the exhibition during its two-month run, and this number included John Lennon and Aunt Mimi. So great was John's pride, Mimi would recall his instruction that she 'look nice' when they went – a rich remark considering she always did and he lived scruffy.

Stuart's piece, half a painting hanging in what the catalogue grandly called 'room V', befuddled Mimi. It was one of many abstract pieces and she couldn't make head nor tail of it. 'What *is* it?' she asked, at which point John hustled her back out to the atrium and said, 'How can you *say* a thing like that, Mimi?' Thumping his chest, he impatiently explained to this 53-year-old (who'd been reading art history for decades, and knew), 'Art comes from *in here*.'[43]

While Stuart waited to find out whether he was in line for one of the prizes, Paul won one. In the last Liverpool Institute Speech Day of the 1950s, in the Philharmonic Hall on 15 December, he had to walk on stage to collect a special 'Prize for Art' – a sweet if nerve-racking moment in his final school year, watched by his proud father in the balcony. It came in what must have been a good period for Paul. For the Quarrymen, the weekly residency at the Casbah was like having their own venue, where they got to entertain out front and also enjoy a life behind the scenes. It was in West Derby, not their own patch but a series of bus journeys away, so they were being seen by people who didn't know them or their history. Pam Thompson was one of the first Casbah regulars to spend time in their company:

Sometimes we had private parties upstairs after the club had closed. Not everyone was there, just a select few. Paul was the nice one – I think everybody liked Paul. George was the youngest and always seemed so. I had a soft spot for him – he was very sweet and naive. John and Paul were so much older and more streetwise whereas George seemed like the little boy among them. John was very charismatic but I was always a little bit wary of him. He came across as being strong, hard, with a good opinion of himself. He kissed me on the cheek once. George got so drunk one time that he turned green: we made him a cocktail of tomato juice and all sorts of awful things to help him be sick, and he was, on the steps just outside.[44]

One of these parties developed into a sleepover because the last bus had gone and there was no way anyone could get home. Quiet was required because Mrs Best's 70-year-old bedridden mother was in the room opposite, but on this night everything was so hushed that Mona became suspicious, as Pete's friend Bill Barlow remembers:

There were about twenty of us – a few with girls – in the front room, and it was two or three o'clock in the morning. Some of us were lying on the floor, the lights were off and it had gone quiet, people sleeping. Paul was with a young lady and Mrs Best came in, put the lights on and said, 'Paul, what are you doing?' and this head popped up and said, 'Nothing Mrs Best! Nothing Mrs Best!' I knew the young lady he was with, so I can imagine what was going on.[45]

If Paul was having any joy it was more than George, whose success in the sex department was, at most, what Liverpool lads cunningly called 'finger pie'. His abiding memory of these late-night parties was of all but breaking his hand trying to get beyond bras and corsets that appeared to be made of reinforced steel. 'I'd be snogging with some girl and having a hard-on for eight hours till my groin was aching – and not getting any relief. That was how it always was. Those *weren't* the days.'[46]

Also in John, Paul and George's orbit at the Casbah was Neil Aspinall. Paul and George hadn't seen him for months, not since he'd left the Institute in the summer, but West Derby was his patch – he lived close by. Neil now got to know John Lennon and enjoy the Quarrymen, and he also came into contact with the Best family for the first time, striking up a firm friendship with Pete.

It was at the Casbah, one evening towards the end of 1959, that John and Paul laid eyes on a sweet-faced blonde dancing a few feet away from them. Both made a beeline for her at the next break; she was Dorothy Rhone, a 16-year-old from Childwall who'd just left Liverpool Institute High School for Girls. 'They were so fast on their feet, sparking off each other with jokes and cracks, that it was impossible to keep up,' she recalled. 'I liked John's face – I thought he was rugged-looking; Paul was handsome in a softer way. John was also the dominant one, a very different personality ... more compassionate.'[47] John called her 'Bubbles' because she wasn't – she was quiet and innocent, though at the same time not afraid to manoeuvre for what she wanted. When she found John was 'going steady' she switched to Paul. Feigning faintness, she said she needed fresh air and asked him to follow her into the garden; the night ended on a kiss and the promise of a date. They went to the pictures, and as Paul saw her safely on to a bus back to Childwall they agreed to see each other again at the Casbah – and then they were boyfriend and girlfriend, beginning the first long-term relationship either had had.

Another to break into the Casbah scene at this time was Richy Starkey, whose group made their debut appearance there on 29 November when Mrs Best first opened up her cellar on a Sunday. As usual, Al Caldwell was fiddling about with his band's name: after a week as Jett Storm and the Hurricanes they became Rory Storm and the Hurricanes for a Jive Hive appearance on 11 November, and – finally – this one stuck. 'Rory', said Al, came from the London rock musician Rory Blackwell; he and Johnny Byrne had met him at Butlin's, Pwllheli, during the recent summer holiday. It could also be that it came from Rory Calhoun, an American screen actor famous for western roles. The Hurricanes had a thing for cowboys: Byrne was now calling himself Johnny Guitar, from the 1954 western movie of that name, and drummer Richy had passed quickly through the nickname Rings to style himself Ringo Starr.*

Mostly he was Ringo because of his three rings – a variant of his existing nickname – but anyone who followed the cowboy scene knew it well. There was Johnny Ringo, famed for the gunfight at the OK Corral and the film of that name, and especially there was the movie *Stagecoach* in which John Wayne became a star playing fugitive hero The Ringo Kid.

The reasoning behind 'Starr' is less obvious. Richy knew, as did everyone, the American singer Kay Starr, who had number 1 hits in Britain during the 1950s; but more than that, quite simply, he liked the name as an abbreviation of Starkey, and for its twist on 'star'. His definitive statement on the name change is this: 'It was going to be Ringo Starkey but that didn't really work, so I cut the name in half, added an "r" [and] had it put on the bass drum.'[48]

Like anyone who adopts a new name, Richy started off confused when people called him by it, and had to accept strangers addressing him as Ringo because they knew nothing else. But though he was Ringo on stage and in the clubs, he would always be Richy to Elsie, Harry and the wider family, to his fiancée, girlfriends, pals, bandmates and workmates.

He gained not only a new name at this time but also transport. Lugging

---

* It's not possible to say precisely when Richy Starkey became Ringo Starr. His new name first appeared in print in a souvenir brochure for an eight-day jazz festival at the Cavern that began on 10 January 1960. The event was arranged before Christmas 1959 and it's probable the information was received and souvenir brochure laid out before the holidays.

drums on and off buses was beyond a joke, and with the kit paid off and plenty of Hurricanes bookings to bolster his Hunt's wages, Richy got his first car. It was a red and white Standard Vanguard, bought for £50 cash from the Cassanovas' drummer John Hutchinson, known on the scene as Johnny Hutch.[49] Its origin was uncertain. Richy would always say that Hutch built the car from spare parts, and boasted of it being 'hand-painted' as if this was an attraction and not an amateur alternative to spray-painting. Richy didn't care: he loved the car and bragged about it too, even though it wouldn't shift into second gear and had endless tyre trouble.[50] It went places, it looked great, it had a back seat. While he had 'wheels' there were certain things he didn't have, like motor insurance, road tax or a licence to drive, but none of this stopped him. Illegal, yes; unusual, no. Richy knew several who did it.

December 1959 was John and Cyn's first Christmas together, and they'd only just made it in one piece. Though regularly unfaithful himself, John was manically insecure about Cyn's fidelity and one day became so enraged in his belief that she'd considered another man, he slapped her. The exact circumstances have varied with retelling, but it seems John heard Cyn had danced with a man at a party; the next day he followed her into the ladies' toilet at college, accused her, and lashed out. Cyn was found crying by her best friend Phyllis McKenzie – 'Apparently, he'd slapped her face. I thought, "He's a right bastard." And that did worry me. He could be very cruel.'[51]

John commented in 1967: 'I was just hysterical. That was the trouble. I was jealous of anyone she had anything to do with. I demanded absolute trust from her, just because I wasn't trustworthy myself. I was neurotic, taking out all my frustrations on her.'[52]

Cyn was encouraged by friends to break off the relationship, and did for a short while – until John apologised and swore he'd never strike her again. In 2005 she wrote, 'John was true to his word, he was never again physically violent to me.'[53]

That first Christmas she received a fantastic eight-page handmade card. The front featured a Lennon ink drawing of them looking into each other's eyes, profile view: John a self-portrait with Teddy Boy quiff and glasses, check jacket and drainpipe trousers, Cyn with long light locks, hairy coat, black-and-white-check skirt worn above the knee, and high heels. OUR FIRST XMAS! John exclaimed. The backside had a second drawing, rear view this time, their arms around each other, love hearts popping from their heads, above which he wished I HOPE IT WON'T BE THE LAST. The rest of it was simply one long love message, a scribbled outpouring of devotion that could have left Cyn in no doubt: she was loved. As declarations of worship go, I LOVE YOU LIKE GUITARS was unsurpassable.

Another piece of Lennon writing, probably from this time, is the short story 'Henry and Harry', seemingly based on George Harrison's dilemma. On Christmas morning, unwrapping his gifts at 25 Upton Green, George was dismayed to find a set of screwdrivers and electricians' tools from his dad. He felt the implication was clear: Harry expected his youngest boy to make electrics his life's work. Dad had a plan too: George's big brother Harry was a motor mechanic, his other brother Peter was a panel beater, and, ultimately, George could join them as the electrician in a family-owned motor garage; he himself would be the manager, leaving his job as bus driver after all these years. John was 'astoundagasted' on behalf of his young pal: to him, all such jobs came into one category, 'brummer striving', a phrase he'd cooked up to represent dead-end industrial work or bog-standard labour of any kind. Asked in a TV interview in 1968 to define it, John replied, 'Brummer striving is . . . brummer striving – all those jobs that people have that they don't want. And there's probably about 90 per cent brummer strivers watching in at the moment.'[54]

'Henry and Harry' encapsulated George's predicament: the school-leaving son at their 'quaint little slum' expected to follow into the father's business, the dad batting away his son's protests. *Get out!* John was urging his young friend, who little needed the encouragement. *Tell him to fuck off!* George could, but wouldn't, at least not in those words.[55] And it wasn't as if his first experiences as an electrician promised much anyway: given the job of maintaining the lights in Blackler's Christmas grotto, he'd fused them, casting a Scouse Santa and a queue of excited kiddies into darkness. It was something for George and Arthur Kelly to laugh about during Blackler's Christmas dance at the Grafton Ballroom. The finest photograph of these best buddies was taken here, their hair defying all known laws of gravity, two 16-year-old working men wearing smart suits and big natural smiles for the camera before they moved in to check out the birds.

Paul had a job that Christmas too, sorting mail as a temporary worker for the GPO (General Post Office), and it was also his first Christmas with Dorothy Rhone.* Dot, as he called her, was faithfully present at the Casbah every week to watch the Quarrymen entertain the club members. Four months into their Saturday-night residency they were now an established fixture here, but not the only attraction. Some Sunday sessions still featured Rory Storm and the Hurricanes, and a new group made its debut on 20 December. The Blackjacks† were a four-piece: Bill Barlow and Chas Newby (formerly of the Barmen) on

---

* She says Paul disclosed that he wrote Love Of The Loved for her. It was written in this period (as previously noted) but he hasn't publicly mentioned if he had a particular person in mind.
† Like Rory Storm, this name came from Rory Blackwell and the Blackjacks.

guitar along with Ken Brown (still with the Quarrymen) and Pete Best on drums. They mostly did Carl Perkins numbers, and Chas was the singer. Pete was a beginner. He'd shown little musical inclination before now, but an interest in percussion was sparked when someone left a snare drum and a pair of brushes in the house and he'd enjoyed tinkering with them. Mo rushed him down to Rushworth & Dreaper's and bought him a smart-looking Premier kit in blue mother-of-pearl.

According to the *Daily Mirror* headline, Thursday 31 December 1959 was THE GAYEST NIGHT OF THE YEAR. The lemonade fizzed and flowed at its grand Teenage Ball at the Waldorf Hotel in London, graced by celebrities Lonnie Donegan, Shirley Bassey and another Larry Parnes discovery, Vince Eager. Two hundred miles north, Ringo Starr had returned to Maxwell Fyfe Hall – the Conservative Club at Back Broadway, near Norris Green – as Rory Storm and the Hurricanes twanged out the old and sang in the new at Sam Leach and Dick Matthews' latest promotional venture, Chez Jazrok. The decade that began with peace secured by an austere, law-abiding, backward-looking Britain, ended with an ear-splitting dose of American rock and roll.

The Quarrymen had no booking this evening and one can only surmise where they were: Paul probably getting bevvied at his family's annual Aintree knees-up; George maybe at home with his family; John perhaps somewhere in town with Cyn, shouting to make themselves heard in pubs even more uproar-ious than usual because New Year's Eve licences allowed boozing beyond midnight.

And when they all woke up the following morning, it was the Sixties.

YEAR 3, 1960:
COMPETENCE, CONFIDENCE & CONTINUITY

12

The Swish of the Curtain

The new year and decade meant expansion at Nems. Liverpool was a city of strong shopping affiliations, and this record/electrical store was liked and trusted by its customers – a reputation earned, not handed out. Nems had operated solely in the north end until 1957, when – with the energy shot of two new directors, Brian Epstein and his brother Clive, 23 and 21 – the company became suddenly more progressive, opening up on Great Charlotte Street in the heart of town. Now it was taking prime space in a new development on Whitechapel, a four-floor store with offices above, everything to be managed hands-on by the brothers. It was another big step up, a flagship for a family business that stretched back sixty-four years, back to the arrival of a Russian émigré fleeing ethnic genocide.

Born 1877 in Konstantinovo in Lithuania, Isaac Epstein sailed into Liverpool at 19 speaking only Yiddish and praying life would be better here for his children, if he should be so lucky.* Two million Jews were fleeing an extermination policy known as the Pogroms, forcing a mass exodus across Europe and to America. Isaac stopped in Liverpool and started working. By 1900, when he married Dinah Hyman (parents from Poland), he'd opened up his own furniture shop on Walton Road. It served the impoverished suburbs of Walton, Anfield, Everton and Kirkdale, and took off rapidly. Customers' money here was hard-earned, and Epstein's (so called) had a reputation for honest value and modernity.[1]

The shop survived ever-present anti-Semitism and the onset of the Depression, and in 1929 Isaac bought his neighbouring business when its

---

* Konstantinovo also known as Chveydan, and now called Kvédarna. The Epstein family of Liverpool pronounced their surname as 'Epsteen'.

owners decided to sell up. This was Nems (North End Music Stores), established in 1886 to sell pianos, organs and sheet music.* Jim McCartney played a Nems piano. The two companies, Epstein's and Nems, were now in the joint hands of Isaac and his sons Lazarus (known as Leslie) and Harry. Born in 1904, Harry was bright and courteous, educated at one of the city's great grammar schools, Liverpool Collegiate. His destiny, along with that of his elder brother, was decided young – the company name became I. Epstein & Sons and Harry would run the businesses for the next thirty-five years, until 1964. His appetite for work and know-how were matched by his urbanity and ethics: underpinning the Epsteins' success was a family principle handed down generation to generation – 'The fair deal is the right deal'.[2]

In 1933, Harry married 19-year-old Minnie Hyman, known to all as Queenie; her family were from Russia and she was born and raised comfortably in Sheffield. A lively, intelligent young woman, she had a deep passion for the arts; classical music, theatre, dance, literature, paintings, sculpture, antiques and more, Queenie was enraptured by them all.

Despite the ten-year age gap, the Epstein son and Hyman daughter seemed a perfect fit. The businesses were running well, profits were invested in property, they could always afford luxuries, and they had a dynasty within three years. Brian Samuel Epstein was born on 19 September 1934 in a private nursing home on Rodney Street, the Liverpool equivalent of London's Harley Street; his brother Clive arrived there twenty-three months later.† Home was a detached villa at 197 Queens Drive, in the suburb of Childwall – this is Liverpool's ring-road, but traffic hum was quelled within a sumptuous house of five bedrooms, two bathrooms, a drawing room, dining room and library. It was a haven for Harry after closing the shops each day, and an idyllic place for Queenie to raise the boys. (She also had mother's help: a cleaner and live-in nanny.) It was *Queenie's house*, everything refined and arranged *just so*. Brian was already considered special for having been born on Yom Kippur (like a Christian born on Christmas Day), and, being the eldest, he held a position of importance. Queenie thought him the most beautiful boy she'd seen.[3] But beyond the panelled doors and willow trees, trouble was brewing.

Brian was just coming up to five when war began. He and Clive were evacuated – first to Prestatyn, North Wales, and then (along with Harry and Queenie) to Southport, up the coast from Liverpool. They returned home in

---

* There was no definitive way of writing the name – the Epsteins would use both NEMS and Nems. This book uses Nems unless otherwise necessary.
† Brian's middle name came from Samuel Epstein, his great-grandfather, Isaac's father.

1943 and Brian was admitted to Liverpool College, a high-achieving private school in nearby Mossley Hill; what with the war, and other reasons, it was already his sixth place of education – and he didn't last long here either.

Brian had become infatuated by theatrical life. It consumed him. On family holidays, he produced, directed and narrated children's concert parties, with elegantly designed bespoke programmes. Art was his one consistent Grade A school subject. The headmaster of Liverpool College sent Harry and Queenie a programme, drawn surreptitiously in class, that showed dancing girls – the head said the drawings were 'suggestive', Brian said they were showgirls dressed for the stage. The head also said that Brian needed to sharply improve his standards, and Harry agreed: he wanted a focused son with a thorough, broad education to come into the family business. Brian felt the college was bearing down on him, and the Epsteins suspected anti-Semitism. It was certainly everywhere, and not always subtly expressed. Brian's most adored book as a child, one he read again and again from the age of seven, was *The Swish Of The Curtain*, Pamela Brown's tale of six upper-middle-class English children who stage a musical theatre show for charity and yearn to go to drama school. At a particular point in the story, one of the girls hits on a money-raising scheme, suggesting that everyone attending a church garden fete be made to buy a programme, to which her brother laughs and exclaims, 'You little Jew!'

When Brian's work didn't improve, Liverpool College told Harry and Queenie he would have to leave. It was expelling him. Brian had joined with the expectation of staying until 18, but after only a year Harry was sitting him down on one of the sofas at Queens Drive and exclaiming, 'I just don't know what on earth we're going to do with you.'[4]

Which Liverpool homes, and which young ears, were tuned in to the radio on the evening of 26 July 1945? There was a Variety show called *Navy Mixture* with several star names and one newcomer. Halfway through the forty-five minutes, host Jack Watson advanced to the weighty BBC microphone and cheerily announced:

> Stepping off the Liberty boat this week is a bloke who's making his first broadcast, and who, incidentally, has just received his commission – and so it's a double celebration. He's a pianist, and after a great deal of persuasion – during which he held up our producer at the point of a gun – he's going to play a composition of his own, which he calls Prelude. His name is Sub Lieutenant *George Martin* [applause].

Born on 3 January 1926 in Holloway, north London, George Henry Martin was the youngest child of Henry Martin, a craftsman carpenter, and Bertha (née

Simpson). No one in the family was musical but they had a piano. George took six lessons at the age of eight and then wrote his first composition, The Spider's Dance, a short sweet blend of ragtime and classical.[5]

By 1941, the Martins had evacuated to Bromley, in the Kentish south-east suburbs, where George formed his own dance band. First they were the Four Tune Tellers, and then, as a five-piece, George Martin and the Four Tune Tellers – trumpet, sax, double-bass and drums, with an occasional guest vocal by his sister Irene. George played piano. 'I wanted to be George Shearing, and I also modelled myself on Meade Lux Lewis,' he explains.[6] They played in clubs and schools and did all the latest songs from America's Tin Pan Alley. A seminal moment then occurred in George's life when the BBC sent its Symphony Orchestra, under Sir Adrian Boult, to give a concert at his school. He was 15 when he witnessed Debussy's *Prélude à l'après-midi d'un faune* and was wafted to paradise. 'I thought it was absolutely heavenly,' he says. 'I couldn't believe human beings made that sound.'

George left school soon after with distinctions in French and Maths (his ability at the latter was exceptional) and an ambition to design aircraft. He went into the War Office as a clerk, bought himself more piano lessons and began to add to his cache of compositions: 'I was writing imitations of Rachmaninov and Chopin and that kind of stuff.' Then, at 17, knowing that he was about to be called up, he volunteered for the Fleet Air Arm.

George Martin had 'a good war'. He saw no action, he spent time in Jamaica and New York (seeing Cab Calloway and Gene Krupa perform on Broadway), he flew planes as an 'observer' – the captain on three-man practice sorties – and, at its end, he became an officer. To blend with his fellow officers, George consciously sharpened his blunt north London tones and tried to adopt the crisp, cut-glass accent of a young English flying ace. This didn't only serve a purpose in the Fleet Air Arm, it would be useful in civilian life: in an ultra-class-conscious Britain, to speak like a gent would boost his chances of 'getting on', and he had the gentility, civility, good humour, height (6ft 2in) and dashing looks – sweeping fair hair and finely carved features – to carry it off.

The armed forces also provided opportunities to continue his piano playing, which is how the 19-year-old Sub Lieutenant Martin found himself playing Prelude (one of those new compositions) before a London audience – and the BBC microphone – in July 1945.

He demobbed in 1947 with no career qualifications or money to fall back on. During military service, George had corresponded with Sidney Harrison, piano teacher of renown, regular BBC broadcaster, and member of the professorial staff at the Guildhall School of Music in London. Harrison was a great encourager, and arranged an audition for him; George played a few of his compositions, was accepted, and signed up to a three-year teaching course. At home, however, all was suddenly discord. George's mother – in his later words, 'the person to whom I had always been so close' – strongly disapproved of his girlfriend, a 26-year-old from Aberdeen, Jean 'Sheena' Chisholm. She was a leading soprano, and they'd met and sung together while he was stationed in Scotland. Defying his mother's censure, George married Sheena on his 22nd birthday, 3 January 1948; Aberdeen newspaper photos show the groom crisp but solemn in his Fleet Air Arm uniform. His mother travelled up for the wedding, but died of a brain haemorrhage three weeks later, aged 53. George felt responsible and was racked with guilt, and the shadow this threw over his marriage remained long after he and Sheena settled in rented rooms in Acton, west London.[7]

The Guildhall classes were difficult. Piano was George's chosen instrument, oboe his second – and his oboe professor, Margaret Eliot, provided additional tutoring at her apartment on Great Portland Street. As owners of a substantial land estate in Cornwall and members of the House of Lords, her family had an illustrious and centuries-old history; her husband was a brilliant and literate doctor of medicine, Richard Asher. They had three children: Peter (born 1944), Jane (1946) and Clare (1948), all with vivid flame-red hair and showing signs of artistic gifts. The Asher home echoed to the clink of intellectual upper-middle-class culture, with a strong dash of erudite eccentricity, and these visits left a marked impression on George Martin, as they would another young man who followed him fifteen years later. They gave a glimpse of *possibilities*, stimulating a greater sense of ambition and encouraging a further polish of his adopted cut-glass voice. Then the clock would chime and he'd be off home – not, like some of his fellow students, to a bijou residence in Chelsea, but to his financially straitened and already stricken marriage.

Elegance filled and fuelled the expectations of Brian Epstein, the Liverpool boy whose schooling was deeply troubled and who daydreamed of costume designs, music and the stage. After expulsion from Liverpool College, he carried on piling up problems. He went to a Jewish school in Kent, and then left; to a small public school in Dorset, and then left; and finally, at the age of 14, he landed up at Wrekin, a minor public school in Shropshire, where he *loathed* the harsh procedures and continued to excel at Art.

Brian later wrote that it was after Wrekin he found out he was homosexual, but he was certainly exposed to it here, at 15.* All public schools had some

* The word 'gay' was barely in use in this context at the time; the only alternatives to 'homosexual' were crude and offensive.

activity, boys feeling the stirrings of sexual interest while ganged together in dormitories, no girls in sight. But these conditions surely didn't fashion Brian's inclination: it seems to have been latent, at the root of so much unhappiness and unease. It was just his bad timing that what he'd need-loathe-crave in his life was illegal and taboo. When chasing pleasure, which Brian often would, prison was just one of the constant dangers; ahead lay years of fear and veiled behaviour, risking the courts, blackmailers and roaming 'queer bashers'. Brian tried to shut it out, but who knows what was shaking his mind when, here at Wrekin, he inked this dramatic howl of pain in his 1949 pocket diary:

> Help me. I am lost. Help me. I am lost. Help me [if] I am to stop. Give me peace, rest. That world, it's too big for me. O lord God, I've asked these questions before. Where is the answer? Why am I here? Help me. What am I to do? O Lord God tell me where is my faith? Give guidance. This is a hell. A hell of madness.[8]

George Martin's three Guildhall years ended in July 1950 and that was it – his student record card mentions no final examination pass. A month later, he took a clerical job in the BBC's music library, earning extra on the side by playing oboe on a London park bandstand and in the pit orchestra at Sadler's Wells. Then, out of a clear blue sky, fell a job offer from The Parlophone Company Ltd.

Founded in Germany by the Swedish-born Carl Lindström, Parlophone was one of the three big record labels owned by the British conglomerate Electric & Musical Industries, known as EMI. Each had its own marque and Parlophone's was a fancy L (for Lindström), forever to be mistaken for the pound sign, £. The letter to George Martin was sent by its manager, O. C. Preuss, from an address in the St John's Wood district, 3 Abbey Road.

In the 1830s, a luxury private house was built here, complete with bathroom and wine cellar; a century later, EMI bought the property and turned it into recording studios. The old house became the front offices, while the studios – three of them – were built in the spacious back garden. The new facility opened in November 1931 with Sir Edward Elgar conducting the London Symphony Orchestra through his patriotic *Land Of Hope And Glory*. EMI's studio at Abbey Road would always be the best of British institutions.

Oscar Preuss had run Parlophone since 1924, his greatest discovery being the bandleader and dance instructor Victor Silvester. The label had so much work that Preuss needed an assistant – and with retirement approaching, he'd also want a successor. It was only later that George discovered Sidney Harrison's hand in his advancement once more; in the meantime, he grasped the opportunity of an unconsidered new career. On 28 November 1950, wearing his beret, bicycle clips and Fleet Air Arm greatcoat, this rangy 24-year-old cycled through wind and rain from his gloomy Acton bedsit to very nice St John's Wood and reported for duty.

The world he entered was like an old gentlemen's club. The office of Mr Preuss – he was 'Mr Preuss' to all – was at the front of the old house, with flames crackling in the fireplace, a grand piano, thick-pile carpet, easy chairs, a walnut-veneered radiogram and, sitting behind a roll-top desk, the well-regarded gent himself. Facing him was a Miss Lockhart Smith, his elegant young secretary, who looked like Katharine Hepburn and coolly greeted the newcomer in a voice like Princess Elizabeth's. Across the corridor were the offices of EMI's other main labels, Columbia and HMV (the august His Master's Voice), staffed by George Martin's colleagues and rivals, all older. He was very much the new boy.

These other labels had binding, decades-old connections to the major US record companies. It was virtually a one-way street – the British took plenty of American product, the US had little or no need of the British – but it meant HMV and Columbia had most of the big-selling American artists, and Parlophone didn't. Oscar Preuss was a maverick, though, and sharp with it – he licensed relevance and credibility instead, striking deals with the smaller, independent companies across the States, whose ears were closer to the ground. Parlophone was the first British label to issue America's so-called 'Race records', the authentic early stirrings of rhythm and blues. The most exciting and vibrant label in Britain from the 1930s to the '50s was the Parlophone Super Rhythm-Style Series, 78rpm discs with a distinctive deep blue label, that '£' logo and 'R' numerical sequence. Meade Lux Lewis, the boogie-woogie pianist who strongly influenced George's style, was on Parlophone.

Notionally EMI's 'third' record label perhaps, Parlophone was certainly its most diverse and interesting. Preuss had all the funds he needed, he could sign whoever he liked, and he had EMI's extensive (even global) organisation, promotion and distribution behind whatever he issued . . . and George arrived out of nowhere to be second-in-command. On the downside, his wage was the not-so-grand £7 4s a week. On the up, again, he'd be working closely with bands and musicians of every kind, stripe and nationality, from orchestral players to accordionists, from Latin-American rumba musicians to Scottish players by the bagpipe-full (every spring, a team from Parlophone ventured north to record reels, jigs, ballads and pipe bands). It was a mind-boggling learning curve, but these experiences took a bright, gauche young man and produced someone intimate with every instrument and style of music, who could understand, and work comfortably with, singers and musicians of all ages, creeds, colours and personalities (*especially* the personalities). Mr Preuss's Parlophone handed George Martin a palette of colours with which to paint a career.

He slipped easily into the working ways at Abbey Road, where it was always suit-and-tie, except for the occasional Sunday session when sports jacket and slacks were permitted. The times of recording sessions (three a day, 10AM–1PM, 2–5, 7–10) and their output (maximum twenty minutes of completed record-ings per session) were regulated by the mighty Musicians' Union, a 'closed-shop' organisation, membership compulsory if you were a jobbing player. The term 'record producer' didn't exist – George was an 'A&R manager' (short for 'artists & repertoire'), a 'recording manager', an 'artiste manager' or 'artist manager'. The title varied, but other things didn't: it wasn't practice to be credited any-where, and there was no question of any royalty payments. As George mostly worked with small bands and orchestras, he generally used Number 2, the medium-sized studio: smaller than 1 but bigger than 3. He moved between the studio floor, where technical engineers in white lab coats pre-positioned the equipment, and the control room, where a balance engineer operated the knobs, buttons and levers on the recording console, and an assistant handled the phys-ical recording.*

George timed his arrival to perfection. When Oscar Preuss had entered the business, in 1904, flat shellac discs had just been introduced as an alternative to cylinders; now *two* technological revolutions were happening. One was the manufacture of records from a vinyl compound – lighter, more durable and less breakable than shellac – pressed either as seven-inch single-play discs to revolve at 45, or as ten- or twelve-inch 'microgroove' discs to spin at 33⅓. They'd come to be called 'albums' but at this point (even in America) were long-playing records, long-players, LPs.

The second revolution was the arrival of tape as the optimum medium for recording. It had long been done straight to wax, which meant the sound couldn't be changed once it passed from the microphone through the engi-neer's console. Tape was an *interim* process – it could be edited or electronically manipulated before going to disc. Until now, the sole purpose of recording had been to capture the sound of a live performance as faithfully as possible; tape could do this too, but also, if desired, it could create a dif-ferent sound altogether. Some clever minds were already pushing the possibilities: in America, husband-and-wife musical duo Les Paul and Mary Ford were releasing what would come to be called multi-track recordings, Paul

---

* Number 2 control room was level with the studio, on the ground floor. It was relocated above in 1957, a long wooden staircase installed for access.

playing up to eight different parts on electric guitar, overdubbing layer on layer, and Ford singing several parts with herself. Such wizardry wasn't going to sit well with everyone; musicians said it cheapened the art of performance, making singers and players seem more accomplished than they really were, as well as giving them a sound they couldn't necessarily produce on stage. In the *Musical Express*, pianist-journalist Steve Race railed bitterly against 'devices in the recording studio which make something that isn't'.[9] But such purist objections were too late, because the genie was out of the bottle.

Brian Epstein had two ambitions: to be a dress designer and/or an actor. The one thing he wouldn't do was the one thing expected of him: to go into the family business.[10] There were heated discussions about it whenever Harry and Queenie visited him at Wrekin. Finally, when Harry said he *must*, Brian (by this point 16) removed himself from Wrekin six months before sitting his School Certificate, the decisive exams for which his entire traumatic schooling had been designed. At Christmas 1950 he was home in Liverpool under a black cloud.

Harry felt he knew his eldest son. He said dress-designing wasn't manly; Brian didn't budge. He said it was a ruthless uncertain business; Brian didn't budge. He then said Brian stood very little chance of being the *best*, at least not for a while – indeed it was likely he'd be unemployed. The defences of a boy who'd one day concede 'I loathe being second best at anything' were breached.[11]

He started at I. Epstein & Sons in the opening days of 1951, as a £5-a-week salesman, bottom of the ladder. His *zayde* (grandfather Isaac) was still there at 73, arriving at 6AM every day and holding firm to his ethic, 'The fair deal is the right deal'. Brian was 16, fresh-faced and prone to blushing, but he had sound principles, faith in the shop's stock, was receptive to guidance, and was a nat-ural-born seller. On his second day, a woman came in to buy a mirror and Brian sold her a dining table – 'because I honestly felt she would be better off with a dining table'.[12] He found he was good at gaining people's confidence, that his manners and sincerity bred effective communication and his BBC voice broad-cast it. He also confirmed an instinctive flair for display, rearranging the furniture artfully and seeing the effect of linking presentation to selling. As he put it, 'I think if you show the public something lovely, they'll accept it.'[13]

In November 1952, a manila envelope fell on the carpet at Queens Drive. It was Brian's call-up. Everything in and about his character explains what kind of a time he had during his stint in the British army. Effete, effeminate, slight, shy, elegant, cultured, artistic, cerebral, temperamental, unphysical, dramatic, nicely spoken, middle-class, Jewish, with a history of walking out or being

expelled from schools . . . he was all this and more. He was mentally and physically unsuited to the mind-numbing 'square bashing', to the brutal agonies and
bullying disciplines, and to the rude, crude, insensitive Tommies in his barracks.
Above all, he was oh-so-easy meat for the sadistic regimental sergeant majors
(RSMs). One day Brian was at home in Childwall, the next he was in bleak barracks at Aldershot, and the shock to his system was total.

Out of this grisly period in his life, compensations would emerge. Being
with so many thousands of other men, he heard whispers about homosexual
activity in London. Private Epstein S/22739590 angled for a posting and
got one by spring 1953 – he was moved to Regent's Park Barracks. The bullying was non-stop appalling but the location a dream – a mile from the West
End with its galleries, theatres, art-house cinemas, restaurants, pubs and
clubs. Brian explored the capital for the first time and revelled in its culture.
He'd later say he didn't go near the bars and clubs he'd heard about 'but I
became aware of other homosexuals everywhere I went'. He also wrote that
he had no physical encounters while in the army, and still didn't know 'the
facts of life'.[14]

The Epsteins had relatives in London, in St John's Wood and Marylebone;
when he could, Brian went to his Aunt Freda's apartment off Baker Street for
Friday-night Sabbath dinner, shedding his army tunic in favour of an elegant
suit, shirt and tie, spotlessly shiny black shoes and bowler hat with a furled
umbrella. Returning to barracks late one night in April 1953, he was put on a
charge of impersonating an officer. By new year 1954, Brian had been seen by
five army psychiatrists who concluded it would be best for everyone if this soldier was given an honourable discharge on 'medical grounds'. On 27 January
1954, ten months earlier than due, he sprinted to Euston station and the train
home.

Little by little now, Brian explored Liverpool's other night-life – a necessarily complex, secretive netherworld of diversion and danger. Every city had its
hang-outs for 'queers' or 'poofs': this or that public toilet, specific areas of certain parks, or, for the bold, particular pubs or bars on a given night of the week.
Brian peeled back the lid and joined in. What's known is that he liked younger
men, but the majority of his encounters were with men of violence, often working-class labouring types who might physically as well as sexually assault him,
and sometimes only the first. The slang was 'rough trade', and Brian was a slave
to it. He had an emotional compulsion to take risks, especially if he was drinking (Scotch was his favourite). He was often beaten, several times blackmailed,
and would have very few meaningful relationships in his life, mostly torrid flings
and one-night stands. He was a man of many companions destined always to
be alone. He despised the way he was, sometimes really hating himself for it,

and yet, for all the guilt and pain these moments brought, his appetite was rarely less than voracious. He was usually (to use his own words from a private letter) 'hot for sex'.

This wasn't *all* Brian did. He attended every concert by the Liverpool Philharmonic Orchestra, was a regular at every theatre, and took up amateur dramatics. There was also a shift towards the performing arts at work: Harry wanted him to make a sideways move, literally, from Epstein's to Nems, the shop they owned next door. As well as pianos and sheet music, Nems now sold household electrical appliances and records, and this sector of the business was strongly on the rise in post-war Britain. Nems needed a fresh mind and new energy, and so Brian began his first association with the record business, initially one of acquainting himself with the repertoire, the London companies and their travelling salesmen, ordering stock and bringing his design ideas into the window.

In December 1954, at EMI's annual Christmas party inside the great Number 1 studio, Oscar Preuss picked up the microphone and announced his retirement, effective the following March. He was always telling his assistant 'recording is a young man's business', and now that assistant took over Parlophone. At 29, George Martin became the youngest A&R chief in England. A further piece of Preuss advice would also echo in his protégé's mind: 'With artists, if you ever get any thanks, it's a bonus.'[15]

George's new salary wasn't a whole lot better than before, but he needed whatever he could get. He and Sheena now had a daughter, Alexis; they'd also taken out a mortgage on a semi-detached house – and because it was in Hatfield, twenty miles north of London, he had to buy a car. Funds were so tight, George had considered a job offer from Decca, and might have taken it had he not been promoted.[16]

As head of Parlophone, George Martin would have to cope with rock and roll and all the other 'five-minute fads' (as everyone called them) certain to emerge from America. He'd also have to keep pace with technological change. EMI now issued some LPs as pre-recorded tapes, and there was another disc format, the seven-inch extended-play (EP), which typically featured four songs and, like a miniature LP, sold in glossy picture sleeves with notes on the back. Then, on 4 April 1955, the day George took charge at Parlophone (he had the knack of good timing), EMI demonstrated the 'Stereosonic' LP – records for people with two ears. Mass-market release of stereo was still some time away, but it was coming.

These changes were managed from central London premises rented solely for EMI's record division, on the top floor of 8–11 Great Castle Street, just behind Oxford Circus. Abbey Road was left entirely in the hands of technicians and administrators, and the recording managers shuttled between the two places.

Other EMI changes were also afoot, including the appointment of a new chairman. Joseph Lockwood's business background in international flour mills seemed unsuited to the rigours of running an electronics company with more than thirty thousand employees worldwide, but Lockwood was an industrialist of vision and vigour. One of his first duties was to complete EMI's $8m (£2.8m) purchase of the American company Capitol Records, Inc, which went through in January 1955 to the shock of the music businesses on both sides of the Atlantic.

The takeover was reported in each country with local emphasis. *Melody Maker* enthused, 'A new field is open for a greater distribution than ever before of EMI "popular" records in America.' *Billboard* stressed that Capitol would 'continue to be operated by present management'. And so it was. Though sold to the British in good faith by its founders, there always seemed to be corporate resentment in Hollywood that this hip label should fall into the hands of Limeys, with their sober suits, derbies, umbrellas and *don't you know, old chap.* Capitol Records was American to its core, from its Washington DC logo (four stars orbiting the Capitol dome) to its array of illustrious sophisticated artists. The British were just overjoyed at this rare reversal of musical fortunes. The *NME* glowed that 'the power of England in the American recording industry will be vastly increased. British personalities of interest to Capitol will [have] their discs released in the US ...' This was notice that Capitol would have automatic first pick for America of any contractually available EMI record, a system known as 'first turn-down option'. Turned out to be an apt name.[17]

In April 1955, as George Martin took up the reins at Parlophone, Harry and Queenie Epstein made a substantial investment in their eldest son. Brian was straining at the leash, wanting to hold a position of responsibility, to run things *his* way, so they opened a shop that he alone would manage, fully in charge of its design, policy, purchasing, sales and the hiring and firing of staff. This was Clarendon Furnishing, located in Hoylake, on the west side of the Wirral, and he stocked it with G-Plan furniture, Parker Knoll armchairs and bedding. It was a changing of the guard for the family businesses: Isaac had died in the February and in his place Brian and Clive were appointed directors and shareholders, with Brian also company secretary. They were 20 and 18, and more than capable. The *Hoylake & West Kirby Advertiser*'s report on Clarendon's VIP opening noted the shop's layout, furnishing and decoration and said it 'clearly indicates the influence of an Epstein with a pronounced artistic flair ... and to this may be added a refined technique in salesmanship'.[18]

Clarendon returned a profit in year one, but its young manager remained restless. Outside work, Brian was becoming immersed in the stage, appearing in amateur plays and socialising with the actors at the Playhouse and Royal Court, the big theatres in the heart of Liverpool. He expressed regret to Playhouse actors Brian Bedford and Helen Lindsay that he couldn't be like them, saying he'd left it too late to become an actor; they said he hadn't – he could apply for a place at the Royal Academy of Dramatic Art (RADA), the nation's foremost theatre school, in London. Brian decided he would.

All hell broke loose inside 197 Queens Drive when he told his parents. Clarendon had been designed as Brian's baby, where he would finally settle and justify his worth. Now, after just nine months, he wanted to chuck it in and disappear off to London – *to act!* – discarding his responsibilities as manager, director, shareholder and company secretary. Harry was incandescent; why couldn't Brian be like his younger brother Clive: steady, capable of staying the course? Even Queenie, Brian's ceaseless defender, struggled to understand her son's reasoning (though she soon came round to it).

The full details of what happened next aren't known and probably never will be, but two documents, both dated 21 February 1956, survive to tell the meat of the story. The first is the RADA application form, sent with the prospectus Brian had requested by post a day or two earlier; the second is his handwritten Last Will and Testament, the existence of which exposes the intensity of events, a dramatic direction in this crisis about drama. It's a single sheet of paper on which he bequeathed his 'artistic possessions' (books, records, theatre programmes) to a friend, his clothing to the State of Israel, and the remainder of his estate to his family. He directed that mourning last no longer than seven days, and that Kaddish (the mourning prayer) not be recited in his memory. He ended by wishing that his parents and brother 'know of my eternal love for them'. It's the only will known to have been made by Brian Epstein, but as it wasn't witnessed, it wasn't legal; it remains today what it was then, a cri-de-coeur from a highly strung, emotionally raw young man with suicide on his mind.[19]

How the situation calmed isn't clear, but Brian made no known attempt to kill himself, didn't complete the application, and stayed on as manager at Clarendon. Harry had won the mind games ... but the heart play was another matter: Brian kept the RADA documents at hand, and the thrill and pull of the stage grew ever stronger, especially when he spent his summer Sundays in a spacious flat in Gambier Terrace taking one-to-one acting lessons from Helen Lindsay. In September 1956, Brian initiated new correspondence with RADA, using the Hoylake shop address, and as a result – despite the domestic firestorm it must have rekindled – he arrived in London on the 19th to audition for academy principal John Fernald. He passed the exam and accepted an offered place on a two-year full-time course to start on 1 October.

Brian had frittered his father's trust and support to dedicate himself to studying for the stage. Would he make the grade at last, after years of academic failure? Also crowding his mind was the subject he rarely mentioned: in London, any variety of thrills and dangers lay before him, closet worlds into which he could slip with anonymity. He rented an expensive flat in Bayswater, and (as far as his spotless dress sense would permit) tried to blend into capital life.

George Martin was in the St John's Wood studio most days, learning his trade on Parlophone's panoply of recordings and, whenever he could, experimenting with tape. He produced much classical music (the London Baroque Ensemble and others), jazz (Humphrey Lyttelton, the Kirchin Band and many more), children's music (Mandy Miller's Nellie The Elephant left its imprint on a generation), vocal music (Eve Boswell, Edna Savage and many more), electric guitar (Bert Weedon), light orchestral music (especially Ron Goodwin, the most musically fruitful association of George's career), Scottish music (accordionist Jimmy Shand was his top act), and also comedy and novelty records.

In November 1952, two years after joining Parlophone, George had produced a multi-layered voice recording by the actor and wit Peter Ustinov; it wasn't a hit, but not every issue had to be, and he was allowed to make further such records when he saw fit. When *The Goon Show* took off on radio, its voice artists came to the attention of record labels, and for three of them (Peter Sellers, Michael Bentine and Spike Milligan) that label was Parlophone, an ever-welcoming shelter for unconventional minds. George loved *The Goon Show*, its zany humour dovetailing with his own; together, he and its creators rose magnificently to the challenge of bringing eccentric musings to disc, records that the show's legions of fans would enjoy time and again.*

George also had success with a singer who'd scored a rare British hit in America. That was in 1948, when Dick James was signed to Decca; by 1953 he'd switched to Parlophone and split his career into two elements: performing (stage and studio), when he wore a wig, and publishing (plugging for one

---

* 'George Martin produced the Goons' is a popular misconception. He was behind some Parlophone releases of BBC shows, and he recorded three of the Goons individually or in collaboration, but he didn't produce them as a group – their collective recordings were on Decca.

of Tin Pan Alley's best music men, Sydney Bron), when he was bald. George produced several records of jolly party medleys in which Dick sang old favourites and an audience of happy-clappy Londoners whooped in the background; none charted, but the genre was popular enough for James to have his own shows on Radio Luxembourg, *Sing Song Time* and *Sunday Singsong With Dick James*. Then, out of nowhere, in 1956, he suddenly scored an enduring British hit, singing the theme of the ITV serial *The Adventures Of Robin Hood*. The recording needed the kind of problem-solving George was now doing on a regular basis. 'I really wanted the "William Walton sound" of all those arrows going through the air. I actually got an archer in and put microphones all the way down Number 2 studio and had him fire an arrow past them and into a target at the other end – and it sounded *awful*. In the end we got the right noise by jamming a wooden ruler on the end of a desk, and going "doinngg" with an elastic band on a mike, and slowing it down.'[20]

After a few awkward moments in his early years, George mastered the record producer's greatest challenge: how to bring the best out of artists. He became naturally good at tact, diplomacy and artful flattery, at letting singers and musicians think the great ideas he'd just planted in their heads were theirs. But it was always a win-some-lose-some job, the catalogues dotted with failures. George tried to produce R&B with the Southlanders, a London-based vocal group from Jamaica whom he signed to Parlophone on the industry-standard penny-per-record contract. He rushed them into Abbey Road in April 1955 to record Earth Angel. His wasn't the only cover version of the US vocal hit by the Penguins – it was standard practice that several different recordings of the same song competed for sales. George's production was fair and faithful but it lacked the qualities of the original and so typified almost all attempts, by all British A&R men at all record companies, to replicate what was unmistakably an American sound. You could get singers to sing and musicians to play the dots, and the studio equipment was sometimes worse and sometimes better, but a key ingredient – feel, soul, energy, vitality, all of them in shades – perpetually lacked in the covers. There's really no better way to describe it than 'they sounded *British*' . . . and you knew that could be bad.

The music that people called 'pops' wasn't quite George's forte, but he had to stay tuned in. He kept close relations with publishers, who in turn had connections of their own, and by this method in early September 1956 came a hot tip: George should get himself down to Soho, to the 2i's Coffee Bar, and check out a young cockney singer called Tommy Hicks. George felt the boy's talent was mostly visual, of little use to him in the recording studio, but he did like the backing group and offered them another of those penny contracts . . . which was how George Martin became the first A&R man to sign a skiffle group.

The Vipers' debut session was on 4 October in Abbey Road Number 2 studio, 7–10PM, after they'd worked their day jobs. The sound was rightly rough: this was 1920s Chicago rent party music, call-and-response singing, strummed guitars, plucked bass and fingered percussive washboard. It was George's first session with untrained musicians, just him and a group of coffee-bar players.

Though new to the studio, the Vipers had the swagger of youth and were prepared not to be impressed, but as their guitarist and singer Wally Whyton would recall, they took an immediate and prolonged liking to their producer: 'George Martin was amazing. We were a fairly eccentric bunch and thought we were Jack the Lads. Every night the 2i's was packed out and everybody wanted to see the Vipers, so we were full of our own importance, but George was an absolute gentleman, a toff. He never got fazed if we fell off stools, or were late, or didn't have the money to get home. He was amazing, pulling down a minor salary at EMI and producing all those records.'[21]

The Vipers were seen on BBC-tv and had other publicity, but their first record didn't sell. Skiffle was a slow boom coming – primed, lit, not yet exploding. Of more pressing concern within EMI was the fact that George had missed landing the big fish: under managers John Kennedy and Larry Parnes, Tommy Hicks very quickly became Tommy Steele, Britain's first rock and roll star, all screams and dreams.

Snap decisions about talent were taken all the time by all A&R men, and everyone made mistakes, but this came at a bad moment, because the gossip within the record business was that Parlophone was being shut down. Oscar Preuss had warned George that EMI's top brass might do this one day. Parlophone's viable artists would be assigned to Columbia or HMV and some let go. The general manager of the record division, C. H. Thomas, was actively pushing for it, intending to shift George Martin to HMV as junior producer under Walter Ridley. If he was to stave off the threat, he *had* to come up with more hits.

Brian Epstein was in Soho too, but not at the 2i's. The clubs he patronised were more discreet, where men danced with danger and perhaps, before the night was out, did something that could see them beaten up or behind bars. Though hardly RADA's only homosexual, Brian had no known relationships here, instead finding or contemplating 'trade' in more perilous avenues. He left Bayswater during the term and found necessarily cheaper accommodation – a flat at the southern end of Finchley Road, by Swiss Cottage.

RADA was *school*. Students had to stand and bid good morning to the teacher – a difficult transition for an adult who'd spent six years in business. He was also troubled by the 'conceit, hypocrisy and narcissism' of his fellow actors.[22] Brian's five tutors were pleased with him though. His 'sensitivity' and 'intelligence' were complimented in the written reports, and all agreed that he showed promise as an actor. He was especially good as the playwright Konstantin in Chekhov's *The Seagull*, one tutor saying he played the climactic suicide scene 'with some power and sensitivity'. It was only a year after he'd been actively contemplating his own. Fellow student Joanna Dunham was electrified by the performance: 'It was obviously therapeutic to him, slightly frightening to watch. When Konstantin tore the bandage off his head and raged at his mother it was all too real.'[23]

Students were given five weeks off at Easter 1957; Brian took a temporary job in the record department at book and record shop Ascroft & Daw on Charing Cross Road, bringing the experience gained at Nems and taking away new ideas for presentation and stock control. He spent the Wednesday evening after Easter, 24 April, at the Arts Theatre Club, at the world premiere of Jean Genet's *The Balcony*; afterwards, returning by Tube to Swiss Cottage, something else was urging his mind.

A few hours later, Brian wrote an eleven-page account of just the first stage of a harrowing nightmare, intended to be his explanation of events should he be sent straight to prison and/or (judging from the tone of the text) perhaps take his own life. The document chronicled how he'd found himself irresistibly drawn to a man in a public toilet inside Swiss Cottage station; how he and the man watched each other warily after leaving the station, loitering in the nearby streets; how they eventually talked and discussed a place suitable for action; and how this man, suddenly revealing himself as a plainclothes policeman and joined by a colleague, arrested him for 'persistently importuning'. The likely sentence, as they probably enjoyed telling him, was six months in jail.

It was a standard police trap – and, ever in thrall to danger, Brian had been an easy catch. The constables twisted his arm up behind his back and frogmarched him to a police station where he was charged with 'persistently importuning several men'. 'Several?' the duty sergeant enquired. 'Four,' the arresting officer confirmed. Released on bail, Brian was compelled to appear at Marylebone Magistrates' Court in the morning.

> I do not think I am an abnormally weak-willed person – the effort and determination with which I have rebuilt my life these past few months have, I assure you, been no mean effort. I believed that my own will-power was the best thing with which to overcome my homosexuality. And I believe my life may even have attained a public success.

I was determined to go through the horror of this world. I feel deeply, for I have always felt deeply, for the persecuted, for the Jews, the coloured people, for the old, and society's misfits. When I made money I planned to devote and give what I could to these people.

I am not sorry for myself. My worst times and punishments are over. Now, through the wreckage of my life by society, my being will stain and bring the deepest distress to all my devoted family and few friends. The damage, the lying criminal methods of the police in importuning me and consequently capturing me, leaves me cold, stunned and finished.[24]

After this, Brian's account (composed over several days) varies from the court records: he wrote that he entered a plea of guilty, the ledger confirms the opposite – he was remanded on bail and instructed to reappear four days later. He did this at Bow Street Magistrates' Court, where records show he again pleaded not guilty and was remanded a second time, pending the submission of a medical report. Four weeks after his torment began, Brian was sentenced at Bow Street to two years' probation and directed to have medical treatment – probably psychiatric analysis, possibly electric shock therapy. In the meantime, Brian stayed at RADA for the summer term and tried to put the shattering ordeal behind him.

The 'Parlophone to end' rumours reached their zenith in February 1957, having gained such strength that EMI issued a statement insisting the story had 'no foundation', and that there was no truth 'Mr Martin [would be] leaving EMI'.[25] It was a pleasing denial, but there was no smoke without fire and the directors' vote must have been close. Chairman Lockwood prevailed: he said that as EMI needed to produce more British talent, it would be counterproductive to reduce the number of output labels. George's position and Parlophone's saving came at a cost, though. EMI reappointed the former Columbia A&R head Norman Newell with a unique brief to sign artists and produce records across all the company's labels. No longer would every Parlophone recording at Abbey Road be a George Martin production; and from this point on, more than before, Parlophone was regularly in the charts, having many hits.

George was creating successes with the Vipers, and also with his first rock and roll singer, the actor Jim Dale. The Vipers records were a particular influence on budding skiffle groups, including those in Liverpool. The Eddie Clayton group (Richy Starkey on drums) played several Vipers songs and Roy Trafford painted 'The Cumberland Gap' on his tea-chest bass. In the Quarry Men, John Lennon sang both Cumberland Gap and Maggie May, a necessarily bowdlerised version of the nineteenth-century seaman's ballad about a robbing Liverpool prostitute conducting her business on Lime Street.*

Then there were the records George *had* to make. When the British music business had a few calypso-crazy weeks in spring 1957, a time when London recording studios swung almost solely to the sounds of sweet Jamaica, the head of Parlophone was cutting tracks with his black South African singer Peter Lowe, his British-based Jamaican Ben Bowers, Eve Boswell, Edna Savage (Me Head's In De Barrel), guitarist Bert Weedon, saxophonist Frank Weir (Calypso Romance) and the Kirchins jazz band (Calypso!!). None troubled the charts.†

The Vipers and Jim Dale aside, George's main success in this period was with a humorous novelty jazz record by Johnny Dankworth, Experiments With Mice, which had four weeks in the top ten. Dankworth's music was really better suited to the new LP format, however, which – because of its higher price – was affordable more to adults and so targeted at that section of the market. Record companies expected LPs to be made in a day: twenty-five to thirty-five minutes of music to be rehearsed, recorded, mixed and prepared for mastering. George produced an album by Johnny Dankworth and his Orchestra in under six hours in EMI Number 2 studio in March 1957. It was achievable if the musicians knew their pieces and were adequately prepared; if it *wasn't* achieved, if an LP took longer to make, the A&R manager could be reproached in an internal memorandum.

Amid all this studio work, other areas of George's daily life were complex. Sheena gave birth to their second child (a boy, Gregory) in January 1957, despite which this wasn't and never had been, by all known accounts, a marriage abundant in joy and happiness. There was still a lot of old guilt flying around, Sheena suffered agoraphobia, and George was always working. At some point in this period, George and his secretary began a relationship. Judy Smith, the 'Miss Lockhart Smith' who'd coolly greeted him on his first day at Parlophone, had become his ally, protector and promoter. Where once she'd been Oscar Preuss's secretary so now she was George's, and over time an affair began to develop – not one entered into lightly by either side, considering the consequences. Both parties could be – had to be – terribly discreet. 'Judy had this incredible upper-class accent and George was clearly that way inclined,' says

---

* Since the 1700s, Liverpool prostitutes had been known collectively as Maggie May, meaning 'Maggie will'. The song is very similar – melodically, lyrically and structurally – to the American slavery song Darling Nellie Gray (written 1856), and it isn't known definitively which came first.
† The only calypso to score any success was The Banana Boat Song (Day-O), three versions of which popped into the NME Top Thirty at the beginning of March. This was the time when a 16-year-old boy in Liverpool, John Lennon, wrote Calypso Rock, his first song.

a former colleague. 'She used to say a raised *what?* at the end of sentences. He was dazzled by her and by her upbringing, completely dazzled.' It was an office relationship, kept secret from almost every EMI colleague. George Martin had started to lead a double life.

Brian Epstein's horrendous court ordeal dragged on through the start of the summer term, but he continued to make progress as an actor. Entry to RADA's second year was dependent on success in a Mid-Course Test, and Brian passed it. But he was now weary of the undiluted company of actors. 'Nowhere,' he would write, 'could one discover such phoney relationships nor witness hypocrisy practised on so grand a scale, almost as an art.' The old restlessness was back again. 'Was there, I wondered, no job I could stick for longer than a year?'[26] Only Brian could have engineered such a complete turnaround.

His withdrawal from the second year at RADA annoyed the academy and baffled his parents. Using the security of their wealth to change his mind mid-stream, and mess everyone about, was something he'd done since infancy. They knew the behaviour pattern, but still this was a move they didn't see coming. Brian told them he was returning to Liverpool to stay, to settle down; he wanted to throw himself into the family business 'and make an increasing and lifelong success of it'.[27] And so Harry and Queenie came up with another winning plan, one that might maintain his interest: instead of sending Brian back to Hoylake, Nems would expand into Liverpool city centre for the first time, opening a three-floor shop on Great Charlotte Street, opposite Blackler's department store. It would sell every kind of domestic appliance and boast a sizeable record department: ground floor and basement. British record sales in 1957 were on course to top eighty million – a huge year-on-year increase fuelled by rising teenage spending power.

An attraction for Brian was that Clive (now completing his National Service) would co-manage the shop with him, although Brian would keep exclusive control of the record department. He threw himself into the challenge, designing systems and policy, establishing contacts, choosing and overseeing the shop-fitting, and ordering the stock. Several examples of his business correspondence survive and they all burst with energy, strength of purpose, dedication to duty, clarity of thought, attention to detail and an ability to express himself.

The *Liverpool Echo* display announcement that Brian wrote – NEMS LTD COME TO TOWN! – ran on the front page on 7 December 1957 immediately under a classified ad for a Quarry Men appearance. They were maybe half an inch apart. The grand opening was performed by recording star Anne Shelton, and a photograph shows a large crowd of Liverpool adults pressed keenly forward, while Brian – an elegant young man, stylishly assured – stares with pride into the camera.*

Nems in Liverpool was nothing less than the success it had to be. The business of selling records in the city centre was competitive but Brian quickly generated good profits. He implemented the stock control system he'd observed at Ascroft & Daw, where each record was kept in a separate folder, and as copies ran low staff would let a string dangle, enabling him to see the ordering history at a glance, and which required restocking. Brian's own experience of record shops often left him frustrated – product was frequently unavailable, the customer leaving the shop empty-handed. Brian shaped a policy where not only did Nems rarely run out, but when a customer wanted a record, no matter how obscure, he'd order at least two extra copies, because if one person wanted it, others also might. Nems at 50 Great Charlotte Street was quickly rewarded with a reputation as the shop where a customer could get anything, which made it the first port-of-call for many. After 4PM each day, a steady stream of blazered schoolboys washed in – Paul McCartney, George Harrison and plenty more – to check out the latest sounds in one of Nems' three ground-floor listening booths, known in the business as 'browseries'.

Brian was in the shop from 6AM and left at 10PM or later. On Sundays, when it was closed, he'd be there ordering stock; on Wednesday afternoons, when like most shops in Liverpool Nems had 'half-day closing', he dressed the windows. Clive ran his 'white goods' departments similarly. Male staff wore suits, the women wore white dresses with 'Nems' embroidered on the breast pocket; customers were greeted as 'sir' and 'madam'. There were specific forms of management address too: Clive was Mr Clive, Brian was Mr Brian, and, when he dropped by, Harry was Mr Harry. 'Nems was an honest, hard-working, decent firm, dead straight, very much respected,' says Margaret Cooney, an employee from the start. 'Brian could be temperamental, but he was a good boss. I wouldn't say anything detrimental about him at all. He was always immaculately dressed, and you knew when he was in the shop because it smelled of after-shave.'[28]

One of Brian's routines, self-appointed, was to compile Nems' own Top Twenty chart. He liked dealing with the pop side, and through relations with record companies felt he was maintaining an attachment to show business.[29]

---

* An earlier ad for the new shop (*Echo*, 22 November; also, bizarrely, next to a Quarry Men ad) mentioned 'television, radio and hi-fidelity equipment' as well as a 'tremendous selection of all the newest labour saving devices for the home'. There was ample scope for business, especially by hire-purchase agreements. While the majority of British households now had a vacuum cleaner, only 18 per cent had a washing machine and 8 per cent a fridge.

He gathered fresh sales data and crunched the numbers twice daily, to keep Nems' exhibited Top Twenty bang up to date, and he gave a weekly cumulative chart to both *Melody Maker* and *The Record Mirror*, which processed his ranked 1–20 positions, along with the same data from other shops, to produce national charts. (*The Record Mirror* also showed Nems' chart separately within its spread of shop top tens.)

George Martin's second visit to America, his first after joining EMI, had a pronounced impact. He and Ron Goodwin had come up with Skiffling Strings, a brisk tune combining skiffle with a light orchestra; it did little at home but Capitol picked it up, renamed it Swinging Sweethearts (skiffle being only a British fad), and invited Goodwin over for promotion. George and the publisher Sydney Bron went too. It was October 1957.

The party worked its way across the States, starting in New York, stopping in Philadelphia for the TV show *American Bandstand*, and ending in Hollywood, where George met Capitol Records' director of international repertoire, the producer Dave Dexter, Jr. It was Dexter who received all the records mailed across from England and decided which ones Capitol would release. EMI expected pretty much all of them to be issued, *and* actively promoted, but from the hundreds of discs sent Dexter's way in 1957, he picked just eighteen and supported two at most. (Eight of the eighteen were George Martin productions – he was more 'successful' in this regard than his colleagues.) So pathetically small was the figure, bad blood was already coursing between the parent company in London and its recalcitrant Hollywood teenager. EMI hoped George's visit to the Capitol Tower might put family relations on a better footing, but actually they worsened: from five hundred British masters diligently offered in 1958, only sixteen were selected ... and still some of Dexter's colleagues thought this too many. As he'd note in his autobiography, 'Capitol's sales chief complained that I was releasing "too many damned British dogs".'[30]

Though hopping mad, EMI was fearful of forcing the issue because of anti-trust, the American law that regulates competitive business. Capitol laid it on thick, saying that if EMI was seen to be bossing them about, the English company could incur heavy fines and even be made to surrender its stockholding. Paul Marshall – probably the most respected US record business lawyer of his time, representing many companies – says this was quite false: 'There was no provision in the United States for anti-trust laws which would have prevented EMI from instructing Capitol what to do, but Capitol's lawyer scared the people in London into thinking there might *be* a problem.'[31] With much embarrassment, EMI began offering its Capitol rejects to other labels – a policy announced by the *NME* on 4 July 1958. It was Independence Day for Capitol, and a bad one for EMI, since it was known throughout the US business that any tapes being hawked around the little league had already been rejected by a major.

The day George Martin and Ron Goodwin were at Capitol, Frank Sinatra was in there to finish recording his album *Come Fly With Me*. Feeling like 'the country cousins from England', they watched as 'The Voice', with Billy May and Nelson Riddle, completed a masterpiece, and stood quietly while the star kicked up a stink over the album artwork.[32] Days after returning to England, George set about finding himself a Voice – and quickly landed Jeremy Lubbock, a young London night-club pianist/singer who sounded more like Sinatra than the real thing. George replicated the arrangements and production he'd heard in Hollywood and had no success at all.

He also returned home looking for *zing*, and thought he'd got it with Manchester rock singer Paul Beattie, who played the Cavern and other clubs with his own backing group, the Beats. His first Parlophone single, I'm Comin' Home, was a big brassy number with a honking sax break and heavy echo on Beattie's deep baritone Elvis-like voice. Though derivative (and actually quite strange), it was arguably the best British rock and roll record made to date. This was virgin territory for George – a genuine rock singer, from the north, with a name that didn't need changing, and he'd managed to produce something unusual. He had high hopes for a breakthrough, of having anticipated 'the next big thing', but it didn't come, and it also didn't come with the follow-up, Me, Please Me, or with Beattie's two final Parlophone releases up to 1960.

George hadn't yet made number 1 (he came closest in December 1957 when Jim Dale was at 2 with Be My Girl), but he did still have impressive firsts. With the obvious exceptions of Lonnie Donegan and Tommy Steele, he produced the first skiffle LP, the Vipers' *Coffee Bar Session*, and, in Jim Dale's *Jim!*, the first British rock and roll LP. It was ten inches of vinyl, ten songs, twenty-four minutes of music taped in under a day, everything pseudo-American and poor. Lennon, McCartney, Harrison, Starkey and thousands of other teenagers awed by the genuine American sound were unmoved – British rock records seldom had authenticity or guts, just weak songs sung in a rigid formulaic style and played by session musicians, jazzers, for whom it was one for the money.

Skiffle was soon gone, at least as far as record sales were concerned. The last releases by the Vipers Skiffle Group were credited simply to the Vipers. In true British style, the genre's final hit was a satire, George Martin's production of Peter Sellers' Any Old Iron. More and more, comedy was becoming George's one solo hand. 'I knew I had to make a mark in some way,' he says, 'and my only plan was to find a way of making records that other people weren't making. Ones that would sell. And the way I chose was to go into comedy, because no one was doing it. People were doing it in the States – Stan Freberg, Bob Newhart – but there was nothing in England to speak of. And it seemed to work.'

George made two particular LPs in this period. One was a live recording of the revue *At The Drop Of A Hat* – Michael Flanders and Donald Swann's literate and witty encapsulations of human foibles and modern life. The show became a big success in London and then on Broadway, but its mass popularity came through the Parlophone LP.

The other, with Peter Sellers, was the most artistically satisfying project George had in 1958, and the most enduring. Over the course of just three three-hour sessions at Abbey Road, he produced *The Best Of Sellers*, the first British comedy LP created in a recording studio. George's role was four-fold: to find the right material, to bring the best out of a brilliant but troubled artist, to enrich the recording with the correct texture and colour by his own imagination and invention, and to fashion a comedy record worth listening to even when the joke was known. George would always refer to these productions as 'sound pictures', and *The Best Of Sellers* is a fine early masterpiece, a five-star ten-inch record that spent forty-seven weeks in *Melody Maker*'s Top Ten – Britain's first LP chart, launched in November 1958.

With ample finance and studio time to try things, even the failures could be glorious. One of George's personal favourites was Sparkie The Fiddle, the record he made with a talking budgerigar. The bird was brought into EMI Number 2 studio and George gave it the full works: he hired a writer to script a hokey American film satire about a jailbird, he had Ron Goodwin compose and conduct an arrangement, and the budgie's spoken words entailed a vast amount of editing, hundreds of pieces of tape cut up and kept carefully in order. The result was a Parlophone single that sold about forty-two copies.

Brian Epstein continued to work dawn to dusk at Great Charlotte Street, dedicated to the challenge, and at 23 had never been so fulfilled. He moved crisply between his two record departments – pop on the ground floor, classics on the first – and he kept a shop staff of twenty-eight on their toes. As the original meaning of Nems (North End Music Stores) was irrelevant in the city, Mr Brian and Mr Clive reversed it into a new one they adopted for press ads: Nems Efficient Modern Service. It was, and that's why it was so quickly prospering.

As well as being a lifelong lover of classical music, Brian was actively enjoying the pop side. He went to several of the touring rock shows at the Empire and elsewhere, advertising Nems in the programmes; he also had a speciality trick of memorising record catalogue numbers – customers could name almost any record and he'd know its label and number by heart. His knowledge of the companies, their artists, labels and sales staff, and the complex distribution networks, was formidable. It was his business to know. At the end of April 1958, the American rockabilly singer Marvin Rainwater was number 1 in Britain with Whole Lotta Woman. He happened to be playing Liverpool Empire for a week and Brian was the only shop owner to fix a lunchtime signing session, arranging extra stock with EMI. Queues formed out of the door.

And then, as usual, he was reckless. At 10.30PM on 19 May 1958, cruising in his car along The Strand, in front of the Liver Building, Brian stopped to pick up some rough trade. Both men knew the score; this won't have been the only time Brian did it. He drove out to the pavilion in Sefton Park ... but whether he got what he wanted wasn't made clear in the resulting court case.

What was detailed, under oath, was that the man menacingly demanded £20, and when Brian said he didn't have it on him, he was attacked about the head and face with an empty milk bottle. The glass broke and Brian was cut (though not too badly). The man grabbed Brian's fine cigarette lighter, some papers and ten shillings, and threatened to expose him as a queer unless he also got the £20. Blackmail. He terrorised Brian into agreeing a meeting the next day at the Queen Victoria Monument to hand over the cash.

In a poor emotional and physical state, Brian drove himself to the Royal Infirmary where he had four stitches inserted into his lacerated left ear and was treated for other cuts, abrasions and bruising to his face and head.[33] Though his parents may not have known of the Swiss Cottage incident thirteen months earlier, he'd no way of keeping this from them. In what must have been an explosive and emotional late night, the truth of his sexuality and compulsion to danger was exposed. Queenie already knew it, or sensed it, though whether Harry did isn't reliably recorded. Either way, it was a mess, of great embarrassment to them personally, and potentially ruinous for business. On one matter his parents were adamant: Brian had to go to the police and report the blackmail. It won't ever be known if he divulged that he was still serving probation for the 1957 London importuning, but it must have been at the forefront of his mind: he could now go to jail for *both* offences.[34]

He was at the police station the following morning, 20 May, possibly with a parent or two. He was interrogated, every element of the incident raked over, and he had to sign a written statement. Then the police gave Brian an envelope containing dummy money and lay in wait a discreet distance from the monument. When the packet was seen to be demanded, the police showed themselves and there was a chase through the streets before the man was apprehended. The case came before magistrates the next day and, as the Epsteins foresaw, court reporters were present. Anticipating this, proceedings began with a plea from the prosecution, that because the complainant was 'a man of substance in Liverpool, and relative of another well-known man of substance in the city, he should be referred to throughout as Mr X'. The court agreed. BEAT UP 'MR. X' IN SEFTON PARK, COURT TOLD and SOLICITOR PROTESTS OVER 'NO BAIL' IN MR. 'X' CASE were two of the subsequent headlines.[35] The defendant, a 23-year-old from Old Swan, was remanded three times over the next four weeks, twice held in custody because Mr X feared for his safety.

In the end, the case went to the Crown Court and the assailant was jailed for two years, while Brian, to his immense relief, was never charged. But it had been another deeply shaming episode, and though his name never came up, he was aware of the whispering that put him squarely in the dock (and anonymity wasn't helped by the bandages and black eyes). Psychologically, Brian was traumatised – his family now knew exactly how he behaved. It was a shocking experience and a huge secret for everyone to hold.

Subterfuge lived elsewhere too. Anti-Semitic antagonism, mild to strong by degrees, was a fact for all Jewish people in Britain (and elsewhere), certainly in strongly Catholic Liverpool. Brian and his family's place of worship, Greenbank Drive Synagogue, was devastated by fire in May 1959, when a thief who broke in to steal a record player and records (donated by Nems) maliciously set papers aflame before running away. It was a traumatic incident for the city's Jewish community, especially so soon after the Holocaust; the sacred scrolls, the Torah, were burned to ashes. Harry Epstein, a member of the synagogue council, had a key involvement in the rebuilding programme, and the arsonist was jailed for four years.

It was easier for many to live their Jewishness down, to try to blend in. Brian took two steps to effect this – irrational ones, but he felt them necessary. While many changed their surname to avoid racist persecution, Brian dropped his middle name. Nems' headed notepaper reveals the sensitivity: in the list of directors, Clive John Epstein was C. J. Epstein but Brian Samuel Epstein was B. Epstein. He also changed the way his surname was pronounced. The Liverpool Epsteins had always been 'Epsteens', and would remain that way, but Brian insisted his was said as 'Epstine'.

Friends saw Brian have two girlfriends in these latter years of the Fifties. The first was Sonia Seligson, met through amateur dramatics. They went to the theatre, dinner-dances, ballet and classical concerts, and she loved his immaculate manners, finely tailored clothes and desire for everything fine. She less enjoyed his drinking. On the occasion he proposed marriage, she felt sure it was the alcohol talking; the question fell flat and wasn't revived. For a while, Sonia was puzzled by Brian's desire to travel alone – he'd spend weekends in Paris, a particularly exotic custom at this time – and it was only when finally he confessed his 'other life' that she realised the weekends were for encounters, and the relationship ended.[36]

Brian's other companion was Rita Harris, a Nems employee. She'd been at Great Charlotte Street several months when a deep friendship dropped into place at the company's annual staff dinner-dance, Christmas 1959. He seems to have confided in her from the start: 'He was not a very happy person. He was so lonely. He said no one was really happy but that one should aim to be reasonably content. He admitted he was a homosexual and talked about it frequently: it used to make him very depressed. He hated himself for it, and never remembered being any other way.'[37]

The intimacy of Brian's revelations – his need to confide, and hers to listen – stirred something. Love developed on both sides, though it wasn't consummated. He spoke to Rita of his private life using the record-business term 'new releases' – he once wrote saying, 'The New Release has stopped selling. Trouble is that having sold quite well for quite a time, it's difficult to clear away bad stock.' (This sounds like a longish relationship – Brian had precious few of these.)

Through staff appointments, Brian kept friends close by. Ray Standing, another Great Charlotte Street employee, saw a pattern: 'I think there were nine blokes working at Nems at one time and only three of us were straight. The Walton Road shop was OK because that was his dad's store, but when Brian opened up in town that's when they started to flock in, so to speak.'[38]

Brian had several good friends now, men with whom he was never intimate but who joined him on weekends and adventurous evenings out. Membership of this inner circle temporarily went down by one when Oxford graduate Geoffrey Ellis, known to Brian for two years, sailed from Liverpool to work in America, but then Terry Doran, a car salesman with a sharp mind and ready Liverpool wit, was added. 'I met Brian by chance one day in a Liverpool pub in 1959,' Doran says, 'and just fell in love with him from the beginning.'[39]

Another new friend was Peter Brown, an ex-grammar-school boy from over the water (Bebington, near Birkenhead) – he met Brian in September 1958 at a mutual friend's birthday party, and worked in the same line of business, managing the record department in Lewis's. 'Brian and I messed around, as they say, that first night, but it never went anywhere and we established very quickly we were going to be friends and that was all, and that's how it continued to be – there was never any physical relationship.'[40]

In late 1959, with the Whitechapel expansion project monopolising Brian's time, he offered Peter Brown the job of running the record department at Great Charlotte Street. Peter's parents had reservations about his leaving Lewis's 'to work for a Jewish shopkeeper' but he said yes anyway. His colleague at work, his friend outside it, Peter was well placed to watch Brian's relationship with his parents, especially the crucial axis with his mother:

> The Epsteins were very nice people. Harry was a quiet man, always polite, but Queenie was much more interesting. She was a stylish, charming, attractive woman who liked the theatre and was very well-read. She and Brian were adorable together – they understood one another and liked the same things; they were a very bonded pair. Brian's brother Clive was on his father's level, very different. He had no interest in those things and nor did Harry. Clive was Harry's boy and Brian was Queenie's.

Oscar Preuss died on Christmas Eve 1958 and George and Judy grieved together – she for her old boss, he for the man who'd taught him everything. As George reflected to the *NME*, 'He invariably adopted the most rebellious tactics.'[41]

George had been Preuss's assistant and now he had his own – Ron Richards, whose background in music publishing would be useful for sourcing songs.* Ron shadowed George in the studio for a while and then began to take sessions himself, mostly on the pop side: George divided Parlophone's pop singers between them and Ron was allowed to go out and find new talent. He was 30, and George, at 33, was still the youngest A&R boss in London. Record companies were not yet as they would become, they were still companies that made records, run by old gents in three-piece suits and short haircuts, characters who'd ridden the disc rodeo in distant days and were now disconnected from the pulse. The top brass at these companies weren't night-clubbers, they were captains of industry, like EMI's accomplished chairman, whose services to commerce were rewarded by the Queen in the 1960 New Year's honours list – he arose Sir Joseph Lockwood.

There was scant prospect of George receiving a 'gong', but he did have a new three-year employment contract, to expire in April 1962. His salary was up to £2700, which George felt wasn't enough, especially as his request for a royalty on sales – the kind of arrangement now commonplace in America – was rejected. No British company paid a producer royalty. It isn't coincidence that George wrote his first recorded songs in this timeframe. A&R men had to find

---

* Ronald Richard Pratley (1929–2009). He worked at Chappell and at Boosey & Hawkes as a song-plugger, then joined Parlophone as a record plugger before moving into A&R. All of George Martin's fellow EMI producers acquired assistants around this time.

some way of supplementing their salaries, and it was usually by writing numbers they recorded, earning from the publishing. The cosy production-line relationship between Tin Pan Alley and record company A&R men made such associations easy, and it was hidden from employers by the use of noms de plume. Few restrained themselves completely and some took it to extremes: George's EMI colleague Norrie Paramor, in charge of the Columbia label, had a reputation for giving his artists his own songs to record. Even as B-sides they earned the same 'mechanical' revenue as the A-side, three farthings (three-quarters of a penny) on every record sold. A hit could bring in a sum you wouldn't sniff at.*

George's initial attempts earned just the farthings. He only wrote music, not lyrics, so if a piece was instrumental it was entirely his, and if it had words, he worked in collaboration. His first tiptoe through the twilight was the B-side of a Jeremy Lubbock single, where he simply left his name off. Then he popped up as the arch-foreigner Lezlo Anales, then as John Chisholm (his father-in-law's name), until settling on Graham Fisher, his most regular pseudonym.

Fake names peppered *Songs For Swingin' Sellers*, George's second LP with the much-loved actor-comic Peter Sellers. The collection included a sketch that dug deep at Larry Parnes, essaying the Svengali manager of teenage rock stars Lenny Bronze, Clint Thigh, Matt Lust and Twit Conway, who all lived with him at his luxury Mayfair flat. George also succeeded in finding another Sinatralike: the LP's title was a play on *Songs For Swingin' Lovers!* and its opening track, You Keep Me Swingin' (co-written by 'Graham Fisher'), was a nailed-on parody. The singer was Matt Monro, although George renamed him Fred Flange. He sang so well, and so like Sinatra, that the song attracted heavy BBC radio play and George offered Monro a Parlophone contract that launched a great career.†

George Martin had cracked the art of making hits, but his work was still

* Though records were bought almost entirely on the strength of their A-side, a royalty paid by record companies to the Mechanical Copyright Protection Society (MCPS) was distributed evenly to the composers and publishers of both sides.
† In Forthlin Road, Paul and Mike McCartney 'rolled around the floor' to *Songs For Swingin' Sellers* and also thrilled to the cover photo: the *Swingin'* element was shown by a man who'd hanged himself. The LP also included an Indian music send-up, with Sellers as Mr Banajee, performing Wouldn't It Be Loverly from *My Fair Lady*. (The recording brought sitar- and tabla-playing Indian musicians into Number 2 studio at Abbey Road for probably the first but certainly not the last time.) Banajee was possibly a parody of virtuoso Ravi Shankar, whose records in India were on Parlophone and who became the best-known Indian classical musician in Britain through several 1950s visits, often appearing on TV. Another visitor from 'the subcontinent' was the bearded sage Maharishi Mahesh Yogi, in Britain in December 1959 to explain his teaching of Transcendental Meditation. Years later, Paul would recall having seen him on Granada TV's local news roundup *People And Places*.

divided. When being original, his creativity sparkled with wit and invention; when copying any established formula, especially when operating in the teenage pop market, it flopped. This was still an era when stardom followed the invention of a persona – a new name on a pretty face, rarely much substance – and George couldn't do anything with it. 'It's not so much artistry as individuality which counts today,' he complained to the *NME* in 1959 ... before explaining the qualities that *he* was always seeking: 'In considering new artists, I look for a distinctive sound which, at the same time, is attractive.'[42]

13

'Hi-yo, hi-yo Silver – away!'
(January–May 1960)

The latest in the line of young men offered the chance to become Quarrymen bass player – always provided they bring their own bass – was Dave May, another art school student. John Lennon asked him because he was ready-equipped, albeit with a homemade guitar: he played it with Ken Dallas and the Silhouettes, a group of Buddy Holly fans from Bootle. May recalls seeing John, Paul and George strumming together in the empty Life Drawing room at college. Without bass and drums they were really just half a group. 'They weren't very good. In fact, they were really bad. John knew I played bass and asked if I fancied playing with them but I said, "Sorry, I'm in an established group, a *good* group." Another reason I didn't fancy it was that John had his own ideas and his own thoughts, and they were such a gang of rebels. They didn't care about anything.'[1]

The suggestion that Stuart Sutcliffe buy a bass and join them had been floated before, when it probably dissolved in a pool of cackles: he had no money, little musical ability and was no rocker. But then, in what was nothing less than a miracle of timing, the first obstacle disappeared – and others were swiftly kicked over – when ninety whole pounds suddenly came his way.

During the first or second week of 1960, as *The John Moores Liverpool Exhibition* 2 drew to a close at the Walker Art Gallery, Moores expressed an interest in buying Stuart's exhibited abstract, *Summer Painting*. Whether or not the millionaire benefactor realised it was only half the true work is no more known than it was apparent. Stuart agreed to its sale and soon had £90 burning a hole in his pocket.[2] To him as to his friends, this was a vast sum, nine or ten times the weekly wage for many a working man. No sooner had Stuart deposited the cheque in his Liverpool Savings Bank account than certain of these friends were whispering urgently in his ear about how best it should be spent.

As George Harrison later remembered, they were quite nice about it: they gave Stuart the choice of drums or bass.[3] They weren't fussed – they needed both. They got him squeezed around a table one night at the Casbah and pressed home the point while supping coffees frothed for them by Rory Best. Pete's younger brother can still visualise 'Stuart sort of hemmed in the corner. John and Paul wouldn't take no for an answer, even though Stuart kept saying it.'[4]

If it was to be anything it would be the bass, Stuart said, but he had major reservations, not least because he'd never touched one in his life. The prospect of plucking one, of being in a group, of the disciplined learning of songs – chords, keys and tempos – and of performing in front of people, this was a major move for someone who'd never expressed any such interest. John, Paul and George had been talking chords and harmonies and what was 'great' about this song and 'crap' about that for years; Stuart hadn't. And being in a rock group was guaranteed to be seen by his parents and family, his teachers and fellow pupils as mad, reckless, beneath his class, a wasteful frittering of his per-haps-once-in-a-lifetime windfall.

John could be relentlessly persuasive, however, and his friendship with Stu had become central to them both. As fellow student Helen Anderson says, 'Though it was strange that Stuart got diverted away from his painting, he was *completely* carried away with John.'[5] Of equal strength too, Stuart simply fancied it: he was curious about how it would be to play in a rock group, to pose with a guitar and look cool, to project that image.

So it was that Stuart Sutcliffe stepped into Frank Hessy's on 21 January 1960 and picked out a Hofner 333 four-string bass, plus carrying case. He put down £15 cash and signed up to a weekly drip repayment that would extend into 1961 and bring the total price to £59 15s.[6] It was a big guitar – Paul says it 'dwarfed him'[7] – and with this he was now in the Quarrymen. What, though, had Stuart joined? A group of four guitarists with one amplifier, no drummer, no bookings, no manager, no prospects, and a name they hated. If they'd been on the verge of great things then Stuart's entrée might just have made some sense; as it was, he'd splashed some of his bumper bundle on not much more than a vision.*

Days before he did this, on probably 9 or 16 January, the Quarrymen's long Saturday-night residency at the Casbah Coffee Club ground to a halt. This

---

* Stuart Fergusson Victor Sutcliffe was born 23 June 1940 at Simpson Memorial Maternity Pavilion in Edinburgh. Both his parents were Scottish and spoke with Scots accents. His father Charles (1905–66) was a Protestant, married with four children, when he and Martha 'Millie' Cronin (1907–83) conceived Stuart. She was a staunch Roman Catholic who until falling pregnant had

particular week Ken Brown wasn't well and didn't feel up to playing – he spent most of the evening quietly taking admission money on the door. It didn't bother John, Paul and George, so long as he let them use his amp. At the end of the night, though, Mrs Best insisted on giving Ken his usual quarter of the group's £3 fee. John, Paul and George said no, they should get a pound each. Two intractable forces met square-on.

It's never been said if John, Paul and George told Mrs Best where she could stick her Casbah, or whether they just accidentally failed to show up the following week; what is certain is that they didn't go back. Evidently, they were prepared to walk out on their only booking and source of income. It could also be that the argument was a device to sever the tie with Ken Brown. They were just about get a bass player and so would have numbered five guitarists. No drummer, five guitarists? Something had to give, and it would be Ken. He knew it, which was why he'd already started playing with the Blackjacks. The

---

been studying to become a nun. Charles was an engineer/fitter with literary leanings and talent. Disowned by their families, by 1943 they'd moved to Roby, just east of Liverpool, where Charles became a wartime inspector of aircraft engines. No record of a marriage can be found but they had two further children, Joyce (1942) and Pauline (1944), and they stayed in the area, for the most part residing in council houses in nearby Huyton. Millie became a schoolteacher and Charles a merchant navy engineer who spent long stretches at sea.

Stuart was a naturally bright child who went to grammar school, passed five O-Levels and began at Liverpool College of Art in 1956, leaving home soon after to share nearby bedsits with Rod Murray. The writer Nik Cohn would describe Stuart's mother as 'a fiercely emotional woman who protected and possessed him with quite obsessive energy. A dramatic lady by any standards, she was always convinced she had a genius on her hands. They hoped he'd become a doctor but at 15 he decided he wanted to paint.' (*Observer*, 8 September 1968.) While Stuart's relationship with Millie remained intact he fought to resist her controlling influence and gave the clearest of impressions about this to John Lennon and George Harrison, as John would recall: 'He hated her ... except she gave him twenty ciggies a day and five bob.' Rod Murray says Stuart adored his father – 'He was like a dog with two dicks when his dad came back from sea. He obviously loved him. Mr Sutcliffe would take us out to the Cracke and we'd all get absolutely bladdered before he went home to his wife. He was a larger than life character, ebullient and fun.'

Stuart, who had no discernible Liverpool accent, stayed delicate and never grew tall, reaching no more than 5ft 7in. College friend Jon Hague remembers him as 'very skinny, weak and sick looking', while Rod Murray notes 'He was often unsteady and wobbly. If someone was going to fall over something, he would.' Stuart's musical background was limited: apart from singing in the church choir at nine and ten he had a few piano lessons and a Spanish guitar he rarely touched. Though his youngest sister claims he was always a great rock and roll fan, and a girlfriend claims he was Elvis-obsessed, few of his college contemporaries saw it. The primary record collector and fount of musical knowledge there at the time, Tony Carricker, says 'Stuart was always the most cerebral and intellectual of all of us: I don't remember him being into rock or having records. I once loaned him about ten 45s and they came back warped – the ultimate sin.'

It was as a painter that Stuart excelled. His work was often brilliant. He obtained a first-class pass in the college Intermediate exam in 1958 and exhibited in Bradford and Liverpool in 1959. He was a quiet but determined and utterly committed young man ... and, as Tony Carricker adds, 'He always understood *image*.'

Quarrymen barely gave him another thought after he'd gone, save for the important fact that they missed his amplifier. These four electric guitarists now had only Paul's little two-input Elpico between them. It could be that some further pressure was applied to Stuart at this time – something about also buying an amp? – but if there was then he resisted it.

They did, however, find a new place to dwell. Just before Christmas 1959, the landlady at 9 Percy Street made a snap inspection of Rod Murray and Stuart Sutcliffe's rooms. As Rod remembers, 'She saw a table-leg burning in the grate in mine – I hadn't realised it was antique but she claimed it was – and then she went upstairs to Stuart's room, found that all the furniture was painted and that the fireplace was missing – we'd used that for firewood too – and she evicted us.'[8] Served with a month's notice, the pair hunted for a new place and found one on Gambier Terrace, a first-floor flat facing the art school and the vast hilltop Anglican Cathedral.

The unfurnished Flat 3, Hillary Mansions, Gambier Terrace, was more spacious than any the pair had shared before. It had a large living room/bedroom at the front, a second bedroom at the rear that doubled as an art studio, a third, smaller bedroom, a kitchen, a hall, a toilet and a bathroom with a gas-heated water geyser. The weekly £3 rent was affordable if Rod and Stuart found others to join them: a pair of girls came in from the art school – Margaret Morris and Margaret Duxbury, known as Diz and Ducky (Rod and Diz soon paired up) – and then, probably a short while after moving in, Stuart invited John to share the studio room. It was the moment John Lennon had been waiting for.

John's brittle accord with Aunt Mimi had gone far beyond breaking point. Both were still struggling to cope with Julia's terrible death, and John had never properly replaced the bolt-hole that was Julia's house whenever he felt Mimi bearing down on him, which was most of the time. She was still clutching at vanishing straws, hoping to make him stick to his studies during another vital year in his education. If he bombed out, *then* what? Cynthia Powell says Mimi 'did her utmost to squash' John's plans, but in the end he simply couldn't be stopped.[9]

John's move into a flat was a godsend for his and Cyn's sex life: privacy at last, freedom from prying eyes and moral barriers, whole nights together instead of snatched moments. When Cyn stayed over at Gambier she told her mother she was with her friend Phyllis; Lil Powell remained dead set against her daughter's relationship – it had been running six months but nothing yet had happened to encourage her to think better of John Lennon. Because of him, Cynthia was out late several nights a week 'over the water' doing who-knew-what, and she was turning from a respectable, soberly dressed college student into a vamp. John was modelling Cyn into his very own Brigitte Bardot, perennial object of his sex fantasies. Her mousey hair went blonde through the application of Hiltone bleach, and she wore black short skirts, black fishnet stockings and suspenders, black tight sweaters and pointed high-heeled shoes.

As much as she appreciated the new opportunities presented by Gambier Terrace, Cyn was appalled by the state of the flat. Outwardly, the building was a grand 1830s colonnade built for the mercantile rich, with a stunning Doric porch. It was (and still is) the most handsome terrace of its kind in all Liverpool, manifestly a world away from the slums and back-to-back houses with their outdoor privies – though actually all that was only a few hundred yards away: Liverpool 8 started just beyond the terrace. Even closer to home, though, the building's beauty ended at the front door. Beyond the threshold those high ceilings and cavernous rooms gave way, in terms of decor, to a shambles. Stuart's and John's studio room was plain filthy: a couple of camp-beds on splinter-shedding floorboards, no curtains, grubby windows and a fireplace full of soot, cigarette butts and fish-and-chip papers, everything marooned in painting materials and accumulating daily debris. If they didn't use the fire there was no other heating, and Cyn had to invent reasons for returning home 'from a night with Phyllis' not just looking like a floozy but a *smudged* floozy.

As the registered tenant, Rod Murray paid the rent and had to collect it in turn from his occupants. John was blessed with a particular talent for frittering away his funds (the council grant designed to provide his working materials) and was rarely in a position to pay. As Rod remembers, 'During the week I'd go and have a pint with him and he'd always have money for a beer, but when it came to the day to pay the rent he was always hard up. "Could I owe it to you?" "Would you like this jacket?" One time he paid me with a check Mounties-type Canadian jacket he'd probably nicked from someone else.'

Though they had no bookings, the Quarrymen needed to rehearse. Stuart – John, Paul and George all called him Stu* – worked hard to learn his instrument: Cyn says he spent 'every spare moment practising, hoping for words of praise from John'. John helped coach him, which was something like the blind leading the blind: he was never a technical guitarist and didn't know the bass. George says they taught Stu to play twelve-bar and that the first tune he learned was Chuck Berry's Thirty Days. Dave May was roped in to show Stu a thing or two and in return was allowed to measure up the Hofner 333, which was so much better than the model for his existing homemade bass. He showed Stu how to play Eddie Cochran's C'mon Everybody, which entailed learning three notes.[10]

When George joined John's group two years earlier he'd objected to its

---

* The English pronunciation, as 'Shtyew'.

'surplus' members, but he had no problems with Stu's presence, despite his lack of ability. George just wanted the group to get off the ground – 'It was better to have a bass player who couldn't play than to not have a bass player at all' – and he'd liked Stu from the start.[11] Almost 17, George was now settling into working life at Blackler's, but he hated the daily grind.

Stu's position in the group did not sit well with Paul, however, whose objection ran on two fronts. First, though he'd helped encourage Stu to join, he couldn't really see the point of taking on a bass player who couldn't play bass. It wasn't the only time John had brought an unmusical close mate into his group, but Pete Shotton's inability had been no particular disadvantage in the skiffle days. Now, at a time when other local rock groups existed on a higher plane, and the Quarrymen patently had to improve, it was nonsensical to shackle themselves to someone who didn't know his instrument.

Paul's second objection was more visceral, and sometimes masked by the first. He quickly became jealous of Stu's relationship with John. He felt edged out, rejected, hurt. A fourth player might normally be expected to join a group in fourth position, but Stu came in nearer the top, perhaps even second, and Paul was pushed down. He'd staked the primary claim to John since the end of 1957 and now slipped down the chart. Before, he would sit next to John on the bus, with George alone in the seat behind. Now, John and Stu sat together and Paul was in the back with the boy nine (or so) months younger.[12]

John had engineered this situation; it was by his actions that dissent was in the air, but Paul couldn't be angry with him, only with Stu – so it was Stu who got Paul's snippy remarks and general behaviour that in one way or another cut the ground from under him. John, as usual, observed it and did nothing: it was for Stu to defend himself, if he wanted to. It seems Stu mostly ignored it. Sometimes, John even joined in, and Stu ignored that too. (John had again chosen someone who stood up to him.)

Mixing now not only with John but Stu and his Gambier Terrace flat-mates, Paul was ever more intent on projecting the appearance of a university scholar – smoking a pipe and reading manifestly impressive books at the bus stop. So limitless was Paul's ambition, he could stand under the Mather Avenue bus shelter, huddled next to the shopping biddies, and imagine himself enormously famous, fabulously wealthy and honoured by his country. 'I always had a good imagination. I dreamed of everything standing by the bus stop reading *Room At The Top*. I [would] always think "Lord Allerton . . ." It sounded great. I never thought it would happen in a million years.'[13]

There came a point in early 1960, though, when all Paul's lofty daydreams must have seemed sunk.

Dot Rhone loved being Paul McCartney's girlfriend. He was unusual and a cut above other boys: much better-looking, brighter, sharper, musically gifted, an entertaining mimic. It did entail acquiescing to a few demands – as she recalls, he didn't want her to see any of her friends, he didn't want her to smoke (though he did), and he copied John by insisting on her adoption of the Brigitte Bardot look, the black clothes and blonde hair: 'He gave me a list of rules that I had to stick to. John had the same rules for Cynthia.'[14]

A virgin when they started going out, Dot didn't stay one for long, and perhaps around February 1960 she discovered she was pregnant; the baby was due in September or October. Paul was 17 and still in school, Dot was 16. Jessie Rhone, her mother, was appalled by Dot's behaviour and worried what people would think. Dot relates that her mother decided she must spend the latter pregnancy period with her sister in Manchester and have the baby adopted there at birth, but that Paul offered marriage instead and said she and the baby could join his dad and brother at Forthlin Road. Only those who needed to know were told (Cynthia never knew it), and the situation entered a fraught period during which every aspect of Paul's future was hanging by a thread.

Liverpool's top group, particularly in terms of ambition and presentation, were Rory Storm and the Hurricanes. Their booking at the Cavern's Jazz Festival in January 1960 – a peculiar spot: they played rock, and were pelted with pennies – was just the latest of several highish-profile engagements, enough to earn them a local-lads-make-good piece in the *Reporter* series of newspapers in the north and east of the city.[15] Each member was profiled in turn and the name Ringo Starr appeared in the press here for the first time. In contrast to the others' sporty attributes (Rory played football, swam great distances, did cross-country running and trialled as a middle-distance runner for the 1960 British Olympic team), there really wasn't much to be said about the drummer, except 'He is saving to get married, and his spare time is spent in making plans.' One such strategy, Johnny Guitar would always remember, entailed Richy's religious conversion, from Protestant to Catholic, to satisfy Gerry's family's demands about how they would raise their children. Elsie wasn't at all happy about this and it wasn't in her nature to keep quiet, telling him, 'You'll never have any luck if you marry a Catholic.'*

---

* Ringo was speaking from experience when he told a US news reporter in 1964, 'Say you're a Protestant and the girl's a Catholic, as long as you love the girl and she loves you … [then] the families get on to you. You're quite happy with the girl, and then her family will start picking on her, saying, "What are the children going to be?" or "Is he going to change religion for you?" Then your family'll say, "You'll never have any luck because you're marrying a Catholic!" But if you were just left alone I think there'd be a lot more mixed marriages. They break up because of the other people, they never break up because of the actual pair.' (Interview by Larry Kane, 2 September 1964.)

The Hurricanes were certainly the busiest group on Merseyside, playing several nights a week in the different halls, and so was born 'Rory Storm' – the personality, the hair, the stunts, and the stutter that miraculously disappeared when singing in a hokey American voice. Six-foot-two and eyes of blue, Rory was irrepressible, startling bandmates and audiences alike with extraordinary feats of stage athleticism: jumping off pianos and shinning up pipes or poles and then leaping back down again, still singing. It was all *show* with the Hurricanes and they never missed a trick, whether Rory was jacking his leg up on Johnny's arched back during guitar solos, or Johnny was sticking his head under Ringo's cymbal while he gave it both sticks. Rory liked the slow numbers, when he'd sit on a reversed chair and run a gold comb through his long blond quiff while serenading the girls, but Johnny suffered through them, much preferring rock and roll.

Their set rarely changed. The opening number was Vince Taylor's Brand New Cadillac, after which they played a whole lotta Jerry Lee, Elvis, Johnny Otis, Eddie Cochran, Carl Perkins, Conway Twitty and the Everly Brothers. A good forty-eight-minute recording survives of one of their Jive Hive bookings in March 1960, but though its very existence and preservation is remarkable, and the naturalness of the show is charming, the performance is no great shakes. Like so much about the early period of rock and roll, in Britain especially, Rory's act was a smokescreen of style over substance, personality over panache. The good looks, gold comb and bustling energy mask a merely adequate singing voice: his phrasing is erratic, he drifts in and out of both time and tune, and his American accent grates. Rock was new in 1960, and everything was primitive, but this performance is surprisingly basic given that Rory Storm and the Hurricanes were 'Liverpool's best group'. Surely they couldn't always be so.*

Through Rory's sister Iris, the Hurricanes auditioned for a Butlin's summer season; she'd applied for one herself, as a dancer, and then made enquiries for her brother's group. So keen were they to find a holiday camp booking, they'd already applied to a place on the Isle of Man, and to Middleton Tower in Morecambe (where Alf Lennon had spent several summers washing up), before the Butlin's audition took place. This was at the Grafton Ballroom in Liverpool on 16 February 1960, and seven days later they heard they'd passed: they were offered a full summer season at the Pwllheli camp, from the beginning of June

---

* Made on 5 March 1960, the recording was issued for the first time in 2012 as the album *Live At The Jive Hive*. Though depicted on the front and back covers, Ringo Starr doesn't seem to be present on the tape. Johnny Guitar wrote in his diary that they used a substitute drummer earlier that week after Ringo went down with flu, and the tape strongly suggests there was more than one such occasion. The playing is so poor on some of these tracks that it simply can't be Ringo, whose attributes – his unfussy style and rock-steady timekeeping especially – were always well recognised. When he heard the recording in 2012, Ringo confirmed it wasn't him.

to the start of September, £100 a week between the five of them, less £20 for accommodation. Three months of rock, birds, beer and sunbathing, on great pay, it was a dream booking ... but a problem for Richy. He had a fiancée who moaned about how often he played drums, and even more vitally he was four years into his five-year apprenticeship at Hunt's. Being at Butlin's would mean giving it up, maybe giving them *both* up. As soon as the Hurricanes heard they'd got the nod, he said to Johnny Guitar, 'I don't know whether I want to go.'[16]

The notion that these guys could actually earn a living from playing was something none had considered before, yet as the handful of promoters continued to stage dances in clubs and halls across Merseyside, and it became possible to play more than a couple of nights a week, so the idea took hold. For Johnny Gustafson, 17-year-old bass player with Cass and the Cassanovas, it hit him square between the eyes on the first day of 1960 – an appropriate date to signify the moment when the Liverpool rock scene slipped into a higher gear: 'One of our first gigs was New Year's Day at the Tower Ballroom, New Brighton. I was working in a jeweller's, Bagshaw's, as a packer and gofer, earning £2 10s a week, but at the Tower I got £2 for playing an hour. Within three months I was making more money than my tradesman brother, who indentured. And I was having fun, getting girls, spending all day doing nothing, and I didn't have to say "Yes-sir-no-sir" to anyone.'[17]

None of the groups had management, but the Jacaranda's livewire proprietor Allan Williams was beginning to take an interest. He let Cass and the Cassanovas play in the basement on Mondays, when Lord Woodbine's steel band had a night off, and they also figured on a list of acts he loosely represented as agent. The list covered all types of music, and if he got them work he took 10 per cent of whatever fee could be had.

This was just one of several interests Williams was suddenly running in parallel with the thriving day-night scene that was the Jacaranda. Approaching his thirtieth birthday, he'd been bitten by the entrepreneurial bug and was chaotically branching out in several directions at once. He had his eye on an empty club on Seel Street, which he was thinking of turning into Liverpool's first modern night-club, and he was also about to become the silent partner in the Cabaret Artists Social Club, a striptease venue being opened by Lord Woodbine in a dingy basement among all the shebeens on Upper Parliament Street. Allan Williams loved clubs. If anything fired his imagination more than looking around clubs and sizing up why some worked and others failed, it was looking around empty premises and considering what kind of a club they could become. And it was with all this in mind that he and the honourable Woodbine picked up on an advertisement for a 'businessman's' long weekend to Amsterdam, 29 to 31 January. It was an all-in deal: ten guineas return including hotel, flying from

Speke in an old Dakota. 'See Continental night life' the ad suggestively suggested – and see it they certainly would.[18]

Not only were they going to enjoy Amsterdam's night life, the pair had a plan all their own: instead of returning with the group, they would push on into Germany and come home later. The reason, Williams recalls, is that a few guys from the steel band had upped and gone from the Jacaranda one day without word, only to send him a postcard from Hamburg saying what a great time they were having, playing in a club by the Alster lake. It seems that a German had come into the Jac one night, taken a shine to the West Indians and offered them work back home. Williams hoped to find them in Hamburg – but mostly he wanted to see the city's clubs. His unfettered mind working overtime again, he wondered if he could strike up an arrangement to send other Liverpool entertainers there. If they wanted one act, why not two? With this in view, he got a chap with a Ferrograph reel-to-reel tape recorder to go down the Jac and record some of the acts he notionally represented. Cass and the Cassanovas were one; there was also the Leon Sait Dance Orchestra, singer Hal Graham, and others no longer remembered.

The trip was predictably eventful. Both Williams and Woodbine enjoyed a drink and they spent most of their time in Amsterdam riotously inebriated and making a public spectacle of themselves. Williams was small (5ft 3in), but this could be disguised by his wearing of a black top hat; he'd started doing this in the Jacaranda as a joke, but now he was rarely seen without it, and the effect was given symmetrical vigour by a heavy black beard he'd recently sprouted. It was only after some lively episodes that the pair reached Hamburg by train, taking a room at the Hotel Stein, on the Reeperbahn. They were in the heart of St Pauli, the long-established 'haven of pleasure' for sailors docked in north-west Germany's great port city.

For the keen clubman, St Pauli was heaven on earth. There were places all around, catering for every kind of entertainment. Nothing like this existed in Britain, not even in Soho – London's den of iniquity – which was a children's playground by comparison. Williams acquainted himself with it thoroughly, and branched off the Reeperbahn into the narrower Grosse Freiheit, illuminated by one alluring place after another. Literally speaking, this wasn't the red-light area – all the prostitutes sat in windows on Herbertstrasse, off the other side of the Reeperbahn – but Grosse Freiheit had the ancillary venues: the strip joints, transvestite bars, hostess clubs and music bars. The sound of music drew Williams down some steps and into the Kaiserkeller (Emperor's cellar), a street corner basement which, judging by its nautical decor, was clearly a sailors' bar. He sat at a table, ordered a drink and kept his eyes open.

A live group was on stage, and to Williams' eyes and ears they merely played parrot-fashion what they'd learned from records. Patrons who wanted to dance remained seated and only got to their feet (some of them) during the interval, when records played on the *Musikbox* (juke-box). Grabbing his moment, Williams motioned to a waiter that he would like to see the manager, and was ushered into the office of the Kaiserkeller's owner. He shook hands with Bruno Koschmider, a man of about his height and of a similar age – 33, though he seemed so much older. He was, through an Englishman's eyes, a caricature German, with a square potato head, bulbous nose and a *Klumpfuss* (club foot) that caused him to walk with a heavy gait: a war wound, it seemed. He spoke no English, and as Williams spoke no German a waiter was brought in to interpret a little. Williams remembers:

> I introduced myself and said I was an entertainment agent from England and had he ever considered employing English rock and roll groups? He said he hadn't and I said how great they were and that he could have them for £100 a week, plus £10 commission for me. That was really asking a lot but he didn't blink, so I said, 'I've got a spool of tape here, if you want to listen to it maybe we can talk business.' I was doing a really good selling job, but when he put the tape on his lovely big Grundig machine all we heard was gibberish. Somebody had taped over it or something, I don't know, but it was a balls-up. I said the machine must be *kaput* but he put on one of his own tapes and it was fine. It was *such* a disappointment and I felt I'd blown it.[19]

There wasn't much more to be said, but before Williams rose to leave he witnessed another vital aspect of St Pauli club life, one that made him shudder. 'While I was in Herr Koschmider's office a fight broke out in the club. Hearing the commotion, he pulled a big truncheon from his desk drawer, hobbled out into the club and started knocking shite out of some poor seaman who was already down and out. Then he came back, wiped his truncheon clean, stuck it back in his desk and carried on talking to me as if nothing had happened.'

Through sheer ill fortune, Williams' hopes of brokering a Liverpool-Hamburg clubs alliance had come to nothing. But so be it – he went home, turned his mind to other incredible ventures and gave Hamburg no further thought.

Paul McCartney was now in the decisive phase of his thirteen-year schooling, and all was far from well. He was sitting his A-Levels in June, and yet, despite his talent for Art – enough to win the school prize the previous term – he was losing focus. His English Literature remained on track, thanks to Dusty

Durband, but Paul's attitude had shifted again. Distractions beyond the school wall weren't helping. There was Dot's pregnancy, and there was Stu. As Stu's rival for John's attention, putting his school days entirely behind him seemed pretty appealing to Paul. He somehow failed to notice that it was necessary to apply now for a course at university, or teacher training college, to begin in September. His contemporaries were doing it and discussing it, but Paul would claim not to have realised.[20]

Paul lined up for a Liverpool Institute panoramic school photograph for the final time in March. Where once had been a child of 11 now stood a young man coming up 18, his quiff flopped in the wind. From 17 to 20 February, he'd appeared in an Institute play for the only time: Shaw's *Saint Joan*. Mr Durband, its director, didn't think him a good enough actor for a speaking part, but he was one of the assessors, a Dominican monk nodding and murmuring assent to Joan of Arc's prosecution. With little to do, and six long performances to do it in, Paul got bored, and Durband caught him smoking behind a pillar. His monkish appearance was also undercut by his long hair, causing some untimely titters from the gallery.[21]

It was to John and Stu's credit that they had no problem with Paul and George attaching themselves to their social life – a generosity that gave the younger ones knowledge and experiences beyond their years. They went now to their first all-night parties, designed in advance to last that long, so that, in addition to a bottle of wine, guests took a breakfast egg. One such event was at 22 Huskisson Street, at the house of art school lecturer Austin Davies.* This was a two-in-one party, musicians from the Royal Liverpool Philharmonic Orchestra relaxing upstairs in full evening dress after a concert, while the scruffy students did their thing downstairs. Tony Carricker insistently played Ray Charles' What'd I Say, both sides one after another for hours, which George thought was fantastic. George was also becoming very, very bevvied. He came close to an altercation when the two parties temporarily mixed and he called over to flautist Fritz Spiegl, 'Hey, Geraldo – got any Elvis?' This was probably just before he mumbled to Cynthia, 'I wish I had a nice girl like you,' and threw up.[22]

Paul was acutely aware of himself mixing in a social group beyond his years – 'We were trying to hang in there and pretend we knew what was going on' – so he projected a particular image at these parties, one he hoped would

---

* John probably had no idea he was partying in the same house where his mother had lived at the time she married Alf Lennon. As for Alf, nothing is known of his movements between 1960 and 1962: they're further lost years. From 1960, John's branch of the Lennon family tree was gone from Liverpool: the electoral roll shows new occupants at 57 Copperfield Street for the first time in almost half a century.

encourage some bright twenty-something woman to take an interest in this 17-year-old schoolboy. He chose to pose as a French troubadour, a mysterious muso in a black turtleneck sweater, a Jacques Brel figure deposited in Liverpool 8, strumming his guitar and mumbling a romantic *chanson*. 'It was me trying to be enigmatic,' he would recall, 'to make girls think "Who's that very interesting French guy over in the corner?" I would literally use it as that, and John knew this was one of my ploys.' Despite the effort, Paul never once 'pulled' as a Frenchman ... but the tune he picked out on his Zenith was interesting, in the style of Chet Atkins' Trambone but original and memorable. It had no words, and Paul (not having studied French at school) didn't know any, so he just murmured Gallic-accented *rhubarbe* to carry it along. It joined his little canon of party pieces and hung around for years.[23]

Some Friday nights and many Saturdays, Paul and George stayed over with John and Stu, bedding down where space could be found amid the detritus. It was rough, but part of growing up. In later years, whenever Paul referred to student life, or things being 'studenty', he specifically tuned in to these memories. 'We used to go around to John's flat and stay the night. We thought it was very wild (though it was very innocent) ... I don't think we got an awful lot of sleep, but I remember waking up in the morning, freezing cold, in a chair somewhere, with the eyes burning, and John leaning out of his bed to his Dansette record player and putting on Johnny Burnette.'[24]

Johnny Burnette And The Rock 'n Roll Trio, a 1957 ten-inch LP on the Coral label that John had somehow acquired, became a most important and influential record for the group and was one of very few albums John could abide all the way through without growing restless. The situation was part of it – music triggers memories, and the Nashville reverb sound of Johnny Burnette would always stir up thoughts of sleepovers at Gambier Terrace – but the tracks were magical in their own right too, a combination of out-and-out rock, like the opening Honey Hush, with distorted guitar, and the Sun-flavoured rockabilly Lonesome Tears In My Eyes. Beyond the mad cries of 'Hi-yo, hi-yo Silver!' (the call of cowboy hero the Lone Ranger to his horse), Honey Hush was a truly misogynistic number, a man bossing his woman about, that confirmed all their northern chauvinist attitudes and validated the way John and Paul treated Cyn and Dot: 'Come on into this house, stop all that yakety yak', 'Turn off the waterworks baby, they don't move me no more', and the frightening 'Don't make me nervous, I'm holding a baseball bat'.

A second LP also burned deep into John, Paul and George's psyche at this same time: *Dance Album*, the first British long-player by Carl Perkins, which came out just before Christmas 1959. They'd all admired his original recording of Blue Suede Shoes, which competed with Elvis's cover in 1956, but the rate of his British record releases had slowed before *Dance Album* appeared. From his 45s they knew Honey Don't, Your True Love, Matchbox, Glad All Over and Lend Me Your Comb, and from this LP they were bowled over by Movie Magg, Sure To Fall, Tennessee, Gone Gone Gone, Wrong Yo Yo, Boppin' The Blues and Everybody's Trying To Be My Baby. This was country music with a back-beat, the genuine slapback Sun sound from Memphis, right up their collective alley. For George in particular here was a whole new bunch of guitar solos to cherish and master, to study note by glorious note.

American rock and roll, the real McCoy, was suddenly all around them, and with ideal synchronicity. They all loved (and Paul bought) Eddie Cochran's Hallelujah, I Love Her So, a rock number so good that even the pro-jazz *Melody Maker* had to admit, 'This is hit stuff from the first bar and stands out from the dreary sameness of pop releases.'[25] In fact, Eddie wasn't only *cool*, he was *here*. The record's release coincided with his first visit across the Atlantic: Jack Good put him on his latest TV show, *Boy Meets Girls*, and Larry Parnes added this second great name from *The Girl Can't Help It* to the Gene Vincent tour he was promoting – the first 100 per cent rock and roll tour staged in Britain.

It was an eventful one, to say the least. Mindful of Buddy Holly's plane crash not a year earlier, Cochran was reluctant to do it at all, and only relented when his manager assured him that, apart from flying across the Atlantic, the trav-elling would only be by rail or road. From 14 to 19 March it played six nights (twelve houses) at Liverpool Empire, and so irresistible was this that even John Lennon went along. He'd sat in the Empire for pantomimes but it was his first rock show. George had attended a fair number and Paul a few, but seeing an artist live never appealed to John, not before or after this experience – he was always, as he put it, 'a record man'.

John, Stu and Tony Carricker all took their women (John with Cyn); Paul and George may have been with them but memories are hazy. Some girls screamed during Cochran's performance and John is said to have become angry, shouting at them to 'shurrup' so he could hear the music.[26] Paul was a huge fan of Cochran and (like the others) had already caught his appearances on *Boy Meets Girls*. As he'd recall, 'A lot of the guys would just stand up and swing their guitar around, but we'd look to see if they could actually play, and when you looked at Eddie he could really play. He played the solos and you knew he was writing this stuff.'[27] Cochran's arrangement of Chuck Berry's Sweet Little Sixteen lodged instantly in their memory, so although he never cut it for record and they never heard him do it again, it became the arrangement they them-selves would always perform.

It remains unclear whether Paul did see the Vincent/Cochran stage show –

at different times he's said he was there or insisted he wasn't – but George certainly did. The night he sat just a few feet from Eddie Cochran would be etched forever in his mind, enabling a permanently clear recall of the American's black leather waistcoat, black leather trousers and raspberry-coloured shirt, how he stood with his back to the audience before launching into the opening number What'd I Say, and how he then spun around to show the great Gretsch guitar George had drooled over in all the photos, complete with a black Gibson pickup and Bigsby tremolo.[28]

> Eddie blew me away. He had his unwound 3rd string, looked good and sang good and he was really getting to be a good guitarist ... One moment will always represent Eddie to me. He finished a tune, the crowd stopped screaming and clapping, and he stepped up to the mike and before he said something he put both his hands back, pushed his hair back, and some girl, a single voice in the audience, she went 'Eddie!' and he said 'Hi honey!' ...
> I thought, 'Yes! That's it – rock 'n' roll!'[29]

It isn't known if Ringo Starr saw the show, but Johnny Guitar went, and so did Pete Best and Neil Aspinall. Most of Liverpool's rockers went to pay homage and learn new tricks. And though the *Liverpool Echo* declared, 'Anyone out of their teens has no place in the theatre this week,' at least one older person was present, a man just turned 30 whose eyes widened with every beat and scream. Allan Williams had never been to a theatre rock show before, but because someone told him it might be interesting he left the Jacaranda one evening and went down. 'It really wasn't my scene at all,' he says, 'but I got quite a shock to see the favourable reaction. I thought, "This is the future."'[30]

No one else operated like Allan Williams. Electrified by the enthusiasm and the business possibilities, he instantly decided to put on a promotion just like it. The next morning, he contacted Larry Parnes and asked if the tour had any open dates. Parnes looked and replied yes: Gene and Eddie were making a trip home to America in mid-April but they were returning to England a fortnight later and Tuesday 3 May was free. Williams checked around the local venues and then phoned Parnes again to confirm: he wanted to bring the show back to Liverpool for one further night, at the boxing stadium. A contract was agreed, Williams paying Parnes £475 for Vincent, Cochran and eight other acts, to which he would then add some local Merseyside talent. This was high stakes for a first-time promoter but Williams was intent on staging the biggest rock show Liverpool – or anywhere else in Britain – had ever seen.

*

John Lennon wrote a new song around this time, his first for a year or more. It was a train song, a strongly rhythmic rocker about a girl travelling on the one after 9.09. Cyn has a clear memory of sitting in the Jacaranda and helping him with some of the words of what he decided to call One After 909 – and it seems he needed it because, even to him, they never made much sense. Paul and George didn't get them either and the three always considered the song unfinished because of it, though it was left in that state.*

John, Paul and George (though not Stu) took One After 909 to Percy Phillips' little home studio in Kensington and cut it as a record. This was where they'd made That'll Be The Day and In Spite Of All The Danger in 1958, but while that recording survives, One After 909 does not. Arthur Kelly was at the session: 'It was just the three of them, no Stuart and no drummer, and I didn't play either – I was just the mate, tagging along. I'm 100 per cent certain they did One After 909 and got it cut as a one-sided acetate because I had it for a while. I was allowed to borrow it and played it to my mum and dad.'[31]

Around this same time, maybe a shade earlier, a domestic tape recording was made of John, Stu and Paul rehearsing (there seems to be only three players; George could have been at work). Attaching a precise date to this session is not possible but it's from the early weeks or months of 1960, and they may not even have been the Quarrymen any more. The reel runs about forty minutes and has eight numbers, most of them untitled twelve-bar rambles of an especially unlistenable kind. Stu is audibly a bass beginner, and there is scant connection between the players and a painfully high number of bum notes. Though they'd just completed a four-month club residency at the Casbah – from which it's clear they could play and sing and were especially good at harmonies – this is, inexplicably, a horror of a tape, suggesting they were chronically bad when testimony has them better than proficient. The recording has only two barely redeeming features: one is a tune that might be called Well Darling and could be a Lennon-McCartney Original; the harmonies are decent and it's just about listenable. The second is Cayenne, a twangy guitar instrumental composition by Paul.[32]

This was a group that needed to get out and play, and with no manager or agent to provide push, the only way to get bookings was to write letters. Three examples survive, all drafted in this period of spring 1960 (probably, though not necessarily, resulting in letters being sent). Two are written by Paul and one by

* As Cynthia's every trip to Liverpool entailed a return train journey from Hoylake, and she was involved in the song's creation, one might surmise there was a 9.09 train … but the timetable confirms not. The lyric includes the phrase 'cold as ice', which was in Treat Me Nice, sung by Elvis in *Jailhouse Rock*.

Stu. Paul prided himself on his handwriting and seems also to have had no qualms about being economical with truth and generous with untruths. As he'd come to concede, 'We would lie our faces off to get anyone to notice us.' The first of his letters – addressed to a Mr Low – is a particular joy, allowing a richly detailed insight into the tiny window of time when, as Paul hesitantly expresses it, the group 'is called the ....'[33]

Putting his own name first, then John's, Stuart's and George's, Paul details their instruments as 'guitar', 'guitar', 'bass' and 'another guitarist'; he doesn't say they have no drummer, he simply doesn't mention a drummer at all, clinging to the hope the recipient (despite his evident involvement in the business) wouldn't notice. Just in case he did, though, Paul skirted the point with particular imagination:

> This line-up may at first seem rather dull, but it must be appreciated that as the boys all have above-average instrumental ability, they achieve surprisingly varied effects. Their basic beat is the off-beat, but this has recently tended to be accompanied by a faint on-beat; thus the overall sound is rather reminiscent of the 4 in the bar beat of traditional jazz. This could possibly be put down to the influence on the group of Mr McCartney, who led one of the top local jazz bands (Jim Mac's Jazz Band) in the 1920's.

The rest of the letter was expert blather: Paul said he and John had written over fifty songs, some instrumental, others composed 'with the modern audience in mind', numbers such as One After 909, Years Roll Along, Thinking Of Linking and Keep Looking That Way.* He also named the group members, starting with John and then claiming for himself the advanced age of 18 and a position at Liverpool University, reading English Literature. The potted biographies of George and Stuart are unavailable because by this point Paul had reached the bottom of the sheet and nothing more survives.†

---

* This letter provides the only reference to the song Keep Looking That Way, evidently a Lennon-McCartney Original with words and music. Nothing more is known of it.

† The reference to their sound being recently 'accompanied by a faint on-beat' may be an allusion to Stu, an attempt to make a virtue of erratic timing issues. Paul's suggestion their sound was even vaguely reminiscent of jazz was merely a device to introduce the connection to Jim Mac's Band, a relative piece of trumpet-blowing; it also suggests John didn't see this draft, or that if he did the letter went no further in this form, because jazz was complete anathema to him. Paul being 18 and 'reading English Literature at Liverpool University' was fanciful, but he was there in his head. The letter screams *versatility* but the recipient would have seen they didn't have a drummer no matter how flowery the writing or how undeniably impressive it was that Paul and John had written fifty tunes. (Thirty would have been nearer the truth, but, still, this was remarkable.) Indeed, if sent, the letter achieved no discernible result.

On 27 March, Stuart wrote a letter looking to get the group a holiday camp booking ... and as if in competition, which he was, Paul also wrote one that same day or soon after. Both are indicative of their hopelessness, for – as Rory Storm and the Hurricanes thrillingly knew – summer seasons had already been tied up a month or more. Paul's was another masterpiece of dressing: this time he made no mention of personnel, obscuring altogether the question of a drummer, and added one to every calculation – the boys were 'eighteen to twenty' and had been together four years, time in which they had 'acquired three very important things – competence, confidence & continuity'.[34]

Stuart's letter was also verbose, and more intense. The recipient couldn't have had many letters from rock groups that began 'Dear Sir, As it is your policy to present entertainment to the habitues of your establishment ...' There are four drafts of the letter – finding the right pitch was clearly a problem. In one the group is 'promising', in another 'very experienced'; in one their stated preference is for rhythm and blues, in another rock and roll. Stuart signed the letter 'Stu Sutcliffe (Manager)' which was almost certainly just a ruse to create a good impression – though it *could* be he was actually their manager for a few hours, a moment that came and went and was forgotten by all save for being captured in writing.[35]

The letter caught something else too – the very moment of transition when one name died and another was born:

I would like to draw your attention ~~to a band~~ to the ~~Quar~~ 'Beatals'.

John and Stu came up with the new identity one evening at Gambier Terrace. All four were desperate to find a new group name, and they didn't lack ideas: 'We had about ten a week,' Paul has said, referring to names not good enough to last and never put to use because they had no bookings. Most were jokes, of which only one – Los Paranoias – would lodge in their memory.[36] If they were ever going to get someplace, though, they needed to find a good one and stick to it.

The influence, once again, was Buddy Holly. Not only had he caused John and Paul to start songwriting, his group now inspired a new name, as John would recall: 'I was looking for a name like the Crickets that meant two things, and from Crickets I got to Beetles. And I changed it to B-E-A because it didn't mean two things on its own as B-double-E. So I changed the E to A and it meant two things – when you said it people thought of crawly things, and when you read it, it was beat music.'[37] It was no more complicated than that: Stu and John were talking, up popped Beetles, and John, for whom wordplay was second nature, made it Beatles; a quick two-step process, finished.

Though Stuart preferred to spell it with an -als, as *Beatals*, Paul and George seem instantly to have preferred John's version. Paul has a clear memory of being told it while walking along Gambier Terrace towards Huskisson Street and Upper Parliament Street. 'John and Stu had come out of the flat one night and we were walking towards the Dingle and just chatting and they said, "Oh, we've had an idea for a name – Beatles, with an A."'[38] There seemed no question of changing it again, and it was a name that would have the most desired of effects: when people heard it spoken, it annoyed or repelled them – 'Ugh, Beatles?' – and when they saw it written they queried it. As such, it became an extension of John, Stu, Paul and George: they turned heads everywhere they went, because of their clothes, their hair, their attitude, their presence, and now their collective name stopped people in their tracks.

It also stood out as different by bucking a trend. Most (though not all) of the other Liverpool groups – in a different class to them in terms of proficiency and stage experience – followed a name formula. There was Cass and the Cassanovas, Rory Storm and the Hurricanes, Derry and the Seniors, Gerry and the Pacemakers, Ken Dallas and the Silhouettes, King-Size Taylor and the Dominoes, and more. As George put it, 'All the groups were "Harry and the Somethings" or "Charlie and the Somethings" so we decided we'd just have "The _____" and that's it. Instead of trying to get one of the fellers as the star with the rest in the back we thought we'd just all be together.'[39]

The first place the Beatles played was the art school, which, during spring 1960, provided their only bookings. They still had no drummer, although this wouldn't have been how they expressed it: in their language they didn't lack a drummer they lacked a *fuckindrummer*. But while they remained stuck at four guitars they did have the use of a second amplifier, one that had the necessary two inputs. This was bought by Sulca (the art school Students' Union) at the urging of Bill Harry, who as Stuart's friend was now closer to John and the others than before. Harry was on the committee and pushed through the purchase on the basis that they played the monthly Saturday-night college dance, performing to canoodling couples in the basement canteen (where, two years back, Paul and George had snuck in from the next-door Institute). The amp didn't belong to the Beatles, it was Sulca's property, but as the 'college band' no one else used it but them.

Jon Hague recalls the Beatles' first appearance as a 'complete fiasco – it never took off and the electrics didn't work'.[40] One can only imagine what kind of collective sound they had – close to shambolic, probably. Still, after two or three months' rehearsal, it was a major moment for Stu finally to be playing live, to be on stage performing. He was a fumbling novice but among friends here, playing to people who picked over his deficiencies gently, if at all. It would be worse elsewhere. Shortcomings were anyway partly deflected by his eye-catching appearance: Stuart in the Beatles was not the Stuart people saw every day standing behind the easel, he was a young dude in crepe-sole shoes, tight trousers, light beard, dark glasses and hair fondly recalled by Arthur Kelly as 'a foot high'. The glasses effected *the James Dean look*, or so people thought, but Bill Harry knew better. He ran Sulca's film society, booking mainly continental movies; Stuart had become fascinated by the Polish actor Zbigniew Cybulski, whose adoption of dark glasses had gained him the probably unwanted mantle 'the Polish James Dean'. Stu's sunglasses weren't quite as they appeared anyway: they were shades clipped on top of his standard spectacles. He didn't only look cool, he could see clearly without embarrassment. If John considered doing the same (and he probably did), he opted to stay blind.

Though his influence is unlikely to have been Cybulski, Ringo Starr had also adopted the same moody look provided by sunglasses on stage. It enhanced yet further, and rather madly, the Hurricanes' flamboyance. Rory Storm's group, along with Cass and the Cassanovas, had been invited by Allan Williams to join the Gene Vincent and Eddie Cochran bill at the Stadium. Scruffs from Liverpool on a bill with *Gene fookin' Vincent and fookin' Eddie fookin' Cochran!* They'd even be hanging around with them backstage. It was simply incredible. Then the unthinkable happened.

By Easter Saturday, 16 April, after almost three solid months on the road, Vincent and Cochran had reached the break they'd been longing for. The following lunchtime they were flying home to America, not due back in England until the tour's resumption on the 30th. They had been appearing this week in Bristol and from here it was a straight A-road run to London. A local man, George Martin, offered his driving services at a cheap price, and the two stars, their luggage, Sharon Sheeley (Eddie's girlfriend and sometime songwriter) and a tour manager all packed tightly into a Ford Consul and set off. Though only 20, Martin already had two convictions for speeding, and as his car entered the town of Chippenham he was doing 80mph when he lost control and smashed into a concrete lamp-post. At his trial, the court heard how the car's roof split open and Cochran, Vincent and Sheeley were thrown out. The latter two were badly though not seriously hurt, but Cochran suffered severe head injuries; he died in a Bath hospital on Easter Day, aged 21.

The news dropped in Liverpool like a bomb. All those young rockers counting the days until they'd be playing in the same show as Cochran were just devastated. Ringo was still feeling it fourteen years later, saying in an interview, 'I'll never forgive him [Cochran], even though he's dead.'[41] The disappointment could even, perhaps, have prompted the young drummer to make a vital decision, for in the teeth of vociferous objections at home, and from Gerry, and also from uncles and aunts, he said he was going to abandon both his apprenticeship and his fiancée and play Butlin's with the Hurricanes. The thin walls at 10 Admiral Grove would not have prevented the neighbourhood hearing them all go off.

As for Allan Williams, his ambitious plan for the Stadium show appeared to be in pieces. 'I phoned Larry Parnes to say "I take it it's all over", but he said no, Gene Vincent was OK and was willing to do it. He gave me the choice, I could either pull out or carry on, so I said, "Right then, let's go ahead." That's when I had the idea of adding even more Liverpool bands to the bill.'[42]

Scrapping his first set of flyers, Williams had a second set printed without Cochran, and over the next few days added Jerry and the Pacemakers (Allan was never good with names), Mal Perry, Ricky Lea, Johnny and his Jets, the Connaughts with midget comedian Nicky Cuff, and Derry and the Seniors. The bill now totalled nine 'professional' acts and eight from Liverpool. It would be a single three-hour show and Williams arranged for tickets to be sold from outlets throughout the city. Brian Epstein agreed to sell them from the Nems counter in exchange for the standard small commission and two complimentaries. While Eddie Cochran, in the words of his posthumous single, was taking Three Steps To Heaven, death was never enough to stop Liverpool.

If George Martin hadn't been doing eighty and hadn't crashed, the Ford Consul would have driven Cochran and Vincent through the Berkshire town of Reading – where, oddly enough, John Lennon and Paul McCartney were also headed. In the Easter school holidays they made their way south to spend a few days with Bett and Mike Robbins and their two infant children.

After leading a nomadic working life, Mike had hung up his Butlin's redcoat to become tenant at the Fox and Hounds pub at Caversham, a Thames-side town close to Reading. He and Bett invited Paul and a friend down for Easter, but Paul didn't take Dot and offered the space to John. There probably wasn't room for more than two, so Stu wasn't asked, and George couldn't go anyway because Blackler's wouldn't give him the time off. The trip gave Paul welcome undivided time with John (who in turn had come without Cyn).

Having twice been away with George, this was Paul's first holiday with John – and John's first with either. They hitch-hiked with some difficulty: each had his guitar and Paul also had the Elpico, and drivers didn't want to pick them up (guitar players = delinquents). Once they realised the problem they hid the gear in a bush until finally someone stopped.[43] They had to share a single bed at the pub, where (despite their age) Mike liked to come into their room and bid them good night. They helped out behind the bar, serving drinks and consuming a few too, and in return Mike said that, as they'd gone to the trouble of bringing their guitars, they could entertain his customers on Saturday night – 23 April, St George's Day. They weren't the Beatles this time, or Quarrymen, or Los Paranoias, but the Nerk Twins. Mike thought it was a good name for them, having also been a name from Paul's younger years, used to describe him and his brother. More than that, it was a *Goon Show* name. Paul and John created some handmade posters to advertise themselves.[44]

They sat on high barstools in the Fox and Hounds' tap room – the public bar, more basic and cheaper than the lounge, no carpet on the floor. Paul would recall how their idea to open with Be-Bop-A-Lula was given the thumbs-down by Mike; he suggested something faster, so they played a quick scuttle through Butlin's favourite The World Is Waiting For The Sunrise, the hit by Les Paul and Mary Ford. John played the rhythm and Paul the melody, but of course they weren't equipped to produce a sound like the multi-tracked record. They later did a second song from the same pair, How High The Moon, but nothing else is remembered about the evening: how long they played, what other songs they sang, whether or not they were able to stop people drinking/chatting and pay them any attention. Still, close on three years after their meeting, this inauspicious yet special little performance was the first and only time Lennon and McCartney played in public as a duo. It was nothing more than a moment, here then gone.* Next day, they were hitching home, school and college resuming on the Monday.

As much as it can be known with any certainty, it was at about this time that Dot miscarried her baby. Information is inevitably and appropriately thin, but Dot has said she was about three months gone when it happened. She went into hospital. 'He [Paul] seemed a bit upset but deep down he was probably relieved,' she has reflected, and it would be hard to imagine any other conclusion. He was let off the hook. All discussion of marriage as the honourable thing to do ended, but the relationship continued, and much as before.[45]

George, in the meantime, caught his second and third rock shows at

---

* Asked about it twenty-plus years later, Mike Robbins wondered if the Nerk Twins had also played during the pub's Sunday lunchtime drinking session, but couldn't be certain.

Liverpool Empire in close succession. Dedicated to studying every guitarist going, especially Americans, he went first to see Duane Eddy, and then, on the day John and Paul were heading home from Caversham, he saw the Everly Brothers, who were backed by none other than the Crickets. The Everlys' latest single, Cathy's Clown, was zipping up the charts at the moment of their first visit to Liverpool, after which it spent nine straight weeks at the top, through all of May and June 1960. It was another sublime blending of harmony and melody, of great drama simply expressed; all the Beatles loved it and wanted to perform it.

George also paid a return visit to the Casbah. Mona Best had no qualms letting him in; while George was party to the Quarrymen walk-out, when they let her down, he was pretty much the quiet one, Paul and John doing all the talking as usual. (Never short of a word, those two.) His visit coincided with the breakup of the Blackjacks. They'd played just a handful of times, and Pete Best set aside his drums – and his only experience of being in a group – still very much a beginner.

His group's dismantling coincided with some unusual events at 8 Hayman's Green. In March 1960, just three months before sitting the A-Levels for which he'd spent eighteen months grafting, Pete suddenly quit school and (beyond saying he 'got fed up') never told anyone why.[46] His friends would always be puzzled, but there was perhaps a deterioration in his spirit. Best was a strong and speedy player of rugby union, left wing for the Liverpool Collegiate XV; in March 1959, the school magazine Esmeduna profiled him as 'a powerful wing, tenacious and aggressive: has had a splendid season and is an outstanding prospect for next season'. A year later he was named openly as one of three players '[who] have not touched last season's form' and from whom the team had suffered 'a loss for long periods'. And then he left. Pete's plans to attend teacher training college – he was going to become a PE instructor – were tossed away. He didn't leave to take a job, he just left and stayed quietly at home.

Something else unusual happened about the same time. Since leaving Liverpool Institute, Neil Aspinall had begun training as an accountant. He had a razor-sharp mind with a keen eye for detail and could do the work without difficulty, except that the job and his staid middle-aged colleagues bored him rigid. Earning a steady weekly wage, Neil bought himself a smart Sunbeam Alpine car and spent a good deal of time with the Bests. One day, as Bill Barlow recalls, 'We all had a big trip out together, going up to Southport in various automobiles, and Neil finished up with Mrs Best at the end of the day. It was a great shock and surprise to everyone, quite mind-blowing for kids our age. We were all staggered by it.'[47]

Neil wasn't the only young person powerfully attracted to the magnetic Mona Best, but this went beyond. She was 36 and married, he was 18 and the best friend of her eldest son, to whom she was intensely close. Neil and Mona shared characteristics: both were steadfast, singleminded, mentally iron-strong. They would keep their relationship as discreet as possible, but if it upset anyone (and it did) that wouldn't stop them. It was another family secret – something else for Pete to keep mum about. Neil left his parents and siblings and moved in with Mona, Pete, Rory and Mona's mother Mary Shaw, who was dying of lung cancer.[48] Johnny Best was gone now. Pete and Neil stayed every bit as close as before, so Pete evidently accepted his best mate having a full relationship with his adored Mo, and that they all lived together in the rambling big house in West Derby. As Pete pointed out in a lawyer's interview, taped in New York in 1965, 'We've virtually become brothers.'

It was to Johnny Best's Liverpool Stadium – Britain's first purpose-built boxing hall – that all eyes turned on 3 May, when Jacaranda Enterprises staged its great rock show starring Gene Vincent. From a recently bought secondhand Morris minibus, Allan Williams had been illegally fly-posting the event all over Merseyside and broadcasting the availability of tickets. The Stadium was abuzz with activity the entire day: Larry Parnes was in town and stars were up from London. Brian Epstein, dressed pin-sharp, broke off from planning the imminent Nems shop on Whitechapel to look around, accompanied by his junior manager Peter Brown. Brian was maintaining his now-established policy of checking out all the shows that came to Liverpool. Brown specifically recalls Epstein and Parnes meeting, but knows nothing of what was said.

The stage was the boxing ring, ropes removed, wooden boards covering and stabilising the canvas. The musicians could only face one way, so the audience occupied just half of the arena. It hadn't been a sell-out and Williams made no money, but everyone enjoyed a night to remember: acoustics lousy, atmosphere electric. While an Empire audience knew instinctively about order, the Stadium crowd was disorderly from the start and, inadequately marshalled, became unruly.

Liverpool outfits filled the first half, rock boys flexing their considerable muscle. Inevitably, the Hurricanes had the most eye-catching act. They were already up and playing before Rory made his grand entrance, sprinting to the ring from the boxers' dressing-room. Cheniston Roland, a photographer friend of Allan Williams and Stuart Sutcliffe, took pictures throughout the show. Rory is the action man at the front, his three guitarists fill the second row, and Ringo is behind, sitting at his kit in an oversize matching dark jacket and black bow-tie, a meaty quiff hovering above giant dark glasses – a pose of admirable magnitude. Eight years later, he recalled the night with unchecked enthusiasm – 'It was great. All the Teds were throwing pennies.'[49]

Which Beatles were watching is again unclear. Paul and John never said they were here, and as one or both had seen Gene Vincent only a few weeks earlier they may not have bothered again. (If John *was* here he would have come down the hill from the art school, because it was on 3 May that he re-sat a key part of the Lettering exam he'd failed so dismally in 1959. If he didn't pass this time there'd be no place for him in the next academic year.) Stuart is known to have been at the show because a Cheniston Roland audience photo happens to include him, and George was definitely present. He'd always recall this night for a specific thought, one that – while irrational – was nonetheless common to all the Beatles:

> We were nothing, just out of school, and we were amateur and we were hopeless, and Rory Storm and the Hurricanes came on at the Stadium and he was big. He came on amazing [doing] What'd I Say and the band rocking, all doing the dance steps with the suits on, and he's jumping about like a loony – and even then I just remember thinking *Well, we're better than all them!* even though we hadn't done anything. And it wasn't an ego thing, it was with no qualifications at all, but there was something about us that was *cocky*, that knew something was going to happen. I remember thinking how we'd got to get our band together.[50]

The show's second half had the professional talent, and here at last was Gene Vincent – gut full of liquor, eyes full of mania, body full of pain – throwing himself about the stage in psychotically energetic defiance of his injuries and grief, just seventeen nights after surviving the death crash. Audience compassion spilled into pandemonium, and as people tried to climb into the ring Larry Parnes and Allan Williams – in his top hat – nipped around treading on fingers to keep them off.

When it was all over, performers and Parnes returned to the Jacaranda for late refreshment. It had been an exhilarating night, and educational too, for in the words of Adrian Barber, the lanky young Yorkshireman who was lead guitarist with Cass and the Cassanovas, the Vincent show was the primary force in binding together the individual ingredients of the Liverpool rock scene. 'None of us knew of any other groups until Allan Williams' gig at the Stadium. I'm sure we were vaguely aware there was something going on, but we weren't a community by any means. At that Stadium show we became aware of all the other bands in Liverpool, about twelve in total.'[51]

Parnes was also pleased. He realised that this man Williams, a stranger not a month earlier, was the gatekeeper to a field of unharvested talent – and inexpensive too, because what the Liverpudlian believed to be a good wage was less than a Londoner's. One problem with managing solo singers was the continual quest for reliable backing musicians. Two of his boys, Duffy Power and Johnny Gentle, were – separately – booked to play the ballroom circuit in Scotland in June and both needed a backing group.* Parnes had just seen four in the Stadium show who would fit the bill admirably. He and Williams talked business late into the night, exploring ways they could work together.

Two days later, Mark Forster of Parnes' company L. M. P. Entertainments phoned Williams to say Larry had been having a further think. As he needed a backing group for Billy Fury too – for *Meet The Beat*, his summer season on Great Yarmouth pier – he wanted to return to Liverpool, bring Fury, and see again the same four groups with a view to all three situations: Power, Gentle and Fury. Williams agreed to round them up for an audition session, and a day later the arrangement was fixed by phone: Parnes and Fury would be in Liverpool the following Tuesday, the 10th. It was all happening fast.

It was in the Jacaranda on 6 or 7 May that John Lennon said something that took Allan Williams by surprise: 'Allan, why don't you do something for us?' Williams didn't quite get his drift. 'I said, "How do you mean 'us'? Who's *us*?" So he explained how he and Stuart had a group, and said if there was going to be an audition for Billy Fury then couldn't they be part of it? I felt indebted to Stuart so I said, "Sure. What's your group's line-up?" He told me the line-up and missed out the drummer. I said, "Who's the drummer?" and he said, "We haven't got one." So I said I'd try to find them one.'[52]

When Williams next saw Brian 'Cass' Cassar in the Jac he asked if there were any drummers looking for work. Cass knew one, Tommy Moore, who'd played with a modern jazz band at the Temple in Dale Street and whose hero was Jack Parnell, the drummer-bandleader whose records were produced by George Martin for Parlophone. An older man, Moore had genuine technique, holding the sticks through his fingers in the conventional dance-band manner. He also had a job, working shifts on a forklift truck at the Garston Bottle Company factory. He agreed to play with the Beatles at the audition, and – without referral to Parnes, it seems – Williams went ahead and added them and

---

* John Askew, a 22-year-old ship's carpenter from Litherland, had become Larry Parnes' second Liverpool signing in February 1959. He was good-looking and could sing; Parnes renamed him Johnny Gentle and got him a contract with Philips Records.

also two others (the Pressmen, and Cliff Roberts and the Rockers, both from Wallasey) to the four main groups.

In Liverpool in 1960, Allan Williams was the man who made things happen. With John's one remark the Beatles' fortunes took a decisive upwards turn. They'd been drifting for months, in need of a sharp kick to get them moving, and Williams provided it. Yesterday they were a drummerless group writing awkward and possibly unsent letters in the hope of getting a single booking; today they were preparing to audition for *Larry Parnes*, a beat away from the touring circuit, TV, fame and 'fortune'. It was true the Beatles didn't think highly of Fury, but the opportunity was great regardless. Cyn says John was 'ecstatic' at the prospect and no doubt he was: here was a possible way out of the nine-to-five brummer striving he dreaded but which was looming large in his life. They devoted themselves to concentrated rehearsal.[53]

They also had to get new clothes. Every group strove for the uniform look, and in the available three or so days, despite having very little money, the four Beatles obtained shirts, trousers and shoes that more or less matched: black shirts with silver edging, jean-like trousers with white-edged front and rear pockets, and bumper shoes with a rubber sole and a canvas top with wire netting. As John would remember, the ensemble was 'direct from my art school. We looked arty compared with other groups, who looked like clerks or dockers. We looked like students … so we had a bit of a classy touch straight away, which was different.'[54]

The audition took place that Tuesday 10 May, starting around 10AM. Most of the musicians got time off from jobs, honestly or otherwise; the Beatles were the only school/college students present, the three of them all sagging off (George probably claimed sickness and didn't go into Blackler's). The venue for all the hopes and dreams was the empty Wyvern Social Club, at the top end of Seel Street. Williams had bought the lease for his night-club venture, which he'd decided to call the Blue Angel, after the Marlene Dietrich film. Work to convert the Wyvern into the posh new 'Blue' was suspended for a day; there was no stage, just an area of ground-floor space near the door with a few tables and chairs.

While Mark Forster came up from London on the morning train, Parnes and Fury travelled together on the overnight sleeper – and now here they were, the renowned manager looking sharp in his sharkskin suit and tie, Billy smoking, cool in an open shirt, the collar of his jacket upturned. Really he was one of them, down-home Dingle boy Ronnie Wycherley, Arthur Kelly's cousin, in the same class as Richy Starkey at St Silas primary. But no, he was *Billy Fury*, schoolgirl pin-up, TV hero, chart artist, sports car owner, a source of scandal through his 'revolting sexual antics' on stage. He was a *pop star*, elevated, no longer one of them at all. As Johnny Gustafson recalls, there was much jostling for space in front of Fury and Parnes by the Liverpool rockers: 'We *all* had wild desires to be rich and famous.'[55]

The day included a fair amount of waiting around, and here the Beatles mingled among their contemporaries for the first time, small fry angling to swim with big fish. Though Rory Storm and the Hurricanes had withdrawn from the audition – their Butlin's season approaching, it was pointless going for jobs they couldn't fulfil – Rory and Johnny turned up to look cool, meet Fury and check out the competition. Tommy Moore would be arriving later, after he'd finished work, and as the Beatles stood and wondered what he even looked like, they got talking to the man who'd suggested him, the little hustler that was Brian Cassar. His Cassanovas were all big lads but Cass was a darting pocket dynamo at 5ft 1in, a 24-year-old who'd done his National Service and never wanted for an opinion. When he asked John what his group was called and was told 'Beatles', Cass denounced it as rubbish. It meant nothing and wasn't a *real* group name – it wasn't *Someone and the Somethings*. Unbidden, Cass invented and handed them a new one on the spot, which, in acknowledgement of his age and their subordinate position, they didn't rebuff. Recognising John as the leader, and reaching back for inspiration (as British males often did) to Robert Louis Stevenson's *Treasure Island*, John became Long John Silver, his group's name similarly adapted.

Quite what it added up to is subject to the fluctuations of memory. John would recall the Cass-coined name as Long John and the Silvermen, Paul as Long John Silver and the Pieces of Eight, and also as Long John and the Silver Beatles, George as Long John and the Pieces of Silver.[56] It isn't clear which they settled on for the audition, most likely Long John and the Silver Beatles. However appended or spelled, they were still the only group in Liverpool smart enough to include the word 'beat' in their name.

When he wasn't covering his ears from the amplified sounds bouncing around the empty room, Cheniston Roland took photos of all the groups as they played. One exposure in between acts captured the moment John Lennon handed Billy Fury a drawing and asked him to autograph it. All the time, Long John and the Silver Beatles begged to go on last because Moore hadn't arrived. In the end, when Parnes could wait no longer, they had to plead with Johnny Hutchinson – chisel-jawed 'Hutch' of the Cassanovas – to drum for them. He said yes, but wasn't happy about it. Johnny Gustafson reflects, 'Hutch didn't like them and he showed it. In fact, he hated them and thought they were posers.'[57]

Just such a look, immaculately blended with boredom, is manifest in one of

Roland's photographs, a single shot that caught Hutch as a temporary Silver Beatle. The subsequent exposures – the first photographs of the group for perhaps eight months and the first of the Beatles, or whatever they were called – prove that Moore did eventually arrive from work, lacking their uniform, looking dishevelled, borrowing Hutch's kit and playing with the four guitarists for the first time. Cyn Powell had also arrived at the Wyvern and sat watching from a discreet distance, keeping fingers, arms and legs tightly crossed for luck. 'They were all nervous but they looked so lovely,' she would recall, 'all clean and trying their best. It was wonderful.'[58]

The auditioning groups did two or three numbers. Roland's photos show that in one song John put down his guitar and took the microphone in his hand, à la Elvis; Paul sang lead in another; a third appears to have been instrumental. The photos also show, with comical clarity, Stu Sutcliffe fully turning his back on Parnes, Fury and Forster while he played. It was one thing for them to hear the wrong bass notes, it was another for them to follow his fingers wandering where they oughtn't. Paul claims ownership of the idea that Stu make a deflective feature of his inadequacy by 'doing a moody' – by making it look like he'd *had enough*, that he couldn't be bothered to face the front; it was like exhibiting the reverse side of a painting, and completed the coolly disdainful image already framed by his beard and dark glasses.[59]

Were Long John and the Silver Beatles any good? Probably not, given that they incorporated a beginner bass player and used two drummers, one who didn't want to play with them and the other who hadn't played with them before, arrived late and used the first man's kit. George would remember it as 'a bit of a shambles . . . it felt pretty dismal',[60] and Johnny Gustafson confirms that 'They made an awful racket, a raucous row. George's guitar playing was poor, stumbling – anything with a scale in it and he was finished. They were amateurish, but they could sing. John and Paul's vocals were pretty good, enough for me to notice them, Paul's high-pitched screaming and John's raucous R&B voice.'[61]

The key question was what Billy Fury and the men from London thought, and it's here that the facts become especially murky, regular retelling possibly pulling it further from the truth. Allan Williams' version is that Fury, with Parnes' support, ignored all the groups who really could perform and chose Long John and the Silver Beatles to back him. The prized Yarmouth contract was theirs . . . provided they ditch the guy who couldn't play bass. Faced with this dilemma, between brummer and summer, John manfully stood by his friend and turned it down, barking, 'You take us all or you take none of us.' Lennon was surely nothing if not a loyal friend, but the scenario seems unlikely. John, Paul and George never corroborated it, nor Fury or Parnes, but Williams has always said it's true and it has been supported by Millie Sutcliffe, who recalled, 'He was quite upset, Stuart. He said, "Mother, I think I've let the boys down."'[62]

This particular scenario seems even less likely in view of the fact that Cass and the Cassanovas were chosen by Parnes for the Scotland jobs backing Duffy Power and Johnny Gentle. Were Long John and the Silver Beatles really too good for them, worthy only of the top division, a summer with Billy? No one was, it seems. Parnes had only one further thought about these groups: to consider Derry and the Seniors for a place in *Idols On Parade*, his act-packed summer show at Blackpool.

John Lennon soon shrugged off the Long but they stayed the Silver Beatles maybe another few days, long enough for it to become embedded in Allan Williams' mind as their true name. It would take a while to shift it, and as they never explained the spelling (or, if they did, he forgot), he came to know them as the Silver Beetles. Names were Williams' weakness: he called Paul *John* and John *George* and George *Paul*, and variations thereof, and they always teased him. 'They used to crack jokes about it,' he admits. 'John used to say, "Allan, I'm *Paul*!"'[63] The one he really knew was Stuart, and it was this friendship that gained them all playing access to the Jacaranda cellar; Williams let them use the space for sharpening up their act. It isn't clear if Tommy Moore was now properly their drummer or whether his late minutes at the audition were likely to be the only time they'd lay eyes on him.

As Cyn concedes, the magic of the group when they played in the Jac was 'so indefinable as to be almost non-existent at times'.[64] Their sound was rough and so was the setting: no stage, just a concrete base, and no PA because the steel band didn't need one. While Williams was able to find them a microphone, he had no stand; one day, George asked if he could borrow a broomstick; when Williams next ambled downstairs, Cyn was holding it in front of the singer, the microphone tied to its top.

It was here that Ringo Starr first set eyes on the Silver Beatles. He turned up with Rory and Johnny and paid them little attention, just a quick glance, enough to notice they were scruffy and that they were just three guitarists, two showing the other one how to play bass. The gulf between the groups seemed unbridgeable: Rory & Co were about to head off for their £100-a-week Butlin's season, pin-sharp professionals, while the Silver Beatles were, in George Harrison's words, 'amateur and hopeless'. Ringo flaunted a motor, Beatles queued for the bus.

All the same, Ringo was still prevaricating about Butlin's, and Johnny Guitar's diary entry for Saturday 14 May specifies what seemed to be his final decision: 'Ritchie [sic] says he's not going to Butlin's now, getting married next June.'

With all that pressure from his immediate and wider family, and from Gerry, and from his boss and colleagues at H. Hunt & Son, Richy had allowed himself to be swayed. Elsie was plying the argument her own mother had used on her: 'If I'd had the chances you've had … I didn't have it as easy as you … you young people, you don't know you're born'.[65] All Elsie was asking, pleading, was that he finish his apprenticeship, that he carry on at Hunt's and get the piece of paper that proved he had a trade 'to fall back on', and so break the line of labourers that ran through her family's history. Echoing the words shouted at John by Aunt Mimi, Elsie told her Richy that drumming was all very well as a hobby but he wouldn't earn a living from it.[66] This and more lay behind his statement to Johnny Guitar on 14 May … but meanwhile he was *still* thinking.

This same Saturday, the Silver Beatles made their first appearance in a Liverpool rock venue, a 'jive dance' at the former electric cinema that was Lathom Hall in Seaforth, at the north end of the docks. Brian 'Beekay' Kelly was the promoter here and the Silver Beatles cadged an audition interval spot Cliff Roberts and the Rockers couldn't make. The Lathom was a roughhouse, like most of Kelly's venues, though that was merely the misfortune of operating in this area. Sometimes the fighting began from the stage: Bobby Thompson, guitarist with King-Size Taylor and the Dominoes, would be ashamed to recall how they thought it was clever to pick fights with the audience, starting something off and then jumping from the stage to get stuck in.[67] Of course, it helped that Ted 'King-Size' Taylor was 6ft 5in and weighed twenty-two stone.

It was this giant of a man that the Silver Beatles – in his eyes, wimps – asked to borrow Dominoes drummer Dave Lovelady when they arrived at Lathom Hall. Tommy Moore wasn't showing up, or maybe they hadn't asked him. Opinions are mixed about how good or bad they were. Despite their inadequate equipment, Thompson thought them exciting and impressive, but Taylor insists they were terrible and that later in the evening, when his group performed the star turn, the Silver Beatles 'all sat in a row and took down one line each of all the songs we did – Dizzy Miss Lizzy, Slow Down, Money, all of those – and the next time we saw them they were playing all our stuff'.[68]

It seems Beekay didn't like them either, and yet he did agree to book them for the following Saturday, perhaps on the understanding they have a full line-up and get themselves together a bit more. He took their name to be Silver Beats, which was how he advertised them in the *Bootle Times* of 20 May 1960, an associated blurb hyping their audition as a 'sensational appearance'. It was the first time the Beatles' name (or something close to it) appeared in print ... and yet, when that Saturday rolled around, when their first proper booking in Liverpool lay on a plate for them, they were not in Seaforth but the north of Scotland, 367 miles away.

14

'Where's the bloody money?'
(18–30 May 1960)

The Beatles grabbed their first 'professional experience' not on merit but because no one else could fill the bill and they shifted everything to make it happen.

Cass and the Cassanovas had won the 10 May audition determining who might play Scotland in June with a pair of Larry Parnes boys . . . but seven days later Parnes was back on the phone hoping Allan Williams could help him out of a hole. Johnny Gentle wasn't only working north of the border next month, he was up there for a nine-day sweep around some ballrooms from the coming Friday, the 20th, and didn't have backing musicians. It was short notice, but was there any chance Williams could rush him a group?

A month previously, Williams had got the Cassanovas a regular Saturday-night booking on New Brighton Pier for ten guineas a time. Their spot the coming Saturday. had been formally contracted and advertised and they couldn't be withdrawn, any more than they could pull out of a Cavern booking midway through the next week: they were scheduled to appear with Rory Storm and the Hurricanes in the jazz club's first ever designated Rock Night. (Times really were changing.) Rory and Johnny Guitar confirmed as much when Williams approached them about Scotland. Gerry and the Pacemakers, his third port of call, also couldn't do it: they all had jobs and wouldn't be able to get time off. Likewise the guys in Derry and the Seniors.

So it was – on, now, Wednesday the 18th – that Allan Williams asked Stuart Sutcliffe if 'the Silver Beetles' could do a week in Scotland . . . and be up there by Friday night. There was £75 on the table from Parnes if they could, £15 each for the five of them, but only if there *were* five of them. Tommy Moore had to be found, pronto, and there were several other obstacles to be hurdled.

The next twenty-four hours, 18–19 May 1960, was the turning point in their lives.

It seems John never told Mimi about it. After moving into Gambier Terrace there was even more in his life about which she knew nothing. John didn't need to hear her reaction to the suggestion he cut college during exams and go 'gallivanting' around the Highlands with his guitar, so he didn't tell her. Though further elements of his course work needed to be done, Cyn could do them in his name. Stuart was approaching his Finals, the last exams in a four-year study at which he had dazzled, so he had a tough decision. Millie was livid that he was even entertaining the idea, no matter that he'd be touring his mother country, which she missed so much. Charles Sutcliffe felt the same, branding his son 'a strolling minstrel'.[1] But Stuart was also a rocker now. Deciding he could accommodate a week off and still pass the tests, he announced his availability.

Paul's challenge was greater. He wasn't going to miss out on Scotland, no fear, but he was just a couple of weeks from sitting his A-Levels, a period the school liked to insist was devoted to concentrated revision. More than that, a written paper for his Art exam was to be taken in the coming week and he would miss it.[2] Few greater illustrations exist of what the group meant to Paul McCartney, of his keenness, his confidence in the power of persuasion, and his instinct about how to win over his dad. His ploy was complex: first to fabricate that Liverpool Institute had given all A-Level students a pre-exam week off, and then to praise the restorative powers of fresh air for the tired mind.[3] A trip would do his exam chances the world of good, he said, and everyone knew there was no fresher air than in the Scottish Highlands. *Oh, go on, Dad – all the others are playing!* Only if Jim McCartney was a mug could he have swallowed such deceit, and he was no such thing. Nevertheless, this latest battle with his eldest son ended quickly and, like most others, in defeat and with a resigned shrug. Mary would most certainly have said no and that would have been the end of the matter, but Mary had been gone coming up four years.

The Institute was another thing entirely: The Baz would yield to no tactics of any kind, and in his long years as headmaster had heard them all. There was nothing else for Paul but to feign sickness on the Friday, all of the following week, and probably the Monday after – a scam that might well have entailed an elaborate illness and concluded, on his return, with the forgery of a hand-written letter from his dad. Putting one over on the school was simply too tasty for Paul to keep quiet about. Ivan Vaughan, who'd got him into John's group in the first place, argued with him that exams had to come first, that he mustn't fritter away his Art A-Level like this. Another student, Ian Caulfield, says, 'The conventional wisdom among my classmates was what a stupid idiot he was, ruining his career.'[4]

George had an equally big problem: Blackler's or Beatles? Actually, *no contest*. While it isn't clear if he asked for the time off and was refused, or didn't bother asking because he knew what the answer would be, he arrived with speed at his decision. At the same moment Richy Starkey was on the cusp of chucking in his apprenticeship to go off and play drums in Wales, George chucked in his apprenticeship to go and play guitar in Scotland.

The decision went down badly at home. In post-war Liverpool, where times were never less than tough, if you had a trade you were made and if you abandoned a trade you were mad. There was no accommodation for defeatism, on top of which George had stiff financial commitments; how did he plan to pay off his Futurama without a bloody wage? Harry Harrison was greatly upset, but, as usual, George could not be shifted from his position once his mind was made up – a trait he'd got straight from his dad. As Harry would remember, 'I told George it would be better if he was only a part-time professional, but our George is a determined lad.'[5] He'd been at Blackler's exactly six months when he threw the job back at them with, at most, a few hours' notice.

All this was contingent on Allan Williams persuading Tommy Moore to go with them, which was far from clear-cut. Moore wasn't 'one of them', he was an old man, approaching 29, a factory worker, not the brightest of sparks to join a group of cocky grammar-school kids; but on the almost literal eve of departure they simply had to have him. No drummer meant no booking, so now was not the moment to be choosy.

Moore had to be encouraged to beg time off from the Garston Bottle Company, or feign sickness, but he said yes; £15 was more than he earned driving the forklift and maybe he simply fancied the chance of playing drums for a week, and gazing upon glorious Scottish scenery instead of the factory clock. His woman told him he was a fool but Moore told Williams he was on board. For at least the week ahead, Tommy Moore was a Silver Beatle.*

Or was he? It was in this timeframe, give or take a day or two, that the name evolved once more, when the Silver was dropped and they became the Beatles unadorned. While Stu held out for Beatals just a little longer, and Allan Williams continued to call them the Silver Beetles (and advertise them this way) well into the summer, they were, clean and clear, *the Beatles*.

Williams' role in getting them the Scotland tour and his taking of a

---

* Thomas Henry Moore, born Liverpool, 29 September 1931. He died there in the month he turned 50, having given only a couple of unchallenging interviews about his time in the group.

commission defines the moment when he became the Beatles' manager.* It was a position he acted upon with immediate effect: while they were away he fixed them a string of local bookings for their return. This doesn't mean he was convinced of the Beatles' great potential or had grand ideas about how to make them international stars, rather that there was a situation to be explored for mutual benefit. Mostly it was a relationship rooted in his amity with Stuart and his appreciation of the lads' personal qualities. As he reflects, 'They were rough, and I probably wouldn't have managed them if it wasn't for their personalities: they were a bit more intelligent than most other groups. They weren't the run-of-the-mill average thickie doing rock 'n' dole.'[6]

The Beatles weren't the only group Williams looked after, and he wasn't their first manager; as far as John, Paul and George were concerned, he was their third, after Nigel Walley and Derek Hodkin, and they measured him against that yardstick.

They had, at most, the night of Thursday 19 May to rehearse. Rod Murray remembers a practice session in his front room at Gambier Terrace when Tommy Moore played drums, and this might be it. Then they went home to pack. They didn't have much beyond the single stage outfit got for the Fury audition, and Tommy didn't even have that. They forgot to tell Brian Kelly they couldn't play at Lathom Hall; they probably had a small advance on their fee from Allan Williams, sufficient to buy train tickets; and by Friday morning, while all their mates were at school or work, they were off to Scotland like professional musicians, the first Liverpool rock group to go on tour.

Where we going, Johnny?
    Alloa, boys, to Alloa, the county town of distant Clackmannanshire.
    Where the ———?
    It was a long old journey, plenty enough time for the excitement to rise and fall. Paul had his 1957 guitar still, the Zenith; George had the Futurama he might soon have to surrender back to Hessy's if he couldn't meet the drip; John had his Club Footy and Stu his Hofner bass; the separate pieces of Tommy's kit were carried among them. As for amplification, they didn't have enough, probably only Paul's little Elpico. 'In Scotland . . . they had no amplifiers,' John wrote a few months later, suggesting they'd not been able to bring the art school amp. Begging and borrowing was a permanent state for these boys.
    Johnny Gentle was pretty much unknown to them. In the Parnes stable there were unofficial but clear A, B and C stalls and Gentle was in the last,

---

* Allan Richard Williams, born in Bootle, north Liverpool, 21 February 1930.

sometimes not even mentioned when his manager named his artists in press interviews. If the Beatles had caught Gentle singing on TV it was only once or twice, down the bottom of bills, and it's unlikely they knew his Philips-label records, not one of which had made the *NME* or *Record Retailer* charts and all of which were the kind of sappy 45s from which they instinctively recoiled.[7] Did they even know he was John Askew from Liverpool, born in 1936 off Scotland Road? 'We thought it was a pity we were out on tour with a Gentle,' Paul has said, 'because we'd wanted a Fury or an Eager.' Still, the idea of being 'big time' was intoxicating, as Paul remembers:

> We all thought, 'This is it! We've arrived, we're showbiz people now. He's Johnny Gentle, who do you want to be?' So, in the Larry Parnes spirit, George became Carl Harrison, after Carl Perkins, Stuart became Stuart de Staël, after his favourite painter Nicolas de Staël, Tommy Moore became Thomas Moore – he signed autographs 'Thomas Moore, drums' – and I became Paul Ramon, which seemed to me like a sexy French name. It made us all seem like these great London showbiz guys. When you were in Fraserburgh, instead of saying 'I'm a kid from Liverpool' it suggested there was something more to you. It's an old trick.[8]

John's subsequent insistence that he kept his real name ('because I could never find one I liked better than my own; that was the only thing I ever clung on to, that I never changed my name') has at times been confirmed and refuted by Paul. The proof rests in two sets of autographs from this week, where he signed himself *Johnny Lennon*. This was a tour with two Johnnies.[9]

Their first date was the Friday-night dance in the fine ballroom of Alloa Town Hall, an area of maple floor, big windows, a balcony with seats. Apart from their Carroll Levis dates, John, Paul and George had never played anywhere so grand. There was time only for a half-hour rehearsal ... and during this the bubble of excitement burst. Here they were, meant to be professionals, about to go on stage before a paying audience, and they didn't know the songs Gentle wanted to sing. They *knew* them, from radio or records, but they'd never played them. It was a challenge for all five, but especially for that there de Staël on bass who had no hope whatever of playing songs he hadn't painstakingly been shown. It was a setback they'd fail to overcome to any satisfactory degree throughout the tour.

Though he wouldn't have known them anyway, Gentle hadn't been told who his group would be – partly because their involvement was arranged so late, and partly because these things were always so. It was the lot of solo singers to be shunted from hall to hall and given a pickup band, they and everyone else short-changed in the process. The Beatles, however, were a sight worse than Gentle had encountered before. They had to scrounge the use of an amp, their ability was mixed, and they were scruffy: their stage clothes were also their everyday clothes, quickly showing signs of distress. As George would recall, 'We were like orphans. Our shoes were full of holes and our trousers were a mess, while Johnny Gentle had a posh suit.'[10] Larry Parnes' local man in Scotland was Duncan MacKinnon – he was the promoter who fixed up the seemingly endless cycle of visits north o' the border by the likes of Messrs Gentle, Power and Eager – and he was not pleased with the Beatles. Not at all. He was soon on the phone to London, lodging a complaint which Allan Williams (who heard it secondhand from Parnes) remembers as 'they're a scruffy no-good group'.[11]

Having got the booking at such short notice, the Beatles weren't named in newspaper ads for any of the seven dates they'd be playing – it was always 'Johnny Gentle and His Group'. And there are only three known photographs from the entire week, all taken on the first night here at Alloa.* They feature Gentle of course – white sports jacket and, miraculously, shoes that almost matched the Beatles' – and it's fortunate that one shot happens also to include a member of his backing group. Here is *Carl*, twanging his Futurama, his face tight. Pressed up to the lip of the stage, by the footlights, a row of girls gaze admiringly upon the star . . . and only the star. The Beatles are just His Group. 'We were crummy, horrible, an embarrassment,' George would say. 'We didn't have amplifiers or anything.'[12]

An eyewitness from one of the midweek dances says the Beatles performed three numbers on stage before Gentle made his entrance, John singing them all, and also that Gentle performed a couple of songs from a chair brought on stage for him. The songs the Beatles had to play have never been convincingly remembered. John Askew liked Bobby Darin, Brook Benton, Perry Como and Dinah Washington, but Johnny Gentle's career had been routed down a different track: his records were all 'beat ballads' and the only songs ever mentioned in reviews of his stage work (on the occasions he played the bigger tours) were designed to get the girls cooing, chart hits such as Only Sixteen, Living Doll and A Teenager In Love and oldies like I'm Confessin' and Alright, Okay, You Win. 'Johnny Gentle is one of the new school – good looking, quiet, relaxed,' Jack Good noted in his weekly *Disc* column. While it's possible that in Scotland, away from Parnes' watchful eye, Gentle performed a little more rock – George would remember them doing Elvis's Teddy Bear and Wear My Ring Around Your Neck – there wouldn't have been much: he had to give the

---

* It seems none of the Beatles took a camera to Scotland.

audience what his name suggested and they expected, and as at least three of the week's presentations were called *The Beat Ballad Show* this was clearly the main menu. In all, Gentle performed less than an hour, and they went on stage here in Alloa after a support act, Alex Harvey and his Big Beat Band.[13]

The Beatles didn't know this opening night was the biggest they would play. It was Friday, payday, a good ballroom in a populous area, and the man advertised as a 'Star of TV and Decca Recording Fame' had come to town.* Of the seven dates, Alloa was the only one to receive a local paper write-up: a piece headlined GENTLE ADMIRERS WERE GENTLE was published with a photograph of the Parnes boy draped by nine local lasses. The attendance was 'exceptionally large' and the police prevented a few young females trying to mount the stage and touch the heart-throb. Nonetheless, the audience was more orderly this night than when other beat boys had visited, with fewer 'screaming teenage girls', and the person who threw pennies at the musicians during Johnny's performance had been quickly removed from the hall. There was no explicit mention of the backing group.[14]

Crummy, horrible, embarrassing on stage ... it was generally worse off it, when they were exposed to an absence of care shown them by Parnes and MacKinnon – or, for that matter, Allan Williams. They had to pay for their food throughout the week and find their own accommodation at least twice. Mostly they stayed in a small, respectable riverside hotel in Inverness, but they spent at least one night in a Dormobile van and Paul would return to Liverpool with tales of sleeping in a hayloft.[15] The van, provided by MacKinnon to ferry musicians and their gear/luggage between towns, was papered with posters from his promotions, so everyone knew they were entertainers.

Little is known of how the troupe spent the long off-stage hours, beyond the fact they completely got on each other's nerves. George would recall, 'There weren't enough seats in the van, and somebody had to sit on the inside of the mudguard on the back wheel – usually Stu.'[16] The de Staël desire to be a rock star was put to a severe test during the course of the week, when everyone made his life a misery. Paul played a more open hand than usual, sniping away the entire time, and George played a closed hand, literally hitting him: 'I had a lot of fist fights with Stuart. It was fighting for your inch then. I suppose the reason I was fighting him was that in the ego pecking order he wasn't really a musician.'[17] John weighed in too, of course, mouthing off at his best friend and flatmate, the guy who not four months earlier he'd been so desperate to entice

* Decca, Philips ... it little mattered the advert was wrong, as they all were, the entire week. Larry Parnes wasn't particular about such details.

into the group. 'We were terrible. We'd tell Stu he couldn't sit with us, or eat with us. We'd tell him to go away, and he did. That was how he learned to be with us. It was all stupid, but that was what we were like.' In one town, they heard – or imagined they'd heard – that a circus had not long departed and that a dwarf had slept in a particular hotel bed. They insisted Stu sleep in it; no one else would, so it had to be him.[18]

Even more than Stu, however, the Lennon tongue was directed at Tommy Moore. Here was a verbal cruelty that knew no bounds, especially when his target's weakness – and the unlikelihood of a physical response – had been assessed. He wound up Tommy from start to finish, unrelenting, until the drummer (he liked *jazz*) was utterly sick to death of the Beatles, the van, the tour and life. This 'weakness', as Allan Williams calls it, was nothing Moore could change. 'Tommy was a simple man, not very bright, and he was also much older than them, so he stood *no chance*: John Lennon had no time for anybody who wasn't on his wavelength.' As George would reflect, 'John was very tough. He had that ability to be gentle and soft and lovely but he was acid too. He gave that hard edge to the Beatles.'[19]

Not much of this behaviour was modified by the arrival of Margie. Johnny Gentle brought along his bird, a Berkshire blonde who, they gathered, had modelled for men's magazines *Spick* and *Span*. With her fine features, modish dress and spirited personality, she turned heads everywhere in Scotland, which seemed to all of them several years behind the times. As double-rooms in hotels could only be taken by married couples, it was necessary to pretend they were, and it seems the ruse was extended to the Beatles. In spite of the terrible behaviour among themselves, they demonstrated they knew too their adult-instilled values of politeness by calling her 'Mrs Gentle'.[20]

Alloa was the only date in the south of Scotland. They didn't emerge again from the van until they'd bumped their way 150 miles north, through the Cairngorms mountains to Inverness – George and John returning to a town visited in childhood holidays. Though the 'Silver Beats' should have been at Lathom Hall in Seaforth, they spent Saturday night playing a *Beat Ballad Show* with Johnny Gentle upstairs in the Northern Meeting Ballroom. The management provided an alternative entertainment on the ground floor, where the good folk of Inverness – in their tartan kilts, dresses and ghillies – were dancing jigs, hornpipes, Gay Gordons and reels to Lindsay Ross and his Famous Broadcasting Band. These musicians were celebrating the release of their first record, issued by Parlophone only the previous day. It had been recorded three weeks earlier by a tall, good-looking and wryly amusing young man up from London, George Martin, who was making his annual Scottish sortie to capture the latest sounds.

The beat boys spent the remainder of the week in the van, trundling back and forth between here and Peterhead, mostly driving in their own tyre tracks along the north-east coastal roads. After playing Friday and Saturday, Gentle's next show was Monday night in Fraserburgh, and they spent much of Sunday hanging around Inverness. Paul sent home a postcard saying they were 'going down better than Vince Eager or Duffy Power'.[21] George and John lounged around their hotel with Johnny Gentle. He was an easy-going individual and a fair musician: he played a guitar he'd made during his days as a ship's carpenter, and he wrote songs. Half of the six sides on his three singles were his own words and music. He tells the story of how, here in Inverness, he showed John and George a song he'd written though not yet finished, called I've Just Fallen For Someone.

My song was fine up to the middle-eight: I had one but wasn't happy with it. John started telling me what I needed, which I thought was out of order because I'd been writing songs a year or more and he was some upstart with no professional experience.

But he came up with something, sang me what he had and I was impressed. 'We know that – we'll get by / Just wait and see / Just like the – song tells us / The best things in life are free.' It just flowed, and I thought it was great. I used it in the song.[22]

As Gentle points out, there was no question of Lennon being given a credit for his contribution, let alone payment. It was just one of those things, and the moment passed. John may have forgotten about it, because he never mentioned it.

A clear highlight of the week was the thrill of signing autographs. Two extant sets from this week were obtained in the same place at the same time, when the tour Dormobile collided with a car at the crest of the hill coming down into Banff. It was Sunday evening and the entourage, temporarily relocating from Inverness, was en route to Fraserburgh twenty-four hours early. Gentle had the wheel but rough was the impact: everything inside the van was sent flying, and while most emerged merely shook up, Tommy Moore was hit full in the face, losing teeth and receiving other injuries. The sound of the collision brought people out of their houses, and, seeing from the van's decoration that its passengers were entertainers, two teenage girls ran to fetch autograph books. While waiting for an ambulance to speed Tommy to hospital, everyone signed. These are the first known Beatles signatures, the first of tens of thousands and maybe more. One set extended over five pages:

> The Beatles. Paul Ramon. Johnny Lennon. Carl Harrison
> love Stuart*
> Thomas Moore, Drums
> Love Johnny Gentle
> With best wishes, Margie xxxx

In the other book the autographs are spread across two pages. As the star, Johnny Gentle got one to himself, and the five Beatals (as Stuart has written it) are crowded on to the other: Stuart, Johnny Lennon, Carl Harrison, Paul Ramon and Thomas Moore Drums.

This was stardom. They had made it. *Hi there honey, want my autograph?* Though not too incapacitated to sign his name, Moore was also seeing stars in another sense. The ambulance rushed him down the hill to Chalmers Hospital, and the four guitar-playing Beatles waved it off, not knowing when they'd see him next.†

At the fishing port of Fraserburgh, in the north-east corner of Aberdeenshire, they checked into the Station Hotel for two nights knowing they'd no means of paying the bill. The advance given to the Beatles by Allan Williams had evaporated, and so quickly was the tour arranged they didn't seem to realise they'd only be paid at the end of the week. Larry Parnes would enjoy relating a tale (possibly partly true) of a reverse-charge phone call received from Scotland on the Monday morning – Johnny Lennon asking, 'Where's the bloody money?'[23]

They hung around all day in Fraserburgh before playing in the evening. Paul sent another postcard home – 'It's gear. I've been asked for my autograph'[24] – and Stuart sent one to 'Rod, Diz, Ducky' at Gambier Terrace, omitting any mention of how he was being bullied: 'Going like a bomb, love every minute, Scotland beautiful, here particularly. See you Monday. I hope.' By mid-afternoon, when it seemed they might have to play without a drummer, someone went off to Banff and fetched Tommy Moore from hospital. He sat behind his kit that night battered and bruised, his face inflamed, his lip stitched, his mouth missing teeth – and, as he would relate, every few minutes John turned around and howled with glee at his misfortune. How Moore *hated* him.[25]

---

* In both autograph books Stuart followed his signature with a monogram. Though difficult to distinguish, it doesn't appear to be a blend of *d* and *s* for de Staël; it may be *f, v* and *s* for Fergusson Victor Sutcliffe.

† The crash made the local press. Nestling among news of church jumble sales and the Townswomen's Guild was a brief but detailed description of their Dormobile's collision with a car. The other driver was George Merson, a 'farm grieve' (estate manager). The *Banffshire Journal* of 24 May 1960 became the first newspaper in the world to write about the Beatles ... and not the last to misspell it 'Beetles'.

Away four days now, the bloom of being on the road long gone, the Beatles were missing home comforts and a measure of human kindness . . . but found both here in Fraserburgh, and as a consequence it became the place they would most remember. Situated near the harbour, Dalrymple Hall – a compact ball-room with a seated balcony – was half empty because the town's young men were out on the boats, but there were some particularly enthusiastic young lasses present. Although just 17, Margaret Jack had passed her driving test and had the use of her father's car; it had already been arranged that during the dance she would stand with Mrs Gentle – the object of much attention – and, in the event of any hysteria at the end, drive them away to safety. As the evening progressed, though, Margaret and her friends thought Johnny nowhere near as edgy and exciting as His Group.

After it was over she was waiting behind the wheel for Mr and Mrs Gentle to appear when, chased by an excited pack of girls – and very much loving it – the Beatles came running down the Dalrymple's back stairs and jumped in. Mr George Jack's red and brown Vauxhall Estate was the first step on a road that would lead them, five years later, to a Wells Fargo armoured truck. Margaret ended up taking everyone back to her parents' house, 145 Strichen Road. 'They were highly entertaining and filled the house with music, playing the piano and offering autographs for all the family. I liked Paul most: he introduced himself to me as Paul Ramon and was lovely, a really nice person. I ran them back to their hotel at the end of the evening and made arrangements to see Paul the next day.'[26]

While Paul was out and about with Margaret Jack in her dad's car, John piqued the interest of her friend, 15-year-old Margaret Gauld. She was sitting on a sand dune with another friend who suddenly said, 'Look, there's the group that was on last night.' They made to approach them in a way that seemed casual.

We started chatting and after a while they asked if there was a café nearby. We said we'd show them, then they asked us to join them; I had a chilled orange and so did Johnny Lennon – that's what he called himself – and he insisted on paying for me with what turned out to be his final shilling.

We sat in the café for ages and it was great fun. Johnny was a character, a really funny guy, cracking me up all the time. I told him he looked like 'Sach', one of the Bowery Boys. He said his shirt had been torn the night before by some girls grabbing at him, so I took it home, up to my bedroom, and mended it, and then I went back with some softies [bread rolls] with strawberry jam which I made for them. I was *smitten*.[27]

Paul and Margaret Jack didn't have long together, but she showed him around some local villages and they went to look at Cairnbulg Castle. Here was the fresh air to restore his tired mind. The two had a sweet moment of time together, enjoying each other's company before parting with an innocent kiss. 'He was the perfect gentleman,' says Margaret, 'and when I dropped him back in town he asked if I would go to see them in Peterhead on the Saturday. I said I couldn't because I knew I was going to be away.'

By late afternoon they'd been booted out of the Station Hotel, when it was realised they'd no money. They were moving back to Inverness. Margaret Gauld says, 'My friend Alison and I went to see them leaving Fraserburgh in their Dormobile. John came across and pleaded with me to go with them but I was only 15 and wouldn't have been allowed. They gave me their autographs: *To Margaret, with love Johnny Lennon* and *To Margaret, with love Paul Ramon*.'

The second half of the week had a straight run of engagements: Wednesday night in a small church hall in the distillery town of Keith; Thursday in the sizeable Town Hall ballroom at Forres; Friday in the big Regal Ballroom in Nairn; and then, finally, Saturday back beyond Fraserburgh to Peterhead. Here they played in the compact side-street Rescue Hall, where a furniture exhibition was cleared away just in time for the locals to jive. Margaret Jack in Fraserburgh was very much an exception: young people hereabouts didn't have cars, and because public transport ended early the promoters arranged free buses from the outlying villages and slate-grey dwellings that dotted the farmlands.[28] For many, the bus to the dance was the excitement of the week, getting dressed up and collected from tiny hamlets and taken to a slightly bigger town where a hall was lit up and lively. Musicians passed through week after week after week, and one time it just happened to be the Beatles; it was so low-key it's little wonder there are no more photographs. As George would remember, with only some exaggeration, 'We were playing to nobody in little halls, until the pubs cleared out when about five Scottish Teds would come in and look at us. That was all. Nothing happened.'[29]

The train delivered them back into Liverpool on Monday 30 May, ten days after leaving. Mostly, the tour had been plain awful; George, for one, never had a good word to say about it. But, as Paul would reflect: 'It was a vital experience for us, because after that we knew it was no breeze – you'd have to work hard and sort out where the money was coming from. It taught us a lot of lessons. It gave us an insight into what it could be like.'[30]

The Beatles had played seven times in eight days – more than in the previous five months combined – and they'd learned plenty. They now knew themselves and one another better, and while Tommy Moore remained with them only another week or two, the others stayed put, and where the dust settled was who and where they were.

Two years later, the tour would be described on a Beatles management handout as 'rough and hard stuff, but it led to a beginning'. Less poetically, it *was* the beginning. Unlike the other groups who'd auditioned at Allan Williams' empty Wyvern club, the Beatles had little stage experience, and as a rock group, as a five-piece band with electric guitars and drums, they had none. The tour happened the wrong way round for them: they went on the road and found out about one another before they'd performed any local bookings. It was only now, on their return, that they would play closer to their own back yard.

15

Drive and Bash (31 May–15 August 1960)

The day the Beatles got back to Liverpool, the *Echo* ran a full-page editorial-ad for Nems. The store at 12–14 Whitechapel was the first occupant in a new-build, and Brian and Clive Epstein – but mostly Brian – designed every aspect of the interior in conjunction with architects. A lift and a mahogany staircase reached 'four floors of magnificent showrooms featuring televisions, records and domestic appliances' . . . but the emphasis was on records, Brian's preserve: classical on the ground floor, popular, jazz and 'Continental' in the basement. As the *Echo* stated, 'The ambition of Nems is to supply ANY record that is named – and to produce it almost immediately.' Nems of Whitechapel promised to be the best record shop in the north and, from the moment it opened, it was. Now 25, Brian wasn't interested in second best.

It wasn't just that he knew how to manage, it was the unabashed relish with which he went about it. The boy who'd been such an abject failure academically held his head as high as any who prospered. The ground floor featured a 42ft length of U-shaped counter and a suspended ceiling covered with more than a thousand LP sleeves – it was the first time in Britain such a ceiling had been created and was soon copied by others.

Delegating was always difficult, Brian struggling to accommodate standards that didn't match his own, but he chose staff well. He kept Peter Brown as manager of the Great Charlotte Street branch and among the thirty or so new appointments at Whitechapel was a full-time secretary, Beryl Adams. They all learned, the hard way, to live with his insistence on perfection, and to recognise his mood swings. Mr Brian's behaviour earned their loyalty but kept them ever wary; arrogant and adorable, cutting and charming, flawed but fair, here was a man they could love and hate in the same breath. He operated between the shop floor, a small office in the basement and a big one above the shop: he'd taken a good chunk of the Whitechapel development's upper-storey offices too, enabling him to add the Nems name in four huge letters on the fascia, emphasising (tastefully, of course) its pre-eminence.

Not everyone realised that his RADA London voice, refined air, immaculate appearance, manicured nails and use of male fragrance (at a time when barely no man in Liverpool touched it) indicated a 'queer' – people simply weren't used to thinking that way – but *to those who knew* he was patently identifiable. It was precisely two years since his harrowing ordeal in Sefton Park at the hands of a violent blackmailer, and his assailant had been released from jail. Brian's friend Yankel Feather would never forget a certain conversation they had in the shop: 'I said, "Brian, I wish you would look at me and not over my shoulder when we're talking." He said, "I am looking at that young man on the corner. He has just come out of prison and he is the young man who attacked me." I said, "You'd better ring the police then," and he said, "Oh no, I am taking him out to lunch."'[1]

The opening of the new Nems on 31 May brought traffic in central Liverpool to a standstill. Brian had excellent relations with the record companies (both Decca and EMI provided paid ads for the *Echo*'s special page) and he arranged with Decca for the actor-musician Anthony Newley to make a personal appearance and cut the ribbon. There was a huge turnout, spilling across the width of the street. Brian had met several pop stars but it hadn't quite been his scene before: he was shy, blushed in their presence, and was over-anxious not to bore them. But he got along famously with Newley, and so did Queenie and Harry when Brian drove the Londoner back to Queens Drive for cocktails and dinner. Brian thought it was great that Newley was normal, natural and without pretensions, concluding this was 'how a real star should behave'.[2]

In its first trading month, Nems Whitechapel achieved twice the turnover of the Walton Road store's record counter for all of 1959. Such retail muscle deserved a special discount and Brian made proposals to Decca, EMI and his other main accounts, as a consequence of which he became one of the first visitors to EMI House, the great organisation's new purpose-built London headquarters. A businesslike discussion ensued with R. N. (Ron) White, EMI Records sales manager, Brian asking for a 2.5 per cent discount if Nems achieved EMI record sales over £20,000 a year. White insisted this wasn't company policy but Brian won the day: White consulted the EMI directors and came back with a convenient fudge – they would call it a 'Co-operative Advertising Allowance'. Such was EMI's fear that others in the retail trade might learn of it, prompting a flurry of similar requests, White asked that whenever Brian wrote to him about it he marked the envelope Strictly Confidential. The secret was safe with Brian, whose initiative and polite perseverance saw EMI write a cheque to Nems for £564 at the end of the first twelve months.

Five years after EMI appointed (Sir) Joseph Lockwood as chairman, its image had grown in parallel with its fortune: the British company was a global player in its many fields of operation. At 20 Manchester Square, just off Baker Street, EMI House was among the first office blocks of a new post-war epoch, a bright light Sixties building with eye-catching architectural features, such as an open balcony on each storey that looked down to the main entrance. Once-scattered staff came together for the first time in the offices. The popular A&R departments, formerly in Great Castle Street, occupied a wing of the fourth floor. The Parlophone set-up was typical: George Martin and his assistant Ron Richards were in separate outer offices (as the boss, George's had the piano for routining musical arrangements) and their respective secretaries Judy Lockhart Smith and Shirley Spence shared an office in between. George and Judy maintained, too, their love affair, of now perhaps four years' standing; the utmost discretion remained essential because Sheena was refusing to grant George a divorce.

The man who'd delivered rock and roll to the masses was now out of the army, his tour of duty done. The pelvis-thrusting, hip-swivelling, lip-curling young Elvis Presley who'd sexually terrorised America stood tall as a model patriot, tolerated and for the most part tolerable. He looked leaner and fitter than before, in fact he looked just great, but he just wasn't the Elvis they'd drafted back in '58. Three weeks after returning as a civilian superstar he was in Miami, wearing a dinner-jacket and bow-tie in a TV special with Frank Sinatra, who'd never before had a good word to say about him. Everything was fine now because rock was tamed ... wasn't it?

In Liverpool, diehards were struggling a little: his new single A Mess Of Blues was all right, but it wasn't Heartbreak Hotel or Baby Let's Play House, though *surely his next one'll be great.* Other wonderful records were coming out of America anyway. Rock was missing in action at corporate level, but the robust, vitally unconventional independent labels across the States – the bravura blend of two immigrant classes, blacks and Jews – continued to pump out great new R&R, R&B and more. Prize masters were picked up for Britain by Decca's London label and lapped up in Liverpool, where groups of young men stood in browseries at Nems and elsewhere, absorbing every note before going out to play them in the clubs and ballrooms.

It seems everyone was blown away by Money (That's What I Want) by Barrett Strong. *Disc*'s review half got it – 'Girl group and jungly rhythm group make plenty of noise and half the time it seems as if Barrett's struggling to overcome them'[3] – but more yet was excitement, beat, riffs, an irresistible sparse arrangement, soulful vocals and a lyric that announced the singer didn't want sex, he wanted *money*. The London label revealed the source of the recording as 'Anna, Detroit', and it was only later that the full implication of this was realised: it was the first spark from a new musical expressway, the moment when the black urban Detroit sound jump-started across the Atlantic, a pulsing production line of Motor City rhythm and melody. Money was the second Tamla (or Tamla-related) record released in Britain, and though it wasn't a hit, it was *heard*, and things were never quite the same again.

Money became John Lennon's song, one he always sang, a scarred boy who craved money *and* sex and was injecting passion into every performance. It was almost certainly the lyric of Money, released in April, that prompted him to say the line 'The best things in life are free' when Johnny Gentle had been looking for help with his song in Inverness.*

All the Beatles, but especially George, were Duane Eddy fans, and his ultra-twangy Shazam! lodged in their minds, as did Road Runner by Bo Diddley ('I'm a roooooroad-runner *honey*!'), and they liked Only The Lonely, a richly dramatic record by Roy Orbison, a name new to them though he'd been around in the States for some years. Cut Across Shorty, a storytelling B-side of the late Eddie Cochran's Three Steps To Heaven, was another big one, and Paul was especially enamoured of the Coasters' new take on the 1940s Spanish song Besame Mucho, issued in Britain at the end of April.†

Another hot record was the novelty number Alley Oop, by the Hollywood Argyles. It was a guaranteed crowd-pleaser: part-spoken, part-sung and allowing for lots of audience participation, ideally suited to someone who could sing but didn't have the greatest range, someone who'd never sung on stage before and needed to experience a microphone in front of his face. And so it proved for Ringo Starr at Butlin's, six nights a week in the Rock and

---

* In turn, the Money line likely came from the 1927 song The Best Things In Life Are Free, a hit for several singers and the title of a 1956 Hollywood biopic about its composers, Lew Brown, Buddy DeSylva and Ray Henderson.
† The London label always cited the original US source. The Coasters' Besame Mucho was on Atlantic's imprint Atco (New York), Duane Eddy's Shazam! on Jamie (Philadelphia), Bo Diddley's Road Runner on the Chess imprint Checker (Chicago), Roy Orbison's Only The Lonely on Monument (Nashville) and Eddie Cochran's Cut Across Shorty on Liberty (Hollywood) – all America's musical hotspots covered in one influential sweep.

Calypso Ballroom in the summer of 1960. He'd decided to go, and had gone.*

Iris Caldwell says her brother helped Ringo make the decisive move. Mere days away from leaving for Wales, the Hurricanes needed Ringo even more than he needed them, so Rory generously bought him one or two new pieces for his kit and laid it on thick about all the fun they'd have at Butlin's. More than that, he went to Admiral Grove and pleaded with Elsie and Harry to let Richy go. For at least a short while afterwards, recalls Iris, 'they said Rory ruined his life'.[4]

The ultimate decision, though, was Richy's alone, and after see-sawing since February his mind was made up. He was earning £6 a week at Hunt's and about £8 extra from playing in Liverpool with the Hurricanes, but at Butlin's he'd pocket £16 for twenty-five hours' work a week. *Work?* Just loads of drumming and the time of his life, combined. He'd said in 1958 'This is the job for me', and now, two years on, here was his big opportunity, onwards and upwards to the London Palladium. He told Elsie and Harry the news they dreaded. 'I said I wanted to take the chance – and, in the end, they said, "OK, it's your life, if you want to mess it up. We've tried our bit."' As they would tell enquiring journalists just over three years later, 'We knew it was the one thing that would make him happy.'[5]

Richy quit his apprenticeship with only a year to go. People at Hunt's told him he was stupid. He'd started in the factory a sickly lad coming up 16; he was leaving a tough-minded bugger of almost 20. On Friday 27 May he gave Roy Trafford his T-square, handed in his union card and punched the clock for the last time – and while the Beatles were up in Nairn, playing with Johnny Gentle, Richy was down the boozer with his ex-workmates, sinking farewell ales.

Meanwhile, what of Gerry McGovern? She'd put up with her fiancé's musical sideline all the time they'd been together, and had latterly been making her position clear: *me or the drums*. Richy was blunt: she could hang around and wait for him if she wanted, but he was off to Butlin's and wouldn't be back for three months.

There were a few things to do in what would be his last week in Liverpool until September. Having just relinquished his engineer's union card, Richy went straight into the Musicians' Union. Rory and the Hurricanes had to be members to play at Butlin's – the weekly subscription was one shilling, whether

---

* To Ringo and the rest of the Hurricanes, Alley Oop was just a song. Americans knew it as a syndicated newspaper comic strip, a caveman from one million years BC having time-machine misadventures. The strip led to the song, a novelty number 1 on *Billboard* and *Cash Box* (and a smaller hit in Britain where it was issued on the London label). The recording session was a happily drunken affair produced in Los Angeles by Kim Fowley.

they liked it or not. They also bought matching grey suits and rock 'n' roll shoes and played the Cavern's second weekly Rock Night.

Saturday 4 June was the big day. Rory and Johnny Guitar managed to get the use of a van, and Elsie and Harry waved their Richy off by the Empress pub. By six in the evening the Hurricanes had navigated their way through North Wales to the Butlin's camp at Pwllheli, and were unloading. Johnny's diary records that, to begin with, they didn't stay in the camp but in digs outside, a bus ride away. Johnny shared a room with bass guitarist Wally, rhythm guitarist Chas with Ringo, and Rory had one to himself . . . except that wasn't exactly who they were now: as Rory, Johnny and Ringo all had cowboy names, so Chas O'Brien and Wally Eymond changed theirs too, to Ty Brian and Lu Walters.

Saturday was campers' changeover day at Butlin's and the live band didn't play, but there they were in the Rock and Calypso come Sunday night at eight. Butlin's official photographer lined them up for the camera, five of them *sharp* in big quiffs, broad smiles, grey suits, matching top-pocket handkerchiefs and black-and-white winkle-pickers, watched all the while by the young men and women for whom they were about to rock. They jived and swung until 11.15 and then – before everyone went back to the chalets, though not necessarily their own – they joined with Redcoats and campers to sing (to the tune of Ray Noble's Goodnight Sweetheart) Butlin's nightly closedown anthem. It was going to be a long, cracking and very British summer.

The same day the Hurricanes were heading for Wales, 4 June, an ad hoc group of 2i's rockers calling themselves the Jets were heading for Hamburg. In the last days of May, a squat German with a *Klumpfuss* had journeyed to England look-ing for a group to bring custom to his bar. It was Bruno Koschmider from the Kaiserkeller, and though it's impossible to say for sure, he probably arrived look-ing for Allan Williams, the little entrepreneur who'd visited his bar earlier in the year, talking the talk but playing him a *kaput* tape.* Seemingly, Koschmider didn't know Williams was from Liverpool, or he'd forgotten, or he decided to go to London first. Whichever it was, he hobbled his way to the 2i's Coffee Bar at 59 Old Compton Street, the only surefire place to find rock 'n' roll, where the sound of electric guitars sliced the air in aromatic Soho, shooting up from the cellar.

Talking through a local interpreter, Koschmider fell into conversation with

---

* There are so many conflicting (and missing) details about why Koschmider went to London that the truth will never be known for certain, but it's reasonably safe to assume that if Williams hadn't pricked his interest in the first place it wouldn't have happened.

one of its denizens, Iain Hines, a pianist, and from then on it all happened fast. It took only hours for Hines to put together a scratch group of talented scruffs happy to go to Hamburg and rock for good money, one being a guitarist called Tony Sheridan, as unreliable and temperamental as he was brilliant.* Five guys and their gear took the boat-train over, and on the night of Sunday 5 June, almost on the beat the Hurricanes struck up at Butlin's, the Jets opened in the Kaiserkeller and ballsy British rock 'n' roll was up and running in the notorious red-light area of Hamburg. Here was a cultural turning point of great proportion.

And again that same 4 June, the Beatles were underway on Merseyside at last – they were the resident group for council-run 'Dances For Youth', staged every Saturday at the Grosvenor Ballroom, an attractive red-brick hall in Liscard, Wallasey. It was one of three good contracts – all over the water from Liverpool – that Allan Williams fixed for them while they were in Scotland: there was also a deal with a local dance promoter to present them (and Gerry and the Pacemakers) at the same venue on the coming Whitsun bank holiday, and for six consecutive Thursday nights at a hall in Neston, deeper into rural Wirral.†

There was constant confusion over their name. To Williams they were the Silver Beetles and, because he wrote this into the contracts, the promoters billed them that way. The Whitsun dance was also advertised in the *Liverpool Echo* – the Beatles' first mention in their city's great nightly paper; even though it said 'the Silver Beetles', Paul (or Mike) tore out the tiny classified and kept it always. Given the chance to explain themselves, however, the Beatles made sure it was written properly. A Wirral newspaper reporter spoke to them on their opening night at Neston Institute on Thursday 2 June – the Beatles' first head-lining and advertised performance anywhere – and the resulting article had it right: they were the Beatles with an 'A'. As for their individual names, though, the Scotland legacy was (mostly) lingering on: 'John Lennon, the leader, plays one of the three rhythm guitars, the other guitarists being Paul Ramon and Carl Harrison. Stuart Da Stael [*sic*] plays the bass, and the drummer is Thomas Moore.'[6]

Tommy had yet to lay down his sticks – he continued to put his factory job on the line in pursuit of a little extra cash. John and Stu returned to the art school from Scotland probably unscathed from taking the time off. Paul was

---

* Anthony Esmond Sheridan McGinnity, born Norwich, 21 May 1940.
† The local dance promoter was Les Dodd of Paramount Enterprises, based in Wallasey. He paid the Beatles £10 for the Monday date and £9 every Thursday at Neston Institute. As fees went in Liverpool at this time, these were above average, and Williams didn't always take his 10 per cent commission.

back in a school blazer, a professional musician fibbing his way into Liverpool Institute, delivering the forged letter from his father and reassuring teachers he was feeling much better now thanks, but no, he didn't know about the written Art test that meant he was sure to fail.

Carl had the most miserable task. Returning hungry and broke from a rotten tour was one thing, being idle about the house quite another. He'd thrown away his Blackler's apprenticeship and left without a reference, so finding another job was going to be tough. He had no exam passes, nothing to suggest he was fit for anything other than labouring, and instead of contributing to the household he was back to cadging. Beyond all that, he was falling behind with the sixteen-shilling weekly drip for the Futurama. Harry Harrison was a patient and fair-minded father but he'd always been a hard worker. Also, through his role on the transport employees' social committee, he knew just how tough it was for a man to earn a living from entertaining. How on earth was George going to manage it, playing his guitar?[7] Louise continued to give her youngest child every support, but she also worked industriously; never a shirker, she couldn't approve of George being one. The Harrisons always paid their way honestly.

Get out and get a job, son.

To begin with, George quietly took the heat. He kept his head down and his heels dug in and showed them the shillings earned from Williams' bookings. All the same, demands that he *do something* mounted inexorably until, by about the third week of June, George couldn't stand being got at any longer and got out. He quit, moving out of the family home and into Gambier Terrace.

It was a boldly independent step for a 17-year-old, and obligingly generous of John and Stu to shove aside some debris and make space. Though the studio room was a pigsty, from George's point of view here was sanity, space to think, to smoke, to play his guitar, to be with John and Stu. No one here would be beating his drum about finding a job or telling him what to do. Louise realised the situation had to be handled with care; in the meantime, George was safe with his gang, three Beatles in one room.*

They were pocketing maybe six stage hours a week now and, on the back of Scotland, starting to smooth out a few of the rough edges. Chris Huston, lead guitarist with Wallasey group Bob Evans and his Five Shillings, went along to

---

* It might have been four. George's sister-in-law Irene has said 'the idea was, they were all going to live in this flat' – which seems to suggest Paul also had the option of joining them. Paul already spent most weekends here but stayed at home in the week. There is no further information about this, and there's also no definitive knowledge regarding when George stopped living here and returned to Speke, but he did, probably a week or two into July. He reverted to his previous routine: Monday to Friday at home, weekends in John and Stu's room with Paul and sometimes Cyn.

the Grosvenor every week and remembers them as 'rowdy – a Liverpool group
off their turf, coming to Wallasey. The boundaries of our world were very small,
so if you were a Liverpool group playing the Wirral you felt like you needed a
passport.

> Their stage presentation was totally absent – they just rock and rolled with
> a fury. Stuart was off to the side and obviously couldn't keep up with them.
> He had no image to project yet – in fact, his image was *not projecting*. He was
> very slight, with a big Hofner bass. The lasting impression I have of them at
> the Grosvenor is Stuart standing to one side, sort of on the outside, and the
> others having a rare old time playing Red Sails In The Sunset and Chuck
> Berry, good old rock and roll.[8]

The Grosvenor set-up was common to most town ballrooms in Britain: girls
stood on one side of the hall, boys on the other. Patrons (as managements liked
to call them) might arrive in mixed groups but they'd separate at the door, even
couples. Girls danced together in ones, twos and groups, often around their
handbags, and occasionally went across to fetch their boyfriends to jive with
them. The lads stood in groups, sneering, smoking, posing, eyeing up the birds
and sizing up the next fight. Musicians had to be tough to play such places –
being caught up in battles was always a possibility, merely observing them
enough to turn the stomach. Skirmishes could be ignited in an instant. Paul
recalls one Grosvenor night when a huge fight broke out and he found himself
involved. 'I tried to save my Elpico amp, my pride and joy at the time, and one
Ted grabbed me and said, "Don't move son or you're fucking dead."'[9]

Violence was commonplace in leafy Neston as well as in urban Wallasey. The
Beatles saw plenty of it when they played the Institute those six Thursdays from
June into July. Supporting them here some weeks were Heswall group Keith
Rowlands and the Deesiders, and their guitarist Pete Bolt still remembers the
unique impact made on him by John and Paul, and also the unusual reaction
they got from girls on the dance floor: 'It was the first time I'd heard people
singing in harmony. They weren't just a backing group with a singer out front,
it was the two of them together at the microphone – most unusual, and good.
I was also impressed with their clean starts and finishes to songs, and how they
engaged the audience with a bit of chat, especially some girls who positioned
themselves around the stage.'[10]

The Beatles' routine on Saturdays was to rendezvous at the Jacaranda and
be driven across to Liscard. One time – perhaps the second week, 11 June –
Tommy Moore failed to show. His kit was there but he wasn't. Allan Williams
was at home when Stuart phoned to say they still hadn't left, even though they

were due on stage imminently. Williams had a Jaguar and was, by unconquerable compulsion, a lethally fast driver; he dashed over to the Jac, collected the four Beatles and they roared off to Tommy's house in nearby Toxteth. Their hammering on his door was answered from an upstairs window: it was Moore's woman, shouting, 'What do you want?' Williams said, 'Where's Tommy? He's supposed to be playing,' and the woman gave them all a right Liverpool mouthful: 'Yez can *piss off* – 'e's not playing with yez any more, we've 'ad enough, 'e's at the bottle factory.' Williams and the Beatles sped down to Garston – to 'Brummer Striving Street', factory after strike-ridden factory – and there was Moore, in his overalls, doing the 3–11 shift. They pleaded with him to play but it wasn't on: he was stuck at work and his old woman had made it clear – ditch the group and stick to the job or I'm off.

Williams shot the Beatles through the Mersey Tunnel and up to Liscard, where he dropped them off and returned home. Setting up was a simple affair: you put the amps down on stage, plugged in and started. Soundchecks didn't exist. They set up the drums too, and before the opening number John asked if anyone fancied helping them out. He hadn't reckoned on a great bruising Ted, the leader of the gang, stepping up and having a thrash, nor still his insistent suggestion they use him every week from now on, OK? Williams had to speed back across later in the evening to talk them out of trouble.

Being drummerless was their old, old problem, though their brain-racking on the matter didn't extend to calling on Pete Best, the quiet lad who, they knew, had a kit *and* was idle up at his mum's Casbah. 'A series of drums came and went and came', John wrote of this period a few months later. History doesn't record all the names and the Beatles never remembered them.

With money from their weekly dates over the water, on 14 June the Beatles bought an amplifier at Hessy's. It does seem to have been a group purchase, possibly involving a spot of subterfuge. George was believed by Hessy's to still have a job, so he went down as the main name. Unable to use his mother as guarantor this time, they embroiled Glynne Trower, a mature student at Liverpool College of Art who'd supported the buying of Stu's bass. More than the entire fee from one of the Wirral dates, £10, was staked as deposit on a Selmer Truvoice (fifteen watts, two inputs and a carrying handle), by far the best amp they'd had, and it was put to good use right away when, around Paul's 18th birthday, 18 June, and probably at his house, the Beatles made further amateur recordings of themselves. As Paul remembers, 'Sometimes I'd borrow a tape recorder – a Grundig with a little green eye – [or] John would manage to borrow one, and we'd go around my house and try to record things. I seem to remember recording Hallelujah, I Love Her So, because I had the Eddie Cochran record. They were very much home demos, very bad sound quality.'[11]

It's the second such tape to survive from 1960, and of far greater value than the first. It runs about forty-seven minutes and has nineteen distinct songs or jams, enabling a clearer insight into the Beatles' abilities, ideas and humour, illustrating where they were good and where they weren't. There's no drummer and also little or no George – either he wasn't at these sessions (there seems to have been more than one) or was present only briefly. A few songs feature only John and Paul but mostly it's three guitarists, John and Paul plus Stu.

The performance is unpolished but there's greater confidence and cohesion than before, the result of their stage time. Stu's bass playing has improved, and though he's far from accomplished he's also beyond a beginner: some fingers find the right notes some of the time. His greatest struggles come in the few untitled and uninspiring jams, even though their twelve-bar structure is suited to less technical musicians. In these, the Beatles sound positively bad.

It's when they sing that it works. They do several 'current' numbers. Paul takes Hallelujah, I Love Her So and two good versions of Wild Cat (Gene Vincent, 1959); he also does Les Paul and Mary Ford's The World Is Waiting For The Sunrise, as sung by the Nerk Twins in the pub at Easter. John sings Matchbox (Carl Perkins) and a pair of recently revived oldies, That's When Your Heartaches Begin (recently recorded by Elvis) and I'll Always Be In Love With You (by Liverpool's Bing Crosby soundalike Michael Holliday), and they riff through a couple of Duane Eddy instrumentals, Ramrod and Movin' And Groovin'.

Best of all are the six Lennon-McCartney Originals, including three that were possibly new and would never surface again, seemingly titled Some Days, You Must Write Every Day and You'll Be Mine. Paul sings lead on all three and was the main or sole writer. You'll Be Mine is particularly entertaining – Paul sings like Caruso and John like an Ink Spot, dropping into an outlandish rich-brown spoken section that epitomised their collective love of the absurd and his own fondness for wordplay. There's also the earliest-available recordings of One After 909, I'll Follow The Sun and Hello Little Girl. One After 909 is clearly a diamond in the rough, polished by John and Paul's attractive harmonising. I'll Follow The Sun is Paul alone, guitar and voice, save for someone (probably John) slapping a guitar case. Hello Little Girl is a Nerk Twins treat that sheds welcome light on what John always called *his first song*, written at 17 when the influence of Buddy Holly was palpable.[12]

With their Truvoice amp, tape and regular bookings, the Beatles were beginning to motor, a position they owed entirely to one man. As Rod Murray observes, 'None of them had any business sense, and without Allan Williams I don't think they would have got anywhere.' Williams was the only person getting them work: the other Liverpool promoters didn't even know of their existence, except for Brian Kelly, who was miffed they hadn't turned up at Lathom Hall the other week and would take some persuading before trying them again. It was also very handy they were managed by a man who owned his own café and club – it became their second home, their daily hang-out, and they played here too, in the coal-hole basement, on occasional Monday nights. Girlfriends could tag along if they obeyed the rules: Dot says she and Cyn were allowed to sit with John and Paul when they talked music but they had to stay silent – 'We weren't allowed to open our mouths.'[13]

It was through the Jacaranda that the Beatles found another drummer. Norman Chapman was 22, newly married and working as a picture-frame maker at Jackson's, the art shop opposite the Jac (scene of many a John Lennon 'slap leather' episode since 1957). He also had a £20 drum kit, and – unable to play it at home – had arranged the use of a vacant attic space on the corner of Slater and Seel Streets so he could practise without disturbing anyone. One night, while a Beatle or two were sitting in the Jac wondering how they were ever going to find themselves another *fuckindrummer*, the sound of Chapman's percussion drifted in through the doorway. Paul presented himself at Jackson's the following day and asked if he wanted to play with the Beatles that night, as they had a booking. Chapman did, and stayed.*

Allan Williams remembers the Beatles' latest drummer as 'one of the best they had, a tall and very friendly man, a bit on the quiet side but a very good player'.[14] Chapman joined them in their weekly round of dates at Neston and Liscard, and occasionally at the Jacaranda, and seems to have been closer to them than Tommy Moore ever was, even hanging out a little at Gambier Terrace. ('I went there from time to time. It was something you had to see to believe: ashes in the middle of the floor, cans and bottles, drawings all over the wall.') As much as he was enjoying himself, though, Chapman already knew his days with the Beatles were numbered. Born in 1937, he was among the penultimate batch of young men called up for National Service. His conscription had been deferred while he worked his five-year frame-making apprenticeship, but now that was over and a manila envelope bearing the words On Her Majesty's Service was due any day.

Also dropping into the Gambier Terrace pit was a special guest, Royston Ellis, 'King of the Beatniks'. The bearded bard, who featured in TV documentaries

---

* Norman Chapman, born Liverpool, 31 December 1937. The other Beatles never publicly spoke about him and there are no photos of them together. He died aged 57 and was interviewed only once about it, by Spencer Leigh, the source of the quotes and information used here.

and press articles whenever an offbeat teenage angle was needed, was in Liverpool to read his poetry at the university on 24/25 June, and he swiftly found himself drawn into the Beatles' company. The conduit was George, who (with nothing else to do while John, Stu and Paul were in school) was hanging around the Jac when the wandering coffee-bar poet traipsed in, drawn by hip radar to 'the happening place'. Avowedly 'trying everything', Ellis was an active bisexual in this period of his life and he took an immediate fancy to George: 'He looked fabulous with his long hair and matelot-style striped T-shirt, very modern, which is why I deliberately spoke to him. I was nineteen and he was seventeen and we clicked right away.'[15] George took Ellis, his typewriter and his duffel-bag back to Gambier Terrace to meet John and Stu. A rapport was quickly established and Ellis was invited to 'crash' for a few days – yet another occupant for the filthy back room.

Born in February 1941, Ellis was younger than John and Stu but had broader life experience, having grooved around the country, appeared on TV and radio, been published as a poet and writer, and experimented with sex and drugs. To the *Daily Mirror* he was 'a weirdie from weirdsville' but to John Lennon he was 'England's answer to Allen Ginsberg', speaking something like their language.[16] He'd said young people not seeking work weren't layabouts but 'prospectors', and that no self-respecting teenager should marry a virgin. ('That remark alone generated fees to keep me comfortable for a year,' he recalls.) Also, he was friendly with Cliff Richard and, in particular, with Cliff's backing group the Shadows (formerly the Drifters). They provided a rock soundtrack when Ellis recited his poetry at occasional public readings, sessions he called 'Rocketry'.

His Liverpool University audience didn't dig him at all. The Beatles were much more his kind of people, and – in an unadvertised appearance down the Jac – they stepped into the Shadows' shoes and backed him in a spot of Rocketry. Paul really enjoyed the experience but was taken aback by some of the words, like this stanza from the poem 'Julian':

> Easy, easy,
> break me in easy.
>
> Sure I'm big time,
> cock-sure and brash,
> but easy, easy,
> break me in easy.[17]

Surely this was *queer sex* he was talking about! Paul worried it was about 'shagging sailors' while attempting to find the right guitar notes to set it off.[18]

Ellis's bisexuality was an eye-opener for the Beatles, as he remembers: 'There was an expression, "Do you still love me?", and I think I must have said it to John because all the eyebrows went up … "What?!" And then I gave them a lecture about the Soho scene and said they shouldn't worry, because one in four men were queer although they mightn't know it.' The remark bit deep. As Paul says, 'We looked at each other and wondered which one it was. "[It] must be one of us, because there's four of us … Oh fucking hell, it's not me, is it?"'[19]

Most memorably of all, Royston Ellis gave the Beatles their first drugs experience. Not long afterwards, he would write of his amazement that they didn't know of the Benzedrine-impregnated cardboard strip curled inside a Vicks nasal inhaler, and how it produced a high when chewed.[20] Several were present in the flat, including John, Stu, George, Paul, Rod Murray and Bill Harry, but the idea of taking something to feel euphoric, or in some way altered, appealed most especially to John. He was the closest to Ellis in outlook: he wanted to try everything life could offer, and maybe, only maybe, ask questions later.* His art school friend Jon Hague vividly remembers a night in the Cracke when John poured pint after pint down his throat and remarked, 'If only we didn't have to drink all this liquid' – in other words, 'Wouldn't it be nice if there was a quicker way to get out of your head?'[21]

John always recalled the Benzedrine event with enthusiasm: 'Everybody talked their mouths off for a night and thought, "Wow, what's *this*?"' George was keen too: 'We cracked open a Vicks inhaler, ate it and sat up all night until about nine o'clock the next morning, rapping and burping up the taste.' But Paul was reticent. 'Probably they didn't give me that much, probably they kept it for themselves,' he says, indicating he passed up the opportunity … not entirely, but more or less. He was by nature more cautious than George and considerably more so than John, the great experimentalist who always tried everything with complete abandon. (*Something'll happen.*) Paul knew a little about drugs because his mum had been a nurse, and again he was also mindful of his age in this company. Ellis, although just sixteen months older, seemed far more mature; Stu was no longer a teenager, having turned 20 the week before; and John was on the cusp. George was never concerned by his youth but Paul was. 'I was … thinking "I'm really hanging out with a slightly older crowd here". So I was always cautious.'[22]

---

* John first smoked marijuana in this period. The only knowledge of this comes from an interview he gave fifteen years later: 'Some guy was showing us pot in Liverpool in 1960, with twigs in it, and we smoked it – we didn't know what it was, you know, we were drunk.' (Interview by Jean-François Vallée for French TV, 4 April 1975.) It's not clear who John meant by *us* and *we* but it probably wasn't Paul and George, one or both of whom first smoked dope with John in 1962.

The night passed in a blur of banter. Ellis says he developed a particular rapport with John and Stuart and that they discussed poetry, art and London. When he left, they spoke of doing it again some time: 'We were talking about how I wanted a band to come to London and back me on my Rocketry performances, and they were thrilled at the idea.' Art school studies finished the following Friday, 1 July, marking the end of Stu's fourth year and John's third and last because the college was waving him goodbye. The exam results, when they came through on 1 August, were just as expected: John failed and was out, Stuart passed the NDD, for which he received a certificate. The option was there for him to do a fifth year and attain the highest available qualification, the Art Teacher's Diploma (ATD), akin to a degree and entitling him to become a teacher . . . but both he and John were pondering a period as prospectors, and doing something again with Ellis was a definite possibility.

As for Ellis, so much was he enthused by the possibility of appearing with them again that he soon got the Beatles their first mention in a music paper. It was the 9 July edition of *Record and Show Mirror*, where a supercilious little article about 'the bearded sage of the coffee bars' ended 'he's thinking of bringing down to London a Liverpool group which he considers is most in accord with his poetry. Name of the group? *"The Beetles"!*'[23]

The British summer of 1960 produced endless rain, but that bothered few of Butlin's six hundred thousand happy campers because much of what they needed was indoors. With military precision, coaches transported up to seven thousand fresh faces to the Pwllheli camp gates every Saturday, to replace a similar number heading home. The Hurricanes played a three-hour session here six nights a week, and also every weekday afternoon for an hour in the Player's Bachelor Starmaker Contest. This was where they, the professionals, backed amateur singing talent shooting for pop fame in four daily heats and a weekly final.

It became a nightly feature in the Rock and Calypso for Rory to put aside his gold comb, stop leaping off the piano and announce *Starrtime!* – at which point the drummer tilted his head towards a microphone angled over his kit, found his singing voice (not brilliant but reasonable and characteristic) and bellowed Alley Oop while the band rocked and the jivers called and responded *Alley oop, oop, oop, oop-oop!*, laughing, clapping and cheering. Because few drummers sang, this was a real novelty for the Hurricanes, and Rory either left the stage or tried to blend into the background (never easy for him). When Ringo fancied a break from Alley Oop he sang Matchbox, the Carl Perkins record. As Johnny Guitar would reflect, 'He had a voice like a steamroller, and it went down well. He was a very good drummer and his personality came over when he was singing.'[24]

Ringo, too, was a teenager no more, having turned 20 on 7 July, and he'd been drumming three years now.* He was already hot enough to have played in Liverpool's best two skiffle groups, Eddie Clayton and the Darktown, and been picked by the top rock outfit, Rory's Hurricanes, and it was here at Butlin's that he really hit his stride. He wasn't a technical drummer, he was no Buddy Rich or Gene Krupa, he couldn't even do a proper roll, but he was a rock guitarist's dream. Though he projected *flash*, in his job he wasn't, he was just solid and reliable, metronomic, dead steady in all the requisite styles, tempos and beats, doing precisely what he was there to do and with the attitude that was pure Richy Starkey.

All the Hurricanes signed autographs for the holidaymakers. Those who asked for Ringo's had to be patient. His signature was prefaced with 'The Sensational', then he wrote 'Ringo Starr', then he added the drawing of a little star, then he double-underlined both his names, and then, in the channel between the two lines, to emphasise he was both singer and instrumentalist, he wrote 'Vcl' under Ringo and 'Drums' under Starr. Finally, to leave the fan in no doubt who'd been signing, he added 'Time' after Starr and 'Rory Storm & Hurricanes' underneath everything, underlined. This man was the consummate pro.

Questions about his rings were welcome, questions about his grey streak irritating: Lu Walters would recall him shouting angrily, 'It's natural!'[25] Plenty of girls found him fascinating. And Ringo, he just loved them all ... or as many as he could manage. A juke-box pumped out records when the Hurricanes took a break and he was easily the best jiver in the group, never short of a dance partner. Margaret Douglas, on holiday here from Liverpool, says, 'Ringo was a *brilliant* rock 'n' roll dancer. He knew all the moves.'[26]

That he did. Butlin's meant sex, sex and even more sex, week after glorious week for three solid months. The boy who'd lost his virginity in the Sefton Park grass and then had to make out in his hand-painted Standard Vanguard now enjoyed it between sheets. The Hurricanes had quickly ditched their outside digs and moved into the camp chalets, and though unmarried sex was outlawed, plenty were at it. All was fine so long as one of the parties cleared out before the chalet-maids came to clean. Ringo remembers the joys: 'A new coachload of girls would arrive every week and we'd be like, "Hi, I'm with the

---

* Rory was sorry his birthday was 7 January because he wanted the fuss of a Butlin's celebration, so he moved it six months to 7 July. Ringo never got to be the sole focus there on his special day, and Rory also changed his year of birth from 1938 to 1940, again matching Ringo. By way of revenge, Ringo counted both Rory's yearly birthdays towards his age, which was why, in a 1964 radio interview, he wished his pal 'a happy twenty-ninth'.

band." It was paradise for that. There'd be tears at the end of the week, and then a new coach. In a way it was part of the attraction of rock 'n' roll. I ended up living with a hairdresser in a caravan. It was growing up.'[27]

Butlin's also meant plenty of drinking. The alcohol culture here was strong, and with so many men and quite a number of women legless every night, the entertainers weren't going to miss out. Rory generally held back, too much of an athlete to find booze appealing, but Ringo drank heavily. As well as beer, he liked Scotch and Coke – a flamboyantly modern combination often queried by companions and barmen.

The Beatles had no holiday in 1960. Playing every week left no room for one, and this was all they'd ever wanted to do. On 30 June, a day or two after Royston Ellis's departure, Paul got himself a new guitar to go with their expensive new amp. His Zenith was retired after three years' loving service and in its place came Paul's first proper electric, a Rosetti Solid 7; it was a standard model for a right-hander, so he had to play it upside down and switch the strings around. The body was painted in what the company's *Melody Maker* ad called 'smouldering red', but apart from this and its 'American styling!' not much else could be said for the Solid 7 – it wasn't a very good piece. As Paul would say, 'Dad instilled in me "Never get heavily in debt", as a result of which I bought a cheap guitar.' After putting down a small deposit, weekly ten-bob repayments would bring the total price to £21.[28]

He was also conscious that the Beatles needed to look better. Their stage clothes had been 'off the peg' since the start of the Quarry Men, but now they had something custom-made for the first time. Paul's next-door neighbour – David Richards, at 22 Forthlin Road – was a tailor, and Paul bought some lilac-coloured velvet for him to make into four cool bright jackets. He says John, Stu and George weren't too keen to begin with, but then came to the house to be measured up.[29] The jackets were worn with their usual black 'drainies' and either black or white shirts, and new grey winkle-picker shoes that appeared to be made from crocodile skin. They also had something like uniform hair – greased back high on top, long and thick at the back, almost down over their collars – so with all this the Beatles had a definite *look* ... and they weren't the Hurricanes.

Such improvements, and more, helped lasso the Beatles their first fan. Pat Moran was an intelligent 16-year-old Catholic girl from Wallasey who went to the Grosvenor most Saturdays. Her mother died when she was nine and she was raised solely by her disciplinarian Irish father. 'He wouldn't let me wear any make-up and I couldn't wear trousers, only a skirt, and he'd knock hell out of me if I misbehaved. One time, I came home late from seeing the Beatles and he'd locked me out. He stood in the bathroom above the front door and shouted "You're late" and wouldn't let me in.'[30] Such was Pat's passion for the Beatles, it was all worthwhile.

> I loved their music and the way they played it. My favourites were Tutti Frutti, Long Tall Sally, Cathy's Clown and Whole Lotta Shakin' Goin' On – oh and Red Sails In The Sunset was *beautiful*. I can't say they were great musically because I don't know – my idea of music at that age was inexperienced – but they were certainly entertaining. They played music we knew, that we'd heard on the radio, but to hear them doing it was *different*: when John and Paul sang a rock and roll song together we'd all be dancing. John was the leader. He used to talk to Paul and then they'd play something, but Paul was also the leader in a way because he was very much part of it. Certainly it was between Paul and John as to who took the lead.
>
> Paul was my favourite. I can still picture him at the front with his guitar, left-handed. He was on the left side of the stage, then George alongside him, then John, and Stuart on the right.

Something in the Beatles touched Pat Moran deeply, in a way she'd never experienced or expected. Chatting to Paul at the Grosvenor, she gathered they had hardly any money and spent weekends in John's flat at Gambier Terrace, not always with much to eat. She had a job and wanted to give something back to them for all the pleasure they gave her, so every Sunday morning after church she took the ferry across the Mersey and the bus up from the Pier Head with a wicker basket of food for them.

> Friends went with me, I wouldn't have dreamed of going on my own, and we'd arrive about midday. They were always up – we never arrived to find them unclothed – but the flat was horrible. There weren't even chairs to sit on, so we'd either sit on a bed or stand leaning against the window. We'd just talk for a while, then I'd pick up the empty basket and go home to Wallasey. This happened maybe half a dozen times.
>
> They were so friendly and pleasant, no massive egos. Stuart was lovely: very quiet, gentle, a really nice guy, small with dark glasses, and with fairer hair than Paul. John was nice but *very* different. I got the feeling he wouldn't have bothered having us there if Paul wasn't friendly with me. So John accepted that – he opened the door and let us through. Cynthia was there once but I can't say she spoke to us. George didn't really say anything. He wasn't unpleasant, he used to say 'Hello' and 'What did you think of us last night?', but that was about it.

I mostly spoke to Paul. He was friendly and there was no unpleasantness about him at all – he didn't stand off or anything, he was just a nice boy. There was no sexual relationship between us, we were simply mates and I was a good girl, still a virgin when I married in my twenties. I'm sure others were willing to give themselves to him. He'd give me a hug when we met and we held hands when we walked together, but he treated me right. We occasionally met at the Jacaranda for a tea or coffee. I paid and that was right: I had a job and he didn't.

He was very chatty – he told me he was really McCartney, not Ramon, he talked about his songwriting and we laughed because it seemed such 'a teenage thing'. He talked a lot about the Beatles: how hard they needed to work to earn money and how they hoped to become famous. I always felt the Beatles were *determined*.

Paul called Pat Moran 'our number one fan', accepting her as both their first and their keenest, but her enthusiasm led to some sorry consequences at home. Her father demanded to know what-the-devil a good Catholic girl was doing chasing boys who played filthy rock and roll. And when these same boys began to shape her vocabulary – she started to say 'fab' and 'gear' because they did – he almost hit the ceiling (but hit her instead). In the end, she drove him so mad with her non-stop chattering – Beatles for breakfast, dinner and tea – that he pronounced it *a sin* and ordered the first Beatles fan to seek almighty God's forgiveness at confession. 'I had to tell the priest, "I spend too much of my time worshipping the Beatles." He just ignored me and said, as he always did, "Remember your prayers. Say five Hail Marys and four Our Fathers and you'll be forgiven."'

That mention of 'the Beetles' in *Record and Show Mirror* led, a week later, to a second. A born publicist, Royston Ellis knew how to manipulate a follow-up, writing a letter for publication that clarified a point in the first. He expressed his intention to find a group that would join him on TV appearances with Bert Weedon and the Shadows, and reiterated, 'For some time I have been searching for a group to use regularly, and I feel that the "Beetles" (most of them are Liverpool ex-art students) fill the bill.'

This, it seems, was enough to stir John and Stu into action. Of the many curious episodes that pepper the Beatles' story in 1960, here is one of the most fascinating, if frustratingly inconclusive. It goes something like this . . .

By 10 July, at the end of his three-year art school vacation, John had arrived at a key decision in his life: he would try to earn his living from the guitar. 'I became a professional musician the day I got a red letter from the art college saying "Don't bother coming back next September",' he later said.[31] Cyn would remember, 'John decided that this [music] was very definitely the life for him. All the ideas that everyone else had for him of making an impact on the art world faded into the back of beyond with incredible rapidity, and with almost no regret at all. Aunt Mimi was distraught. Her view of his future couldn't have been blacker at that time.'[32]

These events coinciding, it seems John and Stu decided to head south and hang out with Royston Ellis. Allan Williams is emphatic on the matter: he says John and Stu 'split the Beatles and went down to London'.[33] Norman Chapman would remember Stu asking him for a lift through the Mersey Tunnel one day so he (or he and John) could hitch-hike to London – 'They wanted to go down to London and become involved in this poetry-music scene.'

Beat poets led a nomadic life by definition. Ellis lived for periods in all sorts of places, but his main base was still his parents' house, at 31 Clonard Way, Hatch End, Pinner, Middlesex, a pleasant detached villa with the name Denecroft. This was the address he gave John while staying at Gambier Terrace. When Ellis arrived home one day his mother said he'd missed a visit from his 'beatnik friends from Liverpool'. He never knew how many or who had come, but – as insane as it appears – John and Stu (and/or as Ellis always thought – hoped – George*) had hitched the best part of two hundred miles, taken the trouble of locating his house in leafy Metroland, not stayed or left a message and then gone home again, never returning or making further contact. It makes no sense, but there it sits, illogical and incomplete.

Allan Williams remembers them being 'back in Liverpool within a week, because it didn't work out', at which point the Beatles 'reformed' as if they'd never been away. With bookings only every Saturday, it's conceivable they did all this without missing one, and perhaps that was always the intention. However, while three independent witnesses (Ellis, Williams and Chapman) all remember something happening, none of the Beatles ever mentioned it – though in their interviews they talked with candour about everything. So it must remain in doubt, an intriguing puzzle unlikely to be solved.

There are two additional curiosities which may or may not be incidental. One is that, in the last days of July, a group of Liverpool art school students, apparently including John and Stu, went to London (or tried to go) to see a Picasso exhibition at the Tate Gallery.

Second, and most fascinatingly, a set of photographs taken at this very time

---

* George once referred to Royston Ellis as 'a bearded guy from a suburb of London' (*Fifty Years Adrift*, p95), knowledge that could indicate he too made the long journey to Hatch End.

(mid-July 1960) in Stu and John's studio-bedroom-slum at 3 Gambier Terrace includes several people they knew but not John and Stu themselves – perhaps because they were on the Hatch End trip. It was published on 24 July in the national Sunday rag the *People* in a sensation-splash headlined THIS IS THE BEATNIK HORROR. It's as if a man on a flaming pie was pointing down at Flat 3, Hillary Mansions, Gambier Terrace, Liverpool 1. In six months, three Beatles moved in and the fourth was hanging out, the nation's best-known beat poet had come here to get them high, and now, when a Fleet Street journalist and photographer were looking to substantiate a load of old tosh about dirty beat-niks – reportage that could have been cooked up anywhere in the country – they landed in Stu and John's room.[34]

Though hugely amusing, the feature had one unfortunate side-effect: because the address was given (a 'three-roomed flat in decaying Gambier Terrace in Liverpool') and some of the occupants ('well-educated youngsters') were named, the landlord gave the tenant, Rod Murray, notice to quit. On 15 August, everyone – Rod, Diz, Ducky, Stuart, John and sundry other bodies who'd joined them – would be out on the street.

While all this was happening, the Beatles lost their drummer. Norman Chapman's call-up arrived and he was off. Not for him a backwater barracks posting: he was sent to Kenya for two years to help suppress the Mau Mau uprising. 'That could have been us,' the Beatles might have said, and probably did. They'd missed it by months.

This time, the bother of looking for a replacement was beyond them: the Beatles just contracted to a four-piece and Paul went on drums, a move that coincided with a delicate moment in his life. He'd left Liverpool Institute at the end of the summer term, on 21 July, and faced an unclear future. He didn't have to leave – within a month he'd know his two A-Level results, and there was always the option of retaking anything he failed, staying on yet another year. He hadn't ruled that out in as many words ... but he was never going to do it, just as he'd somehow neglected to arrange a college or university place for September. He wasn't going to be the only Beatle in school. Jim *clung* to the hope Paul would do the right thing and train to become a schoolteacher, but such plans were wafer-thin now. Paul had six weeks to sort himself out, or start looking for a job.

For the moment, drumming was his only occupation. He already had a kit (nominally his brother Mike's), assembled in the Quarry Men and Japage 3 days, and to these he added one or two pieces from Tommy Moore's set, so *carelessly* left behind in the Jac. Paul's kit now had a bass drum, a snare, two fixed toms, a floor tom, two cymbals and a hi-hat – quite the best kit they'd had. It looked pretty cheap but he got a piece of card, wrote *beatles.* on it in individual angular lower-case letters, and stuck it on the bass drum head.

But, as much as Paul liked exhibiting versatility, he was unhappy – he felt he'd been *lumbered*, that his multi-instrumental ability was tying him down. Who looked at the drummer? By rights, his place was out front, especially with his new guitar. Here he was, paying off the Solid 7 at ten bob a week and hardly getting to play it. Jealousy of Stu was stoked: Paul was in the back line while *he* remained out front (even if he was hiding and in dark glasses). One thing was for certain: Paul wasn't going to abandon singing. 'I was drumming with my hands, playing the hi-hat and bass drum with my feet and I had a broomstick stuck between my thighs on the end of which was a little microphone, and I'm singing "Tell me what'd I say ..." It wasn't easy!'[35]

Though John and George took turns behind the kit, enabling Paul to venture forward occasionally, drums was his main position for maybe three weeks, and it was one at which he was certainly accomplished. 'He was quite good at it,' George said. 'At least, he seemed OK. Probably we were all pretty crap at that point.'[36]

John, Stu, George and Paul played the Grosvenor as a quartet probably just once before the weekly dances came to a halt, stopped because of the violence. Though most of the three hundred or so teenagers – Pat Moran among them – caused no trouble, they lost their Saturday fixture and so did the Beatles. Now they had nowhere to play.

They weren't the only Liverpool group suddenly desperate for Allan Williams to *do something*. In mid-June, he'd signed a contract for Derry and the Seniors to appear in *Idols On Parade*, Larry Parnes' summer season in Blackpool. It was a fairish deal, up to six weeks at £75–90 a week between them from 17 July, enticing enough for the Liverpool musicians to quit their jobs. But then, at something approaching the eleventh hour, Parnes withdrew the offer. The relationship between the two entrepreneurs had gone into such a steep decline it was now terminated, which left Derry and the Seniors high and dry. They wasted little time making Williams aware he had to help them – and because there was no work anywhere in Liverpool, and because he was Allan Williams, he said he'd drive them all to London. They could look up his friend Tom Littlewood at the 2i's.

They arrived in Soho hot, hungry, tired and about to get incredibly lucky. Their first piece of good fortune was that the rock acts Littlewood managed, who normally sang in the 2i's tiny basement, were all on tour. With the stage more or less empty, Derry and the Seniors were free to get up and play. Then came a second stroke of luck, which Williams would rightly label 'a million to one chance'. In a coincidence so extraordinary it beggars belief, also sitting in the 2i's at that moment was Bruno Koschmider. He was back in London to find another English group for the Kaiserkeller.* 'It was like Stanley meeting Livingstone,' Williams says, with understandable lyricism. ('Herr Koschmider!' 'Herr Williams!') The great 2i's, wellspring first of British skiffle, then rock 'n' roll, completed the holy trinity by propelling Liverpool groups to Hamburg. As soon as Derry and the Seniors struck up their first number they blew the Londoners out of the room, just like Williams had told Koschmider they would. Bruno liked them, *ja*.

Williams couldn't very well conduct rival business in his friend's club, so he ushered Koschmider out of the 2i's and into Act One – Scene 1: the coffee bar opposite. Locating an interpreter in London's most cosmopolitan village presented no difficulty and soon the two men were shaking hands on the business agreement they'd floated at the start of February, by which Williams would send across to Hamburg any English entertainment Koschmider might want. Having come to London to find work for the Seniors, Williams produced a blank Jacaranda Enterprises contract from his briefcase; having been a stage magician before owning bars, Koschmider produced a Kaiserkeller rubber-stamp from his pocket. Williams wrote out the terms, Koschmider stamped it, and the two men signed. Derry and the Seniors would play thirty hours a week for two months, for £100 a week less 10 per cent for Williams. This was 24 July; seven nights later they were in Hamburg and ready to rock. As sax man Howie Casey recalls, 'We took cabs to Grosse Freiheit from Central Station. At this point, Hamburg just looked like any other city, foreign but still a city, and then suddenly we started to drive into a different area with lights and clubs. These naive boys were being driven into this hell-hole of iniquity – it was *marvellous*.'[37]

Allan Williams had landed a miracle for Derry & Co, but what of the Beatles? There was nothing, really. Those local bookings had dried up. He told them about Hamburg, saying his association with a club owner there might lead to something for them, but that was all he had. With debts mounting and nowhere to play, they needed something *now* ... and so it was that Williams fixed them their oddest job yet: to provide backing for a striptease artiste at his other-other operation, the shady 'private members' club in Liverpool 8 he jointly owned with Harold Phillips, his calypsonian comrade Lord Woodbine.

---

* Koschmider was looking for another group because the Jets had walked out on him. They found him dictatorial and bloody-minded, and he'd made them sleep in the Kaiserkeller, locked into a tiny office. They were offered more money and a better experience by a rival entrepreneur, Peter Eckhorn, a younger man who closed the Hippodrom, his family's old Reeperbahn circus, and on 9 July reopened it as a rock club, the Top Ten.

In bigger venues strippers disrobed to live music, here they did it to discs. A few days into August, though, they were sent a Manchester girl who insisted she'd strip only to a live band. Woodbine told Williams who told the Beatles a small fee was on offer if they'd play while 'Janice' stripped.* It was an indignity, but they were boys 'twixt 17 and 20 so there was only going to be one answer.

The line-up was still John, Stu, George and Paul, a foursome with Paul on drums, all in Mr Richards' lilac jackets. Janice handed them sheet music, including a Beethoven piece and, for her rousing finale, España Cañí, the so-called Spanish Gypsy Dance. In an article he wrote two years later, Paul recalled, 'We said, "We can't read music, sorry, but instead of the Spanish Fire Dance [*sic*] we can play The Harry Lime Cha-Cha, which we've arranged ourselves, and instead of Beethoven you can have Moonglow or September Song – take your pick … and instead of the Sabre Dance we'll give you Ramrod. So that's what she got. She seemed quite satisfied anyway.'[38]

So tiny was the stage, Janice had to romp right in among them. It was an act she prolonged as much as possible, long on *tease* and short on *strip*, but eventually it got most of the way there, down to a G-string. The Beatles feasted their eyes and then played her off as she returned to the coal cellar that doubled as a dressing-room.

Saddened as she was at no longer having the Beatles rock her every Saturday night, the main concern of Pat Moran, their first fan, was for the boys themselves. 'I knew they were hard up, that they weren't earning much or had jobs, and because I had a proper job I sent them money. I folded pound notes in such a way that they couldn't be seen through the envelope, and I also sent stamped addressed return envelopes so Paul would reply. He did, and he wrote *Beatles* in script on the back of them.' Pat had all sorts of plans: she offered to start a petition to get the Beatles more bookings; she offered to have a word with her uncle, Bill Gregson, who led the resident dance orchestra at the Tower Ballroom in New Brighton, to ask if he'd put the Beatles on; she even started to organise them a holiday at a little cottage in Rhyl, for which secrecy from her father was paramount ('He'd have most probably lynched me if he'd found out').

Two of Paul's letters back to Pat reveal pretty much what was going on for the Beatles at this moment. The first was written on Sunday 7 August and posted late on the 8th:

---

* The stripper's name has been reported as Janice, Janine and Shirley. For the sake of convenience, she is Janice here.

If it's OK, George (Carl) and I might be able to come – we fancy the idea of a holiday.

Oh yes! I hope your uncle can fix us up with something, anyway if he can't it'll make us get around and look for some good bookings ourselves – it works both ways. I hope.

Have you got your embroidered sweater yet, No. 1 fan?*

The second letter chased the first into the mailbox late on the Monday:

This note is to let you know that I think everything you're doing for us is great.

I've seen John since I wrote the first letter and he says he can come too if you don't mind. This is very nearly definite. See – we were promised some tours of Scotland, road shows, trips to Hamburg & everything but we don't believe any of them, & a couple of promises have been broken already, so we'll probably be able to come; we can hitch-hike down there. It's not far – is it?

I think it's a great idea about the petition.

You ask me if I'm offended by your giving me all these gear things; well, I'm not – I'm flattered and I don't know what to say! I don't know how you can do all this for us, you must think we're not bad, or else you're just a kind hearted type.

Everything was coming to a head. Individually and collectively the Beatles had drip repayments for equipment they'd no prospect of being able to meet, running the risk of Hessy's reclaiming them; Paul was coming under pressure at home for doing nothing about school or college – he wanted neither but the alternative meant being badgered into a job; George was enduring parental sermons along the same lines; John had mortally wounded Mimi (and aggravated her ulcer, she said) because he was unfit for proper work – plus, he'd pledged his future to a career she hated and which was petering out before it even started; and on top of everything else, John and Stu were being evicted from Gambier Terrace a week from now, had no place to go and no money to get there. They were on the brink.

Paul remembers their attitude at such times: 'We had this way of getting over problems – someone would say, "Well, what are we going to do now?" and

---

* Pat liked embroidery and she and Paul joked that she might make a sweater with *Beatles* and *No. 1 Fan* sewn into the front. (It never happened.)

we'd say, "Well, something'll happen," and the four of us believed that. Nobody would ever go, *"What do you mean, 'Something'll happen'? That's no answer!"* We'd go, "Yeah, something will happen." There was this, like, *faith.*'[39]

A call from Germany came through to Allan Williams at the Jacaranda around the same moment, Monday 8 August or thereabouts. Bruno Koschmider (via a translator) told him business at the Kaiserkeller was booming and now he needed a group for the Indra, a second bar he ran on Grosse Freiheit, where he was ceasing transvestite cabaret and switching to rock. He wanted to reopen in not much more than a week, on the 17th, so there was little time. Williams wasn't the kind to say no. He told the German not to worry, he would supply a group; Koschmider said the booking would be for two months, and because the Jets were a five-piece and the Seniors a five-piece (backing Derry the singer) the incoming group must also be a five. He was a stickler for such details.

In circumstances identical to their Johnny Gentle tour, the Beatles weren't first in line but grabbed the gig. The order of approach isn't known, but Williams went to Rory Storm and the Hurricanes, Cass and the Cassanovas and Gerry and the Pacemakers before turning to the Beatles. They all had drummers. The Cassanovas couldn't do it because they didn't want to go, preferred to stay a four-piece, and had some coming engagements in Scotland. Gerry said no because they were a quartet and didn't want to give up their day jobs, and Rory and the Hurricanes couldn't do it because of Butlin's. Had the British holiday season finished in mid-August and not the start of September, or had Koschmider been prepared to wait two more weeks, the Indra booking would have been theirs – but it didn't, and he wasn't. He wanted a group for the 17th; again the Beatles landed an opportunity because there were no other takers. Something like £18 a week each was on offer, and they'd probably have done it for nothing.

So strong was their determination and so bleak their situation, they said yes right away, though they had to be in Hamburg in about seven days and had to be a five-piece. If Koschmider hadn't been so insistent on this they could have gone as John, Stu, George and Paul; as it was, they had to find a fifth man – a drummer, obviously – and they had to find him *now*. No drummer, no Hamburg, end of story. So it was with real eagerness that they pounced on an *Echo* box-number classified ad that chanced to run, in tiny print, on 10 August: 'DRUMMER, young, free – KP 60 Echo'. They may not have seen it for a day or two (Paul's reply has an *Echo* date-stamp of the 12th), but it seemed to be the answer to their prayers. Paul offered the drummer an audition with the Beatles, said he'd need to be 'free soon' for a two-month trip to Hamburg, and that he could be reached at the Jacaranda club.

But that 'soon' came *too* soon. Allan Williams was telling the Beatles he'd personally drive them to Hamburg in his 'van', that three others would be joining them on the journey, and that they'd be leaving on the coming Monday morning, the 15th. By the time the *Echo* advertiser picked up Paul's letter and phoned the Jacaranda, it was too late – he was told the group called the Beatles had gone abroad with someone else in what might have been his place.[40] In the absence of the mystery drummer's instant reply, the Beatles made the call which everything suggests they'd been trying to avoid.

Pete Best hadn't been doing much since quietly and prematurely quitting school in March. He hadn't played his kit in four months, not with musicians at any rate. Approaching him meant, among other things, reopening relations with his mother. To John, Paul and George, she was the bossy woman who hadn't paid them their due at the Casbah seven months previously (they didn't forget such things), while to her they were the ungrateful wretches who'd walked out on her club after all she'd done for them. Pete they knew only as the boy who kept his head bowed and hardly said a word.

Paul was so emphatically pragmatic about getting him that John and George said he must make the call. Peter wasn't home, but Mrs Best confirmed he still had his drums and wasn't doing much at the moment. When Paul and Pete finally spoke – later the same day, probably Saturday – Paul said they'd been offered two months in Hamburg at about £18 a week each, that they were leaving on Monday, and if he was interested he should bring his drums into Liverpool and do an audition. Pete said yes, he would.

At the time, though, Paul was far from certain he'd be able to go to Hamburg himself, as was the case with most or all of them. He was desperate enough – £18 a week was a lot of money, 80 per cent more than his dad earned. Also, two months in Germany would make him miss the start of the next school year. For Paul this meant *problem solved*, for Jim it meant letting go of Mary's last dreams and aspirations. It was a biggie, so Paul enlisted his brother as an ally. Mike says he got him all shook up with the exciting possibilities – playing abroad! becoming famous! buying him presents! – until he was quite desperate for it to happen. Then Paul said, 'But do you think Dad'll let me go?'[41]

Jim was strongly against it, of course, but Paul chipped away and chipped away, he laid it on thick, he spread it thin, he sold it hard, he sold it soft, he got Mike to join in, he listed many pros and very few cons, he even appealed to his dad as a former bandleader. A betting man, Jim knew he was riding a loser. When he told Paul he would meet their manager, to hear him explain it, Paul saw the winning post just ahead. Yes, sure, he would get Allan Williams to come round and give him every reassurance ... and in the meantime he asked for his birth certificate, to get a passport.

None of the Beatles had been abroad before – unless they counted Ireland, where George went once or twice as a child. They all needed passports and were fortunate that Liverpool, as an international seaport, had a Passport Office open to personal callers and able to process applications fast. The provision of a birth certificate was compulsory with every application ... and Mimi told John she didn't know where his was.

Now he was in trouble. They were leaving Monday morning, the 15th, and when he found this out it was already the 10th or 11th. A passport could be got quickly enough, but if John first had to apply for another birth certificate he mightn't make it.

As Cyn has said, Aunt Mimi's view of John's future 'couldn't have been blacker'. She was simply *desperate* he didn't fritter away his prospects by going off to play silly guitar, and she was furious about his wanton sabotage of the college course she'd encouraged and supported him through. He'd defied her once too often, so when John did his best to fire her up about Hamburg, bragging his guitar would earn him '£100 a week', she refused to be stirred and said sorry, she just couldn't find the birth certificate.[42] While racing around to get a second copy, John heaped a ton of spice into the mix by suddenly moving back into Mendips. He's unlikely to have told Mimi of the Gambier Terrace eviction, but Rod Murray knew little of this hasty departure: John left most of his possessions in the flat and several weeks' rent unpaid – to the tune of about £15. He just scarpered.

It was much easier for George. He was doing nothing at home and not working, so going to Germany and being handsomely paid for it was just fine. Crucially, he had his mother's support to overcome whatever opposition his father might put up, but there wasn't much – Harry had gone abroad himself at 17 and lied about his age to do so; he understood. While Louise worried about George being so far from home (and she'd heard some bad things about Hamburg), she wasn't going to stand in his way.[43] His passport acquisition was plain sailing.

For Stuart, Hamburg was an entirely different kettle of fish. When he'd joined the Quarrymen in January he'd no real idea what he was in for. He wasn't musical and they had no bookings. There was no hint they'd be playing abroad just seven months later, so in deciding to go, as part of his artistic/life journey, Stuart set aside his fifth college year, declining the ATD course. His was the most decisive choice of all, and it may have been something he dwelled on just a little longer than the others: his passport was issued by the Liverpool branch office on the Saturday, when it was open 'for cases of special emergency only'. He could scarcely have left it later ... although John did.

John managed to get a 'short copy' of his birth certificate on the Friday, by which time everything was becoming traumatic at Mendips. What scenes, what noise, what ferocity there must have been there that weekend. Written consent of a legal guardian was necessary for the issue of a passport to a minor, but no matter how much John begged or demanded, Mimi wouldn't give it. After the way he'd treated her, and blown away everything she'd slaved for on his behalf? John now had no idea whether he'd even get a passport, and could only find out on Monday morning, when they were supposed to be leaving. At the moment of deciding to make the guitar his life, was he about to watch helplessly as the group he formed and led went off without him?

In the meantime, there was a spot of dirty work to be done. They decided they needed three amplifiers for Hamburg: the new Truvoice, Paul's Elpico, and, if they could get it, the amp (a Watkins Westminster) owned by Sulca, the art school Students' Union. John got in touch with a committee member – his friend June Harry – and persuaded her to meet him at the college. As she would remember:

> I was the fool who had the key to the cupboard where it was kept. John begged it off me because they were going to Germany. I said I couldn't give it to him because I'd get into terrible trouble, but he said, 'You won't, Hairy June. I'll have it back soon enough, before anyone notices.' He could be quite persuasive. And of course he didn't, and I got kicked off the committee. They said I was 'irresponsible'. In fact, I never saw John again. I left Liverpool in 1961 and finished my National Diploma somewhere else.[44]

This appropriately undignified postscript to John's art school years was hard on the woman who – through her love affair with John's Quarry Bank English master Philip Burnett – had got him there to start with ... but relationships were being cracked all over the place in the Beatles' haste to get to Hamburg. Paul was leaving Dot behind, and John (if he was going) would be leaving Cyn. If Dot hadn't miscarried she'd have been heavily pregnant by now and Paul could have been married and unable to go; as it was, they parted on promises of regular letters and, perhaps, fidelity.

Would John and Cyn be parting too? If so, they said they'd write every day, and somehow she believed he'd be faithful, though Germany did seem so awfully far away that anything was possible – and, with John, certain. Cyn was staying at art school to do the second year of her NDD course and Lil Powell hoped plainly and simply that a period apart would be the breaking of her daughter's infatuation with that Liverpool lout, and that she'd never have to see him or hear about him again.[45]

Now they had to get the drummer. Pete Best's 'audition' took place on the

Saturday evening, 13 August, at one of Allan Williams' clubs, either the Jacaranda basement or the Wyvern (the unfinished Blue Angel-to-be). Williams says he was in charge: 'I didn't know what made a good drummer, so I just asked him to do a drum roll and said, "OK, you're in."'[46] Pete says all the Beatles were present except maybe George; Pete's close mate Neil Aspinall (who wasn't there) always said Paul ran it, being that he was primarily responsible for getting Pete into the group. Neil would also accept the audition was 'an absolute formality – they wanted to go to Hamburg and they needed him'.[47] Pete could not have failed if he'd held the sticks between his toes. He was the vital fifth man, the drummer with a kit, a passport and nothing to hang around in Liverpool for. That he was virtually a beginner and very quiet was not going to alter that. As John straightforwardly remarked fifteen years later, 'The reason he got in the group was because the only way we could get to Hamburg [was that] we had to have a drummer. We knew of this guy who was living at his mother's house, who had a club in it, and he had a drum kit and we just grabbed him – [we] auditioned him and he could keep one beat going for long enough, so we took him to Germany.'[48]

All that remained was to sort out his stage outfit. John, Stu, Paul and George had their handmade lilac jackets, black shirts, black drainies and crocodile winkle-pickers. What did Pete have that might make him look like one of them? He said he had a black shirt and black drainies, and while he had nothing in lilac he could do them a blue Italian – though he'd never drummed in a jacket before and didn't know what it would feel like. He didn't have crocodile shoes but he had other colour winkle-pickers and would bring those.[49] 'Be at the Jacaranda on Monday morning,' they told him, and off they all went.

Unlike Tommy Moore and Norman Chapman, the drummer they were bringing in this time was a good physical match. Pete Best was 18 (younger than Stu and John, older than Paul and George), he was their height, he bettered their build (slender like them, but stronger), he was bright (one more grammar-school boy made five out of five), he had attitude, he was handsome, he had pose, poise and a Tony Curtis hairstyle . . . and he was in the Beatles.

Monday was wet, windy and cool in Liverpool, and just another day.

On Hope Street, at 3 Gambier Terrace, Rod Murray and his fellow artisans barricaded themselves into their first-floor flat and refused to be evicted.

In Woolton, at 251 Menlove Avenue, Mimi was on her knees, physically trying to prevent her nephew leaving the house. Everything she'd fought for – for his sake, for hers – was about to walk out the door. The young man just wriggled free, picked up his bag and his guitar and stormed out, defying her to a new record degree[50] . . . though still wondering whether this inglorious getaway might be followed by an ignominious return. All would become clear after he'd rushed to Water Street, to the fifth-floor Passport Office in India Buildings, and waited as patiently as an impatient young man in a hurry could, praying the 'brummercrats' would understand his situation: dead mother, absent father, er, how could he show adult consent?

In Allerton, at 20 Forthlin Road, Jim Mac ensured his son had enough cod liver oil capsules for two months, and enquired (as he did most mornings) whether the boy's bowels had moved, then he gave him an Englishman's pep talk, making him promise to be a good lad, stay out of trouble, eat proper meals and write often.[51]

In Speke, at 25 Upton Green, Louise fussed around the boy with the tall hair, made him promise to eat sensibly and write often, and gave him a tin of scones she'd baked for the journey, to be shared among his friends.[52] That was always Louise.

In Huyton, at 22 Sandiway, the strolling minstrel, the brilliant painter with the aloof Dean pose, packed a few art materials, pocketed his shades, grabbed his bass, bade farewell to his sisters and fraught mother, and sauntered off; tomorrow to fresh woods, and pastures new.

And in West Derby, at 8 Hayman's Green, Mona Best told her eldest boy that Hamburg was a wild place and he was likely to receive an education broader than anything the Collegiate had taught him. As he would reflect, Mo was 'a marvellous champion of a woman who let me choose my own path in life and has supported me like a pillar whether times have been good or bad'.[53]

Each made his way to the Jacaranda, where Allan Williams had parked what he called his van – the Morris J2 Minibus. It was a tatty old thing, cream-and-green and covered in perishing paper that advertised his Gene Vincent show back in May: he'd 'ballsed-up' and used the wrong glue, so the posters were flaking off in their own time. His wife Beryl was also coming along, together with her much younger brother Barry Chang and, for noble company, the calypsonian Lord Woodbine.* Beryl, a domestic science teacher, prepared food and flasks. While they waited for John to arrive – and to find out whether or not he was even coming – Allan advanced the Beatles £15 against their first Hamburg wages, getting Stuart and Paul to sign for it, and he also got their verbal agreement to refund him £10 apiece towards petrol, boat fares and food.

To John's eternal relief, his passport application was processed once the office opened at 9.30. An official leniently considered the circumstances and

---

* Barry Chang had been a year ahead of Paul and two ahead of George at the Institute.

granted dispensation without written adult consent, issuing a standard five-year passport but with a restriction that it expire after six months, in February 1961, unless the required document was produced.[54] John handed over his photos, signed where applicable, grabbed the precious blue-black document, ran for the lift, broke out on to Water Street, felt higher than that there Liver Building and hared up the hill to Slater Street.

Williams was aiming to catch the overnight ferry from Harwich to the Hook of Holland, and he'd agreed to pick up another passenger in London on the way, so they *really* had to get going. There was the luggage of nine as well as guitars, drums and amps, and they piled as much as possible on the roof-rack. Williams whipped off his top hat, drove round the block to get the balance of all the gear, then eight jumped in – one in the front, seven in the back, sitting on opposite benches that ran lengthways down the vehicle, with yet more gear stacked between them. Pulled by only a 1500cc engine, the J2 would be carrying that weight for 625 miles – a thousand kilometres – through three countries. Mona Best was there to wave Peter goodbye, and, unrealised by everyone, Millie Sutcliffe hid in a doorway down the street, watching and crying as her wee Stuart headed off to who-knew-what.

None of them knew. The Beatles wanted to rock and roll, they hungered to move on and try new things, they all needed a way out, they all wanted to *live*, and they loved the thought of going abroad … but as the minibus emerged from the Mersey Tunnel and Williams took the long A41 south, no one had the first idea what lay ahead.

16

'Mach Schau!'
(15 August–30 September 1960)

Beyond the A41, their route was the A5. When he could, Allan Williams put his foot to the floor and eked 55mph out of the laden bus, but it wasn't often, what with all the traffic lights, roundabouts and town centres to be negotiated on the way south. This was the old Roman road, built seventeen hundred years before the motor car; as would soon become apparent, the Second World War's vanquished had roads much superior to its victor's.

Freshly issued this Monday morning, 15 August 1960, John Lennon's passport was grabbed by everyone – and then they were all out and passed around, photos laughed at.

> John Winston Lennon, student, born Liverpool, 9 October 1940.
> James Paul McCartney, student, born Liverpool, 18 June 1942.
> George Harrison, student, born Liverpool, 25 February 1943.
> Stuart Fergusson Victor Sutcliffe, student, born Edinburgh, 23 June 1940.
> Randolph Peter Best, formerly Randolph Peter Scanland, student, born
>   Madras, 24 November 1941.

Pete Best has spoken of how they took the mickey out of his name.[1] The boy was *Randy* and not entirely Best. It was something he never volunteered and already they knew . . . but this group was no place for secrets, less still anyone sensitive to being laughed at. John had crucified Tommy Moore; how would he be this time? Sizing up the personalities bouncing before his very eyes, Pete must have sensed he had to be careful, but then he was patently no lightweight.

Where we going, Johnny? Beyond even Hamburg, John announced, they were going *to the toppermost of the poppermost!* The trip dovetailed perfectly with the arrival of this new tagline for their two-year-old chant. It came courtesy of producer Dick Rowe and his colleagues at Top Rank Records, who, from 5 August, marketed a series of *Toppermost* LPs with that slogan, 'Toppermost of the Poppermost'. John and the others saw this as their divine destination, and couldn't get over the stupidity of the catchphrase, a dumb line cooked up by some suit-and-tie toff in London who, as per usual, didn't have a blinkin' clue.

The Beatles now skirted that London world for the first time, waving (metaphorically at least) hello, goodbye. The A5 routed southbound traffic down the Edgware Road, and as Williams drove them along Maida Vale they passed, unknowingly, seven hundred yards from Abbey Road. At EMI Studios the following afternoon, Cliff Richard (toppermost beyond dispute) was booked in for a session with the Shadows, the four talented and besuited young 2i's rockers who were suddenly bursting out from under Cliff's wing: Apache, their own first hit, reached number 1 in the *NME* on the presses this same day. It would become the sound of the late summer and autumn, inspiring a glut of groups to play precision-perfect twangy instrumentals, point their guitars upwards and outwards in unison and do choreographed footsteps, left-stop-right-stop. This was the Britain the Beatles would return to after playing hard rock and roll for thirty hours a week in Hamburg. This was the fashion they happened to skip.

The Beatles caught their first glimpse of the 2i's, and of Soho, when Williams eased the minibus down to Old Compton Street and it somehow admitted yet another Hamburg-bound passenger, the bilingual waiter (probably named Steiner) from the coffee bar Act One – Scene 1.* They all got out to stretch their legs, but there was no time to linger if they were going to catch the night boat from Harwich, eighty miles distant.

They met with a setback at the quay. The roll-on/roll-off ferry was a recent invention in 1960, little used as yet. Boats had no direct platform access for vehicles – each in turn had to have its fuel-tank emptied and battery disconnected before being hoisted by crane and lowered into the cargo hold. Allan Williams says the stevedores refused to handle his bus. 'They said the crane wouldn't lift it with all that gear on top. I really had to *plead* with them. If it hadn't gone on we would have been in Shit Street.'[2]

Williams was nothing if not a good *Spieler*. He got the men to give it a try,

---

* Little is known of the Beatles' fellow traveller to Hamburg, except that after translating Derry and the Seniors' contract three weeks previously, Bruno Koschmider offered him a job in Hamburg and it was arranged he could have a lift.

though at his own risk. Barry Chang took some photos of the delicate operation: one happens to catch John Lennon, in his glasses, watching as dockers manoeuvred the vehicle – with their precious guitars, amps and drums on board – up into the air, over the side and down on to the ship. The crane held fast, and also worked fine at Hook of Holland (Hoek van Holland), but there was an irritating four-hour wait while Dutch immigration raised questions about the musical instruments. The officials believed the gear was being brought into the country for resale and insisted import duty was due – if it wasn't paid, everything would be confiscated. Again, Allan Williams was the hero of the moment, insisting these crazy boys were students, just like their passports said: they were going on holiday to Germany and they just *loved* playing.

The peril of driving on the 'other' side of the road was matched by the confusion of navigation and they went wrong instantly. Intending to head north towards Amsterdam, they drove east, straight through the centre of Rotterdam. This direction advanced them towards Arnhem, the scene – sixteen summers earlier, in September 1944 – of one of the last big battles of the war. Williams had a cousin who was injured here and spoke often of his fallen comrades; he wanted to pay respects on his behalf.

The Allied cemetery is in nearby Oosterbeek. In a wood, a quiet space where wind shushes through trees, a clearing gives way to the graves of more than 1750 fallen soldiers. Barry Chang got out his camera and clicked the shutter as the Liverpool tourists paused at the main memorial tablet. The picture freezes a vital moment, a turning point: it's the Beatles en route to Hamburg – and, as if by magic, a caption is etched into its very centre: THEIR NAME LIVETH FOR EVERMORE.*

Chang's photo is particularly good of George: his face is full of character, he's wearing the matelot T-shirt that attracted Royston Ellis, and his quiffed hair is toppermost, remarkably so after twenty-seven hours on the road. Pete Best looks happy and comfortable, a nice lad, visually a perfect fit. Paul is smoking, and eating something probably made by Beryl; his quiff, in a state of collapse, hasn't fared as well as George's. Spirits seem good. Stuart – skinny, now clean-shaven and wearing dark glasses – is evidently more adult than Pete, Paul or George. He's standing in a group to the side with Allan, Beryl and Woody. Allan, with a mop of black hair and heavy black beard, is wearing an expandable shirt-sleeve armband, possibly doubling here as a memorial armband.

As well as Barry Chang, two other passengers aren't in the photo: Herr Steiner, for whom Arnhem may have been a bridge too far, and John Lennon. He never explained his absence, nor was he asked, so it cannot be confirmed if Allan

---

* Ecclesiasticus 44:14 – 'Their bodies are buried in peace; but their name liveth for evermore.'

Williams is right when he says John stayed on the bus because the sight of so many graves, so many people his own age killed in combat, sickened him inside out.

Nonetheless, here were the men who'd fought for their sort; here was what the Beatles were, so far, lucky to have escaped; and here again is a reminder of life's slender threads: among the rows and rows and rows of small white head-stones is one for a Private Peter Best, aged 19.

Afterwards, they drove into Arnhem itself, for a look around. Wandering the city streets, the Beatles' first time in a foreign place, they found a music shop and piled in, keen to see the guitars . . . and, while here, John 'slap leathered' a harmonica. He slipped it into his pocket and showed it to everyone outside; Allan Williams was genuinely appalled – 'I thought, "What sort of *loonies* have we got here? We're not even going to *make* Hamburg!"' Three of them – Paul, George and Stu – knew exactly what kind of a loony they had here, and it was another sharp insight for Pete into the company he was keeping. He remembers John being 'supremely confident . . . he knew what he was doing', and he says John cheerfully played his new instrument – and pulled faces – as the bus bumped along.[3]

Finally, after midnight, more than thirty-six hours since departing Liverpool, the happy wanderers reached Hamburg, located St Pauli, and the Reeperbahn, and turned up Grosse Freiheit.*

The narrow old cobbled street might have reminded them of Liverpool, though only for a second. Strip. Sex. Bars. Clubs. All neon life was here. Eyes stared wide and hard through the dirty windows of a Morris J2. And there, on a corner, was the Kaiserkeller they'd heard about. Pulses raced faster still. They parked, trotted downstairs and exchanged Liverpool greetings with Derry and the Seniors . . . who were distinctly unwelcoming. All they knew of the Beatles was what they'd seen at the Billy Fury audition, when they'd been far from impressed. They were sure the Beatles' arrival would spoil the good scene they had going.

Next, the Beatles met Bruno Koschmider. He led them back up the stairs to show them where *they* would be playing – it was further down the street. Much further. Grosse Freiheit darkened, the places of entertainment thinned, the noise of *action* became a distant echo, until here, at 64, was the Indra. A neon Indian elephant and the words INDRA CABARET marked the spot, stretched high and impressively across the street, big enough (necessarily) to be seen from afar. The club itself was closed, dark, quiet. They were off-Broadway.

Bruno's interpreter explained: tomorrow the club will open and they will

---

* Local pronunciation guide. St Pauli: *Zankt Powlee*, Grosse Freiheit (also written as Große Freiheit): *Grorza Fryhite*, and Reeperbahn: *Rayperbarn*.

play, and in the meantime they will spend the night. While Allan, Beryl, Barry and Woody drove off to a hotel, the five Beatles were left in Koschmider's care. Oddly, there's no certainty where they slept this first night. Paul says it was inside the Indra, curled up 'in the little alcoves, on red leather seats'. George said it was in Koschmider's apartment – 'all in the one bed', amazingly. Still, they'd arrived . . . and to prove it, they were here.[4]

Before playing, there was business to be done. All five Beatles put their signatures to contracts in German and English – the first they ever signed. Hamburg being no place for Messrs Ramon, de Staël and the like, they used their real names. This really *was* The Big Time, and these were the stage hours they agreed:

Tuesday to Friday, 4½ hours. 8.00–9.30PM, break ½ hour, 10–11, break ½ hour, 11.30–12.30, break ½ hour, 1–2AM.
Saturday, 6 hours. 7.00–8.30PM, break ½ hour, 9–10, break ½ hour, 10.30–11.30, break ½ hour, 12–1AM, break ½ hour, 1.30–3.
Sunday, 6 hours. 5–6PM, break ½ hour, 6.30–7.30, break ½ hour, 8–9, break ½ hour, 9.30–10.30, break ½ hour, 11–12, break ½ hour, 12.30–1.30AM.

The contract was for two months, 17 August to 16 October, with Mondays off, and it paid each of them DM30 (Deutsche Marks) for every night of work. It defined the Beatles as a five-piece group and stipulated they couldn't play in any rival venue in Hamburg for thirty weeks after the contract's end. Both parties warranted that if they broke the terms they would compensate the other in full, and Koschmider agreed to obtain the Beatles' work permits.*

There were lots of bureaucratic forms to complete – no easy task because they were in German. John had brought a pocket German-English dictionary

---

* Including pauses, the Beatles had to be in the Indra for six hours Tuesday to Friday, eight hours on Saturday and eight and a half hours on Sunday. The exchange rate was DM11.70 to the pound, so DM30 a night was £2 11s (now £2.55). Earned for six nights, Monday to Saturday, the weekly wage was just over £15 each (which was £3 less than expected, possibly because they'd assumed a seven-night working week). Pay was collected every Saturday from Koschmider's office at the Kaiserkeller – often the only time they saw him – and was free of taxation; it was up to the Beatles to declare their earnings for tax when they returned to England.

The contract called for £10 to be paid to Allan Williams every week, seemingly by Koschmider. However, by a separate accord the two men signed six days later, Koschmider agreed that Williams' commission would be 10 per cent of the Beatles' earnings, deducted from their wages and paid into an account Williams opened in St Pauli with Commerzbank. This meant each Beatle pocketed DM162 a week instead of DM180 – a shade under £14.

In that same 23 August contract – drawn up just before Williams returned to England with Beryl and the others – the two businessmen also agreed to be bound exclusively for five years, Williams providing whatever entertainment Koschmider might need from England.

from home but never bothered to open it, Stuart spoke no German, and Paul and George knew a little from school (which 'wasn't madly useful', according to Paul).[5] Pete was the most adept because he'd passed German O-Level. Koschmider noted the Beatles' particulars, including their ages, and notified them to the Fremdenpolizei ('aliens police'). One thing he didn't do was apply for work permits.

The contract made no mention of accommodation, and this swiftly became a source of trouble between the Beatles and Koschmider. He wasn't bound to provide them with anything, but paying for lodging would have left them with little or no money to live. With *ein bisschen* (a pfennig's worth) of sympathy, Koschmider offered what he felt was a more than generous solution: the Beatles could stay free of charge in rooms at the rear of a tiny cinema he leased, the Bambi. They'd be able to come and go through their own back door, just across from the Indra. (As he'd done with the Jets, Koschmider let Derry and the Seniors bed down in the Kaiserkeller, in an office locked after them for fear they'd steal from the bar. Their lavatory was a communal chamber-pot.)

The Bambi was a dump. They had two rooms that weren't much more than storage spaces: a small one that could accommodate three and had an electric light, and – off the first one – a second, tiny room that could take two, without electricity. Both reeked of the adjacent toilets used by the cinema's customers, which served as the Beatles' washroom. There was no other plumbing, no heating and no decoration of any kind, just unpainted concrete walls thick with dust, and ceilings so low they had to duck their heads. There were no drawers, so they had to live out of suitcases, and only one small window set very high (overlooking a courtyard), so the rooms were dark. Koschmider provided two little camp-beds for the tiny room, and two little beds and a miniature couch for the small room, with hardly any bedcovers. As no one ever came in to clean, the place soon resembled Stu and John's studio at Gambier Terrace.

It was particularly grim for Paul. As usual in first-come-first-served Beatles situations, John had the broadest shoulders and sharpest elbows. The leader bagged the best bed in the marginally better room, followed swiftly by Stu and George, continuing their Gambier arrangement, so by the time Paul got in – and he may have been only seconds behind – he and Pete had to go into the second room. It was a triple-blow for Paul: he was in a dump, he had the wretched feeling of being left out of the fun, and he was lumbered with the new boy, *quiet Pete*, never unfriendly or unpleasant but monosyllabically shy. It was massively irksome and the cause of a prolonged jealousy here in Hamburg, often expressed (to the irritation of others) but never resolved.

Bambi-Filmkunsttheater was the venue's real name, but the Beatles called it 'the Bambi Kino', and 'the pit', and *hated* it from the start. Though closed by midnight, the Bambi screened films at 4, 6.30 and 9PM, the sound from the 4PM film disturbing their late-late sleep, the 6.30 film irritating them Tuesdays to Fridays when they didn't start work until eight. They also had to contend with the noise of people passing by their rooms when exiting the cinema through the back door, and customers using the toilets.[6]

It was at this point that the Beatles' working and leisure hours turned upside down, which was how they'd always remain. With their working day not finishing until up to 3AM, and their winding-down and social time only starting then, day became night and night became day. As Paul explained in a letter to his dad and brother (like all of them, he wrote home often), 'I'm writing now at 10.30, before I go to sleep' – this was 10.30AM.[7]

What with their inadequate washing facilities, soiled laundry and heavy smoking – cigarettes were cheap here and they all smoked up to forty a day – the whole place *stank*, and so, surely, did they. Still, they were all in it together, and at least they had a common enemy in Koschmider. It prompted a key shift in their collective chant, into one that would endure and serve many other purposes in the months and years ahead. Instead of Paul and George asking *Where we going, Johnny?* John flipped the question and asked it of his gang, all of them adopting a phoney American accent as if in a cheapo Hollywood exploitation movie:

> When we were all depressed – thinking the group was going nowhere and this is a shitty deal and we're in a shitty dressing-room – I'd say, 'Where we going, fellers?' and they'd go, 'To the top, Johnny!' in pseudo-American voices. And I'd say, 'Where's that, fellers?' and they'd say, 'To the toppermost of the poppermost, Johnny!' I'd say, '*Riiiight!*' and we'd all cheer up. That was our little mantra that got us through.[8]

This eventful first full day in Hamburg concluded with four and a half hours on the Indra's little podium stage, in front of cabaret curtains that so deadened their sound they turned the amps to max. Koschmider had publicity photographs taken of his new attraction – the first photos of the Beatles as John, Paul, George, Stu and Pete, five Liverpool boys, four guitars on the drip, three amplifiers, and two drumsticks in the hands of Pete Best, the boy with the kit bought by his Mo, a hopeful investment dominated by an outsize bass drum. He's wearing his dark jacket, the other four are in Mr Richards' lilac creations; Paul attracts attention by pulling a face and Stu does so with his dark glasses. They look good, and they're ready to rock.

The Beatles' first night in Hamburg, 17 August 1960, was twenty years ago, today, since the Germans launched their first attack on Liverpool, when Nazi planes dropped bombs on the docks at Toxteth, 17 August 1940. Rock and roll music was taken to Hamburg by the children of the survivors, to be heard in turn by children who'd outlived the Allies' revenge blitz of 1943. Scorned by adult society as a force for evil and the work of the devil, black rhythm music out of America – and, before there of course, out of Africa – was bringing harmony where once had been hatred.

The Seniors' Howie Casey says he managed to get away from the Kaiserkeller for a few minutes to check out the new arrivals from his home town. He was expecting to sneer, but since the Billy Fury audition they'd been on the Johnny Gentle tour and played sixteen good dates on the Wirral. 'My jaw went to the floor. There was such a difference from what I'd seen at the audition. There was something there, a spark, that extra little bit. We did a bit of harmony singing but they were marvellous at it. They were stunning. You knew they were going to go places.'[9]

Those voices, John and Paul and sometimes George and Stu in different combinations, carried the Beatles forward. This had long been their strength, one that was unique among the groups. To begin with, however, no matter how appealing their harmonies, they simply didn't have the repertoire. The longest they'd ever had to play in one stretch was about two hours, now they had to do up to six. They were a *bar band*, and though no customer stuck around all night long, the Beatles set themselves the challenge of not repeating themselves. The result was a brisk broadening of their output, as in 'What else can we do? What else do we know?' So they did the whole first Carl Perkins LP, the whole first Johnny Burnette LP, the whole first Buddy Holly and the Crickets LP, the whole first Elvis Presley LP as well as all of *Elvis's Golden Records*, and the whole first Gene Vincent LP (one of their favourite numbers was his cover of Wedding Bells Are Breaking Up That Old Gang Of Mine). Songs were also spun out – Paul could make Ray Charles' What'd I Say last fifteen minutes without any difficulty, and John did something similar with Elvis's Baby Let's Play House: 'We'd make it last about ten minutes, singing the same verse over and over again.'[10] Paul sang Summertime and Over The Rainbow (both because of Gene Vincent), they did Phil Spector's To Know Her Is To Love Her, they did all the Chuck Berry numbers they knew, all the Little Richard, Buddy Holly, Coasters, Eddie Cochran, Fats Domino and Larry Williams. John sang Hank Williams country numbers like Honky Tonk Blues, they did oldies like Moonglow and The Harry Lime Theme and new tunes like Money, Besame Mucho, Shakin' All Over and Apache (but without the Shadows' dance steps). 'We had to learn millions of songs,' George would say, 'because we'd be on for hours. Hamburg was really like our apprenticeship, learning how to play in front of people.'[11]

With little or no prior rehearsal of these songs, there were plenty of ragged

renditions. The front line didn't lack keenness or energy but there were no vir-
tuosos here. George was the kind of guitarist who perfected things over time,
laboriously. Improvising a dazzling solo was not his forte, and when forced into
that situation his playing could be weak. Paul had a still-unfamiliar and cheap
guitar and his exact role was somewhat 'in between' – George played lead, John
was rhythm … and Paul was rhythm too, though he added lead fills when possible. John was on his way to becoming an accomplished rhythm guitarist but
probably hadn't got there yet; he mostly played by feel, and with unfamiliar
songs would have been busking much of the time. And then there was Stu: a
bass guitarist only seven months, he wasn't far beyond a beginner. It was the
combination of talents that gave the Beatles their spark: what they sounded
like, plus what they looked like, plus their personalities. Left to right and at the
back they were *interesting*.

The first night at the Indra was also the first night of the Beatles with Pete
Best, at least their fourth drummer in thirteen weeks. Though he looked the
part, and projected that studied sullenness observed at the Casbah, he was very
much a novice, with precious little group time under his belt and just a fraction of the stage time experienced even by Stu. None of this was a surprise to
John, Paul and George – they realised all along Pete was a beginner and that
they'd have to carry him, and show him their ways.

It was readily apparent that Pete had trouble maintaining an even tempo –
a common problem for drummers, speeding up and slowing down and generally not noticing the difference. Stuart was of little practical help: the backbone
of a rock group is typically the bass and drums locking together, and both were
erratic. Finding a solution, however, also found the Beatles a style. As George
said, 'We'd often turn around and stamp on the stage, to keep the tempo going
right.'[12] They actively encouraged Pete to keep hitting the pedal of that big bass
drum, *boom-boom-boom-boom*, because it was the one thing he could do at an
even beat. In this way, almost from the start here in Hamburg, the Beatles
became all about stamping feet and clapping hands, to generate noise and
excitement and keep themselves musically together. 'We kept that big heavy
four-in-a-bar beat going all night long,' George said.

For Bruno Koschmider, this triggered an unforeseen problem. There was an
old woman who lived above the Indra; whether or not she'd been troubled by
its transvestite cabaret isn't known, but it hadn't disturbed her night's sleep.
The Beatles had three amplifiers and did all this terrible foot-stomping well into
the wee hours, and she complained. Koschmider's *Geschäftsführer* – day-to-day
manager at the Indra – was an older man named Wilhelm 'Willi' Limpinsel,
and he told the Beatles to cut their volume. Conditions being what they were
at the Bambi, their response was two short words.

Though *boom-boom-boom-boom* suited many of the songs, difficulties arose when the Beatles went for variety. John, Paul and George saw how Pete struggled with other styles and tempos; all they could do was hope it would improve over time. Right now, right here at the Indra, they could get by. They were far from home, having fun, and rocking like they'd never done in their lives.

Every night at 9.45 the house PA broke across whatever was going on, even through the middle of their singing, to announce *'Wir machen darauf aufmerksam, dass um zehn Uhr alle Jugendlichen unter achtzehn Jahren das Lokal verlassen haben müssen!'* On the first night, the Beatles looked at one another, wondered what it meant, then carried on; fifteen minutes later, at 10PM, all young people had to show an identity card and those under 18 were made to leave. It was the *Ausweiskontrolle*, the identification check, and it didn't take long for the pfennig to drop: kids under 18 were being forced to go, and George was only 17. He did his best to look inconspicuous until the *Piedels* shouted *one–two–three–four!* and could carry on stomping.*

In Hamburg for the long haul, they got to know the St Pauli quarter like the back of their hands. Its busiest street was the Reeperbahn (literally, 'a ropemaker's way'), home to the majority of the night-clubs, bars, eating-places and the newly opened Top Ten Club; most of the venues had barkers outside to bring in business, men not easily resisted. The main part of Hamburg had townhouses, fine shops and the great Alster lakes, but St Pauli, the dockside district, was rough, working-class, cosmopolitan, the haunt of gangsters, thieves, prostitutes and pimps, providing entertainment for sailors with a pocketful of back-pay stuffed into their blue bell-bottoms.

Though considered the appendix of the Reeperbahn, Grosse Freiheit ('Great Freedom') had its own action, and a little way down, on the corner with the Kaiserkeller, was Schmuckstrasse, where transvestite prostitutes loitered in the doorways of still bomb-damaged buildings. All this behaviour was tolerated in Hamburg only so long as it was confined strictly to St Pauli. It was like a separate society. Decent Hamburg citizens kept away and insisted their children did likewise; newspaper reports spelled out the dangers. On 20 September, when the Beatles had been there a month, a Grosse Freiheit barman killed a Norwegian sea captain by striking him several times with an ashtray, and the

---

* Germans of a certain age, unfamiliar with English, tend to pronounce English Bs as Ps, so 'Beatle' sounded, to some ears, not unlike *piedel*, an old-fashioned juvenile word for 'willy' or 'dick', more silly than rude even though it formed one of the many German slang words for the condom, *piedeltüte* (literally, 'willy bag'). The widespread assertion that 'the Beatles' means 'pricks' in German is evidently exaggerated, and *piedel* is so little used today it doesn't appear in the main German dictionary, the Duden.

court allowed him to walk free because he claimed self-defence, saying the customer had come at him with a bottle.[13]

It was this violent. The disaffected, the angry, the sadistic and the cruel
gravitated to St Pauli along with boxers, bodybuilders and embittered war-
scarred Nazis, many to become white-jacketed waiters who flew at the chance
to put down their tray of drinks and get stuck into a fight. 'Troublemakers'
were attacked with great brutality and in full view of everyone: there was no
attempt at disguise. One common cause of trouble was the *Nepp*. This was the
process by which a mug was parted from his money with vastly inflated drinks
bills. Most clubs and bars practised it, and every trick was used to make the
scam as slick as possible, 'hostesses' ensuring the punter was properly
fleeced ... and if he protested, he was beaten up. The Beatles thought Wilson
Hall and Grosvenor Ballroom were bad, but they were tea-parties, as George
would recall:

> All the club owners were like gangsters, and all the waiters had tear-gas guns,
> truncheons, knuckle-dusters. They were a heavy crew. Everybody around that
> district were homosexuals, pimps, hookers. Being in the middle of that when
> I was seventeen [laughs] was good fun ... [When] the seamen and soldiers
> came into town they'd all get drunk and inevitably it ended in blood and
> tears. And tears for the band, too, with the gas in our faces.[14]

Sex was everywhere, and figured high on the Beatles' menu. There was no
chance they'd match the fidelity demanded of girlfriends back home. And yet,
because so much happened to the Beatles in Hamburg – and because, supposedly, every excess was available here so easily – detaching fact from fiction
just isn't possible. As John would reflect in 1980, 'There was a lot of heavy *boys'
fun* when we were in Hamburg, but the stories built out of all proportion – over
the years they became like *legends*'[15] ... and, after 1980, those legends would
grow exponentially. To give just one example, Pete Best – an honest man, prone
to understatement rather than exaggeration – has talked of all the Beatles
having sex simultaneously at the Bambi Kino, but George, speaking of the
unforgettable occasion he lost his virginity, clearly describes John, Paul and Pete
being in the room at the same time, in bunk beds, which was a 1961 situation.
Accordingly, as unlikely as this is, it appears George managed to go through the
entire, extraordinary Hamburg experience of 1960 without having sex, despite
the mass of opportunities, a healthy sexual appetite and Stu describing him in
print as a Casanova.[16]

While being cautious of legend, though, it's clear there was plenty of
action – mostly with barmaids and sometimes with strippers. In his own words,

Paul got into being a musician 'to get out of having a job and to pull the birds', and here in Hamburg he fulfilled both desires to an unimagined degree.[17]

Already close buddies at home, the Beatles became very close, tighter than ever, here in Hamburg. There was no privacy and they all witnessed the others in intimate situations. As Paul says, 'I'd walk in on John and see a little bottom bobbing up and down with a girl underneath him. It was perfectly normal: you'd go, "Oh shit, sorry," and back out the room.'[18]

Then there was Herbertstrasse, where prostitutes draped themselves in windows. Hamburg law stipulated that the street had to be blocked off to passers-by, signs prohibiting entry to anyone under 18: every time the Beatles went down there, George had to put up with taunting. Which of them used the whores isn't known for sure, but all kinds of stories have been written as fact, some of which are probably true.[19]

For all these reasons, St Pauli was the perfect place for an ambitious evangelist to preach a few firebrand sermons, to save souls with the words of Jesus. Into Hamburg in September 1960 strode Billy Graham, the Southern Baptist from America, on one of his now-regular international crusades. At the end of one of his rallies, he led a honking motorcade the length of the Reeperbahn and drew to a halt at the top of Grosse Freiheit. Standing on a podium, he looked right down this street of sin, with its neon invitations (as far as that great elephant), taking in its strip clubs, the belligerent drunkards in the bars and the rock and rollers who played for them. *'Repent your sins!'* Graham commanded them, *'Repent your sins!'* A brass band played and everyone sang *Ein feste Burg ist unser Gott*. The Beatles were most likely inside the Indra and missed it all (they never mentioned seeing Billy Graham there), but it's not impossible they were among the crowd described in the *Hamburger Echo*'s report, the 'slightly shivering couples, youths with Caesar haircuts, crash-helmet devotees in leatherneck uniforms and lots of cheerful seamen'.[20]

At the opposite end of the scale from all the prostitutes and strippers, the Beatles also began to attract a few ordinary young Hamburg girls, who took a shine to these exotically foreign rockers and became their first local fans. They were nice girls who for one reason or another were in St Pauli even though most kept away: they grew to love seeing the Beatles at the Indra, though they had to leave at the 10PM *Ausweiskontrolle* curfew. No other group or musicians here had such followers, only the Beatles; the girls offered a little romance and warmth without giving themselves. One of them, Corri, whose family owned the Blockhütte restaurant next door to the Indra, started going out with Paul; a girl called Monika Paulsen was sweet on George, and she says John was friendly with a girl named Renate, and Pete with a blonde called Helga. 'When the musicians wanted scx – or at least more than kisses and cuddles – they could get it elsewhere,' says Monika, 'and we were never jealous.'[21] Stuart turned down several who came his way, telling a former girlfriend that he found Hamburg girls 'beautiful and graceful but lacking in quality'.

Stuart was a prolific writer from Hamburg. In a letter back to Liverpool dated 22 September, he hinted the Beatles might be away beyond October ('I expect to be home about Christmas') and said he planned to leave the group to take up his ATD course in Liverpool in 1961. Of his present position, he wrote, 'I suppose a lot of people consider me a fool, but this is a personal escape which I felt was necessary to free me from a lot of uneasyness [sic] ...' One who certainly thought Stuart a fool, and told him so, was his tutor Arthur Ballard, who was appalled this most brilliant artist had given up his studies, even temporarily, to go and play silly rock and roll for £15 a week. The pair corresponded regularly.[22]

When the Beatles weren't working – Mondays, and in the late hours after they finished (at 1.30, 2 or 3AM) – they usually ate, drank and talked or watched music. To begin with, for the first few weeks, the five of them went around together, but Pete then peeled off. He was, they assumed, seeing a girlfriend – he had a long relationship with a stripper – and most of the time they just socialised without him. The real closeness in the Beatles here was felt by the four friends from Liverpool, not five, just as they were around the art school and Institute. Instead of the Cracke it was Gretel und Alfons, instead of being thrown out at half-ten the place only began to get lively after midnight, and instead of some old gent telling you to keep the noise down if you shouted too much, here you just shouted louder.

Booze was plentiful and the main source of revenue in St Pauli, many customers aiming to get out of their heads as quickly as possible. Foaming beer cascaded from high taps and was guzzled from bottles in rough taverns packed with raucous drunks. The Beatles were at first surprised by and then quickly accustomed to being sent free drinks while playing. A tray of Schnaps or a crate of beer or ersatz champagne would arrive on the Indra's little stage together with a request to sing a particular song. They usually had to toast their benefactor with a *Prost*. Performing blotto and belching, farting, chewing, swearing, smoking, drinking and making lewd signs fast became the norm, the way to do it, done six long nights every week. Rapidly, all the stage time they'd ever had was matched and multiplied.

They still had the niggling problem of volume, but every time Limpinsel asked them to play quieter they imagined (or delivered) two fingers. When feeling particularly hard done by they hit on a work-to-rule strategy: if the Indra had customers, the Beatles stood still, barely moving at all, and when the place was empty they jumped around.

Koschmider fired off a letter to Allan Williams, urging him to make his group see sense or else they might be sacked, and in the meantime Limpinsel did his best to spark them properly into action: *'Mach Schau!'* he roared. The Beatles may have narrowly escaped National Service and the spiteful ranting of regimental sergeant majors, but here they were in Germany being barked at by (for all they knew) a former Nazi. *Mach Schau! Do something! Make a show, come on!** At such decisive moments, all eyes would turn to John.

> When nothing was going on they [the other Beatles] were saying 'There's no leader, fuck it', but if anything happened, whenever there was any pressure point, I had to get us out of it. [When] they said *mach Schau* I put me guitar down and I did Gene Vincent all night, banging and lying on the floor, and throwing the mike about and pretending I had a bad leg. That was some experience. So the Germans kept saying *mach Schau! mach Schau!*[23]

Any of the Beatles could *mach Schau*, but John was the original and the best, taking it several goosesteps further. And because he was often out of his skull, anything could – and did – happen.

All the nightly rocking and stomping and *mach Schau*ing took its toll on the gear. Mr Richards' lilac jackets 'melted' (to use George's word), and those shoes, the crocodile-skin ones? Cardboard, letting in water. Ever the sharpest dresser in this group, George was the first to get new clothes, buying an envied leather jacket from a waiter for a fiver; John and Pete followed by purchasing new leather jackets with a fur inside collar, while Paul and Stuart held back for the moment. George also bought new drainpipe jeans and managed to find some black winkle-pickers to complete a whole new outfit, again with John and Pete close behind. These clothes weren't just for outdoor use, they were also stage gear; for a while again, the Beatles discarded their uniform appearance – not their usual territory. Another piece of gear was also failing to take the strain: Paul's new Rosetti Solid 7 guitar. Beneath the gloss, it was just 'a plank of wood with strings'[24] – one that was now regularly letting down its player and his bandmates.

One of the initial Soho rockers to break British rock in Hamburg, the Jets' Peter Wharton, is adamant that colleague Tony Sheridan was paramount to its development. 'The first night we played there, in June 1960, there were twenty to thirty people in the Kaiserkeller, but by the end of that week the place was

---

* *Mach Schau* is literally 'make a show' in German, and similar to *mach schnell*, to hurry up, do it now.

packed. Tony Sheridan made it. He was the guv'nor. Without Sheridan the Hamburg scene would not have happened.'

Sheridan was the first star the Beatles ever befriended, and they were thrilled to sometimes share a stage with him. They'd often watched him on *Oh Boy!*, when Jack Good made him the first man on British TV to sing and play electric guitar together, and he'd opened the Cochran and Vincent show at Liverpool Empire in mid-March. He was the musicians' musician and everyone learned from him. He had a particular way of standing at the mike, with attitude, legs planted apart and vibrating; he didn't smile like a pop star but sang like a *rocker* and was a fine guitar player. George was thrilled when Sheridan shared some of the techniques taught him just six months earlier by Eddie Cochran. It was like a lesson from beyond, Eddie to Tony to George, three steps from heaven. As Sheridan remembers:

> George latched on to me as soon as we met, asking, 'Why this chord and not that one?' We were obsessed with what we were doing, enthusiasm *way* out of proportion to the gig. It was good to be keen, but George was no virtuoso player and never a 'heavy rocker'. When he played Honey Don't he was Carl Perkins, a country singer who rocked a bit, and I was always trying to get him to play bluesy notes, telling him, 'Even if it's a pop song, George, make it *southern States*.'[25]

Having started with the Jets at the Kaiserkeller, Sheridan had moved on to the new Top Ten Club and was now on the verge of quitting there to play at yet another place, a strip joint called Studio X, next door to the Kaiserkeller. Rock and roll was the new business in St Pauli; following Koschmider's lead, other bar and club owners were looking at it. The man behind some if not all these moves was one of the little tough guys, Horst Fascher. A champion amateur boxer, he was barred from the ring in 1959 after killing a man in a St Pauli street brawl, and spent nine months in jail for 'grievous bodily harm resulting in death'. Born in 1936, Fascher loved the rebellion of rock and roll and the company of British musicians. He knew a little English, spoke like a machine-gun, and steadily edged his way towards the centre of the action, a mover and shaker, a musician's friend and protector. In St Pauli, you needed one.

Selected highlights of all these Hamburg lives made their way into letters back to Liverpool. George wrote to his family and to Arthur Kelly. His best mate, on £4 a week at Cunard, was deeply impressed when, in a postcard sent on 25 August, George said the Beatles were on '£18 a week each and free bed!'

Whatever the rate that converted Deutsche Marks into sterling, the total was bound to impress. Soon after arriving in Hamburg, Paul had a letter from his dad giving news of his A-Level results: as expected, he'd failed Art and passed English Literature. Fine, good, but what Paul wanted to do didn't require A-Levels. Having officially left his education in a state of limbo, he relished his letter to The Baz, in which he coolly informed the headmaster he'd formally left the Institute and wasn't going on to college or university. It's a letter Paul has paraphrased in interviews as 'Dear Sir, I'm sure you'll understand, I'm in Hamburg playing with a group, and we're on £15 a week, so stuff you.'[26]

Dot wrote often to Paul, and he wrote often back. He sent her a set of the publicity photos taken the first night at the Indra, lovingly inscribed on the reverse. Lonely in Liverpool without their young men, Dot and Cyn got together, got themselves all dolled up, went into a photo booth, pulled some seductive poses and sent them the strips of snaps. John sent Cyn a photo-booth sequence as Quasimodo. His gift on her 21st birthday, 10 September, was a telephone call, Hamburg to Hoylake – expensive and not easy to arrange. Cyn says John kept his promise to write every day – 'true to his word he didn't once let me down'. He covered envelopes with hearts and kisses and wrote *Postman, postman, don't be slow, I'm in love with Cyn so go man go.* These were steamy letters, full of sex, passion and cripples. He wrote that he'd bought her a pair of leather pants, adding 'they're not trousers, they're knickers'. Something to be enjoyed on his return.[27]

All five Beatles sent money home for their families, enough to make the occasional repayments on the guitars and amp, and maybe a little extra on top. Documents show that Mimi went into Hessy's to make a payment on John's Club 40. She was still livid with him, but he always knew how to butter her up. He sent a postcard, addressed to 'Mimi Mendip', that said 'Don't worry about me, I'm eating and sleeping well and keeping out of trouble', and she too received a booth photo, John's head tilted to the side and back, his eyes fixed deep into the lens. On the reverse side he captioned it his 'come hither type look'.

There was much in all these letters about food, expressing distaste at its *foreignness*. *Cornflakes mit Milch* was their Hamburg staple, sometimes eaten several times a day, especially by Paul. (Pete recalls that if one of them admitted to becoming tired during sex, the advice was 'eat more cornflakes'.)[28] Their favourite café was Harald's, on Grosse Freiheit – here and in other places they fell into the habit of stubbing out cigarettes in their food. They also went to Chug-ou, a very cheap Chinese place at Schmuckstrasse 9, which made *Pfannkuchen* (pancakes). It wasn't only the transvestites the Beatles had to watch for here, but limbless war veterans – Hitler's bequest, men lacking arms or legs, or blind or deaf, down-and-outs in some or other filthy uniform. Even John Lennon would have been hard pressed to crack jokes at their expense.

It was with relief that the Beatles heard about the British Sailors' Society, at Johannesbollwerk 20, down by the pier. Though dispensing little religion, it was essentially a mission, a shelter for seamen and anyone else from the old country who happened to wander along. It wasn't only a little piece of Britain right here in Hamburg, but a big slab of Liverpool: the building was right underneath an overhead railway, the rattle of its trains drowning out the cawing seagulls and the hammer and grunt from the still bomb-damaged docks, with a dirty river slipping by just beyond . . . except it was the Elbe, not the Mersey. Only a few minutes' walk from Grosse Freiheit, they could eat full fried British breakfasts, read the papers, enjoy familiar accents and play games. The Society even offered accommodation, very cheap at DM4 each per night, but the Beatles – as much as they loathed the Bambi Kino – didn't want to pay, and it wouldn't have been as handy as 'the pit' was for nipping off with a *Fräulein* during their half-hour Indra breaks.

Most of the time, the Beatles got on well. Though full of drink and exhaustion, they could rap on any subject under the sun. Paul's care with money was noted – Pete says that while they all passed their ciggies around, Paul would 'sneak one of his own to himself' – and he was still needling everyone about the Bambi sleeping arrangements, made all the worse now because he was jealous of Pete getting the best girls. George had to process more reminders about being 'nine months younger', and Paul still couldn't stand Stuart. He 'hated him', John said.[29] Still, Paul wasn't the only one to pick on Stu. Attacked much of the time in Scotland by all of them, it continued here in Hamburg. John still taunted and belittled his great friend, and all of them had a fair old crack at Pete.

When he wasn't off with his girlfriend, Pete seems to have enjoyed the Beatles' company, but they were chalk and cheese in terms of personalities. They wouldn't shut up, he wouldn't open up. Asked five years later if he got into any arguments with the other Beatles, Pete replied, 'No violence [but] we used to have what we'd call our "sparring round session" – everyone would just have a roughhouse, but it was all good-hearted fun'; when asked what they argued about, Pete mentioned girls ('I seemed to be very popular with the girls, and if there was any dating to be done I'd be the one they'd aim for') and 'tempos of numbers'.[30]

And of course, every Tuesday to Sunday, no matter what else was going on for them, they *boom-boom-boom-boomed* all night long, sharpening with every session and held back only by what they called 'Hamburg throat', when the hours of singing wiped out their voices.

Three pieces of news reached the Beatles towards the end of September. The first was that their refusal to keep the noise down at the Indra was forcing Koschmider to cut out the rock. The old woman had won the night. The Beatles' last Indra performance would be Sunday 2 October, and the final fort-night of their contract was to be fulfilled at the Kaiserkeller, *on* Broadway.

The second was that there would be a new contract – their Hamburg expe-rience was being extended. Despite the fractious relationship with Koschmider, the Beatles were now a real attraction for him, bringing in business from young men and women, Hamburg's rockers in their zipped, studded leather. Allan Williams was coming back to seal the deal, but it's clear from letters home that the Beatles already knew they'd have the chance to stay longer and had decided to do so.

The third item of news was confirmed in a letter Williams sent to the Beatles on 21 September: Derry and the Seniors were returning home on the expiry of their contract and he was sending another group to replace them. From 4 October, the Beatles would be playing split shifts in the Kaiserkeller with Rory Storm and the Hurricanes.

Alley Oop!

Butlin's had been a blast: three full months of good hard rocking and all that this entailed. A week before the season's end, a newspaper interview with Ringo was published in the local *Liverpool Weekly News* – his first proper 'press'. RICHARD REALISES A BOYHOOD AMBITION was the headline, and was he ever. The youngster who'd had 'twelve operations, several of them major ones' was having the time of his life. '"It's as good as a holiday and we get paid for it," said twenty-year-old Richard Starkey – he lives in Admiral Grove, Dingle. His sun-tanned face broke into a smile as he added: "It's fabulous."'[31] The article ended with the news that, after the Butlin's summer finished, the Hurricanes were hoping to play on the Continent, and in Ringo's considered view this was the right move to make. 'There is too much competition here. Rock and roll is beginning to wane. But I like the life. I certainly don't want to give it up.'

That second sentence was how things looked in Britain at the time and is only laughably wrong with hindsight; the fourth spelled the end of his engage-ment to Gerry McGovern. It had been hanging by a thread since the end of May, and soon after Richy's 4 September return to Liverpool it was cut, fin-ished, Goodnight Vienna. Wedding plans were abandoned and with them any talk of his conversion to Catholicism. He kept the engagement ring that had helped fashion his stage name, but switched it to a different finger.

Gerry was missing out on high times, because Richy had come home loaded. The first thing he did was put money down at Hessy's on a handsome and expensive £125 Premier drum kit – the act of someone for whom drumming was now definitively a *profession*. The second was to dispose of his old hand-made car and buy a three-year-old Ford Zephyr Zodiac, cream and eau-de-nil. His Butlin's savings were boosted by the money he'd put aside for marriage, and he blew the bundle on the dream machine. Still bold about not having a driving licence or insurance, he drove it down to Speke, parked it outside Hunt's and flashed the mouth-watering status-symbol at his former factory colleagues and bosses, the chaps in oily overalls who'd thought him mad. Nice blokes, most of them, but *get this*![32]

Post-Butlin's and pre-Hamburg, Rory and the Hurricanes took a holiday together, a week in 'the smoke'. It was Ringo's first time in London since the age of 15 and now he could enjoy it as an adult. The north/south divide – always evident in Britain – was felt often but most acutely when they went to a dance at the Lyceum Ballroom, just off the Strand. 'No one would dance with us,' Ringo says. 'As soon as we asked, in our Liverpool accents, a girl would say, "Piss off!" The only one we danced with was French.'[33]

On their return home, the Hurricanes played a couple of local bookings and obtained passports – and Ringo was overjoyed to see his occupation given as 'musician'. On 29 September, after he put his new car into a 'lock up' garage for safe keeping, they all left Lime Street station for Hamburg. As well as making their own way, they also had to pay their own fares, for which Allan Williams reproached Bruno Koschmider in a letter. After just one month, the impresarios' five-year business arrangement was beginning to crumble.

At Christmas 1956, Harry Graves had struggled with an old secondhand set of drums from London's Liverpool Street station around to Euston, en route to encouraging his stepson Richy's sudden zeal for tapping everything. The consequence of his efforts was the reverse journey taken by 'Ringo Starr' under four years later, carting his new and best-yet kit around from Euston to Liverpool Street with a little help from his Hurricanes (themselves laden with guitars, amps, suitcases and Rory's gold comb). They caught the train to Harwich, the night ferry to Holland, the express rail to Hamburg and arrived on 30 September. The next day, they too joined in the fun on Grosse Freiheit.

17

A Cellarful of Oiks
(1 October–31 December 1960)

The Beatles knew all about the Hurricanes but the Hurricanes didn't give the Beatles a thought, yet. 'We played one club and they were playing in another,' Ringo recalls. 'It was "hello", that's all. We didn't know them. It was just "Hi, you from Liverpool?"'[1] Beyond these greetings, the first Beatle Ringo spent any time with was Stuart: they bumped into each other in Grosse Freiheit when Ringo, not yet familiar with the area and not relishing the look of all that foreign food, was seeking something that wouldn't offend his delicate stomach. Stuart took him to Chug-ou for *Pfannkuchen*, which meant walking past the odd transvestite soliciting on Schmuckstrasse. They didn't have those in Pwllheli.

The Hurricanes were offered the same atrocious accommodation not enjoyed by Derry and the Seniors: locked into an office in the Kaiserkeller, with Union Jack flags as bed sheets and one chamber-pot in which to let out all that Hamburg food and booze. (Thinking this bad enough, they were shocked by the Beatles' cavemen-like existence at the Bambi.) Pointing to their smart stage suits, the Hurricanes demanded Bruno Koschmider find them something better, and they ended up, all five of them, in one room down at the British Sailors' Society. They couldn't have girls back here, so lust would be spent anywhere that lent itself to the moment.

On Tuesday 4 October, the Beatles joined them at the Kaiserkeller, Koschmider's underground *Tanzpalast der Jugend* ('dance palace of the young'). The Hurricanes' contract was similar (or even identical) to the Beatles' in playing times, now they were simply meshed, creating an earlier start and even later finish: each group played four and a half hours Tuesdays to Fridays, which meant nine hours between them; and the six-hour weekend sessions became a shared twelve. These were usually divided as one hour or ninety minutes for each group in turn, and because Koschmider was fastidious about them not leaving the bar between sets, the nights, and days, were about to get even longer.

At the Indra, the Beatles had felt in competition with Derry and the Seniors, but, stuck down the dark end of the street, they'd little chance of mounting a challenge. Here in the Kaiserkeller, on a rickety stage that seemed certain not to last, they strove hard to be the emperors and achieved supremacy right away. It was only five months since George had been at the Stadium and watched Rory and his boys in the Gene Vincent show; they were Liverpool's top group and the Beatles hadn't been fit to lick their boots, yet George had felt 'We're better than them!' Here, now, they were proving it.

*Mach Schau*ing became essential to the Beatles at the Kaiserkeller: they did non-stop stomping, non-stop four-in-the-bar, non-stop flat-out rock and roll, non-stop comedy, non-stop crips and hunchbacks and Sieg Heils and lying on the floor, non-stop piss-takes, non-stop joy, non-stop insane athleticism. They were a complete music-hall show, all in one, led by John who, says Pete, 'would be jumping off the piano and doing the splits'.[2] As John recalled:

> Paul would be doing What'd I Say for an hour-and-a-half [and we'd be] lying on the floor and banging our guitars and kicking things, always drunk. And all these gangsters would come in, like the local Mafia, and send a crate of champagne on stage, or imitation German champagne, and we had to drink it or they'd kill us. They'd say, 'Drink it and then do What'd I Say.' [Even if] they came in at five in the morning and we'd been playing seven hours they gave us a crate of champagne and we were supposed to carry on. I used to be so pissed . . . I'd be lying on the stage floor behind the piano, drunk, while the rest of the group was playing.[3]

In seven weeks at the Indra, the Beatles had clocked up 205 stage hours – the equivalent of 136 ninety-minute shows at home. They were transformed. The spark was now a flame. Confidence, charisma, dynamism and fantastic unpredictability *exploded* from them. There was no one else like them, not in Hamburg, not in Liverpool, not anywhere in the world. The Hurricanes, marginally but decisively older, were instantly exposed as first-generation rock and rollers, blown away in their matching ties and handkerchiefs.

Three years later, when Paul, George and Ringo filled out the questionnaires that asked for their first impressions of one another, Ringo said he thought the Beatles were 'all good musicians', Paul thought Ringo a 'fab drummer' and George said Ringo 'looked moody but [I] found he was quite different once I got to know him'. He later elaborated on this: 'I didn't like the look of Rory's drummer – he looked the nasty one, with his little grey streak of hair. But the nasty one turned out to be Ringo, the nicest of them all.'[4]

The Beatles came as a complete shock to the Hurricanes. The only other time Ringo had seen them was in May, when he'd glanced at three guitarists stumbling through a shambolic rehearsal in the Jacaranda basement. Since then, they'd had a revolution. 'They were *great* in Hamburg. Really good – great rock. That's when the battle started. We played twelve hours on a weekend night between two bands. That's a hell of a long time, especially when in each set we were trying to top them and they were trying to top us.'[5]

Liverpool competed in St Pauli every night bar Mondays, lads from Allerton, Huyton, West Derby, Speke, Woolton, Broad Green and the Dingle stretching to be seen and heard. Paul rocked and charmed; Stu was the James Dean dude in shades; Pete gave it the bashful boom; George cracked his lop-sided smile and shyly spoke German to the audience; John called them 'Krauts' and 'fucking Nazis' and tore his throat out to give them Chuck Berry; Rory rocked and combed back his blond mane; Johnny, Lu and Ty twanged their guitars; and Ringo Alley Ooped in *Starrtime!* – and it all happened in the Kaiserkeller, a dirty violent *Bierhaus* one floor below street level, festooned with ships' paraphernalia.

Five hundred could crowd in, and through the thick tobacco fog those white-jacketed waiters laid into steaming-drunk seamen with tear-gas, knuckle-dusters and spring-loaded truncheons. The Beatles had a policy: when a fight started, they played and stamped their feet even louder.[6] The atmosphere was never more combustible than when big boats were in port. The night the Beatles began at the Kaiserkeller, two huge American vessels docked in Hamburg, the cargo ship USS *Antares* and the warship destroyer USS *Fiske*, and the impact on St Pauli was tremendous. The *Fiske* alone discharged more than three hundred navy boys, dollar rich, into the strip clubs and bars – and with its nautical theme, the Kaiserkeller was a honeypot. As Japage 3 the previous year, three of the Beatles had come close to playing for an American audience; now they met one for the first time – another foreign tobacco to hammer the back of their throats as they *mach Schau*ed.

Allan Williams, back in Hamburg mid-October, was staggered at how good they'd become, and told them they were now the best, that there was no one to touch them in Liverpool.[7] He saw them *mach Schau* and loved how they turned it on even more for his sake. 'The Beatles were now getting pissed and acting outrageous on stage, effing and blinding, saying "We won the war!" and stuff like that. I didn't encourage or discourage them, I just thought it was part of the fun of being there. I saw John moon his arse on the stage, which the Germans thought was hilarious.'[8]

Deeply unhappy – actually, morally offended – by such antics, Bruno

Koschmider started to keep a behaviour logbook (long lost, regrettably) that could be used against these Liverpool louts if things got seriously out of hand. Still, the Beatles' existing contract was extended during Williams' visit, its termination redrawn as 'the end of this year', which the Beatles took literally. There was also talk within the group of moving on to Berlin in January 1961 – both George and Stu mentioned it in letters at this time: they understood they'd stay there a further two months, until the end of February, and earn DM60 a night each.[9]

Always with an eye for opportunity, Williams had a bright idea while here in Hamburg. An operatic tenor himself, he appreciated a deep, strong voice – and Lu 'Wally' Walters (the Hurricanes' second vocalist) had one which he felt could bring success as a night-club crooner. He suggested they get his voice recorded and he would take a disc or two around the London talent agencies. Lu agreed, and Williams located Akustik Studio, on the seventh floor of an office building opposite the Hauptbahnhof (central station) – Hamburg's equivalent of Percy Phillips' place in Liverpool, where a small music combo could cut a straightforward performance. Lu said he wanted Ringo as his drummer because they worked well together, but otherwise the Beatles, rather than the other Hurricanes, could play with him.[10]

The session took place on Saturday 15 October, but critical observation is impossible because the discs are missing. It's the Holy Grail of Beatles audio: a 1960 recording of John, Paul, George and Ringo, along with Lu; Pete and Stu weren't involved. It's not entirely clear which songs they recorded, though with Williams hoping to promote Lu as a crooner they probably weren't done as rock and roll. A photograph of one side of one disc shows the title Summertime, the *Porgy And Bess* song; Williams says they also did the Peggy Lee hit Fever, which was Lu's big finger-clicking number in the Kaiserkeller, and Lu himself has mentioned a third piece, September Song.[11] A week later, tearing home from Hamburg to Liverpool, Williams stopped in London and took at least one of the records into the Regent Street HQ of the Grade Organisation, the new name for the long-established Lew & Leslie Grade agency, the giants of British show business. Though the focus was on Lu Walters, not the backing group, here were the Beatles all the same, in the realm of the mighty Lew Grade for maybe five minutes, and no one wanted to know.

Williams' relationship with Koschmider seriously deteriorated while he was back in Hamburg. He didn't appreciate having to rebuff the German's suggestion of a reduction in his 10 per cent commission (even though this amount was being deducted from the Beatles' wages), nor the way he was slowing the weekly payments and sometimes not paying at all. In Williams' own words, he was being 'shat on'. He felt no compunction about taking his business elsewhere and started discussions with Peter Eckhorn, owner of the Top Ten Club. Williams said the Liverpool groups could be his instead of Koschmider's, starting with Gerry and the Pacemakers. They'd been hammering on his door, rueing the chance they'd let slip to play at the Indra – the booking the Beatles got; now they were prepared to jack in their jobs and join the 'Pool in Hamburg.

Beyond this, Williams also had another idea, one typical of his fertile imagination: he would open a Top Ten Club back home, and the two, Hamburg and Liverpool, could share talent. Home again from Germany and his lightning trip to London, he set about looking for premises. Williams intended – within six weeks – to be running the first 100 per cent rock venue in the centre of Liverpool, a place for the Beatles, Derry, Gerry, Rory, Cass *et al* to call home.

Home for the Beatles was now at least two more months away. Their Hamburg relationship was love–hate defined: it was wonderful and awful, great and crap, satisfying and sickening. One advantage was the range of musical instruments in the shops. All the Beatles were passionate about American guitars, and now here were those objects of beauty. Stu became the first of the Beatles to buy something made in America, a sixteen-watt Gibson Les Paul amplifier that, in a letter to Arthur Kelly, George joked was bigger than Stu himself. The others had hoped Stu would buy an amp for them at the start of the year, and he'd made good within a few months, albeit at a stiff price: £120.[12] Somehow, despite being a foreigner, and though Herr Koschmider refused to act as guarantor, Stu was able to buy it on the drip (*Ratenzahlung*), paying off about £7 a week.

When word reached the Kaiserkeller's Liverpool enclave that Steinway & Sons had a blue Fender Stratocaster guitar, there was an eruption. Accounts of what happened next became contradictory with retelling, but Johnny Guitar remembered John Lennon and Rory Storm having an actual fight in the shop over who would get it. Rory had the cash and had agreed to lend it to John, but at the last moment he loaned it to Ty Brian instead and John went mad. Members of both groups ended up in a twist and shout, after which they didn't speak for a week or two. The confusion comes because Ringo remembers it being George, not John, who lost out to Ty, and George did later tell how close he came to buying the precious Strat here in Hamburg. He had his heart set on it, and when it was sold to someone else he was crushed. 'By the time I got there it had gone. I was *so* disappointed – it scarred me for the rest of my life.'[13] Maybe it was for the best, though: George sometimes got to play Tony Sheridan's Fender, and Ty's, and instead he held out for the American guitar he *really* wanted, a Gretsch.

Whatever the circumstances, John did buy a new American guitar at this time. He liked the look of a Rickenbacker on an LP sleeve photo, and – when he saw one in a Hamburg music store – knew he had to have it. The Rickenbacker

325 was three-quarter size with a scaled-down neck, in natural blonde finish. The cost was £90–100, 'a hell of a lot of money to me at the time', and he always named it among his most treasured possessions, keeping it and having it repaired when necessary. Again, like Stu, he was somehow able to buy it *Ratenzahlung*, which would cause George to wonder whether the repayments were ever completed. Even better, John also got a new amp to go with it, an eighteen-watt Fender Deluxe costing about £80, so now he had an American guitar *and* amp. These two precious pieces of Los Angeles would make a great impact on Liverpool when he got home.[14]

In greater need of a new guitar than any of them, Paul kept his hand in his pocket. John let his Nerk Twin brother use his Club 40, even allowing him to swap the strings around for a left-hander, but when given the chance to buy it outright, Paul didn't, just as he hadn't bought George's surplus Club 40. John sold it to someone else instead, here in Hamburg, and claimed a profit on it.[15]

Progression of these and other kinds continued to be reported back to Liverpool by post. It happens that most of the surviving correspondence is Stuart's, who made regular raids on the Bruno Koschmider Betriebe (Company) stationery cupboard to update his mother, father, sisters, ex-girlfriends, friends and tutors. To his art school friend Ken Horton, he shed light on his present lifestyle:

> It is now my seventh week here. I came for a reason I do not know. I have no money, no resources, no hopes, I'm not the happiest man alive. Six months ago I thought I was an artist. I no longer think about it. Everything that was Art has fallen from me, no paintings left, thank God.
>
> Last Monday night, my night off, I wandered along the streets here, going mad with the beauty, just wandering and wandering by the docks ... Beggars sleeping in doorways unconsciously scratch their lice-fested bodies. Drunken prostitutes lying on newspapers in the gutters slippery with garbage and ships excrement ...[16]

Within days of penning these aching words, Stuart Sutcliffe's world was turned upside down by an injection of beauty, love and art – and, through him, so too was the Beatles'.

It was the consequence of an argument. On an October evening, probably the 20th, a 22-year-old Hamburg art institute graduate named Klaus Voormann had a dispute with his girlfriend and took himself off alone. He went to the cinema and for a long quiet walk by the harbour, and his return route cut through Grosse Freiheit. He resisted the insistent invitations of barkers to step inside this venue or that, having no intention of stopping anywhere, but his stride was halted by the sound of raw rock and roll; it grabbed at his ankles from a tiny basement window at pavement level. His compulsion to go down and investigate was diffused by the sight of some tough-looking rockers gathered around the door. He walked away, but didn't go far, and eventually plucked up the courage to return and venture into this hard, violent place, the Kaiserkeller, to see who was creating such a sound.

> The first band I ever heard playing rock and roll live was the Beatles, through the window, but when I found the guts to go downstairs into that dungeon it was Rory Storm and the Hurricanes on the stage, doing what I later learned was their Butlin's holiday camp act, like a showband thing with routines they did with their legs and all that. What first struck me about them was that they had a fantastic drummer. He was swinging like shit. Just incredible.[17]

Riveted to his seat, Klaus stayed and watched as this first group went off and another came on to replace them. This second lot made a wholly different impression, and though its members were unknown to him, he was later able to apply names to these initial impressions.

> Stuart came out first. His hair was piled really high and he had dark glasses on, and I thought, 'What's he doing wearing sunglasses in a basement?' – but it was a brilliant entrance, by all of them. They did Sweet Little Sixteen, with John singing, and that knocked me out even more than Rory had done. George came to the microphone and talked German. Paul was talking German also, saying a few words into the mike, and the others were making jokes about him and his little announcements between songs. Then George started singing an Eddie Cochran number and it was great. He was so *fresh*. They were like little boys just rocking along, smiling, grinning and being so excited and so happy! They had an amazing communication between them. It was really very exciting and I couldn't take my eyes off them.

Klaus went straight back to his girlfriend. 'She said, "Are you crazy, ringing the bell at this time of night?" So then we went into the kitchen very quietly and she made tea and I told her all about it. I said, "You've *got* to see this, it's simply fantastic, I've never seen anything like it!"'

Klaus Voormann's girlfriend, Astrid Kirchherr, also 22, had been at the same Hamburg art institute. She'd spent two years studying fashion design and then suddenly jumped into photography, which she passed with the highest grade. Now she was working as one of two assistants to a respected fashion/portrait photographer, Reinhart Wolf.[18] 'Klaus is a loner, a moody type of man, and it really takes something special to make him excited,' she says, 'but after he saw the Beatles he was telling me how *wonderful* they were and how *great* they were, and it was rare to see him like that. He persuaded me to go and see them.'[19]

The following day, when Klaus visited Astrid at Wolf's studio, his enthusiasm for the English rock and roll group sparked the interest of Jürgen Vollmer, another art institute friend and fellow assistant to Wolf.* Jürgen said he would go too.

All had striking good looks: Astrid fair-to-blonde-haired, Jürgen fair, Klaus dark. Infants during the Third Reich era, they were filled with guilt over its appalling inhumanity and so shunned everything their own country had to offer. They looked abroad, to France especially, for their intellectual nourishment and artistic direction. Jürgen led the way: he was the one who'd been to Paris, several times, modelling his entire look upon it. From his underwear to his polo-neck sweaters, everything was bought in the flea market ('The Paris flea market was huge and they had new stuff, not just rubbish'). Jürgen was Monsieur Paris in Hamburg. Expelled from the art institute for, among other reasons, drawing nudes as a single straight line, à la Cocteau, he was a young man of 21 well versed in 'acts of a rebellion against the squares'. One was to fashion his hair differently to everyone else, in the modish Paris student style, combed down and a little to the side. 'We called it the Caesar haircut. I always cut it myself because the barbers in Hamburg were totally square.'[20] Astrid and Klaus followed suit.

The three friends found strength through solidarity when it came to venturing down Grosse Freiheit. Jürgen recalls the first night:

> I went to the Kaiserkeller with trepidation because I always avoided that area – I was afraid of those *Halbstarke* ['half-strong'] – but immediately I was fascinated. It wasn't the Beatles *per se* who got to me, it was the atmosphere, the sexual energy. Hamburg people always looked repressed to me, but at the Kaiserkeller the boys and girls were sexual: feminine girls, macho boys. I'd never seen a rock and roll band before and the music blew my mind. Rory Storm and the Hurricanes were in suits and ties – they looked good but weren't the same as the Beatles, who were *rocker types*.

Jürgen was hooked, Klaus was every bit as amazed by the Beatles second night as first, and then there was Astrid.

---

* Local pronunciation guide. Voormann: *Foourmun*, Kirchherr: *Kirichhair* (the 'r' rolled at the back of the throat and the 'ch' enunciated softly), Vollmer: *Follmer*.

It was a dark and disturbing place for me to go, a very harsh environment. The atmosphere around us was dreadful, the typical Reeperbahn crowd – yobs and thugs with broken noses. Then there was this loud music and all the people standing round talking and drinking and shouting at one another. I saw George first, then Paul, and then John, and after John I thought, 'That's enough, I can't take any more.' Pete was sitting in the back and you could hardly see him, and then suddenly I discovered another boy standing in the corner, and that was Stuart. He didn't move at all, compared to the others who were jumping around and singing their hearts out. He looked delicate and fascinated me tremendously – I fell in love with him at first sight.[21]

The three were dangerously out of place here – bohemians in a cellarful of oiks, beauty amid brutality, sensitivity among menace, clean blow-dried heads in an oil-slick. In St Pauli as in Liverpool, looking different was enough to warrant a beating, and they felt it. While others danced, fought, threw beer or shouted to be heard above the music (with their new amps, the Beatles were getting louder all the time), Astrid, Klaus and Jürgen sat at a corner table they judged the safest and stared only at the stage, taking in every little artistic nuance. When the Beatles finished each number they felt moved to *applaud*. The Beatles couldn't help but notice them.*

Klaus and Jürgen spoke fractured English, not brilliant but enough to make themselves understood; Astrid spoke almost no English at all. Stuart was the one they targeted. Klaus tried John: he showed him a scraperboard design he'd done for a new record picture sleeve and was instantly redirected to Stu, 'the arty one'. And so they talked, and built up a rapport. 'The Beatles called us "the Krauts",' says Jürgen, 'and Stuart always asked me questions about Astrid because they couldn't really speak much.' These Krauts were addicted to the Beatles, and they especially loved Stuart, and after this they went to the Kaiserkeller most nights.[22]

Probably Stuart's first mention of his new friends in a letter to Liverpool was sent to his ex-girlfriend Susan Williams towards the end of October, pages that also contained one other key piece of news:

---

* It is always said Klaus, Astrid and Jürgen were 'exis' (short for 'existentialists'). Jürgen definitely inclined to existentialism more than the other two, but none of them followed it as a philosophical doctrine. It was more a label of convenience appropriated (mostly by others) to explain why they looked different to rockers and to ordinary Germans. Klaus is adamant too much has been made of them being exis. 'It is always completely overstated. We were not existentialists, no way. We had no political engagements whatsoever, no demonstrations. We just looked like them, but that derived from the fact that we'd analysed the French avant-garde and worked around Reinhart Wolf.'

I have definitely decided to pack the band in at the beginning of January. My curiosity is quenched, as far as rock 'n' roll is concerned anyway.

Just recently I have found the most delightful friends in three young artists here, one girl and two boys. What intrigues me however is the fact that they found me, and not I them. Looking like typical bohemians in 'real' suede jackets and jeans, they wandered into the club about a week ago ... They asked me why I was playing in a rock band as I obviously wasn't the type ... Here was I, feeling the most insipid looking member of the group being told how much superior I looked – this alongside the great Romeo John Lennon and his two stalwarts Paul and George – the Casanovas of Hamburg! A little intoxicated with their praise, I was enticed into showing them some drawings I had done while here ... the girl thought I was the most handsome of the lot and begged me to allow her to photograph me, which she did today. How ashamed I felt of the pleasure I experienced, of the contempt I felt for my dashing companions of rock – they who at my side had commented unani-mously on her unique beauty, while I, smugly content, knew of her contempt for them ... It's somehow like a dream which I'm participating in ...

Astrid did two photo sessions with Stuart, with superb results. She was gifted, used a Rolleicord and a tripod, measured the light, considered the set-ting and loved the subject. Stuart, who posed every night on stage, just posed some more, unsmiling, dark glasses, guitar, quiff stacked fantastically high, the photographer's hand-knitted scarf draped around his neck. In another letter, just before the second session, Stuart wrote of Astrid 'I find I love her very much ... Still, after tomorrow I will know for sure, as after a whole day in her company something's bound to happen ...'[23]

It did, and it was love, mutually enthralling, artistically glorious and word-lessly expressed. The only English she articulated to him was 'I am sorry that I can never say something to you' – words given her by Klaus or Jürgen, which she wrote on the back of her own photo and presented to him. It is the defin-itive Astrid Kirchherr image – a captivating, clean, stylish self-portrait taken in an ornate mirror, tree branches (dead but suspended in bud) pointing down to a pale and beautiful face.

Astrid and Klaus became Astrid and Stuart, and it all happened very fast. Stuart worried how Klaus would react and felt guilty about it long after Klaus conceded the situation. This took several weeks, a period dotted with dramatic moments, but as Klaus now reflects, 'I felt happy she'd found Stuart, like a brother would be when his sister finally finds a boyfriend. I was friends with them both and they were friends with me, so it was OK.'

When John wasn't calling Astrid, Klaus and Jürgen 'the Krauts', he named them 'Stuart's angel friends', and Paul was more jealous of Stu than ever. Astrid was artistic, attractive, cultured, an intellectual, from a wealthy middle-class Hamburg family; she even had her own car, a Volkswagen Beetle convertible. The relationship, as Paul expressed it from his personal perspective, 'peeved the rest of us like mad, that she hadn't fallen in love with any of us. [And] it was something none of us had ever seen before. None of our parents had that sort of relationship. It was a wild scene to us.'[24]

While the Hamburg trip was laced with memorable and fun moments, the personal truth for Paul was that little had gone right for him. George and Stu were still in with John at the Bambi and he wasn't – he had to share a room with a bloke who hardly spoke but got all the best-looking birds; his guitar was failing him on stage; and now Stu had fallen into the kind of relationship he envied. Worse, because he 'hated' Stu, it was inevitable that Stu's three new friends would take against him, or at least be less comfortable with him than with the others. Paul has ruefully conceded how, for Astrid, Klaus and Jürgen, 'John was number two, which is understandable, George was number three, which was a little bit miffing, because I had expected at least to get third. I came fourth, just before Pete Best.'[25] It wasn't even this. Astrid says, 'In order, I liked Stuart, John, George, Pete and Paul. I liked Pete but he was so very, very shy that you tended to forget about him. He was on his own really. Paul was so "nice" you couldn't get close. He was like a diplomat: everything had to be nice and calm. I never had a close relationship with Paul like I had with John and George.'

It was all too much, and Paul continued to let everyone know it. In a letter to Rod Murray sent towards the end of October, Stuart detailed in black-and-white the stark truth of the matter: 'Funnily enough, Paul has turned out the real black sheep of the trip. Everyone hates him and I only feel sorry for him.'

Perhaps this contributed to John and Paul writing no songs here, despite months of closeted opportunity. Actually, it had been like this for some time, since Stu had come into the group and perhaps before that. The hot streak that produced all those Lennon-McCartney Originals when their collaboration kicked off in 1958 had long since cooled. They hardly wrote at all now. Not that new songs were needed in the Kaiserkeller: as a bar band, it was important the Beatles played songs people knew or might know. There even came a point every night when Stu stepped up to the microphone and crooned Love Me Tender. Sometimes the Kaiserkeller went quiet for him, and he was applauded.

The Beatles were a long way from perfection, however. Tony Sheridan could see how far they'd come in such a short space of time, but he also identified some shortcomings: 'Stuart may have looked good but the guy really couldn't play bass to save his life. He was 90 per cent image, and the most you want is 50 per cent because the other 50 per cent must be musical talent. It didn't make the Beatles a good group to have a bass player who couldn't play bass, any more than it made them a good group to have Pete in there.'[26]

Pete's erratic timing hadn't improved, or improved enough, and was still exposed every time John and Paul wanted to vary from four-in-the-bar. Ringo was in no doubt that he had, in spades, what the Beatles lacked – 'I knew I was better than the drummer they had at the time'[27] – but then this was only to be expected, considering the gulf in experience between them.

As for Stuart, Klaus insists he was perfectly good enough on bass for the Beatles, but Paul thought like Sheridan: 'I was always practical, thinking our band would be great, but with him on bass there was always something holding us back.'[28] On the other hand, it also worried Paul that with Stuart quitting it looked like he would get the job, and Paul no more wanted to be lumbered with the bass than he'd wanted to be the drummer three months before: 'We always considered bass "the fat guy's instrument", the instrument played by the man standing at the back, and I liked the idea of being more at the front.'[29]

As it turned out, the Beatles were not the masters of their own destiny. On the first day of November, Bruno Koschmider handed them thirty days' written notice to leave. He was aborting their contract a month before its natural New Year's Eve expiry. 'The notice is given by order of the Public Authorities who have discovered that Mr George Harrison is only 17 (seventeen) years of age,' it read, but the Beatles knew there was more to it, and there was. Koschmider had notified the Fremdenpolizei of their birth dates in August, and for that authority not to have processed the document for eleven weeks would have represented a level of inefficiency unique here. Koschmider obviously wanted shot of them, and wasn't short of reasons. They'd been getting under his skin (and he theirs) since arrival, and it was just getting worse and worse. He also claimed their reckless flouting of his demands to play quieter at the Indra had caused the authorities to revoke his venue licence, at a personal cost of DM100,000.[30] Then there was the Beatles' behaviour at the Kaiserkeller. His logbook recorded antics so outrageous that he suspended their wages for a time. Koschmider even claimed the Beatles were attracting an unruly element into his bar. 'We had fights breaking out every ten minutes because of the Beatles,' he said, which might have been true, but blaming the Beatles for starting Grosse Freiheit bar brawls would be like blaming the Poles for the Second World War.

Koschmider also wanted shot of the Beatles because they openly flouted his rule about going into rival clubs. There was such a rule (though it was verbal, not in their contract) and they ignored it. Tony Sheridan was back in residence at the Top Ten Club from 28 October, playing with some of the Jets, and the Beatles would leave Grosse Freiheit during their breaks to watch him – and perhaps, briefly, join him on stage. They liked the Top Ten because it was less violent and because Peter Eckhorn had installed a fantastic sound system, the best they'd ever experienced. It was a real rock club, not a bar with music. As their instruments were still in the Kaiserkeller, any performances wouldn't have amounted to much, but Koschmider was undoubtedly hopping mad about them.

Looked at the other way, Koschmider's decision to serve notice on the Beatles by citing George's age, when it's highly likely the authorities knew it all along, suggests he'd been preventing them from taking any action until it suited him. The actual truth of the contract is that Koschmider had been in breach from the beginning: it was set down that he had to arrange working permits for them, and he hadn't.

Another factor, not without weight of its own, was the state of Koschmider's business relationship with Allan Williams. He'd stopped all commission payments now and it was only a matter of time before the Liverpudlian discovered it. On 11 November, the day after Williams formally offered Gerry and the Pacemakers to Eckhorn for a December season at the Top Ten, and less than three weeks from the opening of his own Top Ten Club in Liverpool, Williams wrote to Koschmider cancelling the five-year arrangement they'd agreed not three months previously. At a time when the Beatles could have had their manager urgently discussing their situation with Koschmider, he was in no position to do so.

This supposes the Beatles wanted to stay with Koschmider, though, and they didn't. If he wanted to end the deal early, he could. *Fuck him.* 'Something'll happen.' It's no coincidence that in a letter home to his mother, undated but written during November, Stuart explained, 'We go to Munich next Wednesday, for a month – more money, I think about 20 marks a week more.' Like the Berlin plan (which seems no longer to have been in the offing), this was probably one of their own fruitless dealings. They also thought they could stay in Hamburg and play at the Top Ten – it would be contrary to their Koschmider contract, but just let him try to stop them.

The fact is, wherever they'd be working, the authorities' knowledge of George's age meant he couldn't be part of it, and that he'd be making his way home.* The same kind of head-scratching that had brought Pete into the Beatles three months previously now turned to who could replace the lead guitarist. Despite Paul having John's Club Footy at his disposal, and maybe George's Futurama, he passed on the idea and they ended up trying to bring someone over from England. Pete suggested his friend Chas Newby, rhythm

---

* Just before leaving, it would seem, George had a brief period of playing with the Beatles only until 10PM. After that hour, they had to play without him.

guitarist in previous group the Blackjacks. It was agreed Pete should write and invite him to join them. Newby replied saying he couldn't, but if they still needed him during the Christmas vacation – in Hamburg or anywhere else – he'd gladly give them two weeks of his time.

One final month of Koschmider meant one final month in 'the pit'. Time had not warmed them to the Bambi Kino's charms, for it had none, and conditions were harsher than ever because the weather had turned. The Beatles came to Hamburg in late summer, mid-August, expecting to stay a month, perhaps two; those were the clothes they'd brought. Now they were staying through the autumn and into the winter. October 1960 was a bitterly cold month in this part of northern Europe, the average daily temperature plunging to 4.8°C/41°F, and it was just a shade higher in November. The unheated, concrete-walled Bambi was *freezing*, and Koschmider provided no additional blankets; they shivered themselves to sleep every night. 'Remember my grey sweater? Well, I wear it in bed, my socks too,' Stuart wrote. Worse yet, the rooms were damp, with water dripping on to their beds.

It was definitely 'brass monkey weather' the night John Lennon posed for pictures in his underpants on Grosse Freiheit. Like all good travelling Englishmen, he had a generous pair of Y-fronts about his person, as well as socks, a pair of sandals, a pullover, glasses, an imported copy of the *Daily Express* and a cap on his head. At least two photos were snapped of him standing by the rear door of the Bambi Kino – and in one he divested himself of his sweater and spectacles to stand naked save for the Y-fronts, feigning intent readership of the *Express* small print.[31]

He was dressed a few days later when the Beatles squeezed tight into Astrid Kirchherr's VW Beetle and she drove them off for a photo session – their first, and hers too. 'They couldn't believe I'd suggested it, and I couldn't believe they were so delighted,' she says. 'They even washed for it!' Her chosen location was Heiligengeistfeld ('the field of the Holy Spirit') in Feldstrasse, on the edge of St Pauli, where the great Hamburger Dom funfair had just taken up its thrice-yearly residence for a month.[32]

Astrid took twelve all-but-identical photos of John, Paul, George, Stu and Pete – with their four guitars and a snare drum – up against the steel of an open-sided lorry and the girders of the great rollercoaster.* The one she subsequently selected as 'best' is both the abiding shot of the Hamburg Beatles and the definitive image of the group before they attained fame. 'I liked the rough

---

* John has his Rickenbacker, Paul holds John's former guitar, the Club 40, restrung for his left-handed use.

surrounding of the rusty steel and bits of iron, and lorries. It fits with the Beatles' scruffiness, but when you look in their faces, compared to the rough surrounding, *that's* the contrast I was after.'

The Beatles had had maybe four hours' sleep since stepping off the Kaiserkeller stage, and under notice from Koschmider their Hamburg experience was unravelling. All that and more is in their faces. This one photograph singlehandedly defined the rock band image: young punks who think, dress and act differently to everyone else; who have ego and ambition to burn, but no future plans.

Astrid's other photos from the Dom are its equal. There's John alone with his Rickenbacker, sitting on the front of a heavy lorry, and John joined there by George and Stu with their guitars. There are fine photos of George; and, best of all, some extraordinary photos of Paul and John, individually, with Stu out of focus in the background. These are high-calibre intimate portraits, free of artifice, photos that probe inside. 'I didn't have to tell them not to smile, they just knew. They only had to look straight into the camera. They were absolute professionals, even when it took a long time to get everything just right. No one got angry or said that they didn't want to carry on.'

Astrid photographed George side-on, aware he was sensitive about his splayed ears, what the angel friends lovingly called his *Segelohren*. ('I tried to capture George's childlike and naive aspects.') Paul is natural, not mugging this time; he shows no trace of his awkward relationship with the photographer, but one eyebrow hovers as if slightly, fascinatingly, questioning. ('I tried to bring out Paul's wit and his airiness.') John doesn't pull a crip but lets Astrid get close, full into his face and deep into his eyes, behind defences to sorrow and vulnerability. ('I tried to capture John's wit and sensitivity.')

Pete slipped away after the group shots and features in no other image, and Astrid never took his photo again. He wasn't with the Beatles when, after the session, she drove them back to her house for something to eat – and another world opened up. Stu had already been to 45a Eimsbütteler Strasse but this was the first visit for John, Paul and George, their first real blessed release out of St Pauli, into the trees and quieter streets of residential Hamburg and Astrid's arty world. They instantly loved it.

Astrid's home was a spacious four-storey Altona townhouse belonging to her maternal family, the Bergmanns.* Three generations lived here in separate spacious apartments: her grandparents on the first floor, her aunt on the second, Astrid and her mother, Nielsa, on the third. Other relatives formerly lived in the

---

* They originate from Sweden. Astrid is a Swedish name; Kirchherr is German, meaning, in English, 'Church-lord'.

attic, and Klaus Voormann – who had no family in Hamburg because he was from Berlin – had lived here too. Astrid's father, Emil Kirchherr, died in 1958; he'd had a good job, as a senior salesman for the Ford motor company, and Nielsa was also of independent wealth, from her father, whose company (Theodor Bergmann) manufactured juke-boxes. There was taste, elegance, culture and a particular cleanliness about the house, aided by a maid. Nielsa was a gourmet cook and bought only the finest meats and fish, so the meal she served the Beatles was the best they'd had in months, and perhaps ever. They had to wait for each other to start, resist wolfing it down in the usual St Pauli manner, and not stub out their cigarettes on the plate afterwards.

Starved of home comforts since August, the Beatles made full use of the big house at 45a: they took baths, had their clothes washed and perhaps even ironed, and enjoyed being in a warm and cultured environment. 'Paul always used to look through my LPs – though I had only classical and jazz – and John always went straight for the books.'

Stu had already been enthusing to them about Astrid's bedroom and now they saw it for themselves. No girl in Liverpool had a room like this. It was *black*. Black carpet, big black velvet blanket on the black bed, black walls on which she and Klaus glued silver foil, and on a table was a silver candelabra. 'It was my Jean Cocteau phase,' she says. 'They were impressed.' Klaus says Nielsa hadn't wanted Astrid to decorate the room like this, 'but whatever Astrid wanted to do she was going to do; she was a pampered only-child who could get anything she wanted'.

Astrid had little difficulty persuading Nielsa to let Stuart escape the filthy and freezing Bambi and move into the apartment.* It was no hardship for Nielsa: she liked the young man, nor was she in the least troubled when, in mid-November, Astrid spoke of marrying him. Stuart expected no such reaction from his own mother. He knew, as Allan Williams knew, 'Millie Sutcliffe's attitude was the one lots of people had in Britain after the war: the only good German is a dead German.'

In an undated letter sent home during November, Stuart wrote:

I want your permission and my father's to become engaged to Astrid when I return to England. The question of when I marry her will be one of one or two years ... I've loved before but never so tenderly and intensely. The last three

---

* George left the Bambi couch and slept in Stu's old bed, Paul and Pete stayed in the second room. Leaving the Kaiserkeller in the early hours every morning, Stu headed for warm, middle-class comfort while his bandmates trooped back to the bitterly cold Kino for the definitive 'toppermost of the poppermost' experience ... a detail they didn't let him forget.

weeks or so have been a dream, but I feel calm and collected about this. She knows that I have to go back to college for a year and excepts [*sic*] it. Please write quickly and tell me what you think, but I've made up my mind anyway.

The last nights with Koschmider were bitter. Chief among their missions was to smash his stage. Only a few inches off the floor, it wasn't much more than wooden planks on top of beer crates, like the bar at a McCartney New Year's Eve party. They'd had trouble with it from the start, but Koschmider ignored all their complaints. They'd show him. Hour after hour the Beatles and the Hurricanes held a *Stompfest*. The Kaiserkeller audience lustily encouraged it, probably unaware of the secret motive. It was Rory who finally managed it, dropping leaden off the piano during Whole Lotta Shakin' Goin' On and sending his feet right through the wood. The deed done, the other Hurricanes and Beatles accidentally joined in rather a lot, destroying it some more. Koschmider was appalled; Rory was first fined and then sacked, and the Hurricanes were put on notice too. He could take no more. The man who'd brought British rock and roll to Hamburg was, within six months, waving the white flag – *er hat kapituliert* – and returning to more easily managed forms of entertainment.

When they weren't arguing the toss about guitars, the Beatles and the Hurricanes became close during their two months together. Every Sunday morning, by habit, they'd stagger out of the Kaiserkeller exhausted and seriously drunk after twelve straight hours of *Schau*ing, eat a late dinner or early breakfast, maybe top up with a bit more booze, and then walk down to the harbour, to wander with glazed eyes round and round the weekly *Fischmarkt*. Only then would they finally fall into their beds at the Sailors' Society and Kino.

It was Rory who inspired the only new Beatles composition to emerge from these Hamburg months. Having had local success with the Shadows' Apache, the Beatles wanted to learn Man Of Mystery, its follow-up and another huge British hit. They'd never heard it, but somehow Rory had, and they tried to get him to sing the notes. He whistled or sang the first few bars and they tried to play them, but then Rory couldn't remember any more and dissolved into his usual chronic stammering. John and George carried on, imagining how it might have gone, Rickenbacker and Futurama together, and the first Harrison-Lennon composition emerged. Mostly it was done to send up Rory, but at the end of the exercise they had themselves their very own Shadows-like twangy instrumental, which they called Beatle Bop.[33]

George's first impression of Ringo – that he looked 'the nasty one' – was shared by the other Beatles, but to know him was to like him; they had good times. Butlin's heavy drinking culture was merely an aperitif for Hamburg, and in the small hours of every morning – when the last group was playing the last session for St Pauli's last customers, and the music was getting slower and *slower* – the Beatles and Hurricanes lounged around, all pissed, and requested songs. If the Beatles were playing, Ringo sat at the front and asked for mournful numbers. Moonglow was one, and Paul fondly remembers him requesting a lowdown Duane Eddy instrumental: 'Ringo used to ask us, in a slurred, drunken voice, to play 3.30 Blues.'[34]

They weren't familiar enough to call him Richy, but John, Paul and George formed a bond with Ringo at the Kaiserkeller. Klaus witnessed it:

> He often came across to the Beatles' table and he always had a joke, and his one joke would trigger off the next person, so every time Ringo came near the Beatles it was happiness.
>
> I know the three of them discussed changing their drummer while they were in Hamburg, because I heard them. It wasn't said too explicitly because you don't just go and steal someone else's drummer, but they *always* liked Ringo.

Four years later, John looked back to 1960 and outlined the Beatles' position at that time: 'We met Ringo in Hamburg and we liked his style, but we'd only just got the other drummer so we couldn't do anything about it.'[35]

Pete was closest to John of all the Beatles, and it was this pairing that performed the most notorious act of the Hamburg trip. John had been indulging in the odd bit of 'slap leather' here – Astrid remembers how he 'would suddenly rub his hands and say, "I know, let's go shoplifting!" It was all fun, you couldn't be shocked'[36] – and the St Pauli extension of this was to steal from a drunken sailor. It was being done all over the place. The term, in English, was to 'roll' someone.

John once spoke about it to a journalist, saying their choice was a British sailor; they plied him with drinks on the promise of an interesting scene with a few birds, until they judged him so drunk they could knock him out – but after hitting him twice, they gave up. Pete says four of them (not Stu) were in on the plan, and the sailor was a fat German; they offered to walk him up the Reeperbahn, intending to rob him in one of its quieter corners. Though Paul and George dropped out, John and Pete carried on, and after felling the man with a rugby tackle, they grabbed his wallet, ran . . . and then dropped it when their victim fired a gas-gun at them. They hared back to the Bambi, slammed the door shut behind them, and for the next few nights watched carefully from the Kaiserkeller stage in case the sailor came for revenge – watched, in John's case, with eyes that could barely see.[37]

An identity parade would have been interesting. Dressing and looking as they did, the Beatles always turned heads in Hamburg. Some St Paulianer called them *beknackt* – literally 'cracked' and figuratively 'crazy'. Their stage gear, which was also their everyday gear and often their sleeping gear, gained greater uniformity during November when Paul bought a leather jacket to fall in with George, John and Pete. Another new addition to the stage uniform was a flat peaked cap, like the blue caps worn by Gene Vincent's group in *The Girl Can't Help It*, only these were pink. Being Liverpool lads, and in celebration of the colour, they called them twat 'ats. Then they went a step further again and bought multicoloured leather cowboy boots that extended halfway up their calves. They tucked their jeans into them, and the wooden heels stomped louder yet on the Kaiserkeller's patched-up stage.

The first to buy a leather jacket, George, was also the first to get the boots, bought from the leather shop Erdmann. John and Pete quickly followed, then Paul a couple of weeks later (Stuart didn't participate in the boots or caps). Dressed now in their pink twat 'ats, black leather jackets, black drain-pipe jeans and vivid Texan boots, they were *a sight*, and completely at odds with the Beatles who'd ducked out of Liverpool and arrived here three months previously. Klaus felt they were just *great*, poetically describing John as 'Rock hair, rock boots, rock clothes and rock jargon. Rock 'n' roll in his fingertips, from top to the tip of his toes, in the stomach but above all his throat.'[38]

On 28 November, Stu and Astrid exchanged rings and announced themselves engaged. There was still no news from the Western Front. Stuart's request for parental permission had not been accorded a reply. 'I assume you are rather annoyed about the whole situation,' he wrote again, on 2 December. 'I don't know what you or my father would have done in the same situation, but I don't feel I've let you down . . .'

By then, everything had changed, because the Beatles' fourteen sensational weeks under Bruno Koschmider ground to a halt even more abrupt than expected. According to statements written for the police in January 1961 by Paul and Pete, the group had an unplanned interview with Koschmider (and his interpreter) in his Kaiserkeller office at 1.30 one morning. For 'interview' read 'showdown'. Their hopes of playing in Berlin had come to nothing, though Munich remained a post-Christmas possibility. In the meantime, Koschmider had got wind of their plan to stay in Hamburg and join Tony Sheridan at the Top Ten. In a rapidly escalating tit-for-tat, Koschmider tried to make the Beatles sign a document agreeing they wouldn't work any other Hamburg venue in December, and when they refused he threatened them with physical violence (broken fingers, Pete remembers) and said he'd not pay their return fares to England.* It was another of those moments when all eyes turned to leader Lennon. He told Koschmider they'd never play for him again, and he could *stuff* the notice period. Koschmider shouted he wouldn't pay them their latest wages, at which point events became so heated he brought the meeting to an end and had them manhandled from his office. The Beatles simply couldn't wait to shift everything over to the Top Ten, their accommodation included, and stick the biggest V-sign ever right up Koschmider's fat nose.

George, though, was going home. The night before, he sat up with John and ran through the lead guitar lines he'd need to know. (Presumably, though not necessarily, Paul was switching to rhythm.) It was a time of torment for George – he was being thrown out just at the moment they had a new booking, and if the Top Ten arrangement extended to Christmas, and then they went on to Munich, who knew when he'd see them again? Would someone else take his place? Was this the end of George Harrison and the Beatles? He certainly thought so. 'I felt terrible . . . I had visions of our band staying on there with me stuck in Liverpool, and that would be it.'[39]

Astrid and Stu drove him to the Hauptbahnhof and put him on the express train to the Hook of Holland. 'He was just standing there, little George, all lost,' says Astrid. 'I gave him a big bag of sweets and some apples. He threw his arms around me and Stu, which was the sort of demonstrative thing they never did.'[40] He faced a lonely and arduous journey, twenty-four hours weighed down by his guitar, an amp and several pieces of luggage, depressed about Hamburg and anticipating the embarrassment of being back in Liverpool without the others. He knew he'd come under renewed pressure from his dad to 'get a proper job', and if it was weeks or months before the other Beatles came home it'd be harder to dig in his cowboy-booted heels and resist.

George might have been placated to some small degree by the inclusion of his name on a letter agreement, that the Beatles would play at the Top Ten for at least a month from April 1961 – a basic document written in Peter Eckhorn's hand and dated 30 November – but then this paper also named Stuart and he'd made it clear he was quitting. In the meantime, the final four could start playing there now, and move themselves into the bunk-bed accommodation at the

---

* Unless there was a superseding contract about which nothing is known, the Beatles had already agreed not to appear elsewhere in Hamburg (though they were planning to disregard it) and Koschmider wasn't obliged to pay their return fares. So much about this period is foggy. Though Pete claims the Beatles demanded their early exit from the Kaiserkeller contract a few days before they quit, a surviving document indicates they were already under notice of termination – though the contract makes no mention of this being necessary.

top of the building.* Tony Sheridan was already here, possibly others too, and the Beatles were welcome to shoehorn themselves in. It was neither the Ritz nor the pits. John was the first to move. Then Paul and Pete went back to the Bambi to grab their gear.

The place was in near darkness, as usual. They had to strike a match to see their way about … and then they decided to leave Koschmider a little gift. Pete had a few 'spunk bags', and he and Paul had the idea to hang them on nails in the wall in the long concrete passageway and set light to them. 'The place was dank and dark,' says Pete. 'They spluttered, they stank, and OK, maybe they singed a tiny bit of tapestry on the wall. It caused nothing but a little smoke and a few scorch marks and then they went out.'[41] It was the ultimate *fuck you, Bruno*, or so they thought.

They got to play one night in the Top Ten, and it seems to have been a good one, pulling business away from the Kaiserkeller, but it was just this one night. Having been shafted once by Eckhorn, when he'd prised away the Jets and Tony Sheridan from the Kaiserkeller, Koschmider wasn't going to sit back and let it happen again. He might also have guessed the Beatles would make some grand gesture for his 'benefit' – they could even have hinted at it – because an inspection was made of the Bambi's rooms very quickly. When the *stinkende qualmende Piedeltüten* were found, he decided to form the view it was an attempt to burn down his cinema, and informed the police.

The chronology of events over the next twenty-four hours is rife with confusion and contradiction, but may have gone something like this. Paul was picked up by the police while walking along the Reeperbahn, taken by car to the Davidwache police station (two hundred metres from the Top Ten) and locked in a cell. Pete and John were also arrested. Koschmider didn't know which of them was responsible for the 'attempted arson', so the *Polizei* rounded them all up. As Stuart wrote in a letter back to Liverpool a few days later:

---

* The Eckhorns owned the freehold at Reeperbahn 136. The Top Ten was on the ground floor in the rear and its toilets were in the basement, which still had stables from when the Hippodrom was a horse circus. The front of the building was a four-storey gabled house; two generations of Eckhorns lived here, and the attic space had a small spare room with bunk beds.

It has never been explained why an agreement for April 1961 was drawn up, even roughly, on 30 November when it was expected they would be playing there until Christmas – an engagement for which there seems to have been no paperwork at all. (While the document is most likely legitimate, it's possible it was written 'after the fact', in 1961, in an attempt to deceive authorities.) Nor is it clear why Eckhorn wanted the Beatles in the Top Ten in the last month of 1960: Tony Sheridan was resident, and Gerry and the Pacemakers were already fixed to come out from Liverpool for eight weeks from 9 December.

I am living in the lap of luxury and contentment. Better than the cell I spent a night in last week. I was innocent this time though accused of arson – that is, setting fire to the Kino (cinema) where we sleep. I arrive at the club and am informed that the whole of Hamburg Police are looking for me. The rest of the band are already locked up, so smiling and very brave on the arm of Astrid, I proceed to give myself up. At this time I'm not aware of the charge. All my belongings, including spectacles, are taken away and I'm led to a cell where without food or drink I sat for six hours on a very wooden bench, the door shut very tight. I fall asleep at two in the morning. I signed a confession written in Deutsch that I knew nothing about a fire, and they let me go.[42]

John was also allowed to go. It was now clear who'd done the dirty deed, and for them the ordeal continued; Paul would always remember the little one-way peep-hole in the door of their detention room, through which he sensed they were watched. It seems he and Pete were then allowed to leave, but a few hours later – early the following morning – they were dragged out of their Top Ten bunk beds and interviewed a second time. Pete suggests they were taken to Hamburg's main prison at Fühlsbuttel, Paul remembers it being 'the *Rathaus* ... it doesn't mean rat house, it just felt like one'. They were interviewed by an official of the Bundeskriminalamt (Federal CID), one Herr Gerkins, and it was definitely inadvisable to snigger. Instead, they requested permission to contact the British Embassy, like people did in the films, and were refused; then they were taken for a car ride. 'We tried our best to persuade him it was nothing,' Paul says, 'and he said, "OK fine, well you go with these men." And that was the last we knew of it. We just headed out with these couple of coppers. And we were getting a bit "Oh dear, this could be the concentration camps" – you never know. It hadn't been that long [since the war].'[43]

Criminal charges were not pressed, but Koschmider, inevitably, had the last laugh. It wasn't a camp to which Paul and Pete were being taken, but the airport – and in handcuffs, according to Stuart. They were being deported, and banned from re-entering Germany unless they lodged an appeal within a month. *Auf Wiedersehen, Piedels!* Handed their passports at the gate, they were put on the London plane, set to fly for the first time in their lives. It then got even tastier for Koschmider because Eckhorn was billed for at least part of the cost of the plane tickets. Bruno must have been rubbing his hands with joy.

At the time all this was happening, George was sailing from the Hook of Holland to Harwich, praying he had enough money for the train into London, for porters (necessary), a taxi to Euston, train to Liverpool and taxi out to Speke. 'I had too many things to carry and was standing in the corridor of the train with my belongings around me, and lots of soldiers on the train, drinking.

I finally got to Liverpool and took a taxi home – I just about made it. I got home penniless. It took everything I had to get me back. I felt ashamed, after all the big talk when we set off for Hamburg.'[44]

Paul and Pete reached Liverpool at more or less the same time. They travelled with no money at all, or possessions. Everything was still at Reeperbahn 136 – musical equipment, luggage, purchases, cash. They had only the clothes they'd thrown on when the police burst in. From London Airport they took a courtesy bus to West London Air Terminal in Kensington and then the Tube to Euston, perhaps dodging the fare. Without money for tickets to Liverpool, Pete phoned home and Mona said she'd wire cash to the station's post office. They had to hang around Euston several hours and it wasn't until early the following morning that Pete finally arrived back in West Derby and Paul in Allerton. Like George, they felt the embarrassment of such ignominious returns.

Mike remembers Paul full of speedy talk about what a fantastic time they'd had and what wonderful things he'd bought for them ... and then he sat down on the couch and revealed legs 'as thin and white as dad's pipe-cleaners'. Jim thought Paul looked half-dead, a skeleton, in dire need of nourishment and rest. 'What an object of art!' exclaimed Mona when she saw Pete in his leather jacket, torn jeans and cowboy boots.[45] Louise wasn't around to greet George – she'd sailed to Ontario, Canada, to see her daughter, son-in-law, grandchildren and one of her brothers, and wouldn't be home for five months; Harry was very pleased to welcome back his youngest boy – and wondered, as did they all, whether these children would finally now 'settle down', having surely got this rock and roll music out of their system.

John and Stu were still in Hamburg. On the same day Paul and Pete were sent home, 1 December, they had to fill in forms for work and residence permits; Stu was planning to stay until January and what John had in mind isn't known. It was moot anyway: when they had a further interview on the 6th, they were told they couldn't work, and that while Stu could stay on temporarily, John had to leave Germany by the 10th. He spent some of these days with Stu, Astrid and Nielsa at 45a Eimsbütteler Strasse and he played with Tony Sheridan in the odd Top Ten session, Rory Storm – sacked from the Kaiserkeller – singing here too.

It all ended on 7 December when John became the fourth Beatle to head home, having flogged clothes to pay for his travel. His journey was the same as George's – train, boat, two or three more trains, maybe taxis – and he was hellishly burdened, shaped into the very hunchback he'd been acting on stage these months. 'It was terrible, setting off home on my own. I had my amp on my back, scared stiff I was going to get it pinched. I hadn't paid for it. I was convinced I'd never find England.'[46] He got back to Liverpool on 8 December 1960, in the middle of the night. There was nowhere to go but Mendips, and John knew very well how this humiliating return would be greeted by Mimi. She made him wait. He had to throw stones up at her bedroom window before she went down to open the door.

Well! Mimi had never-seen-such-a-sight-in-all-her-born-days.

As Paul had defied his dad in the way he'd left school, and breached his every resistance to Hamburg, Jim felt it was time to lay down some rules. Paul was back home in the middle of the academic year, so any resumption of studies – if he could be persuaded, which didn't seem likely – would have to wait until September 1961. Jim saw months of nothing-much stretching ahead and was determined to prevent it. 'Satan finds work for idle hands,' he kept saying.[47]

Paul went down the Labour Exchange at Renshaw Hall and landed a £10-a-week Christmas-period job with SPD Ltd, Speedy Prompt Deliveries. He was 'second man' on a lorry, hopping off to deliver parcels while the driver waited with the engine running. The depot was at 51 Sefton Street, by a scruffy patch of dock road wasteland called the Bally, and Paul had to be down there five mornings a week at 6.30, riding the early bus in the damp wintry darkness with other working men. He fancied himself as one, wearing a donkey jacket and unusually buying the *Daily Mirror*.[48] It was like Hamburg had never happened.

Paul and Dot picked up relations where they'd left off. If she pressed him on the question of his fidelity he had the ultimate answer, a ring for her finger . . . except it was still in Hamburg. George, who had no girlfriend, popped around to see Arthur Kelly and sink a pint or two. As Arthur remembers, 'He came to my house wearing cowboy boots and tight jeans. Going out like that was risky – you could get the shit kicked out of you for it, but I was still as envious as buggery.'[49] Having harboured all those gloomy thoughts about his place in the Beatles, George was hugely relieved to find Paul and Pete home. He was missing out on nothing, which meant he could probably resist his dad's prodding to get a job. No matter what they did next, it would be done together. All they had to do was wait for John to get home, to find out what it was.

They'd no idea he was back in Liverpool, because John was lying low. He was at a crossroads. It was rare for him to consider anything quite so carefully, but five months after deciding to earn his living from the guitar, he took stock of his position. 'I had to think it over. It had been quite a shattering experience to be in a foreign country. We were pretty young. I'd come home on my own, with no money and just carrying amplifiers and guitars. I was thinking, "Is this what I want to do? Is this it? Night-clubs? Seedy scenes? Being deported? Weird people in the clubs?" I thought hard about it: "Should I continue doing this?"'[50]

These were days that must have given Mimi faint hope, a straw to clutch, that John might yet set aside these foolish things and turn his talents to something useful, like *a job*. His decision would dash that once and for all. At least John had Cyn for comfort, and they consumed each other again. The last day of art school before the Christmas break was 16 December and John saw her lunchtimes and night-times.

Pete and Mona were already in touch with Peter Eckhorn, arranging transportation of the gear he and Paul had left behind. John and George had their guitars and amps, but Paul's unSolid 7 was still in Hamburg along with his Elpico amp, and Pete's drum kit was still parked on the Top Ten stage. Pete had recently written BEATLES ROCK COMBO on the bass drum head, his preferred name for them. If they were going to play again – and the Casbah was the obvious place to kick off – they needed the gear back. Eckhorn was as co-operative as Koschmider was obstructive, arranging a shipment that was due in Liverpool before Christmas.

In the Beatles' absence – which wasn't noticed – the Liverpool rock scene had continued to grow. The busiest individual was Bob Wooler, its guiding hand and wit in residence. Telling colleagues 'This is not my station in life', he uncoupled from a steady job as a railway clerk at Garston Docks to become a full-time rock and roll professor and champion. It was a courageous move for a man of almost 35 (though he never admitted his age), but Allan Williams had been at his most persuasive, offering him the top job at the Top Ten: day-to-day manager as well as DJ and MC. Williams hadn't wasted a moment to rush through the launching of the first seven-days-a-week rock club in the centre of Liverpool . . . yet his haste was its undoing. The club opened for business on 1 December (at the very moment George, Paul and Pete were struggling home from Hamburg), and its location was all wrong. One end of Soho Street joined Islington, which wasn't too far from Lime Street, but number 100 was up the top end, close to Everton. It was well beyond easy reach from the city centre and in a part of Liverpool with *a reputation*. Williams knew right away he'd made an error of judgement when he drove around the area in his minibus, making announcements about the club's opening, and people started throwing stones at him.[51]

In too deep, he pressed on. As well as appointing Wooler, he booked good talent from a London agency to appear alongside all the Liverpool groups, he brought in an ultra-violet light that made everyone appear drenched in dandruff, and he hired the most breathtaking Swiss-made juke-box anyone had ever seen. The building attracted much comment too: it was an old wood-built factory with low beams. 'Even I was banging my head on them,' says the 5ft 3in entrepreneur. 'I had to put up signs everywhere telling people to duck their head.'

There was trouble right away with the local toughs, and Wooler also worried about all the electrical apparatus – and so many people smoking – upstairs in a wooden building. Sure enough, after just six nights, half an hour after the club had emptied for the evening, the place burned down. It was gone in minutes.

'Someone got careless with the Bryant & May's,' Wooler always said, one of many to think it *a torch job*, or an insurance job by Williams, but an investigation found overloaded electricity as the cause.

Paul and George went to Soho Street the next day. The fantastic new club meant to establish the Beatles in their home city was smouldering timber. How very strange that, after two of them had been deported for trying to burn down the Bambi – in John's jokey words, the official order was 'Bad Beatles, you must go home and light your English cinemas'[52] – the Liverpool satellite of their favourite Hamburg club burned down before they even got there. Herr Koschmider would have loved that.

The destruction of the Top Ten (which Wooler was already calling 'the Soho Street hotspot') brought out ulcers in Allan Williams and he went into hospital. Beyond his loss, he felt bad about having enticed Wooler to jettison a job for one already gone up in smoke. Williams also asked him to 'look after the Beatles – get them some work'.

George was introduced to Wooler in the Jac on 15 December, when he went to collect a letter Stuart had sent him – and he was very surprised to find John in there too. He was back! In a warm and chatty return letter posted the following day, four pages that spoke volumes for their friendship, George gave Stu the Beatles' latest news and views. They had bookings for Christmas Eve, Boxing Day and New Year's Eve, and a man he called 'some queer bloke' seemed particularly keen to put work their way. George begged Stu to return quickly to Liverpool because Paul would be a 'crumby' bass player – even if he had a bass guitar and amp to use – and George wanted the Beatles to be at their best: 'I would like to have the whole group appearing for our first few bookings at least, so as to go down well from the start. So how about coming home, son. Wouldn't it be good, Astrid's first Christmas in England!'*

The 'queer bloke' in George's letter was surely Wooler – queer probably meant in the sense of being singular. Wooler was a homosexual, but this, like his age, was a secret he guarded deeply and to which he gave no outward clue – it would be surprising if George had already twigged it. Wooler's keenness to find the Beatles work was being executed in good faith: he'd barely or never seen them play and was accepting Williams' assurance that Hamburg had made

---

* In other pages, George gently suggested Stu send him some money because he wanted to buy an echo unit for £34 'or £6 down, the rest when Frank [Hessy] catches me'. Despite being quoted elsewhere saying he had no money, George reported purchases of the Eddie Cochran LP *Singin' To My Baby* and several 45s: Lucille and Like Strangers by the Everly Brothers, Only The Lonely by Roy Orbison, and instrumentals Man Of Mystery by the Shadows and Perfidia by the Ventures, and he was thinking of buying Chariot by Rhet Stoller. As he put it, 'I am learning everything I can get my hands on now!'

them hot. Though not doing anything themselves to bring about this new arrangement, the Beatles would benefit enormously from being taken under Bob Wooler's wing. He was astute, he encouraged, he had everyone's respect and he kept his word.

After the Top Ten fire, Wooler was approached by Brian Kelly. 'Beekay' was now fully switched on to rock, promoting jive dances throughout the north end, two or three a week, and he offered Wooler general charge: booking manager, stage manager, compere and DJ. Kelly ran Liverpool's best circuit, and as the Beatles no longer wanted to play in the Jacaranda coal-hole, they were ideal for Wooler to bring together. But Kelly was also the man they'd let down seven months earlier, when he'd advertised them for a Saturday dance in Seaforth and they rushed off to Scotland without telling him. He'd sworn never to book them again, and it was only because of Wooler's high regard, and some Williams-like persuasion skills, that Kelly grudgingly agreed, adding them to a dance at Litherland Town Hall on the 27th. He did so even after being affronted by the £8 fee Wooler asked for them. Kelly offered £4 and they settled on £6. Wooler took no commission.

'When George and Paul found out [I was home] they were mad at me because they thought we could have been working,' John would say. It was only a week for him, but they'd been home two. Like George, Paul had been 'wondering whether it was going to carry on or if that was the last of it'.[53] Now that John had done his thinking, and he was pointing *forward*, this was where they would go.

Still, they had to get themselves sorted out, and fast. Johnny Gustafson was taken aback to see George in the Jacaranda and even more surprised to be asked to join the Beatles as their new (or at least temporary) bass player. Content in the Cassanovas, he declined.[54] Instead, the Beatles took on Chas Newby as a short-term fix. Pete's friend had already offered himself for the two-week Christmas college break, expecting to replace George in Hamburg; instead, he deputised for Stu in Liverpool.

Their first booking was for the members of the Casbah Coffee Club on Saturday the 17th. The Quarrymen had last played here in January, now they were back as the Beatles and the club belonged to their drummer. As long as Pete was in the group, 8 Hayman's Green would be a useful base and Mona Best an indomitable ally. John, Paul, George, Chas and Pete had a quick rehearsal, the last two using gear borrowed from local group Gene Day and the Jango Beats, Paul perhaps playing his old Zenith. Chas, a left-hander, was new to the bass, and because he wasn't allowed to restring Tommy McGuirk's right-handed Hofner President, he had to play it upside down. McGuirk also loaned him a leather jacket, and though it had a furry collar it just about looked the part. Newby remembers having to learn Wooden

Heart (by Elvis, not yet released in Britain), Red Sails In The Sunset and Hallelujah, I Love Her So.

Pete's regular letters home from Hamburg had assured his best friend and housemate Neil Aspinall of the Beatles' massive improvement since they'd left Liverpool. Neil took the news in good faith, made a poster announcing *Return of the Fabulous Beatles* and pinned it on the club wall. Come the night, he saw his hyperbole fully justified. 'They could have been awful for all I knew. I was upstairs when they started playing, then Rory [Best] came and found me – "Hey, come and see them!" And wow, they were *so* fuckin' good. Their music was *very* different and they were scruffier than ever in twat 'ats, cowboy boots and leather.'[55]

In his own particular dead-straight manner, Aspinall was a Beatles fan from this moment … as was everyone else at the Casbah. Pete remembers, 'We belted it out exactly as we had been doing in Hamburg, and you could physically feel the crowd gasp. It just silenced them. When we finished the first number the place went into rapture, it just exploded.' The Beatles hadn't told Chas their act involved a lot of stomping, and by the end of the night – they closed with a riotous What'd I Say – his feet had lost all feeling. 'It was only a year since I'd seen them as the Quarrymen and they were vastly better. They were much more professional and had a really solid sound. I was frightened to death of making mistakes.'[56]

Between this date and their next on Christmas Eve – back at the old familiar Grosvenor Ballroom in Liscard – the Beatles' ship came in. Pete and Mo went down to the customs shed to retrieve the gear they'd left in Hamburg. Unable to fit the crate into the taxi, they had to dismantle it on the quay, in a bitterly cold wind. Through their efforts, the Beatles were really ready to rip.[57]

The year that began hopelessly ended explosively. They played the Casbah on New Year's Eve, in the cellar of the house in West Derby,* but the moment when things really kicked off for the Beatles in Liverpool, the night that presaged high times, was the one Bob Wooler fixed with Beekay in the ballroom of Litherland Town Hall on Tuesday 27 December.

Here, a mile from the Mersey docks in a northern working-class suburb, the ferocious waiters and angel friends of St Pauli were a world away. No bawdy neon or guttural barkers punctured the quiet, dark night, just two to three hundred young Liverpudlians, loping Lowry-like towards the council ballroom, lasses in dresses, lads in suits, ties and quiffs, some hoping for a scrap. This was home.

Patrons paid three shillings through a porthole to a middle-aged woman cashier; ladies' and gents' cloakrooms left and right, coats exchanged for a

---

* Paul, perhaps for the first time, had to miss his family's annual party.

numbered ticket. Push through double swing doors and into the hall, built for mayoral balls and firms' dances; the smell of a polished sprung dance-floor and cigarette smoke, six great arched windows, seats around the sides and under the high-set stage, a pair of stewards prepared to kick out troublemakers, clutches of girls already dancing around handbags. Refreshments upstairs on the balcony laid on by Mrs Morris, ample wife of the caretaker and mayoral mace-bearer; tea and coffee in cups and saucers, Coke bottles with straws, sandwiches, motherly advice for kids with problems. Bob Wooler in suit and tie, playing records from a deck at the side of the stage while the first group set up behind the heavy curtains. The night's two other groups, almost all teenage lads, lark and cuff backstage in a couple of drab dressing-rooms …

It was the fifth of eight Beekay jive dances over the festive week and no one was expecting magic. Visually and musically presentable, the groups mentioned in the local press ad – the Deltones and Del Renas – mostly played chart songs, the influence and little dance steps of Cliff Richard and the Shadows all-pervasive, guitar twangs posted neatly through an echo box. Then it was the Beatles' turn. Trusting to instinct, Wooler gave them the prime spot, and they had half an hour. He discussed presentation with them, something he alone on the Liverpool rock scene knew to be important. He spoke alliteratively and wagged his forefinger to make the point: it was all about *impact! immediacy! impression!* He'd announce them with the curtain closed, but the moment they heard their name they should start playing, then the drapes would part and they'd be already up and running.

'Direct from Hamburg – the sensational BEATLES!'
   Gonna tell Aunt Mary, 'bout Uncle John! He claim he has the misery but he's havin' a lot of fun!

Paul tore into Long Tall Sally and hit the Little Richard notes right off, the others struck up behind him, the curtains swished open and here they were: Hamburg-hardened rockers in uniform black leather jackets, black drainpipe jeans tucked into gold and silver cowboy boots, pink twat 'ats on top of big quiffs. Here was John's American guitar and amp, not one but three different singers in the front line, unadulterated Chuck Berry, Elvis Presley, Eddie Cochran, Gene Vincent, the first stirrings of Motown and a ballad or two. Here were eye-catching personalities and ear-grabbing harmonies, boom-boom-boom-boom on the big bass drum and stomp-stomp-stomp-stomp from hard wooden heels on a town hall stage. Five of them: John rocking and startling, Paul rocking and charming, George rocking and smiling, Pete rocking and reticent, Chas rocking and *wide-eyed*.

It was meant to be a dance, but the floor emptied. Everyone rushed forward and stood crushed at the front. As Bob Wooler remembered:

> They were transfixed. They were looking up, and I was looking down at the sea of faces. They hadn't seen or heard anything like it before. I'd never seen anything like it. The Beatles were sensational ... They had such a magical influence on people. They put everything into their performance.
>
> People went crazy for their closing number, What'd I Say. Paul took the mike off the stand, shed his guitar and did fantastic antics all over the stage. They were all stomping like hell and the audience went *mad*.[58]

Mad for *Germans*, no less, which was even more amazing – because, as John recalled, 'They all thought we were German. We were billed as "from Hamburg" and they'd all say, "You speak good English."'[59]

Brian Kelly's only local competition, Dave Forshaw, a young rock fan who promoted beat nights in Bootle, was awed not only by the Beatles' magnetism and confidence but by their clothes. Men were allowed into few places without a tie and nowhere at all in working men's jeans, but here, for the first time, was a group *on stage* in leather jackets, jeans and no ties. It was mind-boggling. Forshaw got into their dressing-room afterwards and booked them for three dates. 'I organised them with Pete Best, but Lennon was answering back.'[60]

Sharp to the moment, Kelly told the stewards to allow no one else near them. Only days earlier he'd needed all Wooler's persuasion to book the Beatles when his instinct was to blackball them; now he was the luckiest promoter in Liverpool. 'I was completely knocked out by them. They had a pounding, pulsating beat which I knew would be big box office.'[61] So badly did he want them for himself, Kelly barred his own booking manager: Wooler was kept away from them this night because of his association with other promoters.

When everyone had gone home, Kelly invited the Beatles upstairs for refreshments, got out his 1961 diary and started to talk dates. John, Paul and George, who'd never had any aptitude for organisation, happily conceded the chore to Pete. He knew how to do it, familiar with such dealings through Mona's Casbah enterprise and Johnny Best's boxing promotions. In that instant, Pete became the Beatle who took care of the bookings. It was another asset in his favour, fixing his position when in other ways it was less secure.

Kelly booked them solid, for almost every one of his jive dances over the next three months, at £6 to £8 a time. It was money in the bank. As he well knew, you were lucky if something like the Beatles came along once in a lifetime.

YEAR 4, 1961:–
THE ROCK AGE

18

The Big Beat Boppin' Beatles
(January–March 1961)

Getting to work was a two-bus journey, changing at Penny Lane before jumping off by Edge Hill, at the spaghetti-tangle of railway tracks. After skipping down the dark line-side slipway near the gasholders, Paul McCartney arrived, 8AM every weekday, at the Bridge Road factory of Massey & Coggins Ltd, armature winders and transformer manufacturers, where he imagined himself stepping up to executive status.

Christmas was past and with it went the parcel deliveries, so Jim Mac made his mightiest effort yet at insisting his son had to *knuckle down*. Paul said he already had a job, playing in a group, and they were beginning to go places, but Jim was so resolute that Paul went back to Renshaw Hall and did the jobless shuffle again – a surname and number like twenty thousand others, from the scallies of 15 to the Scousers of 64, many seeking work, plenty hoping to dodge it. 'I went down to the Labour Exchange in me donkey jacket and jeans. The fellow sent me to an electrical engineers firm called Massey & Coggins. I told the boss I wanted a job. I wasn't particular, I said I'd sweep the yard if he wanted. He asked me where I'd been educated and when I said Liverpool Institute he started making big plans.'[1]

The job came his way by chance, but if Paul's aim was to get back at his dad by finding a position diametrically opposed to his talents, he couldn't have arranged it better. Instead of something suited to his bright mind, artistic flair, neat handwriting, five O-Levels and English Lit A-Level, Paul joined a factory, one among the flat-capped working classes punching the clock.

Jim Gilvey, Massey & Coggins' then 39-year-old managing director, would never forget the arrival in his works office of Paul McCartney: 'I interviewed him. He was applying for a job as an electrical apprentice. He would have become an electrician after five years – in the spring of 1966. He never said 'owt to me about being a musician. He called me "Mr Gilvey" and was a very polite young man. I said, "We'll give you an opportunity, lad, and with your outlook on life you'll go a long way."'[2]

Employed against his own wishes maybe, Paul so quickly tapped into a keen, self-motivating attitude that he pictured himself an important man of business not many years from now. 'The group had got going again but I didn't know if I wanted to go back full time . . . I imagined myself working my way up, being an executive if I tried hard.'[3] While John, George and Pete enjoyed long days of leisure, the boss-to-be learned how to wind heavy coils for electric motors, ate jam butties, and played dinner-time football with other fellers 'in a sort of prison exercise yard'.[4] He made and drank a strong brew of tea in the union-negotiated breaks, smoked Woodbines, read the *Daily Mirror*, dashed for the gate when the afternoon hooter went and lived for the weekend and Friday's wage packet (£7 10s, less tax and National Insurance). 'He had to wear a blue boiler-suit and provide it himself,' says Jim Gilvey. 'We had a sort of canteen and all the workers were members of the ETU – the Electrical Trades Union.'

Paul also braved endless jibes about his plentiful hair; and then, after letting out that he was a musician, had to suffer the nickname Mantovani. As boss of the transformer department, Ron Felton had to give Mantovani orders – you must do this, you can't do that – and Paul surely bristled. 'I never liked bosses,' he reflected twenty-five years later, and as he only ever really had one, he probably meant Felton.[5]

Though John also came under labour pressure, from Mimi, he was having none of it, and was genuinely shocked that Paul was prepared to brummer strive after everything they'd been through together. 'Paul would always give in to his dad. His dad told him to get a job and he fuckin' dropped the group, saying, "I need a steady career!" We couldn't believe it.'[6]

Paul didn't drop the Beatles, he just accommodated them alongside the job. The Beatles began 1961 with three bookings a week for promoter Brian Kelly – usually at Litherland Town Hall, Aintree Institute, and Lathom Hall in Seaforth – and as these tended to revolve around weekends, working by day and playing by night caused Paul few problems. Such, anyway, was the adrenalin they generated, the Beatles could have lived without sleep.

They weren't the first Liverpool group back from Hamburg. Derry and the Seniors were, and they hadn't exactly set the place alight. By contrast, the Beatles' return was no less explosive, locally, than the arrival of rock and roll itself in 1956. No one expected it, no one knew who they were or where they came from, they were just suddenly *there*, good beyond belief, so exceptional that everything started to change because of them, and quickly.

In seven extraordinary *mach Schau*ing weeks at the Kaiserkeller the Beatles had doubled the vast amount of stage time already accrued at the Indra. In total, inside just fourteen weeks, they'd rocked Hamburg for about 415 hours – like 276 ninety-minute shows or 830 half-hours – and every night tried not to repeat themselves. No one stopped to realise it, and there was no way of knowing anyway, but the Beatles had to be the most experienced rock group in the world, not just Liverpool. And Hamburg didn't only multiply their repertoire, it toughened their voices, seasoned their characters, enriched their personalities and strengthened their stamina. Four months earlier they would have struggled to play more than a couple of hours, now it was a piece of cake. All the same, witnesses say they played every show with total conviction – St Pauli in Liverpool. The effect was incredible.

First sight of the new Beatles would stay lifelong-sharp in the memory. Wallasey rock guitarist Chris Huston was knocked sideways:

> When they came back from Germany it was like they knew something we didn't. They had this *arrogance*. There was a definite difference: they had cockiness, confidence, a spring in their step, they knew more songs and they had different instruments. I asked John what it was like in Hamburg and he said, 'Fookin' great! They roll up the pavements in Liverpool at eleven, but in Hamburg they're just rolling them out at midnight.' But that didn't answer what I saw, because Hamburg didn't change anyone else the same way.[7]

The Beatles were a foursome for the first time. Stu was in Hamburg with Astrid, though due home soon, and Chas Newby was back in college, his two weeks in the Beatles at an end. Paul was on bass now ... in a manner of speaking. He is remembered for playing his upside-down and broken-down Rosetti with the lead tucked into his pocket rather than plugged into an amplifier – miming, in other words – producing (at best) a few clicks picked up by the vocal microphone. When he did run the Rosetti through an amp it generated an unusual sound because Paul had fitted it with piano strings, three or four of them, snipped surreptitiously from someone's upright with a pair of pliers. The Beatles' overall noise was so loud that hardly anyone noticed the lack of bass. Instrumentally, the Beatles' raw power was coming from three players, not four.

The front-of-house 'mixing desk' was a beast yet to be born: groups provided their own instruments and amps, and promoters hired the microphones and PA. Whenever possible, Pete put a mike close to the bass drum, or even inside it, to kick his four-in-the-bar boom to the distant corners of every dance hall. No one else drummed like this and he quickly had imitators.

Tony Sanders, drummer with Bootle group the Phantoms, was amazed that the Beatles smoked while playing – just one of many visible aspects of an apparent don't-give-a-damn attitude. He says that when Paul sang Elvis's Wooden Heart, Pete played the bass drum with his foot, hit the hi-hat with his right hand and smoked with his left. 'We thought this was tremendous,' Sanders says. 'We were all smoking the next time we went on stage, but it didn't go with our short haircuts and clean boy-next-door image.'[8]

All the groups raced to cover Elvis first, and the Beatles won again with Are You Lonesome Tonight. It came out in Britain on Friday 13 January and they did it the next night at Aintree Institute. Paul set down his guitar, clasped the microphone and did his Elvis act, the great solo star crooning his new slow one. It was already going to pot when he went into the long spoken-word middle section about 'all the world's a stage', which he'd crammed into his brain inside a few hours ... and then John just stopped the group dead.

Refusing to be involved in anything so corny, he completely took the piss out of Paul, ripping his close mate and bandmate to shreds in front of everyone. 'They sent me up *rotten*,' Paul says, 'especially John. They all but laughed me off the stage.' This was the way John dealt with things, and he also knew the Beatles must have a solid front line, not back a soloist. As he said, 'Every group had a lead singer in a pink jacket singing Cliff Richard-type songs. We were the only group that didn't ... and that was how we broke through, by being different.'[9] Another difference was that most groups used an echo unit (all the rage since the Shadows' breakthrough) and the Beatles didn't. In his December 1960 letter to Stu, George had said he was planning to buy one, but he hadn't, and now they decided they *wouldn't*.

Bob Wooler was MC on the night and central to the Beatles' activities in this period. Although Allan Williams was out of hospital, the Top Ten Club fire effectively marked the end of his involvement with rock and roll. His time was consumed by the Jacaranda and imminent opening of the Blue Angel nightclub. Though Wooler tried to stoke Williams' interest, to drag him out to see the Beatles and the effect they were having on audiences, Williams didn't go. He'd moved on. 'I have a mind like a grasshopper,' he says. 'Once I've done a thing, I don't go back.'[10]

Everything experienced by the Beatles in 1960 happened because of Allan Williams; in 1961 it almost all happened without him. His role had been to light the blue touchpaper and withdraw. Though the Beatles' first printed business cards announced that A. Williams had Sole Direction over them, two phone numbers were given: Jacaranda Enterprises' new office at the Blue Angel and Pete Best's house in West Derby, and it was Pete who handled the Beatles' bookings, liaising mostly with Bob Wooler. Williams' management of the Beatles, never defined or set down on paper, simply evaporated. In his place, John, Paul and George came to be more reliant on the Bests than they could ever have imagined. If Pete was busy or out, Mona handled the bookings; the Beatles' amps and drums were kept at the Bests' house; and any one of three Best family friends provided transport, to ensure they and their equipment got to every date. One was Neil Aspinall. Although busy – he had an accountancy job in town and spent most evenings labouring over a correspondence course, aiming for bookkeeping qualifications – he drove the Beatles to the halls and returned to fetch them later.[11]

On Saturday 7 January, Neil took them to Aintree Institute for their first booking at this atmospheric upstairs hall not far from the Grand National race-course. Again, Neil was staggered by how the Beatles made a direct and instant impact on people who'd never heard of them and were expecting nothing out of the ordinary: 'All the people were there as normal and suddenly the Beatles came on and everybody who was anywhere in the hall, anyone who was danc-ing, stopped and came forward, straight to the front of the stage. They stood there with their mouths open. The Beatles caused a lot of trouble because all the Teds who'd brought their girls to the dance got very jealous, and then John did this big fucking *wink*, which really wound them all up.'[12]

Lennon's big wink was a new instrument in his stage armoury, transmitting maximum sarcasm and provocation in one move. It was a music-hall wink, a wink with inbuilt wind-up, with *attitude*, accompanied always by a sideways chasm in the mouth, a great gaping oval. It was seldom impotent, and if a fight wasn't already in the air, this could kick one off – inciting tempests which to John, as blind as a bat, were but a violent blur. Tough nuts at Aintree Institute used as weapons any wooden chairs around the edge of the dance floor that weren't bolted together, and some went up to the balcony and lobbed chairs down from there, causing mayhem.[13]

Considering the ever-present danger, the Beatles were assaulted surprisingly few times. It did happen, but only rarely. Paul was reliably effective in a role familiar and necessary from four years of Lennon friendship: pouring oil on his troubled waters, taking the heat out of his steam, pulling him – and often all of them – back from brinks to which they were so recklessly propelled.

Bob Wooler staged the Aintree dances for Brian Kelly as he did in Seaforth and Litherland. He was the benevolent besuited scout-leader with a twist, a master of the microphone who travelled by bus all over Merseyside with a hand-tooled wooden box full of 45s. Partial to a tot or two of Navy Rum, and smoking sixty a day, he worried how to encourage everyone to do their best, and how to make these groups of youths behave themselves on stage, respecting the audience as well as his meticulous handwritten schedules.

Almost all of the Beatles' bookings in this period were stage-managed by Wooler and he quickly got to know them well – while they in turn tried to find out about him, which wasn't easy. He gave them prime position in every show, not the final spot but the middle one, around 9.30; people would be drifting off by 10.15 to catch the last bus home and the closing group generally played to a fraction of those who'd been in the hall earlier.

It was Wooler who broke the Beatles beyond Brian Kelly's Beekay circuit. A new venue opened in January 1961 in Huyton, on the outskirts of Liverpool. Hambleton Hall was rented from the local council's Parks & Gardens Committee, but there was nothing remotely recreational about the beat nights at this forbidding place. It was in the middle of a housing estate and gang fights always broke out. The promoter was a car salesman, Vic Anton, only 20 and an acquaintance of Brian Epstein, though he wasn't involved in these promotions. Like everyone else, Anton hired Wooler as disc jockey, compere, bookings manager and stage manager.

One of Wooler's many tasks for these promoters was to compose and place advertisements in the *Echo*. Editorially, Liverpool's nightly newspaper didn't go anywhere near the rock scene. Its journalists, mostly middle-aged men, knew nothing of it and wouldn't have considered it worth covering. The only indication of activity was in the paid-for classifieds, where events were itemised in fascinating, amusing and illuminating detail. Everything still ran under the Jazz heading, but these ads, studied in hindsight, represent a daily bulletin of the beat, reflecting and responding instantly to the current pulse and temperature. And while the Teds at Aintree Institute lobbed chairs, Liverpool promoters lobbed text grenades at one another, small-print vendettas needled at five bob a line.[14]

Ads in the *Echo* and in the north end local press provide black-and-white proof of the Beatles' impact. From very soon after they started ripping into the Brian Kelly jive circuit, there was an increase in the number of promoters, venues and groups. Everyone and everything became noticeably busier in the first weeks of 1961, and this built month on month throughout the year and beyond. Having steadily gained momentum in the preceding two years, the Liverpool rock scene suddenly took a mighty leap. Bass player Johnny Gustafson, one of so many to benefit from the increased opportunities, summarises it succinctly: 'The Beatles cracked Liverpool open, and the avalanche came after that.'[15]

These ads also show that the Beatles went straight in at number 1. Their name was placed top almost without exception, sometimes in block capitals, centred, while the groups underneath were in upper and lower case. Wooler's relish for alliteration and liberal use of eye-catching exclamation marks made them, in this first month alone, Dynamic, The Great! The Sensational! and, on the last day of the month, in one of his Hive of Jive ads, the Stupendous, Stompin' Big Beat Beatles.

The man central to most of the spiky ads between promoters was Sam Leach, who'd launched Liverpool's first regular rock dances in 1958. No longer the youngest operator (Dave Forshaw, 18, wore that mantle, and Vic Anton was second), Leach remained the most eager and expansive. He didn't promote at one hall, he was everywhere, and he liked to think *big* ... though his grand ideas could lack sufficient planning. His was a Peter-to-Paul operation – groups might be paid for one show with the takings from another to come – and he regularly annoyed rivals by publicising something he couldn't deliver, or by encroaching on their ideas or slogans. His latest plan was to take over the name Cassanova Club and run rock nights in the Sampson and Barlow ballroom in the heart of Liverpool ... and the moment he saw the Beatles, in their Hambleton Hall debut on 25 January, Leach knew he'd found his headlining act.

> The curtains fell open and *there they were*. Even now, I can still feel the kick. You couldn't mistake how good they were. Even the fighting stopped.
>
> The first thing I said to the Beatles was 'You're going to be as big as Elvis!' Lennon looked up like I was mental and said, 'We've got a right nutter here, Paul.' Paul – who knew I was opening a club in town because he was always in the Jacaranda chasing my girls – said, 'Yes, but I bet you've got some work for us, haven't you, Mr Leach?' I gave them twelve bookings that first night at £6 or more a time.[16]

The Beatles seen by Sam Leach were a five-piece again. Stu arrived home about 15 January and took his place in the group a day or two later. Though he came back for another purpose, and had often written of his intention to pack up rocking, he wanted to carry on.

Stu's days of standing with his back to the audience were past; while he liked to stand side-on, there was no pretence at hiding his guitar work. One year and all those Hamburg hours later, the Dean-like dude in dark glasses could play his bass – albeit not brilliantly, and not well enough to please Paul. He didn't welcome Stu's return, even if it did mean he could stop fiddling with those odd bass notes and stick to miming with his broken guitar.

Primarily, Stu was home because his temporary residence permit in Hamburg had elapsed, and because he was applying for a place on the Art Teacher's Diploma course at Liverpool College of Art, to begin in September 1961 – in other words, to do his fifth and final year there after a twelve-month break. He set this in motion right away and was invited to interview on 23 February. He was going to be in Liverpool at least a month, and after all the years of sharing bedsit flats, lastly in Gambier Terrace, he returned to his family, who were now living in Liverpool. (The Sutcliffes moved from Huyton in autumn 1960 and were renting the ground-floor Flat A at 53 Ullet Road, by Sefton Park.)

This was Stu and Astrid's first separation, and though brief – she was coming to join him in Liverpool for two or three weeks at the start of February – he sent her long love letters ('Tonight I play once more with the Beatles my beauty, and I will play in your jeans, and your blue pullover and your *hempt* and will close my eyes and think always of you. As I play, I think of the days that keep us apart . . .')[17] and realising his fiancée would struggle to comprehend the words, he drew a cartoon self-portrait: dark glasses, high collar, big hair, bigger guitar, hearts as crotchets, I LOVE ASTRID sung sweetly in a speech bubble and floated across Europe by air mail.

Stu wasn't the only one returning from Hamburg in January: Rory Storm and the Hurricanes headed back on the second day of the year. Their three months in St Pauli had in no sense galvanised them as it had the Beatles; the experience had soured after Rory broke the Kaiserkeller stage, and when they tried to open in another venue, on New Year's Day, Bruno Koschmider instantly put an end to it, pointing to the exclusive contract they'd signed with him. As it took a while for their bookings to pick up, they all went on the dole. This meant declaring they'd no other income, though they did. A fair number of the Liverpool rockers took this risk – the so-called rock 'n' dole – but not, it seems, the Beatles. They had no need. Ringo briefly, semi-seriously, looked around for a proper job, one that would enable him to earn by day, play by night and leave him free to go away when necessary, like back to Butlin's or Hamburg. He thought about becoming a freelance hairdresser, and while he wondered how to make it happen, it didn't.

'Welcome home from continental tour,' an *Echo* classified announced on 6 January, advertising the Hurricanes' re-emergence on a scene where they were no longer tops. Save for a few sporadic appearances in September 1960, they'd not played locally in seven months and momentum had been lost. The night before, Rory, Johnny and Ringo went to Litherland Town Hall and discovered the Beatles were still in their Kaiserkeller groove, setting a blistering pace. The Hurricanes' mate and sometime roadie Dave 'Jamo' Jamieson remembers, 'The curtains opened, Paul went into Good Golly Miss Molly, the crowd rushed forward and *that was it* – the place just took off. The Beatles were in leathers and black T-shirts – they were rebels. Richy, Johnny and Rory never said anything about being overtaken, they didn't say anything at all.'[18]

The two groups started to share the same bill, but no matter how much Rory leapt and jumped and climbed and combed there was no doubt who was the fairest of them all. Ringo often left the dressing-room to go out front and watch them. 'I just loved the way they played; I loved the songs, the attitude was great, and I knew they were a better band than the one I was in.'[19]

Plenty of onlookers – John, Paul and George among them – continued to revere Ringo's rock-steady tempo in all styles, and his ability to play evenly with either hand, but Pete believed he now held the upper hand, and would later claim 'Ringo . . . copied our [my] beat'.[20]

The three Beatles saw a wider picture. There was no question Pete's forceful four-in-the-bar drumming was one of the ingredients that ignited their explosion. But, as they'd quickly assessed in Hamburg, he was less convincing when they played anything that wasn't meaty rock. The Wallasey singer-guitarist Jackie Lomax puts it bluntly when he says, 'Pete could only play one drum beat, either slowed down or speeded up.' And as John reflected, 'We trained him to keep a stick going up and down four-in-the-bar, [but] he couldn't do much else.'[21]

Crucial too were the personality differences. No other group was *close* like the Beatles, three of whom functioned as intimate friends with their own short-hand language, humour and complexities. That heart and strength – John, Paul and George – went back to 1957–8 and advanced from there through a thousand shared experiences: they were mates, tight, fine-tuned to a frequency unfathomable to others, which was all right by them. Pete didn't think this way and didn't share their attitudes; to the three of them, quite simply, he wasn't *one of us*, and they knew it now as surely as they knew it when they'd first met him at the Casbah in 1959, and when, out of sheer pragmatism, they grabbed him as their last choice for Hamburg a year later. It was nothing to do with quality of character – Pete was 'a good skin', decent, well brought-up, hard to dislike – it was about fitting in, simple chemistry. 'Pete was a bit slow,' John said. 'He was a harmless guy but he was not quick. All of us were quick minds and he never picked up on the idiom.'

John, Paul and George saw Pete in the halls but rarely beyond, John being the only one who socialised to any extent with him. It was like Hamburg again: they said hello, did the show, then he'd go his own way while they stuck together and did something else as a threesome . . . or foursome, with Stu. There were plenty of exceptions, but this was the general way of things. And Pete's onstage personality also presented difficulties. He'd settled into a role he hardly ever varied, booking after booking, night after night – playing with his head down, avoiding eye contact, not smiling, projecting the study in moody shyness he knew would win girls' hearts. Fine, but it was bound to wear thin for the other Beatles. Sometimes they wanted to see a spark when they turned around, some vibrancy, emotion, an engagement of eyes or mind.

'We were always going to dump him when we could find a decent drummer,' John revealed a decade later. As it was, he, Paul and George lacked the courage of their convictions. They allowed themselves to grow comfortable with the way Pete, his mother and his friends efficiently ensured the smooth running of their group, so all they had to do was turn up and play. They didn't want to deal with it, and they had no one to get rid of Pete for them the way they'd made Nigel Walley dump Eric Griffiths. They continued to grumble in private, but their failure to act meant that Pete's position in the group settled and solidified, and the problem of what to do about it was swept under the carpet.

Bob Wooler would write that the power of the Beatles' performances and old-rock repertoire made them 'explode on a jaded scene', but those who saw them actually heard a broad variety of musical styles – country and western, rhythm and blues, instrumentals, tender ballads, standards and much more.[22] Their set constantly evolved, and so great was its range that people never saw the same show twice. John, Paul and George were always fascinated by the pursuit of new sounds, and in 1961 this still meant *American* sounds. Absent from Liverpool for the last third of 1960, they spent winter days in Nems and other shops, crowded into the browseries, checking out what was happening across the Atlantic, and listening in particular to the labels that licensed excitement from the wonderful American independents – primarily Decca's London imprint and Top Rank, newly acquired by EMI.

As Liverpool groups started to proliferate so competition for songs became more intense. Long Tall Sally and What'd I Say, two of the Beatles' biggest weapons, were done by Rory Storm and Gerry and the Pacemakers respectively, and duplication could be awkward when groups shared a bill. The Beatles, John and Paul in particular, identified a challenge and turned it to their advantage. They decided to find obscure songs the other groups didn't know, numbers they alone would do, to stay different and ahead of the pack.

Their own Lennon-McCartney Originals would have achieved this for them, but they didn't consider them up to scratch, not something to play in front of people – and on the odd occasion they did, they wouldn't announce the songs as their own. So quiet did John and Paul keep the fact that they'd written anything, no one around the Beatles in 1961 (with the possible exception of Bob Wooler) was aware of it, and it appears they wrote no new numbers this year. The Lennon-McCartney partnership was lively in so many ways but as creating composers it was dormant.

Paul's labours at Massey & Coggins gave John plenty of solo time in the city in the early weeks of 1961, and it's no coincidence that the important musical discoveries in this period, the key additions to the Beatles' repertoire, were unearthed and sung by him – and that, as a consequence, he steered a shift in their musical direction. All these were discoveries that existed to John as *sounds*, as records – no image came with them except those formed in his head.

An early obscure find was You Don't Understand Me by Bobby Freeman, an intense and dramatic 'doo-wop' number located on the B-side of a Parlophone 45.* There's no recording of the Beatles playing it, but with this type of song and John's kind of voice it must have been a show-stopping moment.

They also performed Stay, by Maurice Williams, and New Orleans, by US Bonds, rearranging them for exciting interaction between lead singer (John) and backing vocalists (Paul and George). Other additions to the repertoire included Leave My Kitten Alone by Johnny Preston (covering Little Willie John) and the Olympics' rocking update of I Wish I Could Shimmy Like My Sister Kate. John sang these too, sometimes singing the repeated line 'shimmy shimmy' as 'shitty shitty'. It was unheard of for an entertainer, of any kind, to swear on stage, a genuinely daring departure.

John also loved Corrine Corrina by Ray Peterson, an American hit on the New York label Dunes. It was a new version of an old Joe Turner blues shouter, and though no producer was named on the London label, ten years later John was delighted to find it was Phil Spector, working with an orchestra for the first time. It was songs like this, and the Drifters' Save The Last Dance For Me (again sung by John), that presented particular challenges to Pete, numbers where four-in-the-bar just wouldn't do.

It was also at this time that John discovered a record he would eulogise for the rest of his life, Angel Baby by Rosie and the Originals; and he'd always associate that cherished 45 with another vital discovery, perhaps because he found them on the same day or in the same shop – the Miracles' Who's Loving You. Following Barrett Strong's Money (That's What I Want), it was the second time John had been knocked out by a record from the Detroit label Tamla.[23]

Who's Loving You (and its A-side, Shop Around, which John also thought great) defines the moment when a new musical playground opened up for John Lennon, and for the Beatles. A soulful singer and his supporting vocalists deliver a romantic song of melody and rhythm, a lyric that doesn't just say 'I

---

* Licensed from the King label of Cincinnati. The Beatles also performed the A-side – the energetic (I Do The) Shimmy Shimmy – with John and Paul sharing the lead vocal.

love you' but wraps the feeling inside a storyline, one that reached the tender core of a Lennon few saw. More than anything, he loved its *sound*, a style defined in America as rhythm and blues. Shop Around made the top of *Billboard*'s R&B chart, giving Tamla its first number 1 and million-seller. John also loved the way Shop Around had a preliminary section that didn't recur in the rest of the song, like the old 1920s numbers Julia taught him on banjo. He appreciated the name too, the Miracles; they were a group, like the Beatles. 'Robinson' was credited as composer on both sides of the record, but John had no way yet of realising this was also the singer, and that he'd turn out to be that forever hero William 'Smokey' Robinson.

It isn't known if John added Who's Loving You and Shop Around to the Beatles' repertoire, but the songs lived within him regardless and enriched his personal tastes. *R&B!* He loved Elvis, Eddie, Chuck, Carl, Gene, Buddy, Little Richard, Jerry Lee and all the other great Fifties heroes (all R&B- or C&W-style rock and rollers), and now he loved this 1960s black pop music from the northern United States – and when he shared his passion with Paul and George, they loved it too … just as they were all gripped at this time by yet *another* momentous arrival in their lives: Will You Love Me Tomorrow by the Shirelles. This one record effectively launched the 'girl-group sound' – R&B with beat, rhythm, melody and harmony – and no musical force beyond rock and roll was ever as crucial to the Beatles' development.

The Shirelles were four 19-year-old black girls from Passaic High School in New Jersey who came under the wing of Florence Greenberg, the mother of one of their schoolfriends; Greenberg owned her own independent record label, Scepter, based ten miles from Passaic, in New York City. The tapestry of the American music business was already enhanced beyond measure by the creative partnership of blacks and Jews, and a bright new chapter opened with Will You Love Me Tomorrow, the greatest teenage love song of the period and the first record by a black female group to top the US charts.

Greenberg ran Scepter Records from an office at 1650 Broadway and West 51st Street. Her choice as Scepter's in-house producer was Luther Dixon, 29, a black singer-songwriter-arranger; Will You Love Me Tomorrow was written by a composer partnership new to those who studied record labels: the husband-and-wife pairing of Gerry Goffin and Carole King, 21 and 18, words and music respectively. They numbered among an array of talented young songwriting teams who arrived each day at the same building to work for the publishing company Aldon Music. Each pairing, and a piano, were squeezed into neighbouring cubicles in a modern Tin Pan Alley scenario – a *Teen* Pan Alley. Almost all the songs that lit up the first half of the twentieth century were written in similar circumstances twenty-three blocks south of here – tunes for musicals, films, dance fads and hits; now they were being written for seven-inch vinyl discs and the teenagers who bought them.

At 1650 Broadway, and in offices at the Brill Building across and further up Broadway at 1619, it seemed everyone was the child or grandchild of European Jews.* There was Goffin and King, Jerry Leiber and Mike Stoller, Burt Bacharach and Hal David, Barry Mann and Cynthia Weil, Doc Pomus and Mort Shuman, Jeff Barry and Ellie Greenwich, and Neil Sedaka and Howie Greenfield, writing songs for producers like Phil Spector and Jerry Wexler. Sedaka sang the numbers he and Greenfield wrote, but otherwise the pairings created a host of classy compositions for different performers. Often these were black girl-groups, urban teenagers who'd honed their voices and harmonies by singing gospel music in church. And they were girls singing to girls, a revolutionary departure in pop music.

Gender didn't stop the Beatles (or other Liverpool groups) singing these numbers – a good song was a good song and that was enough for them. John grabbed Will You Love Me Tomorrow and Paul and George took the backing vocals, and while there's no recording of them doing it, several say it had extraordinary power and tenderness, like another To Know Her Is To Love Her. To the Beatles, to John and Paul especially, the composer credit Goffin-King would become nothing less than a trademark of quality, sufficient in itself to make them listen to or buy a record, and rarely were they disappointed.

Then they flipped the record over and discovered the B-side, a song called Boys. This wasn't Goffin and King's work but almost entirely the creation of Luther Dixon, who co-wrote, arranged and produced. Dixon was the creator of the Shirelles *sound* that the Beatles loved – another name for them to sleuth on record labels. Will You Love Me Tomorrow works beautifully with strings, Boys is big-beat R&B, the backing singers up front. That's how the Beatles did it. John sang lead and Paul and George gave full support, the two of them leaning in towards the microphone, laughing and harmonising *bop-shoo-op-abop-bop-shoo-op* into each other's faces, or sometimes, on appropriate occasions, *bobwooler-abob-bobwooler*. If they realised it was a girls' song about boys, it didn't matter. While several Liverpool groups did Will You Love Me Tomorrow, the Beatles were one of only three to sing Boys. King-Size Taylor and the Dominoes did it, and so did Rory Storm and the Hurricanes: it became the latest speciality number in Ringo's popular nightly *Starrtime!* spot – and he didn't change the gender either.

---

* Historically, though inaccurately, the term 'Brill Building' has come to define activities in both places, including Aldon Music. Aldon was named after its owners, Al Nevins and Don Kirshner.

No such sounds were being made in Britain, where, by definition, everything was smaller-scale. There were no black songwriters or producers, no independent companies releasing pop records, and the business was fixated on Cliff Richard and the Shadows, and also the new chart-topping Parlophone star Adam Faith. Cliff was Britain's golden boy, his every record in the top ten, several making number 1; the Beatles had a *collective* attitude about him, which meant they had John's attitude: the Shadows were OK to listen to, samey but good, but Cliff was loathed. 'We've always hated him,' John said in 1963 with a degree of outspokenness that shocked. 'He was everything we hated in pop.'[24]

Bigger even than Cliff, though, was Elvis. The post-army Presley was scaling heights far greater than those reached first flush, holding fort atop the British charts most weeks between November 1960 and April 1961. All this was in spite of his films – suddenly the cornerstone of his career – receiving less than great reviews. Asked if Elvis would reject an unsuitable project, his manager Colonel Parker replied, 'For the 500,000 dollars a picture they're paying him, plus 5000 dollars a day overtime, they're going to offer Elvis a bad script?'[25] Yes, they were, and these movies and the songs that came with them were beginning to drive his original fans mad with frustration. The Beatles liked Elvis's new records enough to sing them, but knew they were second rate compared to Heartbreak Hotel and Mystery Train. In his weekly *Disc* column, the TV and record producer Jack Good frequently put the Beatles' thoughts into print. Having reluctantly yet constructively panned Elvis's films, and been disappointed by the records which (bafflingly to him) were selling more than ever, Good wrote his hero an open letter. 'Now that your mission of converting the squares is well and truly accomplished, how about making a few sides for us?' it pleaded. 'Some real, low-down, raunchy, scraunchy rhythm and blues, Floyd Cramer knocking the guts out of the old piano, and D. J. Fontana beating the hide out of his drum kit, and then some uptempo screaming – big dramatic stuff?'[26]

As far as Good was concerned, one of the best records of 1961 was a George Martin production, the atmospheric West Indian folk song Long Time Boy, by Nadia Cattouse, who hailed from British Honduras. Good called it 'the most magical record I have heard for months: this could be sensational' – but it didn't sell enough to chart. It *did* underline how EMI always provided the funds for its label chiefs to record the artists and songs of their choosing, no matter how commercially viable they might be ... and George was also able to claim involvement in one of the five whole tracks picked for US single release in 1960 by EMI's own company, Capitol – selections made in Hollywood by Dave Dexter, Jr. None made the charts, which was no surprise given Capitol's supremely brazen refusal to put any promotional effort behind them. While George didn't always agree on policy with his A&R colleagues, they were united in deploring Capitol's corporate behaviour – and none would forgive or forget it.[27]

This was, though, a breakthrough period in George Martin's career, when his chart successes became regular. The singer Matt Monro arrived as an artist of quality with Portrait Of My Love, and when it peaked at 3 in the *NME* (13 January 1961) it was one of two Martin productions in the same top ten. The other was Goodness Gracious Me! by an Indian-accented Peter Sellers and Italian actress Sophia Loren, whose face and figure adorned many a boy's bedroom wall. One of the great productions of George's career, this also peaked at 3, earned a silver disc, and – with its appealing 'boom-boody-boom' lyric and wobbleboard flexing – captured the enduring imagination of the British public. Then George again made the unfashionable fashionable by recording a 1920s-style jazz band, nine intemperate and wittily original young men who called themselves the Temperance Seven. He produced their Parlophone debut, You're Driving Me Crazy, in EMI Number 2 studio in February, and it was soon heading into the charts.

By the end of January, the Beatles were playing seven bookings a week and life had become much more hectic – especially for Paul, because while the others could lie in bed until the afternoons he had to be at the factory every morning, Monday to Friday. Seven bookings in the first half of the month were followed by thirteen in the second – everything was already accelerating. The Beatles' fee, ranging from £6 to £8 10s per booking, was much more than anyone else earned: few other groups were paid more than £2 and played once or twice a week, so in the table of income the Beatles were easily toppermost. All these engagements were in the north end, which was fine for Pete, but John, Paul, George and Stu had to make a crosstown bus journey or two (usually to the Best house) before going on stage. It was like playing away all the time, and they only saw these places in the dark.

The north end was also *hard*. No part of Liverpool was free from violence, and they'd all had tough experiences in places like the Dingle, Toxteth, Garston and Speke – everywhere, actually – but here they had to be ever mindful of the roughnecks' strict territorial mentality. One night towards the end of January, some Seaforth Teds managed to isolate Stu at Lathom Hall and inflict a bad beating. He was only just home from Hamburg but here he was, right in the thick of it, picked on because he was smaller, or puny, or clever, or not from the local area, or wore dark glasses, or dressed differently, or because some Ted's girl sighed when he crooned Love Me Tender. Any reason would do. When word reached the others that Stu was in trouble, they flew to the rescue. Pete says it happened backstage: 'John and I piled in and managed to stop it, and in the ensuing scrap John broke his finger.'[28] Neil Aspinall related it a little differently:

> I wasn't there because I'd dropped them off and gone home to do my correspondence course. But when I went back to pick them up they said, 'There's been a fight in the bogs.' John had broken a finger, Pete had a black eye, Paul had been dancing around and Stuart had been kicked in the head. It was Liverpool, one of those 'lucky we got away with it' situations. Apparently Stu had been trapped in the toilets by some Teds because their girls had been screaming, and John had probably done one of his *big fucking winks*. They didn't go to hospital.

It might have been, as Neil reflected, just one of those Liverpool situations, but that didn't comfort Millie Sutcliffe. She was traumatised when Stuart returned to Ullet Road battered and bleeding. He refused to let her summon a doctor right away, but she prevailed in the morning – the medical opinion was that no obvious damage had been done and a couple of days' bed-rest would see him right.[29] Stu ignored the advice and was back on stage a few hours later, alongside John who played guitar with the middle finger of his right hand in a splint.

The damage was already receding when Astrid arrived. She'd shown Stuart her Hamburg, he would show her his Liverpool, and they would walk it dressed in each other's clothes. The plan was that she would stay with Stuart and his family, but such was Millie's hatred of Germans, and upset that Stuart was engaged to one, it was a disaster. As Astrid explains, 'She never said she hated me but there was always a horrible politeness, and I could feel the horribleness inside. I felt uncomfortable whenever I was in her company.'[30]

The situation quickly broke down. Stuart told his mother he and Astrid intended to sleep together and she forbade it. In 1961, very few mothers would have said otherwise, but events here became overheated. As Allan Williams remembers, 'Stuart and Astrid arrived at our house [58 Huskisson Street] at midnight and she was crying her eyes out. We let them stay with us, and they slept together. Astrid was a very lovely, gentle person and she got on well straight away with Beryl. I think we turned what was a nasty experience for them into a pleasant one.'[31]

Stuart had become accustomed to people's stares for a while, but it was as nothing compared to the looks he and Astrid got together. Swapping clothes in Liverpool in 1961 was bold beyond belief. Rod Murray couldn't have been happier for his best friend. 'Astrid was very pretty and really avant-garde. She and Stuart looked exotic in their black leather and he was obviously happy. I thought, "What a lucky guy.'"[32]

Astrid's visit was a reminder to the Beatles – not that they needed one – of the possibility of a return Hamburg booking. If the document is to be believed, Peter Eckhorn had scribbled that agreement on 30 November 1960 saying they could come back to play his Top Ten Club in April, for a one-month season extendable to two at his discretion. Deported just hours after that was written, Paul and Pete were instructed they had to appeal within thirty days to stand any chance of ever being re-admitted into Germany. It was a process they began late, in the first week of the year. Realising the deadline would be expired by the time their appeal reached Hamburg, they misrepresented the deportation date, giving it as 5 December, and hoped the Germans wouldn't notice. Not a good start.

Finding some unused pages in the back of an old Liverpool Institute exercise book, Paul drafted a statement which politely insisted that deportation for his and Pete's silly act of burning a rubber in the Bambi Kino passageway was a punishment disproportionate to the crime.[33] Though Allan Williams' link with the Beatles was diminishing, he was still committed to getting them back to Hamburg, and got his secretary to restructure Paul's words into formal statements, one each for Paul and Pete. She then typed them and sent the documents with covering letters to Herr Knoop, the chief officer of the 'aliens police'. His office received the documents on 12 January, days after the deadline; Paul and Pete would be requiring leniency from a bureaucratic German official known to have none.

This wasn't the only hurdle to overcome before the Beatles could return to Hamburg. John knew that unless he could lift the restriction on his passport, he'd also be going nowhere. Limited to six months from 15 August 1960, it was set to expire on 15 February and its extension (while he remained under 21) was in doubt. As usual, left to their own devices, the Beatles bordered on clueless. On top of all that, while sending off his semi-fictional appeal to Knoop, Paul had started work at Massey & Coggins. Even assuming he could get the restriction overturned, the only way he'd be free to return to Hamburg would be to quit the factory and forgo his aspiration of rising through the ranks to executive level.

This apparent dichotomy was highlighted on Thursday 9 February 1961, when the Beatles made their first appearance at the Cavern, the cellar jazz club in Mathew Street.* John, Paul and George hadn't been back since the Quarry Men last played here in spring 1958, when, as John remembered it, they'd received a year's ban for playing rock and roll. New owner Ray McFall was

---

* Like Penny Lane, Mathew Street is named after a slave-ship captain.

becoming steadily more accepting of the electric guitar, however. His Wednesday Rock Nights were doing fair business, and in October 1960 he'd introduced lunchtime sessions – two hours of good records and live rock underneath the city for four days a week, soon extended to five. Sessions ran 12–2PM, members' admission one shilling. There was a clear market for it – and, from January 1961, Bob Wooler became the club's talent booker, compere and DJ, his new catchphrase (taken from George Martin's Peter Sellers LP) coming clear through the loudspeakers: 'Remember all you cave-dwellers, the Cavern is the *best* of cellars.'

It didn't take Wooler long to promote the Beatles. They weren't available on Rock Nights because their Wednesdays were booked by Brian Kelly or Vic Anton, but Wooler added them to a shortlist of groups able to perform at lunchtimes because they had no other jobs. Uniquely in Britain, Liverpool now sustained several professional rock groups, including the Beatles, Derry and the Seniors, Rory Storm and the Hurricanes, Gerry and the Pacemakers (home from Hamburg the first weekend of February) and the Big Three. The last named were Cass and the Cassanovas without Cass, who'd slipped off to London and wasn't coming back.

Wooler offered the Beatles £5 for their Cavern Club debut, a pound each for the five, or twenty-five bob each for the four if Paul didn't turn up. 'I remember the guys – John and George particularly – coming down to this coil-winding factory where I worked and saying, "We've got an offer to play the Cavern," and I said, "I'm not sure, I've got this real good job here, coil-winding, could be a good future in it." And they said, "No, come with us." I bunked over the wall . . .'[34] The wall, as Massey & Coggins managing director Jim Gilvey remembers it, was about fourteen feet high, so this was some bunk. Being too far to run, they took the bus or train into town, likewise Paul's return, and the entire escapade probably ate the best part of three hours out of his working day. His absence was noticed and doubtless some measure of unremembered rebuke meted out, met by Paul's promise not to do it again.

But there would be future occasions, because the moment the Beatles hit the Cavern stage, they were incredible, as Ray McFall remembers:

> When I first saw them I said to Bob, 'How did they get past the door staff?' They were wearing scruffy jumpers and jeans, and I didn't allow jeans in the Cavern. They indicated the wearer might be up for a fight, as he wouldn't mind getting them dirty. We kept out the jeans brigade.
>
> However, the Beatles were sensational and I was smitten. Completely. Absolutely. *Instantly*. I stood at the side, between the pillars, about halfway up the hall, and as soon as they started playing I was captivated by them. My

God, what a group! John started, then Paul, then George, and they alternated. Then there'd be a number with two of them – Paul and George or John and Paul – and I couldn't get over the quality of their music. From that very first day, there was no stopping them. I said to Bob, 'What other lunchtimes have they got? We must have them regularly.'[35]

The Cavern wasn't packed. These were early days for its lunchtime sessions, and for the most part the Beatles were playing to audiences who didn't know them. Right in the middle of the city – in the business district and close to the main shopping streets – the club drew its membership from every point of the compass: all the places in and around Liverpool, the Wirral and other areas of Lancashire and Cheshire the Beatles had never been. Cavern reputations grew by word of mouth . . . and, as usual, the difference between the Beatles and other groups was the lightning speed with which it happened to them.

The Cavern audience was unlike any the Beatles had faced. It was secretaries, clerks, office boys, messengers, telephonists, shop assistants, girls from hairdressing salons and much more. There were no labourers or factory workers because the factories were in the suburbs, and no Teddy Boy drapes because everyone was dressed for work – boys in suits and ties, girls in smart skirts or dresses. It was mostly a working-class and generally intelligent crowd, school achievers rather than dropouts, aged between 15 (the minimum for starting work) and early twenties.

McFall not only kept the Cavern alcohol-free, he provided clubgoers with affordable refreshments. 'Members paid a shilling to spend up to two hours watching the Beatles,' he says, 'and instead of eating lunch in their office they could eat at the Cavern and get the cheapest meal they could wish for – we sold hot dogs for ninepence, a bowl of soup and a bread roll for the same, and tea for fivepence. It was much less than we could have charged but I didn't think it was fair to ask the kids for more.'

Among those at the Beatles' first Cavern performance was 15-year-old Beryl Johnson, who'd already got herself on speaking terms with them at Aintree Institute and was among the first to start following the group around.

I went to Bootle Grammar School, and when I heard they were playing at the Cavern I pretended to have a dentist appointment and rushed down there. (I ended up having loads of 'dentist appointments', much to my mother's annoyance.) That first lunchtime the place was half empty and I sat on the front row with my feet up on stage and talked to them between songs. Anyone could call out a song request.

I liked them doing Memphis, Tennessee, but my favourite of favourites was John singing Will You Love Me Tomorrow. It really touched me. I liked John the best – he had a great sense of humour. Stuart was very nice, a quiet person – I talked to him at Aintree Institute when Astrid was with him. I liked Paul but I wasn't big on him, George seemed kind and caring, more introvert than extrovert, and Pete was *extremely* shy. He'd say 'Hello' and maybe 'How are you?' and that was it.[36]

Because Mona Best was her Peter's greatest champion, all the Beatles fell under her broad wing as she hustled and bustled them forward. In her eyes, they weren't so much the Beatles as 'my son's group', and on 17 February she became the first – and only – woman rock promoter on Merseyside when she held the first in a monthly series of Casbah Promotions dances at St John's church hall in Tuebrook, the adjacent suburb to West Derby. The Beatles starred, one of the occasions when they were advertised by the name Pete liked to use: the Fabulous Beatles Rock Combo. Having fun with the name was something they all seemed to do: a *Liverpool Echo* ad on 8 February called them the Big Beat Boppin' Beatles, which Bob Wooler says was their own idea.*

Mrs Best paid them £7 for St John's and the same when they played the Casbah every alternate Sunday night. While they were in Hamburg, alterations had been made to the cellar to create a bigger performing space (though it was still tiny) and Mona had painted a splendid spider-and-web mural across the width of the back wall. The Beatles always played 'the spider room'; fifty people made it jam-packed, and when the music didn't hit you, the heat did. For all the best reasons, the Casbah had a family atmosphere, and because the Beatles were Pete's group so this extended to them.

Cyn and Dot were often in the Casbah to see their boyfriends play, safer at this venue than any other. This was where Paul and Dot had met and now they were as good as engaged. Dot proudly wore on the third finger of her left hand the gold ring Paul bought for her in Hamburg for 54 marks (about £4 12s). It meant marriage was on the horizon, but it was a distant one – no date was set or, it seems, discussed. Dot was still quiet ('a very nice, simple, shy girl' recalls Mike McCartney, who took some good photos of the couple in this period)[37] and Paul provided all the push in the relationship. The Casbah was a good place

---

* It may have been their response to the Wooler-conceived name Stupendous, Stompin' Big Beat Beatles. It isn't known if BEATLES ROCK COMBO was still written on Pete's bass drum head or if it had been removed by now. All 1961 Beatles photos (mostly taken after the spring) show it as blank.

for meeting girls. Pauline Behan thought the Beatles were great (her favourite song of theirs was Carl Perkins' Lend Me Your Comb), and although initially she was attracted to John, it was George who made a move and the two began a steady relationship, both on the edge of 18.

The Beatles' three weekly bookings at the start of January had rapidly evolved. In February's twenty-eight days Pete had only four empty spaces in his diary and they had thirty-six bookings in total, several nights including what they called 'the double shuffle' – two different venues. When they played Cavern lunchtimes there could be three shows in a day. This was a good period, one they'd always remember with fondness: a time of laughs, when they were kings but owed nothing to no one and operated free of contracts. Away from the stage, much of this fun was being had by George and John as a twosome. Stu was busy with Astrid, Pete at home and Paul at the factory. Winding coils was causing Paul to miss out on whatever the others were doing with John ... so it was inevitable that something had to give.

The Beatles were booked to play another Cavern lunchtime on 21 February and Paul either went over the wall again or phoned the factory and claimed sickness. Whichever it was, he was dicing with dismissal. The following week brought the day of reckoning, the 28th. The Beatles were due on stage at the Cavern at twelve o'clock. If Paul played, it was goodbye Massey & Coggins and hello to the biggest ever revolt he'd mounted against his dad; if he didn't play, it was goodbye Beatles. As Neil Aspinall remembered, John made himself crystal clear on the situation: 'John said to Paul on the phone, "Either fucking turn up today or you're not in the band any more." And that lunchtime, when Paul bounced in – "Hi!" – and got up on stage with them, John said to him, "Right! *You've given up your fucking job.*"'[38] John remembered it too: 'I told him on the phone, "Either come or you're out." So he had to make a decision between me and his dad then, and in the end he chose me. But it was a long trip.'[39]

The last day of February 1961 was Mantovani's factory farewell. He wasn't good at winding coils anyway: 'I was hopeless – everybody else used to wind fourteen a day, I'd get through one-and-a-half and mine were the ones that never worked.' A week later, by post, Paul received his final wage packet, his National Insurance card and his P45 form, recording the income tax he'd paid, to be handed on to his next employer. But there wasn't going to be one. Paul was fully a Beatle, and in his mind would stay one until the group thing flopped or he reached 25.[40]

In the circumstances, it was highly desirable that they push ahead with their hoped-for second trip to Hamburg. If, straight away, Paul started living like the others – hanging around the house, sleeping until the afternoons – while his dad was still upset over Massey & Coggins, he would no doubt hear all about it. Better that he clear off out of the way for a month or two. On this same day, 28 February, all five Beatles filled out visa applications, obtained from the German Consulate in Liverpool. There seemed no reason why George wouldn't be allowed back in – he'd turned 18 three days earlier, freeing him to play in night-clubs after the 10PM *Ausweiskontrolle* – but there remained a legitimate concern that the bar would not be lifted for Paul and Pete. No progress had been made in the fight to overturn the ban on their re-entry, even though Peter Eckhorn was doing what he could in St Pauli and Allan Williams was working away on their behalf in Liverpool.

The Beatles became notably busier once Paul was free of the factory, as if a handbrake had been released. In addition to all their nightly bookings, they played three Cavern lunchtime sessions the week of 6 March and four the following week. Even at this time of the day, Liverpool presented competition for the rock audience. Close on the heels of opening one club, Sam Leach – as was his way – opened a second, taking over operations at the Iron Door jazz club, a music cellar close to the Cavern, at 13 Temple Street. It was presently functioning as the Liverpool Jazz Society (LJS) but Leach put on Liverpool rock and was never reluctant to move into a rival's territory.

Ray McFall and Bob Wooler tried to safeguard their prime asset – *Echo* ads on 4 and 14 March announced that, at lunchtime, the Beatles were *exclusive* to the Cavern – but this didn't deter the insurgent. 'I had no respect for anybody,' Leach says. 'We went down Mathew Street late at night, after the Cavern had closed, and I put up posters right down the street, even over the Cavern door.' He admits also to a friend buying stink bombs from Liverpool magic shop Wizard's Den and chucking them down the Cavern steps. The place was a reeking hole at the best of times, so it's possible no one noticed.

On Saturday 11 March, Leach presented his most impressive venture yet: twelve rock groups played a twelve-hour LJS session, 8PM to 8AM, admission 6s 6d for members and 7s 6d for non-members.* Unsure whether to name it *The First All Night Rock Ball* or *Rock Around The Clock* he'd ended up calling it both, and nothing like this was happening anywhere else in Britain, or even in America. It was the first great gathering of the clans, lads from all parts of Liverpool, friends and rivals, camaraderie and competition, watched

---

* The Beatles, Gerry and the Pacemakers, the Remo Four, Rory Storm and the Hurricanes, King-Size Taylor and the Dominoes, the Big Three, Dale Roberts and the Jaywalkers, Derry and the Seniors, Ray and the Del Renas, the Pressmen, Johnny Rocco and the Jets, and Faron and the Tempest Tornadoes.

by masses of kids squeezed into a filthy steaming cellar with one heavy iron doorway in and out. Leach claims two thousand saw at least part of the action; Johnny Guitar's diary mentions eight hundred and says the place was packed.

Sam Leach *not* featuring the Beatles at lunchtime led to appearances by an ad hoc group he called Rory Storm and the Wild Ones. He says this was Rory, Johnny and Ringo from the Hurricanes joined by others including John, Paul and maybe George from the Beatles. As none of the participants ever mentioned it, a question mark remains over precisely what occurred, but there's no doubt that John, Paul and George were seeing plenty of Ringo again, usually when Pete had taken himself home to West Derby.

While the Beatles were angling to get back to Hamburg, Rory Storm and the Hurricanes were fixed on getting a second summer season at Butlin's. The big date on their horizon was a Butlin's dance in Garston, south Liverpool, on 29 March. If they put in a good show here, another Pwllheli summer was as good as theirs. The paths of the two groups were clearly diverging: the Beatles were musically superior and sensationally scruffy; the Hurricanes, driven by Rory's tastes, were becoming ever more flash. Ringo had recently been measured for a silver lamé evening jacket.

The only rock group regularly booked into the Cavern in 1959–60, the Hurricanes didn't play there at all in 1961 – some long-forgotten incident or disagreement prevented it – but because they spent lunchtimes in the LJS while the Beatles were in the Cavern, so members of both groups often found themselves at a loose end during the winter afternoons. It was like being back on Grosse Freiheit: Gretel und Alfons toasted in the Grapes. Unlike in Hamburg, British licensing laws meant the pubs chucked them out at 2.30 – and in need of something else to do, somewhere else to go to escape the penetrating cold, a popular stop was the Tatler, a tiny cinema at 25 Church Street, in the middle of all the shops. A continuous cycle of films ran here – newsreels, documentaries, Tom and Jerry cartoons, old cowboy prints and shorts starring northern comedians. John, Paul and George loved the eleven-minute comedy *The Running Jumping & Standing Still Film* and this was where they saw it, several times, enjoying the surreal humour of Peter Sellers, Spike Milligan and their director Dick Lester. It played frequently at the Tatler, *Echo* ads proclaiming 'brought back by popular demand'.

The Beatles' blending of 'Goon' humour with their own native Liverpool wit was yet another distinction between them and other groups. Though much of what they did and said was for self-amusement, they were rarely not funny to everyone else. Pop stars liked to mumble (as directed) that they hoped to become 'all-round entertainers' – by implication, a singing career alone wasn't enough – but the Beatles achieved it naturally and while remaining true to themselves and their music. They were never anything so specialist as a comedy-rock group (such combinations did exist), they were simply a group who were incredibly funny, before and after shows, between and during numbers, blessed with consummate timing.

Stresses inflicted on the Cavern's decaying electrical circuits by the PA system, amps, lighting, humidity and sweat often made the fuses blow, plunging the cellar into darkness save for emergency bulbs. When this happened, groups went off to the tiny God-forsaken cubicle that served as the dressing-room, and waited to be summoned back when everything was working again. The Beatles stayed on stage. As often as not, George would go round the back to fix the fault while John and Paul entertained the audience. Paul might sit at the Cavern piano and bang out a few old numbers, including the brief and still-untitled melody he wrote when turning 14 – the one that would eventually become When I'm Sixty-Four. They played all manner of odd things. People remember them doing the theme tune of ITV's children's puppet series *Torchy, The Battery Boy*, and the audience would be embroiled in a rollicking send-up of the long-running BBC people's entertainment *Have A Go*, with John brutally satirising the broad Yorkshireman host Wilfred Pickles – *'ow do, 'OW ARE YER?* They led community-singing sessions that had people in hysterics; some of these were even *themed*, like when one 'eyes' song led seamlessly into the next – What Do You Want To Make Those Eyes At Me For into When Irish Eyes Are Smiling into Ma! (She's Making Eyes At Me) – packed full of ad-lib wordplay and scurrilous but beguiling irreverence. It was so incredibly novel and magical and enjoyable there were always groans when George fixed the fuse . . . but then they'd start up *rocking*.

'It sounds corny,' says Bernadette Farrell, a spring 1961 Cavernite, 'but they got into your *soul*. Before the Beatles I'd been a Cliff Richard fan, then suddenly there was this, so wild and different and exciting. They seemed somehow more mature than the other groups.

> We always requested Paul to sing Long Tall Sally. He used to say, 'I can't do it because it kills me throat,' but then he would. He'd announce, 'I'm doing this one for these two flossies over here,' or something like that. Girls used to say his eyes were like mince pies. He had long eyelashes and would deliberately flutter them, and though you knew he was always aware of himself, he was so friendly to everybody that you couldn't help but like him.[41]

One of the flutter numbers was Over The Rainbow, guaranteed to go down a storm with the girls. The song from *The Wizard Of Oz* seemed a strange choice, but the Beatles considered it valid because Gene Vincent did it. Paul sang it somewhere between the two versions, pausing impressively after the heightened 'Some*where*' and then sweetly rolling down. Cavern girls would get used to the sight: he made his eyes big, turned his face up and slightly at an angle and fixed his gaze above their heads on a brick at the far end of the centre tunnel.*

Sometimes John joined in with fine harmonies, but mostly he took the piss. Pete says that during one Cavern performance of Over The Rainbow, John leaned back on the piano, pointed to Paul, burst into raucous laughter and shouted, 'God, he's doing Judy Garland!' Paul had to keep singing in the knowledge that John was pulling crips and Quasis behind his back or making strange sounds on his guitar to interrupt him. Yet, if Paul stopped in the middle of the number, John would stare around the stage, the essence of innocence.[42] There were always several simultaneous reasons why an audience couldn't take their eyes off the Beatles.

Paul took such behaviour from no one but John, but also he gave it back and was strong-minded enough to carry on doing what he wanted, knowing how much the audience liked it. He sang these songs well, and added one more to the portfolio at this time, the Broadway show number Till There Was You, as covered in a new version by Peggy Lee – or Peggy Leg, as Paul called her. (He was given her record by his cousin Bett Robbins.) John *really* had a go at Paul for singing this – but didn't try to stop him doing it, recognising there was scope for all kinds of music in this group, to please all kinds of audiences . . . just so long as no one went near jazz.

Another number added by Paul in this period was The Hippy Hippy Shake, by the Montana-born singer Chan Romero. Bob Wooler was given the British pressing of this record in 1959 and occasionally played it in the jive halls, between groups. It was a chugging rocker, sung in a high voice that Wooler felt was ideally suited to Paul's range. 'I played it one lunchtime at the Cavern and Paul said, "What's that?" After the session he asked me to play it again. I lent it to him and the Beatles started doing it. He bought me a pint in the Grapes for it.' Paul was great with The Hippy Hippy Shake, screaming and giving it his all like any of the Little Richard songs, and it would become a long-term audience favourite.

---

* There were three arched tunnels at the Cavern. The centre was for music and a seated audience; the right had the cloakroom, snack bar and standing room; the left was for standing or dancing. At the far end of the left tunnel, adjacent to the stage, was the tiny bandroom and the nook from which Bob Wooler played records and made his announcements.

The longer Wooler spent in the Beatles' company, the more fascinated he became with them. He saw how John, Paul and George's humour was *as one*: they would latch on to something or someone and not let go of it until they'd picked it up, examined it, poked at it and made fun of it, richly, mercilessly, unforgettably and often beyond the point of pain to another. As he would recall, from experience, 'The Beatles were terrible when they ganged up on you – all of them, Pete Best as well. Their tongues could be savage.'[43]

This toughness wasn't something they reserved solely for irritating outsiders. New to the set-up, with no appreciation yet of their histories, Neil Aspinall watched John *allow* Paul to bully Stu, even though, clearly, the two were close friends. 'Paul tilted at him in a way that John couldn't argue with, rounding on him for being a crap musician – "For God's sake, Stu, will you practise? You're dragging us all down."' Neil saw John leaving Stu to fight his own battles – if he wanted to stay in the group he had to handle it, survival of the fittest. Paul later realised how he was cast as the fall guy, that the others left him to voice concerns which, at some level or other, they all recognised. 'I felt he [Stu] was holding us back, musically. It was the same with Pete Best. There were very practical reasons for my not wanting Stu in the group, and everyone else knew them and was fully aware, but I was the man who had to say it. It became my role, and if they [the other Beatles] hadn't wanted it . . . All these things were *group* decisions – I was just the tip of the iceberg with Stu.'[44]

Despite the joy of having Astrid around, it had not been a happy homecoming for Stuart. The terrible experience of being beaten up had been followed by the mother of all rows with Millie over Astrid's visit; he'd begun to suffer attacks of heartburn and headaches, and had a grumbling appendix, though he'd been unable to get satisfaction from the local doctor; and then the main purpose of his return – his 23 February interview at the art school – went badly. In spite of his four glory-strewn years here from 1956 to 1960, no place was offered to him on the teaching course for 1961–2. Instead, Stuart decided to make Hamburg his home for a while: he'd go back with the Beatles, or earlier if it could be arranged.

Although his bass playing remained, for some, a contentious drag on the Beatles' musical progress, his artistic influence held strong. Mike McCartney saw him on stage in the Cavern wearing a curious jacket – a collarless design for women, handmade in corduroy by Astrid after the latest Paris design by Pierre Cardin. 'The whole audience, including myself, thought he was a bit daft for doing that,' Mike remembers.[45] This wasn't all. Astrid had also given Stu a new hairstyle – combed down, side parted, grease free – as sported by Klaus Voormann after the look first adopted in their circle by Jürgen Vollmer. It was the Paris style, which Jürgen cut for himself because the Hamburg hairdressers were *all too square*. It's said the other Beatles laughed at Stu's new hairdo, and though this amusement gradually subsided, it wasn't a look anyone rushed to copy.

The Beatles' Hamburg return continued to focus their minds. When Astrid went home she made personal calls to the Bundeskriminalamt to get Paul and Pete's ban overturned, and Allan Williams was still doing what he could in Liverpool. On 1 March he sent a letter to the German Consul in Liverpool, providing his assurance that 'all the musicians have very good characters and come from first class families, and they have never been in trouble with the Police in this Country' – which, amazingly, was true. A contract with Eckhorn was typed on 2 March by Williams' secretary, mostly designed to impress the authorities but also as a means of establishing commission payments to reward his involvement. While their handwritten agreement with Eckhorn provided for a nightly payment of DM35 each, Williams was trying to force through DM40, out of which Eckhorn would deposit £10 sterling (about DM120) every week in Williams' Hamburg bank account. The money would be docked from the Beatles' wages – £2 (about DM23) apiece – but this way he'd get his commission and they'd end up slightly better off than before. Bob Wooler later related how Paul told him that, whatever the nightly rate, they weren't going to pay Williams' commission because they were cutting him out. 'Paul said [to me], "I suppose you're going to tell your mate [Williams] about this." I said, "Too bloody true."'[46] (It isn't clear if or when Wooler did, however.)

The restrictive clause in John's five-year passport that terminated it after just six months was deleted in the Liverpool Passport Office on 3 March, when John went back to India Buildings, Water Street. Finally, Mimi had given her assent to his international travel. The period since his return from Hamburg had been trying for them both. The guitar (from which he would *never earn a living*) had been diverting and distracting John since 1956, but at least he'd always done something else at the same time: grammar school then art school. To see the boy brazenly rejecting all talk of getting a job just so he could play in a silly group was very worrying to Mimi. And the hours! Out every evening, barging in during the middle of the night, waking the lodging students, wanting break-fast after lunchtime . . .

The Beatles made their night-time debut in the Cavern on Tuesday 21 March. Slowly but steadily, the club was giving way to beat. In addition to Wednesday Rock Nights, Ray McFall had created a second window on Tuesdays. The Swinging Bluegenes weren't rock but could play it, straddling several styles including jazz; McFall gave them their own weekly feature,

Bluegenes Guest Night, and booked supporting groups at the smarter end of the rock spectrum. The idea was to produce a halfway-house evening, bringing in a variety of music fans. In this respect, booking the Beatles was like admitting the bull into the china shop.

There were difficulties when they arrived. The Cavern doorman this night was one of the regulars, Paddy Delaney, and he knew his instructions: keep out anyone in jeans. He couldn't believe it when, one by one, the Beatles turned up in jeans, leather jackets and cowboy boots and said he had to let them through because they were playing. He didn't until he'd properly checked. The Bluegenes didn't like the look of them either. Lead singer Ray Ennis says, 'All the bands tried to be like professionals in the way that they conducted themselves, but the Beatles were *smoking.* I remember Stu Sutcliffe sitting on the piano facing Pete Best on the drums and he wasn't even looking at the audience, he just plonked away as though he was totally disinterested.'[47]

Shortly after this, Stuart returned to Hamburg with his bass guitar and amp and moved back into his room at 45a Eimsbütteler Strasse. John and George planned to repeat his journey only a few days later ... but Paul and Pete still couldn't go. Stuart now joined Astrid in pushing an appeal with the Bundeskriminalamt.

John and George, though, were heading off, and for the second time in seven months Cyn was reconciled to waving John goodbye for an extended absence ... though she also agreed to his suggestion of popping over to Hamburg to see him for at least a couple of weeks. Dot would join her, if Paul ever managed to get there. These two girls had been the dazed spectators of a hurricane in the first quarter of 1961. Their boyfriends were busy most nights, very popular and much fancied. Depending on bookings, they might see them only at weekends, and even then just in the daytime. At other hours, the girls were clueless about what their boys were up to, having no idea of what Paul called 'the occasional knee-trembler after a gig' or the females who, as John called it, 'would be *available for functions'.*[48]

John was loafing in the Jacaranda one day when Bill Harry told him he was planning to start a newspaper, like a What's-On On Merseyside, to cover all aspects of sport and entertainment including the local poetry, rock and jazz scenes. The title, he'd decided, would be *Mersey Beat* – named not for its rock content, or to revive memories of the *Echo*'s now-finished local music feature, but because he envisaged a policeman walking his beat, noting all the events. A Liverpool businessman put up £50 capital and found Bill a little office above an off-licence. Bill himself, 22, was still at art school by day, but his girlfriend

Virginia Sowry (they'd met in the Jacaranda) was a full-time employee. Friends through their art school years together, since 1957, Bill and John talked easily, and their conversation turned to the word Beatles. John mentioned (probably with a groan) that people were always asking what it meant and how they'd thought of it, and Bill replied – with *Mersey Beat* in mind – 'Why don't you tell them?'[49]

So John wrote the history of the Beatles, and because he and George were knocking around together, he was on hand to contribute. John had been happy to let Paul help him write a comic piece or two in 1958, notably 'On Safairy With Whide Hunter', now he allowed George to get involved in what became known as 'Being A Short Diversion On The Dubious Origins Of Beatles'.

Once upon a time there were three little boys called John, George and Paul, by name christened. They decided to get together because they were the getting together type. When they were together they wondered what for after all, what for? So all of a sudden they all grew guitars and formed a noise. Funnily enough, no one was interested, least of all the three little men. So-o-o-o on discovering a fourth little even littler man called Stuart Sutcliffe running about them they said, quote 'Sonny get a bass guitar and you will be alright' and he did – but he wasn't alright because he couldn't play it. So they sat on him with comfort 'til he could play. Still there was no beat, and a kindly old aged man said, quote 'Thou hast not drums!' We had no drums! they coffed. So a series of drums came and went and came.

Suddenly, in Scotland, touring with Johnny Gentle, the group (called the Beatles called) discovered they had not a very nice sound – because they had no amplifiers. They got some. Many people ask what are Beatles? Why Beatles? Ugh, Beatles, how did the name arrive? So we will tell you. It came in a vision – a man appeared on a flaming pie and said unto them 'From this day on you are Beatles with an A'. Thank you, Mister Man, they said, thanking him.*

---

* The likeliest spark for 'flaming pie' was the Elvis film *Flaming Star*, which played in Liverpool 12–18 March. Royston Ellis claims he inspired the line (and is therefore the 'Mister Man' mentioned) because he accidentally set fire to a chicken pie he cooked for John, Stu and possibly George in the Gambier Terrace flat in June 1960. This seems fanciful and no one else has confirmed it, and Ellis ties it to his claim to have given them the Beatles spelling with the 'a' – which has been disproved. Paul says the flaming pie reference was purely 'Goon humour and biblical joking, like "The Lord said 'Come forth' and he came fifth." That's *very* Liverpool, very much the humour that was going around at the time.' (Author interview, 7 November 1995.)

And then a man with a beard cut off said – will you go to Germany (Hamburg) and play mighty rock for the peasants for money? And we said we would play mighty anything for money.*

But before we could go we had to grow a drummer, so we grew one in West Derby in a club called Some Casbah and his trouble was Pete Best. We called 'Hello, Pete, come off to Germany!' 'Yes!' Zooooom. After a few months, Peter and Paul (who is called McArtrey, son of Jim McArtrey, his father) lit a Kino (cinema) and the German police said 'Bad Beatles, you must go home and light your English cinemas.' Zooooom, half a group. But even before this, the Gestapo had taken my friend little George Harrison (of Speke) away because he was only twelve and too young to vote in Germany; but after two months in England he grew eighteen, and the Gestapoes said 'you can come'. So suddenly all back in Liverpool Village were many groups playing in grey suits and Jim said 'Why have you no grey suits?' 'We don't like them, Jim' we said speaking to Jim. After playing in the clubs a bit, everyone said 'Go to Germany!' So we are. Zooooom. Stuart gone. Zoom zoom John (of Woolton) George (of Speke) Peter and Paul zoom zoom. All of them gone.

Thank you club members, from John and George (what are friends).

John saw Bill Harry in the Jacaranda a day or two later and gave him the finished piece, by which time the Beatles were set to zooooom.

The group's last performance in this period was at the Casbah on Sunday 26 March. They were booked into the Top Ten Club for a month (or maybe two) from 1 April – the Saturday of the Easter weekend. What an odd Beatles it would be, though: just John, George and Stu, 'The rhythm's in the guitars – mark II'. Paul would be missed, but they knew enough songs to get by, and his guitar was negligible anyway; the absence of a drummer and drum kit was more of a problem, but they'd deal with it somehow. These were details, not enough to stop them going, just as John's passport anxieties the previous August wouldn't have stopped the others making the trip without him.

John and George were travelling by rail and boat this time, not in Allan Williams' minibus. The journey would be quicker, despite having to haul their

---

* The man was Allan Williams. In and out of the Jacaranda when John and George were writing this, he'd just adopted a clean-shaven look for the opening of the Blue Angel on 22 March. The article didn't have a title. 'Being A Short Diversion On The Dubious Origins Of Beatles' was added by Bill Harry for publication – it ran on page two of the first issue of *Mersey Beat*, 6 July 1961, with the byline 'Translated from the John Lennon'.

guitars, amps and luggage by hand. They left on Tuesday 28th on the last train to London, pulling out of Lime Street ten minutes after midnight and arriving at Euston six slow hours later. After breakfast, and killing three hours before the Harwich train left Liverpool Street, they sailed the North Sea and were speeding through Holland when, back home, Rory Storm and the Hurricanes were getting the definitive thumbs-up from Butlin's for their second summer season, to begin in June. The train then delivered the two Beatles into the Hauptbahnhof at 3.16AM on Thursday 30th. They were back in Hamburg.

It was different this time. They had every idea of what was in store, knowing the people, places, food, faces, come-ons, neon, ciggies, cornflakes, cafés, bars, booze, birds, strippers, sex, whores, rockers, sailors, clubs, owners, waiters, truncheons, fists, knives, guns and gas.

And there at the station, despite the hour, were Astrid and Stu – Astrid sleek in a black leather suit, Stu in something very similar. Everything was tight, including the VW Beetle convertible in which she roared them off to the Reeperbahn.

19

Piedels on Prellies (April–June 1961)

Second day in Hamburg, John and George renewed their comradeship with *the Krauts* – and the Krauts were delighted to have them back.

It was Good Friday, 31 March, and the two of them spent several hours relaxing with Jürgen Vollmer and a couple of his friends. They drove the city looking for a bar not closed on this religious holiday and eventually found one in fashionable Mühlenkamp; over beers, they resumed asking Jürgen about his cool Paris clothes and combed-down hairstyle, and managed to squeeze in a crack or two about his nationality. 'There was always a reference to Hitler,' he remembers.[1]

They were a day from playing with Stu as a drummerless trio ... but the two other Beatles *were* finally on their way, having left Liverpool the instant they received a communiqué from the Hamburg police department. Dated 28 March, sent in a pouch to the German Consulate in Liverpool and picked up by Allan Williams on the 30th, this explained that their pardon was temporary and would expire after a year. They were on probation, would have to show their passports at the Hamburg immigration office on arrival, and pay DM195 for expenses arising from their expulsion.

This second Beatles party repeated the journey of the first but two days behind, more quietly and less comfortably. Scrambling on to the midnight train at Lime Street as the whistle blew, Paul and Pete found all the second-class seats taken and ended up in the guard's van. It was only after an uncomfortable hour that they gatecrashed first-class and spent the rest of the ride to London waiting to be turfed out. When they crawled into Hamburg after twenty-eight hours' travelling it was the dead of night, no one was there to meet them, they were definitively cold, wet, hungry and exhausted, couldn't raise anyone at the

Top Ten Club and spent several hours shivering in the venue's turquoise-tiled entry passage with their gear and baggage. Finally, their door-knocking was answered by Tony Sheridan, they grabbed a little sleep, and that night – Saturday 1 April – the five Beatles were back together again to plug in and kick off their second Hamburg season.

They worked much harder this time. In 1960, Bruno Koschmider had them on stage six nights a week, thirty hours in total; Peter Eckhorn made them spend fifty-one hours in the Top Ten across all seven nights and they played for thirty-eight – 7PM to 2AM weekdays, 8PM to 4AM weekends, with a fifteen-minute pause in every hour. This was what they'd been hankering for since the turn of the year?

On the upside, mostly, they were playing with Tony Sheridan, not having to shoulder these marathon sessions alone. Though never a Beatle, Sheridan seemed like one – they backed him when he sang, he often backed them when they sang, and there were usually six musicians on the Top Ten stage. The London 2i's rock sound married the Liverpool rock sound – a fascinating and sometimes fiery shotgun wedding.

But if the Beatles believed they were getting better money, they were mistaken. In 1960, Koschmider paid them DM30 a night each; Eckhorn paid 35, but then, to the Beatles' anger, *Lohnsteuer* and *Kirchensteuer* were knocked off at source – income tax and church tax – the last being a tithe given by the state straight to religious organisations. 'Balls to that,' they probably said, because they soon got rid of it; nevertheless, it meant that, to begin with, they pocketed 215 marks a week each when they were counting on 245.

Eckhorn was sticking to his original agreement and wouldn't pay the Beatles the DM40 per night indicated in the 2 March contract prepared by Allan Williams; in turn, the Beatles confirmed they wouldn't pay Williams any commission – the 'man with a beard cut off' was now the man with his money cut off. Back in Liverpool, Bob Wooler had understood the Beatles to be thinking this way, even before the tax business affronted them, but, whatever the case, two weekly deductions were already two more than enough and they wouldn't countenance a third. As Stuart was Williams' closest friend, he was put upon to write *the difficult letter*.[2]

Quite right too, because Stu had it cushy. He was living in the lap of luxury at the well-appointed Bergmann house in Altona – hot water, a mother's meals, a girlfriend's love – while John, Paul, George, Pete, Tony and Tony's St Pauli girlfriend Rosi Heitmann were crammed into free accommodation above the front of the club, bunk beds and a couple of army camp beds in a small attic considered by George 'a really grubby little room'.[3] This was the place from which, at the start of the winter now ending, Paul and Pete had been picked up by the

Polizei. First time here, Hamburg had grown colder and darker while the Beatles stayed; this time, warmer longer days were coming.

The Top Ten was a cut above what they'd had before: there were fewer louts on the dance floor and the place was a degree less violent than the Kaiserkeller, just as the Reeperbahn – the main drag in St Pauli – was a shade more respectable than Grosse Freiheit. There were still fights, just not *quite* so many, though the waiters would start one when things became too calm. A small section of seats and tables by the stage were reserved (unspoken) for VIPs and friends of the band, particularly Jürgen, Astrid and Klaus. 'We went to see the Beatles every night,' says Jürgen, '*every night*. It actually got embarrassing, so one night we went to the movies instead, but at the end of the film we thought "Let's go!" and went. It was like falling in love, when you want to see the person every day. I'd been into jazz before but not any more – I was now completely a rock and roll fan. It had become the expression of my own rebellion.'

The club was one room, big but not overly so, a comfortable space with the stage set along the side wall and raised only slightly off the ground, in front of which was *die Tanzfläche*, the dance floor. The bar was to the musicians' right, along the back wall, and white-jacketed waiters bustled back and forth with trays of beer bottles and Coca-Cola with straws. There was no distance between the performers and their audience, no hiding place, full exposure.

The Beatles were thrilled to use the Binson echo system installed by Eckhorn on the microphones. They'd spurned the opportunity to buy guitar echo, but this was different, giving them vocal reverb like all the heavenly American records. Beyond council-house bathrooms and Mendips' porch, this was the first place the Beatles heard their voices with reverb, and it was a deep and lasting joy. They feasted anew on everything from Elvis's Baby Let's Play House to Gene Vincent's Be-Bop-A-Lula, and from this moment John Lennon was definitively sold on vocal echo, wanting only to hear his voice dressed this way, and actually uncomfortable when it wasn't.

For these and other reasons, the Top Ten would stick in the Beatles' minds as the best Hamburg club they played. As George reflected in 1969, 'The Top Ten is probably the best one. It was fantastic! Echo on the microphones – it was really a gas.'[4] Tony Sheridan played an electric-acoustic Martin guitar; George played lead; John rhythm; Stu bass; Pete drums; Paul piano. He'd gone to the trouble of bringing his clapped-out Rosetti to Hamburg but had to set it aside after just a week or two. Instead, Paul sat side-on to some of the audience and with his back to most (ironically, just how he'd instructed Stu to stand a year earlier) and hammered out tunes from the Top Ten's not-very-good upright. 'It was a terrible old piano,' he'd recall, 'so to be able to even pick out anything was an achievement.' For Paul, the downside of not buying a new guitar was, as Pete would remember, being 'the target of some good-natured ribbing about being a bit of a meanie', but the upside was a great advancement in his piano skills.[5] Playing up to thirty-eight hours a week added greatly to his natural flair and talent, confirming him as easily the Beatles' best pianist. John was self-taught to a pleasingly basic level and George could pick out some chords, but Paul was now just like his dad: unable to read music but a fine, confident and inventive player.

Then, at one, two, three in the morning, St Pauli's gangsters would walk into the Top Ten: swaggering, loudmouthed, big-shot bastards, drunk and belligerent, with floozies on their arms. They'd sit down next to the stage, their voices bellowing, and send drinks up for the band with the imperative they be drunk. They were. Then, invariably, a gangster would get up and sing. These were men to avoid at all costs, but here they were *with the Beatles* for a few minutes. 'I'd pretend to be busy and try not to get involved,' says Tony Sheridan, 'but Paul always did this thing with them, a syrupy, wide-eyed, extra cooperative attitude, on the basis of "If I'm nice to this guy he's not going to hurt me". *You want to sing?! What would you like to sing?! OK!!* I was never into that and I didn't respect Paul for it.'[6]

There are no photos of the Beatles at the Kaiserkeller and only posed publicity pictures taken first night at the Indra, but several sets exist to show the Beatles in the Top Ten in spring 1961. Among them is a shoot by photo-journalist Gerd Mingram, who caught the Beatles in a *mach Schau* moment: Paul stands with the microphone, laughing and singing to John who's down on one knee and reacting in kind with his Rickenbacker – two Liverpool lads bonded tight through the beat, six-hundred-plus miles from home, watched by an amused George and Stu.

Mingram's camera also caught one of those occasions when a gangster sang with the Beatles. Tony Sheridan was sensible to keep away (he's not in these photos), and harsh to criticise Paul for fawning, for the man is Walter Sprenger, remembered by Sheridan as 'a butcher, a hard-punching man, with arms like thighs'. His police mug-shots were published in *Bild-Zeitung* this same summer under the headline BERÜCHTIGTE ST PAULI-SCHLÄGER BEDROHTEN GÄSTE [INFAMOUS ST PAULI THUGS THREATEN PATRONS] – by which time he had fifteen convictions for grievous bodily harm, though he was still roaming free.[7] Also in the photos is Wilfrid Schulz, the undisputed king of the Hamburg underworld, a beefy bully the press nicknamed Der Pate von St Pauli – the Godfather of St Pauli. He was a known murderer but the police could never make any charges stick. 'Schulz was an animal,' says Sheridan, 'an ultra-violent man known for his bestiality – I saw him in action and he enjoyed hurting people.'

The Beatles had good protection at the Top Ten in the small but feisty shape of Horst 'Hoddel' Fascher. They'd come to know him to some degree on their first visit and now he became part of their circle. Horst had two younger brothers also on the scene, Uwe and Manfred (Fredi), and they were all tough little guys, boxers, cheery hard-fighting men remembered by some Top Ten regulars more for causing trouble than calming it. 'We really got to know these people very, very well,' says Paul, 'and they loved us like brothers.' So they did . . . and this time it was George's turn to steer clear. As friendly as Fascher was – and he seemed to love nothing more than being happy pals with the musicians – he had *a reputation*. 'Horst Fascher was very rough,' George would recall. 'He was known for being in prison for manslaughter. I saw his brother once kick somebody in the head so hard I heard the crack of the guy's skull from about a hundred yards. I kept well out of it, *well* away from that.'[8]

The Beatles were young to be consorting with such adult bruisers – Stu and John were 20 (the same as Tony Sheridan), Pete 19 and Paul and George 18 – so it was necessary they sought kinder company away from the stage. There were frequent visits to Astrid's house, to get themselves and their clothes cleaned, and to sit down politely and entertainingly, as Beatles always could, to another of Frau Kirchherr's white-napkin meals. Everybody went except Pete – he never showed up, maintaining an almost complete detachment from the group when they weren't playing.

One of Paul's off-stage friendships was with the Top Ten's *Toilettenfrau*. A little bespectacled 60-year-old, Rosa Hoffman was known to her extended family of St Pauli clubgoers by at least four affectionate names: Mutti, Mama, Tante Rosa and Röschen.* She was a maternal figure to many, and though she didn't speak English (Paul talked to her in schoolboy German) she was a willing listener, glad to dole out care, consolation and paper towels. Her place of work in the Top Ten was downstairs – one floor below the loud music, dancing and violence – inside the men's lavatory, sitting at a small table with a plate on which customers dropped a few pfennigs. Paul was always kind and solicitous to her and she became very fond of him, making sure he was looked after.[9] And Rosa didn't only manage the toilets, she was part of the St Pauli supply line. Uwe Fascher marvelled at her ability to secure whatever anyone asked for: she found him some particular pornographic books he was after, and she sold the Beatles their drugs.

Tony Sheridan had just been introduced to Preludin when he offered it to the Beatles.[10] The Top Ten nights were very long, especially the eight-hour

---

* Mutti and Mama mean Mummy, Tante Rosa is Auntie Rosa, Röschen an affectionate diminutive of Rosa.

weekend sessions, and Preludin the surest way to last the distance. The Beatles
went through their first Hamburg trip stimulated only by alcohol and momentum, but now most people in the clubs were taking pills: the waiters, the
owners, the underworld gangsters and the musicians. 'I never saw any hash[ish]
or grass or cocaine or heroin in St Pauli,' says Sheridan, 'it was just pills that you
could get from a waiter or the *Toilettenfrau*.'

Preludin was an appetite suppressant, an anorectic drug introduced into
West German society in 1954, when commercial pressures were making women
become more image-conscious. Users maintained an appetite but quickly felt
full when eating, and the reduced intake brought about weight loss. Preludin's
primary ingredient, phenmetrazine, was not an amphetamine but an upper,
giving the user a euphoric buzz. It was soon sold internationally and used recre-
ationally, and though available in Germany only with a doctor's prescription,
obtained from a pharmacist in small round metal tubes of twenty, supply
thrived on the black market. In the Top Ten Club toilets, Tante Rosa kept a
great glass jar full of them which she freely sold for 50 pfennigs apiece. They
looked like little white sweets . . . but these were no mint drops.

Ten months earlier, the Beatles had experienced their first taste of amphetamine, chewing the Benzedrine card inside a nasal inhaler. John, George and
probably Stu took it with enthusiasm, and so did they take to Preludin in
Hamburg. George spoke graphically of how they would be 'frothing at the
mouth . . . we used to be up there foaming, stomping away'.[11] John, as always,
dived straight in, wholeheartedly grabbing another new experience with an
open mouth and no thought of tomorrow. The Beatles called them 'pep pills' –
the commonly used British term of the period – and also 'Prellies'. Tony
Sheridan remembers the Top Ten edict: you took one or two at a time, swallowed with a drink in one big swig, *auf ex* – down-in-one. Two pills a night were
more than enough for most but John frequently took four or five, and in conjunction with hour after hour of booze he became *wired*, a high-speed gabbling
blur of talent, torment and hilarity.

Ruth Lallemannd, a St Pauli barmaid who knew the Beatles from 1960,
recalls an occasion when 'They crushed ten Prellies to powder, put them in a
bottle of Cola and shared it between them. They were always wound up.'[12] But
this wouldn't have been all of them. Stu certainly indulged because Astrid
remembers it – she took Preludin too, and had an easy personal supply because
her mother (who also took it) got them privately from a friendly pharmacist –
but Pete never took them or anything else, not even once. He held strong views
about drugs, perhaps associated with his sporting prowess: he was physically fit
and took proper care of himself, though he could drink alcohol in prodigious
quantities, especially in Hamburg.

The introduction of Preludin into the Beatles' world caused a problem for Paul. In the Gambier Terrace flat with Royston Ellis he'd been reluctant to chew the Vicks inhaler, knowing it was something he shouldn't do, and hearing echoes of his parents' warnings to *be careful*. Hamburg was the same only much more so, and again he tried to hold out. 'When the Preludin came around I was probably the last one to have it,' he remembers. 'It was: "Oh, I'll stick to the beer, thanks."'[13]

Paul wasn't the last . . . he just excludes Pete from his thinking. The five-man Beatles contained a core four, and within this a switched-on trio with their own particular brand of peer-group pressure. John and George wanted Paul to feel what they were experiencing, to share the new knowledge, to be all-in-this-together. For Pete, coercion to take the pills was light and half-hearted, for Paul it was heavy and persistent; John needled him and called him a cissy. 'That was the attitude that prevailed,' Paul says.[14] How long he held out isn't known, but the view was maintained even after he conceded, when he was mocked for taking too few. 'Maybe I'd just have one to last the night,' he says, 'whereas John might have four or five. I was never excessive in that way.'[15]

Preludin small-print advised against its being taken less than six hours before bedtime, in case of sleep disorders. Paul slept fine on just the one pill, John and George didn't. George would recall 'lying in bed, sweating from Preludin, thinking, "Why aren't I sleeping?"'[16] John simply took more: 'You could work almost endlessly until the pill wore off, then you'd have to have another . . . You'd have two hours' sleep and wake up to take a pill and get on stage, and it would go on and on and on. When you didn't even get a day off you'd begin to go out of your mind with tiredness.'[17]

The Beatles were also drinking like fish. 'At times there were more bottles and glasses on stage than equipment,' Pete says. They drank whatever was delivered up, usually by order. Beer was on endless supply, and necessary because Preludin made them thirsty – but, when they had the choice, three of them had started to opt for something different. George really didn't care for cold fizzy German beer, preferring the tastier English ale unavailable here, so Scotch and Coke (one of Ringo's tipples) became his main drink, and John and Paul soon followed.

Finally, after all that – after all the hours of playing and *Schau*ing, all the pills and all the drink – Tony, George, Paul, John and Pete, along with Rosi and perhaps some stray females, would stagger wearily and noisily up three long flights of wooden stairs to their attic room – two painful sets of twenty-three steps and then a final, agonising twenty-one more – rudely awakening the ageing Eckhorn family members as they went. Girls climbed into bunks with boys, but, says Rosi, 'Sex was done without speaking. Tony always wanted it after he finished

playing and we'd try to be up there alone, arranging it to make sure it was a separate time.'[18] George had no such fortune: there were several witnesses to the
moment this 18-year-old Liverpool lad lost his virginity, here in the attic at
Reeperbahn 136. 'My first shag was in Hamburg,' he recalled, 'with Paul and
John and Pete Best all watching. We were in bunk beds. They couldn't really
see anything because I was under the covers, but after I'd finished they all
applauded and cheered. At least they kept quiet whilst I was doing it.'[19]

And then, says Rosi, when they woke, in the early hours of the afternoon,
'John Lennon would clear his throat with a big *hawk*, spit, and line up the
phlegm on the wall, to show what they thought of the dirty hole they were
made to sleep in.'

Rosi never saw a girl in Pete's bed because he conducted his private life privately, as was his way. He went to where the women lived, and was spending
much offstage time with a stripper whose husband was in jail.[20] Once again,
John, Paul and George lived a disconnected existence from Pete here in
Hamburg, similar to the first trip only more so, and like the Liverpool period
just past. This was now the established way of things: Pete was with them only
on stage, and at all other times they functioned without him, as Rosi confirms:

> Pete always went off on his own. I'd see him standing on a corner somewhere
> with his curly hair and his collar up, making the James Dean look for himself.
>
> John, Paul and George were like the Three Musketeers. They were close,
> and there was a bond even though they were all different. They all wanted to
> learn as much as they could – 'Have you seen this place? Have you heard
> about this?' Pete was always doing something else. He didn't fit in with the
> others *at all*. It was clear to us.

Both John and Paul vented anger towards Pete when he fell asleep at the
drums. He was living a different timetable with his stripper girlfriend, and the
triple cross – not enough sleep, seven or eight hours' rocking every night, and
his flat refusal to take a Prelly to keep himself going – meant he sometimes
struggled to keep pace. Paul admits he used to 'get on Pete's case … I remember during tom-tom fills turning round to shout "PETE!" and we would argue
as to whether he'd slept for a split-second or not, so it got a little bit
fraught.'[21]

Such lapses were understandable in the circumstances and could have been
overlooked but for the fact that Pete continued to fall short for them as a drummer. John, Paul and George all spoke of this in later years, though only a little,
conscious of complex personal situations, but Tony Sheridan – on the Top Ten
stage with them the entire time – has no need for self-censorship.

Pete was a crap drummer, you can take my word for it. He was just not competent, and there were discrepancies between his feet and his hands. He didn't care – he exuded a feeling of 'I'm not an interesting person, so don't even bother'. This is not a good attribute on stage: if you're going to play drums you have to do your best. He needed a shot of vitality; I used to *scream* at him. I don't know why he was the Beatles' drummer – they just didn't get on. He didn't talk much and wasn't artistically minded or anything. They were completely different types.

Stu's Top Ten season was different from the others'. Hamburg was his home town now, he was starting to pick up some spoken German, Astrid's circle was becoming his, and they were considering a June wedding, perhaps at the British Embassy. Also, having failed or sabotaged his interview in Liverpool, he was enquiring about enrolling at a Hamburg art school. It was clear to all that his time in the Beatles was drawing to a close, so he was less involved in the everyday laughs and stresses, turning up to play and then going home again. Beyond his usual problem in the group – Paul's jealousy and the associated moans about musical crappiness – Stu's main concern was that he was still suffering from his grumbling appendix and persistent headaches. They won him little sympathy from the others. As Pete recalls, 'He would complain he had headaches and we said "Tough luck". That was our attitude.' The spotlight still dwelled on Stu once a night for Love Me Tender, his moment in the sun. He'd pass the bass to Paul, light a cigarette, stand at the microphone, stare straight at Astrid and sing one for his sweetheart. Such performances were spiked, inevitably, by a babble of bandmate backchat, and one time it got too much to bear. Tearing his gaze from his fiancée, quiet Stu spun round and screamed, '*For Chrissake shut up!*'[22]

Stuart so enjoyed Astrid's black leather suit – the tight trousers and jacket – that she arranged to have an identical pair tailor-made for him. This was done at Hamburger Ledermoden, a smart, expensive leather store downtown, and it cost her DM1500 (about £128). The moment the other Beatles saw it they wanted the same, for wearing off and on stage. The price was beyond them but they learned of a St Pauli *Schneider*, a tailor, who could make the trousers for about DM250 (£21). All this happened within the first two weeks of their return: they ordered black leather trousers and black velvet shirts.

The Beatles' leather look was started on their first Hamburg visit and completed on the second. From head to toe, they wore pink twat 'ats (occasionally) on top of greased quiffs, black leather jackets on top of black velvet shirts or black round-collar T-shirts, and black leather trousers down to pointy black winkle-pickers or tucked at the calves into gold and silver Texan boots. They were a sight: wild leather boys, pumped up on Prellies and stomping with Sheridan through the small hours at the Top Ten. John, Paul and George – buddies, friends and pals, to use their own expression – went up on the roof and posed for photos with *the new look*. Nine months earlier, they were down on their luck, playing in Williams' and Woodbine's Liverpool strip club: they'd come a long way very fast.

When the Beatles arrived in Hamburg, they gave out their business cards to everyone. They'd had no such status symbol on the first visit and liked the way it conferred the sheen of professionalism. This was the card that named A. Williams as provider of the Beatles' 'Sole Direction' – he was their manager. Only, he wasn't. He'd been chopped, and knew it. He'd received Stuart's letter, informing him they weren't going to pay his weekly commission, and he was furious. On 20 April, he sent them a letter by air mail Express Delivery:

> May I remind you, seeing you are all appearing to get more than a little swollen-headed, that you would not even have smelled Hamburg if I had not made the contacts, and by Law it is illegal for any person under contract to make a contract through the first contract.
>
> If you decide not to pay I promise you that I shall have you out of Germany inside two weeks through several legal ways and don't you think I'm bluffing.
>
> I will also submit a full report of your behaviour to the Agency Members Association of which I am a full member, and every Agent in England is a member, to protect Agents from artistes who misbehave and welsh out of agreements.
>
> So if you want to play in Liverpool for all the local boys you go straight ahead and welsh on your contract. Don't underestimate my ability to carry out what I have written.
>
> I don't want to fall out with you but I can't abide anybody who does not honour their word or bond, and I could have sworn you were all decent lads, that is why I pushed you when nobody wanted to hear you.

Williams had actual as well as moral right on his side. The second contract had been made through the first, which by law entitled him to continued involvement; moreover, the Beatles' Hamburg return would not have happened without his efforts. All the key documents that brought it about – from Paul and Pete's post-deportation appeals, to the Top Ten contract that helped convince the authorities to allow them back – originated on the same machine as this letter, typed by his secretary, his sister-in-law Val Chang. The last words in the last letter he'd sent to the German Consul on their behalf had been 'they have a watertight contract'. He'd not counted on the Beatles' ability to spring a leak.

Williams was well placed to carry out at least one of his threats. If he reported the Beatles to the Agents' Association they'd be barred from employment at that level of business throughout Britain. The Beatles didn't think he was a member and reckoned that Liverpool promoters operated outside of the association ... but they couldn't be certain in either case. By ignoring the letter – which is what four of them did – they were hard-nosed enough to risk their very future when £2 each a week would have avoided it.* Being at odds with Williams would also mean being barred from his Blue Angel night-club and, more vitally, from the Jacaranda coffee bar, their social hub since school-days.

In their own minds, it didn't matter what Williams might do to them in the future, any more than they were 'grateful' for what he'd put their way in the past. They were *here now*, and tough luck. And they'd always managed to have a good moan at his expense, taking the mickey out of his voice (making it out to be higher-pitched than it was) and laughing at his baffling inability to get their names right, calling Paul *John* and John *George* and George *Paul*. But it had become hollow laughter, and Williams' cause was not helped by the envelope that enclosed his Express Delivery letter, which was addressed to 'The Beetles'. It's not hard to imagine them saying 'Even *now* he can't get our bloody name right!'

It isn't clear at what point in the Beatles' Top Ten engagement it was agreed they would stay longer, but it may have been now, as a means of locking themselves into a deal Allan Williams might try to undo. They'd gone to Hamburg for a month, perhaps two, and while here it was extended to three. They would be in Germany until the start of July.[23]

In 1960, Astrid Kirchherr shot some superlative photos of the Beatles in Hamburg; she then took none at all in 1961, scaling back her work to focus solely on helping Reinhart Wolf. His other assistant, Jürgen Vollmer, made up for it. Early in this second visit he asked George to go out with him for a few hours for a solo session, and George agreed, slipping into his leather jacket and

---

* Stuart was the only one to reply, sending Williams some money. How much he sent isn't known, but Paul would recall 'he paid something because he already owed Williams money for other things'.

greasing back his quiff. The others showed their intrigue with nods and winks. They knew Jürgen had a crush on George; he sometimes wore an I LIKE IKE badge he'd altered to read I LIKE GEORGE.* 'It was chemical,' says Jürgen. 'I liked George the most. He was very quiet and shy, like me, and also a dreamer.'

This was an experimental day, because Jürgen had never done a photo session before. He was using a Rolleicord camera borrowed from Wolf, probably the same one Astrid had used for her first shoot. The results were similarly excellent. He fired off a roll of twelve black-and-white photos on the Alster ferry, and eight more frames on the landing stage at Winterhuder Fährhaus, and George's character and youth shine fresh from the spring images.[24]

George was well liked by his Hamburg friends. Klaus remembers that they were fond of his long eye-teeth, his *Segelohren* (protruding ears) and the seemingly involuntary way his leg twitched when he played guitar. Jürgen smiles as he recalls, 'Stuart told me that when George got back to the others, after spending the day with me, he didn't say anything except "Jürgen is fab". Just that, nothing else.'

His bandmates' envy over missing out quickly dissipated when Jürgen suggested a group photo session in the Top Ten. He had little chance to train his lens on Pete, whom he considered the best-looking of the five, because the drummer left early, most of the afternoon shoot taking place without him. The session produced some exceptional photos of John, George and Paul closely grouped around the Top Ten microphones, playing the Rickenbacker, Futurama and *kaput* Rosetti; Jürgen also took a very good photo of John and Stu together – the single existing high-quality image of these great friends – as well as John in action on his own and many more solo shots of George. Within five rolls of twelve exposures, Jürgen Vollmer produced the first set of high-calibre photographs of the Beatles in performance, stunning images that revealed much about them and also the consuming passion for rockers they inspired in him.

When he'd taken enough in the Top Ten, Jürgen led the four Beatles to nearby Wohlwillstrasse. Here, between shops, tucked away behind a gated entrance you could walk past and never notice, was Jäger-Passage, an enclosed courtyard with tall arched doorways and graffiti chalked light on pock-marked bricks. It was both atmospheric and perfect for a shy photographer – through the lens it looked like a busy street, but hardly anyone would pass by all afternoon.

Jürgen had a purpose for this shoot and the Beatles were his guinea pigs. 'I

---

* I LIKE IKE was a well-marketed slogan coined for Dwight D. Eisenhower's successful Republican campaign for the 1952 US presidential election.

wanted to experiment with long exposure time. I put John in the doorway because he looked the most *rocker* of them all – to me, he was like Marlon Brando in *The Wild One* – and I made him stand still, then I got the other three to pass by. I put the camera on a tripod and set a long exposure so their bodies were out of focus, but I wanted their shoes to be *sharp* so you could hear the hard steps.'

Here, then, is the definitive leather-jacket Lennon at 20, leaning into the brick of a Hamburg doorway. His old Woolton gang and Quarry Bank pals are home in England – studying hard and hoping to pass, slipping into careers, getting married, settling down – but he's out and about, causing a bit of havoc, drinking and getting pilled, upsetting people, singing for his supper, having a laff and a shout with the lads, a Lennon just like the dad he's not seen in fifteen years, and *his* dad – the first John Lennon – and of course like Julia too. They were all here.

The photos proved to Jürgen that he had talent. Shortly after this, he did a fine session with Astrid and Stuart, placing the chic couple in the ornamental doorway of a Hamburg house; and then, around August, he began to fulfil his rebel dream: he left Germany and went to live in Paris.[25]

Hamburg wasn't West Germany's biggest city or capital, but it was the centre of its recording business. Pre-war, record companies had been based in Berlin, but in 1951 Deutsche Grammophon opened an office in Hamburg – primarily to build up its light/popular label Polydor – and other companies followed.[26] It was to the Beatles' eternal good fortune that Allan Williams chanced to export Liverpool groups to this same city. Talent-spotting recording managers didn't set foot in the Indra or Kaiserkeller but they did go in the Top Ten Club – just as London A&R men scouted the 2i's Coffee Bar. Tony Sheridan, uniquely, was signed up in both places.

Missing information makes it impossible to fix a proper chronology of who went to the Top Ten and when, but it's likely that the first record producer to take an interest in the Beatles was Jimmy Bowien, aged 28 and trying to make a mark in only his second year on the Polydor staff. He paid a visit around the end of April and enjoyed what he saw. 'I liked the Beatles' new attitude and the wild way they presented themselves,' he says. 'I was convinced they were a very good group and really wanted to do something with them.' Bowien had a brief conversation with George and went away, but when he returned a few days later with a colleague, George told him someone else had beaten him to the punch. 'He came over to me and said, "You've come too late – another man wants to sign us, Bert Kaempfert."'[27]

At 37, Hamburg-born Berthold 'Bert' Kaempfert was a major name in his native country as both a producer for Polydor and leader of a famous easy-listening orchestra, and he'd also achieved a remarkable breakthrough in America, displacing Elvis's Are You Lonesome Tonight to reach number 1 on the Hot 100 with a plodding trumpet-led instrumental called Wonderland By Night (Wunderland Bei Nacht); simultaneously, he'd also got top spot on the album chart with *Wonderland By Night* the long-player. As Capitol was always telling EMI in England, Americans rarely went for anything foreign, so this was an unusual situation. The trade magazine *Billboard* said Kaempfert's success presaged a 'Teutonic tune invasion'.[28]

He went to the Top Ten on the basis of two personal recommendations. The first came from one of his closest associates, Alfred Schacht, a lawyer who was general manager of the music publishing firm Aberbach. Having heard that Sheridan was writing songs, Schacht went to hear them; he then told his friend Fips (Kaempfert's widely used affectionate nickname) that Sheridan was worth seeing as a performer too, and so was his backing group.

Another Top Ten visitor was Tommy Kent, a German boy whose American-sounding pseudonym disguised the identity of Guntram Kühbeck, a nationally known *Schlager* (slushy, catchy pop) singer for the Polydor label. Having just turned 18, Kent was able to frequent the St Pauli clubs beyond 10PM and one night he saw the Beatles. 'From the first second, I thought, "What fun they are." I knew they were very good.'[29]

Kaempfert is said to have made several visits to the Top Ten, and he was proposing to sign Sheridan and the Beatles not to Polydor directly but to his own independent company, Bert Kaempfert Produktion, which in turn had an exclusive licensing arrangement with Deutsche Grammophon's pop label. For the moment, however, there was no contract, and no date was set for any sessions. Sheridan and the Beatles simply waited to hear when they would be required, and probably which songs Kaempfert would tell them to do.

How strange it was that Brian Epstein was here in Hamburg at about the same time, as a guest of Deutsche Grammophon. He was among a deputation of thirty British record dealers flown to Germany from London on 24 April who spent three days being wined, dined and shown all aspects of record manufacturing in both Hanover and Hamburg. The invitation came because Nems was one of the company's biggest British customers. As the party also included the editor of the British trade magazine *Record Retailer*, a full report was published including two photos of Brian, one while touring Hamburg docks on a riverboat. 'The evening was spent in a typical German beer house,' the commentary added.[30]

Given the opportunity to explore St Pauli freedoms, and his already confident familiarity with foreign exotica, Brian didn't turn in for the night like most other delegates but went out in search of hotspots. As most of the trip's participants were older, the few younger ones grouped together and some went out with him. Among them was Graham Pauncefort, 20-year-old assistant sales manager at Deutsche Grammophon (Great Britain), who knew and respected Brian from his occasional visits to Nems. Pauncefort clearly remembers three or four of them walking late at night along the Reeperbahn – and, tantalisingly, he's 'fairly certain' they went inside the Top Ten Club for a few minutes.[31] It would have been just a quick look, he says. Had Brian ventured closer to the stage, the Beatles would have recognised him and perhaps he them, a familiar face from Great Charlotte Street and Whitechapel back home. Instead, here was a moment when – though so far from Liverpool – their tracks paralleled mere metres apart but didn't cross.

Beyond the business visitors, the Beatles were also grabbing a local following in Hamburg for the first time. It had happened a little but not much in Bruno Koschmider's bars. Since then they'd amassed a core of devoted fans in Liverpool and now it was happening again. Tony Sheridan, in spite of his talent and achievements, didn't pull in supporters like this, nor did any of the other visiting groups – apart from which, these weren't the usual St Pauli clubgoers. Through the Beatles, the Top Ten wasn't only full of drunken sailors, leather-clad rockers and passing businessmen; it had young men and women, typically of the upper-working and middle classes, late-teenagers, students and office workers and many attractive girls, some who commuted from beyond the city to enjoy the Beatles and dance. A Cavern*ish* audience was developing on the Reeperbahn.

Seventeen-year-old Frank Sellman was one of the Beatles' new fans. He lived in Pinneberg, twenty kilometres north of Hamburg, where word somehow reached him and his friends, all apprentice car mechanics, that American rock and roll was being played on the Reeperbahn.

> It was nothing less than a revolution for children born at the end of the war to be out in such places, a real *liberation*. The strip shows in St Pauli intrigued us, but the big draw was this American music, played by English bands.
>
> We were all very taken with the Beatles, their presence, dynamism and charisma. It was like an addiction: once we'd seen them a couple of times we couldn't get enough of them. John and Paul interacted with the audience and were responsible for creating the sense of show. The other three were very much more background, the quietest being Harrison.[32]

Brigitte Leidigkeit was an apprentice, just turning 18, when a couple of girls from college asked if she'd ever been to the Top Ten Club.

I didn't know what it was, but my friend and I were getting bored with the local dances – all the '*Fräulein, Fräulein*' *Schlager* music – so we dared ourselves to go. If my parents had ever known that I was going to the Reeperbahn! I was getting dressed up in my nice skirt and white blouse and high heels and I was going down to the local dance, wasn't I? Was I heck!

I'll never forget the first time I went. It was the Beatles, and that was it, I was *hooked*. I'd never heard anything like it. We thought they were fabulous and I fell madly in love with Pete Best. I thought he was absolutely gorgeous, though I never spoke to him; I didn't speak to any of them because none of us spoke English.[33]

Memories have stayed distinct and precise for other Top Ten habitués. Ellen Piel, then 18, says, 'Paul was always smiling, a nice guy to everybody, very easy, but John was sometimes dangerous; he used to drink on stage and burp into the microphone.'

Elvi Erichsen, also 18, was a passionate dancer, never happier than when jiving. She says it was common knowledge among her friends at the time that Pete was 'an outsider who didn't get on very well with the others'.

Icke Braun, 24, liked it when John was late returning from a break because Paul would say over the microphone 'Quasimodo, get on the stage!' and John would go into one of his cripple imitations, which made everyone laugh.

Kathia Berger, 22, was deeply in love with Paul.

He looked like an angel with big eyes. He found it hard to say my name so he would play a request for 'the girl with red hair' and sing Till There Was You. I wished that he loved me but I was not his type: he liked small, tender blondes. But he did like me and we talked. I could speak English, which not many could do; I told him the Beatles would be famous and he laughed.

The Beatles were sexy. Very. You couldn't decide who was sexiest. They didn't try to be sexy, they just were, and they were natural.[34]

The angel friends were there too, in their select seats by the stage. Astrid's favourite song was One After 909 – a rare (and possibly unique) instance of the Beatles performing a Lennon-McCartney number in this period. But playing for seven, eight hours every night necessitated regular additions to what was already the broadest of repertoires; Sheridan and the Beatles would respond to the atmosphere, playing fast when the dance floor was packed and slowing right down when the clock edged past two or three. Paul fondly recalls how John sang Lazy River when the mood mellowed. It was yet another pre-rock standard which they considered fair game because Gene Vincent had recorded it – much like Summertime, Paul's Over The Rainbow and John's Ain't She Sweet, which the Germans particularly liked. They sometimes played the Harrison-Lennon instrumental from their first Hamburg visit, the twangy Shadows pastiche they still called Beatle Bop, and Pete says that even *he* sang from time to time, sticking the microphone between his thighs to render Carl Perkins' Matchbox – one of the songs Ringo was doing in *Starrtime!*, back home with Rory Storm and the Hurricanes.

'In the few months we played and lived together the Beatles became probably the best rhythm and blues band I've ever heard,' Sheridan says – high praise in anyone's language and especially his. He was a demanding and volatile leader. As Rosi describes it, 'Tony was always shouting at them, for eight hours a night, "Do it in B-flat minor!" or "Pete, you're too fast!" and "Why can't you play that?"' The Beatles had been thrilled to meet Sheridan on their first Hamburg visit, and they realised the benefits of playing with him here, but they didn't always appreciate his company. One night, in the middle of a song, Sheridan saw someone asking Rosi to dance, and without hesitation he rushed over and knocked the man out; another time, in a fight that involved a broken bottle, Sheridan severed a tendon in the middle finger of his right hand and was taken off to hospital. He had to miss a night or two, and his damaged finger would always protrude when he played. 'It was good to have Sheridan there,' George said, 'but at the same time he was such a downer. He was always getting into fights.'[35]

Tony says it was John who goaded him into fighting Pete. John felt that Pete 'lived a lie' and needed to be taught a lesson ... provided he could find someone to teach it. As John would recall, 'He was always telling us all the fights he'd had, and the people he'd thumped. We'd pretend to be asleep when he came [to the attic] and started to tell us. He also pretended he was a judo expert, which we knew he wasn't.'[36] Sheridan relates what happened next: 'John was saying *fuckin' judo* this and *fuckin' judo* that, and because I was pissed off with Pete when he didn't put enough effort in[to] his drumming, John cleverly manipulated me into fighting him. "Look Tony, if you and Pete don't fuckin' see eye to eye, go outside and have a fuckin' fight or something." And I said, "That's a good idea, John. Come on Pete, when we've finished, two o'clock, *outside*, and we'll see about it."'

The venue was the attractively ornate, turquoise-tiled alley between the front door of the club and the Reeperbahn pavement, possibly closed off at each end to make 'a ring'. It was a chance for Pete to show all he'd learned from the Best boxing dynasty in Liverpool, and for Sheridan to prove, as John Lennon regularly did, that being ex-art school didn't mean you weren't *handy*. Tony says they had maybe twenty to thirty cheering spectators, and while it isn't certain if Beatles numbered among them, John – having shoved Sheridan into this – was expecting Pete 'to kill him'. Pete might have bragged, but he was clearly hard. 'We agreed the fight had to be clean,' says Sheridan, 'no kicking in the bollocks.'

The result would always be a matter of dispute. John said Tony 'shut Pete up without a whimper'; Pete says they beat hell out of each other but that, if anybody won, he did; Rosi thinks it was a draw; and Tony is sure Pete conceded but admits they both suffered – 'The next day we could hardly move.' John probably had a good laugh at both of them.

When Cyn and Dot arrived from Liverpool, they were even more wide-eyed at St Pauli's sights than the Beatles had been the previous August. *Incredible!* It was the first time either had travelled abroad and they left Lime Street with unsuppressed excitement, cheese butties, a hot Thermos and farewell waves from Lil Powell and Jim Mac. John and Paul arranged to rendezvous with their Brigittes at the Hauptbahnhof and they came 'fresh' from the Top Ten stage, dressed in leather, all larks and boots and smoke and booze, shouting and jumping, living on Prellies time. The girls were disappointed, but then it passed; a fried English breakfast at the British Sailors' Society helped settle them in, and they were soon taking Preludin too.[37]

Paul had told Mutti his fiancée was coming to Hamburg, and expressed concerns about such a shy girl sharing the tight Top Ten attic. The *Toilettenfrau*, eager to help the boy she liked so much, suggested he and Dot stay on her houseboat, moored on the Elbe. John arranged for Cyn to stay with Astrid, Nielsa and Stuart at Eimsbütteler Strasse; Cyn gelled with Astrid and marvelled at her style. Astrid's all-black bedroom contrasted sharply with her very English boudoir back in Cheshire, with its standard dressing-table and floral nylon bedspread. Because Cyn's staying here made sex a bit difficult, there were also occasions when the girls slept over in the attic – as remembered by Rosi and also by Pete, who says he and George got the command 'look the other way'.[38]

Cyn and Dot's presence was a mixed blessing for John and Paul. It cramped their style (and there was always the chance the girls would learn of something they shouldn't), but it was also the first time either had been away with their bird. It was like being on a holiday that involved an evening job. Warm spring days were becoming hot summer days and on one of them John and Cyn joined Astrid and Stu in a run out to the coast in her VW convertible. She drove them to Scharbeutz, the Ostsee (Baltic) resort to which she'd been evacuated as a child, and where her family kept a holiday home. It was about an hour away and they had to be mindful of the clock, to be back at the Top Ten by early evening, but they spent a happy day on the beach – despite John suffering sunburn.

Simple snapshots record John and Cyn happily hugging by the water's edge, and two close mates enjoying a moment: John in a T-shirt, Stu in a floppy hat with a ciggie clenched between his teeth, together crafting a piece of art with driftwood and sand.

John and Paul showed Cyn and Dot the Hamburg they knew, from the harbour to the wicked Herbertstrasse. One such day, Stu and Astrid joined them and they climbed the great green-copper tower at Hauptkirche St Michaelis (St Michael's church). Here on the viewing platform, which presented a grand panorama of the metropolis, a wooden handrail would preserve three testimonials to love, carved with care and a pocket penknife: *John + Cyn, Paul + Dot, Stu + Astrid.*[39]

Just as Stuart's entry into the Beatles came through his art, so too was it his exit. Nielsa Kirchherr bought him paints and brushes and her brother made him an easel, and he resumed his primary passion refreshed and with much to say. Then, from the last week of May, he studied under Eduardo Paolozzi, newly appointed as visiting professor for a year at Hochschule für Bildende Künste, the Hamburg College of Fine Arts. Paolozzi was a founder member of the 'Independent Group' of artists in London, fascinated with America's post-war consumer culture; some of his artwork anticipated the coming pop art style, but he had particular renown as a sculptor – and it was as a sculptor, not a painter, that Stuart successfully applied for both a place in the Hochschule and a support grant. Paolozzi thought his new student's work and ideas well worthy of encouragement. As he remarked six years later, 'He had so much energy and was so very inventive. The feeling of potential splashed out from him. He had the right kind of sensibility and arrogance to succeed.'[40]

Stuart was given two non-repayable monthly grants of 100 marks for a summer term beginning 1 June, but he remained determined to complete the Beatles' Top Ten season, to finish on 1 July. Playing all night and working all day was exhausting, however, so he did miss the occasional night, on top of which his health was causing genuine concern: his appendix was troubling him continually and he was alarmingly thin and still having headaches.

Plugging the gap when Stuart was absent, and plugging in, Paul switched from piano to bass, borrowing Stuart's big Hofner 333 and playing it upside down (so the strings were still in the right place when Stuart wanted it). Paul was back in the Beatles' front line at long last, though he remained as reluctant as ever to take over the bass full-time: in spite of Stu's skinny frame, he still considered it 'the fat guy's instrument'.[41] It was clear the Beatles were rapidly approaching a decision, however: back in Liverpool, they'd either have to find a new bass player or slim down to a foursome with John, Paul or George playing it.

Would they even have any bookings, though? Clearly Allan Williams had not been able to bring this Hamburg trip to a halt, as he'd threatened, but perhaps he hadn't tried. The position in Liverpool could be different, however, and that Williams was still angry *was* known to them – it was made clear in a letter Paul received from his dad, in which Jim reported that Williams was seeing a solicitor about the Beatles' refusal to pay his commission. Jim told Paul the Beatles were wrong to have treated their manager this way and encouraged him to make amends before the situation became too difficult.[42] But the Beatles were going to brazen it out; in fact, measures to get around any problems were already in hand.

One of Cyn's main impressions of her Hamburg visit was that Pete was 'a misfit' in the group, 'a loner who brooded a great deal on his own'. It's also true that the same Pete, with his energetic mother Mo, was working harder to secure the Beatles' future than the other four members combined, and he was doing it without their acknowledgement or thanks. The Bests, in their unrewarded role as organisers, were laying the groundwork for the Beatles' Liverpool return, and shooting high. They'd never again play for the scale of fees earned at the start of the year, typically between £5 and £10 a booking. These had already exceeded the earnings of any other group but now they were raising the stakes. Cavern lunchtime sessions that had paid them £5 were pegged at £10, evening bookings at the Cavern and elsewhere rarely less than £15. 'Let's get the cash in!' was the motto, and this tone was set from the start.[43] The Beatles' first post-Hamburg date would be for Mona Best herself – at St John's church hall in Tuebrook on 13 July – and their fee an astronomical £20. The promoters' grapevine glowed red hot. The Beatles pulled in the crowds for these men and now, through gritted teeth, they were going to have to pay for it.

One had already agreed. Pete set up a long-term booking with Wally Hill, to play every Saturday and Sunday night, for £15 and £12 respectively, until at least the end of September. Hill wasn't mad on the Beatles – 'They were dirty: it looked like they never washed their hair'[44] – but he was desperate to block-book them just as Brian Kelly had monopolised them between January and March. It suited the Beatles to be the subject of inter-promoter rivalry.

There was also one other development: Neil Aspinall – Pete's best friend, his mother's lodger and lover, and George and Paul's pal from school – had chucked in his steady job as a trainee accountant, done away with his laborious correspondence course, and was buying a new van. The Beatles were set to become the only group in Liverpool with a driver and assistant who did nothing else but drive and assist, a staunch ally and devoted employee to boot.

*

After an impressively adept week or two with Stuart's bass, Paul played himself into the job he didn't want. As George would remember, this question of who'd become the Beatles' bassman kind of decided itself when two of the three possibilities ruled themselves out of the running: 'I said ... "One of us three is going to be the bass player, and it's not going to be me", and John said, "I'm not doing it either", and Paul didn't seem to mind the idea.'[45] Paul says he was left with no choice: 'I doubt I would have picked up the bass if Stuart hadn't left. I certainly didn't start playing it by choice: I got *lumbered* with it.'[46]

Either Paul didn't want to buy Stuart's bass or it wasn't made available to him, because he went into Hamburg and bought one. His initial intention was to buy a Fender, but he thought the price prohibitive and ended up at Steinway & Sons trying the hollow-bodied, violin-shaped Hofner 500/1. He liked its symmetrical appearance and was pleased to find it light, like balsa wood in his hands, where Stuart's guitar was heavy. Buying a Hofner inside its country of manufacture made it easy to request a left-handed model; although a special order, it was available within days and became the first guitar Paul wasn't forced to play upside down. The price was also appealing – DM360, a little under £31. 'I didn't really want to spend that much,' he'd recall. It was only £10 more than he'd spent on the Rosetti a year earlier, and he'd soon regretted his decision to buy cheap. That guitar fell apart within months, so it remained to be seen how long this 'Hofner Violin' bass would stay in use. As for the old Rosetti, its overdue demise was mourned right there on the Top Ten stage in a heartfelt festival of Prelly-fuelled performance art. As Paul would recall, 'George, Stu, Pete and John – especially John – had a great time smashing it to bits by jumping up and down on it.'[47]

A pair of photographs show Paul and Stu on stage with their basses. At the start of the year the Beatles didn't have one bass player and now they had two, and *comments* were surely passed. Although Cyn would write of how Stu 'restrained himself' when Paul was niggling him, there was one occasion when he didn't, when the Top Ten witnessed an explosion, and yet another fight: Beatle on Beatle this time, Stu on Paul.

The fight's origin is vague or varies in the telling, but everyone agrees that a tease or derogatory mention of Astrid set it off. Klaus says Stuart owed Paul some money, and Paul, nagging to get it back, made a flippant remark about Astrid being able to afford it. As Paul would remember, 'I'd always wondered, if he and I ever had a fight, who would win? He was probably wondering too. I assumed I'd win because he wasn't that big, but the strength of love or something entered into him because he was no easy match at all.'[48]

Everyone was amazed by the manner in which Stu, so manifestly puny, could summon up such power, as if his every muted response to eighteen months of snipes and jibes accumulated in one volcanic eruption. As George put it, 'Stuart suddenly got this amazing strength that Paul hadn't bargained for.' Klaus says Stu 'picked Paul up and put him on the piano'. Pete says Stu 'landed Paul such a wallop that it knocked him off his stool. [They] began struggling on the floor, rolling around locked in the most ferocious battle . . . a fury of flailing fists'. Paul always speaks of it being 'a silly fight – you just stay locked for about an hour, with nobody doing anything. All the old German gangsters were laughing, but it was very serious for us.'[49]

It has never been explained how the fight ended or how they were able to work together afterwards, because this wasn't a skirmish that cleared the air and left the protagonists friends again. The situation remained awkward, and it was just as well Stu's remaining days in the Beatles numbered in single figures. He, not Paul, was now the spare part on stage, and it was Paul, not Stu, who played bass when the Beatles went off to make a record.

Recording session

> Thursday 22* June 1961. Friedrich-Ebert-Halle, Hamburg-Harburg.
> Recording: My Bonnie; The Saints; Why; Beatle Bop**; Nobody's Child; Take Out Some Insurance; Ain't She Sweet**. Order of recording not known.
> By Tony Sheridan and the Beatles except ** the Beatles only. *Possibly also the 23rd.

The Beatles' first recording session took place in a civic concert hall annexed to a high school. This didn't reflect any lack of intent on the part of producer Bert Kaempfert: the auditorium was regularly used for recording, typically when Hamburg's main facility, Musikhalle, was occupied. Friedrich-Ebert-Halle – named after Germany's first president – was in Harburg, twenty-two kilometres south of Hamburg, and the Beatles got there by way of the St Pauli Elbtunnel, which transported vehicles underground by elevator before the road stretched away beneath the great river.

John Lennon, Paul McCartney, George Harrison, Pete Best and Tony Sheridan, with Stu Sutcliffe accompanying them as a spectator, were collected from the Top Ten at 8AM, an hour the musicians usually saw only if they'd not yet been to bed. And they hadn't. They'd come off stage at two, eaten and had a few more drinks, killed some time, and then waited in the already warm early-morning sunshine for their transport to destiny. 'We did the recordings on a Preludin high,' says Sheridan, 'there was no other way we could have done it.' (Pete abstained as usual.)

Sleep was probably beyond them anyway, because here at last was their chance to *make a record* – a prized moment for the five lads whose average age was 19. Sheridan had worked in a few studios in England (including EMI's on Abbey Road) but he'd never been the star. John, Paul and George's only 'studio' experiences had been here in Hamburg eight months previously, when they'd cut some private discs with Wally and Ringo from the Hurricanes, and in Percy Phillips' terraced house in Liverpool, where twice they'd put down pocket money to finance basic sessions. This German situation was completely different: they were working with the nation's best-known producer, a man whose single and album had hit number 1 in America just five months earlier, and what they did with him would be issued on a major label and sold in shops. People might buy it and make them rich and famous. At the very least, back in Liverpool, they'd be able to put a piece of seven-inch plastic on a record turntable and say, 'That's us,' which no other group could do.

Facing the empty stalls and circle of the arena, they set up on the wooden stage as they did at the Top Ten – left to right, Paul, George, John and Tony, with Pete at the back. Kaempfert provided the amplifiers – the musicians didn't bring their own – and replacement gear was delivered during the session after problems developed. The performances were recorded live, no overdubbing, and there was little audio separation between the drums and other instruments; the sound was taped two-track stereo and balanced by engineer Karl Hinze, who sat either in a small basement room or on the stage behind a curtain. No document survives to detail the start/finish times, the order of work, number of required takes, and whether the session took place over one day or two – most likely it was one, and personal recollections refer to it that way, but some papers show it as two, 22 and 23 June.

As soon as they began playing, while Hinze was setting the levels and balance, there was a problem. The producer didn't think Pete's drumming good enough for recording. As Sheridan recalls, 'Kaempfert suggested Pete not play his bass drum, because he used to get too fast ... the tempo was a problem.' Pete was quickly exposed and had no allies: Hinze would later say *der Schlagzeuger das ist doch verdammt mies* – 'the drummer is just bloody awful'[50] – and it's hard to imagine the other Beatles not being desperately disappointed at such a development in their first session. Kaempfert didn't only prevent Pete playing bass drum, it seems he had it physically removed from the kit, and with it also went the tom-tom drum. There's no bass or tom on any of these recordings, and they were missed; Pete had to carry the beat solely with the snare drum, hi-hat and a ride cymbal. He recovered from the setback with admirable tenacity – no drummer could have sounded great with such limited tools, and actually Pete had a fair session.

It was Kaempfert's idea they record My Bonnie Lies Over The Ocean. He'd witnessed them playing it in the Top Ten and felt that, because German children learned the song at school, a modern arrangement cooked up by Sheridan could become a hit. Ray Charles and Gene Vincent had also recorded it, so the lads didn't mind, and they turned in a tight and dynamic performance – London's best rock singer and guitarist, on top form here in both respects, was playing with Liverpool's best group, and it worked. Made in a shade over two minutes, My Bonnie – it took that abbreviated title – bristles with energy and deserves to be considered nothing less than one of the best British rock and roll records of the first era, in the ranks with Brand New Cadillac, Move It! and Shakin' All Over. It's a European union: a Scottish folk song performed by English musicians with that typical British *edge*, and recorded with crisp German clarity. Made in America it would have sounded different, and to the musicians' ears more authentic – but at this time, in the middle of 1961, such explosive rock and roll wasn't being recorded in the States.

'I told George he could play whatever he felt like playing,' says Sheridan, 'but that I would take the solo.* It was a blues solo, nothing to do with the song and not thought out beforehand. I don't remember how many takes we did but they would have been different each time. John had to chug away on rhythm to compensate for the drums, though I still had to instruct him on what was needed: to play sevenths all the time, C7, F7, G7.'

Paul's bass is strong on My Bonnie. He'd been desperate to avoid the instrument for three years, his real experience of playing it extended to perhaps three weeks, and he was using a new and not yet familiar guitar. Taking these factors into consideration, this was a virtuoso performance, the mark of a naturally gifted musician. He didn't play single notes but melodically inventive runs, while at the same time singing energetic harmonies and emitting rhythmic yelps. For a beginner to perform these disciplines simultaneously is difficult, but Paul had them under command; he'd have been the first to say he had much to learn as a bass player, but he'd already found a way to sound very good.

The bass is also distinguished on When The Saints Go Marching In – its title abbreviated to The Saints. This song had Jerry Lee Lewis's seal of approval and Sheridan copied his vocal style here. They also taped passable performances of Why (written mostly by Sheridan in his 2i's days), and two tunes Sheridan sang like Elvis: Nobody's Child and a Jimmy Reed blues, Take Out Some Insurance. On the second of these Sheridan fluffed the start of his guitar

---

* In a letter sent to an enquiring fan in May 1962, George wrote, 'When Tony sings then it is me playing lead, but the break in the middle is Tony playing. The shouting in the background is Paul.'

solo but Kaempfert denied him the chance to redo it. Nobody's Child, the old Hank Snow country tearjerker that had long been Richy Starkey's Liverpool party piece, was recorded here by a trio: Tony on guitar and vocals, Paul on bass, Pete on drums.[51]

John and George were much involved in the recording of Beatle Bop, which Pete says they did at Kaempfert's request. Though no Lennon-McCartney numbers were taped here, they did do this unique Harrison-Lennon instrumental, and Sheridan didn't participate – it's just the Beatles, usefully preserving their sound at the very time they contracted from a five-piece to a four. They gave a fair performance but wouldn't have cared for the bright clean production. Denied the use of his bass and tom-tom, Pete's snare sound is inevitably samey, but George's lead guitar is consistently fine and John's rhythm playing impressive (Tony says John borrowed his Gibson guitar). Paul's inventive bass again belies his novice status, and he screeches himself hoarse in the background, injecting an audibly vocal presence into the instrumental.

The Beatles also had a second number to themselves, the first time they were let loose in the studio to record a vocal track . . . so, of course, it was sung by John.[52] They believed this would be the A-side of their first 45, which made the choice of song important. John didn't go for a Lennon-McCartney Original, he chose Ain't She Sweet. Like My Bonnie, this carried the credibility of a Gene Vincent recording, but still the choice was unaccountably odd. The song was thirty-four years old, a relic of the Roaring Twenties, nor was it something Kaempfert made them do: Ain't She Sweet had been in the Beatles' stage act longer than they were the Beatles, and it may have been one of the songs Julia had played to John on Pop Stanley's banjo.

The Beatles' attitude about this opportunity was typically bullish – according to John, 'We thought it would be easy: the Germans had such shitty records, ours was bound to be better' – but actually they made a curious recording. It's likely that Kaempfert insisted they change the style, because John would later reflect how Gene Vincent's cover was 'very mellow and very high pitched, and I used to do it like that, but they said *harder, harder* – you know, Germans all want it a bit more like a march – so we ended up doing a harder version of it'.[53]

As recorded by the Beatles, Ain't She Sweet is a curiosity. John gives it a good and powerful go, but there's a strange timbre to his voice, as if he was suffering from 'Hamburg throat' while also straining to deliver Kaempfert's brittle sound on a song that didn't suit it. Nor would he have been happy that his vocal was treated with such minimal echo: there's more reverb on the drums than his voice. This drumming, inevitably heavy on the snare, lacks imagination – there's no variance, no extra fills or frills, just the same shuffle sound that Pete played on all these recordings. Paul's bass is accomplished, John again plays Tony Sheridan's Gibson, but George's ten-second solo on his Futurama is below average. He'd had a reasonable session up to now but was probably given only one chance to get this right, and didn't. Rock guitar standards in 1961 were nowhere near as high as they would become, but, judged even in its place and time, this solo wasn't good, and it was George's misfortune that he couldn't take it again.

In short, the Beatles in the studio, Germany 1961, were a mixed bag. Instrumental strengths and weaknesses were clear. Missing were the vocal harmonies by John, Paul and George that had become their greatest asset. Since Pete says it was these harmonies that attracted Kaempfert to the Beatles in the first place, it's all the harder to fathom why the producer didn't use them. Instead, they sang a peculiarly deep, Mills Brothers style of backing vocal that engineer Karl Hinze would describe as 'a whispering Negroid humming'. It's most evident on the song Why and in the two waltz-time introductions recorded for My Bonnie – one in German, the other in English – where Sheridan sings and John, Paul and George provide this weird wordless harmony. It was probably Kaempfert's idea, because they'd not done it before and wouldn't do it again; while it's not bad, it's also not *the Beatles*.

Before the five musicians were driven back to St Pauli for another seven-hour slog at the Top Ten (and yet more Prellies), they were treated to a playback. A subsequent letter written by George suggests the experience wasn't too bad, but at some point, in a time to come, Paul and John and perhaps the others decided they didn't like My Bonnie at all. 'We hated it, we thought it was a terrible record,' Paul said in 1964.[54] It seems the Beatles were underwhelmed generally by their first recording session, and beyond such brief mentions hardly talked about it – mostly because they were so rarely asked.

Alfred Schacht felt sure his friend was disappointed with and unenthusiastic about the session, as was Hanne Kaempfert, a musician professionally involved in her husband's career. This may explain why it was some months before a record was issued, although the Beatles left Harburg with the clear impression that a single featuring their two numbers – Ain't She Sweet c/w Beatle Bop – would be released in America, Germany and Britain within a few weeks. On 28 June, George and John signed contracts with Schacht, vesting in Tonika – his new, privately owned music publishing company – the copyright in their joint composition, a tune which had suddenly assumed a wry new title, the punning Cry For A Shadow. These were standard, pre-printed contracts with specific details added by typewriter, but because they were in German, George and John had no idea what they were signing.[55]

The agreements were made a few days after all four Beatles put their

signatures on their first recording contract, a document signed by Bert
Kaempfert on 19 June 1961. It was a six-page pact with Bert Kaempfert
Produktion (BKP), not a standard document but one typed expressly for the
purpose. The signatures on the last page read J. W. Lennon, James Paul
McCartney, George Harrison and Peter Best – but, again, they were clueless
about what they were signing. Everything was in German and they had no
translation. As Paul would reflect three years later, 'We signed all sorts of contracts when we were about eighteen, because we had no manager and we didn't
know what we were doing.'[56]

In which case they were fortunate, because, in a business infested by sharks,
Kaempfert played it straight and gave them a fair agreement – one-sided, yes,
because this was typical, but not villainous. The Beatles didn't know it any more
than they knew anything, and they blindly agreed to a contract that was effective for a year from 1 July 1961 and subject to automatic renewals unless
terminated with three months' notice; that paid them a royalty in Germany of
5 per cent of the wholesale price on 90 per cent of all records sold, and less for
exports; and that allowed BKP to use a pseudonym for the Beatles – while not
specified in the contract, this would be 'the Beat Brothers'.[57]

BKP took no publicity photos of the Beatles with or without Tony
Sheridan, so if any release was a hit, Polydor would have nothing on file for
press coverage – but each of them was given a sheet of paper on which to
hand-write his personal biography. These documents are fascinating and
revealing on many levels. John, George and Pete wrote theirs in capitals, Paul
used the flowing handwriting he knew counted among his attributes, Pete
alone wrote his in the third-person (PLAYED RUGBY UNTIL HE JOINED
'THE BEATLES') and the difference in John and Paul's characters is crystallised in two sentences:

> Paul: <u>Songs written</u>: With John (LENNON) – around 70 songs
> John: WRITTEN A COUPLE OF SONGS WITH PAUL

Also here, laid out plain, graphite on paper, the 20-year-old who called himself
JOHN W. LENNON (LEADER) stated explicitly what he wanted from life:
'AMBITION. TO BE <u>RICH</u>.'

They finished at the Top Ten on Saturday 1 July, three months to the day after
they started. It was their ninety-second straight night . . . and Stu's swansong.
He'd been with the Beatles through eighteen remarkable months, joining a
group that had no name and no discernible clue, and leaving one that had
acclaim, drive, abundant talent and originality, rich ambitions and a recording

British pop before the Beatles changed everything. George Martin at 30, the youngest A&R man in London, with the 'teenage' acts he's just recorded for a Parlophone 45. To his left, Jim Dale and four of the Vipers Skiffle Group; to his right, the King Brothers. EMI party, Abbey Road, Christmas 1957.

Scoffing scallops and talking rock. Paul, George and John loafing on stage in the art-school canteen. John's friend and fellow student Ann Mason inked this 1958 lunchtime moment as it happened – the participants unaware – and recently found it in a sketchbook.

The debut of Japage 3 (pronounced 'Jaypage'), rocking at brother Harry Harrison's wedding reception in the saloon bar of Childwall Abbey Hotel, 20 December 1958. The rhythm was in the guitars, just two of them. Later, John poured his pint of ale over an elderly lady pianist, announcing, 'I anoint thee David.' Typical John, typical Liverpool.

Liverpool, 10 May 1960 – a composite of two photos to make the Beatles' first group shot. Stuart Sutcliffe has joined John, Paul and George, with fill-in drummer Tommy Moore. They're auditioning to back Billy Fury in a summer season on Great Yarmouth pier. Stuart is a beginner on bass, so Paul tells him to stand with his back to Fury and his manager Larry Parnes.

Summer 1960 at Butlin's holiday camp in Pwllheli, North Wales. Richy has been Ringo since the end of '59, as drummer with Rory Storm and the Hurricanes . . . Liverpool's top group, though not for much longer. Larks here with Ty Brian (left), Johnny Guitar (right) and the irrepressible Rory.

Their Name Liveth For Evermore. The Beatles on the road to Hamburg, 16 August 1960. Their manager Allan Williams – bearded, and briefly without his top hat – stops in Oosterbeek, to pay respects at the Allied war cemetery. Fellow travellers include his wife Beryl, friend Harold Phillips (aka Lord Woodbine), Stuart, Paul, George and the Beatles' new drummer, Pete Best, grabbed at the last minute to secure the Hamburg booking. (John kept out of the picture.)

Deep among trees in a wood by the Elbe, hair up and defences down – Stuart photographed by Astrid Kirchherr, November 1960. She's already the love of his life, he's the love of hers, and wearing her scarf.

The youngest Beatle often led their fashion moves. George at 17, the first to go leather. Photographed by Astrid at the Hamburger Dom funfair, November 1960.

John, also now in leather, with Stuart at the Dom, by Astrid.

Paul (who generally bought things after the others) with Stuart at the Dom, by Astrid.

5-4-3-2-1. Five Liverpool youths, four guitars on the drip, three amps, two drumsticks, one new band. The Beatles at the Indra, first night, 17 August 1960 – fresh in Hamburg and primed to learn, *fast*. They play just along the street from Derry and the Seniors at the Kaiserkeller: Liverpool rock has arrived in Germany.

The Englishman abroad. John, the *Daily Express* and a pair of Y-fronts on Grosse Freiheit, November 1960. He's standing outside 'the pit', two grim back-of-the-screen rooms in the old Bambi Kino they called home for three months.

The Hamburg Beatles defined, Dom '60. John has just bought a new guitar – incredibly, *American* – and Paul is using his old one. This was the only time Astrid photographed Pete. He always looked the part, but an almost complete detachment from the other Beatles was quickly established.

Hamburg again (now spring 1961) and the new look is complete: pink twat 'ats atop greased quiffs, black leather jackets, black leather trousers tucked into gold and silver Texan boots. 'Three Gene Vincents' on the Top Ten roof.

Lennon und McCartney *mach Schau*, couples neck, and then a hard-nut swaggers along. Meet Wilfrid Schulz, right, *Der Pate von St Pauli* (the Godfather of St Pauli), a murderer the police couldn't nail. Top Ten Club, April–June 1961.

contract. He'd mostly taken grief for all his time and trouble, but given hugely, if not so much musically then certainly in terms of attitude and appearance.

By his own admission, Paul was mean to him to the end: 'I was pretty nasty to him on the last day, [but] I caught his eye on stage [and] he was crying. It was one of those feelings, when you're suddenly very close to someone.'[58]

Astrid remembers there being plenty of tears and requests for forgiveness for misdeeds and misbehaviour. Almost everyone was drunk, pilled and emotional, and when it was all over and they'd had something to eat they wandered around and around the *Fischmarkt*, as was their Sunday morning way. Jürgen was in Paris, Astrid had Stu, and Klaus was so emotional at the thought of the Beatles leaving that he asked to return with them to Liverpool and join the group.

> The sun was shining and we were sitting on some wooden planks on Talstrasse, close to the Top Ten. We were stoned and I asked John if I could become the Beatles' bass player. He said, 'Oh Klaus, Paul already bought the bass, it's going to be him.' That would have changed the story – there would have been five Beatles again – but it was clear the Beatles had *a plan*, and they wanted to carry on and pull it through. How many times in life do you find three people like that, in a bunch? They were incredible.

It was also farewell to Tony Sheridan, who was staying in Hamburg. His influence on the Beatles would endure, not least through his guitar techniques, steely intensity and, in John's case, the way he stood at the microphone. Tony planted his feet wide but vibrated his legs, John planted his feet wide and didn't budge an inch. He held his guitar high and his upper body tilted this way and that as he played, knees flexing, shoulders back, head forward – an authoritative presence peering down his bony nose while singing with complete commitment to the blur beyond.

Stu let George return to Liverpool with his Gibson Les Paul amplifier; without this, his Hofner 333 bass was soundless, and shortly afterwards he sold it to Klaus for DM200, his days as a rock musician seemingly over, Klaus's just beginning. As Paul's tiny Elpico amp lacked the power needed for his Hofner Violin, he took over the Selmer Truvoice George had used, and so, once again, the Beatles were returning home from Hamburg better equipped. They were also dressed to shock and smuggling a load of Preludin, stuffed here and there and inside cigarette packets at the bottom of their luggage. They were risking problems at customs in both Holland and England, but John – with his addictive, compulsive personality and zest for talking – wasn't the kind to gulp drugs by the handful for three months and then simply stop.

Ellen Piel happened to be travelling to England on the same train and boat as the Beatles, leaving Hamburg mid-afternoon on 2 July, and she recalls how the three Fascher brothers made the group's departure *boisterous*, shoulder-carrying them high through the Hauptbahnhof, laughing and shouting and grabbing everyone's attention on what was otherwise a quiet Sunday afternoon in the city. Paul had told Peter Eckhorn he'd be in touch later in the year to discuss when the Beatles might come back, but right now they weren't sure they wanted to. As John vividly described it twelve years later, 'Every time [after] we went to Hamburg we said "Never again! Never again!"'[59] Astrid and Stu were at the station too, for fond farewells. There were sincere promises to keep in touch; Stu, George and John said they'd write.

They were exhausted when they reached home, mid-afternoon on Monday the 3rd. Liverpool *was* still home, though they'd spent more time in Hamburg from last summer to this. They were giving themselves a few days off before the nightly merry-go-round started up again, when the kids and dance promoters of Merseyside would witness another riveting transformation. Kings before they left, they'd taken their performance to another, higher level: now a foursome, all in leather, even more dynamic, packing yet more punch and charisma, and bursting with the experience that only another 503 extraordinary hours on the Hamburg stage could have given them.*

---

* The running total from their two Hamburg visits: 918 hours' playing – the equivalent of 612 ninety-minute shows or 1836 half-hours – in just twenty-seven weeks.

20

Soup and Sweat and Rock 'n' Roll
(July–September 1961)

The 21st birthday party in Liverpool on 8 July 1961 didn't only mark a coming-of-age, the vital step up from juvenile to adult – for Richy Starkey it was a celebration of *being alive*, a shindig to show the doctors wrong, for Lazarus to prove he'd beaten the odds and made it to manhood. He and his loved ones had anticipated the moment for years: the infant Richy had spent his seventh birthday in hospital, in a coma, certain to die; the weakling adolescent Richy had pleurisy and tuberculosis on his 14th birthday; so where would he be for his 21st ... or would he *not* be? They'd often talked about it, keeping their fingers crossed and raising a glass to his health.

The young man was fit, strong in his own way, happy and awash with gifts. Elsie gave him a gold identity bracelet; he got yet another ring for his fingers, a fourth, to further embellish his professional name; and an auntie gave him a gold St Christopher, sacred protection from the patron saint of travelling. He treasured these presents. Just as he'd never removed Grandad Starkey's wedding ring, so now he slipped the St Christopher over his head and there it would remain until ripped from his neck.*

He'd travelled just to be here. The 8th of July (twenty-four hours after his actual birthday) was a Saturday, campers' changeover at Butlin's and the Hurricanes' weekly day off, and during the morning he'd sped home from Pwllheli in his Ford Zodiac. Rory and his band were a month into their second

---

* He also got a fifth ring, from a girl. He wore this too, in place of his first, the signet Elsie gave him at 16. He didn't wear more than four, two on each hand.

summer season and flashier than ever. Four days before leaving, they'd swanned along to Duncan (Classic Tailors) on London Road and been fitted with perhaps the gaudiest suits ever seen in rock and roll, which was really saying something: the Hurricanes were in flaming red and Rory in shocking turquoise, with white shirts, slim black bow-ties, and eye-opening cream and black winklepickers. There was no mistaking this lot for undertakers, and the occasion justified the presence of a photographer with colour film.

For Richy, this Butlin's season was preceded by none of the angst experienced in 1960. It might yet all turn to dust, but none of his old factory mates lived like this: birds in the chalet, booze in the bar, three hours' drumming every night and an hour every afternoon. All the same, he was beginning to question his future with the Hurricanes. In his head, he was still shooting for the London Palladium, but was Rory the guy to get him there? Though working hard enough – a note in Johnny Guitar's 1961 diary records '140 appearances, Jan/22 May', in other words, 140 in 142 days – they weren't going forward. With his chiselled features, stacked blond hair, incredible energy and gold lamé shirt, Rory appeared to have all the makings of a star, but Larry Parnes had seen him and been unmoved, and – here at Pwllheli – Rory was again being overlooked by the kind of showmen who never went to Liverpool but regularly dropped into Butlin's. Stars were routinely 'discovered' here, but Rory wasn't. Maybe his offstage stammer put them off; more likely, these talent-spotters saw that he lacked 'that certain something'.

Richy knew it. Johnny, Lu and Ty were content to enjoy the ride, but he was considering options. He'd become good mates with the Marsden brothers, Fred and Gerry, half of the four-piece Gerry and the Pacemakers, and expressed an interest in joining them. Fred was on the drums but they had no bass player and it was decided Richy could be the man. It was a pub idea, a crazy plan seeded in Scotch and planted in pale ale, but it lingered. Richy had never played any kind of guitar but thought he could learn; he fancied standing in a group's front line for a change, and wanted to get back to Hamburg. Rory had no prospect of making a return, but Gerry & Co were heading back to the Top Ten Club on 29 July, to play with Tony Sheridan for a month. In the end, he decided to stay put, letting the Pacemakers head off without him, but still he had the wanderlust, and talk of this kind flowed through his coming-of-age celebration as freely as the liquor. They partied long and hard in Admiral Grove, and the tiny terraced house heaved with family and friends, pressed up to the backyard privy and spilling out on the front 'play street'.

Plenty of musicians were there, among them the Hurricanes, Dominoes, Pacemakers, Big Three and Priscilla White, a girl from Scotland Road whose occasional cameos as Swinging Cilla were being noticed – she'd sung with the

Beatles (once, at the LJS in March), Hurricanes (several times) and was now working with the Big Three. She liked singing Boys, the Shirelles' song, and here at the party did it as a duet with Richy. The two had become good pals. Cilla and her friend Pat Davies were keen to practise hairdressing and Elsie volunteered to be their model; the girls went to 10 Admiral Grove every Wednesday evening to bleach, style, curl, cut and set, and in return she cooked them fried Spam and chips. Richy became friends with Cilla through these visits and had a fling with Pat (who worked at the Jacaranda and later at the Cavern) that lasted several months.[1]

The Beatles weren't at the party. John, Paul and George's absence is more puzzling than Pete's, and there's no known explanation for it. Perhaps they were in Hamburg when the invitations went out, or were engaged elsewhere. This was their holiday week and John and Paul may have gone away for a few days;[2] George, meanwhile, was busy on the domestic front. His mother was home from Canada and they were reunited after eleven months, and he was also trying to hang on to his girlfriend. Gerry Marsden had moved in on Pauline Behan while the Beatles were in Hamburg; George accused Gerry of being 'a flirt', then he and Pauline had one or two more dates before he said she had to choose between them, and she chose Gerry.[3]

This same week also marked the first appearance of *Mersey Beat* – Britain's first regional pop paper – the inside front page of which included 'Being A Short Diversion On The Dubious Origins Of Beatles', that larf-a-line history by John (with a little help from George) written before they left for Hamburg. Except for a poem and drawing in his school magazine, this was John's first time in print; Bill Harry recalls him being so delighted that he loped along to *Mersey Beat*'s office and handed over a scrappy bundle of 250 stories and poems, saying, 'Use whatever you want.'

If *Mersey Beat* was to survive, it needed all the local support Harry could muster. One of its keenest advocates, from even before the start, was Brian Epstein. His 1961 diary notes a 20 June meeting with Bill Harry in the office at Nems Whitechapel. Harry wanted Nems to take a stake in *Mersey Beat*, to put the paper (published fortnightly) on a sounder financial footing, but Brian declined – a decision he came to regret; Ray McFall became its primary investor instead, the paper's unobtrusive owner, with Harry as editor. But Brian did take a dozen copies of the first issue: he displayed them prominently on the serving counter in both of Nems' city-centre stores, and when these sold out he requested more, after which he placed an order for twelve dozen copies of issue two. Promoting local activity was good for everyone's business.[4]

Whitechapel had been open more than a year by this point and its success was greater than anyone might have expected, save Brian himself. His co-management with younger brother Clive was running like clockwork. Brian had also appointed a junior member to his executive team, a 25-year-old married man named Alistair Taylor, who combined general sales duties with the new position of 'Personal Assistant to Brian Epstein'. No other record shop manager had a PA. Taylor quickly became accustomed to his master's cultured voice and imperiously flamboyant manner, and, like most Nems staff, he was drawn into serving Mr Brian with scarcely resistible devotion – even when spitting nails over his autocracy. One day Brian would be refusing with illogical obstinacy the necessary purchase of a £14 filing cabinet, the next he was inviting Taylor to join him on a paid-for trip to the south of France, with personally arranged flights and his own first-class hotel suite.[5]

Brian was scooting around Europe often now, not just going on the record retailers' junket to Hamburg but making private trips all over the place. While his thoughts in relation to Alistair Taylor were strictly those of an abnormally philanthropic employer, his solo experiences in the south of France, Amsterdam, Paris, Barcelona and elsewhere turned always on sexual adventure. He was living as dangerously as ever, and on 5 October 1960 was robbed in Barcelona after behaving (in his own words) 'foolishly and irresponsibly'. Nems was running so smoothly that he'd slip away for odd weeks or weekends. He was already bored at work and in need of fresh risk ... that familiar Brian Epstein pattern. His father Harry could only watch from the sidelines, powerless, knowing his eldest child was again yearning for a diversion beyond the family firm that so thrived on his talents.[6]

Trade was booming for everyone involved in records. The spectacular sales increases of the 1950s showed no sign of abating: teenagers were wielding their spending power. *Record Retailer* reported a 'bumper 1961' with sales 13 per cent up on 1960. George Martin's career certainly remained in the ascendant, his recent successes matched and bettered. Matt Monro's My Kind Of Girl made the British top five *and* the US top twenty – it was George's first American hit and the first time a British singer had done so well there in three years* – and these events followed on the heels of a landmark moment at home, when finally, after ten years at Parlophone, George produced a British number 1.

It came, inevitably, from left-field, with the Temperance Seven's You're Driving Me Crazy – 1920s jazz played with sincerity and solemnity by nine eccentric Englishmen in spats, wing collars, velvet smoking-jackets and Edwardian frock coats. The record entered the *NME* chart on April Fool's Day

---

* Inevitably, the record had been rejected by Capitol; it was issued instead on the Warwick label.

and four weeks later had sped to the top, while the follow-up, Pasadena, peaked at 3 the week the Beatles arrived home from Hamburg. 'They're probably the most phenomenal group to happen this year,' wrote June Harris in *Disc*. 'The Temps' (as people called them) also laid down an important if unconsidered marker, being the first successful Sixties musicians to emerge from art school.[7]

News of his number 1 was delivered personally to George Martin in Cambridge, where he was recording the opening night of a comedy revue called *Beyond The Fringe*, on a short provincial tour prior to its opening in London. It had been the hit of the 1960 Edinburgh Festival, and because George already had a happy working relationship with one of the four performers – Dudley Moore, the jazz pianist and humorist – he'd a head start over any rivals for its recording.

For the next two years, until 1963, the best-known young men in Britain were a four-man group of Soho-suited, sharp-minded Parlophone artists whose original ideas, wit, irreverence and attractive outspokenness detonated a revolution. Oxbridge graduates Alan Bennett, Peter Cook, Jonathan Miller and Dudley Moore brought into everyday use a word that would permeate the rest of the Sixties – *satire*. Their show reformed first the London stage and then Broadway, and they discarded centuries of subservience by sending up every sacred cow: prime ministers, presidents, politics, the police, nationalism, the Empire, royalty and religion. Nothing could ever be the same again, and in their wake, over the next three or four years, Oxford and Cambridge universities produced a line of other intelligent writer-performers to further push back the boundaries. Several would go on to work with George Martin, whose Parlophone recordings of *Beyond The Fringe* remain an invaluable document of a very funny show and a giant step towards the unbuttoning of a stiff-shirted society, essential to this particular history.[8]

The first time the Beatles went to Hamburg, nobody in Liverpool noticed they'd gone. Not so the second time. They were missed, and now they were back, and kicking-on – slimmed down, speeded up, professional, intent on making a go of it.

Thanks to Pete and Mona Best, the immediate future was bright. Instead of being prevented from playing by the still-angry Allan Williams, or pricing themselves out of employment, the Beatles' diary was as full as they wanted it to be. The Cavern booked them as its star attraction every Wednesday night for seven weeks and then extended it to the rest of the year, in addition to two or three lunchtime sessions a week (usually Tuesday and Thursday one week and Monday, Wednesday, Friday the next). They had a weekly Thursday-night date with Mrs Best, the Wally Hill bookings every weekend, and Brian Kelly presented them twice a week.

The Bests' maxim – 'Let's get the cash in!' – was pursued successfully. Most of these were £15 bookings, a level of fee the promoters had determined not to meet. Bob Wooler would remember how these rival men discussed the Beatles' demands and formed a secret cartel to resist them, which then collapsed in acrimony when Ray McFall agreed to pay £15 in the Cavern. From the fact that these bookings continued into August and beyond, it's clear they brought in the public. And once the people were in, the Beatles knocked them flat.

Their hair, still slicked up into quiffs, was longer than ever, the longest of any of the Liverpool groups – and in conjunction with their outfits, the Beatles projected the strongest possible statement of individuality. They were copying no one, and the groups who'd imitated them earlier in the year were a long way behind again. The black leather trousers, jackets and boots caused a sensation: leather was inextricably linked in the public mind with troublemakers, and the Beatles not only knew it, they had the courage and attitude to go on stage and perform in it. As George would recall, 'With black T-shirts, black leather gear and sweaty, we did look like hooligans.' John likened it to homage: 'We dressed in leather suits [and] looked like four Gene Vincents!'[9] Beyond this, they occasionally wore their pink twat 'ats and also, sometimes, pink neckerchiefs.* Having lost both Stu and the piano they'd had in the Top Ten Club, they were now an unfussy foursome – lead guitar, rhythm guitar, bass guitar, drums. They also had the visual appeal of Paul's violin-shaped bass, and his natural talent with it made their sound better and tighter than ever.

Once again, the Beatles had to immerse themselves in the latest American sounds, checking out what they'd missed while in Hamburg. Their main venue of discovery was the basement at Nems Whitechapel, where they flicked through the racks, chatted up the salesgirls and wedged themselves and their opinions tight into a browserie, requesting to hear both sides of every selected 45.

While John, Paul and George still went around almost exclusively as a threesome, Pete sometimes joined them here, needing to perform whatever they were picking for the stage. He recalls how if someone said 'I'm gonna do this one' that song then became *theirs*.[10] Nems' manager, the immaculately attired Mr Epstein, would glare at them from time to time, wondering if (despite what they claimed when he was within eavesdropping distance) they actually intended to buy anything. 'Every afternoon a group of scruffy leather-jacketed lads came in,' Brian would remember. 'Strange and odd but attractive. I

---

* An early Beatles follower at the Cavern, Ann Sheridan, describes their neckerchiefs as 'like a square scarf halved and tied at the back, worn on the outside of their leathers. These scarves were very popular with girls – Brigitte Bardot wore them – and the Beatles had theirs cowboy-style, pale pink, with the triangle coming down the front. No other boys wore pink then.'

thought at one time they were messing about with the girls, and I asked the girls. The girls said they did buy discs and they knew what they wanted. They bought R&B.'[11]

When the Beatles returned from Hamburg in 1960 they found tidy guitar-instrumentals all the rage; this time the rising trend was for trad jazz. It was as if rock and roll had never happened and everyone was back dancing to 1920s Dixieland music, the Temperance Seven featuring strongly. John's hatred of old jazz scaled new heights. Still, there was plenty of new American music to excite them. Quarter To Three by US Bonds was a noisy, distorted, danceable, rocking mush that broke all the rules because Bonds sang it over an existing record. Standing there in the Nems browserie, John was the first Beatle to shout 'I'm gonna do this one'.

It isn't clear who grabbed Buzz Buzz A-Diddle-It by Freddy Cannon but it was probably the title as well as the chugging Bo Diddley-like rhythm that swung it; this and the fact that they were checking out all the imports on EMI's Top Rank label. US Bonds' record also came from this source, as did the latest 45 by the Shirelles; Paul bagged Mama Said, using his high register for the lead vocal, John and George on either side of the other microphone for the girl-group backing. There were no new Goffin-King numbers they wanted to sing but they did perform Time, a similarly styled American-written hit for the young British singer Craig Douglas.

The London label gave the Beatles at least three more songs. They did Livin' Lovin' Wreck by Jerry Lee Lewis (the B-side of his hit cover of What'd I Say) and they did a rousing rendition of a Coasters B-side, Thumbin' A Ride. Paul sang this, as he did other Coasters records Searchin' and Besame Mucho, the last of which he'd rearranged to accommodate comically dramatic 'cha-cha-boom!' shouts by John, George and himself. The real highlight, though, was Stand By Me by Ben E. King. John thought it *a great record* and made sure to nab it first; for the intro percussion shuffle he rubbed together two matchboxes, and he sang it with a fervour and tenderness that captivated audiences – especially girls. As he recalled fourteen years later, 'Stand By Me was one of my big ballads, I used to score a lot of groupies with that one.'[12]

The antithesis of Stand By Me, which inflamed hearts, was the Olympics' (Baby) Hully Gully, which usually stirred up violence. John sang it, and as George would recall, 'Every time we did Hully Gully there would be a fight . . . On Saturday night they would all be back from the pub and you could guarantee *Hully Gully*.'[13]

To have a laugh, and keep their distance from other groups, the Beatles also found more fun numbers. Paul had a record of Fats Waller's Your Feet's Too Big, and it became a big number for them in the Cavern. And George then added three vintage tunes currently performed by Joe Brown: I'm Henery The Eighth, I Am (written 1910), The Darktown Strutters' Ball (1917) and The Sheik Of Araby (1921).[14] They gave the last a sprightly rock arrangement, starting with a twangy guitar intro that badly suggested 'Middle East', and then John and Paul embellished it with several bizarre 'not arf!' interjections. It was odd but done for laughs, and became a staple of the Beatles' act for a year, George's trademark vocal spot in many shows. He usually sang two or three numbers a night, and another new one was So How Come (No One Loves Me), which he learned from the spring 1961 LP A Date With The Everly Brothers. The song's very title made George laugh and sometimes he introduced it to the audience as 'So How Come brackets No One Loves Me brackets', said with a wacker's jagged edge.

Unchallenged and ideal, the Cavern became firmly established as the Beatles' home. While never the club's only act, they became the backbone of Wooler's and McFall's booking schedule ... and with good reason, because no group ever created such excitement. It suited the Beatles too. For the lunchtime shows, Pete would arrive with Neil Aspinall about eleven o'clock and lug the drums and amps down the steep and slippery stone steps; John, Paul and George would rise around ten, ride separate buses into town with their guitars, meet at the cellar at half-eleven and between them set up the gear on stage, ready to play. It was easy, hassle-free and fun.

It was here, for the first time, that the Beatles became central to the lives of their audience. This daylight gathering, the crowd of metropolitan Liverpudlians, were the first members of an inclusive and ever-widening circle, the same people turning up again and again to stand under a particular arch or sit in a specific seat. The stage was only eighteen inches off the floor, easily accessible, so they handed up song requests, many of them written in the style of the Beatles' wit, as if submitting a script to be read and ridiculed. The girls were more vociferous than the boys but the Beatles won their love and devotion equally, to a degree far in excess of any other group.

Lunchtime sessions were really two separate shows, taking into account workers' typical 'dinner-hour' breaks: the first shift began at midday, the group playing from 12.15 until 1PM, then the act would return after a ten-minute break and play again until two.[15] The second shift was the busier, but throughout the session people would be reluctantly tearing themselves away, needing to get back to work ... though always carrying the cellar around with them.

The Cavern stank. In the empty morning, the smell was 'Aunt Sally' disinfectant on top of every-yesterday on top of damp on top of fruit (the neighbouring three- to six-storey warehouses didn't only cast the narrow Mathew Street into permanently sunless gloom, they also packed a lot of produce). Once a session began – lunchtime sessions were hot, evenings hotter – the smell was enhanced by aromas from the men's and ladies' toilets, which regularly overflowed into the general area; from perspiration on top of body odour seeping from the mass of humanity packed into the hot cellar; from the soup- and hot-dog-infused steam rising from the gas rings in Thelma's snack bar; and from the cigarettes smoked by most of the crowd. Speak to anyone who saw the Beatles in the Cavern and two particular comments emerge every time: they wish they'd 'bottled the smell', because it was so intensely evocative, and they could never disguise from their parents, bosses and colleagues where they'd been, because the Cavern clung to their hair, skin and clothes.

'Every time I walked down the steps of the Cavern my glasses steamed over,' remembers Alan Smith, a trainee journalist from Birkenhead who was set on moving to London to work for a music paper. 'People would call from the middle distance, "Hi Alan, how you doing?" and I'd need to wipe off the condensation before I could see who it was.

The walls were literally running – you could have lifted a glass to them and filled up a drink. That's no exaggeration. How people were not electrocuted I don't know. But all that is just the mildly eccentric side of it – the thing is, it was *incredible*. There was love in the air as well. It was like the meeting of a club: the audiences loved the bands and the bands loved the audiences, and half the time they were related to them or were old schoolmates. It was a tremendous place.[16]

It was also dangerous. The conditions in the Cavern would never have been permitted in later years; at this time, 1961, the law had no power to enforce safety inspections, which were carried out solely at the discretion of club owners. In terms of sanitation, there were only three toilets and a single urinal, grossly inadequate for large crowds, and while it was assumed these led to mains sewerage, everything went into the ground, ultimately oozing into the tunnel of Liverpool's underground railway. There was also no fire escape, just one hopelessly narrow way in and out. The consequences of a fire would have been appalling, as was shown all too tragically when a blaze swept through a club thirty miles away, in Bolton, on 1 May 1961: fifteen burned to death, trapped in an upstairs room with no fire escape, and four more died leaping from windows.

The government promised to tighten safety regulations, and there was a test case in Liverpool inquiring into what would happen if a local venue suffered a comparable tragedy. This was the Cavern, which now made the front page of the *Echo* for the first time. The court heard that the cellar, 11 feet below street level, is 58 feet by 39 feet with a stage at one end. The only means of access is a doorway from Mathew Street, then along a passage 3ft 6in wide, through another door 2ft 6in wide and then down 17 steps. As many as 200 and 300 are in the club at lunchtimes and in the evenings 500 to 600. It is a well-run club where teen-agers can resort to listen to the type of music they like and in this respect it has the [Liverpool] Corporation's blessing ... but the Corporation is extremely worried that the one staircase is utterly inadequate as a means of escape in case of fire.[17]

The inquiry found that the Cavern should undergo structural changes, but, while plans were drawn up, a loophole meant they weren't enforced; the premises would remain unaltered until the club was enlarged some years later. In the meantime, it was felt that because the place was entirely stone, there was little that could catch fire.

For Paul, the Cavern was little short of heaven. He was five years from first hearing Elvis, since when his life had taken so many unexpected twists and turns. 'My best playing days were at the Cavern, lunchtime sessions, where we'd just go on stage with a cheese roll and a Coke and a ciggie, and a few requests. And you just sing them in between eating your cheese roll, and no one minded, and afterwards you went and had a drink. That was great. We really got something going in that place, in the Cavern, we really got a rapport with an audience that we never got again.'[18]

There was nothing precious about a Beatles lunchtime session. Anything went. One day Bob Wooler asked them if a young man called Steve Calrow could get up and sing: he had a good voice and was beginning a career as a club entertainer. The Beatles did three numbers with him – two Elvis and one Little Richard – and, says Calrow, 'They were out of this world as a backing group, and naturally funny on the stage.

> There was a shopkeeper character in *Coronation Street* called Leonard Swindley, played by Arthur Lowe. He was courting his assistant, a Miss Emily, and Paul used to do an impression of Swindley that had everyone laughing. Then John would read out requests like 'Will John sing Money because we want to see his face turn red' and 'Will Paul sing Till There Was You because he looks so lovely'. Paul would pretend not to hear and John would say to the audience, 'He's not looking *but he's listening to every word*.'[19]

John and Paul became closer once Stu left the Beatles. He'd come between them for eighteen months and now the rift was closed. John loved Stu as a friend but didn't miss his musical contribution – he'd ended up a fair bass player but Paul overtook him in no time at all. John and Paul forged ahead with ambition, drive, dedication, humour and so much more, even drawing mutual strength from being motherless. It was something only they could laugh at, and they enjoyed watching people squirm when innocent mentions of their mothers would be met with the blunt and straightfaced riposte 'She's dead.'[20]

The lunchtime sessions strengthened Beatle friendships tighter than ever. They didn't only see one another at night, like other groups, but often spent entire days together, best mates. When the Cavern session ended – when Bob Wooler played Bobby Darin's I'll Be There and everyone fetched their coats – the Beatles retired to one of the local pubs. They sometimes went to the wood-panelled back room of the White Star, just around the corner, but mostly they went into the Grapes (at the rear of the Fruit Exchange, plumb opposite the Cavern door) where festoons of carved wooden grapes hung from an ornate mahogany bar. There they downed pints of cider mixed with Guinness – black velvet – and were never quiet.[21] Come chucking-out time, unless they were going on to Nems together, Pete and Neil usually went home to West Derby and John, Paul and George stayed in the city.

Summer afternoons were spent on the streets, smoking, swearing, darting, larking, cuffing, cackling. The sight (and smell) of three young men in leather with either cowboy boots or black winkle-picker boots made people gape or step aside or cross the road or pass the standard judgement – 'I fought the war for you young layabouts!'[22] They sometimes visited Bill Harry, dropping into the *Mersey Beat* office on Renshaw Street; they watched films in the Tatler, ogled the instruments in Hessy's and Rushworth's, and – barred from the Jacaranda – idled away hours in the Kardomah tea rooms, to the disgust of many.

The haul of Preludin brought back from Hamburg was diminishing with some speed, especially as John was sprinkling them around 'to get people talking'. One afternoon, after the Grapes had shut, John and George went with Wooler to a private members' establishment, the White Rose Social Club on South Castle Street, where boozing was legal outside pub hours. Returning to the table after buying a round, Wooler saw two little white pills bobbing in his glass, dissolving but not yet gone. When John and George relented and told him what they were, John countered the suggestion they could be harmful by drinking the glass dry, *auf ex*. Still, Wooler did start taking Prellies from time to time. Because they came in metal tubes, he'd say to the Beatles, with a knowing look, 'Anyone travelling by Tube tonight?'[23]

'It was a glorious age to be young – to be not drinking, not doing anything we shouldn't do, but having such a great time,' says Eileen Robinson.[24] She was among the new wave of Cavernites, all aged between 15 and 20, who tuned right into the Beatles and had with them the closest reciprocal relationships any fan could ever have.

'The Beatles were just mad,' remembers Margaret Douglas.

> They were always chewing – we called it 'chewy' – and John pulled cripple faces, though no one took any offence. Everyone fancied at least one of them, but if they'd asked me out I'd have been too scared to go. Paul was my favourite, and my best friend Marie was friendly with John – she was a fat girl with a brilliant sense of humour and John made a point of talking to her. I found John OK but a bit frightening. He often used to be with Cyndy [Cynthia], who was quite arty. If another group was on, they'd sit together and eat apples while they watched.[25]

Roberta 'Bobby' Brown always tried to get the middle seat on the second row because it gave a grandstand view of all of them ... and Paul in particular. He'd usually acknowledge her and invite requests, and she always asked for Your Feet's Too Big, knowing he'd be doing Till There Was You and Over The Rainbow anyway, 'always with the big eyes and his face turned up, looking above our heads'.

> Paul was my favourite. I really adored him, like lots of us did. George was very quiet and shy but totally honest and truthful, a good person. John was funnier but I couldn't quite get his humour. Pete was sullen, miserable and moody, or at least he looked it – he made no attempt to engage with anyone. Some girls preferred him, for his looks, but my friends and I didn't and couldn't understand why others would.
>
> I remember Paul taking Dot's face in his hand and kissing it. It was so romantic. I thought 'Wouldn't it be lovely to be kissed like that?' but I wasn't jealous – you knew your place. He was out of our reach but always a friend. He'd say to me, 'Dot's coming down tonight, can she sit with you?' Of course she can! My friend Anne and I were thrilled he'd asked us to look after her. Honoured. It meant he trusted us.[26]

Bernard 'Bernie' Boyle was one of the many Cavern lads fascinated by the Beatles – and in his case it cost him his job. Aged 16, he was the tea boy in an architect's office on Water Street when a friend tempted him down to a lunchtime session. 'There were four guys on stage who'd just come back from Hamburg, four guys in black leather trousers playing absolutely spot-on the music I'd bought on 78s and 45s – Memphis, Kansas City, Jerry Lee Lewis numbers. The place was thumping, and at one o'clock in the bloody afternoon.

> I went to every session after that. John's voice was absolutely magic, and their harmonies were superb. I used to ask them to do Memphis and I also liked Dizzy Miss Lizzy, Long Tall Sally, Honey Don't and Three Cool Cats. John chewed constantly, and I often saw him do an exaggerated wink if he was saying something with a double-meaning.
>
> I talked to Bob Wooler and kept saying to him, 'This group's the fucking greatest ever!' – so he introduced me to them. I was over the moon. I looked up to all of them: I was young, naive, wide-eyed, and I thought these guys were the greatest in the world. My one-hour lunch breaks from the office got longer and longer until eventually I went back to find I'd been fired. So I started doing occasional jobs for the Beatles, to help Neil. I'd carry the gear and go to gigs with them in the van. I was just a kid but I wormed my way in and they didn't mind.[27]

There was one instrument Boyle didn't carry. Around late July, George upgraded his guitar for the first time since getting the Futurama in 1959. He'd long set his heart on buying a Gretsch – as featured on the sleeves of his Chet Atkins LPs, and played by the late Eddie Cochran – even though, despite the lifting of Britain's trade embargo, they remained almost impossible to obtain. Then George heard about a secondhand one being sold by a merchant seaman, and he rushed over to see it.[28]

It was *beautiful*. The real McCoy – a black Gretsch Duo Jet with a warm sound and easy action, unlike the Futurama which looked good but was tough to play. The seller, Ivan Hayward, had bought the guitar in New York in 1957 for around $200, and now he wanted £90 for it. He was surprised this 18-year-old lad had the funds, but, as George would recall, 'I saved up for years and years to get a guitar [like this]. I got £70 and felt I was gonna get murdered if anybody knew I had it in me pocket.' Hayward allowed George to take the guitar away after writing an IOU for the remaining £20; it was signed in pencil on the back of the customs bill incurred when Hayward first brought the instrument home. He has it still, because George never returned to settle the debt.[29]

John and George both had *American* guitars now, and American amps to go with them – maximum male appeal – and George clearly adored his new instrument. Fans started to call him 'George Gretsch', and Bernie Boyle remembers how inseparable he was from it. 'George never had a case for his Duo Jet, just a soft bag, and he used to carry it everywhere. We'd go to the Kardomah for a coffee and George would carry the guitar. If we went to a pub he'd have the beer in his right hand and the guitar under his left arm. He took it wherever he went and never left it for a moment.'*

George's big news didn't make *Mersey Beat*, but its second issue broke ground by publishing a local rock group photo for the first time – and it was the Beatles. Astrid's shot from the Hamburger Dom fairground first appeared in print here, adjacent to the front-page headline BEATLE'S SIGN RECORDING CON-TRACT![30] A report of their deal with Bert Kaempfert concluded with news that Stuart Sutcliffe had stayed behind in Germany and the group were continuing as a quartet. Paul supplied Bill Harry with both the news and the photograph, so it was unfortunate he was captioned as 'Paul MacArthy'. John had called him McArtrey in the first *Mersey Beat*, and later in this second issue he merited a further mention in Virginia's column ('Howie of "Derry and the Seniors" says that Paul MacArtrey of the Beatles is a better singer than Cliff Richard') which meant he suffered three different misspellings in just two issues. This wouldn't have gone unnoticed by John.

Nems took its twelve dozen copies, and Brian Epstein must have liked it because he invited Bill Harry back up to Nems, talked about it at length, and offered to write a record review column to begin with issue three, which Harry gladly accepted.

On 25 July, as they stirred from their slumbers for a Cavern midday session, John, Paul, George and Pete received an identical letter in the morning post, a small envelope franked with the name Silverman, Livermore & Co, well-known solicitors in Liverpool. The Beatles were involved in their first legal situation.

Allan Williams didn't report them to the Agents' Association for blocking his Hamburg commission, but he believed he was owed £104 and was prepared

---

* *The Beatles got their American music from shops, not ships.*
While the so-called Cunard Yanks, the Scouse merchant sailors who plied the Atlantic route, have a vital and fascinating history, and played their part in shaping local lives, they had little or none of the influence on the Beatles' music that commentators have always suggested. George's Gretsch guitar is the best of a few examples of how the circumstances worked in their favour ... but, as this book demonstrates, the music the Beatles played, while it came from America, reached them from records licensed by British companies, pressed in Britain and sold in shops like Nems. Ringo Starr had access to the transatlantic supply line, which enriched his collection of country and blues records otherwise unavailable in Britain, but the Beatles didn't, and this fact also applies to many (but not all) of the other Liverpool groups. Bob Wooler was finger-proddingly emphatic on the point, saying, 'There is no evidence – I repeat, no evidence – that the beat groups were perform-ing songs brought over from America by the Cunard Yanks.' Paul McCartney has also said Cunard Yanks had nothing to do with the Beatles knowing American records.

to see them in court for it. (This was £26 each, £2 a week for the thirteen-week season; it seems Stuart received no such demand, because he'd sent Williams money from Hamburg.)

The Beatles don't appear to have been unduly bothered by it – and certainly weren't going to capitulate. Ray McFall advised them to retain a solicitor, suggesting Charles D. Munro, and Paul set up a Thursday appointment as he'd be in town anyway for the Cavern. His leather suit must have shocked in such conservative surroundings, but while Munro's dress-code was strictly pin-stripe, he still agreed to represent them. And it wasn't necessary for all the Beatles to fight Williams: one would do. The role fell naturally to Paul, and – after gathering relevant documents from the others – he returned to Munro's office on Saturday the 29th to do his bit.

'I am a member of the Jazz Group known as the Beatles,' their first ever legal statement began, Munro judging it unwise to mount a robust character defence with the words 'rock' or 'rock 'n' roll' in the first line. Paul said that although Williams had his and Pete's post-deportation appeals typed, to appear more presentable, 'no mention of being paid was ever made'; and he emphasised that when Peter Eckhorn refused to give the Beatles more than 35 marks a night at the Top Ten, they then 'absolutely refused to pay' Williams' commission. The document ended equally boldly: 'If necessary we are quite prepared to defend these proceedings [and] we are not afraid of any bad publicity Mr Williams may give us.'

Which side Munro believed isn't recorded, but he did ask for, and receive in cash, £10 to cover his costs in advance. He then wrote a brisk letter informing Silverman, Livermore that Williams' claim for commission was being rejected on the basis of there being 'no contract between our respective clients'.

There was no acknowledgement of what Allan Williams had done for the Beatles, just a stiff swatting-away of his claim. The Beatles weren't sentimental types. When, for example, they decided someone was taking advantage of them, their response could be uncompromising. This same weekend, they abruptly curtailed their relationship with the promoter Wally Hill. He was the man who'd stolen a march on his rivals by booking the Beatles every Saturday and Sunday for months ahead – paying what, to him, was a steep £15 for Blair Hall and £12 for Holyoake Hall. This was the agreement he'd made by letter with Pete while the Beatles were in Hamburg. Now that they were home – confident they could get other dates if they lost these, and irritated they'd been sold for £12 on Sundays when they could be getting £15 – they let trouble foment and handled it in their own sweet way. As Neil Aspinall remembered, the previous Sunday at Blair Hall 'we were late turning up, five minutes or half an hour, whatever it was. When we finished the last number the curtains stayed open and the promoter said we had to play more, because we'd gone on late. We played another number and he still wouldn't close them, so it was "Fuck you! We'll never fucking play for you again, you cunt." He was saying "If you don't turn up you'll never work in Liverpool again" and all that shit, but we just got in my van and pissed off.'[31]

'Neil's one of those people that clicked as soon as you meet him,' John said in 1964, talking about the Beatles' first and original full-time assistant.[32] He and Neil Aspinall got along very well very quickly; so too did George with his old smokers' corner pal from the Institute; and also Paul, though to a lesser extent. They mostly called him Nell – his nickname since childhood – and the degree to which he fitted into the Beatles' framework is evident from his description of the group as 'we'. He didn't play, but was rapidly indispensable to them, best friend of the quiet one but as tenacious as John, Paul and George. To them, he became *one of us*, and John made sure Neil was man enough to stand up to him. He wasn't just their driver and he wasn't only their roadie, he was their mate and their protector.* They shared plenty of characteristics – they were sharp, blunt, mentally strong, bright, funny, opinionated, mouthy, loyal, honest, and addicted to nicotine. They paid him about £7 a week to begin with, shared between the four.

The three never had much to say to Pete, but Neil became an effective bridge, and it's quite possible his employment helped extend Pete's time in the group when their inclination had been (in John's words) 'to dump him'. Even more than before, the Beatles were clamped to the Bests: Pete and Mona ran their bookings, Neil drove the van bought for him by Mona (their relationship continued), and their amps and bits and pieces were kept in the entrance hall at 8 Hayman's Green – the house where still, when diary vacancies allowed, the Beatles played in the cellar Casbah and had many good times.

Insofar as the Beatles thought of tomorrow, Neil's van was to be their mode of transport for the foreseeable future, a place for fun, games, shouting, eating and sex with girls after gigs. It cost £65 and the hire-purchase agreement was in Mona's name because the garage was unwilling to make a contract with Neil, who was 19 (he was a year younger than John, a month older than Pete and a shade over eight months older than Paul – the same difference as between Paul and George). Because all the Beatles' bookings were in town or north of it, John, Paul and George still made their way by bus, but Neil would run them home

---

* Neil never thought of himself as the Beatles' road manager until the label was thrust on him towards the end of 1962.

afterwards or wherever else they wanted to go. There'd be a dash and a squabble to get the adjacent front seat; behind this was a bench-seat for the other three, and after that – as Bernie Boyle remembers – an empty space. 'That was where they kept all the gear. There was no seat for me but I would wriggle my way into the back and lie on top of the amps. Nothing was strapped down, and when Neil took a corner everything would fly all over the place, me included. The guitars and Pete's kit were in cases but the amps weren't, they were just banging about.'

Good times ... and yet, in the Beatles' minds, it was all becoming a little too easy. They were toppermost but *bored*, John and Paul especially. The local halls were called 'a circuit', and so it seemed: they were going round and round the same places on the same nights, week-in and week-out. This was fine enough for other groups but not for the Beatles. And though Neil stood up to them, no one else did. They'd demanded £15 a night, knowing they mightn't get it, but the promoters paid up – and, as Bob Wooler would recall, the Beatles, paradoxically, weren't overly impressed by this. When obstacles did come along, like Wally Hill, they simply obliterated them. Wooler saw the Beatles two or three lunchtimes/afternoons a week, and most evenings, and he'd always be clear and adamant that the Beatles 'nearly split up in the summer of 1961, because they felt they were getting nowhere'. It's an extraordinary statement.[33]

Paul said they needed some publicity, and it's no coincidence that the Beatles' first *Liverpool Echo* mention (beyond the classifieds) came now, on 10 August 1961. The daily column Over The Mersey Wall, a roundup of folksy news and views, quoted Paul explaining a nice story: a cloakroom girl at the LJS had asked him to buy a doll in Hamburg for a hospitalised, crippled infant; he had, but he'd lost the address and didn't know where to send it. It was true, and a publicity grab ... and also the springboard to Paul's best wheeze. The column's main story this same day – headlined YES, THEY DID SWIM THE MERSEY – explained why nobody had swum from one side of the river to the other since 1923: it was considered too dangerous on account of its shipping and strong tidal current. Paul reckoned that if the forty-year absence of an attempt could make the news, they'd score maximum coverage by actually doing it. As remembered years later, it was never specified whether he or John was going to be the brave, wet Beatle, but Paul did like the idea of a publicity stunt. 'We were trying to think of 'em, because we didn't have a manager, so we'd just sit around, thinking of ones we could do. We were going to get one of us to jump in the Mersey, and swim it ...'[34]

We didn't have a manager. Here was the nub of it. They were rudderless, in need of someone to get them beyond where they were, to open up new opportunities to conquer – for while the Beatles lacked direction, they were never short of belief. As John would say on numerous occasions, they felt they'd the beating of anyone, given the chance. 'We were always thinking we were better than whoever was famous, so why shouldn't *we* be up there? ... In the back of me mind I thought "I'm gonna make it", but I couldn't lay it on the line when and how, I just knew we had *something* ... You always hope somebody will come along – we were always waiting for the big man with a cigar.'[35]

The cigar men were in London, and none saw any need to travel two hundred miles to look for talent ... when they gave Liverpool a thought at all. Locally, such men just didn't exist: there were no potential managers scouting Merseyside for groups to represent. No group had one. Anyway, a think-local man would have been pointless for the Beatles. They were already at their maximum earnings potential, taking home about £25 a week each; there seemed no way promoters could be persuaded to pay them more. Also, the managers the Beatles had heard about – Larry Parnes and his ilk – were known to take up to 50 per cent.

Bob Wooler summarised their problem like this:

> They needed someone to channel their energies, their ideas. It called for somebody who was prepared to put up with the Beatles, and they were such a handful because they were strong willed. They had their own ideas. Whoever took on the Beatles had to knuckle down to the Beatles – and the breed of person who will submit to that sort of control is rare.
>
> The Beatles wanted someone who could further their career in a very positive way: they wanted somebody with nous, somebody with clout, somebody with cash, and somebody who drove a car.[36]

Wooler had 'a bit of nous, no clout outside Liverpool, no cash and no car'. The Beatles liked his humour and erudition, but if he was their manager they'd never have put up with his pedantry; and he, sensitive and easily hurt, would have been sorely bruised by John and Paul.

There were other contenders, as he would relate:

> Ray McFall, Bill Harry and Sam Leach all toyed with the idea of managing them. Ray knew they needed someone, but his personality was very different from theirs and he wouldn't have tolerated their behaviour. I remember him saying to me, 'The Beatles *really* need a manager,' and I thought, 'Then you'll find out how awkward the sods can be.' Bill Harry was too preoccupied with *Mersey Beat* and I think they would have fallen out with Sam.[37]

There might also have been talk of Brian Kelly, but he was too busy with his jive dances and electronics business to manage the Beatles, and it's hard to imagine the Beatles wanting him.

Then there was Mrs Best. In the summer of 1960, Peter had suddenly abandoned his education and was a quiet boy at home, not doing anything; one year on, he was a quiet boy with the hottest group in Liverpool, and – in Mona's adoring eyes – largely responsible for it. By doing everything humanly possible for her eldest son, as she always would, she accomplished more for the Beatles at this time than any of the other parents combined. But did she want to manage them? Pete says she didn't, and Wooler was not alone in expressing certainty that John, Paul and George would never have allowed it.[38]

Brian Epstein's first *Mersey Beat* column appeared at the start of August. He commented on stage and jazz records as well as pops (everyone still called it this), noting the 'good potential' of a forthcoming single by Chubby Checker called Let's Twist Again. He also anticipated big sales for the Parlophone LP *Beyond The Fringe*. Elsewhere in the issue, the Beatles were congratulated for their 'continued success at home and abroad' and for securing a recording contract, and were named in a prominent front-page ad for the Cavern's all-night session on Saturday 5 August.

No matter the talk of boredom and depression, the Beatles still had some wild times. Cavern all-nighters were real occasions, sweltering, rowdy, six-act, ten-hour parties for musicians and audience alike. Behind the snack bar, Thelma Wilkinson was sluicing away sweat, watching out for rats, shouting above the incredibly loud music, brewing endless pots of tea and cooking pan after pan of scouse – onions, carrots, potatoes and meat – to be carried hazardously to a minuscule bandroom jam-packed with musicians. The toilets were overflowing, the ceilings and walls pouring, the fuses blowing, and the musicians lugging their gear – drums, guitars, amps, everything – right through the packed crowd (only the one entrance and exit). Inevitably, the audience parted more reluctantly for heroes, so the Beatles always had a tough time, being kissed and backslapped and questioned and handed requests as they pushed through the throng.

Jazz and rock both featured, and national trad star Kenny Ball was the main attraction. 'You only picked up the trumpet to get the crumpet,' John Lennon told him, needling.[39] At least two of the Hurricanes – Ringo and Lu 'Wally' Walters – were there as spectators, taking advantage of their Butlin's day off to return to Liverpool again. A photo of them flanking George Harrison, who has an arm on their shoulders, appeared in the fourth *Mersey Beat* – the first known occasion Ringo was pictured with a Beatle. An atmospheric action shot of the Beatles in mid-performance – John giving his all at the mike – ran on the front page.

A *Riverboat Shuffle*, staged by Ray McFall three weeks later, was also memorable. These occasional summer soirées were meant to be jazz only, but such was McFall's sway to the beat they too became a combination of jazz and rock. The Cavern was closed on 25 August and everyone decamped to the Pier Head to board the MV *Royal Iris* for a momentous night on the Mersey, more than three hours of music, dancing and mayhem on the muddy water. The Beatles supported star act Mr Acker Bilk, trad's biggest name, about to score his third top ten hit. His trademark was the bowler hat and he gave one to each of the Beatles, which they wore as they worked their way through the crates of brown ale.

A great cream- and green-coloured ferry boat, the *Royal Iris* had a ballroom said to be bigger than the liner *Queen Elizabeth*'s, plus several bars all doing a roaring trade, and a food saloon that provided its Liverpool nickname, 'the fish and chip boat'. Sailings could always be a bit choppy, and this night the boat was buffeted by strong winds. The sailing wasn't too bad going up river but as the captain steered beyond New Brighton the open pull of Liverpool Bay made it start to roll. Microphones swayed, dancers staggered, then there was a rush for the sides and many of the revellers threw up. Bernie Boyle paints an evocative image: 'The Beatles rocked the boat that night. You couldn't squeeze a ten-bob note on there – it was fucking *heaving* – and you were sweating your balls off in the crush. People were drinking and smoking and eating fish and chips and puking – it was an unbelievable night.'

So it went, right through August. Wally Hill's loss on Saturday nights was Brian Kelly's gain – he booked them every week into Aintree Institute, where lads still lobbed chairs but girls gathered at the Beatles' feet. Some pressed up to the stage; others sat on it, their legs dangling back over the edge; a few sat fully on the stage itself. They all looked up, mesmerised, and there were shrieks, excitement bubbling over in reaction to particular songs or movements – though it was never too much and didn't mar the performance. There were shrieks of a different order at Hambleton Hall, the Huyton council-estate venue where the Beatles now played alternate Sundays with the Casbah. 'You never get stung at the Hive of Jive,' Bob Wooler lyricised in his *Echo* ad. He had to be joking, especially when John started singing Hully Gully. These were particularly arduous nights for Neil, who had to get the Beatles' equipment into the hall through a corridor of toughs.

Neil had been a trainee accountant bored by trial balances. Now, when the condensation flowing off the Cavern bricks shorted a Beatle's amp, he'd be unscrewing the plug and sticking the wires straight into the mains with a couple of matches, and holding them there until they finished a number.[40] He'd be effecting repairs while John, Paul and George did a high-kicking Tiller Girls impression as a Shadows piss-take; when John wore a polythene bag over one of his shoes or just leaned back against the piano, picked his nose and stuck spent chewing gum on his amp; and when Paul walked on stage with shredded newspaper sticking out of his trouser legs, acting wide-eyed surprise when the audience pointed it out. It was pantomime time with the Beatles, like one of Aunt Mimi and Uncle George's annual treats for the infant John. *She's behind you!*

Had Mimi seen John chewing gum and picking his nose in the name of entertainment, her reaction would itself have been worthy of the stage. Utter exasperation at his choice of 'career' wasn't Mimi's only source of stress at this time. Just after Cyn returned from Hamburg, her mother sailed off to Canada for a few months and their terraced house in Hoylake was rented out. Cyn stayed at Mendips as if one of Mimi's student lodgers. This brought the lovers properly under the same roof for the first time, which set everyone on their mettle. Mimi would no more allow premarital how's-your-father on her premises than Lil Powell, Millie Sutcliffe or any other of their generation. It was one of numerous tensions that set in, and it was around this time that Mimi decided to see for herself exactly what it was John *did* for a living. She wanted to go to 'this Cavern place', without telling him. Her nephew Stan Parkes, John's cousin, escorted her to Mathew Street and they trod gingerly down the slippery steps and into the subterranean hell-hole ... where Mimi exclaimed with maximum irony, 'Very nice, John. This is *very* nice!'[41]

She wouldn't allow a Mendips visit by the girls from the Beatles Fan Club, who were hoping to gather titbits about John's childhood for an information sheet. The club was launched at the start of August 1961 and had the Beatles' full support from the moment Bernie Boyle suggested it to them. Boyle also shared his idea with Bob Wooler, and the DJ then introduced him to two girls from nearby St Helens who could help him run it, Maureen O'Shea and Jennifer Dawes, devoted Beatles fans from the Cavern and some of the halls. The three joined forces: Bernie was 16, Jennifer 19 and Maureen 21, and respectively they became president, treasurer and secretary of the Beatles Fan Club.

'We were dedicated to working for the Beatles and making them better and more professional,' says Jennifer Dawes. 'They just wanted to play and everything else was irrelevant to them. They were very difficult to organise, but we thought they were marvellous and thoroughly enjoyed spending time in their company: we used to hang around with them and visit them at home. Of course, my mother had *no* idea what we were doing.'[42]

Though the club was Bernie's idea, the girls were better suited to the job, being able to type and happy to spend evenings stamping envelopes, so they effectively took it over between them. They set annual membership at five shillings, produced stencilled application forms and had membership cards printed for '1961–62 Season', running August to August. They had badges made, and commissioned a set of photographs to be taken exclusively for members – 'We said to the Beatles "Look smart, wear clean shirts and be on time,"' says Maureen O'Shea. 'We were quite bossy with them. Of course, they turned up in their black leather and black T-shirts.'[43]

The Beatles' first Liverpool photo session – their first anywhere outside Hamburg – took place in the quiet of the Cavern before a lunchtime show. But, supportive as they were of the fans and their club, they weren't especially co-operative with the photographer. Geoff Williams, a forty-something St Helens man who usually did weddings and commercial work, found the Beatles tricky characters.[44]

Mendips aside, the girls were warmly welcomed into the parents' homes.

> Maureen: The Harrisons were very nice, and interested in the fan club. We went in the evening and they cooked us tea. George asked me where I'd gone to school and when I said 'Notre Dame' he called me 'The Hunchback of Notre Dame'. He also asked me out – he said 'Do you want a date with me?' – and I said no. I was very keen on him but knew I couldn't possibly introduce him to my mother because of his Liverpool accent.

> Jennifer: George's mum was telling us how much he weighed when he was born, and George said, 'I didn't have a guitar then – so it was just me weight, not the guitar.' He was quite thin and skinny was George.

> M: Jim McCartney was very welcoming so we went to Forthlin Road quite a few times. Once, when Jim was at work, we cooked chips for Paul and Mike. Jen and I took time off from our jobs. Mike took us to his bedroom and very proudly showed us his paintings and drawings.[45]

> M: I thought Mona Best was a very exotic woman. I'd never met anyone like her. She had the boys' interests – well, mostly Pete's – very much at heart.

> J: Pete was a pleasant, decent person but we always felt that he lived under rather peculiar circumstances at home. Mrs Best was a difficult character, a hard-nosed businesswoman, and she and Neil were 'very friendly'. Pete lived within her shadow – she always spoke for him.

Bob Wooler was given honorary membership of the club and did all he could to encourage it. He invited Maureen and Jennifer to join him on stage at Litherland Town Hall and tell the audience what the club was for and how they could join. 'The Beatles were on stage at the time,' Maureen says. 'We had our backs to them. George, Paul and Pete were probably smiling and John was probably smirking.'

Wooler had been the Beatles' biggest champion since their first return from Hamburg – 'squarely behind the pivotal moments', as Bernie Boyle puts it. Recognising his contribution to the local music scene, and his precision with words, Bill Harry invited him to write a regular column in *Mersey Beat*, and on 31 August 1961 Wooler kicked off by tackling the subject that was on everyone's lips. The result was the first piece of journalism about the Beatles, an article of rare perception and prescience, deserving of being reproduced here in its entirety.

A Phenomenon called The Beatles!
by Bob Wooler

Why do you think The Beatles are so popular? Many people many times have asked me this question since that fantastic night (Tuesday, 27th December 1960) at Litherland Town Hall, when the impact of the act was first felt on this side of the River. I consider myself privileged to have been associated with the launching of the group on that exciting occasion, and grateful for the opportunities of presenting them to fever-pitch audiences at practically all of the group's subsequent appearances prior to their last Hamburg trip.

Perhaps my close association with the group's activities, both earlier this year and since their recent re-appearance on the Merseyside scene, persuades people to think that I can produce a blueprint of The Beatles Success Story. It figures, I suppose, and if, in attempting to explain the popularity of their act, the following analysis is at variance with other people's views, well that's just one of those things. The question is nevertheless thought-provoking.

Well then, how to answer it? First some obvious observations. The Beatles are the biggest thing to have hit the Liverpool rock 'n' roll set-up in years. They were, and still are, the hottest local property any Rock promoter is likely to encounter. To many of these gentlemen's ears, Beatle-brand noises are cacophonous on stage, but who can ignore the fact that the same sounds translate into the sweetest music this side of heaven at the box-office!

I think The Beatles are No. 1 because they resurrected original style rock 'n' roll music, the origins of which are to be found in American negro singers.

They hit the scene when it had been emasculated by figures like Cliff Richard and sounds like those electronic wonders The Shadows and their many imitators. Gone was the drive that inflamed the emotions. This was studio set jungle music purveyed skilfully in a chartwise direction by arrangement with the A & R men.

The Beatles, therefore, exploded on a jaded scene. And to those people on the verge of quitting teendom – those who had experienced during their most impressionable years the impact of rhythm 'n' blues music (raw rock 'n' roll) – this was an experience, a process of regaining and reliving a style of sounds and associated feelings identifiable with their era.

Here again, in The Beatles, was the stuff that screams are made of. Here was the excitement – both physical and aural – that symbolised the rebellion of youth in the ennuied mid-1950's. This was the real thing. Here they were, first five and then four human dynamos generating a beat which was irresistible. Turning back the Rock clock. Pounding out items from Chuck Berry, Little Richard, Carl Perkins, The Coasters and the other great etceteras of the era. Here they were, unmindful of uniformity of dress. Unkempt-like long hair. Rugged yet romantic, appealing to both sexes. With calculated naivete and an ingenious, throw-away approach to their music. Affecting indifference to audience response and yet always saying 'Thank-you.' Reviving interest in and commanding enthusiasm for numbers which descended the Charts way back. Popularising (more than any other group) flipside items – example, 'Boys'. Compelling attention and influencing, wittingly or unwittingly, other groups in the style, choice and presentation of songs.

Essentially a vocal act, hardly ever instrumental (at least not in this country), here they were, independently minded, playing what they liked for kicks, kudos and cash. Privileged in having gained prestige and experience from a residency at the Hamburg Top Ten Club during the autumn and winter of last year. Musically authoritative and physically magnetic, example the mean, moody magnificence of drummer Pete Best – a sort of teenage Jeff Chandler. A remarkable variety of talented voices which song-wise sound distinctive, but when speaking, possess the same naivete of tone. Rhythmic revolutionaries. An act which from beginning to end is a succession of climaxes. A personality cult. Seemingly unambitious, yet fluctuating between the self-assured and the vulnerable. Truly a phenomenon – and also a predicament to promoters! Such are the fantastic Beatles. I don't think anything like them will happen again.

Mersey Beat definitively brought together all the local personalities within its pages. Wooler's article ran alongside a Nems ad ('The finest record Selections in the North'), John Lennon was identified as the author of a strangely funny poem called 'I Remember Arnold', and Brian Epstein's record reviews ran adjacent to an article about Rory Storm and the Hurricanes, whose photo adorned the front page. Their Pwllheli summer, now ending, had gone so well they'd been offered a repeat booking for 1962; in the meantime, after returning to Liverpool, they were hoping to play on the Continent, perhaps in Italy, France and Germany. Richy was keen for whatever trips could be arranged, but when they weren't – when the hot air evaporated – his itch to travel, and to leave the Hurricanes, returned stronger than ever.

The lure this time was America. It was always America, ever since he'd watched Gene Autry sing South Of The Border and ride his horse through the prairie, when a sickly 10-year-old emerged halfway to paradise from a Dingle cinema. His love of rock and country music had only increased his intent to get there some day, and the end of his hope to do so as a merchant seaman hadn't dented that. Blues music had entered his heart more recently and he'd already amassed a fair collection of import albums. One of these – bought in Hamburg and given to him by Gerry Marsden – was the anthology *Bad Luck Blues*, featuring (among others) Lonnie Johnson, Kokomo Arnold, Sleepy John Estes, Peetie Wheatstraw and Lightnin' Hopkins. They were the real deal, black players from poverty way more crushing than Liverpool 8, most of them born around the turn of the twentieth century. Richy especially liked the two tracks by Lightnin' Hopkins (Highway Blues and Bad Things On My Mind), and investigation revealed connections to Houston, Texas: he'd served prison time there, and eventually made his name with recordings for Gold Star, a local label.

This was enough for Richy. He went down to the American Consulate, in the great Cunard Building at the Pier Head, and picked up immigration forms. He'd need to show he had money and the offer of work, so he wrote to Houston Chamber of Commerce, received a list of local employment agencies and, after further correspondence, picked out a job in a factory. He could always change it once he got there.[46]

While Richy waited for news from America, the Hurricanes returned to the Liverpool scene. As usual, they cut a dash more sartorial than musical: they were the same post-Butlin's as pre-Butlin's, the same in 1961 as 1960. They simply didn't change beyond the occasional inclusion of a new number; *Starrtime!* was one of the few elements of their show relatively up to date.

Inevitably, Rory was taunted for his stammer and mocked for his vanity, but he always received fantastic encouragement at home from his mum. Through her generosity and love of company, Violet Caldwell fulfilled this role for many of the rock and rollers. Any time of the day or night, anyone was welcome to drop into 54 Broad Green Road – the house Rory had named Hurricaneville –

and she'd serve up plates of food, endless cups of tea and lots of laughs through a thick fug of tobacco smoke.[47]

Iris Caldwell remembers the late nights when her brother laboured to express himself and Ringo sat quietly for hours, listening and probably contemplating Houston. 'Ringo's moods varied a lot. Sometimes he'd be very happy and animated and other times miserable and depressed. He had a strong effect on all the others present. If he was feeling happy, they all ended up happy. If he was sad, everyone seemed to be miserable.'[48]

John, Paul and George saw more of Ringo in the Caldwells' back room than they did on the circuit. After five months apart, the Beatles and the Hurricanes were back playing the same bills again once or twice a week, but they hooked up more often late at night, when the groups completed their respective gigs and dropped into either of two late-night venues: Joe's Restaurant – a rockers' rendezvous because it stayed open until 4AM – or here at Hurricaneville in Broad Green.* They knew Vi Caldwell from the days of the Morgue Skiffle Cellar, and George for longer still, from the time of his innocent young fling with Iris – but it was in this period of 1961 that these friendships moved on to a stronger footing.

The three Beatles established a particularly warm and lasting relationship with Vi, the energetic and talkative 53-year-old fondly renamed Ma Storm by Bob Wooler. *Everybody* loved her. Several nights a week – after Neil and Pete had dropped them off and returned home to West Derby – John, Paul and George would be here with Ringo, Rory, Iris, Vi, her husband Ernie and sundry others who dropped in to wolf down her house specialities (cheese barm-cakes or chip butties), gulp gallons of tea and shout to be heard above this very Liverpool hubbub.

The Beatles were the antithesis of the Hurricanes. While Rory's repertoire hardly changed, the Beatles' varied *show to show* – they kept the fans on their toes and themselves in touch with the latest releases coming into Nems. They performed both sides of the new Elvis number 1 hit: the uptempo B-side I Feel So Bad, which Paul sang, and the maudlin ballad Wild In The Country, which became one of the few numbers sung by Pete. No drums were needed, so he

---

* Joe's Restaurant, usually called Joe's café, was at 139 Duke Street, up the hill from town towards the Anglican Cathedral. It was run by the middle-aged Joe Davey, a cheery Liverpool *mine host*, balding, bearded, and with a moustache twiddled to an upwards point on both sides. He and the groups got along fine. In a questionnaire for the *NME* in February 1963, John Lennon gave his favourite foods as 'curry and jelly' and both were specialities *chez* Joe. The suggestion is of a constantly verbal young man speeding, slurping and smoking his way through the menu while Liverpool slumbered.

would step out front and sing while John, Paul and George – who played the only guitar part – sat on the edge of the stage and harmonised. (There are no photos, unfortunately.)

The Beatles weren't averse to doing number 1s – for a short while they sang Del Shannon's Runaway. Mostly, though, they stuck to obscure numbers no other group was doing: George and John sang the frantic Red Hot, found on a 1960 EP by Ronnie Hawkins; John did Watch Your Step by Bobby Parker (again reaping the reward of checking B-sides); and he said 'I'm gonna do this one' the moment he heard I Just Don't Understand. This record was all-original: a rock-waltz tempo, a sexy vocal from the young actress-singer Ann-Margret, a strong harmonica part and a sound like nothing the Beatles had ever heard, *fuzz guitar*, discovered by accident in a recording studio and impossible to re-create on stage; the Beatles also performed it without harmonica because John *had* to sing.

There was one other new record John seized at this time. Chuck Berry had disappeared from the weekly music papers and his record releases had dried up; though details weren't reported in Britain, the star was on bail in America, awaiting the (ultimately unsuccessful) appeal of a prison sentence for violating the Mann Act – the unlawful transportation of a female across state lines for immoral purposes. Then suddenly, in August 1961, he popped up with I'm Talking About You and it was typical Berry, with poetic lyrics and inimitable guitar. Other artists came and went, but Chuck Berry was always part of the Beatles' set – they were still regularly playing Almost Grown, Carol, I Got To Find My Baby, Johnny B. Goode, Little Queenie, Maybellene, Rock And Roll Music, Roll Over Beethoven, School Days, Sweet Little Sixteen, Thirty Days, Too Much Monkey Business and Memphis, Tennessee.

These songs came across stronger than ever now because Paul had got himself a new bass speaker. It came courtesy of the Big Three, who made the loudest sound of any Liverpool group – not just because Johnny Hutch hit the drums hardest but because their lead guitarist Adrian Barber had made a pair of huge loudspeakers for the guitars and voices. When Barber let it be known he could make more of these, for something like twenty-five guineas apiece, Paul ordered one for his Hofner Violin, paying Barber £5 every so often as far as summer 1962. Powered by his Selmer Truvoice amp, this was a vast piece of kit for the Beatles, an immense fifteen-inch loudspeaker inside a wooden cabinet standing five feet tall and painted black – and so, inevitably, it became known as 'the coffin'.

It was a beast to carry, a burden especially dreaded by whoever had to get it into the Cavern. This was usually Neil and Pete – who huffed, puffed and cussed it down the slippery steps, scraping knuckles as they shuffled it round the tight corner at the bottom. The coffin was loud everywhere but never more than here, where the pounding sound broke loose the Cavern bricks' calcium deposits, which then sprinkled on the heads of the audience. The Beatles called it 'Liverpool dandruff'.[49] Paul sometimes turned the coffin to the back wall, away from the audience, which seemed to make it even louder. A Liverpool College of Art student, Peter Mackey, soon to form a group himself, saw a Cavern lunchtime session and was shaken by the experience.

> The combination of Pete's bass drum and Paul's bass guitar, with the bass speaker facing the back wall, smacked me hard in the chest. That had never happened to me before. And their charisma! At nights, a buzz used to go around the Cavern when the Beatles were arriving – 'They're here, they're here' – and we all used to turn around to see them come in. They'd walk through, all in black. I was a complete and utter Beatles fan right from the start. If I hadn't seen and heard the Beatles at the Cavern my life would have gone a different way. I wouldn't have 'chased the dream'.[50]

So much was Mackey knocked out, he allowed the purpose of his initial Cavern visit to capsize. He went there as president of Sulca, the art school Students' Union, to reclaim the amplifier provided to the Beatles eighteen months earlier, the amp John took to Hamburg ... and never brought back. Mackey intended to demand its return, but then he found himself face to face with John Lennon. 'I ventured into the bandroom, introduced myself and said, "We'd like our equipment back." He said, "Oh, we hocked it in Germany ..." and that was it. I didn't ask for reparation, I just let it go.'

Much had happened in a short time. The amp was bought by Sulca because Stuart was in the 'college band'; a year on, he was living and studying in Hamburg and, but for correspondence, removed from Liverpool life. John and Stu wrote often to each other. John told him the Beatles had a fan club, and he expressed frustration that nothing was happening for them – 'It's all a shitty deal. Something is going to happen, but where is it?' There were letters as long as twenty-one pages, with drawings – one showed Christ on the cross with a pair of slippers underneath – and the rawest of raw text, much of it stream-of-consciousness scribble. 'I've got one ciggie till Thursday, so what about that, twat face?' Swinging from prose to poetry, the scrappy pages revealed a troubling insight into the mind of John Lennon:

> I can't remember anything
> without a sadness
> so deep that it hardly

becomes known to me,
so deep that its tears
leave me a spectator
of my own STUPIDITY.
& so I go rambling on
With a hey nonny nonny nonny no.[51]

Stuart was making great progress in his studies at the Hochschule, working under Eduardo Paolozzi. The course didn't only involve sculpture and painting: he was also making experimental films. (He's thought to have made two; few details are known, they haven't been seen and are presumed lost.) Paolozzi never doubted Stuart's talent, dedication or capacity for intense work, but, increasingly, these studies were being interrupted by failing health.

Mersey Beat printed a letter from a girl asking if it was true that this member of the Beatles had been killed in a car crash. But while rumours of Stuart's demise were happily premature, his health was evidently deteriorating at an alarming rate, especially for a young man of 21. A hospital examination in Hamburg revealed gastritis, the grumbling appendix, a shadow on the entrance to his lungs, and swollen glands; he was also moody, neurotic and a nervous wreck.[52]

Most worryingly, nothing took away Stuart's headaches. They were so excruciating that he collapsed at the Hochschule one day and had to be taken home. Klaus Voormann remembers the pain being so severe that Stu created terrible scenes in Nielsa and Astrid's house, throwing food about the room and shouting. When Stu announced he was planning a brief return to Liverpool, to have his appendix removed free on the National Health Service, his mother arranged for him to be analysed with recourse to a whole new set of X-rays. In the end, nothing was done – the NHS wouldn't operate on his appendix without first establishing it was necessary, then Stuart failed to turn up for the X-ray appointment. The consultant surgeon at Sefton General Hospital, who met Stuart on one occasion, wrote to Millie saying the German X-rays showed his condition 'was within the limits of normal', and he added, 'my impression was that most of his symptoms were nervous in origin'.[53]

It isn't known if Stu saw the Beatles during this brief trip home, though it's likely he and John got together, given that they wrote so often. Astrid accompanied Stuart and they had another tetchy time with Millie, which seems to have prompted an early departure back to Hamburg. Before doing so, he discussed the possibility of a Liverpool exhibition of his paintings, which Allan Williams was hoping to mount at the Blue Angel.

As for Williams' legal complaint against the Beatles, all had gone quiet.

Charles Munro had to chase a response from Williams' solicitors, and when it came, on 16 August, it was merely to report that their client had been in London and couldn't be contacted. Munro wrote to Paul saying 'it may be a little time before I can let you have a report of any substance' – and this silence extended right through September. John included a little dig at Williams in the sixth *Mersey Beat*, the 14 September issue, when he parodied the listings entry that read 'Jacaranda – members only' as 'The Jackarandy – Membrains only'.

John called *Mersey Beat* itself *Mersy Boat* and said it was 'selling another three copies to some go home foreigners who went home'. Brian Epstein also adapted the paper's name in *his* column, referring to its readers as 'Mersey-beaters'. And over the page (again adjacent to a Nems ad), Bob Wooler was expressing some important thoughts. As far as anyone knew, *Mersey Beat* wasn't being read in London, but Wooler used his column to implore talent-spotters to visit Liverpool, saying, 'We have the genuine article on Merseyside. We only want the genuine people to discover, groom and promote them for potential stardom. Is that asking too much?'

Mrs Best was still doing what she could. Paying a visit to Hayman's Green, Jennifer Dawes of the fan club witnessed Mona in a determined mood: 'She was standing with her back to the fire one night, saying how the Beatles had to be moved up to a better scale: more money, better prospects. We couldn't do anything better. We had the impression she wanted to manage the Beatles and that the other three wouldn't go along with her.'

Mona had good ideas. One was to get the Beatles on TV for the first time, but her letter to Granada, pitching them for the local news show *People And Places*, met with a non-committal response.[54] Had the reply been positive, however, offering the Beatles an audition or broadcast, a postponement might have been necessary, because the same 14 September *Mersey Beat* also included an important news-line: 'John Lennon and Paul MacArtney of the "Beatles" will be off to Spain for a holiday towards the end of September'.*

John's 21st birthday was a month away, and he knew he was getting money – £100, *cash*, more than he or Paul had ever seen in their lives. It was a coming-of-age gift from his Aunt Elizabeth in Edinburgh, and his idea was to go away with Paul and enjoy it. Bob Wooler was party to their planning, and fought with them:

---

* The running total was now six spellings from six issues of *Mersey Beat*: McArtrey, MacArthy, McCartney, MacArtrey, McArtney and MacArtney.

They were bored, and decided they would go away for a month. I thought this was disastrous because they would be away from the scene too long and lose their fans. Fans were very capricious: they moved from one group to another. And anyway, what about the other two members, George Harrison and Pete Best? What about them, what do they do? We argued a lot about this – we argued in the back room of the Grapes pub to a large extent – and they said, 'Well, we'll go away for a fortnight only.'[55]

Wooler secured for the Cavern a definite undertaking that they would return, which would be advertised in their absence. Nonetheless, John later identified this moment as 'another time when the group was in debate, about whether it would exist or not'.[56]

It was nine months after his previous deliberation, when he'd returned from Hamburg and thought hard about whether or not he wanted to continue. This *boredom*, felt by Paul and particularly by John, was quite a problem now. It was getting to be make-or-break time for the Beatles, and it could be that Wooler's insistence they consider their fans as well as George and Pete helped swing the decision to carry on. Bookings for 15 October and dates beyond were not cancelled, so it was clear when John and Paul were expected back, but all bookings from 30 September to 14 October had to be broken – an unpleasant job for Pete; he and George had to accept losing up to £50 apiece, as well as being left behind. John said George 'was furious because he needed the money', and it's unlikely Paul extended George much sympathy, subsequently conceding how he 'tended to talk down to him ... all the way through the Beatle years'.[57]

Equally, the promoters who paid the Beatles over-the-odds to present them every week had to 'lump it'. Ray McFall was forced to find other entertainment for two Wednesday nights and five lunchtimes in the Cavern, Brian Kelly for two Thursdays at Litherland and probably two Saturdays at Aintree, Vic Anton one Sunday at Hambleton Hall, and Mrs Best one Sunday at the Casbah and two Fridays at Knotty Ash Village Hall, her latest enterprise. To a man, and woman, they were *incensed* by it – but John and Paul hadn't a care. They didn't mean to be rude about it, but basically it was *tough shit*.

It was tough too on Dot and Cyn. Dot simply had to accept the situation, but Cyn had a greater case for grievance. John was heading off without her when he could so easily have waited for the art school holidays. He had money in his pocket, a trip inside his head, and she didn't figure. And she would surely have welcomed the diversion, because life at Mendips had become so intolerable that she'd moved out. Mimi had discovered the bundle of love-letters John sent from Hamburg, correspondence he himself would describe as 'the sexiest letters this side of Henry Miller, forty pages long some of them'. Mimi considered them *pornographic*, and there was a great scene. Cyn was out within hours, moving in with an aunt on the other side of Liverpool.[58]

That John was taking Paul, no one else, accentuates the renewed closeness since Stu quit the Beatles. They were the Beatles' force, an unstoppable and authentically powerful pair. 'Lennon [had] attitude,' said Bob Wooler, 'and, taking his lead from Lennon, McCartney could be similar. At times, they reminded me of those well-to-do Chicago lads Leopold and Loeb, who killed someone because they felt superior to him. Lennon and McCartney were "superior human beings".'[59]

'You'd always see them together, in the pub or walking along the street,' says Johnny Gustafson of the Big Three. 'They were a duo, and seemed each other's equal.' Bernie Boyle, the young lad hanging around with them at every opportunity (and they made him suffer for it), says, 'They were like brothers, with John as the elder, Paul's mentor. They were so tight it was like there was a telepathy between them: on stage, they'd look at each other and know instinctively what the other was thinking.'

They *were* brothers. They were the Nerk Twins, and now they were taking a break from the Beatles and going off to Spain. En route, they'd stop a day or two in Paris, to size up the Brigittes, check out the kind of clothes Jürgen Vollmer wore, and perhaps see Jürgen himself, if he was around.

Gustafson happened to bump into them the day they left, Saturday 30 September. 'They both had bowler hats on, with the usual leather jackets and jeans. They said they were off to Paris, so I walked down to Lime Street station with them and watched them go. They were an incredible pair: always great fun, irreverent, and *so close.*'

21

Les Nerk Twins à Paris (1–14 October 1961)

They meant to hitch-hike, hence the bowler hats. Acker Bilk's freebies would catch the eye of drivers as John and Paul thumbed a ride. But John had £100 in his pocket, so they took the train to London and beyond to Dover, then caught the last ferry to Dunkirk and the first morning train straight to the French capital. They emerged at la Gare du Nord with hope in their hearts and a skip in their step, for nowhere on Earth to the post-war Englishman was ever as exotic, sexy and *risqué* as Paris.[1]

Jürgen Vollmer was lodging in a little place on the Left Bank, the Hôtel de Beaune. Still seeking a job as a photographer's assistant, he'd quickly settled in a metropolis where, with his clean, combed-down hair and *à la mode* fashion, he blended in as the chic young Frenchman he longed to be. Though not at his hotel when John and Paul bustled along, the parties managed to find each other later in the day, in front of the Abbey of Saint-Germain-des-Prés. And then it hit home: this reserved and cultured young German had on his hands two boisterous English tourists expecting to be shown where it was all happening.

They hoped to stay somewhere cheap, perhaps the same hotel – but it was full, and so too, it seems, were the other inexpensive *pensions* in the district. When Jürgen tried to sneak them up to his room, where they could crash on the floor, the concierge appeared in her night-gown and began screaming at them, and as Jürgen protested his innocence, John made fun of him.

Their best chance of finding a room was in Montmartre, where there were cheap hotels used by the area's prostitutes. Jürgen hailed a taxi, told the driver where to take them, and they disappeared off down the street. The Spanish O-Level graduate Paul would do all the speaking in Spain, the French O-Level failure John would do all the *parlez* in Paris ... so they struggled, and were reduced to wandering around exhausted in the early hours, asking prostitutes, 'Avez-vous un hôtel pour la nuit?' As Paul would remember, 'We thought we were so young and beautiful that one of these women would take us back to her hotel pour la nuit, but I'm afraid they didn't. We had to find a little flea-bitten hotel, and we got bitten.'[2]

They decided to stay a second day, which then became a third and a fourth. Spain could wait because this place was full of femmes exotiques whose every utterance aroused the two Liverpool lads. While Jürgen showed them Paris, pointing out the interesting places, John and Paul ogled the birds. They went to the Latin Quarter and drank banana milkshakes on la rue des Anglais; they sipped wine in les Deux Magots, the famous café on the Left Bank, former haunt of Hemingway and Sartre; they went to the Eiffel Tower, but didn't go up because it cost too much; they goggled at the pissoir right there in the street; they laughed at the sight of the Kardomah café by the Louvre, their Liverpool tea company having got here before them; and when Jürgen showed them L'Opéra Garnier they burst into flamboyant song, lifted up their guide and carried him across le Boulevard de la Madeleine – while he, painfully shy, yelled at them in broken English to put him down.

John and Paul loved Paris, John deciding here this week that it was his favourite city in all the world. It would remain his toppermost, or thereabouts, for the rest of his life, the ambience appealing on all levels, especially the artistic and idealistic. 'All the kissing and holding ... was so romantic, the way people would just stand under the tree kissing,' he would recall. 'They weren't mauling each other, they were just kissing. To be there and see them ... I really loved it.'[3]

It isn't known if he and Paul got l'amour in Paris. So numerous were their conquests back home it's hard to imagine them going without on holiday, but this was very much foreign soil. 'John and Paul liked all the girls,' says Jürgen. 'They loved the style of what I called "the bohemian beauties", the pseudo existentialists, girls who looked the part but didn't subscribe to the ideas.' Such girls, though, didn't necessarily like John and Paul.

> I had a great-looking French girlfriend, Alice, who had long black hair, a beautiful figure and a bohemian flair. I raved to her about John and Paul, and I raved about her to them, so we arranged to meet at the Café Royale on Boulevard Saint-Germain. The three of us were sitting there when Alice came along, and I could tell immediately from her face there was something wrong. She didn't want to sit down, then she started to say how dare I bring her together with this kind of wild type. John and Paul had their Elvis hair and leather jackets, and they really stuck out. She was appalled. They were looking

at us not realising they were the cause of this French dispute, and then she left. That was the last time I saw her until years later when we happened to meet and I told her those two guys were John Lennon and Paul McCartney . . .[4]

A day or two later, the situation might have been different. John and Paul had admired Jürgen's cool Paris style since first meeting him in Hamburg twelve months back, and they weren't going to Spain until they'd invested a few francs in some similar gear. As Jürgen says, 'It sounds conceited but it's the truth: they really wanted to look like me.' At their request, he took them to the weekend flea market at Porte de Clignancourt, at the northern end of Métro Line 4. Searching through the racks, John bought a green corduroy jacket like Jürgen's, Paul found an eye-catching patterned polo-neck, and they looked for – though didn't find – the Vollmer style of shoes, 'like half-boots'.

Their most daring purchase was two pairs of flared trousers, similar though different to the bell-bottoms worn by sailors – but the first time John and Paul wore them was also the last. As John would explain, 'They were flapping around, and we felt like fools in anything that wasn't skin-tight, so we sewed them up by hand that very night' – a comment that conjures up the quaint image of Lennon and McCartney working away with needle and thread under a murky light in a Montmartre hotel room. But alteration was essential: they knew precisely how the trousers, if left unchanged, would be received back home. What was OK in Paris would *not* be OK in Liverpool; the Beatles' audience was mixed male and female and they didn't want to alienate either by, in John's words, coming across queer.[5]

Only Frenchmen wore flares at this time, and here too was the collarless round-neck jacket they'd seen worn by Astrid and (made by her) Stuart. It was the Pierre Cardin design, from his spring 1961 Paris collection, and both John and Paul liked it. 'The kids by the Moulin Rouge were wearing flared trousers, in '61, and round-neck jackets,' John would recall. 'Cardin had invented them. We liked the jacket and went to a shop and bought one.'[6]

They were also keen to check out the Paris music scene. The dominant teenage trend in France, strongly centred in the capital, was *yé-yé* – a derogatory phrase coined by the conservative French press for songs with the 'yeah yeah' shouts of rock and R&B. Its style was melodic pop, sweet songs about boys and romance sung mostly by adolescent girls for adolescent girls. *Yé-yé* had a mascot, a *chouchou* (sweetheart), which was a caricature drawing of a young man with a pudding-basin haircut, hair fringed down over his eyes.

Rock had made little impact here since erupting out of America in 1956 – it was a foreign culture sung in a foreign language. But in spring 1961 it suddenly exploded with a French voice in the streets and theatres of Paris, and with it came the same taint of juvenile delinquency that accompanied its rise in America and Britain. John sent a postcard to a Beatles fan back in Bootle saying 'Paris is great, only no "Rock". (Well, a bit of crappy French Rock.)' This was an informed view, because they checked it out for themselves. They went to the Olympia Theatre to see France's top rock star Johnny Hallyday, an 18-year-old who modelled himself on Elvis in the way he looked, sang, spoke and gyrated.

They also saw a poster for a *Festival de Rock* at Bal Tabarin, the famous can-can night-club in Pigalle which had turned (temporarily) from high kicks and bare breasts to rock guitars. Here they watched several groups reminiscent of Rory Storm and the Hurricanes – bequiffed lead singers with choreographed guitarists. Topping the bill was Vince Taylor, the British-born, American-bred rocker who'd recorded for Parlophone with Tony Sheridan, and who now did a carbon-copy of Gene Vincent's act.

Thinking they could do better, the Nerk Twins tried to push themselves into the scene, for at least this one evening and perhaps in the hope of several. They managed to talk to Taylor (maybe raising their mutual connection with Sheridan) and asked him if they could play; Taylor said they should speak to the Bal Tabarin management. As John's French wasn't up to the task, they browbeat Jürgen into having the conversation for them.

I found out who the manager was and said to him, 'I have two great British rock 'n' roll musicians here. They play in Hamburg and we love them. Can they play at the club while they're here in Paris?' It was slightly absurd because John and Paul didn't have their guitars with them, but there was no interest anyway. The Parisian arrogance was such that saying they were 'big in Liverpool and Hamburg' made no difference. For Parisians, only Paris counts.

John and Paul happened to be in Paris during a particularly unstable time: a bomb wrecked the foyer of the ABC Music Hall this same week, and, a few days later, a Ray Charles show at the Palais des Sports was postponed by the detainment inside the arena of six thousand Muslims protesting the enforcement of a night-curfew. All of Paris – all of France – was embroiled in a pivotal moment in Algeria's bloody fight for independence from colonisation; terrorist activity was at its peak, leading to the Paris police shooting dead forty demonstrators during a protest rally. Paul would retain the memory of Frenchmen crowding around a TV shop, watching a speech by President de Gaulle.[7]

But no number of blaring sirens could persuade them to leave and move on to Spain. They were into the second week now, and as they'd promised to be home by 15 October there wasn't any point in going further from it. A two-week trip to Spain, with a brief stop in Paris, became a fortnight in Paris, and they were more than content at that. John celebrated his 21st birthday in the city he'd come to love, and a pact agreed between the Beatles not to give one another presents was maintained, save that Paul sprang for the hamburger and Coke that was John's big-birthday dinner.[8]

Paul had borrowed a camera from Mike, and some fun photos resulted from the trip – of John at the Dunkirk ferry, in dark glasses outside the Louvre and under the Eiffel Tower, and of John and Paul seated at a café table. In one picture, Paul wears his bowler hat while sitting on the bidet in their Montmartre hotel room, fully dressed in his leather jacket and jeans and reading the newspaper upside down. Another shot has them both exposing underpants, with Paul wearing a wig and John's glasses, his jacket askew, while John is in a furry hat, his hand stuck inside his shoe, his eyes shut and tongue poking through in full crip mode. Photos like this, with John and Paul together, were taken by Jürgen. Another shows les Nerk Twins outside the club they'd hoped to play, the Bal Tabarin – though their heads are cut off. 'I didn't know how to use that camera,' Jürgen says. 'They wrote to me afterwards and said, "You're a professional photographer and you've cut off our heads."'[9]

Vollmer was responsible nonetheless for the greatest legacy of this Paris fortnight: it was at the Hôtel de Beaune, two hundred steps from the Seine, that he cut and restyled John and Paul's hair. This was the moment they finally shed the greased quiffs of youth, the Ted hair that had been their image for four or five years, and went instead with the clean, combed-down Paris style.

It wasn't Jürgen's idea, because he liked them as *rockers*. He says they wanted it, 'because they'd have more chance with the bohemian beauties on the Left Bank'. This was true, but it also went deeper. They wanted it because they liked it, because it was new and different, because when they got home to Liverpool they'd be like no one else – this was always their desire, in everything – and because, in having this style, it was, by definition, *not English*. Eight years later, thinking back to being 21 and in Paris, John remarked on his mother country's lack of sartorial elegance with the words 'I was ashamed to go on the Continent and say I was British.'[10]

As they knew only too well, that harridan of a concierge doggedly prevented guests receiving night visitors, but daytimes at the Hôtel de Beaune were different. Jürgen had a small room on one of the upper floors – up steeply winding tile-and-wood steps – and this was where the deed was done. He cut Paul's hair first, because he felt more comfortable with him, and then he did John's. The shorn locks were shovelled under the bed. In Hamburg, Jürgen had called it the 'Caesar' style, combed down and a little to the side with a diagonal parting; it was described well by Paul, though with an unfortunate connotation, as 'a kind of long-haired Hitler thing'.[11] It stayed this way until it was washed and grown out, after which the diagonal parting disappeared and the hair came down straight to a fringe, halfway to one of those *yé-yé chouchou*.

The *Beatles haircut* was born that afternoon, perhaps 12 or 13 October 1961, in the tranquillity of 29 rue de Beaune, a narrow side-street shaded by tall buildings. The quiet was pierced the following morning when the concierge discovered the debris under Jürgen Vollmer's bed. She would not be the last to scream over the Beatles' hair.

Little is known of how the Paris sojourn concluded, save for a comment made by Paul five years later – 'We just flew home at the end; a real lazy hitch-hiking holiday.'[12] Certainly John and Paul were back in Liverpool in time to meet the Beatles' obligations ... but they weren't the same lads who'd left Lime Street a fortnight earlier. They were now even tighter friends, with Paris in their step, continental clothes in their cupboard and, above all else, that new hairstyle. Let people try to copy them now.

22

'Right then, Brian – manage us'
(15 October–3 December 1961)

Neil Aspinall would always remember the moment. 'We went to collect John, and his hair was down. But it was when we went to collect Paul that we realised something was going on, because not only was Paul's hair down as well, but he *skipped* out of his house – in that way that he does – pointing at his hair and generally unable to be subtle about it. His hair was different and we had to notice it.'[1]

The Beatles' first booking after the break was a curious one: a Sunday afternoon Variety concert for charity in a big cinema in Maghull, ten miles north of Liverpool. It was a fair drive, especially as they fetched George from Speke before setting out, so there was plenty of van time to chitchat about bell-bottoms, birds and the Bal Tabarin. But it was a sticky journey: Pete and George were still peeved over being ditched for two weeks, and now John and Paul had come home *different*. Nothing was said, however. Nothing needed to be said. One of them couldn't resist pointing, but things were not spelled out. In this group, you were either hip to the thinking or you weren't.

Matters took care of themselves over the next few days. George altered his hair to join the new look – in fact, he took it further, choosing the full comb-forward style while, for the time being, John and Paul persevered with partings. Pete left his just as it was. In his fourteen months with the Beatles he'd gone full tilt into whatever new look they'd chosen, often picking up on things before Paul, but he was proud of his Tony Curtis hairstyle and didn't want to change. He tried the comb-down once, wasn't happy, restored it how it was, and kept it that way.

Pete would always say the others never asked him to switch – and that, had they done so, he would have gone with it: 'If they'd said they wanted to get some uniformity – could I sweep my hair forward and wear a fringe? – I'd most probably have done it, but there was no mention of it.'[2] This is true, but not the whole truth, because a dilemma had been created . . . and while Pete intimates he was blind to it, his best mate Neil wasn't. 'George changed his style to match John and Paul's but this was a real tester for Pete. It was like a gauntlet had been thrown down. And Pete absolutely didn't want to put his hair down. A decision had to be made – and he decided no.'[3]

The Albany, Maghull, was the biggest stage Pete had played, and the biggest for the others since Manchester '58 as Johnny and the Moondogs; it was their first theatre performance as the Beatles, their first charity show, and the first time they appeared in a printed souvenir programme – there was a short biography of them and a photo (those hairstyles were out of date, though). Their old pal Jim Gretty, the country musician and Hessy's guitar salesman, put the show together to raise money for the St John Ambulance Brigade – the Beatles played for nothing and Gretty hoped they'd attract youngsters to fill the 1400 seats. Comedian Ken Dodd topped the bill and the other acts were a mixed bunch of ageing, willing amateurs, including several operatic tenors.

It was a disaster. The place was cold and only one-third full, the show ran too long, and the Beatles were awful. The front row was full of authority figures John couldn't stand – the local mayor in his chains, the mayoress, aldermen, councillors, chairmen and their wives – and these middle-aged, rock-hating dignitaries saw the Beatles at their worst. They'd no idea how to work the larger stage or project themselves to such an auditorium, no clue about volume or sound balance, and there was actual internal discord. Perhaps anticipating this, show producer George Martin (a local ambulance driver) switched them to go on last. They were fortunate that the *Crosby Herald* reporter (writing what would be the Beatles' first concert review) was young, liked the music and wanted to say something positive. As Alan Walsh remembers, 'There was a kind of stunned silence when the Beatles came on, like "What's this lot doing here?" And compared to everybody else, they were very loud. I wrote, "The Beatles closed the show with their own brand of feet-tapping Rock."'[4]

They did it again – another second-rate show played for nothing – just two nights later, when their fan club tried its hand at promotion. Maureen O'Shea and Jennifer Dawes hired the ballroom of 'the Davy Lew', the David Lewis Club, and hoped for a bumper night, open to non-members too. But because the event's only ad ran in the *Echo* this same evening (after Jennifer's mother lent her the £5), fewer than fifty turned up – not even enough to cover the rental. The Beatles were disappointed; they also wrongly assumed the ballroom would have its own PA system, which meant they had no microphones; and then their amps malfunctioned. As Pete recalls, they spent most of the evening 'sitting on the edge of the stage chatting to the birds'. Jim McCartney was there – one of the first times he saw the Beatles – and he can't have been impressed.[5]

Jim had a good rapport with the fan club girls. Maureen and Jennifer spent many an evening at 20 Forthlin Road, watching TV, chatting easily and singing along while he played piano. When he revealed he'd never been to the Cavern, the girls said they would take him. 'He was absolutely amazed,' says Maureen. 'He thought the Cavern was pretty disgusting but was pleased to see where his son played. He understood what it was about and why young people liked it.' Jim's visits became regular, especially on days when Paul was heading home in the afternoon. The Cavern was only a short walk from Jim's Chapel Street office, cutting through Exchange Flags at the back of the Town Hall, and he'd usually stop at a butcher's and buy sausages or chops for dinner. He'd wait in the bandroom and hand them over to Paul with instructions about how and when to cook them, and at what time he should start preparing the potatoes.[6]

Then, one evening at Forthlin Road, Jim made Maureen and Jennifer a proposition they hadn't seen coming. He said the two girls should *manage the Beatles*. Says Maureen:

> Jim said, 'You're doing the Beatles' fan club, so why don't you manage them?' We just looked at each other. We were both secretaries and had no experience of anything like that. He asked how much we earned – I was on about £11 a week and Jennifer £13 – and he said the Beatles would pay each of us £15, because the boys were getting £15 a night. It seemed like a good deal and was a serious offer: he said it in front of Paul, and Paul wasn't stopping him.

Quite how much the other Beatles knew about this is a little cloudy, but Jennifer is certain 'they went along with it'. 'Paul was the main communicator but the impression we got was that they all seemed quite serious about it – like, "We haven't got anyone looking out for us, so if you want to do it, you can." The Beatles really wanted to get on and felt they should have someone speaking up on their behalf. We were about the same age as them but they seemed to think we were more mature, and we did want them to be a bit more professional.'

The girls went back to St Helens all shook up. Where to start? As Maureen says, 'I don't think anyone explained what we would *do* as the Beatles' managers, and we thought we'd have to learn. I remember going home on the bus saying it would be tough and we'd really have to study.'[7]

John and Paul's crazy first week home continued with some distinction on the Thursday, when the Beatles had an evening booking at Litherland Town Hall on a bill with Gerry and the Pacemakers. Angered by their peremptory cancellation of four dates, Brian Kelly was now limiting the Beatles to one a week. Was it asking too much for them to show contrition?

The Pacemakers played this day's Cavern lunchtime too, and the Nerk Twins went down to watch. The Beatles – especially Paul – considered Gerry and his group the main threat to their supremacy. They were good professionals and showed the experience of two Hamburg seasons with Tony Sheridan. John and Paul didn't usually turn up just to watch others, but they wanted to show the Pacemakers their new look. They were like Mods among Rockers, and knew they'd receive carping comments from their peers – which, naturally, they were more than ready to rebuff.

After the session, and a few swift pints in the Grapes, John and Paul (with the Pacemakers' Les Chadwick and maybe others) accompanied Bob Wooler for a liquid afternoon in Toxteth, in the Mandolin, where they proceeded to get hammered. The Mandolin was a newly opened drinking club with modern touches – ultra-violet lighting on the wall and purple heart amphetamines behind the bar – but it was in an old building, one of Liverpool's earliest cinemas, the Warwick Picturedrome; without realising it, John was gulping Scotch and pills in the hall where both sides of his family used to go for their entertainment.

They arrived at Litherland Town Hall in a highly bevvied state, and one sight of their condition was sufficient to send Gerry Marsden scuttling to the pub around the corner, where, as Wooler put it, 'he got steamed as well'. Far from expressing regret to Brian Kelly over messing him about, the Beatles took exception to his insistence that each group play a full hour instead of forty-five minutes. The Pacemakers felt the same way, and in what Wooler would describe as 'a carefree mutual mood of co-operativeness', they went on stage together. Even he, the epitome of professionalism, allowed himself to be swayed by the moment: he announced *the Beatmakers* and parted the curtains to reveal an eight-piece band – John, Paul, Gerry, George, Les, Les, Pete and Fred. 'They exploded on an astonished crowd with a sound bigger than the Guns of Navarone,' Wooler wrote.[8]

It wasn't only the sound that surprised. Paul wore an old pink nightie given to Fred Marsden by his mum to protect his drums; Fred himself wore a railwayman's tunic; Gerry had George's leather jacket; George was in a hood; and John blew Les Maguire's saxophone. He also joined Paul on top of the piano: they lay on their stomachs and leaned over to strike the notes upside down. The Beatmakers thundered through four numbers – Whole Lotta Shakin' Goin' On, What'd I Say (extended mix), Red Sails In The Sunset and the new Ray

Charles record Hit The Road Jack – during which John, pissed and pilled, slid from the piano and slumped on the stage. It was the Top Ten Club in the Town Hall ballroom. The dancers stood and gaped. As Bob Wooler conceded, 'Brian Kelly was fraught with anxiety over it. It was only a short episode and a bit of a shambles.'[9]

Kelly was more than fraught, he was appalled; and on top of numerous previous insults, their erratic punctuality, and those cancellations, it brought his relationship with the Beatles to an end. If he was annoyed with Wooler for colluding in the prank, the two men could patch that up; of the Beatles, however, he'd had more than enough, thank you. There were four further bookings in the diary but, after those, no more. First Hill and now Kelly ... one by one, the Beatles were cutting ties with the providers of their paid work. If they carried on like this they'd have nowhere left to play – not unless new opportunities could be conjured out of thin air. Here was Maureen and Jennifer's challenge.

Excepting Sunday night at the Casbah, every Beatles booking in the next seven days was in the Cavern, including another eventful Saturday all-night session. And it was probably during this week that Stuart Sutcliffe sent over the initial copies of their first record. It wasn't Ain't She Sweet and Cry For A Shadow, as they'd long been expecting, but My Bonnie and The Saints – not so much them as them backing Tony Sheridan. Bert Kaempfert and Polydor scheduled it for a 23 October release in West Germany, where it stood a fair chance of being a hit.

Still, the Beatles had the unrepeatable thrill of handling and hearing their first real record. It looked *strange* to them, a 45 with orange labels, a large centre-hole and a picture sleeve. Sheridan's photo was on the front and back and the Beatles weren't shown or named: the label credit, on both sides, was Tony Sheridan & The Beat Brothers. Underneath each song title was the word 'Rock' – it was standard practice in mainland Europe to classify the music – and My Bonnie had a German translation in brackets underneath: *Mein Herz ist bei dir nur* ('My heart is with you only').

George showed his enthusiasm in a warm letter to Stu, also enclosing a £5 note in the hope he would send over as many as twenty more. 'They aren't as good as the play-back at the studio, but that was stereo. Everybody thinks it's great. There's that feeling (when speaking to a member [or members] of other groups) "showed you again!", cos I think a lot of people didn't really believe we had made anything, and no matter what anybody says, it's Beatles on a "real" record. I didn't get the hang of "Beat Brothers", though.'[10]

The Beatles' dislike of My Bonnie – Paul's in particular – would be made clear at a later date. For now, they were just thrilled to be on a record. 'I didn't stop playing it for days,' George told the *NME* two years later.[11] Teenage lad Jimmy Campbell would remember Paul running up the stairs at Aintree Institute shouting 'This is our record!' 'He made the DJ [Bob Wooler] put it on and he was bouncing all over the place just listening to himself coming out of the speakers. He was really made up. *Listen to that!'*[12]

The consequence of such grapevine exposure came quickly, mid-afternoon on Saturday 28 October, when a young man from Knotty Ash, Raymond Jones, walked into the Nems shop on Whitechapel and tried to buy the record.

What happened next is the subject of conflicting accounts, though they end the same way. Jones remembers that Brian Epstein, unable to find My Bonnie in any release lists, asked him questions about it, which concluded with Jones saying the Beatles were locals and 'the most fantastic group you will ever hear'. Brian himself, in his autobiography, suggested this additional information only came to him over the following days, and in the raw interview transcript for that book, he said one of his shop-girls noted Jones' order.[13]

Whatever took place, it was because of Brian's policy that Nems obtain *any* record a customer ordered, no matter how obscure, that the enquiry didn't end here as it could and probably would have done in other shops. He said he'd find it, and his determination then doubled when two girls came into Nems a day or so later also wanting to buy it. And this wasn't the first time he'd come across the name Beatles. He remembered seeing it on a poster somewhere, and surely he'd seen it dozens of times in *Mersey Beat* since July. It was an unusual and clever name, one that lodged in the brain.

Brian had only just returned to Liverpool when this Saturday came around. He'd taken his longest-ever break from Nems, five weeks in Spain to soak up the sun, brush up his language, see a few bullfights (an intoxicating new passion) and pursue hedonistic pleasures. He had the shop purring with such efficiency that its management bored him – it was, as he would describe it, 'working too easily'.[14] Restlessness rolled up month on month; he craved a new challenge still unidentified as he set about his My Bonnie enquiries.

He had yet to connect the name Beatles with the leather-jacket lads who loitered in Nems' browseries every few days, consuming all the latest 45s, those kids who knew what they liked – everything American – and usually found something to stoke their excitement. As much as they had a reputation for performing obscure B-sides, all the newest additions to the Beatles' set were US top tens – and chief among them was Take Good Care Of My Baby, recorded by Bobby Vee and written by Goffin-King. Paul added an attractive harmony line but the lead vocal was George's. In the Cavern, he'd dedicate the song 'to Doctor Barnardo's', the well-known charity for abandoned children.

It was probably Paul who sang Elvis's newest British number 1, (Marie's The Name) His Latest Flame, written by Doc Pomus and Mort Shuman, while John handled You Don't Know What You've Got (Until You Lose It) by Ral Donner, a Chicago singer who'd cloned Elvis's voice to an unnerving degree. Donner's record was one of two additions to the Beatles' set picked up from Parlophone, along with the energetic R&B number One Track Mind by Bobby Lewis. Paul sang Hit The Road Jack, Ray Charles' latest hit; he got a good reaction to reviving Fools Like Me (the B-side of Jerry Lee Lewis's memorable 1959 hit High School Confidential); and he enjoyed singing the new country sound of Brenda Lee's Fool #1.

The chances are that Paul first heard Lee's record on *Juke Box Jury*, BBC-tv's single thirty-minute weekly concession to pop. It featured (along with Elvis's His Latest Flame) in the 21 October edition, picked up on the small black-and-white set at 20 Forthlin Road while Paul prepared for the Cavern all-night session. The four panellists included two 15-year-old schoolgirl stars, singer Helen Shapiro and actress Jane Asher, and it was Miss Asher's third appearance in nine weeks: the monochrome picture greyed her flame-red hair but still she was the show's bright new face, instantly becoming the British media's go-to girl whenever 'the teenagers' opinion' was sought. Mike McCartney would recall, 'We watched *Juke Box Jury* religiously, especially when Jane Asher was on ... She was young, beautiful, had a well-cultured, Dad-admired accent and when she smiled the set lit up. Paul and I both fancied her.'[15]

The Beatles' new songs were presented on a nightly circuit visibly contracting in size. Brian Kelly's decision to drop them coincided with Mrs Best's to end outside promotions and limit herself to the Casbah. Desperate to break out of their rut, Paul said they should get back to where they'd had good times, to Hamburg, and John agreed. As he'd reflect, no matter how much they'd vow at the end of a Hamburg season not to put themselves through the ordeal again, time would mellow the memory: '... you'd be home for three months and then you remember the good times, so you say "OK!"'[16] Around the end of October, Paul wrote to Peter Eckhorn announcing the Beatles' availability for a Top Ten season from January 1962.

This time, they'd be steering clear of involving Allan Williams, although his threat of legal action against them did seem to have petered out. The tough rebuttal of his claims by Paul's solicitor had silenced him: there'd been no reply at all and no action taken. 'The Beatles were brazening it out and I caved in,' Williams concedes. He appeared to be softening to the Beatles individually – George said in his letter to Stu that he'd seen and talked to Allan, and he wrote of no ill feelings – but the impresario maintained a sour attitude towards them as a group, banning them from the Blue Angel. 'Everybody came to the Blue,' he says, 'all the groups after they finished work for the night, all the girlfriends – it was their private club, and the Beatles were shut out.'[17]

There was no chance of their current 'managers' shutting them out – they were having trouble getting them into places. Jennifer and Maureen enjoyed being around the Beatles and visiting their homes but were finding it hard to create openings for them. The familiarity of their friendship with the Beatles, established through running the fan club, never quite allowed for practical conversation. As Jennifer remembers, instead of discussing opportunities when they saw John, he was more likely to say, "Eh Jen, can you gerrus a ciggie from somewhere? I'm desperate for a ciggie and I haven't got any. And don't tell Cynthia you've seen me.' He was, she says, 'always trying to avoid seeing Cynthia if he was up to no particular good. John liked a lot of fun.'[18]

Bob Wooler remained the Beatles' chief guide, and they'd profited greatly from his expertise and advice, while also being frustrated by him. A witty man who liked a laugh, Wooler was weighed down by unfathomable secrets, and so steadfastly did he thwart attempts to probe his private life, the Beatles' imagination was running riot, as Paul would remember: 'We used to try and get Bob Wooler to let us in his house. He never would. We used to imagine whips, manacles on the wall, or that it was incredibly dirty. We used to drop him off every night after gigs and he'd never let us in. "*Why* won't you let us in, Bob?"'[19]

John called Wooler 'Dad' – as a joke, perhaps to acknowledge a comfortable familiarity, and certainly to accentuate the gulf between men born in 1940 and 1926 (even if Wooler did pretend it was 1932). One was a literate young punk of 21, the other a literate old gent of 35 (29). In turn, Wooler announced John to audiences as 'The Singing Rage'. 'He could hurt with his remarks and observations,' Wooler said of the many Lennon serrations that hung heavy in the air and left recipients and witnesses feeling grazed or uneasy ... while Paul, George and Pete 'would laugh in a nervous, apologetic way'.[20] John hardly ever said sorry and the others hardly ever muttered it on his behalf: the victim would be left to laugh it off or lick his wounds.

Wooler included John's new appellation in an *Echo* classified in which he had names for all them:

> John Lennon ("The Singing Rage")
> Paul McCartney ("The Rockin' Riot")
> George Harrison ("Sheik of Araby")
> Pete Best ("The Bashful Beat")[21]

... and it was Wooler who created and put into print the first-name order John, Paul, George and Pete. It scanned well, and reflected the lineal imperative: the Beatles were John's group, he started it and was the leader; he brought in Paul, who introduced George, and then they got Pete. It was a hierarchy one had to keep in mind, especially in conversations. Wooler had more with them than anyone, and he was acutely aware that the Beatles had reached a crossroads. If something *was* going to 'turn up' for them, it really had to happen now.

> Things weren't going very brilliantly. Something *had* to be done for this group. They had so much. My Bonnie kept them a bit jubilant but nothing was really happening for them. We had a little confab. I was very concerned because I liked them very much.
>
> They were *definitely* going to collapse as an entity unless something happened for them, and I suggested I write to Jack Good, who was linked with Decca at the time. They admired Jack Good and I thought maybe he would give them an audition.
>
> They were really at desperation stage ... they needed guidance, they needed someone with finesse and with money.[22]

Right on cue, on Thursday 9 November 1961, at the Cavern lunchtime session, the tracks that had been running in parallel for so long finally converged.

Brian Epstein's My Bonnie enquiries had taken him so far but no further. He knew it was a foreign record, probably from Germany, and found it 'very significant' that Nems had received three orders for it.[23] He knew the Beatles were a Liverpool group and for the first time actively searched *Mersey Beat* for their name. The current issue (which, also for the first time, had a Nems front-page ad) included Wooler's report of the Beatmakers' spectacle, and the Beatles advertised for appearances at Litherland, New Brighton and the Cavern.

They were listed three times at the Cavern. Brian had been here when it was a jazz cellar run by its founder Alan Sytner – they'd grown up together, boys of the same age at the same synagogue.[24] Now it was 'a teenage venue', the very thought of which intimidated him ... though not enough to squash his interest. He phoned Bill Harry, who made enquiries and found out the Beatles were playing the Thursday lunchtime session; Harry informed Ray McFall that Brian Epstein of Nems would be coming down to speak to the Beatles; doorman Paddy Delaney was told to expect him – he was to be signed in without a membership card, special dispensation. Going to see live rock music wasn't new to Brian – he'd been to Empire shows and, with his sharp eye for presentation, always found the staging dismal, noticing that few acts projected their personality across the footlights – but going to the Cavern was sure to be a different experience. Brian suggested his PA Alistair Taylor join him: they would go for lunch and drop into the Cavern on the way, to find out more about this My Bonnie record.

The club was just a two-hundred-step walk from Nems, but 9 November was one of those smoggy, cold, early-winter days in Liverpool, so damp that smuts glued to skin, so dark that the sooty buildings lost detail and car headlights couldn't put it back. Flights were cancelled at the airport and foghorns groaned over the Mersey sound: the cawing seagulls and booming one o'clock cannon. The businessmen picked a path through narrow Mathew Street, between Fruit Exchange lorries and their debris, and at number 10 Paddy Delaney showed them along the dimly lit passage and down the greasy steps.

Bob Wooler was in the bandroom when Delaney ushered in their visitor. Wooler recognised him from Nems, though they'd never met. Brian waited for a pause in that cellarful of noise then leaned across and asked, impeccably *RADA*, if that was the Beatles on stage, the group on the My Bonnie record. Wooler confirmed it was: 'They are they, they're the ones.'[25] The visitor made his way to the back of the centre tunnel and watched.

> It was pretty much an eye-opener, to go down into this darkened, dank, smoky cellar, in the middle of the day, and to see crowds and crowds of kids watching these four young men on stage. They were rather scruffily dressed – in the nicest possible way, or I should say in the most *attractive* way: black leather jackets and jeans, long hair of course, and rather untidy stage presentation, not terribly aware and not caring very much what they looked like. I think they cared more, even then, what they *sounded* like.[26]

The Beatles had started the second of their two lunchtime spots. As Brian watched, Ray McFall made a point of introducing himself to the man whose elegance instantly impressed him, and Cavernites consuming cheese rolls and soup wondered about *the natty feller*. Margaret Douglas remembers he was 'standing at the back, near the snack bar. He looked so out of place that people were saying "What's 'e doin' 'ere?" Ray McFall and Bob Wooler always wore suits and ties but they were nothing like Brian Epstein – he always looked like his mum got him ready.'[27]

The Beatles were rocking, smoking, eating, joking, drinking, charming, cussing, laughing, taking requests and answering back; they spoke local, looked continental, and played black and white American music with English colour; John and Paul vied and jibed for attention, George smiled quietly to the side and sang from time to time, Pete drummed and kept his head down. It was another lunchtime session – and not one of their best. They were jaded, losing interest. But Brian saw enough to see beyond:

> Their presentation left a little to be desired as far as I was concerned, because I'd been interested in the theatre and acting a long time – but, amongst all that, something *tremendous* came over, and I was immediately struck by their music, their beat, and their sense of humour on stage. They were very funny; their ad-libbing was excellent.
>
> I liked them enormously, I immediately liked the sound that I heard: I heard their sound before I met them. I think actually that that's important, because it should always be remembered that people hear their sound and like their sound before they meet them. I thought their sound was something that an awful lot of people would like. They were fresh and they were honest and they had what I thought was a sort of presence, and – this is a terrible, vague term – 'star quality'. Whatever that is, they had it – or I sensed that they had it.[28]

He was *hooked*, and his words illuminate ample causes. Perhaps too there was something else – for Bob Wooler was always certain Brian was 'attracted to the Beatles physically'. Twenty years later, it would become received wisdom that Brian Epstein fell in love with John Lennon at first sight, his focus narrowing on the most aggressive of the four young men in tight-fitting leather. It was only one writer's view – which he didn't substantiate with evidence or quotes, an assertion based on an assumption – but it stuck because, given Brian's taste, appetite and the sight that confronted him, the suggestion is plausible. As Wooler noticed, 'John Lennon commanded the stage with the way he stared and stood. His legs would be wide apart – that was one of his trademarks, and it was regarded as being very sexual and very aggressive. The girls up front would be looking up his legs, keeping a watch on the crotch.'[29]

Suggestions that it was *only* homoerotic fantasy that drew Brian Epstein to the Beatles are distortion, however, and perform a malign disservice to both him and them. It may have been part of the mix, but he was, above all else, simply the latest in an ever-lengthening line of people seduced by the Beatles' singular mix of talents: their sound, look, charm, charisma, honesty and humour. They were the complete and original package, and watching them made Brian feel – as it did so many others – elated, enthralled, mesmerised. Bob Wooler witnessed Brian Epstein's Cavern visit and would crystallise it in eight words: 'He came, he saw and he was conquered.'[30]

All this must have come as a complete shock, and he had to collect himself and remember he'd gone there with a purpose, to obtain information about My

Bonnie so he could order copies and satisfy his customers. He spoke to George, who enquired – in that expressively querulous drawl, both sing-song and flat – 'What brings Mr Epstein here?'* Brian wasn't only charmed, he thought George looked familiar to him. 'George knew me from the shop, and I realised he was one of the lads hanging round. I said I would love to hear it [My Bonnie]. George got a DJ called Bob Wooler to play it for me. Bob [announced] there was a rep of Nems in the Cavern.'

Though George would retain little memory of this initial encounter, he distilled his and the other Beatles' earliest impression of Brian Epstein as 'some very posh rich feller'. As first impacts go, it was the best one he could have made.[31]

Later than expected, Brian and Alistair went for their lunch – to the Peacock Buffet on Hackins Hey. It was just a quick bite now because Brian had a tailoring appointment at three and it was already well past two, but there was time enough for him to confide in his PA: he was thinking of suggesting *management* to the Beatles. It was that instant, like it always was with Brian. His life, as his family knew only too well, was a succession of impulsive passions, energetically devoured and then discarded. (It also suggests he'd found out the Beatles didn't have a manager and wanted one.)

But Brian Epstein had never been so certain of anything in all his twenty-seven years. His conviction in the Beatles' qualities was unshakeable from the start. He loved, and he believed, and top of these beliefs – and it does appear that he thought this right away – was that they would be the greatest. 'I knew they would be bigger than Elvis. I knew they would be the biggest in the world.'[32]

As Brian Epstein entered the Beatles' lives, Sam Leach re-entered. Chaotically busy at the start of 1961, the renegade promoter had been quiet of late – the Beatles hadn't played for him since March – but now, as was his way, he was about to get hyperactive. Diving back in with an almighty splash, he staged *Operation Big Beat*.

His venue was the area's biggest dance hall, the Tower Ballroom at New Brighton, Merseyside's pleasure resort, just a short ferry hop from Liverpool. No other rock promoter thought to present shows here. The Tower itself (where George's grandfather, John French, once worked as a commissionaire)

---

* And straight away the surname pronunciation problems began again. Some (including Wooler and – most of the time – the Beatles) said it as 'Epsteen' and others said 'Epstine'. Brian still used 'Epstine', contrary to the rest of his family.

had been an attempt to bring a touch of Eiffel's Paris to the north-west English seaside; it was long dismantled, but a vast and splendid ballroom survived underneath as the centrepiece of an amusement park much loved by day trippers, though an eternal 'white elephant' in business terms, fading and rusting with every year. Leach presented five and a half hours of high-volume high-octane rock here, licked by (in order of billing) the Beatles, Gerry and the Pacemakers, Rory Storm and the Hurricanes, the Remo Four and King-Size Taylor and the Dominoes. Streams of revellers were delivered in hired coaches that crawled through befogged Victorian streets at two miles an hour. While the attendance figure varied from one eyewitness to the next, Leach himself (in an *Echo* ad five days later) gave it as three thousand. Atmospheric photos were taken all evening by Dick Matthews. Suddenly active on the scene again, he definitively photographed the Beatles' all-leather look of summer/autumn 1961 here and at Aintree Institute and in the Cavern.

Leach maintains that he struck a handshake agreement with John and Paul to 'manage the Beatles'. It's unclear when this happened – nothing was on paper, and the handshake was proverbial – but the promoter did hope to capitalise on his renewed association with Liverpool's best group by somehow propelling them, with him, into the big time, and he hoped to do it by putting them on stage in London and getting all the top impresarios to drop by and be knocked out. He learned from Pete that the Beatles were free on Saturday 9 December and told them he'd book a venue: the Beatles were going to conquer the capital. This would happen at the same time as they'd be proving their status in Liverpool. In the 16 November *Mersey Beat*, readers were given the chance to vote for their ten favourite acts in a Popularity Poll; forms had to be received by 1 December. It's said the groups bought multiple copies of the ballot issue and voted for themselves under assumed names; not taking any chances, the Beatles sent in at least a dozen, all with them at the top and Gerry and the Pacemakers at the bottom. As Paul would remember, 'It was a tense moment, because we thought Gerry and the Pacemakers were definitely gonna take it off us. So we bought a few copies and filled them in. I'm sure Gerry bought as many copies as we did.'[33]

In these same days, Brian Epstein was showing recurring interest in them. With his My Bonnie enquiry satisfied, he was now dropping in to see the Beatles with his altogether different purpose in mind. The tailor measuring him for another new suit the afternoon of 9 November may have wrinkled his nose at the Aunt Sally smell clinging to this usually unsullied gentleman, but Brian was going back to the Cavern for more, and more. 'I commenced to go around with them almost a week or so after having first met them,' he told the BBC two years later – suggesting this kicked off approximately the weekend of 18–19 November.[34] No details are known, but perhaps he saw them at Merseyside Civil Service Club or Hambleton Hall (most likely) or New Brighton Tower; he definitely saw them at the Cavern, catching lunchtime sessions and the odd evening date. Bob Wooler watched him from the shadows, unseen in the tiny cubbyhole from which he ruled the record deck and MC's microphone: 'Brian knew straight away he wanted to manage them, but he didn't rush in as he needed a getting-to-know-you period first. He went to a couple of other venues to see what they were like and how they behaved, and he found them very animalistic.'[35]

The more he saw, the more he was sure. As he explained it, 'I never thought that they would be anything less than the greatest stars in the world – and I mean that. I always knew they were going to be tremendous . . . I sensed something big, if it could be at once harnessed and at the same time left untamed.'[36]

He was a beginner, absolutely, but not an absolute beginner. He knew his decision to offer management to the Beatles was 'largely impulse' but it wasn't something of which he had no knowledge. 'I had watched the careers of pop artists under various managements through my sales of records,' he said, and he also felt he had a grasp on the art of *presenting* music.[37] At this precise moment, as he planned the Beatles' management, the British chart included the year's unlikeliest hit, the oddly metred sax/piano jazz instrumental Take Five, by the Dave Brubeck Quartet. Brian wrote about it in *Mersey Beat* and reflected thoughtfully that it was 'a brilliant example of a disc being presented to the public at the right moment'.[38]

Brian believed it vital to swing his family and senior staff to his way of thinking; he would need their support in times to come – and he was also bursting to tell everyone what he'd found. Peter Brown, still running Nems' record department at Great Charlotte Street, remembers Brian first mentioning the Beatles when they dined one evening in the grill room of the Corn Market Hotel, near the Pier Head. Brian then took him down the Cavern where Brown saw none of the attractions so enthusiastically described. 'I thought it was hideous, full of a lot of nasty girls from Tate & Lyle. It was dark, small, sweaty and you couldn't get a drink.'[39] Like Brian before him, Brown recognised the Beatles as lads who hung around his shop; one rainy afternoon they'd come in wearing the Acker Bilk bowlers.

Brown, of course, wasn't only a Nems manager, he was among Brian's closest circle – not lovers, just good friends. So *did* Brian want to manage the Beatles to pursue them sexually?

For me personally at that time, Paul was the most attractive, with his baby-face, but Brian wasn't drawn to his type at all. His type was a working-class boy who was a bit rough, unrefined, with a lot of attitude. John pretended he was rough trade, the Teddy Boy type, and this was certainly more interesting to Brian – but while I'm sure that liking the look of John was an element of Brian's interest, I don't believe for a moment that it was the motivation for him to want to manage them. Brian was far too honest to do that – that would be a Machiavellian thing to do and Brian wasn't like that.[40]

Brian's family approach began with his brother. He and Clive were unalike but always close, and Brian needed him to *understand*. Over lunch at the 23 Club, Brian explained how he'd discovered the greatest act in the world and how he believed he could propel them to the top. He probably blushed when he said it – he always went red when he said such things (though this never stopped him saying them) – and Clive saw his brother's enthusiasm, and that he wasn't in it for the money. There'd be precious little of this to begin with. 'He thought that if there was any money to be made it was just going to be a few pounds a week,' Clive would remember.[41]

Harry and Queenie Epstein were visiting relatives in London at the time, but as soon as they returned Brian took home a copy of My Bonnie (Nems had received stock from Germany) and played it to them. 'Ignore the singer,' he instructed, 'just listen to the backing group.' For a little under three minutes – from Sheridan's German-*sprechen* waltz intro, to the die-away of the last beat – the luxuriously appointed lounge at 197 Queens Drive, Childwall, shook to the Prellies sound of five young Englishmen on stage in a suburban Hamburg hall. It's hard to imagine Mr and Mrs Epstein liking it for even a moment, or being anything other than astonished when Brian announced, 'They are going to be a big hit and I'm going to manage them.'[42]

They'd seen *something* coming, this much was clear from Brian's behaviour in recent months, but such a move was entirely unexpected. And yet these walls had witnessed innumerable shockwaves before, going back to Brian's childhood. As Harry rose to challenge him for what must have seemed (and was) the umpteenth time, Brian stemmed the tide by saying that managing the Beatles – if indeed they accepted his management – would entail little distraction from work, perhaps only two half-days a week (to begin with, at any rate). He would make up the time, and Nems would not suffer.

Further objection was futile: Brian had decided, and would not be budged. Queenie, as ever, pacified Harry, saying Brian must be given the opportunity to pursue his passions, even to the extent of getting mixed up with probably rough and working-class Liverpool boys who played rock and roll. Privately, there was

surely that particular concern too – *please* God let Brian find what he was looking for and not make a fool of himself, or end up in trouble again, or back in
court, or come to harm.

The Beatles knew they were being watched. Brian stood out *a fuckin' mile*, not
just in the Cavern but everywhere. He exhibited class: the finest suits and
Italian shoes, jewellery, gold cigarette case and lighter, the smart overcoat, the
foulard scarf – white spots on dark blue – which he tied like a cravat, and that
crisp RADA voice. He started to speak to them after Cavern lunchtime sessions,
just a few words. Paul told him if he'd been there the night before he'd have
seen him signing an autograph on a girl's arm. 'I always seemed to miss their
greatest moments,' Brian would reflect with genuine regret. It's obvious that he
was, from the start, a fan. He admitted it in an interview four years later – 'I'm
very much a Beatle fan, I've always realised this, right since I've known them.'[43]

They didn't think he wanted to manage them, they just wondered why he
was paying them such attention, and were flattered by it. They judged him by
the standards engrained in the population of a poor, working-class city that
exhibited few signs of conspicuous success: the man was *posh* – said not in the
usual accusatory Scouse sense, to keep an aspiring individual in his place, but
because he actually *was* posh. He was cultured and refined, a gentleman not
a scruff, an efficient and educated man of style who spoke like royalty, owned
the shop they spent so much time in, drove a Ford Zodiac, lived in a big house
and seemed to be rich. As John explained, 'To us he was the expert. I mean,
he had a shop. Anybody who's got a shop must be all right. And a car. And a
big house on Queens Drive . . . I mean, fuckin' hell, you don't care whether it's
his dad['s house] or not, that means *they're it*, aren't they? So we thought he
was *it*.'[44]

They knew he was 'queer'. Brian would labour for months under the delu-
sion they didn't, but they did. There'd be many people in the months and years
to come who'd not realise it, because their minds didn't think that way, but the
Beatles were hip to it, and it didn't particularly bother them.[45] Royston Ellis had
told them one in four blokes was queer and they already counted themselves
fortunate to have bucked that statistic. Brian manifestly *was*, though. Male
grooming in Britain in 1961 just about – maybe for a few – extended to the use
of underarm deodorant (the weekly bath washed away sweat, didn't it?), but
Brian was well scrubbed, shaved and after-shaved, deodorised, and so manicured he wore transparent varnish to give his nails a clean sheen. He had
physical and vocal affectations, he was pernickety about lots of things, and then
there was the way he walked – it wasn't quite a mince but there was a dainti-
ness that begged imitation, and surely got it.

When Brian invited the Beatles to a meeting at Nems Whitechapel on 29 November, it was already clear they could shift records. A box of twenty-five My Bonnies had arrived from Germany (a special import order placed via Deutsche Grammophon's London office) and once he'd put some aside for Raymond Jones and others who'd ordered it, and kept back maybe five more, the rest went on general sale. As Alistair Taylor would remember, 'Brian stuck up a notice in the window of Nems saying BEATLES RECORD AVAILABLE HERE and literally within hours we'd sold out. So we rang up and I think we ordered another fifty.'[46]

The meeting was fixed for early afternoon, after the Beatles' Cavern lunchtime session. The two-hundred-step walk was halted after ten when they stepped into the Grapes. They didn't step out again until closing time, and arrived at Nems tardily, and with Bob Wooler in tow. 'They asked me to go to the meeting – "Come along and see what you think of this feller." They didn't know if he was going to be a con man. There were a lot of con men around. John introduced me [to Brian] as his dad, which threw everybody, including me.'[47] Wooler would recall the Beatles wearing leather jackets and jeans, and that formal introductions were made by the classical counter on the ground floor. He was personally embarrassed the Beatles had turned up late and lubricated, and Brian – a pathological stickler for punctuality – would not have been impressed either. But he wasn't going to be distracted by it. There was much he wanted to say, so he started.

Pete says he was struck by Brian's timidity and hesitant delivery; he noticed him 'choosing his words carefully, unsure if they'd be flung back at him'.[48] The Beatles got his drift the moment Brian asked about their management arrangements. They told him about Allan Williams (though not necessarily all the details) and Pete said he ran the bookings.

Brian also asked how the My Bonnie record had come about … and then explained why he wanted to know. He'd taken the liberty, unasked, of starting a process likely to lead to an audition for a British record company. If this interested them, it was vital he first establish the extent of their commitment to Kaempfert. Brian asked whoever had the contract to bring it into Nems by the following day because he was going down to London and wanted to take it with him. He'd already fixed some record company appointments for Friday, 1 December.

Speaking to them straight, and no doubt with some shyness, Brian told the Beatles that if they let him be their manager it would be a two-way street. He wouldn't be dictatorial but would listen to what they had to say and take their views into consideration. He would be the manager and they the artists, and ultimately there'd be a contract embodying this, but in real terms it would be a partnership, everyone for the same goal. He made his novice status clear by adding 'I'll be quite honest, I've never been engaged in this kind of thing before', and they said something like 'Well, we don't know anything about being managed so we could all try together'.[49]

The Beatles recognised and respected integrity. Anyone who thought he could barge in and tell them what to do and how to be, like a Larry Parnes figure, wouldn't last five minutes with them, and anyone they sensed to be bluffing would be *deaded* (*Goon Show* speak) even sooner. Wooler said the meeting ended with the discussion of management 'on a "getting to know you" basis, as in "If you like me and I like you and we can get on, well OK, we'll clinch it". A sort of probationary period. That was how it was left.'[50]

It also finished with another meeting fixed: Brian said they should return on Sunday at 4.30, when he'd report back to them about London. The shop would be closed but they should knock on the door: he'd be working inside, ordering stock for Christmas, keeping the promise to his parents to make up time.

John, Paul and George had always thought *Something'll happen, something will turn up*, and their mantra had proved right yet again . . . in the closest of all shaves. Without Brian Epstein materialising for them, the Beatles – as Bob Wooler foresaw – 'were *definitely* going to collapse', and this just eleven months after their sensational first return from Hamburg.

Brian was, they felt, a bit 'antwakky' (Liverpudlian for 'antique') but otherwise a cut above the rest. Not counting Jennifer Dawes and Maureen O'Shea – who effectively withdrew the moment Brian arrived on the scene; 'he had class and he had money,' says Jennifer – Brian Epstein would be the fourth manager they'd had, the fourth man to come along and fix things for them, after Nigel Walley, Derek Hodkin and Allan Williams. This was the way John, Paul and George considered it, and in every key respect – contacts, professionalism, clout – Brian was in a different league. He was still *Liverpool*, which was crucial, but he had London connections, knew the record business and had money, which meant he knew both how to make it and how to hang on to it. They'd give him a try.[51]

It's fortunate Brian was a gambler, because the risks were his alone to shoulder. He was the only one who felt sure of a return on his time and investment. The Beatles were damaged goods: they had that reputation for being unreliable, unpunctual, arrogant and bolshie. Their perfunctory, take-it-or-leave-it attitude was so disliked by promoters that two had left it, and several others steered clear altogether. Their fee remained at maximum but their bookings had shrunk – the only promoters who gave them work now were Vic Anton (once a fortnight), Mrs Best (ditto, at the Casbah), Sam Leach (weekly), and the Cavern (as often as possible). Also, they'd signed a recording deal in Germany of which they knew no details because it was all in German, and which could easily prevent them getting another in Britain. But the shirtsleeves of Brian's mind were ready-rolled as he went to work in the final weeks of 1961, with no contract or offer of compensation, or even the likelihood of expenses being repaid. And as he was about to discover, managerial involvement with the Beatles didn't come with any glowing testimonials. Allan Williams remained stoutly bitter about the way the lads he'd helped had given him a drubbing.

Epstein went to the Blue Angel to learn from Williams what had happened between him and the Beatles. Still swearing they'd reneged on the agreement, sufficient for him to have threatened legal action, Williams vented his feelings with characteristic bluntness.

> When he told me he wanted to manage the Beatles I said, 'Brian, *don't touch them with a fucking bargepole.*' He didn't use language like that, but he took it in his stride, as a gentleman would.
>
> He had the class I didn't have, and – with having the music shop – he also had the credibility of some sort of lever. I could tell he wasn't going to manage the Beatles for the money, and that he wasn't a typical showbiz manager who'd rip them off. He loved them. I could see that. Brian Epstein was the best thing that could have happened to the Beatles because he was *devoted.*
>
> In the end, as he was leaving, I called out, 'Just make sure you sign them up, because they'll let you down.'[52]

Nothing could dent Brian's personal commitment. Now they'd properly met, he craved the Beatles' association even more. As he'd recall in 1964:

> I liked them very much indeed. I liked them even more off the stage than on. Everything about the Beatles was right for me – their kind of attitude to life, the attitude that comes out in their music and their rhythm and their lyrics, and their humour, and their own personal way of behaving – it was all just what I wanted. They represented the direct, unselfconscious, good-natured, uninhibited human relationships which I hadn't found and had wanted and felt deprived of. And my own sense of inferiority evaporated with the Beatles because I knew I could help them, and that they wanted me to help them, and trusted me to help them.[53]

'I think if you show the public something lovely, they'll accept it,' Brian said of the stylish and modern way he presented the windows at I. Epstein &

Sons in 1951, when he was 16.[54] Here was what he had in mind with the Beatles. All year long, in Liverpool and in Hamburg, they had stunned audiences and earned the extraordinary devotion of fans, himself included, so why shouldn't this also happen if he was able to project them beyond Merseyside – through the north-west, say, and then the rest of England, Britain, the world? Even at such an early stage, it seems, at the outset of his management, he had in mind the ultimate goal, *America*. As he later said, 'One has thought about America in connection with the Beatles for a long time, because I always thought – I was always *quite sure*, really – that the Beatles would make it big over there.'[55]

And, most vitally of all, both to him and to the Beatles, he intended to strive for these triumphs *from Liverpool*, on their own terms.

The impossibilities were piled high.

Brian went to London on the overnight sleeper train and spent a full Friday with the record companies. Fixing his aim on the two giants of the British business, he had appointments at EMI House and Decca House. Inside his attaché case was the Beatles' original contract with Bert Kaempfert and several copies of My Bonnie. It isn't known if he also had photographs – it was too soon for him to have had new ones taken, but it's possible he had some Jürgen Vollmer shots from the Top Ten Club earlier in the year.

His primary contacts were sales directors. At EMI this was Ron White, now promoted to general marketing manager; he was the man whose office Brian had visited to negotiate Nems' unique and advantageous trading discount. Brian's good relations with EMI extended beyond this too: he was familiar to the records division managing director Len Wood, known in the business as 'L. G.'. 'I knew Epstein very well before he had contact with the Beatles,' Wood later said. 'He used to come down to town, join us at special industry dinners and sit at our table. A good man.'[56]

Brian stopped short of giving White the really hard sell. Managers always said their act was 'the greatest ever' and he wanted to be different. He pushed the Beatles well and politely, as befitting his company, and left a copy of My Bonnie; White promised to bring it to the attention of the company's four senior A&R men – Norrie Paramor, Norman Newell, Wally Ridley and George Martin – and Brian reminded him to ensure they ignore the singer and listen only to the backing group. But even if one of them should want to see the Beatles, and maybe offer a recording contract, nothing was possible until the terms of the Kaempfert deal had been ascertained. White suggested Brian leave it with him and he would show it to a German-speaking colleague.

Next, Brian lunched in the executive dining room at Decca House, over-looking the Thames and the Houses of Parliament. His hosts were the company's sales manager Sidney 'Steve' Beecher-Stevens and his assistant Colin Borland, and Brian was again the youngster in such company.* To emphasise how Decca could profit from this extension of their association, he'd run Nems display ads in the *Liverpool Echo* the two previous evenings (29 and 30 November) in which Decca product was pushed heavily. Whether or not Brian bought the ad space with this motive in mind, it reinforced the message: Decca couldn't refuse to see a group touted by a client who advertised company product and sold £20,000 worth of it per annum.

There was, however, an administrative process to follow. All these record companies ran as efficient bureaucracies: Brian left Decca with the 'Standard Audition Agreement' and the promise his application would be fast-tracked through the Artistes Department. Decca's popular A&R team was about to undergo a radical shake-up – it would be reported in the music press within days – and he could expect news of an audition for his Beatles soon.

His final meeting was an unusual one – still with Decca but in a different building, around the corner from the HQ. Brian had written to the *Liverpool Echo* columnist Disker and been surprised to receive a reply from London, and from Decca. Tony Barrow, alias Disker, had migrated from Crosby to London and taken a job in Decca's sleeve department, writing LP linernotes – a position that fortuitously left plenty of spare time for freelance journalism. During their November correspondence, Brian asked Disker to write about the Beatles, and Barrow had to decline because his column didn't generally deviate from record reviews. He says Brian arrived at his Decca desk in person, this time hoping he could help oil wheels to get the Beatles a contract. Oddly, he insists Brian had with him an acetate disc with a recording of the Beatles in the Cavern, blaming the rough audio quality on its origin as a TV broadcast. Barrow couldn't hear much through the atrocious sound quality but promised to men-tion the visit to his Decca colleagues. He spoke to the marketing department, who will have registered Epstein's pushing of his group a second time.[57]

At the moment Brian Epstein was taking these initial steps to break the Beatles into the big time, the music business, show business, was contorting itself – up and down and round and round – over a new American craze. It started with a song – The Twist, turned into a hit by Chubby Checker – which then detonated

---

* In December 1961, S. A. Beecher-Stevens was 54, L. G. Wood 51, Colin Borland 41 and Ron White 40.

in Britain in mid-November as both a musical sound and a dance fad, simultaneous with identical twin explosions in several other countries, including West Germany (*Der Twist*) and France (the Paris visited a month earlier by John and Paul was now *Le Twiste* mad). Craziest of all was America, where it was embraced by all ages, adults included, and all social classes. The trade press was stupefied by this unexpected development because the Twist was just the hated rock and roll under another name, newly hinged to a dance that, like the music itself, was strongly of black origin, with a lineage back to African slavery. As *Cash Box* exclaimed in an editorial, 'If you spend enough time in our business, sooner or later you're bound to see just about everything.'[58]

The Twist broke big not just because it was a very good R&B record but because of Chubby's dance steps, which anyone could do and everyone *did* do. It could even be done alone, becoming the first popular solo dance; floors were instantly full of people going through motions memorably described as 'drying one's derrière with an imaginary bath towel while pretending to be grinding out a cigarette with one foot'.[59] In the improbable way these things happen, everyone was suddenly Twisting. Rock and roll had never shaken the White House but the American press buzzed over rumours that President Kennedy and the First Lady had danced the Twist at a party. Everyone was doing it, doing it, doing it – and those who didn't do it talked about why they weren't.

The Twist boom would last until summer 1962 and then fade away, and its legacy was to remind the music business in America – and from there Britain and the rest of the world – that novelty dance crazes sold records. In the meantime, record companies indulged in the usual acts of chicanery, attaching the Twist label where it plainly didn't belong – and one example was My Bonnie by 'Tony Sheridan and the Beat Brothers'. Germany (*Billboard* explained) was suffering a bad case of 'Twist-mania', and it was no coincidence that Polydor prepared a rush reissue of My Bonnie with the word 'Twist' plastered across Sheridan's photo and replacing 'Rock' as the classification on the label. Despite some good reviews, the record had yet to take off, and it was hoped this might kick-start some action. At the same time, Bert Kaempfert was hoping to conduct Twist business in America: information from the famous conductor/producer caused *Cash Box* to call Tony Sheridan 'a Twister from England' and say that both My Bonnie and The Saints had been recorded 'in Twist rhythm'. Better yet, America's 'six top record firms' were 'fighting over the master', all no doubt anxious to slay 'em with a bit of Anglo-Saxon Twist. Here was the Beatles' first dalliance with the American record business ... and they knew nothing of it.[60]

EMI found itself in the lucky position of owning the hit in Britain, though actually it had had the song all along: Chubby's recording was a clone of the original version by its writer Hank Ballard, twice issued by Parlophone to no interest whatever. For label boss George Martin, successes always came the hard way. He had another big hit in October/November 1961 with My Boomerang Won't Come Back, in which the TV comedian Charlie Drake was set into an Australian aural landscape using sounds ingeniously conjured from studio equipment. There were also ongoing LP sessions with Spike Milligan and with Michael Bentine that required constant invention (and rare use of the new four-track tape machine at Abbey Road). 'I always try to do something different,' George told *Disc*, a comment that couldn't honestly have been said by another producer in Britain at this time.[61]

One man *not* trying something different was Dave Dexter, Jr, at Capitol Records in Hollywood. George gritted his teeth as he saw his big successes rejected by the company EMI owned but felt powerless to instruct. Drake went to United Artists, and the Temperance Seven's chart-topping You're Driving Me Crazy went to Verve. EMI's other big artists were dotted ad hoc around America, few succeeding, and it was at this point that L. G. Wood decided EMI must pursue an alternative and more focused policy. He reshaped the EMI-owned Top Rank Co-operative into a seemingly independent New York-based corporation, its twin-task to license more American masters for Britain and to find best-possible US labels for British records. EMI's involvement in the as-yet-unnamed company was to remain secret, but one of its first moves was to secure a stronger relationship with the small but vibrant Chicago R&B label Vee Jay. To begin with, EMI licensed its hottest releases for British issue; ultimately, it was anticipated Vee Jay could become a home for some of the British acts rejected by Capitol under its way too literally applied 'first turn-down option'.

George's main bugbear at this time, though, was his pay-packet: £2800 a year plus a small Christmas bonus was a reasonable salary, but the job didn't provide a car and there remained zero prospect of gaining a percentage royalty on sales. Every time George raised it with L. G. Wood, it was flatly rebutted. With his three-year rolling contract coming up for renewal in April 1962, George was seriously considering moving on.

His private life was also at crunch time. His affair with Judy Lockhart Smith remained known to precious few, but after five years something had to give. Amid emotional turmoil for all concerned, George left his wife and two young children in Hatfield and rented a small flat in central London, not far from EMI House. It was handy too for Judy's flat, which was just behind EMI.[62] She shared with two other young women and George often bunked down for the night on a 'chair bed' – a short-term solution for a long-legged man. He became more focused in his activities from the moment he and Judy were united. Left to his own devices, George was happy to amble or lose himself in projects that might satisfy creatively but reward inadequately. Judy was intent on making him more of an all-round success. Already his secretary since 1955, she now took greater direction over George's life and career, easing it into a higher gear, boosting his confidence and self-belief.

One avenue ripe for a bolder approach was songwriting – handily aided by a rather nice grand piano in the corner of Judy's flat. The former Guildhall composition student had been quietly placing tunes on record here and there for some years, usually written as 'Graham Fisher', and now there was an acceleration. Fisher co-wrote Matt Monro's hit Can This Be Love, and there were further tracks in 1961 released by Ron Goodwin and Spike Milligan. As the year moved on, George wrote two short, catchy tunes, Double Scotch and The Niagara Theme, both of which were copyrighted under his real name and assigned to a new music publishing company, Dick James Music. The ace plugger and talent-spotter had left Sydney Bron after eight years and set up on his own. George and Dick had been close almost a decade, from the days when James spent daytimes in the studio and evenings on stage in his wig. George knew James was both a good publisher and hungry for success, and that he would work his songs hard. Double Scotch was 'copyright 001' in the Dick James Music ledger.

Publishing was still the core part of the music business it had been from the start, since before records. It was one corner of the essential triangle, as fundamental as the artist and record company. And it wasn't just records: sales of sheet music, although in decline, were still healthy enough to have their own niche chart in *Record Retailer*, and a big chunk of a publisher's balance sheet came from live and broadcast performances. George Martin's first port of call with almost all his artists was the same as every other A&R man's: Denmark Street – 'Tin Pan Alley' – to find the right songs. Most of the time they came to him: his diary was filled with one lunch after another. Any publisher who couldn't *push* wasn't worth a penny. Plugging, also still known as exploitation, was the name of the game, the essence of the business, and a publisher was frequently more crucial in breaking a hit than the record company.

Dick James had a reputation for honesty, and there was much goodwill for him to succeed – *Record Retailer* called him 'the pillar of the trade', and his long-time American associate Lee Eastman, visiting London from New York, wouldn't have left without dropping by to wish him well.[63] James' determination to make a success of his business was unlimited, at least so long as the £5000 start-up capital lasted. Half came from his own savings and half from his accountant, Emanuel Charles Silver, who recognised the sound investment potential. James found a 'suite' of two small offices on the first floor at 132 Charing Cross Road, right over the corner of Denmark Street, and opened for business on 21 September 1961, the day after Yom Kippur and a week after George Martin's Double Scotch was released on Parlophone by the Ron

Goodwin Orchestra. With so many American companies operating around him, James made a conscious decision to promote British: in a handwritten document lodged with the Performing Right Society (PRS) he set out his mission statement: 'It is the intention of the company to pursue a policy of securing and exploiting works by British writers. It is probable that the company may well publish works of foreign origin but the accent will be on British works wherever and whenever possible.'[64]

On Sunday 3 December, the Beatles had their second meeting with Brian Epstein, to discuss management. It was the day they said *yes*.

Bob Wooler wasn't with them this time, it was just the Beatles, with three hours to spare before a night in the Casbah. Each made his own way by bus to Whitechapel for the 4.30 appointment. John, George and Pete arrived, Paul didn't. Five minutes passed. Ten. *Fifteen.* Brian became edgy. Anyone wanting to get under his skin could guarantee success by turning up late – he was a sensitive character and took it as a personal slight, and he also found it insultingly rude. Beyond this, Paul's non-arrival made things awkward – Brian wouldn't want to say everything twice, so they waited for him to show ... and waited. Brian's irritation couldn't be suppressed, and at least one Beatle was angry too: as Brian would recall, 'George was really cross with Paul because he thought he was going to spoil things.'[65]

'I was a bit put out,' Brian said two years later, more coolly collected. 'I thought, "This is the first meeting, they *want* to do something about management ..."'[66] He had every right to wonder what was going on. Paul was patently ambitious, liked to impress, and the Beatles needed a manager, so why was he doing this to the one person trying to help him, probably the only man in Liverpool who stood any chance of getting him everything he wanted?

After three-quarters of an hour, Brian suggested George phone Forthlin Road to establish when Paul had left for the bus. He returned saying Paul had only just got out of bed, was now having a bath, and would be along when he was done. Brian *blew* ... but ended up being charmed and laughing – the usual Beatle mix. 'I shouted about a bit, and I thought "This is very disgraceful indeed!" and "How can he be so late for an important thing?" and George, with his slow, lop-sided smile, just simply replied – it was very typical of them – "Well he may be late but he's very clean."'[67]

It's unlikely Paul arrived much before six, when Brian finally got to explain in detail the London meetings he'd had on their behalf. EMI and Decca were likely to be back in touch within days, although neither would decide anything until clear on the terms of the Kaempfert contract.

The Beatles' reservoir of self-worth surely filled even higher when Brian expressed genuine surprise on hearing they earned only £15 per night between them. They told him promoters wouldn't pay more, but Brian said their value was greater, and he intended to do something about it. ('I hoped that even if I were not to run their affairs completely I could at least secure a decent rate for their performances.')[68]

Brian agreed to have a separate meeting with Pete at which they would discuss Beatles bookings – leading to a transfer of responsibility, relieving Pete of the job; and he also undertook to look into the Beatles' accounts and tax situation. Before Brian came along, the Beatles had appointed their own accountant, Keith Smith, a reputable young man who worked in one of the top local firms; Brian said he would meet him to establish the current state of affairs.[69] Otherwise, his priorities were to get the Beatles a recording contract and get them photographed.

Brian was, in several ways, the ideal manager for Paul: 'He'd gone to a public school: it was another strata of society, [and] none of *us* had been to RADA.'[70] He also says Brian's religion was an attraction for him, which wouldn't have been the case with John and George, though it also wasn't something that kept them away. 'My dad was quite pleased when we went with Brian because he thought Jewish people had a flair with money, which I think is probably true.'[71]

However, John remembered Paul's attitude to Brian being very different. John was always emphatic that Paul didn't want Brian as the Beatles' manager and presented obstacles to destabilise him, to make his job difficult … like turning up late for meetings. 'Three of us chose Epstein. Paul used to sulk and God knows what … [Paul] wasn't that keen [on Brian] – he's more conservative, the way he approaches things. He even says that: it's nothing he denies.'[72]

Paul's stance may in part have been a reaction to John's, who always made snap judgements and leapt right in. It was a major and constant difference between them. 'John said to me once, "Look, imagine you're like on a cliff-top and you're thinking about diving off. Dive! Try it!" I said, "Like bloody hell I'm gonna dive. *You* dive and give us a shout and tell me how it is, and then if it's great I'll dive." John always had a strong instinct to do that, but it's not my personality.'[73]

Paul has confirmed that he asked Brian most of the questions about the contract: there had to be a signed agreement between them, but there wasn't one yet because Brian was still looking into it. Paul says they didn't know the going rate for a manager's commission – 'We had a little discussion about percentage, whether it was going to be 20 or 15 or maybe 10 perhaps, you know, because isn't that what they charge? We were pretty naive then'[74] – but, having mixed with other artists for the best part of eighteen months, they surely had some idea. They're likely to have heard from Johnny Gentle that Larry Parnes kept him on £15 a week but took 40–50 per cent from his bigger artists.

At seven o'clock the pubs opened and they left the shop and went for a drink.[75] The conversation relaxed, and it might have been at this point that Brian first learned John and Paul had written some songs. It was a while back, but they still had them. It's clear from a letter Brian wrote five days later that he now knew this detail and there's nothing to indicate he knew it before – and, given that he enthused about the quality of one of the songs, he must have heard it in the interim, probably in the Cavern the night of 6 December.

Perhaps it was coincidence, perhaps not, but it was here and now, in the last month of 1961, that John and Paul finally set their old reservations aside and the Beatles started playing Lennon-McCartney songs on a regular basis. The first was Like Dreamers Do, written by Paul in 1959 – he sang it like he sang Till There Was You, Over The Rainbow and The Honeymoon Song, with his face turned up and angled, big eyes fixed on the far end of the tunnel, above the heads of the crowd. John also sang one, Hello Little Girl, the third song he wrote (but the first to stick), from 1957; and within days they added a third, Paul's unusually melodic rock-ballad Love Of The Loved, also from 1959. To begin with, they confined these numbers solely to the Cavern, where they were among adoring family – as John put it, the Cavernites 'still preferred the straight rock but they were very nice to us'.[76] Brian seized on it: this gave the Beatles a unique selling point. Who else among artists hoping for a recording contract could boast their own self-written songs?

For all their ego and self-belief, it was still a shock for the Beatles to hear, as Brian told them, that they would one day be *bigger than Elvis*. George was genuinely taken aback by the remark. 'That is where Brian was good. He knew how to get it happening. We had felt cocky and certain but when Epstein said "You're going to be bigger than Elvis you know", we thought, "Well, *how big do you have to be*? I mean, I doubt that." That seemed outrageous, yet he did have the right attitude.'[77]

History is actually a little muddied about when the Beatles told Brian he had the job. Accounts of what was said at which meeting and where quickly became jumbled, but if it wasn't here on this day, Sunday 3 December (and it probably was), it was very soon after. The decision, of course, was John's. This democracy had a leader and only he approved the moves. It was time for another of his big decisions. His first was to bring in Paul and his second was to allow Paul to bring in George. This was the third. Should he admit Brian Epstein into their partnership, or not?

We certainly weren't naive. We were no more naive than he was. It was a mutual deal. You want to manage us? OK, we'll let you. We *allow* you to. We weren't picked up off the street, we allowed him to take us . . .

It was assessment. I make a lot of mistakes, character-wise, but now and then I make a good one . . . and Brian was one.[78]

Five months earlier, writing his pocket CV for Bert Kaempfert, John was categoric in his stated ambition, scribbling three short words: 'TO BE RICH'. Brian was a man who might achieve it for him. Of all the characters he knew in Liverpool, no one better suggested the possibility. It was plain that Brian had a fragile personality, but he was also intelligent, cultured, a fellow reader and thinker, generous, smart, civilised, cool, edgy, arrogant and, most vitally, a risk-taker. There was enough here for John to decide, and to disregard Paul's games. In time he'd subject Brian to a few tests of character, to find out how he *really* worked – but, for now, John had seen and heard enough.

'Right then, Brian – manage us.'[79]

23

The Boys (December 1961)

The Beatles' fan base followed a steep upward curve through the autumn of 1961 and into what was already set to be the severest winter in a decade. The Cavern was the crucible – this is where it was all happening, and word spread from here by lunchtime and by night, out into the offices, shops and schools of Liverpool. Playing the Cavern between three and five times a week now, the Beatles inspired infinite passions, allegiances and joyful delight in their followers, some of whom also grabbed the easy opportunity to become their acquaintances or friends.

Geoff Davies was an 18-year-old jazz fan forced to 'drop all prejudices' when he caught the Beatles one lunchtime. He went back as often as possible.

> One of my favourite numbers was Money. They always varied the intro – sometimes they'd keep it going for a long time – and then there was John Lennon's voice as he came in with 'The best things in life are free!' No one had ever sung like this before. It was so dirty and horrible, but horrible-great.
>
> They had this 'couldn't care less' attitude, with their style and the jokes they cracked between numbers, but of course they *did* care. It got to the stage where I just loved this lot *so* much.[1]

Fourteen-year-old Linda Ness was a member of the Campaign for Nuclear Disarmament, a badge-wearing beatnik in duffel-coat and desert boots, quite unprepared for the sight of the Beatles.

> They were true all-round entertainers – no other group had members taking the mickey out of each other during songs. They did silly walks, they larked

around, and sent-up records in the top twenty, just a couple of bars but enough. They didn't tell jokes as such, with a beginning and end, but there were *loads* of throwaway gags, typically Liverpool and very original, with word-play and double-entendres.

They also smoked and ate during their set – they'd take a bite from a sand-wich and leave it on top of an amp, sing a song, then go back for another bite. And they stuck lit cigarettes on the ends of their guitar strings – George par-ticularly did that. They were incredibly charismatic . . . and John Lennon in a leather suit *was a sight to behold!*[2]

One of Linda Ness's closest friends was Linda Steen. John called them Lindy and Lou (or Louey) and that's how they stayed. They went to evening sessions together, and Lou also saw some lunchtime shows.

I used to bunk off school and race down the Cavern for lunchtime sessions. Every stitch of my clothes stank afterwards and it was *great*. I didn't care.

We saw every Liverpool band. The Big Three were shit-hot, head-butting rockers but the Beatles were streets ahead. I loved Searchin', Memphis, loads of them, and my favourite was Your Feet's Too Big. Sometimes George's guitar solo would be an awkward moment, but the energy of their per-formances was fantastic: they played proper rock and roll, they enjoyed themselves, and they were drop-dead gorgeous.

John came over as a bit of a hard-case – nice too, but edgy. Paul was the pretty boy: I fancied him and was blinded by the google-eyes – also, he was approachable and never offhand. George was the young one who looked kind of vulnerable, and Pete was like 'I'm a gorgeous simmering sex-god but don't talk to me because I'm too busy playing me drums'. He hardly cracked a smile, but John, Paul and George were always getting the giggles and burst-ing out laughing. Pete was on his own, but he did look good with them. Off stage, no matter how busy they were, they were never rude – they always made time for you. They weren't Little Lord Fauntleroys but they were nice; they could have been right bastards and they weren't.[3]

Freda Kelly was a 16-year-old office secretary. She preferred the second lunchtime spot, but because her 'dinner-hour' finished at two and the Beatles played until a few minutes after, she 'was always running back late'. Had anyone watched Mathew Street in the middle of the day they would have seen many lads and lasses haring back to their schools, shops or offices, incapable of tear-ing themselves away from the Beatles a moment sooner. For Freda, as for so many others, it was love at first sight.

They were messing about on stage and that's what I liked, the fun side of it. Initially, I liked Paul the most, for his looks, but then George spoke to me and I liked him. He was thoughtful, and while the other two were always larking about, George would just say something *dry*. They all had their own following, and Pete had plenty of fans. He was very quiet, though, and wasn't on the scene with them around town, in the KD [Kardomah] and other places. The three of them bounced off each other – there was repartee the whole time – but I don't think they listened to each other much.[4]

Pat Brady was 15 and went to Childwall Valley High School for Girls. It was a two-bus journey to town and going out lunchtimes was forbidden. 'I went to school in my uniform with other clothes underneath. I used to register and then sneak out at morning break, and go back for the end of the day. I got my comeuppance, but I don't regret having done it. It was *such* an exciting time.

> I really liked John, though I found him overwhelming. He would come up really close to you, look you in the eye and say something. I was quite a mature 15-year-old and wasn't stupid so I could quip back at him, which of course he absolutely revelled in. He would just stand there and soak it all up.
>
> I could make George giggle by staring at his feet – he knew I was doing it and it would set him laughing; Paul also thought it was hysterical and that would get me going, so they called me Laughing Annie. John once signed an autograph to me as 'Love to Laughing Pat or Deaf Annie or Happy Ernie from John Lennon xxx'.[5]

The Cavern had no hiding place. On that tiny stage, within arm's reach of an adoring, respecting audience, everyone witnessed everything. Liverpudlians are renowned for seeing through sham ... but the Beatles weren't faking, and their personalities were always in full view. No greater insight into the Beatles at the end of 1961 can be had than from the words of the people glued to their every move.

> The Beatles had a big following of males. Other groups didn't. They didn't follow Gerry and the Pacemakers but they followed the Beatles, which you knew was another good thing for them. (Freda Kelly)
>
> They would say things that would make you think. (Steve Calrow)

When Paul sang Besame Mucho, John used to stand behind him and make cripple faces. He had to: Paul was asking for it. But John wasn't particular – he also took the piss out of George and Pete, mostly by imitations of some kind. (Lindy Ness)

You could tell right away they were into the Goons. John and Paul said things to each other in Goon voices. (Geoff Davies)

You had to be a Paul fan or a John fan or a George fan or a Pete fan – you had to be identified with one Beatle, you couldn't *only* be a fan of the band. (Susan Sanders)

I liked Pete, and he was a great favourite with the fans. He was a very nice boy. I think Paul was number one and then Pete. George was my own favourite, though, and then Paul. (Maureen O'Shea)

When they did Chuck Berry's Almost Grown, John used to do the spastic bit, singing it like 'halmosgrun', and do a club-foot walk around the stage à la Charles Laughton. (Lou Steen)

I could never get on the first three rows in the Cavern. One girl would get there first and save them for about fifteen others. It was a clique and they all used to take turns. The closest I ever got was the fourth row – and I was probably the second person to arrive that day. (Barbara Houghton)

The all-night sessions really heated up but they could begin cold; one time somebody wanted to borrow George's leather jacket but he said no because 'the people will wonder who that skeleton in the corner is' – he thought he was that skinny. (Beryl Johnson)

Pete used to crack a one-liner, not often but every now and then, and make the others laugh. They could hear what he said but we couldn't. But otherwise it was definitely three and one. The impression was that he wasn't there, really, like the invisible man. (Lindy Ness)

One time a rat ran down the stairs into the Cavern. Everyone was screaming and Paddy Delaney was chasing it with a long stick, and then the Beatles came on and you forgot everything. It was *so* exciting. (Bobby Brown)

Paul was my favourite (he had *the eyes*) but Pete was handsome and wonderful. He was sizzling, sexy and quiet – very shy, very understated. He wasn't one of the Beatles in that he kept himself in the background and wasn't a womaniser, whereas Paul and John talked to everybody, especially at the coffee bar. Pete didn't have the humour and he wasn't forthcoming. It was *them* and *him*. (Barbara Houghton)

I never got off with boys at any Beatles show – your whole focus was on the stage. (Lou Steen)

In Memphis, John sang 'Hurry-home drops trickling from her sty' instead of 'trickling from her eye'. But despite all his mucking about, whenever John sang – it didn't matter if it was rock and roll or a love song – he delivered complete emotional intensity. (Lindy Ness)

Lots of girls thought George was lovely, though mostly to mother him. (Liz Tibbott-Roberts)

Their signature tune was What'd I Say, the final number. It often lasted ten minutes or more, with all the fans involved in the frenzied and extended *Huuuuh* and *Hooooh* calls. (Clive Walley)

When they did Honey Don't they used to do a little foot shuffle in the middle. (Lou Steen)

When the Beatles first started to do their own songs there was a *little* bit of hostility, a barrier – playing new numbers is always a bit tricky – but then we were won over. They were breaking down prejudices. (Geoff Davies)

Paul was my favourite because he was so pretty, so angelic. But I watched John. I knew I could take Paul home to meet my mum but if I took John home she wouldn't be best pleased. (Liz Tibbott-Roberts)

George sang [Buddy Holly's] Raining In My Heart as 'raining in the yard'. (Lindy Ness)

When Pete sang, the other Beatles played but from the side, leaving the stage to him. He looked like he used to hate it because he was so self-conscious. (Barbara Houghton)

Paul was my favourite. I went with him to the Grapes, not as his girlfriend although I think he must have fancied me, to ask me like that. I found him the nicest of the four. When he was on his own he could be quiet, but put him with the other three and he was loud, as if he was keeping up with them. (Ruth Gore)

Young Blood was another one where John did a spastic imitation while singing – always the bit where he sang 'Well what's your name?' And during the guitar solo he used to do the cripple walk around the stage. (Lou Steen)[6]

The Beatles were *our secret*. Some of us had a contempt for the fact that people in the 'poncey south' hadn't heard of them, but partly we wanted that secret to be known. (Alan Smith)

I loved Pete. He was so very quiet and moody and handsome and clean-cut. He never actually said anything – I was his fan and I never heard him utter a word – and that's why I liked him: he wasn't as forward as the others. (Vivien Jones)[7]

For those who wanted to be seen and counted, there was the Beatles Fan Club. Despite their best intentions, however, founding officers Maureen O'Shea and Jennifer Dawes never quite got it off the ground. Being offered the chance to manage the Beatles was a distraction, in fact it probably overloaded them because they soon dropped out of both positions. Paul was rightly sharp to the need for such a club, one that the Beatles themselves could be involved in and enjoy, and he offered the job of running it to Roberta 'Bobby' Brown. A bright 18-year-old from Wallasey, she was the girl who looked after Dot on the occasions when Paul's girlfriend went down the Cavern. Fan club secretary was an honorary position, unpaid, but Bobby was flattered to be asked, and up to the task. It meant, of course, constant close access to the Beatles, which was payment enough. 'My friend Anne and I got in free everywhere. The lads would say "They're with us" and Paul would always say to Neil, "Make sure Bobby gets home."'[8]

Bobby took over the Beatles Fan Club during the first week or two of November, just before Brian Epstein became involved. When he did, he almost immediately asked her to suspend its activities. He recognised the club's virtues but wasn't happy with its structure and intended to refresh it with a clear, clean organisation. Bobby, however, was too valuable to lose: she and Brian quickly formed a close working partnership built on trust, respect for each other's abilities and a desire to see the Beatles reach the top.

Straight away, Brian got Bobby to apply a little well-placed tactical pressure with a view to achieving one of his objectives: a British release of My Bonnie. He gave her the name and address of Bert Kaempfert's Hamburg associate, the music publisher Alfred Schacht, and she typed a professional letter of enquiry, stressing the record's 'very high demand from Merseyside's teenagers'. The biggest step towards achieving this goal, however, came on 5 December, the day Brian was able to first introduce the Beatles to someone from a London record company.

Graham Pauncefort, assistant sales manager at Deutsche Grammophon (Great Britain), was making one of his occasional visits to Liverpool's record dealers, but Brian – his biggest seller and already a friend – wanted to talk Beatles. It was Pauncefort who'd been with him in Hamburg earlier in the year, when they'd stepped along the Reeperbahn and, as he uncertainly remembers, probably dropped into the Top Ten Club. Epstein and the Beatles had come fantastically close to meeting that night; now, seven months later, he could speak of little else, and wanted to show off his discovery. Pauncefort has two abiding memories of the moment: he says the Beatles were performing in leather and jeans, and they were 'surprisingly reverential' when Brian intro-duced them. 'I was very ambitious for Polydor to expand into pop and keen to hear what Brian had to say. We had lunch afterwards and he told me about the Bert Kaempfert situation. I said that when I got back to London I would do what I could to help. I dictated a memo to my boss and told him My Bonnie should be issued in Britain, that we should "take it forward".'[9]

The combination of Pauncefort's push and Epstein's commitment to order a large quantity for Nems persuaded DG to schedule My Bonnie for British release on 5 January 1962. The Beatles would have a record on the catalogue, on sale not just in Nems but all over the country. And it *would* be the Beatles – Brian told DG it should say the group's real name after Tony Sheridan's, not 'Beat Brothers'. While he still planned to get the Beatles away from the Kaempfert contract as soon as possible, it would help their prospects consid-erably if My Bonnie was a hit. Given that Polydor had paltry promotional muscle in Britain, he knew this was unlikely, but still it was worth striving for.

Brian Epstein's energies seemed limitless when driven by passion and pur-pose. He juggled the job of managing the Beatles with his responsibilities as a company director, employer of around forty staff, and city-centre store manager in the month of Christmas – the retailer's busiest – and took it all in his stride. He also expected his secretary, Beryl Adams, to do likewise. Brian was a hard boss to work for, always demanding perfection. He generally dictated his letters on to tape (a new office gadget), then she typed them to his particular wishes – his correspondence was clean, contemporary and distinctive.

Simultaneous too was the development of Brian's and the Beatles' personal relationships. There wasn't a great difference between them by age: he was 27, John 21, Pete had just turned 20, Paul was 19 and George 18. Crucially, though, in all that was important to them, the Beatles were war babies, teenagers in the mid-1950s when rock and roll burst through, whereas Brian spent his mid-teens in the dour 1940s, kicking helplessly against the buttoning-up of boarding school. He'd done National Service and they'd escaped it – the list went on and on, and these perceptions pervaded, on both sides. 'Brian was a grown-up, we weren't,' Paul says, 'a major difference.'[10]

Brian's name for them reflected this. Affectionately, conversationally, and in all but the most formal of circumstances, they were *the boys* – and, through his use of this phrase, everyone else in their organisational orbit came to call them 'the boys' too. In turn, they called him Bri to his face and Eppy among themselves, and wanted whatever they could get from him. Pete remembers a night in the Cavern when they said, 'Let's go and buy some Cokes – you're the manager!' and Brian realised he had to pay, like an easy uncle tapped up at the seaside. At all times, though, he showed them only politeness, prefacing every request with 'Could we . . .' and 'Would it be possible . . .', which no doubt is how he first suggested they become more professional in their attitude.[11] If they really did want to get somewhere they had to stop eating, drinking, smoking and cussing on stage and start to put a little more care into their presentation – and, above all else, they had to turn up for bookings *on time*.

It was because of this age-gap perception that Brian visited the Beatles' parents – to introduce himself, explain something of what he had in mind for the group, and answer any questions they might have. History records few details of these meetings, only a positive consensus. One visit was to Mendips. John personally took Brian to meet Mimi, even though, being 21, he was the only Beatle free to make contracts without parental consent. How great was the irony that John was resting his hopes for fame and fortune on a queer Jew, two of the mainstays in his canon of cruelty. From the surname Epstein, at least the latter of the two characteristics was probably realised by Mimi. She found him impressive and charming and expressed one concern only – that management of John could be just a plaything for him, that it might matter a lot less to him than to John and his friends if it all fizzled to nothing.[12]

Brian also paid a visit to Hayman's Green. No parent had done more for the Beatles than Pete's mighty Mo. Whether or not she ever had designs on being their manager, she'd acted as one – and in good faith – since the moment her Peter returned with them from Hamburg twelve months before.

These were momentous times in the Best household. Pete was potentially on the cusp of 'stardom' and Mona, about to turn 38, was pregnant. She'd conceived, perhaps, in the first half of October, while the Nerk Twins were in Paris. A biological clock was ticking, with seven months remaining before Pete got a baby sibling fathered by his best mate Neil. Mona couldn't manage the Beatles now even if John, Paul and George had wanted her to – the possibility was over, and Brian's arrival in their lives was ideally timed. More than this, Mona realised he was just what they needed: 'He was so keen and full of enthusiasm. He was also young and certainly seemed to be the type of person who could do something for the Beatles. I could see nothing but stardom ahead for the group. They were fantastic.'[13]

This manager needed a contract. Brian had two diary appointments on Wednesday the 6th: at 2PM with E. Rex Makin (his solicitor, friend and neighbour) and at 4.30 with Keith Smith (the Beatles' accountant). Makin would always say Brian wanted him to draw up an *unbreakable* contract, so perhaps the heartfelt advice of Allan Williams was still ringing in his ears. Makin said there was no such thing, and was generally high-handed about Brian's commitment, dismissing his enthusiasm as another daft folly ... and, in the process, he floated himself out of a potentially lucrative position.

Brian smarted and pressed on, confident in what he was doing. That same afternoon, he and Keith Smith knocked together the essence of a management contract. Smith is able to provide the earliest reliable insight into the kind of deal Brian wanted to make with the Beatles, and it so surpasses all the expressed opinions of 'fairness' that he was now close to beating himself up. 'We drew up a sketchy Heads of Agreement,' Smith says, 'the nutshell being that he would get something like 10 per cent of any extra income he could earn them. He only wanted a share of whatever he could additionally make them, so we spent time discussing what they might make. I liked Brian. I could see he was going to bring them order and organisation.'[14]

On the Friday of this crowded week, Brian sent a letter to Ron White at EMI, on the pretext of being disappointed not to have had word since their meeting seven days earlier. His real motive was to gee up EMI by summarising events rapidly unfolding without them. The Beatles had been seen by Deutsche Grammophon, and, added Brian – divulging news probably just received – next week, A&R men from Decca would be coming to Liverpool to see the Beatles. 'As you may appreciate,' he added, truthfully or otherwise, 'if we could choose, it would certainly be EMI.'[15] His letter crossed in the post with one from White, returning the original Kaempfert contract together with a typed English translation, provided at no cost as an EMI courtesy. Now Brian could see the extent of the Beatles' commitment to the German producer, and register (as White also pointed out) that if notice was properly served then they would be free of it by the end of June 1962. This was enough for White to reassure Brian he'd now bring My Bonnie to the attention of EMI's A&R men.

Concurrent with Brian's efforts to cajole London music men up to Liverpool, the Beatles played a booking down south, and shrewdly he mentioned it to no one. Sam Leach's plan to show off the Beatles in the capital – as part of his scheme to make them rich and him their manager – went more than slightly askew. On Saturday 9 December the Beatles played for the first time in the south of England ... in the Palais Ballroom, Aldershot. Leach had posters, handbills and tickets printed, booked an ad in the *Aldershot News*, and hoped that, though it was almost forty miles south-west of London, a few star-spotters would drive out to see them. For the Beatles, it entailed a 420-mile round-trip in a clapped-out van and hired car – no motorways, at least nine hours on the road each way. Neil Aspinall didn't go because Leach used his own driver. It was a mad day out, a big fat last hurrah before the Epstein era. By tidy coincidence, before leaving home that morning, Paul had a letter in the post from Charles Munro, his solicitor. Allan Williams' case against the Beatles had lapsed; it was over. From his £10 advance, £2 13s was returned to Paul with thanks. *Managers* ...

The Beatles were supposed to be headlining over three other groups in Aldershot, the evening running 7.30 to 11.30 ... but no one else turned up. Leach had fabricated two of the groups, to make the poster look better, but the main named support act simply failed to show. And so too did the general public. The newspaper hadn't run Leach's ad. All manner of reasons have been given for this, at least some of them fanciful, but the one salient fact for the Beatles was that they'd travelled 210 miles for a £20 gig and no one was there to see them.

By going around pubs and coffee bars announcing themselves, Leach and the Beatles managed to rustle up a few customers – eighteen is the unverifiable number that has gone down in legend – and, to their great credit, the Beatles played almost the entire four hours. Never had so much been played to so few. 'We didn't walk off,' says Paul, 'we did our whole thing for about twelve people. We always did this, on the unspoken understanding that if we ever came back then those twelve would have told other people "I saw this quite good group the other day ..."'[16]

A photo of the Beatles playing while ten people danced and four more stood around was taken by Dick Matthews, who'd come along for the adventure and brought his Zeiss camera. Before the night was out it also captured a shot of

Pete singing and mugging, John and George waltzing around the dance floor, John pulling two monstrous crips, and John, George, Leach and Matthews glugging from bottles of southern Watneys Brown Ale. They were in the middle of a boisterous game of bingo-ball football when the police arrived, enquired who they were and what they were doing there, and ordered them out of town.

From here the story gets especially cloudy. They drove forty miles into central London, perhaps in search of a particular person or a particular Soho club, but it was long after midnight and even here places were bolting their doors. Leach says they went to the All-Nighter Club in Wardour Street and that John and Paul got up on stage and played a couple of numbers. The Nerk Twins Go To London? It's a nice story but maybe not much more.[17]

No food was provided, nor lodging – they slept in the van parked in a lay-by. Leach says the Beatles' driver (his pal Terry McCann) had to siphon petrol to get them back to Liverpool. Pete says Leach was unable to pay the Beatles their £20 and could scrape together just £12, so they ignored him all the way back to Liverpool, 'treating him to one of our Beatle Silences, which could be quite frosty, with solemn, sour faces gazing vacantly into space'.[18] Leach says he still thought the Beatles might choose him as their manager . . . but if they weren't already committed to going with Brian (which they were), the Aldershot fiasco did it for him.

Their Sunday booking was at Hambleton Hall in Huyton, one of their last remaining Merseyside venues, rough but regular. Bob Wooler's *Echo* ad announced Big Beat Beatle Boppin' with three exclamation marks, five support groups and fifteen bus routes helpfully detailed so people could get there. Brian was present too . . . but the Beatles let everybody down. So late back were they from Aldershot, they arrived only a quarter of an hour before the night's end. With quaint symmetry, there were maybe eighteen people left to see them.

Brian was embarrassed and ashamed, Bob knew where to lay the blame ('If you haven't got the organisation to promote something two hundred miles away then it is better not to do it at all'), and Vic Anton joined his fellow promoters in yelling *Enough!* – the Beatles weren't worth either the hassle or the money. Wooler would recall how their £15 fee for these fifteen minutes, which Anton did pay, became 'the talk of the scene – the promoters said, "They're going to demand the moon!"'[19] The Beatles played Hambleton Hall just once more, five weeks later and free of charge, which Brian arranged as compensation for this night, but otherwise it was over. While this wasn't the kind of venue Brian envisaged for the Beatles' future, Anton's withdrawal merely added to his problems. His challenge for 1962 was doubling. On the one hand, he was committed to increasing their nightly earnings; on the other, he'd have to create the opportunities – the venues and promotions – that would pay it.

Apart from the three Lennon-McCartney Originals, the Beatles added two songs to their set in December 1961. One was an unusual choice – the 1930s film tune September In The Rain. The influence here was Dinah Washington, the so-called Queen of the Blues, whose sassy, classy reading of the old number made the American and British charts at the end of the year; the Beatles swapped its orchestral strings for guitar strings and twanged their way through it in the Cavern, with Paul taking lead vocal.

Their other new song crossed the Atlantic with great expectations, was loved by aficionados, bought by almost no one and would remain a favourite for years. Its British label, Fontana, gave no clue to the US origin of Please Mr Postman by a Michigan girl-group called the Marvelettes . . . but it was Tamla, and it had just delivered the little Detroit label its first number 1 on the *Billboard* pop chart, the Hot 100. It became the third Tamla song in the Beatles' repertoire and all were sung by John, with Paul and George head to head at the second microphone to deliver the prominent backing vocals, and all three adding the handclaps high, at head level, as a visual attraction. They immediately made the song *theirs* in Liverpool. Billy Hatton, of the rock and comedy group the Four Jays, says that first seeing the Beatles play Please Mr Postman was 'a *wow* moment. I was struck by how tight they were. As a semi-pro group, the Four Jays would take a month to start playing a new song really well.'[20]

The occasion described by Hatton was probably the Cavern evening session on 13 December, when the Four Jays and Gerry and the Pacemakers were support acts in the Beatles' Wednesday residency . . . and Decca A&R man Mike Smith was in the audience. Brian Epstein would recall the moment, saying it 'caused a tremendous stir. What an occasion! An A&R manager at the Cavern!'[21]

Decca had responded swiftly to Brian's London visit on the first day of the month, and he could justifiably claim a triumph in getting an A&R man up to Liverpool just ten days after John had assented to his management. The timing actually augured well for all sides, because Decca had just announced a root-and-branch revamp of its popular-singles A&R team, 'a dynamic new policy' designed to be more in tune with changing trends and 'increase Decca's success with singles by British artists'.[22] The news was all over the music press: Mike Smith, previously Dick Rowe's assistant, had been promoted to A&R man in his own right, one of a team reporting to Rowe but able to make creative decisions of his own; another member of the team, the one who took the head-lines, was Tony Meehan, who'd quit his position as the Shadows' drummer in order to become a record producer. Smith, then, arrived in Liverpool buoyed by his promotion, empowered to find his own artists and keen to make his mark in the new set-up.

Paul McCartney wasn't so happy that Smith was in the Cavern this particular night, worrying the Decca man would prefer Gerry and the Pacemakers over the Beatles. The smart dinner to which Brian treated the A&R executive before he saw the Beatles may have been timed so he'd miss most of the Pacemakers' set. He certainly saw the Beatles, though, and was impressed: 'It was incredibly hot, crowded, smoky, but very exciting in the Cavern. Everybody's reaction to the Beatles was amazing. It was very early in my career as a producer – they were probably one of the first people I'd seen play live. I didn't have the power to give them a contract that night in the Cavern but I told Brian they should come down to London for a test in the studio.'[23]

The date fixed between the two men was 1 January 1962.

Some of the gloss was then knocked off Brian's delight. Six days later, he received a 'No' from EMI. Ron White had played My Bonnie to EMI's 'Artistes Managers' who'd concluded the company had 'sufficient groups of this type at the present time under contract and that it would not be advisable for us to sign any further contracts of this nature at present'.[24]

With hindsight, Brian must have appreciated that he'd made an error of judgement in presenting the Beatles to EMI by this method. He'd expected it to lead to a personal appraisal, as it had at Decca, but instead they'd closed the door. He might need to try forcing it open at some point, but, for now, with Decca's strong interest, he could afford to leave it be and concentrate his efforts there.

What had happened, though? The official line within EMI, after managing director L. G. Wood reviewed the matter in December 1963, was that Ron White played the record to only two of the company's four A&R men, Wally Ridley and Norman Newell, and both turned it down 'on the basis that it sounded like a bad recording of the Shadows – and apparently it did!' (a strange explanation, given that it didn't sound like the Shadows at all).[25] However, the fact remains that in the only surviving document from the time, White specified he'd played My Bonnie 'to each of our Artistes Managers' and mentioned nothing about excluding Norrie Paramor and George Martin. There's no way of knowing if he was being entirely truthful, but he wrote this when there was no need for anything else.

Such rejections were part and parcel of everyday work, and increasingly now A&R men were having to deal with applications from vocal-instrumental groups. This very week (16 December 1961), *Disc* examined the situation in an article headlined MORE BEAT GROUPS THAN EVER – BUT THEY DON'T STAND A

CHANCE ON DISC. Its author, the venerable music journalist Dick Tatham, wanted to know why groups were flourishing in the ballrooms but couldn't get recording contracts, and he sought answers from two recording managers, including George Martin, who replied, 'A beat group presents far more of a problem than does a solo artist. Many approach me; but I'm not interested unless I hear a distinct sound – one you can recognise right away. I hardly ever get it. Even when I do, there's the snag of finding the right material. For a group, that's most difficult.'

Record companies didn't routinely hold artist management contracts, but it was probably from Decca or EMI that Brian Epstein first obtained a sample document. He never revealed whose it was, only that the terms were 'quite disgraceful: it gave the artists no freedom, hardly any money, and bound them. It was tough.' It could have been a 'weekly wage' contract or the kind that stole as much as 50 per cent of an artist's earnings – they were all one or the other, their every clause shaped solely to the manager's advantage, many of them concealing outright theft of present and future rights and income. Line up every 1950s/'60s pop artist in Britain and America and ask those who weren't screwed by management to raise a hand, and you will see very few hands. This was the lions' den Brian was now entering, intent on being fair.[26]

The Heads of Agreement he'd sketched out with the Beatles' accountant was fine on one level but not enough to do the job properly. Brian knew he and the Beatles needed an actual contract – and, as E. Rex Makin wouldn't handle it, he turned to David Harris, a young partner at lawyers Silverman, Livermore & Co, who had a smart reputation and mixed in the same social circles as his family.

> I'd never done this before so it was a challenge, and good fun. Brian may well have given me something to work from, I don't exactly remember, but he was very keen indeed to ensure that the contract was a fair one. This was the tenor of his instruction: 'I want to be *fair*.' He was a middle-class boy, well educated, well spoken, dealing with lads who were, in that sense and in those days, of an inferior class. And he was very conscious of that, and he wanted to ensure that he wasn't seen to be taking advantage of them because of his position and because he was a director of a record retail company. So it was stated, and understood, and indeed acted upon. It was absolutely admirable.
>
> I did say to Brian that I would be happier if they [the Beatles] were independently represented – on the basis that he didn't want to take advantage of them – but, as I recall it, they didn't want to be. They were perfectly happy for him to let me do it and to accept what we did.[27]

The first fruit of the Harris-Epstein labours was never seen by the Beatles – they saw it only after extensive alterations. Harris extracted the substance from the sample contract, copying its outline terms, and took instruction from Brian on the specifics. He also talked him out of the notion of only claiming a percentage of any additional income he earned them, on the basis that it was unfair to Brian himself. As first drafted, the agreement was between Brian Epstein, the four named Artistes (this was the standard word in such contracts; 'Beatles' didn't need to appear) and also the fathers of Paul, George and Pete because their sons were under 21. It was an exclusive contract for five years from 1 February 1962, paying Brian 10 per cent of all monies received, rising to 20 per cent if their earnings exceeded £1500 each per year (presently, they were earning about £1000–1100). Brian sought sole direction over their advertising, publicity, photographs, clothes, make-up, presentation and construction of acts, and the music they would perform.

One additional clause (7) specified, 'The manager may at any time if he so desires split up the Artistes with whom this Agreement is made so that they shall perform as separate individual performers.' This was probably nothing more than a hangover from the sample contract, or perhaps it reflected Brian's thinking after (as Alistair Taylor alone would claim, without verification) Paul had said he hoped the Beatles would be successful as a group, but, if they weren't, he'd still be shooting for stardom – presumably alone.[28]

The draft went to Brian a day or two before Christmas and he worried about it through the holiday, taking a red pen to lines here and entire clauses there. As much as he'd hoped to have the contract wrapped up by the time the Beatles went down to Decca on New Year's Day, it was clear there'd have to be a second draft in January.

Brian's influence over the Beatles' clothes would become apparent in time; for the moment, he was happy for them to keep their leather image and to promote them dressed that way. He arranged, and paid for, the Beatles' first photo session done expressly for PR – its images would be used for promotion and advertising over the next few months – and instructed his boys to wear their leather suits and black T-shirts; he also got John, Paul and George to hold their guitars and Pete to set up his drums.

The session took place in Wallasey Village on Sunday 17 December. The photographer, Albert Marrion, mostly did wedding and portrait work – in fact he'd already taken portrait shots of Brian. He was a Liverpool drinking acquaintance, had a military bearing, was much older and almost entirely bald – which was why (to Marrion's irritation) John kept calling him Curly. He'd recall how 'John and Paul joked and laughed throughout most of the session, George Harrison was quiet and Pete Best didn't speak almost at all'.[29]

Brian was present, and involved himself in suggesting the different group-ings and set-ups. Except where their faces betrayed a moment of private humour, these were not smiling shots: the Beatles were instructed to keep a straight face and, in most of them, look right into the camera. Brian pressed Marrion to print the photos quickly and returned to select the one main shot he needed for publicity. In this, they're all gazing into the lens, and George seems particularly stern; only Paul shows the slightest trace of a smirk.

Brian's PR buildup for My Bonnie's release was boosted with news, revealed three days before Christmas, that the Beatles had won the *Mersey Beat* poll. The results would be announced in the first issue of 1962, but they'd finished ahead of Gerry and the Pacemakers, the Remo Four and Rory Storm and the Hurricanes. Brian sent Christmas cards to each of the Beatles – his own stock, his home address printed on the bottom – and personalised the message 'With all Good Wishes for Christmas and the New Year' with the words '(especially January 1st)'. He also gave them alarm clocks, writing on each gift tag – the back of his business card – 'My little bit to get you all on in time'. The presents were both practical and symbolic: these were *travelling* alarm clocks. They'd be going places in 1962.

On 27 December 1960 the Beatles had closed a year full of surprises and star-tling progress with a climactic show at Litherland Town Hall. On 27 December 1961 they closed a year full of promise and triumphs as John, Paul, George and Ringo. It was their own special night in the Cavern, advertised as *The Beatles' Christmas Party*, a right rockin' seasonal knees-up with guests Gerry and the Pacemakers and King-Size Taylor and the Dominoes. It was Liverpool's cold-est December night in eleven years (16°F/minus 9°C) and Pete called in sick. Instead of using Fred Marsden of the Pacemakers, or Dave Lovelady of the Dominoes, John, Paul and George decided to get Ringo, although it isn't clear whether they sent word via Jones the Newsagent or if Ringo was in the Cavern anyway – the Hurricanes didn't have a booking and the night did promise to be a good one.

John, Paul and George all liked Ringo, and George was forming the closest relationship. Dick Matthews had just taken another photograph of them together, when the Beatles and Hurricanes shared a bill at New Brighton Tower. They'd enjoyed each other's company since playing alternate sets in the Kaiserkeller in October/November 1960, and spent much of 1961 weaving through each other's lives. At *The Beatles' Christmas Party* they engaged deeper still, as musicians. The Beatles instantly enjoyed having Ringo in the group. It felt good, as George explained: '[When Ringo] sat in with us it felt *complete*. It just really happened, it felt really good. And after the shows we were all friends with Ringo and we liked him a lot and hung out with him, whereas Pete – he was like a loner. He would finish the gig and then he would go.'[30]

Whether Pete's dismissal from the Beatles would come within weeks or months, it was coming. His days had been numbered from the start, but he'd maintained his status through the combination of his being generally invaluable to John, Paul and George, and their being too reticent to deliver the push. It hadn't taken Brian long to work out the situation. He personally liked Pete, though he found him moody, but the others told or gave him the impression that Pete was 'Conventional. Didn't fit in too well as drummer or man. Beat too slow. George thought so. Friendly with John, but Paul and George didn't like him.'[31]

If having Ringo in the group this night put the Beatles in mind of kicking Pete out and bringing him in, that possibility was instantly rendered unachievable because three days later, out of the blue, Ringo quit the Hurricanes and went abroad.

His Houston emigration plan had come to a halt. After completing application forms and jumping through different administrative hoops, what Ringo called 'the really big forms' arrived, enquiring into not only his political allegiances but those of his wider family, questions he would paraphrase as 'Was your grandfather's Great Dane a Commie?' The forms were impertinent; worse than that, they were complicated. 'They were just ridiculous, too crazy to bother with, so we ripped them up and said, "Sod it."'[32] In place of Houston, Ringo went to Hamburg.

Tony Sheridan was to be the star attraction at the Top Ten Club through January and February 1962, and instead of being backed by whatever group was around, he'd have his own musicians – in effect, a temporary Top Ten house band. Needing a drummer, Sheridan and Peter Eckhorn took advantage of a quiet Hamburg post-Christmas to journey to Liverpool, where they were sure to find a good one. Their first choice was Fred Marsden but he said no – then he pointed them in the direction of Ringo's house, across the other side of the Dingle. As Sheridan recalls, 'We spent a while looking for his street and then I took a deep breath and knocked on the door. Ringo invited us in, we told him why we were there and did he want to come back with us to Hamburg? And he said "OK" and did.'[33]

Ringo had been chasing a challenge since the summer, his tenure in the Hurricanes merely an accommodation. There was more to life than this. Rory and the group might not have realised his thinking, but surely they did now – he gave them only twenty-four hours' notice before shooting off to the Continent for a couple of months. Ringo operated like this: he'd made up his mind, and that was it; times had been good and now they were over; he wished them well, he owed them nothing, he was moving on.

His decision marooned the Hurricanes up a creek. Rory and Johnny had to decide whether to find temporary deputies for two months and hope Ringo came back in March, or ditch him and get a real replacement. They elected to wait for his return and pick up a different drummer every night from whoever was sharing the bill. Hindsight would show they made the wrong choice. On the slide anyway, Rory Storm and the Hurricanes floundered. In 1960, by common consensus, they were the biggest Liverpool group; they'd already slipped to fourth in the coming *Mersey Beat* poll, and in 1962 they would plummet, just when everyone else was coming up.

Eckhorn's ulterior motive in going to Liverpool was to book the Beatles for a return season at the Top Ten. Last time he'd become embroiled in their spat with Allan Williams, this time he found they had another manager. Brian knew the Beatles were keen to go back to Hamburg, and he wasn't against the idea, but he felt they'd been selling themselves too cheaply and was determined to fix the right price. Eckhorn had paid them 1225 marks a week in the spring (245 each for five Beatles) and this time kept it about the same, 300 each for the four. Brian insisted on 500; Eckhorn protested and was dragged to 400 but not a pfennig further. They 'provisionally agreed' the Beatles would return to the Top Ten for one or two months from 1 March, subject to continuing the negotiation by phone and post.[34]

Eckhorn and Sheridan left Lime Street station on the 30th with Ringo and his drum kit, starting a horrendous journey back to Hamburg. Britain was now snow- and ice-bound, and all flights from London Airport were delayed or cancelled. Ringo was nervous anyway, waiting to fly for the first time, and here were workers scraping ice off the runway and aeroplane wings. Buddy Holly had been killed in such circumstances. The three young men, all solid drinkers, fortified themselves in the airport lounge, and when Eckhorn tried to sleep he was kept awake by Ringo nervously drumming his fingers on the table.

The Beatles' 'rehearsal' before their Decca recording test was three Cavern dates in four nights, capping a year when they'd played 349 times. Still, London was looming in their minds. Before leaving Liverpool, Eckhorn had an alcoholic night with them and gathered there was 'one thing worrying them – they had a recording test coming up. It was making them nervous. George asked me if I had a tranquilliser to help them do a swinging test.'[35]

They weren't the only Merseysiders heading for 'the smoke'. Alan Smith, the young Cavernite and trainee journalist from Birkenhead who wanted to work for a music paper, had landed a job on the *NME*. The Beatles' last Liverpool show of the year, 30 December in the Cavern, was his too.

Someone said to Paul, 'Have you met Alan? He's joining the *NME* next week.' Paul's eyes widened and he said, 'D'ya think you could get us a bit of a write-up?'

Paul had a passion for the Beatles to be big, and because John's psyche knew no bounds they unquestionably saw themselves as having the world at their feet, once a few buttons had been pressed. That meant getting out of Liverpool. I find it almost impossible to describe the feeling, even though I remember it well, but these guys were something with Destiny written all over them.[36]

South again, for the second time in three weeks. They met 11AM on New Year's Eve at the Jolly Miller, a huge roadside pub in West Derby: John, Paul and George got there by green Corporation buses that slipped and slid over unploughed roads; Neil and Pete had the van (a bigger one, hired for the occasion, Eppy paying); Brian was there in his smart Zodiac but would be travelling south by train. They'd rendezvous again at the hotel he'd booked for them.

Their mecca was Decca, and they were nervous – they hadn't been in a British recording studio before, just the suburban Hamburg auditorium the Germans called a studio. All the same, there was a sense that the prized recording contract was within their grasp. They'd read about Decca's souped-up A&R department, and Mike Smith surely liked them or he wouldn't have invited them to the studio. It was just *sod's law* that their two-hundred-mile journey would be so atrocious, affected by snowdrifts, blizzards, ice, dense fog and abandoned vehicles. Neil did it in eleven hours and they got lost somewhere near Wolverhampton.

Brian's train journey was similarly troubled. He stayed with his Aunt Freda, who still lived in a block of mansion flats in Marylebone, just off Baker Street. He met the Beatles around 10PM, when they arrived at the Royal Hotel on Woburn Place, checking in and then leaving again to find food and action. They climbed back in the van, and Neil – on his first visit to London – was guided by Brian to Charing Cross Road, where four years previously he'd worked in a book and record shop.

While Neil drove off to find parking, the others fell into a pub; then Neil returned with a tale of two men who'd asked if they could 'smoke pot' in the van. Having no idea what they were talking about, he'd said no. They sat down in a café and were shocked at the London prices – six bob for a bowl of soup! – and so persistently did they challenge the waiter about it, he ordered them out. Paul (who was again missing his family's Hogmanay party) has a memory of going to the Nucleus Coffee Bar on Monmouth Street and being amazed to see people passing around speed pills. Neil also said Brian took them to a discreet club in St Giles, and that they went in just for a laugh, knowing it was the kind of place where the 'women' had eight o'clock shadows.[37]

Not even the bitter cold prevented them window-shopping. On Charing Cross Road (just by Dick James Music) was a row of musical instrument shops even better than Hessy's back home – and further down, at 96, was the theatrical and ballet shoe-shop Anello & Davide. Their attention was held by a pair of Spanish flamenco ankle boots, 'Chelsea'-style in black leather, with black elastic sides, a tag at the back, pointed toes and Cuban heels. £3 15s a pair. As they'd shown with the leather suits, cowboy boots and twat 'ats, the Beatles could be collectively enthused about clothing, all wanting to wear it – and here was another such moment. Details were committed to memory, and after returning home they contacted Anello & Davide and ordered four pairs.[38]

The Beatles knew the tradition was to gather in Trafalgar Square at midnight, by the giant Christmas tree, to ring out the old, ring in the new, sing Auld Lang Syne and watch a few hardy souls jump in the fountains – but because of the weather it was the smallest crowd and quietest New Year's Eve in London in more than forty years.

They fell into their beds exhausted, the biggest moment of their lives just hours away. They'd soon be back in Liverpool boasting of a recording contract. Needing to be at Decca's West Hampstead studio before ten in the morning, they set Eppy's alarm clocks and slumbered as 1962 settled in.

YEAR 5, 1962:—
ALWAYS BE TRUE

24

Choices (1 January–5 February 1962)

'We knew we could make it,' John said. 'We simply wanted to be the biggest. We dreamed of being the British Elvis Presleys, and we believed it.'

The Beatles kept their ambitions in focus. They had 'specific little aims, a series of goals: to get a record made, to get a number one . . .' Appropriately, on this ice-cold New Year's morning in London, the next step was the slippiest. 'All we wanted to do was make a record,' George later said. 'We thought, "If we can make a record we'll show Cliff and the Shadows."'[1]

They had only to pass a test, to show once again their dazzling abilities, and they would become – in the words of the day – *Decca artistes*.

A mile north of the EMI studios on Abbey Road, Decca's facility was in Broadhurst Gardens, West Hampstead. Britain's recording business was just as it had been for decades, and staffed by many of the same men: the companies ran their own studios and the contracted talent had no choice but to work there. Daily life functioned more like a government department than a branch of the entertainment business – everyone was on the payroll, producers and balance engineers worked in lounge suits, technical engineers wore white lab coats and janitorial staff wore brown. Decca and EMI were global conglomerates, and so closely did their industrial interests overlap, there was often talk of a merger. The City of London was buzzing with rumours at this precise moment: in the last days of 1961 it seemed EMI would be mounting a takeover bid for its great rival. The story went away a few days later, but the situation would have been the talk of the studio this first morning in January.*

---

* Until 1975, Scotland was the only place in Britain where New Year's Day was a national holiday; in England and Wales it was a normal working day.

There was a problem the moment the Beatles set up. The amplifiers they'd lugged down from Liverpool, banging about in the back of the van, were unsuitable. They were good on stage, loud enough to blast calcium from the Cavern bricks and pin back the brawling Teds at Hambleton Hall, but they didn't sound good here. Studio 2 was 36ft by 21ft – a large oblong basement, windowless but for a same-level control room – and the boom and oomph of a Merseyside night simply wasn't needed; at lower volume, though, the amps hummed. John, Paul and George had to defer to the decisions of the balance engineer assigned to their session, Mike Savage, even though he was only 20: the three guitars were plugged into some studio amps, and they had no control over their sound. Also, Pete had to set up his drums behind isolation screens, so his sound wouldn't dominate the other microphones.

The key word of the day was 'test'. Among themselves, the Beatles seem to have called it 'an audition', but to the studio staff it was a Commercial Test. The Beatles were here because Mike Smith had already assessed them in the Cavern and knew they were good enough; now he wanted to test them in studio conditions. The standard procedure was to record between two and five songs and then usher the artiste off the premises; as the Beatles taped fifteen at Decca, this strongly suggests that (if offered a deal) their first single, and perhaps others after it, would be taken from this tape. It was a long trek down from Liverpool and having a choice of numbers in the can would save hassle for everyone. This situation is further indicated by the session's duration – it began late in the morning and extended after a lunch break into the afternoon. (The precise times aren't known because session paperwork has not survived.)

The Beatles were to start at 10AM with Mike Smith taking charge. Despite his elevated position within Decca's loudly touted A&R revamp, the 26-year-old Smith earned £13 a week and lived at home with his parents. He had talent and good technical training but was relatively inexperienced. As he acknowledged, when he watched the Beatles in the Cavern it was one of the first rock gigs he'd seen. And in the studio, while he was bright enough to have earned promotions, Smith lacked skills common to others in his position. 'I couldn't read music, but nobody at Decca sussed that. The producer was held to be God Almighty and it was taken for granted that I knew what I was talking about.'[2]

God was bigger than the Beatles this bitter Monday morning. He was *late*. As the minutes passed so, inevitably, Brian Epstein took it as a personal slight and got hot under the collar, saying the Beatles were being undervalued. And when Smith arrived he was nursing not only a New Year's party hangover but also cuts and bruises from a car crash three days before Christmas. Suddenly, then, these blokes from Liverpool were standing in front of him, awaiting his instruction. Pete remembers George drawling 'Happy New Year, Mike – we didn't see you in the fountain last night'; and then, with a smile and no more time to lose, the session started. The Beatles were in a basement in London, standing for the first time on their own in a recording studio. They watched from the wooden floor while men behind the glass made technical adjustments, and then the red light went on.[3]

Recording session

> Monday 1 January 1962. Studio 2, Decca, London.
> Recording: Money (That's What I Want); The Sheik Of Araby; Memphis, Tennessee; Three Cool Cats; Sure To Fall (In Love With You); September In The Rain; Take Good Care Of My Baby; Till There Was You; Crying, Waiting, Hoping; To Know Her Is To Love Her; Besame Mucho; Searchin'; Like Dreamers Do; Hello Little Girl; Love Of The Loved. Order of recording not known.

Running to fifteen songs, thirty-five minutes, the Decca tape allows the first real opportunity to listen to the Beatles, to hear them at the moment they were striving for the success they felt their due.[4] But while they'd experienced incredible progress and so many triumphs, this was an instance when they signally failed to put across their magic.

For a band so brimming in confidence and cockiness, they could also fall prey to nerves. John later said of this day that they were 'terrible ... we were terrified, nervous'.[5] They allowed an 'us and them' chasm to come between the studio floor and the control room, failing to adapt to the goldfish-bowl environment, of being judged from behind glass. It was also too early in the day to make music, and they started and stayed physically cold. Outside was the sharpest New Year's morning in London since 1887 (19°F/minus 7°C), and inside wasn't much warmer. They could do nothing to alter or improve any of this, having no choice but to put behind them one below-par performance after another and pitch into the next, almost forcing themselves to go better.

It isn't certain if the Beatles were aware they'd be recording as many as fifteen songs and so chose them in advance, or whether Mike Smith just kept wanting 'one more'. As the years passed, it would become accepted 'fact' that the Decca selection was made by Brian Epstein, riding rough-shod over the Beatles' own opinions. This is untrue, and John made the point clearly: 'We virtually recorded our Cavern stage show, with a few omissions of a repetitive kind.'[6] Eleven of the fifteen still figured when they played an important booking a month later and the other four resurfaced to stay in the Beatles' set throughout 1962. If there *was* a considered plan here at Decca, it might have been to project what the Beatles demonstrated in Liverpool as often as eight times a week: that they were musically versatile and that three of them sang – this was a unique strength, well worth emphasising.

The song selection fell into four categories:

- Five numbers that dipped into the previous five years: the Teddy Bears' harmony ballad To Know Her Is To Love Her; Chuck Berry's chugging Memphis, Tennessee; Carl Perkins' country and western Sure To Fall; Buddy Holly's catchy Crying, Waiting, Hoping; and a nod to the Detroit R&B sound in Barrett Strong's Money.
- Four humorous rock numbers: three by the Coasters – Searchin', Three Cool Cats and Besame Mucho – and Joe Brown's adaptation of The Sheik Of Araby.
- Three recent hits, to show they could cover – and sometimes creatively rearrange – contemporary chart material: Bobby Vee's poppy Take Good Care Of My Baby; Peggy Lee's ballad Till There Was You; and Dinah Washington's bluesy version of the jazz standard September In The Rain. (None of these pandered to the current obsession with Twist records. Probably no other group in the country would have left a Twist song, or an instrumental number, out of a presentation at this time.)
- Three Lennon-McCartney Originals, those songs they'd only just intro-duced into the Beatles' set: two of Paul's from 1959, Like Dreamers Do and Love Of The Loved, and John's 1957 number Hello Little Girl, his first 'keeper'.

If Brian did have a hand in the selection it was surely to impose John and Paul's songs into the fifteen, because they themselves were still hesitant about playing them, especially outside the Cavern. Brian's attempts to market the Beatles as 'something new' would always include a strong push for John and Paul's writing – even though, in the climate that prevailed, he couldn't have been certain of its recognition as a virtue. The current issue of *Disc* had an arti-cle headlined SINGERS SHOULD NOT PEN THEIR OWN SONGS, its writer (Don Nicholl) 'spotlighting a trend that could spell disaster for pop music'. This appeared the same day that veteran bandleader Jack Payne went on TV and complained that pop records were the product of 'souped up sound', that there were too many noises cooked up by studio engineers at the expense of musi-cianship.[7] This was the setting the Beatles and plenty of others had to work against as the third year of the Sixties got underway.

The salient feature about the fifteen songs is that John sang only four – and one of these jointly with Paul. George also sang four, and Paul seven. John's compliance with this is surprising. What undercuts everything, though, is that the *real* Beatles barely turned up at Decca. The Beatles who *mach Schau*ed in Hamburg and grabbed the rapt attention of Liverpool audiences were neither caught rapturously on tape nor much enjoyed through the West Hampstead glass on New Year's Day 1962. This was a lacklustre performance, restrained, subdued, the handbrake on.

Paul's nerves are palpable on Till There Was You, where he seems so hung up on having to put himself across as a romantic balladeer, and budding star, and musician to be reckoned with, that he forgot how to read the song and put across nothing. It would be the number they'd always talk about – John later said Paul's voice went so high 'he sounded like a woman'.[8] Paul is also so careful to enunciate properly that he over-enunciates and introduces odd affectations, singing *musicck* in the line 'and then there was music'. He does it again elsewhere in the session, singing a hard *lookk* (in 'each time I look') in Love Of The Loved.

John wasn't much better. He later said he sang Money 'like a madman'.[9] This could suggest he gave it his usual full-on blistering voice – but actually he meant he was crazed. Far from belting it out, he audibly pulls back, playing safe, ending up neither one thing nor the other, in no-man's land. Where was the Lennon soul, edge, bite? It isn't on Money or To Know Her Is To Love Her or Memphis. Only once in John Lennon's life would he be heard timid, and it was here today.

George performed best. His guitar playing in Besame Mucho is sharp and precise, and his middle-eight solo in Crying, Waiting, Hoping is good. However, at other times his playing was below the standard this questing perfectionist would have wanted from himself: his solo on Searchin' is quite terrible in its stumbling twanginess, and it isn't much better in Hello Little Girl. As a vocalist, George is enthusiastic and mostly free of nerves – Take Good Care Of My Baby is particularly good. However, The Sheik Of Araby is perhaps the most misjudged of the day's work. It required the Cavern audience's response to John and Paul's pulled faces, wacky dances and strange *not arf!* interjections. On tape, in cold surroundings, it just sounds mad.

Worst is Pete's drumming. He, particularly, was on test here, having been shown up in the Hamburg session six months earlier, when Bert Kaempfert found his drumming so poor he stripped away half his kit. Pete hadn't been able to give his guitarists the sound they needed – the sound which, just five days before this Decca test, John, Paul and George had experienced and enjoyed with Ringo in their larky Christmas party. At Decca, Pete had the full kit at his disposal and did little with it. He was just as nervous as the others, and being behind isolation screens must have been strange, but they didn't manufacture his erratic tempo (audible in several places, notably Till There Was You) or his playing of the same tip-tap hi-hat beat and snare-drum shuffle on virtually every song. His drumming on Money is good, but the rest of the time it's weak and rudimentary: there's no cohesion with Paul's bass, and never any *attack* – at no time does Pete's drumming bind the group or drive them on. Mike Savage remembers being deeply unimpressed. 'I thought Pete Best was *very* average, and didn't keep good time. You could pick up a better drummer in any pub in London. If you've got a quarter of a group being very average, that isn't good. The drummer should be the rock, and if the rock isn't good then you start thinking, "No." If Decca was going to sign the Beatles, we wouldn't have used Pete Best on the records.'[10]

The session wasn't *all* bad. No group, first time in a studio, cold and with unfamiliar gear, was going to make fifteen scorching tracks. There was about enough to make a couple of singles. Despite weak moments, Love Of The Loved and Hello Little Girl turned out fairly well, the latter benefiting from a combined lead vocal by John and Paul. The Beatles' harmony unit, always held to be their greatest strength in this period, was surprisingly underused here at Decca, although Paul sings an attractive line towards the end of Take Good Care Of My Baby. They all spark on Three Cool Cats. George's self-created guitar solo isn't great but this is still the real sound of Beatles '61 – John slips into Peter Sellers mode to sing his two lines 'Hey man, save one chick for me!', the first done in an Indian accent, the second in cod-German. It's hokey, but the Beatles could make hokey attractive.

The fifteen tracks were recorded straight, in mono, mostly in one take, though they also had run-throughs of each number to get themselves together and in tune, and to enable Mike Savage to rebalance the instrument and vocal levels. The Beatles were allowed to hear the tape, but not in the control room. 'If we played anything back to them we would have done it on the studio floor,' Savage says. The image is of them standing around the basement studio, smoking hard and experiencing the dubious pleasure of hearing themselves not playing well. 'We didn't sound natural' was John's recollection two years later – words that pinpoint the essence of his disappointment.[11]

'At the end of the session I said to them, "I'll let you know,"' recalls Mike Smith. He knew the decision about the Beatles' contract was going to be delayed at least three weeks. He was supposedly empowered to make such judgements himself, but, this early in the revamped A&R set-up, he'd been told to consult Dick Rowe, and the head of department was busy. Rowe was deeply involved in a Billy Fury film, *Play It Cool!*, and then he was heading straight to America to study the music scene. So many times had trends and ideas broken in Britain secondhand from the States, Rowe was flying to New York to get an early clue to the new direction. Also going was Tony Meehan, the trophy figurehead of Decca A&R's 'dynamic new policy'; Smith was the only one staying home, so he'd be busy.

The following day, amid still-atrocious weather, the Beatles battled the roads back to Liverpool. The Cavern was calling them again – their 1962 bookings diary kicked off with lunchtime and evening sessions on 3 January. They got home to tell their friends and families that Decca had been nerve-racking ... but the arrival of a letter confirming a prized recording contract was surely just a matter of time.

The fourth day of 1962 delivered Vol. 1 No. 13 of *Mersey Beat* and its big front-page headline BEATLES TOP POLL! Here they were, in the photo that would publicise them in the opening weeks of the year: no-nonsense, unsmiling Beatles in rough-looking black leather outfits with three guitars and drums; three young men with their hair down in a modish continental European style, one with it up. There was, oddly, no editorial about the winning group, just a caption under the photo in which (no doubt to John's delight) Bill Harry reverted to calling Paul *McArtrey*.

A day later, Friday 5 January, My Bonnie was released in Britain. The Beatles were a recording group, *fact*, their sound pressed into seven inches of black plastic obtainable in shops nationwide.[12] It picked up coverage in *Record Retailer* and the British column of *Cash Box*, sent to every corner of the United States, and this itself was mentioned in the *Liverpool Echo* by Disker, whose positive review was accompanied by the publicity picture – the Beatles' debut sighting in their city's beloved newspaper. They also made the national weekly music press for the first time. Record-review vocabulary was standard and formulaic: in the *NME*, Keith Fordyce said My Bonnie was 'worth a listen for the above-average ideas', both *Disc* and *Record Retailer* gave it three stars ('Good' and 'Possible' respectively), *Melody Maker* praised both sides and, having assumed Sheridan and the Beatles were a permanent team, concluded 'We should be hearing a lot more of them'; *The World's Fair*, so often best for reviews, called My Bonnie 'a real gone rocker which will please the youngsters', and reckoned it was 'likely to receive steady plays [on juke-boxes]'.[13]

It didn't. My Bonnie failed to crack even the bottom of the paper's Top 100 juke-box chart. In fact, it disappeared from sight virtually on issue, the fate of most weekly record releases. Neither Deutsche Grammophon nor the song's British publisher, Progressive Music, managed to get it a single plug on Radio Luxembourg, the BBC Light Programme or TV programmes *Juke Box Jury* and *Thank Your Lucky Stars*. Launched by ABC-TV in April 1961, *Lucky Stars* (as everyone called it) was a new-style pop show for British television, with performers in the studio miming to their latest chart hit or new release. It was an obvious idea but hadn't been done like this before. The sets were imaginatively designed but the show's scheduling wasn't: it was placed opposite the BBC's *Juke Box Jury*, so the week's only two TV pop shows were on at the same time. John Lennon, a restless viewer at the best of times, spent the early part of every Saturday evening – before going out to be a Beatle – in 'the morning room' at Mendips, jumping up and down from his chair to the set, switching the channels back and forth.

He was probably hoping to catch My Bonnie on one show or the other, unaware it had been overlooked; but he didn't need David Jacobs' pinged bell to know My Bonnie was a hit for *someone* – to the great surprise of all, Mimi thought it a wonderful record. For the first time, she said she understood how John might be able to earn a living from his guitar. This is remembered by one of the university student lodgers, Frank Duckworth: 'Mimi was *very* proud of the fact that they'd made a record of My Bonnie Lies Over The Ocean. She brought it into our room and played it to us. "They've done a record!"'[14]

My Bonnie did achieve some success in Germany, breaking into a few charts, but it didn't sell much in Britain.[15] Brian did all he could to boost it, ordering a hefty quantity to sell at both the city-centre Nems ... and ended up burdened by unsold stock because My Bonnie hardly did a thing. The fans who really wanted it had already bought the German import, and few others bothered because the Beatles were only the backing group, it wasn't *their Beatles*. Two facts emerge from Nems' Top Twenty charts compiled in mid- and late-January 1962, as published in *Mersey Beat*: My Bonnie was selling so poorly that it didn't make even the lowest rung, and Brian held so scrupulously to an avowed principle about 'honest charts' that he resisted giving My Bonnie a false position even though it might have been useful to them and no one could have challenged it.

On Wednesday 24 January, the Beatles signed their management contract with Brian Epstein, to take effect from 1 February. It was the third draft but the only one they saw, and it embodied the concerns of a businessman so determined to be honest and open that he'd deliberately weakened his own position. 'The fair deal is the right deal' was the Epstein ethic passed generation to generation, and Brian was taking it to masochistic extremes.

The legal procedure called for each contracted party to put his signature across a postage stamp. Five sixpenny ones were affixed to the final page, across which flowed four signatures: J. W. Lennon, George Harrison, James Paul McCartney and R. P. Best. J. A. Taylor – Brian's personal assistant Alistair

Taylor – witnessed the contract in five places, but one of his signatures is next to an unmarked stamp.[16] Brian's best explanation for not signing would appear in his autobiography: 'It was because even though I knew I would keep the contract in every clause, I had not 100 per cent faith in myself to help the Beatles adequately. In other words, I wanted to free the Beatles of their obligations if I felt they would be better off.'[17]

It's not certain if the Beatles realised Brian didn't sign. Of equal importance, and unnoticed by everyone, the contract wasn't legal anyway. Against the advice of his lawyers, Brian had ordered the removal of James McCartney, Harold Harrison and John Best as parties to the agreement. Paul, George and Pete were under 21, minors in the eyes of the law; without their parents' involvement the contract wasn't worth even one of those sixpenny stamps. They were present in the first two drafts but not in the third, Brian sabotaging a perfectly good document to give the Beatles an easy way out any time they wanted one.*

As far as John, Paul, George and Pete were concerned, however, they were appointing Brian as their manager for five years, until February 1967, via a contract that could be terminated by either side after one year by giving three months' notice. Paul then raised a late objection to Brian's commission rate. The typed contract stated 10 per cent, rising to 20 if their individual gross annual earnings exceeded £1500, and Paul would later recall how his objection was based on the old tactic of holding out for less no matter what was being asked. 'He asked for 20 per cent and I argued with him. I said, "Twenty, man? I thought managers only took 10 per cent." He said, "No, it's 20 these days." I said, "OK, maybe I'm not very modern."'[18]

It was a point on which Brian was prepared to concede. As signed, the contract has a penned amendment: 20 was crossed out and 15 written instead as the upper limit.

At 10 rising to 20 per cent this would already have been a generous contract; at 10 rising to 15 it was a steal for the Beatles, and they'd no idea how much. It was standard for artists to pay *two* sets of commission, having not only a management contract but, separately, an agency agreement; the managers took their cut for managing, agents took a further 10 per cent for fixing all the paid work. Brian was shooting to do both jobs, providing the Beatles with this ambitious, all-inclusive service for the single 10–15 per cent commission.

The risk was one-way. John, Paul and George had a record of being hard with

---

* Also gone from previous drafts was the clause that would have enabled Brian to split up the group into individual performers. This was never seen by the Beatles and its origin will probably always be obscure.

managers, but Brian – who'd never committed himself to anything for five years – went into the contract demonstrating his belief, investing his money and risking his family's good name ... as well as their wrath for pursuing this distraction from his full-time Nems responsibilities. If the Beatles turned out to be badly behaved, aggressive, unprofessional, not honouring the engagements he secured for them, turning up late or not at all, his reputation was at stake as well as his cash. But Brian believed in them, and knew they wouldn't let him down. More to the point, if any trouble came their way, he'd shield them from it.

Throughout the second half of 1961 the Beatles had held out, instinctively, for someone to represent them as they would have represented themselves, only with the right amount of flair and finesse necessary to open doors. They'd found their man. In Brian Epstein they had a manager who wouldn't buckle at the first misfortune, a manager who wouldn't kow-tow in a business meeting, but who had the belief, arrogance, perseverance and style to push the Beatles' cause, holding firm, but politely, for what they wanted and felt they deserved. They had a Liverpool man with Mayfair manners to give them the best of reputations in the business, and they had someone who would manage their lives and provide direction yet consult them over all the important decisions and not smother them, so they remained free to be themselves. They'd found a partner – or, as master of brevity John Lennon put it, 'one of us'.[19]

Just 10 per cent of their income – and surely soon 15 – got the Beatles all this. At the same time, the Beatles gave Brian his first outlet for genuine creative expression since 1957, when he'd returned unfulfilled from RADA and buried himself in the business of directing and managing shops. As George would reflect, 'We needed somebody to elevate us out of that cellar, and he needed somebody to get him out of the hole that he was in. It was mutually beneficial.'[20]

In January 1962, Brian Epstein opened up the Beatles' business on a number of fronts. There were many days when Beryl Adams typed as many letters for them as she did for her real employer, Nems Ltd. Brian instructed her to type BEATLES in upper case every time they were mentioned, so their name stood proud from the scores of documents that left Liverpool 1 and went all round the nation. Though Brian used Nems Ltd stationery in his dealings with record companies, most of the early correspondence in the Epstein-Beatles file is on his own personal octavo notepaper, the top of each sheet embossed with his monogrammed initials, B and E stylishly formed into an oval.

Using this stationery, Brian obtained and submitted an application for the Beatles to have an audition for BBC radio. As a commitment to public service broadcasting, the BBC gave free auditions to every applying actor or entertainer, and everyone but rank amateurs had the right to be seen, at the expense of studio time and producers' nerves. Applications from Liverpool were sent to Manchester, and – in the case of pop music – landed on the desk of Light Entertainment producer Peter Pilbeam. 'Most of the applications we received had abysmal handwriting,' he remembers, 'but Brian Epstein's was different.'[21] The typed form brimmed with crisp efficiency, and Brian submitted the document with promotional materials and the publicity photo. The BBC was well organised too – Pilbeam granted the Beatles an audition in Manchester on 8 February; pass this and they'd be given a national radio broadcast. It was as easy as that, though the Beatles had never done it for themselves.

Still, the everyday business of management was *the stage*. No 'pop stars' could live off broadcasting fees and only the very biggest of chart stars could live off record royalties, so minuscule were the percentages. No one even tried. The sole object of making records was to attract a bigger profile and so earn higher fees from concert and ballroom shows – and, if the artists were lucky to be chosen, to appear in summer seasons in seaside resorts. Brian's pledge to earn the Beatles more money from broader horizons was his greatest challenge.

Their hectic, frightening, unforgettable nights of playing for the youth of north and east Liverpool were over. It was a 1961 thing only. Anyone there who wanted to see the Beatles now had to hop on a bus and head for the Cavern. This was the one club Brian kept firmly in the Beatles' schedule – in fact, it became the Beatles' base in 1962. Though they could be seen at an ever-wider variety of venues, *the* place to catch them was in the fantastically hot, noisy, smelly, smoky cellar right under the metropolis. Brian formed a mutually respectful, give-and-take working relationship with both Bob Wooler and Ray McFall through which all their and the Beatles' needs were met. McFall knew times were changing when Brian invited him to lunch at his club, the Rembrandt, merely to show goodwill; no one else had ever done such a thing.[22]

From now on, the Beatles rarely saw cash for their night's work. The period of being paid in door money, collected by Pete then divvied up in the van, was over. They really were professional now – their money was taken by Brian or Neil, mostly as cheques, and each Beatle collected cash in a pay-packet from Beryl's office every Friday. Here again was Brian's skill as an administrator: every penny was accounted for in typed individual statements that deducted group expenses and his commission from 'group fees received' to make a total that was then divided equally by four; any individual expenses were then subtracted to leave each Beatle with a unique *Nett* total that matched the content of his pay-packet.

Despite the loss of old opportunities, Brian had the Beatles equalling and then exceeding their previous earnings within about three weeks. There was no more effective way of keeping them content in a period of such change. As George would recall, 'We got £25 a week when we were first with Brian Epstein, when we played the clubs. But £25 a week each was quite good. My dad earned £10 a week, so I was earning two-and-a-half times more than my father.'[23]

Among the Beatles, George paid the closest interest in Brian's way of doing business, setting in motion a reputation for being especially attentive about their money. In spite of later protestations of unfair branding – 'The press once had me as "The Business Beatle" because I asked Brian Epstein how much we got paid for one gig!' – it was George's mother who effectively fixed this reputation in print. Louise would recall how 'He was always very serious about his music, and the money. He always wanted to know how much they were getting.'[24]

A second sheet of typed paper, and often a third, would be attached by Beryl to the pay statements: Brian's list of their coming week's engagements by date and venue, along with any additional commentary or instruction to emphasise why a booking was important and worthy of their best efforts and *punctuality*. He also set out their playing time. Except at the Cavern, most of the Beatles' new engagements were fixed by a formal contract in which the duration of their performance was specified. This was business.

Brian preferred them to play sixty minutes but frequently agreed to two sets of forty-five. He told the Beatles they must have a *programme*, the night's music decided in advance, the right number of songs for the duration, paced for impact. They didn't need much telling. It is no coincidence that at least seven set-lists survive from 1962 in a Beatle's handwriting (mostly Paul's), whereas in the five years before this there are one and a half. It's also no surprise that the Beatles continued to play a different set in every lunchtime and evening performance, such was their astounding repertoire.

Neil was given maps and printed route instructions that enabled him to drive the van into uncharted areas, places where the Liverpool rock scene had barely infiltrated, if at all. The week the management contract came into force, when January slid into February, the Beatles played Monday night in a beach-side club in Southport, reaching a mostly untapped market in this north-west coastal resort; they played Thursday in a small dance hall in the Wirral town of West Kirby; and on the Friday they left the area altogether. It wasn't the *Liverpool Echo* that showed where the Beatles were playing this night, it was the *Manchester Evening News*. They were at the Oasis, the club's ad announcing FOR THE FIRST TIME IN MANCHESTER, POLYDOR'S GREAT RECORDING STARS.[25]

Brian was also booking them well into the future. They were fixed with Liverpool University to play all three Panto Week dances, a prestigious gig; and he arranged two nights where they could gain invaluable big-stage experience, at Floral Hall in Southport and at Liverpool's Pavilion Theatre, the renowned 'Pivvy'.

That particular opportunity was to happen on 2 April, and the Beatles were free then because the plan for them to play a season at Hamburg's Top Ten Club from the start of March fell through.

Peter Eckhorn was a young man in a hurry when, in mid-January, he phoned Brian to finalise terms for the Beatles' Top Ten return. Word had reached him of a coming rival, Manfred Weissleder – a tough man, with fortunes made from sex clubs – who was going to open a new rock venue slap on Grosse Freiheit. As usual, the instigator was Horst Fascher, the disqualified little boxer who just loved these crazy English rock and roll musicians and liked to shield them from St Pauli's violence by whatever force necessary. The new club would open in mid-April in a converted cinema, a big place with ideas and budgets to match. When Eckhorn found out Fascher was leaving for Liverpool, to sign up some groups and, particularly, to get the Beatles for the opening season, he phoned Brian and found the accord they'd been unable to reach at the end of December: the two men settled on a compromise DM450 a week ... but nothing was yet in writing.

Fascher arrived in Liverpool with his interpreter Roy Young, the singing pianist who was taking a few days off from Eckhorn's club – he was in the Top Ten house band with Tony Sheridan and Ringo Starr – so he could do business for his rival. It was, as usual, dog eat dog in St Pauli. Fascher and Young enjoyed a happy reunion with the Beatles, though were dismayed to hear that any discussion about Hamburg would have to be had with their *manager*. Brian Epstein and Peter Eckhorn had got along, but Horst Fascher was different meat. When Brian told him he'd verbally agreed a deal with Eckhorn, Fascher hinted that if this happened there wouldn't *be* a Top Ten Club.

The Beatles' Hamburg return was quickly agreed: they'd play for seven weeks, from 13 April to 31 May, keeping long hours in the club but working on stage a lot less because other acts would also be on the bill. They'd receive 2000 marks a week between the four of them – 500 for each Beatle before the subtraction at source of Brian's commission left them with 425. While the Top Ten made tax deductions, the new club wouldn't.*

To seal the deal, and do things the St Pauli way, Fascher pressed a new 1000-mark note into Brian's hand. There's no proof of what he did with it. Perhaps

---

* At now 11.2 Deutsche Marks to the pound, 2000 was approximately £179; 500 was £45; 425 was £38; 1000 was £89.

he shared it out among the group, or perhaps he used it to part-offset the out-of-pocket expenses he'd incurred since late November – he took no cut of the Beatles' money before February, saying their bookings were 'contracts from contracts', not of his making, even though this wasn't entirely true. Fascher has written that Brian 'put it in his pocket without a word – the Beatles never saw a penny of it. That's what Epstein was like,' but he doesn't say how he knows this or why he's so sure.[26]

John, Paul, George and Pete knew 'Eppy' wasn't managing them to make money. They hoped to become rich, and therefore he would too because he was part of the team, but they knew it wasn't his motivation. Being them, though, they still put him through the wringer and let him feel their personalities.

Brian was, for example, the first Jewish person central to their lives. None of the Beatles was anti-Semitic but they sometimes made anti-Semitic comments because, given the opportunity, people would. In Britain (as elsewhere), anti-Semitism was perennially there or thereabouts, rising or falling depending on external events but never not present – especially in strongly Catholic Liverpool.

Like so much else, Brian's views of religion were *shaped* by being with the Beatles. As he said in 1964, 'I am Orthodox by general Jewish standards. I went home for festivals and still do. Only when I met the Beatles did I realise where I stood. Like them I am a non-believer. The Beatles have crystallised each other's thoughts and mine. We seem to bring out the best in each other.'[27]

There's not much evidence, but it seems George had an uninformed ambivalence about Jews, one that went back to his primary school days, or earlier. It was not untypical. The standard slur that everyone knew (and most said) concerned 'Jews and money'.

A couple of episodes would be remembered within the group. One evening, while Brian drove George to a hall where the Beatles were playing, George enquired how much they'd be getting. When Brian told him, George replied that he should have held out for more. Sensitive to what George might have been thinking, and with his own shoulder-load of insecurities, Brian looked over at him and said, 'You mean Jew, you.' Paul also recalls having an anti-Semitic thought one night when they were out with Brian and one of his friends, Terry Doran, the car dealer with a wicked sense of humour. (As the Beatles got to know Brian so they also got to know friends like Doran and Peter Brown.) They were in a Liverpool pub called the Old Dive when an argument bubbled up over whose packet of cigarettes was on the table. They were Brian's, but Paul found something 'very Jewish' in the way he claimed them; he worried about whether he wanted this man as his manager ... and, as John would later point out, Paul actually didn't. He was still to be convinced that Eppy was the right man for the job.[28]

Fan club secretary Bobby Brown witnessed the Beatles' relationship with Brian throughout the year and heard only light-hearted jesting about his religion.

> They used to say 'Do you fancy a bacon buttie, Brian?' and Brian would blush and laugh. I thought they had a smashing relationship. They were always respectful of Brian. I wasn't in on their meetings but I never saw any evidence of friction. John would tease him, but John teased everybody; he'd always find something about you to tease. With Brian being Jewish, he'd say, 'What are you doing here, Brian? It's Saturday. You're not supposed to be doing anything.'[29]

There was always the other side of the coin, when John's humour turned and he would lash out. According to Pete (though no one else), there was an ugly incident during the Decca session, when Brian made a remark about something John was singing or playing, and he shouted back, 'You've got nothing to do with the music. You go back and count your money, you Jewish git.' Brian apparently seethed and blushed and left the room for twenty minutes. It would have been another of those heavy, awkward Beatle moments, when everyone looked at their feet and then carried on like nothing had happened.[30]

But it was also typical of John Lennon that he would lacerate with one breath and forget it the next, and still have a close rapport with that person. And in the Epstein-Beatles axis, the core, essential relationship was always that of Brian and John.

> I liked Brian and I had a very close relationship with him for years, because I'm not going to have some stranger running the scene. I also like to work with friends. I was the closest to Brian – as close as you can get to somebody who lives a sort of fag life and you don't know what they're doing on the side. But in the group I was closest to him, and I did like him – he had great qualities and he was good fun. He had a flair. He was a theatrical man rather than a businessman, so in that way I liked him.[31]

Brian realised that when a decision was needed, he had to get John on his side, because the others always looked to see which way he jumped. In the words of Les Chadwick, a Liverpool photographer who worked with the Beatles and Brian later in the year, 'If you wanted to go from A to B you had to tell John why, and that's what Brian did, very skilfully. The first person he spoke to was John, always, and once he had John on board the rest would follow.'[32]

Inevitably, John did to Brian what he'd sort of done with Bob Wooler and doubtless others – he used pills to 'get him talking', to have Prelly Conversations that went deeper. As he later revealed, 'I introduced him to pills ... to make him talk, to find out what he was like. I was pretty close to Brian because if somebody's going to manage me I want to know them inside out. And there was a period when he told me he was a fag and all that. I remember him saying, "Don't ever throw it back in me face, that I'm a fag." Which I didn't.'[33]

Paul had to accept John's closeness to Brian and that, once again, he was further down the pecking order than he wanted to be – not that he and John weren't themselves incredibly close. Paul believes John 'was wise to the possibility' of being the man to whom Brian turned first, and made sure to secure that position. 'Also,' he adds, 'I'm sure Brian was in love with John. We were all in love with John, but Brian was gay so that added an edge.'[34]

It was through John that Brian floated most of the changes he thought essential if the Beatles were to make it. Some battles he won, others he didn't; some the Beatles accepted easily, others not.

Brian failed to curb John's cripple act on stage. He pointed out that while plenty in the audience responded well to it, his actions also caused offence, even if just to one person.[35] John may have toned it down a degree but he didn't cut it out – crips were part of his personality and his personality was on the stage, always. Brian also failed to stop John's rampant chewing through every performance, though he did cut down.

He had more success in other avenues. He got the Beatles to quit onstage smoking and swearing (off stage, both remained rife) and to stop addressing comments to only the first few rows of an audience: Brian said this alienated everyone else, making people feel disappointed at missing out on something. He also asked them to stop gulping down food during Cavern lunchtime sessions. As John would remember, 'Epstein said, "Look, if you really want to get into bigger places you have to stop eating on stage, stop swearing, stop smoking." It was a choice of *making it* or still eating chicken on stage ...'[36]

They stopped.

Clause 2(b) in the contract allowed Brian the right to advise the Beatles on their music. He didn't, at least not in relation to songs and how they were played: John apparently made it clear at Decca, and perhaps on other occasions, that his opinion wasn't welcome. In general terms, however, two alterations to the constitution of the Beatles' music were made in these opening weeks of his management, and this may not have been coincidental. Not only did they first brave playing Lennon-McCartney numbers as soon as Brian came along, but, in January, George was promoted to equal singing status, handling as many songs as John and Paul. This can only have happened if they all agreed to it, but Brian was constantly reaffirming their push for a *group* image – something else that marked them out as different. Surviving 1962 set-lists confirm a structure unknown in 1961: John, Paul and George worked in strict rotation as lead vocalist.

Brian didn't try to change everything. In fact, in his mind, this wasn't even the right word for it. 'I didn't *change* them,' he would maintain, 'I just projected what was there.'[37] He recognised the appeal of John, Paul and George's continental-style hair and worked only to improve it, getting them to have it cut in a way that emphasised it. Fastidious about his own hair, Brian had a man he went to maybe three times a week, to have it tidied, and now his stylist became the Beatles'. Jim Cannon, born in 1920, was one of six white-coated hairdressers employed in the basement salon within the tailoring shop Horne Bros, on Lord Street in the centre of Liverpool. The Beatles didn't like having haircuts – George especially hated it – but, for two heady years until the start of 1964, Cannon kept them all in trim. Because their hair fell into a fringe, and almost everyone else (like Pete) swept it up off the forehead, people said they had long hair when really they didn't.[38]

It was at this time that Bill Harry had a visit from John, asking for the return of some photos he'd previously handed over – like the ones of him standing on Grosse Freiheit in his underpants. John had thought Bill might want to publish them in *Mersey Beat* but Bill evidently steered clear: they'd have been out of place on his pages and out of step with the times – such photos simply weren't published in this period. Brian had no doubt impressed on John that it would be better if they were removed from the hands of a newspaper editor, and, though he could have said *fuck off* – as he frequently did to Brian, the other Beatles and everyone except Mimi – John saw the sense of it and retrieved them. As he said five years later, 'We've always been in control of what we're doing ... [but] Brian was a natural guide.'[39]

Another battle won – but not unanimously, it seems – was getting the Beatles to bow on stage. This was phased in over several weeks in early 1962. In a later age, bowing would seem deeply anachronistic, but it was established procedure for all performers, and looked good. Cliff Richard and the Shadows played a chaotic show at Liverpool Empire on Sunday 21 January and Brian got the Beatles first-house tickets. Cliff and his group bowed after every number to a mass of screaming girls, while the Beatles were no doubt cracking untold numbers of sarcastic remarks ... though noticing its effect. Brian took them to the stage door afterwards and asked if they could talk to the Shadows, and at least one of them (drummer Brian Bennett) came out to say hello.

George, who seems to have been the most entrenched in his dislike of Cliff and his group, was unhappy at the prospect of bowing on stage – he saw it as 'a showbiz thing' – but he was persuaded.[40] They all did it, inevitably imbuing their Beatle bows with a dose of *Beatle personality*. Paul certainly saw its merit: 'I was a great believer in that. Brian's RADA experience came into play a little bit there and I would tend to agree with some of his stagey ideas. I don't think any of us had a problem with that, or else one of us wouldn't have done it. We actually used to count the bow . . . we'd do this big uniform bow all at once.'[41]

Brian's mission in this crucial first stage of Beatles management was to ensure that the people they needed to impress didn't recoil from their appearance or habits. They might be able to do anything once they were accepted, but to begin with they had to get through the door. It was no more complicated than that. And of all the suggestions Brian made, those rejected and those accepted, none had a greater impact than his views about their stage outfits. He told the Beatles a truth, which was that while he saw a fantastic future for them – *bigger than Elvis*, no less – they wouldn't get off the starting blocks unless they smartened up. He had no more wish than they to look square, but they did need to look *sharper*.

Brian certainly had nothing against the leather – he fell in love with them dressed that way and was still keenly promoting them with that image – but it was obvious they'd never get on *radio* dressed like that, let alone TV; and that theatres wouldn't book them dressed like that, so they'd get no tours; and that they could even be denied the chance to make a record. The Beatles wanted all these things, so to hold out against change was self-defeating.

They had anyway begun to work it out for themselves. As John would recall, wearing leathers 'was all right in Liverpool and around there but as soon as we went anywhere else they didn't want to know'. They were in leather for that first out-of-town date in Manchester, which seems to have stupefied the audience; and when, on 24 February, they played for the first and only time in Hoylake (Cynthia's home town), the audience laughed and jeered them for looking so slovenly.[42] This was, then, a look they were ready to drop, as Paul would recall eighteen months later in a BBC-tv documentary that centred on them: 'It was a bit old-hat anyway, all wearing leather gear. And we decided we didn't want to look ridiculous because, more often than not, too many people would laugh. It was just stupid, and we didn't wanna appear as a gang of idiots. We just got rid of the leather gear.'[43]

The change was gradual and, Brian said, not entirely of his making. 'I would say it was due to the five of us rather than to me. I encouraged them at first to get out of leather jackets, and I wouldn't *allow* them to appear in jeans after a short time, and then after that step I got them to wear sweaters on stage – and then, *very* reluctantly, eventually, suits.'[44]

*

Suits. Should the Beatles have *sold out* and worn suits, or should they have stayed in their leather and been *true to themselves?* John most pointedly raised the issue. 'Brian put us in suits and all that, and we made it very, very big – but we sold out,' he exclaimed in the midst of a wider rant in 1970. His words appear irrefutable, though his concluding remark was formed from an accumulation of emotive factors, not just the suits.[45]

But *sold out?* Hindsight's perfect vision is seldom clouded by context, and the question is largely meaningless anyway, on the basis that if they'd stayed in leather they wouldn't have become anyone's topic of conversation. After this, the Beatles should be the judges of their situation … and, despite John's comments in 1970–1, it seems they not only went into suits, they went *eagerly* into suits. Brian used the term 'very reluctantly', but it's unclear where this reluctance lived.

> John: Epstein said, 'Look, if you wear a suit you'll get this much money.' All right I'll wear a suit – I'll wear a fucking *balloon* if somebody's going to pay me! I'm not in love with the leather *that* much.
>
> Everybody wanted a good suit – a nice, sharp, black suit. We liked the leather and the jeans but we wanted a good suit, even to wear off-stage. We allowed Epstein to package us, it wasn't the other way around.[46]

> Paul: He [Brian] quite wisely said, 'If I get a huge offer, they won't take you in leather,' and I didn't think it was a bad idea because it fitted with my 'Gateshead group philosophy', that you should look similar. And because we got mohair suits it was a bit like the black acts.
>
> I was attached to the leather as much as anyone, but it was time to change to the mohair suits. It wasn't just me – we all loved those suits.[47]

> George: I didn't really see it as selling out. I just saw it as playing a game: if it takes suits to get us on the television, and if we need to be on television to be able to promote ourselves, then we will put on suits. We would wear fancy dress, whatever it took to get the gigs. The only thing we didn't like about the suits was [that it was like] Cliff and the Shadows.[48]

There were suits and there were suits. Rory Storm did his thing in vivid turquoise and his Hurricanes flaming red, Gerry and the Pacemakers had their royal blue blazers with a G/P crest and gold buttons, Faron's Flamingos had royal blue velvet jackets with black corduroy trousers, the Undertakers dressed in funereal suits and top hats, black and heavy. The Beatles, as usual, went the other way. They decided to make their suits *cool.* These were tailored creations, and they demanded – and had – a voice in their design. The afternoon of Monday 29 January, Brian took them all over the water to Birkenhead, to the establishment of master craftsman Beno Dorn, where they were attended by senior tailor Walter Smith.

> We were the best tailors in the north-west – we had cloths other tailors hadn't even seen, and we had exclusive rights on several brands. This brought in a very good clientele and Brian Epstein was a regular customer, as was his brother Clive. One week Brian said to me, 'I'm going to bring you four lads in next week, musicians. I'm managing them.' He said they were called the Beatles which I thought was a damn stupid name, associating them with the insect. But we had girls working upstairs and they said the Beatles were *fab*.[49]

The Beatles hadn't done this before, so it was great fun; there was much riffling through racks and raising of voices as they considered cloths and styles. Smith remembers them having 'very strong views about the kind of suits they wanted – in fact, they were very lively lads all round, and their swearing was appalling. I had to remind them they were in a tailor's shop and should moderate their language.'

They finally settled on a dark-blue mohair, single-breasted, three-button suit with especially narrow lapels. The cloth wasn't plain but had a little weave, and the general look was Italian – progressively becoming Mod fashion in London but cutting-edge for Liverpool in 1962. As Walter Smith recalls, 'They insisted the lapels had to be narrow and they wanted their trousers *extremely* narrow – we reduced and reduced the legs about three times before we got them the way they wanted.' Older men still wore turn-ups but the Beatles' suit trousers went straight down to the Cuban-heel Spanish flamenco boots that now became even more integral to their appearance.

'The price was twenty-eight guineas but we ended up charging twenty-three,' says Smith. 'Brian was telling us the Beatles would be big and we'd get more orders when that happened.' The bill then went higher because they also ordered matching white shirts, cuff-links, slim black ties and collar pins. Each Beatle was expected to pay for his own outfit, putting down a deposit to show good faith; the balance would be invoiced to Brian Epstein (and then deducted) when the finished articles were ready for collection – though, because of all the alterations, this would take longer than expected. In the meantime, they continued to perform in their leathers or, for certain shows, leather jackets or jumpers and ordinary trousers. By the time the suits were finished, they were ready for them.

*

The Saturday before this Monday tailoring appointment, *Liverpool Echo*'s Disker had again written about the Beatles. Tony Barrow's day job at Decca gave him the inside scoop on A&R deliberations, and the word he heard was that everything looked positive there for the Beatles. On top of this, the BBC audition was coming up, and the university triple engagement, and so much else. Everything looked rosy. When Brian was invited to lunch at Decca, he boarded the overnight London train with only one expectation, that he would be returning to Liverpool with a contract.

But he didn't, because Decca had chosen to turn the Beatles down.

25

'A tendency to play music'
(6 February–8 March 1962)

Two months after Brian Epstein first told Decca about the Beatles, he was back in the same executive dining room on the Thames south bank. If his account of events is true – and this cannot be said with certainty – the bad news came with coffee.

With him, probably, were the head of A&R Dick Rowe and sales manager Steve Beecher-Stevens with one of his assistants, Arthur Kelland. The presence of sales staff, and the executive lunch, reflects Decca's awareness that Nems was an important company client; they didn't want Epstein's group but they valued the business he put their way.

Two years later, in his autobiography, Brian quoted Rowe saying, 'Not to mince words, Mr Epstein, we don't like your boys' sound. Groups of guitarists are on their way out.'[1] Rowe always denied being at any such lunch and saying those words – understandably, given every subsequent event and his continuing role in signing artists and making records. And perhaps he wasn't and didn't, for not only was it a terrible prediction, guitar groups had never been *in*. The Shadows were the only British band of significance, but vocal-instrumental groups, beat groups, didn't appeal to record companies and the public at large didn't even know they existed.

What seems certain is that any Rowe forecast was based not on British trends but American. The Beatles decision followed hard on the heels of his fact-finding mission to New York, a twelve-day trip to see where the music was heading, and the *Billboard* Hot 100 current during his visit had no noticeable use of electric guitars at all and nothing even vaguely like the Beatles' self-contained sound of three vocals, three guitars and drums. It was a chart dominated by solo acts ... and one record flying the flag for Britain: George Martin's production of *My Boomerang Won't Come Back*, which went on to reach 21.

Brian was cut to the quick by Decca's decision. The Beatles were his obsession, and getting them a recording contract was the single most important thing in his life at this moment, and perhaps ever. He flourished at them a copy of *Mersey Beat* – the one headlined BEATLES TOP POLL! – and told Rowe and his colleagues what they'd be missing. 'You must be out of your mind. These boys are going to explode. I am confident that one day they will be bigger than Elvis Presley.'

Elvis was unassailable. The Decca men knew this better than anyone in Britain – and, according to Brian's autobiography, they said to him, patronisingly, 'The boys [Beatles] won't go, Mr Epstein. We know these things. You have a good record business in Liverpool. Stick to that.'[2]

Whatever was said, it was strange that Decca's Beatles rejection came at the precise time the company was blowing trumpets about its A&R department's 'dynamic new policy' and focused pro-British approach. The current (3 February) issue of *Disc* – perhaps carried and read on the London train by Brian – included an interview with Rowe headlined DECCA GET READY FOR BIG POP DRIVE. Among many interesting comments, Rowe explained how he (and thereby Decca, with a 40 per cent market share of the British record business) analysed the singles market three years into the Sixties:

> I think there are about five separate markets for discs. We talk about teenagers but even that section is divided into three.
>
> Those between twelve and fourteen are not romantically inclined, and like the thumping rock style best.
>
> Those between fourteen and eighteen are romantically minded and enjoy the ballad style of people like Presley and Cliff Richard.
>
> Those between eighteen and twenty-two go for artists like Sinatra, and people older than that have other tastes.

Rowe also told *Disc*'s Nigel Hunter how his A&R team was working unhampered by directives from on high or by budget limitations; he said his colleagues were free to follow their ideas with artists and material without reference to him. But he very much interfered in the decision of his A&R junior Mike Smith. The man who'd twice seen the Beatles had also auditioned another vocal-instrumental group, Brian Poole and the Tremilos. Smith says (and his colleagues support him on this) that he wanted to offer Decca contracts to *both* groups but Rowe said he could have only one and must choose between them. 'I took the band that had been better in the studio – it was the only measure

I had,' Smith says, though this isn't quite true because he'd also seen the Beatles live, amid the hot excitement of the Cavern.[3] But certain facts spoke for themselves. Poole and his group were so much more *tidy* than the Beatles – they'd played American air bases and a 1961 Butlin's summer season and made two hallowed *Saturday Club* radio broadcasts; they had smart suits, Mayfair management, were paid-up members of the Musicians' Union, and claimed to own £2500 worth of musical equipment. When *they* went into Decca they were allowed to use their own amps.

There were also geographical factors. Smith planned to put his signed group to regular use, not just in making their own records but contributing to other sessions as backing singers and musicians. This was unworkable with a band two hundred miles away in Liverpool, but Poole and the Tremilos lived around the corner from Smith, in Barking, on the eastern fringe of London. They were friends and saw one another socially – Smith says that after they'd signed Decca's contract they came round to his mum's house for Sunday tea . . . and there was also a comical, extra connection: both Poole and Smith wore heavy black horn-rim glasses (like Buddy Holly and Hank Marvin) and it was their optician who'd brought them together. It made a good press story – and was used as one.

For a multitude of reasons, then, when Rowe forced Smith to decide between the Beatles and the Tremilos, there was only going to be one winner.[4]

Almost certainly, Brian Epstein knew none of this. He was still at lunch, devastated, smarting, but fighting his corner. He pushed so hard that Rowe looked for a possible compromise. He suggested Brian speak to the new star name in Decca A&R, ex-Shadows drummer Tony Meehan, about producing the Beatles by private arrangement. For a fee approaching £100, Meehan would make their record and Decca would put it out. Rowe's own quoted analysis had the Beatles down, at most, as something for 12- to 14-year-olds, so Meehan, all of 18, had what Rowe called 'first-hand experience of what the teenagers want'.[5]

Brian was tempted and insulted by turn, but it was *some* kind of concession. Rowe said Meehan would be in the West Hampstead studio the next day, and offered to make the introductions. It meant Brian staying in London another night, which would greatly irritate his father.

And so the tale of 'Decca turning down the Beatles' gathers yet another layer of complexity.

Meehan's recollection of events was straightforward enough – there he was at 18, trying to handle an orchestral session, when Dick Rowe walked into the control room and interrupted.

He said, 'There's a chap here I'd like you to meet. I know you're busy but can you fit him in? He's a very, very interesting man and he's got another one of these groups.' That's exactly what he said, 'another one of these groups'. Dick seemed more interested in Brian Epstein than the Beatles, for some strange reason.

I just said, as any professional person would do in the middle of their work, 'Look, I'm busy, contact me later and I'll be available.' That's all that happened. Dick never told me anything about them, and I never discussed them with Brian.[6]

Brian's own account had it that he and Meehan *did* discuss the Beatles, and the young producer was brisk: 'Mr Rowe and I are very busy men . . . phone my secretary and make sure that when you want the session I am available.' A letter written by Brian at the end of this week may indicate that he left Decca this day saying yes, he was prepared to pay close on £100 to finance the Beatles' first real record.[7]

There *could* be more to it than this – but (almost inevitably) all the accounts conflict. Paul McCartney would remember Meehan being in the studio with them on New Year's Day, though they didn't meet him, and he says the subsequent bargaining confirmed for him some previously half-heard tales of sordid show-business life in London.[8]

George would always bitterly resent the way the Beatles were treated by Decca. While he spoke often and with pleasure about how cocky he, John and Paul were, no matter their youth and inexperience, he held a grudge against Meehan for being arrogant and young. (Despite all he'd achieved in the Shadows, Meehan was five days younger than George, born in March 1943.) 'Tony Meehan was *really* cocky,' George would say. 'He was the star and he decided he could choose who would be on the label or not . . . and he was this kid!' George's bitterness about Meehan, unshakeable even in the face of enlightening evidence, would one day be manifested when he had the chance to tell Meehan, and at some length, *just* what he thought of him.[9]

John more or less agreed with Paul. Thirteen years after the event, he spoke in some detail, and with certainty, that it was Meehan who made the thirty-five-minute tape that has gone down as the Beatles' Decca test: 'Tony Meehan was a producer and we paid £15 or something to make the tape. We made it in a Decca studio but it was an independent production.'[10]

In the end, by definition, Decca didn't turn down the Beatles. Brian Epstein rejected Decca. Back in his office on 10 February (*What are you doing here, Brian? It's Saturday. You're not supposed to be doing anything*) he dictated a letter to Dick Rowe, copied to Beecher-Stevens and Kelland, in which he expressed thanks for Rowe's 'kind offer of co-operation in assisting me to put the Beatles on records', but then stated, 'Whilst I appreciate the offer of Mr Meehan's services I have now decided not to accept.' He concluded with a bluff designed to make Decca regret everything: 'The principal reason for this change of mind is that since I saw you last the Group have received an offer of a recording Contract from another Company.' Had they heck.

The bottom line seems to have been that Brian couldn't accept the Beatles' records being made by someone who didn't appreciate them and was doing it only for the money. In a perfect world they would come under the wing of a man who, like him, could see their potential and was interested in adding his talents to theirs. He also didn't agree with the idea of being forced into paying for the chance to be commercially creative. Other managers might have been prepared to accept Decca's crumbs, but Brian didn't, because it wasn't right.

Brian walked away from the Decca experience with the bitter taste of rejection ... but, preciously, a spool of tape comprising some or all of the fifteen recorded songs. Such a goodwill gesture wasn't normal practice but, says Mike Smith, 'who ever knew what Dick Rowe got up to?' Life carried on and Decca management had no cause yet to dwell on events. But it wasn't long before they realised with horror that not only had they missed out on the Beatles in Britain, their US subsidiary London Records had lost the Beatles for America, Decca's other companies had lost them around the world, and their in-house publishing company Burlington Music had probably missed out on Lennon-McCartney's songs.

Stupidity had ruled, as it did at most record companies. If Brian Epstein was such an important company customer to warrant Decca twice seeing his group (and this was always suggested as the reason the Beatles were considered in the first place), what purpose was being served by rejecting them? And what anyway was the block that stopped Decca giving them something for nothing? Almost no one was given an advance or signing-on fee, and Brian would have accepted the offered contract, the industry-standard one-penny royalty on 85 per cent of records sold, payable in arrears. It also can't have been because of costs, since Decca's recording, pressing and distribution were all self-owned, the charges internal and not even computed. Naturally, Decca couldn't sign everyone (not even at the outset of their heralded backing-British campaign), but if they rejected the Beatles because their records might not sell, here was a manager whose shop would order enough copies to give them an instant profit.

Logic also cannot explain why Decca rejected a group who'd won a newspaper popularity poll, had a fan club and were the biggest band in Liverpool and Hamburg, playing 350 bookings a year, sometimes to as many as three thousand people a night, but then signed and issued records by several semi-professional, non-performing nonentities during 1962, one of whom they promoted as a singing decorator. And . . . Decca spent more money treating Brian Epstein to lunch to tell him they weren't signing the Beatles than it would have cost to sign them. As Tony Meehan summed up, speaking from long experience in the business, 'It was just a complete mess, as things generally are – a dreadful corporate blunder.'[11]

John, Paul and George were shocked, stunned, by Decca's rejection. They'd had no real setback in eighteen months, since they first went to Hamburg, and, such was their self-belief, they weren't expecting one. This was a low point, the lowest they'd known – and how ironic that 'toppermost of the poppermost', the cynical call-and-response chant that rallied them at such moments, was a Dick Rowe catchphrase and they didn't realise it.

Paul has said how they thought the rejection 'was really very short-sighted . . . I think it just heightened our determination', but John marked it differently. He knew the Beatles had under-performed on the day, and he also wondered if they'd shot their bolt. Both of Britain's two great record companies, EMI and Decca, had slammed the door on them. 'We really thought "that was it", that was the end. They always said it was too bluesy or too rocky. "Too much rock 'n' roll and that's all over now," they used to keep telling us.'[12]

It was a tough one to swallow. Rock was what they did, what they loved, what they believed in; being refused a contract was bad enough but it was a double-blow to also realise that the people who decided these things were against what they did. This was the wall they had to vault, and it wasn't obvious how they could.

John was also gloomy about being *too old*, because stars were made young. As Tony Meehan was five days George Harrison's junior (but already in the second phase of his career) so Cliff Richard, at 21, was five days younger than John Lennon and had been famous almost four years. As John would recall, 'I was thinking "I'm too old. I've missed the boat. You've got to be *seventeen*." A lot of stars were kids, much younger than I was.'[13]

Pete Best had no opinion on the Decca rejection, because John, Paul and George decided not to tell him. Having already waited close on six weeks before getting the verdict, they just told Pete, whenever he asked, that they were still waiting. Their purpose in doing this has never been revealed, but clearly *something* was in their minds. Whatever the actual reason, or reasons, it's plain that the three-and-one rift within the Beatles was becoming wider than ever, that conversations were being had by John, Paul and George that ended when Pete walked in the room.

They could, at least, get on the BBC. During the evening of 8 February, the day Brian returned from his meetings at Decca, the Beatles were in Manchester for a second time in six days. Their destination now was the Playhouse Theatre in the southern suburb of Hulme, where they auditioned for radio producer Peter Pilbeam. At 33, Pilbeam wasn't enamoured of rock either (he preferred big band), but the job had befallen him to audition groups and he was up for the challenge. 'Lumbered was usually the word,' he says. 'With some of the groups, where noise could replace musical values, it did – I used to get home semi-deafened. Most groups also did lots of hip thrusts and gyrations you wouldn't see on the radio, but there was a lot of talent too – there always has been in the north.'[14]

Brian had suggested Pilbeam hear three of the Beatles sing, but, on the night, only John and Paul were vocal and Pilbeam assessed them separately. They had a half-hour slot in which to tune up and allow the studio manager (engineer) to get a good sound balance on his tape, then they played four numbers.* These were all songs done at Decca the month before – Like Dreamers Do, Till There Was You, Memphis, Tennessee and Hello Little Girl – and Paul was again not at his best, probably suffering from the nerves that seemed to strike him on testing occasions. Pilbeam marked him down as NO but gave a YES to John. He also noted a 'good solid backing' on Memphis, that John and Paul sang Hello Little Girl as a duet, and that (unusually for the period) the Beatles didn't play him any instrumentals. All this was written on the blank back page of Brian's typed application, and Pilbeam concluded with a summary he remembers as defining 'high praise': 'An unusual group, not as "Rocky" as most, more C&W, with a tendency to play music. YES.'

Where Decca had kept the Beatles in suspense almost six weeks, Pilbeam was quick to offer them a session on national radio. The date was fixed by phone with Brian inside the next forty-eight hours and a BBC contract was sent to Liverpool shortly after: the Beatles would record in front of an audience back in the same theatre, the Playhouse, on 7 March, for a programme to be broadcast the following afternoon in the Light Programme. Here was instant success . . . and the prospect of catching the ear of at least two million listeners.

While George didn't get to sing for the BBC, he did have most of the new numbers in the live set, which brought him parity with John and Paul as vocalists. The choice of songs demonstrated again the Beatles' refined/unusual musical tastes. Their ears always pricked at an interesting melody, no matter its

---

* Audition tapes weren't kept, and this recording is certainly lost.

age or genre: if it was good, they noticed it, and influences came just as easily from the BBC Light Programme as the Nems browseries. Two of George's new songs at the start of 1962 were Dream, written in 1944 by Johnny Mercer, and Blue Skies, written in 1926 by Irving Berlin. Dream is intriguing because it could be the only example of the Beatles taking a song from Cliff Richard . . . and it's also one of the two numbers the Beatles can be *seen* singing and playing in their earliest-known film. Around thirty seconds of 8mm home-movie footage was shot – in colour, but without sound – at one of their shows in February 1962. Precise date/place identification remains elusive but the songs (discernible through close study) indicate it was at this time, and the Beatles were still performing in leathers and black T-shirts, the suits not yet ready. Only the front line is visible; John and Paul play while George sings Dream, although Paul's bass work is so animated that he attracts the eye. In the second number, George and John sing the backing (and John chews constantly, which would have wound up Brian if he was there) while Paul sings Gene Vincent's Dance In The Street . . . or, more likely, the Beatles' short-lived contemporary adaptation, Twist In The Street.[15]

The Twist couldn't be ignored. It was *the* dance of the period and the Beatles' primary role was still to play for dancing. They especially needed Twist numbers when they worked at new venues, where a good part of their set had to be songs in vogue. Twist In The Street was one of three Twist songs the Beatles did – and both the others were unusual. Pete had sung with the Beatles in times past – Matchbox, then Wild In The Country – but he'd been silent for a while before Brian (under pressure from Mona Best to give Pete microphone time) proposed his singing spot be reinstated and the others went along with it.[16] His new number was Peppermint Twist, theme song of the worldwide Twist HQ, the Peppermint Lounge night-club in New York City. Pete came out front to sing it and do a little dance while Paul relished a few minutes behind the drums and George picked up Paul's left-handed bass and tried to find the notes as a right-hander. It was a cabaret moment.

The Twist also provided the inspiration for Paul to write a song – his first since 1960 or 1959. This breakthrough came with no apparent involvement from John. Paul would recall writing it so that the Beatles had its exclusive use, solving the perennial problem in Liverpool of many groups drawing from the same musical well. Pinwheel Twist wasn't recorded, didn't spend long in the Beatles' set, and not everyone would recall it with fondness. Neil Aspinall said it was 'a fucking awful song – it had a waltz middle-eight when the song suddenly *dragged*. It really didn't work. I hated it.'[17]

Along with the vintage numbers and transitory songs, this period at the start of 1962 marked yet another important shift in the Beatles' chosen music. Ever receptive to the latest sounds, eager to adapt to changes, they enthused for the new – and there was one casualty in particular, a man whose culling would once have been heresy.

Elvis would always be their God – the 1956–8 Elvis – but the Beatles couldn't swallow his Hollywood sugar any more. The lead single from his latest film *Blue Hawaii* – Rock-A-Hula Baby c/w Can't Help Falling In Love – was a 45 of note in that the Beatles *didn't* perform it. Not that they routinely sang all of Elvis's records (they'd ignored several), but they never performed any new Elvis material again. Anything of his they played now was an *oldie*, often announced as such – and, as usual, they were of one mind about the rightness of their thinking. 'I went off Elvis after he left the army,' Paul said. 'I felt they tamed him too much. It was all wrong, *GI Blues* and *Blue Hawaii*.' John, who wore an Elvis badge (button) on occasion through the rest of his life, remarked, 'They cut his bollocks off in the army. They not only shaved his hair off, I think they shaved between his legs too … The rest of it was just a living death.'[18]

The new messiah was Luther Dixon, the producer behind the Shirelles' sound. John sang Will You Love Me Tomorrow and Boys, Paul did Mama Said, and now John grabbed their latest release, Baby It's You, out on EMI's Top Rank label at the beginning of February. It wasn't written by Goffin-King but was in their style, being a modern girl-boy love song wrapped in a sparse, quirky, jerky beat. The songwriting credit was Bacharach-David-Williams: music by Burt Bacharach, who also arranged it, lyric by Mack David (older brother of Burt's usual lyricist Hal) and, masquerading as Barney Williams, Luther Dixon. It was the sound of New York 1962 and that vital immigrant mix, black singers and producer with Jewish songwriters and record company.

So attuned were John, Paul and George to this sound that they even picked up on something unexpected: a British song and recording which resembled Goffin-King. Jackie Lee & the Raindrops' There's No One In The Whole Wide World was New Bond Street, not New York – it was recorded in London for the British qualifying heat of the Eurovision Song Contest, where it flopped dismally. A second English song the Beatles added at this time was What A Crazy World We're Living In, a cockney comedy piece by chirpy Joe Brown and the Bruvvers, written by a young Londoner named Alan Klein. George sang this, and he also picked Open (Your Lovin' Arms), a bouncy pop song by the Texas country singer Buddy Knox. The Beatles claimed this before anyone else in Liverpool, and they earned bragging rights to Roy Orbison's new single Dream Baby by doing it better than anyone else. As the Searchers' drummer Chris Curtis would remember, 'There were so many groups living in each other's pockets when it came to songs that the first week Roy Orbison came out with

Dream Baby *everyone* did it. Paul McCartney was the best, he was up for it, he was really right for the song.'[19]

And last, though really first, the Beatles' most extraordinary new song was If You Gotta Make A Fool Of Somebody, by James Ray – first heard by Paul one afternoon in the original city-centre Nems, the smaller one on Great Charlotte Street. It was, he says with evident enthusiasm, 'the first time we ever heard *waltz* done in R&B!'[20] This one had the lot – it was rhythmic and bluesy with the wow combination of tuba and wailing harmonica, plus it had stirring lead and harmony vocals, was done in 3/4 time and checked out inside two minutes. James Ray – a name not known to them, with no image either – was instantly a hero, as was the source of his magical sound, the also unheard-of New York independent label Caprice. Everything about this 45 was dark, even the deep turquoise and gold-lettered Pye International label, and Paul spoke for all the Beatles when he said such records represented 'exciting little black moments for us'.[21] They absorbed every nuance of both sides, and particularly liked the B-side's title, It's Been A Drag – a useful new American meaning for an old English word.

Stuart Sutcliffe was back in Liverpool for a few days around the third week of February. He'd not been home since August, when he'd returned for some hospital tests; now he was back to visit his mother who'd just had an operation. But while she was on the mend, he wasn't.

Stuart's recent letters home told of continuing strong headaches, and an 'evil temper' that was upsetting Astrid. He ascribed this to his family's characteristic, but clearly his mental state was being aggravated by acute pain. The letters didn't only spell out a portrait of ill health, they showed it: his spelling had become erratic, some sentences were vague, and his handwriting – previously a handsome script – was sinking into scribble. Towards the end of January, Stuart had suffered a convulsive fit and was signed off college for at least three weeks. No doctor, not even a senior specialist, could find the cause. He stayed home with Nielsa and Astrid, he wrote long letters to John, he painted like a man possessed – canvas after canvas of a truly fantastic intensity – and, surprisingly, he borrowed a bass guitar and played a few dates with a Hamburg group called the Bats.[22] Then he made his trip back to Liverpool . . . alone. Astrid knew she wouldn't be welcomed by mother Millie.

The Beatles were shocked by Stuart's condition. He went to see them in the Cavern and socialised with them at least a couple of times. He had a warmly pleasant time at George's house in Speke; he told John he'd thought of jumping out the window, causing John to worry his friend was going mad; he told Mike McCartney he felt something bad would happen when he went back to Hamburg, and Mike realised Stuart 'was obviously worried and nervous'; and when he said goodbye to Pete at the end of his visit he said, 'This'll be the last time I see you.'[23]

Allan Williams had a strange evening with Stuart and some or all of the Beatles at a bowling alley. Ten-pin bowling was the big new American craze sweeping Britain in 1961–2 and all the groups frequented the Liverpool lanes because the place sold booze and stayed open until 4AM. The Beatles often went, and this time they took Stu, with Williams joining them. It was the first time they'd seen their former manager since he'd started legal proceedings against them the previous summer, though that had fizzled out and was beginning to be forgotten. He took one look at his close friend Stuart and said, 'Christ, you look really ill.' 'He looked like death,' Allan remembers. 'He had a death pallor.'[24]

From the Beatles' old manager to the new: Stuart also met Brian for the first time. Little of this is known for certain – it's said they had dinner, which is credible, but subsequent claims that Brian so enjoyed Stuart's company he offered him a percentage of the Beatles' management, perhaps in consideration for Stuart becoming the Beatles' 'art director', are unproven and less believable. Stuart wasn't hanging around in Liverpool – he was going back to Hamburg to regain his health, paint, hopefully resume his studies and be married to Astrid by the start of the summer.

When Brian Epstein first considered managing the Beatles he assured his parents – his infuriated father especially – it would distract him from Nems no more than two half-days a week. In his mind, since he saw the Beatles being the greatest stars ever, and was even thinking *America*, this statement was merely a sop to get them off his back. Just weeks into taking on the task, Beatles management had become a second full-time job. As well as running the family stores and their staff, and being the director of a company with multiple operations, Brian was pounding the London pavements one or two days a week and running around Liverpool trying to make things happen. This seriously tested the support of Queenie and Clive and the patience of Harry, who had every right to tell Brian – and certainly did – he was neglecting his responsibilities. They could see he'd become caught up in something, but still he had *duties*. And because Brian couldn't abide being second best at anything, he was burning the candle at both ends, every working week. Something, inevitably, was heading for meltdown.

At the same time he was racking up out-of-pocket expenses – headlined by travel bills, hotel bills, entertainment bills and legal bills – that so outstripped his weekly Beatles commission of about £22 he had to fund the difference from his wallet. He was, in every sense, investing in a group of mentally tough rock and roll boys who, when he hurried to spend time with them, teased him, tested him, popped pills in his drink, and didn't rush to say thank you.

By mid-February, Brian's plans were plotted and progressive. The Beatles were about to play their three important dates for Liverpool University, and on the 20th they were booked into Floral Hall, Southport, a 1200-capacity ballroom. Brian had designated this a flagship night not only for the Beatles but for his own ambitions. His personal scope was broadening at the same pace as everything else: he wanted to put on shows like this himself and needed to observe how it was done, so he got Ric Dixon of the Dixon Agency (and Manchester's Oasis Club) to promote it and let him enjoy a close involvement. 'I sometimes had the impression Brian was trying to find out, through me, the bits he didn't know,' Dixon recalls. 'Concert promotion is a money-motivated business but I never felt money was Brian's motivation – living his dream was more important to him. He was the exception, and not the kind of man you expected to be involved in the music business, which was mostly full of sharp and untrustworthy operators.'[25]

The Floral Hall night was key to the future life of Brian *the promoter*. By mounting his own shows he could try out ideas for presentation and staging, controlling the environment to achieve maximum effectiveness for the acts. And some of these would be under his sole direction, because within three weeks of obtaining the Beatles' signatures, Brian began offering his management package to others. Why not? Liverpool was awash with talent and no one else was doing much.

He took advice from Bob Wooler about the people and personalities, finding out who was reliable and who wasn't, and during February showed interest in signing at least five groups – Gerry and the Pacemakers, the Remo Four, Johnny Sandon and the Searchers, the Undertakers and the Four Jays. Along with the Beatles, this represented four of the top five in the *Mersey Beat* poll plus those placed tenth and twelfth (the top-five exception was Rory Storm and the Hurricanes, who, with Ringo still in Hamburg, were sliding, and didn't appeal to Brian). He had no contracts for anyone yet, but to show goodwill he got them bookings and took no commission. Brian wouldn't allow any of this to distract him from advancing the Beatles, and these other groups realised the Beatles would always be uppermost in Brian's thinking and attention. Still, if anyone could improve their bookings and earn them more money, it was Brian Epstein, so they weren't about to turn him down.

His principal involvement in the Floral Hall night was two-fold: to help sell the 1200 tickets and to book the talent that would provide continuous dancing for four hours – five groups headed by POLYDOR RECORDING STARS, THE BEATLES. He circulated typed leaflets among Beatles fans and on the record counters at all three Nems shops, announcing affordable coach trips: fans could pay 8s 6d for return transportation, admission to the hall and, afterwards, the chance to mingle with the musicians and get their autographs. These special all-in tickets were sold only in the Whitechapel shop, outside which the chartered buses would leave. The Beatles were taking a Liverpool audience with them for a night out up the coast.

When he first became involved with the Beatles, Brian suspended the activities of their fan club; now he was preparing to relaunch it to his own specifications. Retained as its volunteer secretary, Bobby Brown began a memorable period of close co-operation with the Beatles and Brian. 'He was determined the club should be run well,' she says, 'so I was able to get proper stationery and membership cards printed, and when I told him about some unpaid bills I'd received from before my time, he gave me the money to settle them.'[26] Grand relaunch plans were in place by mid-February: Brian booked the Cavern as a 'private let' for the night of Thursday 5 April and announced a show called *The Beatles For Their Fans*. At a cost of 6s 6d they would see a special performance, be given a glossy photograph for autographing, and could register for a year's free club membership. Members would be sent newsletters that kept them in touch with Beatles events and detailed the ways in which they could support and encourage the group. Everyone would be happy: the Beatles, the fans and Brian himself, who would gain an invaluable mailing list for marketing use as well as sufficient start-up capital for the club. He hoped it would break even financially – it wasn't designed for profit because the membership fee had to be kept affordable for all; and if the club made a loss, he would cover it.

Overriding every plan, though, was Brian's imperative: to get the Beatles a recording contract. They weren't going to be bigger than Elvis without one. His April 1961 visit to Hamburg and Hanover as a guest of Deutsche Grammophon had already proved fruitful in getting My Bonnie released in Britain, and now it paid dividends a second time. Another delegate among the thirty-strong deputation was Robert Boast, manager of His Master's Voice (HMV), the self-proclaimed world's largest record store, situated on Oxford Street in the heart of London. After Decca's rejection, Brian took the opportunity to renew Boast's acquaintance; he had no obvious plan in mind, but Boast was an address-book contact and he was exploring every possibility. Brian had with him the Beatles' Decca tape and sat in Boast's office saying his boys would become very big stars if only someone would take a chance with them. 'He said he'd had a very wearing two days visiting record companies. It seems they just weren't prepared to listen. I was, though it was beyond my powers to help him. But at that time we had a small recording studio on the first floor, where budding artists could make 78rpm demonstration discs. I took Brian there and introduced him to our disc cutter, Jim Foy.'[27]

It made sense for Brian to pitch the Beatles from discs rather than a reel of tape. Every recording manager had an office gramophone (as they were still called), not everyone had a tape deck. As Jim Foy remembers, he and Brian Epstein chatted while a lathe cut the Beatles' sound into 78rpm acetate discs of heavy black lacquer.

> I remarked that the tape sounded very good, to which he replied, rather proudly, that some of the songs were actually written by the group, which was uncommon. I asked whether they had been published, and when he said they hadn't I told him that the office of Ardmore and Beechwood, one of EMI's music publishing companies, was on the top floor of the shop. Should I fetch the general manager, Sid Colman? He said yes, Sid came down, listened to the tape and he too expressed interest. When I'd done the cutting, he and Brian went back up to the office.[28]

It was here that the Beatles' Decca recording of three Lennon-McCartney Originals turned up trumps. If they hadn't sung those songs, Brian would not have been sitting in an oak-panelled, fourth-floor office over the hum and thrum of Oxford Street, having his first discussion about an element of the business still little known to him. He knew record companies and enjoyed memorising their catalogue numbers and titles, but music publishers were just names on record labels or sheet music, familiar in themselves while their workings, the business strategies behind them, were not.

At 56, Sid Colman was a wise old bird of the song trade, in the business since 1937 and now installed by EMI as general manager of its publishing operation. As Decca had Burlington Music and Philips had Flamingo Music so EMI had Ardmore and Beechwood, formed in 1958 as an extension of Capitol Records' publishing businesses. Whatever the country, the idea was the same: owning music copyrights reaped a tidy income, and so much the better if it was from the company's own record product and every revenue stream flowed into the same pool.

Colman was interested in Ardmore and Beechwood publishing these Lennon-McCartney songs, which was good news ... except that Brian wanted a Beatles recording contract. A publisher would give the songs to someone else to record and he wanted the Beatles to have first use of them. Colman understood and told Brian he'd see what he could do to help; in return, Brian gave his word that if Colman could assist in obtaining the Beatles a recording contract, Ardmore and Beechwood would get the publishing.

Precisely what propelled Brian from here to the office of George Martin may never be known. George would always say, naturally, that Colman picked up the phone, told him about Brian and suggested they meet, but Colman's indispensable right-hand man throughout this period, a music plugger who called himself Kim Bennett, insists this was not the case, and that George was the very *last* person Colman would have called because he strongly disliked him. Whatever the reason, George Martin's desk diary for 13 February 1962 includes Judy Lockhart Smith's lightly pencilled untimed entry for 'Bernard Epstein'.

Brian was chancing his arm at EMI, trying to wrest a Yes where there'd been a No. The recording managers had already turned down the Beatles on the basis of their appearance on the Tony Sheridan disc; Brian must have been hoping this wouldn't be remembered, and that he might score a better result with a personal approach and different product. It could also be that he was after *any* appointment at EMI House and George Martin was the only man available – two of his three A&R colleagues, Norman Newell and Norrie Paramor, were on holiday this week.

George wasn't there when Brian arrived, so the first person he met was Judy. She would always remember appreciating how well dressed, well mannered and well spoken he was, not at all like the other managers who came into the office, while Brian would later write, genuinely, of how he and Judy developed 'an instant friendship'.[29]

George's day was filled with appointments, and when he arrived he wouldn't have been able to give his visitor much time. The two sat across a desk – one man aged 36, the other 27, both in smart suits and ties, and with polite, cultured voices that had benefited from self-improvement. Brian was desperate but trying not to seem so, George was tolerant, pleasant and in a position of power. Brian told him about the Beatles, saying how big they were in Liverpool and affecting surprise when George said he hadn't heard of them. This somewhat riled his host: as George would reflect, 'I almost asked him in reply where Liverpool was – the thought of anything coming out of the provinces was extraordinary.'[30]

In interpreting the way Brian remembered the meeting, there was probably time to hear only one of his new-cut records – a ten-inch 78 acetate with Hello Little Girl on one side and Till There Was You on the other. He'd written the essential details on the labels in blue fountain pen. With limited space, and constantly keen to demonstrate the Beatles had more than one singer, he wrote that Hullo Little Girl (*sic*) was John Lennon & The Beatles – adding too the songwriting credit Lennon, McCartney – and that Til There Was You (*sic*) was Paul McCartney & The Beatles. Brian's recollection two years later was that

'George liked Hello Little Girl, Till There Was You. Liked George on guitar. Thought Paul was the one for discs.'[31]

It would be a long time before anyone else got to hear the Decca recording of Till There Was You, and express wonderment first that Brian had selected it – this was the number where John said Paul 'sounded like a woman' and Pete's timing was all over the place – and second that George Martin, from this, thought Paul best for recording and liked George's guitar playing. This was perhaps George's worst guitar work of the day. (Hello Little Girl was reasonable, though.)

If this isn't perplexing enough, George Martin would remember the meeting quite differently. In his first lengthy quote on the subject – a *Melody Maker* interview nine years later – he specifically mentioned Your Feet's Too Big being on the tape (*sic*) Brian played him, and added, 'I wasn't knocked out at all – it was a pretty lousy tape, recorded in a back room, very badly balanced, not very good songs and a rather raw group.'[32] This strongly suggests he wasn't listening to the Beatles' Decca test but a recording of which nothing else is known.

So, the meeting came to an end with George not 'knocked out at all'. He kept the acetate and might have said he would get in touch if he was interested in hearing more, but he wasn't and he didn't. It was just another disappointing encounter for Brian, one of way too many for his liking. He was having a far harder job selling the Beatles than expected.

The line may well have ended here but for the involvement of Kim Bennett. He'd been out when Brian sat in Sid Colman's office – busy plugging Ardmore and Beechwood's latest songs, lunching with a radio producer here or hustling around a bandleader's office there, trying to get a broadcast or a ballroom performance. Bennett was a twenty-four-hour worker and known for a dogged persistency greater than anyone else's in the business.

Thomas (Tom) Whippey was his real name, but he was still using the professional identity given him when he'd hoped to become a singing star. Until 1958, Kim Bennett had been a crooner of average looks and ability; he toured with the great but fading bandleader Ambrose, appeared a few times on radio and TV and was signed to Decca. He had four 78s/45s released in 1955–6 but they didn't sell and Decca didn't renew his contract, saying the market had changed. He worked as a Butlin's Redcoat for a season and then slipped into a new career in music publishing. While Sid Colman ran Ardmore and Beechwood (and was also its accountant), Bennett – at 31 much more contemporary than his boss – advised on all matters concerning the acquisition and exploitation of songs. He was the person whose job it was to harry them into the hit parade so Colman consulted him on all creative matters, and that included the Beatles.[33]

Soon after Brian Epstein had left the building, Bennett returned to find his boss keen to play him one of those new 78s from the Personal Recording Department. It was Like Dreamers Do, written by Paul McCartney when he was 17. 'I said, "I like that. What do they call themselves?" and Sid said *the Beatles*. "Oh bloody hell, what a name to use!" He told me the song was available if we could get them a record release and I replied, "I like it very much, Sid. I like that sound. If we can get them a record, and then if we can get it played, I think it could go into the charts. It's different."'[34]

As Bennett would remember it, at some time over the following days Colman took Like Dreamers Do across Oxford Street to EMI House in the hope the song and its sound would appeal to one of the A&R men – Paramor, Ridley, Martin and Newell – only to return with the news that no one was interested. 'His actual words were "Nobody over there wants to know" and, as he didn't qualify that remark, I took "nobody" to mean that he'd seen everybody.'

Kim Bennett, being persistent, was both disappointed that a promising lead had so quickly amounted to nothing and reluctant to let the matter drop. He remained free to kindle the interest of other record company A&R men, but such a path was doomed to failure. It was obvious to everyone that if Ardmore and Beechwood was touting something around the business then it had already been rejected by EMI, to whom they were bound to turn first. It was just like the situation in America, where companies knew that if EMI was trying to place a record with them, it had already been spurned by Capitol.

> I mused about it for a while and then had a thought. 'Why can't *we* make the record?' I knew we weren't allowed to, but I couldn't see why not. So I went back into Sid's office and said, 'Look, you've given me permission to spend *x* amount on plugging a song, so could I make a suggestion? Why don't you go across to [EMI Records managing director] Len Wood and say that if EMI give us a record, we will pay for its cost. Because it's a group it'll be a straightforward studio production, no orchestra; we'll have got two copyrights for the next fifty years plus maybe a royalty on the record.'
>
> Sid agreed, and it was only some time later that I heard the result, which was that Len Wood, while sympathetic to our situation, said we should stick to publishing and leave EMI to make the records.
>
> Sid was fed up with the bloody-mindedness of it all, and so was I. And, at this point, that seemed to be the end of it ...

Managing the Beatles entailed attention to a thousand tiny details and some not-so-tiny personalities. Problems could flare up for Brian without notice, as happened on Friday 16 February, when they were set to perform the last of their three dances for Liverpool University and there was an issue with Paul.

More and more now, Brian was picking up John, Paul and George in his Zodiac and taking them to the night's venue. As well as being of benefit to them, it was his hands-on way of ensuring they arrived on time. Like him, they all lived in the south end of Liverpool, while Pete, in the north, would make his own way to the hall with Neil and the vanload of gear. The Beatles had a double-shuffle this night: the final university date, at the Technical College Hall in Birkenhead, and then a late headline booking for Sam Leach at New Brighton Tower. Brian stopped in Woolton to collect John (he was about the only visitor Mimi welcomed through the front door – he didn't have to go around the side), he dropped down to Speke for George, and then he turned back to Allerton for Paul. But when George knocked on the door at 20 Forthlin Road, Paul shouted, 'Tell Brian I'm not ready and I'll be a while.'

Brian's response was the one Paul could have anticipated: 'Well he *should* be ready. I said I'd be here at eight and it's past eight.' George gave Paul another knock and told him to hurry. After a further wait, Brian said George should tell Paul they were going into town for a quick drink before taking the tunnel to Birkenhead: Paul would have to get himself there by other means. Brian, John and George went to the Beehive and John used a public box to call Paul, returning with the message 'He says he's not coming.' Brian must have been *apoplectic*: they'd be unable to play the booking, letting down the university and their paying audience, embarrassing him, ruining their chance of a rebooking, and undoing his repair work to the Beatles' old bad reputation. He went back to his office to phone Paul, but Paul refused to speak. Jim informed Brian that Paul said he wouldn't be turning up, and that was that.[35]

Recalling the night five years later, Paul told of how, having discovered Brian and the others hadn't waited outside his house for him, he decided 'Fuck them – if they can't be arsed waiting for me, I can't be arsed going after them. So I sat down and watched telly.'[36] Jim was unable to persuade Paul to change his mind. Paul said he felt he'd always been 'the keen one', so now he'd go sharp the other way and make no effort at all.

John saw a bigger picture, and it would be surprising if it wasn't equally obvious, or made obvious, to Brian and George. He likened Paul's enduring snag with Brian to his other long-standing difficulty: '[Brian] and Paul didn't get along – it was a bit like [Stuart and Paul] between the two of them.'[37]

Inevitably, this wouldn't be the only dispute to arise between Brian and a Beatle in their years together, but it is one of the few to be known, and its timing is telling. Brian devoted more than a page to it in his autobiography, saying how 'worried, angry and upset' he was. The university triple booking was giving the Beatles prestige, earning them good money and presenting them to new audiences in good venues, and Paul had chosen *this moment* to make a stand.

John took a benign view. He might deal with it his own way – probably a knowing word to Paul at some point – but he also wanted to see how Brian reacted, unaided, to being tested. John's cruelty was bruising and obvious, Paul's dissent cutting and concealed, which made him trickier to manage. The testy way his and Brian's relationship had started in late 1961 was the way it set. Brian crystallised it in 1964 as 'our clash of personalities – Paul can be temperamental and moody and difficult to deal with: he is a great one for not wishing to hear about things'. (Not that Brian was always an angel himself.)

The Beatles' non-appearance was reported in the students' paper *Guild Gazette*. Instead of becoming only the second newspaper to review a Beatles show – and probably the first to give them more than two lines – it noted how 'the organisers were besieged by bedecked totties demanding the Beatles or their money. They got their money.' (The dance was open to all and had been advertised in the *Echo* two nights back.) Brian hastened to offer a make-good Beatles appearance, squeezed in the following Friday and played for nothing. Paul did allow himself to be persuaded out to the Tower late this first evening so they didn't also let down Sam Leach's customers.

Harsh words were had, and it's clear that Paul's test of Brian's resolve did, however briefly, endanger the Beatles' future. Brian's commitment to the cause of creating their fame and fortune could not have been more emphatically established before Paul threw his spanner in the works, so he felt steeled to talk sternly. While he later wrote of how he 'toyed' with the idea of saying he'd quit if this was the way they were going to behave, Paul's brother Mike said he actually *did* tell them: 'The Beatles were still turning up late and missing their spot every now and again, mostly because of Paul. Brian Epstein stood this for a while then he issued an ultimatum – they must improve their attitude or he was abandoning their management.'[38]

The next few days turned up further intriguing events. The Floral Hall show went well the following Tuesday, but it would be remembered for another reason – because it was here, in the dressing-room, that two of the Beatles smoked marijuana.

Pete kept well out of it, and it's unlikely Paul tried it on this occasion because he never mentioned it, but John and George – the usual two experimenters – were game. John had already smoked 'pot' once, around 1960, but this was the first time it was had by a couple of them together. It was grass, from the drummer in another group. Whether it was the weed's influence or not, they were soon doing the Twist, madly, in the dressing-room, while shouting, 'This stuff isn't doing anything!' George later likened it to the old joke about two hippies at a party, floating on the ceiling and saying, 'This stuff doesn't work, man.'[39] John, however, talked it down in his one interview comment about the occasion – 'A guy brought us some grass but we didn't know anything about it and anyway we were already pissed.'[40] It would be a while before they had the chance of a repeat experience.

The following day, two of the Beatles were sitting in the Kardomah café. Their Wednesday-night Cavern residency was preceded this week by a lunchtime session, and John and Paul were still in the habit of staying in town on such days, idling away afternoons in 'the KD'. This time they were chatting to one of John's old mates from art school, who then said, 'I believe Brian Epstein is managing you – which one of you does he fancy?' It was just a bit of lads' banter, something that often came up behind Brian's back, along with digs about him being Jewish.

Nothing more would have been said about it if one of the two Beatles (or both) hadn't then relayed the comment to Brian's face. He was mortified. It was a stain on his character; it was combustible, in view of homosexual acts being illegal; and, because he was still denying this side of his life to the Beatles, it was a direct challenge for him to respond. Forty-eight hours later, Brian turned the matter over to his lawyer; and seven days after passing the comment, John's friend from art school was dumped deep in it.

> We have been consulted by Mr Brian Epstein who instructs us that on the 21st February last in the Kardomah Café, Church Street, Liverpool, you uttered a certain highly malicious and defamatory statement concerning him to two members of the Beatles.
>
> We are instructed that in the course of a conversation you said, 'I believe Brian Epstein is managing you. Which one of you does he fancy?' The unwarranted innuendo contained in that remark is perfectly clear and is one to which our client takes the gravest possible exception and the damaging nature of which has caused him considerable anxiety and distress.
>
> He is not prepared to tolerate the utterance of such remarks by you and we accordingly have to require that we receive by return your written apology together with an undertaking that this or similar remarks will not be made by you in the future.

The apology and undertaking arrived by return of post and that was the end of the matter – but it was another hard and damaging episode for Brian. The man who craved 'rough trade' for gratification was being fulfilled, mentally, by managing the Beatles ... while, physically, he continued to risk life and limb by cruising for it – the rougher and straighter the better. He'd just rented a bachelor flat on Falkner Street in order to conduct private liaisons, and it would be naive to think his overnight London visits on the Beatles' behalf didn't include sex. These trips essentially replaced the overseas expeditions that had been a feature of his life in 1960 and '61, trips he was now having to postpone because, in 1962, it was Beatles before Barcelona. It also happened that they (inadvertently) put paid to Brian's closest female relationship. Rita Harris, his platonic companion for two years, could no longer accept playing second fiddle to his Beatles absorption and stormed off one night, wounding him by announcing, 'I'm not going to compete with four kids.'[41]

Towards the end of February, Richy Starkey returned from his gig in Hamburg. He got back a little earlier than expected, having played seven weeks instead of two months.

After that initial delay at snowbound London Airport, Ringo began his stint as drummer in the Top Ten house band on New Year's Day, just as the Beatles were reversing their van away from Decca's back entrance. It was his second time in Hamburg, but now he was the only Liverpool boy in town, part of a four-strong English line-up with pianist Roy ('England's Little Richard') Young, bass player Colin Crawley and Tony Sheridan. The singer-guitarist had been in Hamburg since the summer of 1960 and his girlfriend Rosi Heitmann had given birth to their baby, Richard, in October 1961, the same month My Bonnie was released. The record had put Sheridan in the charts but this didn't pay the bills – he still bunked down with his musicians in the attic above the Top Ten, the Beatles' quarters the spring before. The line of John Lennon's caked-on green gob had *probably* since been cleaned off the wall by Mutti, the caring *Toilettenfrau* and Preludin peddler.

Ringo – like John, Paul and George – found that a diet of booze and Prellies was the only way to fulfil the Top Ten's playing time, seven or eight hours a night, and still have energy left for experiences outside. He coped easily with this new lifestyle. More so than being here with the Hurricanes, more than any Butlin's season in north-west Wales, Ringo felt *free*. 'It was tough but we didn't give a damn; it was fabulous. This was opening your eyes, this was leaving home, this was leaving the country. Hamburg was fabulous. To me, Hamburg felt like Soho.'[42]

Soho was a *little* like that, but its white-jacketed waiters didn't gang up on customers and drag them outside for vicious beatings, not routinely anyway; and no Soho criminal brandished his lethal weapon quite as openly as his St Pauli counterpart. One of Ringo's main memories of these Hamburg weeks was watching gangsters in the Top Ten cleaning their guns while the band played.

As he'd recall, when one of these hard men shouted '*Spielen* What'd I Say' it was pointless shouting back 'We've just played it' because the response would be, in a noticeably stern imperative, '*Spielen What'd I Say!*'[43]

Then there was Tony Sheridan himself. George had seen how he was 'always getting into fights' and now Ringo saw it too: 'If anyone in the club was talking to his girl he'd be punching and kicking all over the place while we'd just keep on jamming. Then he'd come back and join us, covered in blood if he'd lost. But he was a really good player.'[44] Sheridan, in turn, came to appreciate Ringo's talents, not having known him much before now: 'Ringo was a very good drummer with us, though he seemed perpetually bored. He was slightly depressed all the time, a melancholy character, but he had his own charisma in a way.'[45] Colin Crawley also enjoyed playing with Ringo – 'He was the best drummer we'd had, not because he was technically gifted but because he could keep the beat like clockwork.'[46] It was what everyone who played with him always said.

The weeks passed in St Pauli's boozy blur of sex, drugs and rock and roll. Ringo learned a new musical trick – how to play boogie-woogie piano, though he could only do it with his left hand. This was taught him by Roy Young, who also went away for a few days with Horst Fascher on that trip to Liverpool, the one that clinched the Beatles for Hamburg's new venue, opening April. When Peter Eckhorn realised what was happening, he tried to prevent Sheridan defecting by getting him to sign up to a DM6000 penalty clause if he broke his Top Ten contract. Such a sum, it would soon transpire, was chicken feed to the coming Mr Big-Shot, Herr Manfred Weissleder.

The worst part of Ringo's Hamburg stay was the January–February weather. He was used to the cold and damp of home, but this coldness was damn persistent: the temperature barely rose above freezing throughout the opening weeks of the year, and then, in catastrophic circumstances, climatic events brought his stay to an end. The night of 16–17 February 1962 would be infamous in Hamburg's history: hurricane-force winds over the North Sea brought flooding to large areas of the city, buildings collapsed, twenty thousand people were made homeless and 343 died. The British Sailors' Society, that popular musicians' hub, was deluged, and though the water never reached the Reeperbahn (it was uphill) there were power failures, food shortages and fears of typhoid. After a night or two when the musicians played acoustically by candlelight, the Top Ten closed for several days. Ringo might have stayed, extending his two-month contract, but he took the opportunity to go home, because his beloved grandmother had died.

Annie Starkey, tired out at 72, had a fatal heart attack on 7 February. Richy may not have been entirely sorry to miss her funeral – the horror of grandad

Johnny Starkey's burial had never left him – but Annie would be a big loss in his life. She was there at his birth, her hot toddies and witchy remedies had tended him through his sickly childhood, her singing and playing had enlivened family parties, *and* she was the superstitious 'voodoo queen of Liverpool' who'd turned him from a left-hander to a right-hander, the switch that had given him his unusual drumming style, what he would call his 'rock lope'. His left hand was just staging its fightback (being dominant in his boogie-woogie piano playing) when she died.

Her death brought Richy face to face with his dad for the first time since his infancy. The elder Richy Starkey was 48 now, remarried, living in Crewe, working part-time as a confectioner and part-time as a window-cleaner. His son's anger over being deserted had subsided somewhat as he'd grown older, and the two men stood side by side together and looked at Little Richy's big Ford Zodiac. A few simple and not unfriendly remarks were exchanged, they parted, and (as far as is known) never met again.[47]

Now he was back, Richy didn't rush to rejoin the Hurricanes. They'd been using 'dep' (deputy) drummers since he left them at the end of December, and they could continue using them. A third consecutive Butlin's summer season was coming up in June, although it wasn't yet clear where, and Rory and Johnny were trying to get them a gig playing American air bases in France. Richy might join them for these. For the moment, he just hung around, marking time – he signed back on the dole; he again contemplated becoming a freelance hairdresser, or perhaps even opening his own salon; and he went on long late-night solo drives with no particular place to go.[48]

It probably wasn't until March that Pete found out they hadn't got the Decca contract. Brian told him the news, and assured him he was doing everything he could to get them a deal somewhere else. When Pete asked John, Paul and George why he'd not been told this earlier, they said they'd felt he would take the news badly, and they didn't want to dishearten him.[49] Pete divulged these details in later years but not how he rationalised his bandmates' behaviour; he suggested only that he felt secure in his position through his popularity among the fans. He continued to turn a blind eye to the ever-present scenario, which was that it was a royal pain for the Beatles' front line to be whooping it up on stage only to turn around and find their drummer with his head bowed, unsmiling, making no eye contact, bringing to the stage the disconnectedness that existed off it.

Bob Wooler would describe how 'At times, Pete would be like a zombie on the drums: it was as though he was saying "Do I have to do this?" He had no show about him – he always looked bored.' *Mersey Beat* editor Bill Harry wasn't about to rock the boat in print, but what he actually saw was that 'Pete never said anything. He'd sit by himself. If somebody talked to him, he'd just grunt or nod – but I always liked him.' And Neil Aspinall certainly recognised how his best mate operated outside the core: 'John, Paul and George were always *a three. They* were the tight ones.'[50]

They were the same tight ones who'd shown no tact or remorse when dumping Pete's pal Ken Brown – he was never really 'one of the group' and they'd considered him musically limited – and now they compelled Brian to address the Pete situation. In his autobiography, Brian said that John, Paul and George wanted to sack Pete 'sooner or later', and that he urged them 'to leave the group as it was'. This was no time to upset the applecart. He said he'd have a quiet talk with Pete about his drumming, 'without hurting his feelings'.[51] Brian knew nothing about drums but was probably fed some words; Pete made no noticeable change afterwards.

It was yet another tricky situation for Brian, who was finding group management more complex than he could ever have anticipated. What he understood well, however, was stability and timing. Much was going on for the Beatles, in every sphere, not least that he was selling them around London as *this* award-winning four-piece group as shown in *this* publicity photograph. It would have been unhelpful if they suddenly differed from what he was marketing.

It was also only just over a month until their seven-week season in Hamburg, its signed agreement specifying the names Lennon, McCartney, Harrison and Best. It was a good contract which they should honour, not try to amend. Not only that, Brian had booked air tickets for them and for himself – this was fixed once Horst Fascher confirmed that groups would be able to use the still-unnamed-club's own amplifiers, meaning the Beatles would have to take only their guitars and drums. Each Hamburg trip represented a progression: a cramped minibus the first time, boat and train the second, air travel the third. This was *style*, and this was Brian Epstein, though it also required nerve. Still relatively early in the history of passenger aviation, a week rarely passed without news of a fatal crash – the headline splashed across the front page of the *Liverpool Echo* on 1 March 1962, just when Brian booked the Beatles' tickets, was 95 IN CRASHED JET: NO SURVIVORS.* The Beatles (George in particular) would be edgy fliers for some time to come.

---

* A Boeing 707 had plunged from the sky shortly after leaving New York for Chicago and Los Angeles. Among the dead was Louise Eastman, wife of music business attorney Lee and mother of their four children. The eldest, John, was at Harvard, and in the summer vacations he was a yacht

Brian had yet to decide if they should take their suits to Hamburg – but so many times had the jackets and trousers been sent back for alteration, they still weren't ready. He'd hoped they would wear them at Floral Hall, but instead they played this important show in leather jackets and jeans, Brian lifting his ban against them. This was their usual outdoor gear too . . . and a look that, to *considerable* amusement, had latterly been sported by Brian himself. The longer he spent in their company the more self-conscious he'd become about being so conventional when they were so casual, standing out when he wanted to blend in. So at the same time as encouraging the Beatles to get smart and wear suits, Brian turned up once or twice in jeans and leather jacket – though where theirs were well worn and broken in, his were clean and new. Bob Wooler looked at Brian and thought, 'There's another Beatle.' The Beatles themselves found it hilarious, and not all their laughter was behind his back. Brian rapidly ditched his new outfit, but did occasionally, like they did, wear a polo-neck sweater, or a leather jacket over shirt and tie.[52]

The suits were finally ready on Tuesday 6 March and they trooped over to Birkenhead once more, to Beno Dorn's shop. Walter Smith again had to remind them to curb their language, and he also had the malodorous task of supervising the final fittings. 'The Beatles' boots had a lining,' he remembers, 'and with them sweating so much on stage, their feet stank to high heaven. I had to spray air freshener after they'd left the shop.' The four young men did so carrying a zipped red tartan-pattern plastic suit-bag with a handle. The Beatles had a *new look.* *

It was on display the next day, when, back at the Playhouse Theatre in Manchester, they made their debut BBC radio recording. The show was called *Here We Go* – informally known as *Here We Go With The NDO* because the last three words were said in the opening announcement. The NDO, Northern Dance Orchestra, were the show's mainstays, nineteen sight-reading musicians playing punchy big band pop – in this particular edition it was Twist Around The Clock. BBC producer Peter Pilbeam remembers the men being 'initially displeased at the prospect of sharing the airwaves with untutored beat musicians, but it was bread and butter, keeping them in work; we kitted out the

---

instructor in wealthy East Hampton, where his parents had just bought a house. Their second child, Linda, 20, had enrolled at the University of Arizona, in Tucson, but she spent more time riding horses than studying, and had just 'dropped out' when the crash occurred. She fell pregnant within days, married her boyfriend – geology student Melville See – on 18 June, and gave birth to their daughter, Heather, on 30 December 1962.

* John also got new glasses about this same time, thick black horn-rims like those worn by Buddy Holly and Hank Marvin (and Brian Poole). John's were decidedly *not* for public use, so he stayed stage-blind.

NDO's different sections with different colour chunky sweaters, to make them look like teenagers'.[53]

In this period, *Here We Go* went out on Thursday afternoons at five in *Teenagers' Turn*, the Monday-to-Friday half-hour slot that featured 'live' BBC music sessions. There was still only the Light Programme radio network to showcase 'pops', under eighteen hours' airtime a day shared with other kinds of music that the entire population, all ages and tastes, expected for their licence fee – and such fare was shoehorned into the schedule along with comedies, drama serials, topical talks, religious programmes, enriching children's entertainment, magazines, news and sport.

Britain first heard the Beatles within a show that was part of the typical daily pop diet of about two and a quarter hours. The BBC would be justifiably accused of steering pop too safely down the middle of the road – its staff, like record company A&R men, were detached from what *moved* young people – but it was powerless to solve what would one day become its main criticism: to provide pop with more airtime. It wasn't within the BBC's influence to conjure up new stations, and it was already running at the maximum end of the 'Needletime' restrictions imposed by record companies and the Musicians' Union. Despite all the difficulties, however, the BBC always made room for artists to perform live ... and for a Liverpool rock group without a recording contract to be given national bandwidth *and* be paid for it.

Pilbeam had the job of producing *Here We Go* on a £75 budget, and the Beatles were paid more than a third of this, £26 18s, plus expenses. It was more than they got for playing to 270 people in Liverpool, but if they expected greater reward for entertaining 2.7 million radio listeners, they never said anything. Pilbeam remembers the Beatles this day as 'just four Liverpool lads chuffed with the fact they were getting somewhere and had been recognised by the national broadcasting organisation'.[54]

On 7 March 1962, 250 young and youngish Mancunians were dressed up for an evening out and had free BBC tickets for the Playhouse. They were the first to see the Beatles in their narrow-lapel, tight-trouser dark-blue mohair suits with bright white shirts and slim ties. With the greaseless, clean, combed-forward, fringe-falling hair worn by three of them and the Cuban-heel flamenco 'Chelsea' boots worn by all four, no band of musicians looking like this had ever stepped up to the microphone in the BBC's forty-year history.

Mike McCartney was again in the right place at the right time. He climbed the electricians' gallery at the side of the stage, just behind the house tabs, and took a photo of John, Paul and George standing poised while Pilbeam addressed the one main vocal microphone ... to which a BBC badge was clipped, reminding the performers *where they were*.[55] The Beatles were to record four songs –

Hello Little Girl, Memphis, Dream Baby and Please Mr Postman – as agreed between them, Brian and Peter Pilbeam. Three (omitting Hello Little Girl) would be broadcast. Brian had successfully lobbied Pilbeam to relent from his original rejection of Paul as a vocalist and let him take one number, and show host Ray Peters gave him a broadcast name-check as the singer of Dream Baby. With Roy Orbison only entering the *NME* chart the day of the broadcast, the Nashville song was unknown to almost everyone, but the Beatles were already tight and confident with it.

The Beatles' spot on *Here We Go* didn't appear to herald anything exceptional. It wasn't anticipated in the music press, they received a name-only billing in the BBC's programme journal *Radio Times*, and the broadcast won no retrospective notice as a special moment. But it was. After identifying John Lennon as the singer of Memphis, Tennessee, presenter Ray Peters labelled it 'a rhythm and blues version'. Such words would have been unfamiliar to the studio and listening audience – in fact, so seldom was R&B heard on the BBC that, for many, this would have been their initial exposure to something new. And when John sang Please Mr Postman it was both the first time this song had been broadcast and the first time *anything* from Tamla had been played on BBC radio. Without even realising it (and they'd have been thrilled to know), the Beatles broke the Detroit 'Motown sound' to the British listening public.

Plenty of teenagers *didn't* turn to *Here We Go* at five the following afternoon. Some were playing outside, or still getting home from school, or doing homework, or watching television, or couldn't listen because there was only one 'wireless' in the house and an adult was tuned into something else. Pete says John and Paul were at his house to catch the broadcast through Mona's radiogram, which received the better-quality VHF (FM) mono signals. The Beatles' three numbers gave them six minutes of national airtime, and the recording shows a group on their best behaviour, packing more vitality than in their Decca test but still clearly in their early days as professionals. It's also significant that, at first grasp, they won over an audience that didn't know them: the Playhouse crowd cheered, clapped along and – at the end of all three songs – girls screamed.

It sounded just great through the speakers at Hayman's Green, and was a major moment in their lives. 'We were jumping about in the living-room listening to it,' says Pete. 'We weren't just recording stars but *radio* stars!'[56]

26

'Us against them' (9 March–10 April 1962)

The suits were put away after the broadcast and kept hidden. Brian Epstein wanted their first Liverpool exposure to be a *moment*, maybe four weeks hence in *The Beatles For Their Fans*. For now, most of those fans were unaware of the coming change. Late at night on 9 March, Lindy Ness wrote in her diary: 'Beatles on at Cave. Got there just before 7.30. Had to run miles. Got seats at the front. They were great, especially John. He sang Baby It's You again. Paul was cute, and George and Pete. John had a brown shirt on and black pullover and blue jeans. He was acting the fool with Paul. Paul said at the beginning of Dream Baby, *"Here We Go With The NDO!"'*

Some Liverpool groups had some female fans but the Beatles were producing addicts by the legion – supporters inspired to passion, devotion, wit and imagination, girls who loved all of them but one of them just that bit more, and whom the Beatles protected like brothers with kid sisters. Lindy's diary for 6 March reads: 'Went to the Cave. When I got there it was 4s 6d [to get in] and I only had 3s 6d. I saw John coming up with Cynthia. I asked him for a shilling and he lent me a shilling. Pete sang Matchbox and John sang Baby It's You. I still owe him a shilling.'

Neil tried to keep the Beatles' van nondescript, but failed: the bodywork was daubed with lipstick love messages, some of them rude. On the odd nights when John, Paul and George went straight home after a show, rejecting a late drink or some passionate activity, fans like Lindy and her friend Lou Steen, who lived in Woolton and Allerton, would be treated to a ride with their heroes. All the gear would be piled in the back and then, as Lou remembers, she and Lindy would clamber inside.

Nell drove – he was very nice – and otherwise it was John, Paul, George and us. I don't know where Pete was. Nothing sexual happened, not even a kiss – when they dropped us off they'd just say 'Bye girls!' We were fourteen and they were like grown men, a generation apart, so we never realistically thought we had a chance of shagging one of them. In those days you had to be reckless or brave to do it, and most of us were still virgins when we left school. Riding the van was fun anyway – the Beatles were always dead funny, and quite hyper after they'd done a gig.[1]

Cyn and Dot still made sporadic appearances at the Cavern, standing in their place under the first arch on the left, closest to the stage and bandroom, but it was beginning to get precarious – jealousy could prompt unwelcome gestures, more verbal than physical but sometimes both. Brian was also beginning to apply pressure on the Beatles to keep their girlfriends hidden – this certainly became his thinking as 1962 ran its course. It was a policy universally applied in the music business and reached back to Hollywood's earliest days, when the popularity of male stars could be preserved only if they were seen to be *available*. The point had been proved as recently as 1959–60 when the hits of Larry Parnes' boy Marty Wilde all but dried up the day he stepped down the aisle. The Beatles were a way yet from having hit records, but Brian asked them to maintain the illusion of availability. The logic seemed fair – it was nonsensical to shut down a key part of their audience – and it became another of Brian's wishes which the Beatles, principally John and Paul at this point, could have rejected but didn't. In the Cavern, anyway, there *were* no secrets.

Standing tall among the Beatles' newest fans was Malcolm (Mal) Evans, a 26-year-old Post Office telephone engineer and Elvis nut who fell very keenly for the group after chancing on a Cavern lunchtime session. The first person he spoke to was Bobby Brown, and he and the fan club secretary became friends. 'Mal was a really, really nice person, and because he was often saying how much he loved the Beatles and wanted to meet them, I introduced him to Paul. They got chatting, and every time after that Mal would either sit with me or stand on the side, close to them; Paul always spoke to him and then the others got to know him too.'[2]

Mal was unmissable: he stood 6ft 2in but was gentle and wore glasses, and John, Paul and George quickly cottoned on to those inevitable Elvis requests. I Forgot To Remember To Forget was his favourite, which George sang, lamenting 'I'm so bloody lonely' in place of 'I'm so blue and lonely'. They usually prefaced their songs for Mal with a play on his name – 'This one's for Malcontent' or 'This one's for Malfunctioning' or 'This one's for Malodorous'.

In spring 1962, the Beatles' world was not the globe but an underground club in Liverpool – but already here was an extraordinary domination, one that went far beyond the bounds of four young guys playing music. The Beatles were influencing and changing others around them, without even trying. They were stars to the next generation of Merseyside groups, like the just-formed Mersey Beats, and they caused people to go around doing *the Beatles' voice* – not Scouse but a laconic Liverpudlian, cynical, droll, flat, hard, sharp, funny. Another act new to the scene, singer Lee Curtis, says, 'They were so individual that they had their own way of talking, their own hairstyle, their own clothing . . . they had so many things *worked out*.'[3]

This was happening unaided by any hype and untainted by any commercialism – it was developing authentically, and so right was it that people naturally fell into copying it. As Bobby Brown remembers:

> The Beatles looked German, French, more cosmopolitan than Liverpool lads, and they influenced how the Cavern people dressed. Because of them, most of the girls wore black – black polo-neck sweaters, black straight skirts, black stockings and flat shoes. Nothing was agreed between us, we just all wore the same. Then, because Paul had a corduroy coat and John had a corduroy jacket, a lot of people started coming in wearing corduroy. I bought a green corduroy dress.
>
> I also went and had my hair dyed blonde. I wondered what the Beatles would say about it, and they were on the stage winking and pointing at me. A lot of us were blonde because the Beatles liked blondes. It wasn't only done to please the Beatles, it was an image they set.[4]

Here was every kind of inspiration. Celia Mortimer, just turning 17, was newly enrolled at Liverpool College of Art and had a passion for making clothes. Exposure to the Beatles sent her straight to the sketchbook.

> In my first year at art college everyone was wild about trad jazz, but then word came up the hill that 'things were happening' at the Cavern; a few of us went down one lunchtime to have a look – and there were the Beatles. They wiped out all interest in trad: their music was a blast of the new – all that great R&B stuff – and so were they. It was the first time anyone in Britain had the black polo-neck, black corduroy, existentialist look. I instantly took their lead and started to make hip black corduroy things to wear.[5]

The Beatles also continued to influence Brian Epstein. By March/April, he wasn't only dressing something like them, he was preaching their musical views. He wrote 'Top Ten Tips' for *Mersey Beat* to run alongside his Nems chart, and here were John, Paul and George's opinions of the latest black records, channelled

Juke Box Jury-like through an impressed new receiver. The Marvelettes' Twistin' Postman (the follow-up to Please Mr Postman) was 'Probably not meant for the British charts but listen to it'; the rhythmic gospel of Etta James' Something's Got A Hold On Me was 'a super spinetingler'; Summertime by New York girls the Chantels was 'Another good American group who can't make it here – in any case this is the wrong song . . .'; and the Miracles' What's So Good About Goodbye was 'double-sided brilliance – a collector's gem'.[6]

What's So Good About Goodbye was something else too – it was the inspiration for John to write a song, which he called Ask Me Why. Discounting the instrumental Cry For A Shadow, it was his first new number since One After 909, written in the grimy Gambier Terrace days of spring 1960, and it followed closely Paul writing *his* first new number in a while, Pinwheel Twist. With interesting melodic key shifts and a Latin lilt, Ask Me Why was written in the first person: the singer so loves a girl that he could cry with joy. The lyric is corny but tender, never cloying or syrupy, and John's literacy shows in the line 'I can't conceive of any more misery' – not many songs used the word *conceive*.[7]

Several, however, had *misery*: it could have come from 'Oh misery, misery . . .' in Buddy Holly's Raining In My Heart, sung on stage by George, but more likely it was from 'All I've known is misery' in What's So Good About Goodbye, which also happened to include the words 'tell me why'. Ask Me Why had other echoes of Smokey Robinson's artistry: both songs opened with similar guitar figures and had verses that ended in falsetto. But this wasn't plagiarism; Smokey was just the springboard to John's creativity, his song ending up different. The Beatles learned Ask Me Why in a private afternoon rehearsal in the Cavern (one of the benefits of Brian's good business relationship with Ray McFall and Bob Wooler), and though it didn't go into the regular set just yet, there's an unconfirmed suggestion it was played in one of their last pre-Hamburg shows, at the start of April.

Further refinements to the Beatles' developing sound were added in March courtesy of two records. One was the poppy Hey! Baby by Bruce Channel, recorded in Texas; the other – from Muscle Shoals, Alabama – packed the deep R&B groove of Arthur Alexander. His single, You Better Move On c/w A Shot Of Rhythm And Blues, came out on Decca's London label on 9 March and rooted itself in many fertile minds around Britain, not just in Liverpool.

A US number 1 and British number 2, Hey! Baby was more than just a good, catchy, danceable, bluesy pop song, it was yet another contemporary American recording to feature harmonica. There was suddenly a little glut of them, and the Beatles liked them all. For nine months, since Paul stopped playing piano and took up the bass, they'd kept strictly to three guitars and drums, but Hey! Baby changed that: Paul sang it and John introduced harmonica into the Beatles' sound, reconnecting with one of his perennially favourite instruments.*

The harmonica added a new dimension to Beatles performances, one that few other groups could muster – it kept them different as well as current. While they didn't go back and use it on If You Gotta Make A Fool Of Somebody or I Just Don't Understand, the harmonica refreshed a 1956 song that, until now, the Beatles had played only occasionally: Clarabella, by the Jodimars. Paul sang this with fantastic energy, like one of his electrifyingly good Little Richard numbers, and John added bluesy harmonica where, on the original, there'd been saxes. They created, instantly, a new audience favourite and a track no other group even knew.

Arthur Alexander's record was a hit in America but not in Britain, and it came with no information. Like James Ray before him, he was just a name on a record label, two songs without data or image but a sound most wonderfully black. He was in fact from Sheffield – Sheffield, Alabama – and he was John's age, 21. One person remembers John singing You Better Move On in the Cavern, but it didn't linger in the Beatles' set. The B-side, A Shot Of Rhythm And Blues, stayed and became one of their best 1962 stage numbers. They weren't the only Liverpool group to do it but they always felt they played it best: unable to replicate the original's saxes, they recast it without a middle-eight – their version was carried by John's powerful vocal, Paul's harmonies, and a couple of guitar motifs by George.[8]

For connoisseurs, this Arthur Alexander bloke became the topic of fevered conversation. At this moment – as Paul would recall – the Beatles almost wanted to *be* Arthur Alexander: 'If the Beatles ever wanted "a sound" it was R&B – that was what we used to listen to, what we used to like, what we wanted to be like. Black. That was basically it. Arthur Alexander. It came out whiter because it always does – we're white and we were just young Liverpool musicians: we didn't have any finesse to be able to actually *sound* black.'[9]

The Beatles weren't alone in calling this R&B. What else could it be if the record company and the music press said it was, and the song was called A Shot Of Rhythm And Blues? But an argument that it *wasn't* R&B, not at all, was made public after Jack Good used his 17 March *Disc* column to advocate a WE CHOOSE RHYTHM AND BLUES campaign. So fired up was he by James Ray's If You Gotta Make A Fool Of Somebody and this Arthur Alexander B-side

---

* There's no certain information about the harmonica John played in this period – it may have been the one he 'slap leathered' in Arnhem in August 1960, as the Beatles passed through the Netherlands on their way to Hamburg.

(Good's and the Beatles' tastes were always uncannily though coincidentally similar) he was lobbying the BBC to broadcast more of it. Two weeks later, though, the same paper printed a letter that challenged Good over whether this was R&B at all.

> 'Rhythm and blues' seems to be a term which needs defining, judging by Jack Good's column.
>
> It is a genuine blues style, evolved directly from the earlier, less sophisticated country blues. R and B in turn gave birth to a commercial offspring, universally known as rock 'n' roll. Billy Fury is a rock 'n' roll singer – not an R and B vocalist.
>
> I listened to all the records quoted by Jack Good in his article, and all except one were rock 'n' roll records. The one exception was the Barbara George disc I Know.
>
> Please will somebody play Jack Good a Muddy Waters or a Howlin' Wolf disc so that he can hear what R and B really is?

The letter was sent in by *Disc* reader Brian Jones, of Cheltenham, Gloucestershire, and a week later Good posted a full response, part of which declared 'It must be nice to be a purist, you don't have to think or feel, you just apply a rule of thumb'. He wasn't against what either man labelled R&B: Good welcomed every interesting musical development. Just the previous week, his main headline was about a new venue – the Ealing Club, in west London – devoted entirely to R&B, and this week he reported news that, from May, the man behind that place, blues guitarist Alexis Korner, would also be playing a weekly residency at the Marquee Club in central London, until now a jazz stronghold.[10]

It was at the Ealing Club, on 7 April – the same date as Jack Good's printed response to Brian Jones – that the fervent 20-year-old blues fan from Cheltenham met two 18-year-old blues fans from Dartford, Kent – Mick Jagger and Keith Richards. They'd come across London to check out the sounds, and Jones was in the capital every weekend from Gloucestershire to crash with Korner and play with his band, Blues Incorporated. This week their line-up included jazz drummer Charlie Watts and a singer calling himself P. P. Pond, both 20. Styling himself 'Elmo Lewis', Jones sat hunched over a guitar and played some slide: Dust My Broom by Mississippi bluesman Elmore James. A surprisingly accomplished musician, Jones made a deep impression on Jagger and Richards. They went back to Dartford, to their non-gigging group Little Boy Blue and the Blue Boys, with something to think about.[11]

Two similar events happened that night, Saturday 7 April 1962, and neither

made any headlines. Seventeen steps beneath Liverpool streets, in a club running with condensation, the Beatles treated a packed audience to a farewell
session before leaving for Hamburg's red-light district. Two hundred miles
south, sixteen steps beneath London streets, in a club running with condensation, Brian Jones told Mick Jagger and Keith Richards (as he told everyone he
met) he'd shortly be moving to London and forming a band. They'd play none
of that rock 'n' roll shit but stick to the real thing: Muddy Waters, Willie Dixon,
Jimmy Reed, John Lee Hooker, Howlin' Wolf. Within a month, in the 2 May
issue of *Jazz News*, Jones advertised his intention:

RHYTHM AND BLUES
Guitarist and Vocalist forming R.&B. Band, require Harmonica and/or
Tenor Sax, Piano, Bass, and Drums. Must be keen to rehearse. Plenty of
interesting work available.
BOX No. 1277.[12]

The slow but steady rise of R&B groups in the south of England was no more
noticed by recording managers than the surge in 'beat group' activity up north.
In December, Brian Epstein had enticed a Decca man to Liverpool and got the
attention of EMI . . . then EMI folded, Decca rejected, and he was never again
able to get anyone to so much as *look* at the Beatles. 'There was a lot of heavy
grind for Brian in the early days,' John once remarked, and he probably didn't
know the half of it. 'He never stopped,' says Bobby Brown, 'he was *always going
somewhere*.' Brian himself would recall the period by saying, 'I did everything
I could. Everything. I shouted from the rooftops.'[13]

Some days he was consumed with anger over his treatment, and on others
his morale hit the floor and he questioned his abilities. Bob Wooler would
describe occasions when, after a Cavern midday session, Brian took him to his
favourite lunch café, Peacocks, and metaphorically cried on his shoulder. 'He
would say, "What am I doing wrong? Why aren't the record people responding?" All I could say was, "I can't believe it, Brian. They should come and see
what the Beatles are doing to audiences." He was so disappointed – but he was
persistent and determined to make a breakthrough. Of course, his family
couldn't see it – they were saying, "Give up, Brian. You've given it a go, now give
it up."'[14]

Brian wouldn't give up. In 1962, EMI and Decca had 80 per cent of the
record market between them, with four or five other companies sharing the rest.
He saw them all. The list of men who rejected the Beatles but signed the flimsiest of inexperienced talent on the strangest of whims is longer than will ever

be known – it was so quickly something none dared admit . . . but (to a greater or lesser degree) it encompassed the A&R staff at Pye, Philips, Ember and Oriole Records.*

There was more to these rejections than an inability to hear the Beatles. Londoners were sniffy about Liverpool – they always had been and always would be. Brian's and the Beatles' undiluted determination to achieve their breakthrough *from Liverpool*, on their own terms, was not doing them any favours in the capital. Less than a year later, interviewed for Peter Cook's Soho-based arts magazine *Scene*, Brian remembered, 'London agents said we'd never do it from Liverpool, we'd never get the TV exposure and all that. It was hard getting them work.' Clive Epstein would recall how his brother 'put up with rudeness and indifference and doors being slammed in his face'.[15]

Brian was also continually told *Change the name Beatles*. It was preventing their progress. Ditch it, call them something more sensible, less unpleasant. Bob Wooler was again the confidant. 'They said, "What do you mean by *the Beatles*?" Brian would spell it out for them and they said, "What a ridiculous name!" He said to me, "They're suggesting that as the name Beatles doesn't mean anything they'll have to change it." I reassured Brian the name was positively valid, not just because they were known on the local scene but because it was a short name and, when you put it on posters, the shorter the name the bigger the print.'[16]

The Beatles took all this news badly. They were steamed up about Londoners' patronising attitude to Liverpool, and became all the more determined to show them. But how? After EMI, Decca, Philips, Pye, Oriole and Ember, there was nowhere else; the few other record companies that existed were niche-specialists with no chance of charting a record. John, Paul and sometimes George would meet Brian off the London train, a four-hour-plus run from Euston. They sat in the Punch and Judy, a 'greasy spoon' caff down the slope outside Lime Street station, and when Eppy walked in with a long face they knew he was home empty-handed. When Brian's London meetings took him past six o'clock he'd be aboard the night's final train, the 8.45, pulling into Liverpool at 1.45 after a change at Crewe. They'd retire to Duke Street and

---

* In this period when the Beatles couldn't get a contract, record company signings followed the pattern established over many years. Philips snapped up a Canadian singing wrestler, Frankie Townsend, and a middle-aged London housewife singer, Mary May; Oriole signed a singing builder's labourer they renamed Brett Ansell; Mike Smith at Decca produced house-decorator singer Vern Brandon; Wally Ridley at HMV signed ten-year-old schoolboy singer Stephen Sinclair; Norrie Paramor at Columbia signed Welsh council draughtsman singer Peter Harvey, plus 'pint-sized' 15-year-old schoolboy singer Ian Vint, and four singing-trumpeters called the Bell-Tones. And so on, ad infinitum. Here was the rut of *old show business* – and not one electric guitar anywhere.

digest the news over one of Joe's late-late curries. As John would describe it, 'He used to come back from London and couldn't face us because he'd been down about twenty times and come back to say, "Well, I'm afraid they didn't accept it again." And by then we were a bit close with him and he was really hurt. He'd be terrified to tell us that we had not made it again. He did all that – he went around, smarming and charming everybody.'[17]

Those were retrospective remarks. Bob Wooler would remember Beatles irritation over Brian's failures, and how 'John lost patience with him from time to time, which didn't help'. John admitted to this: 'We did have a few little fights with Brian. We used to say he was doing nothing and we were doing all the work. We were just saying it, really. We knew how hard he was working. It was *Us against Them*.'[18]

At the end of the line was a laugh, as there always was. In his autobiography, Brian related the tale of a despondent night in Joe's Restaurant when every record company had turned them down and every idea had been explored. 'Right. Try Embassy,' John suddenly said. Embassy was Woolworth's budget label, cover versions of chart hits performed in the style of the originals by singers and session men under other names. Embassy records sold well but didn't qualify for the charts, and the label was artistically moribund: it didn't sign creative talent. They laughed long ... and hard ... because, really, where were they? 'It was,' says Paul, 'all a bit *bloody hell, what are we gonna do?*'[19]

John and Paul were openly gloomy about their chances of success. 'We didn't think we were going to make it at all,' John recalled two years later ... before adding that they hadn't *all* been so pessimistic: 'It was only Brian telling us we were going to make it, and George. Brian Epstein and George Harrison.'[20] So this one time when the seemingly indefatigable Lennon and McCartney felt defeated, their young friend George stayed optimistic. He rallied them, he showed them that while *they* might be thinking the worst, *he* was remaining hopeful. Wasn't 'Something'll turn up' the Beatles' mantra? Such was the depth, and the strength, of the personalities in this group.

The rejections put a crimp in Brian's management expansion plans. In mid-March, he wrote to the other groups he'd said he would handle – anything between two and five of them, including Gerry and the Pacemakers and the Remo Four – to withdraw his offer. He had to get the Beatles a record deal, and would branch out into wider management later. Despite this, he decided to set up a separate company for his entrepreneurial interests – his stewardship of the Beatles, his developing ideas to become a promoter, and, eventually, the management of other artists. It would be a proper business on a proper business footing, with its own office, staff, banking and stationery. His idea was to involve Clive as much as possible: Brian considered his brother 'the businessman of the family: calm, cool and efficient', and working in tandem would give him a layer of protection against their father's opposition.[21]

This time, there was a vital difference in Brian's message to his father: he was transparent in his commitment to doing *just this*, being an impresario, and therefore he'd be taking a reduced involvement in the shops. Clive would remain hands-on, but Brian wouldn't be, not so much; he would promote Peter Brown from Great Charlotte Street to become manager of the Whitechapel record department, to handle the responsibility he was relinquishing. Harry's objections were understood and noted, but Brian pressed ahead. He had his lawyer process an application to the Board of Trade for the formation of a company called BC Enterprises Ltd – BC for Brian and Clive, styled this way, no spaces or stops. He expected everything to be up and running by the time of his return from Hamburg, after he'd overseen the Beatles' first week or so there ...

... which was a trip that almost didn't happen. It suddenly materialised during March that Paul and Pete needed official, individual clearance letters to get back into Germany. The legacy of their 1960 deportation, that crazy Bambi Kino incident, was rearing up again. The police dispensation they'd scrambled to get at the last moment the previous March, so they could play the Top Ten season, was for twelve months only and would expire on 28 March 1962, two weeks before their Hamburg return. Just like Allan Williams before him, Brian suddenly found himself jumping through bureaucratic hoops at the German Consulate in Liverpool, filling out forms and begging and scraping to get the troublesome Messrs McCartney and Best back into Deutschland. He was successful, but future restrictions were enforced even tighter: permit applications would have to be made on a trip-by-trip basis.

They'd soon be seeing Astrid, Klaus and Stuart again. On 3 February, just before Stuart's trip to Liverpool, these close friends were photographed together during a carnival at Stuart's Hochschule. It was a dressing-up event: Klaus wore a velvet shirt with medieval ruffle, and Stuart wore tight black leather trousers, black winkle-picker shoes, and a black shirt tied like a blouson halfway down his chest, showing his navel. He looked well, confident, the same hip individual he'd been since landing in Hamburg eighteen months earlier. It was one of several fine, recent photos. Stuart *was* ill, but in short interludes of better health Astrid was able to photograph him. He could have stepped back alongside John any time. With the combed-forward fringe, boots, black T-shirt, waistcoat and skinny tie, he was the Altona Beatle, not yet 22. Astrid took his picture in Reinhart Wolf's studio, and in Stuart's artist's garret at the Kirchherr-Bergmann house, standing by the easel that held yet another brilliantly intense new canvas. In one photo, the left side of Stuart's face was illuminated by the light streaming through the attic window, and the right side, to the room, was in shadow.

The camera loved and tragically lied. Stuart wasn't well at all. Around mid-March, his headaches became dramatically more violent – he suffered vicious, debilitating attacks that lasted hours and sometimes days. As Astrid remembers, 'He didn't know what was happening to him. He went from one doctor to another and they couldn't help him. If he was writing a letter, his handwriting would get very weird when the attack was at its highest point. He'd keep holding the pen but it was just lines and scribble. He was a very, very controlled person and was trying to get the pain under control . . .'[22]

Nielsa Kirchherr paid the medical bills, which included a course of spinal massage. After one session Stu and Astrid passed an undertaker's window displaying coffins: Stuart said he didn't want the standard one, he wanted pure white wood. Nielsa rebuked him for saying such things. To his own mother, Stuart started letters he never completed, the barely legible ones described by Astrid, half-formed words calling himself 'a very sick little boy' scratched across the pages.

Hamburg's imminent new rock 'n' roll venue now had a name: the Star-Club. It had picked itself – the biggest stars would work its stage, and Manfred Weissleder could make use of the giant, five-pointed yellow neon star erected over the entrance when it was the Stern-Kino (Star-Cinema). It was at Grosse Freiheit 39, in the heart of the action, and Peter Eckhorn knew his reign running St Pauli rock was finished. Half his Top Ten house band had already been lured across, first Roy Young and then Tony Sheridan. Eckhorn could count his contractual release money while staring at an empty stage.

Since the new band needed a drummer, Sheridan got back in touch with Ringo. He was offered a year's contract, running to April 1963 – he'd get about £30 a week, an apartment and the use of a car. It was his best deal yet. Had he not left Hamburg in February, it would have been a cinch. If Hamburg's fatal floods hadn't come and Granny Annie hadn't died, he'd probably just have switched clubs like Sheridan and Young did – *alley oop*! As it was, he'd gone home and picked up other offers, new adventures to explore, not old ones to repeat. While he'd had a great time in Hamburg and was very tempted to return, he said no. As Sheridan and Young stayed in St Pauli more or less continuously from this point, year after year until later in the decade, Ringo's instinctive decision was crucial to his future.

Sheridan's was just one of four offers Ringo received in the space of about three weeks. The second was to join Howie Casey and the Seniors on the road, and the third was the one he accepted – to rejoin the Hurricanes. It wasn't so much that he craved their company or musicianship, though they were all still mates, it was what they were doing that interested him: they were off to France for a month or more, to play to the soldiers at a United States Army base.

Only four months after Ringo reluctantly ended his Houston emigration plans, he'd be inside the little American enclaves that dotted the post-war European landscape, enjoying access to PX shops full of amazing American goods. And as it also happened that the Hurricanes' return from France would lead into a third straight Butlin's summer season, running from the start of June to early September, Ringo would be back with Rory another six months before considering his next move.

The US Army contract had one stipulation: the Hurricanes had to have a female singer. The GIs didn't want to sit looking at men all night long, they wanted *a broad*. Richy failed to persuade Swinging Cilla to make the trip (her dad wouldn't let her go), but they found their girl in Vicky Woods, an attractive blonde who sang in a double-act with her mother in Liverpool's other thriving entertainment scene, clubland – the working men's, church, social and political clubs that ran parallel to the rock/jive business but rarely crossed over. With Vicky on board, Rory & Co were ready once more to put their passports to good use, and Ringo's return gave them the boost they'd been lacking since he left – in his *Echo* ad for their booking at New Brighton Tower on 23 March, Sam Leach announced they were 'back to their top form'. Ringo was in the groove, the man of the moment, respected by and in demand from fellow musicians ... and it was just days after committing to France that he got his fourth offer. Liverpool's number one group wanted him.

The Beatles had between eight and ten bookings a week and sometimes someone was ill and couldn't play. Gerry Marsden deputised for George one lunchtime; Gerry was about five inches smaller, so John and Paul found an orange box from the Fruit Exchange and made him stand on it. Gerry was always up for a laugh and he knew the numbers well enough to make a proper contribution. On Monday 26 March, the Beatles had a lunchtime session in the Cavern and an evening booking at the Kingsway Club in Southport, and, late in the morning, Pete phoned in sick. One name came to mind: the man they'd enjoyed playing with at their Christmas party three months earlier. The Beatles instructed Brian to fetch Ringo.

It was already midday, Cavern starting time, when Brian knocked at 10 Admiral Grove. Elsie left him waiting outside while she went upstairs and rapped on her Richy's bedroom door. He was in bed. He came down and Brian said the Beatles wanted him, and they had to leave immediately. Ringo said he was more than happy to play with the Beatles but wasn't going anywhere until he'd put on some trousers and drunk a brew of tea. Aware of the clock, Brian was no doubt fit to burst, but he had to wait. The two had exchanged a brief hello once or twice in past weeks, when Ringo had gone along to see the Beatles play, but their first proper meeting was in Brian's car as he sped Ringo down the hill to the Cavern. As Ringo would recall, 'I didn't know much about him, except how strange it was that the Beatles had a manager, because none of us had a real manager.'[23]

The Beatles were in uncharacteristic disarray – Cavernites were shouting they'd have to be getting back to work soon, so were they gonna start playing? The drums were assembled around Ringo (by Neil, presumably) only after they finally started, and it was twenty minutes before he had a full kit. But when he did, the four of them gelled as a musical unit just as they'd done in December. As Ringo said, 'They were doing really great tracks – Shirelles tracks and Chuck Berry tracks – [and] they did it so well. They had a good style. There was a whole feel about Paul, George and John. And Pete Best – it's no offence, but I never felt he was a great drummer. He had one sort of style, which was very good for them in those years, I suppose, but they felt, I think, that they wanted to move out of it more.'[24]

Ringo wasn't familiar with *all* the songs, but his bandmates were more than happy with the way he played. Paul said he was particularly pleased with his work on What'd I Say, John loved the way he 'went to the toms [tom-tom drums]' in the middle-eight of Rock And Roll Music, and George simply enjoyed the complete experience, commenting, 'Every time Ringo sat in, it seemed like "this is it".'[25] George admired Ringo: he liked his drumming, his attitude, their chemistry, and that he didn't rush away afterwards but was looking for the same good time they were. 'Pete would go off on his own and we three would hang out together, and then when Ringo was around it was like a full unit, both on and off the stage. When there were the four of us with Ringo, it felt rocking.'[26]

They had Southport in the evening. Pete would have gone home for a few hours, but John, Paul, George and Ringo were tight together through an afternoon's drinking in the Colony Club, Lord Woodbine's dicey establishment off Upper Parliament Street. It was right around the corner from the children's playground factory where 16-year-old Richy had apprenticed to become a fitter. The talk now was of a different job. 'George was saying, "Would you like to join the band?" I was saying, "Yeah, I'd love to, but you've got a drummer . . ." and he started to instigate it with the other two, saying to them, "Why don't we get Ringo in the band?"'[27]

The Beatles weren't only best, they were top dollar: Ringo pocketed £9 from these two shows. Brian's steady pushing meant they now earned £12 for a

Cavern lunchtime and £24 in Southport, sums that were off-the-scale compared to other groups: a typical 'top' Liverpool group in spring 1962 got £5–7
a night, and if the Hurricanes bettered this it wasn't by much. This would be
divided among all the musicians and a roadie, and few lads walked away with
more than a pound a night – not always enough to meet the hire-purchase payments on the guitar or drums. Nine pounds for two shows made a deep
impression on Ringo.[28]

The number of times Ringo deputised because Pete didn't play with the
Beatles would become exaggerated. 'Pete used to be off all the time, he used
to keep being ill and not showing up,' George would claim, which was as untrue
as Pete's insistence it happened twice.[29] There were four gigs: 27 December
1961, two here on 26 March, and one more a couple of days later, when Ringo
played the Cavern's Wednesday lunchtime session before Pete resumed in the
evening. Whatever the number, though, what was relevant was that George
started to initiate getting Pete out and Ringo in. 'I was the one responsible for
getting Ringo in the group,' he would reveal. 'Every time Ringo played with us
the band really swung. I conspired to get Ringo in – I talked to Paul and John
until they came round to the idea. They all had their reasons [for getting rid
of Pete] too.'[30] Pete always said he knew nothing of this, and as he only saw
them on stage and backstage there wasn't much opportunity to notice whispers
or glances.

In the meantime, George and Ringo shared a moment they'd always treasure. While drinking on the Monday afternoon, George mentioned he was
buying a car and needed to get to Warrington to collect it. Ringo offered him
a lift. It happened some time over the next two days, just before Ringo left for
France.

George was the first Beatle to buy a car. Paul was having lessons but hadn't
yet taken the driving test, and no one ever considered John would drive – the
roads in Liverpool would have been a lot less safe if he had. Like his brothers
and his dad, George had a strong interest in motors; he took driving lessons and
passed the test first time, probably during March. So keen was he to drive that
he got a car right away, even though the Beatles were about to go to Hamburg.
He bought it from Brian's friend Terry Doran, who worked at a dealership in
Warrington – it was a secondhand two-door blue Ford Anglia 105E Deluxe and
even had a *radio*. George bought it 'on the knocker' – a cash deposit followed
by weekly payments – and Terry gave him a good price and asked George to
advertise where he'd bought it.

George had been a Formula One fan since boyhood, and within months he'd
picked up two cautions for speeding (one more and he'd be disqualified for a
year). This first day he got away with it. George and Ringo raced back from

Warrington to Liverpool, Ford Anglia against Ford Zodiac, Beatle versus Hurricane. When a slow car held them up, George squeezed a narrow overtake, put his foot down and pulled clear. Ringo just couldn't get by and was 'right up his arse' when a dog ran into the road, the driver hit the brakes and Ringo, as he later put it, 'smashed right into him and broke the fuck out of my car'. He was by a garage and limped in, but because he'd no licence or insurance he was in a spot of bother. George tore home, the winner, checking his rear-view mirror and wondering where Ringo had gone. He wouldn't see him again for four months or more, but he had him in his sights all the way.[31]

Ringo went overseas with the satisfaction of knowing the Beatles wanted him, but it may quickly have receded in his mind. His destination was the USA6 base at Fontenet, in the Charente-Maritime department of south-west France, about ninety kilometres from the Atlantic coast. Rory, Johnny, Ty, Vicky and their luggage filled a car, so Ringo and Bobby Thompson (replacement for Lu Walters) went by train. It was a marathon journey dragging drum cases – train to London, across London, train to Dover, boat to Calais, train to Bordeaux, then taxi – and there was police trouble in Paris when they were mistaken for Algerian independence terrorists. They arrived at the camp the night of Sunday 1 April, exhausted and wishing they hadn't bothered . . . and yet here they were with their instruments and their bright red suits, and for at least a month – three hours a night, six nights in every seven – they'd be the English musicians pumping rock and roll back at the people who'd exported it, their American audience in the Enlisted Men's Club.[32]

The Beatles first wore their suits in Liverpool on 29 March, in the long, narrow basement of the Odd Spot coffee bar on Bold Street. Brian said that this booking – and up to three others in the immediate period – was too important for them to wear anything else, although he and the Beatles were still planning a dramatic unveiling of the new look in a week's time in the Cavern during *The Beatles For Their Fans* show. He asked a friend, Alan Swerdlow, to take some live action photos in the Odd Spot, but they didn't turn out well. Brian also needed studio photos, and these were taken towards the end of March by Harry Watmough, 28, who had a studio in Moorfields, in Liverpool's business district.

Watmough found the Beatles, and Brian, awkward customers, full of opinions about what they wanted him to achieve. He worked in black-and-white and must have shot several rolls of film, though only six images are known. Brian picked three of them for 'throwaway cards'; Watmough added 'The Beatles' underneath in Gill Sans Bold and printed a thousand. The vast leap in the availability of Beatles autographs in spring/summer 1962 owes not only to their growing popularity and accessibility but also to these thousand cards, plus a further thousand of the Beatles in their leathers – the best of Albert Marrion's photos. John, Paul, George and Pete took some to every show to give away, proffering their signatures if not asked. They'd been signing as 'stars' since May 1960, but not too often; from this point in spring 1962, giving autographs became a forever fact of life.

They took the cards with them when, on 31 March, they played their first real date in the south of England, organised by Brian with London-based promoter and musician Jack Fallon. The booking was in Stroud, 150 miles from home, and the Beatles were outsiders here, Liverpool accents in Italianate suits – although, just as much as the southern audience was watching the northerners, the northerners were sussing the southerners, especially the southern girls, forming opinions to be succinctly expressed in the van going home. The birds and lads here spoke with a Gloucestershire burr but they weren't hicks when it came to rock. Stroud was an out-of-the-way place and its grand Subscription Rooms ballroom an unlikely venue, but, through Fallon's efforts, the Saturday-night hops usually had 'name' headliners. Paid £30 for their night's work, the Beatles broke into a new circuit here, drawing the same kind of attendance as others – 466 – because people went to 'the dance' no matter who was on.[33]

One of the 466 was Bob Lusty – local DJ, knowledgeable music aficionado and record shop assistant – who didn't work at 'the Subs' but went every week to check out the groups. The area around Stroud was home to a sizeable number of European migrants and Lusty's record shop specialised in continental labels like Polydor. He knew My Bonnie and, when he read the Beatles were coming, gambled on an order of two boxes of twenty-five, taking them to the dance in the hope of selling them. Getting there early, his enquiries revealed the Beatles had arrived and were in a café across the street.

> I told them who I was and what I did, and asked if I could talk to them. I sat with them for ages and wish I'd had a tape recorder or written it down. I realised right away they were unlike any other group I'd seen, that they had a lot of experience. They'd been around and had old heads on their shoulders. They were quite amazed someone in this neck of the woods knew about them, and said, 'Are you going to sell all those records tonight?' I said I'd try.
>
> I sold them *all*. (My shop manager was amazed.) The Beatles created a lot of excitement – most of the groups who came to Stroud sang chart stuff but the Beatles varied it. They did some current hits but they also played Little Richard and things like The Honeymoon Song and Besame Mucho, which I knew to be continental songs, and they were *harmonising*. A lot of people stopped dancing and stood and watched. I thought to myself, 'I *like* this group.'[34]

Then, on 5 April, came the Fan Club night, every bit as eventful and memorable as Brian and the Beatles had wished. The buzz started at the Cavern's entrance table – five hundred were getting into both a show and an exciting new club. Many had already completed the application form, printed on the reverse of the admission ticket, and Brian was there to help hand out the free glossy photo of the Beatles in leathers, and to explain that everyone would be sent a membership card within days, receive a newsletter from the Beatles in Hamburg, and be notified of other exclusive offers. Bob Wooler (advertised as the Beatles' favourite compere) was DJ on this special night, and the Beatles chose the funny rocking Four Jays as their guest act, to keep the laughs going.

As soon as the Four Jays opened proceedings, the Beatles opened a show of their own in the minuscule dressing-room. The Cavern was 'dry' but they'd smuggled down some booze and were getting stuck in. For Bobby Brown, after so much detailed planning and work, the Fan Club night was about to come unstuck. 'I was watching the show out front with Mike [McCartney], then we went into the bandroom. I was a fairly quiet person and John was always trying to get me to talk more; he knew I never drank but he kept saying, "Come on Bobby, have a drink!" So I did. I don't know what it was, but he kept encouraging me to drink it up . . .'

The Beatles played their first spot in the outfits everyone knew and loved, what John called 'the leather suits', and as the drink and atmosphere took effect the event zipped merrily along . . . though a little *too* merrily for Bobby on her big night.[35]

Mike knew I really liked Paul and dared me to kiss him when he came off stage. Because I'd had a drink I threw my arms around him and we had a necking session. Half the other girls wanted to tear my hair out, and Paul was looking at John as if to say 'What have you *done* to her?'

Soon after that, I was being sick with my head down the toilet, crying. Paul was so lovely – he came to see if I was all right, he fetched my coat and bag and looked after me. My mum would have gone mad if I'd gone home in that state so I went to a friend's house and phoned to say I was ill – and I was.

The Beatles peeled off their leathers during the interval and Bob Wooler prefaced their return to the stage with a big announcement: 'The Beatles will be appearing in their *new suits*!' This was the moment of change. Four months earlier, John and Paul had dared play their self-written songs to the Cavern crowd, knowing they'd find the softest landing here, and now came another test of favour from the faithful. Some 650 witnessed it, subsequently explaining their thoughts as if they were felt universally. 'When they appeared in the suits everybody *screamed* because they looked so handsome,' recalls Barbara Houghton. 'I still liked them in the leathers but the suits were good.' Bernadette Farrell felt disappointed: 'It was a surprise, to say the least – they didn't seem to feel right in them, and everybody thought "They look smart but it's not *our Beatles.*"[36] Not even the Beatles could please all the people all the time – but this was their special audience, and their special audience wasn't rushing for the exit.

Having brought a camera from home, Lou Steen took the first Cavern photos of the new apparel ... as well as capturing the instant when Pete Best fell in love. He came to the front to sing Peppermint Twist and danced on stage with Walton girl Catherine (Kathy) Johnson, one of a group of dancers called the Kingtwisters who were organised and encouraged by Bob Wooler. John, Paul and George extended the song, turning the middle-eight into a middle-eighty, and Pete and Kathy twisted themselves into love. It was his happiest night in the group, and Lou's camera snapped him, microphone in hand.

Lou also photographed her heart-throb on the drums – Paul, blurred in the background, his hair plastered down by sweat, jacket off, tie pulled loose, top shirt-button undone ... and grinning from ear to ear because he was having such a fantastic time and because it was his little friend Louey taking the photo. She froze a turning-point in Paul McCartney's life – in a suit in the Cavern for the first time, things *really happening* for him now.

It was an incredible night, and when it was all over, and everyone was put in mind of catching the last bus home, the Beatles quietened the audience for a special parting message, one they'd considered in advance and were keen to transmit: 'Don't forget us.' This was their penultimate Cavern show before leaving and they'd be gone within a week, not returning until June. Nothing fazed the Beatles, people said, but there was always a certain vulnerability. They worried the avalanche of goodwill they'd amassed since July 1961 might melt in their absence. As Lindy Ness remembers, 'They said, "We're going to play seven weeks in Hamburg and we don't want you to forget us while we're away. It'll be nice if you write to us." And they gave out the address of the club. They thought we'd forget them and move to some other group! My friends and I split the Beatles between us: Suzy wrote to George, Louey wrote to Paul and I wrote one letter to George and many to John, and we all got letters back.'

Then the Beatles stepped down from the stage and this fantastic night – arguably their best of the year, written up in the next *Mersey Beat* as their 'greatest-ever performance'[37] – ended in a mass scrum. They were engulfed, swarmed over for kisses and backslaps and autographs, every inch the phenomenon people described.

All this time, Lindy Ness was drawing closer to John. They were photographed together outside the Cavern two nights later, and she went back to Woolton with him in the van, driven by Neil. John's interest wasn't romantic or sexual, which was just as well since she'd only just turned 15; he just enjoyed her personality and sharp sense of humour and didn't mind having her around. Literally so, because before Lindy walked home from Menlove Avenue, John invited her and Lou to Sunday afternoon tea with him and Mimi. This was a first.

Lindy's diary for 8 April is headlined HAPPY DAY, recording the time she went to Mendips and had tea with John, his 14-year-old cousin David Birch, Mimi, and Lou. John himself poured her what he called 'a tup of twee'. She was surprised to see him wearing glasses. They talked, ate cake, supped their twee and watched TV. While the diary states 'His aunt is weird', Lindy only remembers Mimi as kind and engaging company. Lou recalls being 'Extremely excited. I remember going through the porch and finding it dark inside, though it was bright outside. They had proper cups and saucers, and Mimi was small and dead chatty.'

It was Mimi's first real encounter with Beatles fans, and her enduring opinion of their collective character was based on the visitors this spring Sunday afternoon. When, in 1977, she wrote 'There is a big difference in intelligence and lively outlook in the girls who like John and those who go for the other Beatles – this has long been clear to me from the very beginning', she was (a) being typically snobbish; (b) broadly correct; and (c) thinking of Lindy and Lou.[38]

Along with the other important developments in spring 1962 was the arrival of a point in the lives of John, Paul, George and (to a lesser extent) Pete when girls started hanging around outside their houses, knocking on doors, and phoning with Cavern song requests or to grab a one-to-one moment. And when the objects of desire were out, it became something for Mimi, Jim, Louise and Harry and Mona to handle. This *thing* their boys had been doing all these years, this 'it'll never last' music that kept them busy most nights of the week, was beginning to amount to something, taking on a new shape – a fact that they too had to deal with.

Lou went to the Casbah that Sunday night for what the home-stencilled poster correctly called THE BEATLES' LAST PERFORMANCE IN LIVERPOOL BEFORE GOING TO GERMANY. Ironically, George had come down with German measles (rubella) and Brian wouldn't let him play in case it set back his recovery. The symptoms were known to pass quickly but it was already apparent George wouldn't be fit to fly two days later. Brian said John, Paul and Pete should go on as booked and he would wait a day or so, by which point George might be strong enough to travel.

John and Paul were back at 8 Hayman's Green the morning of Tuesday 10 April. They'd left their guitars here Sunday night and now loaded them into the van with Pete's drums, while John carried the harmonica in his pocket; Neil then drove the three of them to Ringway Airport, Manchester. There were no direct flights to Hamburg – they had to fly to Amsterdam and change – but where their road and boat journey in 1960 had taken more than thirty-six hours, and their train and boat journey in 1961 twenty-six hours, by the modern miracle of air travel they were in Hamburg mid-afternoon. Pete condensed their initial excitement in a letter home: 'From the airport we got a taxi to the club and moved into our rooms. These are OK and we have our own bath and shower and hot water. After this, the trio moved into the club to see what it was like and believe-you-me it's really something. This club is an old converted picture house and has a massive great stage and a fantastic lighting system. It also has an upstairs where people can sit . . .'[39]

That night, they were treated to drinks and steaks by the new bossman, the flash, crop-haired Manfred Weissleder. It would have been foolish to refuse. John seems to have made no attempt to contact Stuart yet – but it would have been too late anyway.

They had no idea that Stu had suffered a violent convulsive fit at noon this same day, that it lasted thirty-five minutes, that he slipped into a coma, that Nielsa Kirchherr summoned Astrid home from work, and that, at 4.30PM, in an ambulance speeding him to hospital, Stuart died in his fiancée's arms.

27

'He could easily have been *the* Beatle'
(10–13 April 1962)

The news reached Liverpool in reverse: a telegram from Astrid to Millie Sutcliffe saying Stuart had died came before another saying he was dangerously ill. The truth was clear and appalling. He was 21 years and 10 months.

Millie was shattered. Stuart was the eldest of her three children, the only son. Things had started going wrong the day he became a *strolling minstrel*, plucking his rock and roll, chucking his final year at Liverpool College of Art to play with the Beatles in Germany, getting engaged to Astrid Kirchherr and making Hamburg his home. Millie had hardly seen him in twenty months – and now her boy was *dead*.

Charles Sutcliffe, Stuart's father, couldn't be reached. A naval second engineer, he'd sailed for South America two days earlier. 'He has a weak heart and we cannot radio his ship to tell him,' Joyce Sutcliffe (Stuart's eldest sister, 20) told the *Liverpool Echo*, while the *Prescot & Huyton Reporter* reported that a padre would meet him when the ship docked in Buenos Aires after three weeks. Stuart's death was in all the local press, not because he was Stuart Sutcliffe (he had, as yet, no public reputation) or because he'd been in the Beatles (the *Echo* journalist wrote 'Stuart went to Germany 18 months ago with a Liverpool skiffle group') but simply because it was a newsworthy tragedy.[1]

Allan Williams was distraught. He too received word direct from Astrid. Allan and Beryl had provided a haven for her and Stuart during their stormy visits to Liverpool – and they'd be instrumental again in keeping warring parties at bay. Allan's memory is that he broke the news to Millie before the arrival of those telegrams. 'She was heartbroken. She always called him "Wee Stuart" and he was the love of her life. Then I contacted Brian Epstein. I knew he was flying to Hamburg and said, "Will you travel over with Millie?" I paid her fare and they travelled together.'[2]

As Millie would remember, the first Beatle to hear the news was George, who'd stayed in Liverpool after the others travelled ahead. 'Brian said he'd call for me to travel to Manchester airport with them in his car. And that was when George burst into tears, on my doorstep. He cried like a child. Brian had apparently cabled the Beatles confirming his arrival and asking them to meet the flight. He said I was in the party – but didn't tell them why. Presumably, he thought they'd already heard the news.'[3]

John, Paul and Pete were at Hamburg airport to greet them. Manfred Weissleder had loaned them a driver and his big American car, a Chevrolet Impala with built-in record player and cocktail bar. On the way, they felt on top of the world; on the way back, that world had caved in. At the terminal, waiting for George and Brian, they saw Astrid and Klaus, who'd come to collect Millie. 'Where's Stu?' they asked – and it was here and now that Astrid told them he was dead. 'Paul tried to be comforting; he put his arm around me and said how sorry he was. Pete wept – he just sat there and cried his eyes out. John went into hysterics. We couldn't make out, in the state we [Klaus and I] were both in, whether he was laughing or crying because he did everything at once. I remember him sitting on a bench, huddled over, and he was shaking, rocking backwards and forwards.'[4]

John went out of control, just like when Uncle George, his surrogate father, had died when John was 14, and when his mother was killed when he was 17. Everybody *died* on John. 'John didn't laugh when he heard Stuart died, as people have made out,' Paul insists, indicating a reaction far more psychologically complex.[5]

For Paul himself, Stuart's death was tough in a different way. He was shocked and saddened, but he also had to reconcile his position within the unfolding scene. He'd openly teased, taunted, irritated and derided him for two years or more, his jealousy of Stu's friendship with John sustained; the last real time he'd seen Stuart was when he'd so needled him, Stuart was finally goaded into a fight, on stage, in front of an audience. It was declared a draw, but everyone talked of how surprisingly strong Stuart was; Paul had started the scrap and not won. When Stuart was in Liverpool in February, he'd mostly avoided Paul. There are quotes about that trip from John, George, Pete and Mike McCartney, but not Paul; Mike had exchanged letters with Stuart and was now being quoted in the *Echo* talking about him, Paul wasn't.

The upshot was that, aside from the other Beatles, Paul was disliked by the people who loved Stuart – notably Astrid, Klaus, and Stuart's family – and Stuart's death slammed a lid on it. As Paul would concede, 'It was really sad for me because I hadn't liked him and it's kind of too late when someone dies – you can't go back [and say] "Hey, Stu, I was only kidding ..." His mum and his sister never felt too good about me.'[6]

Millie Sutcliffe said John averted his eyes when she entered the arrivals hall, but there was rarely much affection between the two of them and none by the time (1970) she made this remark, so the truth is hard to establish.[7] It was, of course, simply a horrible time for everyone. Millie and Astrid, the two principal mourners, had the worst relationship of all, but here they were, thrown together in grief and a thousand angry questions.

Millie had formally to identify her son's corpse. A gruelling scene was played out in private at the morgue, enough to establish further polarisation between Millie on one side and Astrid and Klaus on the other. Millie also had to arrange transportation of the body back to England, for the funeral. She wasn't going to let him be buried in Germany. Her anti-German feelings had blanketed everything these past twenty months. As Allan Williams had noted, she held the opinion shared by many in Britain while the two world wars were in living memory: 'The only good German is a dead German'. First Germany had bombed Millie's Britain to near-bankruptcy, now her son had died there, with no doctor preventing it. She thought the worst of everyone and everything.

A post-mortem gave the cause of death as a blood clot on the brain. A forensic pathologist, who asked to keep the brain for further examination, added that Stuart had suffered a haemorrhage. Astrid was also told he'd had a rare condition, where the size of his brain was gradually increasing and pressing against his skull. No equipment had yet been invented to diagnose any such symptoms. She further learned that, had Stuart survived the convulsive fit that plunged him into a coma, 'he would have been blind or almost a zombie, and that there wouldn't have been any cure for it. To him, that would have been worse than death.'[8]

It would also be said by several of Stuart's Liverpool art school friends that he'd never been robust – he is remembered variously as weak, sick-looking, delicate, puny, prone to falling over, and vividly foreseeing his early death. Twenty years afterwards, an additional idea also gained ground: that there was a link between Stuart's brain haemorrhage and the night in late January 1961 when he was attacked by Teddy Boys, the incident at Lathom Hall in the north end of Liverpool when John fractured a finger rescuing him. Although the association of these two events would become an accepted truth, it cannot be more than theoretical.[9]

The funeral of Stuart Fergusson Victor Sutcliffe was held on 19 April 1962, the day before Good Friday and the start of the Easter weekend, at St

Gabriel's Chapel of Ease in Huyton. This was where the Sutcliffes had settled after leaving Scotland three years into the last war. Stuart had been a
member of the church's youth club and a choirboy here from nine or ten until
his voice broke.

John, Paul, George and Pete were in Hamburg and sent neither flowers nor
words of sympathy. Cynthia attended, as did Stuart's closest art school friend
Rod Murray. Louise Harrison was present for George. Astrid and Klaus were
there, so too Allan and Beryl and Allan's father, Dick Williams, but not many
others, and few family members. Rod Murray says there was just 'a small room-
ful' of mourners. Stuart was buried in the quiet cemetery across from the
church. Air-transport specifications prohibited the white coffin he'd wanted.
The family's memorial notice, posted in the *Echo* and the local press, said he'd
died 'After much suffering bravely borne' and ended with words from the Book
of Job: 'God hath given and God hath taken away'.[10]

Astrid clung to Beryl for moral and physical support – although, for some
reason, she stayed with Millie and her daughters in their flat on Sefton Park.
They all endured a highly testing time that, says Astrid, climaxed when
Millie accused her of *murdering* Stuart. As she'd done before, Astrid sounded
the alarm and Allan and Beryl rushed over, rescued her from the troubled
waters and let her stay with them in Liverpool 8, where Klaus was already
staying.

The death of Stuart Sutcliffe was heartbreaking in every way.

The variety, quantity and quality of his art had been breathtaking. He was
dead at 21 but had crammed a lifetime's work into a few short years, leaving a
prodigious legacy of landscapes, life studies, abstracts, collages, charcoals and
monotype drawings, executed in an array of styles and all with the utmost commitment. The work of his final months was prolific, intense and dazzling. He
was, by any definition, a real talent.

It soon became impossible to detach Stuart Sutcliffe's life and work from
the swamping shadow of *the Beatles* – but art critics had noticed his gifts years
earlier: he was the art school star scholar and the 19-year-old exhibitor in *The
John Moores Liverpool Exhibition 2*, an accolade put beyond doubt when
Moores personally bought the piece. Eduardo Paolozzi, the British painter and
sculptor who taught Stuart in Hamburg, reflected in 1968, 'If he'd lived he
could easily have been *the* Beatle. He was imaginative, ultra-intelligent, and he
was open to everything, not just to painting or pop but to every media and
experience possible.'[11]

Every experience possible – this was Astrid's loss, a devastating burden to
carry at the age of 23. 'Stuart was somebody very, very special. He had a wisdom,

and the ability to give so much, as far as feeling and love was concerned. We were young and innocent and Stuart gave all he had – he wasn't the type of person who could hide anything. He gave everything fully, not only to me but in his devotion to art. We had loved from first sight and he's the only man I met who I was sure would be "the one" – he would be me and I would be him.'[12]

Stuart played a crucial role in shaping the Beatles. He was Stuart de Staël, with an intuitive understanding of image, essential to their development in 1960–1. He and John together cooked up the Beatles name, and without Stuart they may not have taken the Paris fringe haircuts and collarless jackets and the long black scarves. That these were also Astrid's influences was another vital contribution: he was the bridge that delivered them the inspiration and style of Astrid, Klaus and Jürgen. The Beatles wouldn't have looked continental without their 'angel friends'.

The three Germans loved the Beatles for many reasons, and the Beatles were arty and receptive enough to tune in for themselves. However, it all sprang from their initial fascination with the boy whose bass playing had started off ropey but ended up good, and whose stage presence was *magnetic* – the fragile James Dean dude in dark glasses, the little man in black leather with his big bass guitar and expressive Love Me Tender. Stu had been a Beatle because his soul mate, John, wanted him up there by his side, and he'd left only because his life was no longer in Liverpool, not because they'd kicked him out. They had often been horrible to him, John included, but that was just *life* . . .

The loss to John was incalculable. He and Stu had shared a kinship and rarefied degree of honesty. Five years later he'd say, 'I looked up to Stu. I depended on him to tell me the truth, the way I do with Paul today. Stu would tell me if something was good and I'd believe him.'[13] John never said any more about Stu than this – but while that appears to indicate an almost unique desire to keep his feelings clamped down and private, actually it was because no one asked.* Klaus Voormann observed of John and Stuart's friendship that John was content not to hold the upper hand: 'John looked up to Stuart. It might not come across that way but that's what I felt. And Stuart looked down to John – not in a bad way, but natural. John was more on the funny side of life, making jokes all the time, and while Stuart could be funny he was also serious about things. I've seen the letters between them

---

* John Lennon wasn't one to shy away from a question, but not once in his hundreds of interviews did any journalist or broadcaster bring up the subject of his one-time best friend, the Beatle who'd died so young and so talented at 21.

and you get the feeling of a wise man talking to somebody who's a little help-less: that was Stuart and John respectively.'[14]

Just how much Stuart's death affected John would be seen in the Beatles' seven-week season in the Star-Club. This terrible event cast a gloom over their Hamburg return; but, for everyone else, rock was about to roll Grosse Freiheit once more, and with a vengeance. The Beatles were in the ideal place to work through their latest tough experience. Last time here, Stuart was one of them; this time he was *gone*, and they simply had to get on with it.

'Stuart died loving the Beatles, having hope and faith in everything they did,' Millie would say.[15] On Friday 13 April, with their friend not yet buried, they plugged in once more, yelled *one–two–three–four!* and put that hope and faith to work.

28

You Better Move On (13 April–2 June 1962)

The Beatles In Germany, Brian Epstein's report of the Star-Club opening, went out by post to fan club members and was printed verbatim in *Mersey Beat*. A typed bulletin of 250 words set the scene on 'an exciting season' . . . and Brian made sure to end with breaking news: that the Beatles' first British appearance post-Germany would be in the Cavern on 9 June. They *were* coming home.

The report didn't mention Stuart. He'd not played in Liverpool since March the previous year, and, as few of the fans knew him, it seemed pointless to darken the club's premiere despatch with such shocking news.* In Hamburg, of course, it couldn't be avoided. Astrid stayed away from the opening night, unable to face it and having to keep Millie company at home, but Klaus went. This was Friday and he was flying to England the following afternoon with Millie, Astrid and the coffin. Klaus hadn't seen the Beatles in nine months, and the five-piece group he loved had shrunk to a quartet. Some things never changed, though, like how you couldn't take your eyes off one Beatle in particular.

> That first night at the Star-Club, John came on stage dressed like a cleaning-woman, doing his cripple act and carrying a long wooden plank. He walked across the stage and knocked over the microphones and some of the drum kit, then he went up and cleaned the microphones. He cleaned under Paul's armpit, and George's. The people in the club were laughing – they didn't

---

* Word had reached the grapevine anyway. Lindy Ness's diary entry for 12 April 1962 reads: 'Went to Cave. Joined again. Group called Dakotas on. Kate told us Stu of the Beatles has died.'

know Stuart had died. They didn't know Stuart. It gave me shivers to watch it, but this is what clowns do, bring humour to tragedy. It was hilarious.[1]

There would be quite a few more Lennon incidents to come, enough to form the impression of a young man derailed by the deaths that kept afflicting him. In a time to come he might have been diagnosed as suffering post-trau-matic stress disorder, but in 1962 such terms didn't exist, therapy wasn't offered, and the only pills were little white ones called Prellies. He was fortu-nate to be in one of the few places in the world (the only one in *his* world) where he could be *Lennon* without landing himself in much trouble. For three months Brian had had the Beatles putting miles on the clock, spreading them-selves further from Liverpool, but for the next seven weeks, give or take the odd excursion, John and the others would spend their lives on one short stretch of neon-lit Grosse Freiheit – playing, sleeping, eating, drinking, pissing, shitting, shouting, loving, preaching, puking.

Pacing was the key – pacing in Preludin, booze, hard living and perform-ance – and it was generally remembered the hard way. At the Indra and Top Ten, the Beatles had been the only band on the bill, playing all night long, and at the Kaiserkeller they'd been one of two; here at the Star-Club they were one of two or three and sometimes four, playing in rotation. At the start, as John explained in a letter to Cyn, they played three hours one night and four the next, 'so it doesn't seem long at all really', but eventually they were doing just an hour in the run-up to midnight (usually before 10PM, so under-18s could see them before having to leave) and an hour some time after midnight. Whatever the demands, the Beatles went at them full tilt, hammering their vocal cords and instantly suffering 'Hamburg throat'. A letter written by Pete three days into the season said John, Paul and George had all lost their voices.[2]

It was useful, then, that they sometimes had a fifth man working with them. Roy Young sang and played piano and electric organ in the house band and also did cameos with the other acts, the Beatles included. He was good value – he performed standing up, was almost always grinning, and the side of his grand piano shouted his name in large glittery letters. As Pete didn't have the Beatles' name on his bass drum, they looked like the Roy Young Band.[3]

Horst Fascher was in charge of getting the groups on and off stage on time, the man who put the punch in punctuality. He tells the tale of drinking with John and Brian very late the first night. Brian grew tired and after a few drinks dozed off at the table. John, who'd gulped several more Prellies than anyone else and wasn't only awake but *wired*, poured a half-litre glass of beer over Brian's head and neck. Brian woke up in distress, he and John had a shouting match, and then Brian retired to his hotel, defeated, while John roared on for several more hours, gabbling hysterically. This was something else Brian didn't mention in his report for the fan club.

From its launch night, the Star-Club was Hamburg's number one rock venue. The Top Ten stayed open and staged interesting bands for many years to come, but the Star-Club always stole the headlines and headliners. It wasn't a bar or a dancing club with live music, it was a rock hall – or, in its 1962 vernacular, Rock 'n' Twist (in Hamburg, as in so many parts of the world, any music with a beat was 'Twist' even when it wasn't). There hadn't been a venue like this before, so the Star-Club – dominated by rock groups from Liverpool, England – planted an acorn for change in West Germany's youth culture. It wouldn't have happened without the Kaiserkeller, Indra and Top Ten making it possible, and everything could be traced back two years to Allan Williams turning up in Bruno Koschmider's bar with a tape that wouldn't play. Also, as far as the Beatles were concerned, those earlier venues were more crucial to their development ... but the ultimate recipient of all the Hamburg honours in the Sixties, and when the period was viewed from history, would be the Star-Club.

Diagonally opposite here was the Kaiserkeller, scene of the Beatles' great 1960 *punkfest*, and this was at the end of the block that housed the musicians' accommodation, one floor above a strip club at Grosse Freiheit 30. The Beatles had the use of a room with two bunk beds – Paul and John in one (Paul on top), George and Pete in the other – and though they had a bathroom in Hamburg for the first time, eliminating the need to use Astrid's house or public baths to clean themselves, the room soon became rank.

The Beatles were the highest-paid act in the club's first weeks, top of the bill. Once a week they went to sign for their pay, each pocketing 425 marks in cash, about £38. This was even better than their Liverpool fees, plus their travel had been paid for and the accommodation was free. They all sent money home, and for themselves had only to buy sustenance. Though much of their drinking was done for free in the club, meals were pricey. Star-Club owner Manfred Weissleder deducted Brian Epstein's 15 per cent commission at source (the Beatles' DM425 originally being 500), so Brian too, while he was with them here in Hamburg, signed and received payslips, four lots of DM75 totalling 300 a week. When he wasn't around, the amount accumulated until it was paid as a lump sum.

Weissleder employees enjoyed a level of protection rare in St Pauli. This was invaluable for the British musicians, who – being young, far from home, with mates and heavily partaking of drink, sex and pills – often got into scrapes. Anyone threatening violence towards them faced retribution from the Fascher brothers, Horst, Uwe and Fredi. Horst prided himself on being able to knock people out, and Fredi loved head-butting. He was only small and had to stand on tiptoe, but his aim was true. Victims (who may have done little more than query an inflated bar bill) would be sent reeling in a bloodied mess. Yet the three brothers were all good boys who loved their mother, and they say Mama Fascher washed the Beatles' underwear and shirts by boiling them up in a big pot.[4]

It was the Faschers who had to cope with pressure situations created by John Lennon, whether it was Fredi calming customers who didn't appreciate being called *fucking Nazis* or Horst having to pay John's way out of a police cell. 'Scarcely a day went by without something strange happening,' Horst says, 'more than in all the previous years put together.'[5] Some of the stories would be embellished and 'romanticised' with time, but John did teeter alarmingly close to sanity's edge here. George was second only to John in the swallowing of Prellies and knew better than most the sum effect of taking too many for too long, how the combination of pills plus booze plus several sleepless days caused hallucinations and extreme conduct. He'd describe one occasion when he, Paul and Pete were lying in their bunk beds, trying to sleep, only for John to barge into the room in a wild state. 'One night John came in and some chick was in bed with Paul and he cut all her clothes up with a pair of scissors, and was stabbing the wardrobe. Everybody was lying in bed thinking, "Oh fuck, I hope he doesn't kill me." [He was] a frothing mad person – he knew how to have "fun".'[6]

Handling John was something his friends were well used to doing. If he didn't murder them in their beds there was no greater buddy. They might fear for their lives but they loved him still. No way would they walk out and join another group. John was just *John*, and Paul and George's hero-worship stayed fully intact.

Any calming influence Cynthia might have had was out of reach (although she too was mostly at a loss to control such excesses). Girlfriends weren't invited to join the Beatles in Hamburg this year. Twelve months back, three couples had climbed the great green tower at Hauptkirche St Michaelis and carved their names into the wooden handrail, *John + Cyn, Paul + Dot, Stu + Astrid*; now Stu was dead, Astrid was at his funeral, and Cyn and Dot weren't welcome. However, there was good news coming. When John left Liverpool, Cyn was preparing for her final, fifth-year art school exams and actively looking for somewhere to live, probably a bedsit. She was leaving the easy security of her aunt's house for what would be her first place of independence: John knew that when he returned at the start of June she'd be waiting for him in a room as snug as austere 1962 rented furnishings would allow. Wherever it was, no landlady was going to let them be together unmarried, so he'd remain with

Mimi; all the same, the flat would elevate his and Cyn's relationship to a new level after three years. Just a week into his Hamburg trip, she wrote to say she'd taken a room in a house on Garmoyle Road, off Smithdown Road, and that Dot might move in with her, for company and to share costs.

All the Beatles wrote home, and they also all wrote to the girls who wrote to them. Within three or four days of arriving in Hamburg, they started to receive letters from some of their fans, the correspondence openly courted from the Cavern stage on Fan Club night. They'd brought to Hamburg a stack of that night's throwaway photos and used them as postcards, writing around their printed names. They also brought writing paper and envelopes. Many of these epistles survive, conveying a vivid image of the Beatles – Paul especially – sitting down every day and patiently writing letters that would become treasured possessions for their excited recipients back in Liverpool. His were properly polite and funny notes that started with thanks to the writer for hers, moved on to give an expurgated snapshot of the Beatles' Hamburg life (which never quite said as much as the first glance suggested), often included a cartoon or two, and ended something like *Ta-Ta for now. Love, Paul xxx.* From these letters – to Louey, Suzy, Lindy, Anne, Susan and others – comes extra flavour: 'The club we're playing in is good but not as good as Liverpool. The boss is good but we'll still be glad to get back . . . The money's the best bit . . . George is feeling fine now . . . I think we'll be making some records soon, and we'll get them released in Liverpool as soon as possible . . . I'm not getting married to any German girls, nor are the others.'

Brian Epstein was in Hamburg for a week after the Star-Club opened. St Pauli was his pleasure garden too, a chance to enjoy a European city for the first time since taking up the Beatles' management. He's likely to have taken in all the cultural highspots – the art galleries and classical concerts – as well as the lowdown joints around the Reeperbahn.

He also had Hamburg business to do. Though he wasn't Gerry and the Pacemakers' manager, Brian fixed them a Star-Club season from the middle of May, as a goodwill gesture, on a nominal commission of DM50 per week. And he met Bert Kaempfert to discuss the Beatles' July 1961 recording agreement. In March, Brian had served in writing the required three months' notice of termination, and he'd asked Kaempfert to let them go early in case the German contract hindered the acquisition of one in England. Kaempfert accepted this, requesting only that they make some new recordings backing Tony Sheridan before leaving Hamburg at the start of June. However, there's also proof that, once the two men got together here in Hamburg, they discussed the possibility of the Beatles making an entire *album*, on their own, without Sheridan.[7]

A surviving document indicates a plan for them to record twelve tracks in a Hamburg studio on 28/29 May, dates probably fixed at the end of April or beginning of May, after Brian left Hamburg. Kaempfert's signature on the paper presumably indicates his involvement as producer: somebody had to do it, and he was an American star after all. The session's cost was estimated as DM1500 and, as the Kaempfert contract was expiring, it's probable Brian intended to finance it himself and own the recordings, although this isn't specified. The Beatles' Hamburg correspondence confirms they knew a recording project was coming up and that Brian had told them he'd do whatever he could to get the tracks issued in Britain. Further details, like the songs they would do, weren't reported.[8]

George Martin's world had shifted in spring 1962. He was out of his broken marriage and committed to Judy Lockhart Smith, his mistress of several years and secretary at Parlophone. There was, though, no prospect of stresses easing – Sheena Martin still wouldn't grant him a divorce, he was heartbroken at leaving his two young children, and his EMI salary was stretched thin by maintaining his family and renting a London bachelor flat. George and Judy continued to keep their relationship absolutely secret from everyone and there seemed no question of them cohabiting before marriage because people didn't do that. They saw each other every day in their fourth-floor office at EMI House and made the most of the few opportunities for closeness that came along.

George had also reached a decisive moment in his work. His three-year EMI employment contract was about to expire, and perhaps enough was enough. Parlophone had been his playing field since 1950 and his responsibility since 1955, but he was constantly unhappy over the company's refusal to consider even the tiniest of producer royalties. George had begun to branch out, boosting his income by composing theme tunes and other songs, and finally fulfilling a childhood ambition to work in film. But while these were interesting and engaging activities, they didn't pay enough for him to jack in his job at EMI.

In his recordings, George's work brimmed with excellence and originality. All the 'pops' on Parlophone – all the teenage fodder for the singles market – was handled by his assistant Ron Richards or by fellow A&R manager Norman Newell and his aide John Burgess; George no longer touched or considered it except as head of the label. He stayed focused on an exotically diverse range of recordings and was enjoying consistent success. His standout hit at the start of 1962 was The Hole In The Ground, by the revue and film actor Bernard Cribbins, which drilled its way through all the Twist and trad to crack the top ten.

George poured weeks of work into The Hole In The Ground, and the result was a first-class production, loved by buyers and listeners of all generations: it was concise (1.50), catchy, clever and rhythmic, a modern-day music-hall number that tapped into the British love of class ridicule; a satire of the flat-capped working man putting one over a bowler-hatted official. EMI chairman Sir Joseph Lockwood was charmed: 'The record is magnificent and everywhere I go I hear people talking about it, particularly in the City,' he declared in a 21 March memorandum to his Records division managing director, concluding, 'We ought to make an L.P. of this artist.' But L. G. Wood's desire to satisfy his master's voice was stymied by Cribbins' producer. A flurry of memos culminated with George Martin's assertion that such an LP could not be hurried and 'must be allowed to blossom of its own accord like a rare desert flower'. Producers putting artistry above commerciality was anathema in a business geared to making swift capital of success.[9]

Though it would remain an engrained myth that Parlophone was the impoverished laughing stock of the record business, the perennial last pick in the playground, it had long been (and by spring 1962 clearly was) the most eclectic, diverse and fascinating record label in Britain and the world. For artists of imagination and originality, Parlophone was *the* place to be, reflecting the man who assembled its artist roster and the kind of work he wanted to do – George Martin's signings were dissidents, madcaps, fools, wizards, fine singers and talented musicians. He also made a record of his own, released under the pseudonym Ray Cathode. The A-side, Time Beat, married a Latin rhythm to the automated beat of a BBC-tv time signal created in the laboratories of the Radiophonic Workshop. Though most of the recording's instruments were conventional, the *NME*'s news story about it was headlined ELECTRONIC SOUNDS and, to emphasise this futuristic angle, George posed for EMI publicity photos next to a computer. Keen to push his project, he told *Disc*, 'Electronic or "concrete" music is not new in itself, but it is on pop discs. It is concrete music reinforced by musicians – so we're calling it reinforced concrete music.'[10]

The *Juke Box Jury* panellists who voted Time Beat a Miss were right, which wasn't always the case, but it became another staple of the BBC Light Programme, picking up almost as much radio play as Double Scotch, The Niagara Theme and the records of Cribbins, Drake, Bentine, Milligan and Sellers. The British public was finding the ideas and creativity of George Martin – as composer, producer and originator of sounds – very much to its liking.

While all this was happening, George completed his first two film scores. *Take Me Over* was a quaintly arty, low-budget trifle that featured the music of the Temperance Seven; *Crooks Anonymous* was a sprightly British crime comedy with a good script and cast. Neither contract paid very well, £100 and £200, but they let George explore a new medium, composing incidental music and stings as well as title songs. All this was indicative of Judy's increased influence – she not only gave George confidence, she also had contacts: the projects came to him through her father, Kenneth Lockhart Smith, who'd been in the British film industry since the late 1920s and was chairman of the Film Producers Guild.[11]

Such projects were small-fry, however, compared to the extramural activities of Norrie Paramor. George took strongly against his EMI colleague for having fingers in so many pies and hiding behind no fewer than thirty-six fake identities for the songs he forced on to his artists' B-sides. He felt it was morally unjust. George was also jealous of Paramor's ability to reach number 1 with almost every record he issued, and envious of the way Paramor swanked his successes. The two men drew similar EMI salaries, but while George was just keeping his head above water, Norrie had a seaside summer-house in Sussex and a motor-boat in the harbour, zipped around in a new E-Type Jaguar, employed his own publicity agent and bought a property in The Bishop's Avenue, one of the most desirable and expensive residential streets in London, leading to Hampstead Heath.[12]

In March, when George was contacted by a young TV researcher seeking background information about the workings of the record business, he didn't hold back. David Frost was 22, fresh out of Cambridge and working on the London AR-TV current affairs programme *This Week* – his latest assignment being to investigate a possible feature on LPs. George Martin was the one record producer known to all the sharp blades emerging from the universities, so Frost got his number, treated him to a modest £1 1s 6d lunch, and started asking questions. He learned a few things about LPs ... but was more interested to hear how certain people, and one EMI producer in particular, inveigled themselves on to their artists' records. The moment had come, George felt, to expose his colleague. *This Week* found no space for its LP item, but Frost scooped up the spilled beans for possible future use.[13]

In spring 1962, George Martin sat down with L. G. Wood to discuss the renewal of his contract – or not. 'I *always* felt we should have a royalty,' he says. 'I was prepared to take a lower salary if I could have a proportion of what we sold, like the salesmen did. I was very angry about it and nearly didn't sign the contract renewal.'[14]

George mostly respected his managing director, but they had a testing relationship. Len Wood was EMI's headmaster, a shrewd stickler for the rules, a genial and decent man and good ex-soldier who played everything properly, couldn't comprehend rebels and didn't appreciate challenges to a system that evidently worked. He had on his desk a new three-year contract for 36-year-old George Henry Martin and, as far as he was concerned, certain elements were non-negotiable. The salary was close to £3000, and during the course of its three years would surpass it. Though George fought to add a royalty, battling every inch, Wood held firm on the company's behalf, doing his job. Giving in would be the thin end of the wedge – American record companies might pay 'points' but no British firm wanted to open that Pandora's box. Yield now and they'd only be pushed into conceding something else later.

When George played his last card – 'I'll have to leave, then' – Len Wood coolly responded, as George would relate it, 'If you feel like that, be our guest.'[15]

George *couldn't* leave. He needed every penny of his salary. He had obligations, and even a short period out of work would have been disastrous. 'I re-signed with EMI for another three years,' he says, 'which took my contract to 1965.'[16]

Over the weekend of 23–25 March, in the midst of all these events, George had an unusual booking in his diary: representing EMI at a 'festival of live and recorded music', at which audiences attended illustrated talks about records. It took place at Norbreck Hydro, a vast resort hotel on the cliffs above Blackpool. George had three hits in this week's *NME* chart (Bernard Cribbins at 7, Matt Monro at 15 and The Dr Kildare Theme by Johnnie Spence at 19), which was great except that Norrie Paramor had four, including the top two places.[17] George stood at a lectern, with a 'gramophone player' to hand, and delivered *Humour On Record*, outlining incidents from his projects with wits from Michael Bentine to Peter Ustinov. The speech gained George his first front-page coverage in *Eminews*, EMI's staff journal, which said he also described how the Indian Embassy helped him find a sitar player for *Songs For Swingin' Sellers*. What the paper *didn't* report was that this was one of those rare occasions when George felt he could legitimately bring along his secretary, when they could share a measure of closeness less easily achieved in London. Somehow or other, though, L. G. Wood got to hear about it, and he wasn't happy. He was a churchgoer, a principled man of 51 who led an upright life; he wasn't only upset that George and Judy were conducting an adulterous affair, he was offended it was happening under his nose. One of their A&R department colleagues recalls it as 'a red-hot scandal'.[18]

Mr Martin had been a lot of bother to Mr Wood in recent weeks. The managing director was unhappy about being pressed so hard over the no-royalty policy, indeed by the entire tenor of that contract renewal process; he was unhappy with the way he'd been so airily thwarted over the Bernard Cribbins LP, causing him to disappoint the chairman; he was now irate to discover

Martin was having a liaison with his secretary; and he may even have picked up on that particular attitude to Mr Paramor.[19]

Dismissal was out of the question – George Martin was brilliant at his job and personally respected by Sir Joseph – but Wood did find at least some small way to show his disfavour. It came during a routine meeting with Sid Colman, general manager of EMI's music publishing company Ardmore and Beechwood. Colman asked again why Wood had blocked the suggestion – conceived by his plugger, Kim Bennett – that they be allowed to make a recording of the Liverpool beat group, the one which wrote its own songs. Wood, as was his way, still held firm about it . . . but an alternative thought, a compromise, developed in his mind, as Bennett explains:

> Time went by since I'd floated my Beatles idea. Weeks. Then one day Sid came to my office door with a grin on his face, and rubbing his hands. He said, 'I've just been talking to Len Wood on the phone: we're going to get our record made after all.' After a short, stunned silence, I asked, 'Oh? Who's gonna do it then?' [and he said] 'George Martin.'
>
> The Beatles record was going to be made as a *gesture* to Sid, to give Sid Colman a sop. Len was going to bow to our wishes at last.[20]

Wood's motive, as Bennett noted, was not to give the Beatles a recording contract so much as to grant Ardmore and Beechwood the means to get what it wanted, the copyright on Like Dreamers Do, the Lennon-McCartney song that Bennett happened to feel had hit potential. The upshot was that one of EMI's A&R managers would be recording the Beatles, which meant putting them under contract, and George Martin was the man Wood singled out for the chore. No matter who at EMI signed them, the cost was still the company's to bear, not the A&R man's personally, but the sum was trivial and there might be publishing income as well as record sales.

It was a little embarrassing for George, but no big deal. He hadn't seen the Beatles and 'wasn't knocked out at all' with what little he'd heard of them – but, instructed 'You have to sign them', he would. Ron Richards was aware of the situation: he knew George's arm was being twisted into taking the Beatles 'because of his affair with Judy'. And Norman Smith, a balance engineer at Abbey Road, heard it too: 'L. G. Wood didn't approve of people having affairs, and he certainly didn't approve of George going off with his secretary. Not at all. I think it offended his moral standards. L. G. virtually ordered George to record the Beatles.'[21]

None of this would have happened without what John Lennon called Brian Epstein's 'smarming and charming everybody' in London – specifically, in this instance, his visit to the HMV shop where he had discs cut, and his no doubt politely hopeful meetings with Sid Colman and George Martin. But while Brian remained determined to make *something* happen to get the Beatles a record contract, those particular labours were receding in his mind – they were February events and it was now the end of April, beginning of May.

And yet, for this whole fantastical and fortuitous combination of reasons – which Brian possibly never knew and the Beatles certainly never knew – the door of Parlophone Records previously closed to them once, and maybe even twice, was sliding open.

When Astrid returned home from Liverpool and the ordeal of Stu's funeral, John and George went to see her, visiting again the tall, spacious house at 45a Eimsbütteler Strasse in the suburb of Altona. Pete didn't go because he didn't go anywhere with them and had never been to the house; Paul didn't go because he *couldn't*.

Astrid showed them Stuart's painting studio, and the photo she'd taken of him here, one side of his face illuminated by light from the attic window, the other in shade. John said 'Could you take a picture of me there?' and Astrid did. He stood in the very same place and posed like his dead friend; she directed him to turn his head until the angle matched and then triggered the shutter on this most moving of stills, a then-and-almost-then photo that will always speak volumes.[22]

Several other remarkable photos were taken this afternoon – of John sitting alone, his face in half-shadow; of George the same; of John and George standing together, and George standing while John sat, their Beatles haircuts and style looking very sharp. Astrid surveys the photos today and sees truths. John was 'a little lonely feller' and George, 19, 'had so much strength in his face, like he was saying to John "I'll look after you"'. She gave them prints which, John said, 'made Paul mad with envy'.[23]

Astrid didn't go back to work for two months, but George and John encouraged her to drop into the Star-Club to see them play. 'The first time I saw them on stage without Stuart they did all they could to make me laugh,' she remembers, 'and John sang Love Me Tender that night, which Stuart had sung.'[24] In the depths of their suffering, John and Astrid conversed more now than at any other time, and she found further qualities his abrasiveness tended to obscure.

We had long, long talks about life, about relationships, about him and Stuart, about our loss. He said to me, 'You have got to decide: either you die with Stuart or you go on living your life. Be honest and decide. You can't just cry all the time, you've got to *get on*.' It was the real John talking – he said it not nice and sweet but very straight, with a strong voice, and he made me *think about it*. He really helped get myself together again. It was the first time he really showed his love for me.[25]

Astrid also craved warmth with Millie Sutcliffe. Their terminally bad relationship flickered into life for just a brief moment after the funeral. She wrote letters to Millie and her daughters, asking them to excuse her English, which, while fractured, was impressive considering its non-existence a year earlier. She drew them pictures, described herself to Pauline and Joyce as 'your big sister' and called Millie 'mum'; in one letter she wrote 'So mum I hope you not angry with your little Astrid. I have not do anything wrong.'

> John – O mum he is in a terrible mood now, he just can't believe it that darling Stuart never comes back. He just crying his eyes out. The Beatles specially John and George are very good friends of Stuart. They try so hard to give me a bit of happiness. I never know that I had so many good friends. Cynthia writes to me all the time very beautiful letters but John is marvellous to me. He says he know Stuart so much and he love him so much that he can understand me. Klaus still looks after me for his friend Stuart. He never let me go out alone.
>
> George's mum hath tell him all about the funeral and send the papers. I think George still can't believe it. Why can't we go for other people to heaven? John asks me that – he said he would go for Stuart to heaven because Stuart was such a marvellous boy and he is nothing.[26]

John didn't mention Stuart in his numerous despatches to Lindy Ness. She received an immediate reply to her first letter, and their friendship fast gathered another interesting dimension through correspondence. Her letters were full of wit and wordplay and John could respond in kind, scribbling the kind of pages he'd sent to his lost friend. It gave him continuity, and only slightly did he moderate his language for a 15-year-old girl, though she was smart enough to take it and wasn't going to complain or be offended. John sent her several written rambles packed with non-sequiturs, jokes, funny lines attributed to Negroes, Jews, cripples and God, deformed drawings and crucifixion images. One cartoon showed a little figure on a huge cross, with a salesman looking up to enquire *A size smaller sir?* At the bottom of the cross was a door.

In his first letter, John also wrote, 'It's a drag this Hunland – well its not all that bad. I bet there'll be hardly any Beatle fans when we get back – maybe you und Lu (Louy? Louie? Louey? Lumpy).' He was, as usual, fretting that the girls might stray in their absence; Lindy assured him they wouldn't and reported that some Beatles fans had set up an informal meeting group every Wednesday evening in the Odd Spot coffee bar, to swap photos and compare the letters and cards they'd received. Collectively, as members of the fan club, they'd all got a Hamburg bulletin; individually, they scrutinised one another's letters for extra information, compared the numbers of kisses and jostled to be top of their idols' affections. 'Give my love to the Odd Spotters,' John said in one of his numerous postcards. 'I hope you can read this – I was away for writing.' Odd Spotter Margaret Douglas sums up the way they all felt: 'We thought it was lovely that the Beatles wrote to us like that, drawing us funny faces and everything. It was very considerate of them. We'd talk about the letters and cards we sent them, discuss what we'd say to them when they came home, and imagine how they must be loving it in Hamburg. We assumed they were living in luxury there, and it was a long time before we found out they were hell-holes.'[27]

As the weeks passed in sinful St Pauli, the Beatles reconnected to previous feelings of having had enough. Their only escape was the occasional run out to the coast. Manfred Weissleder loaned them his third car, a Fiat, and, while the weather wasn't warm enough for swimming, they tootled around the beach and cleared Hamburg from their nostrils. 'George or I drive,' Paul explained in a letter to Bobby Brown, which meant they squabbled over the ignition keys; Paul hadn't passed his driving test, so George generally won, speeding them along the German highway in their little Italian car.

Pete was never part of these road trips and continued to exist independently. On their first Hamburg visit, the other Beatles might have understood that new boy Pete would want to peel off and do his own thing. By their second trip, he'd been in the group long enough for them to know this was simply the way he was. Another year on again, in spring 1962, the pattern was set rock-solid. Even their common off-stage interests – drinking and women – were pursued separately. Odd occasions excepted, Pete drank with birds, not Beatles.

Sex was easily had. Pete called the Star-Club 'good turkin' ground' (a phrase from 'turkeys' and 'stuffing'), but there were always three concerns. One, as he remarked frankly in a letter to a Liverpool friend, was VD: 'Over here you have got to be so damn careful if you go for your oats. The only snag is that, the way they throw it at you, it's just impossible to resist – especially after you have got a few bevvies inside of you. Anyway I'm trying my best at the moment not to bring home any "you know whats" – come to think of it, it's worth the risk because I'm dreading coming home to those "things" that call themselves girls in the clubs.'[28]

The second fear was pregnancy, although little care was taken to avoid it.

Paul cooked up a long-term stew during this Hamburg trip when he was intimate with a St Pauli waitress named Erika Wohlers, also 19. In December 1962 (two months prematurely, it would be claimed) she gave birth to a daughter, Bettina, and two years later she insisted Paul was the father. It would transpire that he wasn't, but could so easily have been.*

The third concern was Horst Fascher. For all the supposed liberality of St Pauli, German statute books still contained an old law called the *Kuppeleiparagraph*. This gave courts the power to punish anyone caught facilitating sexual intercourse between unmarried individuals, like those who rented or owned the building where the act occurred. Vigilance was exercised only sporadically but one such period appears to have been spring 1962. Out on sex-sentry duty one night, Fascher caught John screwing a girl in the Beatles' apartment. Apparently unable to separate the horizontal couple by any other means, he unzipped himself and urinated on them, peeing on a *Piedel*. John jumped up livid – but, even in the heat of the moment, knew better than to square up to a man who'd been jailed for manslaughter.[29]

The prime meeting place for musicians and the girls who *did* was a little area of the Star-Club demarcated by the girls themselves. 'There were maybe twenty, twenty-five of us,' says Marga Bierfreund, 'and we stood in a place near the stage we called *Ritzenecke*, or "Cunt Corner". The bands changed every month and before they knew what happened we'd sort them out between us – "I'll have him, she can have him."'[30] Marga didn't care much for the Beatles – she found them bad-mannered and scruffy and didn't understand their sense of humour – but plenty did.

There were also the Star-Club barmaids, who generally stayed in their own zone and kept clear of the *Ritzenecke*. Several were close with Beatles. Paul was with Heike Evert, known as Goldie, and John struck up a situation with Bettina Derlien. Known to the English musicians as Big Betty, she was beautiful and massive: for reasons never definitively established, her weight had ballooned to twenty stone (280lb; 127kg). Pete says she used to put his head between her enormous breasts – 'It was a nice way to go deaf for a few seconds' – and Bettina herself always spoke of the way Paul got her to comb his hair, every night, again and again and again. But John was the love of her life, her special one, and

---

* Several such instances would arise in the years that followed, most of them batted away with confidence, others dealt with more circumspectly. Because of the strong possibility Erika Wohlers' claim was legitimate, maintenance money was paid (without prejudice or admission) from about 1966. The arrangement remained confidential until the daughter went public with it in 1981, seeking much greater reward. She demanded Paul McCartney take blood tests – he did, and was found not to be the father.

rumours about them became the talk of the town. People seemed to think the relationship was one-way, that mostly it was Bettina lusting after John, but no one really knew. As Tony Sheridan says, 'I never thought they were lovers, but then nobody could figure them out. People would say to me, "What's he *doing* with her?"'[31]

Bettina was big in every way: she had a giant beehive hairstyle, a huge personality, spoke a bit of English, had a strong sense of humour and a voice that boomed across the room, bar to stage, surfing all other sounds. She also had money, buying John clothes, shoes and Prellies . . . and every once in a while his voice would call out over the Star-Club microphone, a dirty, throaty, smoky, innuendo-pregnant 'BETTINAAAHHHH!'

There's no reliable guide to the songs they were singing here. In a long letter to Bobby Brown – incorporated in the fan club's *Newsletter No. 1* – Paul reported that 'The Germans like mainly rock tunes – What'd I Say, Say Mama, Dizzy Miss Lizzy, Hey! Baby etc', the last of which indicates that John played harmonica to the Hamburg audiences. For the first time in their three visits, the Beatles had the benefit of a musical lifeline from home – Brian sent them the *NME* every week and *Mersey Beat* every fortnight and he also sent records. As usual, the Beatles intended to catch up on all the missed new releases by crowding into a browserie at Nems when they got back, but there were two new-minted 45s Brian felt confident in mailing out to them, by the Shirelles and Joe Brown and the Bruvvers.

It was through this despatch that the Beatles introduced A Picture Of You into their set. It was the fifth Joe Brown song they played, though this wasn't a comedy record but a catchy, attractively rhythmic country and western number. George sang it, of course, and was thrilled to read he'd soon be meeting his musical hero: in a letter enclosed with the record, Brian said he'd booked Brown and the Bruvvers to play two shows on Merseyside in July and the Beatles would be the main supporting act.

The other 45 sent across from Liverpool was just as much a banker – it was another blast of double-sided dynamite by the Shirelles, produced and co-written by Luther Dixon. John's urgent need for something new meant that he grabbed both songs: the A-side was Soldier Boy, in which a girl promises to be faithful while her army boy is away (the Beatles didn't bother to alter the gender), the B-side was the Ray Charles-like groove Love Is A Swingin' Thing.

The arrival of the post was an important moment in every day, bringing the Beatles not just records, papers and news from Brian but letters and cards from parents, girlfriends and fans. Whoever woke first would pad across to the club and fetch it, and mid-afternoon on Wednesday 9 May it was George who made the trip. He returned clutching a telegram with the most fantastic news of all time: *they'd got a recording contract.*

The Beatles' absence from Liverpool allowed Brian uninterrupted focus on their future.

He was realising his ambition to become a promoter of his own shows: those two July nights showcasing Joe Brown and the Beatles would be preceded, five weeks earlier, by his first venture, a 21 June dance at the huge New Brighton Tower Ballroom starring the American star Bruce Channel. The Beatles would be second on the bill again, their name featuring almost as prominently in the advertising materials. He was also filling the Beatles' diary with bookings right through June and July, six or seven nights a week, and piecing together a skeleton itinerary as far ahead as October – and he was doing all this singlehanded, because his personal assistant, Alistair Taylor, left Nems during April.[32]

In a letter to Neil Aspinall on Monday 7 May, Brian had two hot pieces of information. One was that he'd got the Beatles another booking from the BBC in Manchester, which meant they'd be appearing on national radio a second time. The other was that he was about to visit the capital again – 'I am going to London this week to see EMI and very sincerely hope that when I see you on Friday I'll have good news.'[33]

The Parlophone office had been in touch, suggesting Brian come down for a meeting, and his wording suggests he went in anticipation of a positive outcome (though he can have had no idea why). The appointment was with George Martin, Wednesday, 11.30, at Abbey Road.

It was three months since the two men had met, the time when George had been unmoved by the Beatles' sound and got a little miffed with Brian at one point, though he hadn't disliked him.

This time, George said, he was able to break some good news: he was going to give the Beatles a contract to record for Parlophone.

The facts behind this 9 May meeting would be glossed over so effectively that neither man talked much about it, but some elements of what happened can be pieced together with certainty.[34]

First, it's evident – and vital for all that would follow – that George Martin thought well of Brian Epstein and Brian Epstein thought well of George Martin. There was a sustained mutual appreciation of purpose, methods, ethics and articulacy, and it started in this meeting. Having said that, George wasn't thinking *future.* It wasn't his decision to sign the Beatles and he intended to hand them straight over to Ron Richards. The meeting was short, under forty-five minutes, and there were several things he needed to explain.

Most of the time was taken up by George outlining to Brian the essentials of the contract there would be between them. It would be EMI's standard recording agreement – the same one issued to Cliff Richard, the Shadows, Adam Faith, Helen Shapiro and almost everyone else, and much the same as that used throughout the business.

- EMI committed to recording a minimum of six 'sides' (pieces of music) in the first year, typically to be issued as three singles. EMI would own the recordings and have sole right of production and reproduction.
- All recording costs, including studio time, would be paid by EMI.
- There was no 'advance' on royalties. The royalty rate was one penny per 'double-sided record' (single) on 85 per cent of sales, paid quarterly.* LPs were calculated proportionately, usually as six or seven singles.
- It was a four-year contract, but EMI was bound only for the first. If the company chose to renew, the royalty would be increased by farthing increments to a ceiling of 1½d.
- The contract was for the world. Half the prevailing royalty would be paid for record sales outside Britain.

If George didn't actually say to Brian 'Nobody ever gets rich from a recording contract' there was no need. Everyone in the business knew it, and a calculation would have confirmed it. In the Beatles' case, this penny they'd get on 85 per cent of sales would have to be divided five ways: 15 per cent to Brian, the rest split between John, Paul, George and Pete. If they sold a thousand records, they'd get fifteen bob each, and if they ever managed such a famous, gilded, pinnacle-of-career accomplishment as a million-seller, they'd each get £750. If this happened in America – which was, quite obviously, *ludicrously* unlikely – it would be £375.

The contract explanation over, the two men compared diaries and set the Beatles' first recording date twenty-eight days distant, on Wednesday 6 June. It would be a standard three-hour session, 7–10PM, for which they should arrive in good time. Brian was breaking into the Beatles' holiday period but knew they'd have bitten George Martin's hand off for the chance. They could even rehearse for a couple of days beforehand, to be properly prepared.

Such groundwork would be essential, because George told Brian he wanted to assess the Beatles' singing abilities individually. All he'd heard of them so far

---

* The missing 15 per cent was 'to cover records returned and/or damaged in transit and/or used for demonstration or advertising purposes'.

was the acetate with Hello Little Girl on one side and Till There Was You on the other. The labels, in Brian's handwriting, assigned the first to John Lennon & The Beatles and the second to Paul McCartney & The Beatles, and George Martin needed to determine which way he would make the Beatles go. After all, every vocal group was *Someone and the Somethings*. It isn't known if he explained this thinking to Brian, but Brian did leave the meeting conscious of George's wish to test the singers one by one. It seems George also asked to hear them doing other songs, different to the ones he'd heard before, which – as he would say – hadn't knocked him out at all.

Finally, they discussed promotion. Living in Liverpool, the Beatles were a long way from EMI's publicity set-up, so George told Brian he'd arrange for one or more photographers to be present on 6 June to take some shots while they were recording.

That was it. The meeting was over. Brian and George shook hands, and George said he'd set the wheels of bureaucracy in motion. Brian could expect to receive the contract for signing within two weeks.

This was it! Brian's excitement spilled out. Getting a recording contract was his first promise to the Beatles, the biggest step towards making them the very greatest of stars he knew they would be. This day, 9 May 1962, was six months exactly since he'd first seen them in the Cavern, on 9 November 1961; half a year had led them to this moment. The contract, Brian would write, was 'the ultimate – this, to us, was the greatest thing that could happen'.[35]

Bursting to tell, he came out of the studios, crossed Abbey Road by the adjacent zebra crossing and walked straight to St John's Wood Post Office on Circus Road. He phoned his parents and he sent two telegrams. One was to Bill Harry, for announcement in *Mersey Beat*:

HAVE SECURED CONTRACT FOR BEATLES TO RECORDED FOR EMI ON
PARLAPHONE LABEL 1ST RECORDING DATE SET FOR JUNE 6TH. BRIAN EPSTEIN

Whether its errors were caused by Brian's excitement or a clumsy telegraphist isn't known; another message went to the Beatles in Hamburg, sent care of the Star-Club. Though lost soon afterwards, its wording would be remembered by Pete five years later as:

CONGRATULATIONS BOYS EMI REQUEST RECORDING SESSION PLEASE
REHEARSE NEW MATERIAL[36]

It was a busy day for telegram boys. As Brian would remember it, he received messages from at least three Beatles.

[John] WHEN ARE WE GOING TO BE MILLIONAIRES
[Paul] PLEASE WIRE TEN THOUSAND POUND ADVANCE ROYALTIES
[George] PLEASE ORDER FOUR NEW GUITARS[37]

George expressed their feelings in a pair of letters he sent to girls back home, fans who'd written to him and were rewarded with fulsome replies. In one, a three-page note to Margaret Price, he said: 'We are all very happy about Parlophone, as it is a big break for us. We will just have to work hard & hope for a hit with whatever we record. (We don't yet know what the producer will want.)'

George was making a crucial point. It was already perplexing that they'd landed a Parlophone contract, knowing the EMI labels had previously turned them down, but – however it came about – now they had one, what songs would they be directed to do? The Beatles' knowledge of the London recording business came from what they read in the weekly press and gleaned from chatting to other musicians, and this told them that record companies always chose the material. Parlophone could want the Beatles to record one of the stage numbers they performed best, or else they'd be given a song to learn – perhaps something old, a chestnut their A&R man fancied them doing, or something new, *written* by their A&R man maybe, or by a Tin Pan Alley songwriter.

As much as they could, John and Paul decided to take matters into their own hands. 'Please rehearse new material,' Brian's telegram said. They chose to interpret this as 'please *write* new material' and, in this instant, the Lennon-McCartney songwriting partnership was effectively reborn.

The three self-written songs John and Paul had finally, reluctantly and self-consciously started playing at the end of 1961 were all old, from 1957–9. They'd written again recently – Paul had Pinwheel Twist, John had Ask Me Why – but everything else was ancient. They hadn't composed together in two years and most of their material was older still: it was in 1958 that they filled a school exercise book with words and chord-letters formed 'eyeball to eyeball' in Paul's front parlour and John's front porch. Lennon-McCartney Originals they had called them, but there'd been few since.

All that changed in the second week of May 1962. This was the moment when John Winston Lennon (21 years, 7 months) and James Paul McCartney (19 years, 11 months) looked each other full in the face and saw that *something*, saw white-hot ambition, determination, daring, craving, personality, talent and ego, and went for it.

Three weeks later, when they left Hamburg, they had two more numbers ready to take to London on 6 June, songs not only scribbled down on paper but rehearsed – one of them, or even both, they hoped good enough to be accepted by Parlophone for the Beatles' first record.

They eased themselves back into business by revisiting an oldie. John and Paul felt Love Me Do was the best of their early songs, though it wasn't one they'd chosen to revive before now. It was mostly Paul's number, written in 1958 under Buddy Holly's magic spell. By 1962, Paul and John had a whole other body of love songs to inspire them – the rhythm of Tamla and soul of Smokey Robinson, the buoyant melodies of Goffin and King, the grooves of Luther Dixon's Shirelles, and, vital in this particular instance, the blues of Arthur Alexander and the mouthorgan sound of James Ray and Bruce Channel. In '58 Love Me Do was Holly, in '62 it was harmonica; everything was still America but they'd migrated from country to city.

Originally written in the higher key of A, Love Me Do was retooled in G which instantly made it bluesy – even though (but for its three-note bass line) the song remained acoustic. The unfussy first-person lyric – essentially, 'please love me because I'll always love you' – was embellished with a new bridge, 'Someone to love, somebody new / Someone to love, someone like you', and when asked about the song nine years later, John vaguely remembered contributing it.[38] They also worked out a simple vocal arrangement: Paul and John sang together in harmony, Paul holding the higher register.

John explained in a 1963 *Melody Maker* interview that there was clear method in their thinking when it came to the mouthorgan: 'It was just after Hey! Baby came out – [and] we were hoping to be the first British group to use harmonica on record.'[39] The instrument radically altered Love Me Do's sound.

Another important difference was the tempo: what had once been a lively, Hollyesque rhythm was now slower, befitting its blues feel, though they did also opt for a little variation. The work on Love Me Do was done during downtime hours in the Beatles' lodging, and because it was important they all learned it, Pete was there. He made a particular contribution they agreed to pursue. 'The idea was to make the middle-eight different from the rest of the tune,' Pete remembers, 'and I said, "OK, we put the skip beat in."'[40] The 'skip beat' was a fluctuation in tempo, an acceleration to lead into the vocal bridge and again later, before the instrumental middle-eight. It was a strange idea, but must have sounded good enough in the moment for John and Paul to accept.

After Love Me Do, in the space of a week or so, another new song emerged, PS I Love You. This was Paul's creation ... 'but,' qualified John, 'I think we helped him a bit. He was trying to write a Soldier Boy, like the Shirelles track.' The main influence of Soldier Boy was the format: PS I Love You is a letter sung aloud – the writer is away, sending a love note to his girl back home.[41] Paul may have sprung his opening line, 'As I write this letter', from Pat Boone's ballad hit I'll Be Home, the McCartney family's favourite song when they moved into their new house (20 Forthlin Road) in 1956, a happy summer that preceded autumn's horror, when his mother died. Instrumentally, PS I Love You is lightly Latin, a rhythm much evident in pop music at this time and favoured by Paul through his singing of Besame Mucho, The Honeymoon Song and Till There Was You. John liked it too: it was an influence on Ask Me Why, the song which – with Love Me Do and PS I Love You – gave them three new numbers to play to Parlophone.

Some of this activity was witnessed by Gerry and the Pacemakers when they arrived from Liverpool to start their own seven-week Star-Club season. ('All 24 of us sleep in the same room but we're English,' John wrote in a postcard to a fan.) They drove over in their van, bringing with them Bernie Boyle, the Beatles' young pal – he'd thrown in a job at the Fruit Exchange to spend a few weeks in Hamburg, having first asked Brian Epstein if he could work at Nems when he got back; Brian said he could. The presence of other Liverpudlians in Hamburg added to the fun and sharpened the Beatles' competitive spirit, making John feel he had to become even more outrageous. He figures strongly in two more crazy tales that happened during the last three weeks of May – one being the incident when he 'pissed on nuns'.

Eleven years later, John would write a letter mentioning 'a few Hamburg incidents concerned with urinating publicly and otherwise – [which] I won't go into as the "myths" are more interesting (stories abound there)'.[42] Talk of such happenings, sufficiently magnified by 1973 for John to describe them as 'myths', would become much multiplied in the years afterwards, with truth a distant casualty. But … something *did* happen.

They've all talked about it. Paul acknowledges some accuracy in the wider story but mostly dismisses the main headline: '"Beatles Pissed On Nuns" is one story that wasn't true at all. We were staying in this place where you had to go down about five flights of stairs to go to a toilet, so sometimes we'd piss out the window – a good old English medieval habit! And one day, right down the road from where we were pissing, there happened to be some nuns. They didn't see us, but somebody did, the papers picked it up, and it went from being a joke to being a fact.'[43]

George supported some of this, saying, 'John didn't piss on the nuns – we peed over a balcony into a deserted street at about 4.30 in the morning,' though he also added, blithely, 'We were free to piss on anyone we wanted to, if we wanted, although we never actually did.'[44]

Pete – or, quite evidently, his Fleet Street ghostwriter – zoomed in on John's participation and helped enlarge it into legend. He spoke of John's 'anti-clerical demonstration' against 'four gentle nuns' and said 'Lennon unzipped and sprinkled the four sisters with a mini-cloudburst out of a cloudless sky'. Poetic stuff.[45]

Few of the numerous other observations are from people who observed it, but there was one other witness, Bernie Boyle. 'I was there for the "pissing on nuns" incident, but I've no idea whether he hit any nuns or not – he was just pissing into the street from the balcony of their apartment on a Sunday morning as people were going to church. It could be the story was embroidered, but *something* happened because I saw it.'[46]

John went into most detail about it in an interview in 1971: 'There's all big exaggerated stories about us in Hamburg, about us "pissing on nuns" and things like that. What actually happened was we had a balcony in these flats and one Sunday morning we were all just pissing in[to] the street as people were going to church. And there were some nuns over the road, going into the church. It was just a Sunday morning in the club district, with everyone walking about, and three or four people peeing into the street.'[47]

While 'three or four' of them were relieving themselves, legend would attach the tale solely to *Lennon*, and this seems to have happened quite quickly. The key then became not so much 'did he or didn't he?' but who objected to it? Horst Fascher, who says he was present, explains that the nuns called the police and Manfred Weissleder smoothed everything over 'by paying five hundred marks for the people to get their dress clean' ('people' meaning nuns and 'dress' meaning habits). Pete says there was no trouble at all beyond two almost-laughing policemen giving John 'the mildest of rebukes'.[48]

Actually, nothing happened. Then, later, the incident was mentioned to Pastor Albert Mackels, the priest of St Joseph's church, whose order of St Elizabeth nuns had been dampened or dangled before, and he would – in the fullness of time – take action over it.

Less doubt or misinformation surrounds the other wild tale. For Bernie Boyle it was just part of the entertainment: 'In the Star-Club one night John came on stage with a toilet seat around his neck, and a cape on, and a hat. He was out of his fuckin' brain.' John himself said it happened 'when Gerry and the Pacemakers and the whole of Liverpool was over there. We'd *really* get going then. I'd go on with underpants and a toilet seat round me neck, and all sorts of gear on, and out of me fuckin' mind. And I'd do a drum solo, which I couldn't play, while Gerry Marsden was playing.'[49]

In the light of all this jollity, it could be easy to forget the Beatles were a professional band. They had a new record contract and were under signed agreement in Hamburg to do a top-of-the-bill job of work for two or more hours a night, which they did. And, in spite of all the puke and pills and drink and girls, they were better than good. As the Pacemakers' Les Maguire concedes,

'When you watched the Beatles you knew you were seeing something special, even if you didn't know what it was. They were *different*. There was always competition between the groups, and we knew there was a gap between them and us.' The Beatles did great business for Manfred Weissleder, more than enough for him to say he wanted them back again soon. (They told him he'd have to discuss it with their manager.)

Some budding young talents were also watching. Hamburg's first own beat band, the Bats (for whom Stuart Sutcliffe had played), were now followed by a second, the Rattles. From their names and musical style – guitars and vocal harmonies – the influence was obvious. Frank Dostal, later to join the Rattles as guitarist, tuned into the Beatles right away. 'They were relaxed on stage but at the same time energetic and humorous. They had a special mixture of rock 'n' roll and black music that was more or less unknown to German audiences. In Germany you could not get records by black groups like the Shirelles, so nobody knew of them.'

Another future Rattle, drummer Reinhard 'Dicky' Tarrach, says the Beatles 'were the first guys I had seen who talked to the audience. All the other bands said, "Thank you, the next song is …" but the Beatles made jokes on stage. They were very intelligent and as they had German girlfriends they spoke mixed German and English words. John Lennon had a toilet seat round his head. They were laughing about these things and that inspired us to do little stories and be talking with the audience.'[50]

Tarrach felt the Beatles played well with Roy Young but not with Tony Sheridan. 'It didn't work for me,' he says. 'Sheridan was like the old world and they were on the way to the new.' Only one half of the old knockout combination was moving on up … however, first they had some final studio business to complete.

The last 'Sheridan and Beatles' recordings were made at this time, on 24 May. While Brian Epstein's other plan was scotched – events in London meant there was no need for the Beatles to cut an LP independently in Hamburg – Bert Kaempfert did want his one last go before releasing them from their 1961 contract.

Recording session

> Thursday 24 May 1962. Studio Rahlstedt, Wandsbek, Hamburg.
> Recording: Swanee River; Sweet Georgia Brown. Backing tracks only;
> order of recording not known.

Give or take the odd night in 1967 or '68, there was never a more throwaway or forgettable Beatles session than this, their final spin for an expiring contract, a bizarre last tango in Hamburg with the 38-year-old German orchestra leader-arranger-producer Bert Kaempfert.

The Beatles had buzzed for the June 1961 recordings but now didn't need to be here at all. And Kaempfert, for his part, made such strange decisions that either he didn't know what to do with them or was persuaded to do almost nothing. There's no proof of this, but perhaps he discussed the session with Brian Epstein and Brian expressed a wish that little of any substance be recorded – because this, emphatically, sums up what happened. Kaempfert used the Beatles less in 1962 than 1961, though they were top of the bill at the Star-Club and EMI had found them worth signing.

John and Paul didn't show Bert their new songs and Bert showed the Beatles only very old ones: they were to *beat up* two great American standards, Sweet Georgia Brown and Swanee River, for Tony Sheridan to sing. Oddly, however, Kaempfert and Sheridan had already recorded these numbers – they were on the just-issued *My Bonnie* album – and no purpose was served by remaking them when they could have done something else. Kaempfert died in 1980 without being asked to explain his reasoning. To compound the oddness of it, paperwork was generated showing the two tracks would be issued as a 45, then it didn't happen: the tape of Swanee River was lost before it was ever released; and the Beatles' Sweet Georgia Brown, while issued, would always be hard to find – it appeared on a West German EP and as a 45 in Greece.

The session was at Studio Rahlstedt, a new sound-recording facility in the borough of Wandsbek, close to the city centre. For reasons unremembered, Sheridan almost certainly wasn't present (he overdubbed his vocal two weeks later, on 7 June), but there were still five performers: John, Paul, George, Pete and Roy Young – along with bystander Bernie Boyle. Swanee River can't be assessed because the tape is lost, but Sweet Georgia Brown indicates what was done: the musicians made a backing track, with Paul on bass guitar, John playing a bit of rhythm, Roy on piano and Pete hitting a snare drum; George didn't play but he and Paul sang some backing vocals.

The session's sound was all but identical to what had been achieved in both June 1961 and the subsequent recordings Kaempfert made with Sheridan: it was *Bertbeat* – crisp, sharp, ordered, clinically clean. The musicians turned in a perfectly competent backing track ... except Kaempfert again denied Pete most of the drum kit. This time he didn't even get to touch the cymbal, only the snare. (He did well though, and his timing was fine.)

Since working with Pete in 1961, Kaempfert had also exercised discipline with other drummers – most 'Beat Brothers' recordings were percussively limited and he clearly didn't care for bass drum on his sound – but making Pete use just the snare was something he'd done to no other. This was the third time out of three studio dates when Pete's work wasn't trusted or appreciated. Roy Young observed that 'Pete really could not cut it as a recording drummer'. He also says John, Paul and George had already canvassed his opinion of Ringo, knowing they'd played together in the Top Ten house band at the start of the year. 'One night we were sitting around having a drink and they asked what I thought about Ringo. I told them obviously he was a great drummer. Ringo was a metronome.'[51]

The following day, 25 May, five ink signatures were applied to a single sheet of typed paper: Kaempfert, JP McCartney, G. Harrison, J. W. Lennon and R. P. Best. It was the last legal document the Beatles would sign without the presence of management ... and it was on this same day, or tightly thereabouts, in Liverpool, that Brian Epstein put pen to paper on a *new* recording contract, one that would prove altogether more historic and robust: the agreement with EMI.

George Martin had little time or reason to reflect much on his imminent signing, 'the Beattles'. He was overseeing further excellent sessions with Matt Monro; he was working hard on yet another 'oncer', getting Bernard Cribbins the right follow-up to The Hole In The Ground; he was planning more *Beyond The Fringe* recordings; he had 23 May set aside to tape a conceptual LP with Spike Milligan, Peter Sellers, Peter Cook and Jonathan Miller, a satire of the war film *The Bridge On The River Kwai* that became an epic project all its own; and he was making his first foray into 'pops' for many a moon, trying to emulate the success of actor John Leyton's Johnny Remember Me, which raced to number 1 on the back of a TV soap opera appearance. George's hopes were pinned on 24-year-old Leo Maguire from BBC-tv's *Compact*. A storyline was developed in which his character was remodelled into a pop star; Maguire's hit song would be Crying For The Moon and the real recording was produced by George in Abbey Road Number 2 studio on 15 May. On screen, the big star moment was coming on 5 and 7 June, with the Parlophone 45 released the next day. Plumb at the time of the Beatles' first session on the 6th, George Martin looked set to achieve the one thing to have eluded him in five years, a real pop hit.

Amid all of this, on Friday 18 May, he requisitioned a recording contract for the Beatles – and, as their name was typed this way twice, it was what he thought they were called. Six days later, EMI's administration department at Hayes sent back a freshly typed four-page document for his despatch to Liverpool. The contract was between The Parlophone Company Ltd and Brian Epstein – as the manager of 'a group of instrumentalists professionally known as THE BEATTLES'.

It confirmed the outline Brian received verbally two weeks earlier, although he might have been amused to see the records it specified were still 78rpm, which remained standard contract terminology for several years after the format was phased out. The Beatles' agreement would start on 6 June 1962 and expire on 5 June 1963, with the three extensions in EMI's option running those same dates in 1963–4, 1964–5 and 1965–6. Royalties were to be paid during the currency of the contract 'and thereafter during the life of the Manager or for 25 years from the date hereof whichever is the longer' – that is, no monies would be paid after 1987 if Brian Epstein was dead by then; otherwise, they would be paid until his death. (This clause was eventually removed.)

Brian picked up his fountain pen, put a line through the second 't', turning BEATTLES back into BEATLES, and added his signature to the final page, that florid Epstein flourish across the Queen's sixpenny stamp. In need of a witness, he didn't turn to his brother or to Beryl Adams but to Bob Wooler – and, so historic was the moment, the DJ signed with his rarely revealed true first initial, F. Wooler, completed with his characteristic jagged-lightning underscore. Brian returned the contract to EMI (where it would be dated 4 June 1962) and then sent off another unpunctuated telegram to the Beatles:

EMI CONTRACT SIGNED SEALED TREMENDOUS IMPORTANCE TO ALL OF US WONDERFUL[52]

Though the contract was drawn up in Brian's own name, the company he was forming to embrace his entrepreneurial life had almost reached fruition. His request to call it BC Enterprises Ltd had been rejected by the Board of Trade as being too similar to a company called C&B Enterprises Ltd; on his return from Hamburg, Brian had to think again, and about 13 May he settled on Nems Enterprises Ltd. Its successes could only enhance Nems' long-established goodwill. The one name-conflict now would be with Nems Ltd, and this was resolvable with the permission of Harry Epstein.

It must have been yet another difficult family moment when, on 24 May, Harry signed a letter of authority permitting the new name . . . but, from here, everything slipped smoothly into gear. Nems Enterprises Ltd would be a standard £100 company owned evenly by Brian and Clive. They were also its directors, and Clive was company secretary. A bank account was opened: Midland Bank in Kirkdale, Liverpool, was getting the Beatles' business. A stylish range of stationery was designed and printed, not just letterheads but engagement contracts and accounts sheets for Brian's groups – the Beatles and others who'd soon be signed. The company also appointed its first employee, Beryl Adams, who left Nems Ltd and moved across to the new set-up with identical functions: secretary, typist, payroll. The registered office was the same as Nems Ltd, the original shop in Walton Road, but otherwise the companies were wholly separate; all the day-to-day business would be conducted at 12–14 Whitechapel. It was from here – from the medium-sized suite of offices above this provincial new-build shopping parade – that Nems Enterprises Ltd, directed by Brian Epstein, planned to help the Beatles become bigger than Elvis.

Bob Wooler was privy to all the plans and eager to play his part. On behalf of Cavern owner Ray McFall, he agreed terms for the Beatles to be presented exclusively at the Cavern for almost two weeks after their return from Hamburg: they would start on 9 June with a celebratory *Welcome Home* night and then play six further nights and five lunchtimes before appearing anywhere else. Everything would be *cooking* after twelve shows in the Cavern cauldron, then their following date would be the big Bruce Channel night at New Brighton Tower. Brian's posters instantly announced the Beatles as 'Parlophone Recording Artistes' and said this was 'A Bob Wooler Show'. Horst Fascher got all the lads sharply on and off stage by intimidation, Wooler with a wagging finger and everyone's respect.

The Channel show was announced via an *Echo* classified on 1 June, the Cavern bookings – called a 'fortnight season' – on 19 May. Two further agreements were not advertised: the Beatles would have private use of the Cavern for two afternoons on their return, so they could rehearse for EMI, and Ray McFall had assented to a further hike in the Beatles' fee. Brian was using their June return as the platform for another good increase, putting even greater financial distance between them and any rival. Their Cavern price was to be £25 for their usual Wednesday-night residency, and £30 for a Sunday-night residency to begin on 1 July. Brian aimed to have the Beatles collectively earning £200 a week soon after their return; few other groups took as much as £20.

It was Bob Wooler who enticed Rory Storm and the Hurricanes home early from France. They'd been six weeks on *le continent* when suddenly they were rushing back to Liverpool ... desperate not to miss the chance of appearing in a show with Jerry Lee Lewis. The hard-livin' Louisiana rocker was making his first return to Britain since 1958, when he'd been drummed out in disgrace for marrying his 13-year-old cousin. Who could miss *this*?

In Liverpool, this wasn't the only unexpected comeback, because Allan Williams – a year after losing the Beatles – was returning to rock promotion, and on Wooler's advice booked Jerry Lee Lewis for a night at New Brighton Tower. Williams knew who the star was but, bad at names, kept referring to him as Jerry Lewis; Wooler just got on with assembling a vast cast, eighteen supporting acts, fast on and fast off the Tower's triple-tier stages. Resigned as he was to being without the Beatles, he did get Rory Storm and the Hurricanes. They were in Orléans (north-central France) when they heard about the show, and fired off a telegram saying they were scooting home, *tout de suite*.

By then it was 14 May and they'd been in France since the first day of April. Having had a torrid time just getting there, Ringo would remember this period of his life mostly in a series of grumps. 'The French don't like the British – at least, I didn't like them,' he said five years later. He'd recall the trip as a failure, saying they played United States Army bases 'in the wilderness', 'weren't paid', stayed in 'doss-houses' and that food cost them 'a fortune'. But Johnny Guitar's diary tells of a happier six-week sojourn.[53]

Their first month was at USA6, Fontenet. NOT THE BIGGEST BUT THE BEST shouted the sign outside the camp gates; Rory and the Hurricanes posed there for a blurry photo snapped by the lovely Vicky Woods. The audience of four hundred in the Enlisted Men's Club were mighty appreciative of sweaty rock and sweet eye-candy: the shapely blonde Vicky, who sang five numbers a night, had to stay on stage throughout. They played six nights a week, 7.00–10.45 with four fifteen-minute breaks, and found the Americans friendly. One soldier claimed an association with night-clubs in Miami and said he'd book them there, but it didn't materialise.[54]

They slept in town hotels and were meant to be at the Fontenet camp only at night – but often they snuck in by day too, trying to stay one step ahead of the military police who were meant to throw them out. Johnny Guitar's diary says they managed to enjoy the bowling alley and movie house, and Ringo's best memory is of filling their stomachs with Hershey bars and real American hamburgers, so vastly superior to their flabby English imitations. And when Rory ran an ad in the *Echo* announcing the Hurricanes' surprise return, he promised they'd appear in 'fabulous new American fluorescent suits' – so it seems they also made imaginative use of the quartermaster's store. It was ever the Hurricanes' lot to be draped in Rory's desire to dazzle.[55]

On the downside, there were far too few women around (and it isn't known if anything happened with Vicky). On the up, Fontenet was ninety minutes' drive to the coast. They caught suntans on the beach at Royan and had days off in La Rochelle, Rochefort, Saintes and Cognac. Ringo, who generally drank Scotch, developed in this quaint old town a taste for brandy.[56]

But a month was enough. Refusing an extension of their Fontenet contract, they moved 325 kilometres north to the US Army base at Orléans, where they had mixed fortunes before their sudden departure. Johnny's diary says three veteran committee members expelled them for performing rock 'n' roll *and* for doing it too loudly. They played instead at the nearby Saran base and drew so many Orléans soldiers that they were allowed back. Two weeks in, though, came news that Jerry Lee was coming to Liverpool and they were hotfoot back home.

It was worth it. Bob Wooler would report another momentous night in the mighty Tower, with a record-breaking attendance of 'nearly four thousand'. Brian Epstein was there to learn about promotions, and – amid the crush, crowds and chaos that defeated even Wooler's finger-wagging – Mike McCartney took a photograph of Jerry Lee Lewis screaming at everyone to *get off the fuckin' stage* so he could start playing.[57]

The Hurricanes lacked the proper planning skills of a good manager, but Rory and Johnny were always good at creating opportunities. After Jerry Lee's show they quickly fixed up four more Tower bookings before heading straight off for their third consecutive Butlin's summer season. This, they now learned, was not to be in Pwllheli as before but at the Skegness camp, on the bracing east coast of England; the pay was £100 a week less £10 agency commission, leaving the five with £18 each. They set off in their cars on Saturday 2 June. Ringo's Zodiac – just repaired after crashing in the race against George Harrison's Anglia – carried him and his Premier drum kit 166 miles across England's midriff while the Beatles' plane was flying overhead, bringing them home from Hamburg. They wanted him, but he was gone again and not due back until September.

The same man who sent Jerry Lee Lewis to England – the heavyweight manager/promoter Don Arden – also lured Little Richard out of an Alabama church for both a British autumn tour and a short season at the Star-Club, and he sent Gene Vincent to Hamburg. The deeply pained Virginia wildcat arrived at the Star-Club for a two-week season on 28 May, overlapping with the Beatles for four days, and they were overjoyed to meet an American idol for the first time. *Disc* rightly called Vincent 'the star who doesn't need hits' – he was Be-Bop-A-Lula, Ain't She Sweet, Summertime, Over The Rainbow, Say Mama, Dance In The Street, Bluejean Bop and so many more. As John expressed it, 'It's hard for people to realise just how thrilled the four of us were just to see any great American rock 'n' roller in the flesh. We were almost paralysed with adoration.'[58]

It wasn't so much the chance of seeing Vincent in action that John found exciting – he stayed a 'record man', never much bothered about catching even his favourites playing live – it was being able to hang out with him, the chance of getting to know him, that was so thrilling. And here at the Star-Club, the Beatles hung out with Vincent in ways they wouldn't forget.

They found out straight away he was a serious drinker, rarely without a bottle of Scotch in his hands. Wanting his company and his whisky, the Beatles ensured he didn't drink alone. Bernie Boyle was there too, punching above his weight: 'Don Arden, Gene Vincent and their tour manager Henri Henriod had a booth at the Star-Club and everyone squeezed in, including the Beatles and me. John had something of the Vincent in him, the style and the persona. Vincent was a horrible drunk, on the hard booze, a bottle of whisky being shared around, no ice, no water, straight Scotch.'[59] While the Beatles could still get up on stage and play, Boyle was out cold. 'I was absolutely fucking *hammered* and passed out in the street. They carried me up to the flat and rearranged the furniture so I not only woke up with puke all over me, I couldn't fathom where I was. Paul took one look at me and said, "For God's sake go and clean yourself up, you look awful."'

Other elements of Vincent's character they were less keen about. For some reason, he zeroed in on Paul and kept offering to knock him out cold by touching two pressure points on the back of his neck, a trick he said he'd learned while serving in the Marines. Paul didn't fancy this one little bit, and though Gene kept insisting he'd only be unconscious for a few seconds, Paul made sure his neck stayed beyond the American's reach.[60]

Then there was Vincent's fascination for guns. In America, he toyed with the real thing; in England, where there were hardly any weapons, it *was* just toys; in Hamburg, weapons could be bought easily and Gene was very quickly back in his strange comfort zone. One moment George was in the Star-Club with him, the next they were speeding in a taxi along the Reeperbahn to Vincent's hotel, where he suspected his wife was having it off with Henri Henriod. 'He opened his coat and handed me a gun saying, "You hold this." He started banging on the door, shouting, "I know you're in there!" . . . I was holding the gun he was about to shoot her with. It was just like that – one minute you're somewhere and five minutes later you're in *that* situation. I quickly gave the gun back to him and said, "No thank you, see you around, squire," and left.'[61]

Vincent also liked knives. (Would *all* their American heroes be like this?) Intriguingly, John would recall how 'Everyone was always stabbing, everybody had knives . . . really wild scenes it was.'[62] There are photos of the Beatles and Vincent from these few days and one shows John and Pete brandishing knives. Pete does so with a laugh but John's eyes are wide, his tongue is pushed hard inside his cheek to effect another crip face, and he appears like the arch pantomime villain, about to plunge his dagger deep into Vincent's chest. The American, who would have been loaded on pills and whisky, seems oblivious; John looks off-his-trolley, like he does in another photo that shows four Beatles and two tubes of Preludin. Pete points enthusiastically to one (though he'd not taken the pills), Paul, George and especially John broadcast an intimate knowledge of them.

This is the only known photograph explicitly tying the Beatles to 'drug taking', and it's from a set of at least fifteen shots that are their earliest colour photos, probably taken by Manfred Weissleder. They pose with a smiling Horst Fascher in one, and there are eight excellent stage pictures. Pete looks happy, as do they all – and here too is the Star-Club audience, dancing and standing close to the stage, Hamburg's young couples dressed for a night out at St Pauli's raucous new club. The Beatles had opened it in memorable style and now they were leaving – having added something like 144 hours to their St Pauli stage experience.*

Previously, they'd left Hamburg with better guitars and amplifiers, this time they had nothing like that – but they had some new clothes, Paul had bought a Rollei camera for his brother, and John had Stuart's art school scarf, the only one of his friend's possessions he'd wanted from Astrid. He was also smuggling as many Prellies as he dared salt away in his luggage, which was quite a lot. They were going home to unfamiliar arrangements: John to find Cyn in her bedsit, Paul to Dot in the adjacent room to Cyn, and Pete to a domestic life-and-death situation – his mother was more than seven months pregnant, but her mother, Pete's live-in grandmother, there throughout most of his life, succumbed to cancer four days before his return, on 29 May.

More than anything, the Beatles were leaving Hamburg with a tangible sense of being on the verge of something. Klaus Voormann would recall one last Fiat drive out to the coast with George and Paul, when George talked about how he was going to make plenty of money: 'He was going to buy a house and a swimming pool, and then he'd buy a bus for his father, as he was a bus driver.'[63]

They were flying back as *EMI artistes*. Four days after getting home they had a London recording date they did not want to foul up, and five days past that there was another BBC broadcast. It was turning-point time for them all – not least John Lennon and Paul McCartney, who had new and exclusive songs ready to roll and were going to put them firmly on the line for the first time. Hamburg's 'exciting season' was finally over. Once again, they needed to calm down and step up.

---

* Because the Beatles' playing time varied on this trip, and the nightly specifics aren't known, it isn't possible to calculate their stage hours with any certainty. If 144 hours over forty-eight nights is about right, it made the Hamburg running total something like 1062 hours in thirty-four weeks, or just under four and a half hours every night for almost eight months.

29

Under Marching Orders (2–6 June 1962)

It was so different this time. On their first return from Hamburg the Beatles were in disarray: two kicked out, two sent home, no bass player, only half the gear, the leader unsure he'd carry on. Second time, they came back a man light to rejoin a violent north Liverpool jive circuit they'd already conquered. Third time, this time, they returned to organisation, order and promise.

Late evening on Saturday 2 June, when Neil collected them at Manchester airport, he handed each Beatle a large manila envelope from Brian. These contained the latest *Mersey Beat* (reporting news of their EMI contract) and two typed sheets listing line-by-line their bookings for the next forty days and nights. Weekly bulletins would follow with fuller details and instructions, this was only an overview: thirty-one engagements (the odd gaps would be plugged by eight more) plus a secondary list of four notable dates on the horizon. At Christmas, Brian had given them travelling alarm clocks; this document, as John would describe it, was another kind of wake-up call: 'Brian put all our instructions down neatly on paper and it made it all seem real. We were in a daydream till he came along. We'd no idea what we were doing, or where we'd agreed to be. Seeing our marching orders on paper made it all official.'[1]

First on the list was a two-day private rehearsal in the Cavern – as much as three and a half hours on Sunday afternoon and however long they wanted on the Monday night, when the club routinely closed. They'd gone to Decca with no proper rehearsal except gigs, this time there was concentrated preparation.

Brian hadn't known John and Paul were returning from Hamburg with new material, fresh Lennon-McCartney numbers they wanted put on top of the pile – but, as an eager advocate of their songwriting, he'd have been delighted, and equally keen to see them given prominence. With a mixture of pride and amusement, Paul would always be able to imitate Brian's exact reaction whenever he or John played him something they'd just written, emitting a theatrical mid-range *Uh!*, words alone being insufficient for Brian to express his pleasure. This could have been the first of many such great moments.[2]

Brian also talked to John, Paul and George about what other songs they could play to Parlophone. The intent was to impress, so they assembled a strong list of thirty-three that defines the best of the Beatles at June 1962 and distils their tastes at the time Lennon-McCartney resumed writing songs. There's pop, rock, R&B, rockabilly, dance, comedy and ballads, with harmonies throughout, six of the songs coming from long before the rock era; it's the music of nineteen artists from America, two from Britain and one from Italy.

Brian jotted down all the titles and the result was a two-page document, typed on crested BE notepaper, that he gave or quickly sent to George Martin's office. Because the producer said he wanted to assess the Beatles' singing individually, the list showed who sang what, and its first item was a 'Suggested opening medley' of Besame Mucho, Will You Love Me Tomorrow and Open (Your Lovin' Arms) – Paul, John and George singing strong numbers in turn.[3] Otherwise, the most rehearsed numbers in these two Cavern sessions were PS I Love You, Love Me Do and Ask Me Why.

They set out for London on Tuesday the 5th, a repeat of their New Year's journey except darkness and blizzards had yielded to summer brightness and a rare June heatwave. It still took about seven hours, sweltering their way down England's spinal A-roads, slowed by every urban hindrance. Brian travelled by train and met them at the Royal Court Hotel, where he'd booked them into twin-bed rooms for two nights. How they paired isn't remembered, but the idea worked so well that twin-bed rooms would be the way for most of the Beatles' travels from now on. The hotel was on Sloane Square, in a part of London they hadn't seen before; Belgravia lay behind them and Chelsea before, starting just across the square at King's Road. It wasn't yet the King's Road of later renown but there was an essence, enough to catch an inquisitive provincial's eye: bespoke shoe shops, restaurants, pubs, clubs and one or two fancy boutiques for wealthy young gals. Bazaar, where Mary Quant was turning out designer clothes, was just down there on the right, and beyond that, on the left, was Chelsea Manor Studios, haunt of artists and photographers.

The EMI session wasn't until 7PM Wednesday so they had more than twenty-four hours – a day and two nights – to explore 'the smoke'. Their free time in London at New Year had been spent sheltering from Siberia, but on 5–7 June 1962 London stretched before the Beatles in vivid colour: black taxis, red buses, green trees on leafy squares, smog-free streets in Derby Day sunshine, office secretaries in summer dresses, the capital at its glorious best. Prosperity was evident here in a way Liverpool never saw; London's bombsites were almost all gone – they were not the open sores of home but new offices, houses and flats, many furnished with consumer luxuries. Poverty-free cities do not exist and much of the housing in London was bad, but its people – by and large, and as Prime Minister Macmillan so famously declared – had never had it so good.

Here was the promise of something new, the Beatles' first visit to London in the knowledge their contract would be returning them at least twice more ... and, if Brian achieved his goals, at other times too. To begin with, however, it was intimidating. The Beatles were never hicks but they were outnumbered, enough to provoke an even greater closeness than usual. As Paul would remember it, 'We didn't know London and we didn't know anybody *in* London, so we really did stick together. It was like fellows down from the north for a coach trip.' John would recall their first London visits as 'pretty nerve-racking – we were all putting on the "we're from Liverpool and we're tough" bit [said while squaring his shoulders] but there were some hard knocks down in London'.[4]

The Beatles always wanted to know what was going on, and they and Brian were late-night people, never the staying-in kind. What could London offer them? Paul says of these initial visits that they were excited to explore places known to them only by name – Kensington, Chelsea, Soho, Tottenham Court Road and especially around Tin Pan Alley: 'Whenever we came to London we went to Charing Cross Road for the guitar shops. It was like going to Santa's grotto.'[5] Otherwise, where they went and what they did on 5, 6 and 7 June would become blurred by everything that followed.

They certainly didn't find rock music, because there wasn't any – not unless someone happened to be strumming down the 2i's Coffee Bar, which was still the only such venue in town. London had nothing like the Cavern and no live scene like Liverpool. Society Londoners danced the Twist to a buttoned-up band at the Saddle Room club, just off Park Lane; well-heeled Londoners danced the Twist to a buttoned-up band at the Peppermint Lounge, a Trafalgar Square imitation of the New York niterie; hoi polloi Londoners danced the Twist to buttoned-up bands in their local *palais de danse*.

London's music landscape was changing, however. At La Discotheque, in Wardour Street, revellers danced not only to live bands but sometimes to records spun by a DJ – a novel idea. And while the post-war jazz clubs had been able to resist rock, in summer 1962 they were conceding ever-greater stage time to R&B. The new sounds arrived in the West End at the start of May, when the Marquee, which advertised itself as the London Jazz Centre, gave Alexis Korner's Blues Incorporated a Thursday-night season. The group's manager was Ronan O'Rahilly, an original, enterprising 22-year-old Irishman bustling round the Soho scene, and their guest vocalist this first night was a young beanpole who called himself Long John Baldry. Two weeks later, *Disc* reported that a 19-year-old London School of Economics student, Mick Jagger, had joined them to sing and play harmonica.[6]

It happened with speed. By August, *Melody Maker* was headlining R&B BOOM HITS LONDON CLUBS – prematurely perhaps, but something was rumbling. The piece named the main men (including drummer Ginger Baker and bass guitarist Jack Bruce) and quoted Korner predicting 'there'll be a hell of a lot more R&B bands by the end of the year'.[7] One new one (as yet unnamed) had been started by Brian Jones, who was rehearsing with Mick Jagger and his mate Keith Richards.

The Beatles' EMI arrival also coincided with timely record business developments. The supremacy of the 45rpm single was confirmed in June 1962 when EMI and Decca deleted every last 78rpm disc from the catalogues. Shellac – the sole format from the 1920s to '50s – was dead, gone, and vinyl was king. And on the day of the Beatles' first session, 6 June, the *NME* launched its album chart.

Lagging behind *Melody Maker* and *Record Retailer*, the *NME* gave its newcomer no fanfare, but the arrival of LPs in the bestselling music paper underscored a slow-rising status of the format and slight shift in its marketplace – not much, but a perceptible twitch. 'No adult over here ever buys a single,' avowed Capitol Records' Dave Dexter, Jr, in one of his hundreds of individual letters rejecting British EMI masters in America – and, right across the world, the reverse was also true: teenagers seldom bought albums. They were priced beyond pocket money and their content was pitched mostly at grown-ups. But the times were changing: the first number 1 on the first *NME* album chart was Elvis.

One new release that didn't trouble the charts, on either side of the Atlantic, was Bob Dylan's debut album (*Bob Dylan*), out late March in America and 29 June in Britain. But it was noticed – the *NME*'s weekly US column, Nat Hentoff's American Airmail, gave Dylan his first name-check in Britain on 25 May: '... folksong fans watch out for the release of a CBS album by Bob Dylan. He's the most startling of all the American city folk singers.'

Any one, or none, of these matters might have figured in George Martin's mind at lunchtime on Wednesday 6 June as he walked in his shirtsleeves down a hot dry Oxford Street with Ron Richards. They could also have been discussing the prospects of Leo Maguire's record, about to be unveiled on TV. They definitely discussed the Beatles, the Liverpool beat group George had signed to Parlophone unseen, and who were coming in tonight. Ron says George delegated the session to him but said he'd drop by at some point to take a look. They really did need to establish how they'd restructure them, which of the two contenders to make lead singer. 'I desperately wanted my own Cliff,' George says. 'I was so hidebound by Cliff Richard and the Shadows that I was looking for the one voice that would carry them.'[8] Ron would retain a clear memory of their conversation as they strode along, suit jackets slung over shoulders in the sunshine: 'George and I were walking along, talking about what the group should be called. Was it going to be John Lennon and the Beatles or Paul McCartney and the Beatles? We still weren't sure. I remember saying to George, "Bloody silly name that is, Beatles. How corny can you get?"'[9]

The group with the corny name were on their way. Neil steered the van from smart Chelsea to leafy St John's Wood. EMI commissionaire John Skinner, straight-backed and strait-laced in his worsted uniform and polished war medals, guided them through the gates. 'They pulled into the car park in an old white van,' he'd remember. 'They all looked very thin and weedy, almost undernourished. Neil Aspinall, their road manager, said they were the Beatles, here for a session. I thought, "What a *strange* name."'[10]

Recording session

> Wednesday 6 June 1962. Number 2 studio, EMI, London.
> Recording: Besame Mucho; Love Me Do; PS I Love You; Ask Me Why.

The entrance was up front steps, but because the Beatles helped Neil lug in the gear they entered the building down the left side, behind the old house. A turn right, a turn left, and they were in Number 2 studio, 60ft by 38ft, a big room with a high ceiling, no windows, parquet flooring (covered in places by rugs) and all the technical necessities of a recording session. For Paul, and the others to some extent, Decca's brittle anxieties made an unwelcome return. '[It had] great big white studio sight-screens, like at a cricket match, towering over you, and up this endless stairway was the control room. It was like *heaven*, where the great gods lived, and we were down below. Oh God, the nerves.'[11]

They were in the Beno Dorn suits, but still there was enough about them to startle the staff. Norman Smith, the balance engineer assigned to the session, peered through the control room glass at the activity below and muttered *Good God, what've we got 'ere?* 'It was,' he would remember, 'a double-take job: you'd look and have to look again.' His colleague, technical engineer Ken Townsend, recalls how 'they dressed a bit differently and all had what we thought was very long hair. They had broad Liverpool accents. We didn't have many people from Liverpool recording at Abbey Road.'[12]

Despite George Martin saying one or more photographers would attend the session to take publicity shots, none did, and no pictures are known to exist. If they did, what happened this evening might be clearer, because its details are somewhat fogged, like so many aspects of the Beatles' early EMI days. This relationship had started obscurely and would continue so, and these two facts are related; it was only after five more months that everything would become transparent and straightforward.

The first of several long-lingering debates about this 6 June session would centre on what kind of an audition it was – an Artist Test or a Commercial Test? Several interested parties remember it one way and several the other, both views apparently stemming from paperwork pinned to the Abbey Road staff noticeboard. But the crucial documents are clear beyond doubt and can dispel any misleading information for whatever reason it existed: this was no audition at all – the Beatles were at EMI because they already had a contract. George Martin, for understandable reasons, considered the session little more than a look-see, a chance to assess the group he'd signed blind, but the Beatles and Brian believed they were there to make their first record, and the studio was set up to do it – the gods in the upstairs control room would be sending the Beatles' sound to two quarter-inch tape decks.[13]

The extent of George Martin's involvement this evening would also be subject to competing claims, but what's clear is that Ron Richards started the session. It isn't known if Brian was told George would be mostly absent, so this may have come as a disappointment – and, with that, a sense of being slighted.

The session had barely started when it stopped. The Beatles had good instruments – John and George both played their superior American guitars, the Rickenbacker and Gretsch, Paul had his inexpensive German violin-shaped Hofner bass, and Pete a perfectly adequate Premier drum kit – but their backline equipment was tatty, still the amps Decca hadn't liked on New Year's Day. Brian was aware of the need for better equipment and had done nothing about it; the reason for this is unclear, though it could be that, since amps had been the Beatles' domain long before he came along, it was something he left them to sort out for themselves, with the increased money they were earning … except that they hadn't. Paul's old Truvoice amp and mighty bass speaker – the five-foot-tall 'coffin', as grunted up and down the Cavern steps several times a week by Pete and Neil – just weren't suited to recording, and this was clear the second Paul played a few notes so Smith could get a recording level. The studio didn't carry spare guitar amps, but the problem was solved by technical engineer Ken Townsend, in a white laboratory coat, bringing a heavy Tannoy speaker up from a basement echo chamber.

The object of the session was to make the Beatles' first single. No one noted how many songs they rehearsed before the red light went on and the tapes were set rolling, or whether they bothered to play the rehearsed 'opening medley', but Ron Richards selected four numbers for recording – Besame Mucho, Love Me Do, PS I Love You and Ask Me Why – from which the final choice of two would be made. This was most odd. The fact that three or perhaps even all four of these songs matched the Beatles' own choices underlines again what an uncommon situation this was. Recording artists *always* had to do what they were told, to perform only songs chosen and ready-arranged for them – yet here were the Beatles, at their debut session, putting forward their preferred material and having it chosen. They weren't only signed unseen, they'd been brought in for a session without being given songs to learn and without the involvement of an arranger or session musicians. Disregarding the R of A&R, George Martin was treating it like the test it wasn't, albeit with one proviso . . .

What the Beatles never knew, and no one was discussing, was the pressure exerted behind the scenes by Sid Colman and Kim Bennett. Ardmore and Beechwood expected to publish one or both sides of this Beatles record – which was why they'd prompted the Parlophone signing in the first place. While the song that lit their interest, Like Dreamers Do, fell unregarded by the wayside before or during the evening, it was manifest that at least one Lennon-McCartney song *had* to be chosen from those recorded. Discreetly, George Martin was getting the measure of what these two Liverpool boys could give him.

Documents show that Besame Mucho, Love Me Do, PS I Love You and Ask Me Why were recorded in that order, and as it was standard procedure for producers to take the most promising number first, Ron Richards patently favoured the old Spanish song for the Beatles' first A-side. The session tape, which would include variant takes and revealing banter between the numbers, was not kept, but two of these 6 June recordings – Besame Mucho and Love Me Do – survive as acetate discs and the former is merely an average performance, nothing startling.* Richards stopped John and George's backing vocals, omitting even their usual *cha-cha-boom*s, and he was taken aback by Pete's drumming, where an unnecessarily relentless tom-tom pounding was interspersed by weak snare-drum fills and shuffles rather than the required *attack*. 'Pete Best wasn't very good,' Richards would always recall. 'It was me who [later] said to George Martin, "He's useless, we've got to change this drummer."'[14]

George Martin didn't much care for the Beatles' Besame Mucho. While the

---

* Both were released in 1995 on *The Beatles Anthology 1*.

evidence is contradictory, he seems to have arrived at the session when they were playing Love Me Do – possibly after being fetched by Chris Neal, who was operating the tape machines. Neal would remember, 'After they'd run through a couple of tunes Norman and I were not all that impressed with, all of a sudden there was this raunchy noise which struck a chord in our heads. It was Love Me Do. Norman said to me, "Oi, go down and pick up George from the canteen and see what he thinks of this."' George walked into the upstairs control room – the Beatles couldn't see him and didn't know he was there – and was attracted by something they were doing. 'I picked up on Love Me Do mainly because of the harmonica sound,' he would remember. 'I loved raw harmonica and used to issue the records of Sonny Terry and Brownie McGhee.'[15]

Though George liked the harmonica, he wasn't crazy about Love Me Do and instantly homed in on a problem with its arrangement. The Beatles' Hamburg and Cavern rehearsals ought to have prepared them for every eventuality, but at four junctures during the song there was an awkward moment when John sang the title line and, in the same split-second of completing the last word 'do', resumed playing his harmonica. The head of Parlophone came down from the control room, exchanged hellos with the Beatles for the first time, and explained the problem. As Paul recalls:

> George Martin said, 'Wait a minute, there's a crossover there. Someone else has got to sing "love me do" because you're going to have a song called Love Me *Waahhh*. So, Paul, will you sing "love me do"?'
>
> God, I got the screaming heebegeebies. We were doing it live and I was suddenly given this massive moment on our first thing, where everything stopped, no backing, the spotlight went to me and I went [in trembling tones] *love me dooooo*. I can still hear the shake in my voice when I listen to it.[16]

Paul's heebegeebies are certainly audible on the recording, constricting his voice not just at those four places but throughout the song, big-moment nerves afflicting him here as they'd done at Decca and the BBC, and in his first appearance with the Quarry Men, and right back to when he collected school prizes. And beyond the shaky vocal, the recording affords other insights. At this point, Love Me Do was arranged slower than it would become, with a bluesy emphasis. To John and Paul this meant *integrity*, and their pushing of Love Me Do over, say, Hello Little Girl or Like Dreamers Do, which sounded more obviously 'commercial', reveals their initial approach to the business of making records. Their aim was to make something catchy and *worthy*.

However, the most ear-grabbing aspect of this Love Me Do – the first recording of a 'new' Lennon-McCartney song – is a negative one. Pete's skip beat was disastrous. It triggered eccentric tempo changes that made the Beatles seem tentative and even amateurish. It's strange that his bandmates, John and Paul especially, ever considered it a good idea, although maybe Pete had executed it better in the Cavern. Here at EMI, his failure to keep the correct time forced the others to speed up with him, and then he hesitated at the start of the middle-eight, initially playing it straight before suddenly shifting up into that skip. It isn't known how many takes of each song the Beatles recorded, but it's a compelling thought that the preserved Love Me Do, complete with flaws, may have been the best of several – it was customary for only the 'best' record-ing of a song to be pressed as an acetate disc. George Martin and Ron Richards were distinctly unimpressed. They were used to working with precision drum-mers, timekeepers who bound the sound of their fellow musicians. Both men decided that Pete was unsuitable for recording, not to be used on future occa-sions. It was the fourth time in four sessions he'd been rated not good enough – at least once too many.

PS I Love You and Ask Me Why aren't available for study, but Richards would remember being little impressed by either. His view of the former was that he wouldn't consider it for an A-side because it shared the title of a well-known song. Norman Smith's interesting last analysis of the recordings was that 'it was twenty minutes of torture – they made a dreadful sound! – and then they came up to the control room'.

It took twenty possibly torturous steps to get them there, a flight of wooden stairs that led the Beatles into a recording studio control room for the first time. They hadn't got this far at Decca. Making themselves as comfortable as pos-sible, standing and leaning against unfamiliar big machines, they and the seven others squeezed into the small room fogged the air by lighting up – everyone here was a heavy smoker. Pete says they listened to a playback of the recordings and that he at least thought them good, then George Martin spoke to them, saying what would be required of them as Parlophone artists, and clarifying cer-tain technicalities.[17] 'He was giving them a good talking to,' says Ken Townsend, 'explaining about the studio microphones being figure-of-eight – in other words, you could stand on either side of them as opposed to stage mikes which were one-sided.' Norman Smith says the Beatles stayed quiet all this time. 'They didn't say a word back, not a word. They didn't even nod their heads in agreement. When he finished, George said, "Look, I've laid into you for quite a time, you haven't responded. Is there anything you don't like?" They all looked at each other for a long while, shuffling their feet, then George Harrison took a long look at George and said, "Yeah. I don't like your tie."'

George Martin did not instantly appreciate the joke (he was, he says, rather proud of his tie, black with a red horse motif, bought at Liberty's) and the younger George would remember a fleeting tension: 'There was a moment of *ohhhhh*, but then we laughed and he did too. Being born in Liverpool you have to be a comedian.' Paul recalls 'a little tense second and then everyone laughed', and Smith's account would prevail: 'It cracked the ice, and for the next fifteen to twenty minutes the Beatles were pure entertainment. When they left, George and I just sat there saying, "Phew! What do you think of that lot then?" I had tears running down my face.'[18]

Two parties who'd come together for a combination of reasons never discussed, converged here for the first time and found the experience inspiring. When Brian Epstein met the Beatles he was bowled over by their music and their magnetism; George Martin wasn't yet appreciative of the first, but the second had him hooked. As he'd say, 'I did think they had enormous talent, but it wasn't their music, it was their charisma, the fact that when I was with them they gave me a sense of well-being, of being happy. The music was almost incidental. I thought, "If they have this effect on me, they are going to have that effect on their audiences."'[19]

The Beatles always spoke of how they felt intimidated by George Martin's cultured speaking voice – the adopted crystal that cut through his London clay, suiting his personality as if to the manner born. Being British, and especially coming from Liverpool, they were bound to feel second-class by comparison. As Paul describes it, 'We hadn't really met any of these London people before, these people who talked a bit different. George Martin was very well spoken, a little above our station, so it was a little intimidating, but he seemed like a nice bloke.'[20] George Harrison would say, 'We thought he was very posh – he was friendly but schoolteacherly, we had to respect him, but at the same time he gave us the impression he wasn't stiff – that you could joke with him.'[21] And as George Martin would add, 'It was love at first sight. John, George and Paul – I thought they were super. They had great personalities, and they charmed themselves to me a great deal. George was probably the most vociferous of the lot. Pete Best was very much the background boy – he didn't say much at all, he just looked moody and sullen in the corner.'[22]

While three ebullient Beatles relaxed into gags, Pete was silent. 'I never entered into any conversation with him [George Martin],' he said in his autobiography, and Norman Smith confirmed it: 'Pete Best didn't say *one word*. I got a feeling something wasn't right between them – it wasn't only that George and Ron found fault with him as a drummer.'[23] George Martin felt Pete was 'almost surly', although this personal opinion had no bearing on his professional judgement, which was to use a session drummer – a hired hand – next time the Beatles came in to record. He voiced this to Brian, John, Paul and George at the end of the session, while Pete was out of the room.[24]

No Beatle ever said if he drove away from Abbey Road dreading the prospect of their evening's work being issued, or excited that two of the four songs would soon become their first single. Brian had told *Mersey Beat* the record would be issued in July, so what would Parlophone pick? Given that John would tell *Melody Maker* 'We were hoping to be the first British group to use harmonica on record', they seem to have wanted their first 45 to be Love Me Do, Lennon-McCartney's earnest little R&B number.[25]

There was, plainly, so much they still didn't know. First, George Martin and Ron Richards were not done with their deliberations over which Beatle to make lead singer. On the basis of the music recorded, they seem to have favoured Paul because he sang two and a half songs at the session to John's one and a half. Whatever they'd heard of George was enough to rule him out. As George Martin explains, '*Still* I was thinking "Is it John Lennon and the Beatles or Paul McCartney and the Beatles?" I knew it wasn't George. And then suddenly it hit me that I had to take them as they were, which was a new thing. I was being too conventional – but then, I hadn't really heard anything quite like them before.'[26]

No one had. The record business had no template for the Beatles. At the start of July 1962, the *NME* – routinely keen to analyse its own Top Thirty – reported its 'Chart-points race' for the year's first six months. Elvis was 1, Cliff 2 and Chubby Checker 3, and beyond them were soloists, duos, trios, orchestras and the like. The only 'groups' in the Top 75 were the Karl Denver Trio at 5, the Shadows at 8 and B. Bumble and the Stingers at 15 – respectively, a yodelling Scottish country trio, an English instrumental quartet, and an instrumental American novelty act. Groups like the Beatles, rock bands, didn't figure.

There *were* no groups like the Beatles. Three guitars and drums, all three front-line guitarists singing lead and harmonies, a group who wrote their own songs – it was simple, direct and not done. George Martin's decision to accept them this way, as a leaderless unit, was, correspondingly, a first too – and precisely what they'd hoped for and Brian had been trying to help them find. They'd lucked into the only producer in London who shared their resistance to convention, the only man with a reputation for sound experimentation and a strong knack for the unusual . . . and he'd lucked into the Beatles.

But it was just as well they were already under contract, because on the strength of this first session George Martin wouldn't have signed them, not on their musical performance at any rate. Unhappy with both the drummer and the material, he decided to issue none of these first recordings, sweeping the session under the carpet. They could start again another time, though with one important caveat: their contract required Parlophone to record six 'sides' and they'd already done four.

As George Martin had told *Disc* in December 1961, 'A beat group presents far more of a problem than does a solo artist ... there's the snag of finding the right material.' George knew too the Ardmore and Beechwood imperative – that their first record had to include at least one number by Lennon-McCartney, ideally the A-side, and yet he didn't consider even the best of them good enough. As he reflects, 'I was looking for a hit song and didn't think we had it in Love Me Do. I didn't think the Beatles had *any* song of *any* worth – they gave me no evidence that they could write hit material.'[27]

George instructed Ron Richards to find a song for this Liverpool group – to keep his ear to the ground in Denmark Street, Tin Pan Alley – and, when he found it, to consult him and then send it up to Brian Epstein for the Beatles to learn. Love Me Do could be the B-side of whatever Ron found, and if this process took weeks, or even months, so be it: he was in no hurry.

30

The Undesirable Member
(7 June–18 August 1962)

Everything reignited on Saturday 9 June with the *Welcome Home*. Four acts supported the Beatles in a four-and-a-half-hour show that cost Cavern members 6s 6d and non-members 7s 6d – if any could get in. June had always been the quiet month for Liverpool music clubs, but not any more. 'It felt like there were a thousand in there,' says one of the blissfully compressed, Barbara Houghton. 'The place was *heaving* and the atmosphere more than electric. What a night, *what a night!*'[1]

The Cavern fuse-box always blew on such occasions – the only time Bob Wooler lost the power of speech. The hot crowd stood wedged in not-much emergency light but knew not to panic as there was only the one narrow doorway to the slippery staircase out. The Beatles had just left the stage when it happened; they'd worked their audience to a frenzy and were back in the bandroom with the numerous gifts brought by fans, including a cake several sponges high baked by Lindy Ness, Lou Steen and their friend Susan Woolley. 'John was made up,' Lindy noted in her diary, along with 'Wrote the above in Paul's house because we spent the night there.'

It was all still innocent – and highly exciting. When they left the Cavern, George peeled off without the others, keen to test the bird-pulling appeal of his new Ford Anglia; Pete went out with his girlfriend Kathy; and John and Paul let Lindy and Lou return with them in Neil's van to the south end of Liverpool. Instead of being dropped off home, the girls stayed with them, went to Paul's house, and watched them write a song.

Please Please Me was John's baby, conceived inside the forty-eight hours they'd been home from London. It was fair to say that Ask Me Why, Love Me

Do and PS I Love You hadn't gone down brilliantly well at EMI – here was one they could play them next time. He'd remember how the words and tune came together in 'the other bedroom in my auntie's place at Menlove Avenue: I remember the day and the pink eiderdown on the bed'.[2]

The motivation was EMI, the muse elsewhere. Lyrically, the spark came from a song called Please, a US number 1 for Bing Crosby eight years before John was born. He was intrigued by its opening wordplay – 'Please, lend your little ear to my pleas' – and let it inspire his song's title and recurring lyric. Musically, the primary influence on Please Please Me was Roy Orbison. John said he'd heard him 'doing Only The Lonely or something' – but most likely he didn't use any particular number for reference, just Orbison's style and dramatic, octave-vaulting crescendos.[3] It was a love song, but not the kind of 'moon in June' treacle ladled over the charts through John's life to date. This was a Liverpool-Lennon love song: beyond the politeness of the first word, he's urging his girl to please him *like he pleases her*.*

John always said the song was entirely his, and Paul confirms it, but still they were both involved. Late night on 9 June, Lindy and Lou watched them refine it, seated side by side at Jim Mac's upright piano in Paul's front parlour. Lindy recalls them 'mostly working on the chord changes, with a lot of joking and messing about'. The two 15-year-old girls stayed through the night (their mothers thought each was at the other's house) and, later, dozed under the piano while Lennon-McCartney explored chords above their heads. 'They asked us what we thought of it,' Lou remembers, 'and we said it was great. It was certainly great to see them writing, and that they didn't mind us being there – but they were always dead casual about things like that.'[4]

Please Please Me wouldn't emerge into daylight for a while, but a Lennon-McCartney song was broadcast on BBC radio for the first time six days later, making an initial strike on 1.8 million listeners. It was Ask Me Why and it opened the Beatles' second *Here We Go* appearance, recorded in Manchester on 11 June for national broadcast on Friday the 15th. This time, in keeping with their daily stage repertoire, they went consciously for *group projection* – John took the first song, with harmonies by Paul and George; Paul sang the second with backing from John and George; George took the third with backing from John and Paul. It was, again, something never heard on radio before, and impressive enough for producer Peter Pilbeam to retain them on his list of acts to rebook.[5]

---

* Commentators like to assert that it was a plea for oral sex. It could be, but it needn't be, and John never mentioned it.

Here too was an application of polish to shine their versatility. Besame Mucho was an energetic zip through what the announcer called 'a Spanish classic'. A Picture Of You, sung brightly and with impressive confidence by George, was a current hit, in the top five this week and about to give Joe Brown his first and only number 1 – the Beatles' broadcast may even have helped get it there.

Best of all was Ask Me Why. George Martin had found cause to look askance at it, but his opinion was folded within broader downbeat views. Actually, there was plenty of interest going on here, and its appearance pinpointed the critical shift in the Beatles between March and June 1962. In their initial broadcast, they were responsible for the first exposure to the mass British public of a Tamla (Motown) song; three months later they were the first band to play their own new number *inspired* by a Tamla record. And yet, while Ask Me Why was sparked by Smokey Robinson, here was no clone: it emerged through the Lennon-McCartney filter as a melodically complex piece, an attractive and intriguing folky song with a light Latin rhythm, sung by John with a strong harmony from Paul. There was no frippery, no phoney American or mid-Atlantic accents, just two Liverpudlians letting the sincerity and quality of their voices carry an interesting tune. Whether or not any of this registered with even a handful of the 1.8m listeners, the moment can be seen as a milestone in the development of twentieth-century song.[6]

The audience in the Playhouse Theatre clearly liked the Beatles. The surviving recording reveals much clapping along, some between-songs screams and, just before A Picture Of You, a plainly audible flutter as one of the Beatles did something he shouldn't on BBC radio. There's also laughter during the song's instrumental middle-eight, as if John, Paul and George had gone into a little jig. It was like a seven-minute eavesdrop into Liverpool that happened to have been transported thirty-five miles to Manchester – and with good reason, because about a fifth of the audience were Beatles Fan Club members brought on a coach chartered by Brian. He and Jim McCartney travelled with the fans to Manchester, and John, Paul and George jumped aboard to ride home.

It was an interesting night for Pete, and he'd often speak of it. He said he was engulfed by adoring fans as they left the theatre and that he in particular was trapped, pinned back by a sea of admirers after the other three Beatles had wriggled free. Jim Mac, for one, took the view that Pete brought the situation upon himself – he apparently remarked, 'Why did you have to attract all the attention, why didn't you call the other lads back? I think that was very selfish of you.' Pete says he later raised this with Brian, who said he'd query it with Mr McCartney, but nothing more is known; what Pete didn't say was that he wasn't going to catch the coach anyway. It's also been written (although without attribution) that someone said to Pete this same evening, 'They're thinking of getting rid of you, you know, but they don't dare do it.'[7]

This informant, whoever it was, was 50 per cent right. They *were* getting rid of him and they *were* daring to do it. Pete's time in the Beatles was coming to an end.

EMI had been the final straw. Pete's poor performance at Decca was one thing, but they were *signed* to EMI and now George Martin didn't think him good enough either. George would often be asked about this and always give replies consistent with a legal letter he was obliged to write in mid-August 1965:

> I told Mr Epstein that I was not satisfied with the performance of their drum-mer Mr Peter Best, and as far as my recordings were concerned I would prefer not to use him on the actual record but that I would use a session drummer.
>
> Pete Best did seem to be 'an odd man out' and while the other three were very unified in their performance and enthusiasm, he did not seem to be a true part of the group.

The Beatles felt the same. If they kept Pete, they'd be lumbered with a hired drummer not just at their next session but at every session after that, on all their recordings. They'd be having to make music with men they'd never met, cyni-cal 'professionals' (said with a spit) of varying ages who didn't know the songs, probably didn't appreciate the style and sound, who weren't from Liverpool and with whom they'd no emotional connection. They wanted to look one another in the eyes with confidence, understanding and ambition, ready-rehearsed and coordinated, *a band* (a phrase George often used). And what was the point of using a session man anyway? They'd be playing live shows with these songs – in dance halls, maybe even theatres, on radio and TV – so their drummer had to be able to play the tracks to match the records, ideally because he'd helped make them in the first place. As Paul would explain, 'It had got to the stage that Pete was holding us back. What were we gonna do – try and pretend he was a won-derful drummer? We knew he wasn't as good as what we wanted.'[8]

Pete's dismissal would require the axe-swinging confrontation that John, Paul and George – as verbally cutting as they could be – had been reluctant to face for eighteen months. And they weren't going to face it now either. As George said, 'Being unable to deal with the emotional side of that, we went to Brian Epstein and said, "You're the manager, you do it."' Brian's business card said he had Sole Direction over the Beatles, but it was never the case. He still wanted them to keep Pete – 'I was very upset when the three of them came to me one night and said they didn't want him. It had been on the cards for a long time, but I'd hoped it wouldn't happen.'[9]

Brian also didn't like the idea of Ringo as Pete's replacement. 'I thought he was rather loud – I didn't want him,' he'd reflect two years later.[10] This first impression dated back to March, from Brian's mercy dash to Admiral Grove to fetch Ringo as a five-minutes'-notice Cavern lunchtime fill-in – only for the drummer to stubbornly insist on going nowhere until he'd drunk his tea.

But Brian's protestations, if he voiced them, were futile. Flexing the muscle they always had, John, Paul and George brooked no debate over Ringo's merits. It was the strength of their conviction that persuaded Brian to press ahead, and *his* strength that he accepted it: 'They liked Ringo and I trusted the boys' judgement. If they were happy, so was I.'[11]

The way they made Brian sack Pete strongly echoed the way they'd got Nigel Walley to dispose of guitarist Eric Griffiths four years back. However, while that had been a painful if brief conversation, cut and dried, this wasn't. The Pete Best situation was complicated by signed agreements – shakeable in themselves but still not without implications. Brian was under contract to John, Paul, George and Pete: he'd committed in writing to securing them paid work. There was provision for termination of the entire agreement after one year by either party, but not for the sudden removal of one of the signatories; and while the contract contained elements that could have been used to call the whole thing void (the weaknesses deliberately inserted by Brian), he'd subsequently signed for them, as their manager, the recording agreement with Parlophone. The situation was tricky, and to disregard the possibility of legal consequences clearly foolish.

Around 18 June, Brian raised his concerns with David Harris of Silverman, Livermore & Co, who'd drafted the management contract. After mulling the position over, Harris replied to Brian in writing on the 22nd – and because confidentiality was necessary, he referred to Pete not by name but (logically, if unfortunately) as 'the undesirable member'.[12]

Harris explained that, legally speaking, the Beatles were a partnership. Any group of people associated with a common purpose and sharing common loyalties are partners, and Lennon, McCartney, Harrison and Best were partners in the business of being Beatles. As the management contract allowed no means for the expulsion of a single member, Harris could see only one realistic solution: the Beatles must break up and then re-form without the undesirable member, signing a new management contract that excluded him. Brian would still be tied to Pete under the original agreement, however, and remain obliged to provide him with paid work. If he didn't, Pete could take action over loss of earnings, or worse.

Pete knew none of this, but all kinds of conversations were suddenly taking place behind his back. As Paul says, 'We talked amongst ourselves and talked with Brian and took a lot of advice on it all ... We said, "Oh God, I don't know how we're going to do this.'" All the same, Brian didn't have an easy time trying to stem their bulldozing desire for *instant-action-now*. Why didn't Eppy just go ahead and *do it*? 'It was,' Paul continues, 'a very fraught period.'[13]

It was, in addition to everything else, a summer of secrets and lies – for while options were explored and considered, argued and suppressed, everything seemed unaltered. Ringo was in Skegness with the Hurricanes, Pete was in the Beatles, and his best friend Neil was driving them everywhere, lugging their gear, being their minder and mate. He too knew nothing of the unfolding situation, and was yet another problem for which there was no obvious resolution – John, Paul and George wanted shot of Pete but hoped to keep Neil.

In the circumstances, it was right they stopped playing at the Casbah. They still appeared here some Sundays, but 24 June was the last time. The place shut down very soon afterwards, if not this actual night – Mo Best had just lost her mother and was eight months pregnant, no time to be running a teenagers' club. This tiny but magical venue, quite possibly the salvation of John, Paul and George's musical relationship when they were its opening act in August 1959, was closed by the Beatles a little under three years later. They'd remember it with warmth . . . but that's all it would be, a memory.

From one end of their exclusive twelve-date Cavern season to the other, the Beatles scattered several hot new songs into their set. Brian had mailed them a couple of 45s in Hamburg and now they worked their way through others, pressed into the Popular Department browseries at Nems Whitechapel, in the far left corner of the busy basement, picking especially on the British labels that issued American masters. From this singleminded sieving of some nine weeks of vinyl, a good half-dozen nuggets went straight into the set.

Don't Ever Change was one of the new songs that defined the Beatles' evolving sound in mid-1962, and it reunited them with the Crickets, who'd inspired their name and for whom they had an abiding affection. Death had barely diminished Buddy Holly's popularity in Britain, his loyal fan base being dripfed a diet of new issues and reissues, but Don't Ever Change had nothing to do with the Crickets' former leader and everything to do with its composers, Gerry Goffin and Carole King. It was yet another excellent number from the New York duo – a bright, richly melodic and uplifting pop love song performed by the Crickets in Everly Brothers-like voices. It could have been written just for the Beatles, needing no adaptation or rearrangement and embracing a joyful combination of major and minor guitar chords – with one in particular, an E-augmented, that they'd put to good use again and again. It was also a perfect vehicle for Beatle harmonies: while George sang lead, Paul had the talent to hold the high line throughout, effecting an impressively strong duet.

Another new number, Sharing You, was cut of the same cloth – Goffin-King wrote it, and Snuff Garrett produced it for the Hollywood label Liberty, released in Britain through EMI – except it wasn't by the Crickets this time but Bobby Vee. They were all working the same groove: Vee had already had a hit with Goffin-King's Take Good Care Of My Baby, which George had sung in the Beatles. George also took Sharing You, with Paul adding harmonies again – except they did it as Shaving You, to keep the laughs high.

Just a cubicle or two along from Goffin and King at 1650 Broadway was a second husband-and-wife pairing, Barry Mann and Cynthia Weil; their Where Have You Been grabbed the Beatles hard in June 1962. It was Arthur Alexander's second 45 for the Dot label (in Britain it was on London), and John again seized the lead vocal. The song was a heavy chunk of R&B, rising slowly to a dramatic finale, and its piano solo was adapted for guitar by George.

They played its B-side even better. Soldier Of Love became a big new hit in the Beatles' repertoire from June 1962, a song of integrity that showcased them at their best both melodically and harmonically.[14] Written by two young Nashville musicians, James 'Buzz' Cason and Tony Moon, the lyric skilfully fused romance with military vocabulary, a boy begging his girl to stop fighting him, lay down her arms, and surrender peacefully to his love. Alexander sang it as a slow blues but the Beatles quickened the tempo and used guitar instead of sax. John again sang lead, Paul harmony, and George stepped forward now and again to join Paul at the microphone and do the female backing voices like the Shirelles or Marvelettes. The combination was a song of tremendous verve and excitement that went down fantastically well with audiences.

Another exciting number was Mr Moonlight, a boisterously rhythmic Latin piece they found on a B-side by the oddly named American band Dr Feelgood and the Interns. Although Paul weighed in with a robust harmony, this was very much John's song and he was particularly explosive at the start. Mr Moonlight opened with a big, lusty vocal that modulated in clean air for five seconds before the instruments kicked in. There'd be a buzz of anticipation as audiences wondered if John would hit the right note. As it was often their opening number, this meant they'd commanded their crowd's attention before playing so much as a second – a useful device, as Neil Aspinall would remember: 'Mr Moonlight was great because there would be this moment of tension in the audience. The song would be announced and everybody knew John would have to start on *that* note – *MISTER!* Moonlight. There was no chord to precede it, he had to get it right from *nothing*.'[15]

Of these new songs, though, one above all others defines Beatles '62: Richie Barrett's Some Other Guy. More compelling than even Soldier Of Love and Don't Ever Change (and blisteringly unstoppable with them), this was the quintessential Beatles rocker, fantastic for male fans as well as female, a blast from first to last and a particularly powerful number for those competitive Nerk Twins. As Paul would explain, 'John and I both wanted to do it, so we ended up *both* doing it, like a double track.'[16] Night after night – and plenty of lunchtimes – this pair of American R&B fanatics stood at adjacent microphones for two minutes and sang the lead in unison, full on, both of them striving to be the first to achieve Barrett's wondrous tooth-whistle on the word 'Some', but never managing it.

They also added their own new numbers to the set. Please Please Me was kept untested, but Ask Me Why stayed in the repertoire after the BBC show and they sometimes played Love Me Do and PS I Love You. A degree of hesitation did remain, however. Geoff Davies, big Beatles fan and Cavern regular, remembers how the audience continued to prefer 'the R&B stuff' to any original numbers: 'When they played PS I Love You we'd think "what's this soppy love song?" but then we got used to it and were won over.'[17]

Around midnight on 15 June, John spent several hours talking to Lindy Ness, and the subject of ambition – and the need for 'fresh challenges' – featured strongly. 'He spoke of *getting away*,' she says, 'of not restricting himself to one place all his life. He didn't see himself staying in Liverpool forever. He talked about that a lot. I remember him saying he needed to "be somewhere bigger, less provincial".'[18]

It was just the pair of them on a pavilion bench in Sefton Park, lit by the night sky. A short distance away, George and a conquest were steaming the windows of his Anglia – and yet, despite the obvious opportunity to initiate an encounter of his own, John did nothing but talk, and listen while Lindy, 15 years 3 months, talked to him. 'People assumed we were having a sexual relationship,' she says, 'and he'd brag to other lads that I was his "jail bait", but actually he was protective. I was very nervous – I didn't know *what* was going to happen to me – but he treated me really well. I was in safe hands and it was also very interesting. I was on a steep learning curve.

> We spoke about our Woolton childhoods and where we used to play, though we didn't really have to explain it because it was understood – like John, I was a *Just William* child. We talked about God and religion and about drawing. He liked my drawings – I was a budding artist and he seemed to regret not going more down that road himself; he talked about me going to art college and said something like 'Don't screw it up like I did'. But it wasn't all serious conversation – we also had a laugh, told jokes, imitated people. I was very cynical, so we had that in common too.

Cynthia rarely saw John in these hours. It's with mathematical as well as figurative accuracy that Lindy reflects, 'I don't think she knew half of what was going on in his life.' Only occasionally now did Cyn go to Beatles shows – and when she did he largely ignored her, people remember. Also, she and John rarely slept together overnight. They wanted to, but her landlady locked the front door before retiring. John usually popped in by day and at weekends – though, even then, Cyn had to maintain stealth at all times. Having a man in her room transgressed the British landladies' code of 'keeping a *respectable* house', and discovery meant eviction.

When they chose their moments, though, the house at 93 Garmoyle Road finally yielded Cyn and John the opportunities for closeness in short supply since their Gambier Terrace nights two years earlier. Taking no more precautions against pregnancy than ever, they grabbed what they could despite the grubbiness of the surroundings. Externally, the house was a typical south Liverpool upper-working-class red-brick terrace, pleasant enough; inside, Cyn's £2 10s a week rent gained her a side-facing upstairs room with a single bed, moth-eaten chair, one-bar electric fire and one-ring cooker, plus shared use of a landing bathroom (hot water by appointment with crossed fingers).

Paul's girlfriend Dot had moved into the smaller room next door. While Cyn had solid reason to be here (her mother was only now returning from a long trip to Canada, would shortly be going back, and their house in Hoylake remained rented out), Dot's parental home wasn't much more than a mile from Garmoyle Road; she moved in partly to keep Cyn company and partly for the chance for more intimacy with Paul. They'd also been going together coming up three years but had only limited opportunities for bed.

So it was that, for a few weeks in the summer of 1962, Lennon and McCartney both had birds in neighbouring rooms beyond parental regulation. When they weren't being Beatles together on stage, or riding to venues in the van, or rifling through racks of records, or hanging out in Brian's office or in cinemas, coffee bars, pubs and drinking dens, or sitting somewhere writing songs together, they would descend on the same house and retire to adjoining rooms for worldly pleasures. These boys were *close* . . . so close they also partnered in an X-rated photographic enterprise at this same time. Their bedroom models weren't their girlfriends but a pair of obliging young ladies who didn't rush back to a job after Cavern lunchtimes; one of them lived in a top-floor flat in a large house on Prince's Road, close to the Rialto Ballroom – the houses built by George's paternal grandfather; John and Paul got them to stand topless (or better) in 'arty' Romanesque poses while they operated the camera Paul had just given his brother . . . and immediately borrowed back.

Mike's camera also saw plenty of Beatles action, adding a wealth of new shots to his already priceless archive. A purpose-made session took place on the entrance driveway of Allerton Golf Course – the walking or cycling short-cut between John's and Paul's houses. It's *Beatle time in leafy suburbia*: John, Paul and George, three leather jackets and jeans, grouped around the Anglia. Terry Doran's Warrington garage, Hawthorne Motors, used the best picture for promotion, as part of the deal by which George got his car cheaper; it ran as a *Mersey Beat* ad on 12 July: LIKE GEORGE HARRISON OF THE BEATLES YOU CAN BECOME THE PROUD OWNER OF A FIRST-CLASS CAR. The picture also tells another story: Pete. His absence here is a perfect illustration of three Beatles going about Liverpool without him; they're the same tight threesome of old, Japage 3, a quartet only on stage.

Mike also took a fine photo of John and Paul with Gene Vincent, when their hard-living Hamburg hero shared a Cavern bill with them on Sunday 1 July; and he took several pictures aboard the MV *Royal Iris* when, five nights later, the Beatles again played as supporting act to trad jazz star Mr Acker Bilk on a *Riverboat Shuffle*.[19]

This was an important period for Mike McCartney, now 18, who found within the space of weeks both a profession and a revelatory new mode of life. The job was a three-year apprenticeship in hairdressing, taken on the advice of family matriarch Auntie Gin, herself a hairdresser before the war. The lifestyle was surrealism, inspired by a TV programme about Dalí and Buñuel. Mike started behaving curiously, like going around Liverpool with a handkerchief stuffed in his mouth. His older brother suggested he 'stop it' as it was getting embarrassing, but Mike carried on. With such thoughts, and in conjunction with the spur of Paul's camera gift, Mike was suddenly a second young McCartney in Liverpool being productive and creative ... and their ambitions dovetailed when Paul urged Mike 'make me look famous'. Mike would bluntly reflect 'He didn't give a bugger about me and my photography, he just wanted photographs of himself', but he obliged all the same. In the weeks around Paul's 20th birthday (18 June), they staged a number of attempts at pictorial artiness, indoors and out; Paul was after a strong image he could use alongside Astrid's recent half-shadow photos of John and George – the session he was still sore about missing.[20]

The *Royal Iris* booking fell on the fifth anniversary of John and Paul's meeting, a youth coming up 17 singing Come Go With Me to a lad just turned 15. They didn't remember the date (or probably even the year) but still they were tight together, driving forward and now writing songs again as Lennon-McCartney ... or, as Paul was actively considering, Lennon-James. With the Beatles clearly on the cusp of *something* – soon to issue their first record, soon to be mentioned in the press – Paul contemplated taking a professional name.

Almost every star had one. 'I remember being in the back of Brian Epstein's Zodiac – his big, posh Ford car – and talking about whether Paul McCartney was the right name. He felt it was a bit of a mouthful and I did too – we wondered how people were ever going to remember it. People had never really remembered it at school. So I was going to become Paul James, from James Paul.'[21]

How long they deliberated isn't recalled, but it was days or weeks, not minutes – until finally they decided to leave the name unchanged. As Paul explains, 'In the end we just thought, "No, let them remember our names."' It was just a small decision among so many big ones in summer 1962, but the conclusion would come to be of great importance: these three Beatles were striving for the big time as themselves, with their genuine, everyday names.

They'd also have better equipment. John and George – pacesetters since the start in terms of progressing their musical gear – bought new British-made Vox guitar amplifiers: George got an AC-30 (thirty watts) and John an AC-15. John's cost £133, George's even more, and Brian was their guarantor for the weekly drip repayments with Hessy's that stretched ahead to June 1964.[22] They also picked out new guitars, and made their biggest investments yet by ordering identical Gibson J-160E electric-acoustics, the affectionately named 'Jumbo Gibson' that could be played as it was or plugged into an amp. A special order was sent to America for them by Rushworth & Dreaper (Hessy's main rival) and the cost was immense – £161 1s each, including hire-purchase interest. Brian was again the guarantor and Paul didn't join them in the acquisition – he'd borrow theirs.

Brian also advanced them a new 'van'. Pete was about to be pushed out, so Neil's future employment remained very much in doubt and they didn't want to be also without wheels. Terry Doran guided them to a Ford Thames 800 Express Bus, cream-coloured, which seemed to suit all their needs. It seated eight, with the option of two more fold-down seats in the rear, enough space to accommodate five and their gear without much fuss. Nems Enterprises shelled out the money and repaid itself from the Beatles' weekly income; the 'Group Expenses' column of their typed weekly Accounts Statements carried a £4 deduction in addition to Neil's £8 wage. This Thames 800 would be the Beatles' transport well into the future, getting them to all the places up and down the country where opportunities opened up.

One of these, Brian hoped, would be the Granada Television studios in Manchester. Contact was made with this first-class ITV company, one that proudly boasted 'From the North' on its programmes, and the first person who journeyed across to Liverpool was Dick Fontaine. Aged 23, he was one of a bunch of savvy Cambridge graduates being given the opportunity to come up with interesting ideas for films, and then make them; he was introduced to John and Paul in the Cavern on a night they weren't playing, then went out for a drink with them and was surprised to be impressed.[23]

While Fontaine set about thinking how to frame something around the Beatles, his fellow graduate at Granada, Leslie Woodhead, was working on *Know The North*, a series of short TV films about local contrasts. One edition was about music, and having already filmed the Brighouse and Rastrick Brass Band – sturdy, traditional Yorkshire open-air music – he was looking for a counterpoint when Fontaine mentioned the Beatles in their Liverpool cellar. Woodhead arranged to meet Brian Epstein in the lobby of the Adelphi Hotel and saw no one there resembling everyone's image of a shifty rock and roll manager. It was quite some time before he established that a fastidiously groomed young man 'so improbably smart it surely couldn't be him' was his host for the evening. Brian took him to the Cavern, where Woodhead was pinned back by the sheer noise, and then they went for a drink with the Beatles.

> It was plain that they had something about them. They were charming and caustic in a way that only working-class Liverpool kids could be. Paul was a jaunty young man with the eyes of a spaniel, implacably confident of his charm, and John stuck in the odd barbed word. He was obviously wickedly funny but didn't look like the kind of guy you'd want to mess with. George was a rather shrinking presence and I've no recollection of Pete at all, or whether he was even there. And Brian was all charm and affability, cool but very enabling – he was going to make this Beatles thing 'happen'.[24]

But the Beatles' staple work was always the stage. Radio and TV were shortcuts to audiences, money was earned and word-of-mouth spread through the daily diary. Before Brian, they operated entirely on Merseyside; now, the Beatles' calendar was a patchwork-quilt of places new. In their first seven weeks back from Hamburg, they had six days off. Tuesday was usually the breather, although when special engagements arose, they were placed here. Bookings stretched months ahead, something that Star-Club boss Manfred Weissleder was keenly aware of when writing to Brian on 10 July. Contracts were made for two further Star-Club visits before the end of 1962: for two weeks at the start of November, and for the year's final fourteen days, concluding on New Year's Eve. In November, they'd be sharing the bill with one of their all-time heroes, the great god Little Richard.

Brian didn't only book the Beatles into the Star-Club – he also agreed terms for the second group he managed, the Big Three. Stifled in the spring, his expansion ambitions blossomed in the summer and kicked off with Liverpool's

hard-rocking trio. Bassist Johnny Gustafson says they were signed on the rec-
ommendation of John Lennon; they came under Brian's 'sole direction' in early
June and put their signatures to a five-year contract with Nems Enterprises Ltd
that began on 1 July.

Why was Brian signing artists beyond the Beatles? Because Liverpool was
teeming with talent that deserved a broader audience, and he was establishing
a framework to make it happen; because he intended to stay in Liverpool, and
management of several artists would give him some clout when battling
London's forces – its record companies, promoters and agents – from two hundred miles away; because having a talent roster would enable him to put
together stage bills dominated or even completely filled by them; and because
it made sound business sense: the Beatles were the pacesetters, the hot property, and from now on, when he had to tell enquiring promoters they were busy
on a requested date, he could offer an alternative group and keep the work in-
house.

The Big Three's contract reflected a fact that had become pressing since
Brian signed the Beatles in January: that his remuneration for being both manager and agent, 10 per cent rising to 15, was barely enough to meet costs, let
alone give him a living income. He was stuck with the terms of the Beatles contract for the time being but wasn't going to repeat the mistake – Nems
Enterprises' commission on the Big Three's income was 15 per cent if they
earned up to £50 a week each, then 25 per cent. Considering how he could
boost their income, they were still going to be much better off than before.
Lead guitarist Adrian Barber (who made Paul McCartney's 'coffin' loudspeaker)
would recall, 'When Eppy appeared on the scene everyone wondered what a
manager did, and then we saw that thirty shillings a night was going to be £25.
That was a big, big difference. You can't argue with that.'[25]

But they did. The Big Three and Brian argued constantly. They signed the
contract agreeing he could advise them on their stage wear, and then they hated
him for it. Thrown off course, without the working coalition he struck with the
Beatles, Brian made misjudgements. The Big Three were tough nuts, so wilful
in their projection of *hard* that they fought him over everything, especially the
clothes, and if they weren't already difficult enough to handle, their first trip
to Hamburg, in July, worsened everything by several degrees. They returned to
Liverpool minus Barber, who, Gustafson says, *flipped* through all the drugs,
booze and sex – he stayed in Hamburg and took a job as the Star-Club's sound
technician. 'We returned to Liverpool with new guitarist Brian Griffiths, even
louder and more raucous,' Gustafson says. 'The group Brian signed had very
quickly changed.'[26]

Brian sent the Big Three to Hamburg to replace Gerry and the Pacemakers,

who drove back to Liverpool in late June and promptly became his third signing. They too put their signatures on a five-year Nems Enterprises contract
effective 1 July, so within the space of days Brian went from handling one group
to handling three – and it would have been four if the Four Jays hadn't been
reluctant to give up their day jobs and turn professional. It's hard to imagine
Paul being best pleased about all this – he'd long worried that Gerry and the
Pacemakers might overtake the Beatles as the 'Pool's top group, and that they'd
get their big break first, and perhaps now Brian would be pushing them as hard
as he was pushing the Beatles. He had nothing to fear: Brian was always crystal clear on the hierarchy of his signings – and so was everyone else.

Managing three groups was enough to land Brian local dominance. Proof of
Nems Enterprises' power first appeared in the *Echo* on 13 July with an ad for
the huge Grafton Ballroom's inaugural rock night, on Friday 3 August – all
three star attractions were Brian's, listed in the order that confirmed rank: the
Beatles, Gerry and the Pacemakers, the Big Three. Advance tickets were available from Nems and vouchers for discount admission were mailed to Beatles
Fan Club members. Brian was starting to sew up the Liverpool scene – its top
end, at any rate – earning the resentment of the promoters who, until just a
short time earlier, had operated quite happily without him. Now he'd come in,
was running the best talent, raising group fees to record levels, and staging promotions for which he was attracting patrons' spending money and selling
tickets from his own busy shops slap in the centre of town. (The footfall benefited the business of Nems Ltd, too.)

One of these rivals, Sam Leach, saw a demonstration of the newcomer's
steel. In late June, Don Arden struck an agreement to promote an October
British tour starring Little Richard, before his season at the Star-Club. The
American star had never been to Britain and would be big box office. Leach
called Arden from a public phone box and made a verbal accord to present him
at New Brighton Tower Ballroom on 12 October for £350. Though it was subject to written confirmation, Leach instantly ran an *Echo* ad announcing the
sale of tickets he hadn't yet printed for the show he hadn't yet contracted. Brian
was already conversant with Arden and had probably met him by now; he
offered (says Leach) £500 for the Little Richard show and Arden gave it to him
instead. All was fair in love and promotion – these events happened days after
Leach's wedding, at which Brian was a special guest, making a warmly generous speech to toast the happy couple.[27]

For Brian, Little Richard would be more than *just a show* – he prized it as
the crowning glory in his promotional plans for the second half of the year, a
night ripe for his particular brand of prestige. He hired Bob Wooler to help
organise, stage-manage and compere it, and – in place of the tour's usual

supporting cast – Brian would book all his favoured local acts. The Beatles, naturally, were to head that particular list, their name writ as-large-as-one-dared next to their fabulous American idol's.

So it was too when they played second to Joe Brown and the Bruvvers on 26 and 27 July, the first at the theatre-like Cambridge Hall in Southport, the second in the ballroom at New Brighton Tower. Despite the 'Nems Enterprises presents ...' label, these were 50:50 promotions with Allan Williams, the Beatles' second manager working in harmony with the first. The long old spat between Williams and the Beatles evaporated in this period of co-operation, to the extent that he lifted the ban preventing their entry to his Blue Angel nightclub. As he recalls, 'Brian came and pleaded with me, and I relented. I said to him, "Tell them they can come in tomorrow night," and he said, "Well they're outside now." So they came in, threw their arms around me and that was the end of our difficulties.'[28]

Cambridge Hall was demonstrably *a big night*, drawing the great and the good. Leslie Woodhead from Granada TV was back to take another look, Queenie and Harry Epstein saw the Beatles here for the first time, and it was also the first time the Beatles had the services of Mal Evans as their protector. The 27-year-old telephone engineer from Mossley Hill, married with a baby son, was dropping into Cavern sessions and growing friendlier with them all the time; he was also genuinely impressed by having such proximity to stage stars. George had recently taken him home to Speke, where they'd listened to records, and then he had the bright idea that Mal should become one of the Cavern's team of doormen. As Mal would recall, 'George said, "Look, Mal, you're big and ugly enough, why don't you get a job as a bouncer? Then you can get paid, get into the bandroom *and* meet the bands."' So Mal did just that. He'd classify himself 'a middle-class bouncer ... an ardent coward', more intent on talking people out of trouble than swinging his fists, but his sheer bulk – tall and broad with it – put most people off any idea of causing trouble, which was why Brian offered him the job of 'chief bouncer' at his Joe Brown night in Southport.[29]

The long-established presentation format was for top-billed artists to go on last and for 'second-top' to go on before the interval, but at Southport and New Brighton, Brian placed the Beatles as the penultimate act, just before Brown closed the show. 'The idea of doing that,' says Brown, 'is that you get the audience standing up and screaming so much that the main act can't get on. The Beatles *were* a real hard act to follow but we did it – to our credit we did do it.' John and George had first use here of their new Vox amps, and at New Brighton George got to wear, momentarily, a guitar he'd never seen and instantly coveted, Joe Brown's slim, twin-cutaway Gibson. It would be twenty years before Brown discovered that, while he nipped out to the toilet, George posed with it for Mike McCartney's camera.[30]

Afterwards, the Beatles (minus Pete), and Joe Brown with some Bruvvers, decamped to the Blue Angel where the late-drinking licence extended past midnight, and it was during these hours that Brian invited Bruvvers drummer Bobby Graham to join the Beatles. He can't have been offering the position permanently – John, Paul and George were clear they wanted Ringo – but Ringo was at Butlin's until early September and Leslie Woodhead had told Brian that a Granada camera unit would be filming the Beatles in the Cavern on 22 August. This put a point on matters – the contractual situation with Pete was tricky enough as it was without him appearing in their TV film, especially as he'd be gone by the time it was shown. Brian wondered if Graham could bridge the gap between Pete's departure and Ringo's return, but the drummer declined: 'I didn't want to leave the Bruvvers to join a group no one had ever heard of, and I was twenty-two and lived in Chingford – I didn't want to move to Liverpool.'[31]

When the Big Three crashed back from Hamburg, Brian made the same offer to Johnny 'Hutch' Hutchinson, and he too turned them down. His reason was different: he'd despised the Beatles since first setting eyes on them at the Larry Parnes audition in 1960, when he'd reluctantly sat in as their drummer. *Pansies.* John, Paul and George all knew Hutch was hard but he was also strong behind the kit, the only man on Merseyside who did solos. John said he was the best drummer in Liverpool, with Ringo second. Paul says he liked Hutch because he spoke in a mad hip lingo, saying things like 'You drive me *berdzerk*, man' – but Hutch was also prone to acts of harm: just recently he'd beaten up the Beatles' young pal Bernie Boyle and put him in hospital. So it was with mixed views that they let Brian offer him the chance to join them for a while – and it's entirely appropriate that Hutch's only published remark about it was 'I told Brian I wouldn't join the Beatles for a gold clock'.[32]

It was at this same time, around the end of July, that – probably – a strange incident took place, when John and Paul made a 332-mile return road trip to talk to Ringo at Butlin's. Paul had just passed his driving test but had yet to buy a car, so they went in the van – Neil would remember them taking it, and reliable witnesses saw them at the camp, including Johnny Guitar and Rory Storm's mother Vi Caldwell, who was on holiday there at the time. But it all lacks clarification. Paul could have phoned Ringo from home, but the suggestion is that he and John (who was 'navigating') made a mystery trip along England's winding A-roads, west coast to east coast, like *The Nerk Twins Go To Lincolnshire.* There's also no explanation why George, who'd instigated getting Ringo into the Beatles, didn't drive them to Skegness in his car. And while witnesses have insisted it all happened, the story is short on verification from the key parties: Ringo has never mentioned it, John never did, and Paul (asked about it in 2011) has just 'a vague recollection'.[33]

By the end of July, Rory Storm and the Hurricanes were two-thirds of the way through their three-month season, playing six days a week in the Rock Ballroom (Saturdays excluded) from 8 until 11 or 11.15 every night and 3.30 or 4 until 5 every afternoon. Their £18 weekly pay for twenty-five or more hours' stage time wasn't as enticing as it had been – each Beatle was clearing double that amount – but the usual Butlin's compensations were on tap, chiefly the stream of lasses looser with their elastic because they were on 'oliday. Rory and the Hurricanes were pictured in Butlin's printed weekly programme for the first time, although as the season progressed the drummer took on a different appearance: Ringo now had a chinstrap beard that joined up to his long sideburns.[34]

The summer of 1962 was a newsworthy one at Butlin's Skegness – the camp's elephant, Gertie, walked into the outdoor swimming pool and drowned (this made a national splash), and the camp's head chef received a fatal electric shock in the kitchen. Not making the news, the camp's rock drummer accepted an invitation to join King-Size Taylor and the Dominoes. They were at the Star-Club, but on returning to Liverpool at the start of September would be losing their drummer and guitarist; Ted Taylor wrote to Ringo and Bobby Thompson to suggest they switch groups, and they agreed. Having left the Hurricanes once before, Ringo felt no compunction about doing so again, and Rory and Johnny Guitar were resigned to finding a permanent replacement.[35]

It's unclear why Ringo said yes to the Dominoes after George had already asked him to join the Beatles. Insecurity possibly, or not. Certainly, he didn't yet know *when* he'd be needed in the Beatles, whereas the Dominoes' position would open as soon as the Butlin's season closed. But it probably explains why two of the Beatles might suddenly have driven all the way over to Skegness, to make sure they got their man. Johnny Guitar would remember their arrival: he and Ringo were sharing a caravan off-camp after being caught with girls in their chalet, and it was here that John and Paul fetched up around ten o'clock one morning.*

On the basis of what would transpire, it's fair to surmise that Ringo was left

---

* There were few vacant dates in the Beatles' calendar when such a trip could have been made, and it's useful that the Hurricanes' friend and sometime roadie Dave Jamieson is sure it was a Sunday. The Beatles were resident in the Cavern every Sunday except 29 July, which was also free of any other booking. Since Johnny Guitar said they knocked on the caravan about 10AM, John and Paul had probably driven through Saturday night. Their next booking was Monday lunchtime in Liverpool.

assured the Beatles did want him, and soon, and that they'd phone to summon him when the moment came ... which was just as quickly as Brian and his lawyer gambled on a way to sack Pete. Would it *really* come down to the Beatles breaking up and re-forming? Whatever the method, now that Granada was coming to film them in the Cavern on 22 August, there was a deadline – Pete was to be out and Ringo in by that date.

The longer it dragged on, the greater chance there was that the man still being referred to obliquely as 'the undesirable member' would find out his fate ... which more or less happened when Joe Flannery – 'manager and producer' of his brother Lee Curtis and backing group the All Stars – paid a home visit to Pete and mentioned that he'd heard rumours Pete would soon be looking for a new position. Flannery and Brian were old friends, and Brian had shared his Best dilemma in strictest confidence ... but the self-styled 'Colonel Joe', shootin' high and hoping to get Pete to join the All Stars, couldn't resist disclosing it. Pete didn't challenge John, Paul and George over what he'd been told, but he did ask Brian, saying, 'Are there plans to replace me in the Beatles?' Brian, who must have hated every second of his predicament, blushed and stammered a denial.[36]

Such gossip jostled for space in Pete's mind along with earth-shattering domestic events, because on 21 July – right there in the house on Hayman's Green – his adored mother Mo gave birth to a baby boy. She was 38 and her sons 20 and 17; on the cusp of their adulthood, Pete and Rory had gained another brother. All three boys had a different father, for though the baby's birth certificate named 'John Best, professional boxing promoter' in this position, and gave no indication he lived elsewhere, he was long gone and this was Neil Aspinall's child. They had – they were – a family. The big detached house in West Derby already harboured its share of secrets and here was the biggest yet – and further intrigue would follow when, with the baby seven weeks old, Mona registered the birth and gave his name as Vincent Rogue Best; when the registrar queried the spelling of the middle name he was assured it was correct.*

No sooner was all this excitement bubbling away than another big one popped up: Cynthia fell pregnant. She and John had been trusting to luck for three years, and it had run out. She was suffering morning sickness, had missed a period and was fearing 'the dreadful truth' when her best friend Phyllis McKenzie fixed an appointment with her lady doctor. Cyn's reward for braving

---

* The child grew up using the name Roag, still pronounced as 'Rogue'. The Bests' middle-name tradition was thus maintained: Pete was really Randolph Peter (Scanland), Rory was John Rory and Mona was Alice Mona.

the moment, and blurting out the symptoms through a curtain of tears, was confirmation of her condition . . . and then a high-handed moral lecture. Later the same day, Cyn also learned that she'd failed one of her art school final exams. What would have been a major decision – to re-sit the test or abandon plans to become a teacher – paled compared to a new, chart-topping worry. *John.* Soon-to-be-a-dad John Lennon. How would *he* react?

She broke the news in the place where the seed was sown, her room at 93 Garmoyle Road. 'I watched his face drain of all its colour, and fear and panic creep into his eyes. He was speechless for what seemed like an age. "There's only one thing for it, Cyn, we'll have to get married."'[37]

The conversation was had at the beginning of August, and the baby was due at the end of March 1963, so there was little time to lose: Cyn didn't want a bulge on her wedding day any more than she fancied people figuring the arithmetic after she'd given birth. John, in his own words, 'didn't fight it' but would stand tall and 'make an honest womb of her'.[38] He'd have to tell Mimi, but – certain she'd give him one of her brisk lectures – put off doing it as long as possible.

If they timed it right, Cyn's mother would miss the wedding. Lil Powell had just returned from Canada when these events erupted, and she was booked to sail back again on 22 August. Her opposition to Cyn's relationship with John had been unremitting through three hellish years – and yet, says Cyn, she took the news surprisingly well. Perhaps she didn't expect to be around very much; she would anyway welcome the grandchild.

Brian also had to be told. The Beatles had already acquiesced to his suggestion that girlfriends be kept in the background, and it certainly wasn't part of his plans that one of them would marry at this time. Nothing is known of where or when John broke the news, but there was naught Brian could do about it: the situation would just have to be accommodated – and kept quiet, which perfectly suited John and Cyn. Whatever other feelings Brian had, clouded by the complexity of his own affections for John, he was his manager and friend: he offered to organise the marriage licence and book the registrar's office. In consultation with the bride and groom, he arranged the wedding for 23 August, the day after Lil Powell's departure and the Beatles' first date with TV cameras. Pete would be out and Ringo in by this time . . . so one madly busy week was shaping up.

Paul and Dot could also have married, but instead they broke up – not for the first time but decisively the last. Cyn would write about a flaming row they had when Paul arrived at Garmoyle Road unexpectedly, catching Dot looking less than glamorously ready for him, but Dot's own recollection would be more circumspect: 'Paul said we'd been going out so long that it was either get married or split up. He said, "I don't want to get married, so even though I love you we'll have to finish." I could see that Paul was growing away from me. I knew what was coming. All these years he had been having his bits on the side and it was getting so easy for him. He was young and he couldn't resist.'[39]

Dorothy Rhone had been 16 at the start of her romance with Paul, a shy slip of a girl at the Casbah; now she was coming up 19, still a shy slip of a girl. Very little is known publicly about a relationship that lasted two and a half years, but it was over. She moved back in with her parents, and Paul was even freer to fancy his chances.

George, meanwhile, was enjoying a steady relationship of his own, one that lasted throughout the summer. Marie Guirron was a fan – she went around with Lindy Ness, Lou Steen and their friends, going to the Beatles' houses and claiming most of the Cavern front row.

> We wore everything black for the Beatles. Black jackets, black polo-necks, black jeans, total beatniks. I fell for George the first time I saw the Beatles, in Birkenhead, so I always sat on the far left at the Cavern because that's where he stood; Lou was in the middle with Paul, and Lindy was on the end with John. A couple of times when other people sat in those seats John said to them, 'Could you move? That's not your place.' They noticed *everything*.[40]

George noticed Marie. She was a slim attractive blonde, 18 and clearly older than the others. Lindy and Lou were still in school but Marie worked. 'Where?' George asked, one lunchtime in the Cavern, and when she replied 'the Cotton Exchange', he said, 'Oh, do you know Jim McCartney?' She did, both from work and a drop round to Paul's house. So they carried on chatting, then George announced he'd pick her up in his car when she finished work that afternoon at half-past five. 'That's how it began,' she says, 'we just started going out. I was soon head over heels for him. I thought he was the best thing since sliced bread. He was handsome, had great charisma and was very gentle.' George and Marie spent most evenings together for the next three and a half months. 'It was all good fun,' she says, 'and a tremendous introduction for me both to growing up and to a new era of music.'

Marie became the first long-term beneficiary of the Ford Anglia. 'George was thrilled to have his own car – he wanted to be independent, to get himself from A to B without having to rely on anyone else.' He drove her to Beatles shows and gave her the keys when they arrived; afterwards, she'd wait by the car while he signed autographs, then they'd drive off for something to eat, or go bowling. She lived in a nice house in Prenton, on the Wirral, and no longer had a parental curfew; he'd drop her home in the early hours and then speed back through the Mersey Tunnel as fast as the Anglia allowed, racing through Liverpool's deserted streets like his great Argentine hero Juan Manuel Fangio or British world champ-to-be Graham Hill.

John made no reference to George and Marie's relationship in his letters to Lindy Ness, nor to the many dramatic developments in his own life. Lindy was spending the first month of her school summer holidays visiting family in Norway and they corresponded through the last part of July and into August. To begin with, the letters were scribbled in John's omnipresent fountain pen ('For you sad Lindy I scrape this metal tipped plastic finger . . .'), but during August he got hold of a portable manual typewriter from Bobby Brown – he told her he wanted to type new songs – and then Lindy received a letter patiently but Lennonly typed on the reverse side of one of Brian's weekly 'Details of engagements'.

John had always liked typewriters. He'd been a happy tapper from his early teens, hammering out the humour one arfingly mishit word at a time. Paul was very impressed to see John typing on his first visit to Mendips. With his original 'Imperial' model long broken or unavailable, John gratefully seized the chance to borrow Bobby's, and it accompanied (probably prompted) a new and sustained surge of poetic creativity. If he wrote at home, John read his papers in the van or car on the way to gigs – to the great delight of Paul and George who readily chipped in with contributions of their own. It was a laugh a minute with John Lennon; material created on the road might then be typed up (as best it could be remembered) on his return.

Two typed stories were published in *Mersey Beat* right away, but only two. The first, 'Small Sam', was awash with John's repetitive humour, the second was an updating of 'On Safairy With Whide Hunter', the piece John and Paul wrote together 'in conjugal' in 1958, one of the early Lennon-McCartney Originals. At the rate they were being created, John's writings could have appeared in every *Mersey Beat* from here on, but he stopped handing them over. He was distressed that a stack of some 250 pieces he'd given Bill Harry the year before had been carelessly lost during an office move – Bill says they were thrown in the bin by his fiancée Virginia. As only two pieces had been published, 248 irreplaceable Lennon originals had gone, lost forever. 'We had to let John know and met him that night at the Blue Angel,' Bill says. 'When we told him, he broke down and cried on Virginia's shoulder.'[41]

Creativity was confined to laughs at this time because, as songwriters, Lennon-McCartney were temporarily stalled. They'd come up with four new numbers, two each, but until Parlophone let open the creative valve, there was no great incentive to write more. Meanwhile, the Beatles' repertoire progressed once again, embracing a further clutch of new songs – performances first seen, heard and enjoyed by their ecstatic audiences when July tipped into August 1962.

Top of the pile was I Remember You, which Paul sang while John played harmonica – the fourth such combination in the Beatles' set. It was a 1941 number, freshly revived by Frank Ifield, an English-born Australian singer who had the blow-waved looks of a matinee idol, and, in producer Norrie Paramor, the ideal man to give him sound guidance. The combination of harmonica and a yodelling country-music voice (copied from Slim Whitman) greatly appealed to the British public, who kept I Remember You at number 1 in the *NME* for eight straight weeks. It went down 'amazingly well' with audiences, says Paul, but it was also a blow to the Beatles. They'd been hoping to be the first British group to use harmonica on record; as Ifield was a solo singer this was still possible, but while waiting for Parlophone to get them back into the studio their chance of seizing the initiative was slipping away.

The summer charts showed Twist had turned: while the dance itself would long endure, the record fad was fading. The genre's last major hit in America was Twist And Shout by the Isley Brothers, a musical family from a poor black district of Cincinnati. It sold next to no copies in Britain but hit bullseye with the Beatles, combining as it did the pedigree provenance of New York label Wand (a Scepter subsidiary from 1650 Broadway) with impeccable production by Luther Dixon. Here was high energy in action: a full band in a big brass groove, a rousing crescendo where the song just took off, and a strong lead vocal from Ronnie Isley with backing from brothers Rudy and Kelly – their falsetto *wooohs* sung in unison.

The Beatles' front line really went for it. John took the lead vocal at his most full-throated, *ripping* into the repeated line 'Shake it up baby!' Paul and George doubled at the second mike and threw everything into the high *wooohs*. John's and George's guitars put beef where the brass had been. And they created their own simple but exciting arrangement for the vocal crescendo – John started it alone at his microphone, George arrived at the second to add his voice, then Paul joined him to make the third. Better yet, where the Isleys' original had only one crescendo, the Beatles put in a second where the record faded to a finish. Twist And Shout was Medley-Russell arr. Lennon-McCartney-Harrison; it was America arr. England; and though the Beatles didn't play it every night, when they did, the halls *shook*.

The Beatles' intense drive to stay one step ahead of every rival (and they were already at least fifty clear) was taken to extremes by Paul in July/August 1962 when sleuthing songs unknown or unconsidered by others. A good find was Nobody But You, a B-side by a group from Towson, Maryland called the Lafayettes. Beyond a mawkish introduction, this was a strong call-and-response number in the style of Kansas City. Paul also resurrected a couple of interesting numbers from the old, old days – Hey! Ba-Ba-Re-Bop, the swing blues by Lionel Hampton's orchestra that in 1946 topped *Billboard*'s 'Most-Played Juke Box Race Records' chart, and the 1930 Marlene Dietrich torch song Falling In Love Again, which he rearranged as a rock waltz, a bit like If You Gotta Make A Fool Of Somebody. Paul invented a new lyric and sang it impressively, but the song's success hinged on how well George delivered the middle-eight solo, which could be hit or miss.

Until the last day or two of July, George Martin was silent on the Beatles. He was in no hurry to get them back in the studio. They were the beat group (from Liverpool, of all places) he'd been corralled into signing against his own judgement, whose self-written songs he considered substandard (though he was being forced to issue at least one of them), whose backline gear was poor and whose drummer he'd have to replace. He'd enjoyed their personalities, and maybe some good would come of it in the end, but he had more pressing concerns.

One was Spike Milligan's spoof of the epic war film *The Bridge On The River Kwai*, recorded with a full wash of George's most decorative sound-scenery. After its recording, the film's producers got wind of it and said they'd sue if the LP was issued. All looked bleak until George suggested shifting the action from Burma to Wales and calling it *Bridge On The River Wye*. To achieve this, he and an engineer had to go through the master tape and splice, with razor blades, the K off every Kwai. The resulting album (which sold poorly) was almost as labour-intensive as the construction of the infamous bridge.

So little came easy. On 29 June, Parlophone released Bernard Cribbins' follow-up to The Hole In The Ground. Here again was George's perpetual problem: after a comedy hit, what next? Novelty discs only succeeded if the ingredients were right, which meant starting afresh with new ideas every time. In this instance, the old creative team came up with Right, Said Fred – another show of hands in Britain's class struggle, another enduring airplay hit, and another bestseller, peaking at 10 (*Record Retailer* chart) at the start of August.

It still remained apparent – embarrassingly so, sometimes – that George Martin flopped when he followed a formula. His attempt to make a twee pop star out of *Compact* actor Leo Maguire was an unmitigated failure, dead within days . . . but when he was original, George excelled with triumphs beyond any other producer in the business. Just when his bête noire, Norrie Paramor, was celebrating the enormous success of his Australian singer Frank Ifield with I Remember You, George worked with the Australian all-round artist Rolf Harris to record the extraordinary Sun Arise.

It was another example of George's matchless invention in the studio. Lacking a didgeridoo, he replicated its tones with two cellos, a double bass, a piano and Harris's own mouth-sounds; by artful manipulation of two-track quarter-inch tape, he had Harris double- and triple-track his own voice, giving it a rich tonal quality and some impressive harmonies; then, in the final mix, George drew an aural landscape every bit as impressive as one of Harris's canvases. Twenty years before the dawn of the phrase 'world music', a seemingly authentic piece of Aboriginal sound from the outback of Australia was recorded (along with its B-side) inside a brisk four hours in St John's Wood . . . and, once again, the public strongly said *yes*. The record grew slowly, but by December 1962 only Elvis stood between George Martin and his second number 1.

All this time, the Beatles were but a background thought. Two months had elapsed since their Abbey Road session. In May, Brian Epstein had expected the release of the Beatles' first record in July. By late June this had become 'towards the end of August', and now he was reduced to hoping for September. Such delays were unhelpful – he'd be assembling a marketing-bookings strategy to follow the first record and needed to know the date.

Then, as July ebbed away, a one-sided, seven-inch acetate disc arrived at Nems Enterprises, mailed from the Parlophone office in London. The song's title, as written on the label, was How Do You Do, which was cordial but incorrect because really it was How Do You Do It. The story of that song encapsulates the twin components of the music business at the time the Beatles were making their first record: the business of songs, ruled by publishers, and records, the domain of record companies.

In this scenario, the main player was a breezily confident 22-year-old Londoner by the name of Lionel Stitcher. In summer 1961 he bought a ukulele, taught himself to play, and started to compose pop songs (words and music). Inventing himself the professional name Mitch Murray, he quickly bagged a few minor and unsuccessful A- and B-sides, and on 4 May 1962, at his parents' house in the north London suburb of Golders Green, wrote a song he first called How Do You Do What You Do To Me, which was its top line. He recorded a basic demo version five days after that, and three months later it was being reworked by the Beatles and set to become their first record. This was how it happened . . .

The standard music business procedure was three-ply: (1) The composer would try to get a publisher to take his song copyright; (2) the publisher would try to stir interest in the song with a record company A&R man; (3) the A&R man would get it recorded by one of his artists. Murray was shrewd, however: he'd hand over copyright only when a recording was certain, ideally as an A-side, and he himself did the shopping around – before writing songs he'd been a travelling salesman, so he knew the selling spiel. How Do You Do It was turned down for Adam Faith by his manager Evie Taylor and turned down for Brian Poole and the Tremeloes by their producer Mike Smith. When Murray visited EMI House on 7 June, Parlophone's Ron Richards liked the song and a week later confirmed his intention to record it. On the 19th, Richards played the demo to Dick James, the ex-Parlophone singer turned music publisher who regularly dropped into the office; Mitch Murray's diary mentions an enthusiastic 20 June call from James, but Murray held out – he wouldn't assign the copyright until sure of his song's fate. Nonetheless, from this point, Dick James would remain involved.

A further month passed before the Beatles entered the picture. James was back at EMI House on Friday 27 July, the same day or thereabouts that George Martin decided to give How Do You Do It to his Liverpool group. ('I thought it was a good song,' he says, 'no great work of art but very commercial.') In a conversation he'd be asked to repeat countless times in the future, James replied, 'Liverpool? You're joking. So what's from Liverpool?'[42] George then did what everybody had to do with the name Beatles – spell it out. He told James they were 'unusual types', quirky, with long hair. The other side of that weekend, on 30 July, James relayed the good news to Mitch Murray: his song was going to be recorded by a new group. 'I said to him, "What do you mean, *group*?" I didn't know what "a group" was. Was it a singing group? Was it an instrumental group? In 1962, the word *group* didn't mean very much at all. Dick had to explain to me that they sang and played at the same time.'[43]

They did, and they didn't like How Do You Do It one little bit. Brian passed the acetate over to the Beatles with the same message he was given: that, finally, they had another recording date – Tuesday 4 September – and that this song would be the A-side of their first record. Dropping the stylus into the groove, they were horrified to hear the kind of light white English pop to which, in their browserie reveries, they attached their most brutal verdicts. 'We hated it,' Paul remembers, 'and didn't want to do it. We felt we were getting a style, the Beatles' style, which we were known for in Hamburg and Liverpool, and we didn't want to blow it all by suddenly changing our style and becoming run of the mill.'[44]

They could kick, they could scream and they could whinge to Brian – and they did at least the last of these – but resistance was useless. They had to learn the song and, more than that, they had to work on improving it. It was insubstantial as it stood. The kernel of an appealing number was inside – as George Martin, Ron Richards and Dick James all realised – but if the Beatles *had* to record it then they'd spruce it up first. Paul recalls the moment: 'We said, "Well, what are we gonna do with *this*?"'[45]

The acetate had been recorded with Adam Faith in mind, so it was a skippy little ditty in the key of F#. John and Paul switched it to G; they also wrote a new intro, the final D chord of which was repeated at the end of each verse as a transition; Paul added a harmony vocal that ran constantly above John's; George came up with some lead guitar lines and a middle-eight solo which, while unspectacular, was at least well thought-out; they tweaked some of the lyrics; and they dumped the half-step modulation in the demo's final verse. This technique, where the key suddenly shifted up (in this instance to G#), was rife in the kind of pop the Beatles hated. Even with all these alterations, the song was nothing like what they wanted to do, especially for their first record, but where it lacked passion they were at least giving it a little polish.

All this rearranging of How Do You Do It was done by John and Paul, with a little input from George on the guitar lines. They chose not to involve Pete. It was pointless – he'd be gone before the recording session, and even if he wasn't, he wouldn't be there.

The problem all along for Brian was his contract to give Pete paid employment. Ending this would leave him exposed to the possibility of legal action, which could hinder the Beatles' progress. Brian decided his strategy in early August – six weeks after first discussing options with his lawyer, David Harris. He'd get Pete into another group and offer them management. If he took the position, all well and good; if he rejected it, *he* was breaking the contract, not Brian.

As both the Big Three and the Pacemakers had drummers integral to their line-ups, the solution wasn't obvious. Brian had to create a situation to achieve it – and it was with this at least partly in mind that he arranged Nems Enterprises' first tour. It would begin on 26 August, run for eight days, stay entirely in the north of England and star the hit singer Mike Berry. Brian fixed it all, including the venues and supporting groups, one of them placed there for a specific purpose.

The Mersey Beats were new to the scene, and young – the two main guys were lads, Tony Crane and Billy Kinsley, 17 and 15 – but they were good and already beginning to go places. They were open in their admiration of the Beatles, who clearly influenced their style and repertoire, and the Beatles were friendly and helpful to them in return. Brian started getting them some local bookings, not as their official manager (there was no contract and he took no commission) but on a goodwill basis – something he did for a few of the local acts. His plan was to make Pete Best the Mersey Beats' drummer and, as their big-name player and older man, de facto leader. They already had a drummer, a lad who worked in a butcher's shop, but he was about to join another group and would also have problems getting time off for the tour. When Brian had *the difficult meeting* with Pete – which was now just days away – he'd be able to offer him this alternative position, with the tour representing immediate employment. It was a gambit, not brilliant but not without merit either. (What a nuisance it all was, though. Other groups hired and fired people all the time without any fuss or difficulty.)

The ball was set rolling on 14 August when Brian phoned Butlin's Skegness and asked for 'Ringo Starr' to be paged over the public address. It was the summons Ringo had been waiting for, and the detail remained fresh in his memory when asked about it in New York two years later. 'Brian Epstein phoned me up on a Tuesday and said, "Would you join the Beatles?" I said, "Yeah." He said, "Well, can you get home tonight?" And I said, "I can't leave the other group just like that, I must give a *bit* of notice." So I said, "I'll be there Saturday."'[46]

Fellow Hurricane Bobby Thompson was having coffee with Ringo in the Butlin's canteen when the PA crackled its message. He'd recall it was 'the Beatles' on the phone, not specifically Brian, which may tie in with a call Brian would describe John making, where he said, 'You're in, Ringo, but the beard will have to go. You can keep your "sidies" though.'[47]

Until this moment, Thompson had still been hopeful Ringo would join him in the switch to the Dominoes, but it wasn't to be. 'Ringo turned around to me and said, "Sorry Bob, I can't turn this down," and I said, "That's all right – I only wish it was me." And that was that – Ringo didn't join King-Size after all.'[48]

With his arrival set for Saturday, Brian made Thursday the day for his crunch meeting with Pete. It wasn't fair to leave it any later. The Beatles did have three bookings in the interim, and Brian believed Pete would honour them ... though if he didn't, they could always use the drummer from another group. It was far from ideal, but these were exceptional circumstances. On Wednesday they twice played the Cavern, lunch and night, and between the two Brian phoned the house in Hayman's Green and said he wanted to see Pete and Neil in the office at eleven the following morning. Neither thought any more of it and Neil's brow knotted in puzzlement only as they left the Cavern that night. It was no big deal that they asked him to leave the amps on stage – it was a deviation from old practice, but happening often now for rehearsals – but as he was packing away Pete's drums, Neil asked John to confirm the time he'd collect him the following evening. They had a gig in Chester. John said he didn't want a lift, that he'd get there on his own, then he turned and rushed off in a way that made Neil think something was up.[49]

The details of what occurred the following day would always be skewed by dint of being publicly related by only one party. Pete would be asked about it for the rest of his life, whereas the Beatles and Brian had a number of reasons for not discussing it. One was that they rapidly left it behind, another was that

Pete would indeed, just as Brian feared, legally challenge his dismissal, a move that automatically choked open discussion.

The following transcript, from audio of an interview Pete had with New York lawyers in 1965, is a relatively straight if incomplete account of what happened after he and Neil arrived at the Nems Enterprises office in Whitechapel, Liverpool, on Thursday 16 August 1962.

> So the next morning two of us went in. Epstein was sitting behind the table and he was fidgeting with papers and moving ink-stands – he couldn't look me in the face. He talked about how the group had been going on, and how did I think the group was doing, and I told him 'Fab' and then, like a bolt out of the blue, he just turned around and said, 'I've got some bad news for you: the boys and myself have decided that they don't want you in the group any more, and that Ringo is replacing you.'
>
> I was flabbergasted. I said, 'What's the reason behind this?' And he said 'mainly because they think you're not a good enough drummer' and also because at EMI Studios George Martin said 'the drummer isn't good enough'.
>
> I said, 'What's going to happen to me, then?' He made me business offers. He said that as long as I was still under contract to him he'd pay me the present wage that I was earning, which was about £50–60 a week. He'd also put me in another group and make me the leader of it.[50]

It isn't obvious why Brian asked Neil to be present – his employment with the Beatles wasn't addressed, and Brian's strategy was not to raise it but to see on which side of the fence Neil came down. Brian *had* gone to the trouble of sounding out a possible replacement if Neil left, but that man (Johnny Booker, roadie for the Undertakers and sometimes the Mersey Beats) says he turned it down because he was Neil's mate.[51]

Neil was taking it all in. He was angry Pete was being treated this way and admired him for his acceptance of the news: 'He said that if the three other Beatles didn't want him in the group then he would go. He had a contract with them and could have insisted on staying.' Neil also felt sympathy for Brian himself, who patently had been put in this horrible position: 'None of this was Brian's fault. I don't think he wanted to get rid of Pete. It was John, Paul and George, and they kept right out of it and made him do their dirty work.'[52]

Finally, Brian asked Pete if he would stay on till Saturday, doing the Beatles' three Thursday/Friday bookings, and Pete said he would. Then he and Neil left, and in doing so walked straight past Billy Kinsley and Tony Crane of the Mersey

Beats. They'd arrived for an appointment with Brian – to discuss the Mike Berry tour, they thought, though very likely Brian was hoping to tell them about Pete joining their group as leader and him becoming their manager. But Brian had retreated into his office exhausted, and the lads were told to come back another time.[53]

Pete and Neil went to the pub. There wasn't much to do except drink: Pete was numb and Neil could be silent for unusually extended periods when turning things over in his mind. One point above all others was bothering Pete. He'd been in the Beatles two years almost to the day – 13 or 14 August 1960 to 16 August 1962 – so surely there had to be *another* reason for his dismissal, one they weren't telling him. Otherwise, why would it take them all that time to say he wasn't good enough?

What with this, and the timing, and their cowardice, Pete was hurting. 'I knew the Beatles were gonna go places, I knew we were going to be a chart group – and to be kicked out on the verge of it actually happening upset me a great deal. And the fact that they weren't at the dismissal hurt me a lot more. It was vicious and back-handed and I felt like putting a stone round my neck and jumping off the Pier Head.'[54]

Brian somehow gathered himself during the afternoon and got down to business. He spoke to David Harris and then dictated a letter that confirmed their conversation. This formally closed the door on Pete's time in the Beatles and opened it for Ringo; it also set down the framework for a new and more robust contract between him and the Beatles which would cover all activities as far as 1967.

16 August 1962.

Dear David,

Confirming our telephone conversation to-day, would you please prepare the new contract for THE BEATLES based similarly to their previous contract with the following exceptions:–

1. That the name Richard Starkey* replaces that of Pete Best. I understand he is over 21 years of age.
2. That you provide for the signature of both Paul McCartney's and George Harrison's fathers.

---

* R. Starkey was typed, Brian replaced the R. with RICHARD by pen.

3. That the contract is for five years and may be terminated by either party at the end of each contractual year.

4. That you include clause four as in the contracts relating to THE BIG THREE and GERRY & THE PACEMAKERS.*

5. The rate of commission [is] to be changed in that the management receive 20% when the total earnings of an individual artist exceeds £100 per week, and that the management receive 25% should their earnings, individually, amount to more than £200 per week.

I would be obliged if you would please prepare four draft copies of this contract for the group's approval.

Yours sincerely,
For NEMS ENTERPRISES LTD.
Brian Epstein, Director

Pete and Neil went home to find Mo in fighting mood. She'd heard the news from Neil, phoning from a public box, and was ready to spring to her eldest boy's defence in every way. As for Neil, while Pete would maintain that he did his best to persuade him to carry on working for the Beatles, Neil would remember a different version of events: 'When Pete was sacked he wanted to drink with me all through the afternoon, but I said, "No, I have to drive the van tonight." He said, "But I've just been sacked!" and I said *"You've* been sacked, Pete, *I* haven't been sacked. I've still got a job to do."'[55]

Pete didn't play that night after all – he just couldn't face seeing the others and no longer saw why he should work with them. Neil did. He was staying on, and not going to keep his mouth shut. 'They all looked at me and said, "Er, how's Pete taking it?" and I said, "Never mind about how Pete's taking it, how are *you* taking it?"'[56]

John, Paul and George had feared they'd never see their 'Nell' again, so his arrival in Chester this Thursday night came as a huge relief. He was, they already knew, a man to be reckoned with, and this only confirmed his remarkable mental toughness, because he was going to balance being the Beatles' right-hand man while staying in a domestic relationship with the Bests. The essence of pragmatism, the soul of discretion, as unbending as old boots, Neil

---

* Clause 4 (paraphrased): The manager is responsible for the collection of all monies and shall pay them out, after deducting expenses and commission, and the Artists shall have at all times the right to demand production of statements of account.

could stay loyal to both sides, lifelong. He went up even higher in the Beatles' estimation as a result, and his personal relationships, with John and George especially, strengthened. His faithfulness was also rewarded financially: they raised his £8-a-week wage to £10. (Neil was employed directly by the Beatles, never by Nems Enterprises, but Brian paid his wage and deducted it from their statements.)

The line-up at Chester, the first of three consecutive Thursdays here, was assembled by Brian: this week it was the Beatles, the Big Three and Bob Wooler. In the dressing-room, when Wooler pointedly asked John, Paul and George what he should say if people asked him where Pete was, everyone kept their heads down. Meanwhile, the Big Three's presence on the bill meant that Johnny Hutch did drum with the Beatles again after all, playing through a veil of scorn, hitting the drums hard and ruminating that he was doing them a bloody big favour, which he was. And when the night was over, Neil took the Beatles' guitar amps back home to the Best house and parked them in the hall for safe keeping, as he always had, and always would.

They did it again the next night too: the Beatles had a pair of bookings for Sam Leach, independent promotions in Birkenhead and New Brighton, and Hutch again bridged the gap. He'd a berdzerkly busy night because the Big Three also had a booking, back over the water, and he had to dash between the three halls. 'I said to Eppy, "I can't do this no more, it's killing me!"'[57] He wouldn't have to.

Ringo finished with the Hurricanes just as he'd promised. The Butlin's Friday ended as usual at 11.15PM with the jolly holidaymakers joining in to sing God Save The Queen, Auld Lang Syne and the campers' anthem, 'Drown your sorrow, bring the bottles back tomorrow' ... and when that tomorrow came Ringo was out of that caravan, into his Zodiac and haring home, leaving his flaming red suit for the next man and expecting to be paid for it. The future was unknown, but he wasn't coming back.

August 1962 was dull and dismal on Merseyside, and Saturday the 18th sent clouds and light evening rain. Elsie was delighted to have her Richy home three weeks early, doubly so when he announced he'd be able to give her £5 a week housekeeping from now on instead of twenty-five bob. It was an enormous sum. Then Richy stood at the kitchen sink in this tiny terraced house in Liverpool 8 and did as John had bid – he shaved off his beard, then tried to flatten down his hair. With the drums in the boot of his car, he drove down the hill into town for a private first rehearsal in the Cavern.[58]

Tonight's Beatles booking was back on the Wirral, in the beautiful self-contained village of Port Sunlight. The Horticultural Society's annual show took place all afternoon in the smart L-shaped Hulme Hall, and a dance always concluded the day. Brian agreed the Beatles could play between sixty and eighty minutes for £30; they'd be the main act, supported by their friends the Four Jays. In mid-June, at the time of an easy and polite negotiation, it was merely going to be the Beatles' second appearance at this venue, but life had intervened to make it *the start of something*.[59] Hulme Hall was fit for it, with beautiful blooms everywhere, their bouquet just sustaining through the ciggie smoke.

Around the Beatles were flowers, flowers everywhere, but not entirely peace. Ringo was on high alert, expecting trouble from Neil. He didn't know him very well but knew he was Pete's mate, so when Neil seemed to refuse to set up the drums for him, Ringo went into a loud strop, accusing Neil of being petty and mean-minded. As Neil would explain, Ringo misinterpreted the situation:

> I didn't know how to set up a drum kit. Pete always set up his own because he knew how he wanted it. So when Ringo came into the band I just let him do his own thing and he thought I was thinking 'Fuck you' because he'd taken over from Pete.
>
> Ringo didn't have anyone set up his drums in Rory Storm's group but as soon as he got with the Beatles he was Big Time, like 'We've got a road manager, he'll do it.' But he had no intention of telling me *how* to fucking do it.[60]

When finally set up, the kit showed RINGO STARR on the bass drum, not THE BEATLES. Pete hadn't had anything printed on his drum for the longest time and (surprisingly) nobody seemed to care very much.

There are no photographs of the night and no one can think what the Beatles wore – it would have been matching but Ringo didn't yet have a suit like theirs. Also, no one remembers what songs were played … but what *is* recalled is that they were, right from the off, a better, tighter band than before. In May, when the Shadows replaced bassist Jet Harris, Hank Marvin reassured *Melody Maker* readers 'It won't alter the group one bit', but when the Beatles sacked Pete and got Ringo they *wanted* it to alter them – their sound especially – and it did. As the Four Jays' bass player Billy Hatton says, 'The Beatles said to us, "What do you think?" I said I thought it sounded better than they'd been. It wasn't the sound they'd had with Pete, it was different. Pete had a tendency to speed up and slow down, Ringo didn't, and he had charisma. But we felt sorry for Pete all the same.'[61]

Bobby Brown was thrilled to see the Beatles she loved take on a new dimension. 'I really liked Ringo from day one, at Hulme Hall. As soon as he got up there I thought he was great. He was full of personality. He wasn't this moody James Dean-like person at the back. Pete never smiled and Ringo *always* smiled.'[62]

Saturday 18 August 1962 defines the start of Liverpool's famous 1960s. In the afternoon, Liverpool Football Club resumed playing in the top division after an eight-season absence, kicking off a period of unforgettable national and international domination. In the evening, the Beatles became the four the world would know and love.

More so than John and Paul, it was George who brought Ringo into the Beatles, and he always knew the rightness of what he did. 'We were all very happy to have him. From that moment on, it gelled — the Beatles just went on to a different level.'[63]

Neil Aspinall, even to the detriment of his own best mate, also knew the score. 'They'd had a succession of drummers through the years and finally now they found one who integrated, someone who fitted. Until this point it was always "John, Paul, George and a drummer" – now it was John, Paul, George and Ringo.'[64]

31

Some Other Guy
(19 August–4 October 1962)

> *How come you suddenly threw Pete Best out of the group?*
> Because he couldn't play very well.
> *Is that why?*
> Sure. Why else?

John Lennon's reply to a caller on a 1971 New York radio phone-in truthfully answered a question that had hung around for nine years and would continue to linger: why *did* the Beatles get rid of their drummer?[1]

John, Paul and George weren't sentimental types. This was their decision; they'd taken it and they'd live with it. If anyone didn't like it, that was a pity; and if they really didn't like it, that was *tough*. There were also grounds for keeping quiet. Going into detail couldn't have reflected well on Pete; also, the central position of Neil Aspinall and his family called for discretion both here and far into the future. However, this reluctance to explain even the primary reason for Pete's dismissal created a vacuum into which tumbled a blizzard of whispers and rumours.

Twenty-four hours from Port Sunlight, the Beatles had their usual Sunday-night residency in the Cavern, and the cellar was crackling with the hottest of news. They'd sacked Pete! *What? Why?* Half-truths and falsehoods to flourish for decades were seeded this night in nothing more substantial than the tattle of teenage girls – as one of them, Liz Tibbott-Roberts, would remember: 'It was all rumour. One word going round was that Pete "wasn't good enough for them". Another said he was just so handsome that they'd got rid of him out of pure jealousy. Rumours just start, and it never dawned on 15-year-olds to stop and say, "Yes, but how do you *know* that?" You just took it all in like a sponge, then unwittingly spread it.'

> We heard they got rid of Pete because Paul was jealous of the adulation he got. (Joan McCaldon)

> We heard Paul wanted Pete out because he didn't fit in, because he never went around with them, like at the Blue Angel and so on. (Beryl Johnson)

> My friends and I heard 'Brian got rid of him', so we hated Brian for that. The reason was that Pete was so nice looking, the others were jealous. This was the whisper going around – and it could well have been started by one of Pete's fans. We didn't know one drummer from the next, whether he was good or not, so we automatically assumed it had to be jealousy. (Margaret Chillingworth)

Gossip was rife among older heads too. Mal Evans heard Pete was booted out because he wouldn't smile. Others said it was because he wouldn't change his Tony Curtis hair into a Beatle fringe.

> People were saying John Lennon was to blame, that he'd had a row with Pete. (Thelma Wilkinson, who ran the Cavern snack bar)

> I was always led to believe the Beatles got rid of Pete to be free of Mrs Best. (Margaret Kelly)[2]

Very occasionally, when pressed, the Beatles responded to the most persistent of these allegations, that Pete was sacked because Paul was jealous of the attention he received (though no answer would ever quieten the conspiracy theorists).

> John: There was always this myth being built up that he [Pete] was great, and Paul was jealous of him because he was pretty, and all that crap. They didn't get on that much together but it was partly because Pete was a bit slow.

> Paul: I wasn't jealous of him because he was handsome. He just couldn't play! We wanted him out for that reason.

> Paul: What's the truth about why Pete Best was sacked? Because George Martin wouldn't have him, is one good reason. And Ringo was better, was the other prime reason.[3]

Pete would always contend there had to be additional reasons for his dismissal, one or more causes to remain everlastingly unknown to him as to everyone else. This both preserved his dignity and left him room for manoeuvre. Asked about it thousands of times – as he was – he would say variations of 'They said my drumming wasn't good enough but the real reason is a mystery'. Neil knew better and was very much around for the asking, and it's telling that Pete and Mona didn't challenge John, Paul or George about it, only the people around them. Mo even phoned George Martin. Though doubtless bemused at the enquiry, he confirmed his decision not to use Pete on Beatles recording sessions; whether or not the group retained him outside the studio wasn't his business.

Mona disregarded such clear statements about her son's deficiency on the drums, would forever maintain the Beatles had perpetrated 'a dirty trick' against her boy, and left Brian in no doubt she knew why:

> I said to him, 'It's jealousy, Brian, jealousy all the way, because Peter is the one who has the terrific following – he has built up the following in Liverpool for the Beatles.'
> I think it was for that reason that Peter had to be got rid of, at that stage – because if it wasn't, and they went national and international, Peter would have become the main Beatle with the others just the props.[4]

One upshot of all the anger was that Pete rejected Brian's offer to become leader of the Mersey Beats. Brian cannot have been too surprised that a 20-year-old freshly out of the Beatles didn't want to join a group of young lads with a junior position on the scene – but while Bob Wooler would speculate that Brian was counting on this, Brian knew the rejection left Pete free to take legal action.[5]

None of this situation was of Brian's making, but he was a convenient target for the vitriol. The Cavern was a tricky place for a few days and on one visit he accepted Ray McFall's offer of protection from a doorman. Paint-stripper was poured over Brian's fine Ford Zodiac, an act he associated with the Pete Best sacking though it wasn't necessarily so.

Ringo was another innocent party in the thick of it. Movement among groups was routine stuff and he just happened to have landed the hottest seat in the house, as was his right. Asked thirty years later if he'd ever felt sorry for Pete, Ringo delivered a dose of the Liverpool straight-talk that showed him the match of his new bandmates: 'No. Why should I? I was a better player than him. That's how I got the job.'[6]

Ringo was a stranger to most of the Beatles' audience. Some knew him – those who caught any of the four times he'd deputised for Pete – but plenty had never seen him before. The Beatles were metropolitan, the Hurricanes still

suburban: the Cavern hadn't booked them since June 1960 and they mostly frequented the north Liverpool jive halls the Beatles had left behind; Ringo had
also spent most of 1962 in Hamburg, France and Skegness, playing Merseyside
no more than seventeen times since December '61.

> I thought Ringo was rough, a boy from Liverpool 8, the kind of lad who,
> if he hadn't been a Beatle, could well have been a crook. They went from
> having a god to *that*. (Margaret Chillingworth)

> That first time in the Cavern, people were shouting 'Pete forever, Ringo
> never' and stamping their feet in unison like at Saturday-morning pic-
> tures. They were shouting it right in front of Ringo. The Beatles just
> started playing Some Other Guy but the chanting went on quite a while
> and no one seemed concerned it might upset Ringo. (Brenda Murphy)[7]

All these things happened, but while a posse of disgruntled teenage girls did
make their feelings known, the situation was never quite as inflamed as hindsight would suggest. Pete had plenty of fans but never the majority, and while
Ringo himself would sensationalise by claiming there were 'riots in the streets'
over his appointment, this storm passed quickly: broad consensus confirms it
was all over between one and two weeks later.

> Pete Best was very handsome but he never looked as if he belonged to the
> Beatles. I wasn't that bothered when he left. Ringo had the right person-
> ality, if not the looks. I could understand why they'd done it. (Sue Wright)

> New drummer in Beatles – Ringo Starr. He is nice. Sweet – better than
> miserable Pete Best. Paul asked us if we liked Ringo and we all said yes.
> (Diary entry of Sandra Marshall)

> Pete was just a pretty guy. He never had anything to say and didn't match
> their personalities at all. He just used to go home, disappear, very subdued,
> whereas Ringo was Mr Showman. (Marie Guirron, George's girlfriend)

> I used to love Pete and was heartbroken when they sacked him. It was a
> dreadful feeling at the time – *how can they do that?* But it soon passed and
> was as if he'd never been there. They were *much* better with Ringo, with-
> out a doubt. He gave them that solid backbeat – he's a great rock 'n' roll
> drummer – and he fitted in brilliantly. (Elsa Breden)[8]

As it was with the suits, so it was again now: every young voice had an opinion, pro and anti vying for attention – 'Pete forever, Ringo never' or 'Ringo forever, Pete never' – but no one headed for the exit. The Beatles lost no fans in sacking Pete, and were in fact still gaining them.

Three days later, at lunchtime on Wednesday 22 August, the Beatles appeared before TV cameras for the first time. They needed little of Eppy's encouragement to look good, choosing matching dark velvet waistcoats, suit trousers, knitted ties and the Chelsea boots. It was a primitive shoot. The Cavern was so gloomy, the camera could only see when the place was brightly lit, which made it even hotter than usual; the sound was so loud that Granada's single microphone often distorted; the film stock was black-and-white;* cutaway shots – Beatles close-ups and multiple views of the audience – were achieved with a mute clockwork camera that had to be wound up and ran for twenty-four seconds before the charge dropped away to nothing. But through it all, there is a film, one that its maker Leslie Woodhead evocatively describes as 'like something smuggled out of Eastern Europe'.[9]

Factually speaking, it's the second piece of Beatles moving image – predated by the short, silent 8mm colour sequence shot six months earlier – but this is the earliest proper footage of the Beatles, their first with synchronised sound, their first TV coverage and the only film of them in the Cavern. Two complete takes survive of Some Other Guy (played at Woodhead's request), along with a mute cutaway of the end of Money – music from New York and Detroit sung hard in a Liverpool cellar.

So here they are – on film, with sound, at last, *the Beatles*. They do not disappoint. Ringo lays a solid, bricklaying beat behind a powerful three-guitar sound; John and Paul pitch full tilt at the lead vocal, side by side, intense and in harmony. Just like everyone says, they're *themselves*, charismatic and dynamic performers, no faking. Except for a change of clothes and drummer, this is what Brian Epstein saw when he dropped into a lunchtime session nine months earlier, and here's why he was hooked. John sings straight, strong and true, his right hand chopping out the rhythm, the audience but a short-sighted blur. Paul sings with the same total commitment but is more self-aware, mostly looking up at the ceiling, making only occasional eye contact with the audience. George, off to the side, is solidly good on guitar and can't suppress one wry shy smile. Ringo is doing his job mostly in shadow, but

---

* Colour TV in Britain started in 1967 but the two main channels didn't change until the end of 1969. Colour sets first outnumbered black-and-white in 1976.

close-ups catch him laughing and enjoying himself. Looks pass between them, they're confident with who they are, where they are and what they are, and they're ready to fly.

The context is captured well. Screams of enthusiasm and delight sound at the start of Some Other Guy, then are drowned by the sound. Bob Wooler's voice is characteristically crisp in his introductions, and one of the films just catches him crawling back inside his tiny stage-side hole, leaving the Beatles to get on with it. And in a perfect moment of audio-vérité, someone yells out 'We want Pete!' both before and at the tail-end of one of the takes – a young man's voice, not a girl's.

Though the camera didn't see him, Pete *was* in the Cavern for this session. 'I sneaked in and sneaked out again,' he wrote in his autobiography.[10] Leslie Woodhead remembers 'a dozen or fewer Pete Best fans seething above ground, really unhappy that he had gone and Ringo was there', and Granada's clock-work camera filmed a young lad reading the 23 August *Mersey Beat*, hot off the press with what it touted as an 'exclusive story' headlined BEATLES CHANGE DRUMMER! The piece was tucked away on page eight and said 'The Beatles comment "Pete left the group by mutual agreement. There were no arguments or difficulties, and this has been an entirely amicable decision"' – which, insists editor Bill Harry, wasn't his own independent journalism but a typed quote given him by Brian that he didn't challenge. It was whitewash – hogwash, from Pete's perspective – and made little impact. The story also said, truthfully, Ringo had 'admired the Beatles for years ... [and] is tremendously excited about the future'. It concluded with news that the group would be flying to London on 4 September 'to make recordings at EMI Studios'.

The Beatles were back in the Cavern a few hours later – Wednesday night, as usual – after final preparations for John and Cyn's quiet next-day wedding. She was at the docks to wave her mother off to Canada again, and John went home and finally broke the news to Mimi: 'I said Cyn was having a baby, we were get-ting married tomorrow, did she want to come?' Mimi shouted 'You're too young!' at the boy who'd never been so, and vowed both her own absence from the ceremony and any other family member's.[11] There'd be no Stanleys pres-ent and, naturally, no Lennons. John hadn't seen his dad in sixteen years and assumed him to be still sailing the ocean waves as a merchant seaman; he was unaware that Alf Lennon was stomping Britain's byways as an itinerant worker and waif, his happy carefree world since release from prison in 1950.

Thursday 23 August, mid-morning, Brian collected Cyn from Garmoyle Road so she could be driven to her wedding in style – or as much style as could be had in a Ford Zodiac over which someone had maliciously poured paint-stripper. Their destination was the register office on Mount Pleasant, where they found John huddled in a corner of its drab waiting-room with Paul and George, each dressed in black suit, white shirt and black tie as if at a funeral. (Ringo and Neil hadn't been invited and didn't know about it.) They were *all* nervous, Cyn would write. Otherwise, there was only her brother Tony and his wife Marjorie in the room, so the total number attending this wedding, bride and groom included, was seven. Nobody had thought to bring a camera and there isn't a single photograph of the day.

So solemn was the registrar, it might indeed have been a funeral – and, shortly after the ceremony began, a pneumatic drill started up in the adjacent back yard and no one could hear a thing. The couple barely caught the vows they needed to repeat – 'To have and to harm, till death duty part' – and John first knew he'd become a husband when Brian (his choice of best man) nudged him and said it was time to kiss the bride. Then they signed the register. John Winston Lennon, 21, 'Musician (Guitar)', had married Cynthia Powell, 22, 'Art Student (School)'. Their signatures were witnessed by James Paul McCartney and Marjorie Joyce Powell. The great event over, they emerged from the building into a heavy downpour, and burst out laughing.[12]

Tony and Marjorie left after the ceremony so it was just the five of them who ran down Mount Pleasant in the rain to the wedding celebration: lunch at Reece's. As they went, they passed opposite the Vines, the huge ale house where Alf and Julia Lennon celebrated their register office wedding twenty-four years earlier (and there were no photographs of them either).

The Beatles' habit of not giving one another gifts was well set, but Brian gave the newlyweds free use of his private flat for as long as they needed it; 36 Falkner Street was where Mr and Mrs Lennon would begin married life – and where, hopefully, Cyn would see through the last seven months of her pregnancy. It was a typically generous gesture, and both a surprise and great relief to John and Cyn, who'd done nothing to fix their own accommodation and would otherwise have been sleeping apart for the time being, she back in her crummy bedsit, he at Mendips. Cyn so genuinely overflowed with gratitude and emotion, Brian blushed crimson.

For the first time since bunking down in the student flat in Gambier Terrace two years before, John left Mimi and moved into a place of his own. It seemed completely suitable: he and Cyn had the full length of the ground floor in a smartish townhouse, with use of a small walled garden at the back. On the downside, their toilet and bathroom was in the hall and shared with the house's other occupants, and their bedroom fronted a street that was often threateningly noisy. Falkner Street was a violent place. John and Cyn were, appropriately enough, close to the end by the art school, but beyond their front door – the deeper Falkner Street extended into Liverpool 8 – the greater its decay and social malaise, and trouble often spread along its length.

It was strange for a man whom have everything and a wife to boot. A month earlier, marriage hadn't been in John's mind, now he had a dependant, with a second on the way, and nothing could ever be like it was, even if he pretended it to be. His new status was going to take considerable adjustment: 'I did feel embarrassed being married. Walking about married, it was like walking about with odd socks on or your flies open.'[13]

John thought it could be the end of the line for him and the Beatles if people found out – it was what everyone kept telling him, so he believed it – and Ringo was among those he kept in the dark. As he said in 1965, 'I didn't want it to get around and I didn't know how well I could trust him to keep a secret.'[14] They didn't tell Neil either. He needed to know something had changed because he'd be collecting and dropping off at Falkner Street every night instead of Menlove Avenue, but John didn't mention marriage, only that he was living in sin.

Cyn's appearances at Beatles shows, already diminished, ended completely. Awkward questions were to be avoided at all costs and she certainly didn't want to be seen with John when her pregnancy was visible. Despite such precautions, however, the first *married* rumour quickly took root. Apparently, one of the Cavern snack-bar staff had seen John and Cyn leave the register office . . .

Lindy Ness was just home from Norway and made a point of seeing John at the 24 August lunchtime session. He'd asked her to bring him back a gift and she brought a wooden troll with trousers round his ankles, sitting on a potty. She found John, with George, by the bandroom, and had a conversation audible only to its participants: 'I'd already heard rumours that John had got married, and as he unwrapped my present George said something like "Are you going to put it with all the toasters?" John said, "Shut up!" When they saw what it was, George said, "Oh I thought it was another wedding present," and John said, "SHUT UP!", and then he looked at it and said, "What's this, Norwegian wood?"'[15]

John and Lindy resumed their friendship where they'd left it earlier in the summer, and during a number of good conversations over the following weeks he conceded that the rumour about him being married was true. 'He talked about Cynthia "expecting", and – while I don't remember exactly what he said – I got the clear sense he wasn't happy about becoming a father. I also got the impression he loved Cynthia very much.'

He did, and another of John's ways of preventing people thinking him married was to carry on carrying-on. For a short while longer, he kept up his fling with the girl who'd posed for his sexy photos, and he also started a new situation, with a dark-haired, Juliette Gréco-like beauty called Ida Holly. Just turned

16, she was one of few unmarried girls who didn't live 'at home' – she flat-shared with a friend in (of all places) Gambier Terrace. John and Ida began a friendship that extended deep into 1963, one he was surprisingly open about: almost everyone in Liverpool seemed to know it.

All the Beatles were now in settled relationships. Having ended with Dorothy Rhone, Paul played a broad field without hindrance, sparking flames old and new, and he also (from August 1962) found himself a special new 'steady'. This was Thelma Pickles – John's art school lover before he got together with Cynthia. Paul had always liked Thelma, and happened to see her in Liverpool while driving his car – his proud and precious Ford Consul Classic, which he bought new ('on the never-never') in early August.[16] She'd married, had a baby boy and then separated from her husband. Approaching 21, Thelma lived in a Prince's Avenue bedsit as a single parent and was trying to resume her art school studies, a talented young woman ... and here in her life arrived Paul McCartney.

> He was no longer a slightly plump young schoolboy but very much his own person. I only like visual art, I'm not into music, so I had just a vague notion that John and his group were still going. Paul said he'd pick me up later to see them play at the Cavern. It was a jazz club when I'd last been there.
>
> It was full of raw energy. Girls were screaming and boys liked them as well. I'd only ever watched *Six-Five Special* and this was different. I hadn't believed what Paul said about their increasing fame – being brought up working-class in that era, we were given to believe 'our sort' couldn't become successful.[17]

George, meanwhile, was still going steady with Marie. On the rare evenings when the Beatles weren't playing, he'd take her to the bowling alley or the pictures or they'd go for long drives, sometimes heading into Wales, and she also went back to his house, where he showed her his collection of Chet Atkins LPs.[18]

These visits coincided with the Harrisons' last days at 25 Upton Green. Having hated Speke from the moment they moved in, on New Year's Day 1950, their application to be rehoused was finally granted, and during late August this family of now four – Harry (53), Louise (51), Peter (22) and George (19) – moved to 174 Mackets Lane, a new 'overspill' council development on the border of Hunt's Cross and Woolton. It was close to Menlove Avenue and the Harrisons always said it was 'in Woolton'. This was the nicest house they'd had: bigger, semi-detached, with a driveway and garage that enabled Peter and George to keep their cars off the road and on their own property for the first time. It wasn't exactly luxury – the floor in George's bedroom was always bare lino, cold and hard – but it was blessedly removed from Speke's social and alcohol troubles, of which, after close on thirteen years, they'd had enough.

Ringo got himself a new steady girlfriend within days of joining the Beatles, and she too was a fan. Mary 'Maureen' Cox was a Cavernite who'd already been out with Paul – they dated after a friend dared her to kiss him, which she did. 'Maureen was my girlfriend before she was Ringo's,' Paul says. 'I went out with her a couple of times. She was a nice girl and a lot of fun but we weren't really going to hit it off and then Ringo said he seriously fancied her so I left them to it.'[19]

Maureen was training to become a hair stylist, and studying at evening classes. She and her friend Jackie were cutting through Mathew Street on their way back from college when Ringo came out of the Cavern, got in his car and was about to drive off. Maureen tapped on his window and asked for an autograph. She was never sure why – she was generally cool and laid-back, not the star-struck type – but Ringo signed as asked, and as he was driving away called out, 'Coming to the Cavern Sunday?'

Each was an only child and both had a confusion of names. She was Mary, known to some as Maureen and also as its diminutive Mo, though most knew her as Mitch. This was what Ringo first called her (a poor speller, he wrote it 'Mich') and she called him Ringo until he asked her to say Richy, like all his family and loved ones did. It was for Richy and Mitch that romance blossomed, though initially brighter for her: the Beatles had loads more girls around them than the Hurricanes and Ringo was determined to take advantage of the widespread opportunities; but Maureen kept imposing herself and got him to give her and Jackie a lift home at the end of Cavern nights. As he'd recall, 'There was always that Liverpool thing: "I'll take you home, love." – "Sure, can you take my friend too?" – "Er, all right." Then one day you'd ask, "Can we go out alone?"'[20]

Their relationship began to fire on Monday afternoons, which she took off work. He introduced her to his Madryn Street friend and mentor Marie Maguire and took her home to meet Harry and Elsie. Harry was still happily singing round the local pubs and clubs, with Cole Porter's Night And Day one of his favourite numbers – it became Richy and Mitch's 'special song'.*

Finding a steady relationship helped Ringo settle, because jumping into the Beatles – earning place and space in the tightest, brightest band – was a formidable challenge. John, Paul and George had been ultra-close since schooldays,

---

* Mary Cox, no middle name, was born 4 August 1946 at Walton Hospital. Her parents were Liverpudlians: Joseph, known as Joe (born 1912, a barman on merchant ships, like Alf Lennon and Harry Harrison, at sea for long stretches), and Florence, known as Flo (née Barrett, also born 1912, who worked as a packer in Liverpool's huge sugar refinery). Though devoutly Catholic, the bride was expecting at the time of Flo and Joe's marriage in February 1946. When Mary was born they lived with Joe's widowed mother, just off the dock road, and by the time Mitch met Richy they were living in a flat around the corner, 56a Boundary Street.

sharing everything from outlook to income. They were of one mind on life, and all the stronger for arriving at their unanimity from individual perspectives. Ringo knew he had to tune in, as would they to him. Two years later he told *Melody Maker*:

> I was lucky to be on their wavelength when I joined the group. I had to be or I wouldn't have lasted. They all have strong personalities and unless you can match it, you're in a bit of trouble.
>
> I'd sat in with them before they offered me the job fully, so I knew them. But those sit-ins were really for kicks – as a stand-in. When I finally joined them I had to *join* – join them as people as well as a drummer.[21]

The three Beatles were keen to accommodate a fourth. It wouldn't be plain sailing but they wanted it and had chosen him. They were bringing in not just a drummer but an attitude, something fresh into the mix. What they knew of Ringo, they liked. He was a risk-taker, hungry for new experiences, forthright, never afraid to stand up for himself; he was funny and courageous and had a Big Time ego, as shown by his first-night row with Neil. (It lasted a few weeks before Neil 'got over it', Ringo says.) The Beatles' chemistry with Pete had never been right because they needed boldness, brashness, openness, someone with strengths and vulnerabilities similar to theirs, a tough-minded individual and a team player with personality. It was a heavy load for slender shoulders and Ringo felt his way gradually. 'Emotionally,' he'd say, 'I had to earn my way in.'[22]

He took a friend around with him in these initial weeks, someone he could lean on while he found his feet. Step forward again Roy Trafford, his best mate since their time as apprentices at H. Hunt & Son: Richy the fitter, Roy the joiner. Their careers had taken different tracks but the friendship endured, and it so happened that at the time his pal joined the Beatles, Roy and his fiancée had broken off their engagement and he was free in the evenings. Richy grabbed him.

> It was useful for Richy to have me there, because he was new in the group and felt a little bit on edge because of the Pete Best thing. Pete was a good-looking lad and Richy struggled – with himself, I think – to be accepted. He wanted people to accept him but felt uncomfortable for a while. Not that he was shy – he was older than them and the other Beatles looked up to him in a way. They also didn't know which way to take him: although he was very funny he could also be a bit feisty at times, and he's nobody's fool.[23]

Roy was sitting alongside Richy in the Zodiac when Maureen Cox tapped on the window and asked for an autograph, and he rode with the Beatles – in their cars and in the van with them and Neil – for a few weeks from the end of August. 'I didn't know them much before that. I'd had no contact with them since the Quarry Men days, and not much then. I thought Paul was a gentleman, I hardly heard George speak, and John was just *great* – we'd be in the back of the car and he was reading out his poetry. He was such a funny man, changing the names of things as he went along. Some of that stuff was hilarious.'

Though Richy to Elsie and Harry, and to his local cluster of aunts, uncles and cousins – also to Roy and now to Mitch – he was Ringo to the other Beatles. In time, sometimes, they'd call him by his family name, but it never came as easy, and when they had occasion to write it they failed to notice the way he wrote it, using instead Richie or Ritchie (which would also be the way everyone else assumed it was written). He was also their 'Dingle Boy', a name they teased him with if he was exhibiting behaviour a little more salty than theirs, but it was more endearment than indictment. He was from the south end of Liverpool like them, and to some extent they could talk the same streets, shops, pubs and parks, which they'd not been able to do with Pete.

Still, he *was* different. Where the Beatles had been four grammar-school boys, now they were three and one who'd hardly been to school. Where they'd been four musicians all using their real names, now they were three and one with a stage name. Where they'd been four standing an inch or two short of six feet, now they were three and a dwarf (as John called him, at least once), Ringo being some three inches shorter. And yet, while firing Pete lost the Beatles a few uniformities, taking Ringo gave them a different and more appealing feature – *contrast*.

Brian Epstein was soon 100 per cent behind it. 'Ringo's coming into the group was one of the Beatles' most brilliant doings,' he said in 1965. 'It was something they wanted and that I carried out. It was, for so many reasons, a quite brilliant move.'[24]

It was a move brought about by George, and consequently his and Ringo's friendship was a viscerally close and fundamental bond. 'Ringo's relationship with George was always vastly different to what he had with Paul or John,' Neil Aspinall said. 'He felt he *owed* George.'[25]

Neil would often emphasise (sometimes finger-proddingly) that there was one essential key to understanding the Beatles' psychological constitution, as true in 1962 as it would be in the twenty-first century. He called it 'the Chain'. John brought in Paul, and Paul brought in George, and George brought in Ringo. *John, Paul, George and Ringo* doesn't just trip nicely off the tongue, it was (is) a natural order, and connections of great intricacy wend within and without its links.

It was vital the newcomer quickly acquire a sense of John Winston Lennon – the temperaments, crips and the exquisitely or brutally facetious humour. Actually, though, the leader of the gang viewed Ringo with some sense of awe. Their patience with fools was similarly brittle and their verbal despatches likewise brusque. Both had survived the trauma of absent fathers, and where John had been churned through the grammar-school system and come out the other side with no tangible reward, he was impressed by Ringo's innate intelligence and a sharpness that belied his missed classroom years. As John put it, 'To be so *aware*, with so little education, is rather unnerving to someone who's been to school since he was fucking two onwards.'[26]

It took only a little time for Ringo to revere, respect and love John the same way Paul and George did. They were all close, but John was the glue, the one each had his best relationship with. Paul was much closer to John than he was to George, and George was a fair bit closer to John than he was to Paul. George's girlfriend Marie Guirron saw it. 'There was something strong between George and John. Paul was always bouncy but John and George were deeper together.'[27]

'Ringo was intimidated by the rest of the Beatles at the beginning,' says Paul.[28] On the one hand, a big one, Paul was full of admiration for the kind of man Ringo was and what he'd achieved, and the fact he was 22 (the Beatles had sequential ages when Ringo joined, with John 21, Paul 20 and George 19). Age was an important yardstick for Paul and first impressions always the ones that stuck: he looked up to John because he was older, and he looked and talked down to George because he was younger. Ringo was even older than John, by three months, and Paul would always see him in this light: 'He's a grown-up, Ringo – always is, always has been. I suspect when he was about three he was a grown-up.'[29] On the other hand, while venerating Ringo's age and worldliness, Paul paraded the pre-eminence he felt from being a Beatle, and from being an O- and A-Level achiever when Ringo's education had been ruined by illness. As Paul would say a few years later, 'When Ringo joined us I used to act all big time with him because I'd been in the business a bit longer and felt superior. I was a know-all. I'd been in the sixth form and thought I'd read a bit, you know. I began putting him off me, and me off me.'[30]

Dates aren't detailed for many of the anecdotes and episodes from Ringo's opening weeks in the Beatles: they float unfixed between his joining and the end of the year, glimpses of a wider story that will never be known. It was, for example, some time in this period that he showed them his first song. John and Paul both wrote songs, now Ringo came up with one – the Beatles' third songwriter. Showing real guts, he revealed for their approval a little country and western ditty he called Don't Pass Me By.

Roy Trafford started it, unwittingly. He and Richy had always been big fans of country music, sharing an array of favourites like Hank Snow, Buck Owens, Ernest Tubb and Merle Haggard – names Ringo now began to introduce to the other Beatles, who, being more into C&W than pure country, were mostly unaware of them. Roy had an American album called *Midnight Jamboree* by Grand Ole Opry star Ernest Tubb and His Texas Troubadours, and among the guest vocalists was Linda Flanagan singing a new number called Pass Me By. She sang with the accompaniment of Tubb's band, including a country fiddle player. Roy liked it so much, he learned it and played it at a party at Richy's house in Admiral Grove.

In Pass Me By, a girl asks her former sweetheart not even to say hello to her – 'don't you stop and make me cry' – because her heart would break all over again. Don't Pass Me By was thereabouts: from its earliest days it had the chorus 'Don't pass me by / Don't make me cry / Don't make me blue'. Ringo's song probably didn't last more than a minute, and its melody was pure country; he wrote it on a piano (he knew a few chords as well as boogie-woogie), which might account for his comment that when he played it to John, Paul and George they had hysterics and said it was a rewrite of a Jerry Lee Lewis B-side.

Ringo making John, Paul and George laugh was essential in cementing his place. They loved oddballs and eccentrics and he certainly was one. They didn't always know which way to take him, but they made light of his gruffness or dour countenance ('I'm quite happy inside, it's just the face won't smile') because they could pick on his big nose and that weird streak of grey in his hair. They were fascinated by his strictly simple diet and all the things his weakened stomach couldn't tolerate; they were amused by the fallout from his fractured education, like his phonetic spelling and enjoyment of the weekly kids' comics; they laughed when he signed LOVE AND LUCK above his autograph – his latest winning phrase; and they *always* cracked up at his strange sayings, like when he asked a restaurant waiter for 'slight bread' because he wanted only a small portion. They came to call these things Ringoisms and, in time, as Paul would remember, 'keep tabs on them, almost like writing them down: they were quite handy'.[31]

He also popped Prellies with them, smoked with them, swore with them, womanised with them and enjoyed late starts and late nights with them, hanging out after work at the bowling alley or Blue Angel, Joe's caff or Ma Storm's. Their religion was different – John, Paul and George all had Irish blood and were the not-so-common fruit of Catholic–Protestant marriages, Ringo was pure Protestant – but his antipathy towards churchgoing was identical. And where Pete had been solidly into sport, with his boxing background and rugby talent, in Ringo the three of them found just about the only other male on Merseyside utterly indifferent to it. The Beatles now beat sport 4–0.*

But though they didn't give a toss about football, all four of them started doing the football pools when Ringo joined. Every week of the soccer season, from August 1962 to May 1963, they each gave five bob to Ringo's stepdad Harry who filled in their coupons and posted them off.[32] It was done for laffs (they never won a penny) and symbolises how fast the Beatles' revised line-up fell into the habit of doing all things altogether. Three was turning into four, at last. They were on their way to becoming the closest of brothers – and Ringo, the sick only-child who'd stared through the window, longing to go outside and find someone to play with, couldn't get enough of it.

They made him their equal from the start, on a full quarter share of the money, just as Pete had been. It made no difference that they'd established reservoirs of goodwill before Ringo joined, that they'd got themselves a management contract and record contract and, uniquely, were paid London-type fees in Liverpool: Ringo was in the band, he was one of them, he got the same.

This was his first experience of management. The Hurricanes' recent chaotic episode in France was fairly typical of their adventures, and suddenly now he had Brian sorting everything for him, a measure of organisation impeccable by any standards. Along with his pay, accounted for with honesty and transparency, came instructions telling Ringo where to be and at what hour, how to look his best, what to do and sometimes what not to do. There were also short- and long-term itineraries plotting the excitingly progressive opportunities for them all. Ringo's fantasy of playing the London Palladium – an impossible dream in 1957, but he dreamed it all the same – came sharper into focus; he was with Brian Epstein and he was with the Beatles, and if any mates could help him get there, it was them.

Ringo knew Brian hadn't warmed to him at first, but they soon got beyond an initial wariness to find a mutually appreciative relationship. It made a deep and lasting impression on Ringo, and while he could be as sparse with praise as his new bandmates, a compliment such as 'Brian was great: you could trust Brian' speaks volumes.[33]

Ringo would describe the four as being 'three-and-one' for some time to

---

* Ten-pin bowling, and George's interest in motor-racing, somehow didn't count – the Beatles themselves said they were completely non-sporty. Most of the lads in the other groups were into football – Rory Storm was a regular at Liverpool (as was promoter Sam Leach) and Gerry Marsden supported Everton. Alone in the Beatles' camp, Neil Aspinall loved football and was a lifelong Liverpool FC fan.

come, such is the nature of insecurity and such was the complexity of these relationships. In many ways, though, his integration occurred with remarkable speed, and John, Paul and George clearly invested heavily in making it happen. One of them was thinking with particular wisdom: George brought Ringo into the group but chose not to room with him when they stayed at hotels in order to avoid the possibility of the Beatles falling deeper into two divisions, with them in one and John and Paul the other. He suggested Ringo share with Paul, and then, after a period of doing this, with John.[34] They all accepted it and had brilliant times in every combination. Core robust relationships were critical to the Beatles' strength and durability, every permutation of allegiance binding them tight.

It was also George who took a black eye for the pleasure of having Ringo in the group, or so the two of them readily believed. The Cavern (alcohol free 1957–70) was a friendly place; the few difficulties that arose were dealt with quietly and non-violently by one of the door staff – but at the lunchtime session on Friday 24 August, six days after Ringo joined, there was an altercation by the bandroom and George was smacked in the face. The result was a bruise across the bridge of his nose and around his left eye, one that stayed many days and went multicoloured.

Several saw or heard the fracas but accounts differ in the key details. George himself said he was hit after losing patience with a few people in the audience who were *still* calling out 'Pete forever, Ringo never'; he told them to 'bugger off' (or two other words to that effect), and later, as he stepped out of the bandroom, someone dealt him a head-butt, the popular Liverpool move that Paul once saw George himself deploy in the Institute playground. Others are doubtful. 'George was bopped in the Cavern by some guy jealous for his girlfriend,' Paul says, and at least one other person agrees. And it does seem that the assailant – 19-year-old Denny Flynn – hit out not for Pete but because he enjoyed it. One of the Cavern regulars, Dave Spain, is certain it had nothing to do with drummers: 'Denny Flynn wasn't a relative or friend or even a fan of Pete Best, he probably just wanted to stretch his muscles. He was notorious in Liverpool as a hard-case.'[35]

Yet while it's unclear if George sticking up for Ringo *did* lead to someone sticking one on him, it didn't matter to the two of them – they were certain of the connection and it became another of the thousands of layers in their kinship. 'George fought for me!' Ringo would say, proud and laughing.[36]

George's big-blue-job shone beacon-like through a long period without a break. The Beatles worked solidly from 28 August to 17 September, setting foot in towns and counties they'd not been before, where the concept of who they were

Casual for the camera, the Beatles in the Cavern, summer 1961, when the grungy Liverpool cellar became their second home.

Summer 1961: Paul and John with Bob Wooler, their favourite local DJ, drinking buddy, pills sharer and important early champion. Wooler was the *dean of the scene*, a perpetual encourager of Merseyside's young music talent.

Ringo and Johnny Guitar in the Hurricanes' second Butlin's summer, Pwllheli, 1961. Their chalet nights – birds in adjacent beds – got them kicked off the camp.

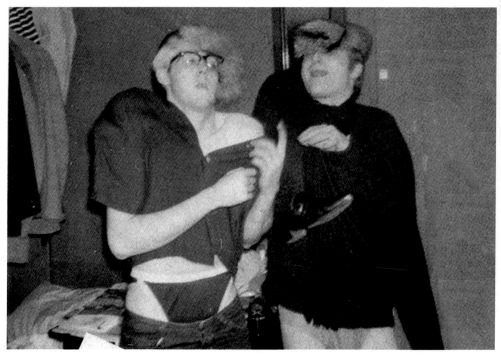

The complete 'crip' mode. Les Nerk Twins à Paris, October 1961.

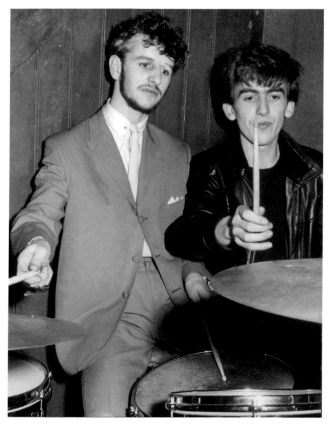

Friendly from the start: Ringo and George at the Tower Ballroom, New Brighton, 24 November 1961, during one of Sam Leach's epic rock promotions.

John, George, Paul and Pete at their initial photo-studio session, 17 December 1961. It was arranged by their new manager, whose nick-of-time arrival prevented the Beatles' breakup. The leather look was central to Brian Epstein's strategy at first . . . but had to go, and they all agreed.

A change of suits, leather to mod: the Beatles display the new threads they've helped to design. March 1962.

John and Lindy Ness outside the Cavern, 7 April 1962. 'He'd brag to other lads that I was his "jail bait", but actually he was protective. I was in safe hands.' Photo by Lindy's schoolfriend and big Paul fan, Lou Steen.

Rory and the Hurricanes in France, playing rock for American servicemen, May 1962 – with Vicky Woods, a temporary addition because the soldiers demanded *eye-candy*. By this time, Ringo has played with the Beatles, loved it, and George has invited him to join them permanently. Pete's time in the group is ending.

The Saturday-night hop in Hulme Hall, Port Sunlight. It's 7 July 1962 and everything is coming together fast. When they next play here, on 18 August, they're John, Paul, George and Ringo.

If every picture tells a story, this one's an exhibition. The boys, snapped by Brian Epstein on the tarmac at Liverpool Airport, 4 September 1962, en route to making their first record in London.

A few hours later, in Abbey Road, to record How Do You Do It and Love Me Do – an afternoon rehearsal in Number 3 studio before a torturous evening recording in Number 2. George is trying to hide his black left eye.

Great early colour, capturing probably George's first appearance with John and Paul. Taken on 8 March 1958 by 14-year-old Mike McCartney, at the wedding party of cousin Ian in Huyton. George has just turned 15 and is eight ('nine') months younger than Paul; John is 17 and, says Paul, those flushed cheeks indicate a *bevvied* state.

John and Cynthia on Hope Street, spring 1960, her mousey hair bleached into the requisite Bardot-like blonde. Fellow art student Jon Hague's Ford Model Y takes the weight of four. He kneels behind Cyn; behind John is Tony Carricker, the record collector and music enthusiast who introduced John to some joyfully authentic American R&B.

The Hurricanes in flaming red, Rory in shocking turquoise. Heading off to play their second Butlin's season, they stop at Duncan's, Liverpool's 'Classic Tailors' on London Road, 29 May 1961.

Hamburg, late-May 1962 – the only known photo explicitly tying the Beatles to drugs. Paul, George and particularly John broadcast an intimate knowledge of the speedy slimming pill Preludin – 'Prellies' to the Hamburg and Liverpool cognoscenti.

28 September 1962, a week from the release of Love Me Do – with history beneath their feet. The Beatles on a strip of land between Saltney Street and Dublin Street, up the dock road. John has no idea he's standing right where the Lennons settled in Liverpool three generations back, another stricken family fleeing Ireland's desperate famine.

and what they were trying to achieve was alien not only to their paying customers but also to the promoters who booked them. It sometimes happened that a single vocal mike was set up for them, because this was all acts usually needed. One place the Beatles weren't playing was London: Brian's experiences of pushing the Beatles in the capital were so consistently bleak, he'd resolved to make no London bookings until they had a big hit record, when there would be demand. His focus instead was on a continuing push out of Liverpool into new regions. Wherever they went, audiences expected to hear or dance to songs they knew, songs from the charts, so while Don't Ever Change and I Remember You were highspots, the Beatles faced a downturn when they went into their obscure American R&B numbers. Liverpool audiences had come to appreciate these songs but no one else knew them. As Neil would remember, 'People would be shouting out for Cliff Richard songs as if the Beatles were just another fuckin' covers band, and we wanted to give them things they'd never heard of. "You want Cliff Richard? OK, well here's If You Gotta Make A Fool Of Somebody by James Ray."'[37]

The toughest call was when one of them – almost always Paul – stepped forward and announced, 'Here's a number we've written ourselves.' But no matter their reception, John and Paul were back writing and not stopping. They all had another Cavern rehearsal the afternoon of Monday 3 September, the day before their hugely anticipated EMI return, and Paul had a new number for them to learn. John wrote Please Please Me with this recording session in mind, Paul had Tip Of My Tongue. It was an upbeat and bubbly song written first-person: the singer is struck by shyness but knows one day he'll get the words out, romance his girl and take her to the altar. It had an interesting verbal trick – where the last word of one line, *lonely*, rhymed with the first of the next line, *only* – but otherwise Tip Of My Tongue was a thin creation, its hooks never quite catching.

They rehearsed it all the same – and, uniquely, John didn't play guitar but maracas, from Ringo's kit. It was added to the stockpile of EMI-ready songs and they played it on stage: Tip Of My Tongue was in the Beatles' set for a few weeks from the start of September.* Another addition, though for days rather than weeks, was How Do You Do It, which they rehearsed here one last time, ready for its (*ugh*) next-day recording.

*

---

* Cavernite Sue Houghton remembers, 'A girl called Kathy brought in a big sombrero hat and gave it to John, and he wore it when they did Tip Of My Tongue – he had his guitar loose and played the maracas shoulder high. When the song goes "to think of things I want to say to you, oooh-ooooohh" they sometimes sang "Yabadoo!" instead.'

The big day dawned wet and windy, and it wasn't far past sunrise when the Beatles had to be up, out and gathered at Speke for their first ever flight from Liverpool Airport. This was still the same unimproved strip where Paul (and probably George) had spotted planes as a child and where John worked the 1958 summer holiday as a kitchen assistant, spitting in the sandwiches. Brian had promised to write a *Mersey Beat* report about the recording session and started off by taking a photo of the Beatles on the runway. The combination of the wind, the rain, the appallingly early hour (8.10AM), the old Viscount pro-peller plane they were about to board, Ringo's strange hairstyle and grey streak, George's unmissable shiner, bad haircut and particularly protruding ears, and four distinctly unsmiling faces waiting for Eppy to *get on and take the bloody thing*, makes for one of the least flattering but most intriguing of all Beatles photos. If every picture tells a story, this one's an exhibition.[38]

Neil had driven down overnight with the van, so Brian guided the Beatles from London Airport to the Royal Court Hotel in Sloane Square – they'd stayed here two nights in June and now were back for one, again putting the twin-bed philosophy into practice. Their attitude was to dress up for an engage-ment, so they changed into their stage suits, with white shirts and dark ties, grabbed a quick bite to eat, then set out to join with Neil at EMI.

Recording session

> Tuesday 4 September 1962. Number 2 studio, EMI, London.
> Recording: How Do You Do It; Love Me Do.

The Liverpool group scanned the posh avenues of Maida Vale and St John's Wood from the windows of their London black cab and arrived ready for the 2PM start. As it was in June, so it was again: all heads turned to look at them. The four northern lads with the strange group name and weird haircuts were considered rough scruffs on their first visit – now they had a different drummer with a big hooter and what looked like grey dye on one side of his head, and the lead guitarist had been in a fight.

They were booked in for two sessions, not one. Three hours of unrecorded rehearsal in Number 3, the smallest studio, between two and five o'clock; three hours of recording in Number 2 between seven and ten – during which, accord-ing to the EMI studio 'red form', they were expected to record four 'sides', four completed masters. Two of them would be taken for their debut 45, to come out the first Friday in October, a month distant.

Two consecutive sessions was an irregular arrangement, but the Beatles' early relationship with EMI *was* abnormal. The 6 June session had been mentally written off, so this was a clean start for everyone. The afternoon rehearsal gave George Martin and Ron Richards – the pair of them here together – the opportunity to re-evaluate this beat group who'd become Parlophone artists; it was a chance to assess material and musicians, including the new drummer. Brian had notified the change to Judy Lockhart Smith, so no session player was present; but would the old drummer's replacement be any better suited to recording?

The primary account of the day's events is Brian Epstein's report for *Mersey Beat*. He didn't write everything, and not everything he wrote was right, but it seems mostly reliable, and he says that six numbers were rehearsed during 'a long and hard afternoon's work'. He didn't specify titles and no EMI document preserves them, but – taking all indications into account – the following list (in any order) is likely to be correct: How Do You Do It, Tip Of My Tongue, Ask Me Why, PS I Love You, Love Me Do, Please Please Me. If this is right, it's obvious that the Beatles' and Brian's push for Lennon-McCartney songs could not have been stronger. That they promoted all five of their new numbers at the expense of any other they did so well – Soldier Of Love, Some Other Guy, Baby It's You, Twist And Shout and the like – is the strongest indication of their wanting a uniquely new take on success: earned on their own terms with their own sound and music.

From the Parlophone point of view, the most important number was How Do You Do It: George Martin and Ron Richards needed to hear how Mitch Murray's demo had been progressed . . . and, in spite of themselves, the Beatles had actually done good work with it, turning an adequate acetate into an appealing song, albeit one that remained way too light and white for their liking. Parlophone's A&R men had no doubts: it would be the A-side and quite possibly a hit. They'd record it in the evening session.

George and his assistant were less impressed with the other songs, one of which they'd be choosing as the B-side – with two more after that, maybe, selected for the evening's third and fourth recordings. They felt the arrangement of Tip Of My Tongue needed work (John again played maracas on this); PS I Love You and Ask Me Why they'd heard before and didn't particularly enjoy; and, while the 'skip beat' in Love Me Do was gone, George remained impervious to the song's merits, liking the harmonica and little else. Please Please Me didn't excite him either: 'They played me Please Please Me but it was very slow and rather dreary. I told them if they doubled the speed it might be interesting.'[39]

One further piece of George Martin criticism would help retool John's song into something more dynamic – 'I told them what beginning and what ending to put on it' – but he said they were to make such improvements in their own time, not EMI's. 'We were a bit embarrassed that he had found a better tempo than we had,' Paul says ... and this wasn't the only embarrassment arising, because during this Please Please Me rehearsal Ringo suddenly had a moment of madness. 'I was playing the bass drum and the hi-hat, and I had a tambourine in one hand and a maraca in another, and I was hitting the cymbals as well, [like] some weird spastic leper, trying to play all these instruments at once.'[40]

It was all too much. Ringo felt pressured to outperform his predecessor and not let down his bandmates; it was his first time in anything like a proper studio, it was his first time in London in two years and his first meeting with the schoolteacherly George Martin, whose voice seemed even more upper-crust and intimidating than Brian's. In an uncharacteristic panic, Ringo lost his head and started hitting everything with everything. It did not go unnoticed. There are no supporting quotes from the studio staff, but they must have ridiculed such amateurishness; the Beatles' last drummer hadn't uttered a word, this new one was crazy. Five years later, carefully measuring his vocabulary to outline his initial view, George Martin conceded, 'I didn't rate Ringo very highly.'[41] His opinion was formed for at least one other reason too: the producer discerned that Ringo couldn't play a drum roll. There would be unhappy repercussions.

Recording started at 7PM in Number 2. Ron Richards had gone, it was just George Martin, assisted by balance engineer Norman Smith and a tape operator. The red form says the session was to be recorded in mono and stereo but only mono was used and George decided on a safety-first approach, getting the Beatles to make a good rhythm track before adding the vocals; this was achieved by doing a tape-to-tape 'bounce' – superimposing voices as the tape was copied from one deck to another. The Beatles would record this way at EMI only one other time.[42]

The most important recording was done first. The red light went on inside and outside the studio, Norman Smith's voice gruffed 'How Do You Do – Take 1' into their headphones, and they were *On*. Information is scant, but they seem to have had little difficulty getting it right. John played a borrowed acoustic, Paul bass, George the Gretsch (most audible on the twangy solo he created, which passed muster but barely taxed his ability), and Ringo drummed well from an opening cymbal sizzle to the dying beat. It lasted a shade under two minutes and was done in two takes. Then, as the tape was bounced to a second spool, John sang the lead vocal and Paul the harmony, and they did some handclaps in the middle-eight. It wasn't difficult, just disagreeable ... they'd advanced to the brink of release a song they strongly did not want out. (Nothing is known about if or how they showed this – yet.)

George Martin selected Love Me Do as the B-side. It was the most developed of the five Lennon-McCartney numbers and, chiefly because of its harmonica, had the most appealing sound. He didn't see much merit in it or consider it A-side material ('Love Me Do, I thought, was pretty poor'), but it was fine for the B-side.[43] Flip-sides, as they were also called, hardly ever picked up airplay and many record buyers ignored them completely, playing only the song they knew and liked. The Beatles thought differently, knowing that B-sides could pack gems.

It turned out to be more difficult than anyone could have imagined. Something derailed them, and it isn't fully clear what, but the recording took hours. Instead of the session finishing at ten, when the studio typically shut down for the night, it went way over. The red form gives the finishing time as 11.15, Brian's report said midnight. Just when the Beatles had seemed to be hitting their stride in the studio, they were stumbling again.

Despite the struggle, though, it *was* good. Compared to everything that followed, How Do You Do It and Love Me Do would inevitably sound 'first session' – a bit simplistic, even quaint. However – emerging in its context, September 1962 – here, undeniably, was something new. Apart from all their other attributes, the Beatles sang and played the instruments they put down on tape, and so would be able to perform their record the same way for live audiences, and this made them highly unusual in 1962. With Love Me Do, they were among *very* few acts even trying a blues groove in a British studio. This was not the rock and roll sound that defined the Beatles on Merseyside or in Hamburg, but one single element of their stage act, one they'd chosen to represent themselves on record. All they needed to do was relax, tune into the studio environment, establish what they wanted to achieve, and progress to a more proficient level . . .

Except there was one more thing. They didn't want How Do You Do It released. And someone had to tell George Martin – right here, right now, last chance.

The way it's mostly related, the Beatles went together to register their protest. All the quotes about it (and, given the import, there are many) start with 'We said . . .' – but George Martin is sure only John did the talking. 'When the dirty work came, I had to be leader,' John would say. 'Whatever the scene was, when it came to the nitty-gritty, I had to do the speaking.'[44]

As George Martin would describe it, 'John came to me and pleaded with me. He said, "Look, I think we can do better than this."'[45]

John himself remembered the moment in an interview twelve years later (saying 'we' throughout): 'They forced us to do a version of How Do You Do It. We wouldn't let 'em put it out. We said, "We'd sooner have no contract than put that crap out" – all the tantrums bit. We thought it was rubbish compared with "love, love me do". We thought ours had more meaning.'[46]

'I suppose we were quite forceful really, for people in our position,' Paul says. 'We said we had to live or die with our own song, Love Me Do. We knew it wasn't as catchy [as How Do You Do It] but that was the way we had to go. We couldn't face the people back in Liverpool laughing at us. We were trying to keep the integrity – a blues group with harmonica on our records.'[47]

It was an extraordinary situation. Artists did not stand up to their producers, they had to do and accept what they were told. The Beatles had no rank at all to challenge George Martin's authority, and the risk was huge. Their future hinged on his reaction, which they certainly couldn't presuppose; it could even have spelled the end of doing *this* for a living instead of having 'a proper job'. John stood strong and said what needed to be said.

But it appeared to be futile. George Martin dismissed his protests out of hand. 'I said, "If you write something as good as that song, I'll let you record it, otherwise that's the song that's going out."'[48] And since he felt they hadn't written a song as good as Mitch Murray's, the dialogue ended there, as did the session, and four low Beatles left EMI and walked out into the St John's Wood night.

The Beatles' How Do You Do It was ditched between the following (Wednesday) morning and Friday afternoon. They would always believe George Martin had graciously yielded to their request, sympathetically accepting that the song *wasn't really them*. Having already decided he was a great bloke, they now knew he was: he wasn't stubborn or pig-headed, he was someone they could work with, and forever had their gratitude. But How Do You Do It was scrapped for reasons the Beatles knew nothing about.

The first gainsayer was Ardmore and Beechwood. The Beatles wouldn't have had a recording contract without Sid Colman and Kim Bennett, two men whose professional interest was set in obtaining one or more Lennon-McCartney song copyrights. They weren't remotely in the frame for How Do You Do It and signalled their anger at being fobbed off with its B-side.[49]

Dick James heard the Beatles' acetate of How Do You Do It in George Martin's office and didn't like it at all. In view of Colman's objection, George then played Love Me Do and asked James if he'd allow the Mitch Murray song to be its B-side. The publisher said no, the song was too good for that. He felt sure Murray wouldn't let it be buried in such a fashion, and, as he still hadn't secured the copyright, he didn't want to be seen advocating it. Love Me Do itself? No, the publishing was already locked up.[50]

On the Friday, Mitch Murray heard the B-side request – and the acetate –

and that was the end of the matter: he refused to allow it out. He felt sure How Do You Do It was hit material, he had a publisher interested and a record producer interested, so he didn't want it lost on a B-side. He also didn't like what the Beatles had done to his song.

It was pointless progressing it any further. George Martin remained certain the song had hit potential and intended to push it forward again as the Beatles' second record – but, with regret, for their first, it couldn't be the A-side and it couldn't be the B-side. He was stymied, and displeased: against his better judgement, he had to let a Lennon-McCartney song be the Beatles' first single – two songs in fact, both sides – and he washed his hands of it, not of the Beatles but of their troublesome first record. They'd done two sessions, recording four songs and then two, and all he had to show was one side of a 45 he didn't think good enough. Now they'd have to come in *again* to record a B-side, and Ron Richards could finish the job. Tuesday was the Beatles' next free day and they were booked back in for a half-session, 4.45 to 6.30PM.

The Beatles rehearsed in the Cavern on Sunday (before their evening session) and/or Monday (after their lunchtime session), intent on being at their sharpest. Since arriving home from EMI, John and George had taken delivery of their expensive new Jumbo Gibson guitars, shipped to Liverpool all the way from Kalamazoo, Michigan. These became integral to the faster, harder reworking of Please Please Me and also figured in whatever other songs were rehearsed, perhaps including PS I Love You. Only one number was needed for the B-side, but, as usual, the Beatles had alternatives.

The new week began like the old. Neil drove to London on Monday night and the Beatles were at the airport again Tuesday morning, though catching a later flight. Brian took another photo on the tarmac – not for any particular purpose, more to complete the circle. Only John is smiling, sort of; George, his black eye not quite gone, looks deeply disgruntled. After their plane bumped its way to London, they checked back into the Royal Court, changed their clothes and headed off once more to Abbey Road. Twice in a week, three times in three months – it was becoming familiar.

Recording session

Tuesday 11 September 1962. Number 2 studio, EMI, London.
Recording: PS I Love You; Please Please Me; Love Me Do.

As the four Beatles stepped into Number 2 studio, they saw a kit all set up and a drummer ready to roll. The spectre of being forced to work with 'a session man' – one they thought they'd banished with Pete's sacking – returned to haunt them, with Ringo the casualty. They were shocked, and he was devastated.

George Martin and Ron Richards held Ringo at least partly accountable for the problems of the previous week, and were taking no more chances – the recording of this first single *had* to be completed within the next hour and three-quarters and it would be done by John, Paul, George and Andy. This was Andy White, proficient in all styles, a proper pro drummer who held the sticks through his fingers and wasn't fazed by the studio red light.[51]

Ringo took it badly. 'I was highly upset – *highly* upset. It blew my brain away.' He bristled at the fakery of it all: the record business was such a *sham*, just like he'd heard, with anonymous musicians creating the sounds others pretended were theirs. He would neither forgive nor forget, and pinpointed George Martin as the cause of his misery. 'I was devastated [he] had his doubts about me … I hated the bugger for years.'[52] In most respects, it wouldn't take long for Ringo and George Martin to strike up a harmonious, enduring and genuinely warm give-and-take working relationship, but – on a deeper level – Ringo never excused George for causing him such heartbreak and would rarely pass up an opportunity to remind him of it. Regardless of all Ringo's positive experiences in the subsequent years that could have obliterated the ache of 11 September 1962 – and despite all the apologies, acknowledgements and explanations – he continued to hurt, and made sure George knew it.

Here at the session, George probably didn't seem responsible for it at all. As involved as he was behind the scenes, he wasn't in the studio to personally inflict this humiliation; Ron Richards was in charge, and they had work to do. The red form says they were expected to record two 'sides' in these 105 minutes, although – given the abbreviated duration and the fact that only one number was required – this could have been an error. Either way, the objective was to record a B-side, and the song selected was PS I Love You. It isn't known who chose it, but its recording commandeered the first part of the session.

For the second and last time at Abbey Road, the Beatles recorded solely in mono, though it seems they played everything live in this session, instruments and vocals together. PS I Love You was completed by take ten (some were probably false starts or breakdowns), with John's Jumbo Gibson plugged into an amp, George playing his Gretsch, Paul the bass, and Andy White on drums. Ringo shook a pair of maracas. As Richards would recall, 'Ringo was sitting next to me in the control box, not saying anything, so I said "Go and play the maracas" and off he went to do it. He stood next to Andy and the drum microphone picked up his sound.'[53]

PS I Love You was a good piece of work, with a particularly imaginative vocal arrangement – Paul singing lead, and John and George chiming in on certain words, tricky parts they'd worked out in the Cavern rehearsals. It was well crafted, catchy and performed with confidence, making for an effective and beguiling B-side. They were finding their stride.

This showed again when they went for a second number. The session had started at 5PM, not 4.45, so time was especially tight when they turned their attention to Please Please Me, now in its new, uptempo arrangement. A short, focused period of rehearsal came first, giving engineer Norman Smith time to adjust the microphones and mixing-desk settings, for Andy White to get acquainted with the rhythm – it included a number of fills – and for Ron Richards to properly attend to his A&R functions, tidying up the composition where necessary. He made one such change to the lead guitar part, which repeatedly riffed the melody and vocal line. 'George was playing the opening phrase over and over and over throughout the song,' Richards would recall. 'I said, "For Christ's sake, George, just play it in the gaps!"'[54]

This first known recording of Please Please Me – preserved on acetate disc – was by some distance the most exciting and dynamic work the Beatles had done in the studio so far. It isn't known how many takes they did before the one labelled 'best', but into a fast-flowing two minutes they crammed a chocolate box of hooks, licks, flicks and tricks, their ingenuity overflowing. A flurry of short verses are sung strongly and in challenging harmony by John and Paul, there are ascending chords, descending chords, appealing vocal crescendos and falsettos, and everything is given heightened impetus by fast doubled guitar chords. Please Please Me was a complex density of clear ideas, and well exe-cuted – John again used the Jumbo Gibson plugged into his Vox amp, George played the Gretsch, Paul added an inventive bass line, and Andy White did a good job. Ringo had no audible role in the recording.

Please Please Me was so good that, here and now, the possibility was floated that it become the B-side of Love Me Do – this is shown by the existence of the acetate. However, while the new arrangement was strong, it retained too many rough edges to go out just yet, needing more studio time than this session had. There was also an overwhelming feeling inside the Parlophone office to get the Beatles record *out*. This business had been dragging on for months and there was no desire anywhere for yet another quandary, yet another delay.

With the session coming to an end, Ron Richards suggested another remake of Love Me Do, thinking they might improve on the previous week. It was com-pleted quickly, with John pulling the harmonica from his pocket for the only time this late afternoon, and Richards getting Ringo to stand next to his usurper and play tambourine – and so hog the microphone that his tapping went down louder than Andy's beat. This now third EMI version of Love Me Do was an impressive job, confident and competent, but (apart from a slightly quicker tempo) in no material sense different to what was laid down the week before. As Ringo would rightly point out, Andy White didn't do anything *he* hadn't done. George used his Jumbo Gibson this time, not the borrowed guitar, and it was probably done entirely live because there are no handclaps in the middle-eight. By the end of the session they'd cut three songs in 105 minutes – less than the time it took them to labour through Love Me Do seven days earlier.[55]

At last, the Beatles' first Parlophone record could be issued. The coupling would be Love Me Do and PS I Love You, which George Martin greatly resented being forced to issue, didn't expect to succeed, and would aid with little support. The release date would be Friday 5 October – and, as Ringo was relieved to discover within the next two or three weeks, the chosen version of Love Me Do was the one with him on drums, not Andy White. It was the better of the two recordings, but George Martin and Ron Richards could never remember if they selected it on purpose or in error.*

The Beatles and Brian may not have realised that EMI's obligation to them was now ended. Their contract required Parlophone to record a minimum of six sides, and six had been done, the titles inscribed in a ledger at EMI's Hayes offices: *1*, Besame Mucho. *2*, Love Me Do. *3*, PS I Love You. *4*, Ask Me Why. *5*, How Do You Do. *6*, Please Please Me. Adjacent to the last of these, in a column headed 'Balance of Guarantee', was written the word 'Complete'. The Beatles didn't appreciate just how important it was that Love Me Do did well: their first record could have been their last.

George Martin *was* aware of the contract situation . . . and he was on their side. He now knew the Beatles, liked them, and believed their unusual 'group sound' could get them a hit – provided they recorded the right song. Success surely wasn't going to happen with Love Me Do, but that would soon be behind them and he'd make sure they fared much better with its follow-up.

The Beatles were standing at the foot of a new ladder, in the knowledge they had a core of popularity in north-west England to give them a good leg up.

---

* The five completed recordings from the 4 and 11 September 1962 sessions are all available. The 4 September Love Me Do became the single (and is now on the compilation *Past Masters*), and an edited version of How Do You Do It is on *The Beatles Anthology 1*. From the 11th, PS I Love You became the single's B-side, and both this and Love Me Do are on the *Please Please Me* album. The song Please Please Me itself, this early take with Andy White on drums, is on *The Beatles Anthology 1*.

The surest way to differentiate between the two September recordings of Love Me Do is to listen for tambourine. The version with Ringo on drums doesn't have it, the Andy White version does, and Ringo shook it so hard it's difficult to miss.

They'd also succeeded in getting their own songs used, Lennon-McCartney numbers on both sides of the record. Soon after that latest Abbey Road session, Brian received from Ardmore and Beechwood a single-sided sheet of paper that was the publishing agreement for Love Me Do and PS I Love You.

It was made out in Brian Epstein's name – 'for and on behalf of "LENNON/McCARTNEY"' – and gave to EMI's music company, in perpetuity, 'the full copyright for all countries'. It wasn't a rip-off contract more than any other, it was a template agreement – the industry-standard '10:50:50' deal – in which the specific details were added by typewriter. Ardmore and Beechwood agreed to pay the composers 10 per cent of the retail price on sheet music sales (after the first five hundred copies), 50 per cent of the publisher's receipts from the sale of records that contained either song (known as mechanical rights), and 50 per cent of royalties received from any sub-publishing deals outside the UK. The usual token sum, a shilling, was paid as an advance against the first royalties; standard agreements like this gave publishers no options on the writers' future compositions; and, for reasons unknown, the document was backdated to 7 September 1962.

There were ten pre-printed clauses in all, but Brian got Beryl Adams to type an eleventh, two colliding lines squeezed into the narrow space above his signature (which she then witnessed):

> 11. That were [sic] sheet music, records, publicity etc is concerned credit will be given to "LENNON/McCARTNEY".

Brian showed the contract to John and Paul in his Falkner Street flat, still being used by John and Cyn. In such surroundings took place an informal meeting of great consequence, because it was here that John and Paul agreed to solidify their old teenage pact to credit their songs jointly, irrespective of contribution – a deal that gained a second dimension in autumn 1962: they'd also share the money. Songwriting was about to start generating them a revenue stream distinct from the Beatles' group income; they didn't know how much, but agreed to divide it evenly. Historically, joint-songwriter agreements enumerated splits of 90:10, 85:15, 80:20, 75:25, 67:33 and every other fiddly fraction down to 50:50, but John and Paul went halves all the way, closeness and ambition shared and matched. Decided with the purest of motives and best of intentions, this accord reached in a Liverpool 8 flat in September 1962 would have lasting ramifications.

There was only one proviso: they agreed that the order of the song's credit would indicate its principal author. They'd continue to work on songs together, one bringing his ideas to the other, but where John was main creator, it would be Lennon-McCartney, and where Paul was main creator, it would be McCartney-Lennon. The credit for 50:50 collaborations would be decided if and when there were any (there'd been none since 1958). Accordingly, as Love Me Do and PS I Love You were mostly Paul's songs, Brian took a pen to the Ardmore and Beechwood contract and amended part of the inserted clause:

> 11. That were [sic] sheet music, records, publicity etc is concerned credit will be given to ~~"LENNON/McCARTNEY"~~ "McCARTNEY/LENNON".

The meeting then broadened out, leading to the discussion of a long-term agreement where Brian would become manager and agent for John Lennon and Paul McCartney as songwriters. Here and now, the three agreed all the outline terms, after which Brian gave David Harris instructions to prepare a contract. The lawyer was currently drafting the pukka management agreement between Brian and the Beatles, to run five years from 1 October; this second agreement – the tripartite one, John and Paul with Brian – would begin the same date and run for three.

Eleven months later, interviewed on BBC-tv, Paul described his and John's songwriting 'as a sort of sideline', but it was always more.[56] The reality is that, from 1 October 1962, unstoppable twin energies – the Beatles, and Lennon-McCartney – were running strong, together and separate, side by side and neck and neck, parallel missions that intertwined, mutually reinforcing.

Three copies of the Lennon and McCartney draft agreement (this was the name order as typed, but it represented no hierarchy) were sent out by Harris on 10 September, one for each party, and its terms were barely altered before the finalised contract was presented for signatures. John and Paul – 'The Composers' – agreed to appoint Nems Enterprises Ltd as their sole and exclusive manager and agent until 30 September 1965 on a 20 per cent commission. The document said nothing about the name order – Lennon-McCartney or McCartney-Lennon – and it would never be put into writing.

It isn't clear what George and Ringo knew of this second contract, or if they knew – neither would ever intimate knowledge of it in any public forum. By carving up the songwriting, John and Paul were effectively excluding them from this source of income. In the natural scheme of things, whenever they brought a song to the group, everyone would chip in with suggestions, George in particular contributing solos and other ideas, and this would continue – but he'd receive no credit or reward for it. Paul would explain the decision: 'It was an option to include George in the songwriting team. John and I had really talked about it. I remember walking up past Woolton Church with John one morning and going over the question: "Without wanting to be too mean to George, should three of us write or would it be better to keep it simple?" We decided we'd just keep to two of us.'[57]

It was from around this time – possibly right now, though probably not – that George perceived a subtle shift in the Beatles' chemistry. On stage, he was still singing as many songs as John and Paul, and they remained the closest bandmates imaginable, a strong all-for-one-and-one-for-all, but, as George would put it, 'An attitude came over John and Paul of "We're the grooves and you two just watch it". They never said that, or did anything, but over a period of time . . .'[58]

By September there had never been so many self-written songs in the Beatles' set. Though they still weren't doing Please Please Me, there was Love Me Do, PS I Love You, Ask Me Why, Tip Of My Tongue and two other new ones. The first was I'll Be On My Way, a Hollyesque number from Paul's harvest of '59. Then, it was a sweet melody written on his old Zenith, but not much more; now it was developed into a Beatles group number, inspired by the new sound of the Jumbo Gibsons. John played one here, while George came up with a middle-eight solo on his Gretsch and incorporated into a new intro the magical E-augmented chord from Goffin-King's Don't Ever Change. Though John sang lead vocal with Paul, side by side in harmonised duet, he never liked I'll Be On My Way, and revealed this when they got to the line 'this way will I go' – he pulled a crip face and hunched himself Quasimodo-like around the microphone. Paul had no choice but to ride the laughter.[59]

The second new song, Hold Me Tight, was another McCartney-Lennon – Paul's contributions to the partnership were easily outnumbering John's. He'd remember them developing it together in the front parlour at Forthlin Road, and also that it was 'a failed attempt at a single'. Please Please Me and Tip Of My Tongue had been written with an EMI *session* in mind but Hold Me Tight was possibly the first time one of them wrote specifically for a 45. It never made it. There's no information about what the song sounded like at this point, but it was probably similar to the recording made a few months later, a frenetic piece with a pulsating bass line, a tempo to match the newly fast Please Please Me and a vocal arrangement that was, as Paul would describe it, 'A bit Shirelles'.[60]

In 1958, the notion of 'Lennon and McCartney' came from Rodgers and Hammerstein, Lerner and Loewe and the other songwriting duos of renown, but by September 1962 it was much more Goffin and King, the young New York husband-and-wife team whose songs, all post-1960, John and Paul revered like no others. They were of the same generation, lyricist Gerry Goffin born the year before John, musician and singer Carole King born four months before

Paul. Goffin and King had mastered the difficult balance of craftsmanship and commerciality, writing songs that made listeners buoyant and happy even when the words weren't obviously so. In these vital respects, their influence on the music of Lennon and McCartney – especially the songs of the next couple of years – would be pronounced. John could not have made the connection or aspiration any clearer when he said (in 1971), 'When Paul and I first got together, we wanted to be the British Goffin and King.'[61]

In September, the Beatles put a sixth Goffin-King song into their set. The Loco-Motion was a million-selling US number 1 and British number 2 for the singer Little Eva, a dance-floor smash that urged people to snake around ballrooms in a long train. The legacy of the Twist, which made the record business and much of the public dance-mad, was still holding sway. John and Paul sang its lead vocal in unison, as they did in Some Other Guy, and George stepped forward to join Paul at the second mike, head to head, for the girl-group backing vocal – but there's no recording and no further information to say if they rearranged it.

Other new numbers in the set were nabbed by George, maintaining their year-long format of stage equilibrium, one vocal from each of the front line in turn. He added two in September and, strangely – and in a timely fashion – the first was by Buddy Holly and the other was very Holly-like. The second of these was a song called Sheila, strongly reminiscent of Peggy Sue but written and sung by the Atlanta-born Tommy Roe; it made number 1 in America and 2 in Britain (where, like The Loco-Motion, it was kept off the top by the Tornados' space-age instrumental Telstar). The Beatles didn't rearrange it but stuck to the record and did it virtually as a two-hander: George sang and played guitar and Ringo hit the toms fast from start to finish. Ringo had yet to sing with the Beatles, but – piece by piece, song by song – the Beatles' set was evolving into one that was exclusive to his drumming, numbers Pete hadn't played.

The new Buddy Holly song was Reminiscing, which happily combined for the Beatles two blasts from the past: great Holly music, to remind them who they were and *why* they were, and also the sound of the Coasters. King Curtis – who played sax on Yakety Yak, Besame Mucho, Three Cool Cats and Young Blood – did so again here on Reminiscing, recorded in 1958, five months before Buddy Holly was killed at the age of 22, and unissued until now. George introduced it as 'Reminiscing-ing-ing-ing', which always got a laugh, and he replicated Curtis's sax solo on his Gretsch, using the lower strings to produce a more rasping sound than the Beatles usually featured.[62]

Through all this time, Brian was having difficulties with Granada TV. He wanted to build promotion around the broadcast of the Cavern film, but the company wouldn't schedule a date and Brian felt his enquiries were being fobbed off. Granada's problem, concealed for the moment, was that the essential contrasting element in this edition of *Know The North* – film of the Brighouse and Rastrick Brass Band – would be too expensive to screen. Only belatedly had Granada realised that showing it would necessitate paying Musicians' Union fees to every one of the thirty bandsmen – a budget-busting proposition. Without this contrast, there was no other vehicle for showing the Beatles, and when Brian demanded to know what was going on, Leslie Woodhead was forced into confessing the problem. As he recalls, 'I said in desperation, "I'll try and get the boys in the studio to do something, as a kind of consolation prize," and this led to their first appearance on *People And Places*.'[63]

While the Cavern film was shelved indefinitely, Woodhead urged his colleague David Baker – producer of Granada's live evening magazine show – to see the Beatles. He drove from Manchester to the Cavern on 3 October and booked them on the spot to broadcast two weeks later, the 17th. It would be another vital breakthrough: the Beatles' first TV appearance, plugging their new record at tea-time right across the north of England.

If it was possible for Brian to exert himself even more, now that Love Me Do was scheduled, he did. His focus was Friday 5 October, and through the second half of September he built a runway so it could take off.

The emphasis was on publicity – by way of photographs, press materials and promotions. Brian himself (anonymously) wrote the Beatles' first biography, two pages run off on a duplicator and mailed out by the score. He didn't know the history terribly well and relied on them to tell him the background facts – and since they were never good at remembering their own details, some of it went down wrong (e.g., they met in 1956), was used by journalists, and would stay wrong for at least the next twenty years. As only two types of band – instrumental groups and vocal groups – were familiar in the music business or understood by the media, Brian had to fashion a sentence to describe what the Beatles did: 'They form essentially a vocal group but at the same time they comprise musicians of the first order.'

He also got Beryl Adams to type two further pages headed WRITINGS OF JOHN LENNON, three pieces that showed off the Beatles as not just a beat group but an *offbeat* beat group. Brian put on top the one that explained the origin of a name everyone still thought very strange and off-putting, a name that, not many weeks earlier, London people were telling him should be ditched or they'd never be successful ('Many people ask what are Beatles? Why Beatles? Ugh, Beatles, how did the name arrive? So we will tell you. It came in a vision – a man appeared on a flaming pie and said unto them "From this day on you are Beatles with an A". Thank you, Mister Man, they said, thanking him').

The press materials were rounded out with four questionnaires, similar to a weekly *NME* feature called Life-lines, where the Beatles showed themselves individually, each detailing his personal information, likes, dislikes, hobbies and interests.

All this was good as far as it went, but Brian sensed he needed more. EMI, Decca, Pye, Philips and the lesser companies were issuing vatfuls of vinyl every week, very few of which became hits. Between January and the start of September 1962, the magazine of Brian's business, *Record Retailer*, listed 4500 new singles, an average of 128 a week (the LP figure was almost eighty a week and rising fast), so Love Me Do would drown unless it was noticed. Once again, Brian approached the convivial Tony Barrow, who combined freelance journalism with a full-time job at Decca, writing LP and EP sleevenotes.

> Brian was meticulous and comprehensive in the way he launched the Beatles. He said to me, 'I've done this and I've done that ... is there anything else you can think of, as a record reviewer yourself, that I could be doing?' I said that apart from the bumf I got from record companies, I also received material from one or two independent PRs, the doyen being Les Perrin. I suggested he might hire an independent PR to put out some press information. He then said, 'Could *you* do that for me?' I said yes, I could.[64]

Barrow was 26, newly married, prolific and hungry – and, vitally, though he lived and worked in London, he remained closely allied to his home town as 'Disker' in the *Liverpool Echo*, the column he'd written every Saturday since he was 17. He couldn't openly work for Brian, plugging an EMI record from a Decca desk, but he'd do it anonymously: he agreed to write the Beatles a first-class independent press package and reckoned he could get hold of a mailing list detailing every record reviewer in the country. His provider was Tony Calder, who'd just left Decca's press office to set himself up as an independent publicist and promoter, based in Soho. Barrow guessed right: Calder had taken for himself a copy of Decca's master mailing list. 'I cut a deal with him that we put his address on the press release – Tony Calder Enterprises, 15 Poland Street, London W1 – and then I wrote it, designed it and got it printed and he sent it out to everyone. Brian paid me £20, I gave some to Tony, and he passed any resulting enquiries on to me.'

This affiliation with Calder would be fortuitous because the young man was also a DJ, spinning records at some of London's busiest ballrooms; if he liked Love Me Do, he'd play it, effecting the Beatles' first thrust into the capital. For now, he just mailed out Tony Barrow's press pack, an impressive five-page document called Introducing THE BEATLES, with a photographic cover printed on pink card so it stood out from the pile – a trick he'd got from the doyen Perrin.

Every relevant media outlet received the first, second or even third press mailing announcing the Beatles' arrival. The third was EMI's, a densely typed three-page biography that drew largely on the other two but also added unique material, particularly some interesting quotes by Brian Epstein. Here occurs the first simplified redressing of how the Beatles had got their Parlophone contract: Brian explained he'd wanted some tapes transferred to disc at the HMV record shop and . . . 'As soon as the people there heard the tapes they advised me to get in touch with George Martin.' As unaware as Brian probably was of the fullest facts, this was clearly an easier story.

Like Brian had done before him, so again now EMI press officer Syd Gillingham pointed out what made the Beatles musically different from everyone else – he went for the underline key to explain that they were 'singers and instrumentalists'. It was also of interest that two of them – just two, John and Paul – specified their ambitions: John's was 'money and everything', Paul's 'money, etc'. Here was an honesty rarely, if ever, seen in a pop PR handout, where the common ambition was 'to become an all-round entertainer'. Finally, Gillingham made much of another unusual aspect of the Beatles – that they were from the north. He mentioned Liverpool twelve times in three pages.

This concerted push to be different – we're from Liverpool: yeah, *Liverpool* – was given great weight by publicity photos that set the Beatles hard on the dock road in bleak industrial surroundings, pictures that showed them as they were: four unaffected, bright working-class lads. This was a time when pretty much every pop publicity photo was formulaic and studio-bound – groomed star pretending to be on phone, groomed star checking tie in mirror, groomed star holding record or a disconnected microphone – but here, suddenly and by unmissable contrast, was a set of black-and-white images like stills from *Coronation Street* or a gritty new northern film.

Three locations were chosen by Les Chadwick of the Liverpool photography company Peter Kaye. The first was Sefton Street, by Brunswick Dock, at a bleak, still-unimproved Second World War bombsite called the Bally. Nature had kindly provided a burned-out car in the middle and the Beatles stood about it, with and without their instruments. It was a weird new experience – standing in the rain, having photos taken, holding poses – but they were definitely on home turf. As they worked, a bunch of scallies sagging off school (just like they'd done) threw stones at them from behind a wall. 'We were all shouting at them to fuck off out of it,' Chadwick says.[65]

He'd chosen the location purely for its visual impact, but connections and history are everywhere in Liverpool. The Bally was next door to where Paul had a job the Christmas before last, second man on a parcel-delivering lorry for SPD Ltd. One building beyond that was the ship repair company J. W. Pickering &

Sons Ltd, where Johnny Starkey had worked – Ringo's beloved and bereaved grandad, who'd loaned his 'bloody Noddler' the cash for his first real drum kit, and whose wedding ring in death became the lad's third in life, prompting the stage name that earned him his living.

The next location was going to be the Pier Head, but Chadwick stopped just short, at the moored SS *Salvor*. It was a salvage boat of the kind sailed by John's late grandad, George Stanley. Chadwick wanted photos with the Liver Building rising proud in the misty background, and went aboard to get the captain's permission to take a few photos with them there four young fellers. On they all went, leaning over railings, balls frozen in the Mersey's bitter wind, posing on deck while the *Salvor*'s muscly seamen – wisecracking wackers in oily overalls – stood behind them and queried their gender.

The last of the three stops was wasteland in front of a vast brick-stone warehouse up by Clarence Graving Dock. Photos for London, shot two hundred miles north in narrow-fitting suits on a strip of cold rubble between Saltney Street and Dublin Street. It must have felt a long way from glamour.

The location's significance was unknown to John. He had no idea of the history beneath his feet, that he was standing exactly where the Lennons had settled in Liverpool not much more than a hundred years earlier: great-grandad James Lennon from County Down, one among the multitude of disease-ridden Irish fleeing famine and death at home. The Lennons were *here*, in the shit-stinking cholera-infested court-housing of which only about now was Liverpool finally free.

Brian studied the contact sheets, said the photos were excellent and ran a chinagraph pencil around several, expecting Chadwick – who'd never done this kind of thing before – to make prints and throwaway cards by the hundred. He also had to make throwaways of the four individual Beatles, for which Paul and Ringo had done special sittings – a protracted business all its own.[66]

In the midst of all this activity, Brian stopped writing *Mersey Beat*'s record review column, and fell out decisively with Sam Leach in a manner symbolic of severing an umbilical cord. The pioneering Liverpool promoter maintained his reputation for paying the debts of his last show with the proceeds of his next, and Brian decided it had happened once too often. The Beatles did a £35 booking for Leach at the Rialto Ballroom in Toxteth on 6 September, but when the night was over he could only find them £16; as Brian accounted to the Beatles in full every Friday, he was left personally out of pocket – for longer than was right. Leach had booked the Beatles again for New Brighton on the 14th, and beforehand, in the dressing-room, Brian demanded both that night's £35 and his still-owed £19. When Leach said he couldn't pay, Brian said they wouldn't play. He hated letting down the public and would try to make it up to them, but the problem was not of his making. Leach looked appealingly to the Beatles to carry his defence, but they didn't – at least, not enough to make the difference they could have made.

There was no one but Brian to shoulder the burdens. On 25 September, the post delivered him a Letter before Action. It came from Fentons, an old established firm of Liverpool solicitors, and said that unless their client was paid an unspecified amount of compensation he would be suing Brian for 'unwarranted and unjustifiable dismissal'. More than a month after being drummed out, Pete Best was making it a legal affair.[67]

Fentons claimed that the management contract of 1 February 1962 bound Mr Epstein to their client Mr Best, that he was legally liable to provide their client with paid engagements, that he was in breach of contract by dismissing their client, and that if he didn't pay their client damages, he would take action.* Brian turned the letter over to David Harris and the lawyer hit a forehand back into Fentons' court: 'The position is that your client was not dismissed by the company, which has always held itself out to provide engagements for your client, and he was so informed. Indeed, Mr Epstein was in the position of making necessary arrangements for him to be placed with another group ...'

This first volley (which alluded to Brian's attempt to put Pete in the Mersey Beats) would soon be followed by two other lines of attack. One (citing George Martin's objections) was that Pete 'had not proven himself to have the necessary talent to fulfil his obligations'; the other was that 'With regard to the Beatles, there was no question of dismissal. Your client agreed to leave, and the group reformed itself.'

Here then was the fallback position so carefully considered between June and August, when the issue of how to dismiss Pete had been assessed. The Beatles had split up and re-formed. It was a strange one, a moment that occurred only in the blink of a legal eye, but, this lawyer argued, it *had* happened: the Beatles had broken up, voiding the management contract, then added Ringo and instantly got back together again.

The timing of all this was odd, because it happened just after Pete joined another group, Lee Curtis and the All Stars, managed by Brian's friend Joe Flannery. It was Colonel Joe who'd jumped the gun in June or July, dropping big hints to Pete about his imminent dismissal from the Beatles even though he'd learned the news in confidence. Once the deed had been done, he went back and offered Pete a job.

---

* With some possible bearing on the legal situation, Pete was also wondering whether the recordings of Love Me Do and PS I Love You shortly to be issued by Parlophone were from the 6 June session, with him on drums. He wouldn't establish the facts of this until a few days into October.

Pete made his All Stars debut at the Majestic Ballroom, Birkenhead, on 10 September, and *Mersey Beat* was soon quoting him enthusing 'I've never enjoyed playing so much', a statement as unbelievable as the one saying he'd left the Beatles amicably. The truth was, it would never be a position that brought him much pleasure. Lee Curtis loved the limelight – he was the singer, the hunk out front, advertised by his brother Joe as 'Merseyside's biggest heart-throb!' – and he didn't appreciate seeing his name trumped by a drummer, as in Joe's newest ads:

> We've Got The Best!
> Yes – Great Ex-Beatle Drummer

This was both the first time anyone would be referred to in print as an 'Ex-Beatle' and an annoyance to Pete. 'I often spoke to Joe Flannery about it,' he'd say. 'There was no way I wanted to be tagged an *ex-Beatle*.'[68]

He'd find the link inescapable. As well as the Majestic and the Cavern, the All Stars played the jive circuit the Beatles had left behind, places like Blair Hall, Holyoake Hall and Litherland Town Hall, which advertised his appearance as 'Welcome Home Pete'.[69] Like the Colonel, Pete hoped his Beatles fans would follow him across. Lee Curtis remembers him saying, '"Curtis" – he often called me Curtis – "let's see who gets the most fans now then." I thought he meant between him and me, but later I analysed it and thought maybe he meant between the Beatles and the All Stars.'[70]

It didn't happen. Plenty had loved Pete in the Beatles and been upset when he went, but they didn't follow him – they stayed with the Beatles and he became a drummer much like any other, in a group much like any other. Vivien Jones was one such fan, a girl who'd loved Pete but never saw him again: 'I was upset when the Beatles got rid of Pete (the rumour I heard was that he was "too handsome") but then I got over it. It wasn't a big deal really: we still carried on seeing the Beatles and I didn't follow Pete any more, and nor did any of my friends.'[71]

A lesson was learned from Brian's legal difficulty with Pete. The management contract as revised had a clause unconsidered way back in January – it allowed for one or two members of the Beatles to be kicked out at the desire of two or more other members of the Beatles, though only with Brian's approval. It needed to be there, but no one had any plan to use it. Otherwise, the new contract was substantially the same as the original agreement of 1 February, varied by Brian's letter of instruction of 18 August, the one he dictated immediately after Pete's firing.

There were two parties – Nems Enterprises Ltd, called 'the Manager', and the four named Beatles, called 'the Artists' (as Paul and George were under 21, their fathers were parties to the second part). The Artists appointed the Manager for five years from 1 October 1962, an appointment that could be ended by either party with three months' written notice.

In return for continuing the job he'd started, the Manager would take 15 per cent commission if the Artists collectively earned up to £400 a week, 20 per cent between £400 and £800, and 25 per cent above that. The unwritten sub-text was that, as Brian would also be fulfilling the duties of an agent, no further commissions were due anyone else – these percentages would be the Beatles' total outlay.

It was a clear and concise document, six pages followed by space for signatures. Everyone gathered in the Whitechapel office for the big moment, standing round Brian's desk behind which he'd pinned a huge wall map of Great Britain as if planning a national campaign – which he was.

There are no photos of the signing. Copies of the bound contract began to circulate, receiving the signatures of Brian Epstein and C. J. Epstein as director and secretary of Nems Enterprises Limited, the second serving as witness to the first; and also of John W. Lennon, George Harrison, James Paul McCartney and Richard Starkey, and of Harold Hargreaves Harrison and J. McCartney, those six signatures all witnessed by Beryl Adams.

Either at this session or privately, the separate agreement between Nems Enterprises, John Lennon and Paul McCartney was also signed and witnessed, the one covering the songwriting 'sideline'. All this – the record, the contracts, everything – was happening precisely a year after the Nerk Twins' exclusive sojourn to Paris. It had been a fantastic twelve months, and the future seemed even brighter.

There was, however, one last thing nagging away at Brian. The Beatles' launch was covered with no fewer than three press releases aimed at all branches of the record business and its consumers, but he'd no mainstream PR, nothing to get them into the daily papers. One night at the end of September, in the Blue Angel night-club, he mentioned this to Allan Williams, and Williams said he might have the answer – he offered to introduce Brian to his friend William (Bill) Marshall, the *Daily Mirror*'s northern correspondent.

A boozer and hell-raiser of genuinely extreme proportions, Bill Marshall could usually be found in the Liverpool Press Club, the city's best late-late boozing establishment, opposite Lime Street station. Membership of this male-only fug was theoretically limited to journalists – to the local scribes and provincial stringers for the nationals – but it also extended to those whose face fitted, including Allan Williams and the Chief Constable of Liverpool (which meant the place was never raided). Stepping into the Press Club was a big risk for Brian because policemen were here, as well as journalists from the court gallery when he was 'Mr X' ... but he liked risks, ventured inside, and – in a stupefyingly drunken night with Marshall and a second man, *Daily Mail* photographer Len Ford – discussed the possibility of setting up a company Marshall wanted to call Publicity Ink. Brian recalled the moment a couple of years later in his autobiography, describing the 'two Rabelaisians' who would pull 'stunts, gimmicks, rows, scenes – anything to get the name of my artistes in the papers'.

Publicity Ink would be a rare deviation from Brian's customary upright path ... and then the next morning's black coffee sobered him. That way was fake sensations, phoney rumours, lies, scams and 'rubbish like that'. That way was the old way, the way of Larry Parnes and his ilk; that way would have debased the Beatles.

Brian's way was truth and integrity, and he would never regret it. As his ghostwriter Derek Taylor put it in 1964, artfully capturing his master's voice, 'I'm glad now, for it enables me to say that I never pulled one stunt to publicise any of my artistes.'[72] Of course, Brian knew too he was completely in tune with his boys: the Beatles didn't want any of that pretence or artificial nonsense either.

The overnight death of Publicity Ink meant the Beatles would be going out to the nation like no one else: with their own sound, their own songs, their own style and look, their own personalities – challenging the way things were done by doing things *their* way, honestly, as themselves.

32

Friday 5 October 1962 – The Sixties Start Here

1. Pop music is not despicable, it is simply immature

The 56-year-old no-nonsense aunt who told John Lennon he could never earn a living from the guitar heard in Love Me Do no reason to change her mind. John took the record to Woolton and played it for his ex-guardian, asking, 'What do you think, Mimi?' As she'd enjoy remembering, 'I told him, "If you think you are going to make your name with that, you've made a big mistake!"' Mimi liked My Bonnie, and how many had *that* sold?[1]

In other houses across Liverpool's south end there was celebration for Paul, George and Richy, and family pride – the boys were really on their way now. Misgivings were maintained at the Epsteins', however, where two parents and two sons gathered in Queenie's cut-glass lounge so Brian could put Love Me Do on the gramophone. After it finished, his heart engaged his tongue for a new spin on the year-old message: his boys 'were going to be bigger than Elvis' and Love Me Do was the first giant leap towards it. Even Clive, his biggest supporter, had to accept it all seemed highly improbable.[2]

For John, Paul, George and Ringo, it was a satisfyingly *single* moment. Here, from Friday 5 October, was a disc seven inches in diameter that said and played Beatles: black plastic, red labels, silver lettering and Parlophone's seemingly patriotic £ trademark. They stared at it so long they memorised the catalogue number, R4949. It was also, of course, an extra-special experience for the fans. Elsa Breden had just shelled out for her precious purchase when she ran into George. 'I said to him, "I can't believe you're on a record!" and he said, "Neither can I!"'[3]

For Ringo it was *'The* most momentous moment – that we had a record out, that we had a bit of plastic with us on it. Just the idea of being on a bit of plastic was really incredible after all those years of playing. My God, a record that you hadn't made in some booth somewhere ... you don't *believe* how great that was.'[4]

Back in May, when somehow they'd got hitched to Parlophone, the Beatles had hoped to be the first group to put R&B-like harmonica on record. And despite the interim hits by Frank Ifield and Brian Hyland – and the long, long while from May to October – they'd succeeded. Ringo was also relieved to have proof he *was* the drummer. It still hurt that he was merely shaking maracas on PS I Love You, but Love Me Do was easily the more important side. The Parlophone labels did carry an error, though, a big one, one that completely screwed up the just-taken decision about composer identities. Contrary to Brian's instructions on the publishing agreement, Love Me Do and PS I Love You had been credited not to McCartney-Lennon but to Lennon-McCartney.

It is (and is likely to remain) intriguingly unclear whose error this was. The Parlophone office's? EMI's label-printing department at the Hayes factory? Brian's, for not returning the contract in time? Ardmore and Beechwood's, for not notifying Parlophone in time? Whichever, Paul had to accept being named second when both the songs were substantially his. He was at least spared one further and much worse blunder: on the 250 advance/promotional copies of the record he'd been McArtney. (Paul James really *would* have been so much easier.)

The release of their first record bump-landed the Beatles in the business – two businesses to be exact, music (publishing) and records. Both were set and shaped long before the rise of the electric guitar, and what would become 'the rock industry' hadn't yet been catapulted into existence; this was still very much old-showbiz, a bizarre body of limbs of which pop was the leprous leg. In the words of Norman Jopling, 18-year-old office boy and fledgling writer on *New Record Mirror*, 'Pop was seen as a branch of show business you were expected to "grow out of", whether you were a fan or a performer. It wasn't felt to have *any* artistry or creativity.' The *Daily Express* pop/entertainment writer Judith Simons reflects how 'Everyone looked down on pop, no doubt about it. They thought it was yobbos singing for yobbos.'[5]

This was also George Melly's conclusion, printed in *New Society*. Perfectly timed to analyse a seismic decade, the weekly sociological journal was launched on 4 October 1962, and in its third issue the Liverpool-born jazz singer wrote an astute paper on the workings of pop. According to him, the artists and consumers were *despised* by the record business that made its money from them – a fact denied in public, naturally, but which he'd heard spoken in private. Melly announced they were wrong to think this way, shrewdly observing, 'Pop music is not despicable, it is simply immature.'[6]

EMI's records division was but one part of its global business, pop one part of its records division, and Love Me Do one of its ten new releases on 5 October. Success was defined as two or three of the ten becoming hits, and while every record was pushed, some were pushed more – and the Beatles weren't favoured with any priority.

Love Me Do lacked support inside EMI House. George Martin says that when he mentioned the name 'Beatles' to colleagues – to his fellow A&R men, sales managers and promotion staff – there were gales of laughter. 'It was,' he would concede, 'a *silly* name. They all thought it was another of my Goon jokes, a comedy record, and that I was spoofing them. Nobody believed in it [Love Me Do] at all.'[7] This apathy extended to George himself, who broke down no walls to push the record he didn't like and which Ardmore and Beechwood had forced him to issue.

Success required exposure, and this meant getting Love Me Do played on radio and television. The BBC, one of Britain's two TV channels, gave pop music thirty minutes a week: *Juke Box Jury* early on Saturday evenings. The job of getting Parlophone records played on here belonged to Alma Warren, the only female 'exploitation man' in the business, and she had no success at all, just as she also failed to get Love Me Do into any BBC radio show. The Light Programme played a shade under thirteen hours of 'popular records' a week – the lion's share of the BBC's 'Needletime' allowance as set down by record companies and the Musicians' Union.* Almost every one of these records was what would eventually be known as MOR – middle of the road music. Warren went to see the various programme producers and got the same reaction everywhere. As she would recall, 'The Beatles' very name was anathema to the BBC. "*Beatles?* What's *that* supposed to be?"'[8] It wasn't only the BBC that thought this way – Warren was also unable to persuade any commercial TV programme to play the record, failing with the one and only networked pop show *Thank Your Lucky Stars*.

The sole remaining way of getting Love Me Do to a mass audience was commercial radio – and this meant Radio Luxembourg. The policy of the

---

* In October 1962, the BBC was in the process of negotiating an easing of Needletime restrictions, from the existing twenty-eight hours a week for the domestic radio services (twenty-two hours for the networks and six for the regions) to a whopping seventy-five, which would have enabled a complete rethink of its approach to playing records. The Musicians' Union was having none of it ... and under the agreement finally reached in November 1963, the BBC ended up paying more for no extra hours. It would remain this way until other circumstances forced changes in 1964 and 1967.

station's British service was (as it had been for some years) to relinquish much of its airtime to 'sponsored programmes', wherein record companies hired big-name DJs to showcase new releases. EMI put on twenty-three such shows a week, recorded in Mayfair and flown out to Luxembourg for transmission back. Records were faded early to discourage home-taping and encourage actual sales.

EMI's promotions department decided the number of Luxembourg plugs to apportion each record per week, the maximum being seven; Love Me Do was granted two each for three weeks, six in all – after which, if it hadn't started to swim, it was considered sunk. EMI would pump Love Me Do's heart no more from the end of October. There was one interesting decision, though: in the second week, one of the two Luxembourg spots was to be in a programme where the Beatles made a personal appearance.

No one noted the precise moment a Beatles record was first played on radio, but there was a colourful Harrison household anecdote about it. It happened in the week ending Friday 5 October; George told his mum and dad it might be on and asked if they'd listen because he had to go and play a gig. They waited for hours, inevitably experiencing the ordeal of every Luxembourg listener, when the 208 medium-wave frequency went a-wandering off to 207 or 209 or paused for a cigarette at 212. Harry had an early shift on the buses and went to bed, and Louise followed when George returned home. He burst into their room a short time later, clutching the radio and shouting, 'We're on! We're on!' 'Who's brought that noisy gramophone in here?' Harry grouched. For George, it was one of life's biggest moments. As he'd say more than thirty years later, 'First hearing Love Me Do on the radio sent me shivery all over. It was the best buzz of all time.'[9]

Then there was the press. The trade magazine for the British music and record-shop businesses was *Record Retailer*, and suddenly, out of nowhere, EMI splashed a full-page ad to announce the Beatles' arrival. This was hardly ever done . . . and Brian had paid for it, not from Nems Enterprises funds but Nems itself, the retail company which had a prosperous two-way account with EMI. But when Brian wasn't injecting Nems' money, EMI barely bothered. Love Me Do wasn't in the company's pan-label ad that ran in prime position next to the *NME* Top Thirty, and it wasn't even reviewed in EMI's own monthly *Record Mail* – a particularly odd omission. EMI advertised the record in only one other place, *The World's Fair*, to be seen by juke-box operators. There were eleven thousand juke-boxes in cafés and coffee bars around Britain and Love Me Do would pick up steady action; the paper reviewed records to help box-stockists make their choices, and the best appreciations of Love Me Do, two of them, ran here.

A most promising first disc from a Liverpool combination. I have already been asked for this in Liverpool and it is a pleasure to be able to buy it solely on merit. Good luck boys.

Commercial folksy sound, not unlike the very successful Springfields. Quite a catchy little tune, which strongly features the now almost inevitable harmonica. Sounds very much like a big hit to me.[10]

The week the Beatles' first record was released, the charts featured nothing remotely like them, and nothing sounding like Love Me Do. The NME Top Thirty had the Tornados' zippy instrumental Telstar at number 1, and after that it was solo artists all the way down to 23, which was another instrumental, by the Shadows. Buddy Holly was at 18 with Reminiscing, Karl Denver yodelled some country music at 30, and that was about it. Seen in this light, Love Me Do – with melodic harmonies, acoustic guitar, bass, drums and harmonica, an appealingly bluesy little love song that wasn't happy and also wasn't sad – stood out far from the crowd.

The Beatles never said if they were surprised that London people didn't *get them* right away. The four weekly music papers, the ones they'd all read or leafed through since schooldays, took a while to tune in. Despite being mailed the record and up to three press releases, *Melody Maker* and the NME didn't review Love Me Do; the other two did, but they made a point of logging all new records.

Disc. The Beatles sound rather like the Everlys or the Brooks [Brook Brothers] according to whose side you're on. But in Love Me Do they have got a deceptively simple beater which could grow on you. Harmonica backing. PS I Love You weaves a little Latin into itself as the boys sing a letter ballad of everyday sentiments. (From Disc Date with Don Nicholl, in a section of brief reviews headed Short and Sharp. Rated two stars, meaning 'Ordinary'.)

New Record Mirror. Harmonica again starts off Love Me Do and then this strangely-monikered group gets at the lyrics. Fairly restrained in their approach, they indulge in some offbeat combinations of vocal chords. Though there's plenty happening, it tends to drag about mid-way, especially when the harmonica takes over for a spell. Not a bad song, though. Fairly straight-forward group handling of a poorish arrangement for the flip. The song stands up well enough but things don't happen frequently enough to make us interested. (Writer not identified. Rated three bells, meaning 'Average'.)[11]

Love Me Do's most positive and supportive review was by Tony Barrow in the *Liverpool Echo*. Under the headline BIG DATE FOR THE BEATLES, illustrated with a session photo, he enthused about both sides, pointing out the 'refreshing do-it-yourself approach' – the Beatles wrote it, they played it, they sang it. The most grudging critique ran in *Mersey Beat*. Brian had recently stopped reviewing for Bill Harry's paper and these words ran without a byline: 'Although Love Me Do is rather monotonous, it is the type of number which grows on you, and I have found that whilst I felt disappointed when I first heard it, I enjoyed it more and more each time I played it. Of the two numbers, PS I Love You is the side I prefer.'[12]

The most perceptive review was in *Record Retailer*, which (thanks to the press releases) flagged that the Beatles 'already have a strong following'.[13] Certainly this was worth mentioning. The Beatles were the first recording artists post-war (and probably pre-war as well) launched with an already thriving sales base. The business had never been geared this way – singers were always 'discovered' and then promoted in the usual clichéd ways. Britain's biggest star by far, Cliff Richard, was a new performer with a new name when he made his first record in 1958; he had no pre-established fan following and almost no stage experience. The Beatles couldn't have been in greater contrast: they'd done everything in every way for years, and in Liverpool had a core of support the envy of anyone, a lovingly loyal battalion of fans who swiftly made their presence felt. As Ringo would enjoy remembering, with only slight exaggeration, 'The whole of Liverpool went out and bought it, en masse. They were proud of it: a group from Liverpool. It was fantastic – there's a lot of that in Liverpool, they're very close.'[14]

A few fans did hold out, gutted to think the Beatles would become famous and leave them, but the great majority couldn't stop themselves and rushed right in. As Bobby Brown says, 'I bought it at Nems. It was really exciting to buy "a Beatles record". We wanted *everyone* to buy it.' Club member and newly appointed Nems Enterprises secretary Freda Kelly was also among the first in line: 'All the Cavernites bought Love Me Do. I bought it and didn't even have a record player. People bought it to get it in the charts.'[15]

Love Me Do began to sell the moment the boxes were opened – not just at Nems but all over Merseyside, and not just on Merseyside but in pockets of the north-west, in places the Beatles had played and places they hadn't. This great news was conveyed to Brian by a regular business contact, John Mair, rep for the record distribution firm Lugton's.

I was in Liverpool the day Love Me Do came out and was walking along Whitechapel as Brian was getting out of his car. I knew the record was already selling in box quantities but it was too soon yet for him to have heard this, so I broke the news to him. His face *beamed* – it was going to be a hit! I told him it was selling across the north-west – even in Lancaster, Morecambe, Barrow-in-Furness and Kendal – and it was, and he was delighted to hear it. 'Oh really? That's *wonderful!*' He was *so* excited – suddenly he was not the cool, imperious, arrogant Brian I knew, he was like a schoolboy. His reaction was one of 'Oh my God, I've been *right*.' It was one of the nice moments in my career.[16]

North-west sales this first Friday and Saturday – with the epicentre in Liverpool – sent Love Me Do straight into the Top Fifty, the one compiled for the following Thursday's *Record Retailer*. It snuck in at 49. Big locally, small nationally – but enough to get them in and get them noticed. It was a dent, and a recognised victory: the Shadows hadn't made the chart with their first record, or the Tornados. Brian called all these moments *ultimates*, and their rate was increasing . . . the contract, the record, getting into the chart.[17]

So freakish was all of this, rumours quickly took grip that Brian was *hyping the chart*, buying in boxes of Love Me Do to fake its position. The strongest story had him buying ten thousand. It was a rumour that clung despite Brian trying to shake it off – no one would believe he hadn't, and denial only fed suspicion – and it wouldn't be long before the whole business was talking about it, unfairly casting a blight on his integrity because it wasn't true. As John Lennon would explain, 'It [Love Me Do] sold so many in Liverpool the first two days – because they were all waiting for us to make it – that the dealers down in London thought there was a fiddle on. "That Mr Epstein feller up there is cheating." But he wasn't.'[18]

Many in Liverpool felt sure of it too. As the Beatles began to go national, so Brian began to find he'd fewer friends than he thought. Gossip about 'the ten thousand' was traded maliciously and without proof by people jealous of his success or keen to claim 'insider' status. No one considered Brian's membership of a committee (within the Gramophone Record Retailers Association) that challenged suspicions of chart malpractice, or his resistance to faking My Bonnie into even his own shop's published Top Twenty, or – most striking of all – the fact that, in 1962, it made no difference how many copies a shop sold of any record because the charts weren't computed that way. Nems had been a 'chart return' operation for years – it still provided data to *Melody Maker* and also now to *Record Retailer* – but those papers' weekly phone calls or printed questionnaires didn't ask for sales figures, only for a shop's bestselling records ranked from 1 to 30; the papers awarded thirty points to the number 1 record down to one point for the number 30, and calculated an overall national total.

All the charts were produced this way, as they still were in America. Brian Epstein had no need to buy ten thousand Love Me Dos to fake it into the charts; he didn't even need to buy one. He *did* buy a couple of thousand copies, because the majority of Beatles fans wanted to buy it from Nems' three stores, and because he was the manager and agent of this band and EMI had sent him one free copy.[19]

Beyond all the mud-slinging, however, one important fact remained, the one that counted: the Beatles were in the charts. They had a foot on the ladder. It was one small step, but they were going national.

2. Nuneaton, North Cheam and New York – it happened right here

The day the Sixties broke out, the Beatles were in Nuneaton, playing the art deco Co-op Ballroom. They were in the Midlands, a hundred miles south of Liverpool: different accents, another dot on Brian Epstein's campaign map. It was standard format that at least one local act would flesh out the bills and on this occasion it was a Rugby-based group called the Mighty Avengers; as their drummer, David 'Biffo' Beech, would relate, the Beatles dropped into their world as if from another planet. 'We did our little bit – covers of Cliff and stuff like that – but as soon as they came on, the whole place stopped. They sounded so different to blokes like us who were doing the usual thing. People just stood there and thought, "Crikey, who are *these?*"'[20]

One hundred and twenty miles further south again, at the same moment, a rhythm and blues group called the Rolling Stones were playing their tenth gig. It was, just, their first outside London, performing for two hours to an audience of two people in the back room of a pub in North Cheam, Surrey – a place called the Woodstock. Their £15 fee was split five ways, and the booking was fixed by Brian Jones because they didn't have a manager.

The music papers wrote only about chart acts, so the Beatles didn't know of the Rolling Stones – or the Rollin' Stones as Jones preferred it – but the Stones were about to hear the Beatles and experience a shock. On a black-tie New York night twenty-five years later, when Mick Jagger made the speech inducting the Beatles into the Rock and Roll Hall of Fame (an institution ludicrously improbable in 1962), he said:

> England was a real wasteland. England had nothing really to offer as far as pop music was concerned. The Stones were playing little clubs in London – doing Chuck Berry songs and blues and things – and we thought we were

totally unique animals, [that] there was no one like us. And then we heard there was a group from *Liverpool*. They had long hair, scruffy clothes and a record contract, and they had a record in the charts, with a bluesy harmonica on it, called Love Me Do – when I heard the combination of all these things, I was almost sick.[21]

R&B's popularity had been building steadily through 1962 in London and a few halls to its south and west – an area that would soon be coined 'the Thames Valley Cottonfields'. The sound was as pure black as these white English boys could play it, not music from New York or Detroit but the hardground Delta states. The young northerners and young southerners in England shared an affinity for Chuck Berry, Arthur Alexander and Bo Diddley, but preferences beyond here deviated down the two accepted definitions of R&B over which Brian Jones had publicly argued in *Disc*: the kind the Beatles did and the kind the Stones did. The Beatles went for Motown, the Stones for Chess; the Beatles for Goffin-King, the Stones for Howlin' Wolf; the Beatles for Richie Barrett, the Stones for Jimmy Reed; the Beatles for Luther Dixon, the Stones for Willie Dixon.

Alexis Korner was R&B's focal point. A year to the day after Peter Cook opened his satirical comedy club the Establishment, the 5 October issue of its offshoot arts magazine *Scene* profiled Korner and his band, concluding, 'They are, you might say, on the brink of a trend. What will happen next depends on the public outside of Central London. Alexis thinks they will like the music – once they get used to it. If so, the group could go a long, long way.'

But it wouldn't be Blues Incorporated taking it the distance, it would be the group whose first booking filled their absence. Back on 12 July, Korner and Blues Inc made their debut radio broadcast, live in session on the BBC Light Programme's *Jazz Club*. It was a Thursday night, Marquee night, so this week another group took their place, one the club's *Jazz News* ad called 'Mick Jagger and the Rolling Stones'.

Jazz News continued to be the only R&B soapbox, and it was this magazine that announced the birth of the Rolling Stones. In an 11 July piece headlined MICK JAGGER FORMS GROUP (which must have galled Brian Jones), the singer and harmonica player leapt instantly to allay any fears their name might spark regarding their musical direction. The result is that this first-ever published quote by Mick Jagger about the Rolling Stones is 'I hope they don't think we're a rock 'n' roll outfit'.[22]

This same Friday 5 October, EMI released its first Beach Boys record. It's there in the company's *Record Retailer* ad, facing Brian Epstein's full-page splash for

Love Me Do. The song was Surfin' Safari, an upbeat chunk of Chuck Berry-like guitar rock with appealingly unusual vocal harmonies. West coasters both, Los Angeles and Liverpool, the Beach Boys and Beatles were having simultaneous breakthroughs; they also shared some influences and were similarly self-contained, playing their own instruments and singing their own songs. Surfin' Safari was written by Brian Wilson and Mike Love; Wilson – an exceptional talent at 20 – was the eldest of the three brothers at the heart of the five-piece, and their father was the manager. Murry Wilson agreed the Beach Boys' contract with Capitol Records on 10 May, the day after George Martin, in London, offered Brian Epstein a Parlophone contract for the Beatles.

In America, the Beach Boys' first Capitol 45 was issued in a colour picture sleeve showing them as five young lads with clean, well-brushed hair a little shorter than the Beatles', wearing uniform blue check shirts over white T-shirts and jeans, and carrying a surf board. No advertising or publicity value was perceived in electric guitars, and the 'surfing sound' – in tandem with music for driving Hot Rod cars – had become big in southern California: guitar rock (mostly instrumental) for the idyllic male teen lifestyle of sunshine, surfing, beaches, cars and girls.

Surfin' Safari caught on big in America, reaching 10 in *Cash Box* and 14 in *Billboard*, and EMI picked it up for British release. It attracted similar press reviews to Love Me Do – generally positive, hardly overwhelming – and had the same battle to be heard. Beyond a couple of Radio Luxembourg spins, it wasn't, and it didn't crack the charts, but it did confirm a change to the vocabulary. *Record Retailer* had the Beatles in mind when it commented on the Beach Boys being 'Another group that is new to us'.[23] It was a crystal-ball moment: *groups* were coming . . .

Flying high (at 13) in the *Cash Box* Top 100 of 6 October 1962 was If I Had A Hammer, by the acoustic guitar and vocal trio Peter, Paul and Mary – but theirs was mostly a different market, a little older, one that had money to buy albums. The trio's first long-player was in its second week atop the *Cash Box* chart – and a style of music that had been around forever burst right into the mainstream with a resounding strum. The coming buzzword was 'hootenanny', though when that odd appellation went away it would be recognised as the great breakthrough of folk music in America. Not pop, not rock, not R&B, not electric at all, but poetically written protest songs, songs acoustically performed for a literate and socially conscious audience, songs of dissent against the world's ills and injustices, intelligently articulated in college campuses and coffee houses. Folk was a musical explosion that detonated in San Francisco and in Greenwich Village, New York; it was music for beatniks – now, inevitably, *folkniks*. Peter,

Paul and Mary were the first to have the hits, but another artist (like them, managed by Chicago-born entrepreneur Albert Grossman) was already shaping up to be its hero: 21-year-old Bob Dylan.

On Friday 5 October, Dylan was top of the bill at one of his earliest important New York shows, *The Traveling Hootenanny*, at the Town Hall on West 43rd Street. One could quibble about time differences, but Nuneaton, North Cheam and New York were in sync this night, united by voice, guitar and harmonica, played differently in each arena but from the heart at all, the sound of music young audiences hadn't even known they wanted. The last of Dylan's four numbers was new and not yet recorded, A Hard Rain's A-Gonna Fall. His future biographer Robert Shelton was present and would write, 'Those who doubted Dylan's poetic gift began to see what all the fuss was about.'[24]

Folk was already on the rise in Britain. Most of the new US recordings were picked up for release, where they were reinvigorating a centuries-old and always active indigenous scene, a fair number of the songs having old-world roots to begin with. The 13 October *Melody Maker* reported strong growth in the British folk circuit, with an estimated 150 clubs dotted around the country. On both sides of the microphone and on both sides of the Atlantic, the first post-war generation – young adults now – was ready to tell it and speak it and think it and breathe it.

33

'We've got it, and here we are with it'
(6–31 October 1962)

Ringo: We went round to them at first, didn't we?

John: We went and said, 'We're a group and we've got this record out. Will you . . .'

George: And then the door would slam.[1]

Southerners aren't mad about Scousers. It's a fact, and often felt more forcefully the other way. Traipsing around London newspaper offices promoting Love Me Do, the Beatles met a sneering negativity they'd not forget. The hard times Brian had getting them a deal were bad enough, this latest reception toughened them again. They'd show these bloody softies . . .

John: When we came down we were treated like provincials by the cockneys . . . looked down upon as animals. We were *hicksville*.

Paul: We were told, 'You'll never do it from Liverpool, you'll have to move down to London.' We stayed in Liverpool quite a long time just to defeat that rule.

George: In London they'd say, 'From Liverpool? Khaziland!'*

Ringo: People were saying, 'What's your name, Beatles? From Liverpool? You'll never make it. Get out of here.'[2]

---

* Khazi – English slang for toilet.

They were in London for thirty-six hours on 8 and 9 October, taking in John's 22nd birthday. It was the Beatles' first time in 'the smoke' for something other than recording, and because Eppy still wasn't fixing them London book-ings until demand was proven, they were unknown here, able to move freely on the streets and stop in shops, pubs and cafés. After checking into the Royal Court Hotel they headed out to Marylebone, to Manchester Square, to record a personal appearance in one of their record company's Radio Luxembourg shows, *The Friday Spectacular*.

This being 1962, no one thought it odd to have a mime programme on radio. It wasn't long since the biggest shows in America and Britain starred a ventriloquist's dummy. The *Friday Spectacular* format was clear enough: it was pre-recorded every Monday evening in the ground-floor conference room at EMI House; eighty to a hundred young Londoners – mainly girls, most with autograph books in their handbags – were given tickets along with access to a free Coca-Cola bar (bottles with straws) and encouragement to dance. A tem-porary floor saved the parquet from stiletto heels. They took part in competition spots, and applauded when two or three guest stars mimed their records from a small stage.

As almost every act was a solo singer, the mime situation was inevitable, but how the Beatles did it without instruments, and what they did when the record faded out, is lost knowledge. Here they were, though: surreally, the Beatles' first stage performance in London was miming-with-nothing. It was also their first commercial radio show, reaching around three million. After the music stopped, one of the two main hosts, Muriel Young or Shaw Taylor, announced, 'And now let's meet the Beatles in person!' – but no recording sur-vives, so it isn't known who spoke or what was said when they first had the ear of the people.

When the show was over, the tapes were edited for air-despatch to Luxembourg and the girls and boys came forward with autograph books and the Beatles' new Parlophone throwaway cards. Signing was standard on these occasions, and though a new experience for the Beatles in London, it was one they'd long mastered in Liverpool. At least one of them wrote *To* ——; boys got a plain *from*, girls got a *love from* with usually three kisses; the first to sign would also write *The Beatles* – a reminder for people of who and what they were – and one or two of them might also draw an inky doodle beetle. All this would be crowded on a single pastel-coloured page in every book. They were *a band*.

The same point was emphasised on the Tuesday, when they plugged Love Me Do to the press. The Beatles' guide around the London streets and offices was Tony Calder – 18, small, sharp, glasses – the ballroom DJ and independent publicist and plugger working the scene from a shared top-floor office in Soho. He set up a few journalist appointments for them at hourly intervals, allowing thirty minutes for each session and then a cab ride or walk to the next one. 'Brian Epstein asked me to do it,' he says, 'and I was pleased to get involved because I liked the record.'[3]

The day's itinerary is lost, but three appointments are known: one very friendly, one friendly, one very unfriendly. They set out to meet columnists on the Fleet Street national dailies – *Mirror, Sketch, Mail, Express* and *Herald* – but no pieces resulted. 'Many journalists that day treated the Beatles badly,' Calder says, though he himself was much impressed by them.

> The Beatles were a breath of fresh air in everything they did. There was no crap. They were wearing leather jackets, not suits, and must have been on speed because they had an energy I'd never seen before.
>
> Wherever we went, Paul and John sat in the two main positions and did the talking, George was sparkly eyed but hardly said anything, and Ringo didn't say a word. Lennon was the gruffer edge, and McCartney just talked and talked all day long. His chat was fantastic – I'd never heard any artist go straight into it like that; it didn't matter what the question was, he knew what he was going to say and he said the same thing in every meeting. He was phe-nomenal – it was full-flow bullshit that ended each time with a look at me and 'Have we gotta go, Tone?' Then up they'd get. 'Sorry but, you know, we've only come to London for the day . . .'

Ringo wasn't quiet in a Pete way – it was because the Beatles' history was theirs not his. As he would realise and describe, the price of his silence was a reputation for moodiness.

> People kept asking questions about the early days of the Beatles [and] I wasn't in a position to talk about it. I hadn't been with them long enough. I knew the story pretty well but I didn't want to make any mistakes; it was like joining a new class at school where everybody-knew-everybody except me. So I thought, 'Keep your mouth shut and you'll be all right. Play it nice and safe' . . . and they all used to say, 'Well, look at him, isn't he miserable? He won't talk to anyone.'[4]

While Ringo was saying nothing, though, and George was quietly taking it all in and forming views, whichever Beatle talked spoke for them all. Theirs was constantly a united group message – particularly, on days such as this, when they hoped to meet the musical press.

The weekly music papers were doing better-than-ever business. The *NME* (many still called it the *Musical Express*) had a 217,000 circulation – more than its rivals combined. *Melody Maker* sold about 78,000 but took solace from its discerning readership, *Disc* wasn't far behind, and *New Record Mirror* (secretly owned by Decca) sold only about 25,000 but was on the rise. Between them, these papers provided comprehensive coverage of pretty much every recording artist, their work, and the music and record businesses. From hard facts to hot gossip, little eluded them, and their weekly news reporting was obsessively strong, giving every reader the tools to be fully informed, and providing history with the richest of repositories.

What these papers lacked was criticism, scepticism, sarcasm, bile, bite. There wasn't none, as history likes to suggest, but *very* little. Their tone naturally reflected the times – in many respects still vital, polite, positive, everything supported, everyone encouraged. This was (superficially, at least) a more innocent world, written in quips and exclamation marks, far less cynical than it would become.* The Beatles were ever-keen readers of the music press but had a heightened sensitivity to fakery. When Cliff Richard said he 'couldn't have girl friends because the fans wouldn't like it', and when he and other stars announced they didn't smoke or drink, the Beatles knew it was nonsense. 'We used to think they were soft,' John said – anything 'soft' in their eyes being crap, finished, down the nick, *fookin' LAST*. As George would explain, they never had any intention of going down that well-trodden, misbegotten road: 'We've always disliked the phoney "star image". We'd much rather be ourselves. We always came out as ourselves, and we thought, "If they don't like us how we are, then hard luck", and they did. People like natural better, I think.'[5]

The Beatles hoped to meet *Melody Maker, Disc* and *New Record Mirror*, but, as no pieces appeared, they may have been turned away – though the last two did see them on a second promo visit a month later. Alan Smith extended the Beatles the warmest welcome of this first promo day, when they dropped into the *NME* office at 23 Denmark Street. To them, he was Liverpool-in-London, a home reporter on away turf; for him, it was a chance to deliver in person the

---

* In America, *Billboard* (*Billboard Music Week* at this time) and *Cash Box*, the two main trade journals, claimed circulation figures of 20,265 and 10,258 respectively. There was still no music consumer press – the only artist coverage was in Hollywoodish teen 'zines, pulp print with pin-up photos and scarcely believable PR spin about the likes of (in October 1962) Bobby Vee, Bobby Rydell, Frankie Avalon, Fabian, Rick Nelson, Richard Chamberlain, George Maharis, George Chakiris, Troy Donahue, Paul Anka, Paul Petersen, Patty Duke, Annette Funicello, Ann-Margret, Brenda Lee, Connie Francis, and one British artist – the child actress and singer Hayley Mills.

group he'd been mocked for supporting, the object of some 'Cockroaches' cracks and 'northern' gags.

As it turned out, whatever Smith wrote of their session wasn't used – the Beatles hadn't yet broken into the *NME* Top Thirty, and the paper's successful editorial policy was 'chart acts only'. An account of the visit popped up in a couple of November issues of *Mersey Beat*, for which Smith was now 'London correspondent'. The Beatles told him they didn't think much of Londoners, the final quote being 'If they know you come from the north they don't want to know.' Smith remembers how 'The Beatles took the "We'll show you!" view about all that ... but, on another level, the overwhelming sense I got from them was that buttons had been pressed and they were going to *happen*. It was like "We've got it, and here we are with it".'[6]

If the *NME* was the Everest of the music press, *Pop Weekly* was its hillock, and a riotously overused promotional tool for its co-owners Albert Hand and Robert Stigwood. Hand was a Presley fan, owner of *Elvis Monthly* and other curious low-end pop-mags published, improbably, in Derbyshire.* Stigwood was a savvy Australian impresario in London who'd signed a number of young actors, found them songs, put them in the studio, and produced, licensed and sometimes published their records. Stigwood's 'stars' were everywhere in *Pop Weekly* but groups didn't figure in his thinking. It was so much easier to manage soloists; he had them sculpted as plaster of Paris busts and sent them to journalists for favourable publicity.

With all that, and its colossally arch hip-speak ('Remember we go-go-go every week to Digsville now, like Wow!'), *Pop Weekly* really was a peculiar little thing ... but it did run an ad for Love Me Do. It was the *Record Retailer* situation again: EMI wouldn't pay for it, so Nems did. Brian responded positively to a direct approach from *Pop Weekly*'s ad manager Sean O'Mahony, who remembers: 'EMI gave me Brian's number and I called him. I was used to dealing with rough managers who didn't want to spend money but Brian was very different. We had an extraordinary phone call – he was so nice, so easy, so charming.'[7]

Love Me Do went on to figure in *Pop Weekly*'s Top Thirty, but, for once, the placing of an ad didn't earn them any editorial space. It might have done, but the Beatles' personal visit here confined it to the spike. The magazine was put together in a little section of Robert Stigwood's office, above a shop on a busy but run-down stretch of the Edgware Road, near Paddington.[8] As Tony

---

* The Beatles didn't buy *Elvis Monthly* but Mal Evans usually had the latest issue in his pocket and they looked at his.

Calder remembers, the young journalist who interviewed the Beatles 'was a horrible, Bri-Nylon white-shirted guy with acne and supposed power because he worked for a magazine "people wanted to be in". He made it clear he didn't really feel like giving the Beatles his valuable time, and said to them at the start, "Guitar groups are finished. It's over. It'll never happen again."' After a few minutes of hard answers to soft questions, John Lennon unilaterally terminated the interview. 'John just couldn't take any more of it. He looked at me and said, "Let's fucking get out of here, the cunt" – and, as he rose, he managed to accidentally-on-purpose tip up the man's desk, which knocked over and broke one of Stigwood's plaster busts. Those busts summed up the state of the business at the time the Beatles arrived – it was a symbolic moment.'

The *Pop Weekly* drop-in was also important in other ways. The Beatles had seen the name Robert Stigwood from reading the music papers; he was one of the major-ish players in the business. But when they came to his Edgware Road HQ it was a wooden staircase up off the street, leading to an office above a shop. *Their* manager had one of those, *and* he owned the shop – so just how much bigger was Robert Stigwood than Brian Epstein, apart from one being in London and the other Liverpool? If this was 'the glamorous London pop biz' it didn't amount to much and they didn't need to be awed by it.

At one point during the brief visit, it was suggested the Beatles go and meet Mr Stigwood – but then word came back that he was too busy. They didn't like it, and at least one of them (probably all four) mentally marked his card on an open-ended basis. As Paul told *Melody Maker* ten years later, 'It was the very first thing we did when we came to London, going to Robert Stigwood's office – and he wouldn't see us. Never been struck on him since.'[9] It was a nothing episode that would boomerang with a vengeance.

The only article actually resulting from the Beatles' day-long debut slog round London was in *Dance News*, a lively weekly that served the ballroom business from an office in Southwark Street, on the Thames' south bank. Its writer, Derek Runciman, liked the Beatles and what they had to say, and it was here (in the 1 November issue) that they were first quoted in a national publication. John was identified in print as 'leader and founder of the group' (which they'd agreed to say, if anyone asked) and this time, on his 22nd birthday, he did all the talking.[10]

When Runciman enthused to the Beatles about Love Me Do (he told readers 'If you haven't heard it you are really missing something'), John produced the first printed intimation of what had always been his group's hallmark – the speed with which they moved on, putting a present-day achievement fast behind them, even choosing to diminish it, in their dash to the next: 'We weren't expecting big things with Love Me Do, in fact we aren't so fond of it now. We've already recorded our follow-up and think it's great.'[11]

Noting all this and also their 'different, unEnglish style clothes', Runciman saw enough in the Beatles to stick his neck out. His piece, published under a good-size photo of them in front of the Liver Building, includes two things – the first London recognition that things were stirring *oop north*, and some bold predictions: 'These four gentlemen from Britain's beat capital, Liverpool, are a big threat to the big names in the instrumental and vocal world. I know it is an easy thing for critics to say, "Oh yes, they're going to make it big" and then later say, "Well, you can't always be right." But I shall herewith forecast that the Beatles are going to be very big and in time become one of the country's top starring attractions!'

Dance News ran its own weekly Top Ten, charting the most-played records in forty ballrooms around Britain. More so than through radio or TV, great numbers of people had exposure to new releases in the dance halls, played between a bandstand orchestra's live music sessions. It was a flourishing scene, and only Tony Calder would have thought to bring the Beatles to *Dance News* because it was the paper of his business: he was London's youngest DJ, working the Lyceum and three more ballrooms in the suburbs (Ilford Palais, Streatham Locarno and Tottenham Royal), and Love Me Do was one of the records he featured.

Calder and his associates – Jeff Dexter, and the top dog, Ian 'Sammy' Samwell – also pushed Love Me Do hard by sending it around to other DJs and putting the cost on Brian Epstein's bill. 'Record companies didn't supply ballrooms,' Calder says. 'Ballroom managers had to buy the records they played, usually by having an account with a local shop. We sent Love Me Do to every Mecca and Top Rank venue on the list. It was unusual, but we knew that because the Beatles were from Liverpool and sounded different, they weren't going to be played unless we did something.'

According to Dexter, the first ever public play of Love Me Do (in the capital, at least) was in the Lyceum, spun a week or two before its release by Sammy Samwell. The man who'd written British rock's original great record, Cliff Richard's Move It!, was the first to play the Beatles in London. 'We took our initial copy of Love Me Do – a one-sided white label test-pressing – straight to the Lyceum on a Tuesday,' Dexter says. 'Sammy played it three times that night and people came to ask us what it was.'[12]

Samwell played Love Me Do to two thousand dancers in London every Tuesday and Sunday night, and dropped it into his DJ box for the Lyceum's 'lunchtime disc sessions' every weekday but one. Liverpool's young office and shop workers had live music in their dinner-hour, London's had a daily hour of dancing to records ... and the Beatles were starting to migrate.

Love Me Do was issued only in Britain for now. Just as the Beatles had to break out of Liverpool to reach the rest of the country, so they'd have to break out of Britain to reach the rest of the world. In America, Capitol Records turned them down flat. It isn't known how much the Beatles knew of the background, but it will have hurt them and Brian to be rejected. George Martin expected nothing less, so routine had Capitol's dismissal of its English owner's product become. Music that sold strongly in Britain and often several other countries continued to be roundly dismissed by Dave Dexter, Jr, Capitol's 47-year-old director of international A&R, and George always suffered: of the mere *six* British 45s picked by 'Dex' for Capitol release in 1962, none was his.

The Beatles first landed in America in a carton postmarked 'London W1', one of eighteen records despatched from EMI House in Manchester Square to the Capitol Tower on Hollywood and Vine. Love Me Do didn't stay long on Dex's deck. Interviewed twenty-two years later for a US radio documentary called *From Britain With Love*, the then-retired Capitol executive ruminated briefly on his act of turning down the Beatles for America: 'I didn't care for it at all because of the harmonica sound. I didn't care for the harmonica because I had grown up listening to the old blues records and blues harmonica players, and I simply didn't ... I nixed the record instantly.'[13]

The fact that Chicago's Vee Jay label was having a huge national hit with Frank Ifield's I Remember You – a harmonica record Dex had nixed a couple of months earlier – prompted no circumspection, and neither did the success Capitol was having with another self-contained vocal-instrumental group, the Beach Boys. Dexter had no love for the British and a neat way of showing it. Though he rejected the Beatles, the Shadows, Cliff Richard, Adam Faith, Helen Shapiro and Matt Monro, he *did* issue Bobbikins, a piano instrumental by Mrs Mills. Gladys Mills was that most British of discoveries, an ample, 43-year-old, heavy-wattled housewife who chopped out party singalong numbers on a saloon-bar-like piano. After finding sudden TV fame late in 1961, she was signed to Parlophone by Norman Newell, but while her debut single was a hit, the follow-ups weren't – and it was one of these failures that Dex decided America needed.

In view of his reproving words to EMI in 1961 – 'No adult over here ever buys a single' – only two conclusions can be drawn. Either Dexter felt American kids would flock to Mrs Mills' Bobbikins, or this was one huge finger up to *England's EMI* – a policy colluded with at all management levels inside Capitol up to the president.[14] The record sold precisely seventy-two copies throughout

America, failing almost as miserably as Dexter's five other 1962 picks, one of which was tartan singer Andy Stewart – again, not exactly teenage pin-up material. And after this (but for one further small-time exception), Dexter managed to ignore *everything* sent from England for another nine months, until deep into an intensely dramatic 1963.

What happened next is a little cloudy, but the upshot was that Love Me Do wasn't released in America. EMI's procedure was to send some of Capitol's rejections to its newly opened and secretly owned New York enterprise, Transglobal Music, Inc. It was essentially British EMI in America, given the twin task of (a) licensing good independent-label US 45s for UK issue, and (b) finding US labels to take the records Capitol turned down. EMI Archives holds a single document showing that Transglobal's president, Joseph E. Zerga, was sent samples of Love Me Do to tout around some labels, but (apart from a late flurry of activity at Liberty Records, in December) there's nothing to indicate which companies might have rejected it.[15] Chances are that it saw little action, given that it was never heavily pushed by London.

The Beatles' sole focus was Britain, and the important thing was progression . . . which Love Me Do provided. People who heard the record – on Radio Luxembourg, on juke-boxes and in ballrooms – were snagged by something in the sound. There would soon come a temptation to exaggerate, for people to say they 'knew right away' the Beatles were special, but many *did* find Love Me Do interesting in 1962. Even if they didn't buy it, the recording stuck in the ears of listeners: it was engaging, appealing, unusual, audibly different to everything else around.

With all the nerves and tightness of their studio struggle on 4 September, it's easy to understand why (as George said) they did Love Me Do better on stage than on the record.[16] They played it and PS I Love You in every show, never failing to mention it was their new release and that people could go and buy it. At the same time, as usual, the Beatles made sure their set had other fresh appeal. The basement Popular Department at Nems, Whitechapel, was selling the Beatles' 45 in high numbers but still they used the place as customers, the four of them crammed into browseries after a lunchtime session, keeping up with the newest American sounds – records that, for the first time now, in a funny way, were the opposition.

It was here that they heard a black teenage girl-group from Michigan and their sweetly bewitching Devil In His Heart. The Donays made only this one record before breaking up, and it wasn't a hit in America or Britain, but the Beatles heard it, loved it, sang it and did something they didn't always do: switched the gender. It became Devil In Her Heart, a two-against-one vocal number – George sang of the reasons his girl was wonderful, John and Paul urged sense from the sidelines ('She's got the devil in her heart / She's gonna tear your heart apart').

A second new song was A Taste Of Honey, a mellifluously melodic number that met with less than unanimous approval within the Beatles. Paul heard the record (by Lenny Welch), fancied he'd like to sing it, bought it, learned it, and wanted it in the set … but there was resistance, most vociferously from John, that it was *soft*, not the sort of thing they should be doing. It would become a sustained point of contention between them, but they decided to put it to the test, to play it to audiences and watch the reaction. Ringo used brushes instead of sticks, Paul slightly varied the chorus words and also, just as he did in Till There Was You, introduced a strange vocal affectation, singing 'sweeter than wine' as 'schweeter than wine'.

One of the first times the Beatles played it was at the Rialto Ballroom on 11 October; the Mersey Beats were on the same bill and were with them again five nights later at a Nems Enterprises *Showdance* in Runcorn. John and Paul were still arguing about A Taste Of Honey, so Paul went off in search of a second opinion and nabbed the Mersey Beats' bassman and singer Billy Kinsley:

> Paul came up to me and said, 'What did you think of that song we did the other night, A Taste Of Honey?' and I said, 'I was knocked out by it. Superb.' Paul grabbed hold of me and said, 'Go and tell the others that.' He took me into their dressing-room and John said, 'Go on then, what do you think?' I was fifteen and very nervous because there was Big John Lennon asking me what I thought of a song he didn't like. Paul said, 'Come on, just tell the truth.' I told him I thought A Taste Of Honey was great. Paul said, 'Ha-ha, there you go!'[17]

There was also one other new song, one they didn't play, a Lennon-McCartney number written (mainly or entirely) by John in the Falkner Street flat. The spark was a precious infancy recollection of his mother serenading him with I'm Wishing, from Disney's *Snow White And The Seven Dwarfs*. 'Want to know a secret? / Promise not to tell? / We are standing by a wishing well.'

Do You Want To Know A Secret was the firstborn of John and Paul's parallel calling, the songwriting agreement with Brian (which itself may have been a secret from George and Ringo). Rarely lacking motivation anyway, the agreement was spurring Lennon and McCartney to step it up as composers, to generate songs the Beatles could use in the studio. If a surplus developed, Brian, as manager, would offer them to record company A&R men in the hope of making hits for other artists.

John gave his creation a slow, easy introduction that didn't recur ('You'll never know how much I really love you . . .'), which was a staple feature in so many of his favourite 1930s and '40s numbers and also a device used by Goffin-King. Then, soon after he'd written it, John realised it suited George's vocal range more than his, and handed it over.[18] It couldn't yet have been clear how this would work out – the Beatles purposely kept the song under wraps for a long time (not playing it on stage this year), so there were no opportunities for George to sing it. Perhaps they thought it might make the B-side of their next Parlophone record, but there's nothing to confirm it was ever a contender. The song was simply set aside for some future use – becoming the first of a stockpile.

With God-given timing, a golden idol dropped into the Beatles' world at the moment of their transition from local stars to first-step national. In May they'd spent mad Hamburg hours with Gene Vincent, in September they had a fresh boost of Buddy in their tank, and now a huge hero was on hand to top up their rock treasury. The Beatles twice shared Merseyside backstages with Little Richard in October, and in November they'd be spending close on two weeks together in Hamburg.

Everything was larger-than-life about little Richard Penniman. Audiences on his British tour never quite knew if they'd be getting the great old songs they'd paid to hear, or what to these young secular minds was religious clap-trap. Since renouncing rock in 1957 to become a preacher and evangelist, Richard had sung only gospel numbers, having no hits after 1959. Judging by the musical accompanist he brought with him, Britain was going to get God's word. Billy Preston was a 16-year-old organist from Los Angeles, a child prodigy steeped in the Church and gospel music. For the duration of their European visit – England then Hamburg – Richard was Preston's legal guardian.

Don Arden promoted the tour on the agreement the star sang ROCK. As Richard would relate it, he'd said yes only after explaining that God was going to punish Arden for putting temptation his way: 'I've always believed it's somebody *evil* that's gonna bring me back.'[19] Arden – who'd recorded religious records himself until the mid-1950s, in Hebrew – would be called much worse, and he was also no fool: he had the sense to bring over a strong supporting star, soul singer Sam Cooke, and to set the tour's first night at the Gaumont, Doncaster. Off-off Broadway.

Richard opened with a gospel number, the second was gospel, and the third, and then he did a quick rock hits medley. All hell must have gone on in the dressing-room between shows, because in the second house the preacher gave his disciples what they *really* wanted. It wasn't wholly rock and it wasn't wholly holy, but there were exhilarating full versions of the old greats – Long Tall Sally,

Lucille, Rip It Up, The Girl Can't Help It, Tutti Frutti and others – and that's the way it stayed. Billy Preston was shell-shocked. His only previous tours had been with Mahalia Jackson and the Reverend James Cleveland, and now he was on stage (along with Richard's British backing group Sounds Incorporated) watching goggle-eyed at the screaming rebirth of the pre-ministry Penniman, an eruption of action in a baggy white suit, a life-loving lunatic yowling the devil's music in woman's make-up, jiving on a grand piano and scaring audiences with a faux fatal collapse . . . before shrieking Good Golly Miss Molly into the fretful silence and leaping up like a defibrillated demon. Little Richard was off the wagon and out of his tree and the *NME*'s reviewer conceded defeat in his opening paragraph, saying, 'How do you describe the most fantastically exciting and shatteringly dynamic stage offering you have ever seen?'[20]

The night Brian Epstein brought Little Richard to Merseyside was the exact fifth anniversary of Richard's rock renunciation, when he flung four showy diamond rings into Sydney's Hunter River, declaring, 'If you want to live for the Lord you can't rock 'n' roll too.' Was the Good Lord looking down on New Brighton the night of Friday 12 October 1962, on the great coastal ballroom by the Ferris wheel, ferry boats and football stadium, the helter skelter, chippies and palmistry booth? God's Little Acre it wasn't. Little Richard took the risk and tore the place apart, splattering sweat over his brethren. 'Man, I *electrified them!*' he announced afterwards to *Mersey Beat*'s Alan Smith.[21]

Little Richard At The Tower was a five-and-a-half-hour, eleven-band rave. The star went on seventh, after which the crowds began to drift away for last transport home. Brian staged the show and Bob Wooler ran it, and they put the Beatles on sixth, one before the peak, so Little Richard would have to top their response. He watched them through a gap in the curtain, and the Beatles and Brian were hotfoot to know what he thought. Brian so blushed at the idea of asking that he got Billy Kramer's amiable manager Ted Knibbs to make the enquiry, and was able to use the quote 'Excellent, quite excellent' in publicity; but Alan Smith got the real scoop, scribbling in his notebook Little Richard's unqualified praise: 'Man, those Beatles are fabulous! If I hadn't seen them I'd never have dreamed they were white. They have a real authentic Negro sound.'[22]

When Richard was doing his whole thing on stage – backed by Billy Preston and Sounds Incorporated – each Beatle in turn tried to pose by the curtain on the far side, so that Mike McCartney could get an action shot with a Beatle in the distance. He never managed it. As it was, Richard kept turning round to smile at Ringo. It was an 'I fancy you' smile, says Mike. It came as a tremendous shock to the Liverpool musicians (and a crushing disappointment for some) that their great rock idol was not-as-most-men. So much was he queening around backstage, making lewd lascivious remarks about boys and scribbling in his giant bible (which he let no one see), he was obviously *one of them*.[23]

All sorts of other fun was going on backstage, where fifty rock lads mingled. John, Paul, George and Ringo were the kings, the professionals with a record in the chart, and here's where they had their first face-to-face with Pete Best since his sacking in August. They were going on stage as Lee Curtis and the All Stars were coming off, and Pete says no word or look passed between them. Bob Wooler was also wandering around offering bets that the Beatles would be bigger than the Shadows within six months, and Paul was bothering Les Chadwick to get a proper picture of them with Little Richard. The photographer went along to the star's dressing-room and asked if he minded; Richard answered, 'Why sure!' – he'd *loved* the Beatles and was only too happy to oblige.[24]

It's an important shot – a kneeling John clasps Richard's left hand, George, Ringo and Paul have his right, and everyone grins. They've not known him long, but they do now know him – and will soon become much better acquainted in Hamburg. It's the last photo in which the Beatles are second feature, grouping themselves around the star as the world would forever group around them; and though John would later reflect, 'All the performers I ever saw from Little Richard . . . I was always disappointed; I preferred the record,' he still showed himself the complete fan by getting Richard to autograph the souvenir programme. As was his way, the great American also added his home address – something he did for girls as well as boys, because in Little Richard World everyone was welcome to drop by: *For John, May God bless You always, Little Richard. 1710 Virginia Rd, Los Angeles, Calif.*[25]

It was a huge night for Brian, his showpiece promotion of the year, organised with an exemplary degree of detail. The event's main purpose – what it could do for the Beatles – took priority over profit, which was just as well since it didn't make one. The ballroom was packed and noisy but not full. Little Richard's £500 fee, plus fees for the ten support acts, the hall hire, heavy advertising and the design and printing of two thousand souvenir programmes, forced Brian to charge 10s 6d for tickets compared to six shillings for his Joe Brown promotion, and the extra expense was always likely to keep some people away.

Would he make any money sixteen nights later, when he did it all again at the great Empire Theatre? First advertised the day after the Tower event, this promotion had no place for the lesser Liverpool groups: Brian folded the Beatles and Little Richard into a line-up of other chart names, including Craig

Douglas, Jet Harris and Kenny Lynch. His priority once again was that the Beatles gained maximum prestige and experience from what would be their first major theatre show. With its twice-nightly houses and hierarchical bill, this kind of venue and set-up had to be their future.

The week of Love Me Do's release, Frank Ifield topped the bill at the Empire and Brian went along to see how such shows were managed, and to ask for tips about the touring circuit. Ifield advised him to contact Arthur Howes, who promoted most of the major package tours and had an exclusive arrangement with several top artists, Ifield included. Soon afterwards, as Howes would always enjoy relating, he received a phone call at his home in Peterborough from Brian Epstein, asking if he had space in a show for the Beatles. 'As soon as I heard the name *Beatles* I thought "Oh Gawd!"' he'd remember.[26] But on the basis of Love Me Do's chart entry, he was prepared to put them into a Frank Ifield concert in Peterborough; it would be two houses the evening of Sunday 2 December, no fee but expenses, and Brian accepted.

Through it all, Brian's planning for the Beatles was maintaining a cyclical structure – an intense participation in the present; an evolving mid-term strategy towards distant, greater goals; and the constant need to overcome niggling problems.

It isn't clear how much the Beatles knew, back in July, of the two contracts Brian made for them with the Star-Club, one for the first fortnight in November, the other for the last two weeks of the year. Probably they were told of them, but the dates seemed so far away. Now they were close – and the Beatles said they weren't going. Love Me Do was on the chart and sure to fall without their hands-on push. Besides which, they'd *done* the Star-Club, didn't like repeating themselves, and would achieve nothing by going there again. Paul had baulked at playing a February booking for Liverpool University, which caused Brian much embarrassment; this time it was group revolt, led by John and George: they simply didn't want to play the Hamburg clubs any more. So strong was the feeling, John could still tap into it nine years later: 'If we'd had our way, we'd have just copped out on the engagement. We didn't feel we owed them fuck all.'[27]

They didn't have their way. Brian must have understood, but he also had to be strong. If they broke the contracts, they'd damage their reputation now and potentially long-term. It might have taken most of October for him to change their mind, but he did. They said they'd go, grumping about it of course, but also clear and united on the need to honour agreements. The Beatles could be royally obstinate but were always realistic. Would all *four* of them make the trip, though? Further worrying Brian was the possibility that Paul might not be able to go to Hamburg anyway – that John, George and

Ringo would have to pick up a 'dep' bass player, a temporary, for both the coming Star-Club seasons.

The fallout from the Bambi Kino prank was still plaguing Paul two years on. Post-deportation, his two applications for German re-entry had been tough to swing, and so it was proving again now. Brian collected four sets of visa and work permit forms from the German Consulate in Liverpool and submitted them typed and tidy, but while the office stamped the passports of John, George and Ringo, Paul's was refused. This was on 9 October, and it was only after Brian pressed the consulate for an explanation that he learned Manfred Weissleder would have to make a special case for Herr McCartney at the Bundeskriminalamt in Hamburg. Brian explained the 'very urgent' situation in a letter flown to St Pauli on 17 October, just two weeks before the Beatles were due in the Star-Club ... and the matter would stay unresolved most of that time before, finally, Paul achieved approval.

Management was never an easy ride. Brian was finding the Big Three more trouble than their worth – they continued to defy his instructions and he was also forced into apologising for their behaviour – but he *was* able to stir record company interest in them.[28] At Christmas, after returning from another Hamburg season, they'd be seen by Decca. Gerry and the Pacemakers were also in line for a Decca audition after their return from Hamburg, and Brian was working towards having all three of his groups signed to record labels by early 1963.

He remained reluctant to take on further talent for the time being, but kept a close eye on the strongest candidates. The main one was singer Billy Kramer, nicknamed Golden Boy on account of his all-gold stage suit. Another was Thomas Quigley, who sang under the stage name Tommy Quickly. In both cases, Brian made his long-term managerial intentions clear, and monitored progress. He encouraged Bob Wooler to book them for the Cavern and added them to Nems Enterprises promotions in the last months of 1962. There were no contracts, no commissions, but Brian was ensuring their experience, prospects and income rose a few degrees.

All this activity was taking place in a city that still made the national news for only wrong reasons. A Home Office report singled out Liverpool as England's worst for drunkenness, with arrests in 1962 up by a third on 1961; the number of young unemployed was greater here than anywhere outside London, and higher than at any time since 1940; and it was estimated that two hundred thousand – almost a third of the population – would quit Liverpool during the next twenty years in search of a better life. The great city was in tragic, open decay, its cries for capital investment ignored. Poverty was endemic, fifty thousand houses had no bathroom or inside toilet, everywhere was soot-black, and so voluminous was Liverpool's derelict land – its unimproved bombsites and slum clearances – that the city's greatest champion, the MP Bessie Braddock, stood up in the House of Commons and begged the Minister of Housing to pay a visit, 'because there are no words to describe the state of the central area in Liverpool'. The university's student paper *Guild Gazette* summed up a perennial fact of life: 'Whatever the cause of her slums and distress, Liverpool deserves better than what she has to contend with at present. For she does have her virtues. The trouble is that only those who are, or have been, emotionally involved with her, can see them.'[29]

While dealt the roughest of hands, Liverpudlians preserved their fierce passion for life, and during 1962 this vitality and humour flowered into further forms of artistic expression. There was the rock scene and also now the painting, poetry and performance-art scenes, which emerged more or less together in the last months of the year and had a fair connection to the Beatles. The hub was Hope Street, Liverpool's bohemia, with the vast Anglican Cathedral at one end and the building blocks of a strange, launchpad-shaped Roman Catholic cathedral just being laid at the other. Starting in Liverpool 1 and morphing into Liverpool 8, Hope Street was John, Paul and George's past playground, by the Institute and art school, Gambier Terrace, the Phil and the Cracke . . . and now something else was stirring here.

A second *Jazz To Poetry* event was held at the Crane Theatre in Liverpool on 5 March 1962, with performances by Adrian Mitchell and sax player Graham Bond (both up from London) and local poet Roger McGough, whose verses were rich in wit, colour and pace. McGough connected with several like-minded denizens of Hope Street, including the boldly original poet-painter Adrian Henri, painter Sam Walsh, poet Brian Patten, and John Gorman, a Post Office engineer by day and crazy diamond by night. He was the main organiser of the *Merseyside Arts Festival*, which ran in the last quarter of 1962 at several venues though mostly in the basement of a cinema on Hope Street. The place was called the Everyman but locals knew it by its former name, Hope Hall – inevitably 'the Hopey'.

Filtered through a strong English-Irish-Welsh-Jewish-Liverpool sensibility, the Mersey poets took their cue from Allen Ginsberg and the original San Francisco beat scene: plain recitation was rejected in favour of direct action and audience involvement. Henri called their programmes 'Events' and they were similar to the Happenings gathering pace in metropolitan intellectual America – mixed-media performance art with poetry, playlets, music, paintings and dance, loose in structure, often impromptu and, here, rich in Liverpoolese.

The *Merseyside Arts Festival* was underway when Mike Weinblatt – artist, saxophonist and Gorman's friend – said to his colleague at the André Bernard hair salon, Mike McCartney, 'You're interested in these arty-farty things, aren't you? Do you want to come to this Event at the Everyman?' Mike went, and soon got talking to McGough and Gorman, who invited him to do a comedy sketch. 'I thought one show-off in the family was enough and said, "No, I don't do that kind of thing." They said, "Neither do we, let's do it for a laugh." I took the sketch home and went back and read the part of an old man. Not only did I enjoy it but so did the audience – it immediately got a laugh and at the end they all applauded. I was hooked, so now there were two show-offs in the family.'[30]

Mike felt right at home with the poets and painters. His passion for surrealism, sparked by Dalí and Buñuel, was propelled by the wittily evocative words of new friend Roger McGough and the challenging imagination of new friend John Gorman. The younger McCartney was entering a whole new scene, full of clever minds and merry English nutters ... but, sensitive to the increasing reputation of 'our kid' (big brother Paul), he decided not to use his surname. When Gorman began planning a second arts festival for 1963, Mike was named on the letterhead as Michael Blank, kicking off an extended period of semi-anonymity as a talented stage performer in his own right.

John Gorman says Mike made a suggestion one day that his brother's group might play for an Event. They had, after all, backed the beat poet Royston Ellis. When Gorman asked what sort of group they were and Mike replied 'rock and roll', Gorman said, 'Come off it, Mike, we're artists – we don't want to be messing around with musicians like that.' The Liverpool poets' preferred accompaniment wasn't rock or jazz but Mississippi-Mersey R&B, and the band who claimed pole position were the Roadrunners – musicians, singers, artists, poets and all-round bright cool guys from Birkenhead. They'd started out as the poppy Tenabeats, but as their inspirational leader Mike Hart later wrote, a pair of bookings as support to the Beatles had a profound impact. The Beatles, he said, 'resulted in a complete change of approach, a mad rush for Chuck Berry records and a resolution to try a bit of humour'.[31]

The Roadrunners turned pro in October 1962, their first paid gig was the art school's Saturday-night dance, and they became Sunday regulars in the Hopey basement, playing Muddy Waters between (and sometimes during) sketches by the poets and artists. 'The speed of change was really something,' their drummer David Boyce says. He'd been, and still was, a great Beatles fan in the Cavern, and now the Beatles – or some of them – were coming to see him. 'George and Paul used to come to Hope Hall on Sunday nights. George always got on well with Mike Hart, and Paul often came along to see what his brother was doing.'[32]

*

Liverpool 8's other resident poet had no involvement in the scene shaping about him – and he was just about to leave the area. John Lennon was still making up his witty verses while going to or from the nightly bookings, and was also now scribbling on scraps of hotel-room stationery. He wrote several pieces in this period, including 'No Flies On Frank', an extended (six-hundred-word) tale of a man upon whom no flies had landed, although plenty gathered on his wife after he 'had clubbed her mercifully to the ground dead'.[33]

John's merry lines always made Cyn laugh, and she knew from long experience not to take things too personally. They were actually one of the few bright spots in her increasingly hemmed-in life. Cynthia Lennon, married two months and pregnant for four, was no longer studying or teaching or going out to see the Beatles or doing anything but lying low in Falkner Street and watching her stomach grow; or washing, ironing and repairing John's shirts; or endeavouring to cook meals for whatever late hour he returned. Her speciality was reconstituted Vesta beef curry and rice, garnished with fresh sliced banana, but she served some to Ringo one night unaware of his delicate stomach and was crushed by his indelicate rejection. John still hadn't told Ringo he was married or that Cyn was pregnant. She hid it, and says Ringo blanked her and viewed her with suspicion for some time to come.[34]

John was away more than before, and while the Beatles were being sneered at in London on 8 and 9 October, Cyn was in Liverpool losing blood. She took a bus to the doctor's surgery, was told she might be miscarrying, returned to the flat by bus and lay there alone and scared out of her wits, using a bedside bucket because the toilet was too far away. She didn't miscarry, but rest never came easy on the ground floor at 36 Falkner Street. In this rough neighbourhood she was often scared, a feeling only partly alleviated by the surprise, temporary residence in the basement flat of Paul's former girlfriend Dot Rhone, seemingly making one last, unsuccessful play to get back into Paul's life. Even when John was home, they were terrorised – a couple of thugs all but broke down their front door late one night, certain they were harbouring someone.[35]

Falkner Street was always troubled but the worst of it came in waves, and one rolled up during October 1962. FALKNER STREET UNITES IN PROTEST announced the *Liverpool Weekly News* front-page headline, reporting that two young lads had glassed a milkman with a broken bottle, that windows were being kicked in every night, that a boy was robbed at razor point, and that criminality was aided by almost total night darkness because the streetlights were smashed. 'Violence and vandalism is holding the area in a grip of fear,' the paper reported ... so this was clearly no place for a pregnant Cynthia Lennon to be alone when, through the first half of November, John would be in Hamburg.[36]

In the last days of October, John asked Mimi if he and Cyn could move into Mendips. Mimi said yes, despite the fiery conclusion to the last time this was tried, twelve months back. They were married now and could have the downstairs while Mimi switched most of her life upstairs. This could only be done ad hoc until Christmas, because until then she also had three lodging students; after that, they'd have more space to do it properly, especially if John made a decent contribution to the household purse. So John thanked Eppy for the use of his flat and they moved to Menlove Avenue ... where Cyn no longer feared being alone but did have to contend with Mimi's mercurial temperament. She also worried that the lodgers would see her bump and work out she'd been pregnant longer than married – so even here, 'at home', she thought it best to carry on hiding it.[37]

John's return to Woolton took him back to the house outside which Julia had been killed four years ago, back to Mimi's cats, back to proper meals and laundry, and back to local habits and friends. Lindy Ness was able to enjoy a closer connection to John than she'd had for some time, and even found herself privy to his short-lived first set of driving lessons. Paul, George and Ringo had cars, and John – as cack-handed and technically uncoordinated as he was – didn't want to miss out. He practised in the Beatles' van, tutored by Neil, as Lindy remembers: 'He used to pick me up and then drive along Menlove Avenue on the way to collect Paul. He wore his glasses, but wasn't a good driver, wasn't a good pupil and certainly didn't inspire me with any confidence. In fact he was absolutely *horrendous*. Neil would be trying to show him what to do and what not to do and John would be shouting "Fuck off!" all the time, and "Stop telling me what to do Nell 'cause I'M FUCKIN' DOING IT!"'[38]

The other Beatles were all keeping busy private lives. Ringo and Maureen – Richy and Mitch – had been going together a couple of months now. George had broken up with Marie Guirron but they stayed friends and she still sometimes went with them in the van to north-west bookings.[39] He'd no shortage of female admirers and had started dating another Cavernite, Bernadette Farrell, a blonde 17-year-old hair stylist who worked in a salon above Nems' Great Charlotte Street shop. She had one date with Paul, then George made a more decisive move and she went with him, getting to stand in the Cavern's first arch.

Paul and Thelma Monaghan had also cooled: he'd so much choice now, women were in and out of his life all the time. He had two main girlfriends in the last weeks of 1962 and neither knew of the other. One was Celia Mortimer, 17, the strikingly attractive redhead from art school who designed her own clothes and was a big Beatles fan in the Cavern.

Paul was attractive, intelligent, arty, all the things that appealed to me, plus he was good to be with: a gentle, genuine person who wanted to please. He was the complete opposite of John, who was snarly and grumpy and incredibly, incisively funny; Paul was the nice one. We started to go out, but things were still quite innocent. Because I lived some way out of Liverpool there weren't many places we could go, except to sit in his dad's front room or my friend's front room, or the cinema – we saw the first James Bond film.[40]

Paul's other girlfriend was Iris Caldwell – Rory Storm's witty, pretty, blonde sister; George's first love; the 18-year-old daughter of Ma Storm, whose house, Hurricaneville at 54 Broad Green Road, was central to the Beatles' late-night social scene. 'He had a beautiful voice and puppy-dog eyes,' Iris says, 'and he was much more interested in me than I was in him. I wanted more than a tuppence-ha'penny guitarist of a Liverpool group.' Iris's professional dancing career had taken off and she was as busy as Paul, working summer seasons and London shows and touring around the country: they could only see each other when their diaries dovetailed, and just as Paul was with Celia when Iris was out of town, she was secretly going out with Frank Ifield.

> Paul was very funny – he used to call me Harris, though I never found out why, and he called himself Pool McCooby or 'our kid'. He said I wasn't to go to any Beatles gigs because Brian Epstein wouldn't like us going around together – it was important that stars had to be 'available' – but wherever we went Paul liked to be the centre of attention. He was always doing impressions of people, and because he liked being seen at the pictures we'd always sit in the front row of the circle. One night he took me to the Empire to see the pianist Joe Henderson. The show was called *Sing Along With Joe* but the only person in the theatre who was singing along was Paul – very loudly, at the top of his voice.[41]

Iris always knew that a big part of the attraction for anyone going out with her or Rory was the chance of extended time at Hurricaneville, to hang longer around her dad Ernie and especially her mum, Vi. Ma Storm was a great Liverpool character, and visitors collapsed over the mad things she said and did. She didn't try to be funny and didn't tell jokes, but her off-the-cuff remarks had people doubled up. She was particularly close to George and Paul, and they didn't always call her Ma Storm – Paul nicknamed her Val-and-Vi and George called her Violent Vi, and both loved her dearly. Vi's was the ultimate 3AM open-house for chat, char, ciggies, cheese barm-cakes and chip butties. 'Mum never chucked anyone out,' Iris says. 'We were all late-night people apart from me dad, who the Beatles called "the Crusher" because he had exotic nightmares and ate household objects. He used to go to bed early, and when they came round he'd be calling downstairs, "They're all down there burning my electricity."'

It was six years since Paul's mother had died, and Vi Caldwell was one of the women who tried to fill the breach. She made him food and drink, took his stage-soaked shirts and washed and ironed them, and shared easy intimacies. 'Paul used to like her combing his legs,' Iris says. 'He had really hairy legs and he'd come in from the Cavern all tired, roll up his trousers and she used to comb his legs. How ridiculous can you get? But he adored my mum and my mum adored him.'

Vi was a chain-smoking, apron-wearing Scouse housewife who spoke to Paul straight, giving him the kind of genuine, affectionate grounding he otherwise accepted only from one or two aunts and cousins. She challenged the certain views he held on many subjects; he was an adamant atheist and she agnostic, and they debated religion. She rebuked him countless times for never having any cigarettes and always scrounging hers – it was amusing to begin with, but then irritating ('He would *never* give you any cigarettes, he was terribly mean over them') – and she saw how, every once in a while, Paul arrived at Hurricaneville in an altered mood, leaving everyone uncertain about where they stood.[42]

The secret the Caldwells kept from Paul – that Iris was also seeing Frank Ifield – came out in unusual circumstances after Paul turned up with a pair of tickets for his Empire show. It was the same one Brian attended to glean managerial information. Iris couldn't very well tell Paul she was seeing Ifield on the side, or that Paul was himself the sideshow to an internationally famous star, 24 years old, tanned, quiffed and big in America. *Hit Parade* said Frank had a new Ford Capri, the coupé version of Paul's Ford Classic. The cars didn't compare, and neither did they.[43]

Unusually, instead of sitting front circle, Paul's tickets took them to the second row of the stalls, so Iris hitched her hopes on a change of appearance. 'Frank liked me very feminine when we went out, all curly hair and sticky-out frocks, but Paul liked me in a straight skirt with the hair in a bun, so that's what I wore, hoping Frank wouldn't recognise me.' All was good until Ifield went off for his 'false tabs' (suggesting the show's end but hurrying back for an encore) and returned to sing the Jim Reeves hit He'll Have To Go. He stood beyond the footlights and sang it straight at the hand-holding young couple squirming in the second row, a song that ended with 'And you can tell your friend there with you, he'll have to go'. As Iris remembers, 'Paul was going "The cheeky bugger! The cheeky bugger!", but I said to him, "There's no point being jealous, Paul, you don't understand – it's *show business*, it's about being *professional*.'" Little did either suitor know that, thanks to Brian's backstage visit here, they'd soon be appearing on the same bill.

It was to Hurricaneville that the Beatles scooted the evening of Wednesday 17 October, to wolf down chip butties and tea and get Vi's instant reaction to their first TV appearance. This was a great occasion: they were seen coast-to-coast across the north of England on Granada's *People And Places*, hosted by genial Dubliner Gay Byrne – or, as John wrote it, Granarthur's *Peckle And Braces* hosted by Gray Burk.[44] For the Beatles in 1962, 'making it' meant a car, a record in the charts, and radio and TV broadcasts, and they'd bagged the lot. And because the British had square eyes, being 'on the telly' branded them *stars* – 405 black-and-white lines of fame, flickering but forever.

They had about five minutes' airtime, engaging in brief light-hearted banter with Byrne and playing Some Other Guy and Love Me Do. Everything was done live, and as it wasn't filmed or video-taped in the studio, the Beatles' first TV appearance vanished into the ether on transmission, never to be seen again, not so much lost as never had. It *was* preserved on amateur audio tape, and as a written description in a Beatles scrapbook kept by Jenny of Birkenhead: 'They looked fab and were their own selves (acting the fool) but sound effects were not as good as they could be.'[45]

The fool-acting came at the end of Some Other Guy, when, by mad arrangement, John and Paul threw their hands above their heads and started whooping. They played and sang the number with impressive strength, choosing it because the Cavern film hadn't been shown and this was still the song they wanted to put across. Love Me Do was confident and good and included a boisterous bridge where Ringo kept the guitars strongly on the beat and brought them back into the next verse; there's every possibility this somewhat more rousing arrangement was the one they were performing regularly on stage.

Jenny's mention of inferior 'sound effects' referred to the overall audio quality, which was poor. This was how it had been for every performer since the dawn of rock and roll – and earlier. Television's technological infancy was another reason why miming was rife: studio sound-mixing facilities were so basic that a decent balance was nigh-on impossible to achieve, and technicians still hadn't figured how to mike a guitar amplifier. Beyond all that, at the receiving end, domestic television sets were housed in small wooden cabinets with one lo-fi mono speaker, and the sound was beamed through the skies with that in mind. The Beatles came a good couple of decades too early for stereo TV and they would always hate their small-screen sound and do everything in their power to improve it, a feeling first shaped here in Manchester.

Apart from the moment of contrived silliness, what the Beatles *were* was self-restrained. This TV debut arrived at a time when the front line were switching their stage manner, becoming noticeably less animated. It wasn't suggested by Brian, it was their own idea. They'd *mach Schaue*d and messed around for a long time and now were trying something different. As John would explain, 'Gradually, we cooled it and cooled it, and used less energy. We had a choice between dancing about, creating havoc, and playing. So we concentrated on the playing.'[46]

They still acted up between numbers, and John still cripped, but during the songs (except when going to and from the mikes) John was now stock still, legs astride and grounded, robotically moving his torso and neck; George was motionless except when kicking out one foot or the other involuntarily – what he'd call his 'Liverpool Leg'; Paul's feet still tapped out the beat and he moved around a little, but not much. Personality was conveyed by attitude, looks, humour and natural charisma: they were still having a great time and it still showed, just differently. On TV, though, unfamiliar with the cameras wheeling about them and zooming in for close-ups, they probably underplayed too much. The change certainly came as a shock to Granada's Leslie Woodhead, whose efforts had brought about the TV booking (for which he says Ringo made a point of thanking him) – he thought the Beatles 'incredibly tame' compared to what he'd seen in the Cavern.[47]

The Granada booking happened because they'd impressed the *People And Places* producer in the Cavern, but Brian had yet to do anything about getting them on BBC-tv. There was no alternative to going down the audition route – trying, waiting, hoping – and it all seemed slightly pointless because there was no programme to appear on. This was either not known or not considered by David John Smith, a sharp 16-year-old musician and fan who began what amounted to a postal campaign to push the Beatles in particular and Liverpool groups in general. To this day, he's not quite sure why he did it: 'I wasn't a letter writer by nature, but I suppose I just wanted to get the Beatles some exposure – even though, like many fans, I was afraid of losing them.'[48] Smith wrote to two BBC producers in London, urging them to give the Beatles a chance on TV – 'Believe me, if you took an interest in this very talented group of lads you would not regret it at all.' He had a reply within four days: his letter had been forwarded to the BBC-tv Auditions Department ... and so another train was set in motion.

The Beatles quickly came to appreciate David John Smith's contribution to their progress – John nicknamed him 'Letters' and Paul asked Brian to give him a job at Nems Enterprises – but someone else was plugging away on their behalf too, a man they knew nothing about and to whom they owed so much. Kim

Bennett – professional manager at music publisher Ardmore and Beechwood, in charge of 'exploitation' – was making relentless efforts to promote Love Me Do. Partly this was because being persistent was his very particular nature, mostly it was for another reason: because it had been his idea that got the Beatles their Parlophone contract in the first place. Bennett and his boss Sid Colman were Lennon and McCartney's first believers in London, saying yes when all around them (including their parent-company colleagues at EMI) were saying no ... and now he was battling to vindicate his faith.

Parlophone's plugger Alma Warren hadn't got anywhere with Love Me Do. It had six quick spins on EMI's Radio Luxembourg shows but nothing else, and she'd since turned her attention to other records. Bennett also had other songs to plug but was still beavering away on Love Me Do, doing the rounds and phoning contacts. Though success was elusive, no one in the business was more unflagging than this 31-year-old ex-crooner from Crystal Palace, the man confusingly called Kim though his real name was Tom Whippey. He was a toiler, pushing and pushing – and pushing again – when others gave up.

> It was a *bastard* to get Love Me Do played, because no one wanted to know. I believed in it – to me, the sound was different and needed to be heard – but all I got was 'I'm not having that bloody noise in my programme, thank you.' I got that attitude *everywhere*. 'Oh bugger off, Kim, it's a load of bloody rubbish and I'm not using it.' When it made the charts I phoned around and said 'It's starting to move you know ...' and got the same verbal darts as before. 'You're not *still* going on about that Love Me Do are you?' But I felt it necessary to persist because I needed to prove I'd been right. I'd say, 'Look, I honestly think this record is better than you've given it marks for. What about it? Have another listen.'[49]

Bennett was unable to get Love Me Do on *Juke Box Jury* or *Thank Your Lucky Stars* but he got it played on *Lunch Box*, a music-themed weekday TV show for Midlands housewives; he got on well with the producer, Reg Watson, who usually played one disc a day and allowed Love Me Do as a personal favour.[50] Bennett also tapped one of his lunch companions, BBC producer Brian Willey, to give the Beatles their first radio recording in London. As negotiated with Brian, they'd be taping an appearance in *The Talent Spot* ten days after returning from Hamburg.

Bennett's best achievement was to persuade producer Jimmy Grant to play Love Me Do on *Saturday Club*. It was the ideal showcase for the Beatles' target audience, averaging ten million listeners a week, but just days before the broadcast the record was suddenly excluded, having fallen foul of sensitivity about bogus record requests. So many postcards were arriving at the BBC from Liverpool, all asking for Love Me Do, that Grant smelled *hype*. It had to be, because whoever heard of a brand-new act being so popular? Bennett went back to the drawing-board wondering what else he could do to get Love Me Do noticed. As he would reflect, 'It was a case of "Where do I go now, please?"'[51]

While Bennett was pondering his problem – and looking to his passport – Paul McCartney was half a mile away, a solo Beatle in London town. He was without the others but with Celia Mortimer … and a new song. It was Tuesday/Wednesday 23/24 October, the Beatles' sole two-day break of the year, and Paul decided to leave his car at home and have an adventure: he and Celia hitch-hiked to London to see Ivan Vaughan. Paul loved hitching but he'd only done it with George or John, never with a girl. Celia – intelligent, chic, a pretty redhead – made it thrilling in a different way. And it was to see the brilliant Ivy, his Institute mate and John's boyhood pal. Having introduced Lennon to McCartney in Woolton five years earlier, he was now in London and mixing with the likes of Peter Cook, Dudley Moore, Barry Humphries and Lenny Bruce. Vaughan was doorman at the Establishment Club in Soho, earning himself a few late-night pounds while reading Classics at University College.

The new song was I Saw Her Standing There, though it had no title as yet. Its melody and structure skidded into Paul's head late on Monday as he drove back from a Nems Enterprises *Showdance* in Widnes. This was a sophistication of delivery he'd never experienced, inspiration so excitingly hot that when he got to Hurricaneville he grabbed an acoustic guitar and started working it out. He had chords, changes and the first two lines, 'She was just seventeen / She'd never been a beauty queen'. It was truly a magical moment for Rory Storm, who'd never seen anyone write a song before. Vi and Iris would always maintain that he asked Paul if he could have it, exclusively, and Paul said yes – but as Rory didn't have a record contract it's unclear why he asked, and Paul may have said yes only to regain some necessary peace and quiet.[52]

He and Celia hitch-hiked to London the next day – a bus to the busiest road, then a succession of lorries. 'It was a real adventure for both of us,' she says, 'a wild, arty thing to do. I told my parents I was staying with a college friend, then off we went. We ate in the Blue Boar at Watford Gap and arrived in Soho well after midnight.'*

The Establishment cabaret had finished – they'd just missed seeing Eleanor Bron, John Bird and John Fortune – but Paul bought Celia a bitter lemon, and

---

* The Blue Boar was Britain's first motorway service station. Situated in the Midlands, it marked the start (at this time) of the M1 road to London.

a Scotch and Coke for himself, and they danced into the night. They slept in Ivan's digs, a tiny room in a well-appointed flat on Great Portland Street – he had a single bed and they had the floor, which was incredibly uncomfortable. But the best part, says Celia, was the next day.*

> We had an amazing time, just wandering streets in the sunshine, looking at London, holding hands and having fun, and Paul had the melody of what became I Saw Her Standing There going round his head all day, humming it and singing it and fleshing out the words. I remember walking around some lovely, elegant squares – I think Fitzroy Square was one – while he made up rhyming lines and asked me what I thought of them. He said, 'What rhymes with "We danced through the night"?' and I came up with 'We held each other tight', which was really quite naff, but he used it. He'd worked out a fair bit of the lyric by the end of the day.[53]

I Saw Her Standing There would be completed by Paul and John in the front parlour at Forthlin Road after the Beatles got back from Hamburg, but it kept its subject, the singer dancing through the night with a girl of 17. 'It felt like the song was about us,' Celia reflects, 'but it wasn't said. It was implicit, but difficult to state openly because it would have made things terribly intimate. But I was very flattered, and it became for me an abiding memory of our trip to London. It was only a quick thing – we went home that night because I had to get back to college and parental control, and the Beatles were getting busier and busier . . .'

All this time, Love Me Do continued an ascent – slow but steady – of now several charts. Airplay starvation killed the chances of other records but this one had booster rockets, like the Beatles' strong northern following, their twenty-three live shows in October, their Radio Luxembourg and Granada TV plugs, their dance-floor action in Liverpool and London and ballrooms everywhere, and their juke-box plays. The record's instant debut at 49 in the *Record Retailer* Top Fifty had been followed by rises to 46 and 41, it went into the *Melody Maker* Top Fifty at 48, and into *The World's Fair*'s Juke-Box 100 at 51

---

* Ivan lived in Flat 6, Seaford Court, 220–222 Great Portland Street. It was, as always, a fantastically connected world. Paul could have spent the night at any one of several million London addresses, but was in the building where George Martin had received oboe lessons from Margaret Asher fifteen years earlier. She and Dr Richard Asher were living in Flat 2 at Seaford Court throughout the time they had their children. Peter, Jane and Clare grew up here, before the family moved to 57 Wimpole Street in 1957.

(positions in this chart were suspect below 5, but they're fascinating lists). Sales were also holding up locally: Liverpool's Own Top 5, in the *Echo*, placed Love Me Do at the top in its first week, followed by a second week at number 1 shared with the Tornados' Telstar, and then a week at number 2 shared with Little Eva's Loco-Motion. All this action was to the good, but Love Me Do was about to take a leap and arrive in the *NME* Top Thirty – it went in at 27, and this altered everything.

Primary experiences shine everlasting. Just as George would describe first hearing Love Me Do on radio as 'the best buzz of all time', and Ringo would call its release '*the* most momentous moment', so Paul has retained every joyful detail of how it felt to see the Beatles break into the *NME* chart. It was Thursday 25 October and he was just back from hitch-hiking to London; as he puts it, 'I remember exactly where I was when we actually thought we'd *arrived*.

> I was on my own at home that morning, and when I looked at the *NME* and saw we were in at 27 I was delirious. 'There it is! There we are!' I was *shaking*. We'd been reading those charts for years – seeing hits come and go, up and down – and finally we had a little place on the ladder. I went out in my Ford Classic, and as I was driving by the Grafton Ballroom I wanted to wind the windows down and shout at everyone, '*We're number 27! We've made it! I'm a hit! A hit! Number 27 in the NME!*' I was sure they'd understand. Twenty-seven was the *height*.[54]

Brian instantly used it to push his pursuit of full national tours, and also to hike the Beatles' nightly fee – their standard ballroom rate, for playing forty-five or sixty minutes, jumped by two-thirds from £30 to £50 – and now, for the first time, proper national interest was developing. He also negotiated another Cavern increase, to £35 for nights and £15 for lunchtimes, with a written guarantee to 'refrain from requesting an adjustment before January next year'.[55]

Love Me Do's success prompted George Martin to liaise with Brian about getting the Beatles back down to EMI, to record their second single: they fixed the session for Monday 26 November, 7–10PM at Abbey Road. The hit also prompted *People And Places* producer David Baker to invite them back; he wanted them on 2 November, but, as they'd be in Hamburg then, it was agreed to pre-record on 29 October. They were returning to Granada's Manchester studio just twelve days after their debut.

Breaching the *NME* chart was a trigger point in so many ways. It meant the Beatles could finally feature in the paper itself – Alan Smith's first piece ran this same week, a factual article headlined LIVERPOOL'S BEATLES WROTE THEIR OWN HIT, illustrated with four head shots. It also meant their activities would now be reported on the news pages. From this point on, a comprehensive rolling Beatles news service ran in the four music papers, accurate and reliable and shining revelatory light on all manner of unfolding events. This very week, reporting what Brian mailed them, the *NME* and *Melody Maker* informed readers throughout Britain that the Beatles would spend the first half of November at the Star-Club, have a *Welcome Home* night in the Cavern on the 18th, that they were featuring in Friday's edition of the BBC's *Teenagers' Turn* (their third broadcast, Ringo's first), and would be showcased with Little Richard at Liverpool Empire this coming Sunday.

Two weeks after the Tower night, the Beatles were back with their American hero and bearing a gift: the photo of them together, blown up into a large print, signed to him and framed. Little Richard told the man from *New Record Mirror* it would hang 'in the gold room' at his house (by which he meant the lavatory) and that he wanted a second shot to go with it: 'I'm going to have a picture taken of Sounds Inc on one side of me and the Beatles on the other, and next time I invite Elvis over I'll show it to him and tell him they are the two best groups in Britain.' Little Richard praising the Beatles to Elvis? – hot air maybe, but the stuff of dreams no doubt. The paper also quoted Richard saying to them, 'I think your record Love Me Do is great. Please don't be offended, but I think you sound like a coloured group. Very few white people have that sound. You should come to America and be famous – you'd go big in the States.'[56]

Richard's tour had been a major success but this was the final date and he'd had enough: he hadn't sung like this, twice a night every night, for five years, and his voice was hurting. Hamburg still loomed, but he was set to quit rock a second time and stick to gospel. He'd considered withdrawing from this Liverpool Empire show and wasn't at his sparkling best, but still he was potent enough for Jim McCartney. At the Empire to see the Beatles' biggest night yet, he realised that Paul's screaming voice, which he'd always considered ridiculous, was actually a great impersonation.[57]

It was, to the day, the first anniversary of Raymond Jones walking into Nems for a copy of My Bonnie, and now Brian was a manager, agent and promoter and the Beatles had a recording contract and were in the charts. Still this was only the start. Countrywide theatre tours were suddenly in the pipeline for early 1963 – Brian was entering talks with three national promoters – and that was what this Empire show was really about, to give the Beatles their theatre debut, to introduce them to the decades-old business and structure they'd soon be having to embrace. Every single star toured this way, from the greatest to the smallest – there was no known alternative.

There were eight acts on this Empire bill; the Beatles went on third and got a more-than-usual twelve minutes. During the afternoon rehearsal, the representative of another artist – 'some cockney manager of one of the so-called stars' as Ringo would sourly describe him – wanted either to cut their time or cut them out of the show completely. 'We all went crying to Brian,' Ringo says. Brian had appointed Bob Wooler stage manager and left him to resolve the issue, but with one clear instruction: 'The Beatles will *do* their twelve minutes, even if you have to cut Little Richard's act.'[58] They were also to stay on stage to back the fourth act, singer Craig Douglas – who, billed second-top, closed the first half.

Nervous before most new stages in their career, the Beatles were uneasy both at the thought of appearing before so many people (potentially, two houses of 2348, although neither sold out) and playing for just twelve minutes instead of an hour. They'd still to decide which numbers to play and who would sing the first one – and, yet again, Bob Wooler was witness to a private situation. 'In the Beatles' dressing-room it was "Who will open the show?" – and then they [John and Paul] were a bit brutal and said, "George, *you* will open the show." George was sort of the Laurel of Laurel and Hardy, *told* he would open the show. He hardly ever opened the show when they were in the local halls and now little George, the junior Beatle, had to open the show.'[59]

There'd be time for four, maybe five songs and some friendly if haltingly nervous between-numbers banter from Paul. George would open with Carl Perkins' Glad All Over, then they'd do Besame Mucho, PS I Love You, perhaps one other, and close with Love Me Do. But the first-house performance opened in shambles: the curtain went up and the spotlights and footlights picked them out but they weren't ready, and Ringo hadn't finished setting up his drums. It was a horrible moment, singled out by him in a questionnaire a few months later as the worst in his professional career. George opened the show 'very well but terribly nervously,' Wooler said, 'but all the fans were rapturous.' These fans weren't grouped together but spread around the theatre, those in the cheaper seats clapping their hands, the rest of them ratifying their adoration from the circle. Still, it just didn't feel right for the Cavernites. Freda Kelly, who was watching from a private box provided by Brian for his staff, remembers 'Paul singing Besame Mucho with the spotlight on him: I couldn't believe they were on *the Empire*. But then, the Beatles weren't *the Beatles* on the Empire.'[60]

Certain things were familiar. When Paul hesitantly announced to the audience 'In the next song you can clap your hands', John went into his cripple act, bigger now for the bigger stage, thrusting his hands together spasmodically, madly casting his eyes, pushing his tongue into his cheek and bawling *clapppp-yerandz*; and when Paul added 'or you can stamp your feet', John thrust out his back leg and stabbed it several times convulsively into the stage, cripping *stammpyerfeet*. It didn't matter that this was the biggest show of their lives –

John just did it more, naturally expressing himself, keeping things grounded, pricking the tension, prompting taut laughter. And what he found, here in the mighty Empire in 1962 as everywhere else, was that no one said *you can't.*

It was all over in twelve minutes and ran smoother in the second house. They also backed Craig Douglas. The Beatles weren't particular fans, but they'd sung two of his hits, Time and When My Little Girl Is Smiling, and knew the material well enough. There was no way Douglas could have appreciated that, here in Liverpool, a form of patriotism existed unlike anywhere else, so that even a generous closing remark could be held against him. As Beatles fan Joan McCaldon explains, 'He said to the audience, "Please give a round of applause to my backing group, the Beatles," and we thought, *"Your backing group?"'*[61]

Outside the back of the Empire, there seemed no doubt who the stars were, Bernie Boyle witnessing a breathless incident on Pudsey Street. 'The Beatles left through the stage door and had to walk to their van, and then suddenly people were running after them and I was running with them and they'd become *pop stars.* The groundswell in our community was that great now: things had really started happening.'[62]

It was the Beatles' final show before leaving for their two reluctant weeks at the Star-Club. On the eve of their last trip they'd played the most incredible hothouse date for the fan club, one of the great, great Cavern nights. Worried about being forgotten, they'd asked from the stage for people to write to them. That was April and this was October, when (with the letters coming ever faster) their final pre-Hamburg bookings were the Empire Theatre and a second shot on TV.[63] So much had advanced in these six months: Parlophone, John and Paul's rebirth as songwriters, Pete out, Ringo in, two strong new contracts, a record issued and on the charts . . . every development pursued with barely a day off, feet down on the gas.

So now, by way of a rest, they were going off to play the Hamburg red-light district.

34

'Show me I'm wrong' (1–15 November 1962)

The Beatles' two original Hamburg trips squeezed 918 stage hours from them in only twenty-seven weeks, so this fourth time, playing a couple of hours a night for two weeks, was a pushover ... and had their complete contempt. They were doing it under duress, and the same was true of the forthcoming fifth visit, at Christmas. Their collective attitude was summed up by John: 'We'd outlived the Hamburg stage and wanted to pack it up. We hated going back those last two times ... but Brian made us go to fulfil the contract.'[1]

Certain aspects were welcome. This was their first Hamburg season with Ringo in the group. He'd been a Hurricane here in 1960 when the four became mates; now John, Paul and George finally had a drummer who went around with them and didn't keep sloping off to do his own thing. It was also great to see old friends again. Jürgen was settled in Paris but Astrid and Klaus were here to welcome the Beatles back with open arms. Stuart had been dead six months and emotions were still raw, but time was beginning to dull the worst of them. They were back too with friendly faces Icke Braun and Kathia Berger; back at Gretel und Alfons, the British Sailors' Society and the Sunday morning *Fischmarkt*; back with the Fascher brothers, foaming glasses and Prellies; back among the brutality and bare breasts, sadism and sex trade.

Nothing had changed except where it counted. The Beatles were on their best-yet Hamburg pay, pocketing DM510 a week each (just under £46) – on a par with their money at home, and with many expenses paid.* They also had

---

* Their actual wage was DM600, but Manfred Weissleder deducted Brian's 15 per cent management commission at source.

better digs: a pair of twin-bed rooms in the Hotel Germania, a small pension on Detlev-Bremer-Strasse, five minutes' quietening walk from Grosse Freiheit. George's idea that John or Paul should room with Ringo was maintained: it had been Paul, here it was John. The hotel was nothing to write home about, but Weissleder paid the bill and acknowledged Brian's insistence on accommodation appropriate for respected artistes, no more of that four-to-a-room nonsense.

Several acts were billed below the Beatles these two weeks: Tony Sheridan, Roy Young, Davy Jones (an American singer; the Beatles had backed him in Liverpool in December 1961) and, from home, Gerry and the Pacemakers and King-Size Taylor and the Dominoes. The starring attraction was Little Richard. Once again, the Beatles were keeping company with the queenly king and his travelling retinue of Billy Preston and Sounds Incorporated.

Here was the trip's one real highspot: John, Paul, George and Ringo had the finest view of the great man's twice-nightly ritual, from stage-side or anywhere else they fancied. 'He'd show off a bit in front of us – he'd want to know we were in the wings,' says Ringo, but it's hard to know how Richard could possibly have shown off any more than usual, because his Star-Club act was Grade A outrageous.[2]

Just three weeks earlier, this Seventh Day Adventist from Alabama had vowed to stick with gospel music and never rock again. He said it here in Hamburg too. But twice a night on Grosse Freiheit the minister was rocking over limits. His high energy act included, every time, a fantastic striptease down to bulging bathing trunks, done while standing on the lid of the grand piano. He started in his tuxedo, white shirt and bow-tie and gradually peeled off almost everything, flinging each article into the audience.

The Beatles hung out with him. They sat in on his backstage bible-study classes, that particular *Penniman* edition of the scriptures, his wild southern-States revivalist oratory sprinkled with their Lancashire spice, tears of laughter folded into the mix. Richard would tell his biographer he liked the Beatles but didn't care for the way John farted, wafted the smell around the room and celebrated when he scored a double,[3] but Billy Preston had no such complaints.

> Right from the start, I fell in love with the Beatles. I was probably their first American fan and friend. John was great – he was funny, he was so smart and clever. I admired him instantly for his wit and manner. You just knew he was special; genius, I suppose, stood out even then, and even to me, a very naïve kid.
>
> He took the time to teach me how to play the harmonica. I learned Love Me Do and reciprocated by making sure that he, George, Paul and Ringo ate.

They didn't get any meals from the promoter, but Richard – being the big American headliner – got steaks and chops and a fabulous spread nightly, so I made sure they [the Beatles] were well fed and watered.[4]

For Preston to play, Manfred Weissleder must have been at his most persuasive with the St Pauli authorities. The *Ausweiskontrolle* hadn't changed, so anyone under 18 had to leave the club at 10PM. George had fallen foul of this law in 1960, when he was 17; Billy was 16 (and 'looked about ten', John said) but here he was, playing Hammond organ on stage with a crazy rocking strip artist on Europe's wickedest street at three o'clock in the morning. He was vulnerable, though, and the Beatles took him under their wing. They made sure he was all right, they dedicated Love Me Do and A Taste Of Honey to him (his favourite songs), and George invited him to join them on stage, to add organ to the Beatles' sound. Preston wanted to but didn't dare: word might get back to Little Richard and 'he'd have got mad'.[5]

Brian Epstein flew in for a few days at the end of the Beatles' first week. He came to see them and also Gerry and the Pacemakers, to handle any difficulties or complaints … and there were *plenty*. The rule of life for the Beatles' manager was, and would always be, that when any of the boys had a gripe he certainly heard about it, and when they were all unhappy he got a complete and utter *belly-aching*. Brian also checked out the Star-Club's other stage talent – he particularly liked the always-impressive Sounds Incorporated – and he conducted business with Weissleder; but when the German wanted to talk about booking the Beatles in 1963, he found Brian evasive, committing to nothing.

Brian enjoyed too some private time among the red lights – like the Beatles, he'd had no holiday this year – but it was a short break. He left Hamburg about 9 November and flew to London, where the job of management was rising through the gears.

To quote his own words, Brian Epstein was keeping the Beatles 'fairly free' from January 1963.[6] He wanted to place them on national tours early in the new year, and any dates still vacant after that would be ballroom bookings – again countrywide. He could achieve this only by limiting Liverpool dates to a few per month. When Bob Wooler and Ray McFall approached him to put the Beatles into the Cavern's 1963 calendar, they found a man keeping his options open. They understood and supported it: they too were dedicated to the cause of making the Beatles national stars … but the Cavern would be the prime casualty.

The Beatles' Cavern pattern of '62 was cast out: Brian wouldn't discuss residencies – not Sunday, Wednesday or any other night – and he ditched the established premise of at least two lunchtimes a week. He had to, because they wouldn't be in Liverpool. He agreed four Cavern bookings in January (two lunchtimes, two nights) and just two nights in February. These six dates for the first two months of 1963 contrast to thirty-nine in 1962.*

Love Me Do didn't progress in the NME Top Thirty – its placing at 27 was a one-week affair – but it was still rising up the other charts and this overall action was enough to make everything possible. Before flying to Hamburg, Brian fixed the Beatles' first tour, of a sort – five ballroom dates in Scotland in the first week of 1963: one hour's stage time a night, played in two thirty-minute bites. He reduced the just-increased £50 nightly fee to £42 in recognition of the block booking, £210 total.

Contracts in 1962 were not complicated. The boilerplate one-page, nine-clause document that booked the Beatles on their first tour had only two typed additions: that Brian would send the promoter publicity materials in advance, and that said promoter – Elgin-based Albert Bonici – was given 'the first option to present this attraction in Scotland following this booking'. Brian had introduced an entice-and-reward policy, and much the same was available for their national tours – but it was an offer spurned, for one reason or another, by three of the country's top promoters, Don Arden, Larry Parnes and the bandleader turned impresario Tito Burns.

Parnes came closest. He and Brian negotiated a place for the Beatles on a February/March 1963 tour headlined by Joe Brown and the Bruvvers, but they couldn't quite agree terms. If Brian had buckled, or Parnes agreed to an extra £60 a week (just over £4 a show), he could have toured the Beatles again for six weeks up to May 1964 and might have secured further options. The Fifties king could have ruled the Sixties . . . but it wasn't to be. So unarguably synonymous was Parnes with everything dodgy in the old English rock 'n' roll business – all puberty, no probity – it was for the best. The Beatles were new school and the *Expresso Bongo* era was passing into history.

His rivals' loss was Arthur Howes' gain. The 38-year-old was a mogul of the touring scene, no small thanks to the benevolence of the Grade Organisation which put acts and opportunities his way. Howes was also agent to several artists of his own, including the young singer Helen Shapiro, and was arranging a tour for her in February/March 1963. It was an unusually complicated affair, broken into three sections because she was also flying to Nashville to record an album. Brian had already spoken to Howes on the phone and secured

---

* It eventually became six Cavern bookings in January (three lunchtimes, three nights) and three in February (one lunchtime, two nights).

the Beatles a one-night booking, and in mid-November they lunched in London to talk other business. Here and now, because the Beatles were in the charts, Howes agreed to add them to at least two of the three Shapiro tour-legs. They were the first supporting act he signed and announced.[7]

He still hadn't seen them. The Beatles were booked into his Frank Ifield promotion at Peterborough on 2 December when he would evaluate them for further work – specifically, another tour he was promoting, in March, starring the American singers Chris Montez (Let's Dance) and Tommy Roe (Sheila). If he thought the Beatles were up to it, they'd go on that tour; if he didn't, they would stick with Shapiro's for its final leg. Whichever, it was now clear the Beatles would be playing nationwide tours through February and March 1963, working theatres from Sunderland in the north-east to Taunton in the south-west, travelling show-to-show in the artists' coach, paid £30 a night with diary space for more lucrative ballroom dates in between. And with Brian enticing Howes' interest by offering him an exclusive three-year option on further tours after this, his plan to present the Beatles before the whole of Britain was already well on the way to being achieved.

The month between this Hamburg season and the next – 16 November to 17 December – was shaping up different to any before. London was calling the Beatles four times: to audition for BBC-tv (their friend 'Letters' Smith brought this about), to broadcast on BBC radio, to appear on national ITV (Beatles fan Pat Brady helped make this happen), to record their second single at Abbey Road, to go merrily again around the music press, and – suddenly now, and most intriguingly – to have a meeting with George Martin at EMI House.

Ardmore and Beechwood had obliged George to sign the Beatles and release Love Me Do. He didn't like or believe in it, so was surprised to see it on the chart after the first weekend and jolted by its subsequent rises. He'd liked the Beatles as people, and appreciated right away how different and appealing they were. They had personality, originality, talent and a strong core following, and now they also had tours and bigger and better radio and TV spots coming up . . . so perhaps it was time to start *planning*. The Beatles already knew their 15 November return from Germany would be to London and not Liverpool, but Brian's evolving itinerary now incorporated this interesting next-day addition: a 3PM meeting with George Martin in the Parlophone office. Ten days ahead of their recording session, George wanted to talk through some ideas.

None of this was known to the man who'd set the ball rolling, Ardmore and Beechwood plugger Kim Bennett. He was too busy beavering away on Love Me Do, going untold extra miles to justify his belief – and his labours were finally bearing fruit. At last now Bennett got the Beatles' record into vast numbers of ears. The first BBC radio play of Love Me Do was in the midday show *Twelve O'Clock Spin* on 31 October, a couple of hours after the Beatles flew off to Hamburg. The audience was a shade under five million, mostly housewives and industrial workers of all ages, and of the show's ten records, three were on Parlophone, produced by George Martin. The Beatles' breakthrough followed twenty-four hours after the same show gave Bob Dylan his first British airplay, with the wailing old hillbilly number Freight Train Blues. The Sixties was rapping on the door of the BBC Light Programme.

Eleven days later, Love Me Do got into *Two-Way Family Favourites* – heard by the week's biggest radio audience, in excess of seventeen million. Appropriately enough for Remembrance Sunday, it was Kim Bennett's Finest Hour and he'd flown to Germany (two weeks earlier) to earn his stripes. He went over to wine and dine the British Forces Network presenter Bill Crozier, a civil servant who was the military end of the BBC's *Two-Way Family Favourites* every Sunday morning, reading requests from serving personnel for their families back home. This was an extraordinary ordeal just to get a record played on the BBC, but worthwhile if it created a hit: Ardmore and Beechwood, like the other big publishers, had an expenses budget for just such a purpose and Bennett typically worked it a couple of times a year. This time, however, unlike any before, he flew there to *beg*.

> I literally said to Bill, 'I've never grovelled before but I'm grovelling to you now because I need to get this record in this programme to show me I'm wrong. And if I'm wrong, I'll stop working the bloody thing.' I pushed home that point because I felt that unless I was proven wrong by a peak programme, I would never know if I was right. Bill said, 'I'll see what I can do,' and I flew out of Cologne not knowing whether I'd achieved it – but a couple of weeks later, Bill came through for me.[8]

Bennett wasn't wrong. The Beatles worried that Love Me Do would slip down the charts in their absence, but it climbed instead. Sales in the week after *Two-Way Family Favourites* pushed it to its highest position yet, 23, in *Record Retailer*, it was up to 26 in *Melody Maker*, it was now in the *Disc* chart at 27, and up to 28 in *The World's Fair*'s Juke-Box 100. Bennett could never be considered solely responsible for Love Me Do's success, but he made a decent contribution and was, for some time, the only man in London shouting the name Beatles. Other accomplishments would follow ... though not for much longer, because Ardmore and Beechwood was about to be handed a different script.

*

Kim Bennett went to Germany to get the Beatles on the BBC – which the Beatles didn't hear because they were in Germany.* Not being in England, they were *fuckin' missing out*, and letters home made clear their frustration. Paul wrote several. To girlfriend Celia Mortimer he said he was 'tired, tired, tired, and just about keeping awake ... Nothing's happened: a thoroughly uneventful week has passed; Hamburg is dead as far as we're concerned.' To Huyton schoolgirl and devoted McCartney fan Fran Leiper, he said he couldn't wait to get home, there being so little of note happening for them in Hamburg that even if he was minded to write a long letter, 'I doubt I could find anything of interest to put in it.'

John could barely stir himself. He very likely wrote to Cyn, but only one Lennon letter has surfaced from this trip, sent to Lindy. She'd been at Liverpool Airport to see them off, and then followed up by sending him one of her funny despatches – but his reply, unlike those sent from here in the spring, was downbeat to the point of depression.

> Thanks for your lovely letter, you're a gas man. I can't think of anything funny for you 'cause I'm so cheesed off I could bloody cry. I hate Hamburg and I wish I was at home. I loved you being at the Airport, it was very thoughtful or something and your hair was good god. This letter won't be a long one 'cause I'm tired and I don't feel like writing, even to you – I haven't answered any other letters 'cause I'm fed up – everyone will think I'm a bastard but I don't care, so there.

Sent from 'The Shit House, Hamburg', the letter ended with 'PS. Wish I was there' and two new additions to John's religious cartoon series – one of a naked man on a cross, with crucifix-shaped genitals, the other of a guitar being crucified.

Conscious of his less-developed written English, Ringo was always a minimal correspondent compared to his bandmates. Identifying himself 'Ringo-Richy' to cover all eventualities, he sent a postcard to Roy Trafford and family: 'Arrived hear OK. Having a good time. Plenty to drink. The weather is cold. We are with Little Richard – he is fab. See you Sunday.'†

George had almost as many pen-pals as Paul. To Margaret Price he said that

---

* Actually, *Two-Way Family Favourites* was receivable in Hamburg, on BFN, but no young Englishman only just toppling into bed at noon, full of pills and booze, was going to stay awake for *that*.

† Hamburg's average temperature in November 1962 was 4.2°C/39°F, the first indication of a particularly savage winter coming to northern Europe.

while everything was going fine, Hamburg remained 'a "DRAG" – still, only 1 week to go and then back to civilisation'. And he sent a warmly funny postcard to Vi Caldwell (addressed to Mrs Violent Stubb), asking her to make sure she'd have the kettle on for their return. 'To caress your teeth once more would be just heaven, also to hold your lungs in mine and drink T.B. John sends you all his lunch, also Paul and Ring-worm greet too!'[9]

The Beatles' contract stipulated three stage hours a night but only two were needed – one earlyish, so under-18s could see them, and one much later, when the club was all-adult and raucous. Their old Cassanova and Big Three mate Adrian Barber had made improvements to the sound system; the Beatles used the house guitar amps, not having bothered to bring their own, and while Ringo had transported his kit, he sometimes used the one that stayed on stage. The Beatles were sartorially casual – they brought their suits but didn't always wear them, playing mostly in shirts and jumpers or polo-neck sweaters – and they were musically loose.

For the first time, all four Beatles played here under the influence of Prellies. On the spectrum of consumption, John was at one extreme, George and Ringo weren't far behind, and Paul took the fewest, while they all drank booze in large quantities. Musicians could indulge in any vice they liked so long as they were ready at the appointed time, with Horst Fascher always on hand to hit home the need for promptness. 'You had to go on, however bad you felt,' Ringo says. 'I heard musicians saying, "Knock me out, I don't want to go on" [but] they would kick you on stage.'[10]

There are few – perhaps no – photos of the Beatles in the Star-Club on this trip. Some scrappy stage shots exist from their two late-'62 visits, but it isn't obvious which. They partied with Little Richard for twelve days but there are no new pictures, and none with Billy Preston or Sounds Incorporated; Manfred Weissleder didn't get out his camera and hired no photographer to snap the talent together. But the Beatles did have an important photo session elsewhere, with Astrid.

Brian needed studio photos for publicity – well lit, properly framed, something arty. A great admirer of Astrid's work, he commissioned her to do it. This would be her sole studio session with the boys she loved, two years (perhaps to the day) since she'd enticed John, Paul, George, Stuart and Pete out to the Hamburger Dom funfair and created the definitive images of the punk Beatles. Since then, she'd only photographed John and George, grieving for Stuart in his artist's garret.

Astrid was in her element when matching subject to setting, but less comfortable in a studio, which was where she now shot the Beatles. She never felt good about this session. 'I didn't really know what I was doing,' she reflects.

'I think *they* liked it, though I never got round to asking. I sent the prints straight to Brian – he liked the photos very much.'[11] Despite Astrid's reservations, several fine images resulted which certainly did the job for Brian: he had group and individual shots printed up for publicity, photos that would become widely seen and always enhance the Beatles' artistic, cutting-edge image.

A nightly visitor to the Star-Club, Astrid was delighted (during the Beatles' second week here) to make a new friend: fan club secretary Bobby Brown. Few 19-year-olds in 1962 were widely travelled. Bobby took the Mersey ferry every morning and evening, Wallasey to Liverpool and back, but not much more – so suddenly being in Germany, in Hamburg, in neon-bawdy St Pauli, was a huge culture shock. She was, though, keeping experienced company. 'I found Hamburg quite scary, but wherever we walked at night I was with John and Paul, so I felt safe. Doormen were constantly trying to entice people into the clubs and bars, and John would pretend he wanted to go in while we'd pretend to pull him back out – it was like a Charlie Chaplin routine.'[12]

In April, during the incredible Cavern night that was *The Beatles For Their Fans*, John had encouraged Bobby to down a few drinks. She usually kept to the soft stuff and quickly lost her sobriety, necking with Paul, throwing up in the Cavern toilets and leaving her own event early. Her second drunken experience was here in Hamburg, when the villain turned carer.

> John had been really drunk the night before, on and off stage. He was quite depressed and whingeing about wanting to go home to Liverpool. I had my arm around him, trying to cheer him up.
>
> The following night, I had some German beers with Astrid, and after the Beatles came off stage and we were all sitting there together, I suddenly felt ill. I told Paul, Astrid took me outside and I was sick. Now it was my turn to whinge, and John looked after me, telling me how lovely I was and how special I was: 'You looked after me last night, I'm looking after you now.'

Bobby knew she was only part of John and Paul's late diversions. They took her out to eat, they mooched around the streets, had a laugh and then walked her back to her hotel before, as she puts it, 'going off for another kind of night life'. With the possible exception of George, who spent much of his time quietly talking to Astrid, the Beatles again had knowledge of the Star-Club *Barfrauen*. Paul was with blonde Ruth Lallemannd, Ringo fancied Heike Evert – known as Goldie, Paul's girl on their last visit – and John resumed relations with BETTINAAAHHHH. Fat Betty (as George called her) would even claim that John invited her up on stage with the Beatles to sing Fats Domino's Blueberry Hill; it seems plausible, because non-musicians were asked up from time to time. Two of the Faschers, Horst and Fredi, occasionally machine-gunned some old rock number or other, to the amusement of the locals.

Bobby Brown flew home with souvenirs, including a monkey on a stick, bought for her by Ringo at Hamburger Dom; a Polaroid photo of Little Richard giving her a great hug, taken by Paul; an autograph in her Cavern membership booklet – 'To Bobby, A Very Pretty Girl. God Bless You. Little Richard'; and a signed throwaway photo-card across which he'd written his Los Angeles home address in beautiful script. Faced with such overwhelming evidence, Bobby's mother felt justified in accusing her of *having an affair with that Little Richard*. The flight back to London was rough – Paul had to use the paper bag – and Bobby watched across the aisle as he and John wrote on a piece of paper, working on something. 'They definitely needed each other,' she says. 'They always seemed to be laughing together, scribbling on bits of paper and laughing some more.'

The Beatles were returning to an array of new opportunities. After landing at London Airport they checked into their usual hotel on Sloane Square and went out to buy the music papers. Their fears had been groundless – Love Me Do was still going up the charts, and now it was time to push on again.

35

New Look, New Sound
(16 November–17 December 1962)

The Sixties' third year was coming to an end with so much still stuck in the Fifties, but every time the Beatles stepped into London to meet the press, a new fuse was burning. The man from *Dance News* had commented on their 'different, unEnglish style clothes' and now *New Record Mirror* said, 'The Beatles are a very off-beat team. They don't wear pointed shoes or have layers of grease on their hair. Chelsea boots, suede coats and long flat hair styles are more their mark.'

Long flat hair. The first to say it in a national paper was the 18-year-old north Londoner Norman Jopling, the youngest writer on the music press. He'd noticed it the instant a Beatles photo arrived in the office. 'Their look was a cross between art college and modernist. Music hadn't caught up with fashion and film – all the pop singers and instrumental groups were still so old-fashioned, with quiffs. When I saw a picture of the Beatles, I knew things were changing.'[1]

The transformation was confirmed when Jopling met Paul McCartney. The Beatles' main appointment this first day back from Hamburg, 16 November, was three o'clock at EMI House, to find out why George Martin suddenly wanted to see them, but they also had a lunchtime interview at *Disc* and, before that, a mid-morning session slotted in at *New Record Mirror* on Shaftesbury Avenue. John, George and Ringo didn't stir, but Paul was up for it. *Someone* had to get them the desired publicity, and he liked seeing the other side of the business: 'I loved it, breezing around these guys' offices. You'd see them [journalists] on their home territory, get a better idea of who they were.'[2]

The resulting article had a wacky headline, "WE MADE SURE OF APPLAUSE –

WE TOOK OUR FANS WITH US", after Paul explained how Brian bussed Beatles fans to certain out-of town dates. It conjured up a pleasingly surreal image: the Beatles hadn't taken people with them, they'd taken *an audience*, winched up as one. Paul said the Beatles liked to play 'Rhythm and bluesy things' but, noted Jopling, he steered well clear of pigeon-holing: 'They don't call themselves a vocal group or an instrumental group or a rhythm and blues group. They just don't know what they are.'[3]

Paul and Brian met up with John, George and Ringo at *Disc*'s office on Fleet Street. They'd made the paper's chart and were due some editorial space; June Harris – a bright, savvy Londoner of 24 – volunteered to see them and suggested they do the interview over a pub lunch. Her fellow *Disc* writer Nigel Hunter joined them, and they walked together along Fleet Street to Ye Old Cock Tavern – diagonally opposite the Royal Courts of Justice, the highest High Court in the land, where the most complex business disputes were decided.

There was an instant problem with the Cock's cockney managers, Bert and Jean, who wouldn't allow the Beatles into the upstairs dining-room. The regular clientele was lawyers, court clerks and journalists, everyone in regulation suits, so the suede jackets, boots, Liverpool accents and 'long hair' offended. They sat downstairs instead, and across a pub table – over drinks, sandwiches, smoke and management antagonism – June Harris was another writer to scent originality.

> The Beatles were new to London and hadn't really acquired any sophistication or expertise yet, but they certainly struck me as having more substance, more purpose, than a lot of people I'd interviewed. George was very sweet and kind, a nice young man, Ringo didn't say much, Paul was sensible and taking things in his stride, and John just got on with it, like 'I know where I'm going and what I want to do with this group'. The others were deferential to him – he was the leader and had a sense of direction for all of them, and when he had something to say he said it, and why not? He wasn't going to take shit from anyone.[4]

Music press writers used pen-names as well as their own, to make the staff seem more numerous. The resulting piece was bylined 'Jean Carol' and had a hackneyed headline typical of *Disc* and its time, BEATLES FIND SHOW BIZ ISN'T ALL FUN. This came from John explaining how tired they felt only twelve hours after flying in from Hamburg. George was quoted the most, saying John and Paul had come up with 'about another six' songs for their next record, but it would probably be a remake of Please Please Me – even though, he said, that title might change because Brian didn't like it.

This was one of many things they discussed in their three o'clock meeting at EMI House. Though, inexplicably, none of its participants would ever pause to reflect on it, this was very likely the most significant creative meeting of their lives. Here and now, in the fourth-floor Parlophone office at 20 Manchester Square, George Martin and the Beatles set down all the necessary components for a harmonious and adventurous working relationship, one that would serve them all so well.

George's ability to hear a catchy song was usually faultless, but he'd erred with Love Me Do and knew it. Despite his misgivings, and lack of support, it had gone into the charts and stayed there – it was now in its sixth week, still rising, selling in thousands, and being noticed in the business. ('I didn't think it [Love Me Do] was all that brilliant but I was thrilled by the reaction to the Beatles and their sound.'[5]) He'd signed an original act that people were talking about, and the combination of this and his fascination with them as people, as personalities, absolutely motivated him. By the letter of their contract, he'd no need to record the Beatles again – Parlophone's commitment was complete – but he wanted to start afresh, to put all the history and histrionics (of which they knew nothing) behind him. Think – and George did – what might be achieved when working together on a record they *all* liked.

They'd be making their second single ten days from now, and – just for the hell of it, sure of the answer he'd get – George re-raised How Do You Do It. The song would be a success for *someone*, and as they still had first dibs, would they reconsider? The answer came hard, fast and flat. They were rejecting a potential smash ... and George respected them all the more for it. His view of the Beatles as 'very self-opinionated' was reinforced, but this didn't put him off.[6] He generally responded well to such people, and was himself – along with the charming and agreeable persona – seldom short of a firm opinion or shy of expressing it. Such tough characters could only work together with give and take, and the will was present on both sides.

George agreed with the Beatles' wish that their second record be Please Please Me – and, as he personally liked the title, Brian's objection to it was subdued and forgotten. George was confident it could achieve big things: he'd had an acetate of Ron Richards' 11 September production on and off his turntable for two months and knew it was strong and catchy, a hit in the making. He'd told them the original was too slow and been impressed by their rearrangement – and now he had a new suggestion to improve it further: that John should play the harmonica.[7] The Beatles agreed, though how much they had to be convinced isn't known. They had an aversion to repeating themselves, but did recognise that reusing Love Me Do's most distinctive instrument, the one that caught in listeners' minds, would be a handy continuation.

George also said he'd let Ringo drum on the recording. He was at least 50 per cent responsible for the decision that had crushed Ringo last time down, but was giving him another try: surely he wouldn't make such a twerp of himself as he had at his first session, and it was obvious that John, Paul and George had complete faith in his ability. Besides, he was playing on the record currently pushing up the charts.

They'd need a B-side, and chose Ask Me Why. It was manifestly good enough, yet it was another song that, until this point, George hadn't rated too highly, not hearing the unusual qualities that others did. He and Brian then conferred about the release date for this record and settled on the second week of the new year, Friday 11 January. The Beatles would fly back from Hamburg on the first day of 1963 with a solid new single to plug on the national tours, ballroom bookings, broadcasts and interviews Brian was setting up.

This was all great news, and then George Martin floored them with his next suggestion. He wanted to make an LP.*

It was a stunning announcement, genuinely mind-boggling. They'd released *one* record, and though it was now in several top thirties, many top-name artists with bigger hits were never asked to make an album, and almost every Parlophone singer was restricted to singles. The LP wasn't the Beatles' natural market: the twelve-inch format, though tilting towards youth, was still dominated by music for the more mature listener. The top sellers in Britain in 1961–2 – bigger than Elvis, Cliff and Adam – were the George Mitchell Minstrels, who swamped the charts' upper reaches with three LPs of olde-time music from *The Black And White Minstrel Show*.

The LP decision seems mystifying but has the purest and most obvious of explanations. A year and a week after Brian Epstein first was bowled over by the Beatles, George Martin was similarly struck – he, too, the ideal receiver in the right place at the right time. His gift for recognising unconventional artistry, and for cultivating that talent in the studio, had made him the most daring and inventive producer in Britain. No one else operated as he did, beyond the basic blueprint: he was a maverick experimenter, following instincts where others played safe. He'd created a bank of memorable left-field successes – records of above-average intelligence that also appealed widely – and now he'd invest his expertise in the Beatles, to find out what they could make together.

His admiration was announced. 'A&R manager George Martin sees a bright future for the Beatles – a new vocal instrumental group,' reported the Great

---

* LP was the term George and the Beatles used in 1962 and for some years beyond, not album. Same difference.

Britain column of the US trade magazine *Cash Box* on 24 November. The recording session two days later was pre-publicised in *Disc* as well as *Mersey Beat*, and the decision to record an LP was revealed by the *NME* on the 30th, under the headline BEATLES LP FIXED.[8] 'The Beatles will record their first LP next month. Parlophone recording manager George Martin may tape the recent "Love Me Do" chart entrants during a session at Liverpool's Cavern Club. Most of the numbers would be written by members of the group.'

As the *NME* intimated, it was to be a live album. Ten days after this meeting, at the Please Please Me recording session, George explained his ideas to journalist Alan Smith: 'I'm thinking of recording their first LP at the Cavern, but obviously I'm going to have to come to see the club before I make a decision. If we can't get the right sound we might do the recording somewhere else in Liverpool, or bring an invited audience into the studio in London. They've told me they work better in front of an audience.'[9]

A certain amount of hurry-up was involved. George Martin's 1962 diary includes an entry for just two days later – 'Sunday 18 November: 9pm, Cavern, Liverpool'. The Beatles would be playing their post-Hamburg *Welcome Home*, sure to be a crazy mad hothouse night, and George would do a recce. He'd assess the Beatles' performance artistically, gauge their special audience rapport, and consider the technicalities of taking mobile recording gear down the humid cellar. But while the diary entry was never deleted, it didn't happen: the trip to Liverpool was postponed three and a half weeks, rearranged for Wednesday 12 December – so although the *NME* anticipated the LP's recording before the year was out, it slipped into 1963.[10]

This 'delay' would enable John and Paul to write the songs, because – as the *NME* made clear, based on what George told Alan Smith – 'Most of the numbers would be written by members of the group'. Smith went into more detail in *Mersey Beat*: 'George Martin added that the numbers on the disc would probably all be originals written by the group, but this hadn't been finally decided.'[11]

George's idea that the Beatles should make an LP was extraordinary; that he wanted it packed with (and perhaps full of) John and Paul's songs is even more so, and there can be no better barometer of both his transformed attitude and interest in seeing where it would lead. This was the man whose reflection on being shown Love Me Do, PS I Love You and Ask Me Why was, 'I didn't think the Beatles had *any* song of *any* worth – they gave me no evidence that they could write hit material.'[12] Since then, he'd heard Please Please Me and Tip Of My Tongue (much preferring the former) and that was it … but, nonetheless, he'd changed his mind.

No doubt Brian was pushing the songs, as part of his separate management of Lennon and McCartney – but still this was a volte-face of immense pro-portions, *and* it was string-free: these wouldn't be Lennon-McCartney-Martin songs. He wasn't going to be inserting his name into the credit and his hand into the royalties, or pushing his own compositions on to Lennon-McCartney's B-sides, like some other producers he might name.

Accepting the songs of Lennon and McCartney would mean a whole new way of working. The production of pop music was rigidly fixed, and explained well by George Martin in a July 1961 *Record Mail* article. It entailed finding a singer, a song and an arranger; they'd work as a trio around his office piano, select the right key and tempo, then discuss the musical treatment, how it should sound and what orchestration it should have; then he'd book the session players, get the music written out for different instruments, and finally head into the studio. Such archetypal A&R functions didn't apply when it came to the Beatles. Their sessions would start with one or some or all four of them demonstrating how the new song went, George would tidy it up as necessary and then they'd record it (along with at least one other title) in the allotted three hours. By letting the Beatles bring along their own songs, George was clearly accepting they were a self-contained group and not to be messed with – the very thing they most wanted. The songs were their songs and the sound was their sound, with a little help.

'Another thing that's worrying us is the title,' George Martin told Alan Smith. *Us?* Artists never had a say in their LP titles, and no EMI contract mentioned anything about involvement in creative decisions . . . but George invited the Beatles to kick around ideas all the same. As a result, here or soon after, Paul came up with a possible title, *Off The Beatle Track*, and a design idea to go with it. He roughly sketched out a square sleeve that had a photograph of the four of them, head and shoulders, the title running horizontally across the middle, two beetle-like antennae sprouting from the B in *Beatle*.[13] George was entitled to disregard it, and did, but the Beatles made it known they had artwork ideas.

This all made a tremendous impression on them. They had a manager dedicated to making them bigger than Elvis and now they had a recording manager (as they called him) to help achieve it. Even their erroneous belief that he'd never recorded rock and roll was considered an advantage. As John would explain, George Martin's productions with Peter Sellers and Spike Milligan 'made him all the more acceptable'[14] – and beyond these was his cache of unusual and alluring 45s which, though recent, were already engrained in British popular culture, from Goodness Gracious Me! to Sun Arise.

They also liked him as a man, very much, for his poise, presence, humour, talents and posh voice; he was the upright English schoolmaster they could rib, be rude to but still respect. If this meeting existed on film, one would see a group of people comfortable in one another's company, laughing easily and openly, they enjoying his wit and impressions, he enjoying theirs; five men – six with Brian – of one mind, fixed on a common purpose, certain of their own ideas but receptive still to others. George experienced 'a sense of well-being, of being happy' in the Beatles' company; he found them attractive, talented and funny, and cared that they thought well of him. 'It shouldn't really have mattered to me, whether they liked me or not,' he'd explain, 'but I was pleased they seemed to.'[15]

They called him Big George to avoid confusion with their George, and also because he *was*: they were tall but he was taller, over six feet, and handsome, carrying a statesmanlike presence. The combination suggested Prince Philip, so they also called him the Duke of Edinburgh, and he played up to it delightfully. Though George was younger than many of his artists, to the Beatles he was clearly older, an avuncular or even fatherly figure – although, at 36, much more youthful than their uncles or dads. He'd been born in a different era, in London, and fought in the war; he was a grown-up who dressed well but old (turn-ups on his trousers), and who adopted Brian's familial term of affection for them: to George Martin too now, the Beatles became 'the boys'.

So it was all working out. If the Beatles had signed to Decca they'd have had none of this. Chances are, they'd have been saddled with a producer doing a standard job, resistant to their views and pushing formulaic Tin Pan Alley songs on them to the exclusion of their own . . . perhaps until their contract wasn't renewed. But instead of being with *that* multinational giant, they were with its greatest rival. On 22 October, when Decca posted a healthy profits increase, EMI chairman Sir Joseph Lockwood sent a letter of congratulation to his counterpart, Sir Edward Lewis, jokingly beseeching, 'I wish you could show us how to do it in EMI.' Twenty-five days later, the answer was sitting right beneath his feet.[16]

Not that it would be *all* gain for EMI. This fact became apparent in a second stage to the Beatles' meeting, held either late the same afternoon or in the days immediately after. They weren't present – it was just George Martin and Brian Epstein, shaping all their futures. The two men had liked each other in May and communicated well since, respecting each other's integrity. Now they were becoming closer still, establishing a professional and personal rapport that would glue this whole remarkable thing together.

Their meeting focused on how to maximise Please Please Me's potential, and George had a specific suggestion that would reverberate forever: that Brian should give the record's publishing to another music company and not to Ardmore and Beechwood. Brian was already thinking of it. He'd been unhappy with several factors concerning the publishing of Love Me Do and PS I Love

You: there was the unfortunate business of both songs being credited on the record labels to Lennon-McCartney after he'd expressly requested McCartney-Lennon, and there were the BBC disappointments: Love Me Do wasn't in *Juke Box Jury* and had been withdrawn late from *Saturday Club*, which Brian felt was Kim Bennett's blunder.

In fact, Bennett was innocent of the *Saturday Club* situation, *Juke Box Jury* was an impossibility (and he'd had no less joy than Parlophone's own plugger), and Ardmore and Beechwood mightn't have been responsible for the wrong songwriting credit. Crucially, however, Bennett and his boss Sid Colman were not invited to defend themselves, and George Martin wasn't going to do it.

George would say, in print, 'Ardmore and Beechwood . . . did virtually nothing about getting the record [Love Me Do] played', but if he believed this, he wasn't acquainting himself with the available facts.[17] Kim Bennett had moved heaven and earth to help make Love Me Do a hit. No man could have done more, and George himself did a lot less. After extreme efforts, Bennett's successes were beginning to mount up – but, one way or another, Brian would conclude that Ardmore and Beechwood had been lazy and of no use to them, and that he should take John and Paul's business to a publisher who'd actually work hard on the songs.

George was sidelining Ardmore and Beechwood. He needed to draw a line under the past and be free to work with the Beatles on his own terms – because he wanted them, not because he'd been forced to take them. He was, at a stroke, cutting adrift the awkward circumstances that had brought him to this point. It made sense in Brian's mind: Ardmore and Beechwood *must* have been useless because why else would an EMI employee be steering a potentially lucrative contract away from an EMI office? Kim Bennett realised what was happening. 'When a song's been established in the charts, there's no reason to change the publishing set-up [on the next one] unless you want to be spiteful. George was *very naughty* in getting them away from us.'[18]

It was a manoeuvre, no more or less, the kind of thing that goes on in business every day. There's no saying Lennon and McCartney's copyrights would have stayed with Ardmore and Beechwood anyway. Even if Brian had given them Please Please Me and Ask Me Why, he might have switched after that. Publishing assignments were always for individual songs with no options reserved on future work, and only the most astute music men had the wit to keep composers loyal to one company.

Brian was thinking of taking John and Paul's music to the London office of Hill & Range, the American company which (under that and other associated names) published most of Elvis's records. George Martin didn't exactly discourage him but put three other names into the frame: Dick James, David Platz and Alan Holmes. All were good Tin Pan Alleymen with years of experience, who'd published George's own compositions. The key difference was owner-ship: Platz and Holmes ran the London offices of American corporations – Essex Music and Robbins Music – while James was British and proud of it. Born in the East End of London to immigrant parents, he flew the flag for British writers at a time when American domination of London was a red-hot potato up the Alley. While Brian was free to assess his options with any publisher, George clearly recommended Dick James and brought the two parties together over the phone before they first met in person on 27 November – the morning after the Please Please Me and Ask Me Why recording session.

There was no time off from here to their Hamburg Christmas – the Beatles had thirty-one consecutive workdays of every kind, requiring constant van and air travel up and down the country. Their 1963 calendar effectively began on 17 November 1962 . . . and not in the best of shape. Brian had urged them to stay sharp in Hamburg, anticipating the onslaught coming their way, but they'd allowed tiredness and boredom to take root. Stage-wise, not even the meeting with George Martin invigorated them. Their initial booking of this new phase was the Saturday dance in a big Coventry ballroom, their first £50 show. It was one Paul would always remember with a shudder, the night to cite whenever he needed reminding that things could be bad but hard work made them better. 'We weren't always good. You'd have these disastrous nights where you're all out of tune, you forget how to turn the amps up, you forget where your levels are and exactly how near the mike it is you've got to sing. We'd have to do a week of that, in the ballrooms, before we could actually get around to doing any good shows – and then we'd be back in it and could go on forever.'[19]

It says everything for how new-style the Beatles were that their impact this night was still powerful. Pete Waterman, junior DJ at the Matrix Hall in Coventry, would recall, 'We mostly had *stars* playing there, but these guys were swearing, carrying their own gear, totally *un*star. Their personalities just won you over straight away. They were different – Harrison was playing Chet Atkins [records] in the dressing-room and Lennon was wearing Levi's. I'd never seen Levi's before. The Matrix promoter said the Beatles would be the greatest thing the world had ever seen.'[20]

Their popularity was building everywhere, boosted by the sustained success of Love Me Do. Even on Merseyside, where they'd been far and away the most popular group for almost two years, new fans were crowding in to see them. There were a great many boys, but mostly it was girls, kids who hadn't been part of the Beatles' development and were tuning in 'late'. Generally, these girls behaved differently around them: they screamed more and were less respectful of distance, and they didn't have – couldn't possibly have – the same close relationships precious to their predecessors. For some, the many was way too much. Despite her special friendship with John, Lindy Ness decided to look elsewhere for her entertainment: 'When Love Me Do came out there started to be big queues, and Louey and I began to see girls in the Cavern from our school class. These were the girls who'd always pooh-poohed this whole thing, and now they were going along too. When we saw those queues, full of people who'd not been interested before, we just stopped going. We "moved on" ... horrible little girls that we were!'[21]

This week's sales pushed Love Me Do up to 21 on the *Record Retailer* Top Fifty, its highest place yet; it also sustained previous positions on *Melody Maker*, *Disc* and *The World's Fair* and stayed all month in Liverpool's Own Top 5. Unaware of the fate about to befall his project, Kim Bennett was suddenly picking up airplay with relative ease: he'd flown to Germany to beg Love Me Do into *Two-Way Family Favourites* and now it made what Tony Barrow (in his Please Please Me press release) claimed was 'the fastest-ever repeat play'. BBC research indicates that this particular broadcast was heard by almost 40 per cent of the measured audience, 18.8 million, with plenty more listening in West Germany. Then 5.4 million heard another play in *Twelve O'Clock Spin*, an occasion when the Beatles first shared the airwaves with Elvis.[22]

It was for the BBC that the Beatles rushed back to London on 23 November, to take the TV audition brought about by their young Preston friend, Letters Smith. Brian was doing his best to minimise the Beatles' travelling but such demands were the inevitable consequence of running a chart group from Liverpool when virtually everything in the business happened two hundred miles away. Their appointment was close to Hyde Park, in one of the many church halls the BBC hired for auditions and rehearsals. Though no verdict was expressed at the time, Brian soon received a letter saying the Beatles might be offered a second audition 'some time in the near future', in a TV studio. It seemed like a rejection but was actually a standard response, and a few days later the Beatles were invited on a new-talent series, *The 625 Show*, starting in January. It would be aired live from the BBC's Bristol studio – but the Beatles were already booked on the available dates. Their TV exposure would stay solely on the commercial channel for a time to come, because the more dates were in their diary, the harder it was to take advantage of late opportunities. This was Brian's own brand of *inevitable consequence*.

Norrie Paramor got his the following day, when the BBC unveiled its new Saturday-night entertainment *That Was The Week That Was*. Fast, funny, scathing and scabrous, it was the first TV show anywhere in the world to expose and wantonly skewer public figures ... and Paramor was a principal target in the premiere edition, prompted by his EMI A&R colleague George Martin. The host of *TW3* (as it became known) was David Frost, the same young man who, eight months earlier, as a programme researcher, had treated George to a cheap lunch and received rich tales of the way Paramor worked, particularly his tendency to slip his own songs on to B-sides or A-sides. About to become the public face of 'the satire boom', and the first Sixties-made TV star, Frost was determined to set down a marker. He stood before the nation this first night and, in a self-written sketch running almost six minutes, hit Paramor hard: 'Norrie is an *ordinary* man writing *ordinary* tunes with *ordinary* words. During the last ten years, Norrie Paramor has used all his power and all his influence and made everything *ordinary*.'

Those who missed the show – Norrie included – heard all about it. PARAMOR PILLORIED! shouted *Melody Maker*, devoting an entire page to commentary and reactions. It was the talk of the business for months, and the question on everyone's lips was, had an insider dished the dirt? Paramor's secretary, Frances Friedlander, remembers the whole business as 'horrible' and thinks Norrie never found out who was behind it.[23] Little else was discussed at EMI all day Monday, not by the reps on the road, nor at the Hayes pressing plant, the Manchester Square head office, or the St John's Wood studios ... and the gossip was still reverberating when the Beatles swung by to make their second record.

Recording session

Monday 26 November 1962. Number 2 studio, EMI, London.
Recording: Please Please Me; Ask Me Why.

The Beatles' three previous Abbey Road sessions had a hunched-shoulders feel about them, the parties slightly kicking against each other, reined in by restrictions, at odds over material, beset by nerves and frustrations, working ... but not working well.

This was a restart. Love Me Do's impressive run up the charts and the 16 November office confab altered everything – the work was efficient, energetic, exciting and harmonious, the chemistry gelled, the jokes flew, everything clicked, and inside the allotted three hours the Beatles-George Martin production line started rolling. 'It went beautifully,' George said. 'The whole session was a joy.'[24]

The aim was clear: to tape both sides of the second Parlophone record, for 11 January release. The titles were known and the music familiar: these weren't songs that needed much more producer input. Ask Me Why would be remade almost as they'd done it in June; Please Please Me had already been rearranged to everyone's satisfaction and they needed only to play it as best they could and then add harmonica. Number 2, becoming their usual studio, was booked 7 'til 10PM, ample time – and by verbal agreement they arrived at six for an hour's rehearsal and technical prep.

There was no session drummer. The four on the floor, setting up in the far left corner, were John, Paul, George and Ringo. In the upstairs control room, behind the glass, there was no Ron Richards. George Martin was the 'A/M in Attendance' (as the studio red form specified), their usual engineer Norman Smith was manipulating the mixing desk, and an assistant was on hand to start, stop and spool the tapes and make tea. Brian Epstein and Neil Aspinall were present, along with a couple of invited guests: the NME's Alan Smith, who'd be offering a written account of the session to *Mersey Beat*, and Bobby Brown, who'd travelled in the van with Neil while the Beatles and Brian took the train.

Bobby followed them down to the studio, to sit among them as they rehearsed . . . and to receive an unexpected invitation. Would she play piano on Please Please Me? The question was quite apposite – Lindy Ness and Lou Steen had been lying under Jim Mac's piano in June when John and Paul worked on the song, now John wanted a girl to help them record it. His request was specific: that Bobby play certain chords at three junctures, emphasising the fast doubled guitar escalations at 0.12, 0.40 and 1.25. 'John was showing me these chords on the piano, saying, "So Bobby, you can play this . . ." and I just said to him, "You're mad. There's no way I can do this." He said, "But you *can* play piano," and I said, "Yes, but I have to have a piece of music in front of me." It went on like this for some time, and in the end I just said *I can't do it*.'[25] It couldn't have happened anyway. She wasn't in the Musicians' Union and non-union talent was prohibited from recording.

George Martin then cleared the floor of all but the Beatles, so the session proper could start. Having decided to make an album, it made sense to tape them in stereo as well as mono, but George again shied away from using Abbey Road's four-track recorder, opting instead for the twin-track process, recording all the vocals in one mono channel and all the instruments in the other, allowing only a rudimentary stereo mix at a later date.

They did the most important number first. When the red light went on for Please Please Me, John was standing there with the Jumbo Gibson acoustic, plugged into his Vox amp, George was holding the treasured Gretsch Duo Jet, plugged into his Vox, Paul's Hofner Violin bass was plugged into the studio's Leak amp, and Ringo was sitting behind his six-piece Premier kit. Each guitar amp/speaker had a state-of-the-art microphone in front, Ringo's drums had two (one by the bass, one overhead) and there were two vocal mikes. Please Please

Me had never been a stage number – it was purely a studio song – but they played as if on the road, instruments and voices live, a straight performance for as many takes as George Martin considered necessary, which was fifteen.

The song's virtues had been obvious in September's recording – two minutes of exhilarating harmonies, melodies, riffs and runs – only this time they did it so much better and so much hotter, properly finding their feet in the studio for the first time. The vocals are a formidable fusion of John's lead and Paul's high-note harmony, bowling the song along with electric energy. John's quadruple *Come on!* calls are echoed in snappy girl-group sound by Paul and George, rising in pitch to crank the tension. George's playing is solid, John's is buried, and the bass (in spite of its cheapness) proves itself both great for recording and dynamic in Paul's hands. He gives the song its pulsing heartbeat by playing mostly a fast repeated single note, while also tripping into an attractive and intuitive counter-melody. And Ringo keeps the rock beat right on time, full of meaty fills and flourishes – a top performance. The whole thing is high energy until, after precisely two minutes, it skids to a halt with everything still happening at once and falsetto vocals slapped excitingly on top.

Once John had overdubbed the harmonica parts – designed to double George's motif guitar lines – it was done, and it was great. Love Me Do was unlike anyone else's recording and now Please Please Me took that initiative and ran several miles with it. Nothing *remotely* like this had ever been made before, not in Britain or America. The influences were checked – Orbison, Everlys, Isleys, Smokey's Miracles, Goffin and King – but the Beatles had taken them and created something else, something vital, joyful, earthy, throaty, catchy and genuinely uplifting. For the second time, only more so, they had *a new sound*.

Upstairs, George Martin reached across Norman Smith, pressed the talkback key and let his voice boom into the studio below: 'Gentlemen, you've just made your first number 1 record.'[26]

'They laughed at me,' he told the *NME* six months later . . . but, for sure, they knew. Please Please Me had *number 1* stamped all over it. The tape would require just a little tidying, notably an edit to cover where John sang the wrong words (a regular problem of his), but that would be done another day and they didn't need to be there for it. Here and now, mono reference lacquers (acetate discs) were cut – Brian would take some with him when meeting John and Paul's prospective new publishers next morning.[27]

Everyone then had a canteen break and Alan Smith took the chance to grab a few words with George Martin. Being Beatles producer already entailed a writer taking notes at his session and soliciting quotes about plans and prospects, which assured him all the more that he'd found a winner. George told Smith about his ideas for making a live LP in the Cavern, with most of the numbers written by John and Paul; he likened the Beatles to a 'male Shirelles' (which will have delighted them) and, inevitably, he glowed about them as people: 'The thing I like about the Beatles is their great sense of humour – and their talent, naturally. It's a real pleasure to work with them because they don't take themselves too seriously. They've got ability, but if they make mistakes they can joke about it. I think they'll go a long way in show business.'[28]

One of their jokes was about Norrie Paramor. The Beatles hadn't seen *That Was The Week That Was* – they'd been playing Prestatyn on Saturday night, another drawing-pin in Brian's wall map – but the topic was discussed around the canteen table and it was a conversation John promptly collapsed when he called Britain's foremost record producer Noddy Paranoid.[29]

And if, as George said, the Beatles were to 'go a long way in show business', they'd be going there speedily. John noticed Bobby Brown being unusually quiet at the table – she was tired, and intimidated by the company and surround-ings – so he proffered a remedy. 'He took out a pill and said, "Take that,"' she says. 'I took it and didn't notice much difference. It could have been aspirin as far as I was concerned.' It wasn't, of course. Just back from Hamburg, John had a fresh supply of Prellies, some of which were rattling in his suit-pocket. Bobby's experience suggests every likelihood John was speeding at the session, which would also indicate a fair chance he wasn't the only one. The Beatles could play Please Please Me well in every situation, straight or high, but they did it at such a lick here that the effect of a few Grosse Fräulein slimming pills can't be ruled out.

They're not audible on Ask Me Why, the B-side recorded after the break – the Beatles sound relaxed and assured all the way. It's a finely crafted mid-tempo piece, decorative, catchy, melodic, Miracles-ish and ending with an unusual and appealing minor seventh chord. John strums his plugged-in Jumbo and sings lead, Paul handles bass and yet more highly effective co-vocals, Ringo keeps the Latinish beat dead steady, and George plays lead, omitting a few little phrases heard in June's BBC recording, which might have been George Martin's suggestion. It took only six takes to find the 'best'.

Tony Barrow – fed word by Brian – called the session 'unusually smooth and brief' in the following Saturday's *Liverpool Echo*, and it certainly was. Booked for three hours, they finished fifteen minutes under. Ten days before, the Beatles told George Martin they worked better in front of an audience than in the recording studio, but at the instant he was relaying their words to Alan Smith, they'd gone out of date. Tuned in and moved in – the studio had started to be the Beatles' second home.

The session was a triumph for Ringo. He'd taken a hefty kick up the backside on their last visit, suffering the indignity of substitution. Was he going to take it lying down or was he going to damn well *show* George Martin? John, Paul and George knew their man could deliver – it was one of the many reasons they picked him. He played with imagination and skill on both Please Please Me and Ask Me Why, securing a self-confidence in the studio that would never leave him. They all did. *And* their producer was telling them they'd made a number 1.

It's possible he also talked to them of America, because he was certainly thinking it. EMI correspondence makes clear that George Martin believed Please Please Me could break the Beatles in the States. During December, EMI's Licensed Repertoire manager Roland Rennie sent two letters about it to Joe Zerga at Transglobal Music in New York. On the 11th, he wrote, 'George Martin, the A. and R. responsible for producing the Beatles' records, has come up with what we consider to be a smash. Could you please place this record with a company which will really get behind [it]? We here are certain this record will be in the Top five in this country shortly after its release.' And on the 28th: 'we have great faith both in the artistes and in the record because George Martin is really anxious to establish the Beatles on your side of the Atlantic'.[30]

It must have been such sweet music to Brian. He'd set his eyes on America almost the moment he saw the Beatles, and now, only a year on, they seemed an inch from stepping through. These two letters also make it clear that whereas Love Me Do had enjoyed minimal support inside Manchester Square, Please Please Me would have something like maximum.

First, however, the Beatles had to endure the agony of suppressing their sure-fire hit for another five weeks. The shackle would come off in the first days of 1963, and then they'd be pushing Please Please Me hard, everywhere, town to town, all over the country and across the airwaves.

The Beatles' turning-point TV booking – the one that would plug their name, their sound, their look, their personalities and Please Please Me into the eyes and ears of at least nine million possible buyers – was fixed the following day by John and Paul's new music publisher. Brian had two morning appointments on Tuesday 27 November, the first at ten, the second at eleven; the latter, with Dick James, was arranged by phone from George Martin's office, and when Brian mentioned the name of the first man he'd be seeing, the first man who'd be hearing his Please Please Me acetate, James was bold enough to remark that this other publisher would 'take the song whether it's good, bad or indifferent'. He asked for, and received, a fair chance to make a pitch for it himself, despite being the day's second appointment.

He [Brian] said, 'I promise you I will not give the song away before you've had an opportunity to hear it and assess it – and I can see your enthusiasm for it.' He sounded very much a man of his word and I accepted this. Well, I had to. I arranged to meet him at my office at eleven o'clock.

About 10.20, my secretary announced that Brian Epstein had arrived, and she ushered him into my office. I said, 'I thought we were going to meet at eleven?' and he said, 'Well, I've had enough of that. I had an appointment at ten and I was there at ten, and there was [only] an office boy. At 10.10 nobody had turned up and I wasn't going to play it to an office boy. You're good enough to be here wanting to meet me, so here I am and I'm not going back to that [other] publisher.'[31]

Dick James had already canvassed good opinion on the Beatles – from his 15-year-old son Stephen, from BBC radio producer Peter Pilbeam, and from Dick James Music receptionist Lee Perry, who counted Love Me Do among her favourite current records.[32] He was already prepared to publish Please Please Me for all these reasons, and because of George Martin's conviction it was a huge hit, but he wasn't prepared for it to knock him over. He and Brian were sitting in his triple-aspect office plumb over the corner of Denmark Street, opposite Foyle's bookshop; Brian drew the acetate from his attaché case, handed it across the desk, James lowered the stylus, and the Beatles' unbridled exuberance exploded into the room.

Last night I said these words to my girl . . .

James would be asked to recall the moment more times than he could ever count. 'I just hit the ceiling. He said, "What do you think?" and I said, "I think it must be number 1. If we get the breaks and can get the exposure on the record, it must be number 1."'

Exposure was the key, and James delivered a masterstroke. Philip Jones, the producer of his 1950s Radio Luxembourg shows, all those treacly singalong sessions, was now producer of *Thank Your Lucky Stars*, ITV's one networked pop show. James called him and said he should sit tight because he was going to hear something exciting. He held telephone to gramophone and the-coming-sound scorched 110 miles to Birmingham, singing in the wire.

Jones said yes, the Beatles could appear on *Lucky Stars*. The show pre-recorded every Sunday for screening the following Saturday – what was the record's release date? Brian said Friday 11 January. The ideal broadcast was the 12th ... but the previous Sunday the Beatles would be in Scotland. Brian turned a page in his 1963 diary (pocket version) and confirmed they were free to record the following Sunday, the 13th, and the booking was made. It was a fantastic achievement for James to have pulled from the hat. Ardmore and

Beechwood hadn't got the Beatles on *Thank Your Lucky Stars*; Dick James had, in the space of five minutes. He'd proved what he could do, and the only way was forward. Their meeting lasted the rest of the morning and his enthusiasm only grew.

James was about to turn 42 and had more than twenty years' broad professional experience in plugging, publishing, managing, songwriting and performing: he was still one of very few British singers to have achieved an American top twenty hit. He knew Please Please Me was strong and very much liked Ask Me Why. He also knew George Martin was planning to use a batch of the Beatles' self-written songs on their live LP. So what with those to come, these two now, and the pair that Ardmore and Beechwood published, he'd found a rich seam of new material. Brian confirmed it: as well as managing the Beatles he also represented John and Paul as composers, and (as Paul liked to claim) they had a hundred songs tucked away.

With this revelation, the two men strolled to the French restaurant La Maisonette on Tottenham Court Road to talk over lunch. Each acquainted the other with what had brought him to this point, and – listening intently as Brian spoke – James could not have been more impressed. 'He was telling me about the Beatles and what they were like and their sense of humour, and one could see that his admiration, his utter 100 per cent immersion in their career and what they were trying to do . . . this was an incredible attitude I was seeing from him – just as much as he was seeing a very refreshing attitude, a genuine attitude, on my part.'

Among many elements, they connected as Jews. Neither was especially 'observant', but they shared a common heritage, a proud history despite brutal repression. Dick extended Brian an invitation to join him, his wife and son at their house for Friday-night Sabbath dinner any time he liked. Mostly, though, they confined themselves to the issue of how to get the Beatles to number 1.*

Brian knew that as a newcomer in London show business he was vulnerable to rogues; it was critical he involve the Beatles only with those he judged 'the most honest of established experts'. George Martin was one, and through

---

* Dick James was born Isaac Vapnick on 12 December 1920 in Whitechapel, in the East End of London, the youngest of five children of parents who'd fled Poland (near the Russian border) after suffering appallingly in the Pogroms. In the Second World War, entertaining troops with Henry Hall's orchestra, Isaac sang as Johnny Sheridan (and later wrote songs as Lee Sheridan). When he sang with Geraldo in 1945–6 he changed his name to Dick James, and formally to Richard Leon James. His recording career at EMI began at this time, and George Martin produced his solo records for Parlophone from 1953 until they ceased in 1959.

George he'd now found a second. Dick James' secretary, Rosalind (Linda) Duque, says, 'Dick was known to be a man of his word. He was honest, and what you saw was what you got. He was an astute businessman, as he proved, and he was straight down the line.'[33]

Interviewed sixteen months later for his autobiography, Brian said of his new business ally, 'I regard him as a most trustworthy and honest person, and he has tremendous enthusiasm. Although Dick is older than the majority of people around the Beatles I found that he gave me good advice in the beginning and it was useful to have an older person around who knew a lot of people, and I also liked him.'[34]

Brian had found more than a music publisher – he was establishing, loosely speaking, a London representative for his management and artists. The pair formulated a policy over their French lunch. The first important point to understand was that, just as producing the Beatles meant a whole new working routine for George Martin, publishing the Beatles would do away with the stolid practices of Tin Pan Alley. Standard procedure was to plug the song and not the performer – this was why the charts could be clogged with multiple versions of the same number – but Brian made it clear that no one was to record competing versions of John and Paul's songs unless they all agreed it. Publishing the Beatles would require Dick James to *control* the copyrights, ensuring the Beatles' recording was sacrosanct.

Dick's usual remit, plugging the copyrights, now meant pushing the Beatles, exposing the songs by getting *them* seen and heard in all the right places. Brian gave him permission to fix certain radio and TV dates for them, subject to consultation and the contracts being sent straight to him in Liverpool. *Thank Your Lucky Stars* was just the start – Dick had strong connections throughout the business and would begin immediately by trying to get them a session on *Saturday Club*. He'd take no commission for any of this: his reward would come through the publishing – from sheet music sales, PRS and mechanical royalties. The more airplay they had, the more he earned; the more records they sold, the greater his income. Here was every incentive for a hard-working man to help make the Beatles as big as possible.

It was the third great advance for the Beatles in eleven days. First the meeting with George Martin, then the Please Please Me recording, now Brian hooking up with Dick James ... and none of this happened in Liverpool. From the end of November, Dick James Music became the Beatles' first London office, sort of, a place they'd be able to use the phone and the loo, hang around, keep warm, eat, sup tea, be interviewed and chat up the secretaries.

The first agreements were signed after lunch, template documents with the specific details for Please Please Me and Ask Me Why typed in by Linda Duque, who then witnessed the James and Epstein signatures. The contract terms were the standard '10:50:50', and the composer names went down as Lennon and McCartney in that order – correctly so, given that these were almost entirely John's songs. Confusion then resurfaced when Parlophone's record 'label copy' (printing instructions) credited both numbers to McCartney-Lennon. This was either through simple error, repeating what should have appeared on the first record, or was intentional, an attempt to even out the previous mistake, so both writers got their name printed first ... just on the wrong record. A written directive from Brian would have clarified the situation, but no such edict is on the Epstein, James or EMI files.

As he set out to plug his new copyrights, Dick James had the advantage of the leg-up given the Beatles by Kim Bennett. He could push them further and faster partly because Please Please Me was a stronger record, but also because the Beatles were off the blocks, given momentum by Love Me Do's chart action and airplay; and it was Bennett who got the Beatles their work this very afternoon and evening. While Brian was signing the Please Please Me and Ask Me Why contracts at Dick James Music, John, Paul, George and Ringo were making their way to the BBC's Paris Studio, on Regent Street, to rehearse and record an appearance in the Light Programme audience show The Talent Spot.[35]

Keeping Please Please Me tucked up their sleeve, they did Love Me Do, PS I Love You and Twist And Shout – their first recording of the Isley Brothers' song. Though unavailable for review (this is one of the few still-lost Beatles broadcasts), an eyewitness vouches for their storming performance. Alan Smith was in the audience, keeping the Beatles company for the second night in a row, and again being enthralled. He didn't recognise the song – he thought it was Ritchie Valens' La Bamba – but he felt it. They played their brilliant rearrangement, so much more dynamic now with Ringo.

Smith was at the Paris with hot news for his Merseyside comrades. In the NME just rolling off the presses, the Beatles had got into the annual readers' poll – they were voted fifth most popular British Vocal Group and eighth most popular British Small Group.[36] On the strength of one record, it really was impressive. Eleven months after winning the Mersey Beat poll, they'd gone national.

The results were reported in the same 30 November NME in which their LP was announced. The Beatles' star was rising fast ... a point happily underscored when they received their first EMI royalty statement. It accounted for 36,868 copies of Love Me Do sold to wholesalers and retailers in the first eight weeks of the record's life. At the royalty of a penny a record on 85 per cent of sales, Brian was sent a cheque for £130 11s 6d. After deduction of his 15 per cent commission, the four Beatles were left with £111, or £27 15s each. A retirement fund it wasn't, but it was celebrated like one.*

So relentless was their upward progress, blips would be magnified into setbacks in the telling of the story. One of the Beatles' biggest face-slaps was apparently handed them by three thousand Peterborough citizens on Sunday 2 December; this was the time they played in support of headlining star Frank Ifield, when fans of the suave smiling Aussie directed antipathy at the Beatles across the footlights.

The night was a sign of the times. Ray McFall and Bob Wooler let the Beatles off their Sunday Cavern residency without Brian being able to offer an alternative; the Beatles simply dropped out of Liverpool and turned up in the east Midlands for a theatre show that also doubled as a test, so promoter Arthur Howes could see if he'd be adding them to his March 1963 tour with Tommy Roe and Chris Montez. The Beatles played second-top in Peterborough, closing the first half in each of the two houses. They also claimed a page in the souvenir programme. Here is Ifield, the 25-year-old matinee idol handsome in stock studio poses, and there are the Beatles, four keen young long-hairs under a slate-grey Liverpool sky, leaning over the rail of a salvage boat.

'We used to think twenty-five was the end of the line,' Paul remembers. 'Frank Ifield was twenty-five and he was our gauge: we thought, "You can't do *this* beyond twenty-five."'[37] Age, and at what point it became ridiculous to still be playing this kind of music, was a topic the Beatles bantered in the van while Neil was putting another 160 miles on the clock, and it was an exchange with edge because golden oldie Ifield was taking out Paul's girl Iris Caldwell, and they all knew it. Bernie Boyle, along for the ride, remembers a flavour of the chat:

> The whole way there, John was saying to Paul, 'You're banging Frank's girl-friend. What's going to happen when we get in the dressing-room – there's not going to be a punch-up is there? 'E's a big fucker, that Frank.'
>
> After we arrived, we were all in the dressing-room plotting what would happen if Frank came in. We decided we'd all jump on him and beat the crap out of him, before the show even started. But of course, it was all fine.
>
> I remember saying to them, '*Fuck* Frank Ifield – you're going to be bigger than Elvis!' and Paul shushing me and saying, 'Eat humble pie, Bernie, eat humble pie.'[38]

---

* John and Paul's publishing income would come separately – they weren't due their first statement from Ardmore and Beechwood before up to ninety days from 31 December. Brian could already work out, however, that they stood to earn at least £325 – which, after deduction of his 20 per cent commission, would give them £130 each, opening a wealth gap with George and Ringo.

Frank was above it. He was toppermost and the Beatles but a minor irritant, like amateurs in the presence of a pro, scruffs in the shadow of that fine quiff. This was their first theatre gig outside Liverpool and only their second ever. In Eppy's Empire show, their inevitably awkward adjustment to the big stage was excused by an audience of friends, and not even Brian had noticed that without stage make-up they were the biggest palefaces this side of the prairie. It was an error they repeated here first-house, until fellow musician Ted Taylor had a quiet word with them about *pancake*. He demonstrated how to apply Leichner 27 with a wet sponge, and trace a thin black pencil line around the eyes and lips for definition under lights. But divining the correct quantities was tricky: Ringo would remember how, in the second house, they 'pranced on like Red Indians, covered in the stuff'.[39]

When the curtain rose, fingers went to ears. The mixing desk was an invention yet to come: the Beatles had their own gigging amps plus house PA mikes and that was it. The sound balance was bad, everything was way too loud and no one turned it down. 'The drummer apparently thought his job was to lead, not to provide rhythm,' wrote Lyndon Whittaker in the *Peterborough Standard*. 'He made far too much noise and in their final number Twist And Shout it sounded as though everyone was trying to make more noise than the others.' Whittaker ended his assessment with a line that pleased him at the time but friends would forever quote back at him: 'Frank (I Remember You) Ifield is the only one I shall remember.'[40]

Clearly this was a long way from being one of the Beatles' better shows, but the degree to which it was disastrous is buried under conflicting recollections – some say the audience booed, others that they screamed adulation. The Beatles had a drink with Arthur Howes afterwards – it was their first meeting with the man who had an exclusive option to promote their tours until the end of 1965, and they found they could talk to him perfectly well. Howes was as impressed with them as he was with Brian Epstein; he told them they'd have plenty of opportunities to put wrong things right, and one would be the Tommy Roe and Chris Montez tour. The Peterborough night that would go down as a failure was really just a bump on the learning curve: they'd passed the test, and their addition to the tour line-up was reported in *Melody Maker* and *Disc* four days later.

A day after meeting their promoter, they met John and Paul's new publisher. The Beatles were getting to know London in little unjoined pockets, and this area of WC2 was the most familiar, 132 Charing Cross Road, up by the instrument shops and the *NME*, just along from Anello & Davide. Dick James was twice their age, just about Ringo's height, but heavier, wore black horn-rim glasses and had a broad bald channel where, in performing days, he'd flashed a luxuriant toupee. He wasn't a toff like Brian or Big George Martin, he spoke in a thickish East End voice – not the stereotype Yiddisher tones widely mocked in daily British life but recognisably Jewish all the same. If they hadn't realised it already, the Beatles now knew they had a second Jew driving their careers – and while there's nothing to indicate this was a problem, it would have registered as a conscious thought. The Beatles were much more open-minded than most, but it's also true that racist remarks were expressed casually and fearlessly in these times, and as much as they liked and respected Brian, he still had to suffer the occasional barb.

Dick's office also had *talent*. His secretary and receptionist were much taken with the four Liverpool lads suddenly making their quietish place appealingly unruly. As Linda Duque remembers:

Suddenly the Beatles arrived – these scruffy boys with the hair and old suede jackets, flopping down in the office and *hungry*. I went down to the Italian café and got four enormous fry-ups to bring upstairs. They were nice boys, friendly, never abrasive. I thought John and Paul were the clever ones and I immediately had a tremendous crush on John. In time, I found out he was married, but I was 'a nice Jewish girl' so nothing could have happened anyway. Lee had the biggest thing about George *ever*.[41]

'George was my favourite, right from the beginning,' Lee Perry confirms. 'I found John a little distant so I only spoke to Paul, George and Ringo.' George gave Lee a photo (his solo shot, printed from Astrid's recent session) and signed it to her with several kisses; she framed it and kept it on her desk, by the typewriter and telephone switchboard. George was the first Beatle on display in London.[42]

The Beatles didn't drop by only to say hello. J. W. Lennon and J. P. McCartney signed PRS agreements for Please Please Me and Ask Me Why – all part of the administrative process, legal and above-board. There was no alternative to being published, and if the songs were successful the writers would prosper ... albeit not as much as the publisher. It was a business, and businesses exist to make money, in this instance by taking the copyright and marketing it, just as record companies owned the recordings and marketed those. But the plain fact for John and Paul was that, while they'd always be credited as the authors of Love Me Do, PS I Love You, Please Please Me and Ask Me Why, and activity in these songs would always reward them, copyright ownership passed out of their hands.

Years later, Paul's hindsight view would be that advantage was taken of their naivety: 'We actually used to think, when we first came down to London, that songs belonged to everyone, that they were in the air and you couldn't actually own one. So you can imagine: the publishers saw us coming! "Welcome boys, sit down. That's what you think, is it?"[43]

Though Paul came to mourn losing ownership of his song copyrights, it would be surprising if he and John were quite as ignorant as he'd retrospectively suggest – this belies their years of devouring the music papers, LP sleeves, sheet music, and the names and details on record labels, as well as backstage conversations with published musicians. But even if they *did* believe songs were 'in the air', Dick James still didn't 'see them coming'. Being published meant signing contracts, and their contracts were the same as those signed by even the most clued-up and successful of songwriters. There was no subterfuge: the wording made it plain that the publisher took the copyright. Brian – on John and Paul's behalf – was in no position to rewrite the rules of a business run this way globally since 1900, and the lawyer-heavy music industry of the late twentieth century was not the music business of 1962. Here, in real time, no one was taking undue advantage, no party considered it, and everything was smiles. As Paul has also said, 'We loved Dick James ... he was a publisher like in the movies, a publisher who was really interested in us and wanted to publish us, so we were in love with the idea.'[44]

Their publisher had already exhibited one movie-like moment in recent days, when he got the Beatles booked on *Thank Your Lucky Stars*, and now he also got them a session on *Saturday Club*, effecting a powerful double-barrel launch for Please Please Me. It would be one of three BBC dates on 22 January, because they'd also be chatting live on *Pop Inn* and taping another *Talent Spot*; and Dick further managed to get them on Scottish TV at the start of the year, when they'd be up there on tour. Brian was filling the diary as well, with a Manchester radio recording in mid-January and another live spot on Granada TV the day before leaving for their Hamburg Christmas.

They were off to do a radio show now. The office of Dick James Music closed every day at 5.30 sharp: Dick put on his hat and coat and took the bus home to Cricklewood, to be Frances' husband and Stephen's father. The Beatles left the building and headed along Oxford Street to EMI House, to make a second appearance on *The Friday Spectacular* for Radio Luxembourg.

After lip-synching Love Me Do and signing autographs, they got away to a pub just off Manchester Square where Brian had arranged for them to meet Tony Barrow. Tony had written the Love Me Do press release and shaped its promotion, now he was writing the Please Please Me press release, and soon he'd be joining Nems Enterprises as press officer. He didn't know this – it was Brian's idea and so far he'd only told the Beatles – but Barrow's support for what they were trying to achieve was growing all the time. Brian wanted him as part of a select team of first-rate, dedicated professionals giving the Beatles all the support necessary to make them the greatest: Lennon-McCartney-Harrison-Starkey pushed by Epstein-Martin-James-Barrow. Conversations about this would continue in 1963, but Tony was at least notionally on board so it was important he connected with the Beatles. He was another handy Liverpudlian in London – a hungry and hard-working 26-year-old from their own back yard, bright (private school and university educated) and keen to do all he could to push his home-town group. George Martin and Dick James were Londoners and there was nothing Brian or the Beatles could do about that, but wherever possible they wanted to work with their own, with Liverpudlians, guys who understood the mentality, lingo and way of life.

These were Tony Barrow's first impressions of the people he'd come to know very well:

> Paul was the first to socialise, coming over to ask what everyone was drinking. He took all the orders, including the other Beatles', then went to the bar, and when the barmaid said, 'That'll be £2 14s,' he turned round and said, 'Bri! £2 14s for the drinks.' This was Paul, the generous host.
>
> George then made a great impression by being very interested in what I had to say. He had a habit of coming up close, standing a couple of inches from your face, almost nose to nose, and speaking in a quiet and confidential manner. To anybody watching, he might have been sharing some great confidence. He was also interested in the other people with me, genuinely interested on a personal level, whereas Paul was more interested in me because Brian had told them he was hiring me for their PR – though he hadn't told me this.
>
> John I mostly remember for his remark 'If you're not queer and you're not Jewish, why are you coming to work for Nems?' I said, 'I'm not, I'm not, and I'm not!' Ringo didn't come over, I went and talked to him a little bit.
>
> All the traits that came out at that initial meeting were consistent with what followed.[45]

Something big was happening every day now. They had another twenty-four hours in London before heading home and this was when they appeared on national TV for the first time, in the children's show *Tuesday Rendezvous*. It went out live from a Wembley studio, was seen everywhere but Scotland, was most viewers' first exposure to the Beatles' sight and sound, and had a particularly captive audience because much of Britain was blanketed by freezing smog.[46] It was the worst pollution experienced in London for twelve years; the Beatles had great difficulty getting into and out of Wembley in nose-to-tail traffic and gloom. The conditions didn't lift for three days, by which time 340 people had choked to death on the toxic fumes.

For a £25 fee, the Beatles mimed all of Love Me Do and forty-five seconds of PS I Love You, their only TV performance of the song, and they made a strong impression – viewers had never seen a guitar-group who sang, and their long dark hair was effective in the black-and-white picture.[47] The result was yet another spike in business for Love Me Do: it had just slipped from 21 to 26 in *Record Retailer*, but sales this week pushed it back up and into its highest position yet, 19. It was yet another milestone moment, for as George would relate, 'The most important thing in our lives was to get into the top twenty.'[48]

In December 1961, at the moment Brian became the Beatles' manager, John and Paul reluctantly faced up to regularly playing their own songs on stage. Twelve months later, they were motivated at every turn to write new ones and push them into the national spotlight, and it was probably in the last days of November that they completed the one Paul had started a month earlier. Its title would become I Saw Her Standing There but they weren't yet sure of it – they also called it Seventeen, and Just Seventeen, and for a while it had no name at all. Beatles fan Sue Houghton (they called her Sue Cement Mixer, her identity when handing up Cavern requests) remembers it going straight into the Beatles' live set, 'but still without a title. One time in the Cavern, Paul announced, "We're gonna do that I saw her standing there one which we do."'[49]

Paul had been thinking up its lyric on his London day with Celia Mortimer – his girlfriend of 17, the one he danced with through the night at the Establishment Club. However, the song was completed only when he had a front parlour session with John at 20 Forthlin Road. They tried out little bits on Jim Mac's Nems piano but mostly used guitars, working 'eyeball to eyeball' just like when they'd first written together here as schoolboys. Mike took photographs of them sitting by the little tiled fireplace – important, historic images, the only such photos ever taken – so here we see these two sharp, ambitious, tuned-in young men looking down at an old Liverpool Institute exercise book in which Paul has written the words, complete with plenty of crossings-out. John is wearing his black horn-rim glasses and playing his Jumbo Gibson, Paul is playing a cheap Spanish acoustic of unknown history. Another Original, a McCartney-Lennon one, is taking shape right here, right now.[50]

The moment Paul started singing, John stopped him. The opening line, 'She was just seventeen', was good; the second, 'She'd never been a beauty queen', wasn't. 'John went, "What? We *must* change that" ... so we tried to think of another line which rhymed with "seventeen" and meant something. We eventually got "You know what I mean", which means *nothing*, completely nothing at all.'[51]

The song as it emerged from here incorporated a number of ideas. 'John and I used to nick a lot. "We'll have *this* bit from the Marvelettes, we'll have *that* bit from . . ." If you *really* nick then it's a disaster, but [the way we did] it just gets you into the song, and in the end you never notice where it was nicked from. You pull it all together and it makes something original.'[52]

Some nicks are conjectural. 'I saw her standing on the corner' is the opening line of the Coasters' Young Blood, and 'she's too cute to be a minute over seventeen' is from Chuck Berry's Little Queenie – both songs still in the Beatles' set. 'How could I dance with another / Since I saw her standing there' has a similar melody and metre to 'I want to be in that number / When the saints go marching in' – the tune Paul learned on trumpet in 1955–6 and the B-side of their own My Bonnie record. Other nicks are definite. In a 1964 interview, Paul cheerfully admitted to the wholesale lifting of the bass riff in Chuck Berry's I'm Talking About You that runs throughout I Saw Her Standing There: 'I played exactly the same notes as he did and it fitted our number perfectly.'[53] But it wasn't so much the parts that were important, it was what Paul and John did with them. Though the title wasn't settled, their new song was dynamic, catchy, appealing, clever . . . and an instant favourite with audiences.

It was one of four new songs in the Beatles' set, because they also refreshed it with infusions from the standard supply line – American records released by British labels, found in Nems. And it was perfectly in step with their current tastes that two of the three were Goffin-King compositions – interesting melodic love songs with appealing lead and harmony vocals, guitars and a great beat.

George homed in on Chains, by a trio of New York girls called the Cookies – his Liverpudlian accent pronouncing it 'Cookies'. Producer Gerry Goffin's arrangement so suited the Beatles that, once again, they'd no need to alter it. The front line sang – George had the lead, John and in particular Paul supported with upper-range harmonies, and where Goffin used handclaps to edge the beat, so did they: Paul and George clapped at head height, John clapped and cripped. It was another of those perfect Cavern songs – except that opportunities for playing it here were fast running out.

John took the lead on Goffin-King's Keep Your Hands Off My Baby, recorded by Little Eva as her follow-up to The Loco-Motion. Ringo whipped them tightly in time, Paul and George sang harmonies behind John's lead while doing the handclaps again, George played a twangy solo where the original had sax, and – in the Cavern at least – there was a vocal variation: George's girlfriend Bernadette Farrell remembers John singing Keep Your Hands Off My Nigel.

John also grabbed Anna, recorded by their favourite R&B singer Arthur Alexander; it was a minor US hit and did nothing in Britain . . . except thrill several cognoscenti who'd long burn the flame. Named after Ann Alexander (Arthur's real-life wife), Anna is a passionate plea from a man to his woman: she wants to go off with another man, he begs her to stay . . . but says if she *really* wants to leave, she should give back his ring and go. Alexander sang it with soul, Lennon did his best to be black and gave it his usual whole self: when he turned up the heat in the bridge he was electrifyingly close to screaming. It needed a fair degree of rearrangement – the original had piano, the Beatles had guitars, and Paul and George created a sustained *aaaah* backing vocal in place of the original's string section. They loved playing it, and it was a particular favourite of George's: Sue Cement Mixer handed up requests to John that read 'Please sing Anna for George'.

It's not known if they played any of these new songs when George Martin saw them in the Cavern, the night he came to assess conditions for recording the Beatles' LP live in the Mathew Street cellar. George and Judy took the train to Liverpool on Wednesday 12 December, Brian treated them to dinner, and Bob Wooler watched the tall gentleman from EMI 'walking around the empty Cavern, clapping his hands and testing the echo'. Dissatisfaction with this, plus concern at the amount of water condensing off the walls and ceiling, and alarm over general safety – a fainted girl was passed prone over George and Judy's heads while the Beatles played – made George decide this *wasn't* a suitable venue for his needs. 'The Cavern would have been a dreadful place to do it,' he'd explain. 'It wasn't a very good acoustic environment – not a very comfortable environment at all really. Very grotty.'[54]

He confirmed his view the next morning at a meeting in Brian's office . . . where, nonetheless, plans for the Beatles' LP took real shape. They discussed George's second idea, to create a live show in the studio by getting an audience into Abbey Road. He wondered if Brian might bring a Liverpool crowd down to London, members of the fan club perhaps, transported in a string of coaches – travel by Nems Enterprises; cakes, Cokes and tape courtesy EMI.

But very soon, probably now, the idea was rejected and the Beatles album became a studio project straight and simple. Vacant dates in their diaries didn't match in January, and the first that suited both, and also the Abbey Road diary, was Monday 11 February, when the tour with Helen Shapiro was taking a break. The LP would require fourteen tracks and – in Love Me Do, PS I Love You, Please Please Me and Ask Me Why – George already had four. He'd book a double session in their usual Number 2 studio – 10AM to 1PM, 2.30 to 5.30PM – when there was no reason why they couldn't record the other ten. John and Paul knew they had two months to write as many songs as possible.

Disappointed as he was with the Cavern, George Martin's evening was still productive, because – with Brian as his guide – he discovered Liverpool had other promising groups. Brian didn't take him to the Cavern until about nine o'clock; first he drove him through the Mersey tunnel to see Gerry and the Pacemakers play at the Majestic Ballroom, Birkenhead. Though Brian had made arrangements for Gerry & Co to be seen by Decca, here was George Martin, ready and willing to take a look now.[55]

He looked, he listened and he liked, and told Brian to bring them down to the studio in London; he would give them a Commercial Test, and tape it, so their first record could come from it – in which case there'd be a contract. Here and now, the session was set for 22 January 1963 at Abbey Road. And while waiting in the Cavern to see the Beatles, George was also impressed by support group the Four Mosts, formerly the Four Jays. He said he'd be happy to test them in the studio, news Brian put to them a day or two later when also restating his previous offer of a management contract. Still cautious about surrendering qualified jobs for a guitar income, they declined both opportunities.

Despite this, everything was clicking nicely for Brian. The Beatles had recorded a certain smash, Gerry and the Pacemakers seemed well set to join EMI, and the Big Three had a successful Artist Test at Decca just before Christmas, right after returning from the Star-Club. He was also moving ahead with his fourth signing, taking over management of the singer who called himself Billy Kramer. The Beatles supported Brian's decision: one reason he wanted to sign him was that John said he had a good voice.[56]

All this time, Brian was still contending with the Pete Best difficulty, the threat of legal action over his 'unwarranted and unjustifiable dismissal' from the Beatles. After an initial flurry of letters, however, with both sides robustly arguing their case, the exchange was slowing to what Brian's lawyer David Harris would describe as 'a desultory correspondence'. The threat of action wasn't withdrawn and would remain active – but only just, because Pete's level of *push* had gone off the boil.

The heat generated when he joined Lee Curtis and the All Stars had also cooled. Though the group's general popularity was increasing, promoters' ads rarely gave them prominence over others, and after Pete instructed manager Joe Flannery not to advertise him as an 'ex-Beatle' he'd ceased to be mentioned at all. As the Cavern doorman Paddy Delaney remarked to *Mersey Beat* eight months later, 'When Pete joined the All Stars, the limelight he had with the Beatles seemed to go.'[57]

Opportunities did seem to be opening up for him in his new group – BBC and London record company auditions beckoned in November 1962 – but managerial bragging was generally greater in advance of these events than after.

Pete had gone to Decca with the Beatles and returned with nothing (that is, once John, Paul and George finally told him); when he went with Curtis, producer Peter Sullivan tested the singer and the All Stars separately and was interested only in Curtis.

The Beatles continued to process the Pete fallout in their own original way. On the one hand, Brian was glossing over the troubles. On 24 November, when Pete turned 21, Brian sent a telegram to the Majestic, Birkenhead, where Lee Curtis and the All Stars were playing, and Bob Wooler read it aloud to the crowd in front of Pete: CONGRATULATIONS MANY HAPPY RETURNS ALL THE BEST – JOHN PAUL GEORGE RINGO AND BRIAN. So, everything seemed fine between them all. On the other hand, John wrote a poem he called 'Randolf's Party'. He was never asked to explain it, so there's no definite proof it was about Pete, but John was always one to express his feelings artistically, laying it down for all to see, and the piece rings true with Pete in mind. There's the title (Pete's first name was Randolph), the passing reference to a dad not living at home, and the no-word-wasted sentences 'We never liked you all the years we've known you. You were never raelly [sic] one of us you know, soft head.' As a Best biographer would conclude, here was 'the crux of Pete's Beatles career, in one paragraph'.[58]

They saw him on Saturday 15 December, at the *Mersey Beat Awards Night* in Birkenhead. It was the third time Lee Curtis and the All Stars were on a bill with the Beatles since Pete had joined them – and the third time they passed by without a word.[59] Curtis and his backing group were here because they'd come a creditable second in the poll, the Beatles because they'd won it again. The Please Please Me press release said their victory was achieved 'by an overwhelming number', which seems entirely likely.

There'd been no *Awards Night* for the 1961 poll, but this made up for it. Produced by Bob Wooler, it didn't begin until midnight, so all the groups could play their usual bookings first. Brian went on stage to present a special Nems Enterprises Award to Billy Kramer with the Coasters, as Top Non-Professional Group, and he also made a short speech before the Beatles came on. His words weren't quoted and aren't remembered, but a photo shows him saying something funny while Paul looks pensive and John hides mock embarrassment behind George's shoulder, so it was clearly a Lennon comment. The hero of the night, Bill Harry, then presented the Beatles with their awards, and they ended the show at 4AM by playing three numbers. One was Please Please Me, let loose from the vault this one time only, to give people a quick first taste of 1963. All quoted witnesses say it went down great, then it was locked away again for three more weeks . . .

In the meantime, their first record was still delivering in every way. For – amazingly – a third straight month, the Beatles had the thrill of watching the weekly charts to see where it stood. It was now leading a curious yo-yo ride – up and down, up and down – that reflected their TV/radio dates and the nightly van dashes to new towns. Though the published charts were all different, sales in the week ending 15 December put Love Me Do at 22 across the board: it dropped to here on *Record Retailer* and *New Record Mirror*, and it climbed to here, its highest place yet, in both *Melody Maker*'s Top Fifty and *The World's Fair*'s Juke-Box 100; it was out of the *Disc* chart (having peaked at 24) and also *Liverpool Echo*'s Own Top 5, but had only just entered *Pop Weekly*'s Top Thirty and was still rising.

One consequence of this activity was a surge in the amount of mail received by the fan club. It was getting too much for Bobby Brown, so Brian assigned her the help of Nems Enterprises typist Freda Kelly; this keen, 17-year-old Cavernite – efficient, helpful and a friend to all – didn't need asking twice and happily immersed herself in the challenge. Brian also made a surprising and far-sighted move by allowing the creation of a second club purely to serve Beatles fans in the south of England – it was an empty vessel he didn't expect to stay empty for long. The idea was kindled by Bettina Rose, an 18-year-old from Richmond, south-west of London, who heard Love Me Do on Radio Luxembourg and wrote to EMI volunteering her services to the Beatles. She met Brian in London in mid-December 1962 and they decided to go ahead with the new venture. Never slow to put plans into practice, Brian defined the club's adjunct structure, agreed to shoulder its costs, and mailed the *NME* a new classified ad for The Beatles Fan Club (Southern Branch) to run in the first issue of the year.

The Beatles' last British dates of 1962 were at the Cavern and on Granada TV, 16 and 17 December. The atmosphere in Mathew Street was palpably end-of-term. Fan club members had seen a list of the Beatles' bookings in January/February 1963, and these devotees could count just nine Merseyside appearances in those fifty-nine days; it was otherwise full of places like Scotland, Birmingham, Newcastle, Leicester and Oxford. Even Liverpool's 10 January *Welcome Home* show – post-Hamburg and Scotland – was being held somewhere bigger, in the Grafton Ballroom. Still, the Beatles celebrated Christmas early with their fans, smuggling booze into the bandroom and going on stage well oiled and up for a laugh. Pat Hodgetts, a happy Cavernite from the south end of town (the Beatles knew her as Polythene Pat, because she chewed the stuff), has a particular memory of the last great Liverpool night of '62: 'John sang To Know Her Is To Love Her and he had the whole front row sniffling. I noticed that when they finished, he pretended to fiddle with his amplifier, turning his back on us – in truth, he was a bit choked up too. It was dead nice to see he was so affected.'[60]

The Beatles were back at Granada the next evening for another *People And Places* – a million and a half people watching them play Love Me Do for the third time and Twist And Shout for the first – and then they were off once more, resigned to the chore of making their final flying visit to the cold, old streets of Hamburg.

36

And Who Knows! (18–31 December 1962)

There was one huge difference with the Beatles' fifth Hamburg season: they knew it was the last. They were scanning new horizons for 1963, not revisiting old ones – besides which, they'd had a *bellyful* of the place and all its sordid squalor. Those two November weeks had been a real imposition – 'a DRAG', George wrote – and these final two were worse: he told Sue Cement Mixer 'Hamburg's a smelly hole'.

It was paying them better than ever: three thousand marks a week (about £268) was DM637.50 (£57) each, in cash, after the deduction of Brian's commission. Manfred Weissleder's free accommodation was also the best they'd had: four single rooms in the Hotel Pacific on Neuer Pferdemarkt, a ten-minute stagger from Grosse Freiheit. They only had to play two or three forty-five-minute sets a night, and the two weeks entailed only thirteen working days because the club closed Christmas Eve.

They were second top of the bill. Below them were, from the 'Pool, the Strangers and King-Size Taylor and the Dominoes, plus Tony Sheridan and Roy Young in the Star-Club house band, and Carol Elvin, a London girl who sang and strummed electric guitar in a skimpy costume; above them were Johnny and the Hurricanes, the instrumental band from Toledo, Ohio, still big in Germany though the hits had dried up at home and in Britain. Thanks to Adrian Barber's running of the club's sound system, the Beatles brought only their guitars and Ringo used the Trixon kit that stayed on stage.

Hamburg loathing was hardened by the weather. It was bitter throughout these two weeks, by far the coldest they'd known here – the Alster lake froze and the Elbe river was an ice cube fifty centimetres thick. The Beatles arrived unprepared and the arctic temperatures stalled their wanderlust: they mostly stayed in the hotel or the club, cooped up and bored. John and Paul needed to write maybe six more songs for the LP (to be recorded seven weeks from here) but they did nothing at all, pushing the problem into a crowded January. They were all grateful recipients of long black woollen scarves knitted for them by Astrid, identical to the one she'd given Stuart. She'd started to make them before the weather turned bad, so her timing was perfect. They socialised, a little though not a lot, with Astrid and Klaus, and with Icke Braun. Icke drove Paul out to his house, a country cottage north-east of the city, to encounter frozen water pipes, no heating, and – save for a few millimetres – another car: his VW Beetle went into an icy skid and came close to a head-on collision.

The Beatles always had *incidents* in Hamburg – fewer this time than usual, although one would become notorious. They went on stage one night as a trio, lacking John, so Horst Fascher went to hunt him down. In the spring, he'd felt the need to urinate on John while he was *fickte* a *Fräulein*; this time, finding John receiving oral sex in a backstage toilet cubicle, he doused the hot couple in ice-cold water from an adjacent shower. John came bursting out of the stall in a raging temper and Fascher ordered him to *get out zere and verk*; John tore the toilet seat off its hinge and went on stage dripping wet, in Beatle boots, underpants and, around his neck, the toilet seat.*

No incidents are mentioned in letters back to Liverpool – but, again, there were fewer of them than before. George sent the best one, to Sue Cement Mixer, after she visited his parents with flowers and chocolates, got invited in for tea, and offered to wash his car.

> A letter arrived at my house from Hamburg and I recognised George's writing. I thought he'd be saying 'Please don't bother my parents', but no – he'd phoned home, his mum said Sue Cement Mixer had been around, she told him my offer, and he sent me a long letter with a seven-point instruction about how to clean his Anglia. And *when* to clean it – 'about the 8th of January', just as they were getting home from Scotland.
>
> It was a great letter, three pages. I was to wash the car inside and out with warm soapy water, polish it with two separate dusters (in 'a circular motion'), vacuum the carpets, do both sides of all the windows, everything. He timed two tea-breaks into my schedule, and the seventh and final instruction was

---

* It does seem John *twice* went on the Star-Club stage in his undies and toilet seat. Several eyewitnesses persuasively place the incident here, at Christmas 1962, but John spoke of it happening when Gerry and the Pacemakers were in Hamburg, saying he went on like that and drummed with the Pacemakers while Gerry Marsden sang. As the moment was also witnessed by Bernie Boyle (who wasn't here at Christmas, or in November) this must have been May. (See chapter 28.)

'Proceed to 20 Forthlin Rd with about 6 buckets full of dirty muddy greasy water, where a shiny Ford Classic will be seen. Spread contents of the buckets evenly, so as to leave a nice film of muck over the car.' He was suggesting I dump his dirty water on Paul's car![1]

Love Me Do had gone up, not down, last time they were in Hamburg – and now, incredibly, it happened again. *Record Retailer*'s Top Fifty of 27 December (shop sales 17th–22nd) took the Beatles to their highest place yet, 17, and jukebox plays spun it to 19 on *The World's Fair* 100 – again, best yet. This longevity was exceptional. Records that entered the chart after Love Me Do, and went higher, had now disappeared while it still hung around. The Beatles were the first group to have *any* size hit on their debut and here they were in the top twenty, and all this happened without exposure on *Juke Box Jury, Thank Your Lucky Stars* and *Saturday Club*. Sales to the end of November had been an impressive 36,868 and in December added another 30,000, and not even Brian or the Beatles could have expected that. Their second EMI royalty statement (due after 28 February) would be better than the first, and it now seemed certain that Love Me Do would still be on the charts when Please Please Me was released – they'd have two records charting at the same time.

The excitement at this moment wasn't with the Beatles in Hamburg, it was without them in London, building through the Epstein-James axis. Brian was using the James office as his base, and while Dick was busy on one phone, fixing airplay for Please Please Me or for the group themselves, Brian was on an adjacent phone to ballroom promoters around the nation, plugging between-tours gaps in the Beatles' January-to-March diary, and filling April with one-nighters – including, for the first time, headlining shows in London.

Dick James now followed George Martin in using Brian's term of affection for the Beatles – 'the boys' – and it was with his guidance that their nightly fee shot up several times in a short period. On 21 November, when fixing a February contract, Brian asked for £50, just increased from £30. This was already a competitive rate, but on 8 December, negotiating a date in March, he made it £75 with a rider that if Please Please Me went into the *Record Retailer* top five before the show, it would be £100 – and by the end of December the Beatles' fee was a flat £100 regardless of chart performance. This was getting into the upper limit of affordability for promoters, ensuring they had to present the Beatles in bigger venues. Dick was encouraging Brian to be ever more bold, and he could, because – quite evidently – a grass-roots, word-of-mouth reputation for the Beatles was growing fast. For his part, Dick got a promise that Please Please Me would be reviewed on *Juke Box Jury* on 5 January, which must have been another major cause of celebration. As he would recall, 'From when we met in November, an enthusiasm was building up between Brian and myself. I was only too happy to co-operate with him as much as possible, and we were in close proximity all the time.'[2] He'd known Brian and the Beatles under a month and was already experiencing the most excitement in all his years in publishing.

Five months earlier, when George Martin told Dick James he was giving How Do You Do It to a group from Liverpool, Dick had jokingly replied, 'So what's from Liverpool?' Here was what. Through the talents of John Lennon and Paul McCartney he saw a catalogue of new songs – formidable, authentic, British – blossoming before his very eyes. It was quite possibly the publishing opportunity of a lifetime, and also a predicament. These two street-smart young composers had already left Ardmore and Beechwood to come to him, and they could just as easily leave him and wander away someplace else. He had to think of a way of enticing them to stick around.

His solution was to propose a new music publishing company, half-owned by John, Paul and Brian, or however they decided it, and half-owned by Dick James Music. John and Paul would have an exclusive contract with the new company for an agreed period of time, and instead of forfeiting their copyrights, as everyone did and as they had done until now, they'd maintain joint ownership. They would still sign individual agreements for each new song, for the standard royalties on sheet music sales and broadcast and mechanical fees, but, on top of that, they'd be entitled to 50 per cent of the company's profits. The bottom line was that Dick James was giving away half his claim on the copyrights, and half his earnings, in order to keep Lennon and McCartney on his books. The deal would pay them much more than royalties alone, and be tax efficient, allowing them to keep more of what they earned.

Transparency was shown by Dick's suggestion that Brian's solicitor draft the contract. The process was started by David Harris in the days after Christmas, an agreement dated 1 January 1963 but the product of 1962 thinking. It would be considered and tweaked in the opening weeks of the year, but as it stood here and now:

- The new company had no name, but the agreement was between, on one side, Dick James Music, and on the other John Lennon, Paul McCartney and Nems Enterprises, with provision for Jim McCartney to sign for Paul, who was still a minor.
- The company would have £100 capital, divided into 100 £1 shares – 50 'A' shares for Dick James Music, 50 'B' shares divided 20 to John Lennon, 20 to Paul McCartney and 10 to Nems Enterprises. (There was no difference

between 'A' and 'B' shares, it was only for ease of understanding.) Dick James and Brian Epstein would be the directors.

- Dick James Music would receive 10 per cent of the new company's gross receipts for providing its office, staff, bookkeeping, stationery and basic running costs, along with daily supervision and management of its activities.

- John and Paul would assign all their song copyrights for the next three years, not less than eighteen compositions deemed acceptable to the company.

It wouldn't be the first such venture – joint-publishing companies were rare but around – but what *was* a first was that it was offered to songwriters whose biggest chart hit was 17. The speed with which Dick James saw the need for his idea was astonishing, and from John, Paul and Brian's perspective, sensational. Subject to contractual agreement, they were ending 1962 with their own publishing company and a chance to make serious sums of money for the first time.

It's unlikely John and Paul knew of this yet. The Beatles were enduring a Hamburg Christmas they already wanted to forget. George seems to have been the most vocal in his intolerance: whenever fed up with something, he'd miss few opportunities to grumble or wish an end to his ordeal, and in Hamburg this extended even to the date Christmas was celebrated. In a letter to one of his regular Liverpool correspondents, Margaret Price of Edge Hill, George complained about the Germans having it on the 24th, and then concluded, 'We have 5 more days to go, then we'll be away from this place for good [I HOPE].'

It was among these circumstances that, for the only time in their five visits here, the Beatles were recorded on stage. Ted 'King-Size' Taylor happened to have bought a reel-to-reel deck, and Adrian Barber positioned it on a table, plugged in a microphone and set it running over several nights at slow speed (3¾ ips). Other groups were recorded too, but the Beatles dominate. In subsequent court testimony it would be claimed they knew they were being taped and didn't care. 'OK Ted, just get the ale in' is the probably apocryphal line; it would also be sworn they *didn't* know. What's clear is that the recordings weren't made for commercial use – the sound is rough lo-fi and the Beatles were already under exclusive worldwide contract to Parlophone.*

---

* The tape's many 'legitimate' releases are of questionable legality, and in 1998 the Beatles finally asserted their moral/artistic rights; but the recordings have been everywhere for so long (since 1977) that their greatest worth now is not monetary but to history ... and that value is enormous.

At thirty-seven songs and one hundred minutes (with perhaps a little more still unknown), this is the only substantial live recording of the 'early Beatles' known to exist, and certainly the only one in the public domain. Through Taylor's and Barber's efforts, there is this historic and highly welcome tape of the Beatles in performance at the precise moment their first phase was ending, a nick-of-time capture of the Beatles as a rock and rolling club band.

Their playing is adept and hyper-energetic, and the microphone catches many important moments. The tape's value has been downplayed on the basis that the Beatles are musically sloppy and perhaps even lazy, knowing they've one foot out of the door, but this is to ignore its virtues. The Beatles *did* hate being in Hamburg this last time ... but the recording shows them still cutting the mustard on stage. They're sloppy because, here, they can be, but they're not lazy, and they're not playing with extra care because they're being recorded: this is an authentic eavesdrop on their club act, not something fizzed-up for the tape machine.

At least three sets were recorded, and because the Beatles rarely repeated themselves in Hamburg, there are only five duplicates among the thirty-seven songs. The repertoire is a real surprise. The only self-written pieces are Ask Me Why and I Saw Her Standing There (twice), so there's no Love Me Do, PS I Love You, Please Please Me, One After 909 or any of several other possibilities, and there are few of the songs from the spine of their all-conquering 1962 stage sets – no Some Other Guy, Soldier Of Love, Please Mr Postman, Don't Ever Change, A Shot Of Rhythm And Blues, Devil In Her Heart, Baby It's You, Will You Love Me Tomorrow, If You Gotta Make A Fool Of Somebody, Hey! Baby, A Picture Of You, and so on. What's here is an idiosyncratic selection of old rock numbers all played at breakneck speed – Prellies pace. The nights of half-hour What'd I Say marathons are past: everything is high velocity, only three numbers tipping into three minutes. It's Hamburg '62 but could just as easily be Huyton '61.[3]

The line-up throughout is John on rhythm, Paul bass, George lead and Ringo drums, the front line singing solo and in harmony. By nothing more fortunate than microphone placement, John's rhythm guitar is unusually upfront, heard to be a hard, driving engine slicing through the songs. Also here, constant in all hundred minutes, is the difference between Ringo and Pete. Ringo is solid and spot-on in every style, even though – since they'd not played many of these songs in a *long* time – he can't have drummed them with the Beatles before. They weren't doing Red Sails In The Sunset, Nothin' Shakin' and Hallelujah, I Love Her So in Nuneaton, Peterborough or Widnes, any more than they were still playing them in the Cavern. But Ringo knows the numbers, and his musical synergy with John, Paul and George is complete. They can wing it, he can swing it, and their combination defines *tight*.

They sound nothing like the Beatles who calmly and effectively despatched a studio session at Abbey Road only a month earlier – this is the old big-beat Beatles with bum notes and personalities flying. John and Paul duet with great energy on the early Elvis number I'm Gonna Sit Right Down And Cry (Over You) and Ringo is right with them in frenzied overdrive. Paul belts out Long Tall Sally and Kansas City in fantastic voice and does a good Red Sails In The Sunset. Matchbox is sung by John, not Ringo or Pete; there's a cloddy I Remember You with John on 'gob iron', and a messy Falling In Love Again with Paul's made-up words and George's lacklustre solo. There are harmonically tight renditions of Twist And Shout and I Saw Her Standing There, the latter already confident and strong, like something out of the future – though, inevitably, John gets the words wrong almost every time he comes in on a chorus. He makes no mistakes in a blistering Sweet Little Sixteen, and George launches himself into an ultra-fast Red Hot. No other recording shows him as an out-and-out rocker quite as much: he sings lead and then trades fast lines with John, Ringo drums like a man possessed, and here's the first stage recording of keyboards on a Beatles track, when John slings the guitar around his back and plays a solo on Roy Young's electric organ.

All the while, everything is bubbling in a well-seasoned St Pauli soup, the authentic Hamburg flavour of jeers, cheers and drunken hecklers. Here are the Beatles backing the tough little boxers: Be-Bop-A-Lula is sung by Fredi Fascher, and Hallelujah, I Love Her So by his eldest brother Horst. Both sing well and in impressively good English: they're clearly big rock fans, living the life. 'Watte für die Ohren können Sie bei der Toilettenfrau haben,' Manfred Weissleder announces (in a harsh, hard voice) before Horst sings, 'Cotton for the ears can be obtained from the toilet lady.' Here is John's ubiquitous Edinburgh accent and his lecherous macho bay for BETTINAAAHHHH. She's felt but not heard: Paul dedicates Your Feet's Too Big to her, at which she'd have knifed the foam from a beer, nodded her beehived blonde mane, jiggled her vast bust and set the bar lanterns swinging.

This is an important record of John Lennon in Hamburg. He's surely drunk and/or speeding, and there's a beguiling belligerence to his humour, a dominant cynical goading to his between-songs banter and the way he deals with hecklers. Like a stuck record, he several times tells the audience 'I don't know whether you can understand me or not', even saying it twice while Paul is singing Your Feet's Too Big, and on one occasion he concludes it with 'but piss off. You got that? Christmas or no Christmas.' Paul is much more polite: he calms John's storms and speaks German impressively all the way through, vocabulary schooled in the Liverpool Institute's dark Dickensian classrooms and knocked hard into shape under St Pauli neon.

The tape throws great light on the Nerk Twins' chemistry. While Paul is singing A Taste Of Honey, John suddenly shouts 'SHUT UP TALKING!' to someone in the audience, interrupting Paul much more than the chatterbox. Paul knows this, and is pitched into laughter. When he sings Till There Was You, John – just a beat behind – speaks most of the lines in a persistent piss-taking echo: 'No, I never heard them at all' ('No, he never heard them'). Paul chuckles and ploughs on; he can't stop it, and he's not even necessarily cross about it – he knows it'll happen because *this is John*, and John is his fairground hero. It's part of the double-act: the audience try to watch the singer but can't tear their eyes off his mate, who's probably also pulling crips. John couldn't do this to anyone else without risking a thump, Paul wouldn't accept it from anyone else; Paul gets to sing his song, John gets to undermine him. It's just one facet of the complex sibling relationship they've always had, one among so many reasons they're special together.

Back in England, minds were focused on pushing Beatles records abroad. Their first radio play on the American continent was on the Toronto AM station CFRB on either 8 or 15 December, in a weekly show titled *Calling All Britons*. The presenter, Ray Sonin, was a confident cockney émigré who'd edited *Melody Maker* and then *New Musical Express* for eighteen years (1939–57) and whose radio show was the week's essential listen for expats. Whether or not this show stirred the interest, Capitol Records of Canada soon decided to release Love Me Do as a local-press 45: it would be available seven weeks into the new year.[4]

Capitol of Canada operated independently of Capitol Records, its US parent – and, of course, that company was still shrugging off all the records EMI sent over from England in the hope of American release. This now included the Beatles again. George Martin's ambition that Please Please Me would be pushed in America just as soon as possible, maybe even simultaneous with the British release, suffered its predictable stumble when Capitol exercised the standard 'first turn-down option'.

Just as Decca had rejected the Beatles while announcing a campaign for new British talent, so Capitol turned them down while boasting of a strong new interest in foreign records. CAPITOL GEARS FOR ALL-OUT GLOBAL DRIVE. WIDENS BASE OF INT'L OPERATION FOR IN-OUT FLOW headlined *Billboard* on 22 December, atop talk of 'a new business philosophy that the international market is a two-way street'. This was all hooey to Dave Dexter. He'd released Mrs Mills and Andy Stewart records and America just didn't want 'em.

The trigger for Capitol's 'new direction' claim is obvious: it was the shock US success of non-American – and in particular English – product in 1962. The year's bestseller was Stranger On The Shore by Acker Bilk, and the Christmas and New Year number 1 was the Tornados' Telstar, recorded above a shop in north London, now big in North Dakota. *Cash Box* ran two consecutive editorials stressing to its US business readership the importance of the 'global market', many paragraphs summarised in one simple prediction: 'We can expect American firms to keep a constant vigil on successful records abroad.'[5] The Capitol men made their press announcement, then didn't twitch a muscle ... and when they *did* take British product, like George Martin's *Beyond The Fringe* album, they reneged on promotion promises. George raged about this to EMI Records managing director L. G. Wood in a 31 December 1962 memorandum that concluded 'This is a serious indictment of Capitol's ability to promote albums of British artists. I would not wish to recommend Capitol Records to any impresario who was thinking of launching a future British show in the States.'

The Beatles weren't a show, least not in the Broadway sense, but neither was George's anger one-dimensional: he would no longer recommend Capitol to anyone *at all*, and that included Brian Epstein.

So it fell again to Transglobal Music, EMI's discreet Manhattan operation, to place the Beatles on an American label, and to make it happen now. Roland Rennie's first point of contact was usually company president Joe Zerga, but much of the real work was done by the well-respected record business lawyer Paul Marshall, who was never a Transglobal employee but ran his own law firm from the adjacent office at 56 West 45th Street; he was retained by Transglobal (on twice Zerga's salary) to advise and be involved in all aspects of the business. Marshall had the contacts, then he made the contracts, and now he set to label-shopping the Beatles.

They were available on standard US terms:

- No advance was payable.
- The royalty to Transglobal would be 10 per cent of the retail price on records sold.
- There was no stipulation about the number of records to be pressed.
- Options were available on the artist's future product.

The entire fourteen-clause contract took up one side of legal paper. It was a case of *Sign here and take the Beatles for free.*

First chance went to Liberty Records. The Hollywood indie was the third most successful US singles label in 1962, two places better than Capitol, and its management already had close ties with EMI via an exclusive contract to release the Liberty imprint in Britain. The label's big star, Bobby Vee, toured England with the Crickets in November, heard Love Me Do, liked it, and mentioned it when he got home. The result was a telegram from A&R chief Snuff Garrett to EMI asking for a copy of Love Me Do to be mailed for consideration of licensing. Rennie felt he couldn't refuse, but in a letter to Zerga (who sent Garrett the record) he made it clear EMI no longer wanted to push Love Me Do in America, preferring to make Please Please Me the focus. By 27 December, Liberty was also reviewing an advance copy of Please Please Me, and considering an 11 January rush-release with Love Me Do as the B-side ... but then word came back that they weren't interested.[6] The decision was taken by Snuff Garrett, who explains, 'Liberty was a hot label, and getting hotter. We were doing so well we wondered how we'd done it. I liked the Beatles' sound but you can only handle so many records at a time and we had our hands full. It was just "another decision", the kind I had to take about artists every day, and I said no.'[7]

Laurie Records also turned down the Beatles. This was a small New York independent, the twenty-ninth best singles label in the States in 1962.* Like Liberty, it had a good connection with EMI, which had a contract to release Laurie product in Britain on the Stateside label. But its most successful artist, Dion, had just moved to Columbia Records and Laurie was in the doldrums at the time it was considering the Beatles; the office wasn't given a record of Love Me Do, only Please Please Me, and it was declined. Surviving documentation is thin but certain: a letter (4 January 1963) from Zerga to Rennie that states 'and as you know, Laurie has also decided against taking this record'. The label had just signed a deal (with Pye) to release Petula Clark in the US; perhaps one English act was enough.[8]

The next contenders to sign the Beatles for America would be approached simultaneously by Paul Marshall, two fine indie R&B labels, the great Atlantic Records of New York and Chicago's Vee Jay. But these would be 1963 opportunities, contacted in the first days of the year; 1962 ended just how it started, with rejections. On 1 January the Beatles were failing their Commercial Test at Decca; 364 days later they'd been turned down by Capitol, Liberty and Laurie. But where Decca had rejected them on the basis of a mediocre session by a line-up that didn't gel in the studio, the US companies – two Los Angeles, one New York – were spurning an options-loaded free signing of the Beatles for Please Please Me, a new sound on a great record predicted with confidence to be number 1 in Britain. 'We can expect American firms to keep a constant vigil

---

* EMI's Economics and Statistics Department compiled a survey of US record labels and how they fared on the *Billboard* Hot 100 chart in 1962. RCA Victor was the runaway winner followed by Columbia and Liberty. Capitol placed 5th, Vee Jay 10th, Atlantic joint 17th, Swan 20th, Tamla 22nd, Laurie 29th and Motown joint 34th. Tamla and Motown combined would have placed 11th.

on successful records abroad,' *Cash Box* had suggested, along with a reflection on 1962 that concluded, 'It was the first year since rock and roll music came on the scene that everyone agreed rock and roll can last.'[9] Some things, transparently, didn't add up.

Invited in 1966 to look back at this period, Brian Epstein reflected, 'The good thing about my management of the Beatles was my attention to them. This was the new thing as a manager that I did. I *dedicated* myself to doing just that – being their manager.'[10]

Brian had invested extraordinary energy in the Beatles these twelve months, fast-tracking their rise from rough local heroes to the brink of (and it really did seem due) national stardom. They'd matched his commitment and gone along with his plans all the way, their talents blending tremendously well. To coincide with the second *Mersey Beat* poll win, Brian put together a full-page ad titled *1962 – the Beatles Year of Achievement*; never one to miss a beat, he also had it printed as giveaway publicity posters on eye-catching coloured paper (the Beatles signed them). Here are four of Astrid's arty new photos together with a long itemised list of Beatles accomplishments since the turn of the year: the EMI contract, the chart position, the ten TV and radio broadcasts, the poll successes, the trips to Hamburg, the big-name stars they'd appeared with, and some of the towns and cities they'd played. Underneath this was an impressive contact list, five people working to make them a success.* But this wasn't only a list of Beatles achievements, it was an audit of Brian's first year in management, a statement of account that was nothing short of sensational – because 1962 was a year in which the Beatles had been managed quite brilliantly by Brian Epstein.

As he was doing everything for the first time, it would be absurd to imagine Brian made no mistakes, that he didn't think, say and do naive things – but these were already rare and eclipsed by towering achievements. The Beatles *really* didn't want to go back to Hamburg these last two times and they *really* gave him an earful for it, but they also knew where they stood at the end of 1962 – especially compared to 1961, when they'd come so close to breaking up. Brian had been making all the right moves since the start, because this was, from every angle, the very best of associations. As he'd explain in summer 1967, 'One of the most perfect relationships there has ever been, in my experience,

---

* Tony Calder still showed as 'press representative', masking the greater involvement of Decca employee Tony Barrow; addresses were given for Calder, Brian Epstein, George Martin and Bobby Brown, but not (for obvious reasons) Neil Aspinall. Among 1962's specified feats, there was no place for the Beatles' *other* first record: My Bonnie was distant and disowned.

is that which exists between the Beatles and myself. If I'd been domineering or dictatorial they would never have accepted me and it would all have gone wrong. You have to allow for freedom.'[11]

Brian had the ideal marriage of enthusiasm, intelligence and instinctive entrepreneurial flair, swept high by trust, belief and love. He loved the Beatles as people and he loved them as artists: he loved their authenticity, originality, attitude, talent, truth, cynicism and fun, the A Grade alchemy that grabbed him – and many others – 100 per cent. He loved them for their uncompromisingly direct communication, for stimulating and challenging his thinking. He loved their sheer lust for life.

He'd more than tripled the Beatles' income during 1962, from about £80 a week between them to a consistent £250 after his 15 per cent commission – an incredible sum for a Liverpool group. Brian had also consolidated a goodwill fund beyond monetary value and entirely at odds with their previous reputation, and took nothing for his efforts. 'I made a net loss on the Beatles' first year,' he conceded in October 1963. A few months later, he said the most he grossed from any one week in this period was £18.[12] His *Year of Achievement* income was decimated by personal expenditure, but he always took the long view.

Danger signals were visible too. 'The Beatles were the love of Brian's life,' says Freda Kelly, 'and the business *was* his life, and he wasn't one for handing over, for delegating.'[13] Brian's workload was becoming ridiculous. Though he had a PA, a secretary and other help, he took all the decisions, attended every meeting and dictated every letter, and he especially protected his position as sole interface with his artists. He was also gulping Prellies and Scotch and pursuing a compulsively reckless 'rough trade' sex life. None of this interfered with his fever-pitch workload or blunted his commitment, but there was no certainty this would always be so.

Brian's past was littered with obsessions he'd picked up, then tossed away. This time too? There was no sign of it. That old perennially unfulfilled Brian wasn't here. Giving 'Sole Direction' to the Beatles and two other groups, running a thriving Nems Enterprises, promoting shows, and now, inevitably, beginning the process of measuring his entrepreneurial flair against London's biggest operators – these challenges seemed to be the essence of his life. Brian Epstein was living like never before. They *all* were – John, Paul, George, Richy, Brian and the team Brian had built around them. Everything was new, exhilarating, possible.

*

Another group flew into Hamburg from London on 30 December. Cliff Bennett and the Rebel Rousers were a *band's band*: meaty, brassy, burly, rock rolled into

R&B. Joe Meek produced their records and Parlophone released them, but they'd made three singles and not come within a sniff of the charts. Jealous of the Beatles for cracking the top twenty on their debut, they watched them in the Star-Club and failed to stay as coolly dispassionate as intended. Frank Allen, bass player and backing singer, instantly saw the difference between the two groups: 'We may have been all around the same age but we were boys while the Beatles were men. They were well aware of what they had to do to make it and they exuded a natural power and charisma.' Cliff Bennett says, 'I was really taken aback. They were doing a lot of rock 'n' roll standards but they were doing them in three-part harmony, and they did all their own arrangements. It was fabulous. I sat there totally gobsmacked.'[14]

A night later it was New Year's Eve ('Silvester' in Germany) and then it was all over – goodbye to Grosse Freiheit, forever. The Faschers would carry on, BETTINAAAHHHH would carry on, St Pauli would carry on, with its drunks, drugs, guns and *Beat-Gruppen*, and the Star- and Top Ten clubs would have plenty of high old times as the Sixties marched on – but the Beatles wouldn't be part of them. They drew the line on 31 December 1962, having played more than 1100 hours here since the day Allan Williams heroically drove them across from Liverpool in his minibus.* In Hamburg, the Beatles took what they made. They honed their skills, earned their spurs and made true a hundred colourful metaphors, coming of age where wildness was allowed. John summarised it in ten words: 'We went in young boys and came out old men.'[15] It was the end of the Beatles as a club band, for now, and more or less the last time they played without everyone watching.

It was *auf Wiedersehen* to Klaus and to Astrid, and to Stu's ghost. In one of several long, chatty letters to Bobby Brown, Astrid said she didn't expect to see the Beatles again. She drove them to the airport the next day, as did Icke Braun. In recent days, Britain had been hit with the same harsh winter weather as the rest of northern Europe: it was a white-out, and the plane was delayed several hours. The Beatles were heading for London, where Brian had booked them a night in the Royal Court. They'd be flying up to Scotland on 2 January. The itinerary was typed, everything was in place.

There are no photos from this last Hamburg–London flight, or any anecdotes to colour the moment, but here are the four travellers – John Winston Lennon,

---

* They played about twenty hours on this visit, adding to perhaps 1090 from the previous four. As imprecise as these calculations must be, the Beatles' Hamburg total was ±1110 hours in thirty-eight weeks of playing – the equivalent of three hours every night for a full year.

22; James Paul McCartney, 20; George Harrison, 19; Richard Starkey, 22; all of Liverpool, England – flying into a bright white tomorrow. Sometimes in life, things go right; only very rarely do they *all* go right, and so it was now – for them and for everyone and everything around them. The plates were aligned for a cultural earthquake that would start shaking the walls in 1963, one of the century's most remarkable and thrilling years.

That *Year of Achievement* poster assembled by Brian didn't only look back on 1962, it anticipated Beatles headlines for the coming three months – Please Please Me, TV, radio, tours, foreign releases, these would be the biggest events in their lives to date . . . but still just a start; stepping stones, not the destination. Daring to wonder what excitement lay beyond March 1963, Brian's anticipation bubbled through his sign-off words – AND WHO KNOWS!

They did. They always had. It was obvious, and felt among them. As leader Lennon would explain, 'We were the best fucking group in the goddamn world . . . and believing that is what made us what we were. Whether you call it "the best rock 'n' roll group" or "the best pop group", whatever – as far as I was concerned, we were the best. We thought we were the best in Hamburg and Liverpool – it was just a matter of time before everybody else caught on.'[16]

END OF PART ONE

INTERMISSION

Notes

The Prologue: **Another Lennon-McCartney Original** (January 1958)

1 Said by Paul McCartney to Hunter Davies, 3 May 1981. (*The Beatles*, by Hunter Davies, Jonathan Cape, London, 1985 edition, p471.)
2 *The Beatles*, by Hunter Davies (William Heinemann, London, 1968), p35. *Unless otherwise specified, all 'Davies' attributions in this book refer to the original 1968 British hardback edition of his authorised biography.*
3 Interview by Alan Rowett and Geoff Barker for *Paul McCartney's Routes Of Rock*, BBC World Service, Oct–Nov 1999.
4 John Lennon interview by Howard Smith, WPLJ-FM, New York, 23 January 1972. John did say Baby Let's Play House, but while there's a small laugh at its end he may have meant Mystery Train, where Elvis all but breaks up with laughter – something that caused much speculation and discussion among his fans.
5 *Paul McCartney: Many Years From Now*, by Barry Miles (Secker & Warburg, London, 1997), p46.
6 Interview by Jean-François Vallée for French TV, 4 April 1975.
7 Interview by author and Kevin Howlett, 6 June 1990.
8 This couplet is from a rough, jokey recording made eleven years later, one that quickly spiralled into nonsense; the lack of a rhyme here probably was part of the messing about, but the original words aren't known.
9 An off-the-cuff 3 January 1969 recording of John and Paul singing Because I Know You Love Me So is included within the 2003 album *Let It Be . . . Naked*, on the second disc, *Fly On The Wall*.
10 Filmed conversation at Twickenham Studios, 6 January 1969.
11 Interview by author and Kevin Howlett, 6 June 1990. Though John and Paul were inspired by the knowledge that Buddy Holly wrote his own songs, numerous names were listed as composers with no consistent pairing: Holly himself, Petty, Allison, Hardin (a Holly pseudonym, though this wasn't realised yet) and others. Composer credits on Elvis Presley records also varied song by song.
12 Interview by author and Kevin Howlett, 6 June 1990.
13 Ibid.
14 Paul from *The Beatles Anthology*, by the Beatles (Cassell & Co, London, 2000), p23; John from interview by Andy Peebles, 6 December 1980, for BBC Radio 1.
15 Interview by Sandra Shevey, the *Hartford Courant*, 26 November 1972.
16 Interview for Earth News Radio, July 1976.
17 Interview by Chris Hutchins, *NME*, 25 September 1964.
18 Interview by Mike Read, 13 October 1987, for BBC Radio 1.
19 Interview by author and Kevin Howlett, 6 June 1990.
20 The porch measures 5ft 5in by 3ft 10in, the roof 7ft 8in, an area of 21 square feet (165 × 117 × 234cm, or 1.9m²).
21 How Love Me Do was created – whether the tune or the words came first or arrived together – has never been recalled. The title may have been inspired by the Elvis film *Love Me Tender* (in Liverpool in January 1957) or from music press ads for a record actually called Love Me Do released in Britain in February 1957. Such influences are likely to have been subliminal at best, though; Paul probably conceived the title as well as most or all of the words.
22 Interview by David Sheff, 24 September 1980, for *Playboy*. The best-available publication of this Q&A is in *Last Interview: All we are saying – John Lennon and Yoko Ono* (Sidgwick & Jackson, London, 2000).
23 His typewriter was an Imperial Good Companion Model T.
24 Interview by author and Kevin Howlett, 6 June 1990. In this and other interviews, Paul aligned

the mention of Edinburgh and 'a dentist' with a further indication of John's middle-classness: someone in his family 'who worked for the BBC'. BBC staff records do not reveal a John Lennon relative, and surviving members of the Stanley side of the family can't think who Paul meant by this. (The dentist was John's Uncle Bert, second husband of his Aunt Elizabeth, aka 'Mater'.)

25 Interview by Mike Read, 13 October 1987, for BBC Radio 1.
26 Interview by Peter McCabe and Robert D. Schonfeld, September 1971. The best-available publication of this interview is in *John Lennon: For The Record*, by McCabe and Schonfeld (Bantam Books, New York, 1984).

1: **In My Liverpool Home** (1845–1945)

1 Author interview, 6 April 2009.
2 *Daddy, Come Home*, by Pauline Lennon (Angus & Robertson, London, 1990), p29.
3 Letter from Mimi Smith to Kathy Burns, 31 October 1986.
4 Joe McCartney's style of music has been lovingly re-created by his grandson Paul in such tunes as Thingumybob (1968).
5 *Ghosts Of The Past*, BBC1, 8 October 1991, included on the DVD of *Paul McCartney's Liverpool Oratorio*, issued 2004.
6 Paul recorded/issued a version of Eloise – retitled Walking In The Park With Eloise – in 1974.
    In a cluster of buildings on West 28th Street in New York City, immigrants or sons of immigrants from Eastern Europe, mostly Jewish, sat in tiny cubicle offices with pianos, writing the rhythms and rhymes that held unchallenged supremacy in the world of popular song. The collective name for this area and enterprise was Tin Pan Alley.
7 Author interview, 23 October 1987.
8 Penny Lane itself was an otherwise undistinguished road, one of a number of tributaries to the main junction where the buses and trams terminated. Its name harks back to Liverpool's dishonourable past: ship captain James Penny was a key proponent of the eighteenth-century slave trade.
9 *Daddy, Come Home*, p33.
10 *The Beatles Anthology*, p33.
11 Both Louises, George's mother and sister, gave the date of birth as 25 February 1943, which is also how it was registered the next day, and on the baptism certificate soon after, and was always written and celebrated ... until the 1990s, when George decided to announce he'd been born on the 24th.
12 Davies, pp38–9.
13 Davies, p149.
14 Author interview, 11 April 2007.
15 A photo of two-year-old George at a VE Day party, with his three elder siblings, is in *George Harrison: Living In The Material World*, by Olivia Harrison (Abrams, New York, 2011), p14.

2: **Boys** (1945–54)

1 *The Beatles Anthology*, p34.
2 There was an innocent error of chronology here. He also recalled his first day at school, which came before the move to Admiral Grove. The St Silas admission register shows he was still living at 9 Madryn Street when his schooling began. The precise date of the move to 10 Admiral Grove isn't recorded, but it followed soon after. 'Condemned' from *The Beatles Anthology*, p33; thankfully, the terrace still stands, preserving not just Richy's childhood home but an authentic piece of Victorian working-class housing.
3 *The Beatles Anthology*, p33. The V sign at 10 Admiral Grove is still over the door, unmoved despite everything that's happened there since.
4 *Thank U Very Much*, by Mike McCartney (Arthur Barker, London, 1981), p24.
5 From author interview with Harry Harrison's daughter Louise, 30 January 2007.
6 Quoted in the US fanzine *George Gernal*, issue 2, 1967. Family information in these paragraphs from author interview with Louise Harrison (daughter), 30 January 2007.
7 *John Lennon, My Brother*, by Julia Baird (Grafton Books, London, 1988), p11. Gateacre is pronounced by locals as 'Gattaker'.

8 The ad appeared in the Personal column on the front page, Monday 15 April 1946.

9 Author interview, 6 April 2009.

10 *Record Mirror*, 6 March 1971. By 'Smith's' Mimi meant the English chain of booksellers W. H. Smith & Son.

11 Davies, p9. John can be seen doing a quick burst of the Charleston in many Beatles film clips.

12 Information from various interviews.

13 Davies, p24.

14 *Thank U Very Much*, p29.

15 Interview by Mike Read, 12 October 1987, for BBC Radio 1.

16 Paul McCartney's foreword for *Liverpool: Wondrous Place*, by Paul Du Noyer (Virgin Books, London, 2002).

17 Interview by Alan Freeman, *Rock Around The World*, US syndicated radio show, 11 April 1976.

18 Probably two of these three pieces mentioned by John in an interview by Mike Hennessey, *Record Mirror*, 2 October 1971: Swedish Rhapsody (composed by Hugo Alfvén), Moulin Rouge (Georges Auric), and Greensleeves (traditional). All were played regularly on the BBC Light Programme.

19 Interview by Ken Zelig, 27 November 1969. Harold Phillips went on to become a teacher; he died many years ago.

20 The Cast Iron Shore was in St Michael in the Hamlet, situated just beyond the Dingle, heading towards Aigburth. A steep cliff showed children down to the banks of the tidal Mersey, a fatal but popular playground for more than a century. People assumed its name derived from the flotsam and jetsam of shipping washed up on the shore, but actually it was from St Michael parish church, part-constructed of cast iron. Today, Otterspool Promenade and the site of Liverpool's International Garden Festival in 1984 cover the Cazzy's history, but the church is still open.

21 Interview by Elliot Mintz, 18 April 1976; '. . . a piano at home' from a roundtable discussion with the press, USA, April 1997 (it's not clear where this piano was). Steble is pronounced to rhyme with 'pebble'. The baths building – now a sports centre – is one of the few Dingle/Toxteth haunts from Richy's childhood still standing in the twenty-first century.

22 Interview for *Jet* magazine, 11 May 1972 (though this section wasn't included in the published piece). In another interview (by Jann S. Wenner, 8 December 1970, for *Rolling Stone*) John described the instrument as 'a Dobro'. The musician he saw may have been Jim Gretty, who will appear later in this history.

23 Interview by Russell Davies, 3 March 1991; *George On George*, BBC Radio 4, 25 May 2004.

24 John was responding to a questionnaire for the organisation National Book League, for use in the first National Library Week, March 1966.

25 The first was a fourteen-line ditty titled 'The Land Of The Lunapots', published in *Mersey Beat*, 27 February 1964. It begins 'T'was custard time and as I / Snuffed at the haggie pie pie / The noodles ran about my plunk / Which rode my wrytle uncle drunk . . .'

26 Author interview, 5 February 2008.

27 Davies, p39.

28 *John Lennon, My Brother*, p16. This is a rare quote from John's cousin Liela Birch, née Hafez (1937–2012).

29 The official name of the house was Strawberry Field but it was usually referred to as Strawberry Fields, plural. The home accommodated up to forty-eight children between the ages of three and sixteen, at which age they would either return to their parents, or the home would place them in a job. The children called themselves 'Strawbs'. A former Strawb, Carol Rigg, says, 'Everybody has the impression we were bad kids. This is completely wrong. All the children were there for the mistakes their parents had made. So we were never locked in: the gates to the road were always open and everybody went out to a normal school every day and made their own way back.' (Author interview, 14 February 2007.)

The original Strawberry Field children's home was demolished in 1975 and replaced with a modern building (itself closed in 2005). An approximate impression of the original structure can be gained by visiting another Gothic Woolton-sandstone mansion, the former Liverpool Convalescent Home, still standing. Its long entrance driveway is located almost opposite 120a Allerton Road, the house owned for years by George and Mimi, where the infant John lived for the only time with his parents. Mimi worked at this convalescent home in the late 1920s.

For decades, tourists in search of John Lennon's Strawberry Field(s) have photographed the old gates to the home on Beaconsfield Road: it's the last surviving remnant of the original building and the only place where the name is visible. John rarely saw these gates because his approach to the house was always gained over the wall in Vale Road, then through the deep trees that are now a housing estate.

30 Leaves From A Liverpolitan's Log Book, by Peter Claughton, *Liverpolitan*, January 1949.

31 *City Of Departures* (Collins, London, 1946), p36.

32 November 1949.

33 Davies, pp39–40.

34 From 1970s interview transcript of unknown origin.

35 The theft was reported in the London *Evening News* (9 January) but Lennon wasn't named. The shop was Jane Lanwin Ltd, at 265–7 Oxford Street, part of the short stretch between Oxford Circus and Harewood Place. The Marlborough Street court and Wormwood Scrubs prison ledgers are in the London Metropolitan Archives.

36 From author interview with Billy Hall, 6 April 2009.

37 Author interview, 5 February 2008.

38 Paul has described this incident as if he witnessed it, intimating that it happened at Liverpool Institute, but George always said it was while he was at Dovedale Road, and named the teacher; John also mentioned it in one of his last interviews because he was also taught by Mr Lyon at Dovedale.

39 *The Beatles Anthology*, p35.

40 *Liverpool Weekly News*, 26 July 1962.

41 Davies, p151.

42 Davies, p153.

43 Interview by Dave Stewart, *Off The Record*, HBO, 2 May 2008.

44 Interview by Krista Bradford, *The Reporters*, Fox, 22 July 1989 (by 'my parents' he meant Elsie and Harry); '... a bottle of gin and a large bottle of brown' from interview by Tony Prince, Radio Luxembourg, 7 October 1976.

    Nobody's Child was recorded by Hank Snow and issued in America at the end of 1949, authentic C&W with a steel guitar. Richy almost certainly got to hear it courtesy of a 'Cunard Yank' bringing the disc back from the States. His other party piece has been mentioned in one interview, the title given as It's Someone Like You. The likeliest number is Someone Like You, featured by Doris Day in the 1949 film *My Dream Is Yours* and also recorded by, among others, Peggy Lee. The Empress is depicted on the front cover of the 1970 album *Sentimental Journey*, the content of which paid undiluted homage to this period of Richy's childhood and especially to the songs sung by Harry Graves. Elsie's and Harry's photos are included in the artwork.

45 From John Lennon's review of the book *The Goon Show Scripts* in the *New York Times*, 30 September 1973. 'My main influences ...' from interview by David Sheff, 24 September 1980, for *Playboy*.

46 Interview by Dennis Elsas, WNEW-FM, 28 September 1974.

47 Shotton from CD enclosed within *John, Paul & Me: Before The Beatles* by Len Garry (CG Publishing, London, 1997); Hill from author interview, 1 June 2005.

48 John Lennon's audio diary, recorded 5 September 1979.

49 John from Davies, pp13–14; Hill from author interview, 26 May 2005.

50 John from interview by David Skan, *Record Mirror*, 11 October 1969; Richy from *The Beatles Anthology*, p36; George from *I Me Mine* (Genesis Publications, Guildford, 1980), pp24–5; Paul from *Many Years From Now*, pp10–11.

51 'Smelled of old people' from *The Beatles Anthology*, pp18–19. Jim McCartney quote from Young Paul, *Beatles Book* magazine, issue 27 (October 1965).

52 Jim McCartney from Davies, p31. A *Liverpool Echo* photographer happened to be present the day Paul went into the cathedral for his choir audition: he's one of eleven boys in a picture published on 17 April 1953, the first time his photo appeared in a newspaper.

53 Paul's original handwritten essay is held in the Liverpool Record Office and was published facsimile in *The McCartneys: In The Town Where They Were Born*, by Kevin Roach (Trinity Mirror, Liverpool, 2009). Paul's 'rubbery legs' quote is from *Many Years From Now* (p7); 'shaking like a jelly' is from a speech he made at the same venue on 28 November 1984 (broadcast by BBC Radio Merseyside).

54 April 1961.

55 It's unclear why the headmaster was nicknamed The Baz. Ian James, Paul McCartney's Institute contemporary (and from 1957 his friend), says, 'There's been all sorts of theories

about it and you couldn't say any one of them was correct. I think he was also called something else – The Jack? – but he was The Baz to everyone.' (Author interview, 18 July 2006.)

56 *The Beatles Anthology*, p18.

57 Ibid., p26.

58 'Red Lion' and 'struggling up the hill' from interview by Nicky Horne, Capital Radio (London), 13 September 1974; 'She's a dark horse' from interview by Ray Coleman, *Melody Maker*, 6 September 1975. Other quotes from *The Beatles Anthology*, p26.

3: 'Who you lookin' at?' (1954–5)

1 The case of Derek Bentley and his partner in crime Christopher Craig became a *cause célèbre*, related in songs, films, books and TV documentaries.

2 George quote from *Earth News Radio*, December 1975; Paul from interview by Janice Long for *Listen To What The Man Says*, BBC Radio 1, 22 December 1985.

3 Interview by Howard Cosell for *Speaking Of Everything*, US radio, October 1974. John meant 'Forty-Ninth State', not fifty-ninth. Until January 1959, America had forty-eight – prompting the expression used (mostly caustically) in post-war Britain.

4 *In My Life*, by Pete Shotton and Nicholas Schaffner (Stein & Day, New York, 1983), p47. John took up smoking at 13.

5 The influence of Cool Water can be heard in Old Dirt Road, on John Lennon's album *Walls And Bridges*, recorded and released 1974.

6 The general view is that John didn't see Julia for some years, though this is contradicted by what he told David Sheff (for *Playboy* magazine) on 24 September 1980: 'My mother was alive and lived fifteen minutes' walk away from me, all my life. And I saw her sporadically off and on all the time. I just didn't live with her.'

7 Davies, p16.

8 *The Beatles Anthology*, p35.

9 The report is illustrated in Davies, p152.

10 Interview by Elliot Mintz, 18 April 1976. The shop was Park Music & Radio Company at 271 Park Road, since demolished.

11 Ibid. Richy remembers the drum on sale at £26.

12 This is a story that's been told many times; the colours assigned to the instruments understandably vary with retelling.

13 Davies, p40.

14 *Rockline*, US radio phone-in, 10 February 1988.

15 From 1970s interview transcript of unknown origin.

16 Author interview, 21 June 2007.

17 Author interview, 14 December 2004.

18 Questionnaires completed by hand in early summer 1963, sold at auction by Christie's, London, 5 May 2004. Paul quote from *The Beatles Anthology*, p21.

19 *Thank U Very Much*, p37.

20 Pwllheli is pronounced as 'Pull-helly', but such was the Englishman's inability to grapple with Welsh words it was often jokingly referred to as 'Peely-weely'. Mike's photo is best seen in his book *Mike Mac's Whites And Blacks Plus One Colour* (Aurum Press, London, 1986), p9.

21 *The Beatles Anthology*, p18.

22 Ibid., p35.

23 Interview by Horst Königstein, Hamburg, 29 September 1976, for *Ringo und die Stadt am Ende des Regenbogen* (*Ringo And The City At The End Of The Rainbow*), West German NDR-TV, 9 and 16 June 1977 – Ringo's best TV interview by far. *Jigsaw* aired on alternate Saturdays from January 1955. George Fierstone (1916–84), who performed with his Quintet in these TV programmes, was a bespectacled drummer, active since childhood in dance and swing bands; he played for seven post-war years in the Skyrockets, houseband at the London Palladium.

24 Author interview, 27 April 2007.

25 John and Mimi from Davies, p15; Liela from *John Lennon, My Brother*, p23; Paul from interview by Sir David Frost, Channel 5, 28 December 1997.

26 John's manuscript illustrated an article about Mimi in *Fabulous*, 27 November 1965. He slightly anglicised Carolyn Leigh's original lyric 'And if you should survive, to a hundred and five'.

27 Interview by Diane Sawyer, *Good Morning America*, ABC-TV, 30 April to 3 May 2001.
28 Author interview, 12 March 2007; '... the boy Casanova of Speke' from Portrait Of Paul, by Mike McCartney, *Woman* magazine, 21 August 1965.
29 It isn't definitively established on which birthday Paul received the trumpet. He usually says it was his 14th, but other events and situations make it more likely to have been his 13th, in June 1955. 'I can sing better than Frank Sinatra!' from interview by Alan Freeman, *Rock Around The World*, US syndicated radio show, 11 April 1976. Paul's cousin Ian was Henry Ian Harris (b.1938), eldest child of Paul's Auntie Gin and Uncle Harry. Huyton should be pronounced as 'Heighten'.
30 Interview by Tony Webster, *Beat Instrumental*, September 1964.
31 Illustrated in *The Beatles Anthology*, p27, and elsewhere.
32 Author interview, 22 March 2007.
33 Illustrated in *The Beatles Anthology*, p39. The Romford address was 86 George Street.
34 *Liverpool Echo*, 3 November 1994.
35 Interview by Brian Matthew, *Pop Profile*, BBC Transcription Service, 2 May 1966.
36 *The Beatles Anthology*, p28.
37 Illustrated in *Harrison*, by the editors of Rolling Stone (Simon & Schuster, New York, 2002), p19, and in numerous other books. In June 2009, in *Observer Music Monthly*, the photo was dated for the first time: 19 April 1956. No explanation was given for the sudden discovery of this detail.
38 Interview by Charlie Gillett and Johnny Beerling, 14 November 1973, for BBC Radio 1. The identity of John's friend isn't known.
39 Song-by-song notes typed by John Lennon for his LP *Rock 'n' Roll*, spring 1975.
40 Pete Shotton quotes and background information in these paragraphs from *In My Life*, p37 and beyond. The book is recommended for those seeking depth on John Lennon's youth.
41 Interview by David Sheff, 12 September 1980, for *Playboy*. 'I've been drinking since I was fifteen.'
42 Interview by Peter Lewis, for *Release*, BBC2, 6 June 1968.
43 Interview by David Sheff, 15 September 1980, for *Playboy*.

4: **Scufflers to Skifflers** (1956)

1 Based on local wholesale and retail sales (the Nems store in Walton was among the places canvassed), 'Liverpool's Own Top 3' chart appeared in the *Echo* every Saturday, compiled by 'Disker' along with his weekly record review column. Disker was Anthony F. J. 'Tony' Barrow (b.1936), an enterprising young man from Crosby (just north of Liverpool) who will play an important part in this history. He began his weekly *Echo* column in 1954, when 17 and still at school; in 1956–7 he promoted several disc and live music dances (skiffle, jazz, etc) in the north end.
2 Interview on *The Weekender*, BBC Radio 2, 18 January 2008.
3 Interview by Elliot Mintz, 18 April 1976. This is one of Ringo's best ever interviews, and is the primary source of the knowledge around this quote.
4 Interview by Jonathan Cott for *Rolling Stone*, 5 December 1980.
5 Main part of quote from interview by Howard Smith, WPLJ-FM, New York, 10 September 1971; second part from radio programme *Pop Goes The Bulldog*, December 1969; third part from an interview for *Record Mirror* (by Mike Hennessey), 2 October 1971; fourth from interview for the *NME* (by Alan Smith), 30 August 1963. Before all this, John already knew the name Elvis Presley. A Quarry Bank boy, Don Beattie, had pointed it out in the *NME*, showing how Heartbreak Hotel was climbing the US chart. John had only just learned of the existence of charts, was yet unfamiliar with music papers, and didn't care at all for the name Elvis, which put him in mind of Perry Como and Frank Sinatra. He also thought Heartbreak Hotel a corny title. But when he heard it ...
6 First part from interview by Andrew Tyler, *Disc*, 16 December 1972; second from interview by Brant Mewborn, *Rolling Stone*, 30 April 1981.
7 *The Beatles Anthology* TV series. Such ads ran in the *NME* on 30 March and 4 May 1956, the first on an inside page, the second occupying the front page.
8 Interview by Joe Brown, *Let It Rock*, BBC Radio 2, 5 July 1999.
9 Author interview, 26 May 2005. Hill lived at 69 Dovedale Road.

10 From John Lennon to Maureen Cleave, quoted in *John Lennon 1940–1980*, by Ray Connolly (Fontana, London, 1981), p32. The Little Richard 78 was Ronnex 1142, with a bright yellow label; Elvis Presley's Heartbreak Hotel was HMV POP 182, blue label.

11 Interview by Elly de Waard, *Vrij Nederland*, 28 March 1969.

12 First and third quotes from interview by Jann S. Wenner, 8 December 1970, for *Rolling Stone*, second quote from interview by Jean-François Vallée for French TV, 4 April 1975. The best-available publication of the *Rolling Stone* interview is in *Lennon Remembers*, by Jann S. Wenner (Verso, London, 2000).

13 Interview by Alan Smith, *NME*, 30 August 1963.

14 Interview by Bob Rogers, Dunedin, 26 June 1964.

15 Interview by Jerry G. Bishop, 13–24 August 1965.

16 Determining the correct chronology of Paul McCartney's earliest songwriting endeavours is tricky. *Many Years From Now* (pp182–3) confirms that Suicide (so called) was written at 20 Forthlin Road, and Paul has stated that this and what became When I'm Sixty-Four were written on the piano and pre-date the rock and roll explosion: 'Rock and roll was about to happen that year, it was about to break, [so] I was still a little bit cabaret minded.' (Interview by Mike Read, 12 October 1987.) 'Rock and roll hadn't happened yet.' (Author interview, 6 June 1990.) 'I wrote a lot of stuff thinking I was going to end up in the cabaret, not realising that rock and roll was particularly going to happen. When I was fourteen there wasn't that much of a clue that it was going to happen.' (From Paul's narration for an unreleased film, *One Hand Clapping*, August 1974.) Paul never mentioned that he wrote any songs while living in Speke, and – as Heartbreak Hotel entered his world no later than May 1956 – they were probably written shortly after the 30 April 1956 move to Allerton.

The title has been variously given as Suicide, Call It Suicide and I Call It Suicide: when copyright was first registered, in 1970, it was as Suicide; when re-registered in 1977 it was as Call It Suicide with the alternative title I Call It Suicide (and Paul has sometimes referred to it in conversation as I Call It Suicide). Four different 1970s recordings of the song are in unofficial circulation, and about eight seconds of another, pre-dating these, was included on the album *McCartney* in 1970.

17 *The Beatles Anthology*, p18.

18 'Turban' remembered by Paul McCartney in the 2011 film *George Harrison: Living In The Material World*. The school photo also shows Ivan Vaughan, Neil Aspinall, Mike McCartney and other names soon to enter this history (Len Garry, John Duff Lowe, and more). George adapted it for an album sleeve (*Dark Horse*, 1974) but doctored the image in several ways. Repositioned directly beneath him is the hated 'Baz' – Liverpool Institute headmaster J. R. Edwards – the Capitol Records logo imposed on his jacket indicating just how George felt about his US record label at this time. George's favourite teacher, art master Stan Reed, was given the good 'OM' sign.

19 *Going Home*, Disney Channel, 18 April 1993 (mostly filmed in Liverpool in 1992). There's a scene in the 1973 film *That'll Be The Day* where Richy enacts his time as a bar waiter. Imagine it on a boat and the picture is about right.

20 Interview by Tom Snyder, *Good Morning America*, ABC-TV, 25 November 1981.

21 Interview by Barry Miles, 23–4 September 1969, partly published in *Fusion* and *Oz*.

22 Interview by Jean-François Vallée for French TV, 4 April 1975.

23 Quotes from interviews with the author, 2 May 1991, and Alan Rowett and Geoff Barker for *Paul McCartney's Routes Of Rock*, BBC World Service, Oct–Nov 1999.

24 Author interview, 22 March 2007.

25 Davies, pp45–6.

26 Author interview, 28 May 2004.

27 *The Beatles Anthology*, p36.

28 *Love Me Do! The Beatles' Progress*, by Michael Braun (Penguin, London, 1964), p35.

29 Reference a 1936 song by Stuff Smith, If You're A Viper: 'I dreamed about a reefer five feet long . . .' The 2i's group deliberately chose the name Vipers for this reason, though they themselves smoked nothing stronger than Virginia tobacco.

30 Interview by the Rev. Wayne Clarke, BBC Radio Merseyside, 28 September 2009.

31 *Yesterday & Today*, by Ray Coleman (Boxtree, London, 1995), p28.

32 Mary McCartney's mass was at the Church of St Bernadette, Mather Avenue, near the family home on Forthlin Road. The committal was at Yew Tree, the RC cemetery in Knotty Ash,

between West Derby and Huyton. She went into eternity in the same plot as her mother (died 1919), baby sister Agnes (1918), and father's second wife Rose (1948), the stepmother she'd left home to escape.

33 Portrait Of Paul, by Mike McCartney, *Woman* magazine, 21 August 1965.
34 *The Beatles Anthology*, p19.
35 First part of quote ('We'd never heard anybody sing ...') from unknown source, quoted in *The Beatles Anthology*, p11; second part ('The most exciting thing ...') from interview by Barry Miles, 23–4 September 1969, partly published in *Fusion* and *Oz*.
36 Interview by Johnnie Walker, BBC Radio 2, 11 May 2001.
37 As told by Maureen Cleave, *Daily Telegraph*, 14 December 2009.
38 Interview by Jerry G. Bishop, 13–24 August 1965.
39 Interview by Timothy White, *Billboard*, 5 December 1992. Liverpool directories of the period list the names of off-licensees, beer retailers and wine and spirits merchants but there's no entry for anyone named Houghton or Horton or any similar-sounding spellings. Seemingly unrelated to this, George's friend Arthur Kelly remembers going with George to learn guitar from a man at a pub in Edge Hill that they called 'The Cat' – actually the Botanic Hotel on Wavertree Road (junction with Byford Street): 'There was a local guy – mixed race, half-black – who used to give lessons. He had a big mother of a guitar, probably a Gibson, with a pickup and an amplifier. He taught us a few Hank Williams country songs like Your Cheatin' Heart.'
40 Author interview, 27 October 2009.
41 Author interview, 5 February 2008.
42 Interview by Spencer Leigh.
43 Varying a little in retelling by others, this comes from James Graves himself, quoted in the *Evening Standard* (London), 25 February 1964. Graves was described as 'a retired packer and one-time Romford United footballer'. An article in the *Romford Recorder* (21 February 1964) said Graves spoke 'without a trace of any kind of accent' – that is, he didn't speak like a typical East End Londoner.
44 Interview by Elliot Mintz, 18 April 1976.

5: **Guaranteed Not to Split** (January–June 1957)

1 Interview by David Sheff, 24 September 1980, for *Playboy*.
2 Ibid. A transcribing error for the book of this interview turned 'Artsy-fartsy people were despised' into 'Artsy-fartsy people were spies', which seemed logical enough. It also appears this way in *The Beatles Anthology*, p9.
3 Interview by Spencer Leigh.
4 Interview by B. P. Fallon for RTE2 (Ireland), circa 20 October 1987.
5 Vic Lewis will re-enter this history in subsequent volumes as a businessman. His orchestra's drummer for the Haley tour, Andy White, also reappears.
6 Author interview, 2 May 1991.
7 Interview by Spencer Leigh.
8 Unpublished quote from September 1971 interview by Mike Hennessey for *Record Mirror*. Nothing is known of this guitar teacher – neither John nor Eric was ever able to recall the man's name or address.
9 Interview by Brian Matthew, *Pop Profile*, BBC Transcription Service, 2 May 1966. Nothing is known of this drum teacher.
10 Interview by John Wilson, *Front Row*, BBC Radio 4, 18 January 2008.
11 Author interview, 28 May 2004.
12 *The Beatles Anthology*, p102. *Sunday Night At The London Palladium* was on the ITV network, launched late 1955 as an alternative to the ad-free BBC.
13 This and the subsequent quote from an interview by Robert W. Morgan, US radio, 20–21 March 1982.
14 George describes his homemade guitar in some detail in *The Beatles Anthology*, p28. It isn't known which guitar manual George and Paul were reading. Paul later said (and George vaguely implied) it was Bert Weedon's *Play In A Day*, a manual so well known to British musicians it's cited even by those who didn't use it. This may be the case here: it was first published in September 1957, surely after George and Paul's experience.

15 Author interview, 18 July 2006.
16 Interview by Ray Coleman, *Melody Maker*, 24 October 1964. The guitar ad said: 'Full size popular plectrum style, handsome shaded mahogany finished, highly polished. Super treble and full bass, warm responses. Suitable for solo or with band, please play it, don't let us try to describe a gem.'
17 Interview by Howard Smith, WPLJ-FM, New York, 23 January 1972.
18 Calypso Rock mentioned in interview by Mike Hennessey (*Record Mirror*, 2 October 1971). In the full transcript, John said 'Calypso/Rock, Rock/Calypso, I couldn't tell which' – which is open to interpretation. Five months earlier, he'd told Raoul Pantin (*Trinidad Express*, 4 May 1971), 'The first song I ever attempted was called Calypso Rock, because the big question at the time was whether calypso would take over from rock 'n' roll.' (The quote 'What I had to learn to do . . .' is from the published Hennessey interview.)
19 Interview by Spencer Leigh.
20 Davies, p54.
21 *NME*, 18 January 1957.
22 Interview by Alan Rowett and Geoff Barker for *Paul McCartney's Routes Of Rock*, BBC World Service, Oct–Nov 1999.
23 Luxembourg was now embracing a kind of permissible payola system where (as well as carrying regular shows and commercials) its schedule included 'sponsored programmes', record companies buying exclusive airtime as shop windows for product, hiring DJs to spin all their latest discs and encourage people to buy them. Though the signal still washed in and out like the waves on a beach, the station at 208 metres remained the only place for British teenagers to hear the kind of music the BBC had scant space for and sometimes little inclination to play; also, crucially, while the BBC was hidebound by rigorous 'Needletime' restrictions (see footnote, p72), Luxembourg operated free of any such outside control. EMI and Decca sponsored numerous programmes, and because Decca had Elvis, and its London label picked up the choice American masters, theirs were the essential shows, the best one being presented by Tony Hall; the programmes were short, sometimes just thirty minutes, and DJs faded records early to discourage home-taping. Historically, Radio Luxembourg was always more popular in the north of England than the south, and listeners in Liverpool still included Richy Starkey, John Lennon, Paul McCartney and George Harrison.
24 Young Paul, *Beatles Book* magazine, issue 27 (October 1965).
25 Two Berry singles were issued in Britain simultaneously at the end of May 1957: School Day and Roll Over Beethoven. Columbia's display ad for the former announced 'He sings it! He plays it! He wrote it!' This didn't prevent a competing cover version by the British singer-trombonist Don Lang, a *Six-Five Special* regular. Berry got to 24 on the NME chart, Lang 26. Roll Over Beethoven didn't chart.
26 Steeply sloping Elswick Street overlooks the Herculaneum Dock, River Mersey and, on a clear day, the distant Welsh hills. The BBC television sitcom *Bread* was filmed here between 1986 and 1991, at a house just across from where Ian James lived with his grandparents. When Paul McCartney made a cameo appearance on the show in 1988 he knocked on the door and told the occupants he'd learned to play guitar in their house.
27 Seventeen years on, in summer 1974, Paul McCartney was working with a cameraman and director at Abbey Road Studios when he suggested they film him on a little patch of wasteland behind the Number 2 studio echo chamber. The result was a nine-minute short he called *The Backyard* but which might as well have been *Elswick Street*, Paul sitting on a chair in the sunshine, playing an upside-down acoustic guitar and singing some 1950s rock and roll numbers – including Twenty Flight Rock. It remains unreleased.
28 Davies, p46. In 1957, Speke British Legion was using a temporary construction, demolished in 1962 when permanent premises were erected on the same site. The coachloads of tourists brought most days to this unlovely spot are always shown the wrong building. Oddly, the club chairman at the time the Rebels played there was G. Harrison.
29 Author interview, 11 November 2004.
30 The photographer was Leslie Kearney, 29, a design engineer from Allerton who took up photography as a hobby and was retained by Charlie McBain to take photos at his dances.
31 Interview by Barry Miles, 23–4 September 1969, partly published in *Fusion* and *Oz*.
32 Interview by Jon Wilde, *Uncut*, July 2004.
33 3 April 1957.

34	Interview by Alan Rowett and Geoff Barker for *Paul McCartney's Routes Of Rock*, BBC World Service, Oct–Nov 1999. Paul recorded a version of Fabulous that year.

35	*McCartney Rocks!* electronic press kit, 1999. The store was either Wood Brothers at 225 Park Road (that most unlikely of combinations: a bicycle shop that also sold records, and occasionally contributed a chart to *The Record Mirror*) or Park Music & Radio Company at 271 Park Road, where Richy Starkey had first become besotted with the notion of playing drums after seeing a tom-tom in its window c.1954.

36	*The Beatles Anthology*, p36.

37	Photos by Charles Roberts, a friend of Colin Hanton's who'd asked the Quarry Men to perform at the party and written the lettering for his bass drum head (COLIN HANTON. THE QUARRY MEN). His mother's efforts had been key to Rosebery Street being awarded the prize in a Liverpool Corporation street decorating competition, marking the 750th anniversary of King John issuing Liverpool a royal charter in 1207. The party was celebrating this prize. Toxteth wasn't the Quarry Men's native part of town, though Rosebery Street was close to where the Lennon and Stanley families lived earlier in the century.

38	Interview by Andy Peebles, 6 December 1980, for BBC Radio 1.

39	From interviews with and letters to the author, January and February 2006. Philip Burnett lived 1930–95.

6: **Come Go With Me** (6 July 1957)

1	The *Observer* piece (SKIFFLE INTELLIGENTSIA) by Hugh Latimer, 16 June 1957; *The World's Fair* piece by Don Anthony, 29 June 1957.

2	Interview by Stuart Colman, *Echoes*, BBC Radio London, 17 June 1984. The line John sang as 'down to the penitentiary' was actually 'don't let me pray beyond the sea', partly buried by backing vocals in the original recording.

3	Davies (1985), p471.

4	Davies, p21.

5	'... almost standoffish' from *In My Life*, p55. The scout hut has been clearly and consistently remembered as the meeting place by Colin Hanton – e.g., in *The Day John Met Paul*, BBC Radio 2, 26 June 2007.

6	Interview by Mike Read, 23 February 1989, for BBC Radio 1. The first half of the following quote is from an interview by Julia Baird, 1988, remainder from *The Beatles Anthology*, p20.

7	First half of quote from interview by Jann S. Wenner, 8 December 1970, for *Rolling Stone*, remainder from Davies, p35.

8	Interview by Dave Sholin, Ron Hummel and Laurie Kaye, RKO, 8 December 1980.

9	From CD enclosed within *John, Paul & Me: Before The Beatles* by Len Garry.

7: **'He'll get you into trouble, son'** (July–December 1957)

1	Interview by Joan Goodman, for *Playboy*, December 1984.

2	Interview by Anthony Cherry, BBC Radio 2, 28 June 1992. The guitar's advertised price was 14 guineas (£14 14s). Paul has never specifically mentioned that George was with him when he got the Zenith so the Jim Gretty 'jazz chord' anecdote could belong to a subsequent occasion. In his book *Many Years From Now*, Paul said he swapped the trumpet for the guitar at Rushworth & Dreaper; Hessy's is more likely, and this was where Gretty worked.

3	Author interview, 19 May 1987. Born in Poland, Mairants (1908–98) moved to Britain aged five. He owned his own musical instrument shop in London from 1962. Stringent import restrictions were evident throughout the 1950s as countries tried to revive their post-war economies. One such ban prevented the import into Britain of musical instruments made in America (it was lifted in 1959). The Conservative government also applied 30 per cent purchase tax on instruments, and 60 per cent on records.

4	Interview by Anthony Cherry, BBC Radio 2, 28 June 1992; Mike from *Thank U Very Much*, p65.

5	Author interview, 30 September 1987.

6	Portrait Of Paul, by Mike McCartney, *Woman* magazine, 28 August 1965.

7	Interview by Alan Rowett and Geoff Barker for *Paul McCartney's Routes Of Rock*, BBC World Service, Oct–Nov 1999.

8 George sold the Egmond for a pound or two to the son of a man who worked with his dad at Speke bus depot. It sold again at auction in 2003 for £276,000. The date George got the Hofner isn't known.

9 *The David Frost Show* (American TV), 3 December 1971.

10 *Lennon*, by Ray Coleman (Pan, London, 2000 edition), p138; Mimi from Davies, p17.

11 First half of John's quote from interview by Alan Smith, *NME*, 30 August 1963, remainder from *The Beatles Anthology*, p13.

12 *The Beatles Anthology*, p36. In the TV documentary *Going Home* (Disney Channel, 18 April 1993), he says he first played the Cavern as drummer with the Darktown group. As he joined them after leaving Eddie Clayton, and Eddie's group appeared there on eight advertised occasions and probably several more unadvertised, this is in question. A well-written *Liverpool Echo* article (16 September 1957) about the explosion of guitar playing on Merseyside concluded with a music teacher remarking, 'Liverpool was the first city to start the skiffle vogue.' It's likely, though difficult to prove.

13 Interview by Patrick Humphries, *Beatles Book* magazine, issue 283 (November 1999).

14 The photo can be seen in two of Mike's photo-archive books, reproduced particularly well in *Remember: The Recollections And Photographs Of Michael McCartney* (Merehurst, London, 1992). It was also the cover art for a Paul McCartney CD in 1999. Paul and Mike's second cousin, Edward 'Ted' Robbins (b.1955), is a well-known British TV comedian and actor, as is his sister Kate (b.1958). Amy (b.1971), the youngest of three further sisters, is an acclaimed actress.

15 *Remember*, p23.

16 Paul McCartney once rebuked me for saying his stage debut had taken place at the Butlin's camp in Filey, insisting it was Pwllheli. 'Why do people keep saying it was Filey?' he asked, seemingly unaware his brother Mike had placed these 1957 activities there when writing of them, at some length, in his first book *Thank U Very Much* (pp61–3). The conclusive proof is Butlin's printed entertainment programme for the Filey week, which has a photo of Mike Robbins as 'compere producer'.

17 Davies, p26.

18 'Horrible' from *Many Years From Now*, p40.

19 Author interview, 18 July 2006.

20 Author interview, 11 November 2004.

21 *Observer Music Monthly*, 18 September 2005. 'Butting is the first move used by the Liverpool lout,' John Lennon would remember. 'I only tried it once but my opponent moved and I nearly cracked my head open.' (*Love Me Do! The Beatles' Progress*, p37.) In the same book Ringo Starr said that in earlier years his Starkey grandad had threatened to head-butt him 'if I gave him any cheek'.

22 Interview by Melvyn Bragg, *The South Bank Show*, LWT, 14 January 1978.

23 *Many Years From Now*, p30.

24 *The John Lennon Story*, 1982 Australian TV documentary by John Torv. In 1971 John appended some biographical information about himself in a publicity booklet and in the section on his schooling deleted 'No GCEs' and wrote '½'. It's not clear what he meant by this. He may have kept his results secret because he was meant to have passed at least one O-Level as a condition of college admission. The 1957–8 prospectus is clear on this, stipulating too that the student also had to pass an entrance test. If John took this he never mentioned it in later years.

25 Jeans from Davies, p51; blazer from author interview with Pat Jourdan, 10 November 2005.

26 Interview by Kevin Howlett, 6 April 1990. Bill Harry was a first-cousin of June Harry, who'd played such a vital role in getting John into the college; both were students there.

27 Many streets in Liverpool are prefixed 'Back', running behind a bigger street with the same name. Back Broadway is literally behind Broadway (less glamorous than even the worst parts of its New York namesake). Liverpool has unusually distinctive street names. A hill is often a 'Brow' and some short lanes are suffixed 'Hey', from the French word *haie*, meaning land enclosed by hedges. Hackins Hey, which sounds very much like a chest complaint, is an interesting little thoroughfare in the city centre.

28 First part of quote from author interview, 3 November 1994; middle from *The Beatles Anthology*, p21; final section from interview by Roger Scott, Capital Radio (London), 17 November 1983.

29 The photographer was Leslie Kearney.

30 *Evening Express* 28 August, 3 and 5 September 1957.

31 21 September 1957.

32 Letter sent by John in September 1974 in response to an enquiry from a Holly fan, Jim Dawson, who asked him what it was about Holly he liked. Illustrated in *Memories Of Buddy Holly*, compiled by Jim Dawson and Spencer Leigh (Big Nickel Publications, Milford, NH, 1996), p101; also in *Record Collector* magazine, issue 234 (February 1999).

33 2 November 1957.

34 Author interview, 3 November 1994. Black or white from *Arena: The Buddy Holly Story*, BBC2, 12 September 1985.

35 Unknown source, quoted without attribution in *The John Lennon Encyclopedia*, by Bill Harry (Virgin Publishing, London, 2000), p904. The full wording suggests it may be from the type of fan magazine where quotes were routinely manufactured. John never mentioned this at any other time, so without further corroboration it may be unwise to give it too much weight.

36 *Many Years From Now*, p30; weren't even proper banjo chords (John) – from interview by Mike Hennessey, *Record Mirror*, 2 October 1971.

37 *The Day John Met Paul*, BBC Radio 2, 26 June 2007.

38 *Thank U Very Much*, p53; also Portrait Of Paul, by Mike McCartney, *Woman* magazine, 28 August 1965, and Paul McCartney interview by Sir David Frost, Channel 5, 28 December 1997.

39 John from interview by Peter McCabe and Robert D. Schonfeld, September 1971; Paul from author interview, 7 November 1995.

40 It was confusing: Holly had records under his own name, clearly using the Crickets although they weren't mentioned, while the Crickets had records under their name without mentioning Holly, who was clearly the lead singer. 'When we started to record something we didn't know if it was going to be a Crickets record or a Buddy Holly record,' recalls Jerry Allison (Crickets drummer and co-writer of Peggy Sue) in *Remembering Buddy*, by John Goldrosen and John Beecher (Omnibus Press, London, 1996) p59. The same book (p53) has a long quote from the group's rhythm guitarist Niki Sullivan about how they arrived at the name Crickets, saying that when they went through a list of insects they briefly considered Beetles.

41 Interview by Alan Freeman, BBC Radio 1, 6 December 1974.

42 Interview by Spencer Leigh. The uncle was probably Eddie French, who emigrated to Canada in the early 1950s.

43 Interview by John Wilson, *Front Row Special*, BBC Radio 4, 29 August 2005. Bourrée was from the fifth movement of Bach's Suite in E minor for Lute (BWV 996).

44 Author interview, 2 May 1991. The tune often called Pink Champagne was composed as a light orchestral piece titled Bubble (or Bubble, Bubble, Bubble) by George Forrest and Robert Wright. The vocal version, Pink Champagne, was published in 1950.

45 Interviews by Russell Harty, BBC1, 26 November 1984, and Janice Long for *Listen To What The Man Says*, BBC Radio 1, 22 December 1985.

46 Author interview, 5 February 2008.

47 Unrelated to this – and John Lennon wouldn't have known it – a song titled Hello Little Girl was released in America in October 1957 by Lloyd Price, on Atlantic subsidiary KRC. Trade ads announced, 'He wails to a hi-shaking mambo beat.' The lyric includes the line 'I wanna hold your hand'.

48 *Paul McCartney In His Own Words*, by Paul Gambaccini (Omnibus Press, London, 1976), p17.

49 Starting in 1977, Paul occasionally performed the song on radio, TV and in concert. It's on his album *Unplugged: The Official Bootleg*, recorded and issued in 1991. Even with a newly added bridge (the twice-sung 'Well gather round people, let me tell you the story of the very first song I wrote') it runs only 1.14. As well as the clear Buddy Holly musical influence, Paul's vocal includes a Holly hiccup, pinpointing its creation to post-September 1957. As it was written on the guitar, which he only began playing after rock's breakthrough, and as he always said he wrote the two piano songs (Call It Suicide and what would become When I'm Sixty-Four) before rock arrived, I Lost My Little Girl was not his first song but his first *guitar* song – a distinction he, as the creator, was entitled to make.

50 Interview for Friends of the Earth, 15 December 1989.

51 Author interview, 18 July 2006.

8: 'Where we going, Johnny?' (January–May 1958)

1 Davies, p47.
2 Interview by Anthony Cherry, BBC Radio 2, 28 June 1992.
3 Evidence given at the Royal Courts of Justice, London, 6 May 1998; George Harrison, James Paul McCartney, Richard Starkey, Yoko Ono Lennon (as executrix of the will of John Winston Ono Lennon (deceased)) vs Lingasong Music Ltd. John quote from interview by Ray Coleman, *Melody Maker*, 24 October 1964.
4 First and third sections from interview by Jann S. Wenner, 8 December 1970, for *Rolling Stone*; second section from Davies, p48.
5 Said in the 2011 film *George Harrison: Living In The Material World*.
6 Davies, p48.
7 *The Beatles Anthology*, p142.
8 Davies (1985), p471.
9 Author interview, 11 November 2004. Scallops (pronounced 'scollops') are flat, round slices of potato dipped in batter, deep fried and best enjoyed with plenty of salt and vinegar. Situated opposite the Liverpool Institute High School for Girls at Blackburne House, Vaughan's was at 5 Falkner Street (it's now a café). A profile of George in the number 1 issue of *Beatles Book* magazine, August 1963, said he first met John 'in the fish and chip shop by his school'. This was Vaughan's, and it may pre-date any other encounter.
10 Author interview, 14 December 2004.
11 Author interview, 2 May 1991. As ever, there's no confirmed information about arrivals and departures in the Quarry Men. Lowe's addition to the group may have been in February 1958 or at any time in the following few weeks.
12 Interview by Spencer Leigh.
13 Interview by Peter McCabe and Robert D. Schonfeld, September 1971.
14 Mike McCartney has named the photo *John, Paul, George and Dennis*, because a young man standing by Paul's left elbow, holding a glass of stout, is Ian's neighbour Dennis Littler.
15 *17 Watts? The Birth Of British Rock Guitar*, by Mo Foster (Sanctuary Publishing, London, 2000), p184.
16 First and last sections from 1970s interview transcript of unknown origin, middle section from *The Beatles Anthology*, p30.
17 Eric Griffiths joined the merchant navy and was at sea 1958–64. The problem of piecing together the Quarry Men chronology, where so many anecdotes and memories are contradictory, is underlined again by the 2010 discovery of a document showing that Griffiths' first voyage sailed on 14 February 1958. This means it cannot be him holding a guitar in the colour photograph taken a month later … and yet George Harrison recalled instigating Eric's dismissal, and Nigel Walley remembers Eric's distress when he was informed of it. The only way these pieces could fit would be if George joined the group considerably earlier than February, but every account says he didn't and his 'audition piece', Raunchy, was little known before this time – besides which, Eric would have been aware of his maiden voyage some weeks before it happened and wouldn't have been upset at the prospect of leaving the group. Perhaps the sailing record is incorrect and it *is* Eric Griffiths holding a guitar in the March 1958 photo; but if it isn't, there's no clue to who else it was.
18 Author interview, 4 October 2004.
19 *The Beatles Anthology*, p30. George also expressed his displeasure at Institute school dinners in a 1975 interview by Sarah Dickinson for LBC radio (London), reflecting on 'old sort of Liverpool Council cabbage'.
20 Paul quote from his foreword for *The Cavern: The Most Famous Club In The World*, by Spencer Leigh (SAF Publishing, London, 2008); George from Earth News Radio, December 1975; John from *Pop Goes The Bulldog*, December 1969.
21 Interview by Spencer Leigh.
22 It has become part of the folklore that George 'auditioned' for the Quarry Men at the Morgue and wasn't otherwise in the group when they played here, and/or that his vital rendition of Raunchy on the top deck of a bus was after a night at the Morgue. Both seem plausible but for the fact that the club opened on Thursday 13 March and the preceding Saturday, the 8th, George was photographed playing with John and Paul at the McCartney family party.
23 *Arena: The Buddy Holly Story*, BBC2, 12 September 1985.

24 Typed letter sent by John Lennon to Jim Dawson, September 1974. *Memories Of Buddy Holly*, p101.
25 *Guitar Player*, November 1987.
26 Interview by Alan Rowett and Geoff Barker for *Paul McCartney's Routes Of Rock*, BBC World Service, Oct–Nov 1999.
27 Paul quote from interview by Chris Welch, *Melody Maker*, 1 December 1973; George from interview by Joe Brown, *Let It Rock*, BBC Radio 2, 5 July 1999. George said he especially liked Chuck's slide guitar on the blues track Deep Feeling, the B-side of the 1957 single School Day. (It wasn't made clear if George felt this at the time or later.)
28 First half of quote from interview with Jann S. Wenner, 8 December 1970, for *Rolling Stone*; remainder from *The Mike Douglas Show*, US TV, 16 February 1972, when John got to play with Chuck Berry for the first and only time (they did Memphis, Tennessee and Johnny B. Goode).
29 *The Songwriter – Paul McCartney*, PPM RadioWaves, spring 1990.
30 From the opening show in *Ringo's Yellow Submarine*, American radio series, 1983, interview by Dave Herman.
31 Interview by Michael Watts, *Melody Maker*, 7 August 1971.
32 'We thought, "Hey, these are good,"' George recalled in *The Beatles Anthology*, p28.
33 Author interview, 28 May 2004.
34 Eddie Clayton (Eddie Myles) interview by Spencer Leigh.
35 Author interview, 10 April 2007.
36 John Lennon in Davies, p48.
37 Author interview, 30 September 1987. A little more of the lyric is known: 'Well I've been thinking of linking my life with you / Thinking of linking a love so true / Thinking of linking can only be done by two.' Like most Lennon-McCartney Originals in this period it was heavily influenced by the sound of Buddy Holly and the Crickets.
38 Davies, p53. Paul quotes from interview by Julia's daughter, Julia Baird, 1988; *The Beatles Anthology*, p20; *Many Years From Now*, p48.
39 Interview by Kevin Howlett, 6 April 1990.
40 Author interview, 9 October 2010.
41 Author interview, 17 December 2004.
42 All details in these paragraphs about Jeff Mahomed's lifestyle and character are drawn from interviews with Ann Mason, Tony Carricker, Pat Jourdan and Thelma Pickles.
43 Author interview, 27 May 2004.
44 Interview by Leonard Gross, *Look* magazine, 13 December 1966.
45 Interview by Paul Drew, US radio, April 1975.
46 Phillips, aged 62, and his eldest son Frank, 32, ran the studio together and much of their business was in personalised greetings. A contemporary newspaper article (Liverpool *Evening Express*, 15 June 1957) took delight in noting how a man cut a disc pleading for his wife to return. And of course, since the skiffle boom, plenty of groups had been turning up at 38 Kensington, lugging their washboards and tea-chests through the front door. The Byrne/Murphy disc was Butterfly c/w She's Got It, Charlie Gracie c/w Little Richard. The latter song is included on the album *Unearthed Merseybeat* (Viper CD016).
47 Interview by Paul Drew, US radio, April 1975.
48 Every new record on the *NME* chart in 1958 was compiled into a pair of four-CD sets, *1958 British Hit Parade*, issued in 2009 (Fantastic Voyage FVQD001 and 002), and of these two hundred tracks only two ran longer than the 3.30 of In Spite Of All The Danger. Thanks to iTunes it's possible to see at a glance that the median duration of a 1958 chart record was 2.25. (These CDs formed part of an invaluable annual series beginning 1952, intended to extend as far as the fifty-year copyright expiry rule permitted.)
49 *Liverpool Echo*, 24 December 1977 (Phillips, born December 1895, was then a grand old timer of 82). A return visit with extra cash could be where the logbook reference to Arthur Kelly comes in. Duff Lowe apart, the Quarry Men lived some distance from Kensington but Kelly was close by. Paul quote from author interview, 30 September 1987.
50 He kept it until 1981 and then sold it to Paul McCartney. Both tracks appear on *The Beatles Anthology 1*, though In Spite Of All The Danger is edited there by forty-five seconds.

9: **'This is my life'** (June–December 1958)

1 *Liverpool Weekly News*, 26 June 1958. The deleted expletive is theirs. (Newspapers could restrain themselves from printing swear words in those days.)

2 *Evening Express* and also *Echo*, 21 June 1958; *Liverpool Weekly News* 26 June and 3 July 1958. The last of these said Dykins was disqualified from driving for three months, but the court record specifies one year.

3 This explanation of Julia's visit, credible in itself and even more so in the circumstances, is contained in an original document written by Mimi, privately owned.

4 Author interview, 5 February 2008.

5 Author interview, 27 April 2007. The death certificate gives the place of death as 'on the way to Sefton General Hospital' and the cause as 'lacerations and haemorrhage of the brain due to fracture of the skull'. Michael Fishwick was no longer living at Mendips, but was back in Liverpool to oversee the printing of his thesis.

6 Davies, p52.

7 Ibid.

8 Ibid.

9 *John Lennon, My Brother*, p46.

10 17 and 24 July 1958.

11 Interview by Mike Tomkies, *Tit-Bits*, 20 June 1964.

12 The swindle from *Daddy, Come Home*, pp99–100; the heroic refusal from *Tit-Bits*, 27 June 1964. Julia's daughter, Julia, believes that she and her sister Jacqui, and John, received a share of their mother's insurance money – them later, John straight away in 1958–9. Considering his permanently impoverished state, and no art school friend recalling his being flush with any cash ever, this must remain unproven. (And John *certainly* didn't inherit £530 on his 21st birthday in 1961.)

13 Interview by David Sheff, 24 September 1980, for *Playboy*.

14 *Fifty Years Adrift*, by Derek Taylor (Genesis Publications, Guildford, 1984), p181.

15 Interview by Nick Logan, *NME*, 29 March 1969; 'born happy' from interview by Michael Aspel, *Aspel & Company*, LWT, 5 March 1988.

16 Interview by Garvin Rutherford, Sydney, 14 June 1964.

17 Author interview, 28 May 2004. Geraldine from *Rave*, issue 7, August 1964.

18 *Aspel & Company*, LWT, 5 March 1988.

19 Davies, p155.

20 Davies, p53.

21 First sentence from interview by Sir David Frost, Channel 5, 28 December 1997; remainder from interview by author and Kevin Howlett, 6 June 1990.

22 Author interview, 25 April 2005.

23 *A Private View*, by Robert Freeman (Pyramid Books, London, 1990), p155.

24 There were four other Vikings besides Brierley: Glyn 'Gwndwn' Williams (guitar/vocal), Bernard Lee (guitar), Aneurin Thomas (tea-chest bass) and John Diggle (snare drum). Aneurin's dad ran the Queens Hotel and the Vikings played in the saloon bar from time to time, mostly on Saturday nights. In *George Harrison: Living In The Material World* (p42), Paul recalled the names John and Aniron [*sic*] – 'a big Welsh guy' – and '[sitting] in with their band one drunken night in a Welsh pub'. George never mentioned it in any interview.

25 *Many Years From Now*, pp41–2.

26 From 1970s interview transcript of unknown origin.

27 Author interview, 17 December 2004.

28 Author interview, 10 August 2004.

29 Interview by Kevin Howlett, 6 April 1990.

30 *Observer*, 13 December 2009.

31 Author interview, 6 September 2010.

32 From Paul McCartney interview by Paul du Noyer for the *World Tour* programme (1989–90), p9. These were briefly used nicknames, though George had also been 'Hazza' to some friends at Liverpool Institute.

33 *A Twist Of Lennon*, by Cynthia Lennon (W. H. Allen, London, 1978), pp26–7. (Cyn went to the house too.) Paul McCartney interview by Julia Baird, 1988; *John Lennon, My Brother*, p49. George: 'When he [Bobby Dykins] was safely down the road, on the way to his local pub, we

would sneak into the house so that we could all plug our instruments into the back of his radiogram' – *17 Watts?*, p184.

34 Author interview, 15 April 2010. *The Adult Beginner's Guide To Musical Notation* was an instruction manual by Dawson Freer (1953).

35 First part of quote from interview by Edward Seckerson, *Kaleidoscope*, BBC Radio 4, 4 October 1997; middle from interview by Ed Stewart, BBC Radio 2, 14 December 1991; final part from interview by Melvyn Bragg, *The South Bank Show*, LWT, 14 January 1978.

36 Davies, p33. Paul from interview by Janice Long for *Listen To What The Man Says*, BBC Radio 1, 22 December 1985.

37 'On Safairy With Whide Hunter' may be unique among John's published works in that it was subjected to revision. When first published (in *Mersey Beat*, 6 September 1962), its opening paragraph was a recent addition to the original 1958 piece, being a parody of the lyric from The Lion Sleeps Tonight (aka Wimoweh), a hit record in early 1962. (The revision may have been prompted by repeats of the TV series *White Hunter* in the Granada TV region at the time.) Although John always said he never returned to a piece once it was written, this clearly was an exception: he typed the revised version on the back of a document dated mid-July 1962 (currently in the hands of a private collector). The piece first appeared in book form in 1964: *In His Own Write* (Jonathan Cape, London), pp62–3.
    During interviews at that time, John said the book also contained a second piece 'written in conjugal with Paul' but that, owing to an error, it hadn't been denoted. Its identity still isn't known.

38 The fullest account of the Pilchard play, which may never have had a title, is in *Many Years From Now*, p39. Paul's exercise-book pages have never been seen and are believed lost. The *Daily Mail* piece was 1 February 1963: Paul told Adrian Mitchell 'We've written a couple of plays together', but if this wasn't bluster no second piece is known.

39 An off-the-cuff 24 January 1969 recording of Paul and John singing I Fancy Me Chances is included within the 2003 album *Let It Be . . . Naked*, on the second disc, *Fly On The Wall*; the song was copyrighted for this purpose, but as Fancy My Chances With You. One line rhymes 'frock' with 'Loc' (as in Locarno Ballroom) but it isn't clear if Paul made this up on the spot or it was part of the 1958 words.

40 The origin of the name Johnny and the Moondogs is not clear cut. The word Moondog probably came to their attention through its use by the American rock and roll DJ Alan Freed, whose show was broadcast for a while on Radio Luxembourg. It had finished by late 1958 but the word could have lodged, and they might also have heard it said in Freed's films. Alternatively, George Harrison recalled not many years later, 'I think Moondog was the name of a big Red Indian on TV at the time.' British TV was certainly swamped by American westerns in autumn 1958: the BBC had three, ITV showed a different import most days of the week. A check of episode descriptions and character names has not yielded a Moondog but the possibility can't be ruled out.

41 Author interview, 11 November 2004. 'Smashed in half' from interview by John Peel, *Night Ride*, BBC Radio 1 and 2, 11 December 1968.

42 Davies, p63.

43 *Beatles Gear*, by Andy Babiuk (Backbeat Books, London and San Francisco, 2001), p26. Clarke and Nash were both later of the Hollies; Nash also of Crosby, Stills, Nash & Young. *Manchester Evening News* review, 25 November 1958.

44 *The Beatles Anthology*, p31. Graham Nash says that he and Allan Clarke, as Ricky & Dane, won the Manchester contest, singing Conway Twitty's current hit It's Only Make Believe, and that they went to perform in Blackpool as a result.

45 Interview by Spencer Leigh.

46 Interview by Charlie Gillett and Johnny Beerling, 14 November 1973, for BBC Radio 1.

47 '. . . the first three-part we ever did' from author interview, 30 September 1987; Jim's help from *The Beatles Anthology*, p96. All these records were released in Britain by Decca's London label. At this same time, Richy Starkey got the only drum record he ever bought, Topsy, by the black jazz drummer Cozy Cole.

48 Author interview, 20 January 2005.

49 *Remember*, p28.

50 Hodkin's recollection seems to suggest John didn't have a guitar at this recording, but it can't be remembered with any certainty. It's clear, however, that he wasn't playing one at events either side of this.

51 Remembered by Harry Harrison in the film *George Harrison: Living In The Material World*. George's recollection of them being drunk is from *The Beatles Anthology*, p30. Almost the same today as it was in 1958, Childwall Abbey Hotel is one of the best 'Beatles Liverpool' locations, the only surviving haunt of Japage 3.

52 Davies, p61.

53 'I used to drink black velvet – Guinness and cider – and get sick a lot,' Paul told Russell Harty when talking about these parties (BBC1, 26 November 1984).

10: **'A sort of violent Teddy Boy'** (January–July 1959)

1 Interview by Ed Stewart, BBC Radio 2, 14 December 1991.

2 Author interview, 17 December 2004. If there was a fourth player there's no clue who it could have been.

3 Author interview, 20 January 2005.

4 Interview by Alan Smith, *NME*, 30 August 1963: 'I did a bit of freelancing for a while. In fact, at one stage I think I was in about three groups all at the same time.' The Les Stewart Quartet and Japage 3 are two – if there was a third, nothing is known of it.

5 Author interview, 6 January 2005.

6 Author interview, 11 November 2004.

7 *I Me Mine*, p26. Irene gave birth to her and Harry's first child, Paul Harrison, on 15 January 1960 – George becoming an uncle for the third time, the first locally.

8 Author interview, 6 September 2010.

9 Interview by David Sheff, 24 September 1980, for *Playboy*.

10 Davies, pp56–7. The song lyric: 'I used to be cruel to my woman / I beat her and kept her apart from the things that she loved' – Getting Better, 1967.

11 Interview by Sandra Shevey, the *Hartford Courant*, 26 November 1972.

12 'The Teddy Boy ... that was my scene, but it was only a club to belong to at the time' – interview by David Skan, *Record Mirror*, 11 October 1969.

13 *Many Years From Now*, pp49/33.

14 *The Beatles Anthology*, p31.

15 One of many secrets was that his real name wasn't Bob or Robert. He was born Frederick James Wooler. This fact didn't emerge until his death in 2002. His earliest involvement in teenage music was his management of Garston skiffle group the Kingstrums in 1957.

16 *Disc*, 18 April 1959. The paper launched on 8 February 1958. Quickly good, informative and pictorially strong, it covered all types of popular music and comfortably found a niche: not musicianly like *Melody Maker* or as fact-filled as the *NME*, it competed mostly with *The Record Mirror*.

17 Interview by Ray Connolly, *Evening Standard* (London), 9 September 1972.

18 Information from interview with Roy Trafford, 9 July 2010. The rehearsal hall was possibly Mount Carmel RC Boys' Club.

19 John wrote this in 1971 when appending a publicity booklet.

20 Interview by Elliot Mintz, 18 April 1976.

21 *The Beatles Anthology*, p38. Richy Starkey saw Sister Rosetta Tharpe in Liverpool, probably in the Cavern on 12 April 1958, and thought her guitar playing was wonderful.

22 Interview by Tom Snyder, *Good Morning America*, ABC-TV, 25 November 1981.

23 Interview by Alan Rowett and Geoff Barker for *Paul McCartney's Routes Of Rock*, BBC World Service, Oct–Nov 1999.

24 5 June 1959.

25 Interview by Tony Webster, *Beat Instrumental*, November 1964.

26 Mimi Smith, interviewed by TVS, December 1981.

27 Interview by Mike Hennessey, *Record Mirror*, 2 October 1971.

28 'Listen to this song, fellers' from Milwaukee press conference, 4 September 1964; 'Yes, OK' from *Many Years From Now*, p112.

29 *The Beatles Anthology*, p18.

30 Interview by Alan Freeman, BBC Radio 1, 6 December 1974.

31 Davies, p56. Thelma Pickles confirms John's mocking ('Here comes Miss Prim', 'Watch your manners, here's Cynthia') but reckons John had long fancied her. 'I always sensed it, and I was very attuned, but I dismissed it because I thought she'd be far too good for him. She was sweet

and lovely, a very nice, quiet girl who would blush and be embarrassed.' (Author interview, 6 September 2010.)

32 Davies, p51.

33 Interview by Tony Wilson, *Granada Weekend*, Granada TV, 26 October 1984.

34 A *Twist Of Lennon*, p19. Cynthia's answer was a nervous one. She'd been engaged to a Hoylake Romeo (a window cleaner called Barry) but it was over.

35 *The Beatles Anthology*, p103.

36 This is the most likely chronological placing of Paul's job at Lewis's, but not definitely correct. He'd hoped to earn the occasional ten shillings as a golf course caddy but there were always other lads ahead of him. (*Many Years From Now*, p43.)

11: 'Come viz me to ze Casbah' (July–December 1959)

1 Author interview, 17 December 2004.

2 Author interview, 7 February 2005.

3 Interview by author and Kevin Howlett, 6 June 1990.

4 Interview by Alan Rowett and Geoff Barker for *Paul McCartney's Routes Of Rock*, BBC World Service, Oct–Nov 1999.

5 Louise remembered George taking a guitar. As there wasn't much point carrying the Club 40 without an amp, it was probably his old Hofner President.

6 *The Beatles Anthology*, p29. George got Oxo Whitney's name into a piece of John Lennon's prose, written in 1964 – 'The Singularge Experience of Miss Anne Duffield', from A *Spaniard In The Works* (Jonathan Cape, London, 1965), pp24–33.

7 Author interview, 6 January 2005. Ken Brown remembered it all quite differently; specifically, he had no recollection of not turning up for a booking. At most (he told me in May 2010) he may have missed a rehearsal.

8 Rory Best thinks George and Ken did play as a duo – he says they had at least one performance at the British Legion club in Old Roan, near Aintree. As George never mentioned it, and Ken had no such recollection, it has to be filed under unproven.

9 Davies, p74, and *Beatle! The Pete Best Story*, by Pete Best and Patrick Doncaster (Plexus, London, 1985), p20.

10 *The Beatles Anthology*, p45. As the years pass so claims have been made that various parts of the Casbah's decor were painted by John, Paul or George – notably in the book *The Beatles – The True Beginnings* by Roag Best with Pete and Rory Best (Screenpress Publishing, Ipswich, 2002). These claims may well be correct but it's fair to say some have questioned them, including Neil Aspinall, a close friend of the Bests for fifty years and long-time resident at the house, who told me, 'The only room John, Paul or George painted at the Casbah was the one with the stripes. They didn't do any others. People aren't remembering things right.'

11 *Beatle!*, p20.

12 Kenneth Alan Brown, born 30 May 1940 in Enfield, Middlesex, moved with his parents to Liverpool at the age of nine months. He went to Stonebridge Lane secondary modern school in Norris Green and by 1959 had an apprenticeship with tools suppliers Robert Kelly & Sons. He died on 14 June 2010, aged 70.

13 John, Paul and George all used European guitars for the time being, but that would change in the early 1960s, after Britain's dollar-conserving prohibition on the import of American instruments and records was lifted in June 1959.

14 This was how John remembered it during an interview by Brian Matthew for *Pop Profile*, BBC Transcription Service, 30 November 1965. It has also been said in other ways, such as 'The guitar's all very well, John, but you'll never earn a living from it', and 'This is all very well but you'll never earn a living at it', and 'The guitar is all right as a hobby, John, but you'll never make a living at it'.

15 Author interview, 8 December 2004.

16 Indian baptismal (birth), death and marriage records before 1948, when the nation gained independence from the British Empire, are held in the Asian & African Studies collection at the British Library in London. The Shaw–Best marriage was mixed by religion as well as colour: she was Anglican, he Catholic.

17 *The Beatles – The True Beginnings*, p161.

18 Author interview, 10 November 2005.
19 Interview by Peter McCabe and Robert D. Schonfeld, September 1971.
20 *The Real John Lennon*, Channel 4, 30 September 2000.
21 *John*, by Cynthia Lennon (Hodder & Stoughton, London, 2005), pp38–9.
22 A *Twist Of Lennon*, p25.
23 A *Twist Of Lennon*, p35.
24 Interview by David Sheff, 24 September 1980, for *Playboy*.
25 Author interview, 10 November 2005. Reference made to the exhibition of modern American art by '17 contemporary American painters', at the United States Embassy, Grosvenor Square, from 31 October 1958.
26 *John*, p45.
27 *Many Years From Now*, p42. 'Most of my reading' from interview by Melvyn Bragg, *The South Bank Show*, LWT, 14 January 1978; 'Good image' from interview by Janice Long for *Listen To What The Man Says*, BBC Radio 1, 22 December 1985; 'at university' from interview by Richard Williams for *The Times*, 16 December 1981. 'I always used to like being on my own. I used to get on the bus and go somewhere, as a change from being with people' – interview on Boston radio WBZ, London, 30 May 1964.
28 Davies, p77.
29 *The Beatles Anthology*, p31.
30 Davies, p60. George's sister was in Canada. Louise emigrated to Ontario in 1956 with her husband Gordon Caldwell, sailing from Liverpool. All the Harrisons, George included, waved them off. He became Uncle George to a boy (Gordon) born April 1957 and a girl (Leslie) in September 1959, to remain unseen for several years yet.
31 Interview by David Sheff, 24 September 1980, for *Playboy*.
32 *The Beatles Anthology*, p38.
33 5 December 1959.
34 *I Me Mine*, p29; 'darts' from Davies, p60.
35 *The Beatles Anthology*, p81.
36 First part of quote from *The Beatles – The True Beginnings*, p29; second from interview by Roger Scott, Capital Radio (London), 17 November 1983.
37 Author interview, 14 December 2004.
38 Author interview, 4 October 2004.
39 Author interview, 17 December 2004.
40 Author interview, 11 November 2004.
41 A *Twist Of Lennon*, p28.
42 Author interview, 10 August 2004.
43 *Shout!*, by Philip Norman (Hamish Hamilton, London, 1981), p53.
44 Author interview, 11 December 2004.
45 Author interview, 25 April 2005.
46 *The Beatles Anthology*, p53.
47 Quoted on the website It's Only Love (http://sentstarr.tripod.com./beatgirls/girl/html). Dorothy Rhone lived at 39 Beauclair Drive, Liverpool 15, close to John Lennon's first school, Mosspits Lane Primary.
48 *The Beatles Anthology*, p39. Ringo's first personalised bass drum head just had the initials R. S., which handily doubled for both Ringo Starr and Rory Storm.
49 £50 is the most frequently quoted figure but he said £75 in an interview by Roderick Mann, *Sunday Express*, 9 March 1969, and in a 1994 conversation filmed for *The Beatles Anthology*.
50 *The Beatles Anthology*, p38.
51 *The Real John Lennon*, Channel 4, 30 September 2000.
52 Davies, pp56–7.
53 *John*, p51.
54 Interview by Peter Lewis, 6 June 1968, for the BBC2 programme *Release*. 'Henry and Harry' was published in 1964, *In His Own Write*, pp66–7; 'astoundagasted' was a Lennon invention used in speech and in his early poem 'The Land Of The Lunapots'.
55 *The Beatles Anthology*, p31.

12: **The Swish of the Curtain**

1 Information in these paragraphs has been drawn from a variety of sources, including naturalisation records (in the National Archives), birth, marriage and death certificates, early twentieth-century Liverpool local newspapers, business documents and discussions with the Epstein family.

2 Leslie Epstein died in 1946. Isaac and Dinah had six children in all. As the only other son, Harry ran the businesses.

3 Davies, p116.

4 Ibid.

5 George recorded The Spider's Dance for inclusion on a CD packaged with his autobiography *Playback* (Genesis Publications, Guildford, 2002).

6 Unless otherwise attributed, all George Martin quotes in this chapter are from author interview, 31 August 2000. Shearing was the blind London-born jazz pianist, Lewis the Chicago-born boogie-woogie player.

7 *All You Need Is Ears*, by George Martin with Jeremy Hornsby (Macmillan, London, 1979), p27.

8 Brian Epstein diaries and personal papers sold at Christie's, London, 27 April 2000; notes taken by the author prior to the sale. Homosexual activity at Wrekin remembered in *Brian Epstein*, by Ray Coleman (Viking Penguin, London, 1989), p28.

9 10 November 1950. *Accordion Times and Musical Express* had become plain *Musical Express* on 6 February 1948. It became *New Musical Express* on 7 March 1952.

10 Interview by Bill Grundy, 7 March 1964, for *Frankly Speaking* (BBC North of England Home Service, 23 March 1964).

11 Quotes and information in these Brian Epstein paragraphs from the raw transcripts of interviews for his autobiography A *Cellarful Of Noise*, noted and typed by Derek Taylor in April 1964 and printed facsimile in his *Fifty Years Adrift*, pp128–41.

12 A *Cellarful Of Noise*, by Brian Epstein (Souvenir Press, London, 1964), p32.

13 Davies, p119.

14 *The Brian Epstein Story*, compiled by Deborah Geller (Faber and Faber, London, 2000), p8.

15 Author interview, 15 June 1992.

16 Ibid.

17 *Melody Maker, Billboard*, 22 January 1955; *NME*, 21 January 1955.

18 22 April 1955. The *Hoylake & West Kirby Advertiser* was where Derek Taylor began his journalism career in 1949. He grew up in West Kirby. He left the paper in 1955 after completing his National Service, and took a better job with the *Liverpool Echo*.

19 The document was published (typeset, not facsimile) in *The Brian Epstein Story*, pp9–10.

20 Author interview, 15 June 1992. Wheels within wheels: the George Martin production that Dick James sang into the charts was the theme of a serial that marked the TV debuts of Peter Asher and his sister Jane, 11 and 10. They even appeared together in one episode, 'Children of the Greenwood' (London ITV on 29 April 1956). William Walton famously scored Laurence Olivier's 1944 film of Shakespeare's *Henry V*, whose set-piece battle sequence featured a breathtaking whoosh of thousands of arrows.

21 Author interview, 11 January 1985.

22 A *Cellarful Of Noise*, p40.

23 *Brian Epstein* (Coleman), pp41–2.

24 Notes from Brian Epstein's handwritten statement made by the author prior to its sale at Christie's, London, 27 April 2000. It was transcribed (partly) in that auction catalogue, and in *The Brian Epstein Story*, pp18–21.

25 Quoted verbatim in the *NME*, 15 February 1957.

26 A *Cellarful Of Noise*, p40.

27 Ibid., p41.

28 Author interview, 12 December 2005.

29 From the raw transcripts of interviews for his autobiography A *Cellarful Of Noise*.

30 *Playback*, by Dave Dexter, Jr (Billboard Publications, New York, 1976), p157.

31 Author interview, 8 April 2005.

32 *All You Need Is Ears*, p144.

33 This account of Brian Epstein's movements after the attack was stated as evidence in court on 21 May 1958. An alternative version is given by his friend Joe Flannery (e.g., in *The Brian*

Epstein Story, p26): he says Brian left his house before the attack and returned there afterwards, although not in his car, and that he (Flannery) nursed the wounds.

34 According to biographer Ray Coleman, Brian Epstein revealed his sexuality to his family after a Friday-night Sabbath dinner. His father and brother were shocked and unaccepting to begin with, but Queenie understood, having sensed the possibility for some time. She became his confidante, the one family member he could be open with (*Brian Epstein*, pp34–5). This may not be right – though, even if it is, it's unclear when it happened.

35 Liverpool *Evening Express*, 21 and 29 May 1958.

36 *Brian Epstein* (Coleman), pp50–5.

37 *News Of The World*, 10 September 1967. This article is not as salacious as the source would suggest: it's a fair piece of journalism, quoting soberly from letters and providing some dates and background.

38 Author interview, 12 December 2005.

39 Davies, p123.

40 Author interview, 10 April 2005.

41 2 January 1959.

42 15 May 1959.

13: 'Hi-yo, hi-yo Silver – away!' (January–May 1960)

1 Interview by Spencer Leigh.

2 £90 was stated by Sutcliffe himself in a résumé of his art career, handwritten a year later. This is the only accurate record of the sum paid him by Moores.

3 Davies, p65.

4 *The Beatles – The True Beginnings*, p54.

5 Author interview, 25 August 2005.

6 *Beatles Gear*, pp29–31. Andy Babiuk's book is the standard work on the Beatles' musical equipment.

7 *The Beatles Anthology*, p23.

8 Author interview, 10 August 2004.

9 A *Twist Of Lennon*, p38.

10 Cyn from A *Twist Of Lennon*, p29; George from *The Beatles Anthology*, p41. The other home-made bass guitar, started in late 1959 by Rod Murray so he might join the Quarrymen, was never completed. It progressed only to a pleasingly artistic shape, nicely planed but far from finished. He still has it.

11 *The Beatles Anthology* TV series.

12 An actual situation, not merely metaphorical; said by Paul in *The Beatles Anthology* director's cut (an unofficial release).

13 Interview by Michael Parkinson, *Parkinson's Sunday Supplement*, BBC Radio 2, 12 October 1997.

14 From the website It's Only Love, which handily collates in one place published quotes and knowledge about the girlfriends in the Beatles' lives.

15 *West Derby Reporter* (and others), 22 January 1960.

16 From Johnny 'Guitar' Byrne interview by Bob Hardy, May 1999.

17 Author interview, 4 March 2008.

18 *Liverpool Echo* ad, 22 January 1960.

19 Author interview, 11 August 2004.

20 *Many Years From Now*, p40. Paul's memory is challenged by classmates, who remember him making at least a preliminary application to Liverpool University for a teacher-training place. His studies would have entailed a long daily trip into Cheshire, attending the affiliated Chester Training College for Schoolmasters.

21 *Daily Mirror*, 24 May 1985. If John, Stuart and George went to see Paul in the play, they never mentioned it. Only seven months after leaving the Institute, George wouldn't have relished a return, and John would have only caused a scene.

22 Austin Davies' wife was Beryl Bainbridge (1932–2010), part-time actress and, from 1967, prizewinning and bestselling novelist. Fritz Spiegl (1926–2003) was a flautist, broadcaster, humorist and author. Other sources: *The Beatles Anthology*, pp31/198; and author interview with Tony Carricker, 17 December 2004.

23 Paul's French tune included the special chord Jim Gretty had shown him and George at Hessy's. Trambone was another tune they'd practised as a two-hander, like Atkins' interpretation of Bach's Bourrée. 'It was ... my ploys' from *Many Years From Now*, p273, where party host Austin Davies is erroneously given as Austin Mitchell; 'We were trying to hang in there ...' from *The Beatles Anthology*, p198. Paul sometimes says 'we' in interviews when he means 'I'.

24 First part from author interview, 30 September 1987; second part from interview by Alan Rowett and Geoff Barker for *Paul McCartney's Routes Of Rock*, BBC World Service, Oct–Nov 1999.

25 2 January 1960.

26 Remembered by Stu's then girlfriend Veronica Johnson in *Stuart: The Life And Art Of Stuart Sutcliffe*, by Kay Williams and Pauline Sutcliffe (Genesis Publications, Guildford, 1996), p99.

27 Interview by Alan Rowett and Geoff Barker for *Paul McCartney's Routes Of Rock*, BBC World Service, Oct–Nov 1999.

28 *The Beatles Anthology*, p28. In 1963, Paul told Michael Braun (*Love Me Do! The Beatles' Progress*, pp34–5), 'I remember thinking before the [Eddie Cochran] show that I was actually *there*.' (He then went on to relate the antics of a black act on the bill, although there wasn't one.) Twenty-five years later BBC Radio Merseyside presenter Spencer Leigh, who has a specialist knowledge about the Vincent–Cochran tour, asked Paul about seeing the Liverpool Empire show and Paul said he hadn't gone, and could no longer remember why not.

29 First part of quote from interview by B. P. Fallon for RTE2 (Ireland), circa 20 October 1987; middle part from interview by Joe Brown, *Let It Rock*, BBC Radio 2, 5 July 1999; final line from *The Beatles Anthology*, p28. Cochran replaced his standard heavy-gauge 3rd guitar string (steel wire around which was wound a nickel-steel wire) with a lighter 2nd string, just plain steel (hence 'unwound'), which made it easier to bend the strings as he played his trademark solos. George didn't notice this at the Empire, he was told it years later by Joe Brown, who'd been able to observe Cochran at close quarters during the tour.

30 Author interview, 20 July 2006; *Echo* review, 15 March 1960.

31 Author interview, 10 May 2010. In 1970, when Kelly heard One After 909 on the Beatles' album *Let It Be*, he instantly recognised it as the song they'd recorded ten years earlier.

32 An edit of Cayenne was released on *The Beatles Anthology 1*; nothing else from the tape is legally available but the tracks circulate unofficially. Another song might be called I Don't Know and could be a Lennon-McCartney piece. The place of recording isn't known: it may have been the Life Drawing room at the art college or the Gambier Terrace flat. Rod Murray bought a tape deck on hire-purchase in January 1960 and remembers recording them in the flat, but believes the tapes were lost or erased almost immediately. (This could still be it, however.)

33 'We would lie our faces off ...' from *The Beatles Anthology*, p23. 'Mr Low' was possibly the agent and promoter Harry Lowe, based in London but born in Liverpool and still visibly active there. He was really Harry Swerdlow, and his nephew, Alan Swerdlow, was both a friend of Brian Epstein and a student at Liverpool College of Art with John, which may have been the connection that prompted the letter. It is reproduced facsimile in Davies, p68. Again underlining the few degrees of separation in Liverpool, the handwriting of which Paul was so proud was taught him at the Institute by 'Cissy' Smith, brother of John's late Uncle George.

34 Reproduced facsimile in *Thank U Very Much*, p70. 'Competence, confidence & continuity' sounds like a Jim Mac phrase.

35 Letter sold in auction at Sotheby's, London, on 1 September 1983, reproduced in that catalogue and also in my book *The Complete Beatles Chronicle* (Pyramid Books, London, 1992), p18.

36 Los Paranoias mentioned by John in an interview by Tony MacArthur, Radio Luxembourg, mid-September 1969. A year previously, a Beatles studio jam (released on *Anthology 3*) evolved knowingly into an impromptu song called Los Paranoias. 'We had about ten a week' from interview by Dibbs Mather for *Dateline London*, BBC Transcription Service, 10 December 1963.

37 Interview by Jim Steck, 26 August 1964.

38 Author interview, 13 February 1997.

39 Interview by Fred Robbins for *Assignment: Hollywood*, Radio Luxembourg, 10 February 1964. In the mid-1970s it was brought to George Harrison's attention that a scene in the Marlon Brando movie *The Wild One* (1953) has co-star Lee Marvin shouting, 'Johnny, we've been looking for you. The Beetles have missed you. All the Beetles have missed you.' Remembering that Stuart Sutcliffe was a Brando fan, George suggested this could have been the source of the

group's name, and he speculated too that the character Johnny could have influenced John Lennon. As a result, the possibility gained strong currency, especially after George discussed it in *The Beatles Anthology* TV series (1995).

George was seemingly unaware *The Wild One* was banned by the British Board of Film Censors over fears it could incite delinquency, and that it wasn't shown in public cinemas until 1968. There is just one chance Sutcliffe saw it before 1960: on 24 November 1956, the Merseyside Film Institute Society (a private club whose aim was to raise the standard and appreciation of films) held a one-off, members-only screening in the Philharmonic Hall. For George to be right, Stuart would have had to retain for more than three years a piece of dialogue inconsequential when he heard it (and yet not suggest it when they were looking for a name earlier), he would have had to gain access to the screening though at 16 he was too young, and he would have needed to be a MFIS member, and wasn't.

The Wild One is likely to have played no more part in the name Beatles (or Beatals) than, for example, the line 'Do the beetle-bop right, side by side' in Bill Haley's Rock This Joint, in the *NME* chart in February 1957 when Paul McCartney saw them in concert.

40 Author interview, 4 October 2004.
41 Interview by Brian Matthew for *My Top 12*, BBC Radio 1, 6 February 1974.
42 Author interview, 20 July 2006.
43 *Disc*, 27 April 1963.
44 In issue 27 of *Beatles Book* magazine (October 1965), Jim McCartney said of Paul and Mike as children, 'Amongst their friends they were known as the Nurk Twins, but I never did find out why.' Fred Nurke was a minor *Goon Show* character, voiced by Peter Sellers and popping up in only three episodes. It was always written as Nurke in the scripts but, being radio, no one could have known this. The spelling Nerk prevails because it was used by Paul in a postcard sent from Caversham to his brother, so this is probably how it was written on their handmade posters. Background information about John and Paul's visit to Caversham comes from a 1983 author interview with Mike Robbins (a good man, 1928–2009).
45 Again, all information drawn from the website It's Only Love.
46 Davies, p75, supported by Liverpool Collegiate school records which confirm his departure on 11 March 1960. No one else left school that day, and it wasn't end of term.
47 Author interview, 25 April 2005.
48 The Aspinall family home was at 43 Liddell Road, just around the corner.
49 Interview by Alan Smith, *NME*, 23 March 1968. Rory sang three numbers: What'd I Say, Honey Don't and Willie And The Hand Jive. Ringo didn't mention speaking to Pete here, but Pete says it in *Beatle!*, p47.
50 Interview by Alan Freeman, BBC Radio 1, 6 December 1974. Final sentence added from *The Beatles Anthology*, p41.
51 Interview by Spencer Leigh.
52 Author interview, 20 July 2006.
53 *A Twist Of Lennon*, p42.
54 Interview by Peter McCabe and Robert D. Schonfeld, September 1971.
55 Author interview, 4 March 2008.
56 John from letter published in *The Beatles: An Illustrated Record*, by Roy Carr and Tony Tyler (NEL, London, 1978 edition onwards), p3; first Paul from interview by Alan Smith, *NME*, 9 August 1963; second Paul from interview by Mike Read, 13 October 1987, for BBC Radio 1; George from *The Beatles Anthology*, p41.
57 Author interview, 4 March 2008.
58 *The Real John Lennon*, Channel 4, 30 September 2000.
59 A good selection of Cheniston Roland's photos of the Billy Fury audition appear in *How They Became The Beatles – A Definitive History Of The Early Years: 1960–1964*, by Gareth L. Pawlowski (E. P. Dutton, New York, 1989), pp13–22.
60 *The Beatles Anthology*, p44.
61 Author interview, 4 March 2008.
62 Millie Sutcliffe from *The Beatles: The Days In Their Life*, 1981 Canadian radio series. Williams first said it publicly when profiled in *Record Mirror* by Bill Harry (22 October 1966): 'The groups were narrowed down to Cass and the Cassanovas and the Beatles. Billy [Fury] wanted the Beatles and Larry Parnes swung towards the Cassanovas. It was decided that if the Beatles would drop Stu then they could become Billy's backing group. But they refused.'

63 Author interview, 27 May 2004.
64 A *Twist Of Lennon*, p37.
65 Extended from interview by Larry Kane, 13 September 1964.
66 From Ringo Starr interviews by Phil Donahue, 1978 and 1995.
67 Interview by Spencer Leigh.
68 Author interview, 26 November 2005.

14: **'Where's the bloody money?'** (18–30 May 1960)

1 Remembered by Millie Sutcliffe (interview by Nik Cohn), *Observer*, 8 September 1968.
2 'I didn't realise there was going to be a written paper' – Paul in *Many Years From Now*, p42.
3 Davies, p70.
4 *Coventry Evening Telegraph*, 29 July 2005.
5 *Weekly News*, 4 January 1964.
6 Author interview, 27 May 2004.
7 Launched on 10 March 1960, *Record Retailer* was Britain's first trade magazine for the record business. Its weekly Top Fifty was the nation's biggest sales chart, the number of places bettered only by *The World's Fair*'s Top 100 chart of juke-box plays.
8 Author interview, 2 May 1991. Previous quote ('we'd wanted a Fury or an Eager') from the same source, along with Paul's explanation of how the stress in Ramon should be put on the second syllable, French style. 'Paul Ramon: God knows where Paul got that name from!' John Lennon remarked in a 1975 interview. Nicolas de Staël (1914–55), born in Russia with French nationality, worked in collage, illustration and textiles but was best known for abstract landscapes. Stuart's ability to adapt to a variety of painting methods caused some at Liverpool College of Art to call him 'Stu the Style', which may or may not be coincidental.
9 John quote from interview by Paul Drew, US radio, April 1975. Paul McCartney: 'There was no longer any need for John to be Long John because we were on tour with Johnny Gentle, so the Long John name fell by the wayside, thank God' (author interview, 2 May 1991). 'People have since said, "Ah, John didn't change his name, that was very suave." Let me tell you: he was Long John! There was none of that "he didn't change his name": we *all* changed our names' (*The Beatles Anthology*, p44).
10 *The Beatles Anthology*, p44.
11 Author interview, 28 August 2006.
12 *The Beatles Anthology*, p44.
13 The eyewitness was Leslie Bisset, who was at Keith on Wednesday 25 May.
    'Darin, Benton, Como, Washington' from *New Record Mirror*, 23 June 1962. (*The Record Mirror* became *Record and Show Mirror* from 22 August 1959 and *New Record Mirror* from 18 March 1961.) Alright, Okay, You Win was only a relative oldie (1955), recently revived by Peggy Lee. *Disc* piece, 2 January 1960.
    In the BBC Radio 2 documentary *The Beatles In Scotland* (24 September 1996), Johnny Gentle said his act was 'only six or seven songs, and then they [the Beatles] played for an hour after'. This is highly unlikely, given that he was the main attraction. Speaking about it eleven years after the tour, John Lennon recalled, 'We'd only be on [alone] about twenty minutes and he'd be on most of the time' (interview by Peter McCabe and Robert D. Schonfeld, September 1971). Even twenty minutes seems too much – it would have been ten at most.
    Alex Harvey (1935–82) was billed as 'Scotland's own Tommy Steele'. He went on to lead Alex Harvey's Soul Band and, in the 1970s, most notably, the Sensational Alex Harvey Band.
14 *The Alloa Circular and Hillfoots Record*, 25 May 1960.
15 Night in the van recalled by George in *The Beatles Anthology*, p44. Hayloft anecdote by Colin Manley of the Remo Four, who knew Paul (and George) from Liverpool Institute.
16 *The Beatles Anthology*, p44.
17 *Fifty Years Adrift*, p95.
18 Davies, p71.
19 Interview on *Good Morning Australia* (Channel 10), spring 1982. Williams quote from author interview, 27 May 2004.
20 Author interview with Paul McCartney, 2 May 1991. Margie was Marjorie A. Overall (born Maidenhead, 1940). As a first-hand witness to the Beatles' tour with Johnny Gentle she may have interesting memories to relate, but can't be found.

21 *Thank U Very Much*, p70.
22 Interview by Spencer Leigh.
23 Interview by Johnny Beerling, early 1972, for BBC Radio 1.
24 Davies, p71.
25 *The Man Who Gave The Beatles Away*, by Allan Williams and William Marshall (Elm Tree Books, London, 1975), pp53–4. Of course, John wouldn't have been able to see detail without his glasses.
26 Author interview, 20 June 2005.
27 Ibid. Sach was played by Huntz Hall – his photo is on the cover of *Sgt Pepper's Lonely Hearts Club Band*. Peter Blake, who conceived and jointly staged its artistic design, claims to have added Hall to the gallery, though one or two books (while unaware of any connection) ponder if John Lennon was responsible for the choice.
28 The promoters at Fraserburgh, Keith, Nairn and Peterhead were Bert Ewen and Hilda May, a married couple from Inverurie who operated as North-East Dances.
29 *The Beatles Anthology*, p44.
30 *The Beatles In Scotland*, BBC Radio 2, 24 September 1996.

15: **Drive and Bash** (31 May–15 August 1960)

1 Interview by Spencer Leigh. Feather was a Jewish homosexual artist who owned the Basement night-club at 62 Mount Pleasant.
2 *A Cellarful Of Noise*, p43. Newley was headlining this week at Liverpool Empire.
3 2 April 1960, review by Don Nicholl.
4 Author interview, 24 July 2004.
5 *Weekly News*, 11 January 1964. Ringo from interview by Jerry G. Bishop, 13–24 August 1965.
6 *Birkenhead News and Advertiser* (Heswall and Neston edition), 11 June 1960. Fifteen years later, John Lennon – given a copy of the cutting in 1964 and keen ever after to show it around – called it 'possibly the first review of Beatles ever' (see *The Beatles: An Illustrated Record* [1978 edition onwards], p3). It was definitely so.
7 Based on Harry Harrison's remarks to Davies, p59.
8 Author interview, 15 March 2007.
9 Davies, p101.
10 Author interview, 12 August 2010.
11 Author interview, 3 November 1994; audio issued on 1995 album *The Beatles Anthology 1*.
12 You'll Be Mine and an edit of Hallelujah, I Love Her So were released on *The Beatles Anthology 1*. Nothing else from the tape is legally available but the tracks circulate unofficially.
13 Dot Rhone interview by Bob Spitz, *The Globe and Mail*, Toronto, 15 November 2005. Margaret Kelly, Brian's widow, who worked closely with him on the dances, remembers him saying, 'They didn't come and they didn't let me know, and that's *it*.' (Author interview, 25 November 2005.) Rod Murray from author interview, 10 August 2004.
14 Author interview, 28 August 2006.
15 Author interview, 7 October 2004. All subsequent Ellis quotes from this too.
16 Letter written to *IT*, issue 155 (31 May–14 June 1973). *Daily Mirror* piece, 26 November 1959. Royston Ellis was born Christopher Roy George Ellis, in Pinner, Middlesex, 10 February 1941.
17 *Rave*, by Royston Ellis (Scorpion Press, Northwood, Middlesex, May 1960), p17.
18 *Many Years From Now*, p88.
19 First part from *Stuart: The Life And Art Of Stuart Sutcliffe*, p107; last from *Many Years From Now*, p88.
20 Vicks inhalers no longer contain Benzedrine.
 '. . . they didn't even know about getting high on Benzedrine strips from nose inhalers!' – from Royston Ellis essay in *Generation X* (by Charles Hamblett and Jane Deverson, Anthony Gibbs & Phillips, London, 1964), pp143/148–9. Ellis also fictionalised his Liverpool experiences with the Beatles in his novel *Myself For Fame* (World Distributors, London, 1964), pp42–9, where they were the Rhythmettes and the Jacaranda coffee bar on Slater Street was the Panda coffee bar on Tater Street. Ellis's factual exposé of British rock, *The Big Beat Scene* (Four Square Books, London, 1961), contains no mention of the Beatles though he claims a reference to 'the Blanks' (p76) is them. The book was republished in 2010 and in a new afterword Ellis related his tale of being with the Beatles in Liverpool in June 1960, repeating the claim (see below) that he gave them their name.

21 Author interview, 4 October 2004.
22 Paul from *Many Years From Now*, p50; George from *Fifty Years Adrift*, p95; John from interview by Paul Drew, US radio, April 1975.
23 It had the byline P. H. – short for Paul Heppel, who wrote the weekly showbiz roundup Show Pieces. Royston Ellis claims he came up with, or somehow confirmed, the name Beatles for them, but this isn't right. They were using it, and it had appeared in print, a month before they met him. If he told them 'Beatles' was a good spelling and worth sticking with, he was right – it was, and they were going to. In a published letter Ellis wrote about them within three weeks of his Liverpool trip, the word was spelled 'Beetles'.
24 Interview by Spencer Leigh.
25 Remembered by Lu Walters, *Mersey Beat*, 18 July 1963.
26 Author interview, 27 August 2005.
27 *The Beatles Anthology*, p39.
28 Interview by Roger Scott, Capital Radio (London), 17 November 1983. The *Melody Maker* ad was 5 March 1960, and there was another on 25 June, the issue current when Paul made his purchase. The cash price was 18 guineas, well at the cheaper end of the guitar range.
29 'No one was very impressed at first,' Paul told Russell Harty (BBC1, 26 November 1984), referring to the other Beatles. Nothing more is known of this.
30 Author interview, 17 July 2006. All subsequent quotes from this.
31 Interview by Lisa Robinson, 29 September 1980.
32 *A Twist Of Lennon*, p40.
33 Author interview, 11 August 2004.
34 The reporter was Peter Forbes and the photographer Harold Chapman – he also took important pictures of Ginsberg, Burroughs, Corso and others at what was known as the Beat Hotel in Paris.
35 Paul McCartney anecdote to the author during tour of his recording studio, 17 December 1996.
36 *The Beatles Anthology*, p44. *Beatles Book* magazine, issue 3 (October 1963), p9, looked briefly at the Beatles' drumming situation in this period, as explained to journalist 'Billy Shepherd' (Peter Jones) by Paul. It says that he, John and George all learned to play the kit 'reasonably well'. They would all continue to get behind the drums from time to time in the years ahead.
37 Interview by Spencer Leigh.
38 'A Little Bare', *Mersey Beat*, 6 September 1962.
39 Interview by author and Kevin Howlett, 6 June 1990. The notion 'Something'll turn up', or words to that effect, was ever John Lennon's thinking (perhaps inspired by Micawber in *David Copperfield*, which he'd read). The leader led, the others adopted his attitude.
40 This information recalled by the *Echo* advertiser, who prefers to remain anonymous though he did once tell his tale in a newspaper.
41 Davies, p77. Also told well by Mike McCartney in *Thank U Very Much*, p70.
42 Davies, p79.
43 Davies, p76.
44 Author interview, 6 February 2006. June Harry died in 2010, aged 73, while this passage was being written.
45 *A Twist Of Lennon*, p49.
46 Author interview, 20 July 2006.
47 Author interview, 21 June 2007.
48 Interview by Paul Drew, US radio, April 1975.
49 *The Best Years Of The Beatles*, by Pete Best with Bill Harry (Headline, London, 1996), p48.
50 Scene described to the author by Cynthia, 4 June 2006. (She was told it by John but hasn't used it in her books.)
51 Davies, p77.
52 Ibid.
53 *Beatle!*, pp29/13.
54 Courtesy of Yoko Ono Lennon, a facsimile reproduction of John's first passport is on display at Mendips (now open as a National Trust property), accurately illuminating this and other facts.

16: 'Mach Schau!' (15 August–30 September 1960)

1 *Beatle Pete, Time Traveller*, by Mallory Curley (Randy Press, USA, 2004), p22.
2 Author interview, 11 August 2004. Unless otherwise stated, all other Williams quotes in this chapter are from this.
3 *Beatle!*, p32 and *The Best Years Of The Beatles*, p40.
4 Paul and George recollections in *The Beatles Anthology*, p45. Koschmider lived three kilometres away, at 14 Eimsbütteler Chaussee. Allan Williams also thinks the Beatles stayed the first night in Koschmider's flat.
5 Interview by Russell Harty, BBC1, 26 November 1984.
6 The Bambi's actual entrance was around the corner, at Paul-Roosen-Strasse 33. It was not a porn cinema (as is often claimed) and this street was beyond the red-light area. Typical of tiny picture houses tucked away in cities the world over, it showed creaky old films: mostly melodramas and some children's movies.
7 Letter reproduced facsimile in *Thank U Very Much*, p91.
8 Interview by David Sheff, 24 September 1980, for *Playboy*.
9 Interview by Spencer Leigh.
10 Interview by Ray Connolly, *Radio Times*, 18 May 1972. George: 'Although we did repeat ourselves, we used to try not to.' (*Fifty Years Adrift*, p169.)
11 *The Beatles Anthology*, p49.
12 *Beatles Book* magazine, issue 3 (October 1963).
13 *Bild-Zeitung*, 29 September 1960.
14 First part from interview by Mitchell Glazer, *Crawdaddy*, February 1977; second from *The Beatles Anthology*, p53.
15 Interview by David Sheff, 12 September 1980, for *Playboy*.
16 Pete's claims are in *Beatle!*, p53; a further account on p54 describes how four of the Beatles (omitting Stu) had eight women between them – which was more than two each because the girls swapped around. Such descriptions don't square with George remaining a virgin until 1961, but no doubt something like this happened. George describes his 'first shag' in *The Beatles Anthology*, p54.
17 Interview by Paul du Noyer, *Paul McCartney World Tour* programme (1989–90), p86.
18 *The Beatles Anthology*, p54.
19 Also wrapped up in the Hamburg *legend* is the extent of the strip- and sex-club entertainment on offer. The truth is more what George Harrison said: 'There were places where there were donkeys shagging women or whatever – allegedly, I never saw it.' (*The Beatles Anthology*, p54.) While accounts of what went on become more lurid with every telling, it's worth noting that German law forbade women to strip off completely: they had to wear a G-string or panties. As for the live sex shows, it was all suggestion and simulation, and there were no donkeys.
20 *Hamburger Echo*, 19 and 24 September 1960.
21 *"Mach Schau!" – Die Beatles In Hamburg*, by Thomas Rehwagen and Thorsten Schmidt (EinfallsReich, Braunschweig, 1992), pp92/94. (A recommended book, though it's in German only; there's no English edition.) Monika Paulsen had the support of her parents to invite the Beatles home for proper food and a good night's sleep (they were in one room, but comfortable; she and her friends in another); her mother also cooked them a meal the following day before they had to return to the stage (see *"Mach Schau!"*, same pages).
22 *Stuart: The Life And Art Of Stuart Sutcliffe*, pp112–13. Stuart's correspondence has come up regularly at auction (sold by his sister Pauline and others) and numerous examples have been published.
23 Interview by Peter McCabe and Robert D. Schonfeld, September 1971.
24 Interview by Chris Welch, *Melody Maker*, 20 September 1975.
25 Author interview, 18 March 2006.
26 Interview by Terry Wogan, BBC1, 20 November 1987.
27 Daily letters from *A Twist Of Lennon*, p49; Quasimodo photos, pp50–1; leather knickers from *The Real John Lennon*, Channel 4, 30 September 2000. Cyn eventually destroyed the letters.
28 *Beatle!*, p55.
29 Interview by Peter McCabe and Robert D. Schonfeld, September 1971; '. . . sneak one of his own' from *Beatle!*, pp66/94.

30   From recording of legal interview with Pete Best, New York, 1965.
31   25 August 1960. The article, which had no byline, was written by Roy Corlett, who'd been a year above Paul McCartney at Liverpool Institute and was now a trainee journalist.
32   *The Beatles Anthology*, p39.
33   Interview by Chris Evans, *TFI Friday*, Channel 4, 26 June 1998.

17: **A Cellarful of Oiks** (1 October–31 December 1960)

1   Interview by Elliot Mintz, 18 April 1976.
2   *Best Of The Beatles* DVD (Best Wishes Productions, 2005).
3   Interview by Peter McCabe and Robert D. Schonfeld, September 1971.
4   Davies, p86.
5   *The Beatles Anthology*, p49.
6   From Pete Best interview by Spencer Leigh.
7   From Stuart Sutcliffe letter to his sister Pauline, written mid-October 1960.
8   Author interview, 20 July 2006.
9   No more is known of this. Allan Williams ought to have been handling the negotiations but remembers nothing of it. Bruno Koschmider didn't operate in Berlin so perhaps the Beatles were fixing the deal themselves with another club owner. It never happened.
10   Akustik was the recording division of a film advertising company, Ernst Breuel Verlag, and its professionally equipped studio was in the Klockmann building at Kirchenallee 57. Though Ringo recalls the recordings being cut straight to acetates, the multiplicity of discs (see below) must mean they were recorded to tape first.
11   An article in *Mersey Beat* (19 December 1963), with information given by Lu Walters, said the Beatles played on Fever, Summertime and September Song, and that 'the discs are still available in Liverpool and being played regularly'. Several were pressed, it seems: Williams remembers 'five or six'. In *Disc* of 13 August 1966 he claimed ownership of two, though within five years he mislaid them both.
      Despite telling *Mersey Beat* he'd recorded three titles with the Beatles, Lu Walters told me in 1983 they played on only one and that Fever and September Song had the Hurricanes behind him. He also said nine discs were cut but he was aware of only one still in existence, in the hands of a relative in Australia. It has yet to surface, and when asked about it again in 2012 he said he was aware of no surviving copies at all. It's the number one lost recording for Ringo, who often mentions how much he'd love to hear it again.
12   Stuart said this in a letter to Susan Williams; it equated to DM1400.
13   *The Story Of The Fender Stratocaster*, by Ray Minhinnett and Bob Young (Carlton, London, 1995), quoted in *Beatles Gear*, p38. The Steinway shop was at Colonnaden 29, near the Binnenalster lake.
14   The LP sleeve photo John saw was *Shearing On Stage!* by the George Shearing Quintet, recorded by Capitol in 1958 and released in Germany in 1960 (the guitar was played by Toots Thielemans). The Rickenbacker 325 is generally described as three-quarter scale but some guitar experts call it five-eighths. There's conflicting information about which shop John got the guitar from; the figure £90–100 was reported by John in a document detailing his Hamburg expenses; '. . . a hell of a lot of money' from interview by Ray Coleman, *Disc Weekly*, 26 March 1966. It isn't known if John or Stu volunteered customs duty on these Hamburg purchases when returning to England, though not likely. The risk was a sizeable fine, about £60.
15   From interview (probably by Tony Webster) for *Beat Instrumental*, December 1964. John made the final drip repayment to Hessy's for the Club 40 on 31 July 1961.
16   Letter undated, started at the end of September and completed in mid-October. In another letter of this period, sent to Rod Murray, Stuart wrote, 'I don't drink, except the odd Coca-Cola.' No one remembers him being teetotal, but, if true, he was the one sober Beatle on stage in the Kaiserkeller.
17   Author interview, 29 March 2006. Unless otherwise stated, all Klaus Voormann quotes in this chapter are from this interview.
18   Reinhart Wolf (born Berlin 1930, died Hamburg 1988) was a witty, stylish, intelligent and gifted photographer, internationally active in advertising, portraiture and architectural photography. His studio was at Rothenbaumchaussee 3. The art institute was the Meisterschule

für Mode, Werkkunstschule für Textil, Werbung und Grafik (Vocational College for Fashion and Commercial Art School for Textiles, Advertising and Graphic Design).

19 Author interview, 11 March 2006. Unless otherwise stated, all Astrid Kirchherr quotes in this chapter are from this interview.

20 Author interview, 12 March 2006. All Jürgen Vollmer quotes in this chapter are from this interview.

21 Author interview, 3 May 1994.

22 Voormann, Kirchherr and Vollmer have each given their account of these events more times than they care to remember. The same essential truths are ever-present but a few of the lesser details no longer dovetail. The record was a cover version of the Ventures' hit instrumental Walk Don't Run, by the Typhoons, on the Heliodor label.

23 Astrid kept no diary of her photography, and the chronology of events has been told differently in the many accounts given in subsequent decades, so the sequence reflected in this chapter might not be definitively correct. If her first session was indeed with Stuart, and not with the Beatles as a group, it was probably the one at Krameramtsstuben – a seventeenth-century courtyard tucked away not far from the other end of the Reeperbahn – and, perhaps this same day, on Wohlwillstrasse. (An atmospheric double-exposure of Stuart standing in a doorway here is the best known of these images.) Her second solo session with Stuart (it *probably* followed her shoot with the Beatles) was on a rainy Monday in the first half of November, among trees in a wood by the Elbe river.

24 *Stuart: The Life And Art Of Stuart Sutcliffe*, p131.

25 *Many Years From Now*, p64.

26 Author interview, 18 March 2006.

27 *The Beatles Anthology*, p49.

28 *Many Years From Now*, p65.

29 Author interview, 3 November 1994.

30 DM100,000 was the equivalent of £8550 – a strangely large amount in 1960. Koschmider said this in the only recorded interview he's known to have given about the Beatles (for BBC radio, 1972) and wasn't asked to substantiate it.

31 A few years later John gave an original print of the photo to Beatles biographer Hunter Davies and captioned it on the reverse Me sightseeing Hamburg, Nov. 1960 and ONE GIANT PHOTO COMING SOON.

32 *Abendblatt*, 4 November 1960. The Hamburger Dom still operates at the same site three times a year.

33 Anecdote told by Pete Best in *Beatle!*, p104, except he says the Shadows' tune Rory demonstrated was Frightened City. The title Beatle Bop was probably inspired by the dance of that name, as cited by Bill Haley in Rock This Joint.

34 Author interview, 7 November 1995.

35 Interview by Malcolm Searle, Melbourne, 15 June 1964.

36 Davies, p106.

37 Pete Best has told the story in two of his books: *Beatle!* (pp58–62) and *The Best Years Of The Beatles* (pp75–6). The gas-gun is in both, but John didn't mention it in Davies, pp84–5.

38 *Four Track Stories*, by Klaus Voormann (self-published, München, 2005). Erdmann-Lederbekleidung was at Reeperbahn 155, opposite the Top Ten Club. It may be that John, Pete and Paul bought their leather jackets here too.

39 First clause from Davies, p92, remainder from *The Beatles Anthology*, p55.

40 Davies, p93. Monika Paulsen says she and her friend Helga took George to the station to begin his homeward journey, giving him a packed meal prepared by her mother. (*"Mach Schau!"*, p94.)

41 Author interview, 7 March 1985. Pete says (*Beatle!*, p72) there were four rubbers and always speaks of them in plural, Paul speaks of one.

42 12 December 1960, sent to Ken Horton. This letter provides the only suggestion that John was arrested in the roundup; he's not mentioned in other accounts.

43 Interview by Paul Gambaccini, *Rolling Stone*, 12 June 1979. *Rathaus* means 'city hall'. Instead of the main prison at Fühlsbuttel, it's more likely Paul and Pete were taken to the remand prison near St Pauli called Untersuchungsgefängnis (easier done than said).

44 *The Beatles Anthology*, p55; last sentence from Davies, p95.

45 *Beatle!*, p76. Mike from *Thank U Very Much*, p72.

46 Davies, p93.

47 Ibid.
48 Davies, p96. Renshaw Hall was a large hall adjacent to Benson Street, opening on to 63 Renshaw Street.
49 Author interview, 14 December 2004.
50 Interview by Elliot Mintz, 1 January 1976.
51 Author interview, 11 August 2004.
52 'Being A Short Diversion On The Dubious Origins Of Beatles', *Mersey Beat*, 6 July 1961.
53 Paul from *The Beatles Anthology*, p56; John from interview by Barbara Graustark, for *Newsweek*, September 1980.
54 Author interview with Johnny Gustafson, 4 March 2008.
55 Author interview, 21 June 2007.
56 Chas from author interview, 8 December 2004; Pete from *The Best Years Of The Beatles*, p107.
57 *Beatle!*, p82.
58 First part from *The Beatles: The Days In Their Life*, 1981 Canadian radio series; second part from *The Best Of Fellas (The Story Of Bob Wooler, Liverpool's First D.J.)*, by Spencer Leigh (Drivegreen Publications, Liverpool, 2002), p70. This is the only published account of Wooler's life, based on months of Leigh's exclusive interviews with the reticent personality and packed with the subject's insights and witty wordplay. Unless otherwise stated, all Wooler quotes here are drawn from this source, by kind permission.
59 Interview 28 August 1963 for *The Mersey Sound* (BBC-tv, 9 October 1963).
60 Interview by Spencer Leigh.
61 *Mersey Beat*, 4 July 1963.

18: **The Big Beat Boppin' Beatles** (January–March 1961)

1 Interview by Chris Hutchins, *NME*, 25 September 1964.
2 Author interview, 3 March 2007. Jim Gilvey is sure Paul didn't sign the apprenticeship papers, though it would have happened, given time.
3 Davies, p96.
4 Ibid.
5 Interview by Janice Long for *Listen To What The Man Says*, BBC Radio 1, 22 December 1985.
6 Interview by Peter McCabe and Robert D. Schonfeld, September 1971.
7 Author interview, 15 March 2007.
8 Interview by Spencer Leigh. The Phantoms became the Coasters in September 1961, when lead singer Bill Ashton, who called himself Billy Forde, changed his name again to Billy Kramer.
9 Interview for *Pop Goes The Bulldog*, December 1969; '... laughed me off the stage' told to the author, 12 October 1987.
10 Author interview, 20 July 2006.
11 Aspinall worked for J. Oakley Worrall, on the fourth floor of Prudential Buildings, 36 Dale Street.
12 Author interview, 21 June 2007. All Neil Aspinall quotes in this chapter are from this interview.
13 There are several TV clips of John doing the big wink – e.g., in the documentary *Follow The Beatles* (BBC1, 1964), in footage of the Jealous Guy recording session (1971), and at the start of Stand By Me, taped for *Old Grey Whistle Test* (BBC2, 1975).
14 Pete Best clipped out the Beatles ads and pasted them into a scrapbook, and Ringo's parents Elsie and Harry cut out all the Rory Storm and the Hurricanes ads. Looking at the *Echo's* Jazz column was the surest way for parents of Liverpool musicians to know where their sons were on given nights of the week.
      The morning *Daily Post* was even further removed from it all. The *Echo's* only concession to pop remained Disker's very good record review column and local sales chart, published every Saturday. The Disker pen-name still masked the identity of Tony Barrow, who, having moved to London, sent in his 'copy' by mail.
15 *Best Of The Beatles* DVD.
16 Author interview, 4 November 2004.
17 Reproduced in *Hamburg Days*, by Astrid Kirchherr and Klaus Voormann (Genesis Publications, Guildford, 1999), p126. *Hemd* is German for shirt; Stuart wrote *hempt*, which is how it's pronounced in Hamburg dialect.
18 Author interview, 12 August 2004.

19 *The Beatles Anthology*, p57.

20 Davies, p144.

21 Interview by Paul Drew, US radio, April 1975. The two subsequent John Lennon quotes about Pete Best are from the same interview. Lomax from interview by Spencer Leigh.

22 Wooler from *Mersey Beat*, 31 August 1961.

23 John's 1973 homage recording of Angel Baby (with a monster production by Phil Spector) is a bonus track on the 2004 reissue of *Rock 'n' Roll*.

24 *Love Me Do! The Beatles' Progress*, p34. It wasn't entirely true. Both John and Paul liked Move It! and Living Doll, and Paul has related how on one occasion he (and maybe some or all of the other Beatles) saw Cliff and the Shadows in concert at Liverpool Empire.

25 *NME*, 28 October 1960.

26 20 May 1961.

27 Dexter's pick from George Martin's 1960 work was a beaty production of As Time Goes By, by Parlophone singer and Frankie Vaughan soundalike Richard Allan. Jack Good quote re. Nadia Cattouse from *Disc*, 21 January 1961.

28 Interview by Spencer Leigh. The incident happened on either 20, 21, 27 or 30 January.

29 Millie Sutcliffe recalled the circumstances in an interview by Mike Ledgerwood for *Disc and Music Echo*, 31 October 1970. 'I always waited up for Stuart to come home. It was 3AM when he finally came in – without his glasses. He told me, "You've had reason to wait up this morning. We've been attacked. I got knocked out ... OUT unconscious. I was hit from the back. My glasses are non-existent. I couldn't even pick up the pieces. But John got the thug. And he broke his wrist giving him what he'd given me."' Millie also added that Stuart had refused a medical examination – 'He said if I called a doctor, he'd be gone before he arrived.' One fact here is certainly wrong: John fractured his finger rescuing his friend, not his wrist. Also, the book *Stuart: The Life And Art Of Stuart Sutcliffe*, p154, writes convincingly of Stuart allowing himself to be seen by a doctor the following morning.

30 Author interview, 11 March 2006.

31 Author interview, 11 August 2004.

32 Author interview, 10 August 2004.

33 Document reproduced facsimile in *The Beatles Anthology*, p55.

34 Interview for Friends Of The Earth, 15 December 1989.

35 Author interview, 4 July 2005.

36 Author interview, 4 August 2005.

37 *Remember*, p33.

38 Author interview, 21 June 2007.

39 Interview by Peter McCabe and Robert D. Schonfeld, September 1971.

40 'Hopeless' from interview by Chris Hutchins, *NME*, 25 September 1964. Covering letter sent with Paul's final pay and documents is reproduced in *Thank U Very Much*, p80. 'My plan was to go on playing the clubs until I reached twenty-five – a ripe old age – and then go to art college and hang on there for a couple of years,' Paul told Ray Coleman and Chris Roberts in *Melody Maker*, 3 August 1963.

41 Author interview, 26 May 2004.

42 *Beatle!*, pp118/120.

43 *The Best Of Fellas*, p88.

44 First two sentences from *Stuart: The Life And Art Of Stuart Sutcliffe*, p157; remainder from interview by Richard Williams, for *The Times*, 16 December 1981.

45 Interview by Spencer Leigh. Astrid usually says Stu first wore the collarless jacket a few weeks later, at the Top Ten Club, prompting John to say, 'What's all this? Have your got your mum's jacket on?' If Stu did wear it in the Cavern, as Mike McCartney remembers, he (after Astrid) was the first to do so in Liverpool.

46 *The Best Of Fellas*, p147.

47 Interview by Spencer Leigh.

48 Paul from interview by Jon Wilde, *Uncut*, July 2004; John from interview by Tom Snyder, *Tomorrow*, NBC-TV, 8 April 1975.

49 John explained this in his interview by Peter McCabe and Robert D. Schonfeld, September 1971. Bill Harry was the guiding hand and co-producer of *Blues For The Hitch-Hiking Dead*, the north's first *Jazz To Poetry* concert, held at Crane Theatre on 31 January 1961, a seminal event in the development of Liverpool's vibrant 1960s poetry scene, which had taken root at

51 Mount Pleasant, at Streates coffee club. *Mersey Beat's* office was at 81a Renshaw Street. The businessman was Jim Anderson, a civil servant friend of Dick Matthews, who, along with Sam Leach, helped propel Harry into launching the paper.

19: Piedels on Prellies (April–June 1961)

1 Author interview, 12 March 2006. All Jürgen Vollmer quotes in this chapter are from this interview.
2 As mentioned in the previous chapter, the Beatles' decision not to pay Allan Williams his commission was probably premeditated. Bob Wooler may have forewarned Williams of their thinking.
3 *The Beatles Anthology*, p58.
4 Interview by Ritchie Yorke, mid-September 1969.
5 '... meanie' from *Beatle!*, p94; Paul re. 'terrible old piano' – *Many Years From Now*, pp74–5.
6 Author interview, 18 March 2006. Unless otherwise stated, all Tony Sheridan quotes in this chapter are from this interview.
7 20 July 1961.
8 Evidence given at the Royal Courts of Justice, London, 6 May 1998. Horst Fascher was present when George said it. Paul quote – *Many Years From Now*, p63.
9 *The Beatles Anthology*, p58. Paul information also from here.
10 *Beatle!*, p95.
11 *The Beatles Anthology*, p50.
12 *"Mach Schau!"*, p138.
13 *The Beatles Anthology*, p50.
14 Ibid.
15 Interview by Jon Wilde, *Uncut*, July 2004.
16 *The Beatles Anthology*, p50.
17 First section from interview by Paul Drew, US radio, April 1975; remainder from interview by Peter McCabe and Robert D. Schonfeld, September 1971.
18 Author interview, 7 June 2006. All Rosi Heitmann quotes in this chapter are from this interview.
19 *The Beatles Anthology*, p54.
20 *Beatle!*, p96. She is remembered by everyone as a stripper though Pete calls her a waitress in his book.
21 *The Beatles Anthology*, p53.
22 *Beatle!*, p94. 'Tough luck' from interview by Spencer Leigh. British Embassy mentioned by Paul in a letter written on 4 May. It didn't happen.
23 The parameters of the booking are fact but there is no known contract for the extension.
24 Winterhuder Fährhaus was close to Jürgen Vollmer's home at Tewessteg 3, where John and George had spent Good Friday with Jürgen and some friends.
25 This Astrid and Stuart session was at Hartungstrasse 12, another location Jürgen had found from prior research; photos were also taken this day in a doorway somewhere in the Eimsbüttel district.
Fourteen years later, in 1975, John chose one of the Jäger-Passage photos for the cover of his *Rock 'n' Roll* album. The blurred figures walking past are, left to right, Paul, Stu and George. It was the only 'solo album' of the period to feature a Beatles group photo, and no one realised it.
26 *Melody Maker*, 25 August 1951. Deutsche Grammophon was a subsidiary of the German electrical engineering company Siemens & Halske.
27 Author interview, 22 March 2006.
28 5 June 1961. *Billboard* became *Billboard Music Week* from 9 January 1961 and didn't revert to its original one-word title until 5 January 1963 – however, for the sake of convenience, it will be referred to here as *Billboard*. Wonderland By Night reached number 1 in this magazine's charts; in *Cash Box*, it was a number 1 single and number 2 album. Though voted a hit on *Juke Box Jury*, it did not break through in Britain.
29 Interview by Spencer Leigh. Kent's biggest success came in 1959, aged 16, with a German version of Susie Darlin', the US hit by Robin Luke.
30 4 May 1961. The trip was also reported in *Billboard*, 1 May 1961.

31 Author interview, 15 March 2011.

32 Author interview, 1 April 2008.

33 Author interview, 25 August 2007.

34 Author interviews. Piel, 7 June 2006; Erichsen, 19 March 2006; Braun, 17 March 2006; Berger, 8 June 2006. 'Icke' Braun was so nicknamed on account of his accent: he was from Berlin, where the word 'ich' – meaning 'I' – is pronounced with a hard ending, a 'k' sound rather than a soft 'ch'. (The phonetic English pronunciation of the nickname is 'Ikker'.)

35 *The Beatles Anthology*, p59.

36 From interview transcript of unknown origin.

37 'We were all on them,' says Cyn in A *Twist Of Lennon*, p54.

38 *Beatle!*, p100. Mutti's houseboat was probably at Spreehafen, in Wilhelmsburg, a short bus ride from St Pauli.

39 John said this in a 28 March 1975 interview by Frances Schoenberger for the German magazine *Bravo*, unpublished until appearing in *Spin*, October 1988. The wooden structures on the viewing platform have since been removed on safety grounds, so the carvings are gone. The church is just beyond the other end of the Reeperbahn from Grosse Freiheit – close to Krameramtsstuben, the seventeenth-century courtyard (preserved intact at the time of writing) where Astrid took some atmospheric photos of Stuart in 1960.

40 Davies, p107. 'Independent Group' members included Richard Hamilton. Peter Blake (then a student at the Royal College of Art) attended meetings.

41 Author interview, 3 November 1994.

42 Letter, dated 19 June 1961, illustrated in *Paul McCartney World Tour* programme (1989–90), p39.

43 *Beatle!*, p109; Cynthia from A *Twist Of Lennon*, p57.

44 Author interview, 21 July 2006.

45 *The Beatles Anthology*, p62.

46 Author interview, 3 November 1994.

47 Interview by Tony Webster, *Beat Instrumental*, September 1964; 'I didn't really want to spend that much' from interview by Paul du Noyer, *Paul McCartney World Tour* programme (1989–90), p43.

48 First two sentences from interview by Richard Williams, for *The Times*, 16 December 1981; third sentence from interview by Julia Baird, 1988.

49 First sentence from interview by Roger Scott, Capital Radio (London), 17 November 1983; second from interview by Mike Read, 13 October 1987, for BBC Radio 1. Pete from *Beatle!*, p103 (beware of ghostwriter's journalese); George from *The Beatles Anthology*, p69; Klaus from author interview, 29 March 2006. All Klaus Voormann quotes in this chapter are from this interview.

50 Hinze interview by Ulf Krüger for *Die Beatles In Harburg* (Christians Druckerei & Verlag, Hamburg, 1996), p99; Sheridan from *The Beatles: Fact And Fiction 1960–1962*, by Eric Krasker (Atlantica-Séguier, Biarritz, 2009), p128.

51 George played and sang on a 1990 remake of Nobody's Child by his band the Traveling Wilburys, recorded for the orphans' charity Romanian Angel Appeal.

52 In the Paul McCartney biography *Many Years From Now* (p208), author Barry Miles mentions that Bert Kaempfert suggested they make a recording as Paul McCartney and the Beatles. Miles writes that the idea was quickly rejected by the group (though of course John went on to take the spotlight in the same way). This detail must have been provided by Paul himself, since it doesn't appear elsewhere.

53 Interview by Paul Drew, US radio, April 1975. During a July 1969 recording session the Beatles slipped casually into a jam of three Gene Vincent numbers, including Ain't She Sweet which they did more in the Vincent style than the 'march' sound of 1961. It appears on *The Beatles Anthology 3*. '. . . bound to be better' from Davies, p107.

54 Interview on Boston radio WBZ, London, 30 May 1964.

55 Ain't She Sweet c/w Beatle Bop mentioned by the Beatles a day or two later to Bob Hardy, a Liverpool friend who, as a merchant seaman, happened to be docked in Hamburg this week and went to see them play at the Top Ten. Hardy conveyed the information to his girlfriend in a letter sent to Merseyside on 26 June, shown to the author. Schacht re. disappointment from interview by Johnny Beerling, January 1972, for BBC Radio 1.

56 Interview by Tony MacArthur, Brisbane, 29 June 1964.

57 Calculating a royalty on 90 or 85 per cent instead of 100 was standard in the record business throughout the world, based on the premise that shellac discs were so breakable many of those pressed would be rendered useless. The fact that records were now made of much more durable vinyl wouldn't be reflected in contracts for at least another decade.

58 Davies (1985), p37.

59 Interview by Elliot Mintz, 16 April 1973.

20: **Soup and Sweat and Rock 'n' Roll** (July–September 1961)

1 According to *Disc Weekly*, 31 July 1965, Ringo recorded his party duet with Cilla and retained the tape. It has never been heard publicly.

2 In his Paul McCartney biography *Many Years From Now* (p52), Barry Miles wrote that Paul once hitch-hiked to the Isle of Wight, with John, to visit his cousin Bett Robbins and her husband Mike at their pub – they were resident managers at the popular Bow Bars, in Ryde. Paul then touched on it during an interview from the Isle of Wight (with Geoff Lloyd for Absolute Radio, 13 June 2010). There are no obvious spaces in Paul and John's calendar for this trip to have happened except at the start of July 1961, but John never mentioned it, and a letter sent by Mike Robbins to Mike McCartney on 6 July 1961 (reproduced in *Thank U Very Much*, p76) doesn't refer to Paul making any visits. Paul went to Ryde alone in April 1963, and he and John hitch-hiked to the pub the Robbinses managed before this, in Caversham, the Easter 1960 visit when they became the Nerk Twins.

3 They were married in 1965 and remained so at the time of writing this, approaching fifty years later.

4 Brian's regret from the raw transcripts of interviews for Brian Epstein's autobiography *A Cellarful Of Noise*.

5 As told to the author, 14 March 1989.

6 Davies, pp122–3, where Queenie Epstein added that Brian 'also went back to amateur acting again'. Further information about this has yet to be found. Barcelona account from a handwritten note by Brian Epstein, shown to the author.

7 June Harris piece in *Disc*, 8 July 1961.

8 The impact of Parlophone's *Beyond The Fringe* album reverberated for years: it made it possible for people to study the format and learn the show by heart, much in the way that, a decade later, the *Monty Python* albums multiplied the impact and influence of the TV show.

9 John from song-by-song notes typed for his LP *Rock 'n' Roll*, spring 1975; George from *The Beatles Anthology*, p73.

10 *The Best Years Of The Beatles*, p99, and *Beatle!*, p126.

11 From the raw transcripts of interviews for Brian Epstein's autobiography *A Cellarful Of Noise*.

12 Interview by Scott Muni, WNEW-FM, 13 February 1975. John was promoting his new record of Stand By Me, an international hit that spring.

13 *The Beatles Anthology*, p53.

14 The Darktown Strutters' Ball was a Joe Brown single in February 1960; I'm Henery The Eighth, I Am in June 1961. He'd yet to issue The Sheik Of Araby but the Beatles saw him do it on TV.

15 Sometimes the sessions ran 12–1PM, break until 1.15, then live music again until 2.15.

16 Author interview, 1 June 2005.

17 3 August 1961.

18 Interview by Chris Charlesworth for *Melody Maker*, 20 November 1971.

19 Author interview, 1 June 2008. Made in Manchester by Granada, *Coronation Street* was the first TV serial (the term 'soap opera' wasn't yet used in Britain) set in the north of England. It wasn't Liverpool but another part of Lancashire, demonstrably northern working-class. The Beatles were sporadic viewers but saw it often enough to impersonate the characters.

20 Interview by author and Kevin Howlett, 6 June 1990.

21 A 1961 photo of the Beatles sitting with their pints was still (at the time of writing) on display in the Grapes. The pub's interior has altered drastically in recent years.

22 'I don't know why girls were all over the Beatles when they came off stage in their leather gear,' recalls Mike McCartney. 'The stench was *terrible*.' (Interview by Spencer Leigh.)

23 *The Best Of Fellas*, p91.

24 Author interview, 4 November 2004.

25 Author interview, 27 August 2005.

26 Author interview, 5 July 2007.
27 Author interview, 6 November 2007.
28 54 Ferndale Road, off Smithdown Road. The drip repayments for the Futurama were completed this summer in five large chunks, adding up to £30. After posing for photos at home with his collection of guitars, now numbering four, George sold the Futurama.
29 Author interview, 18 June 2007; George from interview by Nicky Horne, Capital Radio (London), 13 September 1974.
30 *Mersey Beat* issue dates spanned its fortnightly appearance, so the first was 6–20 July and this second 20 July–3 August 1961. For the sake of abbreviation, this book will cite only the start date of each issue. The headline BEATLE'S SIGN RECORDING CONTRACT was written that way.
31 Author interview, 21 June 2007.
32 Interview by Malcolm Searle, Melbourne, 15 June 1964.
33 Interview by Bob Azurdia, BBC Radio Merseyside, 19 October 1982.
34 Adelaide press conference, 12 June 1964. Here, Paul related how he *and* John planned to swim the Mersey, though John told the crowded room, 'I don't remember this, actually. He keeps saying it all the time.' Paul countered, 'It's true, John, it *is* true,' and John – king of the last word – told him, 'I think you must have been on your own then.' John also mentioned it during his September 1971 interview by Peter McCabe and Robert D. Schonfeld: 'Paul was more aggressive [to getting the Beatles noticed] – "Let's think up publicity stunts," all jump in the Mersey – I don't know, something like that.'
35 First part from interview by Takahiko Iimura, 15 October 1971; second from Montreal press conference, 22 December 1969; third from interview by Jerry G. Bishop, 13–24 August 1965.
36 First paragraph from interview by Bob Azurdia, BBC Radio Merseyside, 19 October 1982; second from *The Best Of Fellas*, p147.
37 *The Best Of Fellas*, p147. Sam Leach's management interest happens a little later.
38 *The Best Years Of The Beatles*, p90, and *The Best Of Fellas*, pp147–8.
39 Kenny Ball interview by Spencer Leigh.
40 *Eyewitness News*, ABC Channel 7, Australia, 19 November 1995.
41 Davies, p78. Cyn had completed her four-year art school course, attained her NDD and was staying on for a fifth and final year, studying for the ATD, the art teacher's diploma. This entailed being sent into schools to gain classroom experience. In the meantime, during the summer holiday, she took a job on the cosmetics counter at Woolworth's (just along from the Penny Lane roundabout), where John dropped in to see her most days, barging and crippling through the shop.
42 Author interview, 12 May 2010.
43 Author interview, 13 May 2010.
44 *Liverpool Echo*, 24 April 1964.
45 Mike McCartney left school (at 17, in July 1961) with one O-Level, in Art, confidently expecting to follow his rebel hero John Lennon into Liverpool College of Art. The last column in the Liverpool Institute register shows the art school as Mike's destination, but then he found the rules had changed. In 1957, John got in with no O-Levels; in 1961, Mike needed several. Following a period on the dole, he took a job in a tailoring shop, and then, for a short period from April 1962, trudged the streets as an unsuccessful door-to-door salesman of the Catholic bible.
46 There's documentary proof that Ringo pursued emigration to Houston in the late summer of 1961, but, on the occasions he talks about it, he usually speaks of 1958 or 1959, when he was 18 and still working at H. Hunt & Son. It's impossible to reconcile these accounts unless he made two separate attempts to go – but if he did, he's never mentioned it. He planned to emigrate in tandem with a Liverpool friend, whose identity has been assigned to/claimed by more than one person.
47 Rory renamed 54 Broad Green Road 'Hurricaneville' in 1961, perhaps inspired by *Stormsville*, the title of a Johnny and the Hurricanes LP released in October 1960. (As previously mentioned, the name Rory Storm and the Hurricanes could also have come from the American group.) The house-name has often been remembered as Stormsville, even by Rory's sister Iris, but it was registered with the Post Office as Hurricaneville and appeared that way in the phone directory.
48 Young Ringo, *Beatles Book* magazine, issue 28 (November 1965).
49 *Beatle!*, p88.

50 Author interview, 11 January 2005. Pete Mackey became bass guitarist with the Tenabeats; David Boyce (another Cavern Beatles fan) was the drummer, and their guitarist/singer was the poet/writer Mike Hart. They twice played on the same bill as the Beatles in 1961–2; then in 1963, after renaming themselves the Roadrunners, did so again three times, and established a strong Merseyside following as an arty rhythm and blues group. (An important band; more about them in the next volume.)

51 See Davies, p113, for illustration of four of the twenty-one pages.

52 *Stuart: The Life And Art Of Stuart Sutcliffe*, pp182–3. *Mersey Beat* piece from 5 October 1961.

53 Ibid. p190. The dates of Stuart's fleeting return to Liverpool aren't known, but it was the end of August 1961. The Sutcliffes had moved again since his previous visit, to a rented ground-floor flat at 37 Aigburth Drive, a grand house near Sefton Park boating lake.

54 Granada's response, dated 21 September 1961, is reproduced in several books – e.g., *Beatle!*, p123.

55 Interview by Johnny Beerling, 13 January 1972, for BBC Radio 1.

56 Interview by Elliot Mintz, 1 January 1976.

57 Paul from *The Beatles Anthology*, p21; John from interview by Elliot Mintz, 1 January 1976.

58 John's quote from Davies, p95. Cyn's aunt, Celia "Tess" Collins, lived at 7 Ennis Road, West Derby. Cyn lived here until spring 1962, entailing long bus journeys to and from art school every day; John became a visitor here.

59 *The Best Of Fellas*, p67.

21: **Les Nerk Twins à Paris** (1–14 October 1961)

1 'We ended up taking the train all the way,' John told Chris Hutchins, *Disc*, 27 April 1963.

2 Interview by Antoine de Caunes, 22 October 2007, for Canal+ TV.

3 Interview by David Sheff, 12 September 1980, for *Playboy*.

4 Author interview, 12 March 2006. All Jürgen Vollmer quotes in this chapter are from this interview.

5 John quote from interview by Albert Goldman, *Charlie*, July 1971; Paul confirmed his and John's needle-and-thread handiwork in *The Beatles Anthology*, p64. 'Queer' from Davies, p111.

6 Interview by Jean-François Vallée for French TV, 4 April 1975. There are no known photos of John or Paul wearing the collarless Cardin jacket (or jackets) bought in Paris, or of their hand-altered flared trousers.

7 Referred to in Cafe On The Left Bank, a Paul McCartney song on Wings' album *London Town*, released 1978.

8 Sydney press conference, 11 June 1964.

9 Jürgen Vollmer's headless photo of John and Paul outside Bal Tabarin – John wearing his new corduroy jacket bought at the flea market – is one of three or four shots from this Paris holiday included on the poster enclosed within *The Beatles* (the White Album), issued 1968. There's also John in his Acker Bilk bowler, sitting up in bed in their Montmartre hotel room; and another crip session – Paul in a cloth cap and scarf and John in glasses. A photo-booth shot of John may also be from this trip. (Except for when Paul handed him his camera, Jürgen took no photos of John and Paul in Paris.)

10 Unidentified 1969 interview, quoted in *The Beatles Anthology*, p64.

11 Ibid. The theory has formed in France that the Beatles' hairstyle was modelled on the cut worn by Jean Marais in the Jean Cocteau film *Le Testament d'Orphée* (1960). This is wrong – Jürgen Vollmer has photos of himself from 1957 (on a trip to London) with the same style.

12 Interview by Ken Douglas, 16 August 1966. If they did fly home, it would have been Paris to Manchester and then a bus and train; there were no direct flights to Liverpool.

22: **'Right then, Brian – manage us'** (15 October–3 December 1961)

1 Author interview, 21 June 2007.

2 Interview by Spencer Leigh. Also said in *Beatle!*, p123, and *The Best Years Of The Beatles*, p161.

3 Author interview, 21 June 2007.

4 Author interview, 16 February 2007. Alan Walsh's (unattributed) review ran in the *Crosby Herald* on 20 October 1961.

5 *Beatle!*, p120.

6 Davies, p104, and *The Beatles Anthology*, p20; Maureen O'Shea from author interview, 13 May 2010.

7 Author interview, 13 May 2010.

8 *Mersey Beat*, 2 November 1961. Wooler's account of the Beatmakers episode is the only one written at the time and must be considered the most reliable, more so than the many anecdotes quoted after it attained legendary status. 'Steamed' quote from interview by Spencer Leigh.

9 *The Best Of Fellas*, p156.

10 Letter from George to Stu, 17 November 1961 (although, oddly, dated 17 August). It also included an intriguing piece of information – 'I've got a drum kit now, only cheap but O.K. for messing around on.' Nothing else is known about this.

11 Interview by Alan Smith, *NME*, 16 August 1963.

12 Interview by Spencer Leigh. Jimmy Campbell (1944–2007) became an acclaimed musician and composer – a member of the Panthers, the Kirkbys, 23rd Turnoff, Rockin' Horse and a busy solo artist.

13 As the years passed, people began to doubt Raymond Jones' existence, wondering if he'd been invented to effect Brian Epstein's introduction to the Beatles' world. In the 1990s, former Nems employee Alistair Taylor announced that the story had indeed been fabricated, by him, and that if anyone was Raymond Jones, he was. This came as some surprise to the real one, who made himself known to the writer and broadcaster Spencer Leigh (see *The Beatles – Ten Years That Shook The World*, by various writers; Dorling Kindersley, London, 2004, p21, and also http://www.beatlesbible.com/features/raymond-jones-interview/). Jones' story – and Epstein's – is verifiably correct. As Jones concludes, 'People have told me that my name will go down in Beatles history. That may be true, but all I did was buy a record by a group that gave me so much pleasure and enjoyment.'

14 From the raw transcripts of interviews for his autobiography *A Cellarful Of Noise*.

15 First part from *Remember*, p117; second from *Thank U Very Much*, p108. Jane Asher's appearances on *Juke Box Jury* coincided with her transition from child actress to juvenile actress or ingénue (the phrases then in use) – she was now starting to handle more mature stage, TV and film roles.

16 Interview by Elliot Mintz, 16 April 1973.

17 Author interview, 20 July 2006.

18 Author interview, 12 May 2010.

19 Interview by Richard Williams, for *The Times*, 16 December 1981.

20 *The Best Of Fellas*, p88. Wooler borrowed the nickname from the American singer Patti Page – it was as inappropriate for her as it was right for John.

21 Hambleton Hall ad, *Liverpool Echo*, 11 November 1961.

22 Interview by Johnny Beerling, 13 January 1972, for BBC Radio 1. In the light of other events, Wooler didn't write the letter to Jack Good.

23 From the raw transcripts of interviews for his autobiography *A Cellarful Of Noise*.

24 Brian Epstein said of the Cavern 'It was a place that I'm sure I visited before' – *Beatles Book* magazine, issue 5 (December 1963).

25 Interview in *The Beatles: The Days In Their Life*, 1981 Canadian radio series.

26 Interview by Bill Grundy, 7 March 1964, for *Frankly Speaking* (BBC North of England Home Service, 23 March 1964).

27 Author interviews: Douglas, 27 August 2005; McFall, 4 July 2005.

28 First paragraph from *The Mersey Sound*, BBC-tv, 9 October 1963, except for final sentence, from the raw transcripts of interviews for *A Cellarful Of Noise*; second paragraph from Bill Grundy interview.

29 *The Best Of Fellas*, p181; 'attracted to the Beatles physically', p162. Brian falling instantly in love: *Shout!*, p127.

30 Interview by Gillian G. Gaar, *Goldmine*, 8 November 1996.

31 *The Beatles Anthology*, p65.

32 *Love Me Do! The Beatles' Progress*, p46.

33 Interview by Paul Gambaccini, *Rolling Stone*, 12 June 1979. When Hunter Davies visited John's and Paul's homes in spring 1967, to interview them for their biography, they still had the old *Mersey Beat* papers with the voting coupons cut out (Davies, p137). Bob Wooler's 25 November *Echo* ad for Hambleton Hall heralded THE VOTE-CATCHING BEATLES.

34 Interview by Bill Grundy, 7 March 1964, for *Frankly Speaking* (BBC North of England Home Service, 23 March 1964).
35 *The Best Of Fellas*, p156.
36 First part from interview by Larry Kane, August 1964; second part quoted in *Time* magazine, 8 September 1967.
37 Interview by Roy Plomley, *Desert Island Discs*, BBC Home Service, 30 November 1964.
38 4 January 1962. Take Five (composed by Paul Desmond) was on the Brubeck album *Time Out* – a record bought or heard by Paul McCartney in 1963.
39 Author interview, 10 April 2005.
40 Ibid.
41 Interview by Johnny Beerling, January 1972, for BBC Radio 1. The 23 Club was a private dining-room at 23 Hope Street frequented by artists and the Philharmonic Hall classical musicians. Brian and Clive were members.
42 Davies, p131.
43 Interview by Larry Kane, August 1965; 'miss their greatest moments' from Davies, p130.
44 Interview by Peter McCabe and Robert D. Schonfeld, September 1971.
45 *Many Years From Now*, p88.
46 Interview by Ken Sharp, *Beatlefan*, June/July 1989. Bob Wooler helped shift these records. When George received his second supply of My Bonnies from Stuart, he gave one to Wooler who plugged it at every opportunity – and he was now compere and stage manager at eleven live sessions a week. As he told Johnny Beerling in 1972 for BBC Radio 1, 'I used to urge people, "Look, for heaven's sake, go and buy this record. It's called My Bonnie, it's on Polydor and it's by your Beatles. They don't actually sing on it, but they're there on it."'
47 *Celebration: John Lennon – Dream Weaver*, Granada TV, 6 November 1981. There's no reason to disbelieve this anecdote, but both Wooler and Epstein also said they'd met (briefly) when Brian first saw the Beatles in the Cavern on 9 November.
48 *The Best Years Of The Beatles*, p135.
49 Brian details via Pete Best in *Beatle!*, pp126–7, and *The Best Years Of The Beatles*, p135. The Beatles' response is quoted by Ringo Starr in an unpublished 1972 interview seen by the author. He was relating what the others told him after he joined the group.
50 Interview by Johnny Beerling, 13 January 1972, for BBC Radio 1.
51 Sam Leach remembers John and Paul telling him about Brian and saying, 'He's a fucking *millionaire!*' – this preceding an occasion when he says they asked him to go and see Brian Epstein and come back to them with his opinion. 'Antwakky' from *Beatle!*, p127.
52 Author interview, 11 August 2004.
53 Interview by Kenneth Harris, *Observer*, 17 May 1964.
54 Davies, p119.
55 Bill Grundy interview.
56 Interview by Richard Buskin, 9 March 1987.
57 Every aspect of this story is strange. When it was in these few days that Brian Epstein had an acetate cut, where, with which song, and from what source recording, remain unanswered questions. The mention of a 'TV broadcast' was a white lie – the Beatles hadn't appeared on television; and if Brian had an acetate, why didn't he give it to his primary contacts at EMI and Decca instead of or in addition to My Bonnie?
58 11 November 1961.
59 *Let's Twist!*, by George Carpozi, Jr (Pyramid Books, New York, 1962), p11.
60 16 December 1961. Six US record companies might have been fighting over the My Bonnie master tape (that smell is called *hype*) but the skirmish was predictably won by (American) Decca, which issued all the Bert Kaempfert records. For reasons unknown, the label didn't release My Bonnie until April 1962.
   Cash Box previously reported (11 November 1961) that Kaempfert spent five days in New York at the end of October, just before Twist broke big. He said then that Sheridan was his 'sensational new singer from England', so there's a fair chance he took My Bonnie with him on the trip and played it around the business. 'Twist-mania' from *Billboard*, 4 December 1961.
61 *Disc*, 27 May 1961. Abbey Road took delivery of a German-made Telefunken four-track tape recorder in 1959, the first major piece of equipment at the studio not made in EMI's own laboratories. It remained for some years almost the preserve of classical and opera producers, who

used it for spreading the recording of certain instruments, for better sound balance, rather than for multi-tracking.

More information about the machine, along with every other piece of equipment at EMI's Abbey Road studios through the 1960s, and the people who operated them, is in the sumptuous book *Recording The Beatles*, by Kevin Ryan and Brian Kehew (Curvebender Publishing, USA, 2006).

62 George's pied-à-terre was Flat 5, 23 Upper Berkeley Street, a smart terrace which George says belied the flats inside (a bit like Gambier Terrace in Liverpool). Judy's flat was on the third floor (out of four) at 55 Manchester Street and looked straight into the Wallace Collection art gallery across the street. The building has since been demolished, as has EMI House.

63 'Pillar' from Alley-gations column by Brian Harvey, 7 September 1961; Eastman's visit to Britain was mentioned in *Billboard*, 11 September 1961.

64 Document in the PRS archive.

65 From the raw transcripts of interviews for his autobiography *A Cellarful Of Noise*.

66 Bill Grundy interview. Brian Epstein referred to this 3 December meeting as the first, when it wasn't.

67 Bill Grundy interview; 'with his slow, lop-sided smile' from *A Cellarful Of Noise*, p49.

68 *A Cellarful Of Noise*, p50.

69 Keith Smith worked for Bailey, Page & Co, whose office was at 10 Dale Street. Gerry and the Pacemakers used him too, and it's likely this is how the Beatles heard about him. It was necessary they had an accountant, probably because the Inland Revenue had discovered they lived from a cash income. Paul made the first appointment, arriving after a Cavern lunchtime session in about August 1961.

70 Interview by Mike Read, 13 October 1987, for BBC Radio 1.

71 Author interview, 19 May 1987.

72 First part from interview by Jann S. Wenner, *Rolling Stone*, 14 May 1970; second from interview by Lisa Robinson, *Hit Parader*, December 1975.

73 Interview by author and Kevin Howlett, 6 June 1990.

74 Interview by Mike Read, 13 October 1987, for BBC Radio 1.

75 In *A Cellarful Of Noise*, Brian said they went to 'a milk bar'. This is possible, but a pub was the more likely destination. One of Brian's favourite haunts was the Basnett Bar, at 29 Basnett Street, equidistant between the two Nems shops. Derek Taylor (whom Brian didn't yet know) was among the regulars here.

76 Interview by Elliot Mintz, 1 January 1976.

77 *I Me Mine*, p33. This was like someone saying, in later years, his act would be bigger than the Beatles.

78 'We certainly weren't naive …' from interview by Lisa Robinson, *Hit Parader*, December 1975; 'It was assessment …' from interview by Jann S. Wenner, 8 December 1970, for *Rolling Stone*.

79 *A Cellarful Of Noise*, p51.

23: **The Boys** (December 1961)

1 Author interview, 19 January 2008. Davies went on to launch and run the Liverpool record shop Probe (1971–) and from that the equally influential record label Probe Plus (1981–).

2 Author interview, 29 October 2004.

3 Author interview, 12 June 2005.

4 Author interview, 28 March 2003.

5 Author interview, 30 August 2005.

6 The Beatles sang Young Blood in a BBC radio session in 1963, and a recording is on their 1994 album *Live At The BBC*. John was still doing his vocal crip – it comes forty-two seconds into the song.

7 Author interviews – Freda Kelly, 28 March 2003; Steve Calrow, 1 June 2008; Lindy Ness, 29 October 2004; Geoff Davies, 19 January 2008; Susan Sanders, 13 June 2005; Maureen O'Shea, 13 May 2010; Lou Steen, 12 June 2005; Barbara Houghton, 15 January 2008; Beryl Johnson, 4 August 2005; Bobby Brown, 5 July 2007; Liz Tibbott-Roberts, 11 June 2005; Clive Walley, 19 February 2008; Ruth Gore, 27 November 2005; Alan Smith, 1 June 2005; Vivien Jones, 24 July 2007.

8 Author interview, 5 July 2007.

9 Author interview, 15 March 2011.
10 Author interview, 19 May 1987.
11 *Beatle!*, pp130–2. Eppy had also been a school nickname, Brian told *London Life* magazine (23 July 1966).
12 Davies, p134.
13 *Beatle!*, p127.
14 Author interview, 27 August 2004.
15 *The Complete Beatles Chronicle*, p54.
16 Interview by Mike Read, 13 October 1987, for BBC Radio 1.
17 Exactly what happened has been a mystery for decades and is sure to remain so, not least since none of the Beatles ever mentioned going into London after Aldershot or John and Paul strumming this night in the capital for the first time.
18 *Beatle!*, p90.
19 Interview by Johnny Beerling, 13 January 1972, for BBC Radio 1; 'better not to do it' from *The Best Of Fellas*, p157.
20 Author interview, 27 August 2004.
21 A *Cellarful Of Noise*, p53.
22 'Dynamic new policy' from *Melody Maker*, 9 December 1961; 'singles by British artists' from *NME*, 8 December 1961.
23 Author interview, 29 September 2004.
24 *The Complete Beatles Chronicle*, p55.
25 Memorandum from Len Wood to Richard Dawes (EMI main board director), 17 December 1963; illustrated in *The Complete Beatles Chronicle*, p55.
26 Brian Epstein quotes from the raw transcripts of interviews for his autobiography A *Cellarful Of Noise*.
27 Author interview, 9 June 2005.
28 A *Secret History*, by Alistair Taylor (John Blake Publishing, London, 2001), p29. Taylor spoke as if he was present at the first management meeting (or meetings), and perhaps he was, but no one else mentioned him.
29 *How They Became The Beatles*, p42.
30 Evidence given at the Royal Courts of Justice, London, 6 May 1998.
31 From the raw transcripts of interviews for his autobiography A *Cellarful Of Noise*.
32 Interview by Nicky Campbell, BBC Radio 1, 7 July 1992.
33 Author interview, 18 March 2006.
34 Davies (p132) said Peter Eckhorn offered 'around 300 Marks a week' and Brian Epstein wanted 400, but this is incorrect.
35 Interview by David Griffiths, *Record Mirror*, 10 October 1964. 'Tranquilliser' was probably *Record Mirror*-speak: George will have asked Eckhorn if he had any Prellies.
36 Author interview, 1 June 2005.
37 *The Beatles Anthology*, p67. Paul's Nucleus Coffee Bar recollection in interview by Roger Scott, Capital Radio (London), 17 November 1983; pot tale from Davies, pp135–6, and *Beatle!*, pp143–4. Hunter Davies quotes Neil Aspinall saying the Beatles were there when the men wanted to smoke 'pot' in their van, and they were scared because they didn't know what it was – but they did. Pete's memory is more likely to be correct – he says Neil alone had the approach. He also says the men were junkies, looking to have 'a fix' in the van.
38 Pete Best says (*Beatle!*, p123) that John and Paul each bought a pair of the boots in Anello & Davide on their way back from Paris in October. This is unlikely: not only did Paul say they flew home from France, the boots don't appear in any 1961 photos.

24: **Choices** (1 January–5 February 1962)

1 *The Last Resort With Jonathan Ross*, Channel 4, 16 October 1987. Previous two quotes are John's: the first from interview in *L'Express*, 23–29 March 1970 (spoken English, translated into French print, now back to English), the second from Davies, p306.
2 Author interview, 29 September 2004.
3 In *Beatle!* (p144) and *The Best Years Of The Beatles* (p137), Pete relates this differently, saying Brian was angry because the Beatles – not Mike Smith – arrived late for the session, and that John told him to calm down ('bugger off'). Brian was always clear that it was Smith who was

late, and Smith confirmed this to me, but it's possible the Beatles were late and Smith later. George quote also from *Beatle!*, p144.

4 Five of the fifteen are available on *The Beatles Anthology 1*. The complete session tape first surfaced on the bootleg market in 1976–7.

5 Interview by Howard Smith, WPLJ-FM, New York, 23 January 1972.

6 Interview by Paul Drew, US radio, April 1975.

7 Payne made his remarks in *A Pair Of Jacks* (BBC-tv, 30 December 1961) and repeated them to *Melody Maker* (6 January 1962).

8 *Love Me Do! The Beatles' Progress*, p49.

9 Ibid.

10 Author interview, 1 February 2007.

11 *Love Me Do! The Beatles' Progress*, p49.

12 The British pressing had the English-language spoken intro by Sheridan, with John, Paul and George's wordless harmony backing. This probably came as a surprise to them. The same English intro was also used for the January 1962 German re-promotion of My Bonnie that capitalised on its (tenuous) Twist connection.

13 Mentions – *Record Retailer*, 18 January 1962; *Cash Box*, 13 Jan; *Liverpool Echo*, 20 Jan. Reviews – *NME*, 5 Jan; *Disc*, 13 Jan; *Record Retailer*, 4 Jan; *Melody Maker*, 27 Jan; *The World's Fair*, 6 Jan. Only *New Record Mirror* failed to review it.

14 Author interview, 13 April 2007.

15 Paul said in October 1962, and the other Beatles didn't disagree, that My Bonnie 'got to number five in the German hit parade', but this wasn't right. It appeared on an array of different charts, its positions generally skewed by the aggregation of sales of other versions of My Bonnie by different artists. It peaked at 32 in the monthly Deutsche Hit-Parade published in West Germany's main music business magazine *Der Musikmarkt*, and it reached 11 in the 'aktuelle 50' in the monthly *Musikbox* (juke-box) trade magazine *Automaten Markt*. Its highest known position anywhere in this period was 4, in a newspaper chart of popular Twist records in Hamburg (*Bild-Zeitung*, 21 May 1962).

16 Pete has always said the Beatles' management contract was signed in the living-room at his house. Alistair Taylor always insisted it was signed in a small office Brian kept in the basement record department at Nems, Whitechapel.

17 *A Cellarful Of Noise*, p59. The contract's final page, with the Beatles' signatures but not Brian's, is illustrated on p52 of the same book.

18 Interview by Geoff Brown, *Melody Maker*, 30 November 1974.

19 TV news interview, 27 August 1967.

20 *The Beatles Anthology*, p267.

21 Author interview, 4 May 2005.

22 Author interview, 4 July 2005. The Rembrandt was at 14 Slater Street, across from the Jacaranda. Brian also brought club-aficionado Allan Williams here.

23 *The Beatles Anthology*, p206.

24 Davies, p103; George from author interview, 23 October 1987.

25 Exaggerated 'bill matter' was typical of the entertainment business. Situated in a sizeable cellar at 45–47 Lloyd Street, off Albert Square, the Oasis had opened as a jazz venue but become by 1962 Manchester's main beat club. Like the Cavern in Liverpool, it was 'dry', indeed it doubled as a coffee bar.

26 *Let The Good Times Roll! Der Star-Club-Gründer erzählt* (*The Star-Club founder tells*), by Horst Fascher with Oliver Flesch (Eichborn, Frankfurt am Main, 2006), p27. The book has appeared only in German.

27 From the raw transcripts of interviews for his autobiography *A Cellarful Of Noise*.

28 Anecdotes told by Paul McCartney to the author, 12 October 1987. The Old Dive was at 12 Brythen Street, just off Williamson Square.

29 Author interview, 5 July 2007.

30 *Beatle!*, p145. John would have said the Liverpool 'get', not 'git'. Pete's account is the only extant testimony about this outburst.

31 Interview by Peter McCabe and Robert D. Schonfeld, September 1971.

32 Author interview, 10 June 2005.

33 Interview by Jann S. Wenner, 8 December 1970, for *Rolling Stone*.

34 *The Beatles Anthology*, p266.

35 This is known from Bob Wooler's interview by Johnny Beerling.
36 Interview by Jean-François Vallée for French TV, 4 April 1975.
37 Davies, p133.
38 After the Beatles had been going to Jim Cannon for a while they found out he was related to Paul. (The link was a few branches away on Paul's father's side.)
39 *Disc and Music Echo*, 2 September 1967.
40 *The Beatles Anthology*, p105.
41 *Many Years From Now*, p96.
42 Explained in 1984 letter to author from Charles Tranter, who booked the Beatles for the Hoylake dance. Manchester recalled by Oasis Club co-owner Ric Dixon in author interview, 28 November 2005. John from Sydney press conference, 11 June 1964.
43 Interview 28 August 1963 for *The Mersey Sound* (BBC-tv, 9 October 1963).
44 Interview by Bill Grundy, 7 March 1964, for *Frankly Speaking* (BBC North of England Home Service, 23 March 1964).
45 Interview by Jann S. Wenner, 8 December 1970, for *Rolling Stone*.
46 Interview by Lisa Robinson, *Hit Parader*, December 1975.
47 First paragraph from *The Beatles Anthology*, p73; second from interview by Richard Williams, for *The Times*, 16 December 1981. Paul's 'Gateshead group philosophy' refers to his epiphany in 1954 – see chapter 3.
48 Evidence given at the Royal Courts of Justice, London, 6 May 1998.
49 Author interview, 11 November 2004. The shop was at 17–19 Grange Road West, Birkenhead, an unprepossessing two-storey building in which Beno Luciano Dorn ran a business that won him multiple London awards.

25: 'A tendency to play music' (6 February–8 March 1962)

1 *A Cellarful Of Noise*, p55. The raw interview transcript for that book is worded a little differently and includes a shorthand – 'Mr Epstein. We don't like your boys' sound. Groups are out. Four groups particularly and guitars are finished.' The interview was by Derek Taylor who then ghosted the material for publication.

  In a 1981 interview by American writer David Klein, Dick Rowe claimed no knowledge of any discussion with Brian Epstein subsequent to his receiving Decca's standard rejection letter, or of any trip to London by Brian to ask Decca to reconsider, or of saying 'Groups of guitarists are on their way out', or of hearing Brian claim the Beatles would be bigger than Elvis. Rowe said it was all 'lies'.

  The full and true circumstances of the Beatles' rejection by Decca will surely never be known. I have done my best to make sense of much conflicting and confusing information, but it's an imperfect blink in history.

2 *A Cellarful Of Noise*, p56. On that book's publication, in October 1964, S. A. Beecher-Stevens complained to Brian Epstein, 'the paragraphs which refer to our meeting are so far from the truth that I feel I must write you this letter in protest. Far from rejecting the Beatles, I *personally* recommended that they be accepted and recorded. As a marketing man, I was proud of the fact that I *did not* turn them down.' Brian recognised that Beecher-Stevens was objecting to the paragraph beginning 'The boys won't go, Mr Epstein . . .', and in his reply stated, 'I recall that this was implied quite definitely by Dick Rowe and admit that whilst you were present at all these conferences you did not in fact comment as such.' Accordingly, Beecher-Stevens' name was omitted from certain later printings, an action which annoyed him just as much. (Source: Epstein files.)

3 Author interview, 29 September 2004. It's commonly said that Poole and the Tremilos auditioned at Decca the same day as the Beatles. This was first put into print by *Beat Monthly* in August 1963 and has been everywhere since – but Poole is certain it was a different day.

4 Brian Poole and the Tremilos became Brian Poole and the Tremeloes to match Decca's misspelling of the name on the label of their first record.

5 *Melody Maker*, 9 December 1961.

6 Author interview, 6 September 1995.

7 Letter to Dick Rowe, 10 February 1962; *A Cellarful Of Noise*, pp57–8.

8 Author interview, 19 May 1987.

9 Author interview with Tony Meehan, 6 September 1995. ('I met George again in 1968 and for

some reason he was harbouring a grudge against me. He was very, very uptight about it – "You blocked us getting a recording contract …"') First part of George quote from interview by Terry David Mulligan, *The Great Canadian Gold Rush*, CBC radio, 30 May and 6 June 1977; concluding five words from interview for *The Beatles Anthology*.

10 Interview by Paul Drew, US radio, April 1975. I once asked Tony Meehan whether he produced what is known as the Beatles 'Decca session' and he answered with a well-supported no, but one of his then-colleagues says he did and just wouldn't admit to it. Tony Calder, 17 in 1962 and just starting a life in the music business, insists Meehan confessed it to him years later (author interview with Calder, 1 October 2004). If Meehan *did* make the tape, though, where is the recording made by Mike Smith and engineer Mike Savage? They surely did something, but the Beatles only went to Decca once. Taking all factors into consideration, it must be considered unlikely that Meehan worked with the Beatles.

11 Author interviews, 5 November 1984 and 6 September 1995.

12 Interview by Howard Smith, WPLJ-FM, New York, 23 January 1972; Paul from interview by Mike Read, 13 October 1987, for BBC Radio 1.

13 Interview for *Rockworld*, syndicated US radio show, September 1974.

14 Author interview, 4 May 2005.

15 The film's existence was unknown until 1996; it was put up for auction by Sotheby's that September and segments were shown on TV news. Ringo Starr recorded Dream for his 1970 album *Sentimental Journey* – it was among the important songs of his childhood.

16 *Beatle!*, p174.

17 Author interview, 21 June 2007; Paul from interview by Mark Radcliffe, BBC Radio 2, 17 September 2005.

18 John – first part from interview by Jean-François Vallée for French TV, 4 April 1975, second from interview by Andy Peebles, BBC Radio 1, 6 December 1980; Paul from *The Beatles Anthology*, p22.

19 Interview by Spencer Leigh.

20 Author interview, 30 September 1987. It was probably this song's waltz tempo that inspired Paul to put the waltz middle-eight in Pinwheel Twist.

21 Ibid.

22 Stuart played nine Hamburg shows with the Bats over eight consecutive days, 2–9 February 1962, concluding, it seems, with three nights in the Kaiserkeller (research by Thorsten Knublauch and Axel Korinth in their book *Komm, Gib Mir Deine Hand*, privately published, 2008). Astrid was rightly concerned for his health while he did this; indeed Stuart wrote in a letter home on 14 February, 'I have played a couple of times [*sic*] in another band and managed to earn a bit … the day I fell sick I was practically on the stage to begin – that was horrible, I thought I was dying.'

23 George's recollection from *The Beatles Anthology*, p69; John's from reliable private source; Mike from *Liverpool Echo*, 16 April 1962; Pete from author interview, 7 March 1985.

24 Author interview, 20 July 2006.

25 Author interview, 28 November 2005.

26 Author interview, 5 July 2007.

27 Author interview, 14 January 1987. Like all Roberts, Boast (1918–94) was usually called Bob, but he was also known informally as Kenneth, which explains Brian Epstein's mention of 'Kenneth Boast' in *A Cellarful Of Noise*, p60.

28 Author interview, 21 January 1987.

29 Davies, p167, and *A Cellarful Of Noise*, p62.

30 *All You Need Is Ears*, p122.

31 From the raw transcripts of interviews for his autobiography *A Cellarful Of Noise*. I've seen what may be the sole surviving Beatles 78rpm acetate cut for Brian Epstein at His Master's Voice, which is in private hands. Its uniqueness is enhanced by his handwriting on the labels, and the recognition of what it led to, making this one of the rarest and most collectable of all Beatles records.

32 Interview by Richard Williams, 21 August 1971.

33 Colman's names have been frequently misspelled. For the record, he was Sidney Herbert Colman (1905–65) and Bennett was Thomas 'Tom' George Whippey (1931–2004). He was given the name Kim Bennett by his producer at Decca, Hugh Mendl.

34 Author interview, 28 July 2003. All Kim Bennett quotes in this chapter are from this interview.

35 This account is largely drawn from A *Cellarful Of Noise*, pp94–7. The Beehive is a pub on Paradise Street in the middle of Liverpool.
36 Davies, p158.
37 Interview by Peter McCabe and Robert D. Schonfeld, September 1971.
38 Portrait Of Paul, by Mike McCartney, *Woman* magazine, 28 August 1965.
39 *The Beatles Anthology*, p158.
40 Interview by Raoul Pantin, *Trinidad Express*, 5 May 1971.
41 A *Cellarful Of Noise*, p63.
42 *The Beatles Anthology*, p58.
43 Interview by Horst Königstein, Hamburg, 29 September 1976, for *Ringo und die Stadt am Ende des Regenbogen* (*Ringo And The City At The End Of The Rainbow*), West German NDR-TV, 9 and 16 June 1977.
44 *The Beatles Anthology*, pp58–9.
45 Author interview, 18 March 2006.
46 From email to Thorsten Knublauch, 6 February 2007.
47 Davies, p262. Richard Starkey died in a Crewe hospital on 5 December 1981, aged 68. He was proud of his son's success and isn't known to have bothered him or asked for money.
48 Interview by Alan Smith, *NME*, 23 August 1963. 'I'd get the car and just drive around by myself, anywhere really. I used to get a lot of kicks out of it.'
49 *The Best Years Of The Beatles*, p161; *Beatle!*, p145; Davies, p137.
50 Wooler from *The Best Of Fellas*, p167; Harry from interview by Spencer Leigh; Aspinall from author interview, 21 June 2007.
51 A *Cellarful Of Noise*, p68. The suggestion here is that this talk was had in summer 1962, but other information indicates it must have been earlier.
52 'There's another Beatle' from Spencer Leigh interview with Southport promoter Ron Appleby; Beatles laughing at Brian Epstein from recording of legal interview with Pete Best, New York, 1965. Mike McCartney has a photo in which Brian can just be seen wearing a leather jacket over a shirt and tie. It was taken on 17 March 1962 at Sam Leach's engagement party, which followed straight after a Leach dance promotion – a *St Patrick's Night Rock Gala* at Knotty Ash Village Hall starring the Beatles and Rory Storm and the Hurricanes. (The Hurricanes were still without Ringo. It was the Beatles' first appearance at this violent place for four months, and their last; Brian made an exception only because of the special occasion.)
53 Author interview, 4 May 2005.
54 The 2.7m figure comes from the BBC's daily 'Audience Barometer' research, which sampled the listening habits of nearly four thousand people and expressed this as a percentage of the possible total audience of 49m – the entire British population bar under-fives. As the figure was computed only for internal use, and the BBC wasn't a commercial organisation, there was no need for dressing. The 8 March 1962 *Here We Go* was heard by an estimated 5.6 per cent of the 49m audience – 2,744,000.
55 *Remember*, p99; the photo is blurred because Mike didn't use flash, not wanting to distract the moment. A sharper image, from the afternoon rehearsal, is on p98.
56 *The Beatles – The True Beginnings*, p145. The broadcast master tape was retained by the BBC for a few months and then junked; it wasn't feasible to keep everything. The surviving recording was made by a Beatles fan at home with a domestic tape recorder, receiving the broadcast at 247 metres on the medium-wave, an historic moment captured in listenable lo-fi.

26: **'Us against them'** (9 March–10 April 1962)

1 Author interview, 12 June 2005.
2 Author interview, 5 July 2007.
3 Interview by Spencer Leigh.
4 Author interview, 5 July 2007.
5 Author interview, 24 April 2012.
6 *Mersey Beat*, 5 and 19 April 1962. The other side of the Miracles' What's So Good About Goodbye was I've Been Good To You.
7 Paul would describe Ask Me Why as 'mostly John's: John's original idea, and we both sat down and wrote it together' (*Many Years From Now*, p92), but John himself – on probably the only

occasion he was asked about it – said, 'I wrote all of that ... I wrote it.' (From unpublished section of interview by Mike Hennessey for *Record Mirror*, 2 October 1971.)

8 Paul says this in *Many Years From Now*, pp81–2.

9 Author interview, 30 September 1987.

10 The Marquee was still in its first location, 165 Oxford Street.

11 P. P. Pond was Paul Pond, who took the name Paul Jones a few months later. Elmore James was really Elmore Brooks (1918–63), songwriter, singer and electrifyingly good blues guitarist, specialising in slide.

12 *Jazz News*, a Soho-based weekly, was the main magazine to cover the rise of rhythm and blues in south-east England in 1962–3. R&B wasn't jazz but *sort of* emerged from it, as did a number of its movers and shakers (Chris Barber, Giorgio Gomelsky, etc).

13 John from interview by Peter McCabe and Robert D. Schonfeld, September 1971; Brown from author interview, 5 July 2007; Brian from interview for WKYC, Cleveland, Ohio, 15 September 1964.

14 *The Best Of Fellas*, p159, with additional text from uncut interview by Spencer Leigh.

15 From foreword to the 1984 edition of *A Cellarful Of Noise*; Brian from interview by Gordon Williams, *Scene*, 9 February 1963.

16 Interview by Johnny Beerling, 13 January 1972, for BBC Radio 1. Wooler made the same point in *Disc and Music Echo*, 2 July 1966. The Epstein quote, via Wooler, 'they'll have to change it', suggests this was said by promoters insisting they'd change the name Beatles before agreeing to book them. *They* would change it, robbing Brian and the Beatles of any control. He declined, of course.

17 Interview by Peter McCabe and Robert D. Schonfeld, September 1971.

18 Davies, p137; Wooler from *The Best Of Fellas*, p159.

19 Author interview, 19 May 1987. 'Right. Try Embassy' from *A Cellarful Of Noise*, p58.

20 Interview 28 October 1964 by Jean Shepherd for *Playboy*, February 1965.

21 From the raw transcripts of interviews for his autobiography *A Cellarful Of Noise*.

22 Author interview, 3 May 1994.

23 *The Beatles Anthology*, p72.

24 Interview by Robyn Flans, *Sh-Boom*, May 1990.

25 George from *The Beatles Anthology*, p72; Paul from *Many Years From Now*, p172. Ringo told Dave Stewart (*Off The Record*, HBO, 2 May 2008) that after he went to the toms in Rock And Roll Music, 'John turned around and looked at me with great surprise [and pleasure].'

26 *The Beatles Anthology*, p49.

27 From part three of *Ringo's Yellow Submarine*, American radio series, 1983, interview by Dave Herman.

28 'I got £9. I thought it was fantastic – £9 for just one night,' Ringo told Alan Smith (*NME*, 23 August 1963). The Beatles weren't yet on £36 for a single night's work, though it would soon come, and be surpassed. A set of autographs survives from the Kingsway Club night on 26 March 1962 – the first single page to embody the signatures of John, Paul, George and Ringo – and has been sold several times at auction.

29 George from interview by Roger Scott, US radio syndication, 15 October 1987. (Pete has said 'twice' in all his interviews and books.)

30 Ibid.

31 Ringo and George related this memory in a 1994 conversation filmed for *The Beatles Anthology* TV series (not used, but included on the bonus DVD).

32 *The Beatles Anthology*, p39. Bass player Lu Walters had left the Hurricanes to go on tour with the Seniors; Bobby Thompson left the Dominoes to replace him. Such movement was commonplace among the groups.

33 Fee and box office information from the accounts of Jaybee Clubs, which promoted at this venue. The company was jointly owned by Jack Fallon and Bill Fraser-Reid; the latter kindly provided details to me in 1984.

34 Author interview, 7 February 2005.

35 'The leather suits' from song-by-song notes typed by John Lennon for his LP *Rock 'n' Roll*, spring 1975.

36 Author interviews – Farrell, 26 May 2004; Houghton, 10 September 2007.

37 19 April 1962.

38 Letter to Kathy Burns, 26 April 1977.

39 *The Beatles – The True Beginnings*, p159.

27: 'He could easily have been *the* Beatle' (10–13 April 1962)

1 *Liverpool Echo*, 14 April 1962; *Prescot & Huyton Reporter*, 20 April 1962. There were further *Echo* pieces on the 16th and 18th and a death notice on the 13th.
2 Author interview, 11 August 2004.
3 Interview by Mike Ledgerwood, *Disc and Music Echo*, 7 November 1970.
4 *Hamburg Days*, p140.
5 *The Beatles Anthology*, p69.
6 Interview by Mike Read, 13 October 1987, for BBC Radio 1. By 'his sister' Paul meant Pauline; Joyce Sutcliffe has remained private.
7 *Disc and Music Echo*, 7 November 1970.
8 *Hamburg Days*, p138.
9 *Shout!*, p141. Among those who doubted Philip Norman's conclusion was Pauline Sutcliffe, Stuart's younger sister. In April 1990, when Kevin Howlett and I interviewed her for a BBC radio documentary series, she said, 'The connection of Stuart's brain haemorrhage with being beaten up at a Beatles gig is a weak theory. The interval between the two would suggest there was no significance.' She also dismissed outright the very theory she herself would advance eleven years later, in her third book about her brother (*The Beatles' Shadow: Stuart Sutcliffe & His Lonely Hearts Club*, Sidgwick & Jackson, London, 2001, p134), that John had so viciously kicked Stuart in a fight that it led to his death.
10 *Liverpool Echo*, 13 April 1962; *Prescot & Huyton Reporter*, 20 April 1962.
11 Interview by Nik Cohn, *Observer*, 8 September 1968.
12 Author interview, 11 March 2006.
13 Davies, p114.
14 Author interview, 29 March 2006.
15 Interview by Mike Ledgerwood, *Disc and Music Echo*, 7 November 1970.

28: You Better Move On (13 April–2 June 1962)

1 Author interview, 29 March 2006.
2 Pete Best letter sold at Sotheby's, 14 September 1995. Letter from John to Cynthia first illustrated in *John Winston Lennon*, by Ray Coleman (Sidgwick & Jackson, London, 1984), pp165–8.
3 Roy Young says Brian Epstein came to him one day and said the Beatles wondered if he'd help them get a recording deal in England. Young replied that he couldn't because he'd just signed a year-long contract with Manfred Weissleder and was unable to leave Hamburg. It's unclear what this help would have been, since Young's own agreement with Philips had expired and (apart from one 45 on Ember) he himself was out of contract, which was why he was happy to take the work in Hamburg. The conversation has been interpreted by some as an invitation for Young to join the Beatles; mostly, he has been careful not to claim this. The idea isn't credible – they liked him, but didn't want to become a five-piece group with a 'name' pianist/singer, someone not from Liverpool and so much older (born London, 1934).
4 *"Mach Schau!"*, p88.
5 *Let The Good Times Roll!*, pp100–1.
6 *Fifty Years Adrift*, p96.
7 The 1961 recordings were still dribbling out in different parts of the world. The Beatles' first record in America, and also Canada, My Bonnie c/w The Saints, was issued the same day they heard about Stuart's death, 11 April. They were unaware of it and would have been bemused to see themselves on Decca, the label that had so recently turned them down in England. Actually, the two Decca companies had separated years earlier, and because 'American Decca' (as it was known in Britain) had a tie-up with both Bert Kaempfert and Deutsche Grammophon, it landed the master tape as a matter of routine. The repeat of the original German credit, to Tony Sheridan and the Beat Brothers, indicates the absence of consultation with Brian Epstein in this North American release. The single was listed in *Billboard* and reviewed relatively positively in *Cash Box* (issues dated 28 April), although kind words were

found for most records. The placing was more relevant – such mentions were way down among the small print. There was little prospect of either side getting airplay and even less chance of the record selling, which is precisely what happened: it came out and it sank.

At this same time in Germany, Deutsche Grammophon issued Tony Sheridan's debut album, *My Bonnie*. The cover photo – Sheridan on a bicycle, a guitar slung across his back – was taken by Astrid in November 1961. (Stuart was there and can be seen in outtakes.) The album was credited to Tony Sheridan and the Beat Brothers, and the Beatles play on just two of the twelve tracks (the title number and The Saints), their proper name specified on the back cover. The 3 May issue of *Mersey Beat* mentioned the LP and said 'copies will soon be available in Liverpool' – this information was provided by Brian Epstein, who imported copies to sell at Nems.

8　The document is reproduced on p28 of the book that accompanies the definitive CD boxed-set *The Beatles With Tony Sheridan: Beatles Bop – Hamburg Days*, and on p135 of an earlier work by the same author (Hans Olof Gottfridsson), *The Beatles: From Cavern To Star-Club* (Premium Publishing, Stockholm, 1997). It also appears in *The Beatles: Fact And Fiction 1960–1962*, p157, with the most plausible interpretation on p149.

9　Recorded in Number 2 studio at EMI on 22 December 1961, The Hole In The Ground was composed by Ted Dicks (music) and Myles Rudge (lyric), not Tin Pan Alley tunesmiths but writers of stage revue numbers – they said in interviews how George Martin kept sending them away to come up with 'the right song'. An LP (*A Combination Of Cribbins*) finally flowered in November 1962.

10　*NME* headline, 6 April 1962; *Disc* quote, 14 April 1962. By 'we' George Martin was including the song's musical arranger, the pianist Tommy Watt. The Radiophonic Workshop was a division of the BBC, based at Maida Vale Studios, a mile from EMI Studios in St John's Wood. Inventive sounds made by brilliant minds, all for the £4 annual licence fee the press encouraged everyone to grumble about.

11　As George didn't write lyrics, he co-composed the *Take Me Over* title song with Paul McDowell of the Temperance Seven. The lyric of the *Crooks Anonymous* title song – called I Must Resist Temptation – was written by the same band's Brian Innes while the music was co-written by George Martin and Muir Mathieson. It was sung by actor Leslie Phillips and issued as a Parlophone single in May 1962.

12　'I had always been very envious of Norrie Paramor,' George Martin volunteered in *All You Need Is Ears*, p120; 'I was frankly jealous of the seemingly easy success other people were having with such acts, in particular Norrie Paramor,' he added in *Summer Of Love: The Making Of Sgt Pepper* (with William Pearson, Macmillan, London, 1994), p130. 'I did envy Norrie Paramor enormously,' George told his son Giles Martin in the 25 April 2011 BBC2 *Arena* documentary *Produced By George Martin*. 'Did you want to beat [better] Norrie Paramor?' Giles asked. 'Yes. He drove an E-Type Jag,' George replied, laughing at the memory.

13　*David Frost – An Autobiography: Part One – From Congregations To Audiences* (HarperCollins, London, 1993), pp40/49.

14　Author interview, 31 August 2000.

15　*All You Need Is Ears*, p179.

16　Author interview, 31 August 2000.

17　George earned well from Dr Kildare's chart success: he composed its B-side, The Midnight Theme, under his usual pseudonym Graham Fisher.

18　Author interview, 24 August 2011. The speaker didn't wish to be identified out of respect.

19　Wood (1910–2001) died without being asked about this.

20　Author interview, 28 July 2003.

21　Author interview, 16 May 2005; Richards from author interview, 2 August 2007.

22　This technique of light and shade management in a monochrome picture was taught to Astrid by her employer, Reinhart Wolf. It has the technical name chiaroscuro, from the Italian for 'clear' and 'dark', and is also written as *clair-obscur*, from the French.

23　John wrote this when appending a Beatles publicity booklet, 1971. Astrid from author interview, 11 March 2006. In a letter to his brother Mike, started on 9 May, Paul broke the news that he'd bought him a new camera, as a gift. 'I've ordered a Rollei. Exactly the same as Astrid's! It's dear but it's a fab one. You'll give me a go of it, won't you?'

24　Author interview, 3 May 1994.

25　Author interview, 11 October 2010.

26 Letter quoted in *Stuart: The Life And Art Of Stuart Sutcliffe*, p215, and another held in a private collection.

27 Author interview, 27 August 2005.

28 Letter sold at auction by Sotheby's, London, on 12 September 1988; 'good turkin' ground' from *Beatle!*, p156.

29 *"Mach Schau!"*, pp77–8.

30 Author interview, 26 November 2005.

31 Author interview, 18 March 2006; Pete from *Beatle!*, p157; Bettina from *Monographien: Damals In Hamburg*, ARD (West German television), 6 January 1967.

32 Alistair Taylor's wife had asthma and she was advised to leave damp north-west England – they moved to London and he got a job with Pye Records. He handed in his notice to Clive Epstein while Brian was with the Beatles in Hamburg; on his return, Brian was so distraught at losing his PA, at this of all times, that he physically shoved Taylor out of his office.

33 Neil Aspinall didn't go to Hamburg when the Beatles played the clubs, he always remained at home.

34 False claims have been made for so many aspects of the Beatles' story and there are at least three fabrications of how they came to get the EMI contract. For the record, Brian Epstein didn't bribe George Martin; he didn't threaten EMI with not stocking its product at Nems if the Beatles weren't signed; and Paul Murphy, a solo singer from Liverpool, signed (as Paul Rogers) to HMV by Wally Ridley in 1960, didn't put in a word on the Beatles' behalf – or, if he did, it didn't make George Martin sign them. (Murphy would surface in Hamburg in 1963–4 and produce Tony Sheridan's records; he also went on to have legal tussles with the Beatles.)

35 A *Cellarful Of Noise*, p12.

36 Told by Best to Hunter Davies in 1967 (see Davies' Beatles biography, p140). Letters written by George to fans a few days later indicate the Beatles knew much more – specifically that they had a contract with Parlophone, and their first recording session was on 6 June. They'd also been informed (presumably in a letter from Brian) of their second BBC broadcast, to be taped days after getting home.

37 A *Cellarful Of Noise*, pp64–5. *Beatles Book* magazine (issue 6, January 1964) quotes two telegrams – WATCH OUT ELVIS and (from John) HOW SOON SHALL WE BE MILLIONAIRES – from information given by the Beatles in August 1963, though the journalist wasn't necessarily seeking verbatim recollections.

38 'I think I had something to do with the middle,' John said of Love Me Do in his interview by Mike Hennessey, *Record Mirror*, 2 October 1971.

39 Interview by Chris Roberts, 21 December 1963.

40 First part from 1979 interview by Spencer Leigh; second from video interview by Jim Ladd, 1982.

41 First sentence from interview by Mike Hennessey, *Record Mirror*, 2 October 1971; second from interview by David Sheff, 24 September 1980, for *Playboy*. Paul wasn't the only listener mistakenly to think Soldier Boy was written in the form of a letter. Actually, the girl sings to her boy in person, before his leaving.

42 Letter written to *IT*, issue 155 (31 May–14 June 1973).

43 Interview by Tony Fletcher, *Jamming*, issue 14, 1983. A floor-plan of the apartment shows a toilet next to the Beatles' room, and Paul's assertion 'the papers picked it up, and it went from being a joke to being a fact' isn't wrong but is time-leaping – the incident went unreported, only becoming 'a story' much later.

44 *The Beatles Anthology*, p78.

45 *Beatle!*, p158. Great purple prose from Patrick Doncaster.

46 Author interview, 6 November 2007.

47 Interview by Peter McCabe and Robert D. Schonfeld, September 1971.

48 Best from *Beatle!*, p158; Fascher from interview by Johnny Beerling, January 1972, for BBC Radio 1.

49 Interview by Peter McCabe and Robert D. Schonfeld, September 1971. A month later, John told it the same way to interviewer Takahiko Iimura: 'A group was playing in Hamburg and they invited me to go and play with them. And rather than just get up and sing one of my songs I went on in underpants, in a toilet seat, and played a drum solo.'

Paul told Chris Welch of *Melody Maker* (11 February 1973), 'In Hamburg one week Tony Sheridan's drummer got sick and I drummed for him, and for the extra cash, for a week.'

Accurate placement of this is difficult, but (even though the Star-Club pay sheets show no such addition) it was probably late in this spring 1962 season.

50 Interviews by Spencer Leigh.

51 First and third sentences from interview by Spencer Leigh (*Now Dig This*, March 2001); second from *Beatles Gear*, p64. Quote re. Pete Best from interview by Tony Copple of the Ottawa Beatles Site, http://beatles.ncf.ca/roy.html

52 *A Cellarful Of Noise*, p64.

53 Ringo recollections from Davies, p157, *The Beatles Anthology*, p39, and miscellaneous sources.

54 *Mersey Beat*, 19 April 1962.

55 *Liverpool Echo*, 16 May 1962.

56 Vicky Woods' account of six weeks with Ringo, Rory and the other Hurricanes would be interesting to hear, but attempts to trace her have been unsuccessful so far.

57 Mike's photo is in *Remember*, p111. Jerry Lee's wife Myra, now 17, accompanied her husband to Liverpool. They'd lost their three-year-old son in a drowning accident less than a month before. Wooler's 'nearly four thousand' from *Mersey Beat*, 31 May 1962.

58 Interview by Scott Muni, WNEW-FM, 13 February 1975; *Disc*, 7 July 1962.

59 Don Arden had been with John Lennon once before – when Arden introduced the Quarry Men on stage in a Liverpool amateur talent show in 1957. It's unlikely either remembered the other from this.

60 From interview by Spencer Leigh. Vincent had served in the US Navy, 1952–5, before the motor-bike accident that shattered his left leg and left him disabled.

61 *Fifty Years Adrift*, p96. It's also told well by George in *The Beatles Anthology*, p69. The incident was at the Grandhotel Monopol, Reeperbahn 48–52, still there today. Paul has related essentially the same anecdote in interviews, saying he was present too.

62 Interview by Peter McCabe and Robert D. Schonfeld, September 1971.

63 Davies, p140.

29: **Under Marching Orders** (2–6 June 1962)

1 Davies, p132.

2 As told by Paul McCartney to author, 19 May 1987.

3 The three medley songs are similar in tempo and can be stitched together relatively easily with a touch of vari-speed software, using recordings by the Beatles, Shirelles and Buddy Knox. One method takes the opening forty-seven seconds of Besame Mucho, the opening fifty-seven seconds of Will You Love Me Tomorrow and the last fifty-nine seconds of Open, the whole piece running 2.43.

4 Paul from interview 28 October 1964 by Jean Shepherd for *Playboy*, February 1965; John from interview 11 March 1975 by Bob Harris for *Old Grey Whistle Test*, BBC2, 18 April 1975.

5 *Many Years From Now*, p100.

6 19 May 1962.

7 Article by acclaimed jazz journalist Max Jones, 25 August 1962.

8 Author interview, 31 August 2000.

9 Author interview, 23 September 2003.

10 Author interview, 23 January 1987.

11 Author interview, 19 May 1987. The 'big white studio sight-screens' were 'swing-out screens', allowing flexible control over the acoustics. Another distinctive feature in Number 2 studio was the long padded quilts (ceiling to floor, almost) full of eelgrass – like seaweed – designed to absorb sound.

12 Author interviews – Smith, 26 January 1987; Townsend, 22 January 1987. Unless otherwise stated, all other Smith and Townsend quotes in this chapter are from these interviews. The ages of the day's key EMI personnel were: George Martin, 36; Ron Richards, 33; Norman Smith, 39; Ken Townsend, 29.

13 It would *always* be claimed that the Beatles were contracted to EMI as a result of 'passing the audition' on 6 June. Not so, but this easy obfuscation would slip successfully into every telling of the Beatles' story and convince even its participants.

14 Author interview, 18 January 1987.

15 Author interview, 9 June 1995. George Martin picked Hootin' Blues for Parlophone in 1953 – it was by Sonny Terry and Brownie McGhee though actually credited to the Sonny Terry Trio.

George also made harmonica records of his own, notably with Tommy Reilly and Max Geldray. In February 1963, John Lennon named Sonny Terry as his 'favourite instrumentalist' in an *NME* questionnaire. This was probably a recent infatuation because there's no indication of such appreciation before this. Chris Neal quote from author interview, 29 January 1987; George Martin's disinterest in the Beatles' Besame Mucho told to the author by Paul McCartney, 19 May 1987.

16 Author interview, 19 May 1987.
17 Pete Best from author interview, 14 January 1987.
18 George Martin from Davies, p168; George Harrison from *The Beatles Anthology*, p70; Paul from interview by Mike Read, 13 October 1987, for BBC Radio 1; Smith from author interview, 26 January 1987.
19 Author interview, 31 August 2000.
20 Interview by Mike Read, 13 October 1987, for BBC Radio 1.
21 *The Beatles Anthology*, p70.
22 *The Beatles: The Days In Their Life*, 1981 Canadian radio series, part 1.
23 Best from *Beatle!*, p163; Smith from author interview, 16 May 2005.
24 Paul (in author interview, 19 May 1987) said George Martin told everyone his opinion of Pete's drumming, but not Pete himself. Pete 'almost surly' from George Martin interview by Richard Williams, *Melody Maker*, 21 August 1971.
25 *Mersey Beat*, 31 May; *Melody Maker*, 21 December 1963.
26 Author interview, 31 August 2000.
27 Author interview, 9 June 1995.

30: **The Undesirable Member** (7 June–18 August 1962)

1 Author interview, 10 September 2007.
2 Interview by David Sheff, 24 September 1980, for *Playboy* – for which a transcription error turned 'eiderdown' into 'eyelet'.
3 Ibid.
4 Author interviews – Ness, 29 October 2004; Steen, 12 June 2005. Paul's involvement in refining Please Please Me doesn't alter the fact that John composed it solo – a point he was eager to make in a postcard sent to *Melody Maker* (reproduced in the 28 August 1971 issue): 'I wrote Please Please Me alone. It was recorded in the exact sequence in which I wrote it.'
5 The BBC's daily 'Audience Barometer' reported a listening audience of 3.7 per cent for this *Here We Go*, about 1,813,000. The figure was well down on the Beatles' previous broadcast but that first show went out on a cold Thursday afternoon in March and this second one a bright warm Friday afternoon in June.
6 The BBC's internal-use 'programme-as-broadcast' report for the 15 June *Here We Go* was the first time the songwriting credit 'Lennon, McCartney' was put into print. Ask Me Why was mostly John's song, so 'Lennon, McCartney' confirms both the 50:50 partnership and Brian Epstein's projection of it – he provided the information to Peter Pilbeam. The song went down as 'MSS' – meaning *manuscript*, naturally copyright but not yet published.
7 *Beatle!*, p149. 'They're thinking of getting rid of you' appears in *Shout!*, p149.
8 Interview by Tony Fletcher, *Jamming*, issue 14, 1983.
9 Davies, p143; George from evidence given at the Royal Courts of Justice, London, 6 May 1998.
10 From the raw transcripts of interviews for his autobiography *A Cellarful Of Noise*.
11 Ibid.
12 Document in the Epstein files.
13 Interview by Mike Read, 13 October 1987, for BBC Radio 1.
14 The Beatles' album *Live At The BBC* includes 1963 recordings of Soldier Of Love, Don't Ever Change and many other songs mentioned in these pages.
15 Author interview, 21 June 2007.
16 Interview by Stuart Colman, *Echoes*, BBC Radio London, 17 June 1984.
17 Author interview, 19 January 2008.
18 Author interview, 29 October 2004.
19 Stage shot, *Remember*, p75. The advertised picture of John, Paul and George with the Anglia is best seen in *Remember*, p95, preceded and followed by outtakes. The photo of John and Paul with Gene Vincent, all three of them looking cool in leather jackets, is the frontispiece in

Remember. Published photos of Paul and Jim McCartney in the back garden at 20 Forthlin Road were taken earlier the same day, Sunday 1 July.

20 Mike McCartney quote from interview by Evert Vermeer, *Beatles Unlimited* magazine, issue 75 (September/October 1987). These 'make me look famous' photos are dotted around Mike's photographic books. Liverpool handkerchief from interview by Peter Doggett, *Beatles Book* magazine, issue 199 (November 1992).

Mike was employed at André Bernard – upstairs at Ranelagh House, opposite Lewis's and the Great Charlotte Street branch of Nems, just along from Blackler's where George had worked. He was called Peter (his true first name) because there was already a Michael, and his colleagues included two other likely lads who would become big stars – Jimmy Tarbuck (John Lennon's primary school nemesis) and Lewis Collins. In his 9 May letter to Mike, sent from Hamburg, Paul said of the hairdressing job, 'It's gear about André Bernards cos you can start earning good money if you like it. I don't know why I said that, maybe it's because I used to fancy doing it too.'

21 Author interview, 2 May 1991.

22 *Beatles Gear*, pp66–8. Everything one could wish to know about Vox amplifiers, including the Beatles' long-term use of them, is in *Vox Amplifiers: The JMI Years*, by Jim Elyea (The History For Hire Press, Los Angeles, 2008); Beatles chapter, pp570–611.

23 Author interview, 20 February 2004.

24 Author interview, 30 June 2003.

25 Interview by Spencer Leigh.

26 Author interview, 4 March 2008.

27 The wedding was 30 June 1962; Leach's premature *Echo* ad ran on 5 July.

28 Author interview, 20 July 2006.

29 Mal Evans quote from unpublished manuscript.

30 *Mike Mac's White And Blacks Plus One Colour*, p16. Joe Brown quote from interview by Spencer Leigh.

31 Author interview, 18 March 2005. Bobby Graham was really Robert Neate (1940–2009).

32 Interview by Spencer Leigh – one of very few Hutchinson has done. He doesn't like talking about this part of his life, and despises talking about the Beatles. An interview approach for this book was rejected out of hand. John Lennon quote from interview by Paul Drew, US radio, April 1975: 'There were the Big Three and Rory Storm and the Hurricanes and the two best drummers were in those groups. Ringo was the second best drummer in Liverpool.' 'Berdzerk' from Paul McCartney interview by Mike Read, 13 October 1987, for BBC Radio 1.

33 In the midst of a 2007 lunch, Neil Aspinall casually told me that Paul once drove John in the Beatles' van to see Ringo in Skegness. This tied in with the quotes by Johnny Guitar and Vi Caldwell – but when asked for further details Neil said he'd talk about it another time and then passed away before it could happen.

In 2011, during the writing of this book, I asked Paul about it, who emailed in reply, 'I have a vague recollection of the story you mention so I suppose it is true but, quite honestly, I'm not all that clear on the details.' The following McCartney quote, while proving nothing, is interesting in this context. Talking in a 1986 interview about long-distance road travel, he said, 'When you were a kid, if you ever travelled four hours you would have reached Skegness and been at Butlin's.' (Paul had childhood holidays at Butlin's Pwllheli and Filey, never Skegness, and reached them by train; in 1962 he was 20.)

34 A Butlin's photographer took publicity shots of them in which Ringo is holding open the programme and they're looking at their own photograph. The Rock and Calypso Ballroom had finally shed the suffix added in anticipation of the craze that never came.

35 The 23 August *Mersey Beat*, which went to press no later than the 17th, indicated that a replacement drummer had been sought long enough for Rory to be 'inundated with applications'.

36 *Beatle!*, p165. 'Colonel Joe' from *Mersey Beat*, 3 May 1962; 'manager and producer' from his *Mersey Beat* ad, 26 July.

37 A *Twist Of Lennon*, p70; *John*, p120.

38 'Didn't fight it' from Davies, p159; 'make an honest womb of her' from 'Halbut Returb', *In His Own Write*, p71.

39 Cynthia from A *Twist Of Lennon*, p71; Dot from the invaluable website It's Only Love.

40 Author interview, 30 December 2011.

41 From Bill Harry essay in *The Literary Lennon,* by Dr James Sauceda (Pierian Press, Ann Arbor, MI, 1983), p148. The office move was one floor, from the top storey of 81a Renshaw Street to the middle.

42 Davies, p173; George Martin quote from author interview, 9 June 1995.

43 Author interview, 30 April 2002.

44 Interview by Nicky Campbell, BBC Radio 1, 19 November 1991.

45 Author interview, 19 May 1987.

46 Interview by Murray The K (Murray Kaufman), 28 August 1964, for WINS (New York radio). Ringo didn't mention the prior conversations that had brought him to this point.

47 Ringo says only Brian called him, not John: 'I don't remember John calling, which is in some-body's book' (*The Beatles Anthology* TV series). The call was first detailed in A *Cellarful Of Noise,* p70.

48 Interview by Spencer Leigh.

49 Davies, p142.

50 He was earning a little less than £50–60 a week at this time.

51 Interview by Spencer Leigh.

52 Author interview, 21 June 2007.

53 *It's Love That Really Counts: The Billy Kinsley Story,* by Spencer Leigh (Cavern City Tours, Liverpool, 2010), p40.

54 Interview by Spencer Leigh.

55 Author interview, 21 June 2007.

56 Ibid.

57 Interview by Spencer Leigh.

58 Nothing is known about this session beyond the fact that it happened. Another rehearsal was photographed two days later.

59 The Beatles' first appearance here was 7 July 1962 – coincidentally, Ringo's 22nd birthday.

60 Author interview, 21 June 2007. Ringo addressed this in *The Beatles Anthology,* p72, prefacing his quote with the words 'A light-hearted side note'. According to Neil, it was never light-hearted and never a side note: Ringo took it as a snub and didn't forget it.

61 Author interview, 27 August 2004; Hank Marvin from *Melody Maker,* 5 May 1962.
     Ringo's friend Dave 'Jamo' Jamieson recorded some of the show. 'I had a little Philips reel-to-reel recorder, stuck it on the table and let it run. It recorded some of the Four Jays' and quite a few of the Beatles' numbers. A little while later I sold it and all the tapes to my next-door neighbour, and when the Beatles became really big I went back and he'd taped Slim Whitman over it.' (Author interview, 12 August 2004.)

62 Author interview, 5 July 2007.

63 Evidence given at the Royal Courts of Justice, London, 6 May 1998.

64 Author interview, 21 June 2007.

31: **Some Other Guy** (19 August–4 October 1962)

1 WPLJ-FM, 9 June 1971.

2 Author interviews – Liz Tibbott-Roberts, 11 June 2005; Joan McCaldon, 25 November 2005; Beryl Johnson, 4 August 2005; Margaret Chillingworth, 8 June 2005; Thelma Wilkinson, 29 August 2005; Margaret Kelly, 25 November 2005. Mal Evans and 'others' from Davies, p143.

3 John from interview by Paul Drew, US radio, April 1975. First Paul from Davies (1985), p471; second from interview by Richard Williams, for *The Times,* 28 December 1981.

4 Interview by Spencer Leigh.

5 Wooler from *The Best Of Fellas,* p168.

6 Interview by Tom Hibbert, *Q,* June 1992.

7 Author interviews – Chillingworth, 8 June 2005; Murphy, 1 July 2006.

8 Sue Wright later became Sue Johnston, the TV and film actor. Aged 18 at this time, she was a lunchtime Cavernite and Beatles fan who worked as a shop assistant in the Whitechapel branch of Nems. Her interview by Spencer Leigh. Author interviews with Sandra Marshall (17 February 1999), Marie Guirron (30 December 2011) and Elsa Breden (9 June 2005).

9 Author interview, 30 June 2003.

10 *Beatle!,* p172.

11 'You're too young!' from *Lennon*, by Ray Coleman (2000 edition), p282; vow of non-atten-
    dance from *A Twist Of Lennon*, p73; John's words to Mimi, Davies, p159.
12 'To have and to harm, till death duty part' from 'Nicely Nicely Clive', *In His Own Write*, p56.
    Details of the wedding from *A Twist Of Lennon*, pp74–8.
13 Davies, p159; '. . . and a wife to boot' from 'Sad Michael', *In His Own Write*, p35.
14 Interview by Chris Hutchins, *NME*, 19 February 1965.
15 Author interview, 29 October 2004. Lindy Ness makes no extravagant claims for John's
    'Norwegian wood' comment, but swears it's true. She doesn't know if it had any bearing on
    John writing a song of that name three years later, but as soon as her friend Marie Guirron
    (George's girlfriend in summer 1962) heard it, in December 1965, she was certain John had
    Lindy in mind. No interviewer ever asked John to explain his song's title.
16 Author interview, 2 May 1991.
17 Author interview, 6 September 2010, and emails 29 August 2010 and 28 February 2012.
18 Author interview, 30 December 2011.
19 Author interview, 13 February 1997.
20 *The Beatles Anthology*, p163.
21 Interview by Ray Coleman, *Melody Maker*, 14 November 1964.
22 *The Beatles Anthology*, p73; 'got over it', p72. It seems to have lasted about three months, as
    far as November 1962.
23 Author interview, 28 May 2004.
24 *Melody Maker*, 25 December 1965.
25 Author interview, 21 June 2007.
26 *Love Me Do! The Beatles' Progress*, p37.
27 Author interview, 30 December 2011.
28 Interview by Colin Irwin, *Melody Maker*, 1 April 1978.
29 Interview by Paul du Noyer, *Paul McCartney World Tour* programme (1989–90), p37.
30 Interview by Ray Connolly, *Evening Standard* (London), 24 February 1968.
31 Interview by Mike Read, 13 October 1987, for BBC Radio 1; '. . . the face won't smile' from
    interview by Larry Kane, 20 August 1965.
32 *Beatles Book* magazine, issue 3 (October 1963).
33 *The Beatles Anthology*, p266.
34 *The Beatles Anthology*, p86; 'three-and-one' from interview by Horst Königstein, Hamburg, 29
    September 1976, for *Ringo und die Stadt am Ende des Regenbogen* (*Ringo And The City At The
    End Of The Rainbow*), West German NDR-TV, 9 and 16 June 1977.
35 Author interview, 18 July 2006. Flynn himself is unavailable for comment: he died of cancer
    in 1971, aged 27. 'Bugger off' from *The Beatles Anthology* TV series; Paul from author inter-
    view, 19 May 1987. Dedicated George fan Sue Houghton agrees: 'I never thought his black
    eye was anything to do with Pete Best, it was somebody's jealous boyfriend.' Mike Berry, who
    shared a Cavern bill with the Beatles on Sunday 26 August, remembers George saying he'd
    been 'nutted' by a man jealous because his girlfriend had taken a shine to him. Other wit-
    nesses claim, variously, that it was Paul, not George, who cussed at the hecklers in the
    audience; that John fought to protect George; that when George returned to the stage for
    the Beatles' second lunchtime set John and Paul were in hysterics and kept calling him
    'Teddy Boy!'; or that when George *didn't* return to the stage with them John announced it
    was because he was 'feeling a little bit *aye*'. It's Billy Kinsley who maintains the Beatles car-
    ried on as a trio – he says they played songs that didn't need lead guitar, including a number
    his group the Mersey Beats often did, I'll Never Let You Go (Little Darlin'), one of Elvis's
    great Sun records.
36 *The Beatles Anthology* TV series.
37 Author interview, 21 June 2007.
38 The photo dominated the front page of the 20 September *Mersey Beat*, where Brian's report
    was given the headline 'BEATLES RECORD FOR EMI story inside'. Below this was a display ad for
    Nems' three stores: 'We are now accepting orders for the Beatles first record on Parlophone.'
39 Author interview, 9 June 1995.
40 Interview by Elliot Mintz, 18 April 1976. George Martin comment from *All You Need Is Ears*,
    p130; Paul from *The Beatles Anthology*, p90.
41 Davies, p169.

42 Grateful thanks to Kevin Ryan, co-author of *Recording The Beatles*, for carefully analysing and explaining the technical procedure used at this session.

43 Interview by Richard Williams, *Melody Maker*, 21 August 1971. The *NME* chart current at the time of this Beatles session had two harmonica records – I Remember You by Frank Ifield at number 1, Sealed With A Kiss by Brian Hyland at 6.

44 Interview by Jann S. Wenner, 8 December 1970, for *Rolling Stone*. Ringo's support expressed eloquently in *The Beatles Anthology*, p77.

45 Interview by Richard Williams, *Melody Maker*, 21 August 1971. In an interview by Robert W. Morgan (US radio, circa 1982), George Martin again said it was John who went to see him.

46 Interview by Paul Drew, US radio, April 1975.

47 Interview by Nicky Campbell, BBC Radio 1, 19 November 1991; 'quite forceful' sentence from author interview, 19 May 1987.

48 Interview by Keith Skues, BBC Radio 1, 2 November 1970.

49 From author interview with Kim Bennett, 27–28 July 2003.

50 Part information from Dick James interview by Johnny Beerling, early 1972, for BBC Radio 1.

51 White was 32, based in London but raised in Glasgow and speaking with a Scots accent. He was a busy session player who drummed on a range of records across the labels, notably on Jack Good's sessions for Decca. Good used him on Billy Fury's fine 1960 album *The Sound Of Fury* and put him on TV in *Boy Meets Girls*. The Beatles had watched that, and also seen *Drumbeat*, a short-lived 1959 BBC-tv series where White was in the house band; Paul had also watched him drum with the Vic Lewis Orchestra when, as a short-trouser schoolboy, he went to see Bill Haley in 1957. The Beatles might even have seen White's photo in the *Liverpool Echo*, on the occasion of his recent (April) wedding to local singer Lyn Cornell. When White played this Beatles recording session, he and Cornell had just returned from honeymoon, delayed by his nightly employment in the pit orchestra of *Stop The World – I Want To Get Off*, Anthony Newley's London stage musical bound for Broadway.

52 *The Beatles Anthology*, p76; 'highly upset' from interview for Earth News Radio, May 1978.

53 Author interview, 23 September 2003.

54 Author interview, 18 January 1987.

55 Ringo from *The Beatles Anthology* TV series.

56 Interview 28 August 1963 for *The Mersey Sound* (BBC-tv, 9 October 1963).

57 *The Beatles Anthology*, p96. Paul's reference to 'walking up past Woolton Church with John' is an intriguing one. They weren't particularly prone to nostalgia, so it's curious that when discussing what amounted to going into business together, they were at the place of their first meeting, five years on – the only time they're known to have gone back.

58 Interview by Alan Freeman, BBC Radio 1, 6 December 1974.

59 John's microphone antics remembered by Lindy Ness.

60 Author interview, 30 September 1987; 'failed attempt at a single' – *Many Years From Now*, p83.

61 Interview by Raoul Pantin, *Trinidad Express*, 4 May 1971.

62 King Curtis was also credited as the song's composer, but it's likely that Holly was its true author.

63 Author interview, 30 June 2003.

64 Author interview, 26 March 2003.

65 Author interview, 10 June 2005. Chadwick was 23 and had studied graphic design at Liverpool College of Art, two years ahead of John Lennon and one ahead of Stuart Sutcliffe. The Beatles' location shoot was on 28 September.

66 Around the end of August, Paul and Ringo had separate appointments with Les Chadwick at the Peter Kaye studio (top floor of 24 Newington – where an unsatisfactory group session also took place, on probably 20 September). The idea was that these images would match Astrid's classy half-shadow shots of John and George in Altona, Hamburg, in the spring – the ones John said 'made Paul mad with envy' – but the results were more like passport photos than arty portraits. Chadwick was a good photographer but chiaroscuro camera settings and lighting weren't an everyday requirement, on top of which his subjects were ill-at-ease. While John and George had been looking into the lens of someone for whom they'd deep affection, standing in the spot where their bandmate/close friend/her fiancée had just died, Paul and Ringo were in a Liverpool studio with a man they knew only a little, straining so hard not to smile that they ended up stern. Brian invited Harry Watmough to reshoot the session at his studio (top floor of 24 Moorfields) – 'He asked me to photograph them with half their faces in shadow,'

Watmough remembers, 'I did think they had some *strange* ideas' – but the results were no better. In the end, Chadwick's photos were used for the throwaway cards and Watmough's appeared on the cover of Introducing THE BEATLES, Tony Barrow's press release.

67 All documents in the Epstein files.

68 'I've never enjoyed playing so much' quote in *Mersey Beat*, 4 October 1962. *Echo* ad dates: 'Merseyside's biggest heartthrob!', 3 September 1962; 'Ex-Beatle', 19 September. Best rebuke to Flannery from interview by Spencer Leigh.

69 *Liverpool Echo*, 20 September 1962.

70 Interview by Spencer Leigh.

71 Author interview, 24 July 2007.

72 A *Cellarful Of Noise*, p110. Marshall (1926–2003) wrote about Publicity Ink in the Allan Williams autobiography he ghosted in 1975, *The Man Who Gave The Beatles Away* (pp222–3) – a book that indicates the kind of writer he was. Derek Taylor, who ghost-wrote *A Cellarful Of Noise*, also drank in the Press Club and knew and liked Marshall, describing him as 'perilously unpredictable' in *Fifty Years Adrift*, p250. Additional information from author interview with Allan Williams, 28 August 2006; he further says that Brian Epstein became a member of the Press Club and went there regularly. A contemporary example of what would have been Publicity Ink's stock-in-trade for the Beatles hit the *Daily Mirror* front page on 18 October 1962 – four columns in which Bill Marshall (without a byline) reported a stunt bull-fight staged by Allan Williams inside the Blue Angel night-club.

32: Friday 5 October 1962 – The Sixties Start Here

1 Interview by Mike Hennessey, *Record Mirror*, 20 March 1971.

2 Interview by Spencer Leigh.

3 Author interview, 9 June 2005.

4 *Scene And Heard*, BBC Radio 1, 25 March 1970. Final sentence from *The Beatles Anthology*, p77, and interview by Elliot Mintz, 18 April 1976.

5 Author interviews – Norman Jopling, 22 February 2006; Judith Simons, 7 July 2005.

6 *New Society*, 18 October 1962.

7 *The Beatles: The Days In Their Life*, 1981 Canadian radio series, part 2.

8 Interview by Spencer Leigh. Liverpool-born Alma Warren was really Alma Roza, younger sister of Decca's singing star Lita Roza, who was personally close to the Epstein family. Alma sang too, and George Martin signed her to Parlophone in 1954. She had a good voice but none of Lita's success, and after five Parlophone releases up to 1956, all produced by George Martin, she was most gainfully employed by EMI in 'exploitation'.

9 George from *The Beatles Anthology*, p77; Louise from Davies (1985), p19. She described the programme as late-night; the latest-scheduled EMI show on Radio Luxembourg was *Ray's On . . .*, presented by the London-based Canadian DJ Ray Orchard, Mondays to Fridays 11.30 to midnight. The likelihood that this show was the first to play Love Me Do is increased by John detailing it on a scribbled card he gave his Aunt Harrie at this time. (He also mentioned Sam Costa's EMI show, which Luxembourg aired every Tuesday evening.) The card is illustrated in *The John Lennon Letters* (edited by Hunter Davies, Weidenfeld & Nicolson, London, 2012), p59.

10 Both ran in *The World's Fair* on 6 October, the first by Mary Smith of Music Hire (Yorks) Ltd, the second by columnist Joe Bronkhorst. He called the Springfields 'very successful' but they hadn't yet done much in Britain – their main breakthrough at this time was in America. His reference to 'the now almost inevitable harmonica' was also something of a stretch, but after Hey! Baby, I Remember You and Sealed With A Kiss, it was easy for reviewers to intimate a trend.

11 *Disc*, 6 October; *New Record Mirror*, 13 October 1962.

12 *Mersey Beat*, 18 October 1962. Disker's review ran in *Liverpool Echo* on 29 September.

13 4 October 1962. 'A new group from the Liverpool area. Their first record but they already have a strong following and this seems to be the strongest outsider of the week.' (Rated three stars, meaning 'Possibly' in terms of hit potential.)

14 Interview by Los Angeles DJ Elliot Mintz, 18 April 1976.

15 Author interviews – Brown, 5 July 2007; Kelly, 28 March 2003.

16 Author interview, 6 December 2004.

17 A *Cellarful Of Noise*, p12. The Beatles did a record-shop signing session, their first, in Widnes on the Saturday, to capitalise on the fan base they'd created with several local performances; they signed at one – probably two – Widnes shops, and may also have done a signing session in Warrington. There's no known explanation for the Beatles *not* doing a Love Me Do signing session in Liverpool, not even at any of Nems' three stores.

18 Interview by Jim Steck, 26 August 1964. Final two sentences from interview 28 August 1963 for *The Mersey Sound* (BBC-tv, 9 October 1963).

19 Confirmation of the methodology of record chart compilation in Britain in this period comes from an array of senior sources, including John Fruin (EMI sales director), Brian Mulligan (EMI press office and founder/editor of *Record Business* magazine), Derek Johnson (*NME* chart compiler), Norman Jopling (*New Record Mirror*), Nigel Hunter (*Disc*) and John Mair (record distributor travelling salesman). Sight of an original 1962 *NME* chart return form confirms everything – it asked only a shop's bestselling records in ranked order, not sales figures. (The precise process by which *Billboard* and *Cash Box* compiled their charts at this time is explained well in *Record Makers And Breakers: Voices Of The Independent Rock 'n' Roll Pioneers*, by John Broven [University of Illinois Press, Urbana and Chicago, 2009], pp200–2.)

It's also unlikely EMI even *pressed* ten thousand copies of Love Me Do to begin with. It was easy to produce additional records to meet demand, and the initial 'stamper' run – for a debut act of no national renown, and a record EMI certainly wasn't supporting in any special way – would not have been great, probably no more than four thousand. EMI Archives has not retained its Hayes factory documentation that would prove the precise number, but this was standard form.

Some have not only published the hype story but embellished it. *Shout!* author Philip Norman put into print the extraordinary assertion by Joe Flannery (manager of Lee Curtis and the All Stars) that Paul McCartney told him Brian forced the Beatles to pay for the ten thousand records, an act so harsh that it temporarily reduced them to starving penury on the streets of London. A TV producer then allowed Flannery to assert his chart-falsification anecdote in a 'documentary' (*Love Me Do: The Beatles '62*, BBC4, 7 October 2012), where his comments were curiously reinforced by Liverpool musician Billy Kinsley. Such was the editorial desire to push this line, it was then claimed that Love Me Do only 'made a brief appearance at number 17 in the charts [and] dropped out after a couple of weeks'. Its actual chart life was eighteen weeks, October 1962 to February 1963 . . . but saying this would have sunk the story.

Some do have a need to say things, and most people swallow what they hear or read, but the time has come for this half-century-old smear to be definitively dismissed.

20 *Nuneaton Evening Telegraph*, 9 October 1992. The Beatles were the middle act on an advertised bill nominally headed by Buddy Britten and the Regents.

21 Rock and Roll Hall of Fame dinner, Waldorf-Astoria Hotel, New York, 20 January 1988.

22 Their line-up this night, 12 July, was Mick Jagger, Keith Richards, Elmo Lewis (Brian Jones), Dick Taylor, Ian 'Stu' Stewart and, probably, Tony Chapman on drums. They were supported by Long John Baldry's Kansas City Blue Boys. Two hundred miles north, the Beatles were playing the Majestic Ballroom, Birkenhead.

23 4 October 1962.

24 *No Direction Home: The Life And Music Of Bob Dylan*, by Robert Shelton (Beech Tree Books, New York, 1986), p152. The Beatles didn't hear Bob Dylan at this time. Paul had one folk LP, Joan Baez's first, issued in Britain in January 1962. Nearly thirty years later, in 1990, he recorded a strong cover of one of its tracks, the traditional All My Trials – which had exerted a minor influence on a song he wrote with John in 1963.

33: 'We've got it, and here we are with it' (6–31 October 1962)

1 Interview 28 October 1964 by Jean Shepherd for *Playboy*, February 1965.

2 John from interview by Jann S. Wenner, 8 December 1970, for *Rolling Stone*; Paul from interview by Janice Long, for *Listen To What The Man Says*, BBC Radio 1, 22 December 1985; George from *The David Frost Show* (American TV), 3 December 1971; Ringo from interview by Horst Königstein, Hamburg, 29 September 1976, for *Ringo und die Stadt am Ende des Regenbogen* (*Ringo And The City At The End Of The Rainbow*), West German NDR-TV, 9 and 16 June 1977. In late 1963, Paul told writer Michael Braun, 'As soon as people heard "Liverpool" they thought we were all from the docks with sideboards. And the name – practically every-

body who knew told us to change it. "Beatles? What does that mean?"' (*Love Me Do! The Beatles' Progress*, p31.)

3 Author interview, 1 October 2004. All Tony Calder quotes in this chapter are from here.

4 Interview by Ray Coleman, *Melody Maker*, 14 November 1964; last section from interview by Larry Kane, 2 September 1964.

5 Cliff Richard in *Liverpool Echo*, 22 September 1961; John from Sydney press conference, 11 June 1964; George from interview by Larry Kane, 8 September 1964.

6 Author interview, 1 June 2005. His *Mersey Beat* pieces ran in issues 1 and 15 November 1962.

7 Author interview, 2 February 2005. The *Pop Weekly* ad for Love Me Do was in the 6 October issue.

8 Craven House, 234–238 Edgware Road, the east side, close to where the Marylebone Road fly-over would be built (it opened in 1967).

9 Interview by Chris Welch, 11 February 1973.

10 John told Ray Coleman a year later (*Melody Maker*, 16 November 1963), 'People kept coming up and asking who the leader was. We said, "Nobody." They said, "There must be a boss," so the others said to me, "You started the whole thing, you're the leader."' No reminder was necessary, but here was Beatle policy-making in action.

11 He can only have been speaking of Please Please Me, a version of which they taped at EMI on 11 September; John might have thought that recording would be issued, or perhaps he simply meant the song would be their next release, but the decision was not his to take, and at the time he made this remark George Martin still intended to issue How Do You Do It as the Beatles' next record. John seemed quite sure that wouldn't be happening.

12 Interview by Andy Neill, 23 February 2007. Ian Samwell (1937–2003) was one of Cliff Richard's original backing group the Drifters. He wrote hits for many artists and was an important and successful producer.

13 Quoted in *Belmo's Beatleg News*, October/November 1989.

14 Capitol vice-president Alan W. Livingston was promoted to president in October 1962 in place of company co-founder Glenn E. Wallichs, head of Capitol before and beyond EMI's 1955 takeover.

15 Letter from Roland Rennie to Joseph Zerga, 11 December 1962. Formerly assistant to managing director L. G. Wood, Rennie had been promoted to manager of a new department, Licensed Repertoire. EMI was taking this business seriously.

16 Davies, p278.

17 *It's Love That Really Counts: The Billy Kinsley Story*, p54. La Scala Ballroom – Milan meets Runcorn, strictly in name only. John, Paul and George twice played here as Japage 3 in 1959, and Brian twice promoted the Beatles here in 1962.

18 'It wasn't *for* him [George] but soon as I'd written it I thought, "He could do this,"' John told *Playboy* interviewer David Sheff, 24 September 1980. John always claimed Do You Want To Know A Secret as his song, but Paul – in the 1997 book *Many Years From Now*, p95 – said it was 50:50. He also called it a 'hack song', implying it was written to order, but it was composed in a period when it wasn't actually needed for anything.

19 *Dream Boogie: The Triumph Of Sam Cooke*, by Peter Guralnick (Little, Brown, London, 2005), pp422–3.

20 Reviewer, Chris Hutchins; 12 October 1962. Sounds Incorporated were a six-piece instrumental group from Kent, with three saxes.

21 15 November 1962.

22 Ibid.

23 In his biography of Sam Cooke (p427), Peter Guralnick says Richard's constant writing in his big bible intrigued everyone on the nightly British tour. Don Arden sometimes took his children to the shows (David, nine, and Sharon, ten – later Sharon Osbourne, wife of Ozzy), and on one occasion David got to see it. Richard was writing a graphic sex diary in his bible, rating lovers for their skills. See also *The Life And Times Of Little Richard*, by Charles White (Omnibus Press, London, 2003), pp114–15. Mike McCartney from *Remember*, p108.

24 Author interview with Les Chadwick, 10 June 2005. Wooler taking bets described by Karl Terry in interview by Spencer Leigh. Pete and Beatles not exchanging a word or look from *Beatle!*, p175.

25 John from interview by Barbara Graustark, for *Newsweek*, September 1980. The autographed programme is illustrated in Davies (1985), p29.

There's also a second photo, in which Little Richard and the Beatles are joined by Derry Wilkie (Liverpool's original Little Richard-like singer) and two of Liverpool's only black group, the Shades; they were a vocal quintet, doo-wop style, and in November renamed themselves the Chants.

26 Interview by Mike Ledgerwood, *Disc and Music Echo*, 5 December 1970.

27 Interview by Peter McCabe and Robert D. Schonfeld, September 1971.

28 The Big Three interrupted Billy Kramer with the Coasters' set at a Nems Enterprises *Showdance* – see 13 November 1962 written apology from Brian Epstein to Ted Knibbs in *Let's Go Down The Cavern*, by Spencer Leigh (Vermilion, London, 1984), p131.

29 'Liverpool Today' by Nick Nye, 5 February 1963. Details from *Liverpool Echo*, 17 July, 18 July, 18 October, 25 October and 13 November 1962, and from *Sphinx*, Spring 1962. Unemployment in Greater London was 1.1 per cent of the population, on Merseyside 4.8, a figure of 29,602; 4449 local 'youths and girls' had no work. The Minister of Housing, Sir Keith Joseph, spent a day in Liverpool in July 1963 and toured the slum areas. One house he visited – in Upper Canning Street, Toxteth – had thirty-three occupants. Elizabeth 'Bessie' Braddock (1899–1970) was Labour MP for Liverpool Exchange, 1945–70, a remarkable woman and probably the British people's greatest ever Parliamentarian. Her slogan was 'When you need "Bessie" she'll be there', and she was.

30 Interview by Spencer Leigh; *Record Collector* magazine, issue 54 (February 1984), except 'it immediately got a laugh and at the end they all applauded', from interview by Colin Hall, *Shindig!* magazine, issue 8 (January–February 2009).

31 *Mersey Beat*, 11 June 1964. The Tenabeats supported the Beatles at Aintree Institute on 28 October 1961 and St John's Hall, Bootle, on 2 March 1962. Gorman from interview by Spencer Leigh.

32 Author interview, 4 November 2004.

33 *In His Own Write*, pp16–19. It's a fascinating piece, open to interpretation and full of such characteristic Lennon lines as 'Yea, though I wart through the valet of thy shadowy hut I will feed no norman.'

34 *A Twist Of Lennon*, p80, and *John*, p132.

35 *A Twist Of Lennon*, pp78–80.

36 *Liverpool Weekly News*, 11 October and 1 November 1962.

37 *A Twist Of Lennon*, p82.

38 Author interview, 29 October 2004.

39 Marie left Merseyside in 1963 ('Life wasn't the same with the Beatles gone') and went to London where she became a fixture of the music clubs. She bumped into Paul a couple of times, and in 1967 met the Moody Blues' Justin Hayward at the Bag O' Nails club. They married in 1970 and remain together.

40 Author interview, 24 April 2012. The first Bond film was *Dr No*, premiered at the London Pavilion cinema on Friday 5 October.

Thelma Monaghan went on to marry poet Roger McGough and have a flourishing career as a TV producer (among much else, she made the highly successful 1980s show *Blind Date*, with Cilla Black). Her son, Nathan Monaghan, aka Nathan McGough – two years old when she was dating Paul – became involved in the music industry and managed Happy Mondays and White Lies.

41 Author interview, 24 July 2004. All Iris Caldwell quotes in this chapter are from here. *Sing Along With Joe* played Liverpool Empire Monday 17 to Saturday 22 September. The Beatles were free two nights that week.

42 All Vi Caldwell quotes from interview by Johnny Beerling, January 1972, for BBC Radio 1.

43 Frank Ifield played Liverpool Empire from 1 to 6 October. The Beatles were free three nights that week.

44 From 'The Fingletoad Resort Of Teddiviscious', *In His Own Write*, p48. Another name John had for *People And Places* was *Peotle And Plaices*, and Granada presenter Bill Grundy was Big Grunty. The Sex Pistols had much worse names for him fourteen years later.

45 Domestic video recorders hadn't been invented and wouldn't begin to become commonplace until the end of the 1970s. The audio recording of the Beatles' first TV show was made by Adrian Killen, a 16-year-old fan in Kirkdale, Liverpool, on a reel-to-reel deck wired direct to the TV speaker, the tape running at 3¾ ips. (The recording is unissued, not in circulation, and now owned by the Beatles' Apple.) There are no photos to confirm Killen's 'almost certain' memory of the Beatles wearing uniform polo-neck jumpers for their TV debut instead of suits and ties.

46 Interview by Albert Goldman, *Charlie*, July 1971.
47 Author interview, 30 June 2003; George's 'Liverpool Leg' from author interview, 23 October 1987.
48 Author interview, 13 June 2005.
49 Author interview, 28 July 2003. All Kim Bennett quotes from this interview.
50 The broadcast date is unknown and the production files no longer exist, so it isn't clear if this was the *first* TV broadcast of Love Me Do, before the Beatles did it in person on *People And Places*, or a later one. Watson was an Australian, working in England for ATV. He was responsible for starting the company's long-running soap opera *Crossroads*, which starred *Lunch Box* 'hostess' Noele Gordon; he later returned to Australia and created *Prisoner* (aka *Prisoner: Cell Block H*) and *Neighbours*.
51 Brian Epstein blamed Kim Bennett for losing the *Saturday Club* airplay, but in time must have told the Beatles the bigger story, because two years later John said to an American interviewer, about Love Me Do, 'When they [Beatles fans] wrote in requests for it to radio programmes, they wouldn't play it because they thought it was a cheat – because all the requests came from Liverpool.' (Interview by Jim Steck, 26 August 1964.)
52 Rory story told by Vi Caldwell to BBC radio producer Johnny Beerling. 'She was just seventeen / She'd never been a beauty queen' from *Many Years From Now*, p93, and other places.
53 Author interview, 24 April 2012. Paul, for whatever reason, has never talked about this London trip, but it did happen.
54 Paul has told this a few times, with unique details. The quote is collated mostly from interviews by Alan Freeman (*Rock Around The World*, US syndicated radio show, 11 April 1976) and Mike Read (13 October 1987, for BBC Radio 1); the remainder is from an interview by David Jensen (Capital Radio, London, mid-August 1986).
55 Document in the Epstein files.
56 Quoted by Graham Knight, *New Record Mirror*, 10 November 1962. Little Richard further told Alan Smith (*Mersey Beat*, 15 November) that the photo of him and the Beatles was one of the most treasured souvenirs of his British visit. Brian Epstein had two enlargements made: the other hung on his office wall at 12–14 Whitechapel. The photo Little Richard said he wanted, in which he'd be flanked by Sounds Incorporated and the Beatles, never happened.
57 Davies, p33. Little Richard's return to gospel announced in *Disc*, 10 November 1962.
58 Ringo from Davies, p179, and from *Ringo Starr – Going Home*, Disney Channel, 18 April 1993. Wooler from interview by Johnny Beerling, 13 January 1972, for BBC Radio 1. He said Sounds Incorporated were the main problem, demanding more stage time, but – in spite of his exacting reputation – their manager Don Arden isn't likely to have been calling for the Beatles to be cut down or out: he knew the whole show was being staged by Brian Epstein for their benefit.
59 Wooler, ibid.
60 Wooler, ibid.; Freda Kelly from author interview, 28 March 2003.
61 Author interview, 25 November 2005. Douglas and the Beatles probably played five numbers, American hits he'd made into British hits: Only Sixteen (his biggest, a 1959 number 1); A Teenager In Love; Pretty Blue Eyes; Oh, Lonesome Me (his latest record); and When My Little Girl Is Smiling (written by Goffin-King). Craig Douglas was really Terence Perkins, born on the Isle of Wight in 1941.
62 Author interview, 6 November 2007.
63 They performed Love Me Do and A Taste Of Honey for the 2 November edition of *People And Places*, seen by a similar number to their debut, around two million. Though recorded for broadcast, the studio video tape was wiped and reused – common practice at British TV companies in this period. Adrian Killen made an off-air audio recording of A Taste Of Honey only, not in circulation and owned now by the Beatles' company Apple.

34: 'Show me I'm wrong' (1–15 November 1962)

1 Davies, p179; last section from interview by Peter McCabe and Robert D. Schonfeld, September 1971.
2 *The Beatles Anthology*, p78.
3 *The Life And Times Of Little Richard*, p116.
4 *Memories Of John Lennon* (edited by Yoko Ono, HarperCollins, New York, 2005), pp219–20.
5 Billy Preston interviews by Ben Fong-Torres, *Rolling Stone*, 16 September 1971, and Mike

Ledgerwood, *Disc and Music Echo*, 8 February 1969; John from interview by Scott Muni, WNEW-FM, 13 February 1975.

6 Letter to London impresario David Stones, late October 1962, which led to a double-shuffle for the Beatles in Birmingham on 19 November.

7 The news was reported in the 30 November *NME* and 1 December *Disc*.

8 Author interview, 28 July 2003.

9 Illustrated in *The Beatles Album*, by Julia Delano (Grange Books, London, 1991), p22.

10 *The Beatles Anthology*, p78.

11 *Hamburg Days*, pp160/162.

12 Author interview, 5 July 2007.

35: **New Look, New Sound** (16 November–17 December 1962)

1 Author interview, 22 February 2006. Jopling was the first to say this in a national paper but Bob Wooler had mentioned the Beatles' pre-Paris long hair in *Mersey Beat* in August 1961.

2 Interview by Paul du Noyer, *Paul McCartney World Tour* programme (1989–90), p41.

3 *New Record Mirror*, 24 November 1962.

4 Author interview, 6 April 2004.

5 Davies, p171.

6 Ibid.

7 'I encouraged the Beatles to keep using the harmonica sound after Love Me Do' – author interview with George Martin, 9 June 1995.

8 *Disc* also 24 November, though it announced the date of the Beatles' recording session incorrectly as 27 November. *Mersey Beat* had it right in its 15 November issue.

9 *Mersey Beat*, 3 January 1963.

10 George Martin's Liverpool visit has been widely given as Sunday 9 December, but it was three days later.

11 3 January 1963.

12 Author interview, 9 June 1995.

13 Illustrated in *Thank U Very Much*, p113. The Beatles drew this same antennae motif on the backs of envelopes when replying to fans, or else they replicated the inky doodle beetle sometimes drawn in autograph books.

14 From John Lennon's review of Spike Milligan's book *The Goon Show Scripts*, *New York Times*, 30 September 1973.

15 Davies, p168. 'A sense of well-being, of being happy' from author interview, 31 August 2000.

16 Letter in EMI Archives.

17 *All You Need Is Ears*, p127.

18 Author interview, 28 July 2003.

19 Combined quote, from interview by Mike Read, 13 October 1987, for BBC Radio 1, and 1969 interview broadcast by David Pritchard on CHUM-FM, Toronto, May 1970. (Also quoted in *The Beatles: An Oral History*, by David Pritchard and Alan Lysaght [Stoddart, Canada, 1998], p72.) Paul said much the same in a conversation with John, filmed over John's shoulder at Apple on 29 January 1969 and included in the film *Let It Be*.

20 *Sounds*, 6 December 1975. Waterman, who went on to become a music producer and songwriter of 1980s and subsequent successes, was not quite 16 in November 1962.

21 Author interview, 29 October 2004.

22 The Elvis record was his new single, Return To Sender. *Twelve O'Clock Spin* on 22 November 1962 and *Two-Way Family Favourites* on the 25th were the third and fourth BBC plays of Love Me Do.

23 Author interview, 24 August 2011; *Melody Maker*, 1 December 1962. In his autobiography (*Part One – From Congregations To Audiences*, pp52–3), David Frost wrote, 'The tribute to Norrie Paramor ... was tough, in a way the clearest declaration in the whole of the show that *TW3* intended to be different.' *TW3* producer Ned Sherrin said Paramor was furious about it (*That Was Satire That Was: The Satire Boom Of The 1960s*, by Humphrey Carpenter, Victor Gollancz, London, 2000, p219). Paramor died in 1979, his knowledge of who was behind his TV assassination a question apparently unasked by interviewers, though he must have worked it out: George Martin produced the *TW3* theme music as a single in January 1963 and made a cast LP soon after.

24 *All You Need Is Ears*, p130.

25 Author interview, 5 July 2007.

26 *All You Need Is Ears*, p130.
27 'They laughed at me' from interview by Derek Johnson, *NME*, 7 June 1963.
28 *Mersey Beat*, 3 January 1963.
29 Noddy Paranoid remembered by Ron Richards in author interview, 23 September 2003.
30 Letters in EMI Archives.
31 Interview by Johnny Beerling, early 1972, for BBC Radio 1. All Dick James quotes in this chapter are from here.
32 From 2004–05 author interviews with Stephen James, Perry and Pilbeam.
33 Author interview, 11 July 2005. Linda Duque was Dick James' secretary for five years from 1960, starting with him at Bron's. '. . . the most honest' from A *Cellarful Of Noise*, p107.
34 From the raw transcripts of interviews for A *Cellarful Of Noise*.
35 The Paris was a BBC radio studio seating an audience of close to four hundred. Originally an art-house cinema, it was converted to BBC use during the Second World War, its deep position – two floors below street level – an advantage when Berlin's bombs were falling.
36 Categories won by, respectively, the Springfields and the Shadows. The Beatles didn't figure in the World Vocal Group section, won easily by the Everly Brothers. The definition of 'group' was just weeks away from changing forever but at this time still meant anything beyond solo artists. The Beatles' score in the two sections was 3906 and 735, and as every vote was given three points, they'd received 1302 and 245.
37 Interview by Richard Skinner, 14 July 1986, for *McCartney*, BBC1, 29 August 1986.
38 Author interview, 6 November 2007.
39 Davies, p179.
40 7 December 1962.
41 Author interview, 11 July 2005.
42 Author interview, 15 December 2004.
43 Author interview, 30 September 1987.
44 First part from author interview, 2 May 1991; second from interview by Richard Williams, for *The Times*, 28 December 1981.
45 Author interview, 26 March 2003. Brian employed no Jews at Nems; John could have been thinking of Dick James and maybe his secretary. Nems employed several gay men, including Peter Brown and Brian's new personal assistant, Barry Leonard, who started at Whitechapel in the last weeks of 1962.
46 Those not watching TV but listening to the radio, to the BBC Light Programme, heard the Beatles on *The Talent Spot*, making that first broadcast of Twist And Shout. The two programmes coincided. *Tuesday Rendezvous* wasn't recorded – it went out live, its pictures gone forever.
47 So remembers chatty London cabbie Danny, who told me on 12 October 2006 that he saw the Beatles on *Tuesday Rendezvous* and immediately thought 'What on earth's *this*?' He'd never seen a guitar-group sing before.
48 Davies, p171.
49 Author interview, 20 June 2005.
50 'We wrote it on guitars and a little bit on the piano' – Paul to author, 30 September 1987. Mike's photo is best seen in *Remember*, p107. Another 1962 photo he took of his brother playing this guitar (some say it's a Framus) became the cover of the Paul McCartney album *Chaos And Creation In The Backyard* (2005).
      Celia Mortimer's relationship with Paul ended in the last weeks of 1962: 'As the Beatles spent more time in London, Paul was there and not in Liverpool so much, and our situation just fizzled out. There was no time for it.' She went on to become a big player on the London fashion scene, with her own label and studio on Great Portland Street, just along from where she spent a few hours with Paul in 1962. In between times, she went out for a long time with Mike McCartney and was part of the Liverpool poetry scene. (More in volume 2.)
51 First part from author interview, 30 September 1987; second from interview by Derek Taylor, 3 March 1965.
52 Interview by Mike Read, 12 October 1987, for BBC Radio 1.
53 Interview by Tony Webster, *Beat Instrumental*, September 1964.
54 Author interview, 9 June 1995; 'water' from *All You Need Is Ears*, p125; Wooler from *The Best Of Fellas*, p193.
55 A *Cellarful Of Noise*, p72.
56 Ibid., p76.

57 *Mersey Beat*, 1 August 1963.
58 Mallory Curley in *Beatle Pete, Time Traveller*, p22. 'Randolf's Party' published in *In His Own Write*, p29. Telegram illustrated in *Beatle!*, p176.
59 *Beatle!*, p175. The second occasion was a Nems Enterprises promotion at Queen's Hall, Widnes, on 22 October.
60 Interview by Tony Barrow, *Beatles Book* magazine, issue 98 (June 1984).

36: **And Who Knows!** (18–31 December 1962)

1 Author interview, 20 June 2005. Sue and her friend Jenny Bale cleaned George's car on the desired date, but stopped short of lugging the dirty water to Paul's house.
2 Interview by Johnny Beerling, early 1972, for BBC Radio 1.
3 The Beatles were probably recorded on 25 December and days immediately after, but establishing this precisely is a task still taxing expert minds – as is firm verification of the song order. (The original claim, that the tape was made on only one night, 31 December, has been proved incorrect.)
4 The best-researched information about the Beatles in Canada is in a series of books by Piers A. Hemmingsen, *The Beatles Canadian Discography (1962–1970)*, published 2003–11; www.capitol6000.com.
    Zola 'Ray' Sonin was born in London's East End in 1907 to Russian immigrant parents; he died in Toronto in 1991, aged 84, having just recorded his latest *Calling All Britons*. The Queen awarded him the MBE in 1984 'for services to the British community in Toronto'.
    The record-keeping of US and Canadian radio output was (is) so incomplete and scattered that making 'first' claims is a perilous indulgence. But it does seem likely that this *was* the Beatles' first North American airplay.
5 5 and 12 January 1963. *Cash Box* had an invaluable weekly editorial/comment page, *Billboard* didn't.
6 Letters (in EMI Archives) from Roland Rennie to Joe Zerga, 11 and 28 December 1962; Zerga telegram to Rennie, 27 December, and letter, 4 January 1963.
7 Author interview, 3 August 2012. Garrett was born in Dallas, Texas, in July 1938; his given name is Thomas. 'Garrett was the best-known brand of snuff in the South in the 1930s and '40s,' he says, 'so my schoolteacher started calling me Snuff and the name stuck.' Garrett had already made many fine records by 1962 and would continue to do so in a well-respected career.
8 Doug Morris, a 24-year-old record company rookie, was in charge of Laurie A&R when the Beatles were turned down. It isn't clear if the rejection was his idea or that of the label's owners, Gene and Bob Schwartz. My direct question to Morris in July 2012 received no response – which doesn't prove it was his decision. As chairman and CEO of Universal Music Group (1995–2010), he went on to become arguably the biggest chief of the global music industry. He fulfilled the same roles at Sony Music Entertainment from 2011.
9 '… rock and roll can last' from *Cash Box*, 22 December 1962. The comment alluded to the success of Twist music.
10 Interview by Brian Innes, 11 October 1966; unpublished.
11 Interview by Mike Hennessey, *Melody Maker*, 5 August 1967.
12 Interviews by Ray Coleman, *Melody Maker*, 12 October 1963; and Kenneth Harris, *The Observer*, 17 May 1964.
13 Author interview, 28 March 2003.
14 Cliff Bennett interview by Simon Wells, 14 February 2002. John and Paul got a particular kick out of watching Bennett sing because he could replicate Richie Barrett's tooth-whistle in Some Other Guy, the trick that continued to elude them. Frank Allen quote from his autobiography, *Travelling Man* (Aureus Publishing, Cardiff, 1999), pp26–7. He bumped into John Lennon on the Beatles' final night, New Year's Eve, and told him how good he thought they were; John thanked him and then said the Rebel Rousers were good too, but Allen's harmonies were 'fucking ridiculous'. Allen stood with his mouth agape, stunned by this new kind of directness.
15 Interview by Sue Masterman and Anton Korne, *Observer* Foreign News Service, 3 April 1969.
16 Interview by David Sheff, 15 September 1980, for *Playboy*.

An appeal from Mark Lewisohn

Research for *All These Years* – can you help?

Information

I've already uncovered much fascinating material to explore and explain the history of the Beatles, but no one can ever say they've seen everything. There's plenty more out there – in private collections, libraries, archives, attics, everywhere – that could enable this extraordinary story to be more accurately told and understood.

If you have, or know of, anything that could possibly shed new light on any element of the Beatles' history – and that includes their many associated areas and topics – please contact me through the HELP page at www.marklewisohn.net

There's no limit to what these things could be – photos, films, recordings, *anything at all* – but documents are my main priority. Scans, photocopies or photos should be enough to convey the content – you needn't part with anything of value.

I'll be pleased to acknowledge in print the source of any information provided by any contributor (unless they request anonymity).

Witnesses

If you were a first-hand witness to any part of the Beatles years – up to, say, 1980 – or know someone who was, I'd like to hear about it, and might want to include that story in one of these books. Again, please contact me through the HELP page at www.marklewisohn.net

Credits

I work quietly and alone, the fewer distractions the better, but a book like this requires reaching out for support, advice, answers and friendship, for people to share information, laughs and bits of news, and I'm overjoyed so many are there for me. Everyone named below has helped make this book happen – and they have my deep gratitude.

Richard Buskin, Jay Donnelly, Harry Klaassen, Andy Neill, Dave Ravenscroft, Piet Schreuders, Adam Smith and Jeff Walden did me the honour of vetting the draft chapters and offering vital feedback in the form of challenges, corrections, clarifications and titbits of new information. Each brought a particular expertise to the task and came up with unique points, and my confidence in the finished product is due in no small measure to their help. To this list I happily add Thorsten Knublauch, who read everything relating to Hamburg and whose feedback was comprehensive and perceptive. I must also thank Harry Klaassen again for planting the idea of a multi-volume Beatles history in my head in the first place.

I've written books about comedy, but no script or comic ever makes me laugh more than the Beatles. Richard Buskin (*New York Times* bestselling author) is the only person I know to tune into the same tiny, arcane, utterly inconsequential details of the greater story and find them so gaspingly funny. Our years of friendship and laughter are the stuff of life, and they've helped shape my approach to this project.

I'm happy to have many friends with niche knowledge of the Beatles, deeper in places than I've the time or need to go. Many are authors in their own right, like Andy Neill. Andy has an impressive array of specialist areas, and he's also a first-class professional researcher and writer. In the early days of this project, I paid Andy to spend days in the British Library for me when I couldn't be in two places at once. He's the only person I trust to turn the pages of obscure old local UK newspapers and find what I would have found. Beyond that, his deep/wide knowledge of rock music over several decades could well be without parallel and he can back his opinions with research no one else has done. Thanks for all the great finds, Andy!

And all that goes for Jay Donnelly too, my research fellow in the States. We enjoyed a memorable week together at the Library of Congress, and Jay continued the work there and elsewhere after I returned to England. Them thar nuggets of gold delight us both and will be dropped into all three volumes. Great work, sir.

In fact, there are many top-class Beatles scholars in America and I'm delighted to call them friends. They've generously sourced new material for me and responded to my every question swiftly and (that most cherished but elusive of attributes) reliably. All these chaps are Beatles authors in their own right – seek out their books or websites with confidence: Andy Babiuk, Belmo, Brian Kehew, Allan Kozinn, Jason Kruppa, Chip Madinger, John McEwen, Wally Podrazik, Scott Raile, Kevin Ryan, Bruce Spizer and John C. Winn. Separately, because Canada ain't America, my thanks to Piers Hemmingsen. You've all been brilliant, and the beer (ale, of course) is on me in London.

Back home, Dave Ravenscroft has been a monumental help, every day for years. A never-say-die resourceful researcher and collector with a fine analytical mind, his enthusiastic and deeply knowledgeable interest in the *important* minutiae, the musical minutiae especially, has contributed much to this book and been a constant reassurance to me.

Spencer Leigh has been his typical helpful self. A prolific writer and close observer of all popular culture, with his own idiosyncratic weekly show on BBC Radio Merseyside, Spencer's emails and phone calls are an endless source of amusement and revelation. I'm also hugely indebted to Spencer for allowing me use of his interviews. I've met quite a few Liverpool rock and rollers, of course, but there were *hundreds*, many now dead. A prodigious north-west-based interviewer for more than thirty years, Spencer has sat down with scores of them, asking questions of the young lads who'd become middle-aged butchers and bakers and candlestick makers – and he gave me unfettered access to the full transcripts. These people were close-up witnesses to anywhere between one and fifty hectic nights with the Beatles in the Liverpool halls and clubs of 1961–2, forming impressions that stuck fast because the Beatles' rise to fame happened so soon after. Not every anecdote is reliable (some people do talk balls) but those that stand up to scrutiny have slotted perfectly into the puzzle. It's given me much pleasure to use these quotes in context, but don't let that put you off reading them (and plenty more) in Spencer's own books – www.spencerleigh.demon.co.uk is the place to go.

I've had every conceivable kind of useful and enjoyable idea, lead and guidance from several other great friends, all of them researcher-writers: Simon Wells, Mark Cousins, Andy Davis, and (co-authors with me of *The Beatles' London*) Piet Schreuders and Adam Smith. Peter Nash allowed me the privilege of a wander around his abundant Beatles collection, and I'm fortunate to have the friendship of Paul Wane. His company Tracks leads the field in buying and selling Beatles memorabilia, everything right up to top-end material; thanks also to Tracks' accomplished staff, including Gema, Lynsey and Chad, and most especially Jason Cornthwaite – they're the best because, like Paul, they have genuine enthusiasm, the second thing money can't buy. I'm also very grateful to the experts at the London auction houses, who've forwarded my enquiries to sellers and allowed me access to plenty of interesting incoming items. They include, at Christie's (at various times), Helen Hall, Sarah Hodgson, Neil Roberts and Carey Wallace; Stephen Maycock at Sotheby's and now Bonhams; and lone ranger Ted Owen. My thanks also to Stephen Bailey at The Beatles Shop in Mathew Street, Liverpool. He's been brilliant, generously volunteering to show me many fascinating documents and artefacts brought into his shop by local people who've had them stuffed down the backs of wardrobes for fifty years.

This is the first book I've written that needed research and interviews in a language I don't speak – German. I'm grateful to a pair of Irishmen who are also professional translators at work in Germany. My cousin Ian Winick (based in Cologne, www.insight-translations.de) translated an entire book for me, and Stephen Roche (based in Hamburg, www.networktranslators.de) was a first-class companion on my trips to his adopted city. We had nothing but productive and happy times working together, with long hours and good laughs – Stephen set up interviews, was on hand for instant translation, helped with library work (with and without me) and prepared several research reports. I'm also grateful to Thorsten Knublauch for being such a resourceful researcher into all aspects of the Beatles' Hamburg years and so generously sharing his findings because he wanted me to tell the story right; and to Jutta Burgi-Pill (secretary of the West German branch of the Official Beatles Fan Club in the 1960s), who spent a whirlwind afternoon with me in the Bavarian State Library in Munich, whispering English translations whenever I pointed to interesting-looking text or ads in one of Germany's two early-1960s music industry magazines. It was her words I typed frenetically into my Macbook.

I'm very pleased to be able to thank Hunter Davies for supporting this project. Hunter wrote the Beatles' authorised biography, the only one there can ever be because it was done when the four were still together to approve it, in 1967–8. (As such, he becomes part of the story in my subsequent volumes.) Hunter's *The Beatles*, first published in 1968, is a seminal work, especially as he had access to people and places now long gone. You cannot write a biography of the Beatles without quoting it, so all credit where it's due. I'm grateful to Hunter for understanding why I felt my project necessary, and for letting me browse his collection of Beatles artefacts while I, in a quid pro quo, tidied it up and catalogued it for him. I enjoyed our days together.

I do my own typing, but in the project's early days had the help of four people to transcribe some of the interviews. Beth Bellin was the first, my eldest son Oliver (hi Oliver, and hi Tom!) did one, my cousin Ruth Wallington did several, and I also had a delightful approach from Mandy Rees, in Los Angeles, who slogged away on my behalf simply because she can't wait to read the book. Thank you all.

For an array of reasons, I send heaps of alphabetical thanks to friends Arthur Atkinson, Tony Bacon, John Beecher, Roy Carr, Dick Fiddy, Michael Fishberg, Pete Frame, Eric Greenberg, Georgie Grindlay, Paolo Hewitt, Keith Howell, David Hughes, Patrick Humphries, Nigel Hunter, Sean Jackson, David Klein, Fred Lindgren, Barry McCann, Gordon Ottershaw, Andy and Denise Paraskos, Stephen Peeples, Phil Smee, Simon Smith, Brian Southall, David Stark, Derek Taylor (perpetual wisdom from beyond), Joan Taylor, David Tossell, John Walker and Ian Woodward.

I'd also like to thank, mostly posthumously, the proprietors and journalists responsible for Britain's music papers – in this period *Disc*, *New Record Mirror*, *Melody Maker* and the *New Musical Express* (NME). Their news reporting was strong enough to reliably underpin any history of the period. In addition to those national weeklies, written in and focused on London, Liverpool had its own fortnightly *Mersey Beat*, for a long time the only such paper outside the capital. Benignly owned and financed by Ray McFall (who also owned the Cavern), the paper was founded and edited by Bill Harry and he was thinking years ahead of his time. The riches I've derived from poring over every issue have given me welcome background knowledge and fine entertainment. Thank you, Bill, you made quite a contribution.

I've been going to Liverpool since the 1970s but hadn't lived there until spending six hectic months in the city for this project – and, in many ways, multiplying that length of time by researching Merseyside newspapers archived in London. In just these few years, philistines on the council have obliterated more Grade One important places in Beatles history, including the Nems shop and Beatles office (demolished), Litherland Town Hall (completely altered) and Aintree Institute (demolished). I was driving past the Institute one day – glancing up to see it, as I always did – and it was *gone*, a hole in a terrace to match the shape of my mouth, and this on the eve of Liverpool's Capital of Culture year. The Beatles played this atmospheric dance hall thirty-one times, including a string of Saturday nights where things really kicked off … and now the place is gone, for no justifiable reason. Council madness exists everywhere, and they do it particularly well in Liverpool – the Cavern to which tourists flock from around the world is a re-creation because the real one was demolished and filled in to make way for precisely nothing. Through these pages, here and now, I urge all Merseyside councillors to commit publicly to a moratorium, so that demolition of their historic landmarks, this mad slashing of the city's own heritage, can at least be discussed first.

In Liverpool, I look not at today's shopping malls and trendy empty apartments, but for the place of this extraordinary history. It's there – you just have to squeeze your eyes tight and peer *through*. I stood outside Central Station one August Bank Holiday night, bag of chips in hand, forced myself to ignore the loud drunken lads pissing in the street and the loud drunken lasses with virtually nothing on, everyone shouting *focchin* this and *focchin* that … and when I looked *through* there was Jim Mac coming round the corner in his hat, puffing on his pipe, *Echo* tucked under his arm, and Aunt Mimi walking along with young John, berating him but having a laugh at the same time. I looked for the green double-decker bus driven by Harry Harrison, while his youngest son George – wearing something outrageous – nipped out of Blackler's and headed for Frank Hessy's to ogle the guitars. I looked for Paul & Ian and Richy & Roy staring at the records in the window of Nems on Great Charlotte Street, from which Brian Epstein stepped out immaculately on his way to the Basnett Bar – where Derek Taylor had stopped by from the *Echo* for a swift half, passing Mal Evans with his GPO engineer's bag and Harry Graves with his decorating ladder, everyone photographed by Mike McCartney from the hair-salon window above. I looked for Neil Aspinall leaving the Pru building, for Julia en route to the Troc with men wolf-whistling her, and Alf Lennon tripping by Johnny Best's boxing stadium and Jim Mac's Cotton Exchange on his way down to the docks.

I've done everything I can do to steep myself in *that* Liverpool, a Liverpool I never experienced, so as to put it faithfully on the page … and it *is* still there, in the streets and buildings I frame in the lens of my camera. I've had many great photographic walks all over the city and suburbs, sometimes alone and other times with Mike Badger – musician, songwriter, artist, friend. Mike knows what I'm looking for, likes finding it too, and can convey bits of the history; he shares my love of this very particular Liverpool of red-brick Victorian villas and terraced streets, of any old iron signs, tinned-up houses, crumbling light industry, pubs, parks, cemeteries, cinemas and the myriad other delights tucked away in Everton, Wavertree, Toxteth, Dingle, Old Swan, Childwall, Woolton, Kensington, West Derby and Aigburth – in fact every original suburb. I've walked many and want to walk them all. This is *authentic* Liverpool; it isn't always pretty but I find it beautiful.

Mike, Netty, Amber, Ray, Cliff and Ruth Badger are among many Liverpudlians who've become friends on these visits, along with Dawn and Mike Birch (the best B&B in Blundellsands); Roy, Helen, Elena and Grace Boulter; Jamie and Becky Bowman; Mike and Bernie Byrne; Steve and Pat Calrow; Jean Catharell; Debbie and Nigel Greenberg; Colin and Sylvia Hall (custodians for the National Trust of John

Lennon's and Paul McCartney's childhood homes – the very best, dedicated people); Billy Hatton; Pat Molyneux; John O'Connor; Hilary Oxlade; Sol Papadopoulos; Steve Phillips; and Cheniston and Jacqueline Roland. Particular thanks to Henry Epstein, the one and only, a good friend and funster and gateway to roomfuls of Liverpool musicians, poets, artists and wits whose company is always a treat.

This book isn't authorised by the Beatles and all the mistakes are mine, but I'm grateful to Jeff Jones, Cathy Hawkes, Jonathan Clyde and Aaron Bremner of the Beatles' company Apple Corps, for keeping positive interest, and I'm especially thankful to Neil Aspinall. The first non-family I shared my 'three-volume book idea' with was Neil, the Beatles' best and closest mate for more than forty years and their manager for thirty; we'd worked together on a number of projects and I wanted him to know what I was planning. His initial response was the one I've heard ten thousand times and will inevitably hear thousands more: 'Does the world *really* need another book on the Beatles?' I told him why I thought it did, using more or less the same words I've written in this volume's introduction, and Neil got it. A man of solid judgement, he said Apple wouldn't be able to help, at least not yet, and I said I certainly wasn't expecting it – but then he proceeded to give me every personal encouragement. He made assenting phone calls to people who said they'd only speak to me 'if it's OK with Neil'. He was always keen to hear who I'd seen and what I could tell him I'd learned.

In 2007, after Neil retired from Apple, my phone rang and I took another of the great Beatle-calls of my life: 'Hi Mark, it's Neil. I'm now free of the burdens of restraint – you've always wanted to interview me; if you need any insights or whatever, just ask.' We'd lunched sporadically for years and I'd enjoyed a few extended meetings in Neil's Apple office when he stopped talking about the 'pro-ject' in hand and just started talking about the Beatles, but those weren't exactly interviews. Neil didn't *do* interviews ... except now he was saying he would, repeatedly, at length. We had our first session shortly after, a riverside lunch and a long afternoon of yakking. Neil was *mostly* relaxed and I thought it went really well, as you can read in this book ... and then he fell ill and died, just like that, very fast, aged 66.

That great gruff sweary no-bullshit Anfield voice *will* sound in the second and third volumes of this series, but nowhere near as much as we both wanted. Though I've wonderful material for all three volumes, I often find myself thinking how much *more* complete this Beatles history could have been if Neil hadn't – as he'd have put it – 'fucked off, *right?*' But so long, Neil, and thanks.

Interviewees

The following nice people graciously allowed me some – often much – of their time, to talk about the Beatles, and I thank them all immensely. (*With just a couple of exceptions, women interviewed for this book appear with the name they had at the time all these events took place, not by any subsequent married name.*)

Keith Altham, Helen Anderson, Bernie Andrews, Dee Armitage, Neil Aspinall, Julia Baird, Bill Barlow, Rikki Barnes, Tony Barrow, Jeni Beattie, Kathia Berger, Georgia Bergman, Mike Berry, Pete Best, Rory Best, Marga Bierfreund, Pauline Bingham, Harry Birch, Sheila Birch, Pat Blease, Otto Blunck, Peter Bolt, Jimmy

Bowien, David Boyce, Bernie Boyle, Pattie Brady, Tony Bramwell, Hans-Walther Braun, Elsa Breden, Jenny Brewer, John Brierley, Ken Brown, Peter Brown, Roberta Brown, Leslie Bryce, John Burgess, Alaster Burman, Shirley Burns, Muriel Burton, Tony Calder, Iris Caldwell, Steve Calrow, David Cardwell, Tony Carricker, Les Chadwick, Margaret Chillingworth, Maureen Cleave, Mary Cockram, Les Cocks, Margaret Cooney, Hazel Cooper, Roy Corlett, Peter Cottenden, Tom Cross, Nicky Cuff, Geoff Davies, Rod Davis, Jennifer Dawes, Bob Dean, Jeff Dexter, Ric Dixon, Margaret Douglas, Frank Duckworth, Tim Dugdill, Linda Duque, Roy Dyke, Geoffrey Ellis, Royston Ellis, Elvi Erichsen, Everett Estridge, Alun Evans ...

Jack Fallon, Bernadette Farrell, Michael Fishwick, Dick Fontaine, Derek France, John Fruin, Snuff Garrett, Margaret Gauld, Syd Gillingham, Jim Gilvey, Giorgio Gomelsky, Jack Good, Ruth Gore, Bobby Graham, Jimmy Grant, Roger Greenaway, Marie Guirron, John Gustafson, Jon Hague, Bill Hall, Tony Hall, Kevin Harrington, David Harris, June Harris, Mona Harris, Joan Harrison, Louise Harrison, June Harry, Brian Harvey, Billy Hatton, Ivan Hayward, Rosi Heitmann, Michael Hill, Wally Hill, Derek Hodkin, Tim Holmes, Chris Hornby, Barbara Houghton, Sue Houghton, David Hughes, Tommy Hughes, Mike Hurst, Chris Huston, Margaret Jack, David Jacobs, Brian John James, Dawn James, Ian James, Stephen James, Dave Jamieson, Derek Jeffery, Beryl Johnson, Derek Johnson, Ron Jones, Vivien Jones, Norman Jopling, Pat Jourdan, Peter Kaschel, Arthur Kelly, Clive Kelly, Freda Kelly, Margaret Kelly, Gibbo and Tina Kemp, Jim Kennedy, Ian King, Astrid Kirchherr ...

Sam Leach, Brigitte Leidigkeit, Fran Leiper, Joyce Lennon, Bob Lusty, Winnie Mac, Peter Mackey, Donald MacLean, Les Maguire, Shelagh Maguire, John Mair, E. Rex Makin, Paul Marshall, Bryan Martin, Ann Mason, Brian Matthew, Dick Matthews, Mike Maxfield, Joan McCaldon, Angie McCartney, Ray McFall, Leonard Milne, Adrian Mitchell, Pat Moran, Celia Mortimer, Brian Mulligan, Brenda Murphy, Mitch Murray, Rod Murray, Linda Ness, Chas Newby, Mary Newton, Maureen Nickson, Geoff Nugent, Maureen O'Grady, Sean O'Mahony, Maureen O'Shea, David Paramor, Tom Parkinson, Graham Pauncefort, Lee Perry, David Picker, Thelma Pickles, Ellen Piel, Peter Pilbeam, Tom and Beryl Plummer (Tommy Wallis and Beryl), Richie Prescott, Peter Prichard, Sheila Prytherch, Roland Rennie, Ron Richards, Wolfgang Riecke, Carol Rigg, Cliff Roberts, George 'Dale' Roberts, Eileen Robinson, Alan Roe, Cheniston and Jacqueline Roland, Bettina Rose, Keith Rowley, Lita Roza ...

Mike Sarne, Mike Savage, Frank Sellman, Ann Sheridan, Tony Sheridan, Judith Simons, Nevil Skrimshire, Alan Smith, Bill Smith, David John Smith, Keith Smith, Mike Smith, Norman Smith, Walter Smith, Dave Spain, Toni Spencer, Ray Standing, Lou Steen, Les Stewart, Alan Swerdlow, Ted Taylor, Michael C. Thompson, Pam Thompson, Liz Tibbott-Roberts, Roy Trafford, Jan Vaughan, Jürgen Vollmer, Klaus Voormann, Noel Walker, Chris Walley, Clive Walley, Alan Walsh, Harry Watmough, Rosi Weber, Bert Weedon, Bruce Welch, Peter Wharton, Tom Whippey (Kim Bennett), Lyndon Whittaker, Alec Whyte, Thelma Wilkinson, Brian Willey, Allan Williams, Ronald Woan, Leslie Woodhead, Neville Wortman, Walter Woyda, Derek Yoxall.

I've been actively interviewing people about the Beatles since 1983 and other quotes in this book come from vintage sessions, including many with Paul McCartney, one with George Harrison and several with George Martin, and also

Judy Martin, Cilla Black, Bob Boast, Jim Foy, Mike McCartney, Tony Meehan, Bob Molyneux, Pauline Sutcliffe, Alistair Taylor and Wally Whyton. Thanks also to Yoko Ono for opening an important research door, and to Paul McCartney for answering some further questions by email; they didn't have to help, so I particularly appreciate the fact they did.

Other providers of information or assistance

Thanks to the following for helping me in a wide variety of ways (with three cheers for the inventors of email).

Roger Akehurst, Harold Alderman, Ken Ashcroft, Geoff Barker, Andre Barreau, Mark Baxter, David Bedford, Johnny Beerling, Simon Beresford, Leon Berger, Jim Berkenstadt, Roag Best, Rachael Binns, David Birch, Charles Blackwell, Rob Bradford, Steve Braunias, Lizzie Bravo, Mike Brocken, Gordon Brown, Kathy Burns, Linda Butt, Trevor Cajiao, Heather Canter, Jasper Carrott, Chris Carter, Stephen Carter, Howie Casey, Ernesto Juan Castellanos, Leslie Cavendish, William Cavendish, Irwin Chusid, Bob Clifford, Jeannie Cohen, Stuart Colman, Peter Compton, Ray Connolly, David Costa, Sylvia Cowling, Martin Creasy, Michael Crick, Lorre Crimi, John Crisp, Sandra Currie, Reynold D'Silva, Bert Danher, Russell Davies, Julian Dawson, Andrew Dickson, Ed Dieckmann, Claudio Dirani, Peter Doggett, Bert Donn, Paul du Noyer, Joe Dumas, Bruno Dupont, Jim Elyea, Ray Ennis, Gary and Vanda Evans, Lily Evans . . .

Joe Farrag, Horst Fascher, Alison Fiddler, Andy Finney, John Firminger, Bob Fisher, Dave Forshaw, Gerard Fox, Frances Friedlander, Susan Fuller, Gillian Gaar, Paul Gallagher, John Gorman, Hans Olof Gotfriddson, Dale Grayson, Ian Greaves, Margaret Grose, Raymond Hall, Colin Hanton, Bob Hardy, Roger Harris, Bill Harry, Tony Hatch, Dermott Hayes, Mark Hayward, Bill Heckle, Stefanie Hempel, Mike Hennessey, Chris Hewlett, Harold Hill, Jean-Claude Hocquet, Peter Hodgson, Jackie Holmes, Brad Howard, Beth Howells, Kevin Howlett, Gary Howman, Brian Hudson, Jim Hughes, Brian Innes, Ivor Jacobs, Dave Jones, Peter Jones, Serena Karp, Jude Southerland Kessler, Adrian Killen, Marlene King, Raymond Kingsbury, Pat Kinzer, Axel Korinth, Eric Krasker, Jonny Kremer, Jeffrey Kruger, Ulf Krüger . . .

Tony Lacey, Richard Larcombe, Peter Lawson, James Leasing, Cynthia Lennon, Richard Lester, John Lewin, John Lewis, Vic Lewis, Helen Lindsay, Rhoddy Macpherson, Kenji Maeda, John Maguire, Pat Mancuso, Margaret Marsden, Garry Marsh, Dibbs Mather, Harald Mau, Chas McDevitt, Dee Meehan, T. J. Meenach, John Merrit, Ray Miller, Doug Morris, Geoff Mullin, Patti Murawski, Lorne Murdoch, Mark Naboshek, Mary Newton, Michael O'Connell, Staffan Olander, Tony Onslow, Alan Ould, Peter Paetzold, Carl Magnus Palm, Nigel Parkinson, Dave Peacock, Brian Poole, Richard Porter, Andrew Pratley, Simon Prentis, Heather Paige Preston, Celia Quantrill, John Repsch, Geoff Rhind, Tim Riley, Kate Robertson, Joe Robinson, Johnny Rogan, Amy Rossiter and Paul Gurrell, Peter Rubin . . .

saki, Jon Schotten, Henry Scott-Irvine, Peter Seaman, Joey Self, Frank Seltier, Denny Seyton, John Shakespeare (Johnny Carter), Adam Sharp, Colin Shearman, Robbie Shepherd, Anna Sheridan, Trevor Simpson, Andy Smith, David J. Smith, Jimmy Stevens, Pauline Stone, Gerry Stonestreet, John Sugar, Michael Swerdlow, Joan Taylor, Greg Temple, Denise Theophilus, Michael Thornton, Dennis Toll, Mike

Tomkies, Ken Townsend, Josie Tucker, Steve Voce, Jacques Volcouve, Tony Wadsworth, Jens Waldenmaier, Anthony Wall, Ron Watson, Linda Watts, Jean Weir, Alan Weston, Carol Weston, Scott Wheeler, Chris White, Jim Woodley, Ali Zayeri.

Archives and libraries

I'm at my happiest quietly turning pages in archives and libraries, and I've had many fine times discovering information great and small for this project. My thanks to all the people who've accommodated me and allowed me to find what I was looking for, and very often what I wasn't.

Merseyside. Liverpool Record Office (Diane Adams, David Stoker, John Keane and particularly Kevin Roach, who patiently and enthusiastically answered dozens of specific enquiries and is now an author himself); Liverpool Roman Catholic Archdiocesan Archives (Dr Meg Whittle); University of Liverpool (Kate Robertson); Athenaeum Club (Anna Jackson); and Wirral Archives (Emma Challoner). Thanks also to Peter Kennerley, to Barbara Woosey at Mosspits Lane Primary School, and to Brian Davies at Calderstones School, formerly Quarry Bank.

London. My thanks to the staffs of the London Library and the various reading rooms of the British Library at St Pancras and especially the newspaper outpost at Colindale. I've had tremendous times researching the Beatles here since 1979 (when it was still the British Museum Newspaper Library) and will miss the place terribly after its closure. I'd like it proved to me that the service for readers won't suffer as a result of the moves. London Metropolitan Archive (Charlotte Hopkins and especially Julian Carr, a dedicated, knowledgeable, resourceful librarian who made the LMA a great place to research); British Film Institute (Steve Bryant, Carolyne Bevan, Dick Fiddy, Veronica Taylor, Heather Osborn); EMI Archive (Jackie Bishop, Sonita Cox, Hamish Hamilton); the National Archives (special thanks to Yudit Collard Treml); London Borough of Havering Central Library (Simon Donoghue); and RADA (James Thornton).

Also in Britain. BBC Written Archives (Jeff Walden – simply the best); Aberdeenshire Library and Information Service (Judith Legg); Bristol University Arts and Social Sciences Library (Hannah Lowery); The British Institute of Jazz Studies (Graham Langley); Butlin's Archive (Roger Billington); Churchill Archives Centre (Sophie Bridges, Claire Knight); Norfolk & Norwich Millennium Library (Claire Agate); University of Reading Special Collections Service (Nancy Jean Fulford; with thanks to Jean Rose at Random House); and Wrekin College (Serena Kyle).

USA. My thanks to the staffs of the Library of Congress, Washington DC; The New York Public Library for the Performing Arts; the Paley Center for Media (Ron Simon); and Clyde Savannah Public Library (Sue Ayers).

Germany. My thanks to the staffs of the Staats-und Universitätsbibliothek, Hamburg; Staatsarchiv, Hamburg; Bayerische StaatsBibliothek, Munich; and to Rudi, Christa and Olaf at *Automaten-Markt* magazine in Braunschweig, who allowed me to visit and make notes from back issues.

Online. There are tons of great things on the internet. My thanks to *everyone* who posts it. (My website will mention some of these sites in particular.)

Publishing

This project required a leap of faith from my publishers. Contracts were signed in 2004, a time when best estimates pitched 2008, 2012 and 2016 as likely publication years for the three volumes. Being that the agreed essence of the project was (and remains) to get the story right and cut no corners, it soon became clear some elasticity would be required. This realisation more or less coincided with the global recession and a revolution in publishing, away from printed books and towards electronic delivery, with companies contracting fast and bookshops closing everywhere. These events brought about the cancellation of hundreds of valid projects, so the fact you're seeing this book at all owes to the professionalism and belief of a number of key people. They could have pulled the plug but didn't, and they have my heartfelt thanks.

Little, Brown Book Group. The project was commissioned in London by the multi-talented Tom Bromley, who then left, overseen by company CEO Ursula Mackenzie, who thankfully hasn't. Richard Beswick has been a constant supporter, and I'm immensely grateful to group managing editor Vivien Lipski and my editor, the publishing director Tim Whiting, for their endurance and editorial brilliance, and I can also only applaud their appointment of Dan Balado as line-editor – he absorbed the spirit of the project from the start and made a valuable contribution.

It's common for authors to have unhappy experiences with publishers, but this Little, Brown team has been magnificent.

The Crown Publishing Group. My thanks to Kristin Kiser, Steve Ross and Carrie Thornton who commissioned the book in New York, and to Tina Constable and Sean Desmond who took it over and have been fantastically patient while I finished writing it.

Agents. Simon Trewin became my London literary agent at the project's inception and I'll be forever grateful for his advice, belief and the wonderful ride we shared before unforeseen events crashed that day-to-day relationship. Thanks also to his excellent PAs, Claire Gill and Ariella Feiner. In New York, Mark Reiter helped seal the Crown deal, aided by *his* terrific PA Emily Sklar. My thanks too to Christy Fletcher.

My deepest gratitude is to KT Forster, my super-agent, who stepped into a difficult breach and performed miracles to keep this project alive. KT's professional advice and personal friendship have been of the very best, helping me overcome a hundred obstacles and taking weights from my shoulders so I could get on with the work. Simply amazing.

Last on the page is the person who's first always, Anita. Through living with me, she's known every intricacy of this project from Day One: the early starts and late finishes, the frustrations and stresses, the delights and air-punching breakthroughs. The long haul. She was also the first person to hear the manuscript, getting me to read it aloud to her every week, giving ever-insightful feedback and becoming a bit of a Beatle Know-all along the way. Thank you, LOML.

Next challenge: volume two.

Mark Lewisohn
Summer 2013

Picture Credits

Beatles (and associated) photos have been sold, bought, freely traded and lovingly shared by people around the world for decades, and it's not always possible to ascertain who took or presently owns the copyright in certain images. Copyright holders of the photos in this book have been contacted where known; if anyone else can prove ownership, I'll be pleased to credit them in future editions and immediately on this book's website – and, if requested, to make a reasonable payment to them or to a charity, or if they wish to have the photo removed this will be respected where possible.

Jim Mac's Band; *Liverpool Echo* ad (19 October 1923); Richard Starkey; John at Quarry Bank; George at Dovedale Road; Richy in hospital; Japage 3; Beatles at Indra; *Hamburger Morgenpost* ad (18 August 1960); John and the *Daily Express*; Top Ten Club roof; Paul and John with Bob Wooler; Les Nerk Twins à Paris – all courtesy Aarkive Features.
Mary, Jim, Mike and Paul – © MPL Communications Ltd.
Harry and Elsie Graves – © Mealey Photographers, Liverpool.
Harry and Louise Harrison – courtesy Denise Theophilus.
Alf Lennon – © Billy Hall.
Mimi and George Smith; Julia and John – © Mark Hayward (from his fine photo book *The Beatles Unseen*).
Richy at St Silas; Paul at Joseph Williams – courtesy Stephen Bailey, The Beatles Shop, Liverpool.
Brian at Hoylake; Beatles at Liverpool Airport – © the Epstein family.
George and Jenny – © Jenny Butler.
Eddie Clayton Skiffle Group – © Les Kearney.
Quarry Men at Woolton – © Geoff Rhind.
George and Arthur – © Arthur Kelly.
Quarry Men at New Clubmoor Hall – photo by Les Kearney, © the Quarry Men.
George Martin's Top Ten Special – © EMI.
John, Paul and George sketch – © Ann Mason.
Beatles audition for Billy Fury – © Cheniston Roland.
Ringo with Ty, Johnny and Rory; Ringo with Johnny; Rory Storm and the Hurricanes with Vicky; outside tailor Duncan's (colour) – © Iris Caldwell.
Oosterbeek cemetery – © Barry Chang.
Stuart in woods; George at Dom; John at Dom; Paul at Dom; Beatles at Dom – photos by Astrid Kirchherr, courtesy Ulf Krüger, K&K.
Top Ten *mach Schau* – courtesy the late Gerd Mingram.
Casual in the Cavern – photo by Geoff Williams, commissioned by Maureen O'Shea and Jennifer Dawes.
George and Ringo – photo by Dick Matthews, © Apple Corps Ltd.

Beatles in leather suits – photo by Albert Marrion, © Apple Corps Ltd.
Beatles in tailored suits – photo by Harry Watmough.
John and Lindy – photo by Lou Steen.
John, Paul and George at Hulme Hall – © Graham Smith.
Beatles in Abbey Road – photo by Dezo Hoffmann, © Apple Corps Ltd.
John, Paul, George and Dennis (colour) – © Mike McCartney.
John, Cyn, Jon and Tony (colour) – © Tony Carricker.
Beatles and Prellies (colour) – © Horst Fascher Collection/K&K.
Beatles on Saltney Street – photo by 'Peter Kaye' (Les Chadwick), © Apple Corps Ltd.

Endpaper photos of John, Paul and George by Geoff Williams, 1961, commissioned by Maureen O'Shea and Jennifer Dawes; Ringo photo by Butlin's, 1960, courtesy Iris Caldwell.

Very grateful thanks to Richard Buskin and especially to Thorsten Knublauch for cleaning up several of the images for publication.

Index

2i's Coffee Bar, Soho: management, 175; Vipers at, 93, 127, 266; promotions, 121; George Martin visit, 97–8, 265-6; Koschmider visits, 331–2, 347–8; Derry and the Seniors at, 347–8; the Shadows, 359; Sheridan at, 441, 452, 463; venue, 664
The 625 Show (BBC-tv), 805

Abbey Road studios (EMI Studios): opening, 256; layout, 258; working day, 258; George Martin role, 258, 265, 266, 268, 274; staff, 262, 640; Indian musicians, 279n; Sheridan's work, 462; equipment, 529, 878-9; Brian's meeting with George Martin, 646; Beatles contract, 646-7; Maguire recording, 655; Beatles first recording session (June 1962), 667–72, 697, 725; Beatles sessions (September 1962), 724–28, 729-32, 733; Beatles session (November 1962), 782, 790, 806-10, 833; Beatles album session booking (February 1963), 822; Gerry and the Pacemakers, 823; Paul filmed at (1974), 849
Adams, Beryl: Nems secretary, 326, 541, 566; working on Beatles management, 566-8; Nems Enterprises, 656-7, 733, 737, 743
Ain't She Sweet (Gene Vincent), 464, 659; Beatles repertoire, 240, 456; Beatles recording, 461, 464–5, 511, 873
Ain't That A Shame (Pat Boone), 78-9
Al Storm and his Hurricanes, 235–7, 238, *see also* Rory Storm and the Hurricanes
All Shook Up (Elvis Presley), 127; Quarry Men repertoire, 145
Alley Oop (Hollywood Argyles), 329; sung by Ringo, 329–30, 340, 379
Allison, Jerry, 852
American Forces Network (AFN), 71, 85
Anderson, Helen, 143, 362, 282
Anderson, Jim, 872
Anna (Arthur Alexander), Beatles repertoire, 822
Anton, Vic, 414, 415, 426, 499, 524, 545
Apache (the Shadows), 359; Beatles repertoire, 365, 393
Arden, Don: Liverpool amateur talent show, 899; Little Richard tour, 659, 687, 766, 897; Gene Vincent at Star-Club, 659–60; spurns Beatles, 789; management of Sounds Incorporated, 899
Ardmore and Beechwood: Brian's agreement with, 591; Kim Bennett plugs Lennon-McCartney songs, 593–4, 779, 790–1; Parlophone signing, 640, 668, 673, 747, 790; copyright issue, 640, 728; contract for Lennon-McCartney, 733–4, 746; Parlophone label error, 746; Brian's view of, 802–3, 811–12; sidelined by George Martin, 803; *Thank Your Lucky Stars* issue, 811–12; John and Paul's statement, 815n; John and Paul leave, 830
Are You Lonesome Tonight (Elvis Presley), 412, 453; Beatles repertoire, 412

Asher, Jane, 255, 513, 781n, 860, 877
Asher family, 255, 781n
Ask Me Why: writing, 608; available 649, 884–5, 890; played by Beatles, 608; chosen for recording, 651, 663; EMI recording (June 1962), 666, 668, 670; unsuccessful, 670, 674–5; BBC broadcast, 675–6, 809; George Martin's opinion, 676, 725, 799, 800; Beatles repertoire, 681, 735; rehearsed, 725; EMI contract, 732; copyright, 803, 817; chosen as B-side, 799; recording (November 1962), 804, 806-7, 809–10, 813; Dick James Music agreement, 812, 814, 817; Beatles LP, 822, 832; Hamburg recording, 832
Aspinall, Neil: character, 703–4; at Liverpool Institute, 60, 139, 847; friendship with George, 70; O-levels, 220; sees Quarry Men, 243; friendship with Pete Best, 243, 304, 601, 706; sees Vincent/Cochran show, 295; accountancy training, 303; relationship with Mona Best, 303–4, 484, 691, 707, 837n; memories of Beatles, 355, 404, 424, 429, 601, 858, 880, 891; accountancy job, 413, 459, 870; driving Beatles, 413, 424, 540, 666, 815; on Paul bullying Stu, 434; Beatles roadie, 459, 476, 484–5, 544, 666, 679, 888; on Blair Hall booking, 483–4; relationship with Beatles, 484, 707; van, 484, 553, 605–6; on Beatles hair, 507; journeys to London, 553–4, 666; Beatles pay, 567; on Beatles songs, 585, 680; contact with Brian, 646; pay, 684, 704; birth of son, 691; Pete's dismissal, 700–3; response to Pete's dismissal, 703–4; on arrival of Ringo, 705, 706, 717, 718; John and Cyn's wedding, 714; football fan, 721n; on Beatles repertoire, 723; tries teaching John to drive, 774; at recording session, 807
Atkins, Chet, 150, 151n, 293, 481, 715, 804
Atlantic Records, 141, 836, 837n
Autry, Gene, 44

Baby It's You (the Shirelles): sung by John, 586, 605; Beatles repertoire, 725, 832
Baby Let's Play House (Elvis Presley), 3, 328; sung by John, 131, 365, 442
Bacon, 'Eggy' (teacher), 105
Bailey, R. F., 57, 102
Baker, David, 737, 782
Ballard, Arthur, 219, 370
Barber, Adrian, 305, 495, 686, 793, 827, 831–2
Barber, Chris, 69, 82
Barlow, Bill, 229, 243, 246, 303
Barrow, Tony (Disker): background, 819, 846; *Liverpool Echo* columnist, 141, 527, 563, 577, 738, 750, 809, 870; Decca sleevenote writer, 527, 577, 738; press pack for Beatles/Love Me Do, 738; Please Please Me press release, 805, 818; on Beatles, 819; Beatles press officer, 818–19, 837n

Bats, the, 587, 653, 883
BBC, 'Needletime Agreement', 71–2, 603, 747, 849
BBC Light Programme: Paul's childhood listening, 55; content, 85, 563, 843; teenage music, 121; *Saturday Club*, 224; *Pick Of The Pops*, 224; Beatles listen to, 585; Beatles audition, 584; Beatles on *Here We Go*, 603; *Jazz Club*, 753; Love Me Do played, 791; Beatles on *The Talent Spot*, 814, 901
Be-Bop-A-Lula (Gene Vincent), 92, 116, 141, 659; sung by John, 129; sung by Paul, 131; Quarry Men repertoire, 145, 302 Beatles repertoire, 442; Hamburg recording, 833
Beach Boys, 753–4, 763
Beatle Bop (Harrison-Lennon), 393, 456, 461, 464, 465 *ee also* Cry For A Shadow
Beatles: at art school dances, 299–300; Billy Fury backing group audition, 306–10; at Lathom Hall, 311; Grosvenor Ballroom (Liscard, Wallasey) residency, 332, 333–4, 347; at Neston Institute, 332, 334; series of drummers, 335; recordings of themselves, 335–6; drummer Norman Chapman, 337; backing for Ellis, 338; playing for stripper, 349, 449; Hamburg booking, 351–5; Pete Best joins, 352; journey to Hamburg, 357, 358–61; arrival in Hamburg, 361–2; stage hours in Hamburg, 362, 378, 661n, 786, 793, 827, 839n; Hamburg accommodation, 363–4, 377, 390, 392n, 396–7, 441–2, 633, 787, 827; publicity photographs, 364; first performance in Hamburg, 364–5; performances at Indra, 366–7, 370–1, 378; life in Hamburg, 373–4; performances at Kaiserkeller, 378, 379–80; relationship with Ringo in Hamburg, 378–9, 393–4; recording with Lu Walters and Ringo, 380, 462; given notice by Koschmider, 388–9; photo session with Astrid, 390–1, 450; row with Koschmider, 395–6; Top Ten Club agreement, 396, 425; return from Hamburg, 404–5; 410–11; relationship with Wooler, 402–3; Casbah bookings, 403–4; 428–9; at Litherland, 404–6; difference from other groups, 412, 472; transport, 413, 459, 484–5, 568, 595, 684; at Aintree Institute, 413; stage management by Wooler, 414; impact on Liverpool rock scene, 414–15, 418; Stu's return, 415; Pete Best's position, 417–18, 444, 446, 447; variety of styles, 418; first appearance at Cavern, 425–8; relationship with Ringo in Liverpool, 431, 479; Cavern night-time debut, 435–6; second Hamburg season, 441; at Top Ten Club, 442–4; photos in new leather look, 449; photo session with Jürgen, 451–2; first recording session, 461–5; George and John's copyright agreement, 465; contract with Kaempfert, 465–6; return from Hamburg, 467–8; Cavern as home, 476–8; days in Liverpool, 479; in *Mersey Beat*, 487; *Riverboat Shuffle*, 488; first Liverpool photo session, 490; Wooler's article on, 491–2; bookings cancelled, 499; charity bookings, 508–9; drunken show at Litherland, 510–11; reputation, 511, 524; bookings shrinking, 511, 524; first record (with Sheridan), 511, 521, 528, 541; first-name order, 513; meeting with Brian, 516–18; record sales, 523; relationship with Brian, 542, 570–3, 588–9, 612–13, 632–3;

Aldershot booking, 544; seen by Decca A&R man, 546–7; Decca test (January 1962), 547, 552, 558–63, 579–80, 581, 880–1, 883; turned down by EMI, 547; first PR photo session, 549–50; win *Mersey Beat* poll, 550, 563; *Beatles Christmas Party*, 550; Ringo plays with, 550–1; journey to London, 553–4; Decca test, 557–62, 581; British release of My Bonnie, 563–4; set-lists, 568; Hamburg booking, 569–70; turned down by Decca, 577, 578–83; BBC audition, 584; film footage (February 1962), 585; Liverpool University booking, 589, 769; Floral Hall booking, 589–90, 596–7; *The Beatles For Their Fans* at the Cavern, 590; BBC broadcast *Here We Go*, 602–4; demo discs from Decca tape, 591; non-appearance, 595–6; debut BBC radio recording, 602–4; influence in Liverpool, 607; Gerry deputises for George, 616; Ringo deputises for Pete, 616–18; photo session, 619–20; Stroud show, 620; Cavern Fan Club night, 621–2; Stuart's death, 625–30; Star-Club opening, 630, 631–2; life in Hamburg, 632–5, 641–5; album plans, 635–6; BBC Manchester booking, 646; New Brighton Tower Ballroom booking, 646, 657; EMI recording contract, 646–9, 655, 672; 'pissing on nuns' story, 651–2; Kaempfert recording session (May 1962), 653–5; encounters with Gene Vincent, 659–60, 766; photos in Hamburg, 660–1; return from Hamburg, 661; in London, 663–4; EMI recording session (6 June 1962), 647, 666–72, 725; relationship with George Martin, 670–1, 801–2; Cavern *Welcome Home*, 674; Cavern twelve-date season, 657, 679; John's wedding, 692; dismissal of Pete, 551, 677–9, 691, 700–4; first TV filming, 711–12, 736–7; football pools, 721; tour (August-September 1962), 722–3; EMI recording session (4 September 1962), 724–8; EMI recording session (11 September 1962), 729–32; Ringo's drumming, 736; first biography, 737; press pack, 738–9; publicity photos, 739–40; release of Love Me Do, 745–6; TV appearance on *People And Places*, 737, 777–8; promoting Love Me Do in London, 757–61; encounters with Little Richard, 766, 767–8; Hamburg bookings, 769–70; *NME* article, 782–3; at Empire with Little Richard, 783–5; return to Hamburg (November 1962), 786–7; life in Hamburg, 792–5; return from Hamburg, 795; *Disc* interview, 797; meeting with George Martin, 790, 796, 798–802; choice of songs for second record, 798–9; LP plans, 799, 800, 801, 807, 809, 812, 814; Coventry ballroom booking, 804; audiences, 804–5; Cavern *Welcome Home*, 800; BBC-tv audition, 790, 805; recording session (26 November 1962), 790, 800, 806–10; on *The Talent Spot*, 814, 818; *NME* readers' poll, 814; Peterborough show, 815–16; on *Thank Your Lucky Stars*, 810, 811–12, 813, 818; meeting Tony Barrow, 818–19; first appearance on national TV, 819–20; *Mersey Beat Awards Night*, 824; Cavern show with fans, 825; *People And Places* again, 826; last Hamburg season, 827–9, 839; Hamburg recording, 831–4; rejected by US companies, 835–6; return from Hamburg, 839–40

APPEARANCE: impact, 299; matching stage
outfits, 307; lilac velvet jackets, 342, 349, 355,
364, 371; winkle-picker shoes, 342, 355, 371,
448; hairstyle, 342, 474; leather jackets, 371,
395, 404, 405, 406, 436, 516, 523, 574, 576,
602, 758, 869; pink peaked caps (twat 'ats),
395, 404, 405, 448, 474, 554; cowboy boots,
395, 404, 405, 436, 479, 554; quiffs, 405, 448,
474, 505; jumpers and jeans, 426; collarless
Cardin jackets, 434, 503, 871, 876; in
corduroy, 434, 607; Stu's new hairstyle, 434–5;
leather suits, 448, 474, 479, 490, 536, 549,
554, 621; new look, 448–9; pink neckerchiefs,
474; haircut, 505–6, 507; comb-down
hairstyle, 507–8, 563, 573, 603; all-leather
look, 519, 549, 574–5, 621, 874; Chelsea
boots, 554, 603, 711, 796; group image,
572–4; suits made, 574–6, 602; way of talking,
607; first wearing of suits, 619; suits worn at
Cavern, 621–2; dark velvet waistcoats and
knitted ties, 711; filmed in Cavern, 711–12;
TV debut, 778; at the Empire, 574; suede
jackets, 796, 797, 817; long flat hair, 796, 797,
820; scarves from Astrid, 828
AUTOGRAPHS: Scottish tour, 321–2, 323, 324;
Stuart's, 322; Ringo's, 341, 720; Paul's, 522;
John's, 537; for fans at Floral Hall, 590; for fan
club, 590; on 'throwaway cards', 619–20; Fan
Club night at the Cavern, 622; George's, 693;
Maureen's introduction to Ringo, 716, 718;
The Friday Spectacular, 757, 818; at Kingsway
Club, 885; programme, 897; beetle antennae
motif, 900
DRINKING: in Hamburg, 370, 393–4, 446, 598,
632, 633, 634, 643, 793; in Colony Club, 617;
at Blue Angel, 689
DRUGS: first drugs experience, 339;
Benzedrine, 339, 445; Hamburg supply, 444,
445, 598; Preludin (Prellies), 444–6, 449, 457,
460, 461, 465, 467, 479, 571–2, 598, 632, 634,
720, 793, 809, 832; smuggled, 467, 661; photo
of Beatles with Preludin, 660–1; marijuana,
339n, 596
FANS: first fan, 342–3; in Hamburg, 369–70,
454–5; Fan Club, 489–91, 540–1, 590; at the
Cavern, 535–40, 621–2, 825; *The Beatles For
Their Fans*, 590, 619, 635, 785, 794;
screaming, 604, 622, 676, 688, 712, 715,
804–5, 816; girlfriends issue, 606, 692;
relationship with Beatles, 605–6; Hamburg
correspondence, 635, 642–3; pursued by, 785
GROUP DYNAMICS: on Scottish tour, 319–20;
in Hamburg, 370, 374, 434, 447; after Stu's
departure, 478–9; Ringo's arrival, 617, 716–17,
718–22; sharing rooms, 722, 787; effects of
John and Paul's songwriting, 734–5
HUMOUR/COMEDY: onstage, 431–2; savagery,
434; gags at Cavern, 488–9; in Hamburg, 652,
653; joking with George Martin, 670–1; first
TV appearance, 777, 778
MANAGEMENT: by Allan Williams, 316,
412–13; refusal to pay Williams' commission,
441, 449–50, 459, 482–3, 872; Williams' legal
case, 459, 482–3, 497–8, 513, 544, 588; Pete
and Mona handle bookings, 406, 413, 459,
473–4, 484; need for a manager, 485–6;
possible managers, 486–7; Maureen and

Jennifer's attempt, 509, 511, 514, 524;
discussion with Brian, 523–4; agreement with
Brian, 531–4; contract, 564–6; commission,
565, 588, 633, 686, 703, 786n, 814–15, 838;
Brian's problems, 594–8; new contract with
Ringo, 702–3, 741
MONEY: pay for Scottish tour, 313; contracts
fixed by Allan Williams, 332, 335; contracts
with Koschmider, 351–2, 362, 372–3, 375,
441; Litherland fee, 403; Kelly's jive dances,
406; Leach's bookings, 415, 544, 545, 740–1;
Liverpool fees in 1961: 423, 459, 474, 485,
486, 532, 568, 617–18, 657; Cavern Club
debut, 426; Mona Best's pay, 428, 459;
agreements with Eckhorn, 435, 441, 569;
Cavern bookings, 459, 474, 618, 657, 782;
Wally Hill bookings, 459, 483; cancellation
losses, 499; compensation for lateness, 545;
Star-Club arrangement, 569–70, 633, 786,
827; *Here We Go* fee, 603; Stroud booking,
620; Brian's efforts, 657, 782, 829, 838;
standard ballroom rate, 782; weekly income,
684; Hulme Hall booking, 705; ballroom dates
in Scotland, 789; nationwide tour bookings
(1963), 790; Coventry ballroom date, 804;
EMI royalties, 814–15, 829; *Tuesday
Rendezvous* fee, 820; nightly fee, 829; income
tripled, 838
NAME: Buddy Holly influence, 298; Beetles,
298; Beatals, 299, 315, 322; Beatles, 299,
315–16; Long John and the Silver Beatles,
308–10; Silver Beatles, 310–11, 315; Silver
Beats, 311–12; Fabulous Beatles Rock Combo,
428; Big Beat Boppin' Beatles, 428; John's
story of origins, 437, 737; Tony Sheridan &
The Beat Brothers, 511; Beatles (George
Martin), 648
SEX: in Hamburg, 368–9, 370, 373, 446–7, 457,
599, 633, 643–4, 828; in Neil's van, 484
Beatles Fan Club: launch, 489; organisation,
489–91; Beatles management, 509, 540; Bobby
Brown's role, 540–1, 590; suspended by Brian,
540, 590; relaunched, 590; night at Cavern,
621, 635; members transported to Manchester,
676; discount admission vouchers, 687;
Southern Branch, 825
Beecher-Stevens, Sidney 'Steve', 527, 578, 581,
882
Behan, Pauline, 429, 471
Bennett, Brian, 573
Bennett, Cliff, 838, 902
Bennett, Kim (Tom Whippey): career, 593; name,
883; on George Martin, 592, 803; listens to
Like Dreamers Do, 594; plan to arrange
recording, 594, 640; role in Beatles recording
contract, 640, 668, 728; plugging Love Me Do,
778–80, 790–2, 803, 805, 814, 899
Bentine, Michael, 55, 264, 529, 637, 639
Bentley, Derek, 63, 845
Berger, Kathia, 455, 786
Berry, Chuck: in *NME* Top Thirty, 127; Rock And
Roll Music, 149; John, Paul and George fans of,
169, 223, 239; fans, 174, 194, 753; Carol, 201;
influence, 202; Les Stewart Quartet repertoire,
209; Little Queenie, 215; Quarrymen
repertoire, 229, 240, 285; Cochran
arrangement, 294; Beatles repertoire, 334, 365,

Berry, Chuck – *continued*
  379, 405, 492, 495, 538, 617; on bail, 495;
  Beatles recording, 560; Rolling Stones
  repertoire, 752; sales, 772; influence on Paul's
  compositions, 821; John plays with (1972), 854
Berry, Mike, 699, 702, 893
Besame Mucho (the Coasters), 329, 736; Beatles
  repertoire, 365, 475, 538, 620, 651, 663, 676,
  784; Beatles recordings, 559, 560, 561, 666,
  668–9, 732
Best, Johnny, 223, 230, 304, 406
Best, Mona (Shaw): background, 223; appearance
  and character, 223, 230, 304, 490; marriage,
  223, 230; sons, 223, 230, 691; relationship with
  son Pete, 230, 304, 356, 428, 487, 490, 585;
  Casbah club opening, 226, 227, 230;
  relationship with Quarrymen, 229, 283, 303,
  352, 403; Casbah Sunday sessions, 244; drum
  kit for Pete, 247, 364; relationship with Neil
  Aspinall, 303–4, 484, 691, 837n; Pete's journey
  to Hamburg, 352, 356, 357; Pete's return from
  Hamburg, 399, 401, 404, 542; relationship with
  Beatles, 403, 413, 428, 459, 473–4, 484, 487,
  498, 524, 542, 585, 679, 708; promotions, 428,
  459, 499; encounters with fans, 490, 623;
  pregnancy, 543, 679; view of Brian, 543;
  mother's death, 679; birth of third son, 691;
  response to Pete's dismissal, 703, 709
Best, Pete (Randolph Peter Scanland): family
  background, 230, 358; appearance and
  character, 230–1, 355, 358, 360, 507–8, 671,
  708; childhood, 223; education, 223, 303;
  relationship with mother, 230, 304, 356, 428,
  487, 490, 585; meeting John, Paul and George,
  227; drumming with Blackjacks, 247, 303;
  leaves school, 303; drum kit, 247, 335, 364; at
  Vincent/Cochran show, 295; joins Beatles, 352,
  354–5; journey to Hamburg, 356, 357;
  drumming in Hamburg, 366–7; drumming
  criticised, 388, 417, 447–8, 462, 600–1, 617;
  rolling a sailor, 394; arrested for attempted
  arson, 397–8; deported, 398–9; return from
  Hamburg, 399, 401, 404, 542; return of drum
  kit, 401, 404; Beatles organisation, 406, 413,
  459, 473–4, 484; drumming technique, 411–12,
  417; smoking, 412, 572; relationship with
  Beatles, 417–18, 444, 446, 447, 459, 551, 583,
  600–1; appeal against Hamburg ban, 425, 430,
  435; return to Hamburg, 440–1; drink but no
  drugs, 445, 461; sex in Hamburg, 447, 643;
  fight with Sheridan, 456–7; singing, 456,
  494–5, 585, 605; Beatles fans, 535–40; Decca
  test, 558, 561–2; Decca rejection, 583; singing,
  585; on Stuart's visit, 588; finds out about
  Decca rejection, 600; popularity among fans,
  600, 676–7, 742; Ringo deputises for, 617, 618;
  in love, 622, 674; journey to Hamburg, 624;
  Stuart's death, 626; Stuart's funeral, 628;
  'pissing on nuns' story, 651–2; drumming not
  trusted for recording, 654–5, 670; encounters
  with Gene Vincent, 660; return from Hamburg,
  661; grandmother's death, 661; drumming at
  EMI recording, 668, 669–70, 671, 677; George
  Martin's opinion of, 670, 671, 677, 701, 709,
  741; dismissal from Beatles, 551, 677–9,
  699–703, 708, 709; responses to his dismissal,
  707–11, 712; rejects Mersey Beats offer, 709;

joins Lee Curtis and the All Stars, 741–2, 823;
  legal case against Brian, 741, 742, 823;
  performances with All Stars, 768, 824;
  auditions, 823–4; birthday telegram, 824
Best, Rory: birth, 230; relationship with mother,
  223; guitar, 239–40; at Casbah, 282, 404; Neil
  moves in, 304; birth of brother, 691
Beyond The Fringe, 473, 487, 655, 835, 874
Bierfreund, Marga, 644
Big Three, the: formation, 426; Leach's twelve-
  group session, 430n; Cilla with, 470–1;
  loudspeakers, 495; fans, 536; Brian's
  management, 685–7, 699, 703, 770, 823; in
  Hamburg, 686, 689; drummer works with
  Beatles, 689, 704; Decca test, 823
Bilk, Acker, 488, 501, 520, 683, 834
Billboard: on Elvis, 68; on Capitol, 262, 834;
  charts, 330n, 696; R&B chart, 420; on
  Kaempfert, 453; on Twist, 528; pop chart (Hot
  100), 546, 578, 754, 836n; circulation, 759n;
  name, 759n, 872
Birch, David (John's cousin), 623
Birch, Harriet (Stanley, John's aunt), 38, 183, 232
Birch, Harry, 171
Birch, Liela (Hafez, John's cousin), 73, 183
Birch, Norman (Uncle Norman), 183, 232
Black, Cilla ('Swinging Cilla' White), 470–1, 616,
  898
Blackboard Jungle (film), 72, 77
Blackjacks, the, 246–7, 283, 303, 390
Blue Angel night-club: origins, 307, 355; opening,
  412, 438n; Beatles barred from, 450, 513–14;
  exhibition, 497; Brian at, 525, 743; ban lifted,
  688; Beatles at, 689, 694, 708, 720; stunt at,
  895
Blue Moon (Elvis Presley): bought by John, 117;
  played by John and Paul, 10
Blue Moon Of Kentucky (Elvis Presley), 67–8;
  Quarry Men repertoire, 145
Blue Skies (Irving Berlin), sung by George, 585
Blue Suede Shoes (Carl Perkins), 88, 91, 117, 141,
  294; Quarry Men repertoire, 145, 165
Blue Suede Shoes (Elvis Presley), 88, 293; Quarry
  Men repertoire, 145, 165
Bluegenes (Swinging Bluegenes), 137, 167, 212,
  216, 435–6
Blues Incorporated, 610, 664–5, 753
Boast, Robert (Kenneth), 590, 883
Bolt, Pete, 334
Bonici, Albert, 789
Booker, Johnny, 701
Boone, Pat, 78, 88
Borland, Colin, 527
Bourrée (Bach/Atkins), played by Paul and
  George, 150–1, 862
Bowien, Jimmy, 452
Boyce, David, 772, 876
Boyle, Bernard 'Bernie': first sees Beatles, 480–1;
  jobs for Beatles, 481; on George's guitar, 481–2;
  travelling with Beatles, 485; on *Riverboat
  Shuffle*, 488; Beatles fan club, 489; on Wooler,
  491; on John and Paul, 500; in Hamburg, 651,
  652, 654, 660, 828n; beaten up, 689; on Beatles
  as pop stars, 785; on Beatles and Ifield, 815
Boys (the Shirelles), 421; sung by Cilla and Richy,
  471; Beatles repertoire, 492, 586
Braddock, Bessie, 771, 898

Brady, Pat, 537, 790
Braun, Icke, 455, 786
Breden, Elsa, 710, 745
Brewer, Jenny, 76, 93–4
Brian, Ty (Chas O'Brien), 236n, 331, 379, 381, 470
Brian Poole and the Tremilos (Tremeloes), 579–80, 698, 882
Brierley, John, 188–9, 855
British Sailors' Society, Hamburg, 374, 377, 457, 599, 786
Bron, Sydney, 265, 272, 530
Brooks, Neil, 237
Broonzy, Big Bill, 118, 165, 174, 209
Brown, Joe: recordings, 476; Beatles song selections, 560, 586, 645; and the Bruvvers, 645, 689, 789; Brian's promotion, 645, 646, 688–9, 768; hit, 676; tour, 789; on Cochran's guitar, 862
Brown, Ken: Les Stewart Quartet, 208, 226; Quarrymen, 227, 229, 241, 247; Blackjacks, 247, 283; dumped by Quarrymen, 283–4, 601, 858
Brown, Peter, 277–8, 304, 326, 520, 570, 614
Brown, Roberta 'Bobby': on Beatles at Cavern, 480, 538; sits with Dot, 480; Beatles Fan Club, 540–1, 590, 621, 825, 837n; relationship with Brian, 540–1, 590; on Beatles and Brian, 571; friendship with Mal, 606; on Beatles style, 607; on Brian, 611; drink and drugs, 621, 794, 809; Paul's letters, 643, 645; typewriter for John, 694; on Ringo, 705–6; buys Beatles record, 750; in Hamburg, 794–5; friendship with Astrid, 794, 839; at Beatles recording session, 807, 809
Bryden, Beryl, 69, 102n
Burgess, John, 636
Burlington Music, 582, 591
Burnett, Philip, 125, 136, 354
Burnette, Johnny, 293, 365
Burns, Tito, 789
Butlin's: McCartney family holidays, 71, 138–9, 145; Mike Robbins's work, 71, 138–9, 301; Paul applies for work, 180, 188; Paul and George's holiday, 225–6; Rory Storm and the Hurricanes booking (1960), 288–9, 298, 308, 310, 330–1, 340, 351, 375; Rory and the Hurricanes booking (1961), 431, 439, 469–70; Rory and the Hurricanes booking (1962), 600, 616, 659, 690; Ringo leaves to join Beatles, 700, 704
Bye Bye Love (Everly Brothers), 6, 127, 140; sung by Paul and Mike, 135
Byrne, Gay, 777
Byrne, Johnny (Johnny Guitar): with Ravin' Texans, 124, 212; Morgue Skiffle Cellar, 166; recording (1957), 178; Richy/Ringo joins Texans, 213; electric guitar, 214, 235–6; name, 244; on Ringo's profile, 287; on Ringo's absences, 288n; on Ringo's career plans, 289, 310–11; at Vincent/Cochran show, 295; Cavern booking, 313; Butlin's season, 331; on Ringo's voice, 340; on Lennon-Storm fight, 381; on Leach's twelve-group session, 431; career prospects, 470; in France, 658; on John and Paul meeting Ringo, 689, 690; Ringo leaving Hurricanes, 690
Byrne, Tony, 233

Cain, Geoff, 143

Calder, Tony, 738, 757, 761, 762, 837n, 883
Caldwell, Alan (Al Storm, Jett Storm, Rory Storm): appearance, 166, 288, 575; stutter, 166, 288, 470, 493; stunts, 288; Ravin' Texans, 124, 166, 212; first meeting with George, 166; Morgue Skiffle Cellar, 166–7; Richy auditions for, 213–14; name, 235, 244, 246n; Hurricanes, 235–7, 238; buys guitar, 381; sacked from Kaiserkeller, 393, 399; at Top Ten Club, 399; career prospects, 470; home (Hurricaneville), 493–4, 875; football fan, 721n; watches Paul songwriting, 780; see also Rory Storm and the Hurricanes
Caldwell, Ernie, 166, 494, 775–6
Caldwell, Gordon (George's brother-in-law), 399, 859
Caldwell, Gordon (George's nephew), 399, 859
Caldwell, Iris: birth, 166; appearance, 166; parents' home, 166, 494, 775–6; George's courtship, 165–6, 494; on George's guitar playing, 166; hitchhiking with Hurricanes, 236; dancing career, 288, 775; on Richy/Ringo, 330, 494; relationship with Paul, 775, 776–7, 815; relationship with Frank Ifield, 775, 776–7, 815; on Paul's songwriting, 780
Caldwell, Leslie (George's niece), 399, 859
Caldwell, Louise (Harrison, George's sister): birth, 23; education, 60; home, 29, 48; on brother George's birth, 842; married life in Canada, 399, 859; children, 399, 859
Caldwell, Vi (Ma Storm): character, 166, 493–4, 775–6; home (Hurricaneville), 166, 493–4, 775–6; relationship with George, 166, 494, 793; relationship with Beatles, 494, 720, 775; at Butlin's, 689; relationship with Paul, 776, 780
Calling All Britons (Toronto radio), 834
Calrow, Steve, 478, 537
Calypso Rock, 114, 152
Cannon, Jim, 573, 882
Capitol Records: label, 92; EMI's purchase, 262; 'first turn-down option', 262, 529; George Martin's visit, 272, 273; rejection of EMI discs, 272–3, 472n, 529, 594; George Martin's work, 272, 422–3, 763, 835; refusal to promote British discs, 423, 835; George Martin's view of, 423, 835; view of foreign discs, 453, 834–5; publishing businesses, 591; single sales, 665; Beach Boys, 754, 763; rejection of Love Me Do, 763; Dexter's selections, 763–4; president, 763, 897; rejection of Please Please Me, 834, 836
Capitol Records of Canada, 834
Carol (Chuck Berry): sung by John, 201; Beatles repertoire, 495
Carricker, Tony: record collection, 143, 174; friendship with John, 143, 174, 191; Quarry Men disc, 180; on John's career plans, 197; on Cliff Richard, 200; on Japage 3: 207–8; on Stuart Sutcliffe, 211, 283n; on building site with John, 220–1, 222, 228; on Quarrymen, 229; on Pete Best, 231; asked to join Quarrymen, 241; at party, 292; at Vincent/Cochran show, 294
Carroll, Lewis, 3, 45, 55, 123
Casbah Coffee Club: name, 226; decor, 226, 228, 428, 858; opening, 226–7, 228, 231; Quarrymen at, 228–9, 237, 240–2, 246, 282–3, 296, 352, 403; entry, 229–30, 240; combat with

Casbah Coffee Club – *continued*
Lowlands, 230; Pete Best at, 231, 335, 366, 406, 417; parties upstairs, 242–3; Rory Storm and the Hurricanes, 244; Richy/Ringo at, 244; George at, 303; Beatles at, 401, 403–4, 428, 438, 484, 488, 511, 524, 531, 623; Casbah Promotions, 428, 513; Beatles pay, 428; girls at, 428–9; Beatles cancellation, 499; shut down, 679
Casey, Howard 'Howie', 237, 348, 365, 482, 615
Cash Box: US trade weekly, 68; top ten, 71, 330; chart compilation, 896; on rockabilly, 88; on Twist, 528; on Kaempfert and Sheridan, 528, 878; on My Bonnie, 528, 563, 886; Top 100: 754; circulation, 759n; on George Martin and Beatles, 799–800; on global market, 835; on rock and roll, 837
Cass and the Cassanovas: at Temple jazz club, 237–8; at Jacaranda, 289; management, 290, 313; name, 299, 308; Gene Vincent show, 300, 305; Scotland booking, 310, 313; Hamburg offer, 351; Big Three, 426
Cassar, Brian, 237, 306, 308, 426
Cathy's Clown (Everly Brothers), 303; Beatles repertoire, 343
Catswalk, 218
Caulfield, Ian, 314–15
Cavern Club: opening, 107–8, 176; club rules, 194; no-alcohol policy, 107, 427, 621, 722, 881; Quarry Men at, 6, 108, 137–8, 165; Richy and Roy dancing at, 133, 137; summer skiffle competition, 137; Texans at, 166, 214; Eddie Clayton Skiffle Group at, 171; lunchtime sessions, 187, 427, 429, 459, 476, 478, 479, 515, 522, 572, 616; electric guitars policy, 214, 426; new ownership, 238, 426; jazz festival, 244n, 287; Cassanovas at, 313; Rory and the Hurricanes at, 331, 431, 710; Beatles first appearance, 425, 426–8; audiences, 427, 476, 480, 533, 561, 607; Beatles performances, 429, 430, 431–3, 459, 475, 511; smell, 476–7; electrical problems, 432, 488, 674; safety issues, 477–8; snack bar, 477, 487, 708; Stuart's appearance, 434; Beatles night-time debut, 435–6; Beatles pay, 459, 474, 617–18, 657, 782; Beatles as star attraction, 473; Beatles home, 476, 567; all-night sessions, 487, 513; Mimi's visit, 489; Beatles photo sessions, 490, 519; loudspeaker effects, 495–6, 558; Beatles holiday, 499; Jim's visits, 509; Pacemakers at, 510; Brian at, 515–18, 519–20, 522, 523, 533, 542; Beatles bookings, 524, 552, 563; Lennon-McCartney numbers, 533, 560; Beatles fans, 535–40, 693, 772, 774; Beatles Wednesday residency, 546, 597, 788; Mike Smith at, 546–7, 558; *The Beatles Christmas Party*, 550; *The Beatles For Their Fans*, 590, 619, 635, 785, 794; Beatles girlfriends at, 606; Beatles private rehearsals, 608, 657, 662, 663, 669, 704, 723, 729, 731; Ringo at, 617, 618, 678; Beatles in new suits, 621–2; Beatles away in Hamburg, 622; return of Beatles, 631, 657, 679; *Welcome Home* shows, 657, 674–5, 783; Gene Vincent at, 683; doormen, 688, 722, 823; Beatles Sunday residency, 690n, 707, 788, 815; responses to sacking of Pete Best, 707–9, 710, 722; Granada TV film, 689, 691, 711–12,

736–7, 777; All Stars at, 742; Brian's groups, 770; Brian's booking policy for Beatles, 788–9; George Martin recording plans, 800, 808–9, 822–3; Beatles last 1962 dates, 825
Cayenne, 218, 296, 862
Chadwick, Les (bassist), 150, 450, 510
Chadwick, Les (photographer), 571, 739–40, 768, 894–5
Chains (the Cookies), Beatles repertoire, 821
Chang, Barry, 356, 360
Chang, Val, 450
Channel, Bruce, 608, 646, 650, 657
Chapman, Norman, 337, 345, 346, 355
Charles, Ray, 224–5, 292, 463, 504, 513, 645
Chess, 168, 169, 329n, 753
Chillingworth, Margaret, 708, 710
Churchill, Winston, 11, 27, 32
Clague, Eric, 184
Clarabella (the Jodimars), Beatles repertoire, 609
Clayton, Eddie (Edward Myles): forms group, 110–11; guitar playing, 115, 157, 171; loss of guitar, 145–6; singing, 171; bookings, 187–8; end of musical career, 213; *see also* Eddie Clayton Skiffle Group
Clegg, Florence (Paul's grandmother), *see* McCartney
Clegg, Paul (Paul's great-grandfather), 28
Coasters, the: successes, 141, 215; influence on Paul and George, 141, 215; reputation, 146; Paul's record collection, 201; Besame Mucho, 329; Beatles repertoire, 365, 475, 492, 560; award, 824
Cochran, Eddie: appearance, 116–17; in *The Girl Can't Help It*, 116–17; Gretsch guitar, 117, 119, 295, 481; hits, 141, 215; influence on John and Paul, 3, 329, 335; song played by Stu Sutcliffe, 285; songs in Hurricanes repertoire, 288; Liverpool Empire shows, 294–5, 372; techniques passed on to Sheridan, 372; death, 300–1; songs in Beatles repertoire, 365, 383, 405
Collins, Jackie, 199
Colman, Sid: meeting and agreement with Brian, 591–2, 593, 640; plan for Lennon-McCartney songs, 594, 640; role in Beatles recording contract, 640, 668, 728, 779; sidelined by George Martin, 803
Colyer, Ken, 102n, 110
Come Go With Me (the Dell-Vikings), 117, 128; sung by John, 128, 129, 683; Quarry Men repertoire, 145
Comets, the, 68–9, 71, 106
Cooke, Sam, 149, 766
Costa, Sam, 895
Cottenden, Peter, 239
Cox, Mary 'Maureen', 716, 718, 774
Crane, Tony, 699, 701–2
Crawley, Colin, 598, 599
Cribbins, Bernard, 636–7, 639, 655, 696, 887
Crickets, the: name, 298; group sound, 4, 193–4; recordings, 852; influence on John and Paul, 4, 6, 147, 854; That'll Be The Day, 146–7; Oh Boy!, 150; at Liverpool Philharmonic Hall, 167, 168; at London Palladium, 167–8; recordings in 1958: 168; Quarry Men recording, 179; with Everly Brothers, 303; Beatles repertoire, 365, 679; with Bobby Vee, 835

Cronin, Martha (Millie), *see* Sutcliffe (Millie)
Crozier, Bill, 791
Cry For A Shadow, 465, 511, 608, *see also* Beatle
  Bop
Crying, Waiting, Hoping (Buddy Holly), 224;
  Quarrymen repertoire, 240; Beatles recording,
  559, 560, 561
Cumberland Gap, 119, 128, 268
Curtis, Chris, 586–7
Curtis, Lee, 607, 691, 741–2, 824
Curtis, Tony, 63, 355, 507, 708

Daily Express, 38
Daily Howl, 65, 125, 126
Daily Mirror: on IRA, 25; ad for shoes, 62; on rock
  and roll, 96; on skiffle, 97; on calypso, 114; on
  Soho, 121; on Buddy Holly, 207; on 1960 New
  Year, 247; on Royston Ellis, 338; Paul reads,
  400, 410; northern correspondent, 743, 895
Dale, Jim, 268, 269, 273
Dance Album (Carl Perkins), 293–4
Dance News, 761–2, 796
Danher, Annie (McCartney, Paul's aunt), 20, 21
Danher, Bert (Paul's mother's cousin), 21
Danher, Bett (Paul's cousin), *see* Robbins
Danher, John (Paul's great-grandfather), 20
Danher, Mary Theresa (Paul's grandmother), *see*
  Mohin
Daniels, Billy, 53
Darktown, the, 213–14, 235, 237, 341, 851
Davies, Austin, 292, 861
Davies, Geoff, 535, 538, 539, 681
Davies, Hunter, 211, 869, 877, 888
Davies, Pat, 471
Davis, Rod: banjo playing, 108, 109; Quarry Men
  Cavern debut, 108; *Star Search* competition,
  124; O-levels, 124; Woolton fete, 127, 129;
  memories of Quarry Men, 135; leaves Quarry
  Men, 137, 146
Dawes, Jennifer: Beatles Fan Club, 489–91, 540;
  on parents of Beatles, 490; on Mona Best, 498;
  fan club promotion, 508; relationship with Jim,
  509; Beatles management, 509, 511, 514, 524
Dean, James, 211
Decca Records: studios, 99, 554, 557; skiffle
  recording, 99; Rock Around The Clock, 72;
  London label, *see* London label; Radio
  Luxembourg airtime, 117, 128, 849; Coral
  label, 150; signings, 200, 264, 593, 612n;
  Durium label, 224; George Martin's job offer,
  261; *Echo* ads, 327; Nems discount proposals,
  327; Brian's meeting about Beatles, 527, 531;
  sleeve department, 527, 577; A&R team,
  546–7, 553, 579; A&R man hears Beatles, 543,
  546–7; Beatles test (January 1962), 547, 549,
  552, 557–63, 579–80, 584, 677, 880–1, 883;
  rejection of Beatles, 577, 578–83, 590, 834,
  836, 882; tape of test, 582, 590, 591, 593, 883;
  share of record market, 611; disc technology,
  665; number of releases, 738; press office, 738;
  New Record Mirror, 759; Gerry and the
  Pacemakers, 770, 823; profits, 802; 'American
  Decca', 886
Delaney, Paddy, 436, 515–16, 538, 823
Dell-Vikings, the, 117, 128
Dene, Terry, 121
Derlien, Bettina, 644–5, 794, 833, 839

Derry and the Seniors: name, 237, 299; Levis's
  contest, 237; Gene Vincent show, 301; *Idols On
  Parade*, 310, 347; job commitments, 313;
  Hamburg booking, 347–8, 351, 359n, 361, 363,
  378; return from Hamburg, 375, 410;
  professional group, 426; Leach's twelve-group
  show, 430n
Deutsche Grammophon (DG): Hamburg office,
  452; pop label, 453; Brian's visit, 453–4, 541;
  My Bonnie, 523, 541, 543, 563, 590, 886–7
Devil In His/Her Heart (the Donays), Beatles
  repertoire, 764–5, 832
Dexter, Dave Jr., 272, 423, 529, 665, 763–4, 834
Dexter, Jeff, 762
Dick James Music, 530–1, 554, 813–14, 830–1
Disc: launch, 857; profile of Texans, 212; on rock
  decline, 237; on Johnny Gentle, 318; review of
  Money, 329; Jack Good's column, 422, 609–10;
  on Elvis, 422; on Temperance Seven, 473;
  George Martin interviews, 529, 637, 673; on
  beat groups, 547–8, 673; on singer-songwriters,
  560; review of My Bonnie, 563; on Decca A&R,
  579; on R&B, 609–10; Brian Jones's letter, 610,
  753; on Gene Vincent, 659; on Mick Jagger,
  665; review of Love Me Do, 749; circulation,
  759; chart, 791, 797, 805, 825, 896; Beatles
  interview, 796–7; on Beatles recording session,
  800, 900; on Peterborough show, 816
Dixon, Luther: career, 420; Shirelles sound, 421,
  586, 645, 650; Twist And Shout, 695; songs in
  Beatles repertoire, 753
Dixon, Ric, 589, 882
Dizzy Miss Lizzy (Larry Williams), 168;
  performed by Beatles, 168, 311, 481, 645
Do You Want To Dance (Bobby Freeman), 168,
  174
Do You Want To Know A Secret, 765–6, 897
Docherty, John, 110
Domino, Fats, 112, 116, 194, 201, 365, 794
Dominoes, the, 470, 690, 700, 885, *see also* King-
  Size Taylor and the Dominoes
Doncaster, Patrick, 96
Donegan, Lonnie: John's record collection, 10, 83;
  recordings, 69, 103n, 128; influence on George,
  69, 83; Rock Island Line, 82–3, 126; guitar, 83,
  100; skiffle, 93, 102n, 103n, 109, 273; status,
  126; Teenage Ball, 247
Don't Ever Change (the Crickets), 679; Beatles
  repertoire, 679, 680, 723, 735, 832
Don't Knock The Rock (film), 106, 117
Don't Pass Me By, 720
Don't You Rock Me Daddy-O (Lonnie Donegan),
  108–9
Don't You Rock Me Daddy-O (Vipers), 108–9, 127
Doran, Terry, 277, 570, 618, 683, 684
Dorn, Beno, 576, 602, 666, 882
Dostal, Frank, 653
Double Scotch (George Martin), 530, 531, 637
Douglas, Craig (Terence Perkins), 475, 768–9,
  784, 785
Douglas, Margaret, 341, 480, 516, 643
Dream (Johnny Mercer), 53; sung by George, 585;
  Ringo's recording, 883
Dream Baby (Roy Orbison), 586–7; sung by Paul,
  587, 605; Beatles BBC recording, 604
Drifters, the, 200, 338, 419
Dunham, Joanna, 267

Duque, Linda, 813, 814, 817, 901
Durband, Alan 'Dusty', 190, 196, 234, 292
Duxbury, Margaret (Ducky), 284, 322, 346
Dykins, John (Bobby, 'Twitchy'): employment, 33,
    46, 80; relationship with Julia, 33; Julia and
    John with, 35; pretence of marriage, 37, 184;
    council house, 37, 184; daughters, 46, 47, 80,
    183; relationship with John, 64, 80, 152, 182,
    185–6, 195, 855; drinking, 80–1, 181; finances,
    114, 182; arrest for drunk driving, 181, 855;
    loses job, 181–2; Julia's death, 183; new home,
    184, 195; clothes worn by George, 190
Dylan, Bob, 665, 755, 791

Eager, Vince, 247, 317, 318, 321
Eastman, Lee, 530, 601n
Eastman, Linda, 601n
Eckhorn, Peter: Top Ten Club opening, 348n;
    relationship with Williams, 381, 389, 441, 552;
    Top Ten sound system, 389, 442; Beatles
    agreement, 396, 397n, 425, 435; relationship
    with Koschmider, 397, 398; Paul and Pete's
    departure, 398, 401; dealing with Paul and
    Pete's return, 430; contract with Beatles, 435,
    441; Beatles pay, 435, 441, 483, 552; question
    of Beatles return, 468, 513, 552, 569; Liverpool
    trip, 551–2; hires Ringo, 551; Sheridan
    contract, 599; loses house band, 615
Eckstine, Billy, 53
Eddie Clayton Skiffle Group: formation, 110–11;
    Richy's time with, 133, 137, 213, 341;
    rehearsals, 111; debut, 111; bookings, 111–12,
    120, 171, 187–8, 851; winning competitions,
    115; photo, 120; playing Empire talent
    contests, 124; Cavern skiffle competition, 137;
    instruments, 171; repertoire, 268; breaks up,
    212–13
Eddy, Duane, 194, 303, 329, 336, 394
Edwards, John 'Jack', The Baz: headmaster, 59,
    314; nickname, 845; opinion of George, 209,
    220; on Kelly's cheating, 210; Paul's letter to,
    373; treatment by George, 847
Eliot, Margaret, 255, 781n
Ellis, Geoffrey, 277
Ellis, Royston: career, 337–8; meets George, 338;
    bisexuality, 338, 339; attracted by George, 338,
    345, 360; stays at Gambier Terrace, 338–40;
    342; backed by Beatles, 338, 772; on 'queers',
    339, 522; drugs, 339–40, 446, 865; relationship
    with John and Stuart, 340; Record and Show
    Mirror, 340, 344; John and Stu's visit, 345;
    claims about Beatles, 437n, 865, 866;
    fictionalises experiences with Beatles, 865
Elvin, Carol, 827
Ember, 612, 886
EMI: Heartbreak Hotel, 85; penny-per-record
    contract, 98, 200; Move It!, 200; Parlophone
    label, see Parlophone; Abbey Road studios, see
    Abbey Road; Columbia label, 257, 279; HMV,
    257; record division, 261–2; chairman, 262,
    278, 328, 637, 802; takeover of Capitol, 262;
    George Martin's career, 266, 268, 270, 636,
    638–40; A&R head, 268; Capitol relationship,
    272–3, 422–3, 453, 529, 763–4, 834–5; Nems
    relationship, 327–8, 526; London headquarters,
    327–8; Top Rank label, 418, 475, 586; Brian's
    relationship with, 526; Brian's meeting about

Beatles, 526, 531; correspondence with Brian,
    543–4; rejection of Beatles, 547, 583, 592, 611;
    Decca relations, 557–8; music publishing, 591,
    733, 779, 803; record market share, 611; Beatles
    contract, 640, 647–8, 655–6, 732, 801, 888; end
    of 78rpm, 665; Beatles recording session (6
    June 1962), 666–70, 889; How Do You Do It,
    698; Beatles recording session (4 September
    1962), 712, 724–8; Beatles recording session
    (11 September 1962), 729–32, 897; Lennon-
    McCartney songs copyright, 733, 746; press
    officer, 739; lack of support for Love Me Do,
    747, 748–9, 760, 836; promotions department,
    748; Beach Boys, 753–4; Radio Luxembourg
    shows, 757, 779, 818, 849, 895; Transglobal
    Music, 764, 810, 835; Beatles recording session
    (26 November 1962), 782, 806–10; support for
    Please Please Me, 810, 836; royalty statements,
    814, 829; ages of key personnel, 889; Love Me
    Do hype story, 896
Epstein, Brian: family background, 251–2; birth,
    252; childhood, 252–3; education, 253, 255–6,
    259, 542; passion for theatre, 253, 261, 263;
    career plans, 259, 263; family business, 259,
    261; National Service, 259–60, 542; at Nems,
    261; Clarendon Furnishing, 262–3;
    correspondence with RADA, 263–4; place at
    RADA, 264; at RADA, 266–7, 268; work in
    record department, 267, 271; leaves RADA,
    270; co-management of Nems expansion, 251,
    270–1; Nems Top Twenty chart, 271–2; Nems
    record departments, 270–1, 274–5; sale of
    Stadium tickets, 301; meeting with Parnes,
    304; negotiations with EMI, 327–8; in
    Hamburg, 453–4; Mersey Beat decision, 471;
    PA, 472; Mersey Beat column, 487, 493, 498,
    520, 740; response to My Bonnie, 512, 515;
    Beatles meeting, 515–18; thinks of managing
    Beatles, 518, 519–22; discusses management
    with Beatles, 523–4; meeting with Williams,
    525; ambitions for Beatles, 525–6; London
    meetings, 526–7, 640–1; management
    agreement with Beatles, 531–4; visits Mimi,
    542; visits Mo, 542–3; Beatles contract, 543,
    548–9; Decca response, 546–7; EMI response,
    547; journey to London, 553; Decca test, 558,
    559–60; Beatles sign contract, 564–6;
    stationery, 566; BBC audition application,
    566–7; Cavern relations, 567; Beatles
    organisation, 568; Beatles bookings, 568–9;
    Hamburg booking, 569–70, 601–2; work on
    Beatles group image, 572–4; Decca meeting,
    577; Decca's rejection of Beatles, 578–83;
    Decca test tape, 582, 590–1; finances, 588–9;
    concert promotion plans, 589, 613–14, 646;
    interest in signing other groups, 589, 613–14;
    gets discs cut from Decca tape, 590–1, 640;
    meeting with George Martin, 592–3; London
    trips, 598, 612–13; Pete's drumming, 601;
    Beatles girlfriends policy, 606; BC Enterprises
    plan, 614, 656; arranges police dispensation for
    Paul and Pete, 614; fetches Ringo to deputise
    for Pete, 616–17; Stuart's death, 625–6; in
    Hamburg, 632–3, 635–6; booking for Gerry and
    the Pacemakers, 635; discussions with
    Kaempfert, 635–6; EMI sign Beatles, 640–1;
    sends records to Beatles, 645; EMI recording

contract, 646–8, 655–6; Beatles bookings, 646; Nems Enterprises, 656–7; Beatles return from Hamburg, 662; response to Lennon-McCartney songs, 662–3; suggested song selection for Parlophone, 663; response to suggestions of Pete's dismissal, 677–9, 691; view of Ringo, 678; Big Three management, 685–7, 699, 703, 770, 823; management of Gerry and the Pacemakers, 686–7, 770, 823; impact on Liverpool scene, 687; Little Richard show, 687–8; promotions, 688, 699; Beatles drummer question, 689; expecting Beatles record release, 697; dismissal of Pete, 699–703; Mersey Beats plan, 699–700, 709, 741; asks Ringo to join Beatles, 700; endures responses to Pete's dismissal, 709; at John and Cyn's wedding, 712–13; lends flat to John and Cyn, 713–14, 733; Ardmore and Beechwood contract, 733–4; management and agent contract for Lennon-McCartney songwriting, 734; Granada TV negotiations, 736–7; produces press materials, 737–8; hires Tony Barrow as PR, 738; Pete's legal case against, 741, 742, 823; Publicity Ink proposal, 743–4; on Love Me Do sales, 751; chart hype story, 751–2; *Little Richard At The Tower*, 767, 768; Little Richard and Beatles show at the Empire, 768–9; Hamburg bookings, 769–70; raises Beatles nightly fee, 782, 789, 829; in Hamburg, 788; Beatles 1963 bookings, 788–9, 829; entice-and-reward policy, 789; commissions photos of Beatles, 793–4; meeting with George Martin (November 1962), 802–4; moving Lennon-McCartney from Ardmore and Beechwood, 802–4; at recording session, 807; US plans, 810; meeting with Dick James, 810–14; Billy Kramer signing, 823; at *Mersey Beat Awards Night*, 824; *Year of Achievement* poster, 837, 838, 840
APPEARANCE: manners, 259; voice, 259, 327, 522; blushing, 259, 327, 521, 571, 713; slight and effete, 259–60; immaculate, 327, 522; dress, 260, 264, 271, 516, 522, 602
CHARACTER: shy and temperamental, 259; contemplating suicide, 263; sensitive and intelligent, 267; arrogant and charming, 326, 534; management skills, 326–7, 471–2, 512; autocratic, 472; fragile personality, 534; multi-tasking, 541; punctual, 523, 545, 568
DRINKING: risk-taking, 260, 838; marriage proposal, 276
DRUGS: Preludin, 571–2, 838
MONEY: attitude to, 472; management commission, 532–3, 549, 565, 588, 633, 686, 703, 786n, 814–15, 838; investing his own money in Beatles, 545–6, 588–9, 686, 838
RELATIONSHIPS: with mother, 252, 263, 270, 278, 521–2, 588, 861; with father, 253, 259, 263, 270, 521–2, 588, 861; sexual, 260–1, 597–8, 838; girlfriends, 276–7, 598; memories of Beatles in Nems, 474–5, 518; Beatles Fan Club relations, 540–1; with Beatles, 542, 545, 570–3, 588–9, 612–13, 788, 838; with Paul, 531–3, 565, 570, 595; with John, 534, 571–2, 632–3; with George, 570; Beatles management problems, 594–8; with Allan Williams, 688; with Ringo, 718, 721; with George Martin, 802; with Dick James, 812,
817; commitment to Beatles, 837–8
SEXUALITY: at school, 255–6; 'rough trade', 260–1, 597–8, 838; at RADA, 266; arrest and sentence, 267–8, 270; blackmail case, 275–6; girlfriends, 276–7, 598; European trips, 276–7, 472, 512, 598; appearance, 522; legal threat for defamation, 597; London trips, 598

Epstein, Clive: birth, 252; childhood, 252–3; character, 263, 278; career, 262, 263; National Service, 270; co-management of Nems expansion, 251, 270–1, 472; attitude to Brian's sexuality, 861; name, 276; dress, 576; on Brian's Beatles management plans, 521, 588; Brian's plans for, 613–14; Nems Enterprises, 656; listens to Love Me Do, 745
Epstein, Dinah (Hyman, Brian's grandmother), 251
Epstein, Harry (Brian's father): family background, 251–2; character, 278; marriage, 252; Brian's education, 253; Brian's career, 259, 261, 262–3, 270; Nems expansion, 270, 271; synagogue rebuilding, 276; response to Brian's blackmail case, 275; attitude to Brian's sexuality, 861; meets Newley, 327; concern for Brian, 472, 588; response to Brian's Beatles management plans, 521–2, 588, 611; efforts on behalf of Beatles, 611–13; Brian's company plans, 614; Nems Enterprises, 656; first sight of Beatles, 688; listens to Love Me Do, 745
Epstein, Isaac (Brian's grandfather), 251–2, 262
Epstein, Leslie (Brian's uncle), 252
Epstein, Queenie (Hyman, Brian's mother): character and interests, 252, 278; marriage, 252; sons, 252; Brian's education, 253, 259; sons' careers, 262, 263, 270; response to Brian's blackmail case, 275; attitude to Brian's sexuality, 861; meets Newley, 327; response to Brian's Beatles management plans, 521–2, 588, 611; first sight of Beatles, 688; listens to Love Me Do, 745
Erichsen, Elvi, 455
Esquerita, 100
Estes, Sleepy John, 174, 493
Evans, Mal, 606, 688, 708, 760n
Evening Express (Liverpool), 25, 126, 146, 167
Everly Brothers: British releases, 127, 135, 140–1, 149, 224; influence on John and Paul, 6, 169, 808; success, 140–1, 149, 194, 901; songs played by Hurricanes, 288; George sees, 303; songs played by Beatles, 476; Beatles comparison, 749
Evert, Heike (Goldie), 644, 794
Eymond, Wally, *see* Walters (Lu)

Faith, Adam, 422, 647, 698, 699, 763
Falling In Love Again (Marlene Dietrich), performed by Beatles, 696; Hamburg recording, 833
Fallon, Jack, 620, 885
Farrell, Bernadette, 432, 622, 774, 821
Fascher, Horst: background and character, 372, 444; relationship with Beatles, 443–4, 468, 569, 633–4, 644, 652, 828; violence, 444, 633–4; Liverpool trip, 569–70, 599; Beatles agreement, 569–70, 599, 601; role at Star-Club, 632, 657, 793, 795; photo with Beatles, 661; return of Beatles, 786; singing, 833

Fascher, Manfred (Fredi), 444, 468, 633–4, 786, 795, 833
Fascher, Uwe, 444, 468, 633–4, 786
Feather, Yankel, 327
Felton, Ron, 410
Fierstone, George, 73
Fisher, Graham (pseudonym), *see* Martin (George)
Fishwick, Michael, 73, 182–3
Flanagan, Linda, 720
Flannery, Joe, 691, 741–2, 823, 860–1, 896
Fontaine, Dick, 684–5
Fontaine, Eddie, 201
Fool #1 (Brenda Lee), sung by Paul, 513
Fools Like Me (Bobby Lewis), performed by Beatles, 513
Ford, Len, 744
Ford, Mary, 258–9, 302
Formby, George, 44–5
Forshaw, Dave, 406, 415
Forster, Mark, 306, 307, 309
Four Jays, the, 546, 589, 621, 687, 705, *see also* Four Mosts
Four Mosts, the, 823, *see also* Four Jays
Foy, Jim, 591
Freed, Alan, 68, 72, 106
Freeman, Bobby, 168, 174, 419
French, John (George's grandfather), 22, 518
French, Louise (George's mother), *see* Harrison
The Friday Spectacular (Radio Luxembourg), 757, 818
Friedlander, Frances, 806
Frost, David, 638, 806, 900
Fury, Billy (Ronnie Wycherley): background, 199–200; at Levis audition, 197–8; signed by Parnes, 199–200; backing group audition, 306–10, 316, 361, 365, 863; *Play It Cool!*, 562; Jack Good on, 610

Garrett, Snuff, 680, 836, 902
Garry, Len: at Liverpool Institute, 139, 847; Quarry Men, 6, 161; Quarry Men at Cavern, 108, 138; Quarry Men at Woolton church fete, 129, 130; Quarry Men photo, 145; summer job, 180
Gauld, Margaret, 323, 324
Gentle, Johnny (John Askew): signed by Parnes, 306n, 533; Scottish tour booking, 306, 313; Cass and the Cassanovas, 310; Beatles booking as his backing group, 313, 316–17, 351; Scottish tour with Beatles, 317–18, 320–2, 330, 365, 437, 864; girlfriend, 320; songwriting, 321, 329
Gerry and the Pacemakers: at Blair Hall, 237; Gene Vincent show, 301; accountant, 879; bookings, 313; at Neston Institute, 332; Hamburg invitation, 351, 381; Hamburg booking, 381, 389, 397n; repertoire, 418; return from Hamburg, 426; Leach's twelve-group session, 430n; Hamburg booking, 470; at Litherland, 510–11; at Tower Ballroom, 519; *Mersey Beat* poll, 519, 550; fans, 537; at the Cavern, 546–7, 550; stage outfits, 575; Brian's interest in, 589; Brian withdraws offer, 613; Hamburg booking, 635, 651, 652; return from Hamburg, 686–7; signed by Brian, 687; Ringo's contract, 703; Decca audition, 770, 823; in Hamburg, 787, 788, 828n; George Martin sees, 823

Gillingham, Syd, 739
Gilvey, Jim, 409–10, 426, 870
The Girl Can't Help It (film), 116–17, 149, 170, 178, 294
Glad All Over (Carl Perkins), 150, 294; Beatles repertoire, 784
Gleave, Catherine 'Kitty' (Johnson, Richy's grandmother), 25
Gleave, Elsie (Richy's mother), *see* Starkey
Gleave, John (Richy's grandfather), 25
Goffin-King songs: background, 420–1, 735–6; influence on John and Paul, 421, 650, 735–6, 766, 808; Beatles repertoire, 421, 512, 679–80, 735, 736, 753, 821; style, 586
Good, Jack: career, 108, 894; *Six-Five Special*, 108, 118; books Cliff Richard for *Oh Boy!*, 200; books Eddie Cochran, 294; on Johnny Gentle, 318; books Tony Sheridan for *Oh Boy!*, 372; on Elvis, 422; Wooler plan, 515, 877; on R&B, 609–10
Good Golly Miss Molly (Little Richard), 168, 767; performed by Paul, 168, 416
Goodness Gracious Me! (Sellers and Loren), 423, 801
Goodwin, Ron, 264, 272, 273, 274, 530, 531
The Goon Show, 55, 264, 302, 524, 863
Gore, Ruth, 540
Gorman, John, 771–2
Grade, Lew & Leslie, 106, 147, 380
Graham, Bobby, 689, 891
Granada TV: *People And Places*, 279n, 737, 777, 782, 826, 898; Beatles fan club letter, 498; Brian contacts, 684; Fontaine's Cavern visit, 684–5; Cavern recces, 685, 688, 777; Cavern filming, 689, 691, 711–12, 736–7; Beatles first appearance, 777, 778, 781; Beatles second appearance, 818, 825, 826
Grant, Jimmy, 121, 779
Graves, Harry Arthur: background, 53; character, 53, 66; relationship with Elsie, 53; employment, 53; singing, 53, 844; social life, 53–4; relationship with Richy, 53, 66, 104; dress, 62; marriage to Elsie, 66; home, 66, 235; trip to Romford, 76; finding work for Richy, 83, 91; drum kit for Richy, 104, 187, 376; arranges booking for Eddie Clayton Skiffle Group, 171; Richy's name, 244, 718; view of Richy's career, 330, 331, 870; meets Maureen, 716; football pools, 721
Great Balls Of Fire (Jerry Lee Lewis), 6, 150
Greenberg, Florence, 420
Gregson, Bill, 349
Gretty, Jim, 134, 508, 843, 850, 862
Griffiths, Eric: character, 159, 164; Quarry Men, 102, 103, 138; first Cavern performance, 108; guitar playing, 109–10, 144, 157, 848; Locarno Ballroom competition, 115; O-levels, 124; Quarry Men photos, 129, 145, 163, 853; Quarry Men rehearsals, 135; Quarry Men songs, 6; sacked from Quarry Men, 163–4, 241, 418, 678, 853; career, 853
Guirron, Marie: relationship with George, 693–4, 715, 774; on Pete and Ringo, 710; on John and George, 719; life, 898
Guitar Boogie (Arthur Smith and his Crackerjacks), 144
guitars: Antoria, 235–6; Egmond, 78, 94, 100, 851;

Fender, 168–9, 239, 381; Futurama, 239–40, 315, 316, 318, 333, 389, 393, 451, 465, 481, 875; Gallotone Champion, 114, 124, 198; Gibson, 464, 465, 684, 688–9, 729, 730, 731, 732, 735, 807, 820; Gretsch 6120: 117, 119; Gretsch Duo Jet, 481, 667, 726, 730, 731, 735, 736, 807; Hofner 333: 282, 285, 334, 458, 467; Hofner Club 40 (Club Footy), 216, 227, 240, 316, 389, 390n; Hofner Committee, 101; Hofner President, 136, 162, 208, 403, 858; Hofner Senator, 227; Hofner Violin, 460, 467, 474, 495, 667, 807; homemade, 281, 285, 848, 861; Martin, 442; Rex, 112–13, 119; Rosetti Solid 7: 342, 371, 411, 442, 451, 460; Rickenbacker 325: 381–2, 390n, 391, 393, 443, 451, 667, 868; tea-chest, 97, 102, 103, 108, 109, 110, 119–20, 146, 161, 171, 194, 213, 268; Zenith, 134–5, 162, 163, 240

Gustafson, Johnny: earnings, 289; on rockers' ambitions, 308; on Hutch, 308; on Beatles, 309; asked to join Beatles, 403; on impact of Beatles, 414; on John and Paul, 500; on Big Three signing, 686

Hague, Jon: at art school, 143, 165; on John's friendships, 165, 191; asked to be drummer, 241; on Stuart Sutcliffe, 283n; on Beatles first appearance, 299; on John's drinking, 339
Haley, Bill: career, 68; Rock Around The Clock, 68–9, 81, 82; Shake, Rattle And Roll, 71; impact on Paul, 77; guitar, 83; age, 86; 1957 British tour, 106–7, 108–9; Paul sees, 106–7
Hall, Billy, 36–7, 49
Hallelujah, I Love Her So (Eddie Cochran), 335; recorded by Beatles, 335–6; Beatles repertoire, 404; Hamburg recording, 832, 833
Hand, Albert, 760
Hanton, Colin: Quarry Men drummer, 103, 109, 138, 145, 152, 161, 164, 167, 850; Cavern debut, 108; Quarry Men rehearsals, 109; Star Search, 124; Quarry Men bookings, 130, 167; Quarry Men songs, 6, 179; Quarry Men photos, 145, 163, 177; Quarry Men recording session, 178–80; departure from Quarry Men, 180
Harris, David: background, 548; contract between Brian and Beatles, 548–9, 678; Pete Best problem, 678, 699, 702; management agreement between Brian and Beatles, 734; Lennon-McCartney agreement with Brian, 734; Pete Best case, 741, 823; Lennon-McCartney contract, 830
Harris, Gin (McCartney, Paul's aunt), 4, 19, 20, 21, 54, 685, 846
Harris, Harry (Paul's uncle), 107, 846
Harris, Ian (Paul's cousin), 75, 107, 162, 846
Harris, Jackie, 162
Harris, Jet, 705, 769
Harris, June, 473, 797
Harris, Mona, 143, 173–4
Harris, Rita, 277, 598
Harris, Wynonie, 100, 174
Harrison, Edward (great-grandfather), 21#
Harrison, Elizabeth (Hargreaves, great-grandmother), 21
Harrison, George: family background, 21–3; birth, 29; name, 29; childhood, 31; musical influences, 44–5, 78; education, 46, 49, 52, 60; home, 48–9; National Service issue, 58, 81, 120–1; religious views, 61; Liverpool Institute, 69–70, 89–90, 95; smoking, 70, 572; Formula One fan, 75–6, 618, 694; family holidays, 76, 93–4; illness (nephritis), 78; record buying, 83, 402n; Elvis influence, 86, 94, 169; Little Richard influence, 87; musical education, 101; *Rock Around The Clock*, 96; Bill Haley at Liverpool Odeon, 106; seeing live shows, 117–18; booking for group, 119–20; Buddy Holly influence, 150, 167–9; joins Quarry Men, 157–9, 534; Quarry Men rehearsals, 161–2, 171–2; at Morgue Skiffle Cellar, 167; Chuck Berry influence, 169; Quarry Men record session, 179; holidays with Paul, 188–9, 220, 225–6; dislike of school, 190; O-levels, 190, 209; group with John and Paul, 197–8; Johnny and the Moondogs, 198–9; Japage 3: 201–4; Les Stewart Quartet, 208–9, 218, 226; employment, 208; leaves school, 210, 220; playing with John and Paul, 218–19; career prospects, 220, 234–5, 246; apprenticeship at Blackler's, 238–9, 246, 315; Carl Perkins influence, 293–4; at Vincent/Cochran stage show, 295; Beatles name, 299; seeing Liverpool Empire shows, 302–3; at Casbah, 303; Billy Fury backing group audition, 307–10; leaves apprenticeship, 315, 333; Scottish tour, 314–25; moves in with John and Stu, 333; meets Royston Ellis, 338, 345; first drugs experience, 339; Hamburg booking, 353; journey to Hamburg, 356; Hamburg pay, 372–3; letters from Hamburg, 372–3, 380, 622, 649, 792–3, 828–9, 831; under-age, 389; forced to leave Hamburg, 389, 396; return from Hamburg, 398–9; meeting with Wooler, 402; return to Hamburg, 436, 438–9, 440; drugs in Hamburg, 446, 634; drinking, 446; photo session with Jürgen, 450–1; response to first record, 511–12; first meeting with Brian, 518; management agreement with Brian, 531–4; Beatles fans, 535–40; Decca test, 561, 581; on Beatles-Epstein relationship, 566; interest in Brian's business methods, 568; response to Decca, 581; smokes marijuana, 596–7; wants Ringo to join Beatles, 617, 618, 706, 718; car (Ford Anglia), 618, 674, 681, 683, 693–4, 715, 828; car race with Ringo, 618–19, 659; illness (German measles), 623; Stu's death, 626; Stu's funeral, 628; Astrid's photographs, 641; life in Hamburg, 643; 'pissing on nuns' story, 651; return from Hamburg, 661; at EMI recording session, 670–1; at John's wedding, 713; black eye at Cavern, 722, 724; London press visits, 756, 758; opens show at Empire, 784
APPEARANCE: as a child, 35, 60; lop-sided smile, 35, 90, 711; boy playing guitar, 78; quiff, 90, 95, 360; high hair, 90, 162, 246; notions of school uniform, 95, 118, 190; accent, 159, 518; individual dress, 159; splayed ears, 162, 724; with Quarry Men, 162–3, 177; smart suit, 246; long hair and matelot T-shirt, 338, 360; on journey to Hamburg, 360; cowboy boots and tight jeans, 400; comb-forward hairstyle, 507–8; attitude to wearing suits, 575; handsome, 693; filmed playing in Cavern, 711; black eye, 722, 724

Harrison, George – *continued*
  CHARACTER: self-reliant, 35; self-sufficient
    and opinionated, 60; sceptical, 60–1;
    determined, 94, 209; cocky, 158; humour, 158,
    160–1; patient, 208; optimistic, 613; gentle,
    693; interested in other people, 819
  GUITAR: first guitar, 78, 94; practising, 94;
    lessons, 100–1; learning chords, 101, 112, 148;
    studying guitar players, 117; photo of him
    with guitar, 119; playing with quartet, 119–20;
    new guitar (Hofner President), 136, 162, 208;
    electric guitar, 172; guitar influences, 150;
    performing with Paul, 188; buys electric guitar
    (Hofner Club 40), 216; new guitar
    (Futurama), 239–40; playing with Long John
    and the Silver Beatles, 309; playing lead in
    Hamburg, 366; learns techniques from
    Sheridan, 372; buys Gretsch guitar, 481–2;
    new guitar (Jumbo Gibson), 684, 729
  RELATIONSHIPS: friendship with Arthur Kelly,
    69–70, 94–5, 140; friendship with Paul, 101,
    136, 139–42, 188; idolatry of John, 158–9;
    Quarry Men relationships, 159–61, 163–5,
    178, 227; first girlfriend, 165–6; sex, 243, 368,
    447; social life, 292–3; girlfriend Pauline, 429,
    471; relationship with Brian, 570; girlfriend
    Marie, 693–4, 715, 719, 774; friendship with
    Ringo, 718, 722; girlfriend Bernadette, 774
  SINGING: with first group, 120; harmony
    singing, 201, 365, 832; singing Carl Perkins,
    240; in Hamburg, 383; backing vocals, 421,
    546, 585, 654, 668; Decca test, 561; equal
    singing status, 572, 584, 735; singing Elvis,
    606; George Martin's assessment, 647,
    663
  SONGWRITING: with Paul, 172; role, 734–5
Harrison, Harold Hargreaves (Harry, father):
    character, 22, 23, 34, 52, 76, 315, 333;
    employment, 4, 22, 23, 34, 44, 353, 716n, 748;
    marriage, 23; children, 23, 29; homes, 23, 29,
    34–5, 48–9, 715; guitar, 101; record collection,
    44; wartime life, 26; birth of son George, 29;
    George's education, 52, 101, 210; George's
    haircuts, 60; dress, 62; first car, 76; George's
    guitar playing, 101; plans for George's career,
    235, 238, 246; view of George's career, 315, 333,
    353, 399; encounters with Beatles fans, 623;
    signs George's contract, 743; hearing Love Me
    Do on radio, 748
Harrison, George (journalist), 146
Harrison, Harry (brother): birth, 23; childhood,
    29; home, 48; education, 60; motor sports, 76;
    employment, 94, 246; clothes, 95; wedding
    party, 201, 203–4; flat, 210
Harrison, Henry (Harry, grandfather), 21, 23
Harrison, Irene (sister-in-law), 201, 210, 333n, 857
Harrison, Jane (Thompson, grandmother), 21–2
Harrison, Louise (French, mother): birth, 22;
    character, 22, 34, 76, 333; marriage, 23;
    children, 23, 27, 29; homes, 23, 29, 34–5, 48–9,
    715; children's education, 46, 61, 210; family
    car, 76; George's first guitar, 78; George's guitar
    playing, 94, 119, 171; Paul's mother's death,
    173; John's mother's death, 188; *Star Search*,
    198; money for George, 234; view of George's
    career, 333, 353, 356; Canada trip, 399, 471;
    encounters with Beatles fans, 490, 623; on

George's business sense, 568; at Stuart's
    funeral, 628; Love Me Do on radio, 748
Harrison, Louise (sister), *see* Caldwell (Louise)
Harrison, Paul (nephew), 857
Harrison, Peter (brother): birth, 27; childhood, 29;
    family homes, 29, 48, 715; education, 46, 60;
    interest in motor-racing, 76; employment, 94,
    246; fixes George's guitar, 94; playing guitar,
    119; car, 715
Harrison, Sidney, 254–5, 256–7
Harry, Bill: cousin of June, 851; at art school, 142,
    299; on John, 142, 173; friendship with Stuart,
    143, 299; friendship with John, 143; on John
    and Stuart, 191; on Stuart, 300; Benzedrine
    experience, 339; *Jazz To Poetry* concert, 871–2;
    Mersey Beat, 436–8, 471, 479; John's writing,
    437–8, 471, 694; Beatles publicity, 482, 563;
    Brian's record review column, 482, 750; Beatles
    management question, 486; Bob Wooler's
    column, 491; Brian/Beatles contact, 515;
    returns photos to John, 573; on Pete Best,
    600–1; 'Beatles recording' telegram, 648;
    Mersey Beat reporting of Beatles drummer
    change, 712; *Mersey Beat Awards Night*, 824
Harry, June, 125, 143, 354, 851
Harry Lime Theme (Anton Karas), played by
    John, 151, 365
Hart, Mike, 772, 876
Harvey, Ann, 165
Hatton, Billy, 546, 705
Hayward, Ivan, 481
Healey, Peter, 110
Heartbreak Hotel (Elvis Presley), 82, 85, 86, 91,
    94, 114, 328, 422; Quarry Men repertoire, 145
Heitmann, Rosi, 441, 446–7, 456, 457, 598
Hello Little Girl: writing, 4, 152–3; title, 852;
    recorded by Beatles, 153, 336; Beatles
    repertoire, 533; recording, 559, 560, 561, 562;
    radio audition, 584; record, 592–3, 648; BBC
    recording, 604; John and Paul's view, 669
Hennessey, Mike, 38
Henriod, Henri, 660
Here We Go (BBC Light Programme), 602–4,
    675–6, 783, 884, 890
Hey! Ba-Ba-Re-Bop (Lionel Hampton), performed
    by Beatles, 696
Hey! Baby (Bruce Channel), Beatles repertoire,
    608–9, 645, 650, 832
Hicks, Tommy, *see* Steele (Tommy)
Hill, Michael, 57, 58, 65, 86–7
Hill, Wally: career, 212; first venue, 212; second
    venue, 237; Beatles bookings, 459, 473; end of
    Beatles relationship, 483–4, 485, 488, 511
Hines, Iain, 332
Hinze, Karl, 462, 465
The Hippy Hippy Shake (Chan Romero), played
    by Beatles, 433
His Latest Flame (Elvis Presley), performed by
    Beatles, 513
His Master's Voice (HMV): cross-licensing
    arrangement, 85; Oxford Street store, 200n,
    590, 640, 739; EMI label, 257; George Martin's
    career, 266; Beatles discs cut, 590–1, 640, 739;
    signings, 612n
Hit The Road Jack (Ray Charles), performed by
    Beatles, 511, 513
Hodgetts, Pat, 825

Hodkin, Derek, 143, 201–4, 207–8, 215–16, 316, 524
Hoffman, Rosa, 444, 445
Hold Me Tight, 735
The Hole In The Ground (Bernard Cribbins), 636–7, 655, 696
Holly, Buddy: appearance, 147, 168, 169, 580, 602n; songwriting, 841, 894; record credits, 852, 894; influence on John and Paul's songwriting, 4, 5, 6, 10, 152–3, 217, 224, 336, 650, 852, 854; Peggy Sue, 6, 149; John on, 146; British tour, 147; studied by John and Paul, 149; influence on George, 150, 239; at Liverpool Philharmonic Hall, 167, 168; at London Palladium, 167–8; recordings in 1958: 168–9; song recorded by John and Paul, 179; songs played by John, Paul and George, 189, 198; death, 207, 294, 552, 679, 736; releases after death, 224, 679, 749; songs performed by Quarrymen, 229, 240; influence on Beatles name, 298; songs in Beatles repertoire, 365, 560, 608, 736
Holly, Ida, 714–15
Honey Don't (Carl Perkins), 88, 117, 294; played by Beatles, 372, 481, 539
The Honeymoon Song (Marino Marini Quartet), 224; Beatles repertoire, 533, 620, 651
Honky Tonk Blues (Hank Williams), sung by John, 78, 365
Horton, Ken, 382
Hot As Sun, 218
Houghton, Barbara, 538, 539, 622, 674
Houghton (Horton), Len, 101, 848
Houghton, Sue (Cement Mixer), 723n, 820, 822, 827, 828–9, 893
Hound Dog (Elvis Presley), 3, 122, 150; Quarry Men repertoire, 145
How Do You Do It (Mitch Murray): history, 697–8; acetate disc sent to Brian, 697, 698, 830; Beatles response, 698–9; rearranged, 699, 729; rehearsing, 723, 725; EMI recording (4 September 1962), 724, 727; Beatles protest against, 727–8, 798; scrapped, 728–9
Howard, Ira, 88
Howes, Arthur, 769, 789–90, 815, 816
Hughes, Raymond, 78
Hully Gully (the Olympics), sung by John, 475, 488
Hunt, H. & Son: Richy's job, 91; Roy Trafford at, 94, 717; Richy's apprenticeship, 95, 104, 143, 171, 186, 214, 289, 311; Richy's earnings, 95, 171, 245, 330; summer break, 96n; skiffle group, 110; relocation, 187; Richy leaves, 330, 376
Hunter, Nigel, 579, 797, 896
Hurricanes, see Al Storm and his Hurricanes, Rory Storm and the Hurricanes
Huston, Chris, 333–4, 411
Hutchinson, Johnny 'Hutch', 245, 308–9, 495, 689, 704, 891

I Call It Suicide, 89, 847, 852
I Call Your Name, 10, 218
I Fancy Me Chances, 197, 202, 856
I Feel So Bad (Elvis Presley), sung by Paul, 494
I Forgot To Remember To Forget (Elvis Presley), sung by George, 201, 606

I Just Don't Understand (Ann-Margret), sung by John, 495, 609
I Lost My Little Girl, 4, 153, 852
I Remember You (Frank Ifield), 695, 696, 763, 816; harmonica, 695, 763, 833, 895; Beatles repertoire, 695, 723; Hamburg recording, 833
I Saw Her Standing There: writing, 780–1, 820–1; Hamburg recording, 832, 833
I Wish I Could Shimmy Like My Sister Kate (the Olympics), Beatles repertoire, 419
If You Gotta Make A Fool Of Somebody (James Ray), 587, 609; Beatles repertoire, 587, 609, 696, 723, 832
Ifield, Frank: appearance, 695, 776; successes, 695, 696, 746, 763, 816; at Empire, 769, 776; advice to Brian, 769; Beatles booking, 769, 790, 815–16; relationship with Iris Caldwell, 775, 776–7
I'll Always Be In Love With You (Michael Holliday), 336; recorded by Beatles, 336
I'll Be Home, 88
I'll Be On My Way, 218, 735
I'll Follow The Sun, 217, 336
I'll Never Let You Go (Elvis Presley), sung by Paul, 201, 893
I'm Gonna Sit Right Down And Cry (Elvis Presley), 113; Hamburg recording, 833
In Spite Of All The Danger (McCartney-Harrison), 172, 179, 180, 296
Indra, Hamburg: Beatles booking, 351; Beatles arrival, 361–4; Beatles pay, 362n; accommodation for Beatles, 363; publicity photos, 364, 373, 443; first night for Beatles, 366; Beatles performances, 366–7, 378, 411, 632; noise issues, 366, 370, 375, 388; audiences, 367, 369, 370; Beatles last performance, 375; influence, 633

Jacaranda: coffee bar, 175, 450; creation of club, 175, 176; membership, 175–6, 498; acts, 289–90; Beatles rehearsals, 310, 379; Beatles playing in, 337, 403; contact for Beatles, 351–2; Pete Best's 'audition', 355
Jacaranda Enterprises, 304, 348, 412–13
Jack, Margaret, 323–4
Jacobs, David, 224, 224n, 564
Jagger, Mick, 610–11, 665, 752–3, 896
Jailhouse Rock (film), 170, 178
James, Dick: family background, 812n; appearance, 264–5, 816–17; character, 813; careers, 264–5, 530, 812n, 860; name, 812n; relationship with George Martin, 264–5, 530; Dick James Music, 530–1, 554, 813–14, 830–1; How Do You Do It, 698, 728, 830; Lennon-McCartney songs, 803–4, 812–14; Please Please Me, 810–14, 829; meeting with Brian, 810–13; relationship with Brian, 812–13; Beatles bookings, 811–12, 818; Lennon-McCartney agreements, 813–14, 817–18; meeting with Beatles, 816–17; relationship with Beatles, 817, 818, 819, 829, 901; Lennon-McCartney contract, 830–1; new music publishing company, 830–1
James, Ian: home, 112, 849; friendship with Paul, 112–13, 122, 140; guitar, 112–13; playing with Paul, 112–13, 118–19, 122; Dingle boy, 133; on Paul's imitation of Little Richard, 3; musical

James, Ian – *continued*
duo with Paul, 135; on Paul's songwriting, 153; leaves school, 220
Japage 3: formation, 203; management, 203, 207–8, 215–16; drumming, 203, 346; public debut, 201, 203–4, 857; bookings, 207–8, 215, 227, 379, 897; end of, 216, 228
Jazz News, 611, 753, 885
Jazz To Poetry events, 771, 871–2
Jets, the: Koschmider booking, 331, 332, 348n, 351, 363, 371–2; Eckhorn booking, 348n, 388, 397
Jim Mac's Band, 2, 20, 21, 42, 297n
Joe's Restaurant, 494, 613, 720
Johnny and the Moondogs, 198–9, 228, 237, 508, 856
Johnny B. Goode (Chuck Berry), 169; Beatles repertoire, 495
Johnson, Beryl, 427, 538, 708
Johnson, Catherine (Kathy), 622, 674
Jones, Brian, 610–11, 665, 752–3, 896
Jones, Len, 235
Jones, Philip, 811
Jones, Raymond, 512, 523, 783, 877
Jones, Vivien, 540, 742
Jopling, Norman, 746, 796–7
Jourdan, Pat, 143, 175, 191, 231
Juke Box Jury (BBC-tv): origins, 224n; Paul and Mike watch, 513; My Bonnie rejected, 563; scheduling, 564; Time Beat a Miss, 637; Love Me Do rejected, 747, 779, 803, 829; Please Please Me, 829–30
Just Fun, 6
Justis, Bill, 150, 194

Kaempfert, Bert: background, 452–3; Decca relationship, 886; plan to sign Sheridan and Beatles, 453; Beatles name, 873; John's CV for, 466, 534; Beatles first recording session (June 1961), 461–5, 561; contract with Beatles, 465–6, 482, 523, 526, 531, 541, 543, 635–6; record release, 511; American Twist plans, 528, 878; Brian's contact with, 541; Brian's discussions with, 635–6; Beatles recording session (May 1962), 653–5; death, 654
Kaiserkeller, Hamburg: Allan Williams' first visit, 290–1; Jets at, 332, 348n, 372, 397; Derry and the Seniors at, 348, 351, 363, 365; Beatles arrival, 361, 365; Koschmider's office, 362n, 395; audiences, 371; Sheridan's role, 371–2; Beatles at, 375, 377–80, 383, 384, 387, 388–9, 391, 392n, 393, 411, 443, 550, 632, 633; Rory Storm and the Hurricanes at, 375, 377, 379, 384, 393, 399, 550; stage damaged, 393, 395, 416; violence, 442; talent spotters, 452; Bats at, 587, 653, 883
Kansas City (Little Richard), 215; Beatles repertoire, 481; Hamburg recording, 833
Keep Looking That Way, 297
Keep Your Hands Off My Baby (Little Eva), Beatles repertoire, 821
Kelland, Arthur, 578, 581
Kelly, Arthur: friendship with George, 69–70, 75, 94–5, 140, 246, 372; education, 69–70, 118, 190, 209–10; guitar, 83, 119, 160, 172, 848; on George, 90, 169, 190; in George's group, 119–20; on Quarry Men, 160–1; girlfriend, 165;

on Vi Caldwell, 166; Quarry Men recording, 178, 854; photo with Quarry Men, 177; on John's guitar, 198; at Quarry Men audition, 199; employment, 210, 241; on Quarrymen, 229; on George's guitar, 240; asked to join Quarrymen, 241; on One After 909 recording, 296; on Stuart, 300; George writes from Hamburg, 372, 381; George's return from Hamburg, 400
Kelly, Brian 'Beekay': background, 212; promotions, 212, 414; books Beatles, 311; Beatles miss booking, 316, 337; books Beatles again, 403, 406, 410; Wooler's stage management, 413; Beatles bookings, 426, 459, 473; Beatles management question, 487; Beatles cancellation, 499, 510; Beatles drunken show, 510–11; drops Beatles, 511, 513
Kelly, Freda, 536, 537, 750, 784, 825, 838
Kelly, Margaret, 708, 865
Kennedy, John, 266
Kent, Tommy (Guntram Kühbeck), 453
King, Carole, *see* Goffin-King songs
King Creole (film), 193
King-Size Taylor and the Dominoes: name, 299; at the Lathom, 311; repertoire, 421; Leach's twelve-group session, 430n; at Tower Ballroom, 519; at the Cavern, 550; Ringo plays with, 690; in Hamburg, 787, 827, 831
Kinsley, Billy, 699, 701–2, 765, 893, 896
Kirchherr, Astrid: background, 383, 387; appearance, 384, 439; sees Beatles, 384–5; friendship with Stuart, 385–6; photography, 386, 887; love affair with Stuart, 386; car, 387, 390; Beatles photo session, 390–1, 450, 451, 482; home, 391–2, 444; bedroom, 392, 457; engagement to Stuart, 392–3, 395; on John's shoplifting, 394; George's departure, 396; with Stuart, 411; in Liverpool, 416, 424–5, 428, 429, 434; relationship with Millie, 424, 497, 587, 627, 628, 631, 642; makes jacket for Stuart, 434, 503, 871; cuts Stuart's hair, 434–5; return to Hamburg, 435; Paul and Pete appeal, 435, 436; welcomes Beatles back to Hamburg, 439; at Top Ten Club, 442, 455; takes Preludin, 445; wedding plans, 448, 588; Beatles leather look, 448; Jürgen's photos, 452, 872; Cyn's visit, 457, 458; Stuart's farewell to Beatles, 467, 468; Stuart's illness, 497, 587, 614, 615, 883; in Liverpool, 497; photographs of Stuart, 614–15, 641; Stuart's death, 624, 625–6; on Stuart, 628–9; Stuart's funeral, 628, 634, 641; photos of John and George, 641, 683, 894; on John, 641–2; Beatles return to Hamburg, 786; Beatles photo session, 793–4, 817, 837; at Star-Club, 794; knits scarves for Beatles, 828; farewell to Beatles, 839
Kirchherr, Nielsa: home, 391–2, 399; cooking, 392, 444; relationship with Stuart, 392; Cyn's visit, 457; buys paints and brushes for Stuart, 458; Stuart's illness, 497, 587, 615; Stuart's death, 624
Knibbs, Ted, 767, 898
Korner, Alexis, 610, 664, 665, 753
Koschmider, Bruno: appearance, 291; character, 291; first meeting with Allan Williams, 291, 633; London visits, 331–2, 348; books the Jets, 332, 351; Jets walk out on, 348n; contract with

Williams for Derry and the Seniors, 348, 351,
359n; business arrangement with Williams,
348, 362n, 376, 380–1, 389; books Beatles, 351;
meets Beatles, 361–2; contracts with Beatles,
362–3, 375, 377, 380, 388; Beatles pay, 362n,
441; accommodation for Beatles, 363, 390;
relationship with Beatles, 364, 371, 375,
379–80, 381, 388, 389, 393; photographs of
Beatles, 364; noise problem, 366, 370–1, 375;
books the Hurricanes, 375, 376;
accommodation for Hurricanes, 377; contract
with Hurricanes, 377–8, 416; gives notice to
Beatles, 388–9, 391, 393; showdown with
Beatles, 395–6; Paul and Pete charged with
attempted arson and deported, 397–8;
shipping Beatles gear, 401; Beatles second
season, 441
Kramer, Billy, 767, 770, 823, 824, 870

Lallemannd, Ruth, 445, 794
Laurie Records, 836, 837n, 902
Lawdy Miss Clawdy (Elvis Presley), 113; played by
Paul and Ian, 135; Quarry Men repertoire, 145
Leach, Sam: career in promotions, 194, 211, 415;
Mossway Jiving Club, 194; Chez Jazrok, 247;
Cassanova Club, 415; Beatles bookings, 415,
524, 544–5, 595, 596, 616, 704, 740; LJS,
430–1; twelve-group session, 430–1; *Mersey
Beat*, 872; considers managing Beatles, 486,
519, 545; *Operation Big Beat*, 518–19;
relationship with Brian, 687, 740–1, 878, 884;
football fan, 721n; Beatles pay issue, 740–1
Lead Belly, 103n, 174, 209
Leave My Kitten Alone (Little Willie John), 224;
Beatles repertoire, 419
Lee Curtis and the All-Stars, 691, 741–2, 768,
823–4
Lee, Geoff, 101n
Leidigkeit, Brigitte, 454–5
Leiper, Fran, 792
Lend Me Your Comb (Carl Perkins), 168, 294;
performed by Beatles, 429
Lennon, Alfred (Alf, father): birth and childhood,
16; employment, 16, 17–18, 22, 30, 35–6, 288,
716n; relationship with Julia, 16, 17, 18;
singing, 18, 124, 224; marriage, 18, 26, 292n,
713; wartime, 26–7, 30; birth of son, 27;
imprisonments, 30, 49; Julia's affairs and
pregnancy, 30; relationship with son John,
30–1, 36–7, 38, 50, 185, 192; living with
mother, 31, 50; end of marriage, 36, 46, 49–50;
dismissal from Merchant Service, 50; itinerant
life, 50, 184–5, 292n, 452, 712; Julia's death,
184–5
Lennon, Charles (uncle), 184
Lennon, Jacqueline Gertrude (Dykins, half-sister),
47, 80, 183, 232
Lennon, James (great-grandfather), 15, 740
Lennon, John: family background, 15–18; birth,
27; childhood, 29–30, 35–7, 38–9; education,
35, 36, 37, 39, 45–6, 56–7; reading, 3, 38–9, 45;
musical education, 42, 43, 78–9; musical
influences, 45–6; National Service issue, 58, 81,
116, 120–1; Quarry Bank School, 56–7, 64–5,
79, 81, 92, 95, 120, 136; smoking, 64, 81, 514,
572; pop music, 64; uncle George's death,
73–4, 626; record collection, 83, 117, 127; Elvis

influence, 3, 85–6, 92–3, 103, 169; Little
Richard influence, 86–7, 99; Carl Perkins
influence, 88, 103, 293–4; Gene Vincent
influence, 92, 103, 116; *Rock Around The
Clock*, 96–7; forms group, 101–2; Quarry Men,
1, 4, 102–3; career prospects, 105, 125; O-
levels, 79, 105, 106, 124–5, 136, 142, 851, 875;
Quarry Men Cavern debut, 108; *Star Search*
week, 122–4; at Woolton fete, 129–32; first
meeting with Paul, 129–32; Woolton fete
recording, 131–2; asks Paul to join Quarry Men,
132, 142, 533; Liverpool College of Art, 136–7,
142–3, 173, 219, 232–3; Buddy Holly influence,
149, 167–9, 298; George joins Quarry Men,
157–9; Quarry Men rehearsals, 161–2, 171–2;
dismissal of Eric Griffiths, 164; at Morgue
Skiffle Cellar, 167; Chuck Berry influence, 169;
Quarry Men record session, 179; groups with
Paul and George, 194–5, 197–8; Johnny and
the Moondogs, 198–9; Japage 3: 201–4; fails
Intermediate Exam, 219, 232; employment,
220–1, 222–3, 228; persuades Stu Sutcliffe to
buy bass, 282; moves in with Stu Sutcliffe, 284;
at Vincent/Cochran show, 294; Beatles name,
298–9; holiday with Paul, 301–2; Billy Fury
backing group audition, 307–10; Scottish tour,
314–25; fails exams and leaves art school, 340;
career decision, 344–5, 350; London trip with
Stu, 345; eviction, 346, 350; Hamburg passport
issue, 353–4, 356–7, 423, 435; journey to
Hamburg, 355–6, 357, 360–1; Hamburg
performances, 365–7, 371; arrested and
released, 397–8; return from Hamburg,
399–400, 400–1; musical discoveries, 419–20;
broken finger, 424; return to Hamburg, 436,
438–9, 440; holiday with Paul in Paris, 498–506;
first meeting with Brian, 517; management
agreement with Brian, 531–4; Decca test,
560–1, 581; response to Decca, 581; Stuart's
visit, 587; gloomy about Beatles future, 613;
journey to Hamburg, 624; Stu's death, 626,
629–30, 631–2; Stu's funeral, 628; Star-Club
performances, 631–2; life in Hamburg, 632,
634, 643; Astrid's photographs, 641; Hamburg
performances with toilet seat, 652, 653, 828,
888; encounters with Gene Vincent, 660;
return from Hamburg, 661; meeting with
Ringo, 689–90; Cyn's pregnancy, 692, 714;
marriage plans, 692; on Pete Best's dismissal,
707, 708; wedding to Cyn, 712–14; married life
in Brian's flat, 713–14; challenges George
Martin on song selection, 727–8; songwriting
publishing agreement, 733–5; London press
visits, 756, 758, 761–2; moves back to Mendips,
774; driving lessons from Neil, 774; plays
electric organ, 833; Hamburg recording, 833–4
APPEARANCE: short-sightedness, 1, 162, 204;
glasses, 5, 45, 85, 97, 191, 193, 204, 231, 245,
360, 390, 602n, 623, 774, 820; hands, 5;
childhood photos, 39–40; tough face, 85, 120;
'cripple' act, 115–16, 148, 433, 455, 480, 538,
540, 572, 631, 778, 784–5; nose, 120, 467;
photo as a musician, 124; Teddy Boy, 1, 129,
142, 148, 160, 211, 521; art school clothes,
142, 211; photo of Quarry Men, 145; lilac
shirt and jeans, 159; photo with Paul and
George, 162–3; wink, 413, 481, 870; leather

Lennon, John – *continued*
  APPEARANCE – *continued*
    jacket, 452; stance when performing, 467,
    517; clothes bought in Paris, 503, 506; haircut,
    505–6, 507–8; attitude to wearing suits, 575;
    Ask Me Why broadcast, 675; filmed in
    Cavern, 711; farting, 787
  ART: drawings, 45, 64–5, 792; spontaneity, 173;
    painting the Casbah, 227; painting, 233
  BANJO: playing, 5, 78–9, 92, 100, 147–8
  CHARACTER: force of personality, 1–2, 12; love
    of pets, 42, 152; cruelty, 2, 50, 191, 245, 320,
    514, 542, 596; stealing (slap leather), 50, 81,
    127, 198, 227, 361, 394, 609n; gang
    leadership, 50–1; vocabulary, 50–1; humour, 2,
    3, 65, 159–60, 160–1, 191, 719, 773, 787;
    attitude towards Jews and 'queers', 65, 115,
    542, 571, 642, 819; cheating in exams, 81;
    bullying, 81; religious views, 81; attitude and
    behaviour, 105–6, 190–1; obsession with
    deformities, 115–16, 373, 642; violent, 138,
    210–11, 245; sarcastic, 148, 159, 191, 210;
    leadership style, 163, 227, 281, 840; political
    stance, 177; gifted yet troubled, 190–1;
    thoughtful and generous, 193, 641–2, 794;
    rages, 211, 232; possessive, 232; creative, 2,
    233; 'borrows' amplifiers, 354; rolling a sailor
    in Hamburg, 394; 'pissing on nuns' story,
    651–2; ambitions, 681, 739
  DRINKING: teenage, 81; drunk, 1;
    abusive/violent when drunk, 138, 163; after
    mother's death, 185, 211; drunk in Hamburg,
    378, 794
  DRUGS: first drugs experience, 339; Preludin in
    Hamburg, 445–6, 632, 634; smuggled
    Preludin, 467; used 'to get people talking',
    479, 571–2; smoking marijuana, 596–7
  GUITAR: interest in guitar, 78; borrowed guitar,
    100; guitar playing, 5, 100, 109–10, 114,
    147–8, 157, 158, 467; first guitar, 100, 113–14,
    124; vamping, 114; banjo chords, 128; breaks
    guitar and steals another, 198; wants electric
    guitar, 216, 221, 222–3; buys guitar (Club
    Footy), 227–8, 240; buys guitar
    (Rickenbacker) and amp, 381–2; new guitar
    (Jumbo Gibson), 684, 729; rhythm guitar,
    832
  HARMONICA: first harmonica, 43; new
    harmonica, 56; playing, 5, 79; left alone, 216n;
    stolen, 361, 609n; played in Hey Baby!, 608–9;
    played in Clarabella, 609; carried, 624; played
    in Hamburg, 645; Love Me Do, 650, 669, 672,
    725, 727, 728, 731, 749, 753, 763; played in I
    Remember You, 695; lessons for Billy Preston,
    787; Please Please Me, 798, 807, 808
  RELATIONSHIPS: with Aunt Mimi, 9, 38–9,
    45, 64, 79–80, 152, 185, 284, 373, 573;
    friendships, 40, 95, 138, 152, 174–5; sex, 3, 57,
    80, 81, 193, 210, 231–2, 369, 644, 828; with
    mother, 64, 79–81, 92–3, 173; girls flirting
    with him, 64; working with Paul, 147–9, 173,
    196; Quarry Men relationships, 151–2,
    158–61, 164–5, 178, 227; with George, 157–9,
    719; Quarry Men leadership style, 163, 227,
    281; with Mona Best, 173–4; mother's death,
    183–5, 188, 191, 192, 626; friendship with Stu
    Sutcliffe, 191–2, 211, 233–4, 241, 286, 292,
    319–20, 361, 374, 434, 478–9, 587, 629–30;
    girlfriend Thelma, 192–3, 210–11; hitting
    women, 210–11, 245; with Paul, 1, 9–12, 204,
    234, 478–9, 500, 795; with Cynthia (Cyn),
    219–20, 227, 245, 284–5, 293, 337, 354, 373,
    401, 436, 457–8, 514, 634–5, 661, 682, 715;
    social life, 292–3; bullying Tommy Moore,
    320, 322, 358; with Ellis, 340, 345; letters
    from Hamburg, 373, 499, 622, 642–3, 792; on-
    stage banter with Paul, 433, 834; Beatles fans'
    views of, 535–40; with Brian, 571–2; with fans,
    621, 642–3; with Lindy Ness, 622–3, 642–3,
    681–2, 694, 714, 792, 893; concern for Astrid,
    641–2; encounters with Fascher, 644, 828;
    with Bettina, 644–5, 794–5, 833; sexy
    photography, 682, 714; with Ida Holly,
    714–15; with Ringo, 719
  SINGING: voice, 5–6, 79, 103, 131–2, 147, 179,
    240, 309; with Quarry Men, 103, 108, 128,
    178; changing the words, 124, 419, 821; on
    the bus, 145; harmony singing, 201, 334, 365,
    832; singing Chuck Berry and Buddy Holly,
    240; with Beatles, 318; 'The Singing Rage',
    514; Decca test, 561; backing vocals, 585, 668;
    George Martin's assessment, 647, 663
  SONGWRITING: first song (Calypso Rock),
    114, 152; Hello Little Girl, 152–3; with Paul,
    6–7, 153, 196, 533; One After 909: 296, 608;
    Ask Me Why, 608; Please Please Me, 674–5;
    songwriting publishing agreement, 733–5;
    new song (Do You Want To Know A Secret),
    765–6; Norwegian Wood, 893; Lennon-
    McCartney partnership, *see* Lennon-
    McCartney partnership
  WRITINGS: 'The Tale Of Hermit Fred', 11;
    poems, 45; poem for Mimi, 74; 'On Safairy
    With Whide Hunter', 196, 437, 694, 856;
    short story 'Henry and Harry', 246; 'Being A
    Short Diversion On The Dubious Origins Of
    Beatles', 437–8, 471; gives stories and poems
    to Bill Harry, 471; pieces in *Mersey Beat*, 493,
    498, 694, 843; typing, 694; stories and poems
    lost, 694; on origin of Beatles name, 737;
    'Randolf's Party', 824
Lennon, John (Jack, grandfather), 15–16, 452
Lennon, Joyce (cousin), 30–1
Lennon, Julia (Stanley, mother): birth and
  childhood, 17; appearance, 18, 46, 79, 173;
  character, 17, 18, 46, 79, 173, 452; short-
  sightedness, 45, 46, 79; banjo playing, 5, 17,
  78–9, 100, 109, 147, 173, 420, 464; first
  meeting with Alf, 16; relationship with Alf, 17,
  18; employment, 18, 25, 30, 46; marriage, 18,
  26, 713; birth of son, 27; relationship with Taffy
  Williams, 30; pregnancy, 30, 31; relationship
  with son John, 31, 35, 37, 38, 39, 47, 64, 77,
  78–80, 92–3, 152, 173, 765, 845; birth of
  daughter Victoria, 31n; relationship with
  Bobby Dykins, 33, 35, 46; end of marriage, 36;
  birth of daughter Julia, 46; pretence of
  marriage, 46, 184; birth of daughter Jacqui, 47;
  Quarry Men rehearsals, 109; guitar for John,
  113–14, 124, 198; shirt for John, 113, 124, 129;
  music practice with John, 147; Paul's
  admiration for, 173; death, 182–3, 188, 191,
  192, 284, 774, 855; funeral, 183; life insurance,
  184–5, 855

Lennon, Julia (Dykins, half-sister), 46, 47, 80, 183, 232
Lennon, Madge (aunt), 30–1
Lennon, Mary 'Polly'(Maguire, grandmother), 16
Lennon, Syd (uncle), 30–1
Lennon, Victoria Elizabeth (John's half-sister), *see* Pedersen
Lennon-McCartney partnership: songwriting, 7–8, 10–11, 197; early songs, 197–8; writings, 196–7, 694; written in 1959: 217–18; influences, 224, 676, 821, 854; arrangements for Quarrymen, 240; tape recordings, 296, 336, 862; Paul's list of songs, 297; period of no songs, 387, 418–19; secrecy, 418; Hamburg performance, 455; songs in Beatles repertoire, 533, 546, 560, 572, 735, 820, 821; Decca recording, 560, 591; Ardmore and Beechwood interest in publishing, 591, 640; rebirth of songwriting partnership, 649–51, 663, 683; Brian's response to new songs, 662–3; EMI recording choices, 668, 673; partnership name, 683; writing stalled, 694; songs for EMI, 723; songs pushed, 725, 800–1; copyrights, 728, 813, 817–18; Beatles first single, 729, 733; publishing agreement with Ardmore and Beechwood, 733–4, 765; name order, 733–4, 746, 803, 814; Brian's management agreement, 734, 765; George's role, 734–5; George Martin's change of mind, 800–1; publishing agreements with Dick James, 813–14; Ardmore and Beechwood income, 815n; new music publishing company, 830–1
Les Stewart Quartet, 208–9, 212n, 216, 218, 223, 226
Levis, Carroll, 123–4, 197–200, 237, 317; see also *Star Search*
Lewis, Jerry Lee: hero to John and Paul, 3, 420; in charts, 6; Whole Lotta Shakin' Going On, 141; backing group, 146; style, 149; Great Balls of Fire, 150; influence, 161, 194; recording studio, 168, 178; songs played by Les Stewart Quartet, 209; songs played by Hurricanes, 288; The Saints, 463; Beatles repertoire, 475, 481, 513; New Brighton Tower show, 657, 659; wife, 889; influence on Ringo, 720
Lewis, Meade Lux, 254, 257
Lewis, Vic, 106, 848
Liberty Records, 680, 764, 835–6
Like Dreamers Do: influences on, 218; sung by Paul, 533; recorded by Beatles, 559, 560; radio audition, 584; EMI reject, 594; copyright issue, 640; not chosen, 668; John and Paul's view, 669
Limpinsel, Wilhelm, 'Willi', 366, 370–1
Lindsay Ross and his Famous Broadcasting Band, 320
Lishman, K. I., 125
Little Richard: John first hears, 86–7, 99; influence on John, 87, 88, 92, 420; first British single, 99–100; influence on John and Paul, 3, 100; Paul's impersonation of, 3, 100, 106, 127, 131, 136, 139, 148, 168, 202, 229, 240, 405, 783; *Don't Knock The Rock*, 106; *The Girl Can't Help It*, 116, 117; NME Top Thirty, 127; Quarry Men performance, 145; backing musicians, 146; renounces rock for religion, 3, 149, 168, 766, 767; popularity, 161, 194, 215; label, 168; Paul playing his songs, 189; Beatles repertoire, 365, 478, 492, 620; sexuality, 767–8;

British tour, 659, 687–8, 766–8, 783–4; Brian's promotion, 687–8, 767, 768; opinion of Beatles, 767, 783, 787; writing in bible, 768, 897; photographed with Beatles, 768, 783, 898, 899; fee, 768; Hamburg Star-Club season, 659, 685, 687, 766, 783, 787, 792, 793; backstage bible-study classes, 787; photo with Bobby, 795
Littlewood, Tom, 175, 347
Liverpolitan, 47, 48
Liverpool College of Art, 4, 59, 136–7, 142–3, 173–5, 231
Liverpool Echo: Alf Lennon's advert, 36; John's childhood reading, 38–9; 'Liverpool's Own Top 3' chart, 91, 846; Cavern adverts, 108, 137; on National Service, 120; Paul delivers, 130n; Disker's column, 141, 527, 563, 577, 738, 846, 870; Charlie Mac's adverts, 145, 151; Eddie Clayton adverts, 171; on Julia's death, 184; Mersey Beat column, 193n, 436; 'Jazz' classifieds, 212, 414, 416, 870; Gerry and the Pacemakers ad, 237; on Nems, 270, 271n; Quarry Men ad, 270, 271n; on Vincent/Cochran show, 295; Nems ads, 326, 527; Decca and EMI ads, 327; Silver Beetles ad, 332; Beatles drummer ad, 351–2; ads for Big Beat Boppin' Beatles, 428, 545; ads for Beatles at Cavern, 430; on Cavern, 477–8; on Paul, 485; Hambleton Hall ads, 488; ad for Beatles at 'Davy Lew', 508; Beatles ad, 514–15; *Operation Big Beat* ad, 519; on Beatles no-show, 596; on air crash, 601; Rory Storm and the Hurricanes ads, 616, 658; on Stuart's death, 625, 626, 628; Channel show ad, 657; Grafton Ballroom ad, 687; review of Love Me Do, 750; 'Liverpool's Own Top 5' chart, 782, 825; report of Beatles recording session, 809
Liverpool Institute High School for Boys: building, 4, 58, 59; motto, 59; uniform, 106, 118; teachers, 56, 59; Lower School, 59; Paul passes exam, 58; Paul at, 59–60, 65, 67, 70, 86, 90, 92, 95–6, 112, 136, 139, 161, 164, 207; George passes exam, 60; George at, 69–70, 83, 90, 95, 118, 164, 198; buses to school, 70, 89–90; absences from, 172; Paul's O-levels, 180; last day of term, 188, 220; Paul's A-levels, 189–90, 220, 314, 333, 346, 373; George leaves, 220, 235, 243; Paul's prize for Art, 242, 291; school plays, 292; school photograph, 292; Paul's Scottish tour, 314–15, 333; Paul leaves, 346, 373, 409
Liverpool University: Mimi's student lodgers, 9, 42; Paul's claims, 297, 861; audience response to Ellis, 338; Beatles booking, 568, 589, 595; final night disaster, 595, 769
Liverpool Weekly News, 128, 181, 184, 375, 773
Livin' Lovin' Wreck (Jerry Lee Lewis), performed by Beatles, 475
Lockhart Smith, Judy: background, 638; appearance, 257; relationship with George Martin, 269–70, 328, 529–30, 636, 638, 639, 640; Oscar Preuss's death, 278; office, 328; friendship with Brian, 592; Beatles recording session, 725; at Cavern, 822
Lockwood, Joseph, 262, 268, 278, 328, 637, 802
The Loco-Motion (Little Eva), Beatles repertoire, 736
Lomax, Jackie, 417

London label: Little Richard releases, 99, 106; Jerry Lee Lewis release, 141; American licensing arrangements, 168; American releases, 215n, 328–9, 418, 849, 856; Chuck Berry release, 224; Alley Oop, 330n; Spector's work, 419; Beatles repertoire, 475; Arthur Alexander release, 608
London Records (USA), 582
Long Tall Sally (Little Richard), 3, 86–7, 99, 106, 766; sung by Paul, 131, 145, 202, 405, 432, 833; Quarry Men repertoire, 145, 165; Beatles repertoire, 343, 418, 481; sung by Rory Storm, 418; Hamburg recording, 833
Looking Glass, 218
Los Paranoias, 324
Loss, Joe, 104
Love Me Do: writing, 10, 218, 841; rewriting, 650, 888; selected for Parlophone, 651, 668; rehearsing, 663, 725; recording (June 1962), 666, 668–70, 741n; harmonica sound, 669, 672, 725, 727, 728, 731, 749–50, 763, 900; choice for record, 672, 673; Beatles repertoire, 681, 735; recording (4 September 1962), 724, 725, 732n; selection, 727, 728, 731, 732, 737; George Martin's opinion of, 725, 727, 747, 790, 798, 800; recording (11 September 1962), 729, 731–2; publishing agreement, 733–4, 802; press release, 738, 818; Mimi's response to, 745; release, 745–6, 749, 769, 790; writing credit, 746, 803; exposure, 747–8; Luxembourg airtime, 748, 781, 895; advertising, 748, 753–4, 760; reviews, 749–50; sales, 750–1, 764, 805, 814, 820, 825, 829; in the charts, 751–2; chart hype story, 751–2, 896; Jagger's response, 753; London newspapers' response, 756; *Pop Weekly* Top Thirty, 760; *Dance News* article, 761–2; played in Lyceum, 762–3; Capitol's response, 763; not released in US, 764; need for pushing, 769; *People And Places*, 777, 778, 782, 826, 898, 899; plugging, 779–80, 790–1, 803, 805, 814; *Saturday Club*, 779–80, 803, 899; rises in charts, 781–2, 789, 791, 795, 805, 820, 824–5, 829; *NME* Top Thirty, 782, 789; Little Richard's response, 783; Empire show, 784; in Hamburg, 787–8; *Twelve O'Clock Spin*, 791, 805, 900; *Two-Way Family Favourites*, 791, 792n, 805, 900; success boosts audiences, 804–5; unique, 808; lack of EMI support, 810; *The Talent Spot*, 814; royalties from, 814–15, 829; copyright, 817–18; lip-synching, 818; miming for TV, 820; Beatles album, 822; Canadian release, 834; US position, 835–6
Love Me Tender (Elvis Presley), sung by Stuart, 387, 424, 448, 629; sung by John, 641
Love Of The Loved, 217, 246n, 533, 559–62
Lovelady, Dave, 311, 550
Loving You (film), 149
Lowe, Duff: education, 161, 180, 847; piano playing, 161; with Quarry Men, 161, 163, 164, 167; Quarry Men recording, 178, 179, 180
Lowlands, 209, 212n, 216, 223, 228–30, 237
Lucille (Little Richard), 3, 127, 767; sung by Paul, 145
Lucky Stars, see Thank Your Lucky Stars
Lunch Box (ATV), 779, 899
Lusty, Bob, 620
Lyon, Mr H. (teacher), 52

Mackels, Pastor Albert, 652
Mackey, Peter, 495, 876
MacKinnon, Duncan, 318, 319
Maggie May (song), 111, 128, 268–9
Maguire, Annie, 43, 111, 170
Maguire, Leo, 655, 665, 696
Maguire, Les, 510, 652–3
Maguire, Marie, 43–4, 187, 716
Maguire, Mary 'Polly', 16
Maguire, Shelagh, 209, 223
Maharishi Mahesh Yogi, 279n
Mahomed, Jeff, 143, 174–5, 191, 219
Mair, John, 750–1, 896
Mairants, Ivor, 134, 850
Makin, E. Rex, 543, 548
Mama Said (the Shirelles), 475; sung by Paul, 475, 586
Manchester Evening News, 198, 568
Manker, Sid, 150
Manley, Colin, 212n, 864
Marrion, Albert, 549–50, 620
Marsden, Fred, 470, 510, 550, 551
Marsden, Gerry: friendship with Richy/Ringo, 470, 493; relationship with Pauline Behan, 471; drunken performance, 510–11; deputises for George, 616; in Hamburg, 652, 828n; Everton supporter, 721n; *see also* Gerry and the Pacemakers
Marshall, Paul, 272, 835, 836
Marshall, Sandra, 710
Marshall, William (Bill), 743–4, 895
Martin, Alexis, 261
Martin, Bertha (Simpson, George's mother), 253–4, 255
Martin, George: birth and childhood, 253–4; education, 254; piano playing, 254; dance band, 254; employment, 254, 256; war service, 254; Guildhall School of Music, 254–5; oboe playing, 255, 256, 781n; Parlophone label, 97–8, 224n, 256–8; head of Parlophone, 261–2; recordings, 264–5; Vipers signing, 97–8, 265–6; Vipers production, 102n, 266, 268–9, 273; Soho talent spotting, 121; EMI view of, 266, 268; calypso recordings, 269; American trip, 272–3; comedy recordings, 273–4, 696; looking for distinctive sound, 280; recording Scottish band, 320; flat, 529, 636; Beatles question, 526; view of beat groups, 548; meeting with Brian, 592–3; listens to Beatles, 592–3, 647–8; signings, 637; EMI contract, 638–9; Norbreck Hydro festival, 639; told to sign Beatles, 640–1, 790; Beatles recording contract, 646–8, 655–6; Beatles (Beattles) name confusion, 648, 655, 666, 672; discussing Beatles, 665–6; Beatles recording session (June 1962), 667, 668–71; opinion of Pete's drumming, 670, 671, 677, 701, 709; opinion of Beatles songs, 673, 800–1; looking for hit song for Beatles, 673; opinion of Ask Me Why, 676, 725, 799, 800; opinion of Beatles, 696, 799, 800; studio work, 697; gives How Do You Do It to Beatles, 698; Beatles recording session (4 September 1962), 725; opinion of Love Me Do, 725–7, 747, 790, 798, 800; opinion of Please Please Me, 725–6, 798, 800, 808, 810; initial opinion of Ringo's drumming, 726, 799; song selection for first Beatles first single, 727–9, 732; Beatles

challenge him on song selection, 727–8;
Beatles recording session (11 September 1962),
729; fixes EMI recording session, 782; meeting
with Beatles (November 1962), 798–802;
choice of songs for second record, 798–9; LP
plans, 799, 800, 801, 807, 809, 812, 822;
Cavern recce plan, 800; changes mind on
Lennon-McCartney songs, 800–1; meeting
with Brian (November 1962), 802–4; sidelining
Ardmore and Beechwood, 803–4; Beatles
recording session (26 November 1962), 806–10;
US plans, 810; at Cavern, 822–3; arranges test
for Gerry and the Pacemakers, 823
APPEARANCE: accent, 254; height, 254, 320,
529, 802; good looks, 254, 320, 802; dress, 802
CHARACTER: civility and good humour, 254;
amusing, 320; confidence and self-belief, 530
COMPOSITIONS: early, 253, 254; Double
Scotch, 530, 531, 637; The Niagara Theme,
530, 637; Ray Cathode pseudonym, 637;
Time Beat, 637; film scores, 637–8, 887; The
Dr Kildare Theme, 639, 887
MONEY: salary, 261, 278, 529, 636, 638–9;
royalty issue, 278, 529, 636, 638–9;
songwriting, 530; theme tunes, songs and film
scores, 636, 637–8
RELATIONSHIPS: marriage, 255, 269, 529,
636; children, 261, 269; with Judy, 269–70,
529–30, 636; with Capitol, 272–3, 422–3,
472n, 763–4, 835; with L. G. Wood, 639–40;
with Beatles, 670–1, 728, 732, 790, 801–2;
with Ringo, 730; with Brian, 802
SONGWRITING: tunes, 278–9; Graham Fisher
pseudonym, 279; Can This Be Love (Matt
Monro), 530; title songs, 638, 887
SUCCESSES: Vipers, 268; Jim Dale, 268;
Johnny Dankworth, 269; Nadia Cattouse, 422;
Matt Monro, 423, 472; Peter Sellers, 273, 423;
Temperance Seven, 423, 638, 472–3; *Beyond
The Fringe*, 473; Charlie Drake, 529, 579;
Spike Milligan, 529; Bernard Cribbins, 636–7,
696; Rolf Harris, 696–7; reputation, 799, 801
Martin, George (driver), 300, 301
Martin, George (1961 show producer), 508
Martin, Henry (George's father), 253–4
Martin, Irene (George's sister), 254
Martin, Sheena (Chisholm, George's wife), 255,
261, 269, 328, 636
Marvin, Hank, 580, 602n, 705
Mason, Ann, 143, 175
Massey & Coggins, 409–10, 419, 425–6, 429–30
Matchbox (Carl Perkins), 117, 294; sung by John,
336, 833; sung by Ringo, 340, 456; sung by
Pete, 456, 585, 605; Hamburg recording, 833
Matthews, Richard/Dick: photography, 194, 519,
544–5, 550; Mossway Jiving Club, 194; Chez
Jazrok, 247
May, Billy, 88
May, Dave, 281, 285
McBain, Charlie (Charlie Mac), 120, 144, 145,
151, 849
McCaldon, Joan, 708, 785
McCann, Terry, 545
McCartney, Annie (aunt), *see* Danher
McCartney, Edie (aunt), 19, 54
McCartney, Elizabeth (Williams, great-
grandmother), 19

McCartney, Florence 'Florrie' (Clegg,
grandmother), 19, 28, 31
McCartney, Gin (Jane, Ginny, aunt), *see* Harris
McCartney, Jack (uncle), 19, 204
McCartney, James (great-grandfather), 19
McCartney, Jim (father): family background, 19;
birth, 19; character, 20, 34; hearing problem,
19; piano, 19, 42, 54, 147, 161, 204, 252, 675,
807, 820; employment, 20, 28, 31, 41, 99, 693;
musical career, 2, 20, 218, 297; songwriting, 20,
89; wartime life, 26, 28; marriage, 28; homes,
28, 31, 41–2, 51, 88; birth of son Paul, 28–9;
birth of son Mike, 31; family life, 34, 42, 55;
sons' education, 42; piano lessons for Paul,
58–9, 195; dress, 62; ambitions for Paul, 8,
58–9, 139, 346, 352; Butlin's holidays, 71, 138;
trumpet for Paul, 75, 134; wife's illness and
death, 4, 90, 98–9; relationship with George,
101; betting, 118; Paul's O-levels, 118, 139,
148, 180; Paul's first guitar, 134; on John's
guitar chords, 147–8; relationship with Paul,
148–9, 151, 195–6, 314, 400, 429–30; warnings
about John, 1, 4, 11, 148, 161–2; relationship
with George, 161–2; meets Derek Hodkin, 202;
Paul's A-levels, 314; attitude to Hamburg
bookings, 352, 356, 399, 457, 459; concern for
Paul's employment, 400, 409; encounters with
Beatles fans, 490, 509, 623; Cavern visits, 509;
Paul's relationship with Beatles, 595; Beatles
booking in Manchester, 676; signs Paul's
contract, 743; view of Paul's Little Richard
impersonation, 783; Paul's songwriting
contract, 830; listening to early songs, 6; on
Paul and Mike as children, 863
McCartney, Joan (aunt), 54, 98–9
McCartney, Joe (uncle), 19, 54, 98–9
McCartney, Joseph (Joe, grandfather), 19
McCartney, Mary Patricia (Mohin, mother):
family background, 20; character, 34; marriage,
28; employment, 28, 31, 41, 51; homes, 28, 31,
41–2, 51, 88; birth of son Paul, 28–9; birth of
son Michael, 31; family life, 34, 42; ambitions
for Paul, 8, 58, 59; illness, 98; death, 4, 98
McCartney, Michael (Mike, Mick): birth, 31;
childhood, 51; relationship with brother, 51,
55, 58, 70; education, 51, 54, 89, 234n, 875;
photography, 71, 138, 162, 887; move to
Allerton, 88, 89; mother's illness and death,
98–9; on Paul's guitar playing, 135; musical
duo with Paul, 135, 139; broken arm, 138, 202;
opinion of John, 148; first colour photo of
John, Paul and George, 162–3, 177; piano
lessons, 195; drumming with Japage 3: 202,
203; drum kit, 346; Paul's Hamburg trip, 352;
Paul's return from Hamburg, 399; photos of
Paul and Dot, 428; employment, 875; lends
camera to Paul, 505; on Jane Asher, 513; on
Stuart's visit, 587; on Beatles management
problems, 596; photographs Beatles BBC
debut, 603; at Cavern fan club night, 621;
Stuart's death, 626; photo of Jerry Lee Lewis,
659; Paul's gift of camera, 661, 682; Paul uses
camera, 682; photos of Beatles, 682–3, 689;
hairdressing apprenticeship, 683, 772; lifestyle,
683; photos of Little Richard, 767; goes to
Events, 772
McCartney, Mill (Milly, aunt), 4, 19, 54

McCartney, Paul: family background, 4, 11, 18–21, 99; birth, 28; name, 28–9; homes, 28, 31, 41–2, 51, 88, 89; childhood, 34, 55; education, 42, 51, 54–5; musical education, 42, 58–9, 75, 195; National Service issue, 58, 81, 120–1; Liverpool Institute, 58, 59–60, 89–90, 95–6, 139; Butlin's holidays, 71, 138–9; reading, 3, 190, 234; Elvis influence, 3, 86, 96, 100, 113, 122, 169–70; Little Richard influence, 87, 100; Gene Vincent influence, 92, 100, 116; record buying, 92, 116, 117, 201, 223–4, 294; *Rock Around The Clock*, 96; mother's illness and death, 98–9, 188, 651; O-levels, 95, 118, 119, 138, 172, 180, 189, 409, 501, 719; Bill Haley at Liverpool Odeon, 106–7; at Woolton fete, 127; first meeting with John, 128–32; joins Quarry Men, 1, 132, 138, 141, 533; Boy Scouts camp, 138; stage debut at Filey, 139; first performance with the Quarry Men, 144, 157; Buddy Holly influence, 149, 153, 167–9, 298; George joins Quarry Men, 158; Quarry Men rehearsals, 161–2, 171–2; dismissal of Eric, 164; at Morgue Skiffle Cellar, 167; Chuck Berry influence, 169; Quarry Men record session, 179–80; holidays with George, 188–9, 220, 225–6, 301; A-levels, 189–90, 220, 291–2, 314, 333, 346, 373, 409, 719; group with John and George, 194–5, 197–8; Johnny and the Moondogs, 198–9; Japage 3: 201–4; summer job, 220, 223; Christmas job, 246; in school play, 292; Carl Perkins influence, 293–4; letters to get bookings, 296–8; Beatles name, 298–9; holiday with John, 301–2; Billy Fury backing group audition, 307–10; Scottish tour, 314–25; Hamburg booking, 351–2; asks Pete Best to join Beatles, 352; journey to Hamburg, 356; letters from Hamburg, 373, 622, 635, 792; fire at Bambi Kino, 397, 614; arrested for attempted arson, 397–8; deported, 398–9; Christmas job, 400; work at Massey & Coggins, 409–10, 419, 423, 425, 426; appeal against Hamburg ban, 425, 430, 435; leaves Massey & Coggins, 429; return to Hamburg, 440–1; memories of Cavern, 478; holiday in Paris with John, 498–506; response to first record, 511–12; management agreement with Brian, 531–4; Beatles fans, 535–40; Decca test, 561, 581; Beatles contract amendment, 565; response to Decca, 581; Hamburg police dispensation, 614; journey to Hamburg, 624; Stu's death, 626–7; Stu's funeral, 628; life in Hamburg, 632, 634, 643; 'pissing on nuns' story, 651–2; encounters with Gene Vincent, 660; return from Hamburg, 661; Love Me Do recording, 669–70, 672; photography, 682; considers becoming Paul James, 683–4, 746; meeting with Ringo, 689–90; car (Ford Consul Classic), 715; at John's wedding, 713; George Martin selects Love Me Do as B-side, 727; songwriting publishing agreement, 733–5; London press visits, 756, 758; German visa problem, 770; London trip with Celia, 779–80; response to Love Me Do chart success, 782; return from Hamburg, 795; press visits, 796–7; Hamburg recording, 833–4
APPEARANCE: left-handedness, 5, 7, 34, 113, 134–5, 189, 198, 343, 382, 460, 585;
childhood photo, 54–5; chubby stage, 70–1, 138; haircuts, 90, 196; white sports coat, 122, 127, 138, 145; photo as 15–year-old, 138; with Quarry Men, 145; Teddy Boy, 151; photo with John and George, 162–3; long hair, 292; quiff, 292, 360; donkey jacket, 400, 409; eyes, 432–3, 533; clothes bought in Paris, 503; Beatles haircut, 505–6, 507–8; baby-face, 521; attitude to wearing suits, 575; wearing suit in Cavern, 622; filmed in Cavern, 711
ART: drawings, 2, 75, 140; school prize for art, 242, 291; painting the Casbah, 227; design for LP sleeve, 801
CHARACTER: charming and sharp, 2, 152; confident, 2; mimicry, 3, 60, 100, 106, 131; humour, 3, 160–1; nerves, 59, 144, 584, 669; care with money, 374, 445, 819; fails to turn up, 595–6; gloomy about Beatles future, 613; ambitions, 286, 739
COMPOSITIONS: piano, 2, 89, 153, 432; guitar instrumentals, 218, 293
DRUGS: first drugs experience, 339; drugs in Hamburg, 446
DRUMMING: practising, 202; kit, 346–7; with Beatles, 347
GUITAR: confident guitarist, 2; chords, 2, 5, 113, 131, 172; learning on Ian's guitar, 112–13, 119; playing right-handed, 113; playing upside down, 130, 134–5, 145, 189, 342, 403, 411, 458, 460; playing to Quarry Men, 130–1; first guitar (Zenith), 134–5; restringing, 134–5; playing with Ian, 135; Little Richard act, 136; playing with John, 147; electric guitar, 163, 172; playing with Vikings, 189; new guitar (Rosetti Solid 7), 342, 347, 371, 401; borrows John's guitar, 382; guitar and amp returned from Hamburg, 401; playing bass, 411, 458, 460, 463, 474; Rosetti strung with piano strings, 411; buys Hofner violin bass (left-handed model), 460, 474; buys bass speaker, 495
PIANO: watching father, 42, 217; lessons, 58–9, 195; playing, 2, 88, 113; compositions, 2, 89, 153, 432; playing with Ian, 118; playing to Quarry Men, 131; playing rock and roll, 141, 189; playing in Hamburg, 442–3
RELATIONSHIPS: with girls, 75; friendship with George, 101, 136, 139–42, 188; friendship with Ian James, 112–13, 118–19, 122, 135; with father, 148–9, 151, 195–6, 314, 400, 429; Quarry Men relationships, 151–2, 158–61, 164–5, 178, 227; view of Julia, 173; with John, 1, 9–12, 147–9, 173, 196–7, 204, 234, 286, 478–9, 719, 795; sex, 3, 243; with Dot, 243–4, 246, 286–7, 293, 337, 354, 400, 661, 682; with Stuart, 286, 292, 319, 347, 374, 387, 415, 434, 448, 460–1, 595, 626–7; Dot's pregnancy, 287, 292; Dot's miscarriage, 302, 354; engagement to Dot, 428; social life, 292–3; dealing with gangsters, 443; fans in Hamburg, 455; fight with Stuart, 460–1; with George, 499; with Brian, 531–3, 565, 570, 595; sex in Hamburg, 643–4; fatherhood issue, 644; Pete Best's dismissal, 708; with Thelma, 715; with Ringo, 719; with Celia, 774–5, 780–1, 792; with Iris, 775, 776–7, 815; with Vi Caldwell, 775–6

SINGING: voice, 5–6, 59, 131, 140, 147, 179, 240, 309; Little Richard impersonation, 3, 100, 106, 127, 131, 136, 139, 145, 148, 202, 229, 240, 433, 783; for Quarry Men, 131; on the bus, 145; with Quarry Men, 178; harmony singing, 201, 334, 365, 832; singing Elvis and Little Richard, 240; while drumming, 347; backing vocals, 421, 546, 654; Decca test, 561; vocal affectations, 561, 765; George Martin's assessment, 647, 663; PS I Love You, 730; at the Empire, 784

SONGWRITING: I Lost My Little Girl, 153; with John, 6–7, 153, 196, 533, 649; with George, 172; In Spite Of All The Danger, 172, 179; Love Of The Loved, 217, 533; I'll Follow The Sun, 217; A World Without Love, 217–18; I'll Be On My Way, 218; Like Dreamers Do, 218, 533; You'll Be Mine, 218; Pinwheel Twist, 585, 608, 649; songwriting publishing agreement, 733–5; view of copyrights, 817–18; I Saw Her Standing There, 820–1; Lennon-McCartney partnership, see Lennon-McCartney partnership

TRUMPET: first attempt, 75, 107; father obtains, 75; playing When The Saints Go Marching In, 75, 821; abandons, 75, 88, 113; plays with George, 101; swaps for guitar, 134

McCartney-Lennon partnership, see Lennon-McCartney partnership

McFall, Ray: buys Cavern Club, 238; attitude to electric guitars, 426; memories of Beatles, 426–7; no-alcohol policy, 427; snackbar, 427; Beatles lunchtime sessions, 430; bookings policy, 435–6; owns Mersey Beat, 471; Beatles pay, 474, 657; Beatles bookings, 476, 657, 788, 815; advice to Beatles, 483; Beatles management issue, 486; Riverboat Shuffle, 488; Beatles cancellations, 499; Brian's arrival, 515, 516; relationship with Brian, 567, 608, 709; Beatles return from Hamburg, 657

McGough, Roger, 771–2, 898

McGovern, Geraldine (Gerry): religious background, 187, 214, 287; relationship with Richy, 187; engagement to Richy, 214, 236; objections to Richy's drumming career, 301, 311, 330; end of engagement, 375

McGrellis, Micky, 110

McGuirk, Tommy, 403

McKenzie, Phyllis, 220, 245, 284, 691

Mean Woman Blues (Jerry Lee Lewis), 150; played by Duff Lowe, 161

Meehan, Tony, 546, 563, 580–1, 583, 883

Melly, George, 746–7

Melody Maker: editor, 834; on guitar boom, 109; on EMI takeover of Capitol, 262; chart compilation, 272, 751–2; Top Ten chart, 274; on Eddie Cochran, 294; guitar ad, 342, 866; on My Bonnie, 563; on R&B, 665; on Shadows, 705; reviews, 749; on folk circuit, 755; circulation, 759; Top Fifty chart, 781, 791, 805, 825; on Beatles bookings, 783; on Paramor satire, 806; on Peterborough show, 816; John's postcard, 890; interview with John, 650, 672, 897; interview with George Martin, 593, 890; interview with Ringo, 717; interviews with Paul, 761, 871, 888

Memphis, Tennessee (Chuck Berry), 223–4; played by Paul, 224; Beatles repertoire, 428, 481, 495, 536, 539, 584, 604; recorded by Beatles, 559, 560, 561

Mersey Beat: start-up, 436–7; investors, 436, 471, 872; offices, 479, 872; John's writing, 437–8, 471, 493, 498, 694, 843, 856; first issue, 438n, 471; sales, 471, 482; second issue, 482; Brian's column, 487, 493, 498, 520, 740; fourth issue, 487; Bob Wooler's column, 491–2, 498; advertisements, 492–3; sixth issue, 498; Brian sees Beatles mentions, 512, 515; Popularity Poll, 519, 550, 552, 563, 579, 589, 814, 877; Nems Top Twenty charts, 564, 607; photos returned to John, 573; Top Ten Tips, 607–8; on Beatles at Cavern, 622; on Star-Club opening, 631; sent to Beatles in Hamburg, 645; on EMI contract, 648, 662, 672; on George's car, 683; on Beatles drummer change, 712; on Pete's appearances, 742, 823; on Beatles recording session, 724, 725; review of Love Me Do, 750; on Beatles promo visit, 760; on Little Richard, 767; on Beatles LP, 800, 807, 887; Awards Night, 824, 837

Mersey Beats, the, 699, 701, 709, 741, 765

Merseyside Arts Festival, 771–2

Miller, Jonathan, 473, 655

Miller, Mandy, 264

Milligan, Spike: Goon Show, 55, 65, 264; film, 431; George Martin recordings, 529, 637, 655, 696, 801; George Martin compositions, 530

Mills, Mrs (Gladys), 763, 834

Milne, Leonard, 195

Milward, Annie (John's grandmother), see Stanley

Mr Moonlight (Dr Feelgood), sung by John, 680

Moan, Owen, (Paul's great-grandfather), 20

Mohin, Dill (Mary's sister-in-law), 98

Mohin, Mary Theresa (Danher), Paul's grandmother, 20–1

Mohin, Owen 'Ownie' (Paul's grandfather), 20–1

Molyneux, Bob, 131

Money (Barrett Strong), 329, 419, 560; sung by John, 329, 478, 535, 561; Beatles repertoire, 311, 329, 365, 535; recorded by Beatles, 559, 560, 561, 562, 711

Monro, Matt: signed by George Martin, 279, 423; hits, 423, 472, 530, 639; George Martin's work, 530, 639, 655; rejected by Capitol, 763

Montez, Chris, 790, 815, 816

Mooney, Johnny, 213

Moonglow (oldie), 53; played by Quarrymen, 240; played by Beatles, 349, 365, 394

Moore, Dudley, 473, 780

Moore, Scotty, 65, 117, 150, 201

Moore, Tommy: background, 306, 315, 355; joins Beatles for Fury audition, 306, 308–9; plays with Beatles on Scottish tour, 313, 315–17, 322, 324–5, 337; relationship with John, 320, 322, 358; injuries, 321, 322; plays with Beatles, 332–3; leaves Beatles, 334–5; drum kit, 346

Moran, Pat, 342–4, 347, 349–50

Morgue Skiffle Cellar, 166–7, 168, 178, 209, 494

Morris, Doug, 902

Morris, Margaret (Diz), 284, 322, 346

Mortimer, Celia, 607, 774–5, 780–1, 792, 820, 901

Move It! (Cliff Richard), 200, 463, 762, 871

Movin' And Groovin' (Duane Eddy), 336; recorded by Beatles, 336

Munro, Charles D., 483, 498, 544

Murphy, Brenda, 710

Murphy, John, 49

Murphy, Paul, 178

Murray, Mitch (Lionel Stitcher), 697–8, 725, 728–9

Murray, Rod: friendship with Stuart, 143, 191–2, 283n, 322, 387; art work, 176; Percy Street flat, 191–2, 284; snooker playing, 233–4; bass guitar project, 241, 861; art exhibition, 241–2; memories of Stuart, 283n; eviction, 284; Gambier Terrace flat, 284, 285, 316, 346; relationship with John, 285, 353; memories of Beatles, 316, 336, 862; drugs, 339; eviction, 346, 353, 355; on Stuart and Astrid, 424–5; Stuart's funeral, 628

Musical Express, see New Musical Express

Musicians' Union: 'Needletime' agreement, 72n, 603, 747; closed shop, 258, 807; Richy's membership, 330; subscription, 330–1; Poole and the Tremilos, 580; fees, 737

My Bonnie (Sheridan & The Beat Brothers): recording session, 461, 463, 464; disliked by Beatles, 464, 511; German release, 465, 511–12, 598; first Liverpool customer, 512, 783; plugged by Wooler, 878; Brian's enquiries, 512, 515, 516, 519; Brian listens to, 518; Nems stock, 521, 523, 564; Brian plays to his parents, 523; sales, 523; Brian takes to Decca and EMI, 526, 544, 878; reviews, 528, 563, 886–7; Decca US release, 878, 886–7; Twist promotion, 528, 881; British release, 541, 563–4, 590; rejected by EMI, 547; PR build-up, 550; liked by Mimi, 564, 745; German charts, 564, 881; sales, 564, 620, 745

My Bonnie album, 654, 887

My Boomerang Won't Come Back (Charlie Drake), 529, 579

Myles, Edward, *see* Clayton (Eddie)

Mystery Train (Elvis Presley), 113, 117, 422, 841; performed by Paul and Ian, 135

National Service, 58, 65, 81, 91, 116, 120–1

Neal, Chris, 669

Nelson, Ricky, 169, 200

Nems: history of company, 251–2, 270, 274, 276, 304, 326–7, 656–7; music shop, 19, 252, 261; pianos, 19, 42, 252, 820; Brian's career, 261, 267, 270–1, 274, 304, 326–8, 472, 512, 515–16, 566, 588, 838; staff, 271, 277, 326–7, 472, 520, 566, 646, 651, 877, 892, 901; browseries, 271, 328, 418, 474–5, 512, 585, 645, 679; record chart, 6, 91, 146, 271–2, 564, 607, 751; record sales, 271, 327, 453, 512, 526, 821, 887; advertisements, 274, 326, 492, 498, 515, 527, 893; EMI relationship, 327–8, 526, 647–8, 748, 760, 822, 888; ticket sales, 301, 590, 687, 688; *Mersey Beat*, 471, 492, 498, 515; Beatles as customers, 474–5, 479, 494, 512, 587, 764; Beatles sales, 482, 512, 515, 521, 523, 541, 750, 752, 764, 783; Beatles meeting with Brian, 523; Decca relationship, 578

Nems Enterprises: formation, 656–7; staff, 656–7, 704, 750, 778, 818–19, 825; van for Beatles, 684; signings, 686, 687; commission, 686;

influence, 687; promotions, 688, 770, 902; How Do You Do It, 697; first tour, 699; dismissal of Pete, 701–3; Lennon-McCartney agreement, 734, 743; Beatles contract, 742–3; *Showdance*, 765, 780, 898; awards, 824; music publishing company, 830–1; Brian's role, 838

Nerk Twins: playing at Caversham, 302, 336; heading for Spain, 500; in Paris, 504, 505, 510, 543, 743; in London, 545; Some Other Guy, 681; recording, 834

Ness, Linda (Lindy): background, 535, 693; Beatles fan, 535–6, 538–9, 605; friendship with John, 622–3, 642–3, 681–2, 694, 714, 792, 893; on Stuart's death, 631n; *Welcome Home* show, 674; watches writing of Please Please Me, 674–5, 807; witnesses John's driving lessons, 774; stops going to Cavern, 805

New Musical Express (NME, *Musical Express*): charts, 71, 82, 91, 106, 109, 126, 317, 359, 423, 472, 604, 639, 695; Heartbreak Hotel ad, 86; on Little Richard, 116, 215, 767; Top Thirty, 127, 140, 141n, 225, 269n, 672, 748, 749, 759–60, 782; on Buddy Holly, 147; on multi-track recordings, 259; on Capitol and EMI, 262, 272; George Martin quotes, 278, 280, 512, 808; Alan Smith's career, 552–3, 807; review of My Bonnie, 563; on Time Beat, 637; album chart, 665; US column, 665; Life-lines, 738; circulation, 759; Beatles promo visit, 759–60; Love Me Do in Top Thirty, 782, 789; article on Beatles, 782–3; on Beatles bookings, 783; on Beatles LP recording, 800, 814; readers' poll, 814

New Orleans Joys, 69

New Record Mirror: views of pop, 746; review of Love Me Do, 749; circulation, 759; Little Richard interview, 783; on Beatles, 796; Paul's visit, 796–7; Love Me Do in chart, 825

Newby, Chas, 229, 246–7, 389–90, 403–4, 405, 411

Newell, Norman: EMI appointment, 268; Beatles question, 526, 547, 592, 594; Parlophone 'pops', 636; signings, 763

Newley, Anthony, 327

The Niagara Theme (George Martin), 530, 637

Nobody But You (the Lafayettes), performed by Beatles, 695–6

Nobody's Child (Hank Snow): sung by Richy, 54, 69, 77, 464; recorded by Lonnie Donegan, 69; recorded by Beatles with Sheridan, 461, 463–4; recorded by Traveling Wilburys, 873

Northern Dance Orchestra (NDO), 602–3

Nothin' Shakin' (Eddie Fontaine), 201; Hamburg recording, 832

O'Brien, Chas (Ty Brian), *see* Brian (Ty)

Observer, 126

Odd Spot coffee bar, 619, 643

Oh Boy! (the Crickets), 4, 6, 150

Oh Boy! (ABC-TV), 200, 372

Olympics, the, 419, 475

O'Mahony, Sean, 760

One After 909: 296, 297, 336, 455, 608, 832

One Track Mind (Bobby Lewis), performed by Beatles, 513

Only The Lonely (Roy Orbison), 329, 402n, 675

Open (Your Lovin' Arms) (Buddy Knox): sung by George, 586; Beatles selection for recording, 663, 889

Orbison, Roy, 329, 586–7, 604, 675, 808
Oriole Records, 612
O'Shea, Maureen: Beatles Fan Club, 489–91, 540; on parents of Beatles, 490; fan club promotion, 508; relationship with Jim, 509; Beatles management, 509, 511, 514, 524; on Beatles, 538
Over The Rainbow (Gene Vincent), 215, 659; Beatles repertoire, 365, 433, 456, 480, 533

Paolozzi, Eduardo, 458, 497, 628
Paramor, Norrie: signs up Cliff Richard, 200; songwriting, 279; Beatles question, 526; rejection of Beatles, 547, 594; on holiday, 592; signings, 612n; Frank Ifield's work, 695, 696; George Martin's view of, 638, 887; successes, 638, 639, 696, 887; target of Frost/TW3 satire, 638, 805–6, 809, 900
Parkes, Stanley (John's cousin), 56, 64, 232, 489
Parkin, John (Johnny, Richy's grandfather), see Starkey
Parkin, John (Richy's great-grandfather), 24
Parkin, Ma (Richy's great-grandmother), 24
Parlophone label: origins, 256; George Martin's career, 97, 121, 256–8, 261–2, 264, 266, 268–9, 472, 636–7; Vipers signing, 98, 268; new 45s, 224; Southlanders signing, 265; rumours of closure, 266, 268; successes, 268–9, 273–4, 422, 472, 529, 636–7; Ron Richards' career, 278; Matt Monro signing, 279; Lindsay Ross release, 320; offices, 328, 798; Temperance Seven release, 423; *Beyond The Fringe*, 473, 487, 874; songs in Beatles repertoire, 513; George Martin's compositions, 531; originality, 637; Beatles recording contract, 646–8, 655–6, 668, 672, 678, 732, 739, 754, 831; selecting songs for, 650, 651, 663; Beatles recording session (6 June 1962), 666–72; Maguire failure, 696; How Do You Do It, 697–8, 727–8; Beatles recording session (4 September 1962), 724–7; Beatles recording session (11 September 1962), 729–32; Love Me Do release, 745–6; plugging Love Me Do, 747, 779, 803; throwaway cards for Beatles, 757; Mrs Mills signing, 763; *Twelve O'Clock Spin* plays, 791; singles, 799; Beatles recording session (26 November 1962), 806–10; label copy for Please Please Me, 814
Parnes, Larry: signs up Billy Fury, 199–200; Vince Eager discovery, 247; Tommy Steele's career, 266; lifestyle, 279; Gene Vincent tour, 294, 295, 301, 304, 305; meeting with Brian, 304; relationship with Williams, 306, 313, 347; Fury backing group audition, 306–10, 689, 863; hierarchy in his stable, 316–17; reports of Beatles appearance, 318; Beatles pay, 319, 322; Blackpool summer season, 347; non-view of Rory Storm, 470; management commission, 486, 533; Marty Wilde's marriage, 606; management style, 744; Beatles negotiations with Brian, 789
Paul, Les, 258–9, 302
Pauncefort, Graham, 454, 541
Pedersen, Ingrid (Victoria Elizabeth Lennon, John's half-sister), 31n
Peggy Sue (Buddy Holly), 4, 6, 149, 168; performed by Quarry Men, 152
Peggy Sue Got Married (Buddy Holly), 224

Penniman, Richard, see Little Richard
Penny Lane: name, 425n, 842; area, 26; roundabout, 4, 16, 196, 875; bus hub, 88, 212, 409
People, 346
People And Places (Granada TV), 498, 737, 777–8, 782, 826, 899
Peppermint Twist (Joey Dee and the Starliters), sung by Pete, 585, 622
Perkins, Carl: hero to John and Paul, 3; Blue Suede Shoes, 88, 91, 141; Sun sound, 109, 117, 141, 150, 168; rock style, 149; Glad All Over, 150; popularity, 161; Quarry Men recording, 178; Les Stewart Quartet repertoire, 209; Quarrymen repertoire, 240; Blackjacks repertoire, 247; Hurricanes repertoire, 288; *Dance Album*, 293; Beatles recording, 336; Ringo sings Matchbox, 340; Beatles repertoire, 365, 429, 784; Pete sings Matchbox, 456; Beatles Decca recording, 560
Perry, Lee, 811, 817
Peter, Paul and Mary, 754–5
Peters, Ray, 604
Philips Records, 306n, 317, 591, 612, 738, 886
Phillips, Harold (Lord Woodbine, Woody): steel band, 175–6, 289; friendship with Allan Williams, 175–6; name, 176; strip club, 289, 348–9, 449; trip to Amsterdam and Hamburg, 289–90; Hamburg journey with Beatles, 356, 360, 362; Colony Club, 617
Phillips, Harold (student lodger), 43, 843
Phillips, Percy: recording studio, 178, 380, 462, 854; Quarry Men recording, 178–80; Billy Fury recording, 199–200; One After 909 recording, 296
Phillips, Sam, 67–8, 109, 150, 168
Pick Of The Pops (BBC Light Programme), 224
Pickles, Thelma (later Monaghan): relationship with John, 192–3, 210–11; on Buddy Holly's death, 207; relationship with Paul, 715, 774; on John and Cynthia, 857–8; life, 898
A Picture Of You (Joe Brown), 676; Beatles repertoire, 645, 676, 832
Piel, Ellen, 455, 467–8
Pilbeam, Peter, 567, 584, 602–4, 675, 811
Pink Champagne, played by Paul, 151
Pinwheel Twist, 585, 608, 649, 883
Please Mr Postman (the Marvelettes), Beatles repertoire, 546, 604, 832
Please Please Me: writing, 674–5, 723, 735, 890; untested, 681; rehearsing, 725, 726; George Martin's opinion, 725, 800, 808, 810; Ringo's drumming, 726; reworking, 729, 731, 735; EMI recording (11 September 1962), 729, 731, 798; title, 797, 798; plan to remake with harmonica, 798; EMI recording session (26 November 1962), 800, 804, 806–8, 809, 813; publishing company, 802, 803, 810–11, 812; press release, 805, 818, 824; Hamburg performance, 809; EMI support, 810; publishing contract, 814; plugging, 814, 829; PRS agreement, 817; launch, 818; Beatles album plans, 822; played at *Mersey Beat Awards Night*, 824; release, 829; possible chart performance, 829; *Juke Box Jury*, 829–30; Capitol's response, 834; US responses, 836; 1963 future, 840
Please Please Me album, 732n

Pobjoy, Mr (headmaster), 115, 136, 142
Poole, Brian, 579–80, 602n, 698, 882
Pop Inn (BBC Light Programme), 818
Pop Weekly, 760–1, 825, 897
Powell, Cynthia (Cyn): family background, 220n,
    574; character and appearance, 219, 231,
    284–5; at Liverpool College of Art, 143, 219,
    314; engagement, 231, 858; relationship with
    John, 219–20, 231–2, 245, 284–5, 287, 293,
    337, 401, 436, 514, 634–5, 661, 682, 715, 857;
    at Dykins house, 855; at Casbah, 227, 428;
    memories of Paul, 234; memories of George,
    235; on John's influence on Stuart, 241; nights
    in Gambier Terrace, 284–5, 333n, 343; at
    Vincent/Cochran show, 294; memories of
    songwriting, 296; on Fury audition, 307, 309;
    on Beatles sound, 310; on John's career plans,
    345; John's Hamburg trip, 353, 354; letters
    from John, 373, 867; Hamburg visit, 436,
    457–9, 460; on Pete, 459; at Cavern, 480, 605,
    606; stays at Mendips, 489; thrown out,
    499–500; stays with aunt, 500, 876; Stuart's
    funeral, 628; John in Hamburg, 632, 634;
    bedsit, 634–5, 661, 682; writes to Astrid, 642;
    pregnancy, 691–2, 714, 773; fails art school
    exam, 692; marriage plans, 692; wedding,
    712–13; married life in Brian's flat, 713–14,
    733, 773; moves into Mendips, 774;
    relationship with Mimi, 774
Powell, Lillian, 232, 284, 354, 457, 459, 692
Powell, Tony and Marjorie, 713
Power, Duffy, 306, 310, 321
Presley, Elvis: appearance, 68, 82, 86, 328;
    recording studio, 67, 141, 178; first recording
    session, 67; contract, 67; first release (That's
    All Right Mama), 67–8, 69; slap echo sound, 9,
    68, 109; Heartbreak Hotel, 82, 85, 94; national
    TV debut, 82; first US number 1: 85; on Radio
    Luxembourg, 85; influence, 3, 86–7, 92–3, 94,
    96, 100, 113, 117, 122, 135, 138, 140, 169–70,
    172; songs played by John and Paul, 10; guitar,
    100, 149; John singing, 103, 131; songs
    performed by Quarry Men, 103, 115, 129,
    131–2, 145, 229, 240; Hound Dog, 122, 150;
    NME Top Thirty, 127; Paul's appearance, 132,
    140, 229, 412; films, 149, 169–70, 190, 193,
    296n, 422, 437n, 586; in US Army, 170; *Rock 'n'
    Roll*, 189, 365; *Elvis's Golden Records*, 201, 365;
    songs performed by Les Stewart Quartet, 209;
    songs in Beatles repertoire, 318, 365, 403–4,
    405, 412, 442, 444, 513, 586; out of the army,
    328; post-army career, 422, 586; Beatles 'bigger
    than', 518, 533, 574, 579, 590, 657, 745, 801,
    815, 882
Preston, Billy, 766–7, 787–8, 793
Preuss, Oscar, 256–8, 261, 266, 278
Price, Margaret, 649, 792, 831
Prytherch, Sheila, 75
PS I Love You: writing, 650–1; rehearsing, 663,
    725, 729; EMI recording (June 1962), 666, 668,
    670, 675, 741n; Beatles repertoire, 681, 735,
    764, 784; George Martin's view, 725, 800; EMI
    recording (September 1962), 729–31, 732, 746;
    publishing agreement, 733, 746; reviews,
    749–50; BBC radio recording, 814; copyright,
    817; TV performance, 820; Beatles LP, 822;
    Hamburg recording, 832

Putting On The Style (Lonnie Donegan), 126;
    performed by Quarry Men, 128, 131
Pye Records, 587, 612, 738, 836, 888

Quarry Bank High School for Boys: school
    magazine, 11; school song, 57, 102; motto, 57;
    Speech Day, 115; teachers, 57, 65, 125, 354;
    uniform, 142; John passes exam, 56; John at,
    57–8, 60, 65, 67, 70, 190; John's reports, 74, 92;
    John's O-levels, 79, 95, 105, 124–5, 136, 142;
    Quarry Men name, 102–3, 228–9; John's career
    options, 105, 125, 136–7; Quarry Men perform
    at, 114; school photograph, 120; John leaves,
    138, 142
Quarry Men, the (Quarrymen): formation, 1,
    101–2, 342; skiffle, 102, 103, 109, 146, 165;
    members, 102, 103, 110, 129, 137–8, 145, 146,
    164, 178, 229, 853; name, 102–3, 228–9;
    rehearsals, 103, 109, 135, 147; Cavern debut,
    108; management, 108, 109, 144, 151–2, 164,
    165, 178, 316, 524; talent show, 889; bookings,
    114–15, 122–4, 127–31, 137, 147, 151, 165,
    167, 177, 270; at Liverpool Empire, 123–4, 197;
    Paul's first sight of, 128; photos, 129, 145, 163,
    177, 853; songs, 6, 131, 145–6, 268–9; first
    recording of, 131–2; Paul joins, 132; Paul's first
    performance with, 144, 669; stage outfits, 145,
    177; George's arrival, 157–8, 160–1, 166,
    285–6, 853; group dynamics, 160; dismissal of
    Eric, 163–4; recording session, 178–80, 199;
    revival, 228–9; at Casbah, 228–9, 237, 240–2,
    246–7, 282–3, 296, 303, 352, 403; trying to find
    a drummer and a bass, 241; Stu Sutcliffe joins,
    281, 282, 285–6, 353
Quickly, Tommy (Thomas Quigley), 770

Race, Steve, 259
Radio Luxembourg: British listeners, 71, 85, 94,
    748, 849; Decca's airtime, 117, 128; sponsored
    programmes, 849; Dick James shows, 265, 811;
    My Bonnie unplayed, 563; Love Me Do, 747–8,
    764, 779, 825, 895; Beach Boys, 754; Beatles
    personal appearances, 757, 781, 818
Rainbows, the, 197, 228
Raining In My Heart (Buddy Holly); Beatles
    repertoire, 539, 608
Ramrod (Duane Eddy), 336; recorded by Beatles,
    336; played by Beatles, 349
Rattles, the, 653
Raunchy (Justis/Manker), 150; played by George,
    157, 158, 853
Rave On (the Crickets), 168, 198
Ravin' Texans, *see* Texan Skiffle Group
Ray, Johnnie, 64, 85, 170, 187
RCA Victor, 82, 85, 836n
Rebels, the, 119–20, 136
Record and Show Mirror, 340, 344
Record Mail, 748, 801
Record Mirror, 6, 91, 101n, 272
Record Retailer: launch, 864; charts, 317, 530, 665,
    696; Hamburg trip report, 453; on sales
    increases, 472; sheet music chart, 530; on Dick
    James, 530; on My Bonnie, 563; on number of
    singles, 738; Beatles arrival ad, 748, 753–4, 760;
    review of Love Me Do, 750; Top Fifty, 751, 781,
    791, 805, 820, 825, 829, 864; chart compilation,
    751–2; on Beach Boys, 754

Red Hot (Ronnie Hawkins); Beatles repertoire, 495; Hamburg recording, 833
Red Sails In The Sunset (traditional): sung by Alf, 18, 224; recorded by Ray Sharpe, 224; Beatles repertoire, 334, 343, 404, 510; Hamburg recording, 832–3
Reed, Jimmy, 463, 611, 753
Reed, Stan, 190, 847
Reminiscing (Buddy Holly), Beatles repertoire, 736
Remo Quartet (Remo Four), 212, 430n, 519, 550, 589, 613
Rennie, Roland, 810, 835–6, 897
Reveille, 113, 115
Rhind, Geoff, 129, 131
Rhone, Dorothy (Dot): appearance and character, 243–4, 287; meets John and Paul, 243–4; relationship with Paul, 244, 246, 286–7, 293, 301, 337, 354, 499, 661, 682; pregnancy, 287, 292; miscarriage, 302, 354; letters to Paul, 373; engagement to Paul, 400, 428; Hamburg visit plans, 436; in Hamburg, 457–8, 634; at Cavern, 480, 540, 606; moves in with Cyn, 635, 661, 682; breaks up with Paul, 692–3; Cyn stays with, 773
Rhone, Jessie, 287
Rialto Ballroom, 133–4, 682, 740
Richard, Cliff (Harry Webb): signed by Paramor, 200; breakthrough, 200, 583, 750; friendship with Ellis, 338; backing groups, 359, 897; influence, 405, 412, 666, 752; Beatles attitude to, 422, 557, 573, 575, 583, 871; Beatles comparison, 432, 482, 491–2; bowing on stage, 573; fans, 579, 723; Beatles play Dream, 585; EMI recording agreement, 647; chart success, 672, 799; on girlfriends, 759; rejected by Capitol, 763
Richards, David, 342, 349, 364, 371
Richards, Keith, 610, 611, 665, 896
Richards, Ron: background, 278n; assistant to George Martin, 278; office, 328; handles 'pops', 636; on George's affair with Judy, 640; position with Beatles recordings, 646; discusses Beatles with George, 665–6, 672; Beatles recording session (June 1962), 667–8, 670; view of Pete Best, 670; finding song for Beatles, 673, 698; Beatles sessions (September 1962), 725, 726, 729–32, 798; view of Ringo, 730
Ridley, Walter (Wally), 266, 526, 547, 594, 612n, 888
Right, Said Fred (Bernard Cribbins), 696
Rimmer, Freddie, 42
Rip It Up (Little Richard), 99–100, 767
Ritson, Keith 'Ritter', 140
Riversdale Technical College, 143–4, 187, 236
Roadrunners, the, 772, 876
Robbins, Amy, 851
Robbins, Bett (Danher, Paul's cousin), 71, 138, 226, 301, 433, 874
Robbins, Edward (Ted), 138, 851
Robbins, Kate, 851
Robbins, Marty, 121
Robbins, Mike: work at Butlin's, 71, 138–9, 851; Paul hopes for his help, 180, 188, 226; pub at Caversham, 301, 302n; pub at Ryde, 874
Robinson, Eileen, 480
Robinson, William 'Smokey', 420, 608, 650, 676

Rock And Roll Music (Chuck Berry), 149; Beatles repertoire, 495; Ringo's drumming, 617
Rock Around The Clock (Bill Haley and His Comets), 68–9, 72, 77, 82, 106, 107, 117
Rock Around The Clock (film), 82, 96–7, 108
Rock Island Line (Lonnie Donegan Skiffle Group), 82–3, 102n, 109, 110, 126; performed by Quarry Men, 128
Rodgers, Jimmie, 44
Roe, Tommy, 736, 790, 815, 816
Roland, Cheniston, 304–5, 308–9
Roll Over Beethoven (Chuck Berry), 174; Beatles repertoire, 495
Rolling Stones, the, 752–3
Rory Storm and the Hurricanes: name, 244, 288, 299; stage suits, 377, 384, 431, 470, 575, 619, 658; at Casbah, 246; at Chez Jazrok, 247; at Cavern, 287, 313; Liverpool's top group, 287, 288; Butlin's booking (1960), 288–9, 298, 308, 310–11, 330–2, 340–1, 351; at Stadium, 300, 304–5; Ringo playing with, 304–5, 330–1, 705; Musicians' Union membership, 330–1; approached for Hamburg, 351; holiday in London, 376; Hamburg contract, 377–8; playing in Hamburg, 375, 378–9, 383, 384; accommodation in Hamburg, 377; destroy stage, 393; relationship with Beatles, 393–4, 494; return from Hamburg, 416, 426, 456; repertoire, 418, 494; playing Boys, 421–2; Leach's twelve-group session, 430n; Butlin's booking (1961), 431, 439, 469–70, 493; future prospects, 470; *Mersey Beat* article, 493; at Tower Ballroom, 519; *Mersey Beat* poll, 550, 552, 589; Ringo leaves, 551–2; decline, 552, 589; 'dep' drummers, 600; Ringo rejoins, 616; US Army booking, 616, 619; pay, 618; in France, 619, 657, 658–9, 721; playing at Jerry Lee Lewis show, 657–8, 659; Tower bookings, 659; at Knotty Ash, 884; Butlin's booking (1962), 600, 616, 659, 679, 690; Ringo leaves again, 690, 704; audiences, 709–10
Rory Storm and the Wild Ones, 431
Rose, Bettina, 825
Roughley, Jimmy, 213
Rowe, Dick: turns down Marty Wilde, 200n; catchphrase, 359, 583; Decca staff, 546; American trip, 562–3, 578; response to Beatles, 578–81; Brian's letter to, 581–2; memories of Beatles, 882
Royal Iris, MV, 488, 683
Royal Liverpool Children's Hospital, 40, 66, 72–3
Runciman, Derek, 761–2

St Tudno, TS, 90–1
The Saints (gospel hymn): played by Paul, 75, 101, 213, 821; Beatles recording, 461, 463, 511, 528, 821
Samwell, Ian 'Sammy', 762, 897
Sanders, Susan, 538
Sanders, Tony, 412
Saturday Club (BBC Light Programme): Paul listens to, 224; Brian Poole and the Tremilos, 580; Love Me Do, 779–80, 803, 899; Dick James's achievement, 813, 818; Beatles achievements without appearance, 829
Saturday Skiffle Club (BBC Light Programme), 121, 224n

Savage, Mike, 558, 562, 883
Save The Last Dance For Me (the Drifters), sung by John, 419
Say Mama, (Gene Vincent), 214, 659; Beatles repertoire, 645
Scene, 612, 753
Schacht, Alfred, 453, 465, 541
Searchin' (the Coasters), 141, 215; performed by Beatles, 475, 536; recorded by Beatles, 559, 560, 561
Seeger, Pete, 93, 176
Seligson, Sonia, 276–7
Sellers, Peter: *Goon Show*, 55, 264, 863; produced by George Martin, 264, 273, 423, 637, 655, 801; *The Best Of Sellers*, 274; *Songs For Swingin' Sellers*, 279, 639; *Running Jumping & Standing Still Film*, 431
Sellman, Frank, 454
September In The Rain (Dinah Washington): Beatles repertoire, 546; recorded by Beatles, 559, 560
Shadows, the: Cliff Richard and, 338, 359, 405, 422, 573, 575, 666; Bert Weedon and, 344; first record, 751; Apache, 359, 393; dance steps, 365, 405; Beatles parody, 393, 456, 489; Man of Mystery, 402n; echo unit, 412, 492; Tony Meehan leaves, 546–7, 580, 581; success, 578, 672, 749, 768; recording agreement, 647; Jet Harris leaves, 705; rejected by Capitol, 763
Shake, Rattle And Roll (Bill Haley and His Comets), 71
Shankar, Ravi, 279n
Shapiro, Helen, 513, 647, 763, 789–90, 822
Sharing You (Bobby Vee), 680; sung by George, 680
Shaw, Mary, 243, 304, 661, 679
Sheeley, Sharon, 300
The Sheik Of Araby (Joe Brown), 874; sung by George, 476, 514; Beatles recording, 559, 560, 561
Sheila (Tommy Roe), Beatles repertoire, 736
Sheridan, Ann, 474n
Sheridan, Tony: background, 332n; appearance, 372, 467; character, 332; career, 372, 462, 504; age, 444; guitars, 381, 442, 464, 465; arrival in Hamburg, 332; influence on Hamburg scene, 371–2; relationship with Beatles, 372, 388–9, 395; opinion of Beatles, 387–8, 456; at Top Ten Club, 388–9, 395, 397, 399, 441, 442, 470; playing with Beatles, 397, 399, 441, 442, 449, 455; girlfriend Rosi, 441, 446–7, 456, 457, 598; on gangsters, 443; taking Preludin, 444–5; on Pete's drumming, 447–8; songwriting, 453; fighting, 456–7, 599; recording session with Beatles, 461–4; signed up, 452, 453; influence on Beatles, 467; playing with Gerry and the Pacemakers, 470, 510; record with Beatles, 511, 521, 528, 541, 563, 592, 598, 886–7; recruits Ringo for Top Ten house band, 551–2, 569, 598; opinion of Ringo, 599; Top Ten contract, 599; playing at Star-Club, 615, 787, 827; offers Ringo work at Star-Club, 615; recording agreement, 635; on John and Bettina, 645; Paul drums with, 888–9; last recordings with Beatles, 653–4
Shirelles, the: background, 420; sound, 420, 421; Luther Dixon's work, 421, 586, 645; song sung by Cilla, 471; Top Rank label, 475; songs in Beatles repertoire, 475, 586, 617, 645, 680; influence on John and Paul's songwriting, 650, 735; unknown in Germany, 653; George Martin on, 809
Short Fat Fannie (Larry Williams), 141; sung by John, 145
A Shot Of Rhythm And Blues (Arthur Alexander), 608; Beatles repertoire, 609, 832
Shotton, Pete: friendship with John, 40, 56–7, 64, 86, 95, 106, 132, 138, 152; Quarry Bank School, 56–7, 70, 74, 190; memories of Julia, 79, 80; Quarry Men, 101–3, 108, 130, 286; Quarry Men photos, 120, 129; Paul joins Quarry Men, 132; departure from Quarry Men, 137–8, 146, 152; police career, 138
Silver, Emanuel Charles, 530
Silverman, Livermore & Co, 482, 483, 548, 678
Simons, Judith, 746
Sinatra, Frank: song influence on John, 74; Paul's singing, 75; *The Man With The Golden Arm*, 88; Paul's songwriting, 89; *Come Fly With Me*, 273; imitators, 279; appearance with Elvis, 328; fans, 579
Six-Five Special (BBC-tv), 108, 118, 150, 200, 213, 715
Skinner, John, 666
Skinner, Ray, 208, 226
Slippin' And Slidin' (Little Richard), 3, 86, 99
Smith, A. J. (Alf, 'Cissy'), 56, 118, 862
Smith, Alan: on Cavern, 477; Beatles fan, 540; career, 552–3; Beatles promo visit, 759–60; Little Richard interview, 767; NME article on Beatles, 782; George Martin interviews, 800, 801, 808, 809; at Beatles recording session, 807, 808–9; on Beatles broadcast, 814
Smith, Bill, 102, 103
Smith, David John (Letters), 778, 790, 805
Smith, George (Uncle George): appearance, 39, 62; employment, 26, 38; marriage, 26; homes, 26, 27, 30, 31, 38; John's childhood, 35, 39, 45, 489; brother's work, 56, 862; death, 9, 73, 185, 626; clothes for John, 137, 142
Smith, Keith, 532, 543, 879
Smith, Mike: Decca position, 546; sees Beatles in Cavern, 546, 553, 558; Decca test, 547, 558, 559, 562–3, 579–80, 880–1, 883; signings, 579–80, 612n, 698; Beatles tape, 582
Smith, Mimi (Stanley, Aunt Mimi): family background, 16–17; birth, 16; appearance, 38; character, 38–9; employment, 843; sister Julia's marriage, 18, 26; marriage to George, 26; home in Allerton Road, 26, 27; John's birth, 27; sister Julia's family situation, 30; concern for John, 31, 33; home in Menlove Avenue, 31, 35, 38; care of John, 35, 37, 38–9, 185; John's education, 36, 46, 56, 64, 74, 136–7, 142; relationship with John, 9, 38–9, 45, 64, 79–80, 152, 185, 284, 573; advice to John, 8; social class, 11, 37–8, 50–1; finances, 38, 39, 42, 137, 176; student lodgers, 9, 42–3, 109; trips to panto, 45, 489; trips to cinema, 45; support for Strawberry Field, 47; relationship with John's father Alf, 50; wireless for John, 55; death of husband George, 9, 73–4; illness, 74, 350; view of Elvis, 93; attitude to Quarry Men rehearsals, 109, 135; attitude to guitar playing, 9, 113, 114,

193, 228, 311, 435; attitude to John's clothes, 129, 142; John at art college, 136–7, 219, 314, 344–5; death of sister Julia, 182–3, 185; attitude to buying a guitar for John, 216, 221, 222, 227–8, 373; attitude to Cyn, 232, 489, 499–500; attitude to art, 242; John moves out to Gambier Terrace, 284; view of John's future, 345, 350, 353, 355, 410; John's passport, 353, 354, 435; postcard from Hamburg, 373; John's return from Hamburg, 400; Cavern visit, 489; attitude to Brian, 542, 595; response to My Bonnie, 564, 745; encounter with Beatles fans, 623; John's marriage, 692, 712, 713; John moves out to Brian's flat, 713; response to Love Me Do, 745; John and Cyn move in, 774; article about, 845

Smith, Norman: on Beatles signing, 640; on Beatles appearance, 666; on recording session (6 June 1962), 669, 670, 671; recording session (4 September 1962), 726, 731; recording session (26 November 1962), 807, 808

Smith, Reg, see Wilde (Marty)

Smith, Walter, 576, 602

So How Come (Everly Brothers), sung by George, 476

Soldier Boy (the Shirelles), 650, 888; Beatles repertoire, 645

Soldier of Love (Arthur Alexander), 679; Beatles repertoire, 679, 680, 725, 832

Some Days, 336

Some Other Guy (Richie Barrett), Beatles repertoire, 680–1, 710, 725, 736, 832; filmed, 711–12; played on TV, 777

Sonin, Ray, 834, 902

sound equipment: bass 'coffin' loudspeaker, 495–6, 667, 686; Decca studios, 558, 580; Elpico amp, 163, 172, 178, 188, 199, 227, 284, 301, 316, 334, 354, 401, 467; EMI studios, 667, 807; Fender Deluxe amp, 382; Leak amp, 807; Selmer Truvoice amp, 335, 336, 354, 467, 495, 667; Tannoy speaker, 667; Vox amplifiers, 684, 688, 731, 807, 891; Watkins Westminster amp, 354, 496

Sounds Incorporated, 767, 783, 787, 788, 897, 899

Sowry, Virginia, 437, 482, 694

Specialty Records, 141, 168

Spector, Phil, 201, 217, 365, 419, 421

Spence, Shirley, 328

Stand By Me (Ben E. King), sung by John, 475

Standing, Ray, 277

Stanley, Anne (John's aunt), 26, 27

Stanley, Annie (Milward, John's grandmother), 16, 17, 26, 27

Stanley, Eliza (John's great-grandmother), 16

Stanley, Elizabeth 'Mater' (John's aunt), see Sutherland

Stanley, George ('Pop', John's grandfather), 16, 17, 27, 464, 740

Stanley, Harriet, see Birch

Stanley, Julia (John's mother), see Lennon

Stanley, Mary Elizabeth, see Smith (Aunt Mimi)

Stanley, William (John's great-grandfather), 16

Star-Club: origins, 569, 599, 601; opening, 615, 631, 633, 635; Beatles season, 630, 631–2, 652; John's performances, 631–2, 652, 828n; house band, 632, 827; success, 633; Beatles pay, 633; Gerry and the Pacemakers at, 635, 651; Astrid at, 641, 794; sex, 643–4, 794; barmaids, 644–5, 794; Little Richard at, 659, 687, 787; Gene Vincent at, 659–60; audiences, 661; Beatles bookings, 685, 769–70, 783, 785, 793, 839; King-Size Taylor and the Dominoes, 690; Sounds Incorporated, 788

Star Search, 123–4, 198–9, 237; see also Levis (Carroll)

Starkey, Annie (Bower, grandmother): birth, 24; marriage, 24; children, 24; 'voodoo queen', 24, 33, 600; home, 26; relationship with daughter-in-law and grandson Richy, 29; care of grandson Richy, 33, 40, 600; 'cures' Richy's left-handedness, 33, 110; musicianship, 54; takes Richy to Isle of Man, 96n; gives ring to Richy, 236; death, 599–600, 615

Starkey, Elsie (Gleave, mother, later Graves): family background, 24–5; first meeting with Richy, 24; marriage, 25; homes, 26, 34; birth of son Richy, 27; separation from husband, 29, 53; employment, 29, 34, 40, 95; son's education, 33–4, 43; relationship with son, 34, 43, 52, 53–4, 66; son's illnesses, 40, 43, 66–7; friendship with Annie Maguire, 43, 111; relationship with Harry Graves, 53; divorce and remarriage, 66, 104; trip to Romford, 76; son's employment, 77; birthday presents for son, 91, 214, 469; son's drum kit, 187; son's name, 244, 718; son's religion, 287; son's career, 311, 330, 331, 616–17, 704, 870; hairdressing, 471; meets Maureen, 716

Starkey, Johnny (Parkin, grandfather): name, 24; marriage, 24; children, 24; home, 26; relationship with daughter-in-law, 29; relationship with grandson Richy, 24, 29, 33, 43, 187; musicianship, 54; takes Richy to Isle of Man, 96n; money for Richy's drum kit, 187; death, 236; funeral, 236, 600; wedding ring, 236, 469; employment, 740

Starkey, Richard 'Richy' (Ringo Starr): family background, 23–7; birth, 27; childhood, 29, 31, 33, 52–4; education, 33–4, 35, 41, 43–4, 52, 65, 76–7, 719, 720; musical education, 44, 54; National Service issue, 58, 65, 81, 91, 120; mother's remarriage, 66, 104; trip to London, 76; employment, 77, 83–4, 90–1, 94, 95, 104, 186–7; Teddy Boy gang, 84–5; Elvis influence, 86, 169; Little Richard influence, 87; apprenticeship at Hunt's, 95, 143, 289, 301, 314, 330; family holiday, 96n; Rock Around The Clock, 96; Eddie Clayton Skiffle Group, 110–12, 120, 133, 137; dancing and nights out, 133, 137, 144; smoking, 137; Riversdale Technical College, 143–4, 187, 236; dreams of stardom, 170–1; forms own group, 213; playing with Darktown, 213–14, 235, 237; playing with Texans, 213–14, 235; playing with Hurricanes, 235, 237, 304–5, 330–1; death of grandfather, 236; first car, 245, 341, 376; Butlin's booking, 289, 301, 310–11, 329–30, 340; Gene Vincent shows, 300, 304–5; quits apprenticeship, 330; autograph, 341; newspaper interview, 375; second car, 376, 469, 600; holiday in London, 376; journey to Hamburg, 376; Beatles view of, 378–9, 393–4; view of Pete's drumming, 388; considers hairdressing, 416, 600; admires Beatles, 417; 21st birthday, 469, 470–1; Butlin's

Starkey, Richard 'Richy' (Ringo Starr) –
  continued
  season, 469–70; career options, 470; record
  collection, 482n; American emigration plans,
  493, 551, 616, 875; plays with Beatles, 550–1;
  Hamburg Top Ten Club band, 551–2, 589;
  leaves Hurricanes, 551–2; in Hamburg, 598–9;
  return from Hamburg, 598; unemployment,
  600; Hamburg offer, 615; rejoins Hurricanes,
  616; US Army booking, 616; plays with Beatles,
  616–18; car race with George, 618–19; car
  accident, 619, 659; in France, 619, 658; car
  repaired, 659; Butlin's season, 659, 689;
  meeting with John and Paul, 689–90; plan to
  join Dominoes, 690, 700; joins Beatles, 700,
  704; first performance as a Beatle, 704–5;
  audiences' responses to, 709–11; London press
  visits, 756, 757, 758; encounter with Little
  Richard, 767; correspondence, 792; EMI
  recording session (November 1962), 808,
  809–10
  APPEARANCE: left-handedness, 33, 110, 600;
  size, 76, 120, 186; rings, 91, 214, 236–7, 341,
  375, 469; dress, 94, 171, 213–14, 304–5; nose,
  186, 720; expression, 186, 300, 720; grey streak
  in hair, 214, 341, 379, 720, 724; sunglasses on
  stage, 300, 305; hairstyle, 305, 704, 724;
  autograph, 341, 720; sideburns, 690, 700;
  beard, 690, 700, 704; filmed in Cavern,
  711–12
  CHARACTER: blunt and candid, 95;
  contented, 186; religious views, 287; moods,
  494; risk-taker, 717; bold and open, 717
  DRINKING: as a bar waiter, 95; underage, 95,
  186; at Butlin's, 342, 393; Scotch and Coke,
  342, 446; in Hamburg, 393–4;
  DRUMMING: left-handedness, 110, 600;
  interest in drumming, 66, 67, 73, 77; first
  drum, 77; first drum kit, 104, 111–12, 171;
  drumming lessons, 110; first new drum kit,
  187–8; reputation, 213, 341, 599, 655;
  transporting drum kit, 236, 244–5; drumming
  style, 341, 599, 600; *Starrtime!*, 340, 379, 421,
  456, 493; buys Premier drum kit, 375–6;
  drumming admired by Beatles, 417, 617;
  drumming opportunities, 615–16; drumming
  at EMI recording session, 726; replaced by
  session drummer, 730; drumming role in
  Beatles, 736, 832; EMI recording session
  (November 1962), 808, 809–10; Hamburg
  recording, 832
  HEALTH: illness (peritonitis), 40–1, 43; illness
  (pleurisy and TB), 66–7, 72–3, 76; weakened,
  83–4, 95, 720; stabilising, 104; delicate
  stomach, 720, 773
  NAME: 'Rings', 237, 244; Ringo Starr, 244;
  Richy or Ringo, 718
  RELATIONSHIPS: with grandparents, 33, 43,
  110, 187, 236, 599–600; sex, 72–3, 122, 341–2;
  friendship with Roy Trafford, 94–5, 110, 137,
  186, 187, 717–18; first steady girlfriend, 187;
  engagement to Gerry, 214, 235, 287, 289, 330;
  end of engagement, 375; with Beatles, 550–1;
  with Maureen, 715–16, 774; friendship with
  George, 718, 722; with John, 719; with Brian,
  721; with George Martin, 730
  SINGING: in church choir, 77; singing voice,

340; *Starrtime!*, 340, 379, 422, 456, 493
  SONGWRITING: Don't Pass Me By, 719–20
Starkey, Richard Henry Parkin (Richy, father):
  birth, 24; first meeting with Elsie, 24; marriage,
  25; wartime, 26; birth of son Richy, 27;
  separation from wife, 29; move from Liverpool,
  34; divorce and remarriage, 66; meeting with
  son, 600
Starr, Ringo, *see* Starkey (Richy)
Stay (Maurice Williams), played by Beatles, 419
Steele, Tommy (Hicks), 97–8, 136, 265–6, 273
Steen, Linda (Lou): on Beatles at Cavern, 536,
  538–40; getting lifts from Beatles, 605; photos,
  622; letters to Paul, 622; tea with John and
  Mimi, 623; at Casbah, 623; Paul's letters from
  Hamburg, 635; cake for Beatles return, 674;
  watches John and Paul write Please Please Me,
  674–5, 807; at Cavern, 693, 805
Stevenson, W. L., 232
Stewart, Les, 208–9, 229
Stigwood, Robert, 760–1
Storm, Al, *see* Caldwell (Alan)
Storm, Rory, *see* Caldwell, Alan
Strawberry Field children's home, 47, 93, 843–4
Strong, Barrett, 329, 419, 560
Sulca (art school Students' Union), 143, 299, 300,
  354, 496
Sullivan, Peter, 824
Summertime (Gene Vincent), 215, 659; Beatles
  repertoire, 365, 380, 456
Sun Arise (Rolf Harris), 696, 801
Sun Studio: slap echo sound, 9–10, 68, 109, 294;
  Elvis recordings, 10, 67–8, 189, 229, 893;
  George's interest, 117; Jerry Lee Lewis
  recordings, 141, 168; guitar sound, 150; Carl
  Perkins recordings, 168; country songs, 201,
  294
Sunday Night At The London Palladium (ATV),
  111, 167–8
Sure To Fall (Carl Perkins), 294; recorded by
  Beatles, 559, 560
Sutcliffe, Charles, 282n, 283n, 314, 625
Sutcliffe, Joyce, 283n, 625, 642, 886
Sutcliffe, Millie (Cronin): background, 282–3n,
  489; character, 283n; relationship with son,
  283n, 310, 424, 434, 497; view of son's
  Hamburg booking, 314, 357; view of Germans,
  392, 424, 627; son's head injury, 424, 871;
  relationship with Astrid, 424, 434, 587, 627,
  628, 631, 642; son's health, 497; son's death,
  625–7, 630; son's funeral, 627, 628, 631
Sutcliffe, Pauline, 283n, 642, 867, 886
Sutcliffe, Stuart: family background, 282–3n;
  appearance, 192, 211, 283n, 300, 309, 343, 360,
  364, 383, 423, 434–5, 448, 503, 587–8, 614;
  character, 191–2, 211, 234, 343, 428;
  relationship with mother, 283n, 424, 434;
  education, 283n; artistic talent, 176, 234,
  241–2, 281, 283n, 370, 628; musical
  background, 282, 283n; Liverpool College of
  Art, 143, 176, 233, 283n, 332, 340, 353, 370,
  416; friendships, 143, 299, 304; flats, 191–2,
  220, 283n, 284, 285, 346, 350, 363, 416;
  friendship with Allan Williams, 176, 306, 310,
  316, 424, 588; friendship with John, 191–2,
  211, 233–4, 241, 286, 292, 319–20, 361, 374,
  434, 478–9; guitar playing, 241, 285, 296,

299–300, 309, 334, 336, 387–8, 415, 479; painting exhibited, 241–2; sale of painting, 281–2; buys bass, 281, 282, 335; joins Quarrymen, 282, 284, 285–6, 353; shares studio room with John, 284, 285, 293, 333; relationship with Paul, 286, 292, 319, 347, 374, 387, 415, 434, 448, 460–1, 626–7; girlfriends, 294, 370; at Vincent/Cochran show, 294; Quarrymen rehearsals, 296; writes letters to get bookings, 296–7, 298; Beatles name, 298–9, 315; stage debut, 299–300; at Gene Vincent show, 305; audition performance, 309–10; Beatles Scottish tour, 313–18, 322; Beatles relationships, 319–20, 374, 434, 437, 448; Beatles bookings, 332, 334–5, 343, 347, 349; George moves in, 333; Beatles recording, 336; drug experiences, 339, 445; relationship with Ellis, 340, 345; Beatles uniform, 342, 349, 355; Hamburg booking, 351, 353, 356; journey to Hamburg, 357, 358, 360; in Hamburg, 363, 364, 370, 371, 382, 390, 411; singing voice, 365; Hamburg performances, 365, 366, 379, 383, 385, 387–8; meets Ringo, 377; Berlin plans, 380, 389; buys amplifier, 381, 382; friends in Hamburg, 385–7; Astrid's photographs, 386, 390–1, 614–15, 793; relationship with Astrid, 386, 392–3, 416; engagement to Astrid, 395; farewell to George, 396; Hamburg arson story, 397–8, 399; correspondence with George, 402, 412, 511, 513; return from Hamburg, 415–16; Beatles bookings, 415, 423, 436; beaten up, 423–4, 627; with Astrid in Liverpool, 424–5, 429, 434–5; ill health, 434, 448, 497, 587–8, 614–15; return to Hamburg, 436; in Hamburg with Astrid, 439, 441, 448; letter to Allan Williams, 441, 449; Top Ten performances, 442–4, 448; sends money to Williams, 450n, 483; Jürgen's photographs, 451, 452; Cyn's visit, 457, 458, 634; returns to art, 458; place at Hochschule, 458; Paul plays bass, 458, 460; fight with Paul, 460–1; last performance with Beatles, 466–7; sells bass, 467; farewell to Beatles, 468, 482; correspondence with John, 496; Hochschule studies, 497, 614; sends Beatles records, 511; Liverpool visit, 587–8; meeting with Brian, 588; back in Hamburg, 614–15; death, 624, 625–7, 631–2, 634, 786; funeral, 627–8, 641; responses to his death, 628–30, 641–2
Sutherland, Elizabeth 'Mater' (Stanley, John's aunt), 56, 232, 298, 492
Sutherland, Robert 'Bert', 56, 232
Swanee River (backing track), 653, 654
Sweet Georgia Brown (backing track), 653, 654
Sweet Little Sixteen (Chuck Berry), 169, 202; Cochran's arrangement, 294; Beatles repertoire, 383, 495; Hamburg recording, 833
Swerdlow, Alan, 619, 862
Swerdlow, Harry, 862
Swinging Bluegenes, see Bluegenes
Sytner, Alan, 107, 108, 176, 238

Take Good Care Of My Baby (Bobby Vee), 680; sung by George, 512, 680; Beatles recording, 559, 560, 561, 562
Take Out Some Insurance (Jimmy Reed), recorded by Beatles with Sheridan, 461, 463–4

Take This Hammer (Ken Colyer's Skiffle Group), 110
The Talent Spot (BBC Light Programme), 779, 814, 818, 901
Tarrach, Reinhard 'Dicky', 653
A Taste of Honey (Lenny Welch), Beatles repertoire, 765, 788, 899; Hamburg recording, 834
Tatham, Dick, 548
Taylor, Alistair: PA to Brian, 472; Cavern visit, 516; on Beatles record sales, 523; on management meetings, 880; Beatles contract, 549, 564–5, 881; leaves Nems, 646, 888; Raymond Jones identity question, 877
Taylor, Derek, 159n, 186, 744, 879, 882, 895
Taylor, E. R., 57, 74
Taylor, Ted 'King-Size', 311, 690, 816, 831–2
Taylor, Vince, 288, 504
Teddy Bears, the, 201, 217, 560
Teddy Boys, 63, 84–5, 96, 97
Teenagers' Turn, see Here We Go
Temperance Seven, 423, 472–3, 475, 529, 638
Tenabeats, the, 772, 876, 898
Texan Skiffle Group (Ravin' Texans, the Texans), 124, 166, 167, 212, 213–14, 215; *see also* Rory Storm and the Hurricanes
Thank Your Lucky Stars (ABC-TV), 563–4, 747, 779, 811–12, 813, 818, 829
Tharpe, Sister Rosetta, 100, 214, 857
That Was The Week That Was (BBC-tv), 805, 806, 809, 900
That'll Be The Day (the Crickets), 4, 5, 146; played by Paul and John, 146, 147; Quarry Men recording, 179, 180, 296; played by George, 229
That's All Right Mama (Elvis Presley), 67, 69, 113, 141; Quarry Men repertoire, 145
That's When Your Heartaches Begin (Elvis Presley), 127; recorded by Beatles, 336
There's No One In The Whole Wide World (Jackie Lee & the Raindrops), performed by Beatles, 586
These Dangerous Years (film), 133
Think It Over (Buddy Holly), 189, 198–9
Thinking Of Linking, 172, 217, 297, 854
Thompson, Bobby, 311, 619, 690, 700
Thompson, Pam, 242–3
Three Cool Cats (the Coasters); sung by John, Paul and George, 215, 229, 481; recorded by Beatles, 559, 560, 562; Beatles repertoire, 736
Thumbin' A Ride (the Coasters), performed by Beatles, 475
Tibbott-Roberts, Liz, 539, 707
Till There Was You (Peggy Lee), sung by Paul, 433, 455, 478, 480, 533, 651, 765, 834; Beatles recording, 559, 560, 561, 562, 584; Beatles record, 592–3, 648; Hamburg recording, 834
Time (Craig Douglas), 475; Beatles repertoire, 475, 785
Tip Of My Tongue, 723, 725, 735, 800
To Know Him (Her) Is To Love Him (Her) (the Teddy Bears), 201, 217; Quarrymen repertoire, 240; Beatles repertoire, 365, 421, 559, 560, 825
Too Bad About Sorrows, 6
Top Ten Club, Hamburg: premises, 397n, 442; opening, 348n, 367; sound system, 389; Sheridan at, 372, 388, 399, 441, 551, 598–9; Williams' discussions with Eckhorn, 381;

Top Ten Club, Hamburg – *continued*
  Beatles visit, 388–9; Gerry and the Pacemakers,
    389; Beatles plans, 389, 395–6; Beatles at, 397,
    398; Pete's drum kit, 401; agreement for
    Beatles return, 425, 438, 449–50; Beatles pay,
    483; Beatles at, 440–3, 457, 458, 463, 465, 632;
    audiences, 443–4, 454–5, 598; staff, 444; drugs,
    444–5, 598; Pete Best's drumming, 447–8;
    Beatles photo session, 451, 526; talent spotters,
    452–3; Brian's visit, 454, 541; guitar smashing,
    460; Beatles last show, 466; Gerry and the
    Pacemakers, 470; Beatles plans for 1962: 513,
    552, 569, 614; house band, 551, 569, 598, 615,
    655; temporary closure, 599; future, 633, 839
Top Ten Club, Liverpool, 381, 389, 401–2, 403,
    412
Townsend, Ken, 666, 667, 670
Trafford, Roy: employment, 94, 330; friendship
    with Richy, 94–5, 137, 144, 170, 187, 213,
    717–18, 792; plays tea-chest bass, 110, 268;
    Eddie Clayton Skiffle Group, 110–11, 115, 120,
    171, 268; sex, 122; dancing, 133, 144; drinking,
    137, 144, 186; plays guitar, 171, 213; country
    music fan, 720
Transglobal Music, 764, 810, 835
Trower, Glynne, 335
Trying To Get To You (Elvis Presley), 113, 172,
    179; sung by Paul and Ian, 135; sung by Paul,
    138; Quarry Men repertoire, 145
Tuesday Rendezvous (AR-TV), 819–20, 901
Tutti Frutti (Little Richard), 3, 106, 767; sung by
    Paul, 136, 145; Beatles repertoire, 343
Twelve O'Clock Spin (BBC Light Programme),
    791, 805, 900
Twenty Flight Rock (Eddie Cochran), 117, 119,
    141; played by Paul, 130, 131, 849; Quarry Men
    repertoire, 145
The Twist (Chubby Checker), 527–9, 585, 736
Twist And Shout (Isley Brothers), 695; Beatles
    repertoire, 695, 725, 816; *Talent Spot*
    performance, 814, 901; TV performance, 826;
    Hamburg recording, 833
Twist In The Street (Beatles adaptation), 585
Two-Way Family Favourites (BBC Light
    Programme), 88, 791, 792n, 805, 900

Undertakers, the, 575, 589, 701
US Bonds, 419, 475

Vaughan, Ivan: friendship with John, 2, 40, 47, 60,
    64, 129, 132; friendship with Paul, 60, 127, 131,
    132, 136, 234, 314; Liverpool Institute, 60, 234,
    847; Quarry Men, 103, 108, 128, 130; Paul and
    Celia's visit, 780–1
Vaughan, Sarah, 53
Vee, Bobby, 512, 560, 680, 835–6
Vee Jay Records, 529, 763, 836
Vikings, the, 189, 855
Vincent, Gene: hero of John and Paul, 3, 92, 100;
    Be-Bop-A-Lula, 92, 116, 129, 141, 442; guitar,
    100; appearance, 116, 305, 474; *The Girl Can't
    Help It*, 116, 117, 395; George plays his
    numbers, 209; British hits, 214–15, 433; tour,
    294; survives car crash, 300, 305; at Liverpool
    Stadium, 300, 301, 304–5, 356, 378; Beatles
    play his numbers, 365, 405, 433, 455, 464, 585;
    John's performances, 371; My Bonnie, 463,

464; Vince Taylor copies, 504; at Star-Club,
    659; with Beatles in Hamburg, 659–60, 766;
    with Beatles at Cavern, 683; photo with John
    and Paul, 683, 890
Violent Playground (film), 133, 172
Vipers (Skiffle Group): Soho Fair (1956), 93, 127;
    instruments, 97, 102n, 109n; *Daily Mirror*
    article, 97; signed by George Martin, 97–8,
    265–6; name, 98, 103n, 273, 847; Don't You
    Rock Me Daddy-O, 109, 127; debut session,
    266; George Martin's work with, 102n, 266,
    268–9, 273; sales, 266; influence, 268; fans,
    112; George sees, 118; Streamline Train, 128;
    Coffee Bar Session, 273
Vollmer, Jürgen: appearance, 384, 434–5, 440;
    friendship with Klaus and Astrid, 384; sees
    Beatles, 384–5; relationship with Beatles, 385,
    386–7, 440; at Top Ten Club, 442;
    photography, 450–2, 505, 526; in Paris, 452,
    467, 500, 786; John and Paul's Paris visit,
    501–6; cuts their hair, 505–6
Voormann, Klaus: appearance, 384, 434, 614;
    character, 383–4; from Berlin, 392; girlfriend,
    382, 383, 386; first sees Beatles, 382–4; first
    conversation with Beatles, 385; friendship with
    Stuart, 385–7, 614, 629; on Stuart's bass
    playing, 388; on Beatles with Ringo, 394; on
    Beatles appearance, 395; at Top Ten Club, 442;
    on George, 451, 661; on Stuart's fight with
    Paul, 460–1; asks to join Beatles, 467; buys
    Stuart's guitar, 467; on Stuart's headaches, 497;
    Stuart's death, 626, 627, 628; at Star-Club,
    631; in Liverpool, 628; on John and Stuart's
    friendship, 629; care of Astrid, 642; seeing
    Beatles again, 786, 828, 839

Walley, Clive, 539
Walley, Nigel: friendship with John, 40, 47;
    memories of John, 45, 51, 64, 65, 93, 113, 124;
    Quarry Men rehearsals, 103, 109; Quarry Men
    management, 108, 109, 144, 151–2, 164, 165,
    178, 316, 524; memories of Quarry Men, 145;
    dismissal of Eric, 164, 418, 678, 853; illness,
    177–8; Julia's death, 182
Walsh, Alan, 508, 876
Walters, Lu (Wally Eymond): bass guitar and
    singing, 236n; name, 331; on Ringo, 341; in
    Hamburg, 379; recording with Beatles, 380,
    462, 868; Butlin's season, 470; at Cavern, 487;
    Hurricanes replacement, 619, 885
Warren, Alma, 747, 779, 895
Waterman, Pete, 804, 900
Watmough, Harry, 619, 894–5
Watson, Reg, 779, 899
Webb, Harry, *see* Richard (Cliff)
Wedding Bells Are Breaking Up That Old Gang
    Of Mine (Gene Vincent), 365; played by
    George, 166
Weedon, Bert, 264, 269, 344
Weil, Cynthia, 421, 680
Weinblatt, Mike, 771–2
Weissleder, Manfred: background, 569;
    appearance, 624; new club, 569; finances, 599,
    633; Star-Club opening, 615; arrival of Beatles,
    624; cars, 626, 643; Roy Young's contract, 886;
    Beatles pay, 633, 786n; care of Beatles, 633,
    652, 787, 827; wants Beatles back, 653;

photography, 661, 793; Beatles contracts, 685; handling Paul's return, 770; handling Preston's appearance, 788; wants Beatles back in 1963: 788; recording, 833

Well Darling, 296

Wharton, Peter, 371–2

What A Crazy World We're Living In (Joe Brown), performed by Beatles, 586

What Goes On, 217

What'd I Say (Ray Charles), 224–5, 292; performed by Eddie Cochran, 295; performed by Gene Vincent, 305; Beatles repertoire, 365, 378, 404, 406, 418, 510, 539, 599, 617, 645, 832; performed by Pacemakers, 418; Jerry Lee Lewis hit, 475

When I'm Sixty-Four, 89, 218, 432, 847, 852

Where Have You Been (Arthur Alexander), sung by John, 680

Whitcomb, Noel, 97

White, Andy, 730–2, 848, 894

White, Priscilla, see Cilla Black

White, R. N. (Ron), 327–8, 526, 527n, 543–4, 547

White Hunter (TV serial), 196, 856

A White Sports Coat (Marty Robbins), 121–2

Whitman, Slim, 78, 134

Whittaker, Lyndon, 816

Whole Lotta Shakin' Goin' On (Jerry Lee Lewis), 141, 150, 201; performed by Beatles, 343, 510; performed by Hurricanes, 393

Why (Tony Sheridan), recorded by Sheridan with Beatles, 461, 463, 465

Wild Cat (Gene Vincent), 336; recorded by Beatles, 336

Wild In The Country (Elvis Presley), sung by Pete, 494, 585

The Wild One (film), 452, 862, 863

Wilde, Marty (Reg Smith), 200n, 606

Wilkie, Derry, 237, 898, see also Derry and the Seniors

Wilkinson, Thelma, 477, 487, 708

Will You Love Me Tomorrow (the Shirelles), 420; Beatles repertoire, 421, 428, 586, 663, 832

Willey, Brian, 779

Williams, Allan: background, 176; appearance, 290, 360, 438n; marriage, 176; career as entrepreneur, 176, 289; Jacaranda Club, 175–6, 289, 310, 412; management of groups, 289, 313, 316, 347–8; trip to Amsterdam and Hamburg, 289–91; meets Koschmider, 291, 331, 633; friendship with Stuart, 176, 306, 310, 316, 424, 588; Gene Vincent rock show, 295, 300–1, 304–5; relationship with Parnes, 306, 313, 347; finds drummer for Beatles, 306–7; (Silver) Beatles audition, 306–7, 309–10; Blue Angel, 307, 355, 412, 438n, 497; Beatles playing at Jacaranda, 310; Beatles Scottish tour, 313, 315–16, 318, 319, 322, 325; Beatles management, 316, 331, 412–13, 435, 449, 523, 524; view of Tommy Moore, 320; Beatles bookings, 331, 332, 334–5, 336–7, 348–9, 449; driving, 335, 347, 356–7, 358, 359–60, 839; view of Norman Chapman, 337; on John and Stuart split to London, 345; relationship with Koschmider, 347–8, 351, 362n, 371, 376, 380–1, 389; Beatles Hamburg booking, 351–2, 355, 452; journey to Hamburg, 356–7, 358, 359–61, 438, 839; Beatles Hamburg contracts,

362n, 375, 380, 389, 435, 441, 449–50; sees Beatles in Hamburg, 379–80; Hamburg recording session, 380; relationship with Eckhorn, 381, 389, 435, 441, 552; Top Ten Club plans, 381, 389; on Millie Sutcliffe, 392, 627; Top Ten Club opening and destruction, 401–2, 412; in hospital, 402, 412; Paul and Pete's deportation appeal, 425, 430, 435, 440, 449–50, 614; Beatles refuse to pay his commission, 441, 449–50, 459, 872; threats, 449–50, 473, 482; legal action against Beatles, 459, 482–3, 497–8, 513, 544, 588; bans Beatles from Blue Angel, 513–14, 688; advice to Brian, 525, 543; Beatles relationship, 588, 688, 743; death of Stuart, 625–6, 628; Jerry Lee Lewis show, 657; Liverpool Press Club, 743, 895; autobiography, 895

Williams, Beryl: background, 176; journey to Hamburg, 356, 360, 362; relationship with Astrid, 424, 625, 628; Stuart's funeral, 628

Williams, Geoff, 490

Williams, Hank, 44, 78, 79, 365

Williams, Larry, 141, 168, 215, 365

Williams, Susan, 385

Williams, Taffy, 30, 64

Winston's Walk, 218

Wohlers, Erika, 644

Wolf, Reinhart, 383, 384, 385n, 450–1, 868–9, 887

Wood, Len (L. G.): EMI role, 526, 529, 835; age, 527n; on Brian, 526; relationship with George Martin, 529, 638–40, 835; Beatles rejection, 547, 594, 640; Beatles recording session, 640

Woodbine, Lord, see Phillips (Harold)

Wooden Heart (Elvis Presley), Beatles repertoire, 403–4, 412

Woodhead, Leslie, 685, 688, 689, 711–12, 737, 778

Woods, Vicky, 616, 619, 658

Wooler, Bob: background and character, 212, 402, 413–14, 514; name, 857; appearance, 516; disc jockey and MC, 212, 237, 401, 405, 412, 433; career move, 401–2; Top Ten Club, 401–2; relationship with Beatles, 402–3, 412–13, 433–4, 486, 510–11, 514–15, 571, 877; work for Kelly, 403, 404–5, 413; Beatles bookings, 403, 404, 406, 414, 426, 474, 770; at Litherland, 405–6; on Beatles performances, 406, 418, 491–2, 510–11; at Aintree Institute, 412, 413, 512; at Hambleton Hall, 414; Echo advertisements, 414, 428, 430, 488, 514; Cavern route, 426, 430, 478–9, 674, 770, 788, 815; on Beatles refusal to pay commission, 435, 441, 872; memories of Beatles, 479, 485, 498–9, 515, 517, 784; on Cunard Yanks, 482n; on Beatles management, 486–7, 524; Beatles Fan Club, 489, 491; Mersey Beat column, 491–2, 498, 900; names Ma Storm, 494; on Lennon-McCartney relationship, 500; Brian's first encounter with Beatles, 516–18, 520; plugging My Bonnie, 878; Brian's business meeting with Beatles, 523–4; on Beatles fees, 545; relationship with Brian, 567, 589, 608, 611, 612, 656–7; on Pete Best, 600; on Brian's clothes, 602; on Brian's relationship with Beatles, 612–13; Beatles Fan Club night, 621; Kingtwisters role, 622; Beatles twelve-date Cavern season, 657; Channel show, 657–8;

Wooler, Bob – *continued*
  Rory Storm and the Hurricanes, 657–8; Jerry
  Lee Lewis night, 657–8, 659; Beatles *Welcome
  Home*, 674; Little Richard show, 687; Pete
  Best's dismissal, 704, 709, 824; *Little Richard
  At The Tower*, 767–8; bets on Beatles future,
  768, 897; Liverpool Empire show, 784; Beatles
  Cavern bookings for 1963: 788; George Martin
  at Cavern, 822; *Mersey Beat Awards Night*, 824;
  death, 857
Woollam, Louise (George's grandmother), 22
Workman, Tony, 69–70
The World Is Waiting For The Sunrise (Les Paul
  and Mary Ford), 302; sung by Nerk Twins, 302;
  recorded by Beatles, 336
A World Without Love, 217–18
The World's Fair: on skiffle, 126; on That'll Be The
  Day, 146; on My Bonnie, 563; Love Me Do ad,
  748; Juke-Box 112, 781, 791, 805, 825, 829,
  864; reviews of Love Me Do, 748–9, 896
Wright, Sue, 710, 892
Wycherley, Ronnie, *see* Fury (Billy)

Years Roll Along, 10, 297

You Better Move On (Arthur Alexander), 608;
  sung by John, 609
You Don't Know What You've Got (Ral Donner),
  performed by Beatles, 513
You Don't Understand Me (Bobby Freeman),
  played by Beatles, 419
You Must Write Every Day, 336
You'll Be Mine, 218, 336, 865
Young, Roy: interpreter for Fascher, 569; Top Ten
  house band, 598; piano playing, 598, 599;
  moves to Star-Club, 615; advice sought by
  Brian, 886; performing with Beatles, 632, 653;
  recording with Sheridan and Beatles, 654; on
  Pete Best, 655; Hamburg billing, 787, 827;
  electric organ, 833
Young Blood (the Coasters), 141, 540, 736, 821;
  sung by Beatles, 879
Your Feet's Too Big (Fats Waller): sung by Paul,
  475, 480, 536, 593; Hamburg recording, 833
Your True Love (Carl Perkins), 117, 294
You're Driving Me Crazy (Temperance Seven),
  423, 472–3, 529

Zerga, Joseph E., 764, 810, 835–6

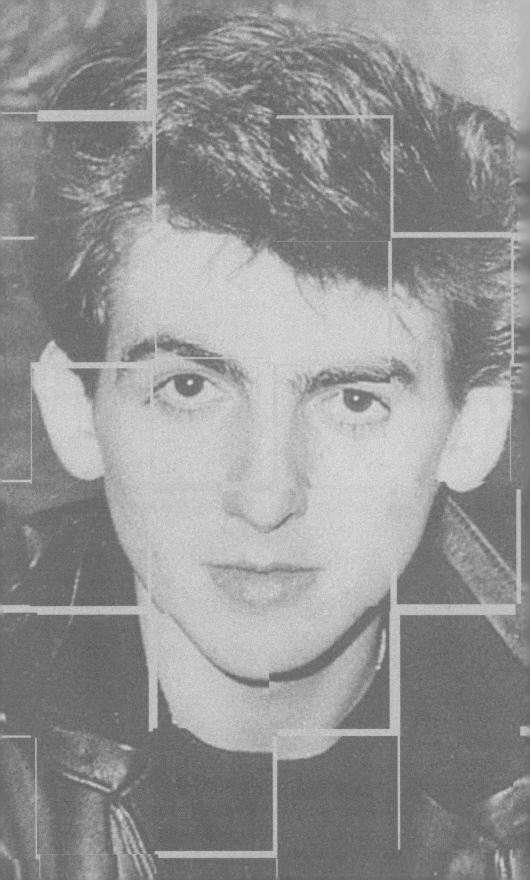